Twentieth-Century Literary Criticism

Topics Volume

Guide to Gale Literary Criticism Series

When you need to review criticism of literary works, these are the Gale series to use:

If the author's death date is:	You should turn to:
After Dec. 31, 1959 (or author is still living)	*CONTEMPORARY LITERARY CRITICISM* for example: Jorge Luis Borges, Anthony Burgess, William Faulkner, Mary Gordon, Ernest Hemingway, Iris Murdoch
1900 through 1959	*TWENTIETH-CENTURY LITERARY CRITICISM* for example: Willa Cather, F. Scott Fitzgerald, Henry James, Mark Twain, Virginia Woolf
1800 through 1899	*NINETEENTH-CENTURY LITERATURE CRITICISM* for example: Fyodor Dostoevsky, Nathaniel Hawthorne, George Sand, William Wordsworth
1400 through 1799	*LITERATURE CRITICISM FROM 1400 TO 1800 (excluding Shakespeare)* for example: Anne Bradstreet, Daniel Defoe, Alexander Pope, François Rabelais, Jonathan Swift, Phillis Wheatley *SHAKESPEAREAN CRITICISM* Shakespeare's plays and poetry
Antiquity through 1399	*CLASSICAL AND MEDIEVAL LITERATURE CRITICISM* for example: Dante, Homer, Plato, Sophocles, Vergil, the Beowulf Poet

---

Gale also publishes related criticism series:

CHILDREN'S LITERATURE REVIEW

This series covers authors of all eras who have written for the preschool through high school audience.

SHORT STORY CRITICISM

This series covers the major short fiction writers of all nationalities and periods of literary history.

ISSN 0276-8178

Volume 38

Twentieth-Century Literary Criticism

Topics Volume

**Excerpts from Criticism of Various Topics
in Twentieth-Century Literature, including Literary
and Critical Movements, Prominent Themes and
Genres, Anniversary Celebrations, and Surveys
of National Literatures**

Paula Kepos
Editor

Marie Lazzari
Thomas Ligotti
Michelle L. McClellan
Laurie Sherman
Associate Editors

 *Gale Research Inc.* · *DETROIT* · *NEW YORK* · *LONDON*

STAFF

Paula Kepos, *Editor*

Marie Lazzari, Thomas Ligotti, Michelle L. McClellan, Laurie Sherman, *Associate Editors*

Ian A. Goodhall, Tina Grant, Alan Hedblad, Grace Jeromski,
Michael W. Jones, David Kmenta, Mark Swartz, Debra A. Wells, *Assistant Editors*

Jeanne A. Gough, *Permissions & Production Manager*
Linda M. Pugliese, *Production Supervisor*
Suzanne Powers, Maureen A. Puhl, Jennifer VanSickle, *Editorial Associates*
Donna Craft, Lorna Mabunda, James G. Wittenbach, *Editorial Assistants*

Victoria B. Cariappa, *Research Manager*
H. Nelson Fields, Judy L. Gale, Maureen Richards, *Editorial Associates*
Paula Cutcher, Robin Lupa, *Editorial Assistants*

Sandra C. Davis, *Permissions Supervisor (Text)*
Josephine M. Keene, Denise Singleton, Kimberly F. Smilay, *Permissions Associates*
Maria L. Franklin, Michele Lonoconus, Camille P. Robinson, Shalice Shah,
Rebecca A. Stanko, *Permissions Assistants*

Patricia A. Seefelt, *Permissions Supervisor (Pictures)*
Margaret A. Chamberlain, *Permissions Associate*
Pamela A. Hayes, Lillian Quickley, *Permissions Assistants*

Mary Beth Trimper, *Production Manager*
Shanna G. Philpott, *External Production Assistant*

Arthur Chartow, *Art Director*
C. J. Jonik, *Keyliner*

Laura Bryant, *Production Supervisor*
Louise Gagné, *Internal Production Associate*
Yolanda Y. Latham, *Internal Production Assistant*

Contents

Preface vii

Acknowledgments xi

Authors to Be Featured in Forthcoming Volumes xv

Detective Fiction

Introduction 1

Representative Works 1-3

The Genesis and History of the Detective Story 3-22

Defining Detective Fiction..22-32

Evolution and Varieties 32-77

The Appeal of Detective Fiction..77-90

Further Reading...90-96

Film and Literature

Introduction 97

Overviews..97-119

Film and Theater...119-34

Film and the Novel...134-45

The Art of the Screenplay...145-66

Genre Literature/Genre Film 167-79

The Writer and the Film Industry..179-90

Authors on Film Adaptations of Their Works............................190-200

Fiction into Film: Comparative Essays.......................................200-23

Further Reading...223-26

Psychoanalysis and Literature

Introduction 227

Overviews...227-46

Freud on Literature..246-51

Psychoanalytic Views of the Literary Process.............................251-61

Psychoanalytic Theories of Response to Literature 261-88

Psychoanalysis and Literary Criticism..288-312

Psychoanalysis as Literature/Literature as Psychoanalysis.........313-34

Further Reading..334-38

Theater of the Absurd

Introduction 339

Representative Works..339-40

"The Theater of the Absurd"...340-47

Major Plays and Playwrights...347-58

The Theater of the Absurd and the Concept of the Absurd 358-86

Theatrical Techniques...386-94

Predecessors of the Theater of the Absurd...394-402

Influence of the Theater of the Absurd 402-13

Further Reading...413-15

Literary Criticism Series Cumulative Author Index   419

Literary Criticism Series Cumulative Topic Index   469

TCLC Cumulative Nationality Index   471

Preface

Since its inception more than ten years ago, *Twentieth-Century Literary Criticism* has been purchased and used by nearly 10,000 school, public, and college or university libraries. With this edition—volume 38 in the series—*TCLC* has covered over 500 authors, representing 58 nationalities, and more than 25,000 titles. No other reference source has surveyed the critical response to twentieth-century authors and literature as thoroughly as *TCLC*. In the words of one reviewer, "there is nothing comparable available." *TCLC* "is a gold mine of information—dates, pseudonyms, biographical information, and criticism from books and periodicals—which many libraries would have difficulty assembling on their own."

TCLC is a companion series to Gale's *Contemporary Literary Criticism*, which reprints commentary on current writing. Because of the different periods under consideration (*CLC* considers authors who were still living after 1959), there is no duplication of material between *CLC* and *TCLC*. For additional information about *CLC* and Gale's other criticism titles, users should consult the Guide to Gale Literary Criticism Series preceding the title page in this volume.

Scope of the Series

TCLC is designed to serve as an introduction for students and advanced readers to authors who died between 1900 and 1960, and to the most significant interpretations of these authors' works. The great poets, novelists, short story writers, playwrights, and philosophers of this period are frequently studied in high school and college literature courses. In organizing and excerpting the vast amount of critical material written on these authors, *TCLC* helps students develop valuable insight into literary history, promotes a better understanding of the texts, and sparks ideas for papers and assignments. Each entry in *TCLC* presents a comprehensive survey of the author's career or an individual work of literature and provides the user a multiplicity of interpretations and assessments. Such a variety allows students to pursue their own interests; furthermore, it fosters an awareness that literature is dynamic and responsive to many different opinions.

Topics Volumes

Every fourth volume of *TCLC* is devoted to literary topics that cannot be covered under the author approach used in the rest of the series. Such topics include literary movements, prominent themes in twentieth-century literature, literary reaction to political and historical events, significant eras in literary history, prominent literary anniversaries, and the literatures of cultures that are often overlooked by English-speaking readers. *TCLC* 38, for example, examines the following four topics: Detective Fiction, Film and Literature, Psychoanalysis and Literature, and Theater of the Absurd. Entries in Topics volumes are generally restricted to the period between 1900 to 1959, and do not duplicate criticism from *CLC*.

Organization of the Book

Each subject entry in a Topics volume consists of the following elements: an introduction, a list of representative works, excerpts of criticism (each preceded by an annotation and followed by a bibliographic citation), a list of further reading on the topic, and numerous illustrations.

- The *introduction* briefly defines the subject of the entry and provides social and historical background information important to an understanding of the criticism.

- The list of *representative works* identifies writings by authors associated with the subject. Arranged chronologically by date of first book publication, the list also indicates the genre of each work. In the case of foreign authors with both foreign-language publications and English translations, the title and date of the first English-language edition are given in brackets. Unless otherwise indicated, dramas are dated by first performance, not first publication.

- The *criticism* is arranged thematically. Entries commonly begin with general surveys of the subject or essays providing historical background information, followed by essays that develop particular aspects of the topic.

For example, the entry devoted to Detective Fiction begins with excerpts detailing the genesis and history of the detective story. These are followed by sections devoted to the definition, evolution, and varieties of detective fiction. The entry concludes with a section on the appeal of the genre. Each section has a separate title heading and is identified with a page number in the table of contents.

The critic's name is given at the beginning of each piece of criticism; anonymous essays are headed by the title of the journal in which they appeared. Many critical essays in *TCLC* contain translated material. Unless otherwise noted, translations within brackets are by the editors; translations within parentheses are by the critic. Publication information (such as publisher names and book prices) and parenthetical numerical references (such as footnotes or page and line references to specific editions of works) have been deleted at the editors' discretion to provide smoother reading of the text.

- Critical essays are prefaced by *annotations* providing the reader with information about both the critic and the criticism that follows. Included are the critic's reputation, individual approach to literary criticism, and particular expertise in the subject under discussion. Also noted are the relative importance of a work of criticism, the scope of the excerpt, and the growth of critical controversy or changes in critical trends regarding the subject. In some cases, these notes cross-reference the work of critics who discuss each other's commentary.

- A complete *bibliographic citation* designed to facilitate location of the original essay or book follows each piece of criticism.

- The bibliography of *further reading* appearing at the end of each subject entry lists further secondary sources on the subject, in some cases including essays for which the editors could not obtain reprint rights, and anthologies of primary sources.

- *Illustrations* throughout the entry include portraits of the authors under discussion; reproductions of important manuscript pages, magazine covers, dust jackets, movie stills, artwork, and maps; and photographs of people, places, and events important to the topic.

Cumulative Indexes

Each volume of *TCLC*, including the Topics volumes, contains a cumulative author index listing all authors who have appeared in the following Gale series: *Contemporary Literary Criticism, Twentieth-Century Literary Criticism, Nineteenth-Century Literature Criticism, Literature Criticism from 1400 to 1800*, and *Classical and Medieval Literature Criticism*. Topic entries devoted to a single author, such as the entry on James Joyce's *Ulysses* in *TCLC* 26, are listed in this index. Also included are cross-references to the Gale series *Short Story Criticism, Children's Literature Review, Authors in the News, Contemporary Authors, Contemporary Authors Autobiography Series, Dictionary of Literary Biography, Concise Dictionary of American Literary Biography, Something about the Author, Something about the Author Autobiography Series*, and *Yesterday's Authors of Books for Children*. Useful for locating authors within the various series, this index is particularly valuable for those authors who are identified with a certain period but who, because of their death dates, are placed in another, or for those authors whose careers span two periods. For example, F. Scott Fitzgerald is found in *TCLC*, yet a writer often associated with him, Ernest Hemingway, is found in *CLC*.

Each new volume in Gale's Literary Criticism Series includes a cumulative topic index, which lists all literary topics treated in *NCLC, TCLC, LC 1400-1800*, and the *CLC* Yearbook.

Each *TCLC* Topics volume also includes a cumulative nationality index which lists all authors who have appeared in regular *TCLC* volumes, arranged alphabetically under their respective nationalities, as well as Topics volume entries devoted to particular national literatures.

Titles discussed in the Topics volume entries are not included in the *TCLC* cumulative title index.

A Note to the Reader

When writing papers, students who quote directly from any volume in Gale's Literary Criticism Series may use the following general forms to footnote reprinted criticism. The first example pertains to material drawn from periodicals, the second to material reprinted from books.

[1]T. S. Eliot, "John Donne," *The Nation and the Athenaeum*, 33 (9 June 1923), 321-32; excerpted and reprinted in *Literature Criticism from 1400 to 1800*, Vol. 10, ed. James E. Person, Jr. (Detroit: Gale Research, 1989), pp. 28-9.

[1]Clara G. Stillman, *Samuel Butler: A Mid-Victorian Modern* (Viking Press, 1932); excerpted and reprinted in *Twentieth-Century Literary Criticism*, Vol. 33, ed. Paula Kepos (Detroit: Gale Research, 1989), pp. 43-5.

Suggestions Are Welcome

In response to suggestions, several features have been added to *TCLC* since the series began, including annotations to excerpted criticism, a cumulative index to authors in all Gale literary criticism series, entries devoted to criticism on a single work by a major author, more extensive illustrations, and a title index listing all literary works discussed in the series since its inception.

Readers who wish to suggest authors or topics to appear in future volumes, or who have other suggestions, are cordially invited to write the editors.

Acknowledgments

The editors wish to thank the copyright holders of the excerpted criticism included in this volume, the permissions managers of many book and magazine publishing companies for assisting us in securing reprint rights, and Anthony Bogucki for assistance with copyright research. We are also grateful to the staffs of the Detroit Public Library, Wayne State University Purdy/Kresge Library Complex, and the University of Michigan Libraries for making their resources available to us. Following is a list of the copyright holders who have granted us permission to reprint material in this volume of *TCLC*. Every effort has been made to trace copyright, but if omissions have been made, please let us know.

Tynan.—Van Dine, S.S. From an introduction to *The Great Detective Stories: A Chronological Anthology.* Charles Scribner's Sons, 1927. Copyright 1931 by Charles Scribner's Sons. Renewed 1955 by Claire Wright. Reprinted by permission of the Literary Estate of S. S. Van Dine.—Wagner, Geoffrey. From *The Novel and the Cinema.* Fairleigh Dickinson University Press, 1975. © 1975 by Associated University Presses, Inc. Reprinted by permission of the publisher.—Wasiolek, Edward. From "The Future of Psychoanalytic Criticism," in *The Frontiers of Literary Criticism.* Edited by David H. Malone. Hennessey & Ingalls, Inc., 1974. Copyright © 1974 by Hennessey & Ingalls, Inc., 1254 Third St. Promenade, Santa Monica, CA 90401. All rights reserved. Reprinted by permission of the publisher.—Waugh, Hillary. From "The Police Procedural," in *The Mystery Story.* Edited by John Ball. University Extension, University of California, 1976. Copyright © 1976 by The Regents of the University of California. All rights reserved. Reprinted by permission of the publisher.—Westlund, Joseph. From "What Comedy Can Do for Us: Reparation and Idealization in Shakespeare's Comedies," in *Psychoanalytic Approaches to Literature and Film.* Edited by Maurice Charney and Joseph Reppen. Fairleigh Dickinson University Press, 1987. © 1987 by Associated University Presses, Inc. Reprinted by permission of the publisher.—Wilson, Edmund. From *Classics and Commercials: A Literary Chronicle of the Forties.* Farrar, Straus and Company, 1950. Copyright 1950 by Edmund Wilson. Renewed 1977 by Elena Wilson. All rights reserved. Reprinted by permission of Farrar, Straus and Giroux, Inc.

PHOTOGRAPHS AND ILLUSTRATIONS APPEARING IN *TCLC,* VOLUME 38, WERE RECEIVED FROM THE FOLLOWING SOURCES:

Otto Penzler: **pp. 30, 81;** Popperfoto: **p. 33;** S.R. Archive: **p. 64;** AP/Wide World Photos: **p. 70;** Frank Serjack: **p. 165;** Culver Pictures: **pp. 183, 282;** The Bettmann Archive: **p. 249;** Photograph by Zoë Dominic: **p. 344;** Courtesy of the German Information Center: **p. 346;** Courtesy of the Cultural Service of the French Embassy: **pp. 348, 357, 379;** Photograph by Wayne Cowart. Courtesy of the Osolo Theatre Company, Sarasota, FL: **p. 350;** Agence de Presse Bernand, Paris: **p. 353;** Photograph by Hank Kranzler. Courtesy of the American Conservatory Theater: **p. 368;** Goethe House: **p. 377.**

Authors to Be Featured in Forthcoming Volumes

Charles Waddell Chesnutt (American short story writer and novelist)—Chesnutt was one of the first black American writers to receive widespread critical and popular attention. He is best known for short stories about the antebellum South that incorporate subtle and ironic condemnations of slavery.

Joseph Conrad (Polish-born English novelist)—Considered an innovator of novel structure as well as one of the finest stylists of modern English literature, Conrad is the author of complex novels that examine the ambiguity of good and evil. *TCLC* will devote an entry to Conrad's novel *Lord Jim*, which examines the failures of a man before society and his own conscience.

Gabriele D'Annunzio (Italian novelist, playwright, and poet)—D'Annunzio, one of modern literature's most flamboyant personalities, is renowned as a consummate stylist who combined the poetic grandeur of Dante and the classical writers with contemporary trends of naturalism, symbolism, and decadence.

Paul Eluard (French poet)—Eluard was a founder of the Surrealist movement in France. His poetry, most often depicting the themes of love, fraternity, and universal harmony, is noted for its purity, lyricism, and highly visual content.

Ford Madox Ford (English novelist)—Ford was a major English novelist and a strong influence on modern trends in both poetry and prose. *TCLC* will devote an entry to *The Good Soldier*, a novel that is often considered Ford's most important.

William Dean Howells (American novelist and critic)—The chief progenitor of American Realism and the most influential American literary critic during the nineteenth century, Howells was the author of three dozen novels, which, though neglected for decades, are today the subject of growing interest. *TCLC* will devote an entry to Howells's best known work, *The Rise of Silas Lapham*.

Henry James (American novelist)—James is considered one of the most important novelists of the English language and his work is universally acclaimed for its stylistic distinction, complex psychological portraits, and originality of theme and technique. *TCLC* will devote an entry to James's study of Americans living in the expatriate society of England and Italy, *The Portrait of a Lady*.

Sinclair Lewis (American novelist)—One of the foremost American novelists of the 1920s and 1930s, Lewis wrote some of the most effective satires in American literature. *TCLC* will devote an entry to his novel *Babbitt*, a scathing portrait of vulgar materialism and spiritual bankruptcy in American business.

Malcolm Lowry (English novelist)—Lowry's novel *Under the Volcano*, the anatomy of a man's psychic and spiritual collapse, is considered a classic of modern literature. *TCLC* will devote an entry to this richly allusive and complex work.

Katherine Mansfield (New Zealand short story writer)—Mansfield was an innovator of the short story form who contributed to the development of the stream-of-consciousness narrative.

Claude McKay (American poet)—A prominent figure of the Harlem Renaissance, McKay was the author of powerful poems of social protest that are considered among the most significant of the early American civil rights movement.

George Meredith (English novelist)—Meredith was a major Victorian novelist whose works, anticipating Modernist trends of the twentieth century, demonstrated a concern with character psychology, social problems, and the development of the novel form. *TCLC* will devote an entry to his most critically acclaimed novel, *The Egoist*.

Ida Tarbell (American journalist and biographer)—A prominent leader of the early twentieth-century muckraking movement in American journalism, Tarbell is best known for her sensational exposé of questionable business practices, *The History of the Standard Oil Company*.

Oscar Wilde (Anglo-Irish dramatist, novelist, and poet)—A crusader for aestheticism, Wilde was one of the most prominent members of the nineteenth-century "art for art's sake" movement. *TCLC*'s upcoming entry will focus on the latest studies of Wilde, particularly his only novel, *The Picture of Dorian Gray*.

Emile Zola (French novelist)—Zola was the founder and principal theorist of Naturalism, one of the most influential literary movements in modern literature. His twenty-volume series "Les Rougon-Macquart" is a monument of Naturalist fiction and served as a model for late nineteenth-century novelists seeking a more candid and accurate representation of human life.

Detective Fiction

INTRODUCTION

For extended discussion of the Sherlock Holmes stories of Arthur Conan Doyle, see the Sherlock Holmes Centenary entry in *TCLC,* Volume 26.

Detective fiction is one of the most widely read forms of popular literature. The beginnings of this genre are usually traced to Edgar Allan Poe's "The Murders in the Rue Morgue," published in *Graham*'s magazine in 1841, and most detective stories adhere closely to the archetypal plot established by this work. A crime (usually murder) is committed; a detective investigates; a number of suspects are considered; the guilty party is discovered and imprisoned, killed, or allowed to escape at the conclusion.

Inaugurated in England by Arthur Conan Doyle's introduction of Sherlock Holmes in 1887, detective fiction especially flourished during a period known as the genre's "Golden Age," from 1918 until about 1930. English detective fiction of this era, which is best represented by the works of E. C. Bentley, John Buchan, Agatha Christie, R. Austin Freeman, E. W. Hornung, A. A. Milne, and Dorothy Sayers, features lavish surroundings, eccentric upper-class characters, and plots that consist of formal puzzles to be solved. Detective fiction by American authors of the same period, such as Jacques Futrelle, Melville Davisson Post, Mary Roberts Rinehart, and S. S. Van Dine, though indebted to English precursors, was strikingly original in some respects, particularly in replacing manor-house exoticism with a greater degree of realism, a trend that culminated in the hard-boiled school.

Originated by Dashiell Hammett in short stories published in *Black Mask* magazine in the 1920s, hard-boiled detective fiction is a distinctively American form of the genre. The hard-boiled detective, exemplified by Sam Spade, Philip Marlowe, and Mike Hammer in the fiction of Hammett, Raymond Chandler, and Mickey Spillane, is a solitary figure who often operates outside the law and moves in a world of sex, violence, and almost universal corruption. Although hard-boiled detective fiction was initially viewed as the ultimate development in the genre, further innovations have included the introduction of women detectives, supernatural elements, and science fiction detective stories. The police procedural novel, focusing on the everyday workings of the police in investigating crime, is the most recent and realistic branch of detective fiction.

Examples of detective fiction have appeared in the literature of nearly every country, yet the genre remains almost exclusively the province of English-language writers. While there exists an abundance of commentary on all varieties of detective fiction, critics remain divided on basic issues of what constitutes detective fiction and whether variations on the prototypical plot of crime-detection-solution mean the development or failure of the genre. Such debate has little effect on the popularity of detective fiction, which retains great currency worldwide.

REPRESENTATIVE WORKS

Allingham, Margery
  Death of a Ghost (novel) 1934
  Dancers in Mourning (novel) 1937
Ambler, Eric
  The Dark Frontier (novel) 1936
  A Coffin for Dimitrios (novel) 1939; also published as *The Mask of Dimitrios,* 1939
Bentley, E. C.
  Trent's Last Case (novel) 1913; also published as *The Woman in Black,* 1913
  Trent Intervenes (short stories) 1938
Biggers, Earl Derr
  The House Without a Key (novel) 1925
Blake, Nicholas [pseudonym of C. Day Lewis]
  The Beast Must Die (novel) 1938
Buchan, John
  The Thirty-Nine Steps (novel) 1915
Carr, John Dickson
  The White Priory Murders [as Carter Dickson] (novel) 1934
  The Three Coffins (novel) 1935; also published as *The Hollow Man,* 1935
  The Burning Court (novel) 1937
  The Peacock Feather Murders [as Carter Dickson] (novel) 1937; also published as *The Ten Teacups,* 1937
  The Crooked Hinge (novel) 1938
  The Reader Is Warned [as Carter Dickson] (novel) 1939
  The Case of the Constant Suicide (novel) 1941
  Below Suspicion (novel) 1949
Chandler, Raymond
  The Big Sleep (novel) 1939
  Farewell, My Lovely (novel) 1940
  The Lady in the Lake (novel) 1944
  The Little Sister (novel) 1949
  The Long Goodbye (novel) 1954
Chase, James Hadley
  No Orchids for Miss Blandish (novel) 1939
Chesterton, G. K.
  The Man Who Was Thursday (novel) 1908
  The Innocence of Father Brown (short stories) 1911
  The Wisdom of Father Brown (short stories) 1914
  The Incredulity of Father Brown (short stories) 1926
  The Secret of Father Brown (short stories) 1927
Christie, Agatha
  The Mysterious Affair at Styles (novel) 1920
  The Murder of Roger Ackroyd (novel) 1926
  Why Didn't They Ask Evans? (novel) 1934; also published as *The Boomerang Clue,* 1935
  Death Comes at the End (novel) 1944
  Five Complete Miss Marple Novels (novels) 1980
  Hercule Poirot's Casebook (short stories) 1984

Miss Marple: The Complete Short Stories (short stories) 1985

Crispin, Edmund [pseudonym of Robert Bruce Montgomery]
The Moving Toyshop; or, Love Lies Bleeding (novel) 1948

Daly, John Carroll
The Snarl of The Beast (novel) 1927

Doyle, Arthur Conan
A Study in Scarlet (novel) 1888
The Sign of Four (novel) 1890
The Adventures of Sherlock Holmes (short stories) 1892
The Memoirs of Sherlock Holmes (short stories) 1894
The House of the Baskervilles (novel) 1902
The Return of Sherlock Holmes (short stories) 1905
His Last Bow (short stories) 1917
The Case-Book of Sherlock Holmes (short stories) 1927

Eberhart, Mignon G.
The Patient in Room 18 (novel) 1929

Fearing, Kenneth
The Big Clock (novel) 1946

Freeling, Nicholas
Double Barrel (novel) 1965
King of the Rainy Country (novel) 1966

Freeman, R. Austin
The Red Thumb Mark (novel) 1907
John Thorndyke's Cases (short stories) 1909; also published as *Dr. Thorndyke's Cases,* 1931
The Singing Bone (short stories) 1912; also published as *The Adventures of Dr. Thorndyke,* 1946
Dr. Thorndyke's Case-Book (short stories) 1923; also published as *The Blue Scarab,* 1924
For the Defence: Dr. Thorndyke (novel) 1934

Futrelle, Jacques
The Thinking Machine (short stories) 1907; also published as *The Problem of Cell 13,* 1918

Gardner, Erle Stanley
The Case of the Velvet Claws (novel) 1933

Hammett, Dashiell
The Dain Curse (novel) 1929
Red Harvest (novel) 1929
The Maltese Falcon (novel) 1930
The Glass Key (novel) 1931
The Thin Man (novel) 1934
The Adventures of Sam Spade (short stories) 1944; also published as *They Can Only Hang You Once,* 1949
The Continental Op (short stories) 1945
The Big Knockover (short stories and novels) 1966

Himes, Chester
If He Hollers Let Him Go (novel) 1945
Lonely Crusade (novel) 1947
Cast the First Stone (novel) 1952
The Crazy Kill (novel) 1959
Pinktoes (novel) 1965
The Heat's On (novel) 1966
Blind Man with a Pistol (novel) 1969

Hornung, E. W.
The Amateur Cracksman (short stories) 1899
The Black Mask (short stories) 1901; also

published as *Raffles: Further Adventures of the Amateur Cracksman,* 1901
A Thief in the Night: The Last Chronicle of Raffles (short stories) 1905; also published as *A Thief in the Night: Further Adventures of A. J. Raffles, Cricketer and Cracksman,* 1905

Innes, Michael
Lament for a Maker (novel) 1938

Knox, Ronald A.
The Viaduct Murder (novel) 1925
The Three Taps: A Detective Story Without a Moral (novel) 1928

Leblanc, Maurice
Arsène Lupin, gentleman-cambrioleur (novel) 1907 [*The Extraordinary Adventures of Arsène Lupin, Gentleman-Burglar,* 1910]

Leroux, Gaston
Le mystère de la chambre jaune (novel) 1907 [*The Mystery of the Yellow Room,* 1908]
Le parfum de la dame en noir (novel) 1908 [*The Perfume of the Lady in Black,* 1909]

Lowndes, Marie Belloc
The Lodger (novel) 1913

Marsh, Ngaio
A Man Lay Dead (novel) 1934
Overture to Death (novel) 1939
Collected Short Fiction of Ngaio Marsh (short stories) 1989

McBain, Ed
Cop Hater (novel) 1956
The Con Man (novel) 1957
Let's Hear It for the Deaf Man (novel) 1973
Ice (novel) 1983
Another Part of the City (novel) 1986

McCoy, Horace
No Pockets in a Shroud (novel) 1937; revised edition, 1948
Kiss Tomorrow Good-Bye (novel) 1949

Milne, A. A.
The Red House Mystery (novel) 1922

Baroness Orczy
The Old Man in the Corner (short stories) 1909

Poe, Edgar Allan
Tales by Edgar A. Poe (short stories) 1845

Post, Melville Davisson
Uncle Abner, Master of Mysteries (short stories) 1918

Queen, Ellery (joint pseudonym of Frederic Dannay and Manfred B. Lee)
The Roman Hat Mystery (novel) 1929

Rinehart, Mary Roberts
The Circular Staircase (novel) 1908

Rohmer, Sax
The Mystery of Dr. Fu Manchu (novel) 1913; also published as *The Insidious Dr. Fu-Manchu,* 1913

Sayers, Dorothy
Whose Body? (novel) 1923
Strong Poison (novel) 1930
The Five Red Herrings (novel) 1931
Murder Must Advertise (novel) 1933
The Nine Tailors (novel) 1934
Gaudy Night (novel) 1935
Lord Peter (short stories) 1972

Simenon, Georges
Au rendez-vous des terre-neuvas (novel) 1931

[*The Sailor's Rendezvous,* published in *Maigret Keeps a Rendezvous,* 1940]

Pietr-le-Letton (novel) 1931

[*The Case of Peter the Lett,* published in *Inspector Maigret Investigates,* 1933; also published as *The Strange Case of Peter the Lett,* 1933]

L'homme qui regardait passer les trains (novel) 1938

[*The Man Who Watched the Trains Go By,* 1945]

La patience de Maigret (novel) 1939

[*The Patience of Maigret,* 1940]

Spillane, Mickey

I, the Jury (novel) 1947

My Gun Is Quick (novel) 1950

Vengeance is Mine! (novel) 1950

The Big Kill (novel) 1951

Kiss Me Deadly (novel) 1952

Stout, Rex

Fer-de-lance (novel) 1934

Symons, Julian

The Immaterial Murder Case (novel) 1945

The Thirtyfirst of February (novel) 1950

The Progress of a Crime (novel) 1960

Tey, Josephine

The Man in the Queue [as Gordon Daviot] (novel) 1929

Miss Pym Disposes (novel) 1947

Van Dine, S. S. [pseudonym of Willard Huntington Wright]

The Benson Murder Case (novel) 1926

The "Canary" Murder Case (novel) 1927

The Bishop Murder Case (novel) 1929

The Casino Murder Case (novel) 1934

The Gracie Allen Murder Case (novel) 1938; also published as *The Smell of Murder,* 1950

The Winter Murder Case (novel) 1939

Wahlöö, Per, and Sjöwall, Maj

Mannee på balkongen (novel) 1967

[*The Man on the Balcony,* 1969]

Skrattande polisen (novel) 1968

[*The Laughing Policeman,* 1970]

Wallace, Edgar

The Door with Seven Locks (novel) 1900

The Arranways Mystery (novel) 1932

The Scotland Yard Book of Edgar Wallace (novels and short stories) 1932

Waugh, Hillary

Last Seen Wearing (novel) 1952

Wells, Carolyn

The Clue (novel) 1909

A Chain of Evidence (novel) 1912

All at Sea (novel) 1927

The Omnibus Fleming Stone (novels) 1932

Murder Will In (novel) 1942

Zangwill, Israel

The Big Bow Mystery (novel) 1892

THE GENESIS AND HISTORY OF THE DETECTIVE STORY

Dorothy Leigh Sayers

[*Sayers was an English writer and critic renowned as an accomplished Dante scholar, a respected writer on Christian themes, and the creator of Lord Peter Wimsey, the sophisticated detective-hero of such acclaimed mystery novels as* Murder Must Advertise *(1933),* The Nine Tailors *(1934), and* Gaudy Night *(1935). In these novels, Sayers attempted to fuse the detective story with the novel of manners, lending literary respectability to detective fiction and pioneering new directions in that field. She is also regarded as a preeminent authority on detective and mystery fiction. In the following excerpt, Sayers discusses the early development of detective fiction, focusing on the seminal works of Edgar Allan Poe and Arthur Conan Doyle.*]

Between 1840 and 1845 the wayward genius of Edgar Allan Poe . . . produced five tales, in which the general principles of the detective-story were laid down for ever. In "The Murders in the Rue Morgue" and, with a certain repulsive facetiousness, in "Thou Art the Man" he achieved the fusion of the two distinct genres and created what we may call the story of mystery, as distinct from pure detection on the one hand and pure horror on the other. In this fused genre, the reader's blood is first curdled by some horrible and apparently inexplicable murder or portent; the machinery of detection is then brought in to solve the mystery and punish the murderer. Since Poe's time all three branches—detection, mystery, and horror—have flourished. We have such pleasant little puzzles as Conan Doyle's *Case of Identity,* in which there is nothing to shock or horrify; we have mere fantasies of blood and terror—human, as in Conan Doyle's "The Case of Lady Sannox," or supernatural, as in Marion Crawford's "The Upper Berth"; most satisfactory of all, perhaps, we have such fusions as "The Speckled Band," or "The Hammer of God," in which the ghostly terror is invoked only to be dispelled.

It is rather puzzling that the detective-story should have had to wait so long to find a serious exponent. Having started so well, why did it not develop earlier? The Oriental races, with their keen appreciation of intellectual subtlety, should surely have evolved it. The germ was there. "Why do you not come to pay your respects to me?" says Æsop's lion to the fox. "I beg your Majesty's pardon," says the fox, "but I noticed the track of the animals that have already come to you; and, while I see many hoof-marks going in, I see none coming out. Till the animals that have entered your cave come out again, I prefer to remain in the open air." Sherlock Holmes could not have reasoned more lucidly from the premises.

Cacus the robber, be it noted, was apparently the first criminal to use the device of forged footprints to mislead the pursuer, though it is a long development from his primitive methods to the horses shod with cow-shoes in Conan Doyle's "Adventure of the Priory School." Hercules's methods of investigation, too, were rather of the rough and ready sort, though the reader will not fail to observe that this early detective was accorded divine honours by his grateful clients.

The Jews, with their strongly moral preoccupation, were . . . peculiarly fitted to produce the *roman policier* ["detective story"]. The Romans, logical and given to law-making, might have been expected to do something with it, but they did not. In one of the folk-tales collected by the Grimms, twelve maidens disguised as men are set to walk across a floor strewn with peas, in the hope that their shuffling feminine tread will betray them; the maidens are, however, warned, and baffle the detectives by treading firmly. In an Indian folk-tale a similar ruse is more successful. Here a suitor is disguised as a woman, and has to be picked out from the women about him by the wise princess. The princess throws a lemon to each in turn, and the disguised man is detected by his instinctive action in clapping his knees together to catch the lemon, whereas the real women spread their knees to catch it in their skirts. Coming down to later European literature, we find the "Bel-and-the-Dragon" motif of the ashes spread on the floor reproduced in the story of Tristan. Here the king's spy spreads flour between Tristan's bed and that of Iseult; Tristan defeats the scheme by leaping from one bed to the other. The eighteenth century also contributed at least one outstanding example, in the famous detective chapter of Voltaire's *Zadig*.

It may be, as Mr. E. M. Wrong has suggested in a brilliant little study [in *Tales of Crime and Detection* (1924)], that throughout this early period "a faulty law of evidence was to blame, for detectives cannot flourish until the public has an idea of what constitutes proof, and while a common criminal procedure is arrest, torture, confession, and death." One may go further, and say that, though crime stories might, and did, flourish, the detective-story proper could not do so until public sympathy had veered round to the side of law and order. It will be noticed that, on the whole, the tendency in early crime-literature is to admire the cunning and astuteness of the criminal. This must be so while the law is arbitrary, oppressive, and brutally administered.

We may note that . . . the full blossoming of the detective-stories is found among the Anglo-Saxon races. It is notorious that an English crowd tends to side with the policeman in a row. The British legal code, with its tradition of "sportsmanship" and "fair play for the criminal" is particularly favourable to the production of detective fiction, allowing, as it does, sufficient rope to the quarry to provide a ding-dong chase, rich in up-and-down incident. In France, also, though the street policeman is less honoured than in England, the detective-force is admirably organised and greatly looked up to. France has a good output of detective-stories, though considerably smaller than that of the English-speaking races. In the Southern States of Europe the law is less loved and the detective story less frequent. We may not unreasonably trace a connection here.

Some further light is thrown on the question by a remark made by Herr Lion Feuchtwanger when broadcasting during his visit to London in 1927. Contrasting the tastes of the English, French, and German publics, he noted the great attention paid by the Englishman to the external details of men and things. The Englishman likes material exactness in the books he reads; the German and the Frenchman, in different degrees, care little for it in comparison with psychological truth. It is hardly surprising, then, that the detective-story, with its insistence on footprints,

bloodstains, dates, times, and places, and its reduction of character-drawing to bold, flat outline, should appeal far more strongly to Anglo-Saxon taste than to that of France or Germany.

Taking these two factors together, we begin to see why the detective-story had to wait for its full development for the establishment of an effective police organisation in the Anglo-Saxon countries. This was achieved—in England, at any rate—during the early part of the nineteenth century, and was followed about the middle of that century by the first outstanding examples of the detective-story as we know it to-day.

To this argument we may add another. In the nineteenth century the vast, unexplored limits of the world began to shrink at an amazing and unprecedented rate. The electric telegraph circled the globe; railways brought remote villages into touch with civilisation; photographs made known to the stay-at-homes the marvels of foreign landscapes, customs, and animals; science reduced seeming miracles to mechanical marvels; popular education and improved policing made town and country safer for the common man than they had ever been. In place of the adventurer and the knight errant, popular imagination hailed the doctor, the scientist, and the policeman as saviours and protectors. But if one could no longer hunt the manticora, one could still hunt the murderer; if the armed escort had grown less necessary, yet one still needed the analyst to frustrate the wiles of the poisoner; from this point of view, the detective steps into his right place as the protector of the weak—the latest of the popular heroes, the true successor of Roland and Lancelot.

Before tracing further the history of detective fiction, let us look a little more closely at those five tales of Poe's, in which so much of the future development is anticipated. Probably the first thing that strikes us is that Poe has struck out at a blow the formal outline on which a large section of detective fiction has been built up. In the three Dupin stories . . . we have the formula of the eccentric and brilliant private detective whose doings are chronicled by an admiring and thickheaded friend. From Dupin and his unnamed chronicler springs a long and distinguished line: Sherlock Holmes and his Watson; Martin Hewitt and his Brett; Raffles and his Bunny (on the criminal side of the business, but of the same breed); Thorndyke and his various Jardines, Ansteys, and Jervises; Hanaud and his Mr. Ricardo; Poirot and his Captain Hastings; Philo Vance and his Van Dine. It is not surprising that this formula should have been used so largely, for it is obviously a very convenient one for the writer. For one thing, the admiring satellite may utter expressions of eulogy which would be unbecoming in the mouth of the author, gaping at his own colossal intellect. Again, the reader, even if he is not, in R. L. Stevenson's phrase, "always a man of such vastly greater ingenuity than the writer," is usually a little more ingenious than Watson. He sees a little further through the brick wall; he pierces, to some extent, the cloud of mystification with which the detective envelops himself. "Aha!" he says to himself, "the average reader is supposed to see no further than Watson. But the author has not reckoned with me. I am one too many for him." He is deluded. It is all a device of the writer's for flattering him and putting him on good terms with himself. For though the reader likes to be mystified, he also likes to say,

"I told you so," and "I spotted that." And this leads us to the third great advantage of the Holmes-Watson convention: by describing the clues as presented to the dim eyes and bemused mind of Watson, the author is enabled to preserve a spurious appearance of frankness, while keeping to himself the special knowledge on which the interpretation of those clues depends. This is a question of paramount importance, involving the whole artistic ethic of the detective-story. We shall return to it later. For the moment, let us consider a few other interesting types and formulæ which make their first appearance in Poe.

The personality of Dupin is eccentric, and for several literary generations eccentricity was highly fashionable among detective heroes. Dupin, we are informed, had a habit of living behind closed shutters, illumined by "a couple of tapers which, strongly perfumed, threw out only the ghastliest and feeblest of rays." From this stronghold he issued by night, to promenade the streets and enjoy the "infinity of mental excitement" afforded by quiet observation. He was also given to startling his friends by analysing their thought-processes, and he had a rooted contempt for the methods of the police.

Sherlock Holmes modelled himself to a large extent upon Dupin, substituting cocaine for candlelight, with accompaniments of shag and fiddle-playing. He is a more human and endearing figure than Dupin, and has earned as his reward the supreme honour which literature has to bestow—the secular equivalent of canonisation. He has passed into the language. He also started a tradition of his own—the hawk-faced tradition, which for many years dominated detective fiction.

So strong, indeed, was this domination that subsequent notable eccentrics have displayed their eccentricities chiefly by escaping from it. "Nothing," we are told, "could have been less like the traditional detective than"—so-and-so. He may be elderly and decrepit, like Baroness Orczy's Old Man in the Corner, whose characteristic habit is the continual knotting of string. Or he may be round and innocent-looking, like Father Brown or Poirot. There is Sax Rohmer's Moris Klaw, with his bald, scholarly forehead; he irrigates his wits with a verbena spray, and carries about with him an "odically-sterilised" cushion to promote psychic intuition. There is the great Dr. Thorndyke, probably the handsomest detective in fiction; he is outwardly bonhomous, but spiritually detached, and his emblem is the green research-case, filled with miniature microscopes and scientific implements. Max Carrados has the distinction of being blind; Old Ebbie wears a rabbit-skin waistcoat; Lord Peter Wimsey (if I may refer to him without immodesty) indulges in the buying of incunabula and has a pretty taste in wines and haberdashery. By a final twist of the tradition, which brings the wheel full circle, there is a strong modern tendency to produce detectives remarkable for their ordinariness; they may be well-bred walking gentlemen, like A. A. Milne's Anthony Gillingham, or journalists, like Gaston Leroux's Rouletabille, or they may even be policemen, like Freeman Wills Crofts' Inspector French, or the heroes of Mr. A. J. Rees's sound and well-planned stories.

There have also been a few women detectives, but on the whole, they have not been very successful. In order to justify their choice of sex, they are obliged to be so irritatingly intuitive as to destroy that quiet enjoyment of the logical which we look for in our detective reading. Or else they are active and courageous, and insist on walking into physical danger and hampering the men engaged on the job. Marriage, also, looms too large in their view of life; which is not surprising, for they are all young and beautiful. Why these charming creatures should be able to tackle abstruse problems at the age of twenty-one or thereabouts, while the male detectives are usually content to wait till their thirties or forties before setting up as experts, it is hard to say. Where do they pick up their worldly knowledge? Not from personal experience, for they are always immaculate as the driven snow. Presumably it is all intuition.

Better use has been made of women in books where the detecting is strictly amateur—done, that is, by members of the family or house-party themselves, and not by a private consultant. Evelyn Humblethorne [featured in Lord Gorell's *In the Night*] is a detective of this kind, and so is Joan Cowper, in *The Brooklyn Murders* [by G. D. H. Cole and M. Cole]. But the really brilliant woman detective has yet to be created. [Sayers adds in a footnote that "Wilkie Collins—who was curiously fascinated by the 'strong-minded' woman—made two attempts at the woman detective in *No Name* and *The Law and the Lady*. The spirit of the time was, however, too powerful to allow these attempts to be altogether successful."]

While on this subject, we must not forget the curious and interesting development of detective fiction which has produced the *Adventures of Sexton Blake,* and other allied cycles. This is the Holmes tradition, adapted for the reading of the board-school boy and crossed with the Buffalo Bill adventure type. The books are written by a syndicate of authors, each one of whom uses a set of characters of his own invention, grouped about a central and traditional group consisting of Sexton Blake and his boy assistant, Tinker, their comic landlady Mrs. Bardell, and their bull-dog Pedro. As might be expected, the quality of the writing and the detective methods employed vary considerably from one author to another. The best specimens display extreme ingenuity, and an immense vigour and fertility in plot and incident. Nevertheless, the central types are pretty consistently preserved throughout the series. Blake and Tinker are less intuitive than Holmes, from whom however, they are directly descended, as their address in Baker Street shows. They are more careless and reckless in their methods; more given to displays of personal heroism and pugilism; more simple and human in their emotions. The really interesting point about them is that they present the nearest modern approach to a national folk-lore, conceived as the centre for a cycle of loosely connected romances in the Arthurian manner. Their significance in popular literature and education would richly repay scientific investigation.

As regards plot also, Poe laid down a number of sound keels for the use of later adventurers. Putting aside his instructive excursion into the psychology of detection—instructive, because we can trace their influence in so many of Poe's successors down to the present day—putting these aside, and discounting that atmosphere of creepiness which Poe so successfully diffused about nearly all he wrote, we shall probably find that to us, sophisticated and trained on an intensive study of detective fiction, his plots are thin to transparency. But in Poe's day they represented a new technique. As a matter of fact, it is doubtful whether there are more than half a dozen deceptions in the mystery-monger's bag of tricks, and we shall find that Poe has got most of them, at any rate in embryo.

Take, first, the three Dupin stories. In "The Murders in the Rue Morgue," an old woman and her daughter are found horribly murdered in an (apparently) hermetically sealed room. An innocent person is arrested by the police. Dupin proves that the police have failed to discover one mode of entrance to the room, and deduces from a number of observations that the "murder" was committed by a huge ape. Here is, then, a combination of three typical motifs: the wrongly suspected man, to whom all the superficial evidence (motive, access, etc.) points; the hermetically sealed death-chamber (still a favourite central theme); finally, the *solution by the unexpected means.* In addition, we have Dupin drawing deductions, which the police have overlooked, from the evidence of witnesses (superiority in inference), and discovering clues which the police have not thought of looking for owing to obsession by an *idée fixe* (superiority in observation based on inference). In this story also are enunciated for the first time those two great aphorisms of detective science: first, that when you have eliminated all the impossibilities, then, whatever remains, *however improbable,* must be the truth; and, secondly, that the more *outré* a case may appear, the easier it is to solve. Indeed, take it all round, "The Murders in the Rue Morgue" constitutes in itself almost a complete manual of detective theory and practice.

"The Father of the Detective Story"—Edgar Allan Poe.

In "The Purloined Letter," we have one of those stolen documents on whose recovery hangs the peace of mind of a distinguished personage. It is not, indeed, one of the sort whose publication would spread consternation among the Chancelleries of Europe, but it is important enough. The police suspect a certain minister of taking it. They ransack every corner of his house, in vain. Dupin, arguing from his knowledge of the minister's character, decides that subtlety must be met by subtlety. He calls on the minister and discovers the letter, turned inside out and stuck in a letter-rack in full view of the casual observer.

Here we have, besides the reiteration, in inverted form, of aphorism No. 2 (above), the method of *psychological deduction* and the solution by the formula of the *most obvious place.* This trick is the forerunner of the diamond concealed in the tumbler of water, the man murdered in the midst of a battle, Chesterton's "Invisible Man" (the postman, so familiar a figure that his presence goes unnoticed), and a whole line of similar ingenuities.

The third Dupin story, "The Mystery of Marie Rogêt," has fewer imitators, but is the most interesting of all to the connoisseur. It consists entirely of a series of newspaper cuttings relative to the disappearance and murder of a shopgirl, with Dupin's comments thereon. The story contains no solution of the problem, and, indeed, no formal ending—and that for a very good reason. The disappearance was a genuine one, its actual heroine being one Mary Cecilia Rogers, and the actual place New York. The newspaper cuttings, were also, *mutatis mutandis,* genuine. The paper which published Poe's article dared not publish his conclusion. Later on it was claimed that his argument was, in substance, correct; and though this claim has, I believe, been challenged of late years, Poe may, nevertheless, be ranked among the small band of mystery-writers who have put their skill in deduction to the acid test of a problem which they had not in the first place invented.

Of the other Poe stories, one, "Thou Art the Man," is very slight in theme and unpleasantly flippant in treatment. A man is murdered; a hearty person, named, with guileless cunning, Goodfellow, is very energetic in fixing the crime on a certain person. The narrator of the story makes a repulsive kind of jack-in-the-box out of the victim's corpse, and extorts a confession of guilt from—Goodfellow! Of course. Nevertheless, we have here two more leading motifs that have done overtime since Poe's day: the trail of false clues laid by the real murderer, and the *solution by way of the most unlikely person.*

The fifth story is "The Gold Bug." In this a man finds a cipher which leads him to the discovery of a hidden treasure. The cipher is of the very simple one-sign-one-letter type, and its solution, of the mark-where-the-shadow-falls-take-three-paces-to-the-east-and-dig variety. In technique this story is the exact opposite of "Marie Rogêt"; the narrator is astonished by the antics of his detective friend, and is kept in entire ignorance of what he is about until *after* the discovery of the treasure; only then is the cipher for the first time either mentioned or explained. Some people think that "The Gold Bug" is Poe's finest mystery-story.

Now, with "The Gold Bug" at the one extreme and "Marie Rogêt" at the other, and the other three stories occupying intermediate places, Poe stands at the parting of the ways for detective fiction. From him go the two great lines of development—the Romantic and the Classic, or, to use terms less abraded by ill-usage, the purely Sensational and the purely Intellectual. In the former, thrill is piled on thrill and mystification on mystification; the reader is led on from bewilderment to bewilderment, till everything is explained in a lump in the last chapter. This school is strong in dramatic incident and atmosphere; its weakness is a tendency to confusion and a dropping of links— its explanations do not always explain; it is never dull, but it is sometimes nonsense. In the other—the purely Intellectual type—the action mostly takes place in the first chapter or so; the detective then follows up quietly from clue to clue till the problem is solved, the reader accompanying the great man in his search and being allowed to try his own teeth on the material provided. The strength of this school is its analytical ingenuity; its weakness is its liability to dullness and pomposity, its mouthing over the infinitely little, and its lack of movement and emotion.

The purely Sensational thriller is not particularly rare— we may find plenty of examples in the work of William Le Queux, Edgar Wallace, and others. The purely Intellectual is rare indeed; few writers have consistently followed the "Marie Rogêt" formula of simply spreading the *whole* evidence before the reader and leaving him to deduce the detective's conclusion from it if he can.

M. P. Shiel, indeed, did so in his trilogy, *Prince Zaleski*, whose curious and elaborate beauty recaptures in every arabesque sentence the very accent of Edgar Allan Poe. Prince Zaleski, "victim of a too importunate, too unfortunate Love, which the fulgor of the throne itself could not abash," sits apart in his ruined tower in "the semi-darkness of the very faint greenish lustre radiated from an open censer-like *lampas* in the centre of the domed encausted roof," surrounded by Flemish sepulchral brasses, runic tablets, miniature paintings, winged bulls, Tamil scriptures on lacquered leaves of the talipot, mediæval reliquaries richly gemmed, Brahmin gods, and Egyptian mummies, and lulled by "the low, liquid tinkling of an invisible musical-box." Like Sherlock Holmes, he indulges in a drug—"the narcotic *cannabis sativa:* the base of the *bhang* of the Mohammedans." A friend brings to him the detective problems of the outside world, which he proceeds to solve from the data given and (except in the final story) without stirring from his couch. He adorns his solutions with philosophical discourses on the social progress of mankind, all delivered with the same melancholy grace and remote intellectual disdain. The reasoning is subtle and lucid, but the crimes themselves are fantastic and incredible—a fault which these tales have in common with those of G. K. Chesterton.

Another writer who uses the "Marie Rogêt" formula is Baroness Orczy. Her Old Man in the Corner series is constructed precisely on those lines, and I have seen a French edition in which, when the expository part of the story is done, the reader is exhorted to: "Pause a moment and see if you can arrive at the explanation yourself, before you read the Old Man's solution." This pure puzzle is a formula which obviously has its limitations. Nearest to this among modern writers comes Freeman Wills Crofts, whose painstaking sleuths always "play fair" and display their clues to the reader as soon as they have picked them up. The intellectually minded reader can hardly demand

more than this. The aim of the writer of this type of detective-story is to make the reader say at the end, neither: "Oh well, I knew it must be that all along," nor yet: "Dash it all! I couldn't be expected to guess that"; but: "Oh, of course! What a fool I was not to see it! Right under my nose all the time!" Precious tribute! How often striven for! How rarely earned!

On the whole, however, the tendency is for the modern educated public to demand fair play from the writer, and for the Sensational and Intellectual branches of the story to move further apart.

Before going further with this important question, we must look back once more to the middle of the last century, and see what development took place to bridge the gap between Dupin and Sherlock Holmes.

Poe, like a restless child, played with his new toy for a little while, and then, for some reason, wearied of it. He turned his attention to other things, and his formula lay neglected for close on forty years. Meanwhile a somewhat different type of detective-story was developing independently in Europe. In 1848 the elder Dumas, always ready to try his hand at any novel and ingenious thing, suddenly inserted into the romantic body of the *Vicomte de Bragelonne* a passage of pure scientific deduction. This passage is quite unlike anything else in the Musketeer cycle, and looks like the direct outcome of Dumas' keen interest in actual crime.

But there is another literary influence which, though the fact is not generally recognised, must have been powerfully exerted at this date upon writers of mystery fiction. Between 1820 and 1850 the novels of Fenimore Cooper began to enjoy their huge popularity, and were not only widely read in America and England, but translated into most European languages. In *The Pathfinder, The Deerslayer, The Last of the Mohicans,* and the rest of the series, Cooper revealed to the delighted youth of two hemispheres the Red Indian's patient skill in tracking his quarry by footprints, in interrogating a broken twig, a mossy trunk, a fallen leaf. The imagination of childhood was fired; every boy wanted to be an Uncas or a Chingachgook. Novelists, not content with following and imitating Cooper on his own ground, discovered a better way, by transferring the romance of the woodland tracker to the surroundings of their native country. In the 'sixties the generation who had read Fenimore Cooper in boyhood turned, as novelists and readers, to tracing the spoor of the criminal upon their own native heath. The enthusiasm for Cooper combined magnificently with that absorbing interest in crime and detection which better methods of communication and an improved police system had made possible. While, in France, Gaboriau and Fortuné du Boisgobey concentrated upon the police novel pure and simple, English writers, still permeated by the terror and mystery of the romantic movement, and influenced by the "Newgate novel" of Bulwer and Ainsworth, perfected a more varied and imaginative genre, in which the ingenuity of the detective problem allied itself with the sombre terrors of the weird and supernatural.

Of the host of writers who attempted this form of fiction in the 'sixties and 'seventies, three may be picked out for special mention.

That voluminous writer, Mrs. Henry Wood, represents,

on the whole, the melodramatic and adventurous development of the crime-story as distinct from the detective problem proper. Through *East Lynne,* crude and sentimental as it is, she exercised an enormous influence on the rank and file of sensational novelists, and at her best, she is a most admirable spinner of plots. Whether her problem concerns a missing will, a vanished heir, a murder, or a family curse, the story spins along without flagging, and, though she is a little too fond of calling in Providence to cut the knot of intrigue with the sword of coincidence, the mystery is fully and properly unravelled, in a workmanlike manner and without any loose ends. She makes frequent use of supernatural thrills. Sometimes these are explained away: a "murdered" person is seen haunting the local churchyard, and turns out never to have been killed at all. Sometimes the supernatural remains supernatural, as, for instance, the coffin-shaped appearance in *The Shadow of Ashlydyat.* Her morality is perhaps a little oppressive, but she is by no means without humour, and at times can produce a shrewd piece of characterisation.

Melodramatic, but a writer of real literary attainment, and gifted with a sombre power which has seldom been equalled in painting the ghastly and the macabre, is Sheridan Le Fanu. Like Poe, he has the gift of investing the most mechanical of plots with an atmosphere of almost unbearable horror. (pp. 9-22)

In [*Wylder's Hand,* by Le Fanu] the detection is done by private persons, and the local police are only brought in at the end to secure the criminal. This is also the case in that extremely interesting book *Checkmate* (1870), in which the plot actually turns upon the complete alteration of the criminal's appearance by a miracle of plastic surgery. It seems amazing that more use has not been made of this device in post-war days, now that the reconstruction of faces has become comparatively common and, with the perfecting of aseptic surgery, infinitely easier than in Le Fanu's day. I can only call to mind two recent examples of this kind: one, Mr. Hopkins Moorhouse's *Gauntlet of Alceste;* the other, a short story called "The Losing of Jasper Virel," by Beckles Willson. In both stories the alterations include the tattooing of the criminal's eyes from blue to brown.

For sheer grimness and power, there is little in the literature of horror to compare with the trepanning scene in Le Fanu's *The House by the Churchyard.* Nobody who has ever read it could possibly forget that sick chamber, with the stricken man sunk in his deathly stupor; the terrified wife; the local doctor, kindly and absurd—and then the pealing of the bell, and the entry of the brilliant, brutal Dillon "in dingy splendours and a great draggled wig, with a gold-headed cane in his bony hand . . . diffusing a reek of whisky-punch, and with a case of instruments under his arm," to perform the operation. The whole scene is magnificently written, with the surgeon's muttered technicalities heard through the door, the footsteps—then the silence while the trepanning is proceeding, and the wounded Sturk's voice, which no one ever thought to hear again, raised as if from the grave to denounce his murderer. That chapter in itself would entitle Le Fanu to be called a master of mystery and horror.

Most important of all during this period we have Wilkie Collins. An extremely uneven writer, Collins is less appreciated to-day than his merits and influence deserve. He

will not bear comparison with Le Fanu in his treatment of the weird, though he was earnestly ambitious to succeed in this line. His style was too dry and inelastic, his mind too legal. Consider the famous dream in *Armadale,* divided into seventeen separate sections, each elaborately and successively fulfilled in laborious detail! In the curious semi-supernatural rhythm of *The Woman in White* he came nearer to genuine achievement, but, on the whole, his eeriness is wiredrawn and unconvincing. But he greatly excels Le Fanu in humour, in the cunning of his rogues in character-drawing, and especially in the architecture of his plots. [Sayers adds in a footnote that "Collins made peculiarly his own the art of plot and counter-plot. Thus we have the magnificent duels of Marion Halcombe and Count Fosco in *The Woman in White;* Captain Wragge and Mrs. Lecount in *No Name;* the Pedgifts and Miss Gwilt in *Armadale.* Move answers to move as though on a chessboard (but very much more briskly), until the villain is manœuvred into the corner where a cunningly contrived legal checkmate has been quietly awaiting him from the beginning of the game."] Taking everything into consideration, *The Moonstone* is probably the very finest detective story ever written. By comparison with its wide scope, its dovetailed completeness and the marvellous variety and soundness of its characterisation, modern mystery fiction looks thin and mechanical. Nothing human is perfect, but *The Moonstone* comes about as near perfection as anything of its kind can be.

In *The Moonstone* Collins used the convention of telling the story in a series of narratives from the pens of the various actors concerned. Modern realism—often too closely wedded to externals—is prejudiced against this device. It is true that, for example, Betteredge's narrative is not at all the kind of thing that a butler would be likely to write; nevertheless, it has an ideal truth—it is the kind of thing that Betteredge might think and feel, even if he could not write it. And, granted this convention of the various narratives, how admirably the characters are drawn! The pathetic figure of Rosanna Spearman, with her deformity and her warped devotion, is beautifully handled, with a freedom from sentimentality which is very remarkable. In Rachel Verinder, Collins has achieved one of the novelist's hardest tasks; he has depicted a girl who is virtuous, a gentlewoman, and really interesting, and that without the slightest exaggeration or deviation from naturalness and probability. From his preface to the book it is clear that he took especial pains with this character, and his success was so great as almost to defeat itself. Rachel is so little spectacular that we fail to realise what a singularly fine and truthful piece of work she is.

The detective part of the story is well worth attention. The figure of Sergeant Cuff is drawn with a restraint and sobriety which makes him seem a little colourless beside Holmes and Thorndyke and Carrados, but he is a very living figure. One can believe that he made a success of his rose-growing when he retired; he genuinely loved roses, whereas one can never feel that the great Sherlock possessed quite the right feeling for his bees. Being an official detective, Sergeant Cuff is bound by the etiquette of his calling. He is never really given a free hand with Rachel, and the conclusion he comes to is a wrong one. But he puts in a good piece of detective work in the matter of Rosanna and the stained nightgown; and the scenes in which his shrewdness and knowledge of human nature are contrasted with the blundering stupidity of Superintendent Seagrave read like an essay in the manner of Poe.

It is, of course, a fact that the Dupin stories had been published fifteen years or so when *The Moonstone* appeared. But there is no need to seek in them for the original of Sergeant Cuff. He had his prototype in real life, and the whole nightgown incident was modelled, with some modifications, upon a famous case of the early 'sixties—the murder of little William Kent by his sixteen-year-old sister, Constance. Those who are interested in origins will find an excellent account of the "Road murder," as it is called, in Miss Tennyson Jesse's *Murder and Its Motives,* or in Atkey's *Famous Trials of the Nineteenth Century,* and may compare the methods of Sergeant Cuff with those of the real Detective Whicher.

Wilkie Collins himself claimed that nearly all his plots were founded on fact; indeed, this was his invariable answer when the charge of improbability was preferred against him.

> "I wish," he cries angrily to a friend, "before people make such assertions, they would think what they are writing or talking about. I know of very few instances in which fiction exceeds the probability of reality. I'll tell you where I got many of my plots from. I was in Paris, wandering about the streets with Charles Dickens, amusing ourselves by looking into the shops. We came to an old book stall—half-shop and half-store—and I found some dilapidated volumes and records of French crime—a sort of French Newgate Calendar. I said to Dickens 'Here is a prize!' So it turned out to be. In them I found some of my best plots." [Wybert Reeve, "Recollections of Wilkie Collins," *Chambers Journal* Vol. IX]

Not that Collins was altogether disingenuous in his claim never to have o'erstepped the modesty of nature. While each one of his astonishing contrivances and coincidences might, taken separately, find its parallel in real life, it remains true that in cramming a whole series of such improbabilities into the course of a single story he does frequently end by staggering all belief. But even so, he was a master craftsman, whom many modern mystery-mongers might imitate to their profit. He never wastes an incident; he never leaves a loose end; no incident, however trivial on the one hand or sensational on the other, is ever introduced for the mere sake of amusement or sensation. Take, for example, the great "sensation-scene" in *No Name,* where for half an hour Magdalen sits, with the bottle of laudanum in her hand, counting the passing ships. "If, in that time, an even number passed her—the sign given should be a sign to live. If the uneven number prevailed, the end should be—death." Here, you would say, is pure sensationalism; it is a situation invented deliberately to wring tears and anguish from the heart of the reader. But you would be wrong. That bottle of laudanum is brought in because it will be wanted again, later on. In the next section of the story it is found in Magdalen's dressing-case, and this discovery, by leading her husband to suppose that she means to murder him, finally induces him to cut her out of his will, and so becomes one of the most important factors in the plot.

In *The Moonstone,* which of all his books comes nearest to being a detective-story in the modern sense, Collins uses with great effect the formula of the most unlikely person

and the unexpected means in conjunction. Opium is the means in this case—a drug with whose effects we are tolerably familiar to-day, but which in Collins's time was still something of an unknown quantity, de Quincey notwithstanding. In the opium of *The Moonstone* and the plastic surgery of *Checkmate* we have the distinguished forebears of a long succession of medical and scientific mysteries which stretches down to the present day.

During the 'seventies and early 'eighties the long novel of marvel and mystery held the field, slowly unrolling its labyrinthine complexity through its three ample volumes crammed with incident and leisurely drawn characters. [In a footnote, Sayers also cites "the stories of Anna Katherine Green, of which the long series begins with *The Leavenworth Case* in 1883, and extends right down to the present day. They are genuine detective-stories, often of considerable ingenuity, but marred by an uncritical sentimentality of style and treatment which makes them difficult reading for the modern student. They are, however, important by their volume and by their influence on other American writers."]

In 1887 *A Study in Scarlet* was flung like a bombshell into the field of detective fiction, to be followed within a few short and brilliant years by the marvellous series of Sherlock Holmes short stories. The effect was electric. Conan Doyle took up the Poe formula and galvanised it into life and popularity. He cut out the elaborate psychological introductions, or restated them in crisp dialogue. He brought into prominence what Poe had only lightly touched upon—the deduction of staggering conclusions from trifling indications in the Dumas-Cooper-Gaboriau manner. He was sparkling, surprising, and short. It was the triumph of the epigram.

A comparison of the Sherlock Holmes tales with the Dupin tales shows clearly how much Doyle owed to Poe, and, at the same time, how greatly he modified Poe's style and formula. Read, for instance, the opening pages of "The Murders in the Rue Morgue," which introduce Dupin, and compare them with the first chapter of *A Study in Scarlet.* Or merely set side by side the two passages which follow and contrast the relations between Dupin and his chronicler on the one hand, and between Holmes and Watson on the other:

> I was astonished, too, at the vast extent of his reading; and, above all, I felt my soul enkindled within me by the wild fervour, and the vivid freshness of his imagination. Seeking in Paris the objects I then sought, I felt that the society of such a man would be to me a treasure beyond price; and this feeling I frankly confided to him. It was at length arranged that we should live together . . . and as my worldly circumstances were somewhat less embarrassed than his own, I was permitted to be at the expense of renting, and furnishing in a style which suited the rather fantastic gloom of our common temper, a time-eaten and grotesque mansion . . . in a retired and desolate portion of the Faubourg Saint Germain . . . It was a freak of fancy in my friend (for what else shall I call it?) to be enamoured of the Night for her own sake; and into this *bizarrerie,* as into all his others, I quietly fell, giving myself up to his wild whims with a perfect abandon. ["The Murders in the Rue Morgue"]

> An anomaly which often struck me in the character

of my friend Sherlock Holmes was that, though in his methods of thought he was the neatest and most methodical of mankind, and although also he affected a certain quiet primness of dress, he was none the less in his personal habits one of the most untidy men that ever drove a fellow-lodger to distraction. Not that I am in the least conventional in that respect myself. The rough-and-tumble work in Afghanistan, coming on the top of a natural Bohemianism of disposition, has made me rather more lax than befits a medical man. But with me there is a limit, and when I find a man who keeps his cigars in the coal-scuttle, his tobacco in the toe-end of a Persian slipper, and his unanswered correspondence transfixed by a jack-knife into the very centre of his wooden mantelpiece, then I begin to give myself virtuous airs. I have always held, too, that pistol-practice should distinctly be an open-air pastime; and when Holmes in one of his queer humours would sit in an arm-chair, with his hair-trigger and a hundred Boxer cartridges, and proceed to adorn the opposite wall with a patriotic V.R. done in bullet-pocks, I felt strongly that neither the atmosphere nor the appearance of our room was improved by it. ["The Musgrave Ritual"]

See how the sturdy independence of Watson adds salt and savour to the eccentricities of Holmes, and how flavourless beside it is the hero-worshipping self-abnegation of Dupin's friend. See, too, how the concrete details of daily life in Baker Street lift the story out of the fantastic and give it a solid reality. The Baker Street ménage has just that touch of humorous commonplace which appeals to British readers.

Another pair of parallel passages will be found in "The Purloined Letter" and "The Naval Treaty." They show the two detectives in dramatic mood, surprising their friends by their solution of the mystery. In "The Adventure of the Priory School," also, a similar situation occurs, though Holmes is here shown in a grimmer vein, rebuking wickedness in high places.

Compare, also, the conversational styles of Holmes and Dupin, and the reasons for Holmes's popularity become clearer than ever. Holmes has enriched English literature with more than one memorable aphorism and turn of speech.

"You know my methods, Watson."

"A long shot, Watson—a very long shot."

"—a little monograph on the hundred-and-fourteen varieties of tobacco-ash."

"These are deep waters, Watson."

"Excellent!" cried Mr. Acton.—"But very superficial," said Holmes.

"Excellent!" I cried.—"Elementary," said he.

"It is of the highest importance in the art of detection to be able to recognise out of a number of facts which are incidental and which vital."

"You mentioned your name as if I should recognise it, but beyond the obvious facts that you are a bachelor, a solicitor, a Freemason and an asthmatic, I know nothing whatever about you."

"Every problem becomes very childish when once it is explained to you."

Nor must we forget that delightful form of riposto which Father Ronald Knox has wittily christened the "Sherlock-ismus":

"I would call your attention to the curious incident of the dog in the night-time."

"The dog did nothing in the night-time."

"That was the curious incident."

So, with Sherlock Holmes, the ball—the original nucleus deposited by Edgar Allan Poe nearly forty years earlier—was at last set rolling. As it went, it swelled into a vast mass—it set off others—it became a spate—a torrent—an avalanche of mystery fiction. It is impossible to keep track of all the detective-stories produced to-day. Book upon book, magazine upon magazine pour out from the Press, crammed with murders, thefts, arsons, frauds, conspiracies, problems, puzzles, mysteries, thrills, maniacs, crooks, prisoners, forgers, garrotters, police, spies, secret-service men, detectives, until it seems that half the world must be engaged in setting riddles for the other half to solve. (pp. 24-31)

> *Dorothy L. Sayers, in an introduction to* The Omnibus of Crime, *edited by Dorothy L. Sayers, Payson and Clarke Ltd., 1929, pp. 9-46.*

Jacques Barzun

[*Barzun is a French-born American man of letters who has produced distinguished works in several fields, including history, culture, musicology, literary criticism, and biography. His contributions to these various disciplines are contained in such modern classics of scholarship and critical insight as* Darwin, Marx, Wagner *(1941),* Berlioz and the Romantic Century *(1950),* The House of the Intellect *(1950), and* A Stroll with William James *(1983). Barzun's literary style has been praised as elegant and unpretentious. In the following excerpt, Barzun outlines the history of detective fiction and suggests that the strict conventions of the genre limited its possibilities for development.*]

Perhaps it is not obvious to all that we moderns have in our time witnessed the greatness and fall of a genre—the detective story. Yet it is the unfortunate truth. The end has come; the genre is extinct though some noble practitioners live on. As I believe its history may entertain the curious and suggest ideas to the critical, I may be forgiven for retracing its course with the eye of a mourning lover. But my reader may be surprised at hearing a type of work called defunct when he keeps finding stacks of fresh specimens on the newsstands: he must remember that a genre dies long before it disappears. For example, English poets used the couplet past Blake's and into Wordsworth's day, and Byron's *English Bards* did not, in 1810, seem as yet a pastiche. As for French tragedy it had to be repeatedly killed—by Stendhal, Hugo, Dumas, Vigny, Musset—before it finally went off the stage.

I am also encouraged to discuss the detective story by the recollection of several studies of it written by critics and poets during its latter days. These writings were generally painstaking and as serious as one could wish, but almost all were trying to account for a queer addiction that the author did not seem to share. Or if he did, he explained too much, by confessing out of his inner life the secret of modern man's appetite for mystery and the chase. The trouble with this is that detection and mystery are not the same, so that all the psychologizing based on the notions of bloodguilt, vicarious killing, sadism, and the like is profundity misplaced. Paradox though it is, comparatively few people seem to know a detective story when they see one, and it follows inevitably that theories of the genre resting on a confused classification must break down.

A detective story, as the name ought to imply, is a tale the chief interest of which lies in the palpable process of detection. This excludes at once those fictions in which the chief interest consists in the complications of crime or the rousing of horror and mystery by whatever means. When Mr. T. S. Eliot calls Wilkie Collins' *Moonstone* "the first, the longest, and the best of detective novels," he permits himself a *mélange des genres* which elsewhere he would firmly reprove. *The Moonstone* is an admirable work, "there is a place for it," but the detection in it is negligible. Even supposing it to be a sort of detective novel, it would not be the first or the best; which leaves the possibility that the critic is right in calling it the longest of some genre not specified.

To be sure, framing definitions is free to everyone and you may give the name of detective story to any tale that presents a secret, a pursuit, and the unmasking of villains or avengers. All are certainly "detected" at the end. But this commits you to including in this class—among others—*Ivanhoe* (because of the mystery of the Black Knight) and *The Three Musketeers* (because of Milady). Many another novel sustains interest by withholding information about identity, and there is a sense in which every novel resolves itself into a game of cops and robbers. The end discloses which side triumphs, or in whom goodness, virtue, and truth have ultimately been detected. ["At least this used to be a principle of suspense," the critic adds in a footnote, "now limited (it seems) to the so-called novels of suspense, as if to show that the rest are predictable in every respect."]

Similarly, the presence of crime or of a character called the detective is no sign or necessary feature of the genuine detective story. One of the finest examples of the true genre, Mr. Dermot Morrah's *Mummy Case Mystery,* has neither. And it would be an abuse of language to call *Hamlet* and *Jane Eyre,* for all their mystery, detective stories. Again, *Macbeth* and *The Brothers Karamazov* deal with crime, but they do not belong to the class; and there are unforgettable detectives in *Bleak House* and *Les misérables,* but they detect outside the novel. Finally, the "tough" tale created by Dashiell Hammett and Raymond Chandler, like the real crime narratives of Edmund Pearson and William Roughhead, have little or no connection with the pure form. All are agreeable works, but none fulfills the precise conditions of the genre.

At this point the reader may think, with some resentment, that he grasps the pedantic reason for all these exclusions. "What you want is one of those mechanical puzzles, in which no literate man can take an interest—a Whodunit, put together solely for the sake of the last ten pages in which 'McMurdo Explains.' " The idea in the term "Who-

dunit" does come closer to the root of the matter, for there must be a problem for detection to seize upon. But though the motive and the suspense come from asking Who?, the chief interest, the artistic interest, springs not from Who but How; and not so much the How the crime as the How of its discovery. In Dorothy Sayers' *Whose Body?,* which by its publication in 1923 may be said to mark the onset of the high period in the genre's evolution, the answer to the question posed by the title is quite unimportant. What matters is how Lord Peter will deal with the many questions arising from the intrusion of the irrelevant corpse. And what engages the connoisseur's attention is the skill and the plausibility with which this investigation advances step by step. Two imaginations are being judged: that of the author who constructed the plot, and that which she ascribes to her detective in unraveling it backward. On either plane, the materials must be sound and their combination economical. Reality as the Realists conceived it is the supreme criterion: that is real which is regular, feasible, normal, even in perpetrating the abnormality of crime.

We are ready then to conceive of the detective story as a strict—indeed rigorous—genre within the wider class of lifelike modern fiction, from which it is set off by one all-important feature: the detective story is a realistic novel turned upside down by scientific curiosity. I use this last phrase to denote an unprofessional, unspecialized, almost a poetic, curiosity about the behavior not of people but of things. In the usual *Passion at Broadacres,* we take the doorknobs and bathtowels for granted. What we want to know is how Edwin sighs for Angelina and whether the old gentleman will stand for it. But in *Murder at Broadacres,* it is people and motives we take for granted and towels and doorknobs that we examine with a new and informed interest. Why? Because the old man has been found stone dead and staring into his whisky and soda and Edwin's fingerprints are all over the decanter. From then on the physical world occupies the foreground of our thoughts as it has the author's from before page one.

This has important consequences. In the ordinary novel, objects furnish the setting of the action and also serve as symbols of character. The reader of novels learns to take in a quantity of small clues which serve as a descriptive shorthand for emotion or habit: a young woman who drops loose hairs everywhere is seldom the lovable heroine, though she might be the strong, careless earth-mother type who turns out more desirable than the prim beauty. In a like manner, prominent teeth or gold-filled ones, the twitching hands of the shady financier, the furniture of the newly-rich, and a hundred other physical signs have been used since Balzac to tell their local tale within the larger one. Sometimes, as in James's story about the girl who was urged to wear the wrong shade of blue, everything hangs on that one detail. But if these things determine fate, they do so by virtue of the social forces they represent or, as in Hardy, by "crass casualty." It is either the working of complex snobberies or else melodramatic accident that embroils human beings with the physical world in its minute detail.

In the detective story we have on the contrary a return to the pure tragedy, in which the protagonist himself prepares his downfall. The fatal flaw in him is the error he makes while committing the crime, an error which comes to light because of inescapable necessity in the workings of physical nature. His acts are embedded in matter and readable by art. The detective's assumption, not without grandeur, is that of science, which says that nature is a faithful recorder of her own history. You cannot erase the deed or cook the account. The action unfolds in a closed system, and from this derive the laws that make the detective story rigorous and fixed in its form—a classic genre. In its construction and in the esthetic pleasure it affords, the detective story is the nearest thing we have to French classical tragedy.

The objections raised against it are to be understood in this light. When Trollope expresses impatience at early examples of the genre because he does not like to bear in mind who was where on the Tuesday afternoon, he means that in his own work the love of detail is for elucidating character, not action. When others complain of repetition in the form, shallowness in the types represented, or artificiality in the circumstances that bring about the investigation, they are resenting the fact that an apparently realistic novel has been made over into a more mathematical species. True, it has been wantonly limited, but thereby made capable of yielding a unique delight to connoisseurs—the delight of a classical effect. In other genres the author as it were writes his own contract and is justified in the sequel. In a classic genre the contract is written ahead of time. The author is to supply a certain pleasure. But the reader must meet this intention halfway by deliberately overlooking the falsity of the conventions. One no more asks, Does every murder in real life take place in a library? than one asks, Did the ancients conduct all their affairs in the courtyard of one palace? The reward of taking the large view of a narrow presentment is that it displays the logic of Nemesis.

The thought charged with this feeling undoubtedly moved the genius who created the detective story at one stroke. That he was a Romanticist only shows that Romanticism is inclusive enough to embrace the classical emotion. When in 1841 Edgar Allan Poe published "The Murders in the Rue Morgue" he had no models for his work, only the barest hints. There was, of course, the ancestral tradition of reading nature by signs. The thoughtful interpretation of clues began with man's need to hunt animals and was reproduced in storytelling, as we can see from the Bible and other ancient literatures. In Greek tragedy, the recognition scene often hinges on physical clues—Electra guesses her brother's presence by some stray hairs and a footprint. And this should be enough to show the permanence—the eternal verity, one might say—of the pleasure inherent in seeing the constructed puzzle solved.

But it was not until the spirit of modern science became a cultural force that the detective story could arise. As E. M. Wrong pointed out, the genre cannot flourish "until the public has an idea what constitutes proof." A hundred years before Poe, Voltaire had made clear in *Zadig* (1748) that his hero's astonishing detective feats owed their validity to his study of nature. But it is all for show—and there is no form. In the year of the American Revolution Beaumarchais, inspired by Voltaire, wrote a sketch which contains the chief features of modern "deduction" from objects, in this instance a lady's evening cloak ["Gaîté faite à Londres," *Oeuvres complètes* (1822)]. Half a century later Balzac's *Etude de moeurs par les gants* (1830) takes

up the idea and expands it in the likeness of a genre popular at the time, the "physiology" of common subjects—business, marriage, and so on. The Romantics' enthusiasm for what might be called the heroism of science was very great. It inspired William Leggett's "The Rifle" (1828), described by Mr. Vincent Starrett as "an incunabulum of detection"; and it was symbolized in the cliché of Cuvier's reconstructing extinct animals "from a single bone." Cuvier himself cites Zadig as a kind of precursor. About the same time, Cooper was popularizing anew the primitive detection of the hunter in his widely translated Leatherstocking tales, and the joy of inference was becoming a familiar literary pleasure.

The outdoors is not, however, the best setting for armchair detection; the detective story is patently an urban, civilized genre—again like French tragedy. Both imply a firmly established order—that of Louis XIV or the modern police. It is significant that Poe's first detective tale coincides in date with the institution of Peel's "bobbies," and that the full-blown form is peculiarly English and Edwardian. For it needs a world in which there is not only respect for law and order but also respectability in the shape of settled habits. To mark off the genre's restricted stage everyone's social orbit must be known—the solicitor must be in full possession of the facts, the numbers of the banknotes must be recorded, and the cabdriver must know where he picked up the gentleman.

Front cover of a paperback edition of Marie Belloc Lowndes's The Lodger.

All this suggests why there is hardly such a thing as a Continental detective. Please do not say "Maigret"—I shall only say "*Mais non*" ["why, no"], and point out that psychology and the *roman policier* are another genre, even though the works of Gaboriau gave impetus to the taste for "reconstructing" crime. But all the French practitioners, through Leroux and Leblanc to Simenon, have been adversely influenced by the memoirs of Vidocq, the convict turned policeman, and by Balzac's Vautrin, who is a sort of Byronic Moriarty. They all, in other words, mix a little detection with much passion, scandal, and legal procedure. The *roman policier* is a monster fit only for newspaper serials, because the drama of trial scenes swamps detection, which in turn interferes with, or is dwarfed by passion.

What Poe's original idea needed in order to blossom was a wider indoctrination of the method of science, so that the taste for reading "The Book of Life" (Sherlock Holmes's phrase) should be general and addressed to physical fact. This came with the great Darwinian controversy which filled the monthly magazines and turned Huxley and Tyndall into popular lecturers. It was in 1880, seven years before Conan Doyle's epoch-making *Study in Scarlet,* that Huxley addressed a London Working Men's College "On the Method of Zadig" and then published his lecture in the widely read *Nineteenth Century.* Huxley's text is that "retrospective prophecy" is a function of science, and this he demonstrates by showing the exact parallel between Zadig's exploits and the method of modern paleontology. "In no distant future," he concludes, "the method of Zadig . . . will enable the biologist to reconstruct the scheme of life from its beginning." In other words, the theory of Evolution is the greatest detective story ever told.

Huxley kept giving the public episodes of it, as in the brilliant lecture (again to workingmen) "On a Piece of Chalk," and Darwin himself ventured to forestall Sherlock Holmes by "deducing" the prevalence of old maids in a community from the luxuriance of clover in nearby fields. Little by little a complete rhetoric of science was taught to the multitude. From it we learned how calm, cool, and collected the scientist always is, how careful yet self-assured his every move, how millimetric his judgments, how beautifully simple his ability to connect the remote principle with the particular fact which the rest of us meet with a dumb stare. After twenty years of this propaganda, the public was ready to follow the fortunes of a hero who was a Huxley with an even clearer social utility—Sherlock Holmes.

That austere figure, an offspring of Poe's Dupin, appeared just before the nineties—one more example of that period's dependence on the earlier part of the century. Yet we must not forget Holmes's marked ninetyish features—his affected nonchalance and addiction to drugs. Conan Doyle had very properly gone back to Poe for the essence of the form, but he energized it with the scientism of Huxley, the Realism of Dickens and Collins, and the current Bohemianism denoting "the genius."

There is today a most unjust tendency to pooh-pooh the Holmes stories because of their implausibility, their transparency, and their unfairness to the reader. The real unfairness is to the man who through these stories taught us to be so hard to please. In him for the first time since Poe (and for a long time to come) detection holds the center of the stage; yet it cannot be said of any of the Holmes tales that it is entirely a puzzle or a trick. Why not rather say this of Maupassant who nonetheless holds a place in literature? Though not profound, there is an air of philosophy about the Holmes-Watson ménage, a sense of the heights and depths of life, of the bustle of business and the oddities of character. Doyle also understood—De Quincey may have taught him—the important maxim that the true atmosphere of crime is the grotesque; the fit intellectual companion of murder is mirth. Doyle has the right humor of style and situation as none of his imitators had until the prewar generation of Chesterton and Bentley. Our own Anna Katherine Greene did her best to develop the long story while keeping to Poe's intention; but read her after Doyle and the abysmal difference appears at once. Her gentility is as unbearable as her idea of violent motives; her settings are vague or overloaded; and Gryce, her detective, is featureless. In Doyle, all is sharp, worldly, adult, contrasted, memorable and, where needed, sinister. And his imagination of the physical is so rich that he leaves one wondering whether the short story is not, after all, the true form of detective fiction.

But the germ planted by Poe was yet to flower in the larger form. The first indications that this was happening came in the first prewar period. Around 1910 appeared the earliest stories of R. Austin Freeman and in 1912 E. C. Bentley's epoch-making *Trent's Last Case.* The book marks the beginning of the great classic period. Like Corneille's *Cid,* it lacks a few of the refinements later achieved, but all the essentials are there, from style and drama to technical virtuosity. Left behind are all the sketches and previsions, the fumbling attempts (to pursue the parallel) of the Jodelles and Rotrous.

On his side, Austin Freeman contributed the elements of exactitude in scientific technique which in time killed off the genre: *The Red Thumb Mark* showed that fingerprints could be forged—and the forgery detected. If Bentley starts from Holmes, Freeman starts from Bertillon [the inventor of systematic techniques in criminal investigation] and the textbook of forensic medicine. Freeman was weak in narrative, and the public did not then recognize what had been offered it. As in other genres and arts, it was not until after the war, in 1920, that the century caught up with itself.

In that year, Agatha Christie published her first, *The Mysterious Affair at Styles,* and Bentley's masterpiece was reissued under its present title. Three years later Dorothy Sayers made her debut with *Whose Body?* and the high genre was fully launched. The notable names come thick and fast: A. A. Milne, John Rhode, Henry Wade, Freeman Wills Crofts, Victor Whitechurch, Margery Allingham, Ngaio Marsh, Ronald Knox, Miles Burton, Ernest Bramah, G. D. H. and Margaret Cole, Georgette Heyer, James Hilton, Raymond Postgate, Dermot Morrah, Nicholas Blake—a full list would be formidable and is better read with critical comments in the admirable studies by H. Douglas Thomson and Howard Haycraft. As for the supreme achievements, they must be left to the choice of each connoisseur; the aim of this retrospect being less to arouse enthusiasm for certain works than to show how they came to exist and to arouse it.

When I call the detective story a classic genre and compare it with seventeenth-century drama, I mean that it is regulated by Difficulty. The result is that the follower of the genre draws pleasure chiefly from the skill with which difficulty is overcome in an original way. As in French tragedy or Italian *opera seria,* the connection of the action with life is secondary, or at least not immediate. The primary concern is with composition—the adept joining of facts and the inspired means, the art, by which they are disclosed and interpreted.

To be sure, thousands of readers pay no attention to these refinements. They gobble up the story to see how it ends or, given the chance, they shudder a little on the way. This is of no moment. They may read Dickens or Tolstoy in the same fashion, and rarely discuss what they read, even inwardly. The point is that the true dilettante does reflect in order to savor, and that a genre must be judged by its fullest capacity to cause rumination. The critics who have interpreted the detective story by its mythic or symbolic qualities err through failing to see that in so doing they have "explained" all the stories in a lump. If "chase" or guilt vicariously atoned is the secret of the appeal, what is the secret of one specimen's superiority over another? The answer cannot be that in this genre alone attention to detail is beneath criticism. A generation that has over and over again dredged that telltale crumb out of Proust's cup of tea can't have the face to mock at the examination of small clues.

It may be objected that the crumb is a clue to Proust's forgotten memories, which are more important than knowing who murdered the cantankerous baronet. No doubt. But, I repeat, it is not the mind of any man, murderer or victim, that matters in our genre, it is the uniformity of Nature and its *legibility.* This is a philosophic concern, indeed an intellectual passion, and we hear it in the narrator's voice. Marking him off from the bewildered crowd, his is the belief in mind, the belief in the orderly life and the eventual triumph, not so much of justice—for the criminal may have his reasons that reason does not know, and escape scot-free—but the triumph of evidential truth. We behold the apotheosis of Voltaire and the Enlightenment, itself a reflection of the classic order attempted in society.

Fed on these deep emotions, the detective story generates its characteristic atmosphere through its precise language, its attractive apparatus, its corpseside manner, and its habit of making fine distinctions. All these produce in the reader feelings of satisfied recognition into which enters a sort of cosmic confidence. As he turns the title page, flanked by a carefully drawn plan of Fittsgrave Manor . . . , he experiences the anticipation of certitude shared by the old theologians who rested their case for revelation on evidence from Design. Indeed, Paley's famous work on that subject contains the prime detective example of the traveler who comes upon a watch in a deserted place. He knows, says Paley, "without intromission or privity" into the mind of the Maker, that this arrangement of wheels and pinions did not come together by chance but has a meaning.

It is a dry faith—classicism tends toward dryness—but it is bracing despite its complacency. And though it is the opposite of Gothic art, in the novel or elsewhere, one can observe the attraction that the idea exerted on some of the great masters of Gothic melodrama—Dickens, Dostoevsky, Henry James. No less than fifteen detectives appear in Dickens' works, and *Edwin Drood,* the last, is the

culmination of a series of three mysteries. In Dostoevsky crime is frequent and the author loves to interpret its ambiguity. And James confesses: "In a recent story, 'The Beldonald Holbein,' it is not my fault if I am so put together as often to find more life in situations obscure and subject to interpretation than in the gross rattle of the foreground."

To be sure, a different end is aimed at through these toyings with uncertainty; the horror of the indefinite which James especially liked is alien to the spirit of detection, going back as it does to the Gothic genre strictly so called—Walpole's *Castle of Otranto* and its successors. In true detective fiction the reader may be sure that no supernatural hand is going to stir up his atavistic fears; the victim himself will be dispatched in a quick and wholesome manner; grief—if any—will remain conventional and unobtrusive; and love will be either excluded or allowed to simmer in the background. By the author's art our mind will be bent upon mightier, impersonal issues, all familiar it may be, but ever alluring: fingerprints and other traces of matter disturbed by human agency, rigor mortis, the state of clocks and watches, the tracks in the lane, the butler who thought he heard a noise, the disappearance of the will, and the significance of the odd marks on the blotter.

What the seasoned connoisseur looks for is Theme and Variation. The problem which will generate themes is or ought to be introduced in the first chapter: beware of laborious tales that begin forty years earlier with a family of planters in the Dutch East Indies. The classic form calls for the three unities, which is why nothing is better than the body in the library by page ten and the denouement on the spot in less than a week. Ships at sea and trains in motion have their appeal, as have school and college campuses, but success in these settings has been rare. It has been nil when the author understood his *donnée* so little as to place his victim in a theater full of people: he might as well hope to hold us with a story of Murder on the Battlefield.

The variations are of two kinds: first the several interpretations of facts as they appear during the search for Reality, and next the version which uncovers it. Both kinds ring the changes upon such fundamental themes as the mode of killing or theft, the "impossibility" of an attested fact (e.g., murder in a locked-and-barred room), the ruses adopted to elicit new evidence, the tangled motives, snags, and dead ends. These gradually raise the dramatic pitch until the demonstration or reconstruction scene whose purpose is primarily the conviction of the reader and only secondarily that of the culprit.

At every point artistic tension arises from the opposite pull of two desired virtues: plausibility and originality. The ordinary reader will doubtless accept any kind of key that seems to fit the stated problem; the devotee of the genre is more exacting. He knows whether the enigma and its particulars have been treated before, as well as every classic solution offered. Access to the premises and the victim, alibis, double bluffs, and the ways of disentangling confusion are so many headings under which he will judge the tale. He will not tolerate repetition, and will insist that new devices be workable in time and space. Novelty and priority matter because the form and its fulfillment are so circumscribed. After *Fatal Descent* no criminal can enlist the aid of barometric pressure on a descending lift. After

Have His Carcase no alibi can depend on hemophilia. After "Brookbend Cottage," high voltage is played out—at least as there employed.

These random examples illustrate the substance of the genre. The art of it resides in the presenting and compounding of the elements. A detective story must be able to withstand close reading; that is, the reader will employ his imagination in lawyer-like fashion as he goes forward and must be able to go back and find that he has not been misled or denied essential information. The discussions between the protagonist and his confidant (as in tragedy) must be full and frank, not to say exhaustive; it will not do to let the reader think of a fact that would wreck the hypothesis of the moment, or worse yet, devise an equally tenable alternative.

To prevent this last calamity (which continually threatens, since there *must* be a tenable alternative to each of the successive false ones), the novelist makes a diabolical use of the "point of view." By taking at face value the ostensible motive or means of the crime, he so fills the reader's mind with material details as to create a presumption of truth. Then under the pressure of a fact that will not fit, he shifts to a new reading and throws an entirely different light on motive or agency or both. In this way the reader sees the central data under two, three, or more aspects consecutively, much as Browning tells the story of *The Ring and the Book.* In other words, the variations on the given themes are paralleled by variations on their connections and meaning, so that the acute amateur enjoys the spectacle of Form as pure as it can ever get.

There are thus very good reasons why the psychology in detective novels is elementary: the variables cannot be multiplied without spoiling the strictness, and—let me repeat—the desired uncertainty belongs to a train of physical, not mental events. Because of this, secondary figures remain traditional, though not necessarily puppets. In good work, such as Dorothy Sayers', they receive just the elaboration required by the total effect—which is exactly what we find, not only in nine-tenths of ordinary fiction and drama but also in certain masterpieces where psychology plays a negligible role, for example in *Robinson Crusoe, Gulliver,* or *Notre Dame.*

In detection people must be as real as, let us say, chairs are in a realistic novel; while the clues, together with the detective's mind must be as vivid and many-faceted as a Racinian heroine. And just as in classical tragedy one does not quarrel with the assumption that honor must be avenged or duty to the state put before inclination, so in our genre one accepts similar conventions about the omnipotent lure of inheritance and the irresistible urge to avoid scandal. Besides, any subtlety or uncatalogued oddity of mind in one of the characters could only be discovered by the detective's intuition and this would violate the rule of fair play toward the reader.

So Mr. Anthony Berkeley's hope of a new style of detection based on the art of the "real novel" can at best only mean the refinement of simple portraiture and better writing at large. The person who suggested to Arnold Bennett (a fair judge of detection) that all of Sherlock Holmes should be rewritten from the point of view of psychoanalysis was either pulling Bennett's leg or betraying his own obtuseness. Detection snaps its fingers at the Id. It would

as soon tolerate the occult or that "poison unknown to science" which has finally been banned from decent literature. Twenty-five years ago, Father Ronald Knox in effect summed up these considerations when he said that in true detection "There must be no Chinaman" [see excerpt below in *Defining Detective Fiction*], adding for the laity's sake: "Why this should be so, I do not know." His expert readers knew, and knew that he knew.

It is not surprising that, being so strict, the detective novel should have exhausted its possibilities in less than forty years. "Strict" implies restricted. The connoisseurs came to know all the devices and their permutations about the time that the authors reached the end of their inventiveness. And this end came especially quickly because the large number of ingenious writers who cultivated the genre willingly supplied the publishers' demand for novels rather than short stories. The shorter form can turn on one original idea—as Poe's four models do and most of Sherlock Holmes; a novel is "ruinously expensive"—to use James's phrase, or else has to be padded. It is easy to see in some writers gifted for detection the rapid drop in quality after the first two or three full-length tales. Not daring to repeat they dilute, and their last works are little more than chitchat over bloodshed, through which wanders a superfluous detective.

One might have thought that since the detective story, like the rest of fiction, furthered our education in one branch of contemporary culture, namely science, the progress of that branch would extend its life. The opposite proved true. The term of life for the Idea of Detection was set by the limits of the nineteenth-century outlook which gave it birth. Science was then the interpreter of matter in its gross, palpable forms, and scientific reasoning was still within the grasp of unspecialized intelligence. Twentieth-century science, as we all know, goes beyond the revelation to common sense of objects and their laws. It deals, if not with a supernatural world of its own making, at least with a suprasensible realm where the best mind is baffled without mathematics. The procedures of actual police work have been sufficiently influenced by this change to make obsolete the artistry of classical detection. If the articles surrounding the dead man have to be taken to the laboratory for analysis, all we can do is wait and be bored by false alarms until "the report" comes in—which is to say that the story has walked out the front door and the detective had better go on the dole.

The farthest point to which scientific detection in this sense can be carried was reached by R. Austin Freeman in his best tales. One does not mind the "drop of Farrant's" on the slide or Polton's lavish photographic enlargements, for something is still left for the naked eye. But when one reads of geiger counters being used on the suspect's boots or learns of a patent taken out in Sweden, by which very faint or very ancient fingerprints can be developed in color by dipping the objects in various baths and drying them in a heat cabinet, the traditionalist loses interest through ceasing to participate. He calls for his insufflator and gray dusting powder; or better still, retreats to pure reason and speculates about that tantalizing affair to which Holmes found the solution by noticing how far the parsley had sunk into the butter.

Nor is it science alone that has betrayed its modest fictional ally. The temper of society also has superannuated classic detection. The genre took for granted a settled, predictable existence which, though it was never true of any class, was at least the ideal and the pretention of the respectable. They trusted and obeyed the policeman on the corner and he called them Sir and Madam. As against this, the modern premise is that the cop on the beat is corrupt and should not say "Sir" even if honest. [The critic adds in a footnote that "modern English writers who try to continue the old genre find difficulty in accommodating it to the presence of thugs, and now that a Scotland Yard man has been sent to jail (Nov. 30, 1955) the prospect is bleak. The attempt at reportage of actual police work (*Gideon's Day*) is dull, and the effort to make tension the chief interest (*Docker Dead*) sounds forced. E. C. Bentley's death early in 1956 may therefore be said to have closed an era."] This democratic view proved especially congenial to American writers, and led by Mr. Dashiell Hammett they developed the hard-boiled detective story upon conventions diametrically opposed to the old.

In the tough tales, police and criminals are hard to distinguish—that is in fact one of the mysteries to unravel. All we are sure of is the integrity of the hero, who is usually a "private eye." To make this sure he is also very much of a private I—he tells the story in the first person and the confidant or Watson is eliminated: it would be too much to ask that two characters be taken on trust. Yet even the hero with whom one is to "identify" is a flawed vessel. That is why he has to refill on whisky continually. He revels in blood, sadism, and loveless promiscuity, and one feels that in the good cause he pursues he enjoys breaking moral and statute law. His whole existence is in fact an attack on bourgeois society, which gives him the pleasure, frequently, of showing up the wealthiest, most respected man in the community as a drug trafficker, vice king, or pervert.

It would be tempting to believe that this return to melodrama came from a desire to show that tales based on law and order do not fully express life, that the world is chaos barely mitigated by law and civilization. But the tough genre is not so much a calculated departure as an angry derivative. The talk imitates Hemingway and the psychology is that of universal obsession. Everybody drinks and fornicates without the slightest taste for living. The obsession is never fiery, never reminds us of

> Vénus tout entière à sa proie attachée

> ["Venus completely attached to her prey"]

but expresses instead the abdication of personal choice. Cynicism is automatic because no one knows anybody else except through status or function, which means that human relations dwindle to mutual contempt. The hero is superior only in his command of the fullest gradation of sneers. In his "detecting" there is no play of mind whatever—merely multitudes of people to see, question, suspect. The pilgrimage takes the reader through the corruption of cities and their artificial paradises—dope, gambling, homosexuality, power, privacy in secret rooms, and the compulsive toying with death.

Owing to the mannered style and painstaking exactitude of dialogue and description, these stories exert a powerful charm. Especially abroad, they have been taken very seriously by advanced critics and novelists as representations of American life, and the genre has found imitators in every European tongue. Over here, Mr. Raymond Chandler, a master of the style, has defended it as a return to reality after the make-believe of bloodless English detection. His somewhat petulant argument is not convincing. All the realism of the tough tale resides in the accessories, and they are real only in Los Angeles and vicinity. Clothes, rooms, bodily characteristics, and vulgarity of speech are photographically rendered. But people's motives and actions are as much make-believe as in the worst of old-fashioned detection. Like a congenital idiot the tough hero invariably goes where he will be "sapped," though by a recurring miracle he is never killed or impaired by concussion. He nurses his faculties on the bottle, which at his typical age of forty-five has left him in perfect physical condition for the dirty fighting that ensues. Though he is hated by every cop and gangster in town, they all receive him in their dens and after some boyish repartee give him the information he needs. Yet so packed with interviews and incidents is the narrative that it is difficult to test its consistency; the final disclosure usually depends on a single lie which the groggy detective has managed to spot. In short, there is no more realism than there is detection, and I cannot agree with the last of Mr. John Loehlin's delightful lines:

> A psychopathic private eye,
> Complete with bourbon, Scotch, and rye,
> And panting wenches running wild—
> Monsieur Dupin, behold your child!
>   ["Whither Homicide?" (1950)]

Rather, I discern under these trappings the outlines of the old Western and the still older thriller of the lone white man's fight against the Indians. All are close kin of the spy story, in which isolation is also important. The new variants on the theme of alienation are in fact the one feature by which the hard-boiled tale does represent one aspect of modern feeling, as Mr. Chandler unwittingly makes clear in his defense of the genre: every hero is convinced that he alone is a good guy in a population of bastards. Many a reader doubtless responds to this pleasant fiction, and is encouraged by what goes with it: the vague proposition that to admit one's faults is much the same as getting rid of them and the safe delights of vicarious drinking, whoring, and shooting.

Perhaps we should rejoice at this high-powered reincarnation of Robin Hood and the Byronic hero. It may show that despite the machine and the city a kind of individualism still survives. But it is regrettable that the old-time defiance has with us turned into a sentimental plaint not far from a whine. The range of tough ideas has proved very small indeed; inventories of clothes and listless sluggings for envelopes do not take one very far. And since by definition all this has to be couched in the language of the gutter, one does not see what untapped levels remain below. If this last muddy drop is the legacy of Romanticism, then let us be done with it as we are done with the Classicism of pure detection. We shall miss the advantage that literature always draws from having at least one fixed genre to satisfy the taste for dilettante concentration; but with both antagonists disposed of, we may regard their passing as the prerequisite and augury of a fictional art that shall be really new. (pp. 304-23)

Jacques Barzun, "From 'Phèdre' to Sherlock Holmes," in his The Energies of Art: Studies of Authors Classic and Modern, *Harper & Brothers, 1956, pp. 303-23.*

Kingsley Amis

[*A distinguished English novelist, poet, essayist, and editor, Amis was one of the Angry Young Men, a group of British writers of the 1950s whose writings expressed bitterness and disillusionment with society. Common to the work of the Angry Young Men is an antihero who rebels against a corrupt social order in a quest for personal integrity. Amis's first and most widely praised novel, Lucky Jim (1954), is characteristic of the school and demonstrates his skill as a satirist. Amis has since rejected categorization or alliance with any literary group and maintains that he is only interested in following his artistic instincts. Throughout his career, Amis has also sustained an interest in science fiction. He was coeditor of the Spectrum science fiction anthologies, and the author of one of the first major critical surveys of the genre, New Maps of Hell (1960). Amis wrote the first James Bond adventure after Ian Fleming's death but did not become Fleming's successor, with critics charging that he made Bond too human. In the following excerpt, he examines the character of the fictional detective.*]

> It is only in books that one finds the brilliant amateur detective X; real policemen are obstinate and hardheaded, are slow and literal-minded, are frequently mean and nearly always narrow: they have to be. They are part of the administrative machine, a tool of government control. . . .

So reflects Van der Valk, Nicolas Freeling's Amsterdam inspector, on his way to try to stop a beautiful female aristocrat and ex-ski champion from ambushing a Dutch businessman with a hunting rifle on a lonely road in southern France. With this adventure, *The King of the Rainy Country,* Van der Valk confirms his status as one of the most promising arrivals on the post-war crime-fiction scene. In his account of real policemen he is actually a little hard on himself. Obstinate and slow he may be, but these are only rude names for the Netherlander's inbred conscientiousness. As for literal-minded, he is given to reflecting self-accusingly that he is too much of a northerner, with his veins full of Ibsen, and is able without difficulty to work out the motivation of a suicide by pondering over the poem of Baudelaire's alluded to in the title. Besides all this, he is intelligent, thoughtful and good-natured—the last of these by no means a standard characteristic of fictional sleuths. (Even Sherlock Holmes has been known to come back at Watson with a quick impatient snarl or so, when the chase is really on.) Van der Valk is an impressive man interestingly rendered. His only shortcoming as a hero, the only thing that robs him of the almost mythical and mystical glamour of a Holmes or a Nero Wolfe, is that he, unlike them, is very much a real policeman.

The point is even clearer with Simenon's celebrated Inspector Maigret. In *My Friend Maigret,* the inspector takes along a Scotland Yard detective called Pyke to investigate a murder on a French island. Pyke—incidentally, an amusing and sympathetic portrayal—is supposed to be studying French police methods. At the end of the book it is suggested that Pyke, apart from having thrown down a good deal of the local wine, has been wasting his time,

because there just are no such methods. None, that is, but the universal ones of interrogation of witnesses, suspects, neighbours and the like, thumbing through records and dossiers, consulting London, Ostend, Zurich and the like, and more interrogation. None of those brilliant intuitions, those miraculous leaps in the dark, those questions about what seem to be insanely irrelevant matters, that are so firmly in the middle of the great detective tradition inaugurated by Poe's Auguste Dupin. And Maigret himself, apart from taking an occasional *calvados* too many, has virtually no characteristics beyond those required to solve his cases. We know all too well that he will never in a million years start playing the violin or suddenly insist on cultivating orchids. That sort of thing is the prerogative of the unreal policeman, or rather the unreal nonpoliceman: Van der Valk's brilliant amateur detective X, who exists only in books. All the sleuths we remember and reverence and take into our private pantheon of heroes are figures not of realism but of fantasy, great talkers, great eccentrics, men who use inspiration instead of hard work, men to whom Venetian old masters mean more than police files and a good bottle of Burgundy more than fingerprints. (Scope here for a scholarly footnote on the parallel with spy fiction: James Bond will still be around long after all the spies who came in from the cold, Ipcress-file-mongers and similar 'real' secret agents have been forgotten.)

Halfway between the policeman and the amateur comes the private investigator, of whom Dashiell Hammett's Sam Spade and Raymond Chandler's Philip Marlowe are typical, plus, in a rather different way, Mickey Spillane's Mike Hammer. Theirs is a fantasy world all right, that of the toughie whose sacred objects are the gun, the boot, the bottle of rye and (less so in Chandler than in the others) the male organ. It has often been objected against the tough school that their values are lopsided or nonexistent, that in regard to ethics, and pretty well everything else, the police and the D.A.'s men are no better than the crooks or the Commies and the private eye is at least as bad as all the others. This loss of moral focusing is felt to be unedifying, even dangerous. Maybe. My own view is that the immoral or amoral hero of this type is bound to forfeit some of the reader's esteem and, along with it, some of his desire to identify with the hero. The story thus goes rather cold. In crime or spy fantasies the interest is partly a fairy-tale one, good versus bad in a rather basic way; James Bond would not mean so much to us if we were unable to feel that he was on the right side and that his cause was just. The toughies have no decent cause. Self-interest is all.

This would probably matter less than it does if these writers wrote better. Spillane is the best of the three cited—an unpopular view, which I would defend hotly. Legitimate shock and horror at the beastliness of Hammer's universe should not be allowed to weigh against the technical brilliance with which the whole thing is stage-managed. Few novelists on any level can match Spillane's skill in getting his essential facts across palatably and without interrupting the action, in knowing what to leave out; and the impression received that the narrative is just tumbling out of the corner of Hammer's mouth at two hundred words a minute is a tribute to real professional competence. With all this granted, what makes the stories finally stultifying is Hammer's total facelessness, or mindlessness. He is a mere network of gristle connecting mouth, fist, trigger, finger and penis. A hero needs more substance than that.

Sam Spade perhaps has a little more. *The Maltese Falcon,* in the period just after its publication (1930), was certainly taken as having opened up an undiscovered area in popular fiction. No doubt the removal of conventional ethics caught the taste of a public who, in mid-Depression, must have been more than ready to believe that almost any cynical view of the world was likely to approximate to the way things really were, and did not care to notice the story's manifold improbabilities. Looking back now, it seems hard to understand what the fuss was about. Spade, the blond Satan with the yellow-grey eyes, grinning wolfishly on every other page and making growling animal noises in his throat nearly as often, the most committed cigarette smoker before our friend 007, turns out to be faintly funny. Where Hammett presents Spade's toughness as real and probable, as the way things are did we but know it, the result is unbelievable; where the toughness is offered as exceptionally cool, exceptionally tough, it just seems corny. And both sorts come down much of the time to mere rudeness and bad temper. All of it is ladled out in low-budget-TV-show dialogue. The gloss and the glow, if they were ever there, have been rubbed out by time.

Raymond Chandler was undoubtedly the most ambitious writer of the tough-thriller school, and for some time was, in England at any rate still is, a toast of the intellectuals. W. H. Auden went on record with the view that: 'Chandler's powerful books should be read and judged not as escape literature but as works of art' [see Further Reading: Secondary Sources]. This advice strikes me as hazardous in the extreme. The books have undoubtedly worn less badly than Hammett's, having had for one thing less time to do so, since they belong roughly to the period 1939-59. Philip Marlowe is an improvement on Spade. Some of Marlowe's toughness does boil down to meanness, unreticent dislike of the rich and indeed of most other groups and individuals, rudeness to servants and to women. On the other hand, there are some things he will not do, he will protect his clients under great pressure, he can show compunction and even sensitivity. What disfigures him is, again, the way he is presented by his creator. The tough catch phrases—'don't kid me, son'; 'quit stalling'; 'on your way, brother'—died with, or before, Bogart. There is also a moral pretentiousness whereby Marlowe is now and again made the vehicle for criticizing the sordid lives of Hollywood's denizens: the perverted producers, the writers drowning in bourbon and self-hatred, the chicks who will do absolutely anything to get a part—all that. Most of this comes ill from a private eye, even a comparatively honest one. Bits of stylistic pretentiousness underline the effect. *The Big Sleep* has bubbles rising in a glass of liquor 'like false hopes' and, after an intermission of four words, a girl's breath being 'as delicate as the eyes of a fawn'. Is this our tough Chandler (let alone a work of art), or has some heart-throbbing female dream-purveyor grabbed the pen?

Perry Mason provides a convenient stopover point. There would be a lot to be said for not noticing him at all, if it were not for the hideous frequency of his appearances in print and on television. I am afraid there can be very few people in our culture who would not know that, although Mason is not in the strict sense a detective, is a mere lawyer employing the Drake Detective Agency to do his legwork for him, he does investigate crimes, ending up ten times out of ten by winning one of those objection-

overruled-objection-sustained rituals in concert with the D.A. and the judge. The TV films faithfully reflect the Erle Stanley Gardner novels in their portrayal of the inevitable three-stage progress from seeing-the-client through seeing-the-witnesses to going-to-court, with an expected unexpected revelation at the end. Mason has an impressive claim to being considered the most boring foe of criminality in our time, which is saying something if we make the effort to remember such cobwebbed figures as Inspector French (in the works of Freeman Wills Crofts) or Philo Vance (S. S. Van Dine). The nullity of Mason is nowhere better displayed than in his relations, or lack of any, with his assistant—I cannot bring myself to say girl Friday—Della Street. Della Street, whose name appears in full every time Gardner mentions her, answers the telephone and listens to Mason telling her that the law is not a rat race unless you run with the rats. Oh, and sometimes she worries because Mason looks so tired. Nothing more; whereas the vital role of the assistant in detective fiction is to encourage and provoke the great man to reveal his hidden inner nature, as we shall see.

I hope we shall see much more than that. The sleuths put up to question so far have admittedly been treated in a rather carping or, as we British say, 'knocking' spirit. My admiration is reserved for the detective who detects, whose claim to fame is his mind rather than his way with a girl or a jury. Heroes of this type show a strong family resemblance. Such a man will show some physical impressiveness, along the lines of Holmes's tall lean figure and

Sherlock Holmes as drawn by Sidney Paget in 1904.

piercing eyes, or Wolfe's vast poundage: 285 of them. If unimpressive, he will be spectacularly unimpressive, small and with an egg-shaped head like Poirot; small, round-faced and bespectacled like Father Brown. He is unmarried, or at least his wife is kept firmly off stage. A crucial point, this. Holmes hit the nail on the head for his group when he declared that he would never marry, lest he biased his judgment. But let Dr Watson spell the point out:

> All emotions, and that one [i.e., love] particularly, were abhorrent to his cold, precise, but admirably balanced mind. He was, I take it, the most perfect reasoning and observing machine that the world has seen. . . . He never spoke of the softer passions, save with a gibe and a sneer. . . . For the trained observer to admit such intrusions into his own delicate and finely adjusted temperament was to introduce a distracting factor which might throw a doubt upon all his mental results. . . . ['A Scandal in Bohemia']

And no doubts must be thrown on any of those mental results. Quite right. But what are we to make of this avoidance of the fair sex, which in Wolfe's case rises, or sinks, to panic at the mere prospect of being alone with a woman? Could there be something a bit . . . you know . . . ? Let us take a look at a famous incident in 'The Three Garridebs', wherein John Garrideb, alias Killer Evans, shoots Watson in the thigh. Holmes promptly disposes of Evans, and then . . .

> . . . my friend's wiry arms were round me, and he was leading me to a chair.

> 'You're not hurt, Watson? For God's sake, say that you are not hurt!'

> It was worth a wound—it was worth many wounds—to know the depth of loyalty and love which lay behind that cold mask. The clear, hard eyes were dimmed for a moment, and the firm lips were shaking. For the one and only time I caught a glimpse of a great heart as well as of a great brain. All my years of humble but single-minded service culminated in that moment of revelation.

> 'It's nothing, Holmes. It's a mere scratch.'

Is it without significance that, whereas the moment of revelation is dated by Watson in 1902, his account of it was held back from book publication until the more tolerant days of twenty-five years later? Answer: Yes. Utterly. Though it might be more fun to believe the opposite, Holmes is no fag. His lack of interest in women, made a positive characteristic to aid in the building up of his character, can be accounted for in at least two innocent ways. Just as the true Western fans in the moviehouse sigh and groan when Destry stops shooting and starts loving—and a large part of our feelings about Holmes are on this sort of level—so we should feel cheated and affronted if the great brain left Watson to get after the Man with the Twisted Lip for a spell and himself started taking Miss Violet de Merville off Baron Adelbert Gruner. Further, although Holmes would not have been difficult to turn into a lover, any adventure featuring him as such could not be a detective story but, as experience of other writers shows, some kind of thriller or pursuit story or psychological melodrama. The magnifying lens and the dozen red roses belong to different worlds.

Holmes is the memorable figure he is because Conan Doyle grasped the essential truth that the deductive solving of crimes cannot in itself throw much light on the character doing the solving, and therefore that that character must be loaded up with quirks, hobbies, eccentricities. It is always these irrelevant qualities that define the figure of the great detective, not his mere powers of reasoning. One thinks of Lord Peter Wimsey's collections of Sèvres vases and early editions of Dante (including the Aldine 8vo of 1502 and the Naples folio of 1477), Poirot's dandified clothes and tiny Russian cigarettes, Dupin's expertise about paving-stones, grasses, astronomy, fungi and probably much more.

In Holmes's opinion, Dupin was 'a very inferior fellow. That trick of his of breaking in on his friends' thoughts with an apropos remark after a quarter of an hour's silence is really very showy and superficial.' I agree. Apart from his irritating mannerisms, all three of Dupin's cases are very shaky. He could never have got ahead of the police in 'The Murders in the Rue Morgue' without their incredible ignorance; his deductions in 'The Mystery of Marie Rogêt' are at least highly dubious at several key points; and in 'The Purloined Letter' he not only again had stupid police to help him out but also a dementedly foolhardy criminal. However, something deeper than professional contempt or jealousy was at work to give Holmes so jaundiced a view of his—rightly or wrongly—famous French predecessor. Holmes was quite intelligent enough to see that Dupin was his predecessor in much more than just the chronological sense.

There are plenty of comparatively minor resemblances between the two detectives: the pipe-smoking, the love of long pedantic monologues (plus, in each case, the presence of a devoted associate who knows just what to break in with or at least stays awake), the hatred of company and intrusions on privacy. Holmes, we are told, 'loathed every form of society with his whole Bohemian soul'; Dupin went so far as to solve the Rogêt case without leaving his armchair, recalling to us a more recent and much fatter detective who makes a point of operating in the same way. More important among Dupin-Holmes resemblances is the possession of vast and variegated learning. Holmes improves on Dupin's astronomy and mycology to the extent of being able to hold forth, in the course of one dinner, about miracle plays, medieval pottery, Stradivarius violins and the Buddhism of Ceylon. As regards the modern world he is frighteningly well informed. It seems that he has always card-indexed the whole of each day's press, 'docketing all paragraphs concerning men and things', a testing task unassisted even for Holmes, 'so that it was difficult to name a subject or a person on which he could not at once furnish information'. Obviously. An occasional pebble from this vast mountain of lore is of course immediately applicable to the case in hand. Just as stuff about grasses and fungi helped Dupin with Marie Rogêt, so Holmes would benefit from the research that went into that unforgettable monograph on the varieties of tobacco ash. But the real point of all this knowledge is much less what you do with it than the simple and memorable fact that you have it.

Knock Dupin as one may, his final and vital legacy to Holmes was what created the detective story as we have known it. However suspect Dupin's chains of inference may be at any particular link, what we are witnessing overall is a convinced demonstration of the power of the human mind to observe and to reason. This is what Holmes is constantly up to. He may, as the story unfolds, deny the reader vital clues and information—or Watson will do it for him, giving him the opportunity, in one of the two stories he narrates himself, to sneer at Watson's habit of contriving 'meretricious finales' by the use of this kind of suppression. A bit hard on poor Watson, this, considering he could only put in as much as Holmes would tell him. Anyway: Holmes may also irk us, or give us the wrong kind of laugh, by overdoing the demonstration, as when he discovers everything that happened at the scene of a fairly complicated crime by working on the footmarks with his lens, or by deducing seventeen separate facts, eleven of them nonphysical, about a man by examining his hat, one of the eleven being that his wife has ceased to love him. (Not all that difficult when you know how: the hat had not been brushed for a long time, and its age would have shown the man was too poor to afford a servant.) But many of the imaginative leaps are valid and thrilling: for instance, the moment when Holmes decides why an elderly pawnbroker has been induced to join a league of red-haired men after a glance at the trouser legs of the old boy's assistant. 'Holmes, this is marvellous!' Watson is supposed to cry when this sort of thing happens, though my recollection is that he never quite does. But he would have been right. It is marvellous.

The deductive prodigies are strongly supported by Doyle's gifts for suspense, horror and action writing, all carried forward on an unfailing flow of ingenious ideas. Holmes founded a dynasty. One of its more unexpected recent members is the Martian detective Syalok, a birdlike creature who wears a *tirstokr* hat, smokes a pipe in which the tobacco is cut with permanganate of potash, and in Poul Anderson's story 'The Martian Crown Jewels' recovers the theft of these diadems by a strict application of Holmesian principles—rather stricter, in fact, than the master often used himself. But Holmes has, in one sense, been even further afield than Mars. His exploits have been the subject of fierce controversy in Russia. I am indebted to G. F. McCleary for the information that some years ago the stories were issued there on a large scale, and that the librarians of the Red Army recommended Holmes to the troops as 'the exterminator of crimes and evils, a model of magnificent strength of thought and great culture'. This, McCleary continues, went down badly with a writer in the newspaper *Vechernaya Moskva,* who thought the tales offended socialist ideology by 'poisoning the minds of readers with false morals concerning the strength of the foundations of private property, and diverting attention from the social contradictions of capitalist reality'. Even Holmes himself might not have been able to deduce that much from the facts.

With few but shining exceptions, the heirs of Sherlock Holmes are an undistinguished lot. Lord Peter Wimsey has never quite survived, in my mind at least, the initial impression given by his righty-ho, dear-old-thing, don't-you-know, chin-chin style of dialogue and his mauve dressing-gown, primrose silk pyjamas, monocle and the rest of the outfit. Here I should in fairness make it plain that Wimsey is no more of a fag than Holmes is: he merely looks and sounds like one, as a certain kind of English aristocrat does to virtually all American, and the vast majori-

ty of British, eyes and ears. As for Wimsey, one might also plead that the bally-fool persona is, at least in part, put on to fool criminals. But what lies beneath the mask, if it is a mask, is hardly more attractive, and certainly less vivid. Lord Peter is just an old connoisseur and clubman who gets asked along to help out upper-crust families or trips over a stray corpse. In his later career the deductive faculty in him ran thin and he would fall back more on luck. He certainly got it, having once happened, for example, to have deposited a bag at a luggage counter where another bag that happened to be the twin of the first one happened also to have been deposited. The second bag happened to have somebody's head in it. In other adventures he got tied up with a ghastly female egghead, thus establishing to some extent his heterosexual bona fides, but at the same time forgetting about crime and talking to the female egghead instead, clear evidence for my rule that love and detection do not mix. Even in his heyday he often seemed to differ from the other people in the story by being merely slow on the uptake while they were moronic or crazed.

Hercule Poirot, Miss Marple, Ellery Queen, Inspector—later Assistant Commissioner Sir John—Appleby deserve, or at any rate will get, shorter shrift from me. I have never understood the fame of the two Agatha Christie characters, both of whom seem straight out of stock—Poirot the excitable but shrewd little foreigner, Marple the innocent, helpless-looking old lady with the keen blue eyes. And although some of the early Christies (*Why Didn't They Ask Evans?* for instance) had splendidly ingenious plots, the later Poirots and Marples have become thinned down, not surprisingly in a writer who has been hard at work for forty-five years. Queen, who has been around just since 1929, has had his ingenuities, too, but he is too slight a figure to sustain more than a tiny corner of Holmes's mantle, acting mostly as a sounding-board for the other characters, a camera for the story, and a mouthpiece when the author wants to chat things over with the reader. Ellery of the silver-coloured eyes is seldom much more than an extension of the plot.

To label as a similar plot device so distinguished a personage as Michael Innes's Appleby may look a little rough, but here I am doing it, and if Appleby could know, he would do no more than shrug his well-tailored shoulders, murmur a quotation from Donne or Hardy and perhaps reach for another modest measure of that liqueur brandy of his that surpasses anything in the Duke of Horton's cellar. Appleby has become an establishment figure, moving in a world that would be anathema to Holmes's Bohemian soul. The Appleby method of detection is to sit back and wait for the unconscious to come up with a solution, though the sitting back is purely mental: there can be plenty of physical rushing about in pursuit of stolen masterpieces, errant scientists with lethal secrets and such. Appleby is mostly the man to whom it all happens; most of it could happen to anybody, or nobody. The opposite is true of the novels of Edmund Crispin, who yet owes something to Innes. Crispin's detective, Gervase Fen, is an Oxford don, an eccentric after the fashion of Holmes or Wimsey, but funnier and in one sense grander than they, in that he seems to create his own kind of adventure. Nobody but Fen could find himself in a room whose occupant had unconsciously re-created the setting of Poe's 'The Raven', or in a situation to which the only clue depends on an intimate knowledge of Edward Lear's limericks. There is ingenuity here, too, including a non-electronic method of eavesdropping on a conversation out of earshot of the eavesdropper.

So far I have tried to anatomize six American and five British detectives, plus a few doubtful cases emanating from the general north-western-European area. This seems fair treatment of an Anglo-American literary form that has always had connections with France and thereabouts. Despite these connections, which go back at least as far as 1828, when the real-life detective François Eugène Vidocq began publishing his famous *Mémoires,* the detective story has flourished typically in the English language. A. E. Murch suggests in her detailed and fascinating work, *The Development of the Detective Novel* [see Further Reading: Secondary Sources], that the law in France among other places is set up in such a way that the public tends to regard the police with some fear and suspicion, at any rate without the instinctive feelings of support common to Americans and British, who thus find it easy and natural to sympathize with a hero working on the side of the police. Possibly. But then all kinds of genre writing, offshoots from the main stem of literature, are largely confined to English: not just the Western novel, but science fiction, the ghost story, to some extent the cloak-and-dagger thriller. Something vague and basic to do with the language? Decide for yourself.

The three great successors of Sherlock Holmes are G. K. Chesterton's Father Brown, Rex Stout's Nero Wolfe and John Dickson Carr's Doctor Fell. The first is British, the second American, the third British again but written about by an American, and so neatly preserving the balance.

Father Brown is not an eccentric in the superficial, violin-playing or orchid-rearing sense. But he is extraordinary enough, more so today than when Chesterton was writing, for Brown's extraordinariness is founded in his religion. Whether we like it or not, the little man's devotion, total courage, human insight and unshakable belief in reason are at any rate statistically uncommon. Some readers have found too much Roman Catholic propaganda in the stories. I feel that the Christian element, which is sometimes built into the plot, is never narrowly sectarian, and that part of it which overlaps with the advocacy of sheer common sense ought to be acceptable to everybody. It would be truer to say that what propaganda there is gets directed against atheism, complacent rationalism, occultism and superstition, all those shabby growths which the decline of Christian belief has fostered, and many, though perhaps not most, readers will sympathize here, too. My only real complaint is that this bias sometimes reveals the villain too early. We know at once that the prophet of a new sun cult is up to no good, and are not surprised that it is he who allows a blind girl to step to her death in an empty lift shaft.

Like Gervase Fen, though on a more serious level, Brown is made for the situations he encounters and they for him. They embody his love of paradox and of turning things back to front, his gift for seeing what is too obvious for everyone else to notice, his eye for the mentally invisible man. Only Brown could have wandered into a house where the recently dead owner's diamonds lay in full view minus their settings, heaps of snuff were piled on shelves, candles littered the tables, and the name of God had been carefully cut out of the family Bible every single time it occurred. And when the owner is dug up and found to be minus his head, only Brown would have taken this as natural and inevitable, the final clue showing that no crime had been committed after all. (You will have to read 'The Honour of Israel Gow' in *The Innocence of Father Brown* to find the answer.)

Rather too often, Brown runs into impersonations, twin brothers, secret passages, unlikely methods of murder: it would take a lot of good luck to succeed first try in dropping a noose round someone's neck from a dozen feet above him, and again to hit your man on the head with a hammer thrown from a church tower. But the good ideas are many and marvellous. The howling dog that gave away a murderer, the trail to an arch crook that began with somebody (guess who) swapping the contents of the sugar and salt containers in a restaurant, the man who seemed to have got into a garden without using the only entrance and the other man who got out of the same garden partly, but not completely—these are pretty standard occurrences in Father Brown's world. That world is vividly atmospheric, thanks to Chesterton's wonderful gift for depicting the effects of light on landscape, so that the stories glow as well as tease and mystify. They are works of art.

It is a goodish step from here to the old brownstone on West 35th Street where Nero Wolfe and Archie Goodwin chew the fat, eat their heads off, infuriate Inspector Cramer and incidentally catch crooks. The weakness of Stout's hugely readable stories is always the story. The idea of splitting the conventional detective into two—Wolfe to do the thinking, Archie the legwork—cuts both ways. It gives great scope for rounding out Wolfe's character, but it inevitably diminishes Archie in proportion. I find Archie faintly unsympathetic anyhow, a bit too effortlessly attractive to women, a bit too free with his fists, a bit too reminiscent of Sam Spade. Certainly, when he goes ferreting for Wolfe at Cramer's headquarters, or Lon Cohen's *Gazette* office, or wherever the crime may have taken place, the interest slackens. We want to be back with Wolfe. I can seldom be bothered with the details of the investigation, which usually proceeds by revelation and discovery rather than by actual deduction. What counts for most readers, I am sure, is the snappy dialogue, Archie's equally snappy narrative style, his relations with Wolfe (he is always sympathetic here), and finally, massively, triumphantly, Wolfe himself.

Wolfe gets about as far as a human being can, much further than Sherlock Holmes, in his suspicion, fear, almost hatred of humanity. We all have such moods, and Wolfe is there to reassure us that these feelings are quite proper for an intelligent, learned, humane and humorous man. This is perhaps the secret of his attraction, for attractive he abundantly is. Along with this goes a marked formidable quality, such that one would, on meeting Wolfe in the flesh, feel grateful for his approval and daunted by his contempt. All really great detectives inspire this reaction, perhaps by acting as some version of a father figure. Brown does it to us, Dr Fell does; even, granted the shift in general outlook since late-Victorian times, Holmes does. Any kind of real policeman does not, and anybody Mike Hammer took a liking to ought to feel a twinge of alarm.

Another part of Wolfe's appeal is his addiction to views and attitudes that seem both outdated and sensible, reactionary and right, the sort of thing you and I ought to think and feel, and probably would if we had Wolfe's leisure and obstinacy. Who has not wanted to insist on never going out, living to an unshakable routine, distrusting all machines more complicated than a wheelbarrow and having to be heavily pressured each time before getting into a car, allowing hardly anybody to use one's first name, keeping television out and reading all the time, reacting so little in conversation that an eighth-of-an-inch shake of the head becomes a frenzy of negation, using an inflexible formal courtesy such that proven murderers are still referred to as 'Mr' and an eighteenth-century style of speech that throws off stuff like: 'Afraid? I can dodge folly without backing into fear' and: 'Madam, I am neither a thaumaturge nor a dunce'? Wolfe is every man's Tory, a contemporary Dr Johnson. The original Dr Johnson was a moralist before everything else, and so at heart is Wolfe. This, I suppose, makes him even more of an antique.

Lastly, Dr Gideon Fell. I must explain at once that, when writing under his pseudonym of Carter Dickson, John Dickson Carr uses a detective called Sir Henry Merrivale, or H. M., who according to me is an old bore. His adventures, however, are as fascinating as any of Fell's, and I should not want to put anybody off masterpieces like *The White Priory Murders, The Reader Is Warned* and *The Ten Teacups*. They are, of course, as are the best Carr novels, minor masterpieces. Perhaps no detective story can attain the pitch of literary excellence. Perhaps it can only offer ingenuity raised to the point of genius. In Carr-cum-Dickson it does, perhaps two dozen times in all, and this author is a first-rate artist. A neglected one, naturally, and likely to remain so while detective fiction remains undervalued, while most of those who should know better remain ignorant of the heights of craftsmanship and virtuosity it can reach. I will offer a small prize to any such person who can read the first chapter of Carr's *The Burning Court* and not in honesty have to go on. Neither Fell nor H. M. nor any great detective features here, only an adequate one. The book is a tour-de-force blending of detection and witchcraft: both ingredients genuine.

To return at length to Dr Fell—it would have been useful in one way to come to him straight after Father Brown. The character of Fell has little to do with that of Brown, but a great deal, especially physically, with Chesterton himself. The huge girth, the bandit's moustache, the box-pleated cape and shovel hat, the enthusiasm for English pubs, beer and roast beef, all these are taken straight from that brilliant and inventive but so often unsatisfactory writer. And more than this. Fell's world is that of Brown made more probable, the wilder flights of fancy brought under control, the holes in the plot conscientiously plastered over and made good. Like Brown, Fell constantly encounters the impossible murder, but Fell shows its possibility more convincingly. Most often, almost always, the victim is discovered in a locked room, last seen in good health, exits and entrances secured or watched or even guarded by responsible and provenly innocent outsiders. Carr boasts that he has devised over eighty different solutions to the locked-room puzzle, and in one of the novels Fell, a monologist with the best of them, delivers a fascinating lecture on the subject. This is *The Three Coffins*, to quote the inexcusable American retitling of the British

edition *The Hollow Man,* which perfectly suggests the macabre menace of the story. That man must indeed have been hollow who, watched of course by a responsible and innocent witness, was seen to enter a room without other access in which, later, there is found the corpse of the room's occupant, but of course no hollow man. This is Chestertonian, or Brownian, though its explanation has a Carrian validity; and another novel, *The Crooked Hinge,* takes as the epigraph of its final section a quotation from a Father Brown story that begins: 'There was one thing which Flambeau, with all his dexterity of disguise, could not cover, and that was his singular height.' On finishing the novel one can see that its whole structure grew out of the implications of that sentence. In fact, an ideal reader would be able to solve the murder at that point without further assistance. The explanation is simple and entirely plausible, but you would just not happen to think of it: Chesterton out-Chestertoned.

The light in Gideon Fell's study is burning low. He still works desultorily at his great chronicle of *The Drinking Customs of England from the Earliest Days,* still gives great rumbling sniffs and plies his red bandanna handkerchief. But without conviction. He makes rare and comparatively ineffectual public appearances now. His heyday came to an end somewhere about 1950, and there died with it the classical detective story, in which all the clues were scrupulously put before the reader, the kind of writing of which Fell's creator has been the greatest exponent.

Elsewhere the picture is the same. Recruitment to the ranks of potential great detectives has fallen to nothing. Real policemen are all the rage. Fell always got on well with them, had no hesitation about saving himself trouble by using their findings, but though they were smart and often nearly right, he was smarter and always right. He would view the activities of contemporary real policemen like Van der Valk with tolerance, even appreciation, but he would have little time for the character who has usurped his place in the sun: the secret agent, the international spy. I can hear him muttering under his bandit's moustache about the sad substitution of brawn for brain as the up-to-date hero's essential characteristic, of action for thought and glamour for decency. I would only go part of the way with him there. But I can sympathize. (pp. 108-25)

Kingsley Amis, "Unreal Policemen," in his What Became of Jane Austen? and Other Questions, *1970. Reprint by Harcourt Brace Jovanovich, Inc., 1971, pp. 108-25.*

DEFINING DETECTIVE FICTION

Carolyn Wells

[*Wells was a popular and prolific American humorist, mystery writer, and critic during the first half of the twentieth century. Her novels featuring the detective Fleming Stone were among the bestsellers of their time. Her study* The Technique of the Mystery Story *(1913), a guide for aspiring writers, was the first book of its kind and is still highly regarded as a sound reference source. In the following excerpt from that work, she defines some principles and facets of the detective story.*]

I. What is a Detective Story?

The class of fiction which we shall group under this head must include all stories where the problem is invented and solved by the author and set forth in such a way as to give an astute reader opportunities for guessing or reasoning out the answer.

An actual detective need not necessarily figure in the story, but detective work must be done by some of the characters.

There must be crime or apparent crime or attempted crime. But whether the problem is one of murder, robbery or kidnapping,—whether it be solved by evidence, deduction or a cryptogram,—it is detected, not guessed, and this is the main element in our classification.

The average or typical Detective Story of to-day is the detailed narrative of the proceedings of an individual of unusual mental acumen in unraveling a mystery.

Strictly speaking, a detective is a member of the police organization or of a private detective agency. But for fictional purposes he may be such, or he may be any one with what is called "detective instinct" or a taste for detective work. (p. 43)

2. Rise of the Detective Story

The Detective Story as we know it was first written by Poe, yet he never used the descriptive word, nor was Dupin a detective, either professional or amateur, for when Poe wrote his immortal Dupin tales, the name "Detective" Stories had not been invented; the detective of fiction not having been as yet discovered. And the title is still something of a misnomer, for many narratives involving a puzzle of some sort, though belonging to the category which we shall discuss, are handled by the writer without expert detective aid. Sometimes the puzzle solves itself through operation of circumstance; sometimes somebody who professes no special detective skill happens upon the secret of its mystery; once in a while some venturesome genius has the courage to leave his enigma unexplained. But ever since Gaboriau created his Lecoq, the *transcendent detective* has been in favor, and Conan Doyle's famous gentleman analyst has given him a fresh lease of life, and reanimated the stage by reverting to the method of Poe. Sherlock Holmes is Dupin *redivivus,* and *mutatus mutandis;* personally he is a more stirring and engaging companion, but so far as kinship to probabilities or even possibilities is concerned, perhaps the older version of him is the more presentable. But in this age of marvels we seem less difficult to suit in this respect than our forefathers were.

The fact is, meanwhile, that, in the Riddle Story, the detective was an afterthought, or, more accurately, a *deus ex machina* to make the story go. The riddle had to be unriddled; and who could do it so naturally and readily as a detective? The detective, as Poe saw him, was a means to this end; and it was only afterwards that writers perceived his availability as a character. Lecoq accordingly becomes a figure in fiction, and Sherlock, while he was yet a novelty,

was nearly as attractive as the complications in which he involved himself.

Detective Story writers in general, however, encounter the obvious embarrassment that their detective is obliged to lavish so much attention on the professional services which the exigencies of the tale demand of him, that he has very little leisure to attend to his own personal equation—the rather since the attitude of peering into a millstone is not, of itself, conducive to elucidations of oneself; the professional endowment obscures all the others. We ordinarily find, therefore, our author dismissing the individuality of his detective with a few strong black-chalk outlines, and devoting his main labor upon what he feels the reader will chiefly occupy his own ingenuity with,—namely, the elaboration of the riddle itself. Reader and writer sit down to a game, as it were, with the odds, of course, altogether on the latter's side,—apart from the fact that a writer sometimes permits himself a little cheating. It more often happens that the detective appears to be in the writer's pay, and aids the deception by leading the reader off on false scents. Be that as it may, the professional sleuth is in nine cases out of ten a dummy by malice prepense; and it might be plausibly argued that, in the interest of pure art, that is what he ought to be. But genius always finds a way that is better than the rules, and it will be found that the very best riddle stories contrive to drive character and riddle side by side, and to make each somehow enhance the effect of the other.

The intention of the above paragraph will be more precisely conveyed if we include under the name of detective not only the man from the central office, but also anybody whom the writer may, for ends of his own, consider better qualified for that function. The latter is a professional detective so far as the exigencies of the tale are concerned, and what becomes of him after that, nobody need care,—there is no longer anything to prevent his becoming, in his own right, the most fascinating of mankind.

Before Poe's or Gaboriau's stories, appeared the *Memoirs of Vidocq.* This work, thought by many to be largely fiction, is the history of a clever villain who became a detective, though never called by that name. He was a Secret Agent, and is called on his own title page, Principal Agent of the French Police. His memoirs are old-fashioned, dull and uninteresting, but they show glimmerings of the kind of reasoning that later marked the Fiction Detective.

Perhaps Gaboriau was the first author to use the terminology, since become so familiar, of detective, clues, deduction, etc.

Poe ascribed to his Dupin, "analytic ability," and this is all that is claimed for the conventional detective of fiction, though perhaps more acutely described by Brander Matthews as "imaginative ratiocination."

Poe goes further in saying Dupin's work was "The result of an excited or perhaps a diseased intelligence." This statement may have mirrored the author's own mind, for, while making no assertion, Professor Matthews observes that he should understand any one who might declare that Poe had mental disease raised to the nth power, and we have long since been told that "great wits are sure to madness near allied."

3. The Detective—Fictive and Real

But it is this very principle that marks the difference between the detective in fiction and in real life. The cleverest detectives in life are not men of diseased intellect, however greatly developed may be their powers of ratiocination. It is just that touch of abnormality, of superhuman reasoning, that makes a Transcendent Detective.

Again, the work of the fiction detective is always successful. Naturally, because his work is planned to this end by the author. The fiction detective plays his game with marked cards. Though seemingly groping in the dark, he is walking a definite path laid straight to a definite end. He is pushed off on false scents, but pulled back and set right again by an adjusting power which does not exist in the case of real detectives.

Indeed, the sooner the writer of detective fiction realizes that the detective of fiction has little in common with the detective in real life, the better is that author equipped for his work.

The real detective, for one thing, is rarely a man of culture or high ideals. The fiction detective is usually an aristocrat, unfortunately impoverished, or working at his art for art's sake.

The real detective, however great his analytic ability, often finds that he cannot apply it to his case. The fiction detective never has this experience; he finds his case ready made and perfectly fitted to his powers.

The real detective finds little or nothing in the way of useful material clues. The fiction detective finds his properties laid ready to his hand at the right moment. Dropped handkerchiefs, shreds of clothing, broken cuff-links, torn letters,—all are sprinkled in the path ahead of him, like roses strewn before a bride.

Even Nature lends a helping hand to the favored detective of fiction. Usually "A light snow had fallen the evening before." This snow is declared by credible witnesses to have begun at one psychological moment, and stopped at another; thus allowing the inevitable display of footprints of certain sizes, shapes and superimposition. Indeed the laws of nature are willing to give way, at need, and vegetation takes on unusual qualities to help along the good work. Sherlock Holmes continually finds his indicative footprints on turf or grass plot, and of course the criminal is identified at once.

But the real detective seldom if ever finds these helpful footprints at the right time and place. In case of his need of them, the obstinate ground is hard and unimpressionable; or the snow is melting and shows only oblong holes; or the grass refuses to present a clear and definite impression; or even if fairly respectable muddy footprints appear on a nice, clean, hard-wood floor, they are so incomplete in outline that they might have been made by any well-advertised shoe.

The criminals and suspects in fiction must presumably wear shoes made for the purpose, with flat level soles that touch the floor at all points and leave an exact working diagram, instead of a shapeless blotch with ragged edges.

Similarly with finger-prints. Though carefully impressed in incriminating places by the fiction criminals, in real life they are rarely found where they can be of use. The finger prints found on the discarded empty frame of the Mona Lisa have not yet led to the recovery of the picture; whereas in fiction they would long ago have put the thief behind bars.

No, the fiction detective is not a real person, any more than the fairy godmother is a real person; but both are honored and popular celebrities in the realm of fiction.

And if one would realize the immense superiority of the fiction detective for fiction purposes he has only to read any of the occasionally published "true detective stories," or even those which are founded on actual cases.

4. Fiction versus Fact

Many years ago, old-fashioned family papers published stories, beneath whose titles a line in parenthesis read, "Founded on fact." Such tales were invariably uninteresting, and at last the editors learned not to publish them.

A true tale of a criminal problem and its solution is uninteresting because it is not planned to be interesting. The technique of the detective story calls for the same kind of planning and preparation on the part of the author as does a successful act of legerdemain. The prestidigitator takes a rabbit out of a silk hat, but unless he had planned for it beforehand he couldn't do it. What he might take, unplanned, out of the hat,—its leather band or gilt stamped lining,—would be of no interest to his audience. (pp. 44-50)

Realism, according to its American master, Mr. W. D. Howells, is nothing more than the truthful treatment of material; and in Mr. Howells' hands this treatment has produced writings of absorbing interest. But it is an equally truthful treatment of material that appears in the Social and Personal column of the *Miller's Corners Weekly Gazette,* or in the Congressional Record, yet we are not interested in either.

But in the plot of a Detective Story, or in the mental make-up of the detective, realism finds little place—as much as you wish in the material details, in the clues, the inquest, or the suspected butler, but the key-note of the story itself is that of pure fiction.

It must *seem* to be true as fairy stories *seem* true to children. You must persuade your readers to believe it, as Peter Pan wheedled his audience into believing in fairies; but "Founded on Fact" or "Elaborated from the Records of a Real Detective," is fatal to the interest of a Detective Story.

Let the argument ring true, let the accessories be realistic, let the situations be logical and the conditions plausible; but let the magic of the unreal detective twinkle through it all as fairies dance in real moonlight. Sustain the interest by a subtly woven chain of events that leads unerringly to the climax in a way the uncertainties of real life can never do. Lead your readers on to the re-solution of the problem, whose terms have been stated in logical sequence straight through the book. (pp. 51-2)

[The] study of the methods of criminal investigation is not entertaining to the reader, unless written as literature,—indeed, as fiction.

A simple description of a crime and the methods pursued in regard to its investigation make dry reading. The setting, the characters, the atmosphere, of a well-constructed story are necessary to make it entertaining. (p. 55)

Carolyn Wells, "Detective Stories," in her The Technique of the Mystery Story, *The Home Correspondence School*, 1913, pp. 43-64.

S. S. Van Dine [Pseudonym of Willard Huntington Wright]

[*Van Dine was one of the most popular detective fiction writers of the 1920s and 1930s, and his novels featuring the brilliant and exotic Philo Vance resurrected the genre as a vital popular form in American literature. In the following excerpt, he examines some characteristics of detective fiction in an attempt to evaluate the reasons for its appeal.*]

There is a tendency among modern critics to gauge all novels by a single literary standard—a standard, in fact, which should be applied only to novels that patently seek a niche among the enduring works of imaginative letters. That all novels do not aspire to such exalted company is obvious; and it is manifestly unfair to judge them by a standard their creators deliberately ignored. Novels of sheer entertainment belong in a different category from those written for purposes of intellectual and aesthetic stimulation; for they are fabricated in a spirit of evanescent diversion, and avoid all the deeper concerns of art.

The novel designed purely for entertainment and the literary novel spring, in the main, from quite different impulses. Their objectives have almost nothing in common. The mental attitudes underlying them are antipathetic: one is frankly superficial, the other sedulously profound. They achieve diametrically opposed results; and their appeals are psychologically unrelated; in fact, they are unable to fulfil each other's function; and the reader who, at different times, can enjoy both without intellectual conflict, can never substitute the one for the other. Any attempt to measure them by the same rules is as inconsistent as to criticize a vaudeville performance and the plays of Shakespeare from the same point of view, or to hold a musical comedy to the standards by which we estimate the foremost grand opera. Even Schnitzler's *Anatol* may not be approached in the same critical frame of mind that one brings to Hauptmann's *The Weavers;* and if *The Mikado* or *Pinafore* were held strictly to the musical canons of *Parsifal* or *Die Meistersinger,* they would suffer unjustly. In the graphic arts the same principle holds. Forain and Degas are not to be judged by the aesthetic criteria we apply to Michelangelo's drawings and the paintings of Rubens.

There are four distinct varieties of the "popular," or "light," novel—to wit: the romantic novel (dealing with young love, and ending generally either at the hymeneal altar or with a prenuptial embrace); the novel of adventure (in which physical action and danger are the chief constituents: sea stories, wild-west yarns, odysseys of the African wilds, etc.); the mystery novel (wherein much of the dramatic suspense is produced by hidden forces that are not revealed until the *dénouement:* novels of diplomatic intrigue, international plottings, secret societies, crime, pseudoscience, specters, and the like); and the detective novel. These types often overlap in content, and at times become so intermingled in subject-matter that one is not quite sure in which category they primarily belong. But though they may borrow devices and appeals from one another, and usurp one another's distinctive material, they follow, in the main, their own special subject, and evolve within their own boundaries.

Of these four kinds of literary entertainment the detective novel is the youngest, the most complicated, the most difficult of construction, and the most distinct. It is, in fact, almost *sui generis,* and, except in its more general structural characteristics, has little in common with its fellows—the romantic, the adventurous, and the mystery novel. In one sense, to be sure, it is a highly specialized offshoot of the last named; but the relationship is far more distant than the average reader imagines.

If we are to understand the unique place held in modern letters by the detective novel, we must first endeavor to determine its peculiar appeal; for this appeal is fundamentally unrelated to that of any other variety of fictional entertainment. What, then, constitutes the hold that the detective novel has on all classes of people—even those who would not stoop to read any other kind of "popular" fiction? Why do we find men of high cultural attainments—college professors, statesmen, scientists, philosophers, and men concerned with the graver, more advanced, more intellectual problems of life—passing by all other varieties of best-seller novels, and going to the detective story for diversion and relaxation?

The answer, I believe, is simply this: the detective novel does not fall under the head of fiction in the ordinary sense, but belongs rather in the category of riddles: it is, in fact, a complicated and extended puzzle cast in fictional form. Its widespread popularity and interest are due, at bottom and in essence, to the same factors that give popularity and interest to the cross-word puzzle. Indeed, the structure and mechanism of the cross-word puzzle and of the detective novel are very similar. In each there is a problem to be solved; and the solution depends wholly on mental processes—on analysis, on the fitting together of apparently unrelated parts, on a knowledge of the ingredients, and, in some measure, on guessing. Each is supplied with a series of overlapping clues to guide the solver; and these clues, when fitted into place, blaze the path for future progress. In each, when the final solution is achieved, all the details are found to be woven into a complete, interrelated, and closely knitted fabric.

There is confirmatory evidence of the mechanical impulse that inspires the true detective novel when we consider what might almost be called the dominant intellectual *penchant* of its inventor. Poe, the originator of the modern detective story, was obsessed with the idea of scientific experimentation. His faculty for analysis manifested itself in his reviews and in the technicalities of his poetry; it produced "Maelzel's Chess-Player"; it led him into the speculative ramifications of handwriting idiosyncrasies in "A Chapter on Autography"; it brought forth his exposition of cryptograms and code-writing in "Cryptography"; and it gave birth to his acrostic verses. His four analytic stories—"The Murders in the Rue Morgue," "The Mystery of Marie Rogêt," "The Gold-Bug," and "The Purloined Letter"—were but a literary development, or application, of the ideas and problems which always fascinated him. "The Gold-Bug," in fact, was merely a fictional presenta-

tion of "Cryptography." (Incidentally, the number of detective stories since Poe's day that have hid their solutions in cipher messages is legion.)

There is no more stimulating activity than that of the mind; and there is no more exciting adventure than that of the intellect. Mankind has always received keen enjoyment from the mental gymnastics required in solving a riddle; and puzzles have been its chief toy throughout the ages. But there is a great difference between waiting placidly for the solution of a problem, and the swift and exhilarating participation in the succeeding steps that lead to the solution. In the average light novel of romance, adventure, or mystery, the reader merely awaits the author's unraveling of the tangled skein of events. True, during the waiting period he is given emotion, wonder, suspense, sentiment and description, with which to occupy himself; and the average novel depends in large measure on these addenda to furnish his enjoyment. But in the detective novel, as we shall see, these qualities are either subordinated to ineffectuality, or else eliminated entirely. The reader is immediately put to work, and kept busy in every chapter, at the task of solving the book's mystery. He shares in the unfoldment of the problem in precisely the same way he participates in the solution of any riddle to which he applies himself.

Madeleine Carroll and Robert Donat in a scene from the 1935 film version of John Buchan's The Thirty-Nine Steps, *directed by Alfred Hitchcock.*

Because of this singularity of appeal the detective novel has gone its own way irrespective of the *progressus* of all other fictional types. It has set its own standards, drawn up its own rules, adhered to its own heritages, advanced along its own narrow-gage track, and created its own ingredients as well as its own form and technic. And all these considerations have had to do with its own isolated purpose, with its own special destiny. In the process of this evolution it has withdrawn farther and farther from its literary fellows, until to-day it has practically reversed the principles on which the ordinary popular novel is based.

A sense of reality is essential to the detective novel. The few attempts that have been made to lift the detective-story plot out of its naturalistic environment and confer on it an air of fancifulness have been failures. A castles-in-Spain atmosphere, wherein the reader may escape from the materiality of every day, often gives the average popular novel its charm and readability; but the objective of a detective novel—the mental reward attending its solution—would be lost unless a sense of verisimilitude was consistently maintained,—a feeling of triviality would attach to its problem, and the reader would experience a sense of wasted effort. This is why in cross-word puzzles the words are all genuine: their correct determination achieves a certain educational, or at least serious, result. The "trick" cross-word puzzle with coined words and purely logomachic inventions (such as filling four boxes with e's—e-e-e-e—for the word "ease," or with i's—i-i-i-i—for the word "eyes," or making u-u-u-u stand for the word "use") has never been popular. The philologic realism, so to speak, is dissipated. A. E. W. Mason has said somewhere that Defoe would have written the perfect detective story. He was referring to Defoe's surpassing ability to create a realistic environment.

This rule of realism suggests the common literary practise of endowing *mises en scène* with varying emotional pressures. And here again the detective novel differs from its fictional confrères; for, aside from the primary achievement of a sense of reality, atmospheres, in the descriptive and psychic sense, have no place in this type of story. Once the reader has accepted the pseudoactuality of the plot, his energies are directed (like those of the detective himself) to the working out of the puzzle; and his mood, being an intellectual one, is only distracted by atmospheric invasions. Atmospheres belong to the romantic and the adventurous tale, such as Poe's "The Fall of the House of Usher" and Scott's *Ivanhoe,* and to the novel of mystery— Henry James's *The Turn of the Screw* and Bram Stoker's *Dracula,* for instance.

The setting of a detective story, however, is of cardinal importance. The plot must appear to be an actual record of events springing from the terrain of its operations; and the plans and diagrams so often encountered in detective stories aid considerably in the achievement of this effect. A familiarity with the terrain and a belief in its existence are what give the reader his feeling of ease and freedom in manipulating the factors of the plot to his own (which are also the author's) ends. Hampered by strange conditions and modes of action, his personal participation in the story's solution becomes restricted and his interest in its *sequiturs* wanes. A detective novel is nearly always more popular in the country in which it is laid than in a foreign country where the conditions, both human and topo-

graphic, are unfamiliar. The variations between English and American customs and police methods, and mental and temperamental attributes, are, of course, not nearly so marked as between those of America and France; and no sharp distinction is now drawn between the English and the American detective tale. But many of the best French novels of this type have had indifferent sales in the United States. Gaston Leroux's *The Mystery of the Yellow Room, The Perfume of the Lady in Black,* and *The Secret of the Night* have never had their deserved popularity in this country because of their foreign *locales;* but *The Phantom of the Opera,* by the same author, which is a sheer mystery story, has been a great success here, due largely to that very unfamiliarity of setting that has worked against the success of his detective novels.

In the matter of character-drawing the detective novel also stands outside the rules governing ordinary fiction. Characters in detective stories may not be too neutral and colorless, nor yet too fully and intimately delineated. They should merely fulfil the requirements of plausibility, so that their actions will not appear to spring entirely from the author's preconceived scheme. Any closely drawn character analysis, any undue lingering over details of temperament, will act only as a clog in the narrative machinery. The automaton of the cheap detective thriller detracts from the reader's eagerness to rectify the confusion of the plot; and the subtly limned personality of the "literary" detective novel shunts the analytic operations of the reader's mind to extraneous considerations. Think back over all the good detective stories you may have read, and try to recall a single memorable personality (aside from the detective himself). And yet these characters were of sufficient color and rotundity to enlist your sympathetic emotions at the time, and to drive you on to a solution of their problems.

The style of a detective story must be direct, simple, smooth, and unencumbered. A "literary" style, replete with descriptive passages, metaphors, and word pictures, which might give viability and beauty to a novel of romance or adventure, would, in a detective yarn, produce sluggishness in the actional current by diverting the reader's mind from the mere record of facts (which is what he is concerned with), and focussing it on irrelevant aesthetic appeals. I do not mean that the style of the detective novel must be bald and legalistic, or cast in the stark language of commercial documentary exposition; but it must, like the style of Defoe, subjugate itself to the function of producing unadorned verisimilitude. No more is gained by stylizing a detective novel than by printing a cross-word puzzle in Garamond Italic, or Cloister Cursive, or the Swash characters of Caslon Old-style.

The material for the plot of a detective novel must be commonplace. Indeed, there are a dozen adequate plots for this kind of story on the front page of almost any metropolitan daily paper. Unusualness, *bizarrerie,* fantasy, or strangeness in subject-matter is rarely desirable; and herein we find another striking reversal of the general rules applying to popular fiction; for originality and eccentricity of plot may give a novel of adventure or mystery its main interest. The task confronting the writer of detective fiction is again the same confronting the cross-word-puzzle manufacturer—namely, the working of familiar materials into a difficult riddle. The skill of a detective story's crafts-

manship is revealed in the way these materials are fitted together, the subtlety with which the clues are presented, and the legitimate manner in which the final solution is withheld.

Furthermore, there is a strict ethical course of conduct imposed upon the author. He must never once deliberately fool the reader: he must succeed by ingenuity alone. The habit of inferior writers of bringing forward false clues whose purpose is to mislead is as much a form of cheating as if the cross-word-puzzle maker should print false definitions to his words. The truth must at all times be in the printed word, so that if the reader should go back over the book he would find that the solution had been there all the time if he had had sufficient shrewdness to grasp it. There was a time when all manner of tricks, deceits, and farfetched devices were employed for the reader's befuddlement; but as the detective novel developed and the demand for straightforward puzzle stories increased, all such methods were abrogated, and to-day we find them only in the cheapest and most inconsequential examples of this type of fiction.

In the central character of the detective novel—the detective himself—we have, perhaps, the most important and original element of the criminal-problem story. It is difficult to describe his exact literary status, for he has no counterpart in any other fictional *genre.* He is, at one and the same time, the outstanding personality of the story (though he is concerned in it only in an *ex-parte* capacity), the projection of the author, the embodiment of the reader, the *deus ex machina* of the plot, the propounder of the problem, the supplier of the clues, and the eventual solver of the mystery. The life of the book takes place in him, yet the life of the narrative has its being outside of him. In a lesser sense, he is the Greek chorus of the drama. All good detective novels have had for their protagonist a character of attractiveness and interest, of high and fascinating attainments—a man at once human and unusual, colorful and gifted. The buffoon, the bungler, the prig, the automaton—all such have failed. And sometimes in an endeavor to be original an otherwise competent writer, misjudging the psychology of the situation has presented us with a farcical detective or a juvenile investigator, only to wonder, later on, why these innovations failed. The more successful detective stories have invariably given us such personalities as *C. Auguste Dupin, Monsieur Lecoq, Sherlock Holmes, Dr. Thorndyke, Rouletabille, Dr. Fortune, Furneaux, Father Brown, Uncle Abner, Richard Hannay, Arsène Lupin, Dawson, Martin Hewitt, Max Carrados* and *Hanaud*—to name but a few that come readily to mind. All the books in which these characters appear do not fall unqualifiedly into the true detective-story category; but in each tale there are sufficient elements to permit broadly of the detective classification. Furthermore, these Œdipuses themselves are not, in every instance, authentic sleuths: some are doctors of medicine, some professors of astronomy, some soldiers, some journalists, some lawyers, and some reformed crooks. But their vocations do not matter, for in this style of book the designation "detective" is used generically.

We come now to what is perhaps the outstanding characteristic of the detective novel: its unity of mood. To be sure, this is a desideratum of all fiction; but the various moods of the ordinary novel—such as love, romance, adventure, wonder, mystery—are so closely related that they may be intermingled or alternated without breaking the thread of interest; whereas, in the detective novel, the chief interest being that of mental analysis and the overcoming of difficulties, any interpolation of purely emotional moods produces the effect of irrelevancy—unless, of course, they are integers of the equation and are subordinated to the main theme. For instance, in none of the best detective novels will you find a love interest,—*Sherlock Holmes* in mellow mood, holding a lady's hand and murmuring amorous platitudes, would be unthinkable. And when a detective is sent scurrying on a long-drawn-out adventure beset with physical dangers, the reader fumes and frets until his hero is again in his armchair analyzing clues and inquiring into motives.

In this connection it is significant that the cinematograph has never been able to project a detective story. The detective story, in fact, is the only type of fiction that cannot be filmed. The test of popular fiction—namely, its presentation in visual pictures, or let us say, the visualizing of its word-pictures—goes to pieces when applied to detective stories. The difficulties confronting a motion-picture director in the screening of a detective tale are very much the same as those he would encounter if he strove to film a cross-word puzzle. The only serious attempt to transcribe a detective story onto the screen was the case of "Sherlock Holmes"; and the effort was made possible only by reducing the actual detective elements to a minimum, and emphasizing all manner of irrelevant dramatic and adventurous factors; for there is neither drama nor adventure, in the conventional sense, in a good detective novel. (pp. 3-11)

A word in parting should be said in regard to the primary theme of the detective novel, for herein lies one of its most important elements of interest. Crime has always exerted a profound fascination over humanity, and the more serious the crime the greater has been that appeal. Murder, therefore, has always been an absorbing public topic. The psychological reasons for this morbid and elemental curiosity need not be gone into here; but the fact itself supplies us with the explanation of why a murder mystery furnishes a far more fascinating *raison d'être* in a detective novel than does any lesser crime. All the best and most popular books of this type deal with mysteries involving human life. Murder would appear to give added zest to the solution of the problem, and to render the satisfaction of the solution just so much greater. The reader feels, no doubt, that his efforts have achieved something worth while—something commensurate with the amount of mental energy which a good detective novel compels him to expand. (p. 37)

S. S. Van Dine [pseudonym of Willard Huntington Wright], in an introduction to The World's Great Detective Stories: A Chronological Anthology, *edited by S. S. Van Dine, Blue Ribbon Books, 1931, pp. 3-37.*

R. A. Knox

[*Knox was an English essayist, critic, translator, and detective story writer who was renowned as one of the most influential Catholic apologists in England. His translations of the Latin New Testament in 1946 and the Old*

Testament in 1949 have been highly praised. In the following excerpt, he discusses several essential characteristics of detective fiction and lists his nine rules for the genre.]

What exactly is a detective story? The title must not be applied indiscriminately to all romances in which a detective, whether professional or amateur, plays a leading part. You might write a novel the hero of which was a professional detective who did not get on with his wife, and therefore ran away with somebody else's in Chapter 58, as is the wont of heroes in modern novels. That would not be a detective story. A detective story must have as its main interest the unravelling of a mystery; a mystery whose elements are clearly presented to the reader at an early stage in the proceedings, and whose nature is such as to arouse curiosity, a curiosity which is gratified at the end of the book. (pp. 181-82)

To put it quite simply, the essence of the detective story is that in it the action takes place before the story begins. Of course, it is well to have one or two chapters at the beginning introducing us to the principal characters and especially to the future corpse or corpses. It is one of the weaknesses of Freeman Wills Croft that he sometimes presents us, in his first two chapters, with the body of a total stranger; at once he has missed a chance of invoking our human sympathies; nor does it make the case any better to discover, as we usually do, at the end of the book, that it was really a totally different total stranger all the time. No, Chapter 1 and perhaps Chapter 2 ought to introduce us to the main characters; but with Chapter 3 or thereabouts the curtain must suddenly go up on a murder or at least a crime already committed, ripe for investigation by the famous detective. The real action of the book is now over. And here is one of the chief difficulties about writing detective stories—to keep the interest alive in spite of the fact that what remains of the plot is, strictly speaking, not action at all, but mere unravelling. There are various ways of solving the difficulty; Mr. A. E. W. Mason, who stands, of course, in the very front rank of detective writers, always manages to get his heroine spirited away by villains early in the story, and Hanaud is careful not to rescue her until she is on the very point of being bumped off. Conscientious detective fans will always have the feeling that this method is a doubtful expedient; for, if the interest of the story is thus kept at a breathless level of excitement, we are apt to forget what the original mystery was about; we are apt, again, so rapidly are we carried along, to miss through carelessness clues that might otherwise have led us to the true solution of the mystery. Roughly speaking, it may be laid down that in the true detective story the elements of horror and violence are already over before the detective appears on the scene; and the story derives its romantic excitement only from the danger of the criminal getting off scot free, or some innocent person being condemned in his place.

It will be seen, therefore, that the detective story differs essentially from every other type of fiction. For the interest of the ordinary romance centres in the question, "What will happen?"—except in the case of the modern sex novel, where the interest centres in the question "When will anything happen?" But the interest of the detective story centres in the question "What has happened?" It is a *hysteron proteron Homerikos*. Ordinary romance was invented, one would think, by a wearied historian, who, finding himself, like most historians, unable to give a true account of the past, and willing, unlike most historians, to confess his inability, sat down to write a kind of literature in which all his characters behaved exactly as he wanted them to, because they had no existence outside his own brain. Whereas one would have expected the first writer of detective fiction to have been a scientist, who, giving up the riddles of his own craft, which either defied explanation or alternatively opened out fresh vistas of problems demanding fresh explanations, determined to set himself a problem which he *could* solve, because he and no other was responsible for the inventing of it. Ordinary fiction appeals to the synthetic in our natures, detective fiction to the analytic. Ordinary fiction works forwards from the conditions of the plot to its consummation, detective fiction works backwards from its consummation to its conditions. Indeed, I am trying to think up a quite new sort of crook film; the crime will be enacted at Hollywood exactly as it took place; but it will be turned into a detective film when it is shewn by the simple expedient of shewing it backwards. (pp. 183-85)

[What] are the rules governing the art of the detective story? Let us remember in the first place that these are rules; and you cannot afford to overlook them, because the detective story is a game. People try to write poetry without rhyme and novels without plots and prose without meaning and so on; they may be right or they may be wrong, but such liberties must not be taken in the field of which we are speaking. For every detective story is a game played between the author and the reader; the author has scored if he can reach the last chapter without letting the reader see how the crime was committed, although he has given him hints all through which ought theoretically to have let him work it out for himself. And there will be no triumph in doing that if the author has broken the rules.

There are nine main rules, which I laid down in a book which nobody read, as long ago as 1924. I will give them here with a slight commentary.

I. The criminal must be someone who has been mentioned in the first five chapters, but it must not be anyone whose thoughts the reader has been allowed to follow. The first half of this rule is often broken by the worst detective writers. What on earth is the use of a mysterious stranger, whose very existence has never been suspected hitherto, turning up in chapter eleven? The second half of the rule is three times almost infringed by Agatha Christie—in *The Man in the Brown Suit, The Murder of Roger Ackroyd,* and in *The Seven Dials,* which is bad; but I think in every case if you read through the story again, you will be inclined to let her off. You did not suspect the criminal, because he seemed to be a person through whose eyes you had looked, and shared with them their mystification; but really Mrs. Christie was not deceiving you, she was allowing you to deceive yourself. The same may be said of *Murder at the Villa Rose.* By the way, one of the tests of a good detective story is that you should be able to read it a second time and enjoy seeing how you were spoofed.

II. All supernatural agencies or preternatural agencies are ruled out as a matter of course. To solve a detective problem by such means would be like winning a race on the river by the use of a concealed motor engine. And here I venture to think there is a limitation about Chesterton's Father Brown stories. He nearly always tries to put us off the scent by suggesting that the crime must have been done by magic. And we know that he is too good a sportsman to fall back upon such a solution. Consequently, although we seldom guess the answer, we usually miss the thrill of having suspected the wrong man.

III. Not more than one secret room or passage is allowable. I would add, that a secret passage should not be brought in at all unless the action takes place in the kind of house where such devices might be expected; the only time I introduced one myself I was careful to say beforehand that the house had belonged to Catholics in penal times. I think Milne's secret passage in *The Red House Mystery* is an unfair one; if a modern house were so equipped—and it would be villainously expensive—all the countryside would be quite certain to know about it.

IV. No hitherto undiscovered poisons may be used, nor any appliance which will need a long scientific explanation at the end. Conan Doyle violates the major principle of this rule, as far as I remember, in one of the later and more obviously spurious Holmes stories. There may be undiscovered poisons with quite unexpected reactions on the human system, but they have not been discovered yet, and until they are they must not be utilized in fiction; it is not cricket. All the cases of Dr. Thorndyke, recorded by Austin Freeman, have the minor medical blemish; you have to go through a long science lecture at the end of the story in order to understand how clever the mystery was.

V. No Chinaman must figure in the story. This principle, I admit, is one merely derived from experience; I see no reason in the nature of things why the Chinaman should spoil a detective story. But as a matter of fact, if you are turning over the pages of an unknown romance on a book-stall, and come across some mention of the narrow, slit-like eyes of Chin Loo, avoid that story; it is bad. The only exception I know is *The Four Tragedies of Memworth,* by Lord Ernest Hamilton.

VI. No accident must ever help the detective, nor must he ever have an unaccountable intuition which proves to be right. That is perhaps rather too strongly stated; it is legitimate for the detective to have inspirations which he afterwards verifies, before he acts on them, by genuine detective work. And again, he will naturally have moments of clear vision, in which the bearings of the observations hitherto made will suddenly become clear to him. But he must not be allowed, for example, to look for the lost will in the works of the grandfather clock because an unaccountable instinct tells him that is the right place to look in. He must look there because he realizes that that is where he would have hidden it himself. I suspect a certain weakness in this direction about Mr. Bailey's detective, Mr. Fortune; it may be that he simply does not take the trouble to explain his working, but it seems to me that he goes a good deal by guess-work.

VII. The detective must not himself commit the crime. This rule may of course be suspended where the detective is introduced as such, not on the author's responsibility, but on the responsibility of one of the characters, who may have made a mistake of identity. I have even read a very bad story in which the coroner was in league with the criminal. That will not do; there must be limits to the area of our suspicion.

VIII. The detective must not light on any clues which he does not instantly produce for the inspection of the reader. Any writer can make a mystery by saying that at this point the great Picklock Holes suddenly bent down and took up from the ground an object which he refused to let me see; "Ha!" he said, while his face grew grave. The skill of the detective writer lies in being able to produce his clues, flourish them defiantly in our faces—"There, what do you make of that?"—and we make nothing. So Holmes, in "Silver Blaze": " 'Let me call your attention to the curious incident of the dog in the night-time.' 'The dog did nothing at all in the night-time.' 'That was the curious incident,' said Sherlock Holmes." Few readers really spot that the man who took the horse out was a man well known to the dog in the stables; yet none can complain that he was not given the chance of guessing.

IX. The stupid friend of the detective, the Watson, must not conceal from the reader any thoughts which pass through his mind. His intelligence must be slightly, but very slightly, below that of the average reader. This rule is only one of perfection; it is not of the *esse* ["nature"] of the detective story to have any Watson at all. But if he does exist, he exists for the purpose of letting the reader have a sparring partner, as it were, against whom he can pit his brains: "I may have been a fool," he says to himself as he lays the book aside, "but at least I wasn't such a doddering fool as old Watson."

These rules were not delivered to us by a revelation; they have been discovered, like most things in our experience, by a process of trial and error. Here, as in most other fields, you will find sentimentalists who commend the *naïf* simplicity of the earlier models. For myself, I should not really be inclined to award the palm to Conan Doyle. Let me apologize for the apparent irreverence of such a statement, and explain what I mean. I am not influenced, I think, by the fact that all his later efforts in this field were, to put criticism at its mildest, unworthy of his fame. He was in his literary dotage; it is a thing that may happen to any man; and the fact that a man cannot write a good story at the end of his life does not prove that he never could. No, greatly as I reverence the earlier stories of the Holmes cycle, I reverence them as old classics, models on which all later work in the same field has been based, and consequently never to be overthrown from their unique niche in literary history. The delineation of Holmes himself, in his best period, is of course irreplaceable; no subsequent detective of fiction has attained the same living personality. But the stories *as stories* have the simplicity of the old masters; and in detective fiction, or at any rate in the great game of reading detective fiction, simplicity will not do. I should like to get hold of a child, and supervise his education so carefully that his eye never lighted on a Holmes story until he had been put through a solid course of Christie, Bailey, and Cole; and then I should like to put Conan Doyle's work into his hands and see whether he could not guess all the mysteries at sight. I may be wrong, but I think he would emerge from the ordeal with credit.

Chesterton simply cannot be placed; he has no characteristic medium, but can make himself at home in any form of literary art, without obeying the rules of any. He is like some great hearty man who goes to the wickets without pads against county-cricket bowlers and hits them all over the field by unashamed slogging. *The Ballad of the White*

Dust jacket for the first American edition of Ronald A. Knox's The Viaduct Murder.

Horse is not like any other poetry, nor *The Man Who Was Thursday* like any other romance, nor *Magic* like any other play, yet he succeeded beyond expectation in all of them. It happened one day (I am told) that Chesterton had no literary work on hand—it seems a strange thing to imagine—and wandered into the office of my literary agent—who was also his—to know if there was any publisher wanting anything done. The reply was "Nothing in your line, I am afraid, Mr. Chesterton; in fact the only thing we have heard of lately is the *Saturday Evening Post* wanting some detective stories." To which he replied, "Oh, well, I don't know," and, sitting down there and then in the office, wrote the first of the Father Brown stories. But are they detective stories? Is it possible to write an impressionist detective story? All one can say is that they are very good Chesterton.

It remains to say something about the future of the detective story. Let me admit at once that this seems rather dark. Nobody can have failed to notice that while the public demand remains unshaken, the faculty for writing a good detective story is rare, and the means of writing one with any symptom of originality about it becomes rarer with each succeeding year. The game is getting played out; before long, it is to be feared, all the possible combinations will have been worked out. Señor Capablanca appealed for brighter chess; he wanted a board with ninety-six squares, or something of that sort. But in what conceivable way are we to enlarge the possible horizons of this far more intriguing game, the solving of detective problems? We have seen how numerous and how stringent are the rules which necessarily govern its construction.

I say the detective story is in danger of getting played out. Even the exterior setting of the thing is by now almost stereotyped. We know, as we sit down to it, that a foul murder has almost certainly been done at a country house; that the butler will have been with the family for sixteen years; that a young male secretary will have been only recently engaged; that the chauffeur will have gone away for the night to visit his widowed mother. If life were like detective stories, we should all feel quite certain of getting jobs, so great would be the demand for young male secretaries; and it would be almost impossible for the father of a chauffeur to insure his life on any terms. We know that the murder—the public more or less demands a murder— will be done either behind the shrubbery in the grounds, or else in the dead man's study; if, however, the victim is a woman, she will be found dead in bed with an empty sleeping-draught bottle by her side. And so on.

But far more serious than this monotony of setting is the growing difficulty, for the author, in finding ways of deceiving his reader without either breaking the rules or using gambits which have been used *ad nauseam* before. I forget where it is that Bernard Shaw describes the growth of naval armaments as a senseless and unending competition between the theory of attack and the theory of defence. A. spends money on torpedoes, and B. has to spend money on torpedo-destroyers; A. invents a new form of mine, and B. has to lay down a new type of minesweeper. So it is with batting and bowling in cricket; so it is with serving and returning serves in lawn tennis; attack and defence improve alternately, each under the stress of competition with the other. And so it is with the great detective game; the stories get cleverer and cleverer, but the readers are getting cleverer and cleverer too; it is almost impossible at the moment to think up any form of bluff which the really seasoned reader will not see through.

Thus, in the old days, when a woman was found very uncomfortably bound to a chair, with her mouth gagged, and possibly only just recovering from the effects of an anaesthetic, we used to suppose, not unnaturally, that she had been tied up like that by the villains. Now we assume as a certainty that she is in league with the villains, and all the tying-up business was only fudge; we have so often had the old bluff worked off on us that it has ceased to take us in. Again, when the room is found covered with fingermarks or the lawn with foot-prints we know at once that these are false clues, arranged by the criminal so as to throw suspicion on an innocent person. That overdose of chloral has long ceased to mislead; there will be a half-empty bottle of it by the bedside, and the stomach of the deceased will be a mass of chloral, but we know for a dead certainty that the poison was administered somehow else—after death, as likely as not. The dead man found in the grounds was not murdered in the grounds; he was murdered miles away, and his corpse was brought there in a motor. The moment we come across any mention of a scape-grace brother who is supposed to have died in

Canada, we know that he did not really die; but is going to reappear either as the villain or the victim, and will get mistaken for the original brother every time. The fact that there were signs of a struggle in the room always means that there was no struggle, and the furniture was deliberately thrown about afterwards; the fact that the window was left open is proof positive that the crime was committed from inside the house. All messages which come over the telephone are fake messages; people who are overheard telephoning in their rooms have never really taken the receiver off.

The possession of a good watertight alibi is perhaps the surest mark of the real criminal; the man who has wandered aimlessly about the streets of London for three and a half hours without meeting anyone who could swear to his identity is no less certainly innocent. Gone, too, are the old familiar tests by which, in the Victorian days, we used to know the good characters and the bad characters apart. Neither age nor sex is spared; the old country squire, who is a J.P. and has for years held his head high among his neighbours, so good, so kind, so charitable—watch him! The heroine, even, the friendless and penniless female who looks up with such appealing eyes into the face of the detective's friend, may quite possibly have done the fellow in; with a good deal of provocation, maybe, but handling the blunt instrument in no uncertain manner. The only person who is really scratch on morals is the aged butler; I do not recollect, off-hand, any lapse of virtue on the part of a man who has been with the family for sixteen years. But I may be wrong; I have not read *all* the detective stories.

It is possible that we shall get into a stage of double bluff, when the author will make his heroes look like heroes and his villains look like villains in the certainty that the reader will get it the wrong way round. Indeed, I did once myself write a story in which the curate was perfectly innocent and the dark, sinister man had committed the murder. I didn't mean it for a detective story; I hadn't written any detective stories then; I meant it for a satire on detective stories. It was rather a good satire, but the public insisted on taking it as a bad detective story. Anyhow, you couldn't play that game often; and you cannot go on to double bluff and treble bluff and so on indefinitely. Is there no change in technique which will rescue the art from becoming stale, and passing out of fashion, like the comedy of manners, through sheer iteration?

One device has been tried lately for altering the formula, which first took shape in *Murder off Miami*. In that book the reader was presented, as far as possible, with facsimiles of the actual clues which the detective had to work on; type-written documents, spent matches, locks of hair and so on; accurate photographs replaced the familiar sketch-map which used to give you the position of the windows, the fire-place, the roll-top desk and the place where the body was found. The experiment, as an experiment, was quite successful; but somehow I doubt whether its technique could ever become general. The public would begin to demand more and more of it, would want to have the mystery enacted under its very eyes, till at last we should be in the position of that blameless military officer in Chesterton's *Club of Queer Trades,* who looked over a garden fence and saw on the other side of it a bed of tulips so laid out as to read DEATH TO MAJOR BROWN—the work of an agency which undertook to supply romance in real life. We should always be getting mysterious parcels with old boots and things in them, which would turn out to be part of the serial we were following at the moment. Reading, in this fatigued age, is exacting enough without having complications like that.

Some hold that the future of the art lies in a closer approximation to the manner of the ordinary novel. The public no longer expects that a detective story should be badly written; and some of Miss Sayers' work, in particular, is so rich in atmosphere that you could almost forgive her if you found out, as the story proceeded, that she was not bothering to put in a mystery at all. May I register, however, one rather hesitant protest? I do not very much like this modern habit of introducing a *motive* which found no place in the earlier stories—there is but a single instance of it, I think, in the Holmes cycle—that of illicit love? Not, I hasten to add, from any Victorian prudery on my part, but simply because I believe that in the great battle of wits between the writer and the reader this intrusion of life's backstairs introduces an element of unfair mystification. Where the nub of the problem seems to lie in finding a motive for the crime, it is unsatisfactory to be told, in the last chapter, that this motive lay in a liaison between two characters, a liaison whose existence the reader has had no opportunity of suspecting. But, even apart from this consideration, I do not myself believe that detective fiction has much to learn from the technique of the ordinary novel. Heaven help us, when the psychological crowd are let loose on it. (pp. 188-98)

R. A. Knox, "Detective Stories," in his Literary Distractions, *Sheed and Ward, 1958, pp. 180-98.*

EVOLUTION AND VARIETIES

Ellery Queen

[*Under the joint pseudonym of Ellery Queen, cousins Frederic Dannay (born Daniel Nathan) and Manfred Bennington Lee (born Manford Lepofsky) cofounded the Mystery Writers of America, edited over 100 mystery and detective short story collections, and coedited* Ellery Queen's Mystery Magazine *from 1941 until 1971 (after Lee's death in 1971, Dannay continued to write under the pseudonym of Ellery Queen until his death in 1982). The two also wrote dozens of mystery and detective novels and short stories, and produced several volumes of criticism of mystery and detective fiction, including* Queen's Quorum: A History of the Detective-Crime Story *(1951) and* In the Queen's Parlor, and Other Leaves from the Editor's Notebook *(1957). The following chapter from the last-named work summarizes three main developments in detective fiction: the "whodunit," or puzzle story, with an emphasis on the process of detecting a malefactor; the "howdunit," with a focus on method; and the "whydunit," with the accent on motive. The essay concludes with speculation about the future direction of detective fiction.*]

If the entire development of the modern detective story, from its birth in 1841 to the mystery novel just published this morning, had to be summarized in three words, the private-eye's progress would best be characterized by these coined terms:

1. whodunit
2. howdunit
3. whydunit

The first stage—the whodunit—stressed pure puzzle. In this type of fictional detection (which has persisted through all the succeeding periods and, glory be, is still vigorously with us) the story usually opened with a provocative and puzzling crime situation; then the detective came on the stage—first, the amateur, and later when realism reared its hard noggin, the professional; the story then spread into criminological investigation, including the discovery of clues, the cross-examination of suspects, the shifting of suspicion, and finally rose to the heights of deduction, culminating in the solution of the mystery and exposure of the criminal. As detective story writers in this stage achieved more and more ingenuity, honing their wits, the question of "who did it" assumed the proportions of a fine art: the writers seemed to ring infinite changes on the least likely criminals (and the least likely the better), with surprise endings (and the bigger the surprise the better) the ultimate 'tec Thule.

After half a century, the whodunit was joined by the howdunit, in which the emphasis swung from the identity of the murderer to the method by which the murder was committed. In the howdunit stage the so-called "medical mystery" gained much popularity, and after the turn of the century the comparatively simple "medical mystery" matured into the more complex "scientific detective story." In 1912 R. Austin Freeman, whose Dr. Thorndyke was the first truly great scientific sleuth (and perhaps still is the greatest), invented the "inverted" detective story—a monumental innovation which led to such outstanding psychological studies of murder as Francis Iles's *Before the Fact* (1932). It was the "inverted" detective story that ushered in the whydunit stage with which so many mystery writers (to say nothing of "serious" writers) are currently preoccupied . . . Years later, in 1939, J. B. Priestley commented in his *Rain upon Godshill:* "For are we not living too exclusively in a narrow world of how-the-trick-is-done, with too much How and not enough Why?"

In the whydunit stage the emphasis veered once more—from Who Killed Cock Robin and How Was Cock Robin Killed to Why Was Cock Robin Killed. This newest approach is psychological and psychiatric (though it should be pointed out that the scientifically psychological method of crime detection was dealt with fictionally as early as 1910, in William MacHarg's and Edwin Balmer's *The Achievements of Luther Trant*). The whydunit does not attempt to find new motives for murder—there are probably no new motives, and surely the old ones are still enormously virile; rather, the whydunit probes more deeply, and more dangerously, into even the oldest of criminological causes (including, these hypnotic days, the ancient ones dredged up through regression).

Thinker to Levers to Trance . . . and will there be a fourth coined word soon? *When*dunit—a fourth-dimensional stage in the development of the detective story? Or, with the boom in science fiction, is a whendunit already oldfangled? (pp. 72-4)

> *Ellery Queen, "Thinker to Levers to Trance,"
> in* In the Queen's Parlor, and Other Leaves
> from the Editors' Notebook, *1957. Reprint by
> Biblo and Tannen, 1969, pp. 72-4.*

Tzvetan Todorov

[*Todorov is a Bulgarian-born French critic. In the following essay, he discusses the conventions of three kinds
of detective fiction: the whodunit, the thriller, and the
suspense novel.*]

> Detective fiction cannot be subdivided into kinds.
> It merely offers historically different forms.
>
> —Boileau and Narcejac, *Le roman policier,* 1964

If I use this observation as the epigraph to an article dealing precisely with "kinds" of "detective fiction," it is not
to emphasize my disagreement with the authors in question, but because their attitude is very widespread; hence
it is the first thing we must confront. Detective fiction has
nothing to do with this question: for nearly two centuries,
there has been a powerful reaction in literary studies
against the very notion of genre. We write either about literature in general or about a single work, and it is a tacit
convention that to classify several works in a genre is to
devalue them. There is a good historical explanation for
this attitude: literary reflection of the classical period,
which concerned genres more than works, also manifested
a penalizing tendency—a work was judged poor if it did
not sufficiently obey the rules of its genre. Hence such criticism sought not only to describe genres but also to prescribe them; the grid of genre preceded literary creation
instead of following it.

The reaction was radical: the romantics and their present-
day descendants have refused not only to conform to the
rules of the genres (which was indeed their privilege) but
also to recognize the very existence of such a notion.
Hence the theory of genres has remained singularly unde-
veloped until very recently. Yet now there is a tendency
to seek an intermediary between the too-general notion of
literature and those individual objects which are works.
The delay doubtless comes from the fact that typology implies and is implied by the description of these individual
works; yet this task of description is still far from having
received satisfactory solutions. So long as we cannot describe the structure of works, we must be content to compare certain measurable elements, such as meter. Despite
the immediate interest in an investigation of genres (as Albert Thibaudet remarked, such an investigation concerns
the problem of universals), we cannot undertake it without first elaborating structural description: only the criticism of the classical period could permit itself to deduce
genres from abstract logical schemas.

An additional difficulty besets the study of genres, one
which has to do with the specific character of every esthetic norm. The major work creates, in a sense, a new genre
and at the same time transgresses the previously valid
rules of the genre. The genre of *The Charterhouse of
Parma,* that is, the norm to which this novel refers, is not
the French novel of the early nineteenth century; it is the
genre "Stendhalian novel" which is created by precisely
this work and a few others. One might say that every great
book establishes the existence of two genres, the reality of
two norms: that of the genre it transgresses, which dominated the preceding literature, and that of the genre it
creates.

Yet there is a happy realm where this dialectical contradiction between the work and its genre does not exist: that
of popular literature. As a rule, the literary masterpiece
does not enter any genre save perhaps its own; but the
masterpiece of popular literature is precisely the book
which best fits its genre. Detective fiction has its norms;
to "develop" them is also to disappoint them: to "improve
upon" detective fiction is to write "literature," not detective fiction. The whodunit par excellence is not the one
which transgresses the rules of the genre, but the one
which conforms to them: *No Orchids for Miss Blandish* is
an incarnation of its genre, not a transcendence. If we had
properly described the genres of popular literature, there
would no longer be an occasion to speak of its masterpieces. They are one and the same thing; the best novel
will be the one about which there is nothing to say. This
is a generally unnoticed phenomenon, whose consequences affect every esthetic category. We are today in the
presence of a discrepancy between two essential manifestations; no longer is there one single esthetic norm in our
society, but two; the same measurements do not apply to
"high" art and "popular" art.

Agatha Christie

The articulation of genres within detective fiction therefore promises to be relatively easy. But we must begin with the description of "kinds," which also means with their delimitation. We shall take as our point of departure the classic detective fiction which reached its peak between the two world wars and is often called the whodunit. Several attempts have already been made to specify the rules of this genre (we shall return below to S. S. Van Dine's twenty rules); but the best general characterization I know is the one Butor gives in his own novel *Passing Time* (*L'emploi du temps*). George Burton, the author of many murder mysteries, explains to the narrator that "all detective fiction is based on two murders of which the first, committed by the murderer, is merely the occasion for the second, in which he is the victim of the pure and unpunishable murderer, the detective," and that "the narrative . . . superimposes two temporal series: the days of the investigation which begin with the crime, and the days of the drama which lead up to it."

At the base of the whodunit we find a duality, and it is this duality which will guide our description. This novel contains not one but two stories: the story of the crime and the story of the investigation. In their purest form, these two stories have no point in common. Here are the first lines of a "pure" whodunit:

> a small green index-card on which is typed:
> Odel, Margaret.
> 184 W. Seventy-first Street. Murder: Strangled about 11 P.M. Apartment robbed. Jewels stolen. Body found by Amy Gibson, maid. (S. S. Van Dine, *The "Canary" Murder Case*)

The first story, that of the crime, ends before the second begins. But what happens in the second? Not much. The characters of this second story, the story of the investigation, do not act, they learn. Nothing can happen to them: a rule of the genre postulates the detective's immunity. We cannot imagine Hercule Poirot or Philo Vance threatened by some danger, attacked, wounded, even killed. The hundred and fifty pages which separate the discovery of the crime from the revelation of the killer are devoted to a slow apprenticeship: we examine clue after clue, lead after lead. The whodunit thus tends toward a purely geometric architecture: Agatha Christie's *Murder on the Orient Express*, for example, offers twelve suspects; the book consists of twelve chapters, and again twelve interrogations, a prologue, and an epilogue (that is, the discovery of the crime and the discovery of the killer).

This second story, the story of the investigation, thereby enjoys a particular status. It is no accident that it is often told by a friend of the detective, who explicitly acknowledges that he is writing a book; the second story consists, in fact, in explaining how this very book came to be written. The first story ignores the book completely, that is, it never confesses its literary nature (no author of detective fiction can permit himself to indicate directly the imaginary character of the story, as it happens in "literature"). On the other hand, the second story is not only supposed to take the reality of the book into account, but it is precisely the story of that very book.

We might further characterize these two stories by saying that the first—the story of the crime—tells "what really happened," whereas the second—the story of the investigation—explains "how the reader (or the narrator) has come to know about it." But these definitions concern not only the two stories in detective fiction, but also two aspects of every literary work which the Russian Formalists isolated forty years ago. They distinguished, in fact, the *fable* (story) from the *subject* (plot) of a narrative: the story is what has happened in life, the plot is the way the author presents it to us. The first notion corresponds to the reality evoked, to events similar to those which take place in our lives; the second, to the book itself, to the narrative, to the literary devices the author employs. In the story, there is no inversion in time, actions follow their natural order; in the plot, the author can present results before their causes, the end before the beginning. These two notions do not characterize two parts of the story or two different works, but two aspects of one and the same work; they are two points of view about the same thing. How does it happen then that detective fiction manages to make both of them present, to put them side by side?

To explain this paradox, we must first recall the special status of the two stories. The first, that of the crime, is in fact the story of an absence: its most accurate characteristic is that it cannot be immediately present in the book. In other words, the narrator cannot transmit directly the conversations of the characters who are implicated, nor describe their actions: to do so, he must necessarily employ the intermediary of another (or the same) character who will report, in the second story, the words heard or the actions observed. The status of the second story is, as we have seen, just as excessive; it is a story which has no importance in itself, which serves only as a mediator between the reader and the story of the crime. Theoreticians of detective fiction have always agreed that style, in this type of literature, must be perfectly transparent, imperceptible; the only requirement it obeys is to be simple, clear, direct. It has even been attempted—significantly—to suppress this second story altogether. One publisher put out real dossiers, consisting of police reports, interrogations, photographs, fingerprints, even locks of hair; these "authentic" documents were to lead the reader to the discovery of the criminal (in case of failure, a sealed envelope, pasted on the last page, gave the answer to the puzzle: for example, the judge's verdict).

We are concerned then in the whodunit with two stories of which one is absent but real, the other present but insignificant. This presence and this absence explain the existence of the two in the continuity of the narrative. The first involves so many conventions and literary devices (which are in fact the "plot" aspects of the narrative) that the author cannot leave them unexplained. These devices are, we may note, of essentially two types, temporal inversions and individual "points of view": the tenor of each piece of information is determined by the person who transmits it, no observation exists without an observer; the author cannot, by definition, be omniscient as he was in the classical novel. The second story then appears as a place where all these devices are justified and "naturalized": to give them a "natural" quality, the author must explain that he is writing a book! And to keep this second story from becoming opaque, from casting a useless shadow on the first, the style is to be kept neutral and plain, to the point where it is rendered imperceptible.

Now let us examine another genre within detective fiction, the genre created in the United States just before and particularly after World War II, and which is published in France under the rubric *"série noire"* (the thriller); this kind of detective fiction fuses the two stories or, in other words, suppresses the first and vitalizes the second. We are no longer told about a crime anterior to the moment of the narrative; the narrative coincides with the action. No thriller is presented in the form of memoirs: there is no point reached where the narrator comprehends all past events, we do not even know if he will reach the end of the story alive. Prospection takes the place of retrospection.

There is no story to be guessed; and there is no mystery, in the sense that it was present in the whodunit. But the reader's interest is not thereby diminished; we realize here that two entirely different forms of interest exist. The first can be called *curiosity;* it proceeds from effect to cause: starting from a certain effect (a corpse and certain clues) we must find its cause (the culprit and his motive). The second form is *suspense,* and here the movement is from cause to effect: we are first shown the causes, the initial *données* (gangsters preparing a heist), and our interest is sustained by the expectation of what will happen, that is, certain effects (corpses, crimes, fights). This type of interest was inconceivable in the whodunit, for its chief characters (the detective and his friend the narrator) were, by definition, immunized: nothing could happen to them. The situation is reversed in the thriller: everything is possible, and the detective risks his health, if not his life.

I have presented the opposition between the whodunit and the thriller as an opposition between two stories and a single one; but this is a logical, not a historical classification. The thriller did not need to perform this specific transformation in order to appear on the scene. Unfortunately for logic, genres are not constituted in conformity with structural descriptions; a new genre is created around an element which was not obligatory in the old one: the two encode different elements. For this reason the poetics of classicism was wasting its time seeking a logical classification of genres. The contemporary thriller has been constituted not around a method of presentation but around the milieu represented, around specific characters and behavior; in other words, its constitutive character is in its themes. This is how it was described, in 1945, by Marcel Duhamel, its promoter in France: in it we find "violence—in all its forms, and especially the most shameful—beatings, killings. . . . Immorality is as much at home here as noble feelings. . . . There is also love—preferably vile—violent passion, implacable hatred." Indeed it is around these few constants that the thriller is constituted: violence, generally sordid crime, the amorality of the characters. Necessarily, too, the "second story," the one taking place in the present, occupies a central place. But the suppression of the first story is not an obligatory feature: the early authors of the thriller, Dashiell Hammett and Raymond Chandler, preserve the element of mystery; the important thing is that it now has a secondary function, subordinate and no longer central as in the whodunit.

This restriction in the milieu described also distinguishes the thriller from the adventure story, though this limit is not very distinct. We can see that the properties listed up to now—danger, pursuit, combat—are also to be found in an adventure story; yet the thriller keeps its autonomy. We must distinguish several reasons for this: the relative effacement of the adventure story and its replacement by the

spy novel; then the thriller's tendency toward the marvelous and the exotic, which brings it closer on the one hand to the travel narrative, and on the other to contemporary science fiction; last, a tendency to description which remains entirely alien to the detective novel. The difference in the milieu and behavior described must be added to these other distinctions, and precisely this difference has permitted the thriller to be constituted as a genre.

One particularly dogmatic author of detective fiction, S. S. Van Dine, laid down, in 1928, twenty rules to which any self-respecting author of detective fiction must conform [see Further Reading: Secondary Sources]. These rules have been frequently reproduced since then . . . and frequently contested. Since we are not concerned with prescribing procedures for the writer but with describing the genres of detective fiction, we may profitably consider these rules a moment. In their original form, they are quite prolix and may be readily summarized by the eight following points:

1. The novel must have at most one detective and one criminal, and at least one victim (a corpse).
2. The culprit must not be a professional criminal, must not be the detective, must kill for personal reasons.
3. Love has no place in detective fiction.
4. The culprit must have a certain importance:
   (a) in life: not be a butler or a chambermaid.
   (b) in the book: must be one of the main characters.
5. Everything must be explained rationally; the fantastic is not admitted.
6. There is no place for descriptions nor for psychological analyses.
7. With regard to information about the story, the following homology must be observed: "author : reader = criminal : detective."
8. Banal situations and solutions must be avoided (Van Dine lists ten).

If we compare this list with the description of the thriller, we will discover an interesting phenomenon. A portion of Van Dine's rules apparently refers to all detective fiction, another portion to the whodunit. This distribution coincides, curiously, with the field of application of the rules: those which concern the themes, the life represented (the "first story"), are limited to the whodunit (rules 1-4a); those which refer to discourse, to the book (to the "second story"), are equally valid for the thriller (rules 4b-7; rule 8 is of a much broader generality). Indeed in the thriller there is often more than one detective (Chester Himes's *For Love of Imabelle*) and more than one criminal (James Hadley Chase's *The Fast Buck*). The criminal is almost obliged to be a professional and does not kill for personal reasons ("the hired killer"); further, he is often a policeman. Love—"preferably vile"—also has its place here. On the other hand, fantastic explanations, descriptions, and psychological analyses remain banished; the criminal must still be one of the main characters. As for rule 7, it has lost its pertinence with the disappearance of the double story. This proves that the development has chiefly affected the thematic part, and not the structure of the discourse itself (Van Dine does not note the necessity of mystery and consequently of the double story, doubtless considering this self-evident).

Certain apparently insignificant features can be codified in either type of detective fiction: a genre unites particularities located on different levels of generality. Hence the thriller, to which any accent on literary devices is alien, does not reserve its surprises for the last lines of the chapter; whereas the whodunit, which legalizes the literary convention by making it explicit in its "second story," will often terminate the chapter by a particular revelation ("You are the murderer," Poirot says to the narrator of *The Murder of Roger Ackroyd*). Further, certain stylistic features in the thriller belong to it specifically. Descriptions are made without rhetoric, coldly, even if dreadful things are being described; one might say "cynically" ("Joe was bleeding like a pig. Incredible that an old man could bleed so much," Horace McCoy, *Kiss Tomorrow Goodbye*). The comparisons suggest a certain brutality (description of hands: "I felt that if ever his hands got around my throat, they would make the blood gush out of my ears," Chase, *You Never Know with Women*). It is enough to read such a passage to be sure one has a thriller in hand.

It is not surprising that between two such different forms there has developed a third, which combines their properties: the suspense novel. It keeps the mystery of the whodunit and also the two stories, that of the past and that of the present; but it refuses to reduce the second to a simple detection of the truth. As in the thriller, it is this second story which here occupies the central place. The reader is interested not only by what has happened but also by what will happen next; he wonders as much about the future as about the past. The two types of interest are thus united here—there is the curiosity to learn how past events are to be explained; and there is also the suspense: what will happen to the main characters? These characters enjoyed an immunity, it will be recalled, in the whodunit; here they constantly risk their lives. Mystery has a function different from the one it had in the whodunit: it is actually a point of departure, the main interest deriving from the second story, the one taking place in the present.

Historically, this form of detective fiction appeared at two moments: it served as transition between the whodunit and the thriller and it existed at the same time as the latter. To these two periods correspond two subtypes of the suspense novel. The first, which might be called "the story of the vulnerable detective" is mainly illustrated by the novels of Hammett and Chandler. Its chief feature is that the detective loses his immunity, gets beaten up, badly hurt, constantly risks his life, in short, he is integrated into the universe of the other characters, instead of being an independent observer as the reader is (we recall Van Dine's detective-as-reader analogy). These novels are habitually classified as thrillers because of the milieu they describe, but we see that their composition brings them closer to suspense novels.

The second type of suspense novel has in fact sought to get rid of the conventional milieu of professional crime and to return to the personal crime of the whodunit, though conforming to the new structure. From it has resulted a novel we might call "the story of the suspect-as-detective." In this case, a crime is committed in the first pages and all the evidence in the hands of the police points to a certain person (who is the main character). In order to prove his innocence, this person must himself find the real culprit, even if he risks his life in doing so. We might say that, in this case, this character is at the same time the

detective, the culprit (in the eyes of the police), and the victim (potential victim of the real murderers). Many novels by William Irish, Patrick Quentin, and Charles Williams are constructed on this model.

It is quite difficult to say whether the forms we have just described correspond to the stages of an evolution or else can exist simultaneously. The fact that we can encounter several types by the same author, such as Arthur Conan Doyle or Maurice Leblanc, preceding the great flowering of detective fiction, would make us tend to the second solution, particularly since these three forms coexist today. But it is remarkable that the evolution of detective fiction in its broad outlines has followed precisely the succession of these forms. We might say that at a certain point detective fiction experiences as an unjustified burden the constraints of this or that genre and gets rid of them in order to constitute a new code. The rule of the genre is perceived as a constraint once it becomes pure form and is no longer justified by the structure of the whole. Hence in novels by Hammett and Chandler, mystery had become a pure pretext, and the thriller which succeeded the whodunit got rid of it, in order to elaborate a new form of interest, suspense, and to concentrate on the description of a milieu. The suspense novel, which appeared after the great years of the thriller, experienced this milieu as a useless attribute, and retained only the suspense itself. But it has been necessary at the same time to reinforce the plot and to re-establish the former mystery. Novels which have tried to do without both mystery and the milieu proper to the thriller—for example, Francis Iles's *Premeditations* and Patricia Highsmith's *The Talented Mr Ripley*—are too few to be considered a separate genre.

Here we reach a final question: what is to be done with the novels which do not fit our classification? It is no accident, it seems to me, that the reader habitually considers novels such as those I have just mentioned marginal to the genre, an intermediary form between detective fiction and the novel itself. Yet if this form (or some other) becomes the germ of a new genre of detective fiction, this will not in itself constitute an argument against the classification proposed; as I have already said, the new genre is not necessarily constituted by the negation of the main feature of the old, but from a different complex of properties, not by necessity logically harmonious with the first form. (pp. 42-52)

> *Tzvetan Todorov, "The Typology of Detective Fiction," in his* The Poetics of Prose, *translated by Richard Howard, Cornell University Press, 1977, pp. 42-52.*

John G. Cawelti

[*Cawelti has written several studies of American popular culture and formula fiction, including* The Six-Gun Mystique *(1971),* The Spy Story *(with Bruce A. Rosenberg, 1987), and* Adventure, Mystery, and Romance: Formula Stories as Art and Popular Culture. *In the following excerpt from the last-named work, Cawelti examines the formula of the classical detective story, drawing examples from the works of Edgar Allan Poe and Arthur Conan Doyle.*]

The formula of the classical detective story can be described as a conventional way of defining and developing a particular kind of situation or situations, a pattern of action or development of this situation, a certain group of characters and the relations between them, and a setting or type of setting appropriate to the characters and action. In "The Murders in the Rue Morgue" and "The Purloined Letter," Poe defined these four aspects of the detective story formula so sharply and effectively that, until the emergence of the hard-boiled story with its different patterns, detective story writers largely based their work on Poe's inventions.

1. *Situation.* The classical detective story begins with an unsolved crime and moves toward the elucidation of its mystery. As Poe discovered in his two stories, the mystery may center upon the identity and motive of the criminal, as in the case of "Rue Morgue," or, with the criminal and his purposes known, the problem may be to determine the means or to establish clear evidence of the criminal's deed, as in the case of "The Purloined Letter" where the detective must determine where the Minister D. has concealed the letter. Poe also defined two major types of crime on which much detective literature bases itself: murder, frequently with sexual or grotesque overtones, and crimes associated with political intrigue. From a formal point of view it is not difficult to see why these should be the favorite crimes of detective story writers. First of all, the significance of these crimes is proportionate to the elaborate parade of mystification and inquiry that the detective story must generate. Though Poe begins with crimes that are self-evidently important, he does not really make the significance of the crimes a major part of his story. We find out very little about the specific political issues and consequences that cluster around the theft of the queen's letter. Nor are we invited to reflect at any length upon the complex human tragedy of the sudden and horrible death of Mme L'Espanaye and her daughter. Instead, in "Rue Morgue," Poe carefully selects as his victims a rather obscure and colorless pair of people in order to keep our minds away from the human implications of their death. This seems to be an important general rule of the detective story situation. The crime must be a major one with the potential for complex ramifications, but the victim cannot really be mourned or the possible complexities of the situation allowed to draw our attention away from the detective and his investigation. A similar rule governs the detective's position in the situation. Poe tells us that Dupin has a personal reason for his involvement in the investigation. In "Rue Morgue" Poe obscurely hints at some prior friendship between Dupin and the prime suspect, Adolphe Le Bon, while in "The Purloined Letter" we are offhandedly informed that Dupin is a partisan of the queen. Neither of these motives amounts to anything in comparison to what continually stands out as Dupin's major interest: delight in the game of analysis and deduction. The classical detective usually has little real personal interest in the crime he is investigating. Instead, he is a detached, gentlemanly amateur. [In "The Detective Story as a Historical Source," *The Popular Arts,* Irving Deer and Harriet Deer, editors, 1967], William Aydelotte suggests that this careful detachment of the detective story situation from the complexities of human life is a fundamental architectonic principle of the formula:

In place of the complex issues of modern existence,

people in a detective story have very simple problems. Life goes along well except for the single point that some crime, usually, in modern stories, a murder, has been committed. . . . From this act follow most of the troubles. Troubles are objectively caused by an external circumstance, the murder, which can and will be resolved, whereupon the troubles will disappear. . . . The mess, confusion, and frustration of life have been reduced to a simple issue between good and evil.

2. *Pattern of action.* As Poe defined it, the detective story formula centers upon the detective's investigation and solution of the crime. Both "Rue Morgue" and "The Purloined Letter" exemplify the six main phases of this pattern: (*a*) introduction of the detective; (*b*) crime and clues; (*c*) investigation; (*d*) announcement of the solution; (*e*) explanation of the solution; (*f*) denouement. These parts do not always appear in sequence and are sometimes collapsed into each other, but it is difficult to conceive of a classical story without them. Sometimes, the story begins with the introduction of the detective through a minor episode that demonstrates his skill at deduction. This is the case in "Rue Morgue," where after a brief characterization of the detective and the narrator we see Dupin "reading" his narrator-friend's mind. Then Dupin explains that he has followed the narrator's train of thought by deducing it from his expressions and gestures. Doyle later developed this initial proof of the detective's skill to a standard convention of the Sherlock Holmes stories. Not only did Doyle try to improve on Dupin's mind-reading trick in Holmes's adventure of "The Resident Patient," but he devised a great variety of such opening proofs of Holmes's miraculous powers: Holmes tells where Watson has been by examining the color of the mud on his trousers; he deduces a complete biography of Watson's unfortunate brother from a watch; he reveals men's occupations by observing the calluses on their thumbs or the characteristic wrinkles in their clothes. These initial tests of the hero are common in many forms of popular literature. The western hero rides a dangerous horse or accomplishes a particularly difficult shooting feat at his first appearance; James Bond often begins his adventures by outwitting the villain in a game, as he defeats Goldfinger at golf and Sir Hugo Drax at bridge. These episodes establish the hero's special competence and give the reader confidence that, however great the obstacles and dangers, the hero will be capable of overcoming them.

"The Purloined Letter" deployed a second way of introducing the detective hero that Doyle also made an important part of the Holmes stories. The narrator is "enjoying the twofold luxury of meditation and a meerschaum in company with my friend C. Auguste Dupin, in his little back library, or book-closet, *au troisième, No. 33, Rue Dunôt, Faubourg St. Germain,*" when the placid calm is suddenly broken by the entry of the Prefect G. from the "gusty evening" outside. This intrusion of the outside world on the serene and reflective calm of the detective's bachelor establishment was elaborated by Conan Doyle into the memorable opening scenes at 221B Baker Street. As he did with many of Poe's inventions, Doyle transformed Dupin's back library into a complex and highly developed scene whose eccentric inventory—tobacco in a Persian slipper, bullet holes in the wall spelling V.R., hypodermic syringe in its neat morocco case—forms an important part of the Holmesian ambience. This same device, though not universal, became one of the standard opening gambits of the classical detective story. One thinks immediately of Dr. Thorndyke's secluded laboratory, Dr. Fell's study, and the house of Nero Wolfe. Even the hard-boiled story has taken over this convention of the detective's retreat, transformed in this case into the shabby offices of Sam Spade and Philip Marlowe. Two considerations probably account for the effectiveness of this kind of introduction to the detective story. First, the sudden disruption of the quiet and secluded retreat is an effective emotional rhythm. The peaceful beginning in the detective's retreat establishes a point of departure and return for the story. The crime symbolizes not only an infraction of the law but a disruption of the normal order of society. It is something extraordinary that must be solved in order to restore the harmonious mood of that charming scene by the blazing fireplace. This manner of introduction also emphasizes the detachment of the detective, his lack of moral or personal involvement in the crime he is called on to investigate. The crime represents a disorder outside the confines of his personal existence, which thrusts itself upon him for resolution. Nero Wolfe goes so far as to refuse to leave his retreat at all, solving the crimes from reports brought to him by his assistant.

Another aspect of the classical detective's detachment appears in Poe's two stories. Dupin stands apart from us and the workings of his mind remain an essential mystery because the story is told from another point of view, that of his devoted but far less brilliant friend. Following Doyle's development of Poe's anonymous narrator into the unforgettable Dr. Watson, this device became a standard feature of the classical detective story. Though sometimes told by an objective narrator who sees partly into the detective's mind, the narrator is often a Watson-figure or a character involved in the story who has an excuse for being close to the detective but cannot follow or understand his line of investigation. There are a number of structural reasons for this practice. First, by narrating the story from a point of view that sees the detective's actions but does not participate in his perceptions or process of reasoning, the writer can more easily misdirect the reader's attention and thereby keep him from prematurely solving the crime. If he uses the detective's point of view, the writer has trouble keeping the mystery a secret without creating unnatural and arbitrary limits on what is shown to us of the detective's reasoning processes. This problem does not arise in the case of the hard-boiled detective because he is not presented as a man of transcendent intelligence or intuition and does not solve the crime primarily by ratiocinative processes. Giving us continual insight into his mental processes does not reveal the solution, for the hard-boiled detective is usually as befuddled as the reader until the end of the story. In the classical story, however, it seems to be important that the detective solve the crime or at least get on the right track from the beginning. In story after story, when the solution is finally revealed to us, we find that the detective immediately established the right line of investigation by making a correct inference from the conflicting and confusing testimony that had baffled everybody else. Of course, if this convention is to be maintained, the writer simply cannot afford to give us any direct insight into the detective's mind. If he decides to drop the device of the Watsonian narrator, the writer must either use a detached and anonymous narrator who sees the detective's actions but does not have

any knowledge of his mental processes, or he must make the crime one that cannot be solved by the normal assumptions and methods of the detective.

There are other reasons for the particular narrative pattern of the detective story: by keeping us away from the detective's point of view, the writer can make the moment of solution an extremely dramatic and surprising climax since we have no clear indication when it will arrive. In addition, the Watsonian narrator provides us with an admiring perspective and commentary on the detective's activity. By using a narrator other than the detective, the writer can manipulate our sympathies and antipathies for the various suspects without forcing a revealing commitment on the detective himself. Moreover, the classical story's narrative method does not encourage an identification between the reader and the detective because the latter's feelings and perceptions remain largely hidden. Instead, the reader is encouraged to relate himself to the Watson figure and to the various suspects. The contrast between this pattern and that of the hard-boiled story is striking. In the Sam Spade and Philip Marlowe type of story, the action is almost invariably narrated from the detective's emotional and perceptual relation to the inquiry.

There is another important narrative tradition within the classical detective story that derives less from Poe than from Wilkie Collins's *The Moonstone* (1868). In this tradition, the story is told by a number of narrators, each of whom moves a step closer to the solution of the crime. Memorable in its few successful examples such as Carr's *The Arabian Nights Mystery* or Innes's *Lament for a Maker,* this technique is very difficult to handle, and most detective writers do not use it. The problem it poses, aside from the obvious difficulties of creating a convincing variety of points of view and coordinating their account of the action, lies in the way it necessarily fragments the process of investigation and the role of the detective.

The second major element in the classical detective story's pattern of action is the crime. In Poe's stories, and usually in Doyle's as well, the description of the crime immediately follows the introduction of the detective. Later writers, observing that this exact sequence was not necessary, found that in some instances it was desirable to present the crime first and then introduce the detective. This practice particularly relates to the use of one of the suspects' point of view as an alternative to the Watsonian narrator. In stories using this device the narrator's involvement with the crime leads to his encounter with the detective. This change in the sequence of the pattern also tends to place greater emphasis on the puzzle of the crime and less on the character of the detective than in the Poe-Doyle treatment of the introductory sequence. In general the classical detective story evolves in this direction, giving increasing importance to the intricacy of the puzzle surrounding the crime and less prominence to the detective's initiative in the investigation.

The effectiveness of the crime itself depends upon two main characteristics with a paradoxical relationship to each other. First, the crime must be surrounded by a number of tangible clues that make it absolutely clear that some agency is responsible for it, and, second, it must appear to be insoluble. With his lucidity and sense of structure Poe created this paradoxical combination with dazzling simplicity in "The Purloined Letter." We have the most tangible physical evidence that Minister D. stole the letter, for the person from whom he stole it saw him. We also know, by equally tangible evidence, that the minister still has the letter, for the catastrophic political consequences certain to follow from its leaving his possession have not appeared. Yet at the same time we have equally certain clues that the letter is not in his possession. The minister's person has been searched several times. His house has been ransacked with microscopes and long, thin needles by the Parisian police. It is certain that the letter is not concealed anywhere. A crime has evidently taken place, and yet it appears to be absolutely insoluble. This is the ideal paradigm of the detective story crime, for it poses a problem really worthy of the detective. Unfortunately, strokes as brilliantly economical as this are rare. The treatment of the crime in "The Murders in the Rue Morgue" is more typical of detective story literature. Here we find a large number of tangible clues that are confusing and obscure but do not reach the ultimate paradox of "The Purloined Letter." The "Rue Morgue" clues, like those of so many other detective stories, combine evidence that some agency has performed the deed with seeming indications that it cannot have been any person we can imagine being involved. The mutilated condition of the bodies, the way things in the room have been scattered about, the evidence of the voices heard by witnesses, make it clear that some person or persons have been involved in the murder, but other clues—the locked window, the apparently superhuman force involved in the murder, the confusion about the language spoken by the second voice—make it impossible to see how any known agent could have been involved. Thus, in the initial formulation of the problem, it is certain that a crime has taken place, but the identity of the criminal remains in doubt. The mystery is not as paradoxical as in the case of "The Purloined Letter" and the solution, when Poe drags in an orangutan to account for the confusion of clues, is correspondingly less satisfying because it seems a way of solving the impasse by introducing a new element into the story. Later writers have generally tried to avoid this necessity by discovering ways to make the paradox of clues eventually point back to one of the initial characters.

The "crime and clues" section of Poe's stories is followed by the parade of witnesses, suspects, and false solutions, which constitutes the investigation as it is presented to the reader. In "Rue Morgue" this section is brief, a sign that Poe had not quite fully articulated the classical detective form as he would in "The Purloined Letter." Nevertheless, Poe did invent two central conventions of this section: the parade of witnesses presented in quasi-documentary fashion and the "red herring" that in "Rue Morgue" takes the form of the obscure clerk Adolphe Le Bon. Remarkably, Poe even seems to have had an inkling of the desirability of having the finger of suspicion point at a character with whom the reader can identify or sympathize. Though Le Bon is too briefly treated to arouse much interest, his name, as Richard Wilbur points out, hints at an implicit moral symbolism. Moreover, we are told that Dupin feels an obligation to Le Bon who "once rendered me a service for which I am not ungrateful." The combined structural and emotional functions of the investigation section are more clearly if not more extensively articulated in "The Purloined Letter." The emotional import of the investigation is provided by the personal and political jeopardy of the queen, which has much more im-

pact than the fate of the obscure M. Le Bon. In addition, through the prefect's account, Poe is able to create that sense of an exhaustive examination of all the material evidence and possible suspects (in this case not people but possible hiding places), which leaves the situation more mysterious than before, thereby paving the way for the brilliant intervention of the detective.

Poe's stories at least partially developed the two major characteristics of the investigation section. Just as the crime and clues must pose a paradox, the parade of witnesses, suspects, and possible solutions, while seemingly moving toward the clarification of the mystery, must really further obfuscate it so that we finally arrive at a total impasse where the reader feels lost in a murky and impenetrable bog of evidence and counterevidence; when this point is reached, the detective is ready to step in. By means of his transcendent intuition, he has been working clearly and rationally toward a solution while the reader sinks into confusion. Second, the investigation usually threatens to uncover or expose the guilt of a character or characters with whom the reader has been encouraged to sympathize or identify, so that the detective's final solution is not only a clarification of the mystery but a rescue of characters we wish to see free from suspicion and danger. The elaboration and expansion of this section of the pattern of action was a major trend in the development of the classical detective story after Poe.

In Poe's stories, the dark confusion and uncertainty reached after the examination of clues and witnesses is suddenly and dramatically superseded by Dupin's announcement that he has solved the crime. Poe evidently took much delight in the staging of these triumphant and surprising revelations, and, as usual, he was particularly successful in "The Purloined Letter" where Dupin responds to the prefect's offer of a check for 50,000 francs to anyone who can help find the queen's letter with the calm statement that the letter is in his desk. It should also be noted that the announcement of the solution is not necessarily coincident with the actual apprehension of the criminal, which I will call the denouement. In "Rue Morgue," Dupin's sudden revelation that "the facility with which I shall arrive, or have arrived, at the solution of this mystery, is in the direct ratio to its apparent insolubility in the eyes of the police" does not lead immediately to the production of the criminal but to the immortal announcement, "I am now awaiting a person who, although perhaps not the perpetrator of these butcheries, must have been in some measure implicated in their perpetration." Then, only after Dupin's explanation of how he has arrived at the solution does Poe finally introduce the mysterious sailor whose orangutan is actually responsible for the crime.

The announcement of the solution is as important as, perhaps in some instances more important than, the actual apprehension and punishment of the criminal. Like Poe, most classical writers make a strikingly dramatic moment out of the detective's revelation that he has solved the mystery. To give just one example, think of that moment in *The Hound of the Baskervilles* where Watson, at the zenith of his confusion, enters the mysterious prehistoric dwelling on the moor to await in darkness the return of the mysterious figure he believes to be the criminal. While he sits there clutching his revolver, he hears footsteps approaching. A shadow falls across the opening of the hut and then: " 'It is a lovely evening, my dear Watson,' said a well-known voice. 'I really think that you will be more comfortable outside than in.' " In the ensuing conversation Holmes calmly reveals that he has worked out the whole thing. This is a paradigm of such scenes: the frantic narrator who is hopelessly lost in the maze of clues and testimony and the supremely calm detective who now takes the action into his hands. We find the same contrast between the desperate prefect who has just about given up the possibility of finding the missing letter and the serenely ironic Dupin who leisurely goes to his desk and takes it out. Naturally, since the action of the classical story focuses on the investigation of a mystery, the detective's calm announcement that he has arrived at the solution is a climactic moment. This is also the turning point of the story in another way. As indicated earlier, the reader has been forced to follow the action from the confused and limited point of view of the narrator. From this point of view investigation leads only to obfuscation. But when the solution is announced, though technically the point of view does not change, in actuality we now see the action from the detective's perspective. As he explains the situation, what had seemed chaotic and confused is revealed as clear and logical. In addition, this is the point at which the detective usually assumes the initiative against the criminal. Throughout the main part of the story the narrator appears to be surrounded by the plots of a mysterious criminal. After the announcement of the solution, the reader joins the detective in his superior position, assuming the role of spider to the criminal fly. Finally, the special importance of the moment of solution presents the classical writer with the opportunity of having two major climaxes or peaks of tension, the moment of solution and the eventual denouement when the criminal is actually captured.

These reflections help to account for the special interest of the next section in the classical pattern: the explanation. Here the detective discourses at length on the reasoning that led him to the solution and reveals just how and why the crime was carried out. To a superficial view it might seem that the explanation section risks being drearily anticlimactic, but I think that most detective story readers will testify that while they are frequently bored by an unimaginative or too detailed handling of the parade of clues, testimony, and suspects, the explanation, despite its involved and intricate reasoning, is usually a high point of interest. Indeed, many stories that get almost intolerably bogged down during the investigation become suddenly fraught with tension and excitement when the detective begins his explanation. Obviously, the explanation is important because in completing the investigation it represents the goal toward which the story has been moving. It also reflects the pleasure we feel when we are told the solution of a puzzle or a riddle. This is a combination of several factors. We are interested because we ourselves have been involved in the explanation and interpretation of the clues presented in the course of the investigation. Therefore a certain fascination hovers about the detective's explanation as we measure our own perception and interpretation of the chain of events against his. How far were we able to go along the road in the right direction? Where did we get off the track? The most exciting and successful detective stories seem to me neither those where the reader solves the crime before the detective announces his solution nor those where he is totally surprised and bamboozled by the solution that

the detective arrives at. When the reader feels confident that he understands the mystery before the detective, the story loses interest. Since many stories are fairly easy to solve, I suspect that most confirmed readers develop an ability to put a premature solution out of their minds so that the story is not spoiled for them. On the other hand, if the detective's solution is a total surprise, that too seems less than satisfactory and the reader feels cheated, because it appears that his earlier participation in the story has been completely irrelevant. When Dupin reveals that the murderer in "Rue Morgue" has been an animal and that he has withheld one essential clue, a tuft of hair from the orangutan, the explanation is far less effective than the brilliant and thoroughly satisfying account of Dupin's recovery of the purloined letter. In that story, the explanation as in the case of all good riddles requires not so much working one's way through a mass of evidence as being able to see the problem from a different angle. Once the new angle or perspective has been grasped, the solution is simple and obvious. When Dupin intuitively recognizes that Minister D. conceived the problem of concealment of the letter not as hiding it in or behind something but as making it too obvious to be seen, his act was like the change of perspective required to solve the old riddle "What's black and white and red [read] all over," where the solution is impossible as long as the guesser interprets the sound "red" as a color. Similarly, the reader of "The Purloined Letter" is unlikely to think of concealment in other than its ordinary meaning of hiding, yet the failure of the prefect makes the reader at least half aware that a new angle of vision is necessary. When the detective supplies the alternative perspective, the reader's feeling, as in the case of a good riddle, is not one of having been cheated and tricked but one of surprise and admiration at the wit of the detective and pleasure and delight at being confronted with a new way of seeing things. Finally, the puzzle or riddle aspect of the detective story depends less upon the reader's own ability to solve the mystery than on giving him enough participation in it to enable him better to appreciate the wit of the detective and to understand the new perspective on which the explanation depends.

Beyond its riddling dimension, the explanation has other sources of interest. One of its special pleasures comes from the satisfaction of seeing a sequence of events not only shaped from a different perspective, but given a different kind of order. (pp. 80-9)

This brings us to the final source of pleasure in the detective's explanation, the sense of relief that accompanies the detective's precise definition and externalization of guilt. It is here that we participate in the culmination of what Northrop Frye [in *Anatomy of Criticism* (1957)] calls "a ritual drama in which a wavering finger of social condemnation passes over a group of 'suspects' and finally settles on one." The parade of false suspects and solutions brings under initial suspicion characters with whom the reader is encouraged to sympathize or identify, thereby exciting a fear that one of them will be shown to be guilty. The reader, in other words, is metaphorically threatened with exposure and shame. Then the detective proves that the sympathetic characters cannot be guilty, or if they are, he establishes by careful explanation that their crime was justified and that they are not guilty in a moral sense. The most popular convention is to externalize and objectify guilt onto the "least-likely person" who is "proved" to be the guilty one. In part, the development of the "least-likely person" as the favorite criminal in the classical detective story was a result of the necessity of displacing the reader's attention during the investigation and thereby keeping him from recognizing the solution. But, in my view, the need to make the criminal a person with whom the reader develops no sympathy or identification is a more important reason for the "least-likely person" convention. For this character is the one who has been kept in the shadow throughout the story, the one to whom relatively little thought has been given. No bonds have been built between him and the reader, and consequently he can serve his role as the personification of guilt without involving the reader's feelings. The relief that accompanies the explanation reflects the reader's pleasure at seeing his favorites and projections clearly and finally exonerated and the guilt thrust beyond question onto a person who has remained largely outside his sphere of interest.

Usually the final section in the pattern of the classical detective story involves the actual apprehension and confession of the criminal. The denouement bears a close relationship to the other climactic moment in the pattern, the announcement that the detective has reached the solution. Sometimes denouement and solution are combined. In many of the Nero Wolfe stories, for example, the solution is announced by means of a trap that both reveals the criminal and apprehends him at the same moment. An alternative treatment of the problem is found in "Rue Morgue" where solution and denouement are distinctly separated. Dupin announces that he has solved the crime and explains it to his dazzled friend before the sailor appears in response to his advertisement. In such cases the denouement serves more as corroboration of the detective's solution and explanation than as a focus of interest and suspense in its own right. In fact, as Poe demonstrated in "The Purloined Letter," the actual representation of the denouement is not essential to the detective story. In that story, Dupin sets a trap for Minister D. by leaving him a false copy of the letter. The reader is assured that this is certain to lead him into a catastrophic political blunder. Poe evidently did not feel it necessary or desirable to stage the scene, perhaps because the elaborate treatment necessary to present such a denouement would have completely taken our attention away from Dupin and made the predicament of Minister D. the real center of the story. Most classical stories do represent the capture and confession of the criminal, but they tend to follow Poe's example by making this section too brief to permit the criminal to upstage the detective. Even in a story like Doyle's *The Hound of the Baskervilles,* where the denouement is full of suspense and excitement, the focus is not on the criminal Stapleton but on the terrible hound that was the means of his crimes. The tendency to make the denouement simply bear out the detective's solution rather than give the reader a more complex interest in the criminal's predicament points to an observation we have already made: the classical story is more concerned with the isolation and specification of guilt than with the punishment of the criminal.

This completes our account of the pattern of action formulated by Poe and followed by the tradition of the classical detective story. All classical detective stories contain these main elements, though not always in the exact sequence given: introduction of the detective, crime and clues, suspects and false solutions, announcement of solution, explanation, and denouement.

3. *Characters and relationships.* As Poe defined it, the classical detective story required four main roles: (*a*) the victim; (*b*) the criminal; (*c*) the detective; and (*d*) those threatened by the crime but incapable of solving it. Later writers have elaborated on these roles and in some cases have mixed them up, but on the whole it seems safe to say that without the relations implicit in these roles it is not possible to create a detective story.

Doing the victim right is a delicate problem for the creator of classical detective tales. If the reader is given too much information about the victim or if he seems a character of great importance, the story's focus around the process of investigation will be blurred. Moreover, its emotional effect will move toward tragedy or pathos, disrupting the relative serenity and detachment of the classical detective formula. On the other hand, if the victim seems insignificant and the reader has no information about him, interest in the inquiry and suspense about its outcome will be minimal. Poe invented two extremely effective ways of striking a balance between the disturbing flow of pity and fear that accompanies tragedy and an indifference to the victim that would keep the reader from caring at all about the investigation of his fate. His first approach as exemplified in "The Murders in the Rue Morgue" was to make his victims obscure, ordinary, and colorless people who meet a grotesque and mystifying end. Consequently their characters do not engage the reader's interest or sympathies, but the nature of their end does. In other words, while Poe tells us nothing about Mme L'Espanaye and her daughter that would make us feel one way or another about what happens to them, he makes the circumstances of their demise so strange and terrifying that we feel a great interest in discovering just what happened to them. In "The Purloined Letter," however, Poe created a victim of considerable importance but kept her almost entirely out of the story, telling us only enough about her predicament to make it clear that Dupin's investigation is relevant. In both instances Poe succeeded in keeping the reader from being too deeply involved in the victim's fate while at the same time providing ample justification and suspense for the detective's inquiry. Detective story writers have tended to follow him in this practice. It is another of the paradoxes of the detective story formula that the victim, who is supposedly responsible for all the activity, is usually the character of least interest.

The criminal also poses a problem of structural focus for, if the writer becomes too interested in his motives and character, he risks the emergence of an emotional and thematic complexity that could break up the formula. The goal of the detective story is a clear and certain establishment of guilt for a specific crime. If we become too concerned with the motives of the criminal, his guilt is likely to seem increasingly ambiguous and difficult to define. It is possible for a detective story writer to create a complex and interesting criminal as Poe did in Minister D., or Doyle in Professor Moriarty, or Michael Innes in the Ranald Guthrie of *Lament for a Maker,* but there must never be any serious question about either the specific guilt or the evil motives of these characters. In short, their motives may be complex and their actions interesting, but they must always be definable as bad.

With the invention of Minister D.—the fascinating but supremely evil master criminal—Poe discovered a way of creating a significant and complex character without permitting him to take over the limelight from the detective. First of all, Minister D. cannot upstage Dupin because the two characters are, in many respects, mirror images of each other. Both brilliant, aristocratic, eccentric, both poets and men of the sharpest reasoning powers; there are even suggestions of an association between the two that goes back many years, to mention just a few of the structural parallels. I cannot help being persuaded by Richard Wilbur's suggestion that in some fashion these characters symbolize two parts of the same soul ["The Poe Mystery Case," *New York Review* (13 July 1967)]. The same kind of relationship, though less profoundly resonant of inner allegory, exists between Sherlock Holmes and Professor Moriarty.

The master criminal is rather exceptional in the tradition of the detective story simply because he is too fascinating, too surrounded with ambiguous fantasies, and therefore extremely difficult to keep subordinated to the detective. One of my students once remarked that the most surprising thing about Sherlock Holmes is that he decided to be a detective rather than a master criminal, a remark that may shed some light on the psychological currents that led Doyle to invent Professor Moriarty as the appropriate means of disposing of a detective in whom his creator had lost interest. Further evidence of the great fascination of the master criminal appears in that type of popular literature where he is an indispensable ingredient, the spy story. Sax Rohmer's Fu Manchu, the secret international organizations of John Buchan, and the super villains of Ian Fleming, lineal descendants of Minister D. and Professor Moriarty, so dominate the spy story's pattern of action with their extraordinary talents and their ambiguous combination of evil and attractiveness that they disrupt the classical pattern of investigation and solution and require a different kind of archetypal structure.

Poe's other solution to the treatment of the criminal established the convention of the least-likely person, which we have already discussed. In "Rue Morgue" Poe rather crudely kept the criminal from engaging the reader's attention by keeping him out of the story until the last moment and then revealing him as an agency the reader was unlikely to expect, an animal. Since the witnesses all testify that they heard voices in the room at the time of the murder, the reader assumes that the criminal was a human being. When it turns out to be an orangutan, the switch seems a bit sudden. Succeeding writers developed the principle of the unanticipated agent into the person who is present throughout the story, but in a very marginal way. As we have seen, this convention has a double structural advantage: it keeps the reader from identifying the criminal before the detective produces the solution and by keeping the person who is to become the embodiment of guilt on the sidelines it prevents the reader from developing much sympathy for him.

Treating victim and criminal as figures without much emotional interest or complexity places the detective story's primary emphasis on those characters who are investigating the crime, the most important of which is the detective. Of all Poe's contributions to the formula of the classical detective story, his invention of the character of

Dupin—with his aristocratic detachment, his brilliance and eccentricity, his synthesis of the poet's intuitive insight with the scientist's power of inductive reasoning, and his capacity for psychological analysis—was certainly the most crucial. This was essentially the same combination of qualities that Doyle built into Sherlock Holmes. With minor differences of emphasis, they have remained the distinguishing characteristics of twentieth-century classical detectives like Hercule Poirot, Dr. Gideon Fell, Mr. Campion, Lord Peter Wimsey, Nero Wolfe, and many others.

Poe introduces Dupin as a man detached not only from society but from the ordinary patterns of human experience. Though "of an illustrious family" Dupin had suffered reverses that reduced him to poverty. Instead of trying to recover his position, Dupin has "ceased to bestir himself in the world, or to care for the retrieval of his fortunes." In contemporary slang, he has dropped out. And not only has Dupin detached himself from the quest for wealth and status, he has rejected the ordinary man's pattern of living—"enamored of the Night," he has rejected the day altogether:

> At the first dawn of the morning, we closed all the massy shutters of our old building: lighted a couple of tapers, which, strongly perfumed, threw out only the ghastliest and feeblest of rays. By the aid of these we then busied our souls in dreams . . . until warned by the clock of the advent of the true Darkness. Then we sallied forth into the streets, arm in arm, continuing the topics of the day, or roaming far and wide until a late hour, seeking, amid the wild lights and shadows of the populous city, that infinity of mental excitement which quiet observation can afford.

This detachment from the ordinary world is a sign of the detective's eccentricity and decadence and of his particular analytic brilliance and insight, which above all takes the form of an ability to read the hidden motives of men.

> At such times I could not help remarking and admiring . . . a peculiar analytic ability in Dupin. He seemed, too, to take an eager delight in its exercise. . . . He boasted to me, with low chuckling laugh, that most men, in respect to himself, wore windows in their bosoms, and was wont to follow up such assertions by direct and very startling proofs of his intimate knowledge of my own.

There follows immediately upon this introduction the first recorded deduction of a fictional detective. After walking in silence for some minutes, Dupin suddenly breaks into the narrator's chain of thought with a comment immediately responsive to the latter's thoughts. The narrator's sudden and terrified reaction demonstrates the particular aura of psychological potency that hovers around this central ability of the detective:

> "Tell me, for Heaven's sake," I exclaimed, "the method—if method there is—by which you have been enabled to fathom my soul in this matter." In fact I was even more startled than I could have been willing to express.

To the enormous relief of the narrator, Dupin explains that he has not actually been able to read his friend's thoughts but only to deduce them from his overt acts and gestures. This incident sums up the detective's essential role in the story. He is a brilliant and rather ambiguous figure who appears to have an almost magical power to expose and lay bare the deepest secrets. But he chooses to use these powers not to threaten but to amuse us and to relieve our tensions by exposing the guilt of a character with whom we have the most minimal ties of interest and sympathy. It is for this reason, I think, that there are such suggestive similarities between Poe's Dupin and Doyle's Holmes and two other characters with whom one would not at first think to associate them: the fictional figure of the gothic villain and the real character of Dr. Sigmund Freud, particularly as that character was articulated in the role of interpreter of dreams and items of neurotic behavior.

When one thinks about it, the close resemblance between Dupin and the gothic villain is immediately clear. Both are demonically brilliant, night-loving figures, and both are involved in plotting out elaborate and complex stratagems. One might interpret Poe's invention of the detective as a means of bringing the terrifying potency of the gothic villain under the control of rationality and thereby directing it to beneficial ends.

Though it has long been common to interpret popular formulas in Freudian terms, the odd analogies between the figure of the detective and that of Dr. Freud himself are

Dust jacket of the 1923 collection of short stories published in the United States as The Blue Scarab.

rather fascinating and have often been noted, most recently in Meyer's delightful *The Seven-Percent Solution.* There is even an odd resemblance between the names sometimes given by Freud to the dreams he discusses and the titles of the cases of Dupin and Holmes, for example "The Dream of the Botanical Monograph" as compared to the case of "The Purloined Letter" or "The Adventure of the Second Stain." The curious analogy between the process of dream interpretation and that of detection as represented in the classical formula can be summarized as follows: a brilliant investigator (Dupin, Freud) is confronted with a series of material clues (footprints, tufts of hair, dream symbols, slips of the tongue) that if properly interpreted are signs of a deeply hidden and disturbing truth. By a combination of method and insight, the investigator overcomes the confusion that attends these clues (the criminal's plot, psychological displacement) and reveals the hidden truth (solves the crime, interprets the dream). The great difference is that where the detective's solution always projects the guilt onto an external character, Freud's method exposes the conflicting motives in our own minds. These analogies between psychoanalysis and the detective story suggest to me a common concern with hidden secrets and guilts that may reflect a cultural pattern of the period. Where the detective story resolved this concern by pretending to find the hidden secret in someone else's mind, psychoanalysis went directly to the root of the problem by exposing and confronting the individual's own inner tension and anxiety.

The detective's terrifying ability to expose hidden secrets also relates to the convention of aristocratic and eccentric detachment from the ordinary concerns of human life. Because his skill threatens to uncover some secret guilt on the part of a character with whom the reader identifies, it is reassuring that, despite this terrifying superiority, the detective is a detached eccentric with no worldly stake in the outcome of the action. Ultimately he uses his powers not to threaten but to uphold the reader's self-esteem by proving the guilt of a specific individual rather than exposing some general guilt in which the reader might be implicated. Thus, the detective story stands in marked contrast to those important late nineteenth- and early twentieth-century novels that explored the lower depths of society and of the individual psyche and returned from their quests with a general indictment of the guilt of the respectable middle classes for their indifference and exploitation of the poor and their illicit and hidden dreams of sex and aggression. The detective may be a reflection of the new nineteenth-century cultural type of intellectual. But instead of laying bare the hidden guilt of bourgeois society the detective-intellectual uses his demonic powers to project the general guilt onto specific and overt acts of particular individuals, thus restoring the serenity of the middle-class social order. Both Freud and Sherlock Holmes are intellectual investigators of the illicit secrets of middle-class society. But where Freud and other social and psychological critics such as Marx and his followers discovered everyone's guilts, Holmes and the other classical detectives absolved society by exposing the least-likely person or the master criminal.

In this perspective the role of the fourth main group of characters in the classical detective story emerges more clearly. This consists of those characters who are involved with the crime but need the detective's aid to solve it. It includes three main types: the offshoots of Poe's narrator, the friends or assistants of the detective who frequently chronicle his exploits; the bungling and inefficient members of the official police, descendants of Poe's prefect; and, finally, the collection of false suspects, generally sympathetic but weak people who require the detective's intervention to exonerate them, the manifold progeny of Poe's Adolphe Le Bon. These characters are usually decent, respectable people who suddenly find themselves in a situation where their ordinarily secure status is no protection against the danger of being charged with a crime and where the police are as likely to arrest the innocent as the guilty. This fourth group of characters represents the norm of middle-class society suddenly disrupted by the abnormality of crime. The special drama of crime in the classical detective story lies in the way it threatens the serene domestic circles of bourgeois life with anarchy and chaos. The official guardians of this order, the police, turn out to be inefficient bunglers, and the finger of suspicion points to everybody. The ordered rationality of society momentarily seems a flimsy surface over a seething pit of guilt and disorder. Then the detective intervenes and proves that the general suspicion is false. He proves the social order is not responsible for the crime because it was the act of a particular individual with his own private motives. Through his treatment of the fourth group of characters, the classical detective writer arouses our fears that sympathetic characters are guilty, then releases that fear when the detective proves that the guilt can be attributed to a specific individual. The importance of this aspect of the classical story is probably the main reason why the criminal and the victim are frequently the least developed characters. It is not the confrontation of detective and criminal so much as the detective's rescue of the false suspects and the police that constitutes the dramatic nexus of the classical formula.

4. *Setting*. In devising the setting for his stories Poe again set the pattern for the classical detective story. Both "Rue Morgue" and "The Purloined Letter" take place in two isolated settings clearly marked off from the rest of the world: Dupin's apartment and the room in which the crime takes place. Around these two curiously delimited and fixed spaces swirls the teeming city of Paris. How often this combination of the isolated place and the bustling world outside is repeated in the classical detective story: the locked room in the midst of the city, the isolated country house in the middle of the strange and frightening moors, the walled-in college quadrangle, or the lonely villa in the suburban town. Mystery after mystery takes us back and forth between the detective's apartment or office and the isolated room full of clues. We are always aware of the threatening chaos of the outside world, but it erupts only rarely into the story, usually at the most suspenseful times, the moment of the crime, and then again at the solution and denouement.

This setting performs many functions. First of all, it furnishes a limited and controlled backdrop against which the clues and suspects so central to the story can be silhouetted. It abstracts the story from the complexity and confusion of the larger social world and provides a rationale for avoiding the consideration of those more complex problems of social injustice and group conflict that form the basis of much contemporary realistic fiction. The isolated setting also fosters that special kind of suspense that

has long been associated with places apart from the busy stream of human affairs. In this respect the classical detective story setting is a direct descendant of the isolated castle or abbey where all those mysterious goings on took place in the gothic novels of Mrs. Radcliffe, "Monk" Lewis, and their followers. But most important, the contrast between the locked room or the lonely country house and the outside world constitutes a symbolic representation of the relation between order and chaos, between surface rationality and hidden depths of guilt. We begin in the serene and rational order of the detective's apartment or in the pleasant warmth and social graces of the country house before the murder. Then we are suddenly transported to the locked room, a mirror image of the detective's apartment disrupted by the chaotic outer world that has penetrated the quiet order and left behind those mysterious clues suggesting the presence of a hidden guilt. By solving the secret of the locked room, the detective brings the threatening external world under control so that he and his assistant can return to the peaceful serenity of his library, or can restore the pleasant social order of the country house.

The isolated setting has remained popular with classical detective story writers for another reason. It establishes a framework for the treatment of manners and local color in a fashion often reminiscent of the great Victorian novelists. Though this tendency is minimal in Poe, it is nonetheless present in his interest in the variety of occupations and responses of the parade of witnesses in "Rue Morgue." Doyle developed this concern into richly atmospheric sketches of Baker Street and its "Irregulars," the London slums, and the English countryside, while in many twentieth-century classical stories local color almost takes over the tale. In Dorothy Sayers's *Nine Tailors* a rural society out of Thomas Hardy by Trollope shares the spotlight with an elaborate discussion of the art of campanology, and Michael Innes enacts an almost Dickensian social panorama in stories like *Appleby's End*. These pageants of local color provide both an air of verisimilitude and an added source of interest to the main theme of investigation. In addition, they symbolize the normally peaceful and serene order of society disrupted by the anomaly of crime and restored when the detective isolates the guilty individual. Many twentieth-century writers of classical detective stories reflect the nineteenth-century novel in their treatment of society in the form of nostalgic fantasies of a more peaceful and harmonious social order associated with the traditional rural society of England. (pp. 90-8)

John G. Cawelti, "The Formula of the Classical Detective Story," in his Adventure, Mystery, and Romance: Formula Stories as Art and Popular Culture, *The University of Chicago Press, 1976, pp. 80-105.*

Julian Symons

[*Symons is highly regarded for his contributions to the genres of biography and detective fiction. His biographies of Charles Dickens, Thomas Carlyle, and his brother A. J. A. Symons are considered excellent introductions to the lives and works of these writers. He remains best known, however, for his detective novels, including* The Immaterial Murder Case *(1945),* The

Thirtyfirst of February *(1950), and* The Progress of a Crime *(1960). In the following excerpt, Symons surveys some innovations in plot, characterization, theme, and technique that were exploited in short detective fiction from the time of the Sherlock Holmes stories of Arthur Conan Doyle until the first World War.*]

The interest of [Sherlock Holmes's immediate successors] lies in the ingenuity with which problems are propounded and solved, rather than in the ability to create credible characters or to write stories interesting as tales rather than as puzzles. The amount of talent working in this period gives it a good claim to be called the first Golden Age of the crime story, but it should be recognized that the metal is nine-carat quality where the best of the Holmes stories is almost pure gold. Yet for those prepared to accept these stories on their own level (as any addict should be) the variety of detectives and ideas offered in them gives enduring pleasure.

At the center of their work was the personality of the detective, who almost always appeared in several series of stories. A number of dichotomies mark these detectives, but the clearest division is between those in the Holmes category of Supermen with no emotional attachments and little interest in everyday life except insofar as it impinges on any particular problem, and the inconspicuous ordinary men who solve their cases by the application of common sense rather than by analytic deduction. The detectives in this second class are private investigators running their own agencies, because that was the fashion of the time, but they often look and sound like policemen. They are Lestrades and Gregsons removed from the official ranks and seen with a friendly eye instead of being made the butts of genius. The Superman is almost always given his accompanying Watson, who may do a lot of the humdrum investigation. The common-sense detective often works alone.

The two most successful Superman detectives of the period were Professor Augustus S. F. X. Van Dusen and Father Brown. Van Dusen was created by Jacques Futrelle (1875-1912), an American born in Georgia, who had a theatrical and journalistic career which was blended with the writing of novels and short stories. Van Dusen's principal appearance is in two collections of stories, *The Thinking Machine* (1907) and *The Thinking Machine on the Case* (1908) [published in England as *The Professor on the Case*]. He carries Holmesian omniscience to the point of absurdity. He is introduced to us when he refers contemptuously to chess, saying that a thorough knowledge of the rules of logic is all that is necessary to become a master at the game, and that he could "take a few hours of competent instruction and defeat a man who has devoted his life to it." A game is arranged between the Professor and the world champion, Tschaikowsky. After a morning spent with an American chess master in learning the moves, the Professor plays the game. At the fifth move, Tschaikowsky stops smiling, and after the fourteenth, when Van Dusen says "Mate in fifteen moves," the world champion exclaims: *"Mon Dieu!"* (he is not one of those Russians who know no language but their own) and adds: "You are not a man; you are a brain—a machine—a thinking machine." From this time onward Professor Van Dusen is called the Thinking Machine. In appearance he is dwarfish, with a small white clean-shaven face, long white flexible hands, and a great domed head taking a size-eight hat, under which is a heavy shock of bushy yellow hair.

The whiff of absurdity is strong, but the Thinking Machine stories are almost all ingenious. The usual Futrelle story falls into two parts. In the first a mystery is shown to us, either by third-person narrative or as told to the Thinking Machine. His assistant, the reporter Hutchinson Hatch, does most of the legwork, and the Professor then solves the case. Among the best stories are: one in which poison is circulated through the application of a court plaster; another in which a man sees in a crystal ball the picture of his future murder in his own apartment some distance away (the basis of the trick is the creation of a duplicate room in the house where the victim sees the crystal ball); and a third in which a car disappears night after night in a lane which has a policeman at each end. The finest of all the Thinking Machine stories is "The Problem of Cell 13," which begins with an assertion by the Professor that anything can be done by the power of thought. Told that nobody can think his way out of a cell, he replies that "a man can so apply his brain and ingenuity that he can leave a cell, which is the same thing." The story shows him doing just that, with some agreeable mystification in the course of it, and then explaining exactly how it was done. (pp. 76-8)

The short detective stories written by Gilbert Keith Chesterton (1874-1936) were as pungent, paradoxical, and romantic as the novels, poems, literary criticism, and journalism that streamed from his occasionally too ready pen. His essential views about the detective story are set down in the first and best of the several pieces in which he discussed various aspects of the form [see excerpt below]. It was, he said, a popular realization of the poetry concealed in city life. The detective crosses a London in which "the casual omnibus assumes the primal colours of a fairy ship," and in which the lights of the city are the guardians of a secret known to the writer but not to the reader. "Every twist of the road is like a finger pointing to it; every fantastic skyline of chimney-pots seems wildly and derisively signalling the meaning of the mystery." The detective-story writer should be regarded as the poet of the city, and the detective as a romantic hero, the protector of civilization. "It is the agent of social justice who is the original and poetic figure, while the burglars and footpads are merely placid old cosmic conservatives, happy in the immemorial respectability of apes and wolves. The romance of the police force is thus the whole romance of man. It reminds us that the whole noiseless and unnoticeable police management by which we are ruled and protected is only a successful knight-errantry."

This was written in 1901, before Father Brown was thought of, and it is admirable special pleading for Chesterton's own detective stories in which reality is made to seem like fantasy and in which Flambeau, the great criminal, soon becomes a detective, like Vidocq. The stories embody also a principle that he announced a quarter of a century later, that "the only thrill, even of a common thriller, is concerned somehow with the conscience and the will." This is true at least of his own very uncommon thrillers, which almost always exemplify a witty paradox about the condition of society or the nature of man. The effect of the Father Brown stories rests partly in the moral point that many of them bring home, but this might appear anodyne but for the witty and subtle way in which Chesterton makes it. He fairly spilled over with good ideas, and they are as evident in his detective stories as in the novels that were the product of his verbal and mental dexterity, like *The Napoleon of Notting Hill* or his metaphysical thriller, *The Man Who Was Thursday.*

Chesterton wrote several other collections of what may loosely be called detective short stories outside the Father Brown series, of which *The Club of Queer Trades, The Man Who Knew Too Much,* and *Four Faultless Felons* all contain good things, but his reputation in this field rests upon the five Father Brown collections. *The Innocence of Father Brown* (1911) was followed by the *Wisdom* (1914), the *Incredulity* (1926), the *Secret* (1927), and the *Scandal* (1935). (pp. 78-9)

It may seem odd to class a man who has difficulty in rolling his umbrella and does not know the right end of his return ticket among the Supermen of detection, but Father Brown belongs among them through the knowledge given to him by God. Logicians of the detective story complained with some bitterness that Chesterton outraged all the rules they had drawn up, that he did not tell you whether all the windows were fastened or whether a shot in the gunroom could be heard in the butler's pantry. But the very merit of Chesterton is his ability to ignore such things, to leave out everything extraneous to the single theme he wants to develop, and yet to provide a clue that is blindingly obvious once we have accepted the premises of the story and the character of Father Brown. A dog whines because a stick sinks in the sea, the red light from a closed door looks like "a splash of blood that grew vivid as it cried for vengeance," the priest of a new religion does not look round when he hears a crash and a scream, and these are genuine clues by which we may solve mysteries. And when we have accepted Father Brown, then we are bound to accept also his right to draw religious and social morals from the cases he investigates.

Often the points he is making are beautifully put. In "The Blue Cross," Father Brown identifies a false priest because he attacks reason, which is "bad theology." In "The Queer Feet," the trick of which rests on the fact that a man in evening dress is indistinguishable from the waiter who is serving him, the criticism is social. "Reverend Sir, your friend must have been very smart to act the gentleman," Colonel Pound says at the end of the story, and the priest replies: "Yes, it must be very hard work to be a gentleman; but, do you know, I have sometimes thought that it must be almost as laborious to be a waiter." The paradoxes at their best are perfect. Why does a man wear a startling purple wig? Because by drawing attention to it he diverts any possible curiosity from his presumedly deformed but in fact normal ear. How can a black man conceal himself in a white country? Why, by posing as a soot-masked nigger minstrel.

The Chesterton short stories are a diet too rich for everyday consumption. Two or three, not six or seven, should be read at a sitting. And they have their faults, which spring from the fact that he was never able to take anything that he wrote quite seriously. Sometimes the detective stories, like his novels, topple into absurdity because the premises of the tale are too fantastic, but this does not happen very often. A comparison with M. P. Shiel's

Prince Zaleski stories, which are never plausible even on their own preposterous grounds, shows Chesterton's skill at this sort of tightrope walking. The first two books are on a higher level than the others but, reading them all again before writing about them, it seemed to me still that the best of these tales are among the finest short crime stories ever written. A personal choice would include "The Queer Feet," which has already been mentioned; "The Secret Garden," with its puzzle of two heads and only one body; "The Man in the Passage," in which a superb comic trick is pulled off with a mirror; the logical exercise in "The Paradise of Thieves"; and "The Dagger with Wings," in which a legend is fulfilled when the body of a man looking like an enormous bat is found spread-eagled in unspotted snow. This last story has some loose ends hanging that will not please academics, but after a dozen readings I feel fresh admiration for the cleverness with which the trick is embodied in the legend and for the brilliance of the central picture.

A reading of Chesterton reinforces the truth that the best detective stories have been written by artists and not by artisans. In considering other Superman detectives of the period, we are dealing with journeymen of letters who do not pretend to art. Some had good ideas and some could construct a good story, but they had no ideas as clever as Futrelle's and no poetic inspiration like that which often touched Chesterton. Originality, certainly, must be granted to the Old Man in the Corner invented by Baroness Orczy (1865-1947). He preceded her better-known Scarlet Pimpernel, and appeared in three collections, *The Case of Miss Elliot* (1905), *The Old Man in the Corner* (1909), and *Unravelled Knots* (1926). The Old Man sits in the corner of an ABC teashop consuming glasses of milk and pieces of cheesecake, endlessly tying and untying knots in a piece of string, and giving his solutions of cases that have baffled the police to a girl reporter named Polly Burton, who seems never to have read the newspapers, since the Old Man has to describe the background of every case to her in detail. "There is no such thing as a mystery in connection with any crime, provided intelligence is brought to bear upon its investigation," he says in characteristic Superman style, and he is never seen to move from his seat, although he mentions attending court hearings in several cases. The misanthropic Old Man is concerned solely with demonstrating his own cleverness. He does not care at all about justice, and it is a peculiarity of the stories that in many of them the criminal goes free. "Hang such a man? Fie!" he cries about one murderer, and of another he reflects only that "there goes a frightful scoundrel unhung." In the last story of *The Old Man in the Corner,* it is a presumption that he has himself committed the murder.

Such a character could be a springboard for all sorts of social comments, but these seem never to have been in Baroness Orczy's mind, and apparently she wrote the stories in this way because they absolved her from any need to turn the Old Man's theories into practical proof of guilt. The writing is quite lively and some of the stories contain ideas put to better use by other writers, like that of two men planning a murder so that the man with an obvious motive has an alibi while his apparently uninvolved companion commits the crime, but they too often depend upon police work so inefficient as to make Lestrade look like a genius. Baroness Orczy was also responsible for a woman detective more disastrously silly than most of her kind,

Lady Molly of Scotland Yard (1910), and for a legal investigator, Patrick Mulligan, who appears in *Skin o' My Tooth* (1928). Lady Molly, really Lady Molly Robertson-Kirk, is "head of the Female Department," and has a husband who is in Dartmoor for murder. She ends up clearing him of the crime after an unexplained five-year delay, and presumably settles down again to domesticity.

Ernest Bramah Smith (1869?-1942), who dropped his commonplace surname for his writings, showed also a stroke of distinct originality in creating the blind detective Max Carrados. The Carrados stories were perhaps a diversion from the mock-Chinese tales about Kai Lung which at one time had an unaccountably large number of admirers, and the blind detective appears in *Max Carrados* (1914), *The Eyes of Max Carrados* (1923), and *Max Carrados Mysteries* (1927). His Watson is an inquiry agent named Louis Carlyle, who changed his name when he was wrongly struck off the solicitorial rolls for falsifying a trust account. Carrados (whose name is really Max Wynn) suffered from a disease called amaurosis, which causes blindness while leaving the external appearance of the eye unchanged. The pair make an agreeable variation on the Holmes-Watson relationship, with Carlyle rather more sophisticated and distinctively characterized than most assistants, and Carrados insistent on the value of having "no blundering, self-confident eyes to be hoodwinked." His supersensitive auditory nerve enables him to hear the cry of a newsboy in the street which is inaudible to other people in a room, and he knows that a man is wearing a false mustache because he carries "a five-yard aura of spirit gum, emphasized by a warm, perspiring skin."

It is a defect of such spectacular discoveries that the reader cannot make them himself, as he can so often make them in the Holmes stories, but the tales about Carrados are well-constructed and interesting. Unlike most crime writers, Bramah sometimes linked his stories to actual social events of the period. Doyle, for instance, although he occasionally dealt with terrorist societies, always placed their activities in some distant country. In "The Knight's Cross Signal Problem," however, the young Indian Drishna responds to Carlyle's indignation about his terrorist act in causing a rail crash by asking: "Do *you* realise, Mr. Carlyle, that you and your Government and your soldiers are responsible for the death of thousands of innocent men and women in my country every day?" A later story, "The Missing Witness Sensation," deals with the kidnaping of a man by Sinn Fein so that he cannot give evidence against them. Carrados handles an unusually wide variety of cases, including in the first volume alone stories about a jewel theft, the railway crash already mentioned, attempted murder, fraud, and the burglary of a safe deposit. Bramah ignored the limiting idea, which had almost become established by the time of his first Carrados book, that every investigation must concern a murder, and the stories are the more interesting for it. Like other Superman detectives, Carrados feels no hesitation about amending the processes of law, in one case to the point of ordering a murderer to commit suicide.

Holmes was a great admirer of Bertillon, but he never concerned himself with fingerprints as he did with tobacco ash, newsprint, and secret writing. Many detectives of this period mention the use of science in solving crimes, but few are seen in the act of using it. The distinction of R.

Austin Freeman (1862-1943) is that his Dr. Thorndyke is actually seen to be a forensic scientist. His square green box covered with Willesden canvas contains a great variety of materials for the detection of crime. When he says, "Will you give me the Vitogen powder, Jervis," or goes to work on footprints with his plaster tin, water bottle, spoon, and little rubber bowl, we are conscious of watching actual and likely processes of detection. Freeman had a firm basis of medical knowledge, and he put this and the admiration he felt for one of his instructors, the great Victorian expert in medical jurisprudence Dr. Alfred Swayne Taylor, to good use.

For a man who began his literary career late, Freeman produced a great many books. The first of them, *The Adventures of Romney Pringle* (1902), published under the pseudonym of Clifford Ashdown and written by Freeman together with a medical colleague who was also a prison officer, is said to be the rarest book of crime short stories. His début under his own name came with *The Red Thumb Mark* (1907) when he was forty-five years old, and he produced an average of rather more than a book a year up to a short time before his death. Many of them were novels, but it is safe to say that with the exception of one or two, like *Mr. Pottermack's Oversight* (1930), they are markedly inferior to the short stories. With Freeman we confront for the first time the crime writer who produced work of no other kind, and whose talents as a writer were negligible. Reading a Freeman story is very much like chewing dry straw. This is how Thorndyke talks as late as the middle twenties:

> "A philosophic conclusion, Jervis, and worthy of my learned friend. It happens that the most intimate contact of Law and Medicine is in crimes against the person and consequently the proper study of the Medical Jurist is crime of that type."

Was ever reader in this manner wooed? If readers were won (and they were), if some remain (and they do), it is because of his accuracy in detail, and because of the originality shown in one collection of short stories. In *The Singing Bone* (1912), Freeman invented what has been called the inverted story. In these stories, we see a crime committed and then watch Thorndyke discover and follow clues that lead to the criminal. There is no mystery, and not much surprise, but the interest of watching Thorndyke at work is enhanced by our own prior knowledge. Freeman never repeated this experiment, which was developed much later and with more skill by Roy Vickers.

It is rather dubiously that one includes Thorndyke among the Supermen, but although he is in character almost anonymous, he has the proper passionless approach to ordinary human affairs. There is less doubt about Uncle Abner, the hero of *Uncle Abner, Master of Mysteries* (1918), by Melville Davisson Post (1871-1930). The stories are set in pre-Civil War Virginia, and Uncle Abner is "one of those austere, deeply religious men who were the product of the Reformation . . . the right hand of the land." He is compared more than once with Cromwell; he carries a Bible in his pocket; he exemplifies the spirit of righteousness in his disorderly society.

The Uncle Abner stories are very highly regarded in America, but comparatively little known elsewhere. No English edition of them has ever been published. This is no doubt because their settings and themes are often distinctively American—"The Edge of the Shadow" contains an argument about the validity of slavery and concerns the murder of an abolitionist, and in the course of "A Twilight Adventure" Uncle Abner stops a lynching for cattle stealing and gives a lecture on the dangers of circumstantial evidence. But the attraction the stories have for Americans simply does not exist for others. To English readers, Uncle Abner is likely to seem a distant and implausible figure, and if one judges in terms of plot the stories have surely been overpraised. They include a farfetched but ingenious locked-room mystery which has already been mentioned, and a cunning story based on phonetic misspelling, but Uncle Abner's deductions are often of dubious validity, like his conclusion that a man followed the left side of a wall "because his controlling side was on the left—because he was left-handed." Some of the other detectives created by Post, like Monsieur Jonquelle, Prefect of Police of Paris, and Sir Henry Marquis, who appeared in *The Sleuth of St. James's Square* and another book, show only that Post was not at home when he was abroad.

The detective as ordinary man is embodied in the Martin Hewitt stories written by Arthur Morrison (1863-1945). The first series of them ran in the *Strand* during 1894, and they were illustrated by Sidney Paget, who had also interpreted the appearance of Holmes. In looks and behavior, Hewitt represents a conscious reaction—and the first reaction, as the date shows—from the Superman detective. Hewitt is a "stoutish, clean-shaven man, of middle height and of a cheerful, round countenance" who "maintains that he has no system beyond a judicious use of ordinary faculties." The first and best of the three Hewitt collections contains some cases with interesting ideas in them, like "The Stanway Cameo Mystery," in which a dealer discovers that the cameo he has sold is a forgery, and steals it back again to save his reputation. There is another story about jewels stolen by a carefully trained parrot, and "The Loss of Sammy Throckett," which deals with the kidnaping of a runner expected to win a handicap race in the North of England, contains sociologically interesting details. But Morrison, who was a journalist and short-story writer concerned with actual poverty and crime (he wrote an admirable book about London slum life, *Tales of Mean Streets,* at the time he was producing the first Hewitt stories), seems always to have been disturbed by the idea of treating crime light-heartedly, and the later collections are rather humdrum.

The stories about Paul Beck and his son, by M. McDonnell Bodkin (1850-1933), do not deserve the total neglect into which they have fallen. Bodkin was an exuberant Irish barrister, and for a short time a Nationalist M.P., who became a judge in the County of Clare. His first detectival creation, Paul Beck, is described as a "stout party in grey" who "don't seem particular bright." He has a ruddy face, curling light brown hair, a chronic look of mild surprise in his light blue eyes, and the appearance of a milkman rather than a detective. Beck does not profess great intelligence. "I just go by the rule of thumb, and muddle and puzzle out my cases as best I can." In saying this, he hardly does himself justice, for *Paul Beck, the Rule of Thumb Detective* (1898) shows him exercising a good deal of native wit, even though the famous detective Murdock Rose is scornful about him. The book had a very good press, and Beck was favorably compared with "the late lamented Sherlock Holmes." *Dora Myrl, the Lady Detective*

(1900) was no less absurd than other stories of the time about women detectives, who retained an impossible gentility of speech and personality while dealing with crime. In *The Capture of Paul Beck* (1909), Dora and Beck end up married after being on opposite sides in a case, and *Young Beck, a Chip of the Old Block* (1911) introduces their son, also Paul. These stories are unusual, in that they are mostly based on young Paul's life at university and just after leaving it, in company with his friend Lord Kirwood, son of the Secretary of State for Foreign Affairs, who is among the sillier Watsons. The cases of Paul, Jr., have great freshness. They include one of the finest card-cheating stories ever written, and one in which Bodkin made good use of his knowledge of the House of Commons. The Becks, senior and junior, are possibly the best Plain Man detectives of their era.

Other Supermen and Plain Men, although not very many of the latter, were at work in the field of the short story during this period, but there seems no need to particularize any of them, except perhaps the prolific Dick Donovan, the pseudonym of J. E. Preston Muddock (1843-1934), who spanned in a curious way the gap between the detective proper and the great flood of penny-dreadful figures headed by Sexton Blake, and including Nelson Lee, Dixon Hawke, and Falcon Swift, which began in imitation of Holmes—but of course an active nonanalytical Holmes always chasing or being chased by a super-villain—in the nineties. In America, a similar development was taking place, as Miss Joan M. Mooney has shown in a valuable, detailed discussion of the Nick Carter and Old Cap Collier stories ["Best-Selling American Detective Fiction," *The Arm-Chair Detective* 3, 4 (January 1970, January 1971)]. The crudity of the few penny dreadfuls I have read precludes them from consideration, but Donovan is a different matter. His plots are often absurdly melodramatic, but the level of his writing is sometimes reminiscent of rather inferior Trollope. He wavers between the undistinguished but readable:

> In personal appearance he was the true stamp of a thorough English gentleman. It might be that there was just a very faint tinge of port wine in the well-rounded cheeks, for if there was one thing that he was more partial to than another it was good old crusted port.

and the totally preposterous:

> "What devil was it that prompted me to listen to your honeyed words, to drink in your gilded lies? Can you undo what has been done! Can you restore to me my girlish innocence?"

The most nearly acceptable Donovan is in the novels told in the third person, some of them recounting the exploits of other detectives like Calvin Sugg, a typical post-Holmes figure, who speaks at least six languages fluently and has been given innumerable medals by various governments, but the most popular were the short stories in which Donovan boastfully recounts his own exploits. Like Holmes, he was thought to be a real person, and received many letters, including one from a woman in Brighton who asked him to shadow her husband. Muddock in his autobiography notes regretfully the preference for his detective stories over his other writings, and says: "I have never been in full sympathy with my Donovan work."

There are two writers still unmentioned whose work should be included in relation to the short story of the time, although what they wrote was nearer to the thriller than to detection. The Arsène Lupin stories of Maurice Leblanc (1864-1941) and the Raffles tales of E. W. Hornung (1866-1921) represent the last flicker for a long time of the criminal-hero tradition. *Arsène Lupin, gentleman-cambrioleur* (1907) introduces him as the leader of a gang of thieves, who masquerades in various disguises and outwits the police of every country, impersonating an English detective at Scotland Yard, making a fool of Holmlock Shears (Herlock Sholmès in the original), and taking charge of the search for Lupin in the Vidocq manner, while posing as the chief of the Sûreté. Lupin is a rogue rather than a villain, and in the later stories he is often on the side of law and order. The short stories about him come off better than the rambling novels, although there is something irritatingly slapdash about them all.

A. J. Raffles is a much more interesting character, even if the interest is partly sociological. Raffles is, on the surface, an image of a perfect English gentleman. He is captain of the school cricket team and later becomes the finest slow bowler of his decade (an amateur, naturally). Apart from playing cricket all the summer, he leads a life of apparent idleness. Apparent: for he really makes a living as a burglar, and *Raffles, the Amateur Cracksman* (1899) records his adventures in collaboration with Bunny, who has worshiped Raffles since fagging for him at school. In one very curious story, Bunny dresses as a woman, and there are suggestions of a platonic homosexual relationship between them.

The series, which includes the later *Raffles* (1901) and *A Thief in the Night* (1905), shows the public-school ethos turned round, with the traditional virtues of sticking to your chums and doing the decent thing used in the service of theft. Raffles sometimes does the decent thing by conventional standards, as on the occasion when he sends a gold cup stolen from the British Museum back to the Queen, and on another occasion he explains to Bunny that it is not a betrayal of hospitality to steal the jewels at Lord Amersteth's house, because he has been "asked for my cricket, as though I were a pro." It is less easy to excuse his conduct in jumping overboard when things become desperate, leaving Bunny to face a long prison sentence, or on the occasion when he burgles the house in which Bunny's girl lives. Bunny's own ethical code is also distinctly odd. After a little initial reluctance, he enters wholeheartedly into burglary, but he refuses to stoop to "personal paragraphs and the baser journalism."

Hornung, who also wrote some indifferent detective and adventure stories, had no satirical intentions. He was Conan Doyle's brother-in-law, and Doyle strongly disapproved of the whole idea of Raffles, saying, "You must not make the criminal a hero." Since Raffles is seen through the worshiping Bunny's eyes, he undoubtedly is a hero, although Bunny often says things like "Raffles was a villain, when all is written," and promises to "paint in every wart." The stories are always lively, although occasionally absurd, and both Raffles and Bunny come through very clearly. They are also often intentionally funny. Hornung was a dexterous punster, as is shown by his remark that "though he might be more humble, there's no police like Holmes," and the Raffles stories contain one excellent pun. When Raffles and Bunny pay a visit to the "Raffles Relics" in Scotland Yard's Black Museum, they see the spectacles and jimmy of Charles Peace, and the master murmurs: "The greatest of the pre-Raffleites." Hornung never sees Raffles as an enemy of the class in which he had been brought up, as an earlier writer would have done, but as a man who adheres to the standards of this class even though he is a crook. For him, as for Bunny, Raffles's sins are canceled out by his heroic death in the Boer War.

The Golden Age of the short story, which began with Holmes, ended with the First World War. The Holmes stories are the best things in the period, but they are not the only things worth remembering. Most of the short story's better practitioners in these years turned to detection as a relief from other work, and partly for this reason much of what they wrote retains its freshness. They enjoyed using a form which, still in its infancy, offered infinite opportunities for variation, and there is a gaiety in the often unsophisticated capers they cut which was slowly lost by the writers who followed them. (pp. 79-90)

> *Julian Symons, "The Short Story: The First Golden Age," in his* Mortal Consequences: A History—From the Detective Story to the Crime Novel, *Harper & Row, Publishers, 1972, pp. 76-90.*

Howard Haycraft

[*Haycraft is an American editor and critic who has written extensively on mystery and detective fiction. In the following excerpt from his highly regarded* Murder for Pleasure: The Life and Times of the Detective Story, *he surveys American detective fiction of the 1920s.*]

There is no denying that until comparatively recent times the American detective story has consistently lagged behind the English. This was particularly true in the early years of the era under present consideration. The Great Revival of the English detective story began almost immediately after the Armistice in 1918. Its American counterpart did not arrive until the better part of a decade later. This is not to say that *no* good American detective stories were written during the intervening years. There were at least a few; but no important technical advance was made, no spontaneous upsurge of popular interest occurred, until well toward the end of the period.

When the Armistice was signed, Arthur B. Reeve was still enthroned as king of American detective story writers; Anna Katharine Green remained active and influential, though well past her prime; and Mary Roberts Rinehart dominated the romantic side of the picture even more personally than she does to-day. A few, but only a few, new authors had arisen or were on the immediate horizon, and most of these followed established patterns instead of striking out in new directions, as their British confrères were doing in the same years.

The works of Isabel Egenton Ostrander (1885-1924) (who also wrote as "Robert Orr Chipperfield," "David Fox," and "Douglas Grant") are all but forgotten to-day, but in the early 1920's they had a very considerable and not undeserved popularity. Essentially a follower of Anna Katharine Green, Miss Ostrander nevertheless made one important forward step of her own, with her *Ashes to Ashes*

(1919), praised by Dorothy Sayers as "an almost unique example of the detective story told from the point of view of the hunted rather than the hunter." In most of her novels, in fact, the careful plot-work will repay the student who can survive the out-dated femininity of her prose.

As far back as 1914, Frederick Irving Anderson (1877-   ), one of the best known "magazine authors" of his generation, had turned his attention to crime with the episodic adventures of *The Infallible Godahl.* A later series of related short stories dealt with the career of *The Notorious Sophie Lang* (memorialized in several cinema incarnations). Neither of these efforts represented pure detection, but the seed was planted. A character who had appeared in both series was Deputy Parr of the New York police. Beginning in 1921, Parr was given a series of his own in *The Saturday Evening Post.* The stories covered a leisurely decade and then were collected in *The Book of Murder* (1930). Because of his small output between permanent covers, Frederick Irving Anderson has escaped the attention of many devotees of the form; yet it is no exaggeration to say that he has shown perhaps the greatest mastery of the American *short* detective story of any writer since Melville Davisson Post, whom he greatly resembles in ingenuity, command of plot, and the carefully integrated backgrounds of his work. Like Post, also, his stories have a quality of timelessness which makes them as readable to-day as when they were written. It can only be regretted that Mr. Anderson has never essayed the detective novel—the detective short story seems unfortunately on the decline, for reasons to be discussed in a later chapter—and that he seems to have retired entirely from the writing field in favor of his Vermont farm. (But the New England locales found in so many of his stories derived from an earlier home in the Massachusetts Berkshires.) These factors have combined to limit the influence and recognition of one of the finest natural American talents of the era.

Another magazine writer who contributed to the genre in this period was Octavus Roy Cohen (1891-   ), best known for his humorous tales of American Negro life. His stories of the private agent Jim Hanvey (white) appeared first in *The Saturday Evening Post* and were collected later in several books. Ponderous, uncouth, but ingratiating Jim Hanvey has entertained a wide circle of readers for many years. Yet it must be confessed that his cases are too often better examples of "slick" magazine formula-fiction than of detection within the purposeful meaning of the act.

Among other authors who enjoyed above-the-average popularity during these years may be mentioned: Ernest M. Poate and his Dr. Bentiron; James Hay, Jr. (1881-1936) and his Jefferson Hastings; Lee Thayer (1874-   ), and her Peter Clancy, who still figures in an investigation or two each annum; and Hulbert Footner and his Madame Storey, a favorite of so particular and experienced a reader as Christopher Morley. Mr. Morley's own single mystery, the delightful *Haunted Bookshop* (1919), only sharpens every reader's regret that he has never turned his hand to bona fide detection. Most of the numerous novels of Natalie Sumner Lincoln (1881-1935) belong to the romance-mystery category, but a few qualify as detection for its own sake. Kay Cleaver Strahan's (1888-   ) early works won considerable favor, despite some particularly atrocious Had-I-But-Knowning; but she seems to have ceased

writing almost altogether. Vincent Starrett (1886-   ) has produced from time to time some ingenious examples of plain and fancy sleuthing, though without endangering his greater eminence in the field as the devoted biographer of Sherlock Holmes; this, after all, is as one would wish it. Ben Ames Williams (1889-   ) has written excellent tales which escape being detection by only a narrow margin. Another "border-liner" of the era was Arthur Somers Roche (1883-1935), whose works considerably resembled those of Louis Joseph Vance before him. Harvey J. O'Higgins (1876-1929) supplied the form with its only passably believable boy hero to date in his Barney Cook stories (based on the actual methods of the Burns agency); while his later Detective Duff is equally singular as the only psychoanalytical sleuth of any prominence. A variation of the psychological mode motivates T. S. Stribling's (1881-   ) single and too little known volume of Poggioli tales, *Clues of the Caribbees* (1929). Charles Honce remarks that the concluding story "is positively thunderous; it will knock you right out of your seat."

Special mention must go to Frances Noyes Hart (1890-   ), who "covered" the famous Hall-Mills case and turned the experience (though not the facts) into an unforgettable but unrepeatable tour de force in her *Bellamy Trial* (1927), in which the detective action takes place in a day-by-day account of a murder trial. Her later *Hide in the Dark* (1929) is credited with popularizing the parlor game "Murder" (or vice versa), but was not otherwise important, and she has written nothing new for some years.

These authors were all "good" authors, and there were others in the same period who were at least competent. But no one of them (save possibly Frederick Irving Anderson with his quiet excellence and Mrs. Hart with her brilliant solo flight) was doing work to compare with the exciting developments that were taking place in England. The American detective story stood still, exactly where it had been before the War. Suddenly, in 1926, came the long-overdue "break," with the publication of *The Benson Murder Case,* the first of the epochal Philo Vance novels by "S. S. Van Dine" (Willard Huntington Wright, 1888-1939). Overnight, American crime fiction came of age. (pp. 159-63)

[Wright's] *The Benson Murder Case,* presumably suggested by the murder of Joseph Bowne Elwell, the New York bridge expert, was for the first few weeks principally a succès d'estime among the chosen few. One must remember that in 1926 in America the pastime was still regarded a little apologetically and cautiously. But gradually the word spread that something unusual had happened in the detective story, and sales began to pick up. The second Vance investigation, *The "Canary" Murder Case* (another roman à clef, based this time on the "Dot" King murder), magnificently smashed the old tabus into fine smithereens for all time. Serialized in *Scribner's Magazine* prior to book publication, it became a sort of national *cause,* rivaling Floyd Collins, Mah Jong, and King Tut as a popular fad.

The book, published in 1927, broke all modern publishing records for detective fiction and was translated into seven languages. Hollywood's interest was engaged, and each succeeding story was filmed shortly after it appeared in print, with a sizable list of silent and talking screen heroes making Vance for a few years, the best known fictional sleuth on the globe. Needless to say, each novel earned Wright more money than all his serious books together, and the picture rights brought him a fortune. Paradoxically, Vance's vast popularity made it impossible for his creator to stop writing—though he had once declared that no one author "has more than six good detective-novel ideas in his system," and had intended to confine his own output to that number. In all, he wrote twelve; and, as if in proof of his contention, nearly all critics have agreed in pronouncing the last six inferior to the first.

Aside from the brilliant plot-work of the initial novels, two factors contributed principally to the success of the Van Dine books: the great literacy with which they were written, matching the hero's—at first—impressive learning; and a high degree of verisimilitude, so carefully worked out in every detail that in the early years numerous uncritical readers thought the cases had really occurred, while Vance, District Attorney Markham, Sergeant Heath, and the Watsonian chronicler became the household familiars of thousands of their countrymen. To these attributes of popularity, certain unkind critics have added another: the undeniable aura of pictured ostentation which (say these scoffers) destined the stories for sure success in a decade which measured its own success in terms of yachts or silk shirts, as the case might be.

Whether or not this was the case, it is unfortunately true that the many superlative qualities of the novels were accompanied by a heavy pretentiousness and lack of humor which became increasingly obtrusive as tastes changed. Philo Vance "dates" to-day much as Calvin Coolidge and Jimmy Walker symbolize a past which seems many years dead. (Van Dine's one embarrassing attempt to cope with change—his next-to-last book, *The Gracie Allen Murder Case*—is most charitably forgotten.) Likewise, Vance's very erudition began to grow thin and wearisome as the series progressed. In the early tales it had served a legitimate function in the plots and had contributed causatively to the solutions. In the later novels it was too often introduced in large and gratuitous chunks, without essential relationship to the criminal problem under consideration. In such circumstances, even its "snob appeal" eventually faltered, and it became faintly ludicrous, almost a burlesque of itself. . . . Another strength-turned-to-weakness was Van Dine's repetition of his "formula." Gilbert Seldes once went so far as to say he could detect the murderer early in a Vance novel, because he always entered the story on the same page!

At any rate, much of Vance's popularity had evaporated, rather unjustly on the whole, before Wright died of thrombosis in 1939, at the age of fifty-one. (pp. 165-67)

In a few short years [Wright became] the best known American writer of the detective story since Poe; he had rejuvenated and re-established the genre in his native land; and his name and that of his sleuth will endure—for all their joint pretentious faults—among the immortals of the literature.

For all his wide and undeniable influence and achievements, "S. S. Van Dine" was essentially a developer, an adapter and polisher of other men's techniques, rather than a true innovator. In this, though scarcely otherwise, his position was not unlike that of Conan Doyle a generation earlier. By contrast, his almost immediate chronologi-

cal follower, Dashiell Hammett, acknowledged founder of the realistic or "hard-boiled" division of detective writing, must be called a *creator* of the first rank, deserving to sit with such diverse comrades-at-arms as E. C. Bentley, Francis Iles, and the small handful of others who brought something really new to their chosen field of effort. Van Dine's Philo Vance novels—to continue the comparison—were epochal in the sense that they raised the detective story to a new peak of excellence and popularity in the land of its birth; they were American in the narrow sense that their milieu and subject matter were American; yet in method and style they departed no whit from the well established English tradition. On the other hand, Hammett's lean, dynamic, unsentimental narratives created a definitely *American style,* quite separate and distinct from the accepted English pattern. (So separate and so distinct, in fact, that to this day certain short-sighted formalists refuse to admit they are detective stories at all! But with such narrow parochialism the truly eclectic student can have no traffic.) (pp. 168-69)

Hammett had been writing for the pulp market (he is the most notable of the numerous "alumni" of *Black Mask*) and reviewing detective fiction for the New York *Post* for some time before he published his first novel, in 1929. It was called *Red Harvest* and was a loosely constructed blood-and-thunder yarn with more gangsterism than detection, even of the Hammett definition, in it. *The Dain Curse,* published the same year, showed a substantial improvement and crystallization of his talent and technique. He reached his zenith (and one of the all-time high points in the detective story) with *The Maltese Falcon* (1930). This novel holds the unusual distinction of being the only contemporary detective story to date to be included in the carefully selected Modern Library series. *The Glass Key* (1931), ranked by most critics as only below *The Maltese Falcon* (though it is Hammett's own first choice among his books), was a worthy successor. But *The Thin Man* (1932), the most popular of his works, paradoxically marked (in the opinion of the initiated) a distinct softening of the author's talents. A film version with William Powell and Myrna Loy in the leading rôles was sensationally successful and has been followed by a number of cinematic sequels with the same actors. The affluence which the series has brought Hammett is probably the reason that he has produced no published work in many years. Nevertheless, *The Thin Man,* while his least typical and least important contribution, is not without significance on its own account, as one of the first works to bring humor, and of a distinctly native brand, to the detective story in this country.

Because of their startling originality, the Hammett novels virtually defy exegesis even to-day—though their external pattern is by now all too familiar by process of over-much imitation. As straightaway detective stories they can hold their own with the best. They are also character studies of close to top rank in their own right, and are penetrating if often shocking novels of manners as well. They established new standards for realism in the genre. Yet they are as sharply stylized and deliberately artificial as Restoration Comedy, and have been called an inverted form of romanticism. They were commercial in inception; but they miss being Literature, if at all, by the narrowest of margins.

The *Bookman's* comment in 1932 that "it is doubtful if even Ernest Hemingway has written more effective dialogue" may seem a trifle over-enthusiastic to-day, but only a little. And Hammett's talents in this direction are, if anything, exceeded by his ability to delineate character by sharp, frugal, telling strokes admirably suited to the form. He is at his best in depicting his central figures, invariably private inquiry agents (drawn from life, he has intimated): brutal, grasping, lecherous "heels"; each, however, with his own hard and distinct code of Hemingwayesque courage and fatalism and a twisted sort of personal integrity incomprehensible to conventional minds. His secondary characters are not always realized with equal care, but some of them (as the tormented baby-faced gunman of *The Maltese Falcon* or the gorilla, Jeff, in *The Glass Key*) give new and unforgettable inflections to the word "sinister."

The action of the novels is machine-gun paced and so violent that, in the first two books particularly, it occasionally defeats its purpose by exhausting the reader's receptive and reactive capacities. Some of the incidents, also, by the extremity of their sadism, tend to stand out too strongly from the main thread of the story and thus to imperil the unity and balance of the novel as a whole: too often they are merely stunts in realistic narration and definitely impede the progress of the plots in which they occur. (This is no moralistic objection, but a statement of the recognized fact that artistic excesses bring their own retribution.) The prose, except for the few such moments of intemperance, is economical, astringent, and muscular, while the Hammett vocabulary, as might be expected, is consistently and quite properly for the *mores* depicted blunt and outspoken. In fact, *The Thin Man*'s lively success in the bookstores is commonly ascribed in publishing circles to the inclusion of a single usage seldom seen in polite print. But it would be an error and an injustice to dismiss Dashiell Hammett's novels as merely salacious or sensational—even though their author wrote with a keen eye to the box-office and a not-too-reluctant use of some of the more dubious tricks of the trade. For the tremendous impact and virility he achieved transcend the means employed. (pp. 170-72)

[Should Hammett] never write another detective story, it is already safe to say that no other author of modern times—certainly no other American—has so basically changed and influenced the form.

Like all originators, Dashiell Hammett has suffered at the hands of his imitators. But the circumstance does not and should not obscure what he has done to give the American detective story a nationality of its own.

It is perhaps a mistake to insist on too-minute classifications and categories within any literary frame. For example: it would be possible, if one chose, to contend that a mating of the more successful elements of the contrasting Van Dine and Hammett schools was inevitable in the American detective story. The point could be quite readily proved by the accurately titled "adventures in deduction" of and about Fllery Queen (who functions both as author and as sleuth). Less pretentious than the Van Dine *opera* but agreeably livelier, lacking the startling impact but also the mannerisms of the Hammett novels, the Queen tales are nevertheless entirely American in their idiom, and could be easily cited as an example of the successful blend-

ing of the two methods. The only obstacle to so delightfully pat a theory is the purely evidential one that the first Queen novel was "work in progress" well before the earliest Hammett efforts appeared in print. This does not alter the fact, however, that, by accident if not by design, or perhaps as the result of independent developmental trends, the Queen stories *do* fall somewhere between the two styles, where they represent some of the most competent writing that has been done on this side of the water in the field of the deductive tale contrived for purely entertainment purposes.

"Ellery Queen" (as author) is a pseudonym covering the identity of two young Americans who are also cousins, Frederic Dannay and Manfred B. Lee. . . . [With] the publication of *The Roman Hat Mystery* (1929), one of the most successful collaborations in contemporary writing was launched. Since then, to quote *News-Week,* "Ellery Queen has been uncovering murders and untangling mysteries with such suavity and sophistication that he has become one of the most popular fictional sleuths extant."

For some years elaborate precautions were taken to conceal the identity of "Queen," who appeared at autographing parties and literary teas wearing a black mask, and likewise of "Barnaby Ross," the name under which Messrs. Dannay and Lee created their second and by no means negligible sleuth, Drury Lane, an ex-Shakespearean actor. . . . Ellery Queen is to-day deservedly one of the two or three best known names in American detective fiction, while the invariably workmanlike stories with which he is associated have recently attracted the attention of new and vastly wider audiences through radio and moving pictures. (pp. 173-75)

Asked to state what they believe to be the cardinal quality that has brought the Queen stories their wide reputation and success, the authors modestly speak of the "absolutely logical" fair-play method of deduction, which, indeed, has been the sign-mark of their work from the beginning. But there is more than this. Although the Messrs. "Queen" frankly and necessarily regard their output as a means of livelihood, they have brought to the detective story a respect and integrity which—combined with their unflagging zest—accounts largely for the high level they have consistently maintained. Unlike other writers who have wearied of the game and too often endeavor to substitute mere cleverness or sensationalism for hard work, the "Queens" have never failed to give their multitude of followers honest merchandise. If the stories have a flaw it is the occasional tendency to too-great intricacy, but even this occurs so rarely as to be negligible.

For the great part, the Queen tales are as adroit a blending of the intellectual and dramatic aspects of the genre, of meticulous plot-work, lively narration, easy, unforced humor, and entertaining personae, as can be found in the modern detective novel. They represent the deductive romance at its present-day skilful best.

Every now and then writers of fiction create characters who strike so universal a note of humanity that they transcend the narratives in which they appear. Dickens frequently did this. So did Mark Twain. So, in the particular field of our consideration, did Conan Doyle. And so did Earl Derr Biggers with his patient, aphoristic Chinese-Hawaiian-American, Charlie Chan, who has probably in-

Lauren Bacall and Humphrey Bogart in a scene from the 1946 film version of Raymond Chandler's The Big Sleep, *directed by Howard Hawkes.*

spired more genuine personal affection in his readers than any other sleuth in recent years. (pp. 176-77)

[In 1925] Charlie Chan made his bow in *The House Without a Key.* (Biggers had a predilection—rather confusing to his readers—for titles using the word "key.") All the Chan novels were serialized in *The Saturday Evening Post* before book publication. There is no Chan short story, to the perennial regret of anthologists. Charlie was not drawn from real life, his author said, although one Chang Apana of the Honolulu police force believed otherwise. "Sinister and wicked Chinese are old stuff," Biggers once explained, "but an amiable Chinese on the side of law and order had never been used." And he added, "If I understand Charlie Chan correctly, he has an idea that if you understand a man's character you can nearly predict what he is apt to do in any set of circumstances."

This pleasantly sound premise, however, must not lead the reader to expect psychological brilliance in the Chan adventures. Rather (like the author himself) they are clean, humorous, unpretentious, more than a little romantic, and—it must be confessed—just a shade mechanical and old-fashioned by modern plot standards. This absence of any novel or startling departure, in fact, is probably the

reason that the first Chan story created no such popular or critical stir as the first Philo Vance case (which, in point of strict chronology, it preceded by a good year). Charlie's fame was of slower growth than the more scintillant Philo's, and it was not until two or three of his adventures had appeared that he struck full stride.

Once started, however, he has been difficult to stop. The stories have been translated into ten different languages, almost a score of Charlie Chan moving pictures have appeared, although the original stories were long since exhausted; J. P. Marquand's later Japanese sleuth, Mr. Moto, who is also cinematically popular, seems more than generically indebted; and Charlie has also figured in numerous radio scripts and . . . even in a newspaper comic-strip. One must believe that Biggers (who died of heart disease at his Pasadena, California, home at fifty-eight in 1933) would scarcely be pleased with some of the posthumous transformations his originally simple and dignified character has undergone at the hands of others. Biggers himself was short, round, and dark, with twinkling eyes and a friendly manner. He was a skilled and genial craftsman who knew his audience and his métier. Nevertheless, his detective stories are remembered less for themselves than for the wise, smiling, pudgy little Chinese they introduced. Conventional as the narratives often were, Charlie Chan's personal popularity played a part in the Renaissance of the American detective story that can not be ignored. (pp. 178-79)

> *Howard Haycraft, in his* Murder for Pleasure: The Life and Times of the Detective Story, *revised edition, Biblo & Tannen, 1968, 409 p.*

Raymond Chandler

[*Along with Dashiell Hammett, Chandler elevated hard-boiled detective fiction into an American art form. His novels describe luridly realistic action in a sophisticated literary style uncommon to pulp mystery fiction. For many readers Chandler's books represent the essence of southern California: the superficialities of Hollywood, crime and vice glossed over with wealth, the cult of glamor, and a certain enduring mystery which eludes precise definition. A number of Chandler's novels were adapted as films—including* The Big Sleep, Farewell, My Lovely, *and* The Long Goodbye—*and for a time Chandler worked as a screenwriter. His screenplay credits include* Double Indemnity *(1944), directed by William Wyler and based on the novel by James M. Cain, and* Strangers on a Train *(1951), directed by Alfred Hitchcock. In the following essay, Chandler criticizes the classical detective story for its distance from psychological and social realities, and argues for the superiority of realistic detective fiction.*]

Fiction in any form has always intended to be realistic. Old-fashioned novels which now seem stilted and artificial to the point of burlesque did not appear that way to the people who first read them. Writers like Fielding and Smollett could seem realistic in the modern sense because they dealt largely with uninhibited characters, many of whom were about two jumps ahead of the police, but Jane Austen's chronicles of highly inhibited people against a background of rural gentility seem real enough psychologically. There is plenty of that kind of social and emotional hypocrisy around today. Add to it a liberal dose of intellectual pretentiousness and you get the tone of the book page in your daily paper and the earnest and fatuous atmosphere breathed by discussion groups in little clubs. These are the people who make best-sellers, which are promotional jobs based on a sort of indirect snob-appeal, carefully escorted by the trained seals of the critical fraternity, and lovingly tended and watered by certain much too powerful pressure groups whose business is selling books, although they would like you to think they are fostering culture. Just get a little behind in your payments and you will find out how idealistic they are.

The detective story for a variety of reasons can seldom be promoted. It is usually about murder and hence lacks the element of uplift. Murder, which is a frustration of the individual and hence a frustration of the race, may, and in fact has, a good deal of sociological implication. But it has been going on too long for it to be news. If the mystery novel is at all realistic (which it very seldom is) it is written in a certain spirit of detachment; otherwise nobody but a psychopath would want to write it or read it. The murder novel has also a depressing way of minding its own business, solving its own problems and answering its own questions. There is nothing left to discuss, except whether it was well enough written to be good fiction, and the people who make up the half-million sales wouldn't know that anyway. The detection of quality in writing is difficult enough even for those who make a career of the job, without paying too much attention to the matter of advance sales.

The detective story (perhaps I had better call it that, since the English formula still dominates the trade) has to find its public by a slow process of distillation. That it does do this, and holds on thereafter with such tenacity, is a fact; the reasons for it are a study for more patient minds than mine. Nor is it any part of my thesis to maintain that it is a vital and significant form of art. There are no vital and significant forms of art; there is only art, and precious little of that. The growth of populations has in no way increased the amount; it has merely increased the adeptness with which substitutes can be produced and packaged.

Yet the detective story, even in its most conventional form, is difficult to write well. Good specimens of the art are much rarer than good serious novels. Rather second-rate items outlast most of the high velocity fiction, and a great many that should never have been born simply refuse to die at all. They are as durable as the statues in public parks and just about that dull. This is very annoying to people of what is called discernment. They do not like it that penetrating and important works of fiction of a few years back stand on their special shelf in the library marked "Best-Sellers of Yesteryear," and nobody goes near them but an occasional shortsighted customer who bends down, peers briefly and hurries away; while old ladies jostle each other at the mystery shelf to grab off some item of the same vintage with a title like *The Triple Petunia Murder Case,* or *Inspector Pinchbottle to the Rescue.* They do not like it that "really important books" get dusty on the reprint counter, while *Death Wears Yellow Garters* is put out in editions of fifty or one hundred thousand copies on the news-stands of the country, and is obviously not there just to say goodbye.

To tell you the truth, I do not like it very much myself. In my less stilted moments I too write detective stories, and all this immortality makes just a little too much competition. Even Einstein couldn't get very far if three hundred treatises of the higher physics were published every year, and several thousand others in some form or other were hanging around in excellent condition, and being read too. Hemingway says somewhere that the good writer competes only with the dead. The good detective story writer (there must after all be a few) competes not only with all the unburied dead but with all the hosts of the living as well. And on almost equal terms; for it is one of the qualities of this kind of writing that the thing that makes people read it never goes out of style. The hero's tie may be a little off the mode and the good gray inspector may arrive in a dogcart instead of a streamlined sedan with siren screaming, but what he does when he gets there is the same old futzing around with timetables and bits of charred paper and who trampled the jolly old flowering arbutus under the library window.

I have, however, a less sordid interest in the matter. It seems to me that production of detective stories on so large a scale, and by writers whose immediate reward is small and whose need of critical praise is almost nil, would not be possible at all if the job took any talent. In that sense the raised eyebrow of the critic and the shoddy merchandizing of the publisher are perfectly logical. The average detective story is probably no worse than the average novel, but you never see the average novel. It doesn't get published. The average—or only slightly above average—detective story does. Not only is it published but it is sold in small quantities to rental libraries, and it is read. There are even a few optimists who buy it at the full retail price of two dollars, because it looks so fresh and new, and there is a picture of a corpse on the cover. And the strange thing is that this average, more than middling dull, pooped-out piece of utterly unreal and mechanical fiction is not terribly different from what are called the masterpieces of the art. It drags on a little more slowly, the dialogue is a little grayer, the cardboard out of which the characters are cut is a shade thinner, and the cheating is a little more obvious; but it is the same kind of book. Whereas the good novel is not at all the same kind of book as the bad novel. It is about entirely different things. But the good detective story and the bad detective story are about exactly the same things, and they are about them in very much the same way. There are reasons for this too, and reasons for the reasons; there always are.

I suppose the principal dilemma of the traditional or classic or straight-deductive or logic—and—deduction novel of detection is that for any approach to perfection it demands a combination of qualities not found in the same mind. The cool-headed constructionist does not also come across with lively characters, sharp dialogue, a sense of pace and an acute use of observed detail. The grim logician has as much atmosphere as a drawing-board. The scientific sleuth has a nice new shiny laboratory, but I'm sorry I can't remember the face. The fellow who can write you a vivid and colorful prose simply won't be bothered with the coolie labor of breaking down unbreakable alibis. The master of rare knowledge is living psychologically in the age of the hoop skirt. If you know all you should know about ceramics and Egyptian needlework, you don't know anything at all about the police. If you know that platinum won't melt under about 2800 degrees F. by itself, but will melt at the glance of a pair of deep blue eyes when put close to a bar of lead, then you don't know how men make love in the twentieth century. And if you know enough about the elegant flânerie of the pre-war French Riviera to lay your story in that locale, you don't know that a couple of capsules of barbital small enough to be swallowed will not only not kill a man—they will not even put him to sleep, if he fights against them.

Every detective story writer makes mistakes, and none will ever know as much as he should. Conan Doyle made mistakes which completely invalidated some of his stories, but he was a pioneer, and Sherlock Holmes after all is mostly an attitude and a few dozen lines of unforgettable dialogue. It is the ladies and gentlemen of what Mr. Howard Haycraft (in his book *Murder for Pleasure*) calls the Golden Age of detective fiction that really get me down. This age is not remote. For Mr. Haycraft's purpose it starts after the first World War and lasts up to about 1930. For all practical purposes it is still here. Two-thirds or three-quarters of all the detective stories published still adhere to the formula the giants of this era created, perfected, polished and sold to the world as problems in logic and deduction. These are stern words, but be not alarmed. They are only words. Let us glance at one of the glories

of the literature, an acknowledged masterpiece of the art of fooling the reader without cheating him. It is called *The Red House Mystery,* was written by A. A. Milne, and has been named by Alexander Woollcott (rather a fast man with a superlative) "one of the three best mystery stories of all time." Words of that size are not spoken lightly. The book was published in 1922, but is quite timeless, and might as easily have been published in July 1939, or, with a few slight changes, last week. It ran thirteen editions and seems to have been in print, in the original format, for about sixteen years. That happens to few books of any kind. It is an agreeable book, light, amusing in the *Punch* style, written with a deceptive smoothness that is not as easy as it looks.

It concerns Mark Ablett's impersonation of his brother Robert, as a hoax on his friends. Mark is the owner of the Red House, a typical laburnum-and-lodge-gate English country house, and he has a secretary who encourages him and abets him in this impersonation, because the secretary is going to murder him, if he pulls it off. Nobody around the Red House has ever seen Robert, fifteen years absent in Australia, known to them by repute as a no-good. A letter from Robert is talked about, but never shown. It announces his arrival, and Mark hints it will not be a pleasant occasion. One afternoon, then, the supposed Robert arrives, identifies himself to a couple of servants, is shown into the study, and Mark (according to testimony at the inquest) goes in after him. Robert is then found dead on the floor with a bullet hole in his face, and of course Mark has vanished into thin air. Arrive the police, suspect Mark must be the murderer, remove the debris and proceed with the investigation, and in due course, with the inquest.

Milne is aware of one very difficult hurdle and tries as well as he can to get over it. Since the secretary is going to murder Mark once he has established himself as Robert, the impersonation has to continue on and fool the police. Since, also, everybody around the Red House knows Mark intimately, disguise is necessary. This is achieved by shaving off Mark's beard, roughening his hands ("not the hands of a manicured gentlemen"—testimony) and the use of a gruff voice and rough manner. But this is not enough. The cops are going to have the body and the clothes on it and whatever is in the pockets. Therefore none of this must suggest Mark. Milne therefore works like a switch engine to put over the motivation that Mark is such a thoroughly conceited performer that he dresses the part down to the socks and underwear (from all of which the secretary has removed the maker's labels), like a ham blacking himself all over to play Othello. If the reader will buy this (and the sales record shows he must have) Milne figures he is solid. Yet, however light in texture the story may be, it is offered as a problem of logic and deduction. If it is not that, it is nothing at all. There is nothing else for it to be. If the situation is false, you cannot even accept it as a light novel, for there is no story for the light novel to be about. If the problem does not contain the elements of truth and plausibility, it is no problem; if the logic is an illusion, there is nothing to deduce. If the impersonation is impossible once the reader is told the conditions it must fulfill, then the whole thing is a fraud. Not a deliberate fraud, because Milne would not have written the story if he had known what he was up against. He is up against a number of deadly things, none of which he even considers. Nor, apparently, does the casual reader, who wants to like the story, hence takes it at face value. But the reader is not called upon to know the facts of life; it is the author who is the expert in the case. Here is what this author ignores:

1. The coroner holds formal jury inquest on a body for which no competent legal identification is offered. A coroner, usually in a big city, will sometimes hold inquest on a body that *cannot* be identified, if the record of such an inquest has or may have a value (fire, disaster, evidence of murder, etc.). No such reason exists here, and there is no one to identify the body. A couple of witnesses said the man said he was Robert Ablett. This is mere presumption, and has weight only if nothing conflicts with it. Identification is a condition precedent to an inquest. Even in death a man has a right to his own identity. The coroner will, wherever humanly possible, enforce that right. To neglect it would be a violation of his office.

2. Since Mark Ablett, missing and suspected of the murder, cannot defend himself, all evidence of his movements before and after the murder is vital (as also whether he has money to run away on); yet all such evidence is given by the man closest to the murder, and is without corroboration. It is automatically suspect until proved true.

3. The police find by direct investigation that Robert Ablett was not well thought of in his native village. Somebody there must have known him. No such person was brought to the inquest. (The story couldn't stand it.)

4. The police know there is an element of threat in Robert's supposed visit, and that it is connected with the murder must be obvious to them. Yet they make no attempt to check Robert in Australia, or find out what character he had there, or what associates, or even if he actually came to England, and with whom. (If they had, they would have found out he had been dead three years.)

5. The police surgeon examines the body with a recently shaved beard (exposing unweathered skin), artificially roughened hands, yet the body of a wealthy, soft-living man, long resident in a cool climate. Robert was a rough individual and had lived fifteen years in Australia. That is the surgeon's information. It is impossible he would have noticed nothing to conflict with it.

6. The clothes are nameless, empty, and have had the labels removed. Yet the man wearing them asserted an identity. The presumption that he was not what he said he was is overpowering. Nothing whatever is done about this peculiar circumstance. It is never even mentioned as being peculiar.

7. A man is missing, a well-known local man, and a body in the morgue closely resembles him. It is impossible that the police should not at once eliminate the chance that the missing man *is* the dead man. Nothing would be easier than to prove it. Not even to think of it is incredible. It makes idiots of the police, so that a brash amateur may startle the world with a fake solution.

The detective in the case is an insouciant gent named Antony Gillingham, a nice lad with a cheery eye, a cozy little flat in London, and that airy manner. He is not making any money on the assignment, but is always available when the local gendarmerie loses its notebook. The English police seem to endure him with their customary sto-

icism; but I shudder to think of what the boys down at the Homicide Bureau in my city would do to him.

There are less plausible examples of the art than this. In *Trent's Last Case* (often called "the perfect detective story") you have to accept the premise that a giant of international finance, whose lightest frown makes Wall Street quiver like a chihuahua, will plot his own death so as to hang his secretary, and that the secretary when pinched will maintain an aristocratic silence; the old Etonian in him maybe. I have known relatively few international financiers, but I rather think the author of this novel has (if possible) known fewer. There is one by Freeman Wills Crofts (the soundest builder of them all when he doesn't get too fancy) wherein a murderer by the aid of makeup, split second timing, and some very sweet evasive action, impersonates the man he has just killed and thereby gets him alive and distant from the place of the crime. There is one of Dorothy Sayers' in which a man is murdered alone at night in his house by a mechanically released weight which works because he always turns the radio on at just such a moment, always stands in just such a position in front of it, and always bends over just so far. A couple of inches either way and the customers would get a rain check. This is what is vulgarly known as having God sit in your lap; a murderer who needs that much help from Providence must be in the wrong business. And there is a scheme of Agatha Christie's featuring M. Hercule Poirot, that ingenius Belgian who talks in a literal translation of school-boy French, wherein, by duly messing around with his "little gray cells," M. Poirot decides that nobody on a certain through sleeper could have done the murder alone, therefore everybody did it together, breaking the process down into a series of simple operations, like assembling an egg-beater. This is the type that is guaranteed to knock the keenest mind for a loop. Only a halfwit could guess it.

There are much better plots by these same writers and by others of their school. There may be one somewhere that would really stand up under close scrutiny. It would be fun to read it, even if I did have to go back to page 47 and refresh my memory about exactly what time the second gardener potted the prize-winning tea-rose begonia. There is nothing new about these stories and nothing old. The ones I mentioned are all English only because the authorities (such as they are) seem to feel the English writers had an edge in this dreary routine, and that the Americans, (even the creator of Philo Vance—probably the most asinine character in detective fiction) only made the Junior Varsity.

This, the classic detective story, has learned nothing and forgotten nothing. It is the story you will find almost any week in the big shiny magazines, handsomely illustrated, and paying due deference to virginal love and the right kind of luxury goods. Perhaps the tempo has become a trifle faster, and the dialogue a little more glib. There are more frozen daiquiris and stingers ordered, and fewer glasses of crusty old port; more clothes by *Vogue,* and décors by the *House Beautiful,* more chic, but not more truth. We spend more time in Miami hotels and Cape Cod summer colonies and go not so often down by the old gray sundial in the Elizabethan garden. But fundamentally it is the same careful grouping of suspects, the same utterly incomprehensible trick of how somebody stabbed Mrs.

Pottington Postlethwaite III with the solid platinum poignard just as she flatted on the top note of the Bell Song from *Lakmé* in the presence of fifteen ill-assorted guests; the same ingenue in fur-trimmed pajamas screaming in the night to make the company pop in and out of doors and ball up the timetable; the same moody silence next day as they sit around sipping Singapore slings and sneering at each other, while the flat-feet crawl to and fro under the Persian rugs, with their derby hats on.

Personally I like the English style better. It is not quite so brittle, and the people as a rule, just wear clothes and drink drinks. There is more sense of background, as if Cheesecake Manor really existed all around and not just the part the camera sees; there are more long walks over the Downs and the characters don't all try to behave as if they had just been tested by MGM. The English may not always be the best writers in the world, but they are incomparably the best dull writers.

There is a very simple statement to be made about all these stories: they do not really come off intellectually as problems, and they do not come off artistically as fiction. They are too contrived, and too little aware of what goes on in the world. They try to be honest, but honesty is an art. The poor writer is dishonest without knowing it, and the fairly good one can be dishonest because he doesn't know what to be honest about. He thinks a complicated murder scheme which baffles the lazy reader, who won't be bothered itemizing the details, will also baffle the police, whose business is with details. The boys with their feet on the desks know that the easiest murder case in the world to break is the one somebody tried to get very cute with; the one that really bothers them is the murder somebody only thought of two minutes before he pulled it off. But if the writers of this fiction wrote about the kind of murders that happen, they would also have to write about the authentic flavor of life as it is lived. And since they cannot do that, they pretend that what they do is what should be done. Which is begging the question—and the best of them know it.

In her introduction to the first *Omnibus of Crime* [see excerpt above], Dorothy Sayers wrote: "It (the detective story) does not, and by hypothesis never can, attain the loftiest level of literary achievement." And she suggested somewhere else that this is because it is a "literature of escape" and not "a literature of expression." I do not know what the loftiest level of literary achievement is: neither did Aeschylus or Shakespeare; neither does Miss Sayers. Other things being equal, which they never are, a more powerful theme will provoke a more powerful performance. Yet some very dull books have been written about God, and some very fine ones about how to make a living and stay fairly honest. It is always a matter of who writes the stuff, and what he has in him to write it with. As for literature of expression and literature of escape, this is critics' jargon, a use of abstract words as if they had absolute meanings. Everything written with vitality expresses that vitality; there are no dull subjects, only dull minds. All men who read escape from something else into what lies behind the printed page; the quality of the dream may be argued, but its release has become a functional necessity. All men must escape at times from the deadly rhythm of their private thoughts. It is part of the process of life among thinking beings. It is one of the things that distin-

guish them from the three-toed sloth; he apparently—one can never be quite sure—is perfectly content hanging upside down on a branch, and not even reading Walter Lippman. I hold no particular brief for the detective story as the ideal escape. I merely say that *all* reading for pleasure is escape, whether it be Greek, mathematics, astronomy, Benedetto Croce, or *The Diary of the Forgotten Man.* To say otherwise is to be an intellectual snob, and a juvenile at the art of living.

I do not think such considerations moved Miss Dorothy Sayers to her essay in critical futility.

I think what was really gnawing at her mind was the slow realization that her kind of detective story was an arid formula which could not even satisfy its own implications. It was second-grade literature because it was not about the things that could make first-grade literature. If it started out to be about real people (and she could write about them—her minor characters show that), they must very soon do unreal things in order to form the artificial pattern required by the plot. When they did unreal things, they ceased to be real themselves. They became puppets and cardboard lovers and papier mâché villains and detectives of exquisite and impossible gentility. The only kind of writer who could be happy with these properties was the one who did not know what reality was. Dorothy Sayers' own stories show that she was annoyed by this triteness; the weakest element in them is the part that makes them detective stories, the strongest the part which could be removed without touching the "problem of logic and deduction." Yet she could not or would not give her characters their heads and let them make their own mystery. It took a much simpler and more direct mind than hers to do that.

In the *Long Week-End,* which is a drastically competent account of English life and manners in the decade following the first World War, Robert Graves and Alan Hodge gave some attention to the detective story. They were just as traditionally English as the ornaments of the Golden Age, and they wrote of the time in which these writers were almost as well-known as any writers in the world. Their books in one form or another sold into the millions, and in a dozen languages. These were the people who fixed the form and established the rules and founded the famous Detection Club, which is a Parnassus of English writers of mystery. Its roster includes practically every important writer of detective fiction since Conan Doyle. But Graves and Hodge decided that during this whole period only one first-class writer had written detective stories at all. An American, Dashiell Hammett. Traditional or not, Graves and Hodge were not fuddy-duddy connoisseurs of the second rate; they could see what went on in the world and that the detective story of their time didn't; and they were aware that writers who have the vision and the ability to produce real fiction do not produce unreal fiction.

How original a writer Hammett really was, it isn't easy to decide now, even if it mattered. He was one of a group, the only one who achieved critical recognition, but not the only one who wrote or tried to write realistic mystery fiction. All literary movements are like this; some one individual is picked out to represent the whole movement; he is usually the culmination of the movement. Hammett was the ace performer, but there is nothing in his work that is not implicit in the early novels and short stories of Hemingway. Yet for all I know, Hemingway may have learned something from Hammett, as well as from writers like Dreiser, Ring Lardner, Carl Sandburg, Sherwood Anderson and himself. A rather revolutionary debunking of both the language and material of fiction had been going on for some time. It probably started in poetry; almost everything does. You can take it clear back to Walt Whitman, if you like. But Hammett applied it to the detective story, and this, because of its heavy crust of English gentility and American pseudo-gentility, was pretty hard to get moving. I doubt that Hammett had any deliberate artistic aims whatever; he was trying to make a living by writing something he had first hand information about. He made some of it up; all writers do; but it had a basis in fact; it was made up out of real things. The only reality the English detection writers knew was the conversational accent of Surbiton and Bognor Regis. If they wrote about dukes and Venetian vases, they knew no more about them out of their own experience than the well-heeled Hollywood character knows about the French Modernists that hang in his Bel-Air château or the semi-antique Chippendale-cum-cobbler's bench that he uses for a coffee table. Hammett took murder out of the Venetian vase and dropped it into the alley; it doesn't have to stay there forever, but it was a good idea to begin by getting as far as possible from Emily Post's idea of how a well-bred debutante gnaws a chicken wing. He wrote at first (and almost to the end) for people with a sharp, aggressive attitude to life. They were not afraid of the seamy side of things; they lived there. Violence did not dismay them; it was right down their street.

Hammett gave murder back to the kind of people that commit it for reasons, not just to provide a corpse; and with the means at hand, not with hand-wrought duelling pistols, curare, and tropical fish. He put these people down on paper as they are, and he made them talk and think in the language they customarily used for these purposes. He had style, but his audience didn't know it, because it was in a language not supposed to be capable of such refinements. They thought they were getting a good meaty melodrama written in the kind of lingo they imagined they spoke themselves. It was, in a sense, but it was much more. All language begins with speech, and the speech of common men at that, but when it develops to the point of becoming a literary medium it only looks like speech. Hammett's style at its worst was almost as formalized as a page of Marius the Epicurean; at its best it could say almost anything. I believe this style, which does not belong to Hammett or to anybody, but is the American language (and not even exclusively that any more), can say things he did not know how to say or feel the need of saying. In his hands it had no overtones, left no echo, evoked no image beyond a distant hill. He is said to have lacked heart, yet the story he thought most of himself is the record of a man's devotion to a friend. He was spare, frugal, hardboiled, but he did over and over again what only the best writers can ever do at all. He wrote scenes that seemed never to have been written before.

With all this he did not wreck the formal detective story. Nobody can; production demands a form that can be produced. Realism takes too much talent, too much knowledge, too much awareness. Hammett may have loosened it up a little here, and sharpened it a little there. Certainly all but the stupidest and most meretricious writers are more conscious of their artificiality than they used to be.

And he demonstrated that the detective story can be important writing. *The Maltese Falcon* may or may not be a work of genius, but an art which is capable of it is not "by hypothesis" incapable of anything. Once a detective story can be as good as this, only the pedants will deny that it *could* be even better. Hammett did something else, he made the detective story fun to write, not an exhausting concatenation of insignificant clues. Without him there might not have been a regional mystery as clever as Percival Wilde's *Inquest,* or an ironic study as able as Raymond Postgate's *Verdict of Twelve,* or a savage piece of intellectual double-talk like Kenneth Fearing's *The Dagger of the Mind,* or a tragi-comic idealization of the murderer as in Donald Henderson's *Mr. Bowling Buys a Newspaper,* or even a gay and intriguing Hollywoodian gambol like Richard Sale's *Lazarus No. 7.*

The realistic style is easy to abuse: from haste, from lack of awareness, from inability to bridge the chasm that lies between what a writer would like to be able to say and what he actually knows how to say. It is easy to fake; brutality is not strength, flipness is not wit, edge-of-the-chair writing can be as boring as flat writing; dalliance with promiscuous blondes can be very dull stuff when described by goaty young men with no other purpose in mind than to describe dalliance with promiscuous blondes. There has been so much of this sort of thing that if a character in a detective story says, "Yeah," the author is automatically a Hammett imitator.

And there are still quite a few people around who say that Hammett did not write detective stories at all, merely hard-boiled chronicles of mean streets with a perfunctory mystery element dropped in like the olive in a martini. These are the flustered old ladies—of both sexes (or no sex) and almost all ages—who like their murders scented with magnolia blossoms and do not care to be reminded that murder is an act of infinite cruelty, even if the perpetrators sometimes look like playboys or college professors or nice motherly women with softly graying hair. There are also a few badly-scared champions of the formal or the classic mystery who think no story is a detective story which does not pose a formal and exact problem and arrange the clues around it with neat labels on them. Such would point out, for example, that in reading *The Maltese Falcon* no one concerns himself with who killed Spade's partner, Archer (which is the only formal problem of the story) because the reader is kept thinking about something else. Yet in *The Glass Key* the reader is constantly reminded that the question is who killed Taylor Henry, and exactly the same effect is obtained; an effect of movement, intrigue, cross-purposes and the gradual elucidation of character, which is all the detective story has any right to be about anyway. The rest is spillikins in the parlor.

But all this (and Hammett too) is for me not quite enough. The realist in murder writes of a world in which gangsters can rule nations and almost rule cities, in which hotels and apartment houses and celebrated restaurants are owned by men who made their money out of brothels, in which a screen star can be the finger-man for a mob, and the nice man down the hall is a boss of the numbers racket; a world where a judge with a cellar full of bootleg liquor can send a man to jail for having a pint in his pocket, where the mayor of your town may have condoned murder as an instrument of money-making, where no man can walk down

A gathering of Black Mask *contributors. From top left: Raymond J. Moffat, Raymond Chandler, Herbert Stinson, Dwight Babcock, Eric Taylor, Dashiell Hammett, Arthur Barnes, John K. Butler, W. T. Ballard, Horace McCoy, Norbert Davis.*

a dark street in safety because law and order are things we talk about but refrain from practising; a world where you may witness a hold-up in broad daylight and see who did it, but you will fade quickly back into the crowd rather than tell anyone, because the hold-up men may have friends with long guns, or the police may not like your testimony, and in any case the shyster for the defense will be allowed to abuse and vilify you in open court, before a jury of selected morons, without any but the most perfunctory interference from a political judge.

It is not a very fragrant world, but it is the world you live in, and certain writers with tough minds and a cool spirit of detachment can make very interesting and even amusing patterns out of it. It is not funny that a man should be killed, but it is sometimes funny that he should be killed for so little, and that his death should be the coin of what we call civilization. All this still is not quite enough.

In everything that can be called art there is a quality of redemption. It may be pure tragedy, if it is high tragedy, and it may be pity and irony, and it may be the raucous laughter of the strong man. But down these mean streets a man must go who is not himself mean, who is neither tarnished nor afraid. The detective in this kind of story must be such a man. He is the hero, he is everything. He must be a complete man and a common man and yet an unusual man. He must be, to use a rather weathered phrase, a man of honor, by instinct, by inevitability, without thought of it, and certainly without saying it. He must be the best man in his world and a good enough man for any world. I do not care much about his private life; he is neither a eunuch nor a satyr; I think he might seduce a duchess and I am quite sure he would not spoil a virgin;

if he is a man of honor in one thing, he is that in all things. He is a relatively poor man, or he would not be a detective at all. He is a common man or he could not go among common people. He has a sense of character, or he would not know his job. He will take no man's money dishonestly and no man's insolence without a due and dispassionate revenge. He is a lonely man and his pride is that you will treat him as a proud man or be very sorry you ever saw him. He talks as the man of his age talks, that is, with rude wit, a lively sense of the grotesque, a disgust for sham, and a contempt for pettiness. The story is his adventure in search of a hidden truth, and it would be no adventure if it did not happen to a man fit for adventure. He has a range of awareness that startles you, but it belongs to him by right, because it belongs to the world he lives in.

If there were enough like him, I think the world would be a very safe place to live in, and yet not too dull to be worth living in. (pp. 222-37)

> *Raymond Chandler, "The Simple Art of Murder," in* The Art of the Mystery Story: A Collection of Critical Essays, *edited by Howard Haycraft, Simon and Schuster, 1946, pp. 222-37.*

Philip Durham

[*Durham was an American critic and educator whose studies of American Western and detective fiction include* Down These Mean Streets a Man Must Go: Raymond Chandler's Knight *(1963) and* The Western Story: Fact, Fiction, and Myth *(1975). He also edited, with Everett Jones,* The Frontier in American Litera-

ture (1969). In the following excerpt, Durham provides an overview of the development of hard-boiled detective fiction in the Black Mask *magazine, edited by Joseph T. Shaw, during the decade 1926 through 1936, focusing on the Race Williams stories of Carroll John Daly and the Continental Op stories of Dashiell Hammett.*]

When Henry L. Mencken and George Jean Nathan began publishing, in the early spring of 1920, the *Black Mask*—one of their three pulp magazines—they could not have known that they were creating a medium which became a vehicle for the "hard-boiled" writers, those writers whose heroes acted as rugged individualists while they brought justice to the deserving. The heroes were violent, but their violence was not merely that of sensationalism. It was rather a kind of meaningful violence, sometimes symbolic of a special ethical code or attitude, sometimes an explicit description and implicit criticism of a corrupt society. Thus, in one of America's unique magazines, the *Black Mask* School was created.

The early *Black Mask,* featuring "mystery, detective, adventure, western, horror, and novelty," was patterned along the lines of such first rate pulps as *Argosy,* but the original contributors rarely measured up to the stature of those writers found in the better-known *Argosy.* In those days, however, pulps were money makers, and editors Mencken and Nathan sold *Black Mask* after six months for a nice profit. Under the subsequent editorship of such capable men as Phil Cody and Harry North, *Black Mask* began to take on a specific character, and within two or three years a version of the heroic knight emerged; the Private Investigator was poised and indestructably ready to clean up the cesspools of crime in New York City.

The two heroes who played a major role in the development of *Black Mask* were Race Williams and the Continental Op in tales by Carroll John Daly and Dashiell Hammett. In November 1926, the *Black Mask* acquired a new editor, Captain Joseph T. Shaw, who during a full decade molded the magazine into a medium which made a unique contribution to American literature. (pp. 51-2)

From the vantage point of twenty years, Shaw looked back, in 1946, to the time when he first came to *Black Mask.* He had meditated then, he later wrote, on the possibility of creating a new type of detective story, different from the one established by Poe in 1841 and so consistently followed right down to the 1920's: the tale of ratiocination, of clues, of puzzles, the locked closet had-I-but-known sort of thing. In the pages of the *Black Mask* he singled out the stories of Dashiell Hammett as approximating what he had in mind: "simplicity for the sake of clarity, plausibility, and belief." Shaw wanted action, but he "held that action is meaningless unless it involves recognizable human character in three-dimensional form." With the work of Hammett as the model, the editor began to search for the stories of those men who wrote in a similar vein; the July 1927 issue carried the statement "We are constantly looking for new writers who have the *Black Mask* spirit and the *Black Mask* idea of what a short story should be." The result became known as the Hard-Boiled School or the *Black Mask School* of Detective Fiction, with such chief practitioners as Dashiell Hammett, Raymond Chandler, Raoul Whitfield, Paul Cain, Lester Dent. The characters which the writers created were, admitted Shaw, hard-boiled, but the authors' "style and treatment were something else again." Modern critics identify the style and treatment as objective realism. Shaw was explicit in pointing out that his writers observed a cardinal principle—"in creating the illusion of reality"—by allowing their characters to act and talk tough rather than by making them do it. Instead of telling the reader how infallible the actors were, the authors allowed their heroes to demonstrate their abilities. By achieving ever greater restraint and by carefully avoiding incredibility, the *Black Mask* boys, thought Shaw, "wrote convincingly." (pp. 52-3)

When Shaw became the editor of *Black Mask* it contained, as Erle Stanley Gardner has pointed out, a type and a style. The type was well known through the stories of Daly, but it was left to Hammett to combine the type and style. Short on style though Daly was, one would have a difficult time finding a more effective hard-boiled hero than was his Race Williams, whom the readers did not examine but merely swallowed in great quantities. One of the earliest, latest, and most prolific of the *Black Mask* contributors, Daly turned out Race Williams stories and novels by the score. According to Gardner, editor Harry North once said that when he put Race Williams on the cover, the *Black Mask* sales jumped fifteen per cent.

In both the June, 1923, and April, 1927, issues of *Black Mask* the editors reported interviews with contributor Carroll John Daly, an assured and somewhat flippant writer, who described his hero, Race Williams, as thirty, five feet eleven and one half inches, one hundred eighty-three pounds, with dark brown hair and black eyes. There was nothing "soft-boiled" about the man who admired a clever woman and respected a good one—"when he finds her." He was a Private Investigator, in the business for thrills and money. Here was the original hard-boiled detective, the private eye who, during the next forty years, moved in fiction across the country—from New York to Chicago to San Francisco to Los Angeles. At times he changed into the clothes of a police detective, newspaper man, camera man, undercover man for the Racing Commission, insurance investigator, good-guy gambler, or just plain knight, but he was always, essentially, the same hard-boiled hero. Some of these men were more attractive than Race Williams, although they were like him: indestructible, fearless, courageous; he was violent, often brutal, a dead-shot, killing when he thought it necessary; he was a celibate admired by women and feared by men; he had his own sense of right and wrong by which he lived, meting out his individual concept of justice that more often than not was contrary to the accepted mores or to the law, which was restrictive and too slow. With supreme confidence in his own judgment, this individualist did not think it necessary to play by the book—one who did was often thought naive. In addition to what he said and did, he frequently administered justice by what he did not do: letting a murderer go free if he exhibited an extra measure of guts, or allowing a girl—who had just put a bullet from a small Colt automatic through a two-timing skunk—to escape because she had been victimized, had a good heart, and meant well. The private eye was always on the side of right, but it was his own personal interpretation and definition of "right."

In "Knights of the Open Palm" Race Williams, always the first person narrator, stated his position: "I'm what you might call the middle-man—just a halfway house between the dicks and the crooks. . . . But my conscience is clear; I never bumped off a guy who didn't need it." This credo was elaborated on throughout his heroic career. In *The Snarl of the Beast,* for example, Race restated his position, adding that "right and wrong are not written on the statutes for me, nor do I find my code of morals in the essays of long-winded professors. My ethics are my own. I'm not saying they're good and I'm not admitting they're bad, and what's more I'm not interested in the opinions of others on that subject." Williams, in "The Amateur Murderer," promised the readers that if anything happened to the girl he would "pop" off the offender, and he followed the assurance with his philosophy: "Not good ethics? Not right thinking? Maybe not. We won't go into that." The fact that he was on the side of right in the spirit of individualism justified almost any act. As he threw terror into all evil-thinking men, Williams' reputation became a symbol which allowed his problems to remain comparatively simple as long as he followed his slogan: "I trusted myself. That was what counted."

Opinions on patriotism, nativism, altruism, communism, and politics were all within the scope of Carroll John Daly. With an eye to public sentiment in the 1920's, Daly had Williams speak on the uselessness of senators, from whom one gets nothing at all. A congressman was a little better, for one can at least get garden seeds from him. When in *The Third Murderer* Florence Drummond—The Flame, the good girl with the criminal mind—complained to Race of the state of society by saying "Honesty—the one thing that the rich leave for the poor to fatten on," Race replied, "You didn't bring me here to fill me up on Communism." "No," Flame said, "Communism is a hatred of the poor for the rich—not simply an envy." Appealing to Williams as a "staunch citizen" was the wrong approach, for he did his work only at the right price. Like the big shoe manufacturer and Henry Ford and John D. Rockefeller, with Race Williams it was a business. They did not give away shoes, cars, or oil, but they gave generously to charity. Foreigners from all of Asia and most of Europe were villains per se, and because they were so frequently arch criminals they made excellent antagonists for Race. He favored patriotic Americans, born and raised, unlike Count Jehdo, on American soil. Yet in "Murder Book" when Race acquired the document which might have saved our country and prevented a war, he returned it for the life of The Flame who was being tortured after having been caught acting as an agent of the government. Williams' personal sense of justice, integrity, and loyalty came first.

Daly was not one to miss the value of "reckless courage" even in the villains; he could say admiringly of Mark Yarrow—the number two bad man of "Murder Book"—"He passed out tough." And there was Purdy Young in *Tainted Power* who represented the "new school" of racketeering because he wore a hundred and fifty dollar gray business suit instead of a sweater and cap—"Purdy Young had guts." Daly saved his unstinted praise, however, for the show of guts in the good guys, including one cop: "Good old Sergeant O'Rourke. He had the guts to live no matter what the consequences." The guttiest of them all was, of course, Race Williams himself, admirably summed up by The Flame.

"You made use of just what you always make use

of. It's not your head; it's the animal in you. The courage in you; the thing that drives you on. You're licked—licked a dozen times, over and over. Everybody knows it but you! No, it's not your head."

"If it isn't my head, what is it?"

"Just guts, I guess," she said. "Just guts."

Clichés and sloppy writing characterized Daly's work. He was a "he don't" writer who had Williams say, "I shoved a butt into my face, gave it heat." Williams identified a bad guy on a foggy, dark night by his bloodshot eyes and yellow teeth. Daly employed brutal death in the tough manner: "Joe Gorgon jumped sort of in the air, half spun, fired wildly, and I laid my next bullet smack between his eyes. Just a little round hole, ever growing larger. Joe Gorgon waved his hands once. His right foot came slowly up, like a lad in the slow motion pictures. Then he pitched forward on his face." Some of his most extravagant prose Daly saved for Williams in "I'll Tell the World": "Both my guns had spoken—both roared out their message of death—and, so help me God, but a single hole appeared in Lutz's forehead. I've done a deal of shooting in my day—mighty fine shooting, but never anything like that." Mr. Daly had been reading Dime Novels.

Carroll John Daly was a careless writer and a muddy thinker who created the hard-boiled detective, the prototype for numberless writers to follow. Race Williams was a popular literary hero in the 1920's and 1930's, but no different from the rugged individualists of any other decade who could say with Race,

"I'm a man of action but I can think occasionally."

"I'm sorry if I appear hard boiled or cold blooded . . . but them that live by the gun should die by the gun."

"I'm all for justice and fair play."

Within a few months after the stereotyped, single-minded Race Williams first appeared in *Black Mask,* a relatively complex hard-boiled hero began his career in the pages of "the book": The Continental Op, a far more imaginative character than Race Williams, was created by Dashiell Hammett, who became one of the most successful of all *Black Mask* contributors. After a varied career which included a period of several years with the Pinkerton Detective Agency, Hammett—who knew a man who once stole a Ferris-wheel—began to turn his experiences into stories. With an eye to style and literary effectiveness, he experimented with techniques. Although he was credited with being the leader of the hard-boiled school of detective fiction, and although his hero had the basic characteristics found in the traditionally tough hero, it is no good trying to make Hammett all of a piece; the idea is too simple and his writing is too subtle. The good writers of Hammett's group, as do good writers in any group, experimented with writing techniques in order to determine what was most useful and effective for their own individual expression. They worked with plot, trying to keep it from becoming too obviously stereotyped; they created a character in their developing short stories who would later stand up in longer works of fiction; they agreed on the theme of the rugged individualist righting the social wrongs; they tried both the first and third person to see which would make the style more objective; and they concentrated on their hard-boiled style, hoping to make it as action-packed as possible. Hammett did all of these things and a bit more. Although he may not have been the smoothest and most consistent stylist, throughout his decade of prolific writing, he changed viewpoint and modified his hero several different times in trying for maximum literary results.

Nicely written though it is, there is but little in such an early Hammett story as "The Green Elephant," which appeared in the *Smart Set* in 1923, to draw unusual attention to the writer. Joe Shupe, whose fault was "that he was an unskilled laborer in the world of crime, and therefore had to content himself with stealing whatever came to hand," was suddenly and accidentally the possessor of a quarter of a million stolen dollars. Unable to cope with so much money, Joe walked the streets, couldn't sleep nights, and changed hotels every day. Only after his suspicious actions caused him to be picked up and jailed by prohibition officers could Joe become "his normal self again, both physically and mentally." There was no hero, let alone a hard-boiled one, in this story without even any tough writing, and tales of this kind did not bring for Hammett the acclaim he later received.

Dashiell Hammett soon, however, acquired a reputation, and among the many who eventually gave him unstinted praise for his writing ability, few were more succinct in expressing praise than Raymond Chandler [see excerpt above]. He realized that Hammett continually viewed violence as an act of human courage, and therefore admirable. Violence, according to Chandler, did not dismay the Hammett characters, "it was right down their street." Furthermore, Hammett was writing for "people with a sharp, aggressive attitude to life." It was in the matter of style, however, that Chandler was most critically aware. Hammett had a style, "but his audience didn't know it, because it was in a language not supposed to be capable of such refinements." The "style," which Chandler held did not belong to Hammett or to any particular individual because it is "the American language," could say things that Hammett did not know or feel the need of saying. Hammett "was spare, frugal, hard-boiled, but he did over and over again what only the best writers can ever do at all. He wrote scenes that seemed never to have been written before." The idea that style is the American language—discovered independently by several writers in the hard-boiled genre—is unquestionably one of the most significant aspects of the evolving, hard-boiled tradition. Style, then, is where you find it: not restricted to the drawing room or study, but equally discoverable in the alleys. Stephen Crane went down into Rum Alley, and in *Maggie* produced a first-rate novel; but "tattered gamins" making a "furious assault" on their "antagonist," while they were "swearing in barbaric trebles," is neither alley style nor American style. Hammett went to the American alleys and came out with an authentic expression of the people who live in and by violence.

Although the early *Black Mask* story "House Dick" contained brutality and four killings, it was only a warm-up for what was to come in later works. The Continental Op did not figure in much of the violence, being rather just simply a thoughtful, fearless man, doing his job. As his creator had done before him, the Op carefully and thoroughly checked his evidence, for "from any crime to its author there is a trail. It may be—as in this case—obscure [but] finding and following such trails is what a detective is paid to do." There was in this story, however, early evidence of clipped prose, that which was to become a Hammett trademark: "Picked him up when he got his mail yesterday afternoon." "Got an apartment on Van Ness Avenue." "Packing a gun under his left arm." The statements imply—although the economy of expression purposely controls—action, violence, and excitement. Perhaps the most important contribution of an early *Black Mask* story such as this was the presentation of the nameless fat man with an age varying between thirty-five and forty (based, said Hammett later, on James Wright, Assistant Superintendent of Pinkerton's Baltimore Agency, under whom Hammett worked); the detective performed through dozens of Hammett's pieces for the Continental Detective Agency's San Francisco office. In these short stories Hammett developed his style and prepared his character, the Op, for the novels which were to come.

In "The Tenth Clue," at the beginning of 1924, the Op continued his patient pursuit of evidence and details, but he threw in a little detection hint: "There are many, many murders with never a woman in them anywhere; but seldom a very conspicuous killing." An unusual Hammett story for these years appeared in the middle of January, unusual because of the setting and the switch to third person. In "The Man Who Killed Dan Odams" the Montana scene was vital, and the Odams woman and her son were like the determined, worn, brutal West of which they were a part. The people and the landscape were immeasurably strong, but the strongest of all was Silence. By the spring of 1924 in "Zigzags of Treachery" the Op was an efficient, dependable detective, but as yet not much given to heroics. He did not like eloquence because "if it isn't effective enough to pierce your hide, it's tiresome; and if it is effective enough then it muddles your thoughts." He was not "a brilliant thinker," yet he had "flashes of intelligence." He was a man of action, really, who liked his jobs to be "simply jobs—emotions are nuisances during business hours." Not yet legendary, he accounted for some of his feats after shooting a gun out of Jake Ledwich's hand: it "looks like a great stunt," the Op told the reader, "but it's a thing that happens now and then. A man who is a fair shot (and that is exactly what I am—no more, no less), naturally and automatically shoots pretty close to the spot upon which his eyes are focused." Unlike Race Williams, whose shooting was calculated to overshadow that of Davy Crockett, the Op simply maintained that when a man goes for his gun you shoot at *him* and if you are looking at his gun you might hit that; if you do, it looks impressive.

It was not long, however, before an accent on violence became pronounced in Hammett's stories, although at first the hero observed it with detachment and only later performed it with virtuous reflection. In "The Golden Horseshoe" the story started slowly with "thumbnail gouging into eye," and a head hanging "crookedly, dangling from a neck that had been cut clean through to the bone." The tempo stepped up when Gooseneck fired at Kewpie at the moment she threw a knife at him. Kewpie "spun back across the room—hammered back by the bullets that tore through her chest. Her back hit the wall. She pitched forward to the floor." Gooseneck was in similar trouble as he stopped shooting and tried to speak, while the haft of the girl's knife protruded from his throat. "He couldn't get his words past the blade. He dropped one gun and tried to take hold of the protruding haft. Halfway up to it his hand came, and dropped. He went down slowly—to his knees—rolled over on his side—and lay still." Hammett was beginning to succumb to the literary tricks used by writers trying to squeeze out the full value of violence but who resorted to artificial means for the effect. The knife in the throat, along with the ice pick in the chest, became a common device for increasing the intensity of the narrative, restricting natural movement, and hindering speech. Although it was not dwelt upon with as much pleasure, it was hardly more ingenious than hand-stomping in the Western story.

The Continental Op soon became physically and personally involved in violence, getting smashed up thoroughly in "One Hour." It was not long, as in "Women, Politics and Murder," before he thought violence was sheer pleasure, "I began to throw my right fist into him. I liked that. His belly was flabby, and it got softer every time I hit it. I hit it often." And the mood continued in "Dead Yellow Women" where the Op observed Dummy Uhl, who with "all the middle of him gone—slid down to the floor and made more of a puddle than a pile there." As the Op continued down a hall, "cracking everything" that got in his way and being "cracked" back, he began to enjoy the violence which was technically accentuated by one sentence paragraphs.

> When he crouched above me I let him have it.
> My bullet cut the gullet out of him.
> I patted his face with my gun as he tumbled down
>   past me.

The violence-is-fun technique which Hammett so thoroughly explored in his short stories of the middle 1920's was soon to reach its apex in his first novel.

In the meantime, however, Hammett had not forgotten the complete role his hero was playing in the tradition. In "The Gutting of Couffignal," for instance, the Op's intelligence was questioned because he refused to cut himself in on a big take. He stopped long enough to explain his role and concept of right and wrong: in addition to his honesty and sense of loyalty, he was a detective because he wanted to be one and because he liked the work. He knew he could make a great deal more money doing something else, but "liking work makes you want to do it as well as you can. Otherwise there'd be no sense to it." But being loyal to himself and his employer did not obviate his commenting on social situations. Couffignal was an island owned and ruled by "well-fed old gentlemen who, the profits they took from the world with both hands in their younger days now stowed away at safer percentages, have bought into the island colony so they may spend what is left of their lives nursing their livers and improving their golf among their kind. They admit to the island only as many storekeepers, working-people, and similar riffraff as are needed to keep them comfortably served." Hammett had a social conscience which Carroll John Daly never dreamed of.

The knightly role aspect of the hard-boiled or *Black Mask* tradition was developed in "The Scorched Face," a story otherwise notable for its brutality and smashing tempo—both in content and style. The Op and Pat Reddy, a good young cop, moved in to clean up one of the California "mystical" cults which victimized naive, wealthy women.

The cult operated by first taking compromising photographs of its victims and then controlling the susceptible women through threat of blackmail. Murder was done before the Op and Pat Reddy cleaned out the cesspool. As a policeman Reddy was obligated to turn over the murderer and all evidence, according to law; as an independent detective the Op took a more liberal view, according to his conscience. Because of his obviously higher law, the Op was able to persuade Reddy to cover the whole thing up, to destroy the evidence and let the murderer off—this prevented more suicides and protected womankind.

That Hammett was continuing to explore among literary techniques during the middle twenties can be inferred from "Ruffian's Wife," in which he worked with third person narration—the viewpoint used in *The Maltese Falcon*—and in which he introduced Leonidas Doucas, a fat man who suggested Casper Gutman of *The Maltese Falcon*. Created also in "Ruffian's Wife" was an unusual version of the tough guy. Guy Tharp was "hard-boiled, hard-nerved, to whom violence was no more than addition to a bookkeeper." But under the fat man's pressure, Tharp's image dissolved into weakness; for his wife, the "red wolf of a husband" became only an illusion, and all she had left was his "callous brutality."

The individualistic attitude toward law was made specific in "Corkscrew," wherein the Op, by going from San Francisco to the Arizona desert town of Corkscrew, found himself in the nineteenth-century West. Upon arrival, the Op was warned by the "better element"—which included Miss Janey, the false-toothed, sour-faced school teacher—against the violent element which included both the good and bad guys. The Op, who was not much of a rider, was tested by being given an unrideable horse. Preferring, obviously, the violent element to the better element, the Op attempted to prove himself worthy of his chosen group by continuing to mount the horse as long as his battered body could draw itself into the saddle. Having become accepted by his courageous display of guts, the Op was ready to enlist admirers. One of the most individualistic of these was Milk River, who was willing to work with the Op if he did not have to become a deputy; Milk River would not put himself in a position where, as he said, "I'll have to enforce no laws I don't like." In this "hard neighborhood" where the inhabitants were "hell-bent on proving to everybody that they're just as tough as the next one," the Op found himself a worthy antagonist and explained to the reader the joy of physical contact as he "smacked both hands into his body, and felt happy when the flesh folded softly around them." Not to be outdone, Milk River was "grinning" while he shot another contestant out of the saddle.

This was a different kind of philosophic attitude toward violent death from the one Stephen Crane had expressed a generation before in "The Blue Hotel." In Crane's story the Easterner explained to the cowboy how in every murder there are from a dozen to forty women involved, but in the death of the Swede only five men collaborated, including the poor gambler who wasn't even a noun, only an adverb. The cowboy cried out blindly and rebelliously against this "mysterious theory." There is no mysterious event to account for the violence in "Corkscrew"; Slim merely refused to pay for his meal at the Toad's eatery. Milk River summed it all up with his own brand of amoral humor: "Think of all them folks that were killed and maimed and jailed—all over a dollar and ten cents. It's a good thing Slim didn't eat five dollars' worth of grub. He'd of depopulated the State of Arizona complete!" It was but a short jump from the wild West back across the street to the violence of the big city, and Dashiell Hammett's Continental Op was now finely trained for the biggest criminal affair the country had to offer.

In February and May of 1927 the *Black Mask* carried two of Hammett's long stories—"The Big Knock-Over" and "$106,000 Blood Money"—which were subsequently published together as his first novel. One hundred and fifty of the country's finest crooks gathered together in San Francisco where they simultaneously knocked over The Seaman's National and The Golden Gate Trust. During the noisy affair sixteen cops were killed and three times that many wounded; twelve bystanders and bank clerks were killed; and the bandits lost seven dead and had thirty-one of their number taken as bleeding prisoners. In a case of this size it was decided that the Op could use some help in recovering the money, but two or three additional operatives from the agency sufficed. One was Dick Foley whose rule it was never to waste words. Another was Jack Counihan, "full of the don't-give-a-damn-gaiety that belonged to his youthfulness." And then there was the Continental Op at his coldblooded best, deciding that the most effective way to get to the source and recover the money was to arrange for the hoods to eliminate each other. So within a few hours one house contained fourteen dead, the next six dead, and so on until the St. Valentine's Day Massacre which happened two years later back in Chicago began to look like a teenage tiff. The Op's part in the decimation of the hoods could be thought ethical only in his own eyes; the readers could accept his chicanery and double-cross only after accepting the role of the Op. Among other tricky moves, the Op befriended one of the hoods so he could later shoot him in the back, and at another point he arranged for one of his own operators to be shot. True, the operator had defected, but it was the Op who meted out the justice, with an additional motive of keeping clean the good name of the Continental Agency. Not since the days when eliminating inhuman Indians was a hero's duty had an individual's judgment caused the demise of so many.

If there is such a thing as a poetry of violence, Hammett achieved it, technically at least, in this novel. At the height of a scene of smashing, slashing, and sudden death, the Op was having the time of his life. As he saw a mouthful of teeth smashed in, a blackjack crunch an arm, a side of a face blown away, the Op got with the rhythmical spirit of the occasion: "It was a swell bag of nails. Swing right, swing left, kick, swing right, swing left, kick. Don't hesitate, don't look for targets. God will see that there's always a mug there for your gun or blackjack to sock, a belly for your foot." Without any perspective shots, the author kept the reader on the scene, and by using diction appropriate to the characters, the narrator was not allowed, except physically, to achieve the superiority which would destroy the unity of effect. From this vantage point the Op delivered one of his most poetic lines: "I swayed and broke a nose where I should have smashed a skull."

Short stories of this period, late twenties, continued to show the Op's various roles as the traditional hero. In "The Main Death" he was a knightly hero who got the

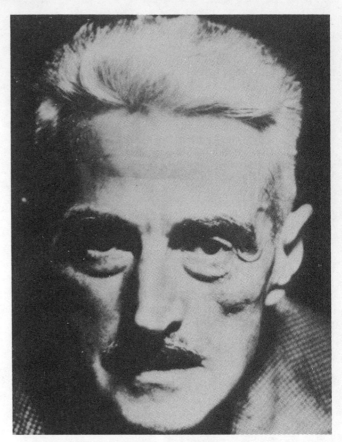

Dashiell Hammett

murderer and collected his fee for it, but he refused to divulge to his client the knowledge of an affair which would implicate his client's wife. In "Fly Paper" the Op was exclusively the hard-boiled hero, with Hammett working his prose for all the violent effects he could squeeze from it. He could use it tight: "Babe liked Sue. Vassos liked Sue. Sue liked Babe. Vassos didn't like that. Jealousy spoiled the Greek's judgment. He kept the speakeasy door locked one night when Babe wanted to come in. Babe came in, bringing pieces of the door with him. Vassos got his gun out . . . Babe hit him with the part of the door that had the brass knob on it. Babe and Sue went away from Vassos's together." Or Hammett could resort to the smashing paragraphs:

> I shot his right knee.
> He lurched toward me.
> I shot his left knee.
> He tumbled down.

During the thirty-two months from November 1927 to June 1930, Hammett's four important novels were published serially in *Black Mask*: *Red Harvest, The Dain Curse, The Maltese Falcon,* and *The Glass Key*. They are critically regarded as his best work, but they were successful only because he had previously worked out everything in them in his short stories. The first two continued the Op as the first person narrator, although he changed character somewhat in the second; the third developed the swaggering Samuel Spade, told in third person; and the fourth created a variation on the character in Ned Beaumont, also with the third person viewpoint.

Red Harvest, originally a group of separate stories referred to under the general title *The Cleansing of Poisonville,* revolved around the Op still at his hard-boiled best, although he was much more concerned with the problems of a collective society than he had been in his first novel. The Op, completely hardened, played everyone off against the middle, and by his own count totaled up one and a half dozen murders. He admitted he could "swing the play legally," but he decided that "it's easier to have them killed off, easier and surer." Allowing himself no sexual diversion, the Op went in only for heavy drinking, the latter presumably because even he occasionally reacted to piled-up violence: "I've got a hard skin all over what's left of my soul, and after twenty years of messing around with crime I can look at any sort of a murder without seeing anything in it but my bread and butter, the day's work. But this getting a rear out of planning deaths is not natural to me."

The slight crack in the Op's armor, barely discernible in *Red Harvest,* broadened to measurable proportions in *The Dain Curse.* He was still the efficient operator, but he had become humanized. The double-crossing and double-dealing were gone. Murder was still present, of course, but it was not the Op's doing; rather it was engineered or performed by Owen Fitzstephan, a man with streaks of insanity. The heavy drinking was cut down to just drinking, and although other people had realistic sexual experiences the Op still abstained. In his most humanitarian role so far, the Op began a benevolent and knightly campaign to save the misused and brutally treated Gabrielle who believed she was suffering from the Dain curse. She doubted her sanity, so the Op soothed her by saying that everyone except the very crazy and the stupid suspect themselves at times. She did not realize that it was her fears, her psychological maladjustment, and her dope habit that rendered her sexually ineffective. The Op consoled her by explaining that there were "a thousand women in San Francisco making the same complaint." As she gradually became convinced that her "differences" were held by other women, and that they could be cured or corrected, Gabrielle still doubted her ability to give up dope. But the Op also scoffed at that thought, saying, "You've been reading the Hearst papers." Well, Gabrielle was rehabilitated, but at what a price. Dashiell Hammett virtually traded a hard-boiled hero for a part-time sentimentalist, a character who could recognize in himself such emotions as might occasionally be acceptable in the traditional hard-boiled hero, but for Hammett it could mean only that his hero had grown old and soft. Long live the Op. He was ready for discard.

With his hero gone soft beyond redemption in *The Dain Curse,* Hammett created a new or at least variant version in *The Maltese Falcon.* Using the third person instead of the first, for a different viewpoint, the author presented Samuel Spade—several years younger than the Op, six inches taller, and looking "rather pleasantly like a blond Satan." Although definitely in the tradition, Spade was a cool hero who was a devil with the women but never called a spade a heart. As the character changed, in part, so did the style. Instead of allowing his hero to act, the author explained the action: "Spade flung his words out with a brutal sort of carelessness that gave them more weight than they could have got from dramatic emphasis or from loudness." This was not Hammett's style at its best, the writing was less objective and the situations too obviously simulated. Spade's role, however, was less impossible and therefore more believable; he was more as the average man romantically imagines himself—brave, heroic, exciting, and irresistible.

Ned Beaumont in *The Glass Key* was another variation of the hero, not a detective but a right-hand man to a big-time racketeer and politician. Perhaps more than any of the Hammett protagonists, Beaumont came the closest to being an amoral character of the kind which was developing in the tradition. Other than for certain loyalties, his motions were mechanical and his emotions were not there. He had a smooth manner and some refinement, but what he did or how seemed not to matter. "I don't believe in anything," Ned Beaumont said, "but I'm too much of a gambler not to be affected by a lot of things." Yet it is difficult for the reader to discover what things affected him. He was smashed to a pulpy mess, won a large amount of money, and became violently ill from too much drinking, without the author giving the reader a clue as to whether any of these acts pleased or displeased the hero. The words Beaumont did not use might have been supplied by Angel Grace who was pulled out of the bay in Hammett's first novel: "Why didn't they let me alone? It's a rotten thing, living."

Some time during the years from 1927 through 1930 Hammett reached his peak—I personally think with *The Dain Curse*—both as a stylist and as a contributor to the tradition of the American literary hard-boiled hero. His stories of the early thirties, published in *Black Mask, The American Magazine, Liberty,* and *Collier's* were quite ordinary. Many of them continued the exploits of Spade, while others were experimental. "Woman in the Dark" presented an unHammett-like hero who although he had chivalry, loyalty, and physical courage was without any of the hard-boiled qualities. Stylistically, a gauzy mellowness was substituted for the clipped prose: "The wind blowing downhill from the south, whipping trees beside the road, made a whisper of exclamation and snatched her scarf away."

There remains little to be said about Hammett's last major effort, *The Thin Man,* which was obviously written under Hollywood influence. The original version of the novel had been planned and begun in 1930, in the style of that period, but only sixty-five pages were completed. The setting was San Francisco and its environs, the viewpoint the third person, and the detective a kind of modified Op. The most interesting aspect of the fragment was the unreal quality that Hammett insisted on attaching to the hero who was referred to as untouchable, as not even a corpse but a ghost, as one with whom it was impossible to come into contact—like trying to hold a handful of smoke. It was three years, one of which was spent in Hollywood, before Hammett returned to his fragment. Unable or unwilling to continue with it he wrote a different novel.

For some, Dashiell Hammett wrote beyond the tradition by specifically expressing the giddy twenties and gloomy thirties. For those readers and critics his private eye spoke for men who had lost faith in the values of their society—during war, gangsterism, and depression. This view, perhaps, can be thought of as analogous to the attitude held by Eric Ambler's protagonist at the end of the thirties;

looking at the body of Dimitrios Makropoulos, Latimer "saw him not as a corpse in a mortuary but as a man, not as an isolate, a phenomenon, but as a unit in a disintegrating social system."

After Captain Joseph Shaw, early in his career as editor of *Black Mask,* had decided on Dashiell Hammett as the leader of the writers who had a new kind of compulsion and authenticity, he set about to find a group good enough to follow the leader. He found them by the dozen, the best of whom he thought would "revolutionize" American literature. Among Hammett's colleagues were several good writers who first published their short stories in *Black Mask,* turned to writing novels, and ended up in Hollywood: Frederick Nebel, Raoul Whitfield, Norbert Davis, W. T. Ballard, George Harmon Coxe, Thomas Walsh, and Lester Dent, among others.

Frederick Nebel had a sound working definition of realism which was not at all hindered by his lack of feeling for humanity. As a writer he thought he should not allow himself any indiscriminate sentiment in viewing human derelicts, but rather he should use the ineffectual man, the "stranded flotsam," as a lesson in "understanding contrasts." He was pleased with one of his heroes who was "*born* hard-boiled," but he was almost equally interested in one of his hoods who was a "man of iron." In *Sleepers East* Nebel wrote a novel of murder and intrigue in politics in which the action is governed by the toughness and weakness in men. The theme, not infrequently appropriated by hard-boiled writers, concerns man's inability to control the incidents of life; man cannot really make the grade, but if he gives it a good try he may get some of what is coming to him if only for the wrong reasons. To live as much and as violently as one can—even for a single night—may be the only way.

The Hollywood setting provided color for much of the work of Raoul Whitfield. He had one big, rough, fearless, frontier-type of hero who rushed to meet danger wherever he sensed it, and he had a private eye who was "cold as hell." Whitfield had a habit of trying to make his hero tough instead of allowing him to be tough, but this was often the result of the hero's compelling drive as a reformer. There was a strong feeling for the joy of violence in the stories of Norbert Davis. Relying on his own sense of justice, the hero—"a gunman, gambler, and soldier-of-fortune"—smashed, shot, and killed all over town; but he was doing it for "good," and those who were maimed or killed were on the side of wrong. The principal character in the work of W. T. Ballard was a good deal like his counterparts in the stories of Whitfield and Davis. A liaison man for the General-Consolidated Studio in Hollywood, Ballard's hero used violence willingly, but only to combat violence; he was indifferent to human life generally, but he sometimes cared about "little people."

The "number one camera for the *Globe*" stood in lieu of the private eye in the *Black Mask* stories of George Harmon Coxe. Coxe's hero had already become what he told a girl she would be if she insisted on working for a newspaper. To the girl, newspaper work was like having a season ticket for the drama of life, but according to the cameraman she would soon become a "hard-boiled, vindictive, loud-mouthed dame with a cigarette throat; without an illusion or ideal—without an honest emotion left in her system." Thomas Walsh wrote tight, fast-moving, energetic

fiction in which he used as hero a "strong, silent, and extremely fortunate man from Chicago," or he did equally well with a plain-clothes-man on homicide. In two of his stories Lester Dent presented a private dick who was as tough and violent as any hero who smashed and ice-picked his way through the pages of *Black Mask.* In his longer fiction, however, he depended on a financially successful man of violence, a man whose violence became sticky at times because of the sentiment behind it: "A door mat, Molloy believed, is good only to be stepped on. It gets nothing out of life but wear and tear. Therefore, Molloy had always fought viciously for what he considered to be his privileges as a human and an American-born."

There was at least one among the *Black Mask* boys whose writing contained something different. The wrappers of the first issue of a novel published in New York in 1933 carried the following statement: "now comes the hardest, toughest, swiftest novel of them all FAST ONE two hours of sheer terror written with a clipped violence, hypnotic in its power." If there ever has been an accurate blurb, this was probably it. *Fast One,* published in part in *Black Mask* in 1932, enjoyed, according to its author Paul Cain (Peter Ruric), a "spectacular critical reception but was not so hot at the box office." When it came out in England, however, it sold like "sixty or seventy."

Among the writers of the hard-boiled genre, there had been an ever-growing awareness of the attitude of negation toward life, a feeling of indifference about humanity which appears to have reached a kind of peak in the early depression years. Humanity was still in evidence around the country, but so were rocks. Again it must be remembered that the awareness of negation was not peculiar to the hard-boiled writers; it had appeared in various forms of literature in America, in the plays of Eugene O'Neill, for example. Nor was it new on the other side of the Atlantic, although a culmination of negation was clearly set forth in *Journey to the End of the Night* by Louis-Ferdinand Céline, published in France the same year that *Fast One* ran in *Black Mask.*

Gerard A. Kells, the protagonist of Cain's novel had the characteristics commonly found in the hard-boiled hero—the brutal, gutty, fearless man. Yet there was something more in Kells, a factor which gave him his violently "hypnotic" appeal. To account for this, one is tempted to turn to the existentialism of Jean-Paul Sartre. Man cannot, according to Sartre, be exclusively individualistic, for whatever man does for himself he does for all men. The one thing man has is freedom, but having it he must constantly make choices. Having no legislator but himself, man must do all the deciding for himself. Whatever choice he makes is acceptable, for he obviously could not or did not make the other. Because the overruling aim in each choice is freedom, man can choose either of two opposite moralities—in matters of choice they are equivalent. Gerry Kells, who appeared unaware of the existence of anyone but himself, was without doubt his own legislator. He also made choices, although to the reader they generally appear as unconscious acts. It did not, incidentally, occur to Kells that he was choosing between "two opposite moralities," for he was amoral. Yet this was not the amorality of Theodore Dreiser, who felt that because man was the victim of his environment and physical makeup he had no moral choice. Kells was aware of his options and alternatives, but being cognizant only of his own existence, he was indifferent even to choices.

Having acquired in the East two thousand dollars and a reputation for knowing how to play "rough," Gerry Kells arrived in Southern California. His reputation made it possible for him to begin taking over the Los Angeles rackets, which he proceeded to do by playing off one racketeer against another and by eliminating a few himself. Double-crossing, smashing, shooting, and ice-picking were all in the act; it mattered not at all to Kells how things went. He accumulated several thousand dollars and lost all of it but seventy cents, and he did not react to that. Like all memorable hard-boiled heroes, he had, however, points of vulnerability—his pride, some small feeling of revenge, and a tiny touch of loyalty brought about his end. He went as he had come, alone, "Then, after a little while, life went away from him."

About an hour before noon on a mid-October day in the 1930's, Philip Marlowe drove through downtown Los Angeles. The sun was not shining, and there was a "look of hard wet rain in the clearness of the foothills." The shabbiness of Bunker Hill made him think of its days of respectability. Soon he headed west on Wilshire Boulevard, through Westlake Park, across La Brea Avenue; turning to the north at La Cienega, he crossed Santa Monica and Sunset Boulevards and found his way into the hills of West Hollywood, to the home of General Guy Sternwood. As Marlowe entered the Sternwood mansion, he looked up to see, on a stained-glass panel, a knight in dark armor rescuing a lady who was tied to a tree. The lady was without clothes, but she was wearing long and convenient hair.

In this fashion, in *The Big Sleep* in 1939, Raymond Chandler introduced his hero, the hard-boiled detective who was to become the epitome of them all. In seven novels during the following two decades, Marlowe drove through the streets of Los Angeles, and the surrounding towns, looking for ladies to rescue, for the little fellow who needed help, for the big man who deserved a shot of old-fashioned justice. "Down these mean streets a man must go," wrote Chandler, and his story was "man's adventure in search of a hidden truth." From the skilled hands of this writer, one of the best literary portrayals of the *Black Mask* hero evolved.

Although Philip Marlowe was not introduced, by that name, until 1939, he had been developing in Chandler's short stories for a half dozen years. Chandler's original private eye, using the name Mallory, appeared in *Black Mask* in December 1933. From that date through 1939, he performed in twenty short stories, usually as the private eye (fourteen times), but occasionally as a detective lieutenant, narcotic squad under-cover man, or hotel dick. He used ten different names and was twice nameless, but always he was a part of the man Marlowe was to become. In experimenting with viewpoint, Chandler used the first person twelve times and the third person eight. Once created, Marlowe was always a first person narrator; this technique kept him on the scene, involved in the lives of others.

Beginning with his first story, "Blackmailers Don't Shoot," Raymond Chandler established his hero as one good enough to compete in the violence found in abundance in the far western city of Los Angeles. The man was tall, with gray eyes and thin nose, and he had a "jaw of stone." He was tough, honest, loyal; women found him attractive and hoods played him carefully. He was a "business man" who got "paid [very little] for his work," part of which was dealing death to those on the side of wrong.

Raymond Chandler's style, at the outset, showed qualities which were to make him one of the best of the *Black Mask* detective writers. The restrained statements, the colorful similes and evocative images, the city of oil wells and jacaranda trees in bloom, the reliable lonely hero—it was all there at the beginning. The third story, "Finger Man," can serve as an example of the Chandler touch. Using an uncomplicated plot, Chandler developed his theme around the idea that when crooked politicians and crime choke a city's moral life, it takes the private eye to make the corrections. The police were willing and helpful, but because they were so necessarily a part of city politics their hands were tied. Only the free, uninhibited, and tough individual was able to move far enough and strongly enough in the right direction. At this early stage in Chandler's writing career, the hero was adequately noble and hard-boiled, but he was not yet the smooth nobleman that Marlowe was to be. In matters of style, however, one can see the similes and images beginning to take their places. Comments like "As a bluff, mine was thinner than the gold on a week-end wedding ring" were to become a Chandler trademark. But images like "I stopped beside a forgotten drugstore that slept behind two giant pepper trees and a dusty cluttered window" contributed to his reputation as a literary stylist. Yet one cannot overlook the fact that in weaker moments he sometimes used a cliché of the trade: "I saw that Canales had fired at least once, because Frank Dorr had no right eye." In the eyes of the knight, the moll was a lady, so she was allowed to escape. And the hero, who was more and more appropriating the role of the humanitarian, said, "It's a shame how little account some folks take of human life."

"Killer in the Rain," a short story Chandler later incorporated into *The Big Sleep*, continued the hero's efforts to help those in trouble. The nameless narrator didn't care about the "trash," but basically good people like Dravec, who had a neurotic daughter, deserved to be saved from a "little heartache," even when it meant ignoring legal requirements. The hero, who saw mankind in a melancholy plight, was provided by the author with a subtle mood through which he observed: "I stared at the window, watched the rain hit it, flatten out, and slide down in a thick wave, like melted gelatine. It was too early in the fall for that kind of rain."

Occasionally a Chandler story had a touch of the old West. The hero of "Nevada Gas" was a good-guy gambler helped by a hotel dick who carried a Buntline Special and said "I'm a tough guy. I used to be a Wells Fargo Dick." The cop in "Spanish Blood," covered for a friend, protected the girl (to whom he said, "Life seems to do nasty things to people"), and lost his badge. One infers that he got his badge back because he was honest and human. He could not help thinking, however, that had it been his grandfather—one of the best sheriffs the county ever had—the case would have been handled "with fewer words and more powder smoke."

Throughout the 1930's Chandler continued to dress his man in the clothes of the traditional hero. Mallory, Carmady, Dalmas, whatever his name, grew harder toward the wrong guys and softer toward the little people. Invariably it was the troubled poor who hired him, so he worked for beans he frequently didn't get. His all-American virility increased with a growing, impatient distaste for effeminate men like Lindley Paul—he had a dimple on his chin in which you could have "lost a marble," and he spoke softly "in the manner of a sultan suggesting a silk noose for a harem lady whose tricks had gone stale." He went to those places where a "hard-boiled redhead sang a hard-boiled song in a voice that could have been used to split firewood," and where a torch singer "sang of something very far away and unhappy, in a voice like old ivory." As he went he drank the "racket" beer which was as "tasteless as a roadhouse blonde."

Drawing from several years' writing experience and specifically from four short stories (three of which were in *Black Mask*), Chandler fashioned his first novel, *The Big Sleep.* The hero, theme, and style came together in a highly successful fruition. "To hell with the rich," Philip Marlowe said, "they make me sick." Yet for a small amount of money, most of which was used on the case, he risked his life many times in trying to help the wealthy Sternwood family. Most of Marlowe's sympathy was spent on old General Sternwood, once virile, now sick and helpless: only "a few locks of dry white hair clung to his scalp, like wild flowers fighting for life on a bare rock." The General's two problems were his two daughters, neither of whom had "any more moral sense than a cat." And Carmen, the younger, was hopelessly psychotic. In his knightly role, Marlowe rescued the ladies, who although beautiful were not very fair. In throwing the naked Carmen out of his bed, the hero brooded over his integrity and moral standards: "This was the room I had to live in. It was all I had in the way of a home. In it was everything that was mine, that had any association with me, any past, anything that took the place of a family." He said, as he moved a piece on his chessboard, "Knights had no meaning in this game. It wasn't a game for knights." Yet he played it as a knight throughout, meeting violence with violence, bringing a little peace of mind to a sick old man, and allowing the murderess to go free. The villains included a dealer in pornography, whose house "had a stealthy nastiness, like a fag party," a blackmailer, and a ruthless killer. They, with several others of their ilk, met justifiable deaths. For Marlowe the "world was a wet emptiness," full of violence and inhumanity, yet he moved through it with dignity and integrity, always, however, alone; in the febrile society in which he operated, the hero never deviated from his code. Occasionally, however, the rain stopped, allowing him to look at "the hard pale wild lilac of the California hills."

During the war years Raymond Chandler published three more novels of high quality in which the hero sought to bring some degree of justice and sympathy to those living in the world of violence. In 1949 *The Little Sister* included a sharp denunciation of Hollywood, and *The Long Goodbye* (1953) insisted on the value of loyalty in society, especially in a superficial society. When Chandler was nearing seventy he published *Playback,* a novel which clearly indicated a lessening of his talents. Feeling sorry for his lonely hero, the author, at the end of the novel, held out the prospect of marriage, although marriage, according to a younger Chandler, was impossible for his detective hero. With Chandler's death, Marlowe escaped a role for which he had never been fitted.

In the pages of *Black Mask* the detective hero contributed to the American myth of the hard-boiled hero. One component of the myth which *Black Mask* School utilized was a special attitude toward violence which provided both an ethical and an aesthetic justification for its employment. (pp. 54-79)

> *Philip Durham, "The 'Black Mask' School,"*
> in Tough Guy Writers of the Thirties, *edited by David Madden, Southern Illinois University Press, 1968, pp. 51-79.*

Ben Ray Redman

[*Redman was an American journalist, poet, and critic. In the following essay, he maintains that gratuitous sex and violence, as exemplified in the detective fiction of Dashiell Hammett, Raymond Chandler, and Mickey Spillane, have debased the genre.*]

Stories of crime and detection have their roots deep in the past. The crime story is as old as Cain, while the tale of detection is at least as old as Daniel's defense of Susanna. Man has always loved a mystery—perhaps murder mysteries best of all—and writers as great as Dostoievsky and Robert Browning have spent the best of their skill and genius on the spinning of such yarns. As for the detective story in its pure form, it might well have begun with Voltaire's *Zadig,* for if that young man had chosen to exploit the deductive powers which he displayed to the Queen's Chief Eunuch and the Master of the King's Hounds he would surely have become one of the greatest detectives of all time. But he did not choose.

So, as all the descendants of Macaulay's schoolboys know, the detective story remained in embryo until Edgar A. Poe brought it into the world in 1841. The exact moment that preceded its delivery was when Monsieur C. Auguste Dupin, strolling at night in the vicinity of the Palais Royal, astonished his companion by apparently reading his mind, and then astonished him still further by explaining that the mind-reading was nothing more than the result of close observation and accurate analysis. Literature's first full-fledged detective was ready and waiting for his first case.

The form with which Poe experimented in "Murders in the Rue Morgue," and with which he fumbled in "The Mystery of Marie Rogêt," was perfected by him in "The Purloined Letter" (1844). He had given a wonderfully fresh lead and a masterly example to his fellow writers and successors, but both lead and example were largely ignored for more than forty years, until 1886, when an impecunious Southsea doctor, by the name of Arthur Conan Doyle, stimulated by memories of Poe and Wilkie Collins and Joseph Bell, sat down to improve his fortunes by writing *A Study in Scarlet,* in which a Dr. Watson would recount the unmasking of a murderer by a certain Sherlock Holmes—an effort which, by the way, was at first rewarded by a publisher's decision that the manuscript was "too long for a story, too short for a book." In the meantime, of course, Gaboriau had flourished shoddily in France, while Collins had flourished brilliantly in England, and Dickens, after putting Inspector Bucket into *Bleak House,* had left *Edwin Drood* unfinished to tease the brains of generations of puzzle addicts. But neither Collins nor Gaboriau nor Dickens belongs in the true Poe-Doyle line that was destined to continue so prosperously and to ramify so unpredictably.

If Poe's example had been neglected, Conan Doyle's was not. The kind of tales that Dr. Watson had to tell whetted the public's appetite for more of the same, and many writers quickly came forward to supply the demand. At first their product was well below the standard of the master, but gradually there began to appear writers capable of advancing and complicating the detective story to a degree unattempted by Conan Doyle. R. Austin Freeman introduced genuinely scientific methods into his tales of Dr. Thorndyke. A. E. W. Mason gave the professional sleuth a leg-up in his contest with the fashionable amateur by introducing to the public the Sûreté ace Monsieur Hanaud. Chesterton made his first collection of Father Brown cases in 1911. *Trent's Last Case* was published two years later. Max Carrados began his blind investigations in 1914. And after that, the deluge.

More and more the detective story attracted writers who had proved their intelligence in other fields. H. C. Bailey was a Classical First at Oxford long before he invented languid Reggie Fortune, whose intuitions so often proved so marvelously right. G. D. H. Cole, co-creator of Superintendent Wilson, was a Balliol man, a famous Socialist economist. Dorothy Sayers took first honors in medieval studies at Oxford, and is a translator of Dante as well as the only begetter of Lord Peter Wimsey. And on this side of the Atlantic, Willard Huntington Wright—who, under the name of S. S. Van Dine, beginning in 1926, did so much to advance the cause of the detective story in the United States—had sufficient belief in the scope and depth of his scholarly attainments to write an unfavorable review of the *Encyclopedia Britannica.*

As the brows of the detective story writers grew higher, so did those of their readers. One by one the world's leaders in statesmanship, in business and the professions, declared themselves to be aficionados of the whodunit school of fiction, until it became an act of incredible daring for any man in the public eye to admit that he did not enjoy detective stories; and many a coward, who honestly preferred to read Aristotle or Tolstoy or Flaubert, was reduced to the expedient of hiding his shameful text within a binding that was stamped with the name of Dorothy Sayers, Philip MacDonald, or Ellery Queen.

For a good many years the detective story advanced steadily on two fronts: it became increasingly ingenious, and it became increasingly well written. Competition flourished, excellence was produced. While some writers worked towards an ever greater complexity of plot, towards bafflingly brilliant crimes and dazzlingly brilliant solutions, others sought to people their stories with characters that were more than puppets, and to lure their readers on with narrative skills worthy of a "serious" novelist. But for the most part, despite wide variations of development and individual practice, the detective story observed certain rules. Not all of them are pertinent here, but a few are. Let me list the few.

1.) Deeds of blood and acts of cruelty should not be exploited for their own sake. 2.) In any story there should be at least as much detection as crime. 3.) The detective should never blunder into his solution. 4.) Romantic involvement of the detective with any woman, or women, should be frowned upon; while sex should definitely be forbidden to raise its fatal head on the detective's side of the fence. 5.) The detective should do most of his work with his brains, rather than with muscles, fists, or firearms.

These, as I say, were a few of the rules by which all self-respecting detective story writers abode until the close of the third decade of the twentieth century. Then, in the United States, which was still lagging behind England in this field of fiction, something happened to the detective story. What happened was a man named Hammett. The impact was terrific. We live today among conditions and convulsions that may be traced directly to the shock.

Dashiell Hammett's first novel, which followed many contributions to the pulps, notably *Black Mask,* was *Red Harvest* (1929). Its hero is a private detective—nameless, fearless, capable of absorbing a vast amount of punishment, and very handy with a gun—who finds himself involved in the murderous doings of a town that has been taken over completely by the forces of lawlessness and disorder. Sadism, in various forms, dominates the novel. Police Chief Noonan knocks hell out of a character called Mac-Swain. An amiable broad, named Dinah Brand, beats up a helpless consumptive with thorough enjoyment; and her house is later the scene of a sadistic free-for-all. The detective-narrator philosophizes: "Play with murder enough and it gets you one of two ways. It makes you sick, or you get to like it." Later the nameless operative finds that he "is getting a rear out of planning deaths." And the novel's climax is an orgy of multiple killings. With *Red Harvest* the hard-boiled school of detective fiction, bound in hard covers, moved out from the back room of the pulps into the bright light of the best bookstores. The private eye was stepping forward to claim his kingdom.

Skipping *The Dain Curse,* also published in 1929, and coming straight to *The Maltese Falcon* (1930), which won its author instant popularity and prosperity, we find the private eye perfectly fashioned and in all his glory. Sam Spade—it is only fair to call him Sam Spade the Great—is the model of countless imitations, and, as will be noted later, exaggerations. Not only is he a fast man with a gun and capable of disarming any opponent who has the drop on him, not only is he tough and ruthless; he is also dynamite with the ladies. When Sam's charms prove obviously irresistible to Effie Perine, Iva Archer, and Brigid O'Shaughnessy it is plain that sex has entered the detective story with a bang—and come to stay. Spade must be credited, too, with firmly establishing the now traditional relationship between the private investigator and the forces of the law. Blessed with a burning ego and an uncontrollable temper, Sam is always at odds with the police and the District Attorney's office, but always able to get the better of them and thereby able to retain the precious license that they are constantly threatening to take away from him. "At one time or another," he boasts, "I've had to tell everybody from the Supreme Court down to go to hell, and I've got away with it."

When Wilmer kicks Spade, and Spade slugs Wilmer, we have a short and snappy example of the kind of sadistic scene that was destined to skyrocket in popularity. When

Spade insists on Brigid undressing in the bathroom, he antedates countless striptease performances that were to clutter American detective fiction. When he turns to Brigid, just before denouncing her to the police, and says tenderly: "I hope to Christ they don't hang you, precious, by that sweet neck," and then slides "his hands up to caress her throat," he is acting a part and speaking lines in which he has been followed by many another actor. Wilmer, the baby-faced killer, has also had his many mimics; the Fat Man has had his obese, sinister imitators; and Cairo and Wilmer have shown the way to other homosexual couples. It would surely seem that *The Maltese Falcon* can, without exaggeration, be called an epoch-making book.

With *The Glass Key* (1931) and *The Thin Man* (1934) Hammett continued to develop the detective story along lines that were to find favor with many followers. In his first book, sex is nicely taken care of by Beaumont and Eloise Matthews; but sex runs second to sadism. A gorilla named Jeff is the boy who hands it out to our hero, Beaumont, who endures a beating from Jeff and an assistant that goes on for pages, and sends him to the hospital. (His hardier successors recover from similar beatings with astonishing rapidity.) At one point Jeff asks Beaumont: "What do you guess it is that makes me get such a hell of a big kick out of slugging you?" Later he delightedly calls Beaumont "a God damned massacrist."

Nick Charles, of *The Thin Man,* is also irresistible to women and incredibly brave and debonair. His heroic drinking, particularly, before breakfast, has proved an inspiration to later sleuths. *The Thin Man* is skilfully spiced with sadism, and there is a brief strip-tease when Nick helps his wife to undress Dorothy Wynant, who is very drunk, and remarks for the benefit of interested readers: "She had a beautiful little body." Later, after Nick has wrestled savagely with Dorothy's mother, his wife asks him a frank question regarding his physical response to the bodily contact, and she receives a charmingly frank answer.

Where Dashiell Hammett left off, Raymond Chandler began. A glance at two of his books—*The Big Sleep* (1939) and *The Little Sister* (1949)—will suffice us. In the first of these, Marlowe—Chandler's private eye, who makes Hammett's Spade and Charles look almost like sissies—successfully resists being brought to bed by the two Sternwood sisters, each of whom is determined to seduce him. The younger is a charming, moronic, epileptic nymphomaniac, who falls into Marlowe's arms at first meeting; the elder remarks to Marlowe that her sister has "a beautiful little body," (note the quote from Hammett, there are many such echoes) but adds: "You ought to see mine." She does her best to have him do so, but he rebuffs her experienced advances and hurries home, only to find the younger sister naked and giggling in his bed. This is no great treat, as he has previously found her nude and drugged in the house of a dealer in obscene books, who is also one half of a devoted homosexual pair. He throws the lady out.

In *The Little Sister* the pace is even faster and more furious. Marlowe meets a Miss Gonzales for the first time. And a few minutes later—"The next thing I knew I had her in my lap and she was trying to bite a piece off my tongue. 'You are a very sweet son-of-a-bitch,' she said. Her mouth was as hot as ever a mouth was. Her lips burned like dry ice. Her tongue was driving hard against my teeth." This is only one of innumerable passages—many of them less decently quotable—in which Chandler proves himself a master of erotic prose. And he also does his best to satisfy the sadists. Marlowe has a genius for walking into booby-traps, getting himself brutally beaten, and blundering towards the solution of his problem. Like Spade, he is always on the verge of losing his license because of his suppression of evidence or other illegal activities, is fearless in the face of danger, and is easily capable of taking a couple of guns away from anyone who has him covered.

One might reasonably think that Raymond Chandler, like the folks in Kansas City, had gone about as far as you can go. One might, if one did not happen to know Mickey Spillane and his private eye, Mike Hammer—the peerless joys of the two-bits reprint market. Three books—*I, the Jury* (1947), *One Lonely Night* (1951), and *The Big Kill* (1951)—will tell you all you need to know about Mickey and Mike, and enable you to decide whether or not you wish to read the rest of the Spillane masterworks.

Just as Marlowe is an exaggeration of Spade, so is Hammer an exaggeration—even a caricature—of Marlowe. More savage than his predecessors, he is even more of a glutton for physical punishment, and he outdoes them in the stupidity that results in his being viciously sapped at regular intervals. But to Mickey's character something very important has been added. He is a killer, with delusions of grandeur; he revels in "the power of the gun and the obscene pleasure that was brutality and force, the

Raymond Chandler

spicy sweetness of murder sanctified by law"; he feels that his .45 is "an extension" of himself; he speaks of "crazy mad hatreds that tied my insides into knots"; and he knows that his emotions make his face "a mask of kill-lust." When he does not kill, he glories in mayhem. ("I grabbed the guy by the neck and hauled him to his feet so I could drag the cold sharp metal of the rod across his face until he was a bright red mask mumbling for me to stop.")

And something else has been added. Spade and Marlowe played hard to get when the girls went after them; but Hammer finds it almost impossible to disappoint a woman. As a result of this compelling streak of old-world chivalry—or should it be called simply satyriasis?—he moves swiftly from bed to bed in a series of concupiscent episodes, on which his creator dwells with amorous emphasis. For Mike is not content merely to kiss; he must also tell, expertly and graphically. He spends much energy, if little intelligence, in running down murderers and in committing murder himself; but he (perhaps the names of Mike and Mickey should here be interchangable) spends no less energy in attempting to demonstrate the truth of the thesis, tunefully enunciated in *South Pacific,* that there's nothing like a dame—more specifically, that nothing is built like a dame.

His devotion to the female form divine is something hardly less than perpetual worship; he has the eye of a Leonardo or a Dürer for anatomical detail, and his reporting on this subject is a model of enthusiastic accuracy. In his own choice words, he is continually "drooling" at the sight, or even the thought, of some choice fleshly morsel. The ladies, more often than not, are highly cooperative, proving themselves deft exhibitionists by suddenly opening a house coat, or dropping another garment, to show beyond doubt—in the immortal words of the *doyenne* of the American stage—"that's all there is, there isn't any more." But when they do not strip themselves, they are stripped by someone else, either willingly or under duress. One of Mr. Spillane's finest scenes is the description of Hammer finding his beautiful secretary stark naked, tied by her wrists with a rope that is in turn tied to the rafters, rotating slowly in the light of an electric lantern, as a man keeps her marvelous body turning with regular blows of a knotted rope, while other men stand around, obscenely fascinated, slobbering—the author assures us—with lust and pleasure at this pretty example of what is yet to come. It is only just, I think, to say that this little episode has everything. Mr. Spillane could hardly top it, unless he chose to flay one of his lovely ladies; and this, perhaps, would not be an improvement, for no less an authority than Dr. Johnson has assured us that the flaying of a woman changes her appearance, surprisingly, for the worse.

Nothing would give me greater pleasure than to support with full, juicy quotations the general description that I have given of Mr. Spillane's works. I fear, however, that this is impossible; that, if I even began to convey passages of Mr. Spillane's richest prose to the pages of the *Saturday Review,* the editors of this comparatively chaste periodical would, with one loud voice, echo Jeffrey's classic verdict—"This will never do." But I trust that even while working in hobbles I have succeeded in communicating some faint idea of the character and quality of Mr. Spillane's art.

He and his fellow-workers—for he is only the most conspicuous, most successful member of a flourishing school—have brought to ripe perfection elements and qualities that were juvenescent in Hammett and mature in Chandler. It is as though their fiction had been bred according to Mendelian laws, so that certain characteristics should be grossly exaggerated while others were suppressed. Detection, in the true sense of the word, has been bred almost out of existence; while crime, on the other hand, has become dominant. Stupidity and brutality have replaced intelligence. Salacity has supplanted ingenuity. Probability is flouted, credibility scorned, absurdity honored. A routine narrative-pattern has been developed in which sadism, exhibitionism, sexual intercourse, and murder recur at regular intervals, while homosexuality, flagellation, or some other attractive perversion occasionally adds zest to the whole.

The frontiers of pure pornography have certainly been approached; whether or not they have been crossed every reader may decide for himself. That this narrative-pattern is giving a vast public exactly what it wants is proved by the enormous sales enjoyed by the writers who make use of it. But there should be a new name for their product. "Detective story" is too ancient and honorable a label for material so debased. If the new school were in complete possession of the field, the detective story would already be dead and buried. Fortunately, however, there are still writers, many of them, whose books deserve to bear that ancient, honorable label; writers who are worthy scions of a distinguished line. May they flourish! But the barbarians are within the gates. (pp. 8-9, 31-2)

Ben Ray Redman, "Decline and Fall of the Whodunit," in The Saturday Review, *New York, Vol. XXXV, No. 22, May 31, 1952, pp. 8-9, 31-2.*

Hillary Waugh

[*Writing under his own name and under the pseudonyms Harry Walker and H. Baldwin Taylor, Waugh has produced several dozen mystery and detective novels. He is a pioneer in the field of the police procedural, which is considered the first significant new development in detective and mystery fiction since the advent of the hard-boiled school in the 1920s. In the following excerpt, he discusses some characteristics of the police procedural novel and compares the police procedural with other forms of detective literature.*]

Lawrence Treat is acknowledged as the first mystery writer to have professional policemen, shown in their natural habitat, solve a crime using authentic police methods. This was his book *V as in Victim,* published in 1945 and followed by *The Big Shot,* using the same characters.

While Larry was first, I doubt that it would be correct to call him the "father" of the police procedural, for this would suggest that a host of other writers were inspired to follow his lead. This did not happen; Larry was ahead of his time and a number of years passed before others began to follow suit. In fact, to quote Larry, "I didn't know I was writing procedurals until somebody invented the term and said that that was the kind of thing I was writing."

If there was a father of the procedural, I think it would have to be the radio program *Dragnet.* Perhaps its success was what created the field, or perhaps the *time* of the procedural, which Larry Treat's books foreshadowed, had finally arrived. In either case, I think the "father" title is deserved for while it is true that no procedural writer I have talked to points to *Dragnet* as a source of inspiration—most not having written their first procedurals until well after *Dragnet*'s demise—I would still regard it as inevitable that the potential of the police-station background was first brought to their attention by Joe Friday and company.

In any case, the police procedural, as yet still unnamed, came into being between the writing and publication of my own first procedural so that, when it appeared in print, it was reviewed as an attempt to translate *Dragnet* to novel form. Though erroneous, such critic reaction is, perhaps, further evidence for the "father" figure.

The police procedural represents the second major change in the nature of the mystery story since it achieved its present "whodunit" form with the advent of the classical detective story. The invention which established the classical period and the "whodunit" form was the shifting of the reader's role from that of observer—i.e., standing at Watson's side watching the great man operate—to that of participant—standing at the detective's side, trying to beat him at his own game.

As a result of this change of viewpoint, the classical detective stories became puzzle tales wherein a detective of outstanding intellect matched wits with a murderer, while the author matched wits with the reader.

The first change in this method of handling the mystery story occurred in the forties and early fifties with the establishment of the private-eye school. Tales in this new approach to the genre retained the puzzle form of the plot, but shifted the story emphasis from thought to action. Prowess took precedence over wits. The detectives in these adventures were for the most part loners, knights errant, fighting a desperate battle for Good against Evil. In the beginning days they were private detectives solving murders to save their clients or themselves. Later they became spies and their problems involved the safety of nations.

Though the classical detective and the private-eye/spy operated in radically different ways, both shared certain common traits. Both, for example, were virtually free of legal restraint; both were laws unto themselves; both operated alone and kept their own counsel.

The police procedural changes all that. The police procedural thrusts the detective into the middle of a working police force, full of rules and regulations. Instead of bypassing the police, as did its predecessors, the procedural takes the reader inside the department and shows how it operates.

These are stories, not just about policemen, but about the world of the policeman. Police Inspector Charlie Chan doesn't belong. (There're no police.) Nor does Inspector Maigret. (There are police, but Maigret, like Chan, remains his own man.)

When we speak of police procedurals, we are talking about the 87th Precinct books of Ed McBain, about the Elizabeth Linington—Dell Shannon—Lesley Egan, Glendale and Los Angeles police novels. There are John Creasey's

Gideon and Roger West stories, there is the Martin Beck series by Maj Sjöwall and the late Per Wahlöö. These are tales about big-city police departments. In the small-town police procedural genre, there may be none other than my own Chief Fred Fellows.

This business of moving toward the police instead of away from the police is a radical shift in the character of the mystery story, and the nature of the procedural can best be understood by comparing it to the other two cited forms. Let us study them in this manner.

I. Realism and the Suspension of Disbelief

"Suspension of disbelief " is one of those awkward phrases that is both hard to say and hard to understand. All it means is: How much *un*reality will the reader endure? How far can a writer go before the reader says, "This is ridiculous!"?

The degree of permissible unreality depends, quite obviously, upon the book. Readers will accept magic spells, witches, and gingerbread houses in fairy tales, but would reject, in disgust, machine guns and electric lights in Civil War novels. The same holds true in the mystery. A great deal more attention to realism is demanded in the police procedural than in the earlier forms. And with reason.

Consider the classical detective story. The moment the reader was brought in on the case and given a chance to solve it, the mystery became a game of wits between author and reader. Authors, therefore, devoted their attention to exploring the possibilities of the puzzle, of finding ways to fool the reader. The result was some of the most elaborately complex plots ever put on paper. Villains, to be worthy foes of the detective, became incredibly clever, incredibly painstaking and, upon occasion, incredibly lucky. The puzzles were exquisite pieces of intellectual architecture.

Such mysteries, naturally, could not pretend a resemblance to reality. Real life murders aren't that elaborately planned. Most actual killings, in fact, are spur-of-the-moment impulses with no more advance thought than will justify the term "premeditation." In real life, the hardest crime to solve is not the one in which every detail has been worked out months in advance, but the unwitnessed, spur-of-the-moment rape or robbery encounter wherein the victim was unknown to the villain.

Such real-life cases, however, would not fit the puzzle mold of the classical mystery. Since puzzle was the aim, reality had to be sacrificed.

As a result, the classical detective story was structured in a language of its own. A large number of wholly artificial devices were accepted as proper baggage. Probably most notable was the traditional denouement wherein all suspects were gathered together and the detective pointed a finger at first one and then another, keeping suspense at its ultimate until, finally, he pointed to the villain and explained in detail how he had found him out. No matter that this is the last thing a real detective would do, the requisites of the puzzle story demanded this kind of approach.

Another was the detective's habit of keeping all the threads of the mystery in his own head, committing nothing to paper, confiding in no one. Keeping the reader in the dark made such behavior obligatory. It also customarily made the detective a tempting target for the murderer and the reader would forgive the lack of reality in favor of the puzzle and the suspense.

Certain artificialities in the form of clues also came to be accepted. These, however, were not born of necessity but stemmed from gross errors of ignorance due to the fact that the mystery writers of the era worked aloof from the police and did not bother to research that aspect of their novels.

One of the most notable was the gospel that fingerprints abound and are readily discoverable on guns. As an adjunct, it was also accepted that fingerprints would be protected rather than smudged if covered with a handkerchief. In point of fact, an identifiable fingerprint is very hard to come by, even on receptive surfaces like mirrors, and the chances of getting a print from a gun are, if not zero, very nearly so.

Other clues of misinformation which these stories circulated were that the expression on the victim's face revealed his emotion (surprise, fear, etc.) at the moment of death; that pathologists could tell almost to the minute how long the victim had been dead; and that headless corpses could readily be *mis*identified.

None of this is true, of course. The best description of the expression on a corpse's face is that there is none. As for times of death, so many variables affect the onset of postmortem changes that an accurate determination is a virtual impossibility without the help of additional evidence. And, of course, the means of identification of bodies by other than facial characteristics are amazingly many. However, for purposes of the puzzle, these gospels of ignorance helped the authors with their clue-planting and readers learned to accept them. The astute reader would, for instance, reflexively know that any body with the face damaged or the head missing belonged to someone else, and that the supposed victim was, in reality, the murderer.

Nor, finally, did murderers ever take the Fifth or deny the accusation, confident that they could never be convicted. Such a concession to realism would make for messy, inconclusive endings and that would not do. When the puzzle was solved, the book had to end.

Mysteries of the classical school might be summed up as follows: Realism is all right so long as it does not interfere with the puzzle.

The private-eye school of mystery fiction is generally accepted as coming to the fore as a revolt against the fantasyland of the puzzle story. It was as if a new breed of author were saying, "This is ridiculous! Let's bring reality to the mystery."

So the stories became more real. The corpses weren't so pretty and death was a matter taken seriously by all concerned, not merely by the detective.

The puzzle could not be as intricate, of course, but that was readily compensated for by having the plot line complicated by an overlay of action rather than one of intellectual obfuscation.

For all that, reality did not really come to the fore. Instead, it became subservient to action. The private-eye of these tales behaved in an extraordinarily unrealistic manner. He customarily arrived on the murder scene ahead of the police, tampered with evidence, pocketed clues, and broke laws with a recklessness that was only justified by the fact that the police in these stories were such bumbling idiots that, had the private-eye abided by the rules, the mystery would never have been solved. It was only because of his law-unto-himself behavior that the villains were ultimately caught.

As time went on, the stories got wilder, reaching the ultimate in the works of Mickey Spillane. Reality was as absent from the mystery as ever.

One might interpret the advent of the police procedural as if a new breed of author were saying, "This is ridiculous! Let's bring reality to the mystery." Except that one might now ask the ultimate question: How much reality can be brought to the mystery? Can it ever be total? And, if it can, is the police procedural the vehicle? Is the police procedural that ultimate form of the mystery that can combine puzzle, action, and total reality into one?

My personal guess is that total reality can never exist in mystery fiction and my definite conclusion is that it certainly can't exist in the procedural.

Consider, first, the narrow field of the small-town police procedural. There is no way total reality can be brought to a series of this kind. In certain areas the reader is obligated to suspend large amounts of disbelief.

Suppose, for example, an author can produce two small-town police procedurals a year—hardly a staggering output. In each there must be one or more confounding murders, problems that strain the resources of both the reader and the police department.

In reality, a town of, say, ten thousand inhabitants, insulated and self-contained, unassaulted by the outside world, would not have a real, honest-to-goodness murder once in a dozen years. That's eight murders a century.

Of these eight genuine murders per century, the chances are that seven of them would pose no problem at all. The police would know who did it ten minutes after they reached the scene and would have the case wrapped up in twenty-four hours.

Inasmuch as the author of the small-town procedural isn't going to write about easily solved mysteries, the stories he will tell are Crime of the Century tales. Except that, in the small-town he's writing about, they will take place twice a year.

If this seems against the odds, add in the fact that the small-town in question is fortunate enough to have a high-powered resident detective capable of cracking these seemingly insoluble mysteries, and we have to pay another homage to Dame Chance.

What about the other side of the coin? What about the big-city procedural? If we want to portray realism, is this not the locale that offers maximum opportunity? In 1966, there were 700 homicides in New York City. Ten years later, the number was almost 1500. A writer in this big city could not turn out books fast enough to cover the 1-in-8 hard-to-solve cases a single homicide detective might handle in a year.

That part of the story might be true to life. Accurate, also, might be the rules and regulations by which the police abide. The jargon can be learned, the difference between street-cops and book-cops can be understood. In time, an interested writer who has entrée can so familiarize himself with the world of real detectives that he will know their dangers and their territory, guffaw at their "in" jokes, understand the way they think and why. His books may be, therefore, rigorously accurate in all details, except . . .

The real-life detective does not do his detecting *à la* Sherlock Holmes. He may observe the way Holmes observed; he may well put the pieces of a puzzle together the way Holmes put them together, but this is not the way most real-life crimes are solved. The real-life murder is solved, not by ratiocination, not by the exercise of Hercule Poirot's little gray cells, but by the accumulation of information. Dozens of people are questioned—hundreds may be questioned—and, bit by bit, pieces of information are gathered which, ultimately, reveal what happened.

That's the hard way.

The easy way is to have the information brought in. Ask a chief of detectives how cases are solved and he won't answer, "clues," he'll answer, "informants" [the critic adds in a footnote that "the term inform*ers* carries ugly connotations and isn't used"]. There is an adage that a detective is only as good as his informants and it is, rest assured, true.

To the mystery writer, this poses certain problems. Consider the following (based upon a true case). There is a shooting in Harlem, one man dead in the hospital, a second man wounded. The wounded man, interviewed by police, tells the story that he and the victim were walking along the street when a man came out of a bar, gunned them down, and ran around the corner. He never saw the man before, he doesn't know why the man shot them. The family of the victim swears he had no enemies, the people in the bar saw nothing, witnesses to the actual shooting don't know who the man was. There is no gun, no clues, no anything.

To an outsider it sounds like a motiveless, unsolvable crime. Even Charlie Chan and Philo Vance would be up a tree.

The police, who are familiar with the local scene, will not be so confounded. They will speculate that it had to do with drugs, that the victim was either a pusher who sold bad junk, or he had robbed a pusher—either act being a killing offense. This gives them motive, but it does not tell them "who." They are not unduly distressed, however, for they anticipate that, later that night—maybe three o'clock in the morning—an informant will slip into headquarters, up to the squad room, and tell the detectives who did it and why. The detectives would then check out the information and, a few days later, make an arrest.

That's the way it usually happens, but it makes for a very bad story. Certain adjustments would have to be imposed upon such a tale to put it into saleable form, to wit: the detective would have to solve the case without the aid of the informant.

But the moment we start doing this, we are moving away from reality again.

II. The Hero

Let us now turn our attention to the heroes of these tales. What are they like and why are they that way?

The detectives of the classical period are all patterned after Sherlock Holmes. They are created as men of giant intellect, towering over their fellows. The only man, in fact, who can come close to matching the hero's intellect is the villain.

Generally speaking, the detective is also separated from the crowd in other ways. Father Brown wears a habit, Nero Wolfe is an obese gourmet, Poirot and Charlie Chan are foreigners, Vance a dilettante, Wimsey a Lord, the early Queen, effete. Every effort is undertaken to make these detectives memorable, to give them the kind of lasting identity that Holmes has. And the ones mentioned above have certainly achieved this distinction.

The homage paid to these detectives and their virtual freedom from the bothersome restrictions imposed on other mortals give them an enviable position. Not for them are there problems about money. They do not have to worry about their jobs, about wives and children. They, like Holmes, are free of all encumbrances, able to devote their great mental prowess exclusively to the murders at hand. It is not difficult for an author to establish reader identification with such a hero.

Let us move on to the hero of the private-eye school. This is a different species of being entirely. This man is a puzzle-solver too, but he is not content to sit and ponder. He is a man of energy and he solves the puzzles through action.

The Saint, James Bond, and Mike Hammer are extreme examples of the type, but they serve as illustrations. These private-eye heroes have more than a touch of Superman about them. They are tough, brave, resourceful, and—as we have noted before—a law unto themselves. They tend to be cavalier, even flamboyant. The qualities that separate them from the rest of the cast are their ability to operate in excess of everyone else, be it the alcohol they can absorb, the beatings they can take, the laws they can break, the women they can handle.

These men are heroes in the genuine sense of the word, meaning that they go out and battle for Right against Wrong, and WIN. They represent the Walter Mitty dream of the frustrated average man whose world has grown too large for an outcome to be affected by his own efforts. The hero's reckless disregard of authority and his success at overcoming obstacles are therapeutic to the reader. He identifies with such a man. He is eager to read more tales of his derring-do.

What happens, though, when an author seeks to create a hero for a police procedural? Immediately he's in trouble, for the attractive superman hero is denied him by the nature of the genre. Not only does realism require that the hero of procedurals be human rather than superhuman, but also the restrictions of his job and the society he is sworn to uphold.

Consider, first, the small-town procedural. Who can be the protagonist of such a story? Certainly not some handsome young cop who drinks a quart of Scotch for breakfast and has to fight his way past the blondes who camp outside his door—not even a handsome young cop who doesn't drink, smoke, or date—not a young cop at all, even if he's home-ly.

When it comes to solving serious crimes, the responsibility goes to the top men on the force, which means the chief of police, the detectives he's got, and the officer in charge of detectives. We're talking about older men, men who are probably married and raising families, men who wouldn't find a blonde in every bed, even if sleepy blondes abounded, because they have too little to offer. They are just struggling, balding, graying, unromantic, plain-looking, ordinary Joes.

It is much harder, obviously, for an author to create a memorable character, one the reader will want to keep reading about, if the character can't do or be anything memorable;—if he can't attain positions of authority until he is past his handsome, dashing youth;—if he can't dine on gourmet foods and know the right wines because he lives on a policeman's salary;—if he has to get to work on time, obey the law, go through all the red tape that real policemen do;—if he has to turn over significant parts of the investigation to others and stay in the good graces of the public and the board of police commissioners.

Such a man can't help being a rather gray, colorless character, leading a gray, colorless life. No single-handedly walking into the nest of thieves for him;—no sneaking into the bad guy's apartment to find crucial evidence;—no keeping to himself bits of vital information so that he can hog the limelight when he really socks it to them at the end.

In the small-town procedural, the solution of a case is not a one-man operation in any case. It can be accomplished by a team of two, but no fewer. Nor can the two be Mutt and Jeff, Johnson and Boswell, or Sherlock and Watson. The disparity must not appear too great. It cannot be me and my shadow, it must be a legitimate team of two.

What about a big-city procedural? In a big-city police force, the number of detectives in a squad will run between twenty and thirty. The problem of creating a hero is not multiplied, however. While many of the detectives may help in various phases of a serious crime—interviewing everybody in an apartment building, for example—and while lab technicians, pathologists, photo, emergency service, and other functionaries may be resorted to, these are information-gathering operations, which information will then be delivered to the detectives in charge, and these would probably again be a team of only two. In a New York City homicide, for instance, the two would be the squad detective who "caught" the case and is therefore responsible for its disposition, and the member of the homicide squad—specialists in this kind of crime—who would be assigned to work with him.

This would appear to make the big-city procedural the same as a small-town procedural, with a pair of detectives carrying the ball. In fact, however, the author of a big-city procedural can go with an individual hero if he wants. If his hero is a member of a specialty squad, like homicide, the detective he'd be assigned to help would be different in each new case and he would remain as the sole, continuing character. In such handling, the rest of the detective squad and the other cases under investigation would be background.

Given this material to work with, what are the tactics for producing memorable detectives? It's not as easy a job as when a writer has the license to invent as he pleases, but the opportunities are still plentiful. The family life of the detectives can be explored—a possibility that was never entertained in the classic and private-eye forms. The relationships of the men with each other can play an important part in the story—an aspect of the mystery that didn't exist when detectives stood head, shoulders, and waist above their associates and communed only with themselves. In fact, the interior of the squad room can become the equivalent of a daytime serial setting—meaning that the readers get to know the people, their personalities and their problems so well that they look forward to the next book as a chance to rejoin old friends.

The hero aspect of the procedural is radically different from the other two forms, but it offers, probably, a much richer vein to mine.

III. Background

Despite the difference in the hero form, it is in the area of background that the greatest distinction occurs between the police procedural and all other forms of the mystery. In the classical and private-eye forms, an author could get away with minimal research, or none at all. Some authors did do research and enhanced their books with information on special skills or backgrounds, giving their stories an added fillip. The research, however, was inevitably directed toward exotic subjects of intellectual interest. The one area that was not researched was the crass, mundane, very nonintellectual subject of how real detectives operated and what the business of solving murders was actually all about.

Of course, there was little incentive. The creators of the classical detectives did not need to know how the police operated, for the only function of the police was to take the murderer away at the end of the story.

Nor was there any particular reason why the writers of private-eye stories should do background research into the way real crimes were solved. If their heroes operated above the law, there was no need for the authors to know what the laws were. In fact, the only effect a knowledge of law would have upon an author would be to inhibit the freedom he was seeking to give his character.

With the police procedural, of course, the situation is totally reversed. Since it sets itself to show realistic-appearing policemen encountering realistic crimes and solving them in a realistic manner, a knowledge of how police forces are actually structured (they vary greatly from city to city) becomes essential. Not only must procedures be known and understood, but also the law. Even a rookie cop has been drilled in criminal law and knows what he can and cannot do, as well as the requirements he must satisfy. The writer, therefore, had better give himself a similar background and know such things as the rules of evidence and how to cope with the Miranda decision.

The writer of a procedural must be true to life in other ways. Since his readership will grant him scant suspension of disbelief, he cannot have his hero overdrink without getting drunk or sick. His hero can't get bashed unconscious without going to the hospital for observation. Everything must be true to life. All kinds of little bits and pieces of annoying trivia will have to be checked and verified, lest readers start complaining.

The problem, then, for the procedural writer is not merely to come up with a compelling story. He has the added obligation and chore of researching.

IV. Puzzle and Fair Play

Lastly, we come to the story that takes place against this procedural background. Here one encounters a situation which poses interesting questions.

In both the classical and private-eye type mysteries, there was a puzzle to be solved, a villain to be caught and, since the reader was engaged as a participant, an element of fair play to be included. The reader had to know everything the detective knew. The reader went through the case at the detective's side.

The puzzle was in greatest evidence in the classical tale. It was the whole point of the story. In the private-eye genre the puzzle played second fiddle to the action, but it was still there.

Does it exist in the procedural?

The answer is, of course, yes. But, depending upon the type of procedural, it can be foremost, as is likely in the small-town procedural where nothing else is happening, or as low as third fiddle in the big-city type of tale, coming in behind both action and background.

It still, however, must be there. The problem cannot solve itself nor, as mentioned earlier, be solved via the unsolicited arrival of an informant. The detectives must work at a solution and the solution must result from their work. And, of course, the reader again is taken along with the detective—at least on the major case—and is apprised of all the information that the detective is privy to.

These qualities, the solving of a puzzle with the reader given all the clues, are the hallmarks of the mystery story and must be present. Omit them and the tale, no matter how mysterious, how murderous, how police-oriented, is not a proper mystery.

Now comes an aspect of the police-procedural tale which, while it has been a matter of moment to me, does not seem to concern anyone else, with the exception, perhaps, of Ed McBain. (See his deaf man, El Sordo, in such as "Let's Hear It for the Deaf Man.") This is the element of the "Fair Fight."

Sherlock Holmes had his Moriarty, a man whose talents were a match for his own. In like manner, the mighty-minded detectives of the classical age had to be similarly tested. In order to don the mantle of super-genius, they had to best the best. This is why the puzzles they had to unravel were so elaborate, why the murderers were so clever, why all the odds had to be stacked in their opponent's favor. Chance could not solve the case for the detective. It could only operate on behalf of the villain, making the detective's problem ever more difficult. The detective, to earn his victory, had to prove his supremacy over both the foe and the odds. There could be no sere leaf on the laurel.

In like manner, the private-eye had to outsmart the gangleader, the nightclub owner or, in the case of the spy, the arrayed forces of the enemy country. The odds always had to be on the side of the opposition, to be overcome along with the foe.

Now we come to the police procedural and we find there is a change in the battle line-up.

Given: One murderer.

And what is there against him?

We can count on at least two detectives devoting full time to his apprehension while, behind them, at beck and call, lie the total resources of the police, medical, and legal systems of the community. Let the villain hole up in an abandoned warehouse and the hero will not go in and shoot it out with him in a one-to-one showdown. There will be dozens of men, all more heavily armed and protected than their quarry. They will have tear gas, searchlights, walkie-talkies, helicopters—an awesome array of tools—creating a maximum mismatch (quite properly) in order to reduce the element of danger to the "good guys" to a minimum.

The disparity is even greater than that. The police detective will be as observant as a Sherlock Holmes by virtue of his training and years of conditioning. If he cannot match Holmes's brilliant mind, he has learned, through long experience, what to look for and where to look, which is almost as good. And the available laboratory facilities can produce, from clues, information the like of which Conan Doyle would never have dreamed.

Meanwhile, against this super-Sherlock stands no Moriarty. The average murderer in real life is below average in mentality. He is motivated by emotion rather than brains. His responses are less planned, his motives less well thought-out. As a physical specimen he would rarely be capable of holding his own against a detective in an even fight. He is more than likely to be one of life's losers. He is outgunned, outmaneuvered, and outwitted every step of the way. The fight is anything but fair.

Does anybody care?

Interestingly enough, I sought, in my own small-town police procedurals, to cope with the problem as follows: The murderers were of better than average intelligence—middle-and upper-middle-class in background (not unreasonable in the small-town genre). Then, due partly to their cleverness, the rest to the luck that fell their way, the whole police apparatus would fail to uncover them. An impasse would be reached, at which point the battle became a one-to-one fight between the chief-of-police hero and the villain. The chief would have to come up, on his own, with the one move or idea that would break the case.

This may well have been a wasted concern on my part, however, for nowhere does there seem to be anyone—reader, critic, or other procedural writer—who has given the matter a thought. Do readers feel a certain sympathy for the outgunned and outnumbered murderer? Do they root for the underdog?

Apparently not. In these realistic days where bodies smell and victims spill blood instead of ketchup, perhaps the readers' desire for justice (or is it vengeance?) is such that they don't care how the killer is brought to bay. Perhaps, as another author suggests, the interest in the police procedural lies not in story but in the fascination of this strange world of the policeman and what it is that sets him apart from the rest of mankind; that makes him advance where others retreat, that makes him the helper instead of the helpless.

Or, perhaps what counts is the satisfaction we feel at seeing a great power for Good overthrow the forces of Evil. Perhaps the police procedural excites that emotion within man that is so evident in war: The desire to annihilate the enemy, and the more overwhelming the victory, the more satisfying it is.

V. Conclusions

A comparison of the police-procedural mystery with its predecessors produces eye-opening results. What comes through most strongly is the close relationship between the classical and private-eye forms, and the separateness of the police procedural. This is evident in the areas we have discussed, but the very difference creates a message of its own.

The classical detective story and the private-eye novel were inevitably described as "light reading." One picked up the former for the puzzle, the latter for the action and the accent was on fun. (The lack of reality helped. Who can take the unreal seriously?)

Reviewers of police procedurals, however, don't talk in terms of "light reading." "Social message" is more commonly the measure of evaluation. The police procedural, by showing policemen as they are, shows, by definition, the social ills they contend against as *they* are. Sometimes the social commentaries revealed by procedural authors are deliberately intended, sometimes the revelations are unconsciously done. In either case, the very nature of the procedural provokes a type of story totally beyond the aim of the other forms.

The puzzle—all-important to the classical story—can sink to the depths of being nothing more than the glue that holds a procedural in the genre. There is little else the new form has in common with the old.

One can only ponder the meaning of the changes in the mystery genre. Perhaps the switch from classical to private-eye seemed, at the time, as enormous as the new switch from them to the procedural. Perhaps we should, therefore, pay more attention to the common ground the procedural shares with its predecessors than the differences. (pp. 164-86)

Hillary Waugh, "The Police Procedural," in The Mystery Story, *edited by John Ball, University Extension, University of California, 1976, pp. 163-87.*

THE APPEAL OF DETECTIVE FICTION

G. K. Chesterton

[*Regarded as one of England's premier men of letters during the first half of the twentieth century, Chesterton is best known today as a colorful bon vivant, witty essayist, and creator of the Father Brown mysteries and the fantasy* The Man Who Was Thursday *(1908). Much of Chesterton's work reflects his pronounced Anglican and, later, Roman Catholic beliefs. His essays are characterized by their humor, frequent use of paradox, and chatty, rambling style. In the following essay, Chesterton offers a defense and analysis of detective fiction as a legitimate form of literature.*]

In attempting to reach the genuine psychological reason for the popularity of detective stories, it is necessary to rid ourselves of many mere phrases. It is not true, for example, that the populace prefer bad literature to good, and accept detective stories because they are bad literature. The mere absence of artistic subtlety does not make a book popular. Bradshaw's Railway Guide contains few gleams of psychological comedy, yet it is not read aloud uproariously on winter evenings. If detective stories are read with more exuberance than railway guides, it is certainly because they are more artistic. Many good books have fortunately been popular; many bad books, still more fortunately, have been unpopular. A good detective story would probably be even more popular than a bad one. The trouble in this matter is that many people do not realize that there is such a thing as a good detective story; it is to them like speaking of a good devil. To write a story about a burglary is, in their eyes, a sort of spiritual manner of committing it. To persons of somewhat weak sensibility this is natural enough; it must be confessed that many detective stories are as full of sensational crime as one of Shakespeare's plays.

There is, however, between a good detective story and a bad detective story as much, or, rather more, difference than there is between a good epic and a bad one. Not only is a detective story a perfectly legitimate form of art, but it has certain definite and real advantages as an agent of the public weal.

The first essential value of the detective story lies in this, that it is the earliest and only form of popular literature in which is expressed some sense of the poetry of modern life. Men lived among mighty mountains and eternal forests for ages before they realized that they were poetical; it may reasonably be inferred that some of our descendants may see the chimney-pots as rich a purple as the mountain-peaks, and find the lamp-posts as old and natural as the trees. Of this realization of a great city itself as something wild and obvious the detective story is certainly the 'Iliad.' No one can have failed to notice that in these stories the hero or the investigator crosses London with something of the loneliness and liberty of a prince in a tale of elfland, that in the course of that incalculable journey the casual omnibus assumes the primal colours of a fairy ship. The lights of the city begin to glow like innumerable goblin eyes, since they are the guardians of some secret, however crude, which the writer knows and the reader does not. Every twist of the road is like a finger pointing to it; every fantastic skyline of chimney-pots seems wildly and derisively signalling the meaning of the mystery.

This realization of the poetry of London is not a small thing. A city is, properly speaking, more poetic even than a countryside, for while Nature is a chaos of unconscious forces, a city is a chaos of conscious ones. The crest of the flower or the pattern of the lichen may or may not be significant symbols. But there is no stone in the street and no brick in the wall that is not actually a deliberate symbol—a message from some man, as much as if it were a telegram or a post-card. The narrowest street possesses, in every crook and twist of its intention, the soul of the man who built it, perhaps long in his grave. Every brick has as human a hieroglyph as if it were a graven brick of Babylon; every slate on the roof is as educational a document as if it were a slate covered with addition and subtraction sums. Anything which tends, even under the fantastic form of the minutiæ of Sherlock Holmes, to assert this romance of detail in civilization, to emphasize this unfathomably human character in flints and tiles, is a good thing. It is good that the average man should fall into the habit of looking imaginatively at ten men in the street even if it is only on the chance that the eleventh might be a notorious thief. We may dream, perhaps, that it might be possible to have another and higher romance of London, that men's souls have stranger adventures than their bodies, and that it would be harder and more exciting to hunt their virtues than to hunt their crimes. But since our great authors (with the admirable exception of Stevenson) decline to write of that thrilling mood and moment when the eyes of the great city, like the eyes of a cat, begin to flame in the dark, we must give fair credit to the popular literature which, amid a babble of pedantry and preciosity, declines to regard the present as prosaic or the common as commonplace. Popular art in all ages has been interested in contemporary manners and costume; it dressed the groups around the Crucifixion in the garb of Florentine gentlefolk or Flemish burghers. In the last century it was the custom for distinguished actors to present Macbeth in a powdered wig and ruffles. How far we are ourselves in this age from such conviction of the poetry of our own life and manners may easily be conceived by anyone who chooses to imagine a picture of Alfred the Great toasting the cakes dressed in tourist's knickerbockers, or a performance of 'Hamlet' in which the Prince appeared in a frock-coat, with a crape band round his hat. But this instinct of the age to look back, like Lot's wife, could not go on for ever. A rude, popular literature of the romantic possibilities of the modern city was bound to arise. It has arisen in the popular detective stories, as rough and refreshing as the ballads of Robin Hood.

There is, however, another good work that is done by detective stories. While it is the constant tendency of the Old Adam to rebel against so universal and automatic a thing as civilization, to preach departure and rebellion, the romance of police activity keeps in some sense before the mind the fact that civilization itself is the most sensational of departures and the most romantic of rebellions. By dealing with the unsleeping sentinels who guard the outposts of society, it tends to remind us that we live in an armed camp, making war with a chaotic world, and that the criminals, the children of chaos, are nothing but the traitors within our gates. When the detective in a police romance stands alone, and somewhat fatuously fearless amid the knives and fists of a thieves' kitchen, it does certainly serve to make us remember that it is the agent of social justice who is the original and poetic figure, while the burglars and footpads are merely placid old cosmic conservatives, happy in the immemorial respectability of apes and wolves. The romance of the police force is thus the whole romance of man. It is based on the fact that morality is the most dark and daring of conspiracies. It re-

minds us that the whole noiseless and unnoticeable police management by which we are ruled and protected is only a successful knight-errantry. (pp. 3-6)

> G. K. Chesterton, "A Defence of Detective Stories," in The Art of the Mystery Story: A Collection of Critical Essays, *edited by Howard Haycraft, Simon and Schuster, 1946, pp. 3-6.*

Edmund Wilson

[*Wilson, considered America's foremost man of letters in the twentieth century, wrote widely on cultural, historical, and literary matters. He is often credited with bringing an international perspective to American letters through his widely read discussions of European literature. Wilson was allied to no critical school; however, several dominant concerns serve as guiding motifs throughout his work. He invariably examined the social and historical implications of a work of literature, particularly literature's significance as "an attempt to give meaning to our experience" and its value for the improvement of humanity. Although he was not a moralist, his criticism displays a deep concern with moral values. Another constant was his discussion of a work of literature as a revelation of its author's personality. In Axel's* Castle *(1931), a seminal study of literary symbolism, Wilson wrote: "The real elements, of course, of any work of fiction are the elements of the author's personality: his imagination embodies in the images of characters, situations and scenes the fundamental conflicts of his nature." Related to this is Wilson's theory, formulated in* The Wound and the Bow *(1941), that artistic ability is a compensation for a psychological wound; thus, a literary work can only be fully understood if one undertakes an emotional profile of its author. Wilson utilized this approach in many essays, and it is the most-often attacked element of his thought. However, though Wilson examined the historical and psychological implications of a work of literature, he rarely did so at the expense of a discussion of its literary qualities. Perhaps Wilson's greatest contributions to American literature were his tireless promotion of writers of the 1920s, 1930s, and 1940s, and his essays introducing the best of modern literature to the general reader. In the following essay, originally written in 1944, Wilson professes not to understand the popularity of detective fiction and pronounces most current works in the genre poorly written.*]

For years I have been hearing about detective stories. Almost everybody I know seems to read them, and they have long conversations about them in which I am unable to take part. I am always being reminded that the most serious public figures of our time, from Woodrow Wilson to W. B. Yeats, have been addicts of this form of fiction. Now, except for a few stories by Chesterton, for which I did not much care, I have not read any detective stories since one of the earliest, if not the earliest, of the imitators of Sherlock Holmes—a writer named Jacques Futrelle, now dead, who invented a character called the Thinking Machine and published his first volume of stories about him in 1907. Enchanted though I had been with Sherlock Holmes, I got bored with the Thinking Machine and dropped him, beginning to feel, at the age of twelve, that I was outgrowing that form of literature.

Since, however, I have recently been sampling the various types of popular merchandise, I have decided that I ought to take a look at some specimens of this kind of fiction, which has grown so tremendously popular and which is now being produced on such a scale that the book departments of magazines have had to employ special editors to cope with it. To be sure of getting something above the average, I waited for new novels by writers who are particularly esteemed by connoisseurs. I started in with the latest volume of Rex Stout's Nero Wolfe stories: *Not Quite Dead Enough.*

What I found rather surprised me and discouraged my curiosity. Here was simply the old Sherlock Holmes formula reproduced with a fidelity even more complete than it had been by Jacques Futrelle almost forty years ago. Here was the incomparable private detective, ironic and ceremonious, with a superior mind and eccentric habits, addicted to overeating and orchid-raising, as Holmes had his enervated indulgence in his cocaine and his violin, yet always prepared to revive for prodigies of intellectual alertness; and here were the admiring stooge, adoring and slightly dense, and Inspector Lestrade of Scotland Yard, energetic but entirely at sea, under the new name of Inspector Cramer of Police Headquarters. Almost the only difference was that Nero Wolfe was fat and lethargic instead of lean and active like Holmes, and that he liked to make the villains commit suicide instead of handing them over to justice. But I rather enjoyed Wolfe himself, with his rich dinners and quiet evenings in his house in farthest West Thirty-fifth Street, where he savors an armchair sadism that is always accompanied by beer. The two stories that made up this new book—*Not Quite Dead Enough* and *Booby Trap*—I found rather disappointing; but, as they were both under the usual length and presented the great detective partly distracted from his regular profession by a rigorous course of training for the Army, I concluded that they might not be first-rate examples of what the author could do in this line and read also *The Nero Wolfe Omnibus,* which contains two earlier book-length stories: *The Red Box* and *The League of Frightened Men.* But neither did these supply the excitement I was hoping for. If the later stories were sketchy and skimpy, these seemed to have been somewhat padded, for they were full of long episodes that led nowhere and had no real business in the story. It was only when I looked up Sherlock Holmes that I realized how much Nero Wolfe was a dim and distant copy of an original. The old stories of Conan Doyle had a wit and a fairy-tale poetry of hansom cabs, gloomy London lodgings and lonely country estates that Rex Stout could hardly duplicate with his backgrounds of modern New York; and the surprises were much more entertaining: you at least got a room with a descending ceiling or a snake trained to climb down the bellrope, whereas with Nero Wolfe—though *The League of Frightened Men* makes use of a clever psychological idea—the solution of the mystery was not usually either fanciful or unexpected. I finally got to feel that I had to unpack large crates by swallowing the excelsior in order to find at the bottom a few bent and rusty nails, and I began to nurse a rankling conviction that detective stories in general are able to profit by an unfair advantage in the code which forbids the reviewer to give away the secret to the public—a custom which results in the concealment of the pointlessness of a good deal of this fiction and affords a protection to the authors which no other department of writing enjoys. It is

not difficult to create suspense by making people await a revelation, but it does demand a certain talent to come through with a criminal device which is ingenious or picturesque or amusing enough to make the reader feel that the waiting has been worth while. I even began to mutter that the real secret that Author Rex Stout had been screening by his false scents and interminable divagations was a meagerness of imagination of which one only came to realize the full ghastliness when the last chapter had left one blank.

I have been told by the experts, however, that this endless carrying on of the Doyle tradition does not represent all or the best that has been done with the detective story during the decades of its proliferation. There has been also the puzzle mystery, and this, I was assured, had been brought to a high pitch of ingenuity in the stories of Agatha Christie. So I have read also the new Agatha Christie, *Death Comes as the End,* and I confess that I have been had by Mrs. Christie. I did not guess who the murderer was, I was incited to keep on and find out, and when I did finally find out, I was surprised. Yet I did not care for Agatha Christie and I hope never to read another of her books. I ought, perhaps, to discount the fact that *Death Comes as the End* is supposed to take place in Egypt two thousand years before Christ, so that the book has a flavor of Lloyd C. Douglas not, I understand, quite typical of the author. ("No more Khay in this world to sail on the Nile and catch fish and laugh up into the sun whilst she, stretched out in the boat with little Teti on her lap, laughed back at him"); but her writing is of a mawkishness and banality which seem to me literally impossible to read. You cannot *read* such a book, you run through it to see the problem worked out; and you cannot become interested in the characters, because they never can be allowed an existence of their own even in a flat two dimensions but have always to be contrived so that they can seem either reliable or sinister, depending on which quarter, at the moment, is to be baited for the reader's suspicion. This I had found also a source of annoyance in the case of Mr. Stout, who, however, has created, after a fashion, Nero Wolfe and Archie Goodwin and has made some attempt at characterization of the people that figure in the crimes; but Mrs. Christie, in proportion as she is more expert and concentrates more narrowly on the puzzle, has to eliminate human interest completely, or, rather, fill in the picture with what seems to me a distasteful parody of it. In this new novel, she has to provide herself with puppets who will be good for three stages of suspense: you must first wonder who is going to be murdered, you must then wonder who is committing the murders, and you must finally be unable to foresee which of two men the heroine will marry. It is all like a sleight-of-hand trick, in which the magician diverts your attention from the awkward or irrelevant movements that conceal the manipulation of the cards, and it may mildly entertain and astonish you, as such a sleight-of-hand performance may. But in a performance like *Death Comes as the End,* the patter is a constant bore and the properties lack the elegance of playing cards.

Still fearing that I might be unjust to a department of literature that seemed to be found so absorbing by many, I went back and read *The Maltese Falcon,* which I assumed to be a classic in the field, since it had been called by Alexander Woollcott "the best detective story America has yet produced" and since, at the time of its publication, it had immediately caused Dashiell Hammett to become—in Jimmy Durante's phrase, referring to himself—"duh toast of duh intellectuals." But it was difficult for me to understand what they had thought—in 1930—they were toasting. Mr. Hammett did have the advantage of real experience as a Pinkerton detective, and he infused the old formula of Sherlock Holmes with a certain cold underworld brutality which gave readers a new shudder in the days when it was fashionable to be interested in gangsters; but, beyond this, he lacked the ability to bring the story to imaginative life. As a writer, he is surely almost as far below the rank of Rex Stout as Rex Stout is below that of James Cain. *The Maltese Falcon* today seems not much above those newspaper picture-strips in which you follow from day to day the ups and downs of a strong-jawed hero and a hardboiled but beautiful adventuress.

What, then, is the spell of the detective story that has been felt by T. S. Eliot and Paul Elmer More but which I seem incapable of feeling? As a department of imaginative writing, it looks to me completely dead. The spy story may perhaps only now be realizing its poetic possibilities, as the admirers of Graham Greene contend; and the murder story that exploits psychological horror is an entirely different matter. But the detective story proper had borne all its finest fruits by the end of the nineteenth century, having only declined from the point where Edgar Allan Poe had been able to communicate to M. Dupin something of his own ratiocinative intensity and where Dickens had invested his plots with a social and moral significance that made the final solution of the mystery a revelatory symbol of something that the author wanted seriously to say. Yet the detective story has kept its hold; had even, in the two decades between the great wars, become more popular than ever before; and there is, I believe, a deep reason for this. The world during those years was ridden by an all-pervasive feeling of guilt and by a fear of impending disaster which it seemed hopeless to try to avert because it never seemed conclusively possible to pin down the responsibility. Who had committed the original crime and who was going to commit the next one?—that second murder which always, in the novels, occurs at an unexpected moment when the investigation is well under way; which, as in one of the Nero Wolfe stories, may take place right in the great detective's office. Everybody is suspected in turn, and the streets are full of lurking agents whose allegiances we cannot know. Nobody seems guiltless, nobody seems safe; and then, suddenly, the murderer is spotted, and—relief!—he is not, after all, a person like you or me. He is a villain—known to the trade as George Gruesome—and he has been caught by an infallible Power, the supercilious and omniscient detective, who knows exactly where to fix the guilt. (pp. 231-37)

> *Edmund Wilson, "Why Do People Read Detective Stories?" in his* Classics and Commercials: A Literary Chronicle of the Forties, *Farrar, Straus and Company, 1950, pp. 231-37.*

Bernard DeVoto

[*An editor of the* Saturday Review of Literature *and longtime contributor to* Harper's Magazine, *DeVoto was a highly controversial literary critic and historian. A man whose thought enraged much of America's literary establishment during the 1930s and 1940s, he was frequently motivated by anger at authors he considered ignorant of American life and history. As a critic, he admired mastery of form and psychological subtlety. His own work is characterized by its scholarly thoroughness and by its vigorous, infectious style. DeVoto was "profoundly interested" in American history and authored several historical works, notably the Pulitzer Prize-winning* Across the Wide Missouri *(1947). In a response to Edmund Wilson's 1944 essay "Why Do People Read Detective Fiction?" (above), DeVoto argues against evaluating detective fiction by criteria more appropriate to serious literature, and offers a defense of the genre.*]

My respect for Mr. Wilson is on record (see for example *Minority Report,*) and extends to nearly any kind of opinion he may see fit to express but not, it has been revealed to me, every kind of opinion. For Mr. Wilson recently found himself obliged to discuss detective stories. The mood in which he approached them might seem to a censorious eye, which I do not profess to have, a trifle lofty, patronizing, and academic. Be that as it may, the standard operating procedure plunged him deep into irrelevance, his professional imperatives threw him out of orientation with his subject, and he brought in a cosmic finding that was almost cosmically cockeyed. I'm sorry, his piece was so wrong that there is nothing to do but correct him and explain what this form of literature is and how we who read it feel about it.

First, Jacques Futrelle belongs to what Mr. Lewis Mumford, if he reads detective stories, calls the paleotechnic age. For first-rate stuff by contemporaries of Futrelle who managed to transcend their time (as Coleridge and Mallarmé did) he should have looked up Frederick Irving Anderson and Melville Davisson Post. As for Poe, he was not even eotechnic. Sherlock Holmes was right when he remarked that M. Dupin's "ratiocinative intensity" was nonsense, and if Mr. Wilson will read Poe's ratiocinative stories without regard to the imposing but irrelevant fact that Poe was a precursor of the symbolists, he will see that those precursors of the detective story are pretty godawful. Moreover, though we revere Conan Doyle as a kind of Tubal Cain we do not think too highly of his stories. When Mr. Wilson finds "wit and fairy-tale poetry" in them he finds something which a critical tradition says is there but which we cannot uncover. The Baker Street Irregulars (I do not belong) and their rituals ought not to impose on Mr. Wilson. The point is that the detective story, as a literary form, has developed with great rapidity, that its techniques have advanced far beyond Doyle, and that to compare Rex Stout with Doyle is equivalent to comparing *Ulysses* with, say, *Rosalind.* Finally, Doyle did not invent "the Sherlock Holmes formula" nor does Rex Stout use it any more intensively than Poe did.

When Mr. Wilson complains about bad writing in mysteries his scale and comparisons trouble me. I too think that Mr. Stout writes better prose than Mr. Hammett but I cannot agree that Mr. Cain is better still. Besides, is there not a question of function? If distinguished prose as such is what Mr. Wilson wants, let him try Mr. Raymond Chandler. In fact, let him try Mr. Chandler on any ground, for he is one of the best mystery writers now practicing, has carried the Hammett subspecies to a distinction its originator never attained, and in a recent movie greatly improved on Mr. Cain's dialogue. Mr. Carter Dickson and Mr. Dickson Carr writes (the verb is correct) excellent prose, so does H. C. Bailey, so do Margery Allingham and Ngaio Marsh and Dorothy Sayers, so do many others. But though good prose as such is a virtue in mystery stories it is by no means indispensable. The mysteries of Erle Stanley Gardner and A. A. Fair are among the very best there are, but the prose is commonplace; some first-rate mysteries are written in tolerably bad prose. Mr. Wilson is accustomed to a similar phenomenon in novels and would hardly require Theodore Dreiser to write gracefully or forbid Scott Fitzgerald to be rhetorical. In mysteries, as in impure forms of fiction, good writing is not exclusively or even fundamentally good prose. Writing is a means to an end; it is good writing when it furthers that end.

And will Mr. Wilson be so good as to stop asking Mr. Stout to be Proust? Will he please stop applying to mystery stories critical criteria which, when applied to them, produce nonsense? He complains that he cannot go slow enough to read Agatha Christie for values because she forces him to hurry on and find out how the puzzle is solved. Yes, and Thomas Nashe's "In Time of Plague" is also excellently achieved in its own terms. He complains that Mr. Stout does not provide sufficient psychological subtlety to absorb his interest, and reduces me to awe and reverence by saying that Mr. Hammett "lacks the ability to bring the story to imaginative life."

See here. Some of us mystery fans, like Woodrow Wilson, have quite liberal ideas; some of us, like W. B. Yeats, are widely acquainted with literature; some of us, like me, know how to use the jargon of literary criticism. But it happens, and without derogation of Proust or of ourselves, that there come times when we don't feel like reading Proust. Live and let live, in the house of literature there are many mansions, and let us be no more magisterial than the context requires. There are many kinds of mysteries.

Some of us don't like some of the kinds; some of us like all kinds; few of us suppose that our preferences represent a law of nature or an imperative of taste. Some like the kind which Mr. Wilson would apparently favor if he liked any kind, those which employ an "ingenious or picturesque or amusing" criminal device. I like a plain shooting, myself, though my enthusiasm Mr. Stout has used a bushmaster and a hoked-up golf club, my enthusiasm Mr. Dickson likes a room locked on the inside and produced one of his corpses with a crossbow, and one of the best of all mystery stories employed a burning-glass. Some of us like them simple, some complicated; some like an additional ingredient of battery or romance or horseplay; some like the mystery undiluted. I suppose we fall into two great classes, those who insist on the puzzle being airtight and rigorous and those who are willing to accept a somewhat less than perfect puzzle if the story is good enough. But all of us insist on a murder, the events that led up to it and those that followed it, and a solution of the mystery it caused.

Well, sinners, no writer who gives us that is going to be able to give us Charlus too. For what he must give us to satisfy our demand is, to get back to the jargon, story. We can have Charlus or we can have story but we can't have both. A writer who is engaged in telling us objectively

what happened and in what sequence and why, in constructing a coherent and accelerating narrative, in giving us both drama and puzzle, is quite unable to be Proust at the same time. Furthermore, it is a principle of fiction that if we had Charlus we would be so deeply engrossed with him that we could not bear to have him killed, by crossbow or Army .45, in Chapter Two.

So that Mr. Wilson, to explain the cult of mystery stories, need not have developed the psycho-metaphysical theory which makes him conclude that the anarchy and especially the insecurity of our time are responsible. It is simpler than that. For nearly a century now the scope of the novel has been widening to include things never dreamed of by Fielding or Smollett: dissection of motive, exploration of psychological states, social analysis and criticism, economic theorizing, every conceivable variety of thesis and crusade. All this has greatly enriched the novel but also it has steadily diminished the element of narrative, of pure story, diminished and sometimes threatened to destroy it. But the element of narrative, which first brought the novel into existence, is indestructible. It expresses a deep and everlasting need which many people bring to literature, and if you heave it out the door it always comes back in through the window.

Dust jacket for an American edition of Dorothy Sayers's Murder Must Advertise.

Coming back in through the window, it has produced the detective story. The detective story, or rather the mystery story (which is the inclusive term), is a thoroughly legitimate form of fiction and it is so popular right now because it is the only current form of fiction that is pure story. Mr. Wilson is under no obligation to enjoy the form but his dislike of it is not a disparagement—he need not suppose that because he is virtuous there will be no more Archie Goodwins or tolerably cultivated people to enjoy them. But if he does not like detective stories, the trade in which he holds a union card nevertheless requires him to understand the form better than he has understood it so far. Let him begin by realizing that it takes a considerable expertness at the art of fiction to write a good one. (pp. 36-7)

Bernard DeVoto, "The Easy Chair," in Harper's Magazine, *Vol. 190, No. 1135, December, 1944, pp. 34-7.*

Edmund Wilson

[In the essay below from 1945, Wilson responds to commentary about his essay "Why Do People Read Detective Stories?"]

Three months ago I wrote an article on some recent detective stories. I had not read any fiction of this kind since the days of Sherlock Holmes, and, since I constantly heard animated discussions of the merits of the mystery writers, I was curious to see what they were like today. The specimens I tried I found disappointing, and I made some rather derogatory remarks in connection with my impressions of the genre in general. To my surprise, this brought me letters of protest in a volume and of a passionate earnestness which had hardly been elicited even by my occasional criticisms of the Soviet Union. Of the thirty-nine letters that have reached me, only seven approve my strictures. The writers of almost all the others seem deeply offended and shocked, and they all say almost exactly the same thing: that I had simply not read the right novels and that I would surely have a different opinion if I would only try this or that author recommended by the correspondent. In many of these letters there was a note of asperity, and one lady went so far as to declare that she would never read my articles again unless I were prepared to reconsider my position. In the meantime, furthermore, a number of other writers have published articles defending the detective story: Jacques Barzun, Joseph Wood Krutch, Raymond Chandler and Somerset Maugham have all had something to say on the subject—nor has the umbrageous Bernard DeVoto failed to raise his voice [see above excerpts from the Chandler and DeVoto essays; see Further Reading: Secondary Sources for the essays by Barzun (1944), Krutch, and Maugham].

Overwhelmed by so much insistence, I at last wrote my correspondents that I would try to correct any injustice by undertaking to read some of the authors that had received the most recommendations and taking the whole matter up again. The preferences of these readers, however, when I had a tabulation of them made, turned out to be extremely divergent. They ranged over fifty-two writers and sixty-seven books, most of which got only one or two votes each. The only writers who got as many as five or over were Dorothy L. Sayers, Margery Allingham, Ngaio Marsh, Michael Innes, Raymond Chandler and the author who

writes under the names of Carter Dickson and John Dickson Carr.

The writer that my correspondents were most nearly unanimous in putting at the top was Miss Dorothy L. Sayers, who was pressed upon me by eighteen people, and the book of hers that eight of them were sure I could not fail to enjoy was a story called *The Nine Tailors.* Well, I set out to read *The Nine Tailors* in the hope of tasting some novel excitement, and I declare that it seems to me one of the dullest books I have ever encountered in any field. The first part of it is all about bell-ringing as it is practised in English churches and contains a lot of information of the kind that you might expect to find in an encyclopedia article on campanology. I skipped a good deal of this, and found myself skipping, also, a large section of the conversations between conventional English village characters: "Oh, here's Hinkins with the aspidistras. People may say what they like about aspidistras, but they do go on all the year round and make a background," etc. There was also a dreadful stock English nobleman of the casual and debonair kind, with the embarrassing name of Lord Peter Wimsey, and, although he was the focal character in the novel, being Miss Dorothy Sayers's version of the inevitable Sherlock Holmes detective, I had to skip a good deal of him, too. In the meantime, I was losing the story, which had not got a firm grip on my attention, but I went back and picked it up and steadfastly pushed through to the end, and there I discovered that the whole point was that if a man was shut up in a belfry while a heavy peal of chimes was being rung, the vibrations of the bells might kill him. Not a bad idea for a murder, and Conan Doyle would have known how to dramatize it in an entertaining tale of thirty pages, but Miss Sayers had not hesitated to pad it out to a book of three hundred and thirty, contriving one of those hackneyed cock-and-bull stories about a woman who commits bigamy without knowing it, and larding the whole thing with details of church architecture, bits of quaint lore from books about bell-ringing and the awful whimsical patter of Lord Peter.

I had often heard people say that Dorothy Sayers wrote well, and I felt that my correspondents had been playing her as their literary ace. But, really, she does not write very well: it is simply that she is more consciously literary than most of the other detective-story writers and that she thus attracts attention in a field which is mostly on a subliterary level. In any serious department of fiction, her writing would not appear to have any distinction at all. Yet, commonplace in this respect though she is, she gives an impression of brilliant talent if we put her beside Miss Ngaio Marsh, whose *Overture to Death* was also suggested by several correspondents. Mr. De Voto has put himself on record as believing that Miss Marsh, as well as Miss Sayers and Miss Allingham, writes her novels in "excellent prose," and this throws for me a good deal of light on Mr. De Voto's opinions as a critic. I hadn't quite realized before, though I had noted his own rather messy style, to what degree he was insensitive to writing. I do not see how it is possible for anyone with a feeling for words to describe the unappetizing sawdust which Miss Marsh has poured into her pages as "excellent prose" or as prose at all except in the sense that distinguishes prose from verse. And here again the book is mostly padding. There is the notion that you could commit a murder by rigging up a gun in a piano in such a way that the victim will shoot himself when he presses down the pedal, but this is embedded in the dialogue and doings of a lot of faked-up English county people who are even more tedious than those of *The Nine Tailors.*

The enthusiastic reader of detective stories will indignantly object at this point that I am reading for the wrong things: that I ought not to be expecting good writing, characterization, human interest or even atmosphere. He is right, of course, though I was not fully aware of it till I attempted *Flowers for the Judge,* considered by connoisseurs one of the best books of one of the masters of this school, Miss Margery Allingham. This tale I found completely unreadable. The story and the writing both showed a surface so wooden and dead that I could not keep my mind on the page. How can you care who committed a murder which has never really been made to take place, because the writer hasn't any ability of even the most ordinary kind to persuade you to see it or feel it? How can you probe the possibilities of guilt among characters who all seem alike, because they are all simply names on the page? It was then that I understood that a true connoisseur of this fiction must be able to suspend the demands of his imagination and literary taste and take the thing as an intellectual problem. But how you arrive at that state of mind is what I do not understand.

In the light of this revelation, I feel that it is probably irrelevant to mention that I enjoyed *The Burning Court,* by John Dickson Carr, more than the novels of any of these ladies. There is a tinge of black magic that gives it a little of the interest of a horror story, and the author has a virtuosity at playing with alternative hypotheses that makes this trick of detective fiction more amusing than it usually is.

I want, however, to take up certain points made by the writers of the above-mentioned articles.

Mr. Barzun informs the non-expert that the detective novel is a kind of game in which the reader of a given story, in order to play properly his hand, should be familiar with all the devices that have already been used in other stories. These devices, it seems, are now barred: the reader must challenge the writer to solve his problem in some novel way, and the writer puts it up to the reader to guess the new solution. This may be true, but I shall never qualify. I would rather play Twenty Questions, which at least does not involve the consumption of hundreds of ill-written books.

A point made by three of these writers, Mr. Maugham, Mr. De Voto and Mr. Krutch, is that the novel has become so philosophical, so psychological and so symbolic that the public have had to take to the detective story as the only department of fiction where pure story-telling survives.

This seems to me to involve two fallacies. On the one hand, it is surely not true that "the serious novelists of today"—to quote Mr. Maugham's assertion—"have often," in contrast to the novelists of the past, "little or no story to tell," that "they have allowed themselves to be persuaded that to tell a story is a negligible form of art." It is true, of course, that Joyce and Proust—who, I suppose, must be accounted the heaviest going—have their various modern ways of boring and playing tricks on the reader. But how about the dreadful bogs and obstacles that one has to get over in Scott? the interpolated essays in Hugo? the leaking tap of Thackeray's reflections on life, in which the story is always trickling away? Is there anything in first-rate modern fiction quite so gratuitous as these *longueurs?* Even Proust and Joyce and Virginia Woolf do certainly have stories to tell, and they have organized their books with an intensity which has been relatively rare in the novel and which, to my mind, more than makes up for the occasional viscosity of their narrative.

On the other hand, it seems to me—for reasons suggested above—a fantastic misrepresentation to say that the average detective novel is an example of good storytelling. The gift for telling stories is uncommon, like other artistic gifts, and the only one of this group of writers—the writers my correspondents have praised—who seems to me to possess it to any degree is Mr. Raymond Chandler. His *Farewell, My Lovely* is the only one of these books that I have read all of and read with enjoyment. But Chandler, though in his recent article he seems to claim Hammett as his master, does not really belong to this school of the old-fashioned detective novel. What he writes is a novel of adventure which has less in common with Hammett than with Alfred Hitchcock and Graham Greene—the modern spy story which has substituted the jitters of the Gestapo and the G.P.U. for the luxury world of E. Phillips Oppenheim. It is not simply a question here of a puzzle which has been put together but of a malaise conveyed to the reader, the horror of a hidden conspiracy that is continually turning up in the most varied and unlikely forms. To write such a novel successfully you must be able to invent character and incident and to generate atmosphere, and all this Mr. Chandler can do, though he is a long way below Graham Greene. It was only when I got to the end that I felt my old crime-story depression descending upon me again—because here again, as is so often the case, the explanation of the mysteries, when it comes, is neither interesting nor plausible enough. It fails to justify the excitement produced by the elaborate build-up of picturesque and sinister happenings, and one cannot help feeling cheated.

My experience with this second batch of novels has, therefore, been even more disillusioning than my experience with the first, and my final conclusion is that the reading of detective stories is simply a kind of vice that, for silliness and minor harmfulness, ranks somewhere between smoking and crossword puzzles. This conclusion seems borne out by the violence of the letters I have been receiving. Detective-story readers feel guilty, they are habitually on the defensive, and all their talk about "well-written" mysteries is simply an excuse for their vice, like the reasons that the alcoholic can always produce for a drink. One of the letters I have had shows the addict in his frankest and most shameless phase. This lady begins by pretending, like the others, to guide me in my choice, but she breaks down and tells the whole dreadful truth. Though she has read, she says, hundreds of detective stories, "it is surprising," she finally confesses,

> how few I would recommend to another. However, a poor detective story is better than none at all. Try again. With a little better luck, you'll find one you admire and enjoy. Then you, too, may be A MYSTERY FIEND.

This letter has made my blood run cold: so the opium

smoker tells the novice not to mind if the first pipe makes him sick; and I fall back for reassurance on the valiant little band of my readers who sympathize with my views on the subject. One of these tells me that I have underestimated both the badness of detective stories themselves and the lax mental habits of those who enjoy them. The worst of it is, he says, that the true addict, half the time, never even finds out who has committed the murder. The addict reads not to find anything out but merely to get the mild stimulation of the succession of unexpected incidents and of the suspense itself of *looking forward* to learning a sensational secret. That this secret is nothing at all and does not really account for the incidents does not matter to such a reader. He has learned from his long indulgence how to connive with the author in the swindle: he does not pay any real attention when the disappointing dénouement occurs, he does not think back and check the events, he simply shuts the book and starts another.

To detective-story addicts, then, I say: Please do not write me any more letters telling me that I have not read the right books. And to the seven correspondents who are with me and who in some cases have thanked me for helping them to liberate themselves from a habit which they recognized as wasteful of time and degrading to the intellect but into which they had been bullied by convention and the portentously invoked examples of Woodrow Wilson and André Gide—to these staunch and pure spirits I say: Friends, we represent a minority, but Literature is on our side. With so many fine books to be read, so much to be studied and known, there is no need to bore ourselves with this rubbish. And with the paper shortage pressing on all publication and many first-rate writers forced out of print, we shall do well to discourage the squandering of this paper that might be put to better use. (pp. 257-65)

> Edmund Wilson, *"Who Cares Who Killed Roger Ackroyd?" in his* Classics and Commercials: A Literary Chronicle of the Forties, *Farrar, Straus and Company, 1950, pp. 257-65.*

Richard Slotkin

[*Slotkin is an American educator, critic, and fiction writer whose works, including* Regeneration Through Violence: The Mythology of the American Frontier, 1600-1860 *(1973), and* The Fatal Environment: The Myth of the Frontier in the Age of Industrialization, 1800-1890 *(1985), reflect his interest in American history and the development of an American mythology. In the following excerpt, he traces the character of the hard-boiled detective to conventions established in American frontier literature and suggests that the attraction of the hard-boiled school lies in the character of the hard-boiled detective, who simultaneously embodies two popular and appealing cultural archetypes: the strong authority figure on the side of the law and the romantically conceived solitary outlaw.*]

In an essay called "The Simple Art of Murder" the American detective writer Raymond Chandler distinguished between two traditions in the writing of detective novels [see essay above]. One he called the puzzle tradition and he identified it mainly with English mystery writers like Arthur Conan Doyle and Agatha Christie. The other tradi-

tion, which Chandler claimed for himself and characterized as American, he called the realist tradition.

In the puzzle tradition the story centers on the resolution of an intellectual problem in the form of a murder which generally is framed in a remote and eccentric setting. The reader is invited to join with the detective in the play of resolution. In the realist tradition, on the other hand, the solving of a simple act of murder engages detective and reader with a real and realistically rendered social environment. The intellectual analysis of clues cannot be pursued in studied isolation. It is complicated by the milieu, and by the cross-conflicts born of family psychology, urban life, social divisions, the struggle between law and justice, and power politics at both the street and the board room level. In brief, where the puzzle tradition reduces crime to an intellectual game, the realist tradition makes the pursuit of the criminal the vehicle for active engagement with social life.

But there is a difference between the realism of the detective novel and the realism of, for example, a Victorian novel or a modern work of naturalistic fiction. The realism of the American detective story is defined not by documentary accuracy but by *hard-boiled* realism, which embodies a view of social life from the perspective of the underworld or, as Raymond Chandler put it, from the perspective of the mean streets. This is Chandler's description:

> The realist in murder writes of a world in which gangsters can rule nations and almost rule cities, in which hotels and apartment houses and celebrated restaurants are owned by men who made their money out of brothels, in which a screen star can be the finger man for a mob, and the nice man down the hall is boss of the numbers racket. A world where a judge with a cellar full of bootleg liquor can send a man to jail for having a pint in his pocket. Where the mayor of your town may have condoned murder as an instrument of money making. Where no man can walk down a dark street in safety because law and order are things we talk about but refrain from practicing. It is not a fragrant world, but it is the world you live in.

Streets in hard-boiled fiction are always mean, whether they are in slums or suburbs. It is their meanness that makes them seem realistic. The central mystery of the hard-boiled detective story is not the discovery of who killed Roger Ackroyd, but rather the discovery that our worst suspicions about our society are true, that behind the facades of prosperity and order the world is really run by criminal conspiracies, driven by greed, establishing themselves through violence: the discovery, as a Chandler character says in *The Long Goodbye,* that "there ain't no clean way to make a hundred million bucks."

What interests me . . . is just why it is that Americans seem to delight in this hard-boiled view which seems to run contrary to our cultural tendency toward optimism and our complacent pride in American democracy and achievements. And with that, I'd like to tell how it was that detective stories became the vehicle for this hard-boiled perspective.

From the beginnings of the American republic, popular culture has provided one of the primary means of public education. Mass-circulation journals and newspapers and popular novels and histories are often the first places where Americans have gone to acquire a knowledge of history and politics. And certainly people spend more time in that kind of reading than they do doing their homework while they're in school. Popular novels are particularly powerful because their teaching is so entertaining, and because the historical and moral concepts they deal with are described in vivid detail and linked to appealing personalities.

One of the earliest and most fundamental of American conflicts was that between settlers and Indians for control of the expanding American frontier. So it isn't surprising that among the most popular types of novel in the early nineteenth century was the frontier romance, as it was called, a genre whose form was established in the 1820s by James Fenimore Cooper. Cooper's novels used the conflict between Indians and whites as a metaphor for the basic conflicts of American society. The racial and cultural conflict between Indians and whites was echoed in Cooper by the opposition between whites and Negro slaves, or by the division in American white society between haves and have-nots, between traditional landowners and the ambitious lower classes that were trying to displace them. According to Cooper, American history can be symbolically represented as a war of races in which white pushes against, and ultimately replaces, vanishing red men. The stakes in the conflict are economic (land and resources) and spiritual, and the struggle is fought on both levels. If white triumphs, then the resources of the New World become the basis of progress; if red triumphs, which the reader knows will not happen historically, then progress halts.

However, the struggle requires certain white men to learn enough of the Indian way so that they can bring about the triumph of civilization. These white men who learn the Indian way become spiritually isolated from the white society; they forget their place in the social hierarchy. Cooper calls one class of these people a kind of evil version of the "squatter" class: those who live like Indians but try to accumulate property by stealing marginal lands from rightful white landowners. In a series of novels, *The Little Page Manuscripts,* which he wrote toward the end of his life, he has a volume actually called *The Red Skins,* in which there are no Indians; the red skins of the title are the squatters, the white-skinned squatters.

The struggle is symbolized by Cooper in the rescue of a captive white woman from the polluting clutch of heathen hands, and the woman symbolizes the stakes of the conflict. She embodies all the civilized and Christian values that ought to dominate in a civilized society. To possess the woman is, in a sense, to control the essence of civilization itself. If this woman falls into Indian hands and is either killed or raped, then the core of civilization has been either lost or polluted, and it is in the nature of the Indian, says Cooper, to try to do exactly this. But Indians are not the only threats to the woman. There are those corrupt squatters and lower-class whites, and even corrupt aristocrats, who would also like to marry or possess the virtuous woman. Cooper's fictional solution is to provide each heroine with a romantic hero of her own race and class to marry. But the problem with this romantic hero is that he doesn't know how to deal with Indians. His hands are too clean. So Cooper invents another character, the character of Hawkeye or Natty Bumppo, who will never get the girl but who understands how to fight the forces that threaten the white woman.

Hawkeye is a white man who has been raised by a particularly noble race of Indians. He has acquired all of their skills and none of the racial vices of the Indians. He is loyal, above all, to his own color because he is by birth a white man. He is a man who lives in both worlds, understands both, but belongs to neither. He criticizes both whites and Indians from an independent moral perspective. His sexual attitudes define his social position: he is too white to fall in love with and marry an Indian woman, so he will never be a savage, and he is too aware of his low social status to propose marriage to any white woman, so he will never become a threat to the romantic hero and the propertied classes. His antipathy for marriage is a metaphor for his attitude toward property. Since he will never own a white woman, he will never own any land either. The two seem to go together. Although he has an Indian companion, this figure is essentially a solitary man who is lonely in his integrity, belonging neither to the Indian nor to the white world but understanding both.

There are real affinities between this figure and the classic private eye. Here is Chandler's description of his idea of the private eye:

> Down these mean streets a man must go who is not himself mean, who is neither tarnished nor afraid. The detective in this story must be such a man. He's the hero. He's everything. He must be a complete man and a common man, yet an unusual man. He must be, to use a rather weathered phrase, a man of honor. He is neither a eunuch nor a satyr. I think he might seduce a duchess, and I'm quite sure he would not spoil a virgin. If he is a man of honor in one thing, he's that in all things. He is a relatively poor man, or he would not be a detective at all. He is a common man or he could not go among common people. He has a sense of character or he would not know his job. He will take no man's money dishonestly, and no man's insolence without due and dispassionate revenge. He is a lonely man, and his pride is that you will treat him as a proud man or be very sorry you ever saw him.

The story, says Chandler, is this man's adventure in search of a hidden truth, and although their environments are different, Hawkeye and the detective have a similar kind of quest in mind: they are both rescuers. They are out to rescue people—usually women—from some kind of threat. They achieve the rescue by following a path of clues (or in Cooper's case of Indian tracks) to the hidden goal. In Cooper's novels there is often a kind of mystery to be solved as well, involving somebody who has been defrauded of an inheritance or is living under a secret identity or something like that. Hawkeye and a Chandler detective are both solitary men who can operate as Indians or as whites, on the common side—the mean street side—or on the polite side. Likewise, they serve a bourgeois society but never compromise themselves by accepting its most corrupting social value. They do not do what they do for money. And they are engaged in unmasking a hidden truth. In Cooper, this is the truth of racial and ethnic incompatibility which will require white and Indian to keep massacring each other until one of them has been wiped out.

At its earliest point of origin . . . the hard-boiled detective story focuses on a similar theme: the idea that society is divided between classes of congenital criminals (white savages) and the rest of the citizens. But the detective story developed toward the discovery of a different kind of social truth.

There are some stages which the story goes through. . . . First does come the frontier romance. Then there is a kind of intermediate stage: stories about adventures that occur just behind the white-Indian frontier, in which semicivilized whites form the basic criminal classes and have to be exterminated in almost the same way that the Indians were. Very often these criminals are represented either as allies of another non-white race, as in the case of Murrell, or as lunatics or psychopaths, as in the case of the notorious Harpe brothers. I call them Harpies (although the name is pronounced "Harp") because you need to think of them as kind of mythological monsters. If gangsters like Murrell and the Harpes could arise in the backwash of the frontier where life is still open and property can still be gotten not by robbing your neighbor but by simply clearing off a small piece of land, what sorts of crime might be expected to occur in cities?

Cities had traditionally been associated with crime and corruption, born of a contrast of haves and have-nots living side by side. Jefferson had even expressed the hope that America might somehow remain a land of farms and plantations, with cities few, culturally insignificant, and fenced off from the rest of society. There was also a popular literature of urban crime whose roots went back to English ballads and pamphlets about London thieves and murderers, collections of which were published in America under the title *Newgate Calendar.* And there were American equivalents, notably the narratives that were appended to execution sermons in colonial New England. However, these stories all center on the pathology of the criminal classes. They do not feature detectives or police officials or vigilantes as heroes. The criminal is usually captured because of his drunken excesses, or because of the routine operations of a faceless constabulary.

The first urban detectives emerged from a hybridization of the frontier romance and the story of the urban sociopath. A key figure here is a man named George Lippard, a best-selling author of sensational fiction of the type now called "bodice rippers," who was also an important spokesman for the Jacksonian labor movement and a writer of patriotic fables. Lippard's novel *Quaker City, or The Monks of Monk Hall,* one of the great lunatic masterpieces of American literature, was published in 1844. Monk Hall is a vast gothic castle or monastery which has somehow grown up in Philadelphia, the city of brotherly love, the model American city. Its presence marks the transfer to the New World of the crime and corruption of the Old. Monk Hall has been built by the wealthy classes as a place for luxurious debauches. And to supply it with prostitutes, the managers of Monk Hall engage in the systematic corruption, seduction, and rape of the virginal daughters of the working and middle classes. As a spokesman for labor, Lippard uses the machinery of the crime novel and the gothic horror tale for ideological purposes. He contrasts the virtues of the so-called producing classes with landlords, bankers, false aristocrats, hypocritical ministers, crooked politicians, and so on. Although the setting is

urban, the plot is the same as that of a Cooper novel, except that this time the wilderness is this huge building. We still identify the enemy by his attempts to capture and rape white women who are the symbols of social and moral value. Lippard emphasizes this structure by describing the inhabitants of the underworld of Monk Hall as "urban savages"—men who might once have been citizens and working men, but who have been so debased by their oppression that they have become both morally and physically deformed.

There are several rescuers who attempt to deal with Monk Hall, one of whom is a kind of urban Hawkeye, a common man of skill and wit who speaks in the vernacular and sees through all hypocrisy. But although Lippard draws on this vocabulary, even his heroes are corrupted by the knowledge that they acquire in the cellars of Monk Hall. Nobody escapes the corruption that lies below the surface of the city of brotherly love. A vision of apocalyptic doom strikes American society at the end of this novel.

After the Civil War, with the increasing pace of industrialization and urbanization, and with rising class tensions now augmented by the fact that many of the working classes were immigrants from non-English-speaking countries or slaves coming up from the South, this imagery of the urban savage becomes very much a part of newspaper language. I will give you just one quotation that sums up this way of thinking. It is a quote from a magazine called the *Nation* (which is still publishing) in response to Custer's last stand (1876).

> There is, among the more rabid country papers just now, a loud demand for the extermination of the Indians, a course for which there is something to be said, if by extermination is meant their rapid slaughter. But if they are to be exterminated, why any longer pauperize them and then arm them? What would be said of the city of New York if, after lodging its thousand tramps in comfortable idleness over the winter, it were to arm them on leaving the almshouse with a revolver and knife and a tinderbox for firing barns? But why should it be worse to do this to savage whites than to savage Indians?

In this environment, with the transfer of the frontier, in a certain sense, to the city, changes occur in popular writing—in the dime novels, for example. Many popular dime-novel figures who began their careers as either Indian-fighters or Wild West figures, begin to be called detectives. Deadwood Dick, for example, is originally the outlaw of the Black Hills but he ends as Deadwood Dick, detective. Buffalo Bill first appeared in dime novels as the man who got the first scalp for Custer, but by the end of his career there are titles like *Buffalo Bill, Detective* and *Buffalo Bill and the Nihilists* (in which he saves a Russian grand duke from an assassination plot).

In this context, in which the race war has now become a class war in the cities, there is one preeminent detective figure who is capable of fighting the urban war as the Indian war had been fought, and this is Allan Pinkerton. He was the head of the first and largest detective agency in the world, and former head of Union army intelligence and counterintelligence during the Civil War—at which he did an absolutely comically execrable job. At one point, he represented General Lee as commanding an army of a quarter of a million men, at a time when there weren't a quarter of a million men under arms in all of the Southern Confederacy. He convinced the head of the Union army that he was perpetually outnumbered. Pinkerton was, however, the nemesis of train robbers and embezzlers, the pursuer of Jesse James, against whom he made his reputation in part. He was the inventor for Americans of the labor spy and of the agent provocateur who broke labor unions. And, not incidentally, he was the author (or the putative author, I should say) of several books, some of which were offered as true accounts, some of which were offered as works of fiction. His most interesting books set the Pinkerton detective against various groups. Of particular interest is one about the breaking of the great coal strike of the mid-1870s, which pits the detective against the Molly Maguires, and *Strikers, Communists, Tramps and Detectives,* which recounts the great railroad strike of 1877.

According to Pinkerton, prevailing practice in the work of police and detective agencies before him had been to set a thief to catch a thief, to use corrupt people as informers. This resulted in an important alliance between law enforcers and the criminal classes. But Pinkerton proposed to train and employ detectives of the highest moral character, chaste men who would forswear drinking and smoking except when on duty! Their task would be to adopt the disguise of the criminal and the working-class malcontent, and to ferret out evil from within society. Pinkerton, in fact, was also running a large-scale vigilante operation. Many of his detectives were involved in fomenting lynch mobs to finish off criminals whose convictions the case would not sustain. The Reno gang in Indiana is one of the first cases of this, but Pinkerton also tried to frame I.W.W. leaders like Bill Haywood. And Dashiell Hammett, who was a Pinkerton man at one time, claimed that he was asked to assassinate a labor leader named Frank Little. But none of this vigilantism ever appears in a Pinkerton novel. His fictional detectives are very straight, they always get their man, and the criminal is always convicted by legal means. In these novels Pinkerton is not an actual operative, but a paternal figure who tells the story and very often gives you his introduction to the life of a detective. He teaches the detective the way to do things and then sends him out to have the adventure.

The heroes, through whose eyes the adventurous part of the story is seen, are also latter-day Hawkeyes. They are men who can live and deal with the criminal classes and seem to be at one with them, but whose pure hearts are firmly on the side of law. McParland, the detective hero who infiltrates the Molly Maguires, is chosen because he's an Irishman. To recruit him, Pinkerton convinces McParland that the Molly Maguires are actually a corrupt extension of a certain type of Irish nationalist group, against whom McParland's family had worked in the Old Country. Much is made of the fact that the Mollies have weird rituals and a kind of tribalist ethic. Pinkerton compares them to the thuggees of India, a sect of supposedly murderous fanatics who worship the goddess Kali. One action wing of the Mollies is called the Modacs, the name of an Indian tribe which had recently been at war with the United States and had assassinated a brigadier general at a peace conference. As Pinkerton's son later wrote, "The case required something more than mere pecuniary reward to secure the right sort of person. McParland doesn't

do it for money. He has to feel he's serving his church, his race, and his country" (just like the Deerslayer).

As a test, Pinkerton requires McParland to do research on secret societies and present a report. The report reveals that McParland is a wretched historian, but that his political prejudice lets him see the Molly Maguires as something after the fashion of the Ku Klux Klan, a group which initially, according to McParland, served a liberating function but which later became an excuse for robbery and murder. McParland disguises himself as a miner, infiltrates the Molly Maguires, and not only exposes them but provokes them to actions that will get them arrested. As the story unfolds, he is tempted by the Mollies—they are his Irish brethren, after all—but he always overcomes the temptation and remains true. This is all, of course, phony. McParland fabricated evidence, as he did again later in his testimony against the I. W. W. But for purposes of the novel, none of this appears. McParland does his job well.

Pinkerton, like Cooper and Lippard, was using a received vocabulary of myths and symbols to create a new model of American society. The stakes in the battle are still the survival of the civilization, with the savage proletariat replacing savage Indians. But where Cooper's story is open-ended and holds open the possibility of a redemptive triumph, the Pinkerton formula story is much more narrow in its possibilities. You can wipe out one criminal, but there will always be a sequel because there will always be another class of criminal to deal with.

The Pinkerton formula story also has the problem of representing only one side of politics and social life in America in the 1880s. It shows only the corporate side. And the fact is that American society in this period was deeply divided between those who sympathized with the position of labor and those who took the point of view of the trusts and the so-called robber barons. If you look at dime novels published in this period, you see a much more representative sample of story types. There is one series called "New York Detective" that, interestingly, included under the title "Detective" stories about both outlaws and detectives. One of their most popular figures is Jesse James, the Robin Hood of the Old West, who stands for justice where law is not equal to bringing justice to society. And on the other hand, there is a man called Old King Brady, an urban detective, a master of a thousand disguises who puts down smugglers, criminals, and gangsters.

It is interesting that as the series unfolds over a span of about twenty years, the stories begin to blend and merge. At first, Jesse James turns up in New York and is pursued by Old King Brady. Then Old King Brady goes out west and pursues Jesse James. Then Jesse James goes to Mexico and discovers a poor but virtuous woman who is being cheated of her ranch by a wicked banker—and Jesse James turns detective. Then Old King Brady turns up facing a situation in which the law is in the hands of gangsters, so he has to turn into Robin Hood in order to solve the mystery. The detective and the outlaw, in other words, over this twenty-year period, begin to inhabit the same space and finally begin to swap roles. And this, for me, is the root of the modern hard-boiled detective story. It is the combination, in a single figure, of the outlaw and the detective. The inner life of the figure is that of the outlaw, whose perspective is that of a victim of social injustice. He has seen the underside of American democracy and capitalism and can tell the difference between law and justice, and he knows that society lives more by law than by justice. Yet he also embodies the politics of the police detective, the belief that we need order, some kind of code to live by if we are to keep from degenerating into a government of pure muscle and money. And he is willing to use force to impose order and strike a proper balance between law and justice.

The modern hard-boiled detective story arises from a combination of the world view of the Pinkerton novel (society is imperiled by conspiracies reflecting class conflict) and the vaguely populist style and ethic of the frontier outlaw-hero. Dashiell Hammett's work bridges the gap between these two worlds, in two detectives particularly—the Continental Op and Sam Spade. Hammett shows each of them as a person who finally ends up doing the work of law, but who stands finally outside and against law as well. In the novel *Red Harvest*, the Continental Op is supposedly a Pinkerton detective who goes into a town which has been taken over by a corrupt partnership of gangsters and factory-owners who have banded together to break a strike. The Pinkerton ends up acting as an agent provocateur not against the union but against the bosses. He turns the Pinkerton story inside out and on its head, to restore justice from the bottom up. It falsifies the history, but it is a wonderful fantasy and shows the potential of the detective. Again, in *The Maltese Falcon*, Hammett's next novel, the detective is described as a blond Satan. The setting is a little more abstract. This time he is a private entrepreneur; he does not work for a corporation. And we are never quite sure which side of the line Sam Spade is going to come down on. He acts like an outlaw, he acts like he could be a criminal—the cops treat him that way, the criminals treat him that way—yet somehow he comes out on the side of law.

For me, this is the essence of the hard-boiled detective and the secret of his appeal. We are in love with authority, we know that on the one hand we need authority and hard lines of value, and on the other hand that authority is often corrupt and misdirected and that those hard lines of value are often blurry. The detective allows us to enjoy both of those features simultaneously, to play imaginatively at being both policeman and outlaw. (pp. 91-100)

> *Richard Slotkin, "The Hard-Boiled Detective Story: From the Open Range to the Mean Streets," in* The Sleuth and the Scholar: Origins, Evolution and Current Trends in Detective Fiction, *edited by Barbara A. Rader and Howard G. Zettler, Greenwood Press, 1988, pp. 91-100.*

Nicholas Blake [pseudonym of C. Day Lewis]

[Lewis, an English man of letters, is linked with W. H. Auden, Stephen Spender, and Louis MacNeice as one of the leftist Oxford poets of the 1930s. Throughout his career, whether in the overtly political statements of his early poems or in the pastoral lyrics of his maturity, Lewis was concerned with the individual's search for selfhood. Although he was eventually named Poet Laureate of England, Lewis is today generally regarded as a minor figure in modern English poetry. In addition to poetry, Lewis also wrote a series of detective novels under the pseudonym Nicholas Blake. In the following excerpt, he discusses reasons for writing and reading detective fiction.]

"Why do we write detective stories?" Many solutions, all of them correct, will suggest themselves to the reader. Because we want to make money. Because the drug addict (and nearly every detection-writer is an omnivorous reader of crime fiction) always wants to introduce other people to the habit. Because artists have a notorious *nostalgie de la boue* ["nostalgia for the mud"], and our own hygienic, a-moral age offers very little honest mud to revel in except the pleasures of imaginary murder. Democratic civilisation does not encourage us to indulge our instinct for cruelty: the quite different attitude of the dictatorships towards this, as well as their different conception of justice, legal evidence and legal proof, must . . . account for the Nazis' banning of all imported detective-fiction and characterising it as "pure liberalism" designed to "stuff the heads of German readers with foreign ideas": a people whose blood-lust was sublimated by reading and writing fiction murders would certainly have less zest for murdering real Poles.

An agreeable monograph might indeed be written on The First Plunge Into Detective Writing. Gone, alas, are the good old days when "without an idea in his head and with no previous knowledge of crime or criminals, Leblanc [creator of the great Arsène Lupin] took up his pen, and his impudent hero sprang into spontaneous being." So expert and exacting is the detection-fan today that the detective novelist must possess a good working knowledge of police procedure, law and forensic medicine if he is to escape severe letters from the public pointing out his errors: (how many plots, I wonder, have been complicated by the writer's need to skirt round some obstacle raised by his technical ignorance?) From what dark incentive, by what devious and secret psychological passages have detective writers—timid and law-abiding persons for the most part, who faint at the sight of blood and tremble when the eye of a policeman is turned upon them—first set out upon the sinister paths of crime-fiction?

The question is enthralling. But it must here be subsumed under my general question: "The Detective Story—Why?" Why, I mean, has the detective story attained such remarkable popularity, rising . . . from a ratio of twelve in 1914 to ninety-seven in 1925 and two hundred and seventeen in 1939, and holding its own even against that most insidious and degraded of mental recreations, the crossword puzzle?

We may imagine some James Frazer of the year 2042 discoursing on "The Detective Novel—the Folk-Myth of the Twentieth Century." He will, I fancy, connect the rise of crime fiction with the decline of religion at the end of the Victorian era. The sense of guilt, psychologists tell us, is deeply rooted in man and one of the mainsprings of his actions. Just as, in the primitive tribe, the idiot or the scapegoat is venerated and the murderer wreathed with flowers, because he has taken upon himself the guilt of the community, so in more civilised times one function of religion is to take the burden of guilt off the individual's shoulders through the agency of some Divine or apotheosised Being. When a religion has lost its hold upon men's hearts, they must have some other outlet for the sense of guilt.

This, our anthropologist of the year 2042 may argue, was provided for us by crime-fiction. He will call attention to the pattern of the detective-novel, as highly formalised as that of a religious ritual, with its initial necessary sin (the murder), its victim, its high priest (the criminal) who must in turn be destroyed by a yet higher power (the detective). He will conjecture—and rightly—that the devotee identified himself both with the detective and the murderer, representing the light and the dark sides of his own nature. He will note a significant parallel between the formalised dénouement of the detective novel and the Christian concept of the Day of Judgment when, with a flourish of trumpets, the mystery is made plain and the goats are separated from the sheep.

Nor is this all. The figure of the detective himself will be exhaustively analysed. Our anthropologist . . . will have been informed that many readers of crime fiction remembered the name of the detective but not of the book or its author. Sherlock Holmes, Peter Wimsey, Hercule Poirot were evidently figures of supernatural importance to the reader: and to the writer, for their creators bodied them out with a loving veneration which suggested that the Father Imago was at work. The detective is, indeed—to change the metaphor—the Fairy Godmother of the twentieth century folk-myth, his magic capabilities only modified to the requirements of a would-be scientific and rational generation. It will be noted, too, that these semi-divine figures fell into two categories. On the one hand was the more primitive, the anthropomorphised type—Holmes and Wimsey its most celebrated examples—in which human frailty and eccentricity, together with superhuman powers of perception, are carried to a supralogical conclusion. On the other hand there was the so-to-speak modernist detective—generally a policeman rather than an amateur—a figure stripped of human attributes, an instrument of pure reason and justice, the Logos of the detective world.

Such may well be, in brief, the theory advanced by posterity to account for the extraordinary hold which the detective novel possessed on the twentieth-century mind. It would be difficult, at any rate, to explain the popularity of a so fantastic offshoot of literature without reference to some fundamental instinct in mankind.

But the general lines of such an inquiry have not been sufficiently adumbrated if they do not include the minor curiosity of class-bias in crime fiction. It is an established fact that the detective-novel proper is read almost exclusively by the upper and professional classes. The so-called "lower-middle" and "working" classes tend to read "bloods," thrillers. Now this is not simply a matter of literary standards, though the modern thriller is generally much below the detective story in sophistication and style. When we compare these two kinds of crime fiction, we cannot fail to notice that, whereas in the detective novel the criminal is almost invariably a squalid creature of irremediably flagitious tendencies, the criminal of the thriller is often its hero and nearly always a romantic figure.

This is, of course, as Mr. Haycraft has pointed out, a natural development of the Robin Hood myth. The detective story's clientele are relatively prosperous persons, who have a stake in the social system and must, therefore, even in fantasy, see the ultimate triumph of their particular social values ensured. It is significant that even the "thrill-ers" most popular with the ruling classes usually represent their hero as being on the side of law and order—the bourgeois conception of law and order, of course (that unspeakable public school bully and neurotic exhibitionist, Bulldog Drummond, is a case in point), or as a reformed criminal (e.g. Father Brown's right hand man); or, like Arsène Lupin, he starts as a criminal character but, after a number of anti-social adventures, gradually goes over to the other side. Not so with the lower ranks of democratic society. Having little or no stake in the system, they prefer such anarchistic heroes, from Robin Hood down to the tommy-gun gangster, who have held to ransom the prosperous and law-abiding. To such readers the policeman is not the protective figure he appears to your politician, your stockbroker, your rural dean: for them his aura is menacing, his baton an offensive weapon rather than a defensive symbol: and therefore the *roman policier* does not give them much of a kick.

The guilt-motive perhaps operates here too. On the whole, the working classes have less time and incentive than the relatively leisured to worry about their consciences. In so far as their lives are less rich, the taking of life (the detective story's almost invariable subject) will seem to them less significant and horrifying. They themselves sometimes kill for passion; seldom, unlike their more fortunately placed brethren, for gain. The general sense of guilt (which is the reverse or seamy side of social responsibility), the specific moral problems which tease the more prosperous classes, affect them less nearly. So, for them, the detective novel—the fantasy-representation of guilt—must have a shallower appeal.

It is the element of fantasy in detective fiction—or rather, the juxtaposition of fantasy with reality—that gives the genre its identity. . . . Carolyn Wells [proposes the] dictum that "the detective novel must *seem* real in the same sense that fairy tales *seem* real to children" [see excerpt above]. By implication, this statement defines very accurately the boundaries of the detective novel. The fairy tale does not reach its greatest heights when—as in the Irish fairy stories—fantasy is piled on fantasy, but by a judicious blending of the possible with the impossible. Similarly, in crime fiction, if we set down unrealistic characters in fantastic situations, we cross the frontier into the domain of the pure "shocker." If on the other hand both our action and our characters are realistic, we produce fiction of the Francis Iles' type which . . . does not come within the strict canon of the detective story.

The detective novelist, then, is left with two alternatives. He can put unreal characters into realistic situations, or he can put realistic characters into fantastic situations. The former method produces the classical *roman policier,* of which Freeman Wills Crofts is perhaps the most able living exponent, where the crime and the police investigation are conducted on strictly realistic lines, and the element of fantasy necessary to the detection novel is achieved by making the characters simple ciphers—formalised simulacra of men and women, that have no life outside the plot they serve. To call this type of novel "mere puzzles" and decry it for its "un-lifelike" characters is to misunderstand the whole paradox of the detective story.

The second alternative, which has produced the at present most fashionable kind of crime fiction, is to place "real" characters in unreal, fantastic, or at least improbable situations. This school of writing covers a wide range. At one extreme we find such books as John Dickson Carr's, where the plot possesses the mad logic and extravagance of a dream, while the *dramatis personae* are roughed in with just enough solidity to stand out against the macabre and whirling background: (Carr's Dr. Fell, incidentally, may be coupled with Rex Stout's Nero Wolfe as the most notable old-style or anthropomorphic detective in contemporary fiction—wayward, masterful, infallible). At the other extreme we get the work of such writers as Ngaio Marsh. Her Inspector Alleyn, like Michael Innes' detective, is gentlemanly, unobtrusive and almost provocatively normal. Her characters have real body, but derive nothing from textbooks on morbid psychology. Where the characters are ordinary people and the plot is neither *outré* nor melodramatic, one might suppose that the element of paradox necessary to the detective story would be missing. But murder is in itself such an abnormal thing that its mere presence among a number of nice, respectable, civilised characters will be paradox enough.

It is reasonable to suppose that this—the "novel of manners" . . .—will remain a predominant type of detective fiction for some time to come. Certainly we can be sure that the general raising of the literary level in the genre has come to stay. Fresher observation, more careful, realistic handling of character and situation are demanded today, and the general level of detective writing is thus improved. But something has been lost in the process. The high fantasy of the old masters cannot now be achieved. No detective novelist today could allow his hero to exclaim, in a moment of strong excitement, "Hold! Have you some mucilage?"

Another interesting line of development is in the detective himself. For some years, the sleuth has been undergoing modification—a toning down from the Sherlock Holmes to the Roderick Alleyn type. Even when, as with Peter Wimsey, his pedigree, family background, hobbies and tastes are diligently documented, he has become a much less far-fetched personality. If this process continues, we may expect in the future a school of detectives without personality at all. I myself rather fancy the idea of a detective who shall be as undistinguished as a piece of blotting paper, absorbing the reactions of his subjects; a shallow mirror, in which we see reflected every feature of the crime; a pure camera-eye. Professor Thorndyke and Dr. Priestley are precursors to this anonymous type. Inspector Maigret is its highest development up to date.

At first sight Maigret, the most formidable embodiment in crime fiction of the "stern, unhurrying chase" of Justice, might seem also the best model for the ambitious writer today. But his influence may well be disruptive of the detective novel as we know it. It is not simply that Simenon breaks the rules, by allowing Maigret to keep so much of his detection-processes under his hat. The real trouble is Simenon's deep and unerring sense of evil, which in practise runs counter to the basic principle of the detective story—that evil must, both for myth-making and entertainment, be volatised by a certain measure of fantasy. In the Maigret stories, evil hangs over everything, as heavy, as concentrated, as real as a black fog. It is a raw wine, which must burst the old bottles. You may remember that remarkable story in which the criminal is so fascinated by Maigret that he cannot keep away from him: he

is like a moth dashing itself again and again into a passive flame. Now this exemplifies a proved psychological truth. As the Greek tragedians knew, crime carries within itself the seed of retribution; some fatal flaw (or saving grace) in human nature impels a wrong-doer to betray himself: that is why even the most painstaking and cold-blooded murderer is apt to leave a glaring clue behind, or talk too much one evening in the public bar.

This is all very right and proper in real life. But the traditional pattern of the detective novel would be disintegrated if writers emphasised the fact that the criminal does, unconsciously, hunt himself down. The fictional detective's occupation would indeed be gone. Perhaps this is the direction we are to move in. Perhaps the detective story, as we know it, will be supplanted by the crime novel. If so, future generations will look back on Simenon and Iles as the fathers of the new genre. It should be some time though, in any event, before we cease to read murder for pleasure. (pp. 398-405)

Nicholas Blake, "The Detective Story—Why?" in The Art of the Mystery Story: A Collection of Critical Essays, *edited by Howard Haycraft, Simon and Schuster, 1946, pp. 398-405.*

FURTHER READING

I. Anthologies

Barzun, Jacques, ed. *The Delights of Detection.* New York: Criterion Books, 1961, 381 p.
    Anthology of short detective fiction including stories by E. C. Bentley, G. K. Chesterton, R. Austin Freeman, John D. MacDonald, Dorothy Sayers, and Rex Stout, with an introduction by the editor.

Green, Hugh, ed. *The Rivals of Sherlock Holmes: Early Detective Stories.* New York: Pantheon Books, 1970, 351 p.
    Reprints short detective fiction by contemporaries of Sir Arthur Conan Doyle. In an introduction the editor offers biographical and critical commentary about the authors included.

Green, Richard Lancelyn, ed. *The Further Adventures of Sherlock Holmes: After Sir Arthur Conan Doyle.* Harmondsworth, England: Penguin, 1985, 272 p.
    Collection of Holmes pastiches with an introduction by the editor.

Greene, Douglas G., and Adey, Robert C. S., eds. *Death Locked In.* New York: International Polygonics, 1987, 553 p.
    Reprints a selection of "locked-room" murder mysteries by detective and crime fiction writers, including Frederic Brown, John Dickson Carr, Arthur Conan Doyle, Jacques Futrelle, Edward D. Hoch, Ngaio Marsh, Ellery Queen, and Cornell Woolrich. In an introduction the editor discusses the appeal of the locked-room mystery.

Queen, Ellery, ed. *101 Years' Entertainment: The Great Detective Stories, 1841-1941.* New York: Modern Library, 1946, 995 p.

Selection of fifty short detective stories in the categories of "The Great Detectives," "The Great Women Detectives," "The Great Humorous Detectives," "The Great Thieves," "The Great Crime Stories," and "The Detective Story to End Detective Stories." The editors supply an introduction characterizing different types of detective fiction.

Sayers, Dorothy, ed. *The Omnibus of Crime.* New York: Payson and Clarke, 1929, 1177 p.
    Collection of short detective, mystery, crime, and horror fiction. Sayers's introduction is excerpted above.

II. Secondary Sources

"The Passing of the Detective." *The Academy* LXIX, No. 1756 (30 December 1905): 1356-57.
    Contends that modern scientific methods of police investigation render the fictional detective implausible and signify the downfall of the genre.

Adams, Donald K., ed. *The Mystery & Detection Annual.* Beverly Hills, Calif.: Castle Press, 1972, 264 p.
    Thirty-two essays and reviews reflecting the year's scholarship.

————, ed. *The Mystery & Detection Annual.* Beverly Hills, Calif.: Castle Press, 1973, 337 p.
    Thirty-one essays and reviews reflecting the year's scholarship.

Aisenberg, Nadya. *A Common Spring: Crime Novel and Classic.* Bowling Green, Ohio: Bowling Green University Popular Press, 1979, 271 p.
    Suggests that the crime novel is linked thematically and structurally to such archetypal literary forms as the myth and fairy tale, and that it serves a similar function—confirming and reinforcing the moral order in which its readers believe.

Auden, W. H. "The Guilty Vicarage." In his *The Dyer's Hand and Other Essays,* pp. 146-58. New York: Random House, 1962.
    Personal appreciation of the detective story that includes discussion of some characteristics of the genre.

Aydelotte, William O. "The Detective Story as a Historical Source." *The Yale Review* XXXIX, No. 1 (September 1949): 76-95.
    Suggests that "the interest of detective stories to the historian is that they shed light on the people who read them. By studying the fantasies contained in this literature, one may gather a description of its readers, in terms of their unsatisfied motivational drives."

Baker, Robert A., and Nietzel, Michael T. *Private Eyes: One Hundred and One Knights—A Survey of American Detective Fiction, 1922-1984.* Bowling Green, Ohio: Bowling Green State University Popular Press, 1985, 385 p.
    Biographical and critical commentary on twentieth-century detective fiction writers and their works.

Ball, John, ed. *The Mystery Story.* San Diego: University of California, 1976, 390 p.
    Commentary by various critics on mystery, crime, and detective fiction. "The Police Procedural," by Hillary Waugh, is excerpted above.

Bander, Elaine. "The English Detective Novel between the Wars: 1919-1939." *The Armchair Detective* 11, No. 3 (July 1978): 262-73.
    Surveys English detective fiction of the period.

Bargainnier, Earl F., ed. *10 Women of Mystery.* Bowling Green, Ohio: Bowling Green State University Popular Press, 1981, 304 p.
    Collects essays devoted to detective story writers Dorothy Sayers, Josephine Tey, Ngaio Marsh, P. D. James, Ruth Rendell, Anna Katharine Green, Mary Roberts Rinehart, Margaret Millar, Emma Lathen, and Amanda Cross.

Barzun, Jacques. "Not 'Whodunit?' But 'How?': First Aid for Critics of the Detective Story." *The Saturday Review of Literature* (New York) XXVII, No. 45 (4 November 1944): 9-11.
    Offers a concise definition of the detective story—"a narrative of which the chief interest lies in the palpable process of detection"—and discusses some characteristics of the genre.

————. "Requiescat." *Chimera* V, No. 4 (Summer 1947): 59-66.
    Attributes a decline in detective fiction to the restrictive nature of the rules governing the genre.

————, and Taylor, Wendell Hertig. *A Catalog of Crime.* Second edition. New York: Harper & Row, 1971, 831 p.
    Annotated bibliography of nearly 3500 novels, short stories, anthologies, magazines, and dramas of detection, crime, mystery, and espionage, as well as the secondary literature on the genre.

Becker, Jens Peter. "The Mean Streets of Europe: The Influence of the American 'Hard-Boiled School' on European Detective Fiction." Translated by Ian E. Oliver. In *Superculture: American Popular Culture and Europe,* edited by C. W. E. Bigsby, pp. 152-59. London: Paul Elek, 1975.
    Assesses the impact of American hard-boiled detective fiction on European detective fiction.

Benstock, Bernard, ed. *Art in Detective Writing: Essays on Detective Fiction.* New York: St. Martin's Press, 1983, 218 p.
    Includes essays on twentieth-century English, American, and French detective story writers.

Bloom, Clive, et al., eds. *Nineteenth-Century Suspense: From Poe to Conan Doyle.* New York: Macmillan, 1988, 139 p.
    Includes essays on Edgar Allan Poe, Wilkie Collins, and Sir Arthur Conan Doyle in a collection of criticism on suspense, mystery, and horror fiction of the period.

Bogan, Louise. "Detective Novels." In her *A Poet's Alphabet: Reflections on the Literary Art and Vocation,* edited by Robert Phelps and Ruth Limmer, pp. 83-7. New York: McGraw-Hill Book Co., 1970.
    Reprints a 1944 essay assessing detective fiction as worthy of consideration within the mainstream of contemporary literature.

Breen, Jon L. *What about Murder? A Guide to Books about Mystery and Detective Fiction.* Metuchen, N.J.: Scarecrow Press, 1981, 157 p.
    Annotated bibliography of criticism.

Brophy, Brigid. "Detective Fiction: A Modern Myth of Violence?" *The Hudson Review* XVIII, No. 1 (Spring 1965): 11-30.

Contends that detective fiction is as strictly patterned and formulaic as traditional cultural mythology.

Browne, Ray B. *Heroes and Humanities: Detective Fiction and Culture.* Bowling Green, Ohio: Bowling Green State University Popular Press, 1986, 141 p.
Explores the role of the hero and the societal view of the hero in the works of American, Canadian, and Australian detective fiction writers.

Butler, William Vivian. *The Durable Desperadoes.* New York: Macmillan, 1973, 288 p.
Critical examination of some protagonists of English detective, crime, and mystery fiction.

Byrd, Max. "The Detective Detected: From Sophocles to Ross Macdonald." *The Yale Review* LXIV, No. 1 (Autumn 1974): 72-83.
Examines variations on the theme of establishing guilt and innocence in detective fiction.

Caillois, Roger. "Order and License: The Ambiguity of the Detective Story." *Chimera* V, No. 4 (Summer 1947): 67-79.
Translated portion of Caillois's *Le roman policier* (1941), exploring the moral ambiguity sometimes found in detective fiction, in which the detective is often a lawless, and the criminal a sympathetic, figure.

Champigny, Robert. *What Will Have Happened: A Philosophical and Technical Essay on Mystery Stories.* Bloomington: Indiana University Press, 1977, 183 p.
Considers ways in which heightened reader interest in the deliberately obscured denouement of mystery fiction affects aesthetic appreciation of the text.

Chandler, Raymond. *Raymond Chandler Speaking.* Edited by Dorothy Gardiner and Kathrine Sorley Walker. Boston: Houghton Mifflin Co., 1962, 271 p.
Reprints selections from Chandler's correspondence on a variety of topics, including his own detective fiction and that of his contemporaries.

Charney, Hanna. *The Detective Novel of Manners: Hedonism, Morality, and the Life of Reason.* Rutherford, N. J.: Fairleigh Dickinson University Press, 1981, 125 p.
Suggests that the detective novel follows the format of the novel of manners: "the long narrative flow that carries pictures of a society that never was but only seemed to be."

Colbron, Grace Isabel. "The Detective Story in Germany and Scandinavia." *The Bookman* (New York) XXX, No. 4 (December 1909): 407-12.
Surveys the works of prominent German and Scandinavian detective story writers of the period.

Connolly, Cyril. "Deductions from Detectives." *The New Statesman and Nation* II, No. 41 (5 December 1931): vii-viii.
Assesses the appeal of detective fiction, which Connolly finds derives from the attention to detail, the attractive settings, and the purity of form that are characteristic of the genre.

Cook, Michael L. *Monthly Murders: A Checklist and Chronological Listing of Fiction in the Digest-Size Mystery Magazines in the United States and England.* Westport, Conn.: Greenwood Press, 1982, 1147 p.
Lists the contents of 130 American and English mystery, detective, crime, and suspense magazines.

Dönötör, Tekla. "Folktales and the Detective Story." Trans-

lated by Elizabeth Tucker and Antony Hellenbert. *Folklore Forum* VIII, No. 1 (May 1975): 335-43.
Considers similarities of style, psychology, and theme in the folktale and the detective story.

Dove, George N. "The Police Procedural." *The Armchair Detective* 10, Nos. 2, 3, 4 (April 1977; July 1977; October 1977): 133-37, 241-43, 320-23; 11, Nos. 1, 2, 3 (January 1978; April 1978; July 1978): 74-7, 150-52, 249-51.
Six-part series detailing the conventions of the police procedural novel.

Eisinger, Erica A. "Detective Story Aspects of the *nouveau roman.*" *The Armchair Detective* 12, No. 4 (Fall 1979): 362-65.
Examines similarities between the French "new novel" of the 1950s and the detective novel.

Freeman, Lucy, ed. *The Murder Mystique: Crime Writers on Their Art.* New York: Frederick Ungar Publishing Co., 1982, 140 p.
Includes essays by Ken Follett, Edward D. Hoch, and Hillary Waugh. Waugh's essay is excerpted above.

Gardiner, Harold C., S. J. "The Barbarians Are Within the Gates." In his *In All Conscience: Reflections on Books and Culture,* pp. 21-5. Garden City, N.Y.: Hanover House, 1959.
Reprises the argument of Ben Ray Redman (see essay excerpted above) that hard-boiled detective fiction is exploitative, violent, and indicative of cultural barbarism.

Geherin, David J. *Sons of Sam Spade: The Private-Eye Novel in the 70s.* New York: Frederick Ungar Publishing Co., 1980, 168 p.
Considers the novels of Robert B. Parker, Roger L. Simon, and Andrew Bergman to be viable, creative variations on the hard-boiled detective formula established by Raymond Chandler, Carroll John Daly, Dashiell Hammett, and Ross Macdonald.

Gerould, Katharine Fullerton. "Murder for Pastime." *The Saturday Review of Literature* (New York) XII, No. 14 (3 August 1935): 3-4, 14.
Asserts the superiority of English over American detective fiction.

Gilbert, Michael, ed. *Crime in Good Company: Essays on Crime and Crime-Writing.* London: Constable Publishers, 1959, 242 p.
New and reprinted essays on crime fiction. Contributors include Eric Ambler, Jacques Barzun, Raymond Chandler, Cyril Hare, and Julian Symons.

Gottschalk, Jane. "Murder, Mystery, and Academe." *The Armchair Detective* 11, No. 2 (April 1978): 159-69.
Surveys detective fiction with an academic setting.

Goulart, Ron. "Dime Detectives." In his *Cheap Thrills: An Informal History of the Pulp Magazines,* pp. 113-33. New Rochelle, N.Y.: Arlington House, 1972.
Study of detective fiction published in pulp magazines of the 1930s, including *Black Mask, Clues, Detective Fiction Weekly, Detective Story,* and *Dime Detective.*

Hagemann, E. R., ed. *A Comprehensive Index to "Black Mask," 1920-1951.* Bowling Green, Ohio: Bowling Green State University Popular Press, 1982, 236 p.
Indexes the contents of *Black Mask* magazine during its thirty-one years of publication.

Hamilton, Cynthia S. *Western and Hard-Boiled Detective*

Fiction in America: From High Noon to Midnight. Iowa City: University of Iowa Press, 1987, 200 p.
> Study of the dynamics of formula fiction that includes examination of detective fiction.

Harper, Ralph. *The World of the Thriller.* Cleveland: Case Western Reserve University Press, 1969, 139 p.
> Examines the psychology of reader involvement in spy and detective fiction.

Hartman, Geoffrey H. "Literature High and Low: The Case of the Mystery Story." In his *The Fate of Reading, and Other Essays,* pp. 203-22. Chicago: University of Chicago Press, 1975.
> Considers the role of Aristotelian literary concepts of *peripeteia* ("reversal"), *anagnorises* ("recognition"), and *tò pathos* ("the suffering") in detective fiction.

Haycraft, Howard, ed. *The Art of the Mystery Story.* New York: Simon and Schuster, 1946, 565 p.
> Collection of previously published essays about mystery, crime, and detective fiction by prominent critics and authors.

Hill, Lew. "The Hero in Criminal Literature." *Pacific Moana Quarterly* 3, No. 1 (January 1978): 33-41.
> Examines the role of the detective as nominal hero in crime fiction.

Holman, Hugh C. "Detective Fiction as American Realism." In *Popular Literature in America: A Symposium in Honor of Lyon N. Richardson,* edited by James C. Austin and Donald A. Koch, pp. 30-41. Bowling Green, Ohio: Bowling Green University Popular Press, 1972.
> Considers reasons for the simultaneous rise of detective fiction, literary realism, and local color fiction in the United States.

Hutter, Albert D. "Dreams, Transformations, and Literature: The Implications of Detective Fiction." *Victorian Studies* XIX, No. 2 (December 1975): 181-209.
> Finds that detective fiction echoes the essential dream process of discovery of a past event.

Innes, Michael. "Death as a Game." *Esquire* LXII, No. 1 (January 1965): 55-6.
> Writer of detective fiction explicates ground rules of the genre.

Johnson, Timothy W., and Johnson, Julia, eds. *Crime Fiction Criticism: An Annotated Bibliography.* New York: Garland Publishing, 1981, 423 p.
> Annotated bibliography of secondary sources

Keating, H. R. F., ed. *Whodunit? A Guide to Crime, Suspense, and Spy Fiction.* New York: Van Nostrand Reinhold Co., 1982, 320 p.
> Essays about the varieties of crime fiction. An annotated list of crime fiction writers and their works rates representative novels on characterizations, plot, readability, and tension. A concluding essay by Philip Graham, "Why People Read Crime Fiction," analyzes the popularity of the genre.

Knight, Stephen. *Form and Ideology in Crime Fiction.* Bloomington: Indiana University Press, 1980, 202 p.
> Examines the social ideologies inherent in selected works of crime fiction.

Krouse, Agate Nesaule, and Peters, Margot. "Murder in Academe." *Southwest Review* 62, No. 4 (Autumn 1977): 371-78.

> Focuses on detective fiction with an academic setting.

Krutch, Joseph Wood. " 'Only a Detective Story'." *The Nation* (New York) 159, No. 22 (25 November 1944): 647-48, 652.
> Assesses detective fiction as "the one clearly defined modern genre of prose fiction impeccably classical in form," and attributes its popularity to its fabular, unified nature.

LaBorde, Charles. "Dicks on Stage: Form and Formula in Detective Drama, Parts I and II." *The Armchair Detective* 11, Nos. 3, 4 (July 1978; October 1978): 214-47, 348-56; 12, Nos. 1, 4 (Winter 1979; Fall 1979): 83-8, 341-47.
> Illustrated survey of stage presentations of mystery and detective dramas.

Lambert, Gavin. *The Dangerous Edge.* London: Barrie & Jenkins, 1975, 271 p.
> Examines the works of crime and detective novelists Wilkie Collins, Arthur Conan Doyle, G. K. Chesterton, John Buchan, Eric Ambler, Graham Greene, Georges Simenon, and Raymond Chandler, and filmmaker Alfred Hitchcock.

Landrum, Larry N.; Browne, Pat; and Browne, Ray B., eds. *Dimensions of Detective Fiction.* New York: Popular Press, 1976, 290 p.
> Collection of essays on various aspects of detective fiction.

Macdonald, Ross. "The Writer as Detective Hero." In his *On Crime Writing,* pp. 9-24. Santa Barbara: Capra Press, 1973.
> Suggests that fictional detectives embody the values of their creators.

Madden, David, ed. *Tough Guy Writers of the Thirties.* Carbondale: Southern Illinois University Press, 1968, 247 p.
> Collects essays on the hard-boiled detective fiction writers of the 1930s. "The 'Black Mask' School," by Philip Durham, is excerpted above.

Margolies, Edward. *Which Way Did He Go? The Private Eye in Dashiell Hammett, Raymond Chandler, Chester Himes, and Ross Macdonald.* New York: Holmes & Meier Publishers, 1982, 97 p.
> Assesses the hard-boiled detective protagonists in the fiction of Hammett, Chandler, Himes, and Macdonald.

Maugham, Somerset. "The Decline and Fall of the Detective Story." In his *The Vagrant Mood: Six Essays,* pp. 91-122. 1933. Reprint. Port Washington, N.Y.: Kennikat Press, 1969.
> Examines several kinds of detective fiction, including stories featuring the police, professional detectives, and amateur sleuths, and suggests that the hard-boiled school represents the genre's ultimate development.

Maurice, Arthur Bartlett. "The Detective in Fiction." *The Bookman* (New York) XV (May 1902): 231-36.
> Classifies different types of fictional detectives and discusses the literary merits of each.

McCarthy, Mary. "Murder and Karl Marx." *The Nation* CXLII, No. 3690 (25 March 1936): 381-83.
> Disparages the tendency to infuse detective fiction with political content.

McLuhan, Herbert Marshall. "Footprints in the Sands of Crime." *The Sewanee Review* LIV, No. 4 (October-December 1946): 617-34.

Suggests that the modern fictional detective derives from megalomaniacal figures in Renaissance literature.

Melvin, David Skene, and Melvin, Ann Skene. *Crime, Detective, Espionage, Mystery, and Thriller Fiction & Film: A Comprehensive Bibliography of Critical Writing through 1979.* Westport, Conn.: Greenwood Press, 1980, 367 p.
Annotated bibliography of literature and film criticism.

Modern Fiction Studies, Special Number: Detective and Suspense 29, No. 3 (Autumn 1983): 387-582.
Essays on detective and suspense fiction by Peter Wolfe, Timothy Steele, T. R. Steiner, William Nelson and Nancy Avery, Thomas M. Leitch, Virginia B. Morris, SueEllen Campbell, Erlene Hubly, JoAnn Cannon, Larry E. Grimes, Keith Newlin, Frederic Svoboda, and David Monaghan.

Montesinos, José F. "Imperfect Myths: Being an Observation on Detective Stories by a Continental Reader." *Chimera* V, No. 4 (September 1947): 2-11.
Discusses the vagaries of the critical and popular reputation of detective fiction in Europe, and considers reasons why the genre is almost exclusively the province of English-language writers.

Moskowitz, Sam. "Crime: From Sherlock to Spaceships." In his *Strange Horizons: The Spectrum of Science Fiction,* pp. 122-59. New York: Charles Scribner's Sons, 1976.
Traces the development of the science fiction detective story.

Most, Glenn W., and Stowe, William W., eds. *The Poetics of Murder: Detective Fiction and Literary Theory.* New York: Harcourt Brace Jovanovich, 1983, 394 p.
Collection of previously published critical essays.

Murch, A. E. *The Development of the Detective Novel.* Westport, Conn.: Greenwood Press, 1958, 272 p.
Insightful history of the genre that offers critical commentary on individual authors and works.

Nevins, Francis M., Jr., ed. *The Mystery Writer's Art.* Bowling Green, Ohio: Bowling Green University Popular Press, 1970, 338 p.
Collection of previously published essays. The contributors include William O. Aydelotte, Jacques Barzun, John Dickson Carr, and Ross Macdonald.

Nicolson, Marjorie. "The Professor and the Detective." *The Atlantic Monthly* 143 (April 1929): 483-93.
Analyzes the appeal of detective fiction to highly educated readers.

Orwell, George. "Raffles and Miss Blandish." In his *The Collected Essays, Journalism, and Letters of George Orwell, Vol. III: As I Please, 1943-1945,* edited by Sonia Orwell and Ian Angus, pp. 212-224. London: Secker & Warburg, 1968.
Contrasts English and American culture through a discussion of the Raffles stories of E. W. Hornung, the novel *No Orchids for Miss Blandish,* by James Hadley Chase, and other detective fiction.

Ousby, Ian. *Bloodhounds of Heaven: The Detective in English Fiction from Godwin to Doyle.* Cambridge: Harvard University Press, 1976, 194 p.
History of the early development of detective fiction in England.

Panek, LeRoy. *Watteau's Shepherds: The Detective Novel in*

Britain, 1914-1940. Bowling Green, Ohio: Bowling Green University Popular Press, 1979, 232 p.
Consideration of the British detective novel during the interwar period known as the "Golden Age."

———. *The Special Branch: The British Spy Novel, 1890-1980.* Bowling Green, Ohio: Bowling Green University Popular Press, 1981, 288 p.
Contains seventeen chapters, each devoted to an individual author of British spy novels. A preface briefly characterizes the genre and a summary recapitulates the history of the genre.

Penzler, Otto. *The Private Lives of Private Eyes, Spies, Crimefighters, & Other Good Guys.* New York: Grosset & Dunlap, 1977, 214 p.
Account of numerous fictional detectives and crimefighters, with illustrations taken from literary sources as well as motion picture adaptations.

———, ed. *The Great Detectives.* Boston: Little, Brown and Co., 1978, 281 p.
Collection of essays about fictional detectives written by their creators. Penzler supplies biographical and critical information about each author.

Porter, Dennis. *The Pursuit of Crime: Art and Ideology in Detective Fiction.* New Haven: Yale University Press, 1981, 267 p.
Examines a number of works of detective fiction in an attempt to determine which characteristics of the genre account for its popularity.

Pronzini, Bill. *Gun in Cheek: A Study of "Alternative" Crime Fiction.* Toronto: Coward, McGann & Geoghegan, 1982, 264 p.
Humorous survey of "the *bad* mystery" by "the *bad* writer," "to provide a different historical perspective on crime fiction."

Queen, Ellery. *The Detective Short Story: A Bibliography.* Boston: Little, Brown and Co., 1942, 146 p.
Bibliography of short detective fiction, providing first publication information, physical descriptions of books, and brief annotations.

———. *Queen's Quorum: A History of the Detective-Crime Short Story as Revealed in the 106 Most Important Books Published in this Field since 1845.* New York: Biblo and Tannen, 1969, 146 p.
Provides a critical overview of the genre.

Raynor, Henry. "The Decline and Fall of the Detective Story." *The Fortnightly* 179, No. 1034 (February 1953): 125-33.
Suggests that the introduction of sordid realism by writers of the hard-boiled school—characterized as a shift from "how" and "who" to "why"—led to the downfall of detective fiction.

Reddy, Maureen T. *Sisters in Crime: Feminism and the Crime Novel.* New York: Continuum, 1988, 172 p.
Argues that feminist writers are creating a countertradition in crime fiction by introducing complex female protagonists.

Reilly, John M., ed. *Twentieth-Century Crime and Mystery Writers.* New York: St. Martin's Press, 1980, 1568 p.
Provides a brief biographical sketch and list of principal works for each of the approximately 620 authors listed.

Rodell, Marie F. *Mystery Fiction: Theory and Technique.* New York: Duell, Sloan and Pearce, 1943, 230 p.
    Guide to technical aspects of mystery fiction composition intended primarily as a manual for beginning writers.

Routley, Erik. *The Puritan Pleasures of the Detective Story: A Personal Monograph.* London: Victor Gollancz, 1972, 253 p.
    Appreciation of the genre, recapitulating aspects of the debate about the appeal of detective fiction.

Ruehlmann, William. *Saint with a Gun: The Unlawful American Private Eye.* New York: New York University Press, 1974, 155 p.
    Critical examination of American detective fiction that offers commentary on what the popularity of the genre reveals about public attitudes toward crime and the legal system.

Rycroft, Charles. "A Detective Story: Psychoanalytic Observations." *The Psychoanalytic Quarterly* XXXVI, No. 2 (1957): 229-45.
    Proffers an explanation for the popularity of detective fiction that derives from Freudian psychosexual theories.

Sayers, Dorothy L. "Aristotle on Detective Fiction." In her *Unpopular Opinions: Twenty-One Essays,* pp. 222-36. New York: Harcourt, Brace and Co., 1947.
    Text of a 1935 lecture suggesting that detective fiction meets Aristotelian specifications for tragic structure.

Scott, Sutherland. *Blood in Their Ink: The March of the Modern Mystery Novel.* London: Stanley Paul and Co., 1953, 200 p.
    Discussion of trends in mystery fiction from 1918 to the early 1950s.

Simon, Reeva S. *The Middle East in Crime Fiction: Mysteries, Spy Novels, and Thrillers from 1916 to the 1980s.* New York: Lilian Barber Press, 1989, 226 p.
    Examines the portrayal of the Middle East and Middle Easterners in twentieth-century crime fiction.

Snow, C. P. "The Classical Detective Story." In *From Parnassus: Essays in Honor of Jacques Barzun,* edited by Dora B. Weiner and William R. Keylor, pp. 16-22. New York: Harper & Row, Publishers, 1976.
    Discusses the origins, salient characteristics, and appeal of classical detective fiction.

Starrett, Vincent. "Some Chinese Detective Stories." In his *Bookman's Holiday: The Private Satisfactions of an Incurable Collector,* pp. 3-26. New York: Random House, 1942.
    Surveys themes and conventions of Chinese detective fiction.

Stewart, R. F. ". . . And Always a Detective": Chapters on the History of Detective Fiction.* London: David & Charles, 1980, 351 p.
    Critical history of the genre.

Symons, Julian. *The Detective Story in Britain.* London: Longmans, Green & Co., 1962, 48 p.
    Outlines developments in the genre from its inception through the mid twentieth-century.

——. "The Face in the Mirror." In his *Critical Occasions,* pp. 149-53. London: Hamish Hamilton, 1966.
    Reprints a 1958 essay setting forth traditions and requisites of crime fiction.

——. "The Crime Collector's Cabinet of Curiosities." In his *Critical Observations,* pp. 131-38. New Haven: Ticknor & Fields, 1981.
    Discusses some "curiosities" of crime fiction, including notable "firsts" in the genre, definitive volumes in different subgenres, and such offshoots as the crime comic strip. The volume also contains critical essays on Agatha Christie, Georges Simenon, Raymond Chandler, and Dashiell Hammett.

Tani, Stefano. *The Doomed Detective: The Contribution of the Detective Novel to Postmodern American and Italian Fiction.* Carbondale: Southern Illinois University Press, 1984, 183 p.
    Examines the use of detective fiction conventions in postmodern American and Italian literature.

Thompson, H. Douglas. *Masters of Mystery: A Study of the Detective Story.* London: W. Collins Sons & Co., 1931, 288 p.
    Provides an overview of the genre.

Todd, Ruthven. "A Trinity of 'Tecs: From There to Where?" *Chimera* V, No. 4 (Summer 1947): 49-58.
    Delineates three types of fictional detectives: the professional, the amateur, and the hard-boiled private investigator.

Van Dine, S. S. "I Used to Be a Highbrow But Look at Me Now." *The American Magazine* 106 (September 1928): 14-31.
    Lists his twenty rules for writing detective fiction.

Warshow, Robert. "The Gangster as Tragic Hero." In his *The Immediate Experience: Movies, Comics, Theatre, and Other Aspects of Popular Culture,* pp. 83-8. Garden City, N.Y.: Anchor Books, 1964.
    Reprints a 1946 essay in which the critic equates the emotional and aesthetic impact afforded by the fixed dramatic pattern of the gangster film with that of traditional tragedy.

Watson, Colin. *Snobbery with Violence: Crime Stories and Their Audience.* London: Eyre & Spottiswoode, 1971, 256 p.
    Suggests that crime and mystery fiction offers clues to the convictions and attitudes of the society that produces it.

Westlake, Donald E. "The Hardboiled Dicks." *The Armchair Detective* 17, No. 1 (Winter 1984): 4-13.
    Surveys the genesis and development of hard-boiled detective fiction.

Williams, H. L. "The Germ of the Detective Novel." *The Book Buyer* XXI, No. 4 (November 1900): 268-74.
    Account of the genesis of the detective novel in France that traces late nineteenth-century developments in the genre in England and America.

Wilson, Edmund. "The Boys in the Back Room." In his *Classics and Commercials: A Literary Chronicle of the Forties,* pp. 19-56. New York: Farrar, Straus and Co., 1951.
    Includes discussion of hard-boiled detective fiction in a survey of California writers James M. Cain, Horace McCoy, Richard Hallas, John O'Hara, William Saroyan, John Steinbeck, and Hans Otto Storm.

Winks, Robin W., ed. *Detective Fiction: A Collection of Criti-*

cal Essays. Englewood Cliffs, N.J.: Prentice-Hall, 1980, 246 p.

Collection of previously published critical essays on detective fiction, including historical overviews, literary analyses, and studies of individual authors.

Winn, Dilys, ed. *Murder Ink: The Mystery Reader's Companion.* New York: Workman Publishing, 1977, 522 p.

Approximately 300 brief essays, both new and reprinted, on a wide variety of topics related to mystery, crime, and detective fiction and nonfiction.

————, ed. *Murderess Ink: The Better Half of the Mystery.* New York: Workman Publishing, 1979, 304 p.

Almost 200 assorted essays relating women to crime and crime fiction.

Film and Literature

INTRODUCTION

For centuries there has existed an interrelationship of and mutual influence between literature and other forms of artistic expression, resulting in painting and music based on works of fiction, drama, and poetry, as well as literary works emulating pictorial styles and musical structures. In the last decade of the nineteenth century, a creative exchange was initiated between literature and a new art form—film. During its earliest stages of development, film seemed more closely related to painting and photography, or appeared to be solely a technological phenomenon similar to the printing press or the phonograph. It soon became apparent, however, that the real potential of the medium lay in the qualities it shared with works of literature, primarily the ability to employ the structures and devices of narrative: a sequence of images on a screen could tell a story in much the same way as a sequence of words on a page. The use of language in film served to establish more firmly its connections with literature.

While acknowledging similarities between the two media, commentators have also recognized characteristics that manifestly distinguish film from literature. For example, in addition to presenting sequential action as in a novel, a film may also present a simultaneous composition of action, images, and words that provides a far more convincing replication of life than that which literature is able to achieve. For this reason, literary works that have their stylistic and thematic basis in a realistic presentation of characters and incidents are the ones most frequently considered suitable for screen adaptation. This practice has all but eliminated poetry as a source for films, while dramatic works—the tradition of realism in the theater notwithstanding—have often been perceived by filmmakers as too enclosed in the scope of their action and too limited in narrative to allow full play to the possibilities of film. Whereas the theater once seemed to be the nearest literary counterpart to cinema because of their common use of actors and sets, critics generally contend that films have their strongest affinity with fiction, specifically novels having a pronounced emphasis on narrative. Although there are numerous and notable examples that contradict this theory, particularly among the works of European and avant-garde filmmakers, it accurately applies to the popular commercial films that predominate in the history of cinema and represent many of its highest achievements.

Beyond the process of adapting works of literature into films, there has been interaction between these two artistic forms at various levels, from the often bitter relations of authors with the film industry to the development of the screenplay as a literary genre. Reciprocating for its extensive use of literary sources, the cinema has in turn exerted an influence on the style and subject matter of such writers as John Dos Passos, Nathanael West, Raymond Chandler, Alain Robbe-Grillet, and Aleksandr Solzhenitsyn. In retrospect, the creative alliance between film and literature may be seen as one of the most valuable and revitalizing developments in the history of artistic expression.

OVERVIEWS

William Jinks

[*Jinks is an American educator and critic. In the following excerpt, he presents a comparison of film and literature, focusing on the parallel artistic devices employed by the two forms.*]

No one would argue that film and literature are the same medium or even the same kind of experience. The primary thrust of literature is linguistic, hence indirect; while the impetus of film is imagistic and immediate. And yet, despite the obvious differences separating these two narrative forms, there are some rather startling resemblances between them.

If the modern film is carefully considered, it becomes evident that it is heavily indebted to other, older art forms. For example, it draws freely upon the tradition of live theater, especially the techniques of staging, lighting, movement, and gesture; from the novel it borrows structure, characterization, theme, and point of view; from poetry, an understanding of metaphor, symbolism, and other literary tropes; from music, rhythm, repetition, and counterpoint; and from painting, a sensitivity to shape and form, visual textures, and color.

Though all these elements are closely interwoven in today's films, they were not much in evidence in the first movies. As Erwin Panofsky points out in his essay "Style and Medium in the Motion Pictures," these early films were produced to exploit a brand new technology, not to satisfy a set of artistic criteria. And they were designed to fill the movie houses of major cities—theaters like Koster & Bial's in New York, the Cinéma Saint-Denis in Paris, and the Kino unter den Linden in Berlin. The audiences that flocked to this new form of entertainment were neither wealthy nor educated; they were composed almost exclusively of lower-middle-class workers and their families.

The sporadic development of the popular film, curiously enough, had much in common with the emergence of the eighteenth-century novel. Similarly, the initial audience for these moralistic adventure novels was primarily the urban middle class. As Martin S. Day suggests:

> The eighteenth century saw a vastly increased reading public, chiefly of the middle class. Practical and down to earth, this class wanted to read about people it could recognize from its own observations and described in the language it employed. It pre-

ferred its stories to end with financial and domestic rewards, its own clear-cut goals in life.

Ian Watt, in *The Rise of the Novel,* contends that as a consequence of the novel's popularity, the middle classes became the center of gravity of the reading public. Like the early movies, the novel was deemed strictly a popular entertainment; subsequently it developed into the significant genre it is today, "largely independent of traditional literary standards [and] unsanctified by established critical canons."

But the parallels went even deeper than similarities of audience. Both the eighteenth-century novel and the turn-of-the-century film relied heavily upon realism as a technique. Furthermore, both showed an unprecedented concern with the daily lives of ordinary people. Thus, any individual was a potential subject for a novel or film. Kenneth Macgowan, in *Behind the Screen,* wrote that the first movie program he saw, in 1897, consisted of two short films: "The first showed a half-dozen men diving into a pool; the other, two girls who leaped out of bed to have a pillow fight that ended with feathers filling the air."

Because of the subject matter they depicted and the audience they attracted, both the fledgling cinema and the early novels were held in low social repute. Panofsky notes that as late as 1905 there was only one movie house in Berlin, and that when the "better classes" ventured inside the theater, it was considered a kind of slumming. And Ian Watt remarks that "The novel was widely regarded as a typical example of the debased kind of writing by which the booksellers pandered to the reading public."

The novel, of course, soon became more acceptable, as men of extraordinary imagination and ability applied their talents to this new narrative form. Daniel Defoe, with *Robinson Crusoe* (1719) and *Moll Flanders* (1722), was one of the first major artists to experiment with the novel. And by 1750, both Samuel Richardson's *Pamela* and Henry Fielding's *Tom Jones* had been published and enjoyed by a wide audience. Throughout the nineteenth century, the novel form was developed and refined into a major medium of literary expression.

By contrast, the development of film techniques progressed at a much faster rate. The reason for this is fairly simple: early film makers were able to draw upon the techniques, conventions, and innovations of literature, specifically the novel. For instance, one of the many apocryphal stories concerning D. W. Griffith, a truly great film innovator, maintains that he always carried a Charles Dickens novel with him when he was on location. Once, when questioned about his unique editing style, Griffith reportedly asked: "Doesn't Dickens write that way?"

The technical, thematic, and stylistic similarities between Dickens and Griffith were discussed at length by the Russian director Sergei Eisenstein in an essay entitled "Dickens, Griffith, and the Film Today." Eisenstein himself, another great innovator, also drew heavily upon literary sources. For example, in his essay "The Organic Structure of Potemkin", he acknowledges that the structure of his own highly acclaimed *The Battleship Potemkin* (1925) was modeled after the five-act division of classical tragedy. (pp. 4-6)

Almost from the beginning there has existed a close rela-

tionship between film and literature. John Huston, for instance, wrote short stories for *The American Mercury* before Samuel Goldwyn brought him to Hollywood in the early '30s. In fact, during the '40s and '50s, many well-known novelists were writing screenplays: James Agee (John Huston's *The African Queen* [1952]), Raymond Chandler (Billy Wilder's *Double Indemnity* [1944], Alfred Hitchcock's *Strangers on a Train* [1951]), William Faulkner (Howard Hawks' *To Have and Have Not* [1944] and *The Big Sleep* [1946]), Graham Greene (Carol Reed's *The Third Man* [1949]), John O'Hara (Michael Curtiz' *The Best Things in Life Are Free* [1956]), Budd Schulberg (Elia Kazan's *On the Waterfront* [1954]), John Steinbeck (Elia Kazan's *Viva Zapata* [1952]). Playwrights, as well, were making their own contributions: Noel Coward (Noel Coward and David Lean's *In Which We Serve* [1942], David Lean's *Brief Encounter* [1945]), Moss Hart (George Cukor's *A Star is Born* [1955]), George S. Kaufman (who collaborated with Morrie Ryskind on Sam Wood's Marx Brothers' classic *A Night at the Opera* [1935]), Harold Pinter (Joseph Losey's *The Servant* [1963]), Gore Vidal and Tennessee Williams (Joseph Mankiewicz' *Suddenly Last Summer* [1959]). More recently, there appears to be a trend among novelists and playwrights to script and direct their own films: Norman Mailer (*Wild 90* [1968], *Beyond the Law* [1968]), Alain Robbe-Grillet (*The Man Who Lies* [1971]) and Susan Sontag (*Duet for Cannibals* [1969]). The interest of novelists and playwrights in the film form is readily understandable, since each form contends with similar aesthetic problems: plot, dramatization of ideas, and highly individualized character studies.

The similarities in origin, narrative devices, and subject matter of the early films and novels are perhaps predictable. What does come as a surprise, however, is the discovery that film maker and novelist attain meaning through similar patterns of organization.

What follows, then, is an extended analogy between the basic structural units of the novel—the word, sentence, paragraph, and chapter—and the elemental building blocks of the film—the frame, shot, scene, and sequence. And though Ezra Pound is very right in asserting that "you can *prove* nothing by analogy. [It] is either range-finding or fumble," the analogy can sometimes make the unfamiliar more accessible by relating it to the familiar. Thus, it is possible to recognize that—even though film is essentially a visual experience and literature a linguistic one—these two "languages" share a remarkable number of similarities. (pp. 6-7)

The word and the image are similar in that they are both visual phenomena—they must both be perceived with the eye. On one hand, the string of letters that make up *farmhouse* demands that the reader convert the lifeless and yet suggestive word into an approximation of what the author intended. Transposing a word to an internalized image will necessarily evoke a highly individualized response, because everyone's experience of a farmhouse differs. To a boy raised in a city slum, *farmhouse* might mean "health," "contentment," "peace"; to a country boy who left home, it might mean "chores," "boredom," "endless, mindless drudgery." In short, the word "farmhouse" will be interpreted by the reader for himself.

On the other hand, it would seem that the film maker is able to exert a greater degree of control over his medium than the writer, since the picture of a farmhouse is much more explicit than the word itself. That is, it is not necessary to *translate* a picture into a mental image—film is literal, concrete, and explicit. The film maker is able to show precisely the farmhouse he has in mind—he doesn't have to trust that the reader will "see" the same farmhouse.

Yet, because his medium is so explicit, the film maker cannot utilize the kinds of ambiguities inherent in language that enable the novelist to suggest more than he says. For example, a novelist might write: "The weathered red barn in back of the house somehow always gave me a comforting feeling of security whenever I looked at it." The film maker can present a barn that is visually attractive, solid in appearance, but he cannot depend on his viewer to perceive the barn as an emblem of security unless he is willing to have an off-camera voice blatantly announce: "Please view this barn as a symbol of security." Yet despite the different degrees of explicitness and connotative control, both artists must work with "languages" that function in a remarkably similar fashion.

For the writer, the most integral unit of creation is the *word*. It is from the word that he creates his sentences, paragraphs, chapters, and ultimately, his book. For the film maker, the basic building block is the *frame*—a single transparent picture on a strip of film. Isolated, both the word and the frame have meaning, but that meaning is imprecise—the word and frame must be set in a context to clarify their meaning.

The word "quiver," for example, could be a reference to either a case for holding arrows—in which instance it would be a noun—or it might describe a particular kind of action as a verb. Even if the reader is able to assume that what he is dealing with is a verb rather than a noun, the ambiguity is still unresolved, for the reader is still unclear as to the nature of the verb. The verb could be indicating the movement that an arrow describes when it comes to rest, or simply the nature of a motion like a shaking movement—a tremor. Even if the reader is further advised that the verb is not describing the motion of an arrow, he still isn't quite sure as to how to perceive the essential character of the quivering movement—the tremor. If this motion, for example, describes a leaf, it is one thing; if it describes, on the other hand, a girl, it is something else again, for the tremor could be simply a reaction to the cold, or perhaps even the reaction to a fright—there even exists the possibility that it might be a combination of both fear and inclement weather.

Again, it might appear that with film, no such problem would exist because of the explicitness of the frame—it provides far more information than the single ambiguous word. And yet notice what happens when a viewer is confronted with the single frame. . . . [The] viewer sees the image of a cabin. The cabin appears to be unpainted pine with a wood-shingled roof, and from the outside the cabin appears to be a single large room. A simple chimney runs up the side of the windowless cabin. The background appears to be bean fields. The image might represent a sharecropper's house during the early depression days; but even if it does, despite the viewer's assurance of *what* he is seeing, there is still some doubt as to *how* to see the cabin. With only the single frame from which to work, it is very difficult to decide in what kind of context the picture needs to be placed, because several possibilities exist.

Perhaps the viewer is supposed to perceive the house as a nostalgic memory of a less complicated, less anxiety-ridden past. In this case, the frame takes on the kind of hard and simple beauty that James Agee captured so well in his *Let Us Now Praise Famous Men*.

The house may appear in a documentary concerning the conditions of poverty in the United States. In this instance, the house is not a remnant of the past, but an eyesore in the present. It is a testimony to the discrepancies that exist between the "Haves" and the "Have-nots." Here the viewer would see the "shack" in the house, would probably feel sympathy or sorrow, perhaps even indignation.

The house may also appear in another kind of documentary—one produced by a government bureau, concerning the history of farming in the United States. Now the cabin represents only a survival of the historic past—an artifact. In this instance, the house (no longer a shack, notice) may well evoke pleasure on the part of the viewer. In comparing the contemporary farm dwellings with the cabin, the viewer is even made to feel proud that the standard of living has been raised so substantially. Just as the reader would need to see "quiver" in the context of a sentence before he could be clear about the meaning of the word, the viewer would need to see the single frame of the farmhouse within the context of the shot.

A sentence typically clarifies the meaning of an individual word, sets it in a more meaningful perspective. In a complete sentence the word "quiver" would attain a more explicit meaning: *She quivered slightly at the coolness of the night air, then proceeded alone up the deserted street.* From this sentence, it is clear that the girl's quivering is the result of the night air, that the motion is a sign of physical discomfort. At the same time, the sentence is colored slightly by the phrase *then proceeded alone up the deserted street.* The additional information—that she is alone, that it is dark, quiet, and chilly—suggests a feeling of fear, of foreboding. Thus, in this sentence the word "quivered" seems to convey both physical discomfort and fear.

In order to provide the same degree of clarity for the film viewer, it would be necessary for him to see a *shot*—a fragment of a film which has been taken, either actually or apparently, in one uninterrupted running of the camera. The shot, in other words, serves the same function for the film maker that the sentence does for the novelist. For example, if a film maker were shooting an important tennis match and wanted to indicate the tension of the contest to an audience, it is very unlikely that he would follow the exchanges of the match like a spectator. That approach would not only be repetitive, monotonous, and dizzying to follow, but it would probably also be completely devoid of tension—the viewer would be so caught up in the very mechanics of watching that the excitement of the match would be lost. To evoke the feeling of tension inherent in the match, the film maker would probably cut extensively during the event. (A *cut* is an instantaneous transition from one shot to another and is usually easy to spot in a film because it is invariably accompanied by a shift of camera position.) He might open with a long shot of the two antagonists facing each other, then cut to a medium shot of the player who was serving, then perhaps to a close-up of the taut face of the player waiting to return the ball. In this instance, the slowing down and breaking up of the action—converting it into shots—has helped to convey the tension involved in the contest.

There is no "average" shot. A shot can be as brief as a single frame. Robert Breer's *Fist Fight* (1964), for example, uses a different shot for almost every frame in the film. On the other hand, the length of a shot is limited only by the amount of film that a cameraman, in one continuous or apparently continuous filming, can shoot. French director Jean-Luc Godard, in his film *Weekend* (1968), reputedly used a tracking shot of a young couple in an automobile that was three hundred meters long (nearly a thousand feet of film).

For the viewer, then, a shot of the farmhouse discussed above is clearly easier to "read" than the single frame—like the sentence, the shot provides an enlarged context. For example, the viewer might first see the farmhouse at a distance of fifty feet or so, then perhaps the camera begins to zoom in toward the house and stops only when the doorway of the house nearly fills the entire screen (both the establishing shot of the house and the succeeding zoom would be considered one shot). Perhaps the camera remains focused on the doorway for a moment, and soon a woman comes to the door carrying a bucket. She wears a torn, ill-fitting cotton dress, and though her body looks young, her face appears drawn and haggard, and her shoulders seem to bend forward slightly. She leans against the doorframe and, for a moment, looks rather vacantly in the direction of the horizon. There is something about her stance that suggests a "bone-tired" kind of weariness. The shot concludes with her standing in the doorway.

This single shot might be as short as ten seconds; yet notice how much information it conveys. First, it becomes apparent that the house and its occupant are not being romanticized—the stark, weary figure of the woman precludes that kind of an interpretation. Second, although it is not impossible, it is unlikely that the footage represents an excerpt from a documentary concerning this nation's farming history. There are clues within the shot itself that suggest what the film maker is doing. The establishing shot (a shot that sets the scene) seems to remain with the house only long enough to suggest location; then it quickly moves to the doorway of the house, implying that it is the occupant or occupants of the house who are the real focus of attention. Also, the woman in the doorway is presented in a very special way. There is the contradiction between her youthful body and prematurely aged face; there comes the realization that she carries the water to the door because she probably has no plumbing; there is pathos in the sudden knowledge that she continues to wear what is clearly a rag because she has nothing to replace it with. These carefully selected details shape the response of the viewer just as surely as the phrase *then proceeded alone up the deserted street* alters and implements the verb *quiver*. Though the question of *what* the word or shot refers to is answered in part by the context, other questions in the reader's and viewer's minds remain to be solved. But expectations of answers have been raised, and these answers can be provided through referring to a broader context.

A paragraph, a series of closely related sentences, typically gives the reader additional information about a particular "key" sentence in it, as in the case of the sentence about the solitary girl:

> The car seemed to be in the throes of death, the way it jerked and stalled. She looked at the gas gauge and discovered the source of her problem—it read empty. She was in a section of town where even the residents stayed behind carefully locked doors at night, and her face showed apprehension as she let the car drift to the curb. After securing the car doors, she stepped out onto the sidewalk. She quivered slightly at the coolness of the night air, then proceeded alone up the deserted street.

This paragraph, it should be noted, is set up much as a film maker might conceive a five-shot scene—an interior close-up shot of the girl being jostled about in the car; an extreme close-up of a gas gauge reading empty, followed by a shot of her tense face; a medium shot of the car drifting toward the curb; a medium-close shot of the girl locking the car and walking up the street of the deserted neighborhood. In this instance, the paragraph has revealed how the girl came to be in this particular predicament, and the paragraph also confirms the implications of fear that previously were only suggested.

A *scene* is ordinarily an action which is unified around a specific action or event and, normally, is also united by considerations of a time and place. The following three-shot scene of the sharecropper's cabin would remove most of the aforementioned ambiguity as to the type of film the audience is seeing:

> Shot #1: Medium shot of the cabin; a slow zoom shot stopping when the doorway of the cabin fills the frame. A woman, walking from the interior, appears in the doorway holding a pan of water. She looks toward the camera.
>
> *cut to:*
> Shot #2: Long shot of a man, perhaps a quarter of a mile away, walking along a dirt road that is lined sparsely with pines. His feet set up small, barely discernible puffs of dust as he walks.
>
> *cut to:*
> Shot #3: The woman, as she was before, looking toward the camera. Abruptly she tosses the water into the yard and returns to the darkened interior of the house.

With this scene, the viewer's speculations are, in part, resolved. No longer is it necessary for him to guess how he should "read" the information he is witnessing. The hardship, the weariness of the people's lives has become readily apparent. It is also apparent, from this three-shot scene, that the film maker is able to exert the kind of artistic control that is ordinarily associated only with the novelist.

In the case of a novelist, there are literally no limitations on what can be described; he can, in fact, set on paper whatever he is capable of imagining. The dramatist, however, has less freedom, for the form with which he works imposes certain restraints upon him. The dramatist cannot, for example, show the husband returning home—this would have to be eliminated or indicated by means of dialogue. In addition, the film maker's control of his material, like the novelist's, is more selective. The dramatist would not be able to forcibly bring our attention to bear on the woman standing in the doorway, as the film maker has done. Rather, he would have to "attract" his audience's attention by means of placement of actors and actresses, staging, dialogue, or perhaps the use of lighting. The same considerations, of course, would hold true for the girl stranded in the forbidding neighborhood. Unless he were willing to go to a great deal of trouble, the dramatist would not be able to stage that particular scene. Again, he would have to employ dialogue to relate this information to the audience. The film maker, however, could easily realize this scene.

Eventually the novelist combines his paragraphs into larger units—chapters. In many respects, the chapter resembles an expanded paragraph; it is usually unified by one central focus. A chapter could derive its unification from a single incident or event; it might cover the events of a particular period of time—an hour, day, year, or even a generation. A chapter could limit itself to a description of a single character. Sometimes unity can be achieved by means of a physical setting: a room, a town, or a country.

In the example of the stranded girl, the episode of her running out of gas might be just one of many similar unpleasant occurrences in the same chapter. Earlier, she may have been threatened over the telephone. Sometime later, an inexplicable fire takes place in the kitchen of her house while she is asleep. While crossing the street, she narrowly averts being run over by an automobile. Finally, she runs out of gas in a dangerous neighborhood. All of these incidents might have one thing in common: the deliberate terrorizing of the girl. Thus, the incidents form a common thread that unifies the chapter into a coherent whole.

Chapters, like paragraphs, are distinct divisions of a novel and are usually characterized by coherence, unity, and completeness. It is difficult, however, to say *exactly* what it is that distinguishes a paragraph from a chapter. Typically, the chapter is much longer than a paragraph, but there are instances of chapters in novels being no longer than a couple of sentences (Laurence Sterne's innovative *Tristram Shandy* and Ken Kesey's *One Flew Over the Cuckoo's Nest* are two obvious examples). The problem is even more complicated when the *sequence*—the film's equivalent of the chapter—is considered.

The film, for example, does not have its narrative neatly divided into chapters (although British film maker Lindsay Anderson, in a film entitled *If . . .* [1969], did utilize an eight-part chapter-like division). The sequence—a series of closely related scenes—is subject to precisely the same criteria as the chapter, namely, unity, coherence, and completeness. In some instances, such as Anderson's *If . . .* , or Stanley Kubrick's *2001: A Space Odyssey* (1969) with its three-part division, the separation between sequences is apparent. In most films, however, it is more difficult to recognize and define the divisions.

The previously described scene of the sharecroppers would, most likely, represent a part of a sequence. The entire film might be composed of three thirty-minute sequences. This scene would be part of the first sequence, depicting the poverty and deprivation of a single family in the rural South. This first sequence might conclude with the family's decision to move north to a large city, and hopefully, a better life. The second sequence might describe their journey to the North, while the third could reveal the protagonists in their new environment. As with chapters in a novel, the possibilities for creating sequences

are virtually unlimited; the artist need merely establish the relationship of one scene to another.

In order to compare the language of film with the language of literature, it was necessary to ignore, for the most part, the very striking dissimilarities of the two genres. Although a metaphor and a simile can enlarge perception by comparing the familiar with the unfamiliar or by examining something in a slightly altered perspective, it is essential to consider the peculiarities of each of the genres in order to determine how they differ from each other.

To begin with, film is a multi-sensory communal experience emphasizing immediacy, whereas literature is a mono-sensory private experience that is more conductive to reflection. A film is usually viewed in the presence of others who necessarily become part of the total gestalt of the film experience. Ideally, each member of the audience respects the presence of others and opens himself to the film. A tall hat, a noisy popcorn chewer, or a self-appointed narrator can adversely affect the impact of the film. The responses of the audience can also affect the perception of a film—an inappropriate laugh can provoke irritation, while infectious laughter can increase delight.

A novel, however, is typically a private experience, in which the relationship between the author and the reader is relatively direct and immediate. The responses of others do not impinge on the novel as they do on the film. The novel is also conducive to reflection, as the reader can pause and consider an important passage or mull over a particular phrase. This convenience, of course, is denied the viewer because the film moves unceasingly toward its conclusion (though developments in cassette television may soon change this).

But the film and the novel are alike insofar as their order is typically linear. For the most part, the movement in the novel as well as the film could be described as sequential—events and scenes are ordered in direct relation to each other. The exception, of course, would be a film like Alain Resnais' *Last Year at Marienbad* (1961), which deliberately eschews causality as well as psychological motivation. However, whether the order be A, B, C or C, B, A, the progression is usually straightforward. This tends to be true even if a film or novel opens with a conclusion (Orson Welles' *Citizen Kane* [1940] or Thornton Wilder's *Bridge of San Luis Rey* come to mind—both open with the protagonist's death); and even though the normal order has been reversed, the narrative will still tend to follow a relatively predictable, sequential path.

One of the exciting features of the film experience is its immediacy—the fact that the film is occurring *right now* before the audience's eyes. Although immediacy tends to promote greater involvement, it also creates certain problems for the film maker. Most of them center around considerations of time.

In order to describe a peculiar habit of one of his characters, a novelist might simply write: "Every day for six months at precisely eleven thirty-two, he would seat himself at a park bench on 27th Avenue and count the busses that passed." The reader unquestionably accepts the suggested duration of time; in other words, to the reader, it seems credible. For a film maker, this sentence would pose a problem. He would have to portray, visually and convincingly, the passage of six months in a relatively short segment of film. This would entail a number of shots of the man on the bench counting busses; it would also be necessary to indicate, within the shots, the passage of time. Typically, this would be accomplished by use of the background: trees blooming, leaves falling, then, finally, the stark, leafless, skeletal trees of winter. The changing attire of the man—short-sleeved shirt to jacket to overcoat— would also support this impression.

Conversely, a novelist might well devote an entire chapter to an event that actually took only seconds to transpire. A man nearly drowns. As he struggles to the surface and subsequently sinks again, the events of his life flit through his mind. Despite the fact that it might take an entire chapter to describe what thoughts race through his mind during this crisis, a reader would have no problem in accepting this chapter as credible. The film maker, however, cannot take advantage of this particular convention. If he moves the scene too rapidly, the viewer loses the density of the experience. If he takes too much time with the scene, its credibility is called into question. Robert Enrico, in his Cannes Film Festival Award-winning short film, *Occurrence at Owl Creek Bridge* (1961), does manage to successfully "stretch" the passage of a second or two into seventeen minutes. In order to do so, he has to introduce some ambiguities that make the viewer realize that time is being altered—but not why. The viewer believes that he is witnessing the miraculous escape of a man who was almost hanged, when in fact he is witnessing the internalized fantasy of a condemned man at the gallows.

It is a relatively easy task for the novelist to manipulate time. He can, for example, employ a narrator who tells a story from two vantage points simultaneously. The narrator can relate events that happened to him when he was seventeen as though he were again experiencing those same events in the present. The narrator, however, is now twenty-seven and the distance from the experience is ten years. Nevertheless, the writer can alternate between these two mentalities, the seventeen-year-old and the twenty-seven-year-old (as, for instance, John Updike does in his highly praised short story, "Flight"), with little difficulty. The film maker, however, will usually select one or the other (though not always, as in Ingmar Bergman's *Wild Strawberries* [1957]). Although it is possible to accompany the earlier scene with the voice of the older narrator, a strikingly different effect than the novelist's dual narrator is produced. The "voice over" (off-camera narration) tends to undermine the immediacy of the earlier scene.

There is, in addition, another curious feature that distinguishes time in a novel from time in a film: technically speaking, film time is always present tense. For example, open a conventional novel to a passage that deals with the past and the verbs alone will signal you that these events occurred some time ago. On the other hand, walk into a theater while a contemporary movie is in progress and try to determine whether you're watching past, present, future, or fantasy. Certainly, given enough time you would figure it out, but the point is that without the additional context, you'd have no way of knowing.

Not only is time employed differently in a film, but space is as well. In the novel, the reader brings his own experience to bear on the novelist's suggestions. If the novelist describes a building, the reader, having had the experience of visualizing a building, will tend to see a structure that conforms not only to the novelist's description but also to his own accumulated experience. Much of Wallace Stevens' poetry, for instance, is "about" or at least deals directly with this convention. In a film, however, the camera sees differently from the eye itself or the mind's eye, and the viewer tends to be more passive than the reader since the *conceptualization* of a scene is provided by the film.

This raises the entire question of conceptualization in the novel and the film. By its very nature, the film tends to be concrete and literal. The novel, on the other hand, is abstract and suggestive. The distinction is an important one, for it means that it is very difficult for the film to deal with abstractions. A brief example might serve to point up this distinction. In one of Macbeth's most famous speeches, he exclaims:

> Tomorrow and tomorrow and tomorrow
> Creeps in this petty pace from day to day,
> To the last syllable of recorded time;
> And all our yesterdays have lighted fools
> The way to dusty death. (Act V; sc. 5)

In the first two lines, Shakespeare has made use of personification; he describes an abstraction—tomorrow—as having the ability to creep, an activity that is usually limited to something animate. Similarly, in the following lines, he suggests that yesterdays (again, an abstraction) have "lighted fools the way to dusty death." The unusual juxtaposition of the abstract with the concrete produces a striking literary trope. A film maker obviously could have an actor deliver Macbeth's speech, but could not possibly film the kind of tropes that the speech includes. How, for example, could a film maker render the following in visual terms: a sea of troubles, a dusty nothing, liberty plucking authority by the nose, a dagger of the mind? The film, of course, through metaphors, similes, and symbols, does deal with abstractions, but it must necessarily render them in concrete images.

The literal-mindedness of the camera also produces other problems. Many writers (Nathaniel Hawthorne in "Young Goodman Brown," Herman Melville in "Bartleby, the Scrivener," and Franz Kafka in *The Trial*) have successfully created characters who are representative figures of mankind. In each of these tales, there is little physical description of the central character, with the result that he becomes "universalized," an Everyman. The camera, however, produces the opposite effect; it tends to wed the character and the role forever. It is very difficult to imagine *La Strada* (1954) without Giulietta Masina; *The Seventh Seal* (1957) without Max Von Sydow; *The Graduate* (1968) without Dustin Hoffman; and *Cries and Whispers* (1973) without Ingrid Thulin, Harriet Andersson, Liv Ullman, and Kari Sylwan. Likewise, it is not enough for a character to experience a particular scene as beautiful or threatening. In order to convince the viewers, the scene must actually be filmed as beautiful or threatening.

Finally, it should always be recognized that the film is a multi-dimensional experience; it combines sight and sound with movement. A film maker who is too "literary," who relies too heavily on dialogue, will produce a film that is "talky." In fact, at times there seems to be a basic conflict between literate or complex language and visual imagery. In Anthony Harvey's *The Lion in Winter* (1968), James Goldman's witty, literate screenplay provides the players with sparkling dialogue, yet the film itself seems almost totally devoid of any memorable images. Cartoonist Jules Feiffer, who wrote the screenplay for Mike Nichols' *Carnal Knowledge* (1971), created a script that was excessively talkative; in order to prevent the audience from being distracted from the characters' speeches by competitive visuals, Nichols was forced to constantly employ darkened and semi-darkened lighting for the interior shots and extreme long shots for the exteriors.

Likewise, a film maker who doesn't understand the languages of vision and movement may end up producing a film that is visually static. Some film makers attempt to avoid this by "opening up" the play with exterior shots and scenes that take place away from the primary setting. Mike Nichols did this in *Who's Afraid of Virginia Woolf?* (1966) with the opening shots of the college campus and later, the roadhouse scene. William Freidkin's *Boys in the Band* (1970), similarly, opened with a montage of short scenes showing what the main characters were doing just prior to their arrival at Michael's apartment.

The dramatist, of course, must confine his action to a relatively small area and restrict the movements of his characters because of the spacial limitations of the stage. In a film, however, "all the world's a stage," and the film maker who ignores this creates a film that seems to the viewer to be unnecessarily restricted and confined. (pp. 8-21)

> *William Jinks, "The Word and the Image: Language," in his* The Celluloid Literature: Film in the Humanities, *second edition, Glencoe Press, 1974, pp. 4-21.*

Jean Mitry

[*Mitry was a French filmmaker and one of the most important critics and theorists of film. In the following essay, he emphasizes the differences in artistic form between film and literature and explains how these formal divergences affect the meanings that a cinematic or literary work is able to express.*]

Today most cinematic production still relies on adaptation. It is obvious, then, that some work exists before the act of filming and independent of the fact of filming, a work which has not only autonomous being but also intrinsic value. The problem is to know if the significations inherent in literary forms are transferable to the cinema, if it is possible to take them as they are, recreating them by means of certain visual forms, or if, on the contrary, the cinema, in this respect, can and ought to be no more than the visual externalization of a drama the essence of which lies entirely in verbal expression. Some maintain that one could translate a tragedy of Racine, for example, by giving it novelistic or filmic form. I believe, on the other hand, that the play would become something altogether different. It would take on another meaning, open onto different perspectives, because the means of expression *in being different* would express different things—not the same things in different ways.

This fact, which remains very difficult for many to accept, is, to my mind, at the source of all the errors and confusions about the adaptation of plays and novels to the screen. We talk as if adaptation were a matter of translation, like passing from one language to another, when in fact it is a matter of passing from one *form* to another, a matter of transposition, of reconstruction. Quite clearly to reduce *Phèdre* or any other tragedy to its dramatic essence would not only strip it of its theatrical elements, but also reduce it to its motivations, to its basic themes, by repudiating its expressive qualities, that is to say, by repudiating everything that makes it what it is, all that gives it meaning and value: *its very form.* Now its form, which is theatrical, lies entirely in its text—and less in the literary or poetic qualities of its text, which are the work of the poet, than in a certain more subtle quality which is included in them, which is the work of the dramatist.

The classical tragedies can be acted in front of a simple curtain. It would be perfectly simple to costume Creon in a tuxedo and no one would pay any attention to it, because the words that he speaks attest to his rank, his personality—even to his appearance—as much as to his thoughts and acts. In a word, the armor of Mithridate, the peplum of Nero, the whole world which surrounds them—all are *in the text,* implied by the words these characters speak and which define them. This phenomenon never appears in the dialogue of a novel or film. While the cinematic "presence" is the formal unity of the person and the world, the theatrical "presence" is the formal unity of the actor and the word: it is the word incarnate. The actor, in the theatre, does not play a role: he assumes a manner of speaking, a character defined entirely by the text.

The dialogue of the theatre is so much the more irreducible to cinema because it explains everything, while the dialogue of film, on the other hand, tends towards a manner of expression which is colloquial, contingent, disengaged from all transcendence. This circumstance does not arise so much from the fact that the word "serves" the image (because the cinema is a "visual" art) as from the fact that there is between the two forms of language a constant desynchronization of the orders of duration. It would, for example, take one or two pages of text to describe the content of a single image. The hero who informs us of his fatigue tells us nothing which his face, his aspect, his bearing doesn't already tell us—except that it adds a few seconds to the signification of something already signified. Hence the constant lag between the rapid rhythm of visual expression and the much slower rhythm of verbal expression. The word, when it does not evoke images, when it signifies by itself, paralyzes the film, ruptures the rhythm. If a time not filled with words is intolerable in the theatre because it is empty, a time filled solely by words is intolerable in the cinema because it is excessive.

One ought in the cinema to begin with the principle which I believe fundamental: *from the moment one puts the idea before the image, the image becomes useless.* Insofar as it is a means of expression, the image exists to *suggest* the idea—at least to develop the narrative in terms of what is to be expressed and what has meaning only in terms of that expression. The role of the image in film corresponds exactly to the role of the word in theatre. A film can therefore be like a play; its content may be founded in the concentration of time and space, provided that the form and the manner of speaking are cinematic. On the other hand, even though the role of the image in the film is analogous to that of the word in a play, the visual development of a theatrical work can only deform it because the possibilities of the image are altogether different. One cannot signify with images what one signifies with words—and *vice versa.* In addition, while time in the theatre is a time of words, time in the cinema has its basis in the process of perception; it is *not* the "time of the action," as people sometimes say. Theatrical reality is *understood;* cinematic reality is *perceived.* It follows that the intellectual process involved is not at all the same. It is obvious, then, that the problem of adaptation is a false problem. It is insoluble in the conventional ways because it is impossible to translate verbal into visual magic, because the meanings, the perspectives, the potentialities are radically different.

Of course one can express visually the tragic sense of any play—*Phèdre,* or *Elektra,* or *Cinna*—but, in doing so, one will give it a completely different meaning. It will no longer be the tragedy of Racine, of Euripides, or of Corneille, but something else entirely, taking its departure from the same theme: a creation, but in no sense an adaptation. To remain "faithful" to Racine is to condemn yourself to illustration; it is to condemn Racine himself, for to replace his words with images is to destroy the sense of his work, to reduce it to a story neither better nor worse than any newspaper item. The only solution is to keep the original work intact and put it on the screen through the *means* of the cinema. But this is nothing more than the use of filmic procedures for the benefit of theatrical expression. As Andre Bazin indicates, "The specific help given here by the cinema can only be described as an added measure of the theatrical." The source of interest in such an adaptation lies in the expansion of duration which the stage does not permit. The play is enriched in all of those moments when the characters do not speak, but move about or reflect in such a way that what they say is made explicit in what they do. But this is useful only in rare moments, for if the filmic realization gives a realistic environment to the tragedy, it also strips the word of all transcendent significance. By the very fact that it gives the hero a concrete existence, temporality causes verbal transcendence to fall into the immanence of lived reality. Thus without ceasing to be tragic, the tragedy becomes a different *kind* of play; the motivations become psychological rather than metaphysical.

While time in the theatre is essentially a time of words, all duration in the cinema which is not sustained by concrete acts becomes dead weight. The conceptual in the cinema is a function of the real, the transcendent a function of the immanent—which is exactly the reverse of what occurs in the theatre. Thus the impossibility of any kind of formal transposition. Not only are the values different, but they work in different ways.

The apparent similarity of progression in the film and the novel (action in time, narration of a more-or-less chronological series of events, etc.) has led cineastes to bring novels to the screen just as the apparent similarity of the spectacle and dramatic structure led them to put plays on film. Yet it is clear that to transpose a work from one mode of expression to another, to "adapt" it, is to assume the equivalence of what is signified despite the difference of the significations; we might as well try to square the circle.

At every moment the adaptor confronts the following dilemma: (1) Either he is faithful to the letter; he follows the procedure of the novelist step-by-step so that the chains of circumstance are exactly the same. But by expressing such facts visually, the adaptor is inevitably led either to signify something altogether different from the novel or to distort the sense determined by the original literary expression which alone conforms to the thought of the author. Thinking only to serve the novelist, the adaptor betrays him consistently with the very elements of his own fabulation. (2) Or he is faithful to the spirit; he expresses similar ideas and analogous sentiments, but arrives at them by slant routes. He inevitably disrupts the novelist's continuity; he transfers the "givens," the circumstances, the characters—and arrives, once again, at a clear case of treason. To speak of "adaptation" in such a case is beside the point, for the film, however interesting it might be, no longer has anything to do with the original work which it is supposed to reflect. And it takes a very curious mentality to believe that one can be faithful to the "spirit" of a work while diverting it from its normal course, changing its givens, and transforming its structure—as if the letter and the spirit of a work were two entirely separate things, which could be dissociated or superimposed, when in fact both constitute an *ensemble* of facts, of expressions and meanings the interdependence of which is constantly manifest. To betray the letter is to betray the spirit, because the spirit is found only in the letter.

Therefore the only possible solutions to the problem are these: (1) Either the adaptor follows the story step-by-step, putting it into images, including nothing which is foreign to it, and signifying nothing through the artifices of language. He does not strive to translate significations, because they are in the words; instead he seeks to reproduce the *things* signified by the words. The film, from that moment, no longer is creation or expression, but only representation or illustration. (2) Or, not troubling to remain faithful to the author, he rethinks the subject, and ends by giving it another development and a completely different meaning. He makes a personal work using the original as a point of departure, as an inspiration. In this case he is in no position to boast of what he has done on behalf of the novel.

In the first case, though the film is nothing more than a vehicle, it can be something better than *Classics Illustrated.* Since purely filmic significations are beside the point, nothing prohibits the adaptor from composing images charged with meaning—images which, at the level of decor or lighting, of plastic structures, of the bearing of the characters, of the action—create an ensemble which conforms to that which it was the mission of the words to evoke. In other words, at the level of *mise-en-scène*—if we define this phrase simply as the creation of dramatic space—the adaptor can compose the world which the novel suggests, its climate, its ambience, and record it with the camera. He records a signified reality, interpreted, which corresponds to the verbal significations insofar as they are limited to description. In all this there is an art which is far from comtemptible, an art which is born in self-effacement, renunciation, and scrupulous fidelity to the original work. If it doesn't get very close to translating any profound meaning of the work or to attaining anything like equal asthetic value, such an art is nevertheless capable of producing a valuable *reflection* of the original. Among the successes of this genre are certainly the Dickens films of David Lean, *Great Expectations* and, especially, *Oliver Twist.* The images seem to burst from the pages of the novel, and sometimes we even catch something like an echo of the style or manner of Dickens.

Among the most obvious and frequently encountered errors of adaptors is transposing a novel in time while retaining the original structure and order of development. This practice indicates considerable distrust of the original work and indicates a total misunderstanding of what characterizes it and constitutes its essential value. When such an adaptor takes on *Thérèse Raquin,* for example, it isn't enough for him to transform the profound meanings by the very act of adaptation; he must attempt to modernize the action as well. Of course he retains the situations and the motives—only slightly altered because of their new context—but reintroduces the characters just as they appear in the novel, with the same mentalities, the same personalities. As a result the contemporaries of Jules Grevy jostle about in 1960. The whole thing collapses because the state of the hero's spirit is characteristic of mores, of manners of being and thinking, which are those of the provincial *petite bourgeoisie* of the 1880's. Lifted from its context *Thérèse Raquin* is no longer *Thérèse Raquin,* but simply the story of two lovers who get rid of an annoying husband and later feel some remorse about it. This is a story which could happen anywhere, in any way, at any time—but we miss what Zola provides, we miss his people whose very existence is a function of the epoch and milieu in which they live and struggle.

This manner of proceeding is evidence again of that false conception which consists of thinking that dramatic action and the stuff of the novel and the character of the hero are unchanging entities and permanent values and that they can be shifted without difficulty onto another infrastructure. The structure which gives the novel its human significance, its psychological authenticity, develops from the infrastructure upon which it is based. Detached from it, the novelistic structure is no longer anything but an abstraction, a theoretical proposition without any real value. Nothing, of course, prevents us from conceiving an analogous drama unfolding in our own time. But this presupposes other conjunctures, other states of mind, and all the implications of a society which is not at all like that at the core of Zola's novel. As a result of all the necessary shifts, such a drama would no longer have anything in common with the original. If one wants to replace an entire infrastructure, it is hardly necessary to study the old one.

One could say the same things about virtually any novel. A novel brings to life something other than abstractions. Solidly lodged in time and space, the people that it creates, their manners, their drama, cannot be separated from the context which determines them without the immediate loss of their authenticity, their value, and their meaning. The same content, of course, may be interpreted in different ways. Such interpretations generate form to the same degree that they depend upon it. One can easily treat the same content in a hundred different ways; each time, however, one will give it another meaning. Of course if one wants to signify something altogether different, or to rediscover and analyze the same "latent" content from other points of view, adaptation ceases to pose any problem. One should simply affirm that it is no longer a question of adaptation, because to adapt a work is to transpose everything in preserving the sense and the meanings, failing which one creates a different work. This is always possible; it is even desirable. But it is not in eluding problems that we solve them.

Bela Balasz in *Theory of Film* says that an adaptor "may use the existing work merely as raw material, regard it from the specific angle of his own art form as if it were raw reality, and pay no attention to the form already given to the material." Of course this is true as long as it is a question of total recreation, of a film resolutely detaching itself from the work which inspires it. But it is no longer true when it becomes a question of adaptation—however little real meaning one can retain in that word "adapt." The position becomes untenable. One cannot consider a work of art—play or novel—as "raw reality" precisely because it is no longer raw reality, but a reality which has been mediated upon and interpreted. It is impossible to avoid a concern with form because it is the form of a work which confers both meaning and impact. Beyond form there is nothing but intention, or a theme or subject which permits that intention to realize itself. To reduce a work of art to its theme negates it as a work of art because at this level it exists only potentially; it is only a quantity of possibilities among which the author must choose, eliminating in order to construct. In choosing to express the same things as the novelist, the adaptor must abandon novelistic form; if he intends to respect it, he will have to content himself with putting an already signified world into images instead of creating his own significations. The transference is impossible.

Leaving adaptations and the false problems they give rise to aside, one can nevertheless say that the cinema comes much closer to novelistic than dramatic structure because film is capable not only of *indicating* duration but of *making it felt,* of translating its deep psychological resonances. Like the novel, film presents characters engaged in a series of events the connections among which are not univocal but contingent, which evoke meanings not simply reducible to themselves. The duration of events isn't merely a matter of opening situations out or of ordering them but also of revealing the individual in all his psychological mobility and ambiguity. An open world succeeds to the closed world of earlier films, and the problem, just as in literary narrative, becomes one of introducing free time into a limited structure. While the short story writer goes directly to the essential, the novelist can wander freely. The course of his work is slow and sinuous—fluvial. A precise and condensed work like *La Princesse de Clèves* is much more a long short story than a novel, because the author retains the right to a leisurely development which turns on itself, clears the perspectives, and brings different points of view into confrontation.

Nevertheless there are—necessarily—irreducible differences between the novel and the film. While space remains conceptual in a literary work, duration is intensely *felt* because the novelistic texture, the linking of circumstances, the evolution of characters, all depend on it and, in fact, generate it at the same time. Time plays, or can play, just as central a role in the cinema. But time in the cinema is always the duration of *something,* of an objectively and geographically situated concrete reality. Therefore this spatial reality must necessarily be established before the duration of which it is the subject. It is difficult to control duration because of the inertia of space, even though it confirms the validity of the time which depends upon it. In other words, time in the novel is constructed with words. In the cinema it is constructed with actions. The novel *creates* a world while the cinema *puts us in the pres-*

ence of a world which it organizes according to a certain continuity. *The novel is a narrative which organizes itself in a world; the film, a world which organizes itself in a narrative.*

In addition, space and time in the cinema compose a continuum analogous but not equivalent to real space-time, a whole which cannot be reduced by any unilateral act of consciousness (spatial or temporal). Cinema perceives an incessant flux, a world at once changing and perpetually present. In this flow the past, whatever exists no more, disappears, though it remains present in the immediate memory; similarly the future, whatever has not yet occurred, disappears. In the cinema, as in real life, there is nothing but the present, a present which is always in the process of evolving. In the moment of perception, the apprehension of a present in the process of realizing itself, we really see only space, space in movement. We cannot grasp onto the duration of space because it is identified with our perception, flows on and changes with it—and with us. In the cinema, no more than in real life, can we perceive and feel this duration which creates itself—unless, of course, the film bores us. The action carries us along with it: we perceive it as action, as movement, not as duration, even though we still have the notion or the consciousness of duration, of something which lasts and which objectifies itself in the time of the drama.

The novel, at the opposite extreme, does permit a unilateral act of consciousness. Everything there is a function of duration. The characters, the decor, the countryside as imagined by the reader, are constantly submitted to the demands of this temporality. Reduced to the necessary authenticity of one place or milieu, space remains conceptual: that is to say, the novel evokes a world which appears and constructs itself around a recognizably valid duration. Moreover the action of a novel always occurs in the past, even when the narrative tense is the present. It is always a question of a reality already established and not of an evolving reality: such a reality must already exist in order for the novelist to describe it. At least if he constructs it with words—as the cineaste constructs with images—it is always already established for the reader. Everything occurs for the reader (always presenting the character to himself and identifying with him) as if "I" in the present (the reader who is also aware that he is a reader) is recalling a "me" in the past (the hero acts—has just acted—in the course of the reading of the phrases). This objectification, which creates temporal distance, brings about a feeling of lived duration; the judgment the reader imposes upon himself (or his alter-ego) attests to this. In the cinema, on the contrary, the spectator identifies with the hero and is always at the point of or in the process of acting with him; his mental projection is in the present. Consequently there is an increase of fascination, of living truth; it is impossible, or at least very difficult, to maintain temporal distance.

This aside, there is nothing to stop the film from developing like a novel, borrowing its structures and movement, ambling to and fro, telling a story which emphasizes the development of the characters at the pleasure of time and circumstance—instead of fixing a momentary drama or a fleeting crisis, braiding and unbraiding the threads of tragedy at will. We need to remind ourselves though that since the means of signifying are not the same, the processes of

signification will not be identical. It is not a matter of *imitating* the novel, but of *perceiving,* in cinema's own way, a certain temporal density, a duration which establishes, opens up, and defines through its multiple perspectives the psychological authenticity of the characters it implicates, a duration which safeguards their free will or at least gives them the appearance of liberty. It is a matter of following the characters according to a logical development through situations which are always contingent, subject to the pressures of chance and the unexpected, instead of directing them, enclosing them, in the constraining limitations of a drama—which always seems artificial to me because the mark of the creator is too visibly manifest. I'm not talking about that "mark" which is style and justifies creation, but about this other thing which intrudes on the givens of a problem because of a premeditated development, about an equilibrium the rigor of which fixes things rather than becoming the constant expression of them. If, then, the film finds itself before the same problematics as the novel, in the sense that it too can be a narrative art, if its development can be analogous to that of the novel, it can neither proceed in the same fashion nor, consequently, signify the same things. (pp. 1-9)

> *Jean Mitry, "Remarks on the Problem of Cinematic Adaptation," in* The Bulletin of the Midwest Modern Language Association, *Vol. 4, No. 1, Spring, 1971, pp. 1-9.*

Joy Gould Boyum

[*Boyum is an American educator and critic. In the following excerpt, she examines the critical position that film and literature are distinct, even antagonistic, art forms, arguing that their functions and aims are in fact complementary and may be identical.*]

Hollywood has never been noted for its literacy. Yet from its very beginnings, it has turned to literature for inspiration and persisted in the practice of translating books to film. Our first and greatest film artist, the man who is variously credited with "inventing Hollywood" and with forging film's distinctive language, typically based his movies on poems, plays, short stories, and novels. True, D. W. Griffith's most famous films are taken from the kind of works which hardly classify as "literature" at all: Thomas Burke's story "The Chink and the Child," which served as the basis for *Broken Blossoms;* Adolph D. Ennery's sentimental melodrama *The Two Orphans,* which he translated into *Orphans of the Storm;* and most notoriously, Thomas Dixon's racist bestseller *The Clansman,* which was both the source and original title of *The Birth of a Nation.* But Griffith—who was evidently more well read than most of his followers and is said to have arrived on the set each day carrying one or another of Dickens' novels—also frequently made use of the classics. He adapted Tennyson in *Enoch Arden,* Browning in *Pippa Passes,* Thomas Hood in *The Song of the Shirt,* Jack London in *The Call of the Wild,* and, in *The Cricket on the Hearth,* his beloved Dickens, whose work is generally credited with inspiring the innovations—the use of the close-up, parallel editing, montage, and even the dissolve—which helped earn Griffith the epithet "father of film technique."

Griffith, however, wasn't the father of adaptation. In bringing classic literary works to the screen, he was merely following the lead of French and Italian filmmakers who had looked to literature for story material as early as 1902. That was the year that Georges Méliès filmed his *A Trip to the Moon* which, loose as its connections to its literary source may have been, still had its origins in a Jules Verne novel, as did Méliès' later film *Twenty Thousand Leagues under the Sea.* More serious attempts at adaptation were made just a few years later: 1908 saw the formation of the Société Film d'Art, a French company formed for the express purpose of translating prestigious literary works to the screen, mostly dramas but also novels by Hugo, Balzac, and Dickens. The Italians, for their part, were attracted to historical works—novels such as Edgar Bulwer-Lytton's *The Last Days of Pompeii* and Henrik Sienkiewicz's *Quo Vadis,* which in 1908 and 1912 respectively made for some of the earliest adaptations, as well as for the movies' first superspectaculars.

What's interesting is that, primitive as these adaptations were in every respect—after all, what can one expect of a five-minute silent version of Zola's *L'assommoir* or a one-reel *Ben-Hur* shot with static camera against a painted backdrop?—they were generally greeted with praise, if not for their aesthetic value, at least for their educational potential. For, like early movies in general, such films were aimed primarily at the lower classes and so were perceived as a promising means of providing these viewers with a share in "the great tradition." Writing in *The Moving Picture World* in 1911, critic Stephen Bush carried such sentiments even further, making the introduction of the literary classics to the masses the very mission of the motion picture:

> It is the masterpiece of the ages that especially invites filming, and the reason for it is very plain. An epic that has pleased and charmed many generations is most likely to stand the test of cinematographic reproduction. . . . After all, the word "classic" has some meaning. It implies the approval of the best people in the most enlightened times. The merits of a classic subject are nonetheless certain because known and appreciated by comparatively few men. It is the business of the moving picture to make them known to all.

"The business of the moving picture" being primarily "business" itself, it's doubtful there were many moviemakers who shared Bush's messianic view. Here and there, a director might have felt drawn to a classic out of some passionate involvement with it, but for the most part, literature attracted filmmakers back then for the same reasons it does today. On the most practical of levels, it supplied motion pictures with a much-needed source of plots and characters. And if the work in question also happened to be either a "masterwork of the ages" or a popular play or novel, it also made for that most valuable of screen assets—the proverbial "proven property." There was another factor at work too: such classic sources gave movies—that suspect, vulgar form which even Griffith had at first held in contempt and which right from the outset suffered from a sense of inferiority regarding its status and respectability—their own touch of class. For to adapt a prestigious work was to do more than merely borrow its plot, its characters, its themes: in the eyes of the movie industry, it was—and in fact still is—to borrow a bit of that work's quality and stature.

Certainly, this is one of the reasons that adaptations have

always held such a privileged place in the movie industry and why at the Academy Awards, it's the adaptation more than any other kind of film on which the industry bestows its honors. Take that stellar movie year 1939, when nearly every competing film was an adaptation—*Wuthering Heights, The Wizard of Oz, Of Mice and Men, Goodbye, Mr. Chips,* and of course, *Gone with the Wind*—and when even the winner of the year's award for best short subject was an adaptation, Disney's version of Hans Christian Andersen's "The Ugly Duckling." Take almost any year in fact, since a list of the movies which have either won or at least been nominated for Best Picture sounds startlingly like a library catalogue: *The Way of All Flesh, All Quiet on the Western Front, Mutiny on the Bounty, Arrowsmith, A Farewell to Arms, David Copperfield, The Informer, A Midsummer Night's Dream, Pygmalion, The Grapes of Wrath, The Magnificent Ambersons, For Whom the Bell Tolls, The Ox-Bow Incident, Hamlet, Henry V, Great Expectations, All the King's Men, The Heiress* (from Henry James's *Washington Square*), *King Solomon's Mines, A Place in the Sun* (from Dreiser's *An American Tragedy*), *Ivanhoe, From Here to Eternity, A Streetcar Named Desire, The Rose Tattoo, Cat on a Hot Tin Roof, Room at the Top, Elmer Gantry, Sons and Lovers, To Kill a Mockingbird, Beckett, Zorba the Greek, Dr. Zhivago, Romeo and Juliet, Tom Jones, A Clockwork Orange, Barry Lyndon, One Flew over the Cuckoo's Nest, Apocalypse Now* (inspired by Conrad's *Heart of Darkness*), *Tess, Sophie's Choice,* and so on. Not to mention such films as *Women in Love, The Prime of Miss Jean Brodie,* and *Being There,* whose stars won awards for Best Performance (outstanding novels, as well as outstanding plays, apparently offering actors equally outstanding opportunities for characterization), or *The Garden of the Finzi-Continis, The Tin Drum,* and *Mephisto* (among other adaptations which have won in the category of Best Foreign Film, first instituted in 1956). What is more, since the industry approval implicit in these awards not only reflects a given film's "quality" but also its popularity—the latter being one of Hollywood's crucial yardsticks of the former—it's fairly clear that in most instances, audiences have also been responsive to these movies.

But if the adaptation has had its supporters, it has also had its detractors. And since most of these have come from the ranks of neither moviemakers nor ordinary moviegoers but of academics, theorists, and latter-day critics—or in other words, from those who tend to put their ideas into print—the fact is that despite occasional early support, most of what has been set down about adaptation has been set down firmly against it. Rumblings were heard even back in those early optimistic days. There was Vachel Lindsay who, passionately taken with this new form and bent on championing "film as art," argued against adaptation on the grounds that it worked against the film medium's uniqueness [see Further Reading]. Virginia Woolf likewise expressed the view that the "alliance" between cinema and literature was "unnatural" and "disastrous" to both forms, though her language makes it clear that she believed it a good deal more disastrous to one than the other and that, unlike Lindsay, her concern was less with the future of movies than with the future of books [see excerpt below]. Railing against the adaptation, she wrote of books as the "prey" and "unfortunate victim," movies as a "parasite" which feeds on them with "immense rapacity," and the movie audience itself (presumably in contrast to the audience for books) as "the savages of the twentieth century."

Lindsay and Woolf were both, of course, writing in the silent days—he in 1915, she a decade later. And though we see in the stance of each the lines along which subsequent arguments against the adaptation have been drawn, these positions were not to become either truly solidified or widespread until movies began to talk and until they also went through a series of dramatic changes in their aesthetics and in their economic and social structures in the years immediately following World War II.

When one considers that the silent film had a lifespan of a mere thirty-five years, its accomplishments are staggering. Still, even in the hands of a Griffith or an Eisenstein, it remained extremely limited as a storytelling medium. For its narrative and dramatic possibilities to be in any way fulfilled, film clearly demanded sound. And sound also brought with it, as moviemakers struggled to come to terms with its use, a host of other technological and stylistic advances. So enormous were the changes that film underwent during the first decades of the sound era (that is, during the thirties and forties) that reviewing them in his essay "The Evolution of the Language of Cinema," André Bazin could go so far as to declare: "the filmmaker . . . is, at last, the equal of the novelist." In the eyes of those who, unlike Bazin, took literature as their primary concern, this hardly seemed the case, but one thing was certain: the filmmaker had become the novelist's competitor. And it wasn't simply that the movies now quite literally had the language of literature at their disposal; it was also that during the first decades of the sound era, movies had become an extraordinarily pervasive medium which now numbered among its audience, together with the uneducated lower classes, members of the middle and upper-middle classes as well.

Movies, moreover, weren't the only mass medium that had come to the fore in this period: the thirties and forties were also the golden age of radio and the era in which comic books and picture magazines like *Life, Look,* and *Coronet* flourished. Thus, by the early 1950s, when the great growth spurt of television began, defenders of traditional culture began to panic. (Actually, they had begun to panic earlier, but more important issues, chiefly World War II, distracted their attention for a while.) Culture was divided up and categorized: into avant-garde and kitsch; highbrow, middlebrow, and lowbrow; mass-cult and mid-cult; the traditional arts and the popular ones; art and entertainment. The aesthetics of the popular arts were explored, the effects of mass culture were investigated; and nearly everywhere with the implicit aim not simply of salvaging the genuine from the ersatz, of rescuing good taste from the onslaught of bad, but indeed of saving culture itself. For thanks to the media (or so certain critics claimed) not only couldn't Johnny read, but with the entertainment industry voraciously feeding on genuine works of art, transforming and making them digestible, there seemed a very real danger that the books he might read (if he could) might themselves be eaten up and destroyed. Such were the fears expressed by numerous defenders of high culture—among them Hannah Arendt, who put the matter this way:

> The entertainment industry is confronted with gargantuan appetites, and since its wares disappear in

consumption, it must constantly offer new commodities. In this predicament, those who produce for the mass media ransack the entire range of past and present culture in the hope of finding suitable material. This material, however, cannot be offered as it is; it must be prepared and altered in order to become entertaining. . . . The danger is . . . precisely that it may become very entertaining indeed; there are many great authors of the past who have survived centuries of oblivion and neglect, but it is still an open question whether they will be able to survive an entertaining version of what they have to say.

It's Virginia Woolf all over again—only a good deal stronger—the metaphor having shifted from the biological one of the "parasite" (which, whatever damage it does to its host, at least has the virtue of proceeding quietly) to the much more strident one of war. On the one side we have the "ransacking" hordes of mass culture; on the other the defending troops of high culture fighting for their very life; with the adaptation emerging as the convenient emblem of the conflict. Why the adaptation? Because, as Arendt suggests, it is here that the gold of art is transformed into the dross of entertainment, and refined, legitimate culture is pummeled into its vulgar mass form. The biases underlying this view are hard to miss: that a work of literature (or anything truly worthy of the name) is by definition a work of complexity and quality which is addressed to an educated elite; that movies, in contrast, are mere entertainment, directed at anyone and everyone; and that to adapt a book to film is thus of necessity to adjust it, not so much to its new medium as to its audience. That is, to the uneducated, undifferentiated mass, with its inevitably limited comprehension and predilection for the homiletic sentiment. Adaptation, in Arendt's view, is synonymous with betrayal. (pp. 3-8)

[The] view still prevails in the literary establishment that the adaptation is a variety of classic comic and that film itself (despite its Ingmar Bergmans and Alain Resnais') is a lesser form. However seemingly sophisticated the works created from it, the "language" of film is still held by many to be an essentially transparent and crude one when contrasted to the "language" of literature. (While everyone has to be taught how to read, we are reminded, no one really has to be taught how to see a movie.) And if the medium isn't simplistic, where are the works that reflect its complexity? Where are the masterpieces of cinematic art? Where are the films, as one defender of high culture asks, that can stand comparison with "the main works of Aeschylus, Sophocles, Euripides, Aristophanes, Homer, Virgil, Dante, Shakespeare, Moliere, Goethe . . . "? So *Citizen Kane* is one of the greatest films ever made. Can the film enthusiast really claim that its symbolism is "in the same league as the iconography of Amiens, the images in Dante's *Commedia* or even the lesser number in *Moby Dick* or *Ulysses;* that the portrayal of a man in *Citizen Kane* is even to be compared with that say in *Le Rouge et le Noir* or *The Great Gatsby"?* So Fellini is one of the great filmmakers. "Is [he] really such an observer as Joyce?" (pp. 9-10)

As the writings of Vachel Lindsay make clear, there were those who regarded movies as a legitimate and significant aesthetic enterprise from the very outset. Still, it wasn't until the late fifties and early sixties that, in this country at least, such a view really took hold. In large part, this reevaluation of film was a function of developments abroad. Immediately after World War II the various European industries began to recover; Italian Neorealism and the French New Wave developed, and suddenly we were importing a type of complex, challenging, even puzzling work that looked like art, felt like art, and was consequently dubbed the "art film" Even more important to this revised perception of film, however, was a development at home—television. Television may have helped spur criticism of mass culture in which movies were inevitably included, and it may have worked economic havoc on the movie industry, but in stealing away movies' great mass audience, it helped to make movies themselves more elite. Moreover, once the studios had sold off their old libraries to this new medium, television suddenly made available the whole of Hollywood's past, evoking a great deal of nostalgia on the one hand, and an enormous amount of serious rethinking and reevaluation on the other.

So we find that during the fifties and sixties, movies began to make a major effort to reshape their image and to reshape it very distinctly in the mold of art. They changed their name, dropping "motion picture" altogether (as in "Academy of Motion Picture Arts and Sciences") and opting for the more connotatively cultivated labels: "film" (as in the newly constituted American Film Institute) and even "cinema." They found a forum at prestigious cultural institutions like Washington, D.C.'s, Kennedy Center and New York City's Lincoln Center. They gave rise, in place of the old fan magazines, to seriously intended publications such as *Film Culture* and *Film Comment.* Their "reviewers" were magically transformed into "critics." More important yet, they began to make major inroads behind the walls of ivy.

But if changing status is one thing, feeling secure about it is another. And film in its efforts to be accepted as art has had to deal not only with such obvious extrinsic burdens as its blatant commercialism and the inescapable trashiness of so many of its products; it has also been plagued with certain intrinsic problems deriving from its very nature. Arguing for film as art, Vachel Lindsay felt it necessary to put forth a case for film's uniqueness, and theorists since his time have felt similarly impelled. But try as they might to isolate qualities truly special to the form, these theorists simply haven't been able to come up with any—beyond, that is, the facts that film is a machine art, depending on mechanical equipment for both its creation and reception, and that it relies on illusion, on our acceptance that such an observer as Joyce?" (pp. 9-10)

Film shares its visual aspect with painting, its dependence on movement with dance, its ability to produce kinetic and emotional effects with music, its reliance on performance and spectacle with theatre, its technological basis with architecture. But the art with which film (or at least narrative film) clearly shares most—from its use of plot, characters, setting, dialogue, and imagery through its manner of expressing theme to its tendency to manipulate space and time—is literature. And so it follows that the effort to assert film's uniqueness involves distancing it from no art so much as the one to which it seems so intimately related.

Here, of course, lies the basis for much of the antipathy cineastes hold toward the adaptation. It's also the basis, significantly enough, for a common approach to the evolution of film itself, one which views film as having struggled throughout its history to free itself from the yoke of literature and its dependence on literary models. It was very much because he saw them as "writer's films," for example, that the young critic François Truffaut took issue with the French films of the postwar period—films which constituted what was known as the "Tradition of Quality" and which were generally based on French classics. That Truffaut didn't criticize them on these particular grounds doesn't matter in the least. (He didn't mind an adaptation, he noted, when it was the work of a "man of the cinema" or, put another way, an *auteur;* while the fact is that when he himself became a filmmaker, he frequently turned to literary sources, whether the works of Henri-Pierre Roche in *Jules and Jim* and *Two English Girls* or of Ray Bradbury in *Fahrenheit 451* or of Henry James in *The Green Room.*) Truffaut's views have nonetheless contributed immeasurably to the negative attitude toward the adaptation—the adaptation being, in the minds of most, inescapably a "writer's film" or, to use a term of even greater opprobrium to cineastes, a "literary" one. An authentically "cinematic" film, in contrast—or so it's widely held—will be free of such roots and connections. It will be originated for the screen and not for the page; conceived in images and not in words; a work that is visual and not linear.

Such a film, as Truffaut proposed, will also be the creation of an *auteur;* and the *"politique"* that issued from this claim contributed in still another way toward the negative perception of the adaptation. For if one of film's difficulties in claiming that it is art lies in its inability to truly determine its cinematic essence, another rests in its peculiar status as a group production—as an art, that is, without an artist. Can such an entity be a work of art at all? The answer for many has been a resounding no. And so, together with the search for the uniqueness of its language and logic of representation, still another of cinema's projects has been to come up with a unique creator—someone conveniently supplied by the *politique des auteurs* in the person of the film director.

Certain films very easily accommodate this view; others, to the contrary, don't. And chief among these, once again, is the adaptation. Consider how much less difficulty there is in thinking of John Ford as the "auteur" of *Fort Apache* than of *The Grapes of Wrath,* where the shadow of Steinbeck looms so large; or in crediting John Huston as creator of *The Asphalt Jungle* than as the guiding sensibility behind *The Man Who Would Be King.* For much as the thriller might owe to W. R. Burnett's novel, it seems to us a good deal less than the classic adventure owes to Kipling. It follows then that in the canon of uniquely cinematic works created by the unique film artist, the likes of *Fort Apache* and *The Asphalt Jungle* would inevitably rank above films like *The Grapes of Wrath* and *The Man Who Would Be King.* And Hollywood's tendency to prefer the latter films to the former only serves to strengthen the auteurist position. Hollywood, after all, is still another of the difficult burdens film must bear in its effort to assert itself as art; and Hollywood's taste (as reflected in the Academy Awards especially) is judged as its very worst to be as vulgar as Hollywood itself, while at its very best, to be naive and misguided—to confuse seriousness of intent with meaningful accomplishment.

Admittedly, not all those who take film seriously subscribe to the arguments of the auteurists. And these arguments certainly don't sit well either with defenders of high culture, who, among other things, have considerable difficulty with the standard auteurist canon—including as it does westerns and thrillers, or, in other words, what is traditionally taken as pulp. There is, however, one argument against adaptation with which nearly all—whether auteurist, nonauteurist, or member of the literati—agree, and which because of this consensus emerges as the most powerful of all: that the adaptation is a lesser form because it lacks originality. Certainly, this is the view that prevails in academia, while it's also the criterion a good number of serious filmmakers would subscribe to as well. "It's hard to think of a truly revolutionary film that was derived from a novel," writes George Linden in his text *Reflections on the Screen;* "I would not want to shoot the adaptation of a novel because . . . to make a film of it is a little like reheating a meal," remarks Alain Resnais; and Jean-Luc Godard notes rather coyly that the only way he could think of filming a novel would be to photograph it page by page. Forget that Godard has in fact adapted both Maupaussant (in an early short, *Une femme coquette*) and Moravia (in his 1963 feature *Le mépris*). Forget, too, that among the "revolutionary films" Professor Linden cites in support of his contention—"films that stand as examples, *par excellence,* of the medium"—are *The Birth of a Nation* (whose source in Dixon's *The Clansman* Linden overlooks) and *The Bicycle Thief* (which he also fails to note was derived from Luigi Bartolini's *Landri de biciclette*). The idea is simply that if film is going to declare itself an art, it must find arguments in its favor. And ironically, perhaps, considering its emphasis on its uniqueness, it has found them not in the unique conditions of the medium, but in the traditional canon of art. Thus, the view that to be truly artful, a film must be the product of a single controlling sensibility; it must have a "language" and "content" of its own; and it must at all costs be a thoroughgoing original. It cannot, then, be an adaptation.

In short, nobody loves an adaptation. Not literary enough in that it proceeds through pictures, not cinematic enough in that it has its origins in words, it finds itself in a no-man's-land, caught somewhere between a series of conflicting aesthetic claims and rivalries. For if film threatens literature, literature also threatens film, and nowhere so powerfully, in either instance, as in the form of adaptation. What makes matters worse is that desperate as both arts are—film for status and legitimacy; literature for mere survival—both overstate their caase. Defenders on both sides fail to see how many of their positions follow from doctrinaire notions about the nature and role of art, from simple bias toward one medium or the other, and from—dare one say it?—sheer hysteria.

Consider the Woolf-Arendt view of the adaptation as threatening to devour and/or destroy its literary source. It's a dramatic notion, but what does it really add up to? It can't be the literal survival of the work that's at stake. Even where a time-honored classic has been reduced to out-and-out kitsch—as in the case of Walt Disney's version of Sir James Barrie's *Peter Pan,* James Whale's adaptation of *Frankenstein,* or the Hollywood *Brothers Karamazov*—the original still exists on the library shelf for those who would read and savor it. Can it mean then, that having seen *The Brothers Karamazov,* the viewer will believe he knows Dostoyevsky's novel and never be led to read it? This certainly seems more possible, but it still

doesn't follow. For the simple fact is that when a film is made of a novel, it tends to encourage reading rather than discourage it—just as the fact that we've read the novel encourages us to see the film. All any of us has to do is glance at a local paperback rack and the books themselves will make the point—all those reissued copies of E. L. Doctorow's *The Book of Daniel* or of Bernard Malamud's *The Natural,* with their respective cover photos of Timothy Hutton and Robert Redford. And this symbiotic relationship isn't a function of the current book-movie tie-in or paperback revolution. Back in 1939, when the film version of *Wuthering Heights* was released, more copies of the novel were sold than in the entire previous near-century of its existence.

Is it then, as Jean-Paul Sartre contends, that the film will somehow stand between us and the book—that if we read *The Natural* after seeing the movie, we will be stuck forever with the image of Robert Redford? This may be true in a sense, but only to the extent that both film and performance are powerful enough to control our reading, or conversely, when the book is not powerful enough to assert its own view. Consider this anecdote related by a thirties film critic who, getting into a taxi one day, noted that the driver was reading Robert Louis Stevenson's *Kidnapped.* The driver had been inspired by the recent movie, and now that he had "the real thing" in his hands, he was absolutely furious at the liberties producer Darryl Zanuck had taken. "There ain't no girl in the book," he informed the critic, "and this David Balfour was a lot older than Freddie Bartholomew." He went on to add, "Why, if I had any dough, I'd sue Zanuck for fraud. They have no right to put over stuff like that on the public." The point isn't to give this driver the last word on adaptation. It's rather to suggest that Sartre notwithstanding—he has been able to see beyond Freddie Bartholomew to the novel's very different image of David Balfour—to read, that is, in ways other than the movie had directed him. Thus even when we see the movie first and read the book after, we still often test the film by the book and not, as Sartre also implies, the book by the film. The novel has a way of remaining the authority.

If the adaptation, then, can't really be seen as destructive to literature, in what sense can it be seen as destructive to film? Does the fact that a film derives from a literary work actually undermine the medium's uniqueness? This could only be the case if it were possible to maintain that the "essence" of cinema lies in its difference from the other arts. But surely, the uniqueness of film, its distinctiveness and special quality, lies in something quite the opposite: in its "melting pot" nature, in the fact that it not only shares each and every one of its qualities with other art forms, but combines the effects of all of them. Looking at film this way—stressing the extent to which it combines the resources of literature, music, dance, painting—we come to understand something of its peculiar power, just as we also come to see there's really nothing that isn't appropriate to cinema or that isn't "cinematic." Not even a movie that's called "a writer's film," not even a "literary" film adaptation. And what is a "literary" movie anyway? Is it a nonstop talkie with not much more than a single set, like Howard Hawks's *His Girl Friday?* A film with a voice-over commentary, like Billy Wilder's *Sunset Boulevard?* A movie pervaded by the sensibility of its scenarist, like poet Jacques Prévert's *Children of Paradise?* Or is it merely a question of origins, of the source of any given film in the first place? Adapted from a Henri-Pierre Roche novel, and so originally conceived for the printed page, is *Jules and Jim* literary? Is Fassbinder's *Effi Briest?* Is even Eric Rohmer's nearly line-by-line rendition of Heinrich von Kleist's *The Marquise of O?* And are they any more "literary" than Bergman's *The Seventh Seal* or Antonioni's *L'avventura?*

And to turn to that most crucial of the arguments against adaptation, just what constitutes originality in a work of art anyway, at least when we apply it as a criterion of value? It can't be a question of a work being the first of its kind—since in film, as in any art, being the first is far from synonymous with being the best or even with being merely good. (We're surely not going to claim that the 1930 *Little Caesar* was a better movie than *The Godfather,* or that the 1903 *The Great Train Robbery* was superior to *The Wild Bunch*—though these first films are much more "original" than those that followed them.) Nor can originality be a matter of mere invention, since a work can be highly inventive and great, or highly inventive and awful. Originality isn't even a matter of a work's materials, of an artist making up his own story or characters, of generating his own subject matter—if it were, we'd have to reject not only Verdi's *Otello* but even *Othello* itself and everything else of Shakespeare's. What it is a matter of instead—given that originality isn't a totally meaningless term and that some films do strike us as fresh, others in contrast as stale—is the way those materials are handled. What makes for the originality (and for the greatness as well) of Sir Laurence Olivier's *Henry V* is the way Olivier "staged" that play on film; just as what makes for the originality of Fellini's *8½* is the manner in which the maestro mounted his fantasies.

It's evident, then, that an adaptation can be as original or unoriginal as any other kind of movie. Can one also claim, however, that an adaptation is equally *necessary?* Why bother to adapt a fine novel in the first place? The only reasonable answer to such a question, it seems to me, is why not? An artist has the right to look anywhere for his materials—and if he finds his stories and characters in books rather than life, if he finds his *donnée* on a printed page rather than in a glimpse of a painting or an overheard piece of conversation, so be it. Besides, there's a natural impulse to want to vivify a work of literature that has moved us and mattered to us. It may even be this challenge itself that excites the filmmaker and that, more often than is generally acknowledged, has inspired him to reach for new techniques, discover new strategies, expand the narrative and psychological possibilities of his art. Indeed, the history of film suggests that adaptations have frequently been quite as revolutionary in their techniques—if not more so—than other types of film.

The history of film also suggests that whatever the limitations of certain current-day adaptations—whether highly controversial and ambitious ones like Stanley Kubrick's *Barry Lyndon* or modest and generally neglected ones like George Roy Hill's *The World According to Garp* or Sidney Lumet's *Daniel*—their flaws and insufficiencies have little to do with those of the *reductio ad absurdum* adaptations of the old days: with the likes, that is, of the Hollywood *War and Peace,* of Martin Ritt's *The Sound and the Fury,* of Minelli's *Madame Bovary.* For movies have done more than change their image: movies themselves have changed, and so have adaptations right along with them. The literary establishment seems not to have noticed, however, given that so many of the arguments it puts forth against adaptation (and against movies themselves) are really arguments about film-as-it-was, rather than about film-as-it-is; about film when it was synonymous with Hollywood and had to submit to the taste of the moguls, the strictures of the star system, and the censoring eye of the Hayes office; about film when it was more of a mass medium than it is today and, consequently, operated with very different notions as to the nature of its audience. Today, most moviegoers clearly are aware, to be more educated and sophisticated than the population at large. As such, they no longer demand the traditional Hollywood sop—among other things, bowdlerizations and happy endings.

And it's not only film's sociology and structure that have changed; its very aesthetic has as well—though once again you'd never know it from those who rail against adaptation. Ignoring the radical artistic changes of recent years, their arguments are about movies before they began to incorporate the innovations of avant-garde filmmaking, the French New Wave, the Italian Neorealists, and other contemporary arts as well. They also tend to be about film before technological developments altered its shape and texture: from the widespread use of color, the development of handheld cameras, and the emphasis on location shooting to the increased pace and tempo of editing.

Earlier, talking about the silent film, I noted the impressive extent of its accomplishments given its very brief lifespan. The same holds true for film in general, whose growth over the mere century of its existence is astonishing. Certainly, the distance between Edwin S. Porter's *The Great Train Robbery* and *Bonnie and Clyde,* between Méliè's *A Trip to the Moon* and *2001* is greater than that between a Greek tragedy and the plays of Ibsen, between the statues of Praxitcles and those of Rodin. And though the distance between adaptation then and adaptations now isn't nearly as huge, it's nonetheless considerable. Made today, *The Grapes of Wrath* could have retained the novel's devastating ending. A modern-day version of the Laurence Olivier-Merle Oberson *Wuthering Heights* would clearly have avoided the use of pasteboard sets and most likely, too, the inclusion of an insistent and saccharine score. A film of *A Farewell to Arms* in the 1980s wouldn't have to marry off Catherine and Frederick. And given the decline of the star system, *Madame Bovary* wouldn't have been forced to feature a Jennifer Jones, *Moby Dick* a Gregory Peck, *The Sound and the Fury* a Yul Brynner (thus sparing it, among other things, the need to transform Jason into a Cajun).

This isn't to dismiss all adaptations made prior to 1960, or to assert that what's new, wide, in color, and sexually explicit is necessarily more effective than what's old, black and white, and implicit. There were worthy adaptations around even in the silent days, just as there are totally miscarried adaptations now. My point is merely to suggest that a great deal of what has always troubled us about adaptations in the past and a good deal, too, of the so-called theoretical talk about them is very much a matter of issues like these—blatant omissions, ludicrous revisions, absurd miscarriages. It's also to say that what may trouble us about the film versions of *The Bostonians* or *A Passage to*

India or the 1984 *1984* is on another aesthetic plane altogether. (pp. 12-19)

[Ideas] about what film can't do that literature can, about differences in the structure and effects of the two media, and above all, about the process of adaptation itself are very much in need of revision. For one thing, there are the prejudices that have prevailed; for another, there are the changes that have taken place in the nature and situation of film. There's also the fact that—since adaptations are likely always to be with us and since film tends to be extremely sensitive to its audience—the more sophistication we as viewers bring to the process, the more effective these adaptations will tend to be. But perhaps the most pressing reason for rethinking these issues and reconsidering this curiously controversial form lies in the essential absurdity of seeing film and literature as mortal enemies. Indeed when the din and dust of the battle die down, when the bias toward print is removed and the need to assert cinema's uniqueness quelled, what becomes manifest is something quite the opposite: that far from being literature's antagonist, film is in a very real sense a form of literature itself. Not simply sharing the very qualities that make literature literature, but making for a system of narration that unites the power of words with the potentially even greater power of the images they aim to create, it might even be considered a natural next step in literature's evolution—a form that Flaubert and Dickens and other writers had somehow envisioned in their mind's eye and, through Griffith, Eisenstein, and other filmmakers, actually helped to create. (pp. 19-20)

> *Joy Gould Boyum, "Biases and Preconceptions," in her* "Double Exposure": Fiction into Film, *Universe Books, 1985, pp. 3-20.*

Robert Richardson

[*Richardson is an American educator and critic. In the following excerpt, he contends that film should be regarded as a branch of literature.*]

The attempt to relate literature and film is anything but new. From the early days of the film, when "classic" novels were first done into movies to the current trend toward *cinéma écriture* or *caméra stylo,* film makers have continually been indebted to literature in a wide variety of ways. So, too, a number of writers, from Pirandello to Nathanael West, have shown that the influence goes both ways. In an essay called "Dickens, Griffith, and the Film Today," Sergei Eisenstein has tried to document the importance of the English novelist to the early American film maker, and he goes on to suggest an even broader connection between film and literature. Eisenstein derides the idea that the film is an autonomous, self-contained, and utterly independent form.

> It is only very thoughtless and presumptuous people [he writes] who can erect laws and an esthetic for cinema, proceeding from premises of some incredible virgin-birth of this art!

> Let Dickens and the whole ancestral array, going back as far as the Greeks and Shakespeare, be superfluous reminders that both Griffith and our cinema prove our origins to be not solely as of Edison and his fellow inventors, but as based on an enor-

> mous cultured past; each part of this past in its own moment of world history has moved forward the great art of cinematography. Let this past be a reproach to those thoughtless people who have displayed arrogance in reference to literature, which has contributed so much to this apparently unprecedented art and is, in the first and most important place, the art of viewing.

Eisenstein's films and his writings both show his own continued and imaginative use of literature, and it may even be urged that Eisenstein's well known "film sense" is actually an expanded version of what has been called the literary imagination.

If one considers literature as the art of words, that is to say, if it is letters or words that give literary activity its peculiar and distinctive character, then of course, we should have to say that film is obviously neither literature, nor even literary, certainly not in the silent era and only marginally or collaterally in the sound era. If it is the primacy of the word that creates or allows literature, then one would have to be content with saying that the film is at most analogous to literature, having, as it does, its own pictorial vocabulary and its montage for syntax. But if one is willing to shift the focus a little, and to describe literature as being, in the main, a narrative art, intent upon creating images and sounds in the reader's mind, then film will appear much more obviously literary itself. This description would seem to argue that the film is only an extension, but a magnificent one, of the older narrative arts.

Both ideas seem to contain some truth. Film works, in its purely visual aspects, in ways that are often analogous to the ways literature works, and, considered as narrative forms, film and literature have some obvious similarities. André Bazin's *What Is Cinema?* contains some highly suggestive writing on this subject and Herbert Read, in a general way, has described this meeting point or conjunction.

> Those people who deny that there can be any connection between the scenario and literature seem to me to have a wrong conception, so much of the film as of literature. Literature they seem to regard as something polite and academic, in other words, as something godforsaken and superannuated, compounded of correct grammar and high-sounding ciceronian phrases. Such a conception reveals the feebleness of their sensibility. If you ask me to give you the most distinctive quality of good writing, I would give it to you in this one word: VISUAL. Reduce the art of writing to its fundamentals and you come to this single aim: to convey images by means of words. But to *convey images.* To make the mind see. To project onto that inner screen of the brain a moving picture of objects and events, events and objects moving toward a balance and reconciliation of a more than usual state of emotion with more than usual order. That is a definition of good literature—of the achievement of every good poet—from Homer and Shakespeare to James Joyce or Ernest Hemingway. It is also a definition of the ideal film [see Further Reading].

Granting that the means or mediums of film and literature are different—though perhaps not so radically different as might be supposed, as we shall see—there does seem to be enough fairly clear common ground between the two to permit the claim that the visual literacy that is still being created and enlarged by the films is an extension, or another and very closely related version, of the verbal literacy that has been associated with literature and literary culture since the Greeks.

Indeed, the currently much belabored split between the word and the image, the announcements of the end of the age of print and the advent of the age of the electronic image, and the diagnoses of post-literate man seem to me vastly to overrate the phenomena in question. The new literacy, the ability to "read" streams of visual images, has indeed, at times, the chaotic, uncontrolled, unsophisticated and exuberant qualities that often accompany a significant innovation or advance, but I think it is beginning to be apparent that this new literacy is not a negation of the older sort of literacy, but an expansion or an enlargement of the idea of literacy itself. And I suspect that the new literacy, if it takes the trouble to recognize and develop its kinship with the strictly verbal sort, will in time create a milieu for works of art that are not inferior to the best of our literary masterpieces.

It also seems arguable that the humane literacy for which George Steiner pleads so eloquently in his *Language and Silence,* and about which he is something less than sanguine, will come about, if it does come about, through some sort of union between the old and the new literacy. Mr. Steiner has spoken of the two principal functions of language as "the conveyance of humane order which we call law, and the communication of the quick of the human spirit which we call grace." Film already shares the second of these functions with literature (the final scene of Fellini's *8½,* in which all the characters from the hero's life join hands to dance in a circle in a splendid gesture of assent, is one of a hundred possible examples) and film may come to share even the first of these two crucial functions.

Many people object, as Herbert Read noted, to attempts to pull the film within the realm of literature, and modern literary endeavor gives some color to this objection. For it is an odd fact, and one that is difficult to explain, that, at a time when the study of literature engages more minds, more time, and more energy than in any previous age, the scope of literary study, particularly that of the modern period, has shrunk drastically. The study of Renaissance literature used to include, and still does to a decent extent, works on theology, philosophy, education, science, history, biography, journalism, manners, morals, and navigation, in addition to poems, plays, and works of fiction. To some degree, this is true of the study of all literary periods up to the present, but the study of twentieth century literature is inexplicably confined to poems, plays, and novels, while in the universities the spread of theatre departments tends to limit the literary people more and more to just poems and fiction. This narrowing of interest to the so-called creative forms ought to favor the inclusion of dramatic films in literary study, and a recent publication by the National Council of Teachers of English called *The Motion Picture and the Teaching of English* seems to point in this direction, but it is not in this spirit that I should like to urge the study of film and literature. I should prefer a climate in which everything written, including of course film scripts, was legitimately considered a part of the study of literature, and it is in this very broad sense that I shall argue that film is a branch of literature. The claim is less

sweeping than it appears, for the argument is simply that certain films and certain kinds of films are similar or related to certain works and genres of literature if we are willing to define literature broadly.

In literary studies, it is customary to regard the novel, the epic poem, the play, and a number of other genres as separate and distinct forms, each having its own qualities and strength, its own demands and controls over its material. A good play cannot be redone as a poem, a good poem cannot be put in novel form. So too, the good dramatic film, the commonest film form, and the one that normally shows a story about people, cannot be successfully done in any other form. There has, of course, been a great deal of "adaptation" work done in the films. Countless plays and novels and even a few poems have been done into film, and a fair amount of critical attention has been paid to the connections between drama and film and novels and film. Such connections may be important, but it is necessary to realize that these connections are neither more nor less than the kind of relation usually referred to as translation, and translation, as opposed to what Dryden or Robert Lowell mean by "imitation," inevitably loses something, often much, in the process. A play may be translated into a film, but this should not obscure the fact that plays and films are not essentially similar. The Russian poet Alexander Blok understood this when he wrote in 1918, in reply to a request:

> I have nothing now ready for the screen but I have more than once thought of writing for it; I always feel, however, that this will have to find a new technique for itself. In my opinion cinema has nothing in common with theatre, is not attached to it, does not compete with it, nor can they destroy each other; those once fashionable discussions 'on cinema and theatre' seem quite unreal to me. I have long loved the cinema just as it was.

What is true of drama and the film is also true, most of the time, of the connection between novels and film, as George Bluestone has taken great care to show [see Further Reading]. Stories can be translated from one form to the other, but what makes a good novel rarely makes a good film. *On the Waterfront* is a good film but poor in its later novel form; Joyce's *Ulysses* is a great novel, but mediocre in its film form. Alain Resnais has put the problem straightforwardly, saying, "I would not want to shoot the adaptation of a novel because I think that the writer has completely expressed himself in the novel and that wanting to make a film of it is a little like re-heating a meal."

Of the various kinds of literature, the modern novel and modern poetry come closest to the forms and methods of the dramatic film. Herbert Read has it that "the film of imagination—the film as a work of art ranking with great drama, great literature, and great painting, will not come until the poet enters the studio." Others indeed claim that this has already happened and that it is still going on. Stanley Kauffmann notes that Bergman, Fellini, Antonioni "and others, including some Americans, have been extending the film into the vast areas of innermost privacy, even of the unconscious, that have been the province of the novel and of metaphysical poetry." Agnes Varda has said that she wanted "to make a film exactly as one writes a novel," and Alain Resnais remarked, apropos of his *Hiroshima mon amour,* that he "was intending to compose a sort of poem where the image would serve only as a counterpoint to the text." Jean Cocteau has made a number of films on this last principle; *Blood of a Poet* and *Orpheus* in particular are remarkable for their extensive reliance on techniques usually associated with modern poetry.

It was also Cocteau who referred to his films as studies of "the frontier incidents between one world and another." The frontier he meant is that between the real and the apparent, between the actual world and the camera's world, between dreams and art, and between death and life. His description may be given another meaning, whether he intended it or not, for his films and those of a number of other gifted men are "frontier incidents" also in the sense that they take place between the world of words and the world of images. (pp. 11-16)

> *Robert Richardson, in his* Literature and Film, *1969. Reprint by Garland Publishing, Inc., 1985, 149 p.*

Morris Beja

[*Beja is an American educator and critic specializing in modern literature. In the following excerpt, he considers the ways in which film and literature can or cannot be compared.*]

In . . . *Literature and Film* [see excerpt above], Robert Richardson makes the interesting and valid point that when we think of a historical period such as the Renaissance, we generally agree that its "literature" includes "works on theology, philosophy, education, science, history, biography, journalism, manners, morals, and navigation, in addition to poems, plays, and works of fiction," yet for some reason we act as if "twentieth century literature is inexplicably confined to poems, plays, and novels." Moreover, if we go further back than Richardson does, we will include works that are not written or printed: everyone agrees that the Homeric epics are literature, yet it was not until centuries after they were composed that anyone ever wrote them down. Had movies somehow existed in ancient Greece—or during the Renaissance—we would surely now be studying them as works of literature.

If, instead of stressing writing or print, we were to argue that it is best to regard literature as a purely linguistic art, one that uses words alone, then no doubt we would have to exclude film—along with the plays of Shakespeare, Sophocles, Shaw, and O'Neill, to be sure. Like drama, film is not exclusively a linguistic art; indeed it is not even primarily so. But when some critics argue that it is exclusively a "visual" art and not *at all* an art of words, one can only wonder when was the last time they went to a movie.

The "literary" art with which film is most often associated, by far, is not the drama, as one might at first expect, but the novel; and the reason for this near universal tendency is above all that both are forms of telling stories, and their modes of telling those stories are comparably open. So basic indeed are these similarities that they overshadow many of the differences. The French film critic Christian Metz even claims, in his discussion of what he calls "the total invasion of the cinema by novelesque fiction," that "the rule of the 'story' is so powerful that the image, which is said to be the major constituent of film, vanishes behind the plot it has woven . . . so that the cinema is only in theory the art of images." (pp. 53-4)

But if narrative literature and film share, indeed by definition, the basic element of the story, they do not "tell" the story in the same way or in the same "language." Many critics have gotten round that fact by in a sense denying it, through elaborate comparisons of verbal and cinematic language. They point out that the basic components of verbal language—that is, of course, what most people think of as language—are words (vocabulary) and the ways in which they are put together (grammar and syntax). The comparable elements in film, say these critics, are the frame or the photographed image (which is parallel to the word) and the editing of the images (parallel to grammar and syntax). Sometimes, just as the word is seen as the equivalent of the frame, so the sentence is compared to the shot, the paragraph to the scene, and the chapter to the sequence.

Such one-to-one analogies, at first glance perhaps intriguing, are in fact basically misleading. If editing is syntax, how do we know when a particular example of a "sentence" (or shot) is "ungrammatical" or "nonstandard"? If frames are words, how can a dictionary be compiled which will "define" each image? Moreover, a fundamental problem in such analogies is that by describing film in terminology which is suitable to verbal language, they inevitably make film seem cruder by comparison; film is not being examined on its *own* terms.

A more fruitful approach has been the newer one associated with semiotics, the study of systems of signs and meanings, which has sought to describe *cinematic* language. According to this approach, film *is* a language, but it is one that is quite different from verbal language. Film is language in the most general sense—it is a mode of communication—not in the more particular sense by which we mean "language" to refer to such highly systematized codes as "the English language," or Italian, or German. Christian Metz, who has been doing important work in this field, has pursued numerous associations and distinctions between film language and verbal language. For example, he points out that the total number of *words* is large but finite, while the number of possible *statements* using those words is infinite; a film image or frame is in that sense like a statement and unlike a word, since the number of possible images is also infinite. Each visual image is comparable to a full sentence in other ways as well. An image of a man and woman kissing each other is the equivalent not of any single word—for example, "kiss"—but, even at the crudest level, of a full sentence, "The man and woman are kissing each other." In addition, words already exist, but at least theoretically each writer creates a statement for the first time. (The words *whose, woods, these, are,* and so on are part of the vocabulary for all of us; the statement "Whose woods these are I think I know" is the creation of Robert Frost.) Each film image is also, again at least theoretically, a new invention.

Moreover, the relationship between each "signifier" (the word or statement on the one hand and the visual image or shot on the other) and what is "signified" is very different. A photograph of a bird has a relationship to the "real" bird which seems closer or more direct than does the word *bird*. Yet the photograph is *not* a bird; it is a picture (a sign, a symbol, a representation of birdness). It is unlike the word in that it is universally recognizable as signifying a bird and because it is *specifically* representational (of a cardinal rather than an eagle, say). Still, neither the word nor the picture will fly, so to speak.

The fact that the relation between signifier and signified in a picture seems undeniably more direct than in the case of a word may remind us that, as everyone knows, one picture is worth a thousand words. But what everyone knows need not always be true. In this case, sometimes it is (indeed, if anything, it is often an understatement), but sometimes it is not. It *is* true when the given conception is best comprehended in visual terms. We shall explore this question of which realms may seem more ideally suited to each art, but first it is important to recognize the possibility of a hidden assumption in asking whether one picture is worth a thousand words in the context of a discussion of film and literature. It is in fact an assumption made by numerous critics: that film employs one rather than the other, pictures rather than words. The problem with the assumption is that, as we have already seen, it is false. Film today is not a "purely" visual medium, but an *audiovisual* one. If one doubts that, one can ask a number of people to name some of the most memorable film moments they can think of. Even excluding musical numbers—indeed, even those not in musicals as such, like Jeanne Moreau singing "Le tourbillon" in *Jules and Jim*—or such nonverbal moments as the devastating one in *The Blue Angel* when Emil Jannings crows like a rooster, an extraordinary number will center on famous lines: Peter Sellers at the end of *Dr. Strangelove* exulting, "Mein Führer, I can walk!"; Al Pacino and Marlon Brando in *The Godfather* referring to offers that can't be refused, or an earlier Brando in *On the Waterfront* claiming to Rod Steiger that he could have been a contender; Lauren Bacall telling Humphrey Bogart in *To Have and Have Not* that if he needs her, he can just whistle; or Bogart himself assuring us in several films that he sticks his neck out for nobody (sometimes the line need not be one actually uttered: "Play it again, Sam"); James Cagney at the end of *White Heat* shouting "Top of the world, Ma!"; or Paul Muni at the end of *I Am a Fugitive from a Chain Gang* whispering "I steal!"

The lines are all short, and they do not come from long speeches, and even as one feels that there is no need to exclude words from the tools at a filmmaker's disposal, one can recognize the artistic dangers in being *too* reliant on words alone, or on too many of them. The novelist Virginia Woolf argued in her essay "The Cinema" that although film "has within its grasp innumerable symbols for emotions that have so far failed to find expression," all "which is accessible to words and to words alone, the cinema must avoid."

Woolf's essay was written in 1926, before the advent of the sound film, but one could still agree that there is little point in a film attempting what can *only* be done in words; however, there will be less universal agreement about what we are thinking of when we talk that way, or about which areas are in fact "accessible to words and to words alone." To put the question in more general terms, can we determine which realms in the artistic depiction of human existence are more or less suited to the genre of film than to other genres? Are there aspects of human experience that are better or worse served by written literature than by film?

In practice, attempts to answer these questions seem in-

variably to talk about the limitations of film, and about what is either "cinematic" or "uncinematic": one rarely hears claims that a given topic is unsuited to print, or that it is either "literary" or "unliterary." Probably the most common distinction is one that sees the novel as more appropriate to the presentation of *inner* mental states, while the film is seen as being better able to show what people do and say than what they think or imagine. The reason is that film depicts what is external and visible, physical and material. In the essay from which we have already quoted, Virginia Woolf contemplates a film adaptation of Tolstoy: "The eye says 'Here is Anna Karenina.' A voluptuous lady in black velvet wearing pearls comes before us. But the brain says, 'That is no more Anna Karenina than it is Queen Victoria.' For the brain knows Anna almost entirely by the inside of her mind—her charm, her passion, her despair. All the emphasis is laid by the cinema upon her teeth, her pearls, and her velvet."

George Bluestone [see Further Reading] begins his *Novels into Film* by saying that "between the percept of the visual image and the concept of the mental image lies the root difference between the two media," and throughout his valuable book he stresses his conviction that "the rendition of mental states—memory, dream, imagination—cannot be as adequately represented by film as by language," since "the film, having only arrangements of space to work with, cannot render thought, for the moment thought is externalized it is no longer thought." But it could be countered that written literature itself has only words on pages to work with, and that putting them there is also an act of externalization—and that, in any case, thought is less exclusively "verbal" than Bluestone's distinction seems to imply.

As a matter of fact, a number of major filmmakers have not been willing to yield their right to the depiction of psychological states so easily. In an essay called "Words and Movies" [see excerpt below], Stanley Kubrick explains his preference for adapting novels concentrating on a character's inner life by saying that it is easier to invent external action which will be—and here he borrows T. S. Eliot's term—an "objective correlative of the book's psychological content" than it is to invent a character and a motivation for action plots lacking them. Much earlier, in 1930, Sergei M. Eisenstein sought out James Joyce, whose *Ulysses* he greatly admired. The two men discussed what Joyce had done in his novel to represent inner thought processes by means of the *interior monologue*, a device or technique used to record the *stream of consciousness*—that is, the current of associations going on uninterruptedly in our minds, the flux of thoughts, sensations, and feelings that we all experience, the direction of which is determined by associative rather than "logical" channels. Contrary to the usual assumption, Eisenstein believed that film, even more forcefully than literature, could make such mental processes accessible, comprehensible, and vivid. Joyce was sufficiently impressed by Eisenstein's ideas to remark to a friend that he could imagine Eisenstein succeeding in his wish to adapt *Ulysses* into film.

When Joseph Strick adapted that novel more than thirty years later, in 1966, his chief device for depicting inner thoughts was the *voice-over*, a term for the use of an off-screen voice heard "over" the scene we are seeing; the voice may be that of a narrator, or that of a character who is in the scene but not talking aloud. Laurence Olivier's *Hamlet* presents a number of soliloquies in this way, and Robert Bresson uses a voice-over to give us the journal entries of the protagonist in *Diary of a Country Priest*. But of course films can also use visual as well as verbal correlatives for mental states: Bergman's *Wild Strawberries* makes extensive use of the voice-over, but we *see* the flashbacks and silent dreams of its protagonist, Isak Borg; the visual world of Wiene's *The Cabinet of Dr. Caligari* seems entirely controlled by the intensely subjective mental perspective of its ambiguously disturbed hero.

Often, verbal means such as the voice-over, narration, and dialogue are used to get round a fundamental limitation within the visual image: it cannot easily and immediately convey abstract concepts. It can show a person in pain, but not the general notion of "pain." It can show a woman and a child, but there is no single visual image equivalent to the word "mother." Nor are there specific yet general visual signs for "love," or "hatred," or "sex," or "violence," or "religion." Such abstractions are of course not completely beyond the capabilities of film so long as film uses words; nevertheless, it does seem true that ideas are more economically treated in written literature than in film.

So much is widely acknowledged; many people believe that a corollary is that while literature is a more "intellectual" medium, film is the more emotional; according to Ingmar Bergman, the reason film has more in common with music than with literature is that both film and music "affect our emotions directly, not via the intellect."

Sometimes a similar but actually quite different generalization says that film is a simple rather than a complex medium (in content, not execution). Such a view is expressed with special frequency by people who have worked as both novelists and screenwriters, such as Budd Schulberg, who says that the film

> . . . has no time for what I call the essential digression. The "digression" of complicated, contradictory character. The "digression" of social background. The film must go from significant episode to more significant episode in a constantly mounting pattern. It's an exciting form. But it pays a price for this excitement. It cannot wander as life wanders, or pause as life always pauses, to contemplate the incidental or the unexpected.

Perhaps the most important if obvious source of this difference is in length; the film of two or three or even four hours simply does not have the time to go into all the details which are possible and ordinary in a novel of two or three or four hundred pages. That is one of the reasons for Alfred Hitchcock's conviction that "the nearest art form to the motion picture is . . . the short story. It's the only form where you ask the audience to sit down and read it in one sitting." The drama is also experienced in a single sitting, of course. . . . [It] is surely worth observing that playwrights such as Shakespeare, Chekhov, Shaw, and Beckett have managed to be quite inclusive, subtle, and complex within works encompassing only a few hours.

It is coming to seem, then, as if all the distinctions we have considered between film and other forms of literature are valid, certainly, and yet are not completely so either; they are both revealing and potentially misleading. Pauline Kael speaks for many others in their response to much film criticism and theory when she asks, in regard to Siegfried Kracauer's discussion in *Theory of Film* of subjects that are either "cinematic" or more suitable to the theater: "Who started this divide and conquer game of aesthetics in which the different media are assigned their special domains like salesmen staking out their territories—you stick to the Midwest and I'll take Florida?" It is surely true that, as Kael goes on to say, "what motion picture art shares with other arts is perhaps even more important than what it may, or may *not,* have exclusively." But the key word, perhaps, is *perhaps.* For the differences among art forms can also be extremely revealing, and no doubt the best stance is to be aware of both comparisons and contrasts. (pp. 54-9)

> *Morris Beja, in his* Film & Literature: An Introduction, *Longman, 1979, 335 p.*

Sergei Eisenstein

[*A Russian film director and screenwriter, Eisenstein is considered a magisterial figure in the history of cinema, both as an innovator in film technique and as the maker of such masterworks as* The Battleship Potemkin (*1925*) *and* Alexander Nevsky (*1938*). *In the following excerpt, Eisenstein asserts that literary works should be studied in order to extract from them what is useful to filmmaking.*]

To write "in imitation of Tolstoi" or "in imitation of Hemingway" is, comparatively, easy. Nor is this so silly as it may sound. For everything begins with imitation. We know instances of writers transcribing entire masterworks. This is not a naïve undertaking. This is a way of finding the *movement* of another, perhaps a classical, writer, and of learning by this means the ideas and feelings embedded in this or that system of visual and aural images, in his word-combinations and so forth.

In ascending to the factors that emerge from movement—from this primary gesture of the writer—there is, on the one hand, complexity, for it is always easier to "skin" than to learn. On the other hand, literature can be treated not only directly, as by literary heirs, but in the interests of its *indirect* heirs; for example, the cinema. (p. 77)

What concerns us here is not this or that writer's work as a whole, but the particular features in his creative work that provide illumination on a particular problem—composition or viewpoint, for example. Obviously, "minor" writers will have less to contribute, and the genius of Shakespeare or Tolstoi will have much to teach us in almost every problem with which we have to deal.

I conducted, in 1928-29, a seminar . . . on Emile Zola. We accomplished a great deal in the examination of several purely cinematic elements in the plastic side of his creative work, drawing attention to a series of compositional peculiarities which in literature are found almost exclusively in this writer, and which are very close in their nature to cinema. Thereupon, without considering why we had chosen the creative work of Zola for study, several comrades, armed with Engels's well-known quotation on Balzac's superiority to Zola, announced a campaign against our project, declaring that we ought to be studying Balzac and that an "orientation" to Zola was "perverse".

In the first place the matter is not one of "orientation", for we were not making an acceptance of the whole canon of Zola's work as a unit; we were studying a series of specific features, illustrated especially instructively in Zola's work. In the second place, Engels's directive on the superiority of Balzac is centred on one specific element: the socioeconomic documentation that interested Engels was less conspicuous in Zola—as with many other writers.

On the other hand we can find in Zola a huge quantity of elements, extremely important to film-makers, that are quite absent from Balzac's writings. Open Zola at any page. It is so plastic, so *visually* written that according to it a whole "scene" could be prepared, starting with the director's indications (the emotional characteristics of the scene), exact directions to the designer, the lighting cameraman, the set-dresser, the actors, everyone. Here is the kind of scene you can find on every page of Zola; it is the opening of Chapter II of *La terre*:

> Maître Baillehache, notary of Cloyes, lived on the left-hand side of the Rue Grouaise, on the way to Château-dun, in a small white one-storey house; from a corner hung the solitary street-lamp that lit up the wide paved street, deserted during the week but loud and lively on Saturdays with the influx of peasants on their way to market. The two professional plates were visible from afar, shining against the chalky surface of the low buildings; behind the house, a narrow garden ran right down to the bank of the Loir.

> On this particular Saturday, in the room to the right of the entrance hall, overlooking the street, the under-clerk, a pale puny lad of fifteen, had lifted one of the muslin curtains to watch the people passing. The other two clerks, an old man, pot-bellied and dirty, and a younger man, emaciated, ravaged with liver-trouble, were busy writing at a double desk of ebonized deal, the only piece of furniture in the room except for seven or eight chairs and a cast-iron stove which was never lighted until December, even if snow fell on All Saints' Day. The pigeon-holes covering the walls, the greenish cardboard boxes, broken at the corners and bursting with yellowed papers, fouled the atmosphere of the room with a smell of sour ink and dust-eaten papers.

Compare this with any of the most brilliant pages of Balzac: its visual embodiment seems so grandiose, so literary, that it is not *directly* transferable to a system of visual images. Read this opening of *La peau de chagrin*:

> Towards the close of October, 1829, a young man entered the Palais Royal at the hour when the gaming houses opened their doors in compliance with the law which protects an essentially taxable passion. Without undue hesitation, he went up the stairway leading to a gambling den known as number thirty-six.

> "Your hat, please sir," a little old man called to him curtly and querulously. His face was cadaverous and he crouched in the shadows behind a railing. Suddenly, he rose, exhibiting a degraded countenance.

That's all very well, I'm told—this is not merely a matter of plasticity; what's basic is the images and characters of people, and in this Balzac is superior to Zola.

Exactly! In seeking characters we turn to Balzac, but for the plastic of film style, to Zola—and first of all to Zola.

But there is another element, closely connected with character, that we can seek in Zola: this is the ability to link man plastically with his environment.

We hear too often of the "incompleteness" of a person as outlined by Zola—compared with the "deep relief" of a Balzac character.

A personage in Balzac, thanks to his manner of exposition, always reminds me of the fat señor painted by Velásquez (perhaps because of a resemblance to Balzac himself!). Old Goriot, and Vautrin, and father Grandet, and Cousin Bette, and Cousin Pons, and Cesare Birotteau all resemble the Velásquez personage—three-dimensional, seen at full height on a pedestal, in boots and sword, characterized to the last ringlet or whisker, mitten or glove.

Zola's characters, as we call them to mind, can invariably be imagined in styles dear to him—expressed by Degas or Manet. Particularly Manet. And, if I may say so, most of all in the manner of his "Bar at the Moulin Rouge". Their incompleteness seems the same as the incompleteness of the painted girl behind the bar. She seems cut in half by the counter. It is also an incomplete figure who looks at her friend, the waitress, from another part of the painting, where the legs are cut short by the picture frame, and the left breast is covered by the round head of a drinking guest.

It would never occur to anyone to think of this girl as, anatomically, a half-girl. Nor do we think of the engulfing shadow on the face of a Rembrandt sitter as being an absence of part of the jaw, the temple, the forehead, or the eye deep in the eye-socket—all this being particularly notable in the etchings.

Obviously, what Manet gives us are "clots" of real detail—the personage in "close-up"—for it is no accident that the painting of Zola's time is linked with those masters of the close-up, the Japanese artists of the wood-block. Though Manet's image may not be fully drawn, it cannot be said to be undetermined. It is rounded off with the counter of the bar, the reflection in the mirror behind the girl, the tankard of beer, and the guest's head, so craftily concealing the girl's breast. Even the image of a subsidiary figure is drawn with the same customary complex of elements that is inseparable from the central personage.

Balzac is no less accurate in defining the elements connected with the habits and actions of a person. But Balzac only *names* these, as if describing the supplying firm, their method of ordering, often with attached prices—you almost expect catalogue numbers. So that Balzac gives you the person and all pertaining to him—objects, habits, setting—all gathered by him into a picture, the legs of his personage hidden by the edge of the table, the personage himself hidden in a detailed description of the wall's upholstery, the objects arranged in methodical order. For our art Balzac's method does not give us much help.

On the other hand Zola takes you *into* the image; for example, Nana at the race meeting—though the race is just as much a race as she is Nana, they cannot be taken apart. And Zola cuts his way into your visual memory with an unforgettable "shot", as when the black figure of Eugène

Rougon casts its shadow across the white sculptures in the Chambre, or when the carnally red tonality flows into Nôtre Dame in the scene of the christening of Napoleon III's son. Les Rougon-Macquart are not merely providing a commentary on a full socio-economic picture of Napoleon III's epoch; they encourage each of us, as we read—especially with such a purpose as ours—to do our own creative work. (pp. 79-83)

So we return to our premises: to ask of each writer that quality that makes him a master. And to leave to the literary critic those matters of academic calculation—such as assigning to each writer his place "in the ranks", or defining his degree of greatness.

No, please: don't confuse the addresses. Don't demand of Flaubert the virtues of Gogol—don't seek in Dostoevski lessons in the art of Tolstoi—and vice versa! That's as unreasonable as to want apples in the spring, or snow in the summer.

What we need is a "cinematographer's guide" to the classics of literature. And to painting, too. And to theatre. And music. How fascinating, for example, to define in detail what can be learned in Repin's work as distinct from Serov's work. What can be learned from Bach as distinct from Wagner. From Ben Jonson as distinct from Shakespeare.

We must learn in the way that Busygin writes with such modesty in his autobiography: "At the Industrial Academy the chief thing I'm learning is—how to learn."

We must study how to read.

This is essential in order to write:

for a writer—the pages of a literary scenario (or treatment).

for a director—the sheets of a shooting-script, or the shots in preliminary sketch, or completed images on the canvas of the screen.

Literature *per se* has as many means and circuitous expositions as there are ways of perception. But without our premises these mingled forms remain closed to us.

For film-writing the responsibility is of immeasurable extent. (p. 83)

*Sergei Eisenstein, "Lessons from Literature,"
in his* Film Essays and a Lecture, *edited by Jay Leyda, 1968. Reprint by Princeton University Press, 1982, pp. 77-83.*

Virginia Woolf

[*An English novelist, essayist, and critic, Woolf is one of the most prominent figures of twentieth-century literature. Like her contemporary James Joyce, with whom she is often compared, Woolf employed the stream-of-consciousness technique in the novel. Concerned primarily with depicting the life of the mind, she rebelled against traditional narrative techniques and developed a highly individualized style. Woolf's works, noted for their subjective explorations of characters' inner lives and their delicate poetic quality, have had a lasting effect on the art of the novel. Her critical essays, which cover almost the entire range of English literature, contain some of her finest prose and are praised for their insight. Along with Lytton Strachey, Roger Fry, Clive Bell, and others, Woolf and her husband Leonard formed the literary coterie known as the "Bloomsbury Group." In the following excerpt, Woolf offers observations on the expressive possibilities of cinema in contrast with those presented by literature.*]

[The picture-makers want to make] an art of their own—naturally, for so much seems to be within their scope. So many arts seemed to stand by ready to offer their help. For example, there was literature. All the famous novels of the world, with their well known characters, and their famous scenes, only asked, it seemed, to be put on the films. What could be easier and simpler? The cinema fell upon its prey with immense rapacity, and to this moment largely subsists upon the body of its unfortunate victim. But the results are disastrous to both. The alliance is unnatural. Eye and brain are torn asunder ruthlessly as they try vainly to work in couples. The eye says: "Here is Anna Karenina." A voluptuous lady in black velvet wearing pearls comes before us. But the brain says: "That is no more Anna Karenina than it is Queen Victoria." For the brain knows Anna almost entirely by the inside of her mind—her charm, her passion, her despair. All the emphasis is laid by the cinema upon her teeth, her pearls, and her velvet. Then "Anna falls in love with Vronsky"—that is to say, the lady in black velvet falls into the arms of a gentleman in uniform, and they kiss with enormous succulence, great deliberation, and infinite gesticulation on a sofa in an extremely well appointed library, while a gardener incidentally mows the lawn. So we lurch and lumber through the most famous novels of the world. So we spell them out in words of one syllable written, too, in the scrawl of an illiterate schoolboy. A kiss is love. A broken cup is jealousy. A grin is happiness. Death is a hearse. None of these things has the least connection with the novel that Tolstoy wrote, and it is only when we give up trying to connect the pictures with the book that we guess from some accidental scene—like the gardener mowing the lawn—what the cinema might do if it were left to its own devices.

But what, then, are its devices? If it ceased to be a parasite, how would it walk erect? At present it is only from hints that one can frame any conjecture. For instance, at a performance of *Doctor Caligari* the other day, a shadow shaped like a tadpole suddenly appeared at one corner of the screen. It swelled to an immense size, quivered, bulged, and sank back again into nonentity. For a moment it seemed to embody some monstrous, diseased imagination of the lunatic's brain. For a moment it seemed as if thought could be conveyed by shape more effectively than by words. The monstrous, quivering tadpole seemed to be fear itself, and not the statement, "I am afraid." In fact, the shadow was accidental, and the effect unintentional. But if a shadow at a certain moment can suggest so much more than the actual gestures and words of men and women in a state of fear, it seems plain that the cinema has within its grasp innumerable symbols for emotions that have so far failed to find expression. Terror has, besides its ordinary forms, the shape of a tadpole; it burgeons, bulges, quivers, disappears. Anger is not merely rant and rhetoric, red faces and clenched fists. It is perhaps a black line wriggling upon a white sheet. Anna and Vronsky need no longer scowl and grimace. They have at their command—but what? Is there, we ask, some secret language which we feel and see, but never speak, and, if so, could this be made visible to the eye? Is there any characteristic which thought possesses that can be rendered visible without the help of words? It has speed and slowness; dartlike directness and vaporous circumlocution. But it has also, especially in moments of emotion, the picture-making power, the need to lift its burden to another bearer; to let an image run side by side along with it. The likeness of the thought is, for some reason, more beautiful, more comprehensible, more available than the thought itself. As everybody knows, in Shakespeare the most complex ideas form chains of images through which we mount, changing and turning, until we reach the light of day. But, obviously, the images of a poet are not to be cast in bronze, or traced by pencil. They are compact of a thousand suggestions of which the visual is only the most obvious or the uppermost. Even the simplest image: "My luve's like a red, red rose, that's newly sprung in June," presents us with impressions of moisture and warmth and the glow of crimson and the softness of petals inextricably mixed and strung upon the lilt of a rhythm which is itself the voice of the passion and hesitation of the lover. All this, which is accessible to words, and to words alone, the cinema must avoid.

Yet if so much of our thinking and feeling is connected with seeing, some residue of visual emotion which is of no use either to painter or to poet may still await the cinema. That such symbols will be quite unlike the real objects which we see before us seems highly probable. Something abstract, something which moves with controlled and conscious art, something which calls for the very slightest help from words or music to make itself intelligible, yet justly uses them subserviently—of such movements and abstractions the films may, in time to come, be composed. Then, indeed, when some new symbol for expressing thought is found, the film-maker has enormous riches at his command. The exactitude of reality and its surprising power of suggestion are to be had for the asking. Annas and Vronskys—there they are in the flesh. If into this reality he could breathe emotion, could animate the perfect form with thought, then his booty could be hauled in hand over hand. Then, as smoke pours from Vesuvius, we should be able to see thought in its wildness, in its beauty, in its oddity, pouring from men with their elbows on a table; from women with their little handbags slipping to the floor. We should see these emotions mingling together and affecting each other.

We should see violent changes of emotion produced by their collision. The most fantastic contrasts could be flashed before us with a speed which the writer can only toil after in vain; the dream architecture of arches and battlements, of cascades falling and fountains rising, which sometimes visits us in sleep or shapes itself in half-darkened rooms, could be realized before our waking eyes. No fantasy could be too far-fetched or insubstantial. The past could be unrolled, distances annihilated, and the gulfs which dislocate novels (when, for instance, Tolstoy has to pass from Levin to Anna, and in so doing jars his story and wrenches and arrests our sympathies) could, by the sameness of the background, by the repetition of some scene, be smoothed away.

How all this is to be attempted, much less achieved, no one

at the moment can tell us. We get intimations only in the chaos of the streets, perhaps, when some momentary assembly of color, sound, movement suggests that here is a scene waiting a new art to be transfixed. And sometimes at the cinema in the midst of its immense dexterity and enormous technical proficiency, the curtain parts and we behold, far off, some unknown and unexpected beauty. But it is for a moment only. For a strange thing has happened—while all the other arts were born naked, this, the youngest, has been born fully clothed. It can say everything before it has anything to say. It is as if the savage tribe, instead of finding two bars of iron to play with, had found, scattering the seashore, fiddles, flutes, saxophones, trumpets, grand pianos by Erard and Bechstein, and had begun with incredible energy, but without knowing a note of music, to hammer and thump upon them all at the same time. (pp. 309-10)

Virginia Woolf, "The Movies and Reality," in The New Republic, *Vol. XLVII, No. 609, August 4, 1926, pp. 308-10.*

FILM AND THEATER

Eugenio Montale

[*Considered one of the greatest Italian poets of the twentieth century, Montale received the Nobel Prize in literature in 1975. He began his career as a poet of landscape, but under the influence of the works of Paul Valéry and the French Symbolists he broke away from the staid conventions of Italian poetry in the 1920s to produce richly symbolic, often cryptic verse. The obscurity of his poems led some critics to name him, along with Giuseppe Ungaretti and Salvatore Quasimodo, as one of the founders of the poetic movement known as Hermeticism. In the following essay, which first appeared in a special film issue of the Italian journal* Solaria *in 1927, Montale expresses his views on the "silent art" of the cinema as contrasted with the theater.*]

Dear Editor, you have asked for my opinion of the cinema and I have done what I could to come up with one for *Solaria's* investigation. I must say, first of all, that I am somewhat afraid that the first response your new review will elicit will be yet another attack on the moribund serious theater—not a new or unpredictable response, but one which by now is a bit pointless. To praise the cinema in order to destroy the theater is an idea that may occur to more than one writer, as it has to me; and I should say it *ought* to occur, for I hope that no contributor to *Solaria* is excessively fond of the dramatic "genre": what the aesthetes of years ago, with compunction, called "good prose" as opposed to the vulgar "opera," operetta, varieties, and now, *horribile dictu,* the cinema. Such is my wish: and I apologize to my friends who are theater critics. But it is a wish that could be denied; and perhaps my colleague Gerbi, who doubted in the *Convegno* (October 1916) whether one writer in thirty could be found in Italy who had anything good to say about the cinema, will find that he has not been excessive in his predictions and that I am the only one, or practically the only one, among those invited to participate who will say that I am in favor of the silent art. Let it be clear then that I am praising the cinema; but let it also be clear that I know very little about it. So little that in order to educate myself on the subject, as well as to fire a few obligatory rounds at the theater, I made a selection a few days ago of right opinions and statements drawn from newspapers and reviews to present "on request," stamped with my seal of approval.

One opinion which pleased me was that expressed by A. S. Luciani in the *Fiera letteraria,* where we read that if today we confine spiritual pleasure to books and visual pleasure to film, it is hard to understand what the devil can be expected from the theater—and why we hesitate to do away with it (the addition is mine). It was easy for me to find other opinions—or effusions—in the above-mentioned *Convegno,* which contains many such by young French writers. There are those who claim, for example, that the worst film is still a film, still signifies something moving and mysterious. Here I was tempted to appropriate this phrase for myself, with a few revisions, and to respond to your request that, while I am ignorant of the aims and problems of the cinema, it expresses something more alive, ineffable, and fertile than the theater, which more and more seems like a "genre" that is irremediably remote from the most authentic spirit of our times. But I managed to resist the temptation, and in the end it seemed more reasonable to agree with Gerbi's conclusion, which does not make the cinema into an art *per se* but a new technique (and we know that no technique is art of itself, even if it is inseparable from art); a technique which can be mastered—the successful examples are not many, but they exist—with art as a result, art *sui generis.* The case of the *auteur*-actor is the most propitious for these results. And the most perfect achievement so far (though not the only one) is Charlie Chaplin's *Gold Rush.*

I too have seen *The Gold Rush* and I share Gerbi's admiration, which is also that of the best foreign writers. However, I must express a reservation in this regard: Chaplin seems to me to be a difficult artist; the Jewish basis of his art and his undeniable sadness, the two- or three-sided nature of his humor, seem hardly accessible to the "public." Does the "public," then, understand what for Chaplin's theoreticians constitutes his *specific* art (cinematographic art, not the actor's art)? Or do most people see only a circus clown projected on the screen?

This should not seem like an empty question. The point, in fact, lies precisely here. The theater (apart from the musical theater) is accused of having strayed from its popular, choral, religious, etc., origins and of having closed itself off within four walls for the benefit of a few initiates; and the cinema is praised as art for everyone, art for the crowd, an entirely timely and current art of the moment—classic, in short, the way popular songs and the fashionable Charlestons are classic. But is it not the case that for the masses the cinema is only a kind of inferior theater, more economical, domestic, and quick than the other; and that its specifically artistic essence, which is found not in the genre itself but only in certain works, is only the solitary perception of a few privileged individuals who are much less numerous than the few haggard admirers of our recent serious theater?

If this were so, no objections of this sort could be raised against that cinematic technique which can be mastered for the purposes of art: an art for the few, a difficult art, but art; and definitions don't matter. But it would be unjust to accuse the theater alone of having betrayed its origins: it would be just as valid to blame it for having risen to the status of art, given that the public runs in droves to the inferior theater (the film) which does not concern itself with art. This is perhaps the truest hypothesis, and the approval which surrounds the cinema is due only in small part to a new cinematographic sensibility, but depends to a much greater extent on practical reasons which it would be easy to enumerate.

It remains to conclude that the true art of today (including the outstanding achievements of the special art of the cinema) is more than ever art by and for the few: and that the collective phenomenon *cinema* belongs to the world of fashion, recreation, etc., but does not fall within the strictly spiritual field. And yet this conclusion, too, which is the most probable, must be considered very premature given the present state of the art of film, which is younger than the other arts by far too much. Time will tell; it will tell if the roar of laughter which greets Charlie Chaplin today as he steps into the abyss is the same that was aroused by the pratfalls of Ridolini [Italian name for the American comic movie actor Larry Semon (1890-1928)]; or whether in itself it contains something sadder and more aware, as some feel, and as I myself sometimes feel.

In this case, an ever more widespread filmic sensibility would be undeniable: a new sensibility which will certainly find nourishment not only in the film of the future but which will lead the "new rich" of the senses to confront the silent art—even that which is not cinematographic—with a new spirit and new needs. On that day the gap which separates the so-called public from so-called serious art might be partly bridged.

But is all this possible, or even desirable? Allow me, . . . —and this may be the only sure statement in a note that threatens to be ambiguous beyond the point of tolerance— allow me not to be entirely convinced. . . . (pp. 217-20)

> *Eugenio Montale, "Report on the Cinema," in his* The Second Life of Art: Selected Essays of Eugenio Montale, *edited and translated by Jonathan Galassi, The Ecco Press, 1982, pp. 217-20.*

Allardyce Nicoll

[*Called "one of the masters of dramatic research," Nicoll is best known as a theater critic whose works have proven invaluable to students and educators. In the following excerpt, he contends that the principal distinction between theater and cinema lies in the possibilities and limitations of character portrayal in each medium.*]

Some few years ago a British producing company made a film of Bernard Shaw's *Arms and the Man*. This film, after a few exciting shots depicting the dark streets of a Balkan town, the frenzied flight of the miserable fugitives and the clambering of Bluntschli onto Raina's window terrace, settled down to provide what was fundamentally a screen-picture of the written drama. The dialogue was shortened, no doubt, but the shots proceeded more or less along the dramatic lines established by Shaw and nothing was introduced which he had not originally conceived in preparing his material for the stage. The result was that no more dismal film has ever been shown to the public. On the stage *Arms and the Man* is witty, provocative, incisively stimulating; its characters have a breath of genuine theatrical life; it moves, it breathes, it has vital energy. In the screen version all that life has fled, and, strangest thing of all, those characters—Bluntschli, Raina, Sergius—who are so exciting on the boards, looked to the audience like a set of wooden dummies, hopelessly patterned. Performed by a third-rate amateur cast their life-blood does not so ebb from them, yet here, interpreted by a group of distinguished professionals, they wilted and died—died, too, in such forms that we could never have credited them with ever having had a spark of reality. Was there any basic reason for this failure?

The basic reason seems to be simply this—that practically all effectively drawn stage characters are types and that in the cinema we demand individualisation, or else that we recognise stage figures as types and impute greater power of independent life to the figures we see on the screen. This judgment . . . may seem grossly distorted, but perhaps some further consideration will demonstrate its plausibility. When we go to the theatre, we expect theatre and nothing else. We know that the building we enter is a playhouse; that behind the lowered curtain actors are making ready, dressing themselves in strange garments and transforming their natural features; that the figures we later see on the boards are never living persons of king and bishop and clown, but merely men pretending for a brief space of time to be like these figures. Dramatic illusion is never (or so rarely as to be negligible) the illusion of reality: it is always imaginative illusion, the illusion of a period of make-believe. All the time we watch Hamlet's throes of agony we know that the character Hamlet is being impersonated by a man who presently will walk out of the stage-door in ordinary clothes and an autograph-signing smile on his face. True, volumes have been written on famous dramatic characters—Greek, Elizabethan English and modern Norwegian—and these volumes might well seem to give the lie to such assumptions. Have not Shakespeare's characters seemed so real to a few observers that we have on our shelves books specifically concerned with the girlhood of his heroines—a girlhood the dramas themselves denied us?

These studies, however, should not distract us from the essential truth that the greatest playwrights have always aimed at presenting human personality in bold theatric terms. Hamlet seizes on us, not because he is an individual, not because in him Shakespeare has delineated a particular prince of Denmark, but because in Hamlet there are bits of all men; he is a composite character whose lineaments are determined by dramatic necessity, and through that he lives. Fundamentally, the truly vital theatre deals in stock figures. Like a child's box of bricks, the stage's material is limited; it is the possibilities in arrangement that are well-nigh inexhaustible. Audiences thrill to see new situations born of fresh sociological conditions, but the figures set before them in significant plays are conventionally fixed and familiar. Of Romeos there are many, and of Othellos legion. Character on the stage is restricted and stereotyped and the persons who play upon the boards are governed, not by the strangely perplexing processes of life but by the established terms of stage practice.

Bluntschli represents half a hundred similar rationalists; the idealism of thousands is incorporated in Sergius; and Raina is an eternal stage type of the perplexing feminine. The theatre is populated, not by real individuals whose boyhood or girlhood may legitimately be traced, but by heroes and villains sprung full-bodied from Jove's brain, by clowns and pantaloons whose youth is unknown and whose future matters not after the curtain's fall.

In the cinema we demand something different. Probably we carry into the picture-house prejudices deeply ingrained in our beings. The statement that "the camera cannot lie" has been disproved by millions of flattering portraits and by dozens of spiritualistic pictures which purport to depict fairies but which mostly turn out to be faintly disguised pictures of ballet-dancers or replicas of figures in advertisements of night-lights. Yet in our heart of hearts we credit the truth of that statement. A picture, a piece of sculpture, a stage-play—these we know were created by man; we have watched the scenery being carried in back stage and we know we shall see the actors, turned into themselves again, bowing at the conclusion of the performance. In every way the "falsity" of a theatrical production is borne in upon us, so that we are prepared to demand nothing save a theatrical truth. For the films, however, our orientation is vastly different. Several periodicals, it is true, have endeavored to let us into the secrets of the moving-picture industry and a few favored spectators have been permitted to make the rounds of the studios; but from ninety per cent of the audience the actual methods employed in the preparation of a film remain far off and dimly realised. "New York," we are told,

> struts when it constructs a Rockefeller Center. A small town chirps when it finishes a block of fine cottages. The government gets into the newspapers for projects like Boulder Dam. It takes Hollywood approximately three days to build Rome and a morning to effect its fall, but there is very little hurrah about it. The details are guarded like Victorian virtue.
>
> There is sound reticence on the part of a community that is usually articulate about its successes. Hollywood is in the business of building illusion, not sets. . . . The public likes to feel that the stork brought *The Birth of a Nation*. It likes to feel that a cameraman hung in the clouds—mid-Pacific—the day that Barrymore fought the whale.

That audience, accordingly, carries its prejudices with it intact. "The camera cannot lie"—and therefore, even when we are looking at Marlene Dietrich or Robert Montgomery, we unconsciously lose sight of fictional surroundings and interpret their impersonations as "real" things. Rudolph Valentino became a man who had had innumerable Sheikish adventures, and into each part she took the personality of Greta Garbo was incorporated. The most impossible actions may be shown us in a film, yet Laurel and Hardy are, at their best, seen as individuals experiencing many strange adventures, not as virtuoso comedians in a vaudeville act.

How true this is was demonstrated by a film, *Once in a Blue Moon,* which has been shown only in a few theatres. The general tone of *Once in a Blue Moon* was burlesque. In it was a "take-off" of certain Russian films, incidental jibes at a few popular American examples, and occasional skits directed at prominent players; Jimmy Savo took the rôle of Gabbo the Great while one of the actresses made up to look like Katherine Hepburn. The result was dismal. In Charlie Chaplin's free fantasy there is life and interest; throughout the course of *Once in a Blue Moon* vitality was entirely lacking. Nor was the reason far to seek. We cannot appreciate burlesque in the cinema because of the fact that in serious films actor and rôle are indistinguishable; on the stage we appreciate it since there, in serious plays, we can never escape from separating the fictional character and its creator. Stage burlesque is directed at an artistic method, generally the method employed by an individual player in the treatment of his parts. To caricature Irving was easy; hardly would a cinematic travesty of Arliss succeed. The presentation of this single film proved clearly the difference in approach on the part of cinema and theatre public respectively. These, so generally considered identical, are seen to be controlled by quite distinct psychological elements.

Charlie Chaplin's free fantasy has been referred to above. This, associated with, say, the methods of René Clair, might well serve to demonstrate the true resources of the film; comparison with the erring tendencies of *Once in a Blue Moon* brings out clearly the genuine frontiers of the cinematic sphere. In *The Ghost Goes West* there was much of satire, but this satire was directed at life and not at art and, moreover, was kept well within "realistic" terms. Everything introduced there was possible in the sense that, although we might rationally decide that these events could not actually have taken place, we recognized that, granted the conditions which might make them achievable, they would have assumed just such forms as were cast on the screen. The ghost was thus a "realistic" one, shown now in the guise of a figure solid and opaque and now in that of a transparent wraith, capable of defying the laws of physics. In a precisely similar way is the fantasy of a Chaplin film bound up with reality. We know that the things which Charlie does and the situations in which he appears are impossible but again, given the conditions which would make them possible, these are the shapes, we know, they would assume. Neither René Clair nor Charlie Chaplin steps into the field occupied by the artistic burlesque; neither are "theatrical." The former works in an independent world conceived out of the terms of the actual, and the latter, like George Arliss in a different sphere, stands forth as an individual experiencing a myriad of strange and fantastic adventures.

The individualising process in film appreciation manifestly demands that other standards than those of the stage be applied to the screen-play. In the theatre we are commonly presented with characters relatively simple in their psychological make-up. A sympathetically conceived hero or heroine is devoted in his or her love affairs to one object; at the most some Romeo will abandon a visionary Rosaline for a flesh-and-blood Juliet. For the cinema, on the other hand, greater complexity may be permitted without loss of sympathy. The heroine in *So Red the Rose* is first shown coquetting with her cousin, suggestion is provided that she has not been averse to the attentions of a young family friend, she sets her cap at a visiting Texan and grieves bitterly on receiving news of his death, and finally she discovers or rediscovers the true love she bears to the cousin. All this is done without any hint that she is a mere flirt; her affections are such as might have been those of

an ordinary girl in real life and we easily accept the filmic presentation in this light. On the stage the character could not have been viewed in a similar way; there we should have demanded a much simpler and less emotionally complicated pattern if our sympathies were firmly to be held.

The strange paradox, then, results:—that, although the cinema introduces improbabilities and things beyond nature at which any theatrical director would blench and murmur soft nothings to the air, the filmic material is treated by the audience with far greater respect (in its relation to life) than the material of the stage. Our conceptions of life in Chicago gangsterdom and in distant China are all colored by films we have seen. What we have witnessed on the screen becomes the "real" for us. In moments of sanity, maybe, we confess that of course we do not believe this or that, but, under the spell again, we credit the truth of these pictures even as, for all our professed superiority, we credit the truth of newspaper paragraphs. (pp. 164-71)

The film has such a hold over the world of reality, can achieve expression so vitally in terms of ordinary life, that the realistic play must surely come to seem trivial, false and inconsequential. The truth is, of course, that naturalism on the stage must always be limited and insincere. Thousands have gone to *The Children's Hour* and come away fondly believing that what they have seen is life; they have not realised that here too the familiar stock figures, the type characterisations, of the theatre have been presented before them in modified forms. From this the drama cannot escape; little possibility is there of its delving deeply into the recesses of the individual spirit. That is a realm reserved for cinematic exploitation, and, as the film more and more explores this territory, does it not seem probable that theatre audiences will become weary of watching shows which, although professing to be "lifelike," actually are inexorably bound by the restrictions of the stage? Pursuing this path, the theatre truly seems doomed to inevitable destruction. Whether in its attempt to reproduce reality and give the illusion of actual events or whether in its pretence towards depth and subtlety in character-drawing, the stage is aiming at things alien to its spirit, things which so much more easily may be accomplished in the film that their exploitation on the stage gives only an impression of vain effort. (pp. 183-84)

Precisely because Æschylus and Shakespeare did not try to copy life, because they presented their themes in highly conventional forms, their works have the quality of being independent of time and place. Their characters were more than photographic copies of known originals; their plots took no account of the terms of actuality; and their language soared on poetic wings. To this again must we come if our theatre is to be a vitally arresting force. So long as the stage is bound by the fetters of realism, so long as we judge theatrical characters by reference to individuals with whom we are acquainted, there is no possibility of preparing dialogue which shall rise above the terms of common existence.

From our playwrights, therefore, we must seek for a new foundation. No doubt many journeymen will continue to pen for the day and the hour alone, but of these there have always been legion; what we may desire is that the dramatists of higher effort and broader ideal do not follow the journeyman's way. Boldly must they turn from efforts to delineate in subtle and intimate manner the psychological states of individual men and women, recognising that in the wider sphere the drama has its genuine home. The cheap and ugly simian chatter of familiar conversation must give way to the ringing tones of a poetic utterance, not removed far off from our comprehension, but bearing a manifest relationship to our current speech. To attract men's ears once more to imaginative speech we may take the method of T. S. Eliot, whose violent contrasts in *Murder in the Cathedral* are intended to awaken appreciation and interest, or else the method of Maxwell Anderson, whose *Winterset* aims at building a dramatic poetry out of common expression. What procedure is selected matters little; indeed, if an imaginative theatre does take shape in our years, its strength will largely depend upon its variety of approach. That there is hope that such a theatre truly may come into being is testified by the recent experiments of many poets, by the critical thought which has been devoted to its consummation and by the increasing popular acclaim which has greeted individual efforts. The poetic play may still lag behind the naturalistic or seemingly naturalistic drama in general esteem, but the attention paid in New York to Sean O'Casey's *Within the Gates* and Maxwell Anderson's *Winterset* augurs the beginning of a new appreciation, while in London T. S. Eliot's *Murder in the Cathedral* has awakened an interest of a similar kind. Nor should we forget plays not in verse but aiming at a kindred approach; Robert Sherwood's *The Petrified Forest* and S. N. Behrman's *Rain from Heaven,* familiar and apparently realistic in form, deliberately and frankly aim at doing something more than present figures of individuals; in them the universalising power of the theatre is being utilised no less than in other plays which, by the employment of verse dialogue, deliberately remove the action from the commonplaces of daily existence.

Established on these terms native to its very existence and consequently far removed from the ways of the film, the theatre need have no fear that its hold over men's minds will diminish and fail. It will maintain a position essentially its own to which other arts may not aspire.

For the film are reserved things essentially distinct. Possibility of confusion between the two has entered in only because the playhouse has not been true to itself. To the cinema is given a sphere, where the subjective and objective approaches are combined, where individualisation takes the place of type characterisation, where reality may faithfully be imitated and where the utterly fantastic equally is granted a home, where Walt Disney's animated flowers and flames exist alongside the figures of men and women who may seem more real than the figures of the stage, where a visual imagery in moving forms may thrill and awaken an age whose ears, while still alert to listen to poetic speech based on or in tune with the common language of the day, has forgotten to be moved by the tones of an earlier dramatic verse. Within this field lies the possibility of an artistic expression equally powerful as that of the stage, though essentially distinct from that. The distinction is determined by the audience reactions to the one and to the other. In the theatre the spectators are confronted by characters which, if successfully delineated, always possess a quality which renders them greater than separate individuals. When Clifford Odets declares that by the time he came to write his first play, *Awake and Sing!* he understood clearly that his

interest was not in the presentation of an individual's problems, but in those of a whole class. In other words, the task was to find a theatrical form with which to express the mass as hero—

he is doing no more than indicate that he has the mind and approach of a dramatist. All the well-known figures created in tragedy and comedy since the days of Aristophanes and Æschylus have presented in this way the lineaments of universal humanity. If the theatre stands thus for mankind, the cinema, because of the willingness on the part of spectators to accept as the image of truth the moving forms cast on the screen, stands for the individual. It is related to the modern novel in the same respect that the older novel was related to the stage. Impressionistic and expressionistic settings may serve for the theatre—even may we occasionally fall back on plain curtains without completely losing the interest of our audiences; the cinema can take no such road, for, unless in frankly artificially created films (such as the Walt Disney cartoon), we cling to our preconceived beliefs and clamour for the three-dimensional, the exact and the authentic. In a stage play such as *Yellow Jack* we are prepared to accept a frankly formal background, because we know that the actors are actors merely; but for the treatment of similar material in *The Prisoner of Shark's Island* and *The Story of Pasteur* cinematic authenticity is demanded. At first glance, we might aver that, because of this, the film had fewer opportunities for artistic expression than the stage; but further consideration will demonstrate that the restrictions are amply compensated for by an added scope. Our illusion in the picture-house is certainly less "imaginative" than the illusion which attends us in the theatre, but it has the advantage of giving increased appreciation of things which are outside nature. Through this the purely visionary becomes almost tangible and the impossible assumes shapes easy of comprehension and belief. The sense of reality lies as the foundation of the film, yet real time and real space are banished; the world we move in may be far removed from the world ordinarily about us; and symbols may find a place alongside common objects of little or no importance. If we apply the theory of "psychological distance" to theatre and film we realise the force of each. For any kind of aesthetic appreciation this distance is always demanded; before we can hope to feel the artistic qualities of any form we must be able to set ourselves away from it, to experience the stimulus its contemplation creates and at the same time have no call to put the reactions to that stimulus into play. This distance obviously may be of varying degrees; sometimes it is reduced, sometimes it provides a vast gulf between the observer and the art object. Furthermore the variation may be of two kinds—variation between one art and another, and variation between forms within the sphere of a single art. Music is further removed from reality than sculpture, but in music there may be an approach towards commonly heard sounds and in sculpture abstract shapes may take the place of familiar forms realistically delineated. Determination of the proper and legitimate approach will come from a consideration of the sense of distance between the observer and the object; the masterpieces in any art will necessarily be based on an adaptation to the particular requirements of their own peculiar medium of expression.

Applying this principle to theatre and cinema, we will recognise that whereas there is a strong sense of reality in audience reactions to the film, yet always there is the fact that the pictures on the screen are two-dimensional images and hence removed a stage from actual contact with the spectators. What may happen if successful three-dimensional projection is introduced we cannot tell; at present we are concerned with a flat screen picture. This gulf between the audience and the events presented to them will permit a much greater use of realism than the stage may legitimately employ. The presence of flesh-and-blood actors in the theatre means that it is comparatively easy to break the illusion proper to the theatre and in doing so to shatter the mood at which any performance ought to aim. This statement may appear to run counter to others made above, but there is no essential contradiction involved. The fact remains that, when living person is set before living person—actor before spectator—a certain deliberate conventionalising is demanded of the former if the aesthetic impression is not to be lost, whereas in the film, in which immediately a measure of distance is imposed between image and spectator, greater approaches to real forms may be permitted, even although these have to exist alongside impossibilities and fantastic symbols far removed from the world around us. This is the paradox of cinematic art.

Herein lies the true filmic realm and to these things the cinema, if it also is to be true to itself, must tend, just as towards the universalising and towards conventionalism must tend the theatre if it is to find a secure place among us. (pp. 185-90)

Allardyce Nicoll, "Film Reality: The Cinema and the Theatre," in his Film and Theatre, *Thomas Y. Crowell Company, 1936, pp. 164-91.*

Eric Bentley

[*Bentley is considered one of the most erudite and innovative critics of the modern theater. He was responsible for introducing Bertolt Brecht, Luigi Pirandello, and other European playwrights to America through his studies, translations, and stage adaptations of their plays. In his critical works, Bentley concentrates on the playwright and the dramatic text, rather than on the production aspects of the play. Thus, in his first important critical study,* The Playwright as Thinker (1946), *Bentley distinguishes between "art" and "commodity" in the American theater, basing his definition of commodity on the premise that most producers are more attentive to box office receipts than to the artistic quality of a play and, as a result, the dramatist is often neglected as a true artist. Some critics consider this approach an attempt to compensate for his unwillingness to accept drama as a form of popular entertainment. Bentley's finest work,* The Life of Drama (1964), *is a comprehensive study of the development of dramatic form, specifically examining aspects of melodrama, farce, comedy, tragedy, and tragicomedy. In the following excerpt, Bentley challenges A. Nicoll's contention that, because the appearance of life can more effectively be created on the screen than on the stage, films have made naturalism in the theater obsolete (see Nicoll excerpt above).*]

When the nineteenth-century invention of the cinematograph led to the twentieth-century invention of the cinema there arose a new art, not to mention a new business, which in many respects could carry out the aims of certain types of dramatic performance much more fully than the theater. Some felt from the beginning that the motion picture would be the dramatic art of the twentieth century, and this opinion was not hard to support even in the days of the silent screen. Before the talkies were a decade old, even the kind of people who had earlier despised the screen began to see in it the successor to the living actor. In this belief, it is said, Clifford Odets left Broadway for Hollywood: the drama was a thing of the past, the future belonged to the motion picture. A more subtle analysis of the relation of stage and screen was given by Allardyce Nicoll in his interesting and informative book *Film and Theatre* [see excerpt above.] He tries to find a place for both stage and screen by assigning to each its proper style. The style of the screen is realism, he says, the theater should accordingly be non-realistic. The argument is worth quoting at length:

> If we seek for and desire a theater which shall possess qualities likely to live over generations, unquestionably we must decide that the naturalistic play, made popular towards the close of the nineteenth century and still remaining in our midst, is not calculated to fulfill our highest wishes.

> Of much greater importance, even, is the question of the position this naturalistic play occupies in its relations to the cinema. At the moment it still retains its popularity, but, we may ask, because of cinematic competition, is it not likely to fail gradually in its immediate appeal? The film has such a hold over the world of reality, can achieve expression so vitally in terms of ordinary life, that the realistic play must surely come to seem trivial, false, and inconsequential. The truth is, of course, that naturalism on the stage must always be limited and insincere. Thousands have gone to *The Children's Hour* and come away fondly believing that what they have seen is life; they have not realized that here too the familiar stock figures, the type characterizations, of the theater have been presented before them in modified forms. From this the drama cannot escape; little possibility is there of its delving deeply into the recesses of the individual spirit. That is the realm reserved for cinematic exploitation, and, as the film more and more explores this territory, does it not seem likely that theater audiences will become weary of watching shows which, although professing to be "lifelike," actually are inexorably bound by the restrictions of the stage? Pursuing this path, the theater truly seems doomed to inevitable destruction. Whether in its attempt to reproduce reality and give the illusion of actual events or whether in its pretense toward depth and subtlety in character-drawing, the stage is aiming at things alien to its spirit, things which so much more easily may be accomplished in the film that their exploitation on the stage gives only an impression of vain effort.

> Is, then, the theater, as some have opined, truly dying? Must it succumb to the rivalry of the cinema? The answer to that question depends on what the theater does within the next ten or twenty years. If it pursues naturalism further, unquestionably little hope will remain. . . .

These are weighty sentences, but are they really unquestionable? One might question whether the drama has always been incapable of delving into those "recesses of the individual spirit," whether the movie, even in the best hands, has in fact shown itself any more capable? But my prime interest is in Mr. Nicoll's remarks about "naturalism." A generation of movies has given to "naturalism" a popular success such as no dramatic style has ever had before. *A Tree Grows in Brooklyn,* movie version, is, one might say, pure Zola. Mr. Nicoll's strongest point, perhaps, is that the screen gives the illusion of actuality itself. The screen actor is not thought to act. He does not act. He is himself and, the argument runs, rightly so, since the screen must seem to be life itself. Such is the power of the camera. In support of his argument Mr. Nicoll adduces the fact that plays fail on the screen, and that movie actors haven't a style that can be parodied as Henry Irving had. The screen play, more than any other form of art, is just such a "slice of life" as the naturalists had always wished to cut.

This is Mr. Nicoll's argument, but does it all ring true? After all, we *do* praise acting on the screen; many of the screen's best actors are also stage stars and they are not always so very different in the two mediums; they *can* be parodied, and a parody of Charles Laughton the filmstar is not very different from one of Charles Laughton the actor; and good plays—witness Shaw's *Pygmalion*—have been successfully transferred to the screen with little alteration. Nor do audiences believe that what happens on the screen is really happening or that it has happened—at least no more than theater audiences do. After all, it was in the theater that the proverbial man in the gallery told Othello to leave the lady alone, and it was on the radio that the announcement of the end of the world was taken literally. These are abnormal responses. Normally an audience does not give full credence to fiction on the air, the stage, or the screen. I have known a movie audience to catch its breath at the sight of wounded soldiers in a newsreel and to be quite unperturbed by the same sight in a fictional movie.

In short, and Mr. Nicoll to the contrary notwithstanding, I think there is no radical distinction between stage and screen illusion. At best the difference is one of degree. The usual Hollywood product does seek to be a convincing illusion of actuality, but so does the usual Broadway product. This is a matter not of stage or screen, but of the style chosen by the director or author or producer. On either stage or screen he may choose, with great effectiveness, to be "naturalistic" or the reverse. It is also a matter of audience. An untrained audience, an audience of children, might want to save Desdemona's life in the theatre, as at the movies it might believe that it is actually present in Greta Garbo's bedroom. That is the trouble with being untrained and childish.

What Mr. Nicoll says is true of current movies and of many audiences, but not of all possible movies and all possible audiences. At present, it is true, we go to the movies to witness certain illusions and to share them. We do not go for imaginative experience. Years ago the Lynds found out how the movie magnates appealed to Middletown, via the *Saturday Evening Post,* in such advertisements as this:

> Go to a motion picture . . . and let yourself go. Before you know it you are living the story—laughing, loving, hating, struggling, winning! All the adventure, all the romance, all the excitement you lack in your daily life are in Pictures. They take you completely out of yourself into a wonderful new world . . . Out of the cage of everyday existence! If only for an afternoon or an evening—escape!

This is not Zola's naturalism in subject matter and aim, for it is frankly "romantic" and remote from everyday life. It is the naturalism of the movies. It is Mr. Nicoll's naturalism. And it stems not, as Mr. Nicoll thinks, from the medium, but purely from social factors. The movie is an extension of gossip and daydream. It influences life as no art ever has because it influences not as art at all but as suggestion, almost as hypnotism. Clark Gable is found to have no undershirt on, and the underwear trade of America suffers a fifty-percent loss for a year. Ingrid Bergman has her hair cut short, and the women's hairdressers of the nation have to send for more scissors. Not that the theater, on its part, has held aloof from such nonartistic matters. Actors and actresses have often been foci of mass emotion and sometimes leaders of fashion. All that Hollywood has done in this, as in so many other matters, is to systematize what had been haphazard and to make a mania out of a tendency.

The escapist realism of the movies is only that of most popular art. William Dieterle's movie *The Hunchback of Notre Dame* is not different in kind from Sardou's play *Patrie.* What is new is that we have in movies an art form so exclusively given over to Sardoodledom that a man can think Sardoodledom ingrained in the celluloid. Sardoodledom—or escapist realism—always consisted of concealing flattering, sentimental hokum in a setting of the most solid and beefy reality, thus conferring upon hokum the status of the actual and the real. This, it is very true, the film can do even better than David Belasco, because its realism can be at once more varied and more intimate. The camera can find the needle in the haystack and the fly in the ointment, and, above all, the camera—like Mr. Lee Shubert's box office—cannot lie. Aided by the camera, and abetted by popular prejudice in favor of the tangible, a director is able to wrap the maximum of nonsense in the maximum of verisimilitude, a combination as dangerous as the atomic bomb.

We must distinguish between the predilections of Hollywood and the nature of the medium. If the screen is able to be more realistic than the stage, it is also able to be more fantastic. If the Hollywood director is a super-Belasco, the Disney cartoon is a super-Punch-and-Judy, and Eisenstein is a super-Gordon Craig.

Mr. Nicoll makes the movie so completely natural that it is no longer art. He takes the "slice of life" theory too seriously. If we want life, we have it without making works of art at all. We need not pay our fifty cents for it; we necessarily pay in our hearts' blood. The *theory* of Zolaist naturalism has nearly always been astray here, though Zola himself was prepared to define art as "a part of life seen through a temperament" and the last three words are an important proviso. There is art only if the material of life is selected and intelligently arranged. Such arrangement is of course artificial. It imposes form on the formless. And the understanding of art depends upon a prior understanding of this fact. Nothing, therefore, that we take for reality can we also take for art. In a good movie, as in any good work of art, we *are* aware of the "artificial" elements—structure, selection, characterization, cutting—or rather, we can be. In actual fact very few moviegoers are aware of any of these things; but the same is true of novel readers and theatergoers.

A more astute way of arguing that film and theater are utterly different is by pointing to the conditions of production. A movie is manufactured in little bits, the bits forming a jigsaw puzzle which is put together later; on the stage the unity of a single complete performance is the director's chief end in view. This distinction between the two media, like the others we have examined, is not a necessary distinction. It is to equate the present doings of studios with the exigencies of the medium. The degree of decentralization that exists in Hollywood is not a technical necessity. Many Russian directors, for example, have done their own cutting. And, for that matter, joint authorship, in the form of impudent revisions perpetrated by hacks and businessmen, and lack of integration in the directing and producing of plays—these are the bane of Broadway as well as Hollywood.

What then *is* the difference between film and theater? Or should one not rather ask: what are the differences? Let us be content with the reply that the screen has two dimensions and the stage three, that the screen presents photographs and the stage living actors. All subtler differences stem from these. The camera can show us all sorts of things—from close-ups of insects to panoramas of prairies—which the stage cannot even suggest, and it can move from one to another with much more dexterity than any conceivable stage. The stage, on the other hand, can be revealed in the unsurpassable beauty of three-dimensional shapes, and the stage actor establishes between himself and his audience a contact real as electricity. From these basic differences one might elaborate many others. Here I wish only to reiterate that there is no such difference as is suggested by the antithesis of realistic and non-realistic theater. One cannot say, with Mr. Nicoll, that undecorated reality suits the screen, and fine words the stage. Such a belief is a hangover from the days of silent films. On the talking screen the aural is not necessarily subordinate to the visual. One could just as easily argue that the *stage* should stick to the natural, since on the stage the possibilities of fantasy are physically limited, while the screen should go in for poetic fantasy, since it can show anything in this world or the next with its cameras and can reproduce the merest murmurs and the subtlest intonations with its sound apparatus. All such distinctions are arbitrary. The truth is that dramatic art is possible on both stage and screen. On both it could fulfill its function of presenting an account of human experience deeply and truly. On both it would require the services of an artist—I think we may say a dramatist—to plan the whole work as a unity beforehand and of an interpreter or director to see that the unity is faithfully reproduced.

Is the film the dramatic art of the twentieth century then, or is it not? If as yet it is not, could it still grow to be so? My answers to these questions, which we started from, must now be evident. The movies as a whole, like plays as a whole, are a matter of business, not of art at all. The occasional artistic movie, like the occasional artistic play, is one legitimate and welcome form of twentieth-century art. It is not the only one. Moreover, while playwrights have demonstrated for centuries the potentialities of the stage, the screen is as yet an only partly explored territory. We have still to learn what its possibilities are. I have acknowledged that they are different from those of the stage, especially in certain kinds of emphasis. But they may not be as different as many have supposed. And there is no reason to assume that the art of the screen is a threat to the art of the stage, naturalistic or otherwise. Let us question Mr. Nicoll's unquestionable proposition. Although the movie industry can threaten the theater industry, the one *art* cannot be threatened by the other. So long as an art is alive it will be cherished and kept going by the minority that is interested in the arts. "The answer," Mr. Nicoll said, "depends on what the theater does within the next ten or twenty years. If it pursues naturalism further, unquestionably little hope will remain. . . ." About ten years have passed since these words were written. Today one of the few live spots in the drama is the Epic Theatre of Bertolt Brecht, which is a new form of realism. That the Epic dramatist believes also in combining the use of stage and screen in the theater is an additional sign that the two media need not part company according to the prescriptions of the doctors. (pp. 9-16)

Eric Bentley, "The Two Traditions of Modern Drama," in his The Playwright as Thinker: A Study of Drama in Modern Times, *1946. Reprint by Harcourt Brace Jovanovich, 1967, pp. 1-22.*

Stanley Kauffmann

[*Kauffmann is one of America's most respected film and theater critics. In the following excerpt, he examines a number of common conceptions regarding the distinctions between film and theater as artistic forms.*]

For a number of years I have spent a lot of time going to plays and films, sometimes one of each on the same day, so the two forms are constantly juxtaposed for me. The experience convinces me that there are some received ideas on the subject of theater-and-film—or theater versus film—that can use a quizzical look. My intent is not hierarchical ranking, which seems to me boneheaded, simply investigation. Here are some notes.

ATTENTION

The art of film lives by controlling attention, we are told, and are told truly except when there is an implication that the theater lives otherwise. The film director controls attention irrevocably; you cannot look at anything in the scene except what he permits you to look at. But the theater director wants to have exactly the same power over you. His job is harder because he has to *earn* your attention. If you look elsewhere than where he wants you to be looking at any given moment, the production is wobbling as badly as when the film in a projector flutters.

The difference between the two arts here is certainly not in intent but in means. Temperament sometimes enables a director to use both sets of means—Bergman and Visconti, for just two instances—sometimes not. Antonioni once told me that he had directed a few plays, and I asked him whether he wanted to do more theater work. "No," he said. "Always the same shot."

The film's ability to vary the shots, to command our shifts of attention with no chance of our demurral, is a happy slavery when the right person is giving the orders. But the notion advanced by some film writers that the very idea of holding attention on specific points for specific lengths of time *began* with film is esthetic and pragmatic nonsense.

TIME

The synoptic powers of film in regard to time are much greater than in the theater. The actor crossing the room on stage has to cross it, step by step; the film actor can come in the door and immediately be on the other side of the room. Film can juggle the present, past, and future effortlessly, and can repeat the moment, à la Resnais. The theater can try all these things to some degree (I have even seen the Resnais effect on stage), but it has to breathe hard in the attempt.

Much has been made, quite rightly, of these temporal powers in film. Much has been scanted, almost as if by contrasting obligation, of the temporal powers in the theater. The strength, not the limitation, of the stage is that, in any given scene, time does elapse there, moment by moment. Obviously, figurative time has been used in the theater—mostly between scenes—ever since the *Agamemnon*; still, a strength of the theater is that you feel and see time passing. This is a component of theatrical structure, enrichment, companionship.

It's interesting that in the film form, which can play with time, few works dare to run over two hours. In the theater, which mostly must accept time as it comes, chunk by chunk, many works run over two hours. To see a picture like the Russian film of *Uncle Vanya,* which, among other barbarisms, chopped the play to bits, is to miss the theater's power of letting lives flow before us in simulated passage, the theater's function as the place where such things can happen effectively.

Also, theatrical time works to the actor's advantage in many cases. A scintillating example was Rosalind Russell's performance in *Auntie Mame.* On stage it was not only a dazzling entertainment but a marathon event. Almost the same performance on screen was less effective because we knew it had been done in bits and pieces over a period of months, and the silent hum of wonder as the evening progressed was missing. Almost the only thing wrong for me with Peter Brook's film of *Marat/Sade* was the fact that I knew it had been made in seventeen days—a whirlwind in film-making time but a far distance from the span of one theater performance.

"OPENING UP"

To continue with a comparison of plays and filmed plays, a relation that is not only commonplace but revealing: the surest sign of the cliché mind in film making is a feeling of obligation to "open up" plays when they become films and a conviction that this process proves superiority, that a play really comes into its own when it is filmed. We can really go to Italy in Zeffirelli's film of *Romeo and Juliet,* so it supersedes place-bound theater productions. We can dissolve and cross-fade more easily in the film of *Death of a Salesman,* so the theater is once again just a tryout place for later perfect consummation. We can go outside the house in the film of *Who's Afraid of Virginia Woolf?,* and once again the theater is shown up as cribbed and confined.

The trouble here is a confusion in esthetic logic, an assumption that we are comparing apples and apples when we are really comparing apples and pears. Fundamentally, the film takes the audience to the event, shifting the audience continually; the theater takes the event to the audience, shifting it never. Just as the beauty of poetry often lies in tensions between free flight and form-as-preserver, so the beauty of drama often lies in tensions between imagination and theatrical exigency, theater form as a means of preservation, of *availability.* To assume that the film's extension of a play's action is automatically an improvement is to change the subject: from the way the theater builds upward, folding one event on another in almost perceptible vertical form, to the film's horizontal progression. The theater works predominantly by building higher and higher in one place. The film, despite the literally vertical progress of the frames, works predominantly in lateral series of places.

The very necessity for the dramatist to arrange to get the right people together at the right time in his one place becomes, for the appropriate talent, a means to beauty rather than a burden. (See any Chekhov or Shaw play.) It is muddled to think that, by "unfolding" these careful arrangements, the film inevitably enlarges the original work. This "unfolding" can be successful when the film maker knows clearly what he is doing and treats his film as a new work from a common source, as in the admirable Lester-Wood film of *The Knack.* But most adapters seem to think that any banal set of film gimmicks constitutes a liberation for which the poor cramped play ought to be grateful.

FRAMING

We often read some version of the following: a difference between stage and screen is that the stage contains all of the place where the event occurs, but the screen frames only part of the film's reality, which continues away from its borders on all sides.

One can see why this idea would grow out of film scenes shot on location. The cowhand who steps before the camera steps out of all Colorado into a tiny portion of it. It is harder to credit this idea when a film actor steps onto a set, even though the camera may eventually go into the next room or outside the house.

The theater audience knows that, literally, what is out of sight is the backstage area. The film audience knows that, literally, what is out of sight—even in Colorado—is a different set of mechanical means: grips, gaffers, reflectors, sound men, and a mechanical omnipresence that the theater never has, the camera.

Seemingly desperate for distinctive esthetics, desperate, too, to formulate a mystique, the film lays claim here to an imaginative exclusivity that is invalid except to the dull-minded. When Barbara Loden in her film *Wanda* roamed through coal fields and coal towns, she did not suggest any realer places out of sight than Ruby Dee in Fugard's *Boesman and Lena* telling us of the towns she had tramped through in her lifetime. In both cases there was a literal frame of mechanics and techniques; in both cases there was an imaginative world that stretched endlessly outside the frame. (pp. 353-57)

WORDS

Many have noted, myself among them, that words often fight films, which is why classic plays are hard to film. Let's define "classic" in old theatrical terms: the classic style is one in which you must play on the line, not between the lines. In films the action usually stops for the words, the words for the action. In addition, the camera brings classic language too close, as the camera brings the singing too close in films of opera. But the facile implication behind this, in much film criticism, is that prolixity doesn't matter in the theater. In fact, as all theater people know, a superfluous line in the theater is, in its own scale, as impedimental as it would be on film.

Further, when language is designed for film and is understood as contributory dynamics, it is as cinematic as any other film element. Bibi Andersson's account of the sex orgy in *Persona,* many of the dialogues in *My Night at Maud's* and *Claire's Knee,* John Gielgud's speeches in *The Charge of the Light Brigade,* Ray Collins's farewell at the railroad station in *The Magnificent Ambersons,* these are only a few of the instances where words, understood and controlled, become *film* components.

Of course there are still some who think that the film art died the moment Jolson sang. A quite valid case can be made to show that the silent and the sound film are esthetically separate; but it is a different case from the one that words are intrinsically and inevitably the enemy of the film. (pp. 357-58)

CRITICISM

The crucial historical difference between theater and film is this: the theater began as a sacred event and eventually included the profane. The film began as a profane event and eventually included the sacred.

No serious person objects to the theater's being judged by sacred standards (as the term is relevant here) because of its origins. But many serious people object to the film's being judged by sacred standards because of its origins.

It is tyrannical and priggish and self-cheating to militate against the profane. But it is a curious critical gift that militates against the sacred, or, more curious, equivocates by insisting that the sacred is *in* the profane. This difference in origin is, at worst, hard luck for the film, not esthetic or spiritual hierarchy. No Dionysus happened to be available when the film was beginning, but, fundamentally, it was born out of the same needs and to comparable ends. Its extra burden is that it has had to fashion its Dionysus as it goes, fitfully, patchily. But what a proof of its power and its potentiality that it has been able to do it. Why should film be reproved or patronized for this? Why should the one art born in this century be scolded for treating *everything* that anguishes and exalts human beings in this century? Or, more strangely, why should some of its devotees apply critical standards that implicitly urge it to aim low? What a price to pay for being apt!

The theater's struggle is not to forget its past. The film's struggle is not to be afraid of its future. (pp. 361-62)

Stanley Kauffmann, "Notes on Theater-and-Film," in his Persons of the Drama: Theater Criticism and Comment, *Harper & Row, Publishers, 1976, pp. 353-62.*

Richard Gilman

[*Gilman is an American educator and critic whose works, including* The Making of Modern Drama *(1974) and* Decadence: The Strange Life of an Epithet *(1979), have been praised for their independence from the standardized historical and theoretical terminology in which literature is often discussed. In the following essay, Gilman asserts the superiority of the films of the 1960s to the plays produced during that decade, finding that the works of such directors as Michaelangelo Antonioni and Alain Resnais are more effective artistically and are more convincing as representations of modern life than their counterparts in the theater.*]

The Sunday *New York Times Magazine*—that repository of everything that has been said better elsewhere—recently carried one of those "debates" about the theatre and the movies which leaves us wondering if our cultural despair is as deep as it should be. Tyrone Guthrie argued for the stage and Carl Foreman for the screen, each man displaying an extraordinary masochistic yearning to make the other look good. Mr. Guthrie said that theatre was more "live," that the movie actor "can't pull out all the stops and stun an audience . . . battering it like a typhoon," and that he personally had never seen a movie that wasn't mere journalism. Mr. Foreman said that films were more visual, that plays were just full of "words, words, words," and that since the movies were so much cheaper you could bring the children.

Any more such interchanges and the end is of course in sight, but penultimately we may find it desirable to choose. As for me, despite the fact that as a drama critic I might have been expected to have lined up behind Guthrie, I found myself rooting for Foreman—or being willing to root for him had he exhibited a grain of sense and had the game been rather different; had it been, that is to say, not a question of which medium was intrinsically better or more important but which was giving us more present satisfaction, more truth and more art. Posed this way, I think the debate can have only one outcome: the movies, whatever they may have been or may become, are currently filling the emptiness left by our theatre's abdication from anything we can recognize as our experience. And only snobbism, professional investments or myopia can prevent us from seeing that.

A handful of movies are filling the space: six, eight, perhaps a dozen in the last few years. Three or four are filling more of it than the rest. As for the bulk of films, someone has said that mass tastes belong more to sociology than aesthetics, a dictum as applicable to Broadway as to Hollywood. Most plays are bad, most movies are bad; it has simply been my observation that almost nothing in the recent theatre has been nearly so good as some of the films of the new Frenchmen, of Bergman, Kurosawa and Fellini, especially of Resnais and Antonioni.

Before going on, I should set down some propositions. The first, which should already be clear, is that the movies are an art, full-fledged, conscious, of legitimate birth and needing no more defenses or rationales. The second is that, while cinema is not so different from theatre as is sometimes thought, what does separate them is important enough for us to be able to locate in it some of the reasons for the movies' present superiority. And the third is that it may be possible to maintain an admiration for the contemporary screen without fatal prejudice to a belief that drama possesses the means to affect us more radically and more durably, whatever its almost complete failure in recent years to affect us at all.

Still, I wouldn't line up any trumpets to proclaim this belief in the theatre's historical and renewable powers. Thirty years ago Antonin Artaud, writing about the kind of theatre he wished to compel into being, said that it "did not intend to leave the task of distributing the Myths of man and modern life entirely to the movies." If we shift to a less apocalyptic plane in order to substitute the word "metaphors" or "recognitions" for myths, we who love the theatre remain in the same position as Artaud, except that we have so little of his at least partially efficacious thunder. The movies are more than ever undertaking our commerce, conducting our transactions, while our desire to get back into the field grows more pious and statutory every day.

I write from the boundless unhappiness and ennui induced by a theatrical season in which I saw more than a hundred plays and spectacles only three of which roused me to a more than temporary acknowledgement of some isolated and hermetic act of skill or passion. There were times when there came over me the raw craving to see a movie: in one mood, *any* movie, as on those Saturday afternoons in childhood; in another, a movie that might be able to put me back in touch with the world, after the deracinations and exiles of our theatre of repetition which cannot find a new tone or gesture in any of its bags.

In any but one, I should have said, and such poor hope as we possess comes from it; it contains the only objects we can dare pit against those beautiful and strange new films that have occupied the strategic angles of our vision. I am growing more and more to dislike "Theatre of the Absurd" to describe the kind of play that breaks, by means of new languages, parody and mockery, innocence, despair and painful fantasy, with everything that is moribund or dead in our theatre—which means nearly everything besides itself. But the term helps isolate what I mean.

"Meta-theatre," "anti-theatre," perhaps "infra-theatre," if we have to have a name. It doesn't matter, except that the "absurd" invites the foolish, asking for Arthur Kopit and Gelber's slipping out of his connection, and that such theatre is only absurd, on the occasions when it is, if you use an old logic to measure it by. In any case, this sort of drama, whatever its future (and I believe the theatre itself has none unless it is somehow along these lines) provided me with the few evenings on which I didn't feel suffocated, when the air was stirring around me so that I didn't have to go to the movies to discover that new and original dramatic shapes are still possible to make.

What is so suffocating about almost all theatre today is its unshakable attachment to and nearly unbroken consecration of what has ceased to exist. The stage throws back at us gestures, inflections, rhythms and grammars that have lost their right to serve as descriptions of ourselves—we are no longer like that, even if the forms persist mechanically. At best, nostalgic reminders of our past; at worst, deadly repetitions of a present we are seeking the means to shake off. Unless we want to note that the theatre also sends us Chayefsky or MacLeish-style mythograms, which are messages from the future, dispatched from areas of aspiration none of us has any intention of ever occupying.

There is a future which we do want art to colonize: the area of our next moves, our forthcoming utterances. The art of the present is always partly predictive, since it tells us what we are about to be. Artaud wrote that the theatre can renew our sense of life by being the arena where "man fearlessly makes himself master of what does not yet exist, and brings it into being." But that is exactly what certain movies are doing instead. When I first followed that long, disconsolate, abandoned search in *L'avventura,* that arc of despair that led to truth, I knew that it traced what I had been prepared to feel next; that from then on it would be impossible not to see existence with the same narrowed, dry-eyed, precipice-crawling intentness as Antonioni.

La notte takes us to the same place, by a different route. Here Antonioni leads us into the city, into concrete, walls and reflections in glass, after the rocks, great spaces, sea and terraces of *L'avventura.* And here the search (or movement; films *move,* are a tracing of movement, and in Antonioni, as in Resnais and the best moments of the others, the movement is everything—events, narrative statement, meaning) comes to the same end, or a fractional distance beyond. The acceptance is made of what we are like; it is impossible not to accept it as this film dies out on its couple shatteringly united in the dust, because everything we are not like, but which we have found no other means of shedding, has been stripped away.

I think this stripped, mercilessly bare quality of Antonioni's films is what is so new and marvelous about them. The island criss-crossed a hundred times with nothing come upon; the conversations that fall into voids; Jeanne Moreau's head and shoulders traveling microscopically along the angle of a building; unfilled distances; a bisected figure gazing from the corner of an immense window; the lawn of the rich man across which people eddy like leaves; Monica Vitti's hand resting on Ferzetti's head in the most delicate of all acceptances; ennui, extremity, anguish, abandoned searches, the event we are looking for never happening—as Godot never comes, Beckett and Antonioni being two who enforce our relinquishments of the answer, the arrival, two who disillusion us.

When Antonioni visited the studio of Mark Rothko he is reported to have told the artist that "your paintings are like my films—about nothing, with precision." An alarming remark, calculated to throw the film theoreticians and the significance mongers into a cold sweat. (Film criticism has always struck me as mostly having the tone of Samuel Goldwyn trying to talk his way in to see Immanuel Kant.) Yet there is no reason to be dismayed. Antonioni's films are indeed about nothing, which is not the same thing as being about nothingness.

L'avventura and *La notte* are movies without a traditional subject (we can only think they are "about" the despair of the idle rich or our ill-fated quest for pleasure if we are intent on making old anecdotes out of new essences). They are about nothing we could have known without them, nothing to which we had already attached meanings or surveyed in other ways. They are, without being abstract, about nothing *in particular,* being instead, like most recent paintings, self-contained and absolute, an action and not the description of an action.

They are part of that next step in our feelings which art is continually eliciting and recording. We have been taking that step for a long time, most clearly in painting, but also in music, in certain areas of fiction, in anti-theatre. It might be described as accession through reduction, the coming into truer forms through the cutting away of created encumbrances: all the replicas we have made of ourselves, all the misleading because logical or only psychological narratives, the whole apparatus of reflected wisdom, the clichés, the inherited sensations, the received ideas. In *L'avventura* the woman says: "Things are not like that . . . everything has become so terribly simple. . . . "

Irony, parody, abstraction, reduction: they are all forms of aggression against the traditional subject, against what art is supposed to deal with. They are, much more than the direct violence which we also use, our most effective means of liberating our experience, releasing those unnamed emotions and perceptions that have been blockaded by everything we have been taught to see and feel. What excites us about these new movies, what causes us to call each other up about them as we no longer do about plays, is the sense they communicate, in one degree or another, of extending the areas of freedom—troubled freedom because a price is paid when you are always half engaged in repudiating your erstwhile captors—that we have gained from the other arts.

I don't think it too much to say that the movies, having come into their maturity, are giving us more, or more useful, freedom than any other form. It may be evanescent, or simply data for more permanent structures to be created by other means, but it is being given to us, a week scarcely passing without some new accession. It ranges from the narrowest and most preliminary liberation such as is bestowed by British movies like *Room at the Top, Saturday Night and Sunday Morning* and *A Taste of Honey,* with their mostly traditional procedures but temperamental and thematic rebelliousness, to the far more solid and revolutionary, because more purely cinematic, achievements of Antonioni.

In between are the films of the Frenchmen, Chabrol, Godard, Truffaut, with their neo-existentialist adventures, proceeding by non-motivation and arbitrary acts, the camera jiggling or running along at eye-level or freezing fast, in not entirely successful visual implementation. And there is Bergman, with his new, not entirely convincing legends, his preachy discontent but also his powerful and clean images and isolations of immortality in a context of abrasive psychology and harsh weather. And Fellini, whose *Dolce vita* I thought vastly overrated because of its obviousness and mechanical application of its ideas, but some of whose earlier films—*I vitelloni* and *La strada*— were full of lucid, plangent vision.

I want only to add, passing over so many others and not even touching on the purely abstract film or the work of the American underground (I am an amateur moviegoer, with no compulsion to study everything and no breviary of the medium), a word about Alain Resnais. He seems to be only just below Antonioni, perhaps not so central, but doing with time what the latter does with space, if the distinction is admissible, since film is preeminently the fuser of time and space. But as metaphors the words might serve.

L'année dernière à Marienbad, Resnais has said, is "a mechanism differing from the usual spectacle, a kind of contemplation . . . it is about greater and lesser degrees of reality." And the reality is that of time, of memory and anticipation, the mechanism distributing our ordinary categories, mixing past, present and future, the images from each realm advancing and retreating, fading, reemerging, repeating, coalescing and finally coming to exist simultaneously, the way the mind actually but unavowedly contains them. It is a great film, a "new kind of fiction," as Robbe-Grillet has remarked; when its heroine asks, "What life would you have me live?" we are ready to answer, "This one, because it is truer."

If the movies are providing us with this truer life, this more real fiction, I don't think it has anything to do with the boldness of its themes compared with the theatre's. I think the reason lies, beyond the accidents of genius or circumstance, precisely in the fact that the screen is more abstract than the stage. That is to say, I see the decline of the theatre as rooted in its profound physicality, its being of all the arts (dance is speechless drama) the most nearly incarnate, the most committed to the palpable gestures and the actual word. And it is there, in our gestures, our emotions really, and our speech that we have become most atrophied, most devitalized and false.

What this means for drama is that, being wedded to our bodies and our language, it finds it all but impossible not to drag along with us, imitating our spent movements and utterances. But the film is only the reflection of our movements and statements, and reflections can be *arranged,* selected, reanimated through juxtaposition, interpenetration, *editing.* André Malraux wrote that "the means of reproduction in the cinema is the moving photograph, but its means of expression is the sequence of *planes.*" And planes are outside us, geometries beyond our power to turn into clichés.

When the movies obey their highest nature, turning from being merely another teller of stories to the creation of visual equivalents of our experience, records of our presence among objects and patterns of our occupation of the world, they enjoy a freedom and an authority that the stage has almost lost. Whether it will recover them is not easy to say; there is no magic in our protests that the theatre is perennial, that its loss would be unthinkable, and so forth.

Because our theatre depends so heavily on language, in which so much of our ineffectuality, deceitfulness and untruth is locked, I think it will have to be redeemed mainly by language, despite Artaud's fiery wish that it be redeemed in other ways. And the theatre cannot create a new speech by itself, especially when there is almost nobody willing to listen.

The three plays I saw last season that give me any hope were all works which while not bereft of a reinforcing *mise en scène* were primarily achievements of language, parodic, ironic and outside our formulas. They were Beckett's *Happy Days,* N. F. Simpson's *One-Way Pendulum* and Kenneth Koch's *George Washington Crossing the Delaware,* and none ran for more than a few weeks. I know it is being said that anti-theatre is on the way out. But I can't imagine what will replace it, except something that has learned from it and continues its general action. And I believe we won't have a "total" theatre, the kind of positive, multi-leveled new Elizabethan age certain tiresome critics keep calling for, until we have gone through a great deal more fragmentation, narrowness, indirection and painful jest. Nor will true theatre be anything but a minority enterprise for a very long time.

Meanwhile the movies, with their distance from our skins and breath, their power to make our reflections obey a transforming and arranging will, their eyes less jaded than our own, are beginning to reconstitute our experience. Far-flung, anonymous, their meetings held in shadowy caverns, they are becoming the community of vision that theatre once was. Actuality may be the highest good; when actuality becomes unreal we will settle for true shadows. (pp. 30-7)

> *Richard Gilman, "About Nothing–with Precision," in his* Common and Uncommon Masks: Writings on Theatre, 1961-1970, *Random House, 1971, pp. 30-7.*

David Denby

[*Denby is an American film critic. In the following excerpt, he contrasts film and drama from the perspective of a "theaterphobe."*]

The moviegoer won't put up with too much goodness. And often in movies there's a kind of deep-down nihilism, a surly, alienated indifference, a thoroughly cynical crappiness, that satisfies the big-city moviegoer's most luxuriously pessimistic moods. The basis of Clint Eastwood's appeal, and not just to the displaced but to middle-class intellectuals, too, is his exaggeratedly despairing view of America—a country, in Eastwood's movies, divided between vermin scum and their victims, with only a few righteous avengers staving off complete social collapse. Gangster films have always drawn on disgust for nine-to-five jobs, and horror films assume an open love of bizarre cruelties and ghoulish fantasy. In all these films a "negative" view of life is part of the subtext, part of what's *understood.* Movies, a dreamlike experience in the dark, appeal to "everyone," but especially to the solitary person, the loner, the reader of novels, the reader of horror comics and pornography, and also the teenager, who generally feels misunderstood and out of it; the morose tone of the cinema is part of the reason that the audience trusts it. Theater, on the other hand, appeals to the social-minded, the positive and explicit people who make this country go, and the tone of the theater, all too often, is didactic and public-spirited. Pessimism, even nihilism, is certainly possible in the theater, but such a mood would be so explicit that it would constitute an *issue.* In the theater almost everything must be spelled out, but in a movie the most powerful meanings may emerge principally from the atmosphere, the relation of characters to the world; and that is why a cynical, violent Clint Eastwood movie is hip in a way that a pessimistic and "challenging" Broadway play cannot be. Culturally the movies are both above and below the theater—more subtle, more intricate, at the upper end of the scale (Renoir, Bresson, early Welles), and cruder, more debased, at the lower end. . . . Even at their most

nihilistic, the movies are never vulgar in the way that the theater is. The movies leave us alone: they rarely appeal to the better part of our nature, they rarely force affirmations or responsibilities on us. We can just sit there, safe in the dark. (pp. 39-40)

I still haven't recovered from something I saw more than fifteen years ago: Maurice Evans lighting a cigarette on the stage. The play was an adaptation of Henry James's great novella *The Aspern Papers,* and Evans was the lead, the "publishing scoundrel" who tries to trick an old lady out of her prized possession—a set of letters from her long-dead lover, who was a famous poet. As I remember, Evans, playing this highly presentable, worldly man, selected a cigarette from a silver case and then put the case back in the inner pocket of his morning coat. He threw out his left arm, thrusting his hand well past the cuff so that we could see the cigarette in his fingers, placed the cigarette in his mouth, struck his match with a tremendous flourish, lit the cigarette, inhaled deeply, and swept the match into the fireplace with one hand as he drew the cigarette out of his mouth with the other, exhaling as fervently as Vesuvius. My God, that cigarette was *lit.* The whole action had a formal grandeur suitable for the signing of the Declaration of Independence. And what was he doing? Evans gave us a metaphor for a Victorian man of the world engaging in cigarette smoking as an exercise in social power.

Of course, a portentously struck match is not unknown in the movies. But how different the tonality of a movie cigarette! Hands cupped, his hat at a slight angle, Bogart lights an unfiltered cigarette, and as the smoke, slowly exhaled, passes into the glossy black nether regions of the frame (Warner Brothers' chiaroscuro offering the perfect setting for this sort of thing), we see the remarkably liquid quality of Bogart's ambiguously "hurt" eyes, the eyes of a man of sensibility who has suffered. The cigarette was a sign of his bitter knowledge of the world, of his willingness to accept defeat as the price of knowledge. In the movies of the thirties and forties cigarette smoking by men was associated with experience and heroic vulnerability. A woman who smoked was sexually available—think of Dietrich, or Bette Davis lighting up and batting her eyes, or Lauren Bacall in *To Have and Have Not,* turning a bit of repartee about lighting a cigarette into a whole scene of seduction. The range of these metaphors is, at their best, intimate and romantic, at their worst, no more than naughty—silly and borderline campy, whereas the theater light-up is just self-important. Surely someone will object that a second-rate classical stage actor like Evans should not be compared with the great naturals of the screen. My point, however, is not merely that Bogart and Bette Davis were better actors than Maurice Evans, or even that the meanings yielded by their devastating work with butt and match are smarter and funnier than those suggested by Evans's hopeless bit of stage pomp. Yes, certain kinds of meanings are possible in movies and not in the theater, and I'm partial to the more intimate, funnier tone of those meanings. But I think that in the end the reason for that partiality is that the movie cigarette scenes carry less of a burden. The movie scenes are primarily about a man or a woman lighting up; the meaning arises only secondarily and rather modestly, suggested by the context. As in a good literary narrative, metaphorical implications are produced by the accumulation of concrete details; they aren't simply imposed on the narrative.

In the theater almost everything . . . is a metaphor, and almost every meaning is imposed. That is why for us theaterphobes the allegedly electrifying "presence of the live actor" may often be a burden, an intrusion, and a presumption. The theater actor exists at a higher level of intensity, a faster speed, than a person in life. Trying to reach the back of the house with his inner torments, he often creates too much meaning, or too obvious meanings. And not just the actor. Every prop is also a metaphor. Whether elaborate or simple—a huge, double-tiered set (*Sweeney Todd*) or a pair of ash cans (Beckett)—the stage set cannot re-create reality but can only evoke some small portion of it. A sole chair on an empty stage, precisely because it is yanked out of its normal relations with other chairs or a table or a sideboard, is a portentous symbol. If it is accompanied by the table and the rest, it still has the quality of a metaphor—surrounded, as it is, by a proscenium overhead and doors to the side and back through which actors enter and exit. Well, so what? Aren't there good metaphors and bad? And isn't there good staging and bad? Good acting and bad? Yes, of course, but what I'm trying to get at is the basic *uneasiness* that some of us feel in the theater, and I think some of our pain may derive from an unacknowledged notion of the proper relation of representation to metaphor and symbol. In the movies if you turn on the camera, you can photograph trees, or city streets, or the grimy stacks of a steel mill, and all these things are blessedly free of any extra significance. Representing nothing more than themselves, they have a weight and beauty that is almost moral. The solidity of the physical world in a film can be immensely moving: the rain, the streets, the smokestacks, give off a kind of hum—not an actual sound, of course, but a sensation as palpable as the rustling of the woods on a summer night. That sensation is the knowledge, both thrilling and heartbreaking, that the world exists, that a thing in the world is itself and not another thing.

It's commonly said that theater requires more of the spectator's imagination (the implication being that movies are for the literal-minded). But is this really true? On the stage nearly everything—themes, characterization, humor, emotions—is more explicit, and only the settings are "incomplete." In any case, some of us would rather not complete the work of a mediocre playwright. We would rather look at a picture of something.

I hope I won't be misunderstood: I'm not arguing that a shot of rain on the street, by itself, is art; and I'm not arguing for realism, as against artifice, as a cinematic mode. (Artifice can give off a hum too, though of a different kind.) I'm only trying to explain why theaterphobes can sit through routine movies without experiencing real boredom: we're happy, at some level (however much we're aware of the mediocrity of the film), looking at the Paris cafés or the waves breaking behind the kids in a beach-party comedy—whereas a bad play makes us feel trapped and miserable. For a moviegoer, the theater is often an experience of sensory deprivation. There they are, the actors and the empty stage and the goddamn chairs! There's nothing else to look at, and it's all so murderously *significant.* Unless a genius like Beckett has written the play, and has used the meagerness of the spectacle as a way of evok-

ing life's flirtation with nullity, the pretension of the bare stage is unendurable. At the other extreme, when the stage is full, with sets rapidly wheeled on and off, lights flashing, music blasting, the sense of strain is overwhelming. One wonders how they did it rather than enjoying [it]. . . .

Everyone knows that the presence of the camera encourages the actor to calm down and just exist in the role; and everyone also knows (I hope) that this existing for the camera can be a remarkable form of acting. What's not so well understood is the point that the great French critic André Bazin made in his essays on film and theater (in *What Is Cinema?,* Volume I): in the movies the actor doesn't have to carry as heavy a burden as he does on stage; a large part of the drama is derived from his relation to his surroundings. The actor matters, but so do the peculiar clouds passing overhead, the wide-beamed floor, the cars parked on the street. That is why the argument always used in favor of theater and against cinema—"the presence of the live actor"—is a little beside the point. In the movies many things are "present," and all these things, large and small, animate and inanimate, exist on an equal plane. (pp. 40-1)

Since Ibsen and Strindberg and Shaw, and certainly since the rise of the movies, anyone who has thought seriously about the matter has known that staging realistic plays on realistic sets (life with the fourth wall missing) is problematic at best. A few great playwrights have continued to work as realists, but for the avant-garde, the theorists, and the advanced critics, "illusion" has become the province of the intellectually timid, because the only thing "real" in the theater is the actors holding the stage and the audience watching them. Isn't that why almost every clever modern play seems to be about the theater itself? What else can a smart modern play be about? The self-reflexive strategies of modernism have produced poetry devoted to the process of making poetry, and painting as a commentary on art history, but these are still examples of experimentation. What has figured in the other arts as experiment has become part of the *mainstream* of the theater. By necessity. All those musicals about putting on a show (from *42nd Street* to *A Chorus Line* and beyond) deal with the problem of representation in the most direct way: in a musical about a musical, the playwright needn't struggle to explain why people are standing on a stage. In other kinds of plays he must, and this struggling has made the theater a wretchedly uneasy and self-conscious art form. How many plays hailed as "theatrical" turn out to be devoted to the mechanics of illusion and representation, the ontology of the spectacle itself? The nature of theater forces an obsession with basic aesthetic questions, and even grander matters than that: modern theater visionaries like Artaud and Grotowski, tormented by the question of what to put on the stage, turn the theater into an arena of metaphysical speculation. Devising an acceptable mode of being on the stage becomes a philosophical, rather than a dramatic, problem.

The uneasiness of theater as spectacle encourages a fetish of radical solutions: the middle ground has been burned away, and the avant-garde doubtless feels that it must revolutionize the theater merely to exist in the theater. Expressionism, surrealism, alienation effects, the ritual theater, the silent theater, Artaud's shock tactics, Orson Welles's actors firing blanks at the audience—*anything* to get away from the bourgeois disgrace of realism, the philistine humiliation of representation and imitation. Every successful modern play (aesthetically successful, that is) reinvents the theater. For a while the theater, rescued from intellectual disgrace, can exist again, but then the avant-garde, having defined a new reality onstage, repeats itself, or the imitators and epigones take over, and soon someone has to come up with a new definition of theater. Beckett, it turns out, devised the perfect title not only for his play but also for twentieth-century drama: *Endgame.*

The great inventors of modern drama are heroic figures, and perhaps we theaterphobes need nothing more than outstanding productions of Brecht and Pirandello and Beckett to shake us out of our hostility. (p. 42)

The first act of David Mamet's [*Glengarry Glen Ross*] is thrilling. I don't know when I've heard on a stage words so eager to be spoken, so charged in rhythm, so juicy to play, so completely "overheard" yet poetic. The act consists of three short scenes, each with two men, all set in a dowdy Chinese restaurant. In the first a sixtyish real-estate salesman who is losing his grip tries to get the office manager to give him some leads. What are leads? Are they pieces of property for sale or names of prospective clients? (The latter, it turns out.) Mamet doesn't tell us much; the desperation of the salesman is all the context we get, but it's more than enough. This man is so anxious, and split so many ways about how to proceed—boasting of past prowess, insulting, propitiating, begging, bribing—that he speaks in fragments, changing direction every few words, knocking himself out against a wall of indifference. As we listen, we realize that Mamet has discovered a new mode of American speech—a language of pure intention, which darts ahead, anticipating objections and refusals, and then collapses anyway at the first sign of resistance.

In the second scene two more salesmen meet. A rancorous, hard-nosed type leads the other man, an imitative weakling, through a litany of the company's sins. The company has exploited them for years, given them meager commissions, set the salesmen in brutal competition with one another. To punish the bastards, the first man says, someone should break into the office, steal the leads, and sell them to a rival firm.

> "Are you actually *talking* about this?" says the second man, getting nervous. "Or are we just . . . ,"
> "No, we're just . . . ."
> "We're just *talking* about it."
> "We're just *speaking* about it. [*Pause*] As an *idea.*"

In the third scene still another salesman subjects a silent fellow at the next table to an astonishing monologue that turns out to be a sales pitch. But what a pitch! The salesman reviews his entire life, passing through a kind of Socratic dialogue with himself, each answer leading to another question, constructing a kind of ethos of the business civilization in which every value is equal to every other value. What's so funny about this monologue is that the man's ideas, delivered so forcefully, invariably run into a thicket of equivocation; he is copiously, self-confidently indefinite. Ethics are just a memory, a set of poses, as useful or useless as anything else. Yet the salesman's antinomian philosophy makes him happy; it gives him freedom to operate, to *sell,* and that is the only thing he cares about.

Each of these scenes drives ahead with a fierce inner logic—cruel, exact, hilarious—that makes the audience laugh from the opening words. The second act, set in the real-estate office the morning after it has been robbed, isn't quite so miraculously concentrated. You can feel Mamet making theater, working up conventional suspense, throwing in surprises—but the language keeps forging ahead. Hard and impervious, harsh, narrowly defined, *Glengarry Glen Ross* is as precise as *Death of a Salesman* is vague and rhetorical. Mamet shares nothing of Arthur Miller's pained, sorrowfully disapproving attitude, his Old Testament lamentations over lives devoted to false ideals. These men love to sell, just as warriors love to fight, and Mamet celebrates the go-ahead American business energy—the desperation, the lies, the flamboyance and courage of a really outrageous shuck. Mamet is the true heir to Chandler and Hammett, and to Ben Hecht and Charles MacArthur, whose play about the exhilarations of yellow journalism, *The Front Page,* is an American classic. He sticks to his business, giving you the shoptalk, the insiders' jargon, the way the men feel about their lives. He doesn't have to tell us that they're corrupt; we can see that, and both enjoy and deplore that part of their appetite which links up to our own. He raises no larger issues, but what the play says about the tendency of our business civilization to slip into fraud is devastating and unanswerable.

The language that Mamet has developed in *Glengarry Glen Ross* is really a great discovery—a find comparable in importance to a biochemist's ordering of the elements in a newly isolated molecule. Mamet may have heard evidence of something momentous—perhaps a change in the American character. I would guess that he heard it not only in offices (for a while in his youth Mamet worked in Chicago real estate) but also in such prime records of American felony as the transcripts of Nixon's talks with Dean, Haldeman, and Ehrlichman. In those weird, disintegrating dialogues, a mass of crooked intentions, literally unspeakable, broke language into semi-coherent shards, with only a glint of fact shining through the vague surface of allusion and deception. The President and his advisers, men with an ostensible commitment to legality, *spoke* about covering up crimes—they alluded to the subject suggestively—without actually talking about it. That way they could indignantly deny that the subject ever came up.

When the transcripts were published, people were shocked not only by the meanness of spirit they revealed but also by the manic slovenliness of the talk. The transcripts were like rubble heaps of broken furniture: no one phrased anything gracefully, or even accurately; no one ever completed a sentence. Clearly, something is happening to American speech, and the artists are on to it. In such works as *Mean Streets* and *Taxi Driver* the film director Martin Scorsese made something anguished and heartbreaking out of verbal trash. Though flawlessly clear as emotion and psychology, the first great scene in *Mean Streets* between Robert De Niro and Harvey Keitel (two Little Italy punks) is hopelessly disorganized as language. As generations of screenwriters looked on in dismay, the two actors, improvising around a few basic script ideas, constructed an intricate, highly charged web of implication, allusion, denial—all of it exhilaratingly obscene and funny—out of fragments. In *Glengarry Glen Ross* Mamet has achieved the same degree of spontaneity with written-out dialogue.

The Broadway production of *Glengarry Glen Ross* is very simple, but it's fully adequate for what Mamet wants to accomplish. The *language* is the set, the lighting; the drama; and for the moviegoer, it burns away the embarrassment of stage representation. My reference to Scorsese's great films was more than casual. *Glengarry Glen Ross* is a moviegoer's play: it has the hard, cool, nonsymbolic quality, the violence, the fullness, of a great American movie.

For moviegoers like myself, the theater seems caught in a gigantic double bind. The closer it comes to realistic representation, the more it betrays how inadequate it is next to the cinema; the further away from representation it moves, the more it loses contact with what interests us in the world and becomes preoccupied with the means of its own existence. And yet . . . I know that a few plays each year will transcend this bizarre predicament. It turns out that when I began going to the theater . . ., I was looking for something . . . : not "good theater," or even "good drama," but the *word*. For it is the word that has been banished from the cinema. As the audience for American movies has shifted downward in age, young film-school graduates, often without any literary or theatrical training at all, have taken over the directors' seats. For these young men and women, and also for the studio executives and marketing experts who back them, the screenplay has lost its earlier standing (admittedly shaky) as a complicated narrative with reasonably developed characters and perhaps a few memorable lines. The screenplay is now a "concept"—a salable idea. It's a Hollywood commonplace that Robert Towne's masterly screenplay for *Chinatown* (1974) would not be produced now, and that *Citizen Kane* and *All about Eve* wouldn't even be read. In recent years only one original screenplay of note—Barry Levinson's *Diner,* which he also (luckily) directed—has made it into the movie theaters. . . . [The indifference to writing has] reached such a pitch, even among critics, that a film as parched, cautious, and essentially *unwritten* as Robert Benton's *Places in the Heart* was hailed all over the country as a great picture.

But in the theater language still reigns. David Rabe's . . . *Hurlyburly* is a bad play—nuttily repetitive, rancid, and even rather cheap. Yet Rabe, like Mamet, has made some serious discoveries about the way Americans speak. Set amid the crumb-bum screenwriters, actors, and casting directors of Hollywood—the fourth-raters and hangers-on—the play is about callous people who fill the gaping space where their emotions should be with an elaborate kind of California psycho-babble. They all know that in certain situations they should feel something; their language represents the enfeebled California superego at work—the homage that words pay to the *idea* of feeling, a discourse about emotion in place of having any. As I say, the play isn't a success, but Rabe is definitely onto something; and as the long, peculiar sentences unfold, the audience hardly breathes. Rabe and Mamet have achieved mastery of language, and not for its own sake, or merely as a vehicle for actors, or even as the essence of "the drama," but as a sign, as a trace—a bit of spoor, actually—of the great beast lurking outside. Neither *Glengarry Glen Ross* nor *Hurlyburly* is a play about the resources of the theater, but the theater is the indispensable lens that brings them both into focus. (pp. 48, 50)

David Denby, "Stranger in a Strange Land: A Moviegoer at the Theater," in The Atlantic Monthly, *Vol. 255, No. 1, January, 1985, pp. 37-48, 50.*

FILM AND THE NOVEL

Donald F. Larsson

[*In the following excerpt, Larsson examines the "transformation" of themes, aesthetics, and ideology in adapting novels for film.*]

From at least the 1920s on—the time when "Hollywood" had secured its hegemony over cinematic practice—the novel has not only had to share or cede its position as the dominant American middle class narrative form, it has also had its texts appropriated and transformed—adopted and adapted—by its rival. Comparison of films and novels, especially in the examination of the process of adaptation, has long been a subject for family talks, after-movie barroom conversations, reviewers' tirades, authors' laments, and learned conferences and publications. Yet too often these comparisons, whether on the personal, the popular, or the professional level, have returned to the same old (not necessarily compatible) clichés: that Hollywood automatically degrades anything it touches by reducing it to the lowest common denominator; that great novels make only mediocre films; that film and literature are so different that they cannot be justly compared at all. More recently, a new set of clichés has come into being, based on the fact that the novel and the commercial film are both narrative forms; that film inevitably follows the novel in the presentation and affirmation of humanistic values, especially of the triumph of man over machine and of the recovery and representation for the viewer of a previously lost, unmediated reality; and that the film is essentially just another branch of literature.

All of these clichés, like most clichés, contain some elements of truth, but that truth is worn away by overuse, obscured by metaphysical baggage, and confused by an essentialism that regards both film and novel as single, ahistorical, ideal entities. Moreover, as Charles Eidsvik has pointed out, "film" the medium—the strip of celluloid running through the projector—is usually confused "with its dominant genre, the narrative." (Unfortunately, Eidsvik himself goes on to confuse literature with the medium of print.) It should be clear enough by now that the novel and the narrative film are indeed both means of telling stories, but that they also both have histories and are in turn grounded *in* history, particularly the histories of the American and European middle classes.

Within narrative forms, as Christian Metz and Jonathan Culler have both reminded us, there is a system of codes and conventions—what we might call "literature" in general and what Metz specifically labels as "cinema"—and the *working* of codes in texts—the individual novel or film. Seeing the two narrative forms as analogous—that is, that "cinema" as a set of codes and conventions is to literature as the individual film is to the novel—we should be able to intelligently apply what the screenwriters have always told us—that a novel must be translated to the screen in cinematic terms. I say "intelligently apply" because the problems and motivations of translation from one medium to another are far more complex than even the translation of poetry from one language to another. The conventions and codes of narrative film do derive much—as Eisenstein told us—from those of the novel. Yet they also derive from many other sources in theater, art, photography and mass culture, as we have learned from Erwin Panofsky, John Fell, and Keith Cohen. With this wealth of resources incorporated in the narrative codes of film, there is no reason that any novel should be impoverished by its translation from page to screen.

Such impoverishment does occur, though, and is more often than not expected. The reason it occurs and the reason why (though we expect it) we are continually disappointed is that both literary and filmic texts are grounded in and part of daily social practice. Both adaptors and spectators have certain assumptions about adaptations which derive from their places in time and society and which are not always directed toward the same goals. A text has its birth in relation to its time and retains at least vestiges of that meaning, but its meanings and its significance beyond the page or screen change along with the society beyond the page or screen. In turn, in the adaptation of any novel into film, these changes are inevitably manifested within three broad areas. One of these is the historical matrix within which the text has its origin, its popular reception, its critical study, and its conversion to film. Another is the aesthetic intent of the adaptor in conjunction with market pressures to produce a saleable commodity. Finally there are ideological constraints, both covert, manifested in sociological and psychological subtexts, and overt, resulting from direct pressures to bring a text into conformity with dominant moral and political practices.

Of course, these classifications are an oversimplification since all three areas are inseparably intertwined, often overlapping and sometimes congruent; still, they provide a set of guidelines by which to begin a measure of the process of adaptation. In providing keys to understanding the motivations, possibly conflicting, which underlie various adaptations, we should be able to read the process of transformation as well as the texts being transformed.

The historical matrix of any given novel affects how it is read and changed by its adaptor(s) in two ways. First, any reading is affected by time and by the changes that any reader brings to a text. Professional literary historians have problems enough in trying to reproduce an accurate reading of a work according to its origin in history, so the problem is even more acute for the reader who comes to the work without scholarly knowledge or a professional air of detachment (if, in fact, such knowledge is ever complete and true or such detachment completely possible). We do not have to agree completely with Harold Bloom and insist that all readings are misreadings, to recognize that one's personal, lived experience as well as those dislocations of modern consciousness represented by evolution, Marxism, depth psychology, relativity, and feminism have changed and continue to change (to varying degrees, of course) the ways in which we look at novels produced before these dislocations. This intellectual "distortion" is

greater the more distant culturally and historically the adaptor is from his or her source. Thus, although Martin C. Battestin generally praises the adaptation of *Tom Jones* by John Osborne and Tony Richardson, he does conclude that the film lacks Fielding's moral vision—necessarily so, because a modern mass audience will not share the same attitudes and beliefs which Fielding could assume in his readers. As a more modern instance, no present-day filmmaker could share the naiveté of D. W. Griffith in believing that bringing Thomas Dixon's *The Clansman* to the screen as *Birth of a Nation* was not a racist act.

Second, the degree of historical distortion in an adaptation is complicated further by the *cultural* history of the novel. Only rarely does a well-known work escape a popularization which incorporates the text as a part of general mass culture with little or no regard for its actual content. In these cases, the text which is brought to the screen is less the novel itself than the novel as bowdlerized for public school texts, as fitted out for touring stage presentations, as enshrined in lovable characters (and even lovable authors) from the canons of Acceptable Literature. This enshrinement in the classic Hollywood film is perhaps most obvious in those films which open with the cover, title page, and perhaps opening page of the book itself. This device functions to assure the spectator that the movie is a "faithful" adaptation of the novel (whether it is or not). Of course, the same device was often used in adaptations of contemporary best sellers as well; in either case, the audience is being promised the prestige of the novel. Gregory Ratoff's 1949 *Black Magic* goes one step further. The film opens with a conversation in which Alexandre Dumas's *père* complains to his son (appropriately referred to as the author of *Camille*) about the block he is having in writing about the magician-hypnotist Cagliostro. As the author begins to recount the details of Cagliostro's career, there is a dissolve into the main narrative of the film which itself concludes with a dissolve to a hand, writing: "The End. Alexandre Dumas." A bit of black magic has also taken place here. A verbal recounting of a story has given way to its dramatic representation which has in turn become the novel itself, all sanctified by the seeming physical presence of one of the great Romantic storytellers.

Canonization of the text within the realm of mass culture helps to explain the scandalous adaptations so many works have had. Nowhere is this more apparent than in the treatment of those dark and subversive works which have been cleaned up and banished to the realm of Children's Literature—notably, *Gulliver's Travels*, *Huckleberry Finn*, and *Alice in Wonderland*. Norman Z. McLeod's 1933 version of *Alice*, for example, is wonderfully cast but literally enshrines its subject by making all the actors wear masks modeled after the Tenniel drawings. (The Disney version has more to do with Mickey Mouse than Lewis Carroll.) Clearly, works which raise fundamental questions about the nature of humanity (like *Gulliver*), about duty to a personal moral vision over social moral conventions (as in *Huckleberry Finn*), and about the logic and justice of education and authority (as in *Alice*) will very rarely find full expression in a centralized, industrialized mass medium. This, though, is the realm of ideology, which is yet to be discussed.

Aesthetic considerations in adaptations may be the most difficult to deal with, though they seem the simplest. It is the aesthetic response of the individual filmmaker to the novel which is usually found wanting by the weekly popular movie reviewers, and it is either the failure of that response or the technical obstacles to a satisfactory adaptation that are the focus for so many discussions of adaptations. What makes the aesthetic actually so difficult to deal with, though, is not just the problem of knowing the personal and subjective response of an adaptor to a novel, but the fact that that response is itself incorporated in the historical matrix of the novel and bound up in ideology. For the moment, however, we can isolate three varieties of response by the adaptor to the text: first, a desire to "reproduce" the text, to bring the novel to the screen—what is usually called a "faithful" adaptation; second, a more or less significant alteration to the work to fit the adaptor's own artistic purposes; and finally, a conscious effort to criticize, subvert, undercut or deconstruct the novel itself, even to the point of altering it entirely. All three responses may themselves spring from a variety of motivations— some even at odds with each other—and none of these responses guarantees that the completed adaptation will be adequate to the response.

The reason for the different motivations underlying these aesthetic responses has to do with the perennial question of film authorship. Most basically, it is the writer who is responsible for transforming the novel into the screenplay, but we are all aware of the transformations which even a screenplay can undergo in filming. The director is most often responsible for the final product, but in a Hollywood-type system, final responsibility may be removed from the director and assigned to a studio editor or may even be relegated to the producer. The problem is obvious enough, but I mention it once more just to draw attention to the fact that the process of adaptation can rarely be neatly held to a uniform set of circumstances, the simple fusion of two consciousnesses resulting in a final product. Even though, for the sake of time and space, I will refer mainly to the "adaptor" without specifying a specific role for that individual, we must be aware that the dialectics of film and print are considerably more complicated.

The "faithful" adaptation is probably the one most desired and demanded by the popular critics, the one we think of as being the ideal adaptation, but immediately a question arises: "Faithful to *what?*" Like the Law, novels are said to have a "letter" and a "spirit," and it is considered better to be faithful to the spirit than to engage in a "slavish" following of the original text. The "spirit" of the novel, though, is precisely what changes in the historical matrix within which we read the novel. Some works simply cannot be read completely in their original "spirit"—if, in fact, that entity can ever be isolated—and not only because we misread but also because an "accurate" reading would be intolerable.

Faithfulness to the "letter" of the novel seems easier; seemingly, all one has to do is reproduce the characters, the events and the dialogue, but we have all seen enough movies to know that is not sufficient either. First, there are the constraints of time and money within commercial exhibition practices. Few adaptations can completely cover a work in the time of a feature-length film and few producers are willing or able to put up enough money to finance a complete adaptation (though the occasional successes of television mini-series like *Shogun* may change this prac-

tice). Secondly, faithfulness to the "letter" may be impossible because it *is* the letter. Those adaptations which have been judged most disappointing are usually of works in which language and narrative technique are heavily foregrounded. Unless the cinematic narrative and image are foregrounded in similar ways, unless cinematic tropes are substituted for literary ones, the result is Martin Ritt's *The Sound and the Fury,* from which the play of consciousness in Benjy, Quentin, and Jason has disappeared; or Paul Newman's *Sometimes a Great Notion,* which straightens Ken Kesey's revelatory, insistent, continually looping, multi-voiced narration into just another family saga; or Joseph Strick's *Ulysses,* which becomes, as Pauline Kael puts it, "readings from the book plus illustrated slides."

To ask, "Faithful to *what?*" also requires a recognition that most adaptations are made to assure a profit. It was not simply an innate desire by early filmmakers to bring favorite stories to life that prompted them to adapt novels, short stories and plays for the screen; it was also the need for a product. Once it was discovered that stories on film drew audiences, there arose a need for more and more stories to consume. Novel rights are bought by producers not from love of literature, but because a successful or prestigious book can assure a good return, and if the work in question is a classic in the public domain, so much the better. In addition, submitting a work to the rationalizing and conventionalizing processes of mass culture usually overrides any question of faithfulness to a text. Adaptors and producers who see the novel as a consumable product, who envision *Crime and Punishment* as a swell detective story, are legendary in the folklore of Hollywood.

Even in Hollywood, though, there are exceptions, and there have been and are filmmakers whose avowed purpose was or is to bring the novel to the screen in a completely faithful production. But still the question asserts itself: "Faithful to *what?*" Eric von Stroheim, David O. Selznick, and Robert Bresson all claimed utter fidelity to the text when they made, respectively, *Greed, Gone with the Wind,* and *Diary of a Country Priest.* Each is a very different book, adapted for very different reasons, resulting in very different films. Even when an adaptation is successful in conveying a book to screen, we are still obligated to examine the source and motivations of that adaptation, to ask for what purpose this film was made. Stroheim's insistent naturalism, Selznick's apotheosis of Hollywood style, and the elliptical quietness of Bresson cannot be equated simply because each adaptation is "faithful." A simpleminded notion of faithfulness, whether to letter or spirit, only serves to obscure the works and the process and remove them from history while isolating them from ideology.

A second response by filmmakers to individual texts is to make the work faithful to *themselves,* to recast it and adapt it to conform to their own obsessions and personal visions. Obviously, this form of adaptation is employed most fully by those directors whose identifiable body of works and continuing themes and concerns label them as *auteurs.* With *The Grapes of Wrath,* for example, Nunally Johnson and John Ford transform John Steinbeck's nascent socialism into a nostalgic populism typical of Ford's other films. Orson Welles in *The Magnificent Amerbersons, The Trial,* and *The Immortal Story,* is at least as much concerned with his own continuing depiction of the results of lost innocence, of personal corruption, and of the redemptive powers of story-telling as with an accurate depiction of the individual worlds of Booth Tarkington, Franz Kafka, and Isak Dinesen. The adaptor's vision may be as much a sociological one as an artistic one. Taking Richard Brooks's postwar novel, *The Brick Foxhole*—a badly confused expression of antimilitarism and psychological and sexual insecurity—Dore Schary and Edward Dmytryk fashioned the film *Crossfire*—a tightly constructed thriller which attacks anti-Semitism and makes an overt left-liberal appeal for social justice. Babette Mangolte, in her production of Henry James's *What Maisie Knew,* literally reshapes the text to her—in fact, the camera's—vision. Discarding most of any plot (not just James's) and setting the film in a contemporary urban apartment, Mangolte uses a subjective camera to recreate a child's vision while bringing the viewer's vision into question at the same time. Again, there is a wide divergence of motives and means in adapting novels. Filmmakers who reform the work to their own desires are certainly not offering faithful adaptations, but such adaptations would likely be less powerful and coherent if they did not reform to answer new questions and to fit into a new context.

That context may sometimes be a questioning, undermining, or deconstruction of the original novel itself. Mangolte's *Maisie* certainly points in that direction, as does the production of *Sigmund Freud's Dora* by Anthony McCall, Claire Pajaczkowska, Andrew Tyndall, and Jane Weinstock. Though *Dora* is not a traditional literary text, the film uses Freud's account of his patient to demonstrate how he himself in fact did read her as a text and subverts that reading by placing the narrative of the original in a variety of visual and narrative contexts which undermine Freud's own reading and open up new questions. Novels may have been undermined by Hollywood adaptors for their own, mostly commercial purposes, but that process is an obscuring and covering of the original text. The radical filmmaker, on the other hand, wishes to undercut the novel in order to expose its underlying assumptions and basic premises, often to substitute new assumptions in a radical rereading of the text. Keith Cohen has shown how Sergei Eisenstein tried to do precisely this in his plans to adapt Theodore Dreiser's *An American Tragedy.* Taking an already radical American novel, Eisenstein intended to probe even deeper and offer a truly Marxist analysis of the capitalist class relationships in the novel. It almost goes without saying that Eisenstein's version was never filmed; the project instead went to that arch-aesthete, Joseph von Sternberg. Cohen, though, holds up Eisenstein's project as a model for *all* adaptations and makes a convincing case for the necessity of a sense of purpose beyond the mere adaptation itself: "The adaptation must subvert its original, perform a double and paradoxical job of masking and unveiling its source, or else the pleasure it provides will be nothing more than that of seeing words changed into images."

Such a conception and such a project of adaptation was perhaps impossible in the classic Hollywood era, but one place in which research is needed is the determination of whether it was in fact impossible. So much has been said about inadequacies in Hollywood's approach to novels that we may be overlooking cases in which the adaptation did in fact go beneath and beyond the text. Such films certainly were possible by the 1950s, even if they were not performed with the rigor and purpose an Eisenstein might bring to them. Genre films may be most prone to such textual rereadings; certainly, two prime examples have come from the realm of the detective film. Robert Aldrich's *Kiss Me Deadly* is completely different in attitude from a more traditional version of Mickey Spillane like Victor Saville's *I, the Jury.* In the Aldrich film, Mike Hammer is exposed as a thoroughly contemptible creature—a bully, liar, blackmailer, and petty sadist whose greed leads to the detonation of an atomic bomb and his own destruction. On a somewhat more subtle level, Robert Altman's *The Long Goodbye* outraged Raymond Chandler fans by the transformation of Philip Marlowe, Chandler's knight of chivalry patrolling the mean streets of modern society, into an anachronism in the sensual, high-tech world of 1970s Los Angeles—such an anachronism that he finally forgets his personal code of honor and stoops to murder and revenge.

This last category of aesthetic response to the printed text—the subversion or undermining of the text—leads naturally into our final area of concern, that of ideological constraints. A conscious ideological purpose like that of Eisenstein has the special virtue of providing a solid theoretical framework within which to adapt a work, but when the ideology in question is that of the dominant society within which the adaptation is made—the capitalist, bourgeois society which founded and sustained Hollywood—*conscious* ideology disappears or seems to. Here we are in the realm of ideology as redefined by Louis Althusser, as the way in which people live the relationship between themselves and the conditions of their existence. Ideology, then, is the continual procession of daily events which confirms and naturalizes all human relations. Obviously, cultural media play an extremely important role in such naturalization. The upper middle class is elevated and displayed as the norm; sexual relationships are placed within a patriarchal framework with little or no question paid to the place of woman; the individual is always given priority and ascendence over the group.

When both novels and films are produced within ideology, without self-awareness, then they usually unquestioningly reproduce that ideology and it is the task of the reader or spectator alone to undermine these texts by concentrating on the contradictions, gaps, and fissures that inevitably occur within the narrative. Of course, the historical matrix is in process here too. A change in lived relationships produces changed perceptions and changed readings. Films like *Stella Dallas* and *Mildred Pierce* insist even more forcefully than the novels from which they came that women who seek personal satisfaction and financial success over duty and subservience to a man will lose everything (including themselves in the form of their adored daughters), but fewer people today than ever before are willing to accept such a covert message and more can recognize it *as* a message. The ideology of the text eventually loses its invisibility and stands exposed, even though it is replaced by new ideologies and new forms of ideology.

A separate, though related, problem is that of the ideology of the image. Much of the important film scholarship of the last decade has called into question and examined the nature of the film image, especially its claimed ability to reproduce or represent reality. Noting the origins of the movie camera in the *camera obscura* which ordered and rationalized vision in painting for the rising middle classes of the Renaissance, critics associated with the *Cahiers du cinéma* in France and the British journal *Screen* have seen the function of the film image as the placement and even construction of an individual, seemingly autonomous spectator-subject. The critique of this film image has begun, both by critics and by filmmakers, but what is also needed is an examination of the ideology of the film image in adaptations in relation to the ideology of the real which is subsumed within the texts from which the films derive. Such a project can only be suggested here, but it is one more item for future film study.

Finally, we must remember that ideology also functions overtly, censoring and editing in the name of moral, economic, and political righteousness. The Hays Office and the Production Code were the most obvious manifestations of this sort of control, but even they are too often forgotten as we look at the shape a novel took in making its way to the screen. Less obvious, and needing a more detailed history, are direct interventions in movies for political reasons, such as that which Constance Pohl has detailed in regard to *For Whom the Bell Tolls*. As Gerald Peary and Roger Shatzkin remind us, ideology can be quite conscious as well as unconscious, and it is one of the duties of scholars and critics to deal with the interrelationships of both and to recognize their functioning. (pp. 70-80)

To study the process of adaptation is to undertake several things at once: a consideration of the nature of narrative art, a theoretical view of high and popular culture, a history of the commerce of images and narratives. We do need to understand what makes an adaptation effective—the concern of most writing on adaptation so far—but that effectiveness itself is a far less tangible entity than is at first apparent. As mass culture ever more voraciously seeks out images and narratives for processing and consumption, adaptation will become increasingly important. The text will lose its boundaries as it shifts from book to movie to television series to comic book to novelization in serial form. To understand the future, which is already with us, we must understand the past and present, and we must see how we ourselves may become the texts unless we are aware. (p. 81)

> *Donald F. Larsson, "Novel into Film: Some Preliminary Reconsiderations," in* Transformations in Literature and Film, *edited by Leon Golden, University Presses of Florida, 1982, pp. 69-83.*

Leon Edel

[*Edel is an American critic and biographer who has been highly acclaimed for his five-volume biography of Henry James. In the following excerpt, he observes that, as a form of narrative, films have advanced in popularity at the expense of novels.*]

Novelists have sought almost from the first to become a camera. And not a static instrument but one possessing the movement through space and time which the motion-picture camera has achieved in our century. We follow Balzac, moving into his subject, from the city into the street, from the street into the house, and we tread hard on his heels as he takes us from room to room. We feel as if that massive "realist" had a prevision of cinema. A movie camera would "shoot" this same business in a montage of a few seconds. What we lose in the process is the power of the Word. We are confronted instead with the power of the Picture.

Wherever we turn in the nineteenth century we can see novelists cultivating the camera-eye and the camera movement—Tolstoy not least in those brilliant racing sequences, near the opening of *Anna Karenin,* with a superb sense of montage. The country-fair scene of *Madame Bovary* is well known. Flaubert's "cinema" was prophetic—he panned, he closed up, crowds, individuals, glimpses, and used not only sight but sound—for Emma and Rodolphe on their balcony listen to the windy oratory of the prize presentations, and the clichés mingle with the clichés of Rodolphe's love-making. They even serve as editorial, as when the word *merde* crashes into a particularly banal *mot d'amour.* Under the guise of his "picture" and "scene" Henry James was also a camera-eye. What else is "point of view"? Maria Gostrey scans Strether's countenance, and Strether scans Maria's. The reader becomes Maria; then Strether. And then he is allowed to move a short distance away so that he may see the two together, face to face. A great anomaly in the history of painting and fiction is that the painters tried very hard to get away from the camera, where the novelists sought by every possible means to embrace it.

And yet to say this is to simplify and exaggerate a matter requiring considerable refinement. What we know is that, with Balzac, "realism" came to the novel, and novels were discussed increasingly—and still are—as if they were "real" (never more so than by psychoanalysts who talk of Emma as if they had her on the couch, or of Anna as if she had been under observation for years as a manic depressive). So great was the "reality" of these nineteenth-century fictional personages that we often forget that they never lived: that they are poetized archetypal figures, figments of imagination. The real and the imaginary-real have become confused. *Ulysses* is cinematic—Nighttown especially, with its phantasmagoric "dissolves," its perpetual montage, and its faithful adherence to Dublin real rather than Dublin imaginary. Did not Joyce write to an aunt or sister to count the number of steps of a given stoop so that his word-picture would be photographic? Where James invented Woollett to avoid the need for specification, Joyce gloried in recording Dublin signposts, real names, real people. *Ulysses* is all camera and sound track. And this confusion of reality with the imagined real is being further compounded in our time by Mr. Mailer's flirtation with the cinema; and Susan Sontag, after her flirtation with fiction, now attempts visual fiction. Before them Robbe-Grillet tried to turn his novel into a series of camera shots and cultivated the banishing of affect from his language (as if this were possible). He also gave us his scenario-film *L'année dernière à Marienbad.*

The camera was invented so soon after the invention of the novel that the two have come down to us like a pair of siblings, each intent on asserting itself and capturing the attention of the world. Richard Stang in his book on nineteenth-century fictional theory quotes a paragraph from the *Westminster Review* of 1841—very early indeed—a comparison of camera and fiction:

> There is an instinct in every unwarped mind which

prefers truth to extravagance, and a photographic picture, if it be only of a kitten or a hay-stack, is a pleasanter subject in the eyes of most people (were they brave enough to admit it) than many a piece of mythology.

The early critics of realism often invoked the camera, understandably; but we also know that the votaries of realism in fiction thought of themselves as far more richly endowed than the limited little black box, which had to be manipulated and called for so much tranquil posing before any picture could be obtained. The camera was a presence, and for some a threat; certainly for the painters, since it was a question of one kind of visuality versus another. Yet even the impressionists, who went in search of light and air and sought out their subjects directly—leaving the studio for the rivers and fields—in a certain way also emulated the camera. What else is Claude Monet being when he paints the façade of Rouen cathedral at different hours of the day? It is as if he were putting on canvas a series of snapshots—in color. Here too, recognizing this, we must refine our problem. It is more complex than a mere competition between two recording media.

Without tracing the novel's comparatively short history, we know that it achieved its greatest heights of "realism" in the nineteenth century with Flaubert on the side of art and Tolstoy on the side of "reality"—the difference being that of "shaped" and unshaped reality. The Russians, slower in evolving a formal literature, brought great perfection to the novel-form and made it life-like and gave it extraordinary emotional power. The French moved in what seems a logical evolution from Balzacian realism to the extended documentary realism of the naturalists—and then to the counter-revolt of the symbolists, comparable to the revolt of impressionism in painting. In England, the novel began with exuberant and often jocular pictures of life, and much caricature and wit; it sought social and moral substance, with a characteristic disregard for "technique." The English novelists cultivated largely the mode of happy amateurs telling good stories. It was left to an American, who in his youth had disassembled novels as other children treat trains or carriages or automobiles, to try to establish "ground rules" or modes for the art, and to possess the "know-how." This was perhaps the most American side of Henry James. He disassembled the novel and then rose brilliantly above it, into a freedom of his own. With a detached and yet passionate Olympianism he wrote "the art of the novel" as Bach wrote, late in life, "the art of the fugue." When an art reaches this point in its history—the point of codification—we may assume that it is nearing its end. Where has it to go? It may take other shapes, but it has run its course, it has tested most of the permutations and combinations. The symbolist novel brought us Joyce's two idiosyncratic and labyrinthine performances which indeed stand outside the evolution of fiction, being strange Rabelaisian (though without the *joie de vivre* of Rabelais) or Swiftian books, called novels only because they were written in prose (*Ulysses*) and a mixture of prose and poetry (*Finnegans Wake*). In technique the novel has not moved far beyond the "stream-of-consciousness" of our time, save for certain ventures into the discontinuities of surrealism or chance effects. Virginia Woolf and William Faulkner were the last authentic practitioners of subjective narrative, thus bringing the novel in English around to where Goethe had said it should have

started—without influencing very much the development of the novel in his own country. Goethe had recognized from the first that in the novel "reflection and incidents should be featured; in drama, character and action." The novel, he further said, had to proceed slowly, and "the thought-processes of the principal figure must, by one device or another, hold up the development of the whole." Mann would, with his strong Germanic intellect, achieve this: but it was Proust who would create the greatest novel of sensibility that at the same time would embody a picture of an entire society.

The changes in our time have been in the direction of simplification of the novel-form or of its thematic content—absurdity, alienation, dissociation. This is reflected in the novel of discontinuity or, at the other extreme, intense inner-directed personalism. It has yielded works as different as *The Stranger,* or the tropisms of Nathalie Sarraute, Ralph Ellison's *Invisible Man* or the Mailerian strut which emulates the strut of Hemingway, but which now moves fiction into the realm of that other reality, *reportage*; as Truman Capote, achieving the greatest incongruity of all, has attempted to report truth and call it fiction. We have ended with simplifications, imitations, or film. Novelists are now at the point the painters reached long ago.

The painters had their *crise* of the camera early; it wasn't perhaps a conscious or specific crisis, but the camera was one of the determinants of the course painting took in our time. Since the art of the brush is visual, it had to contend with the direct objective visuality of the camera: and it found its solution by warning the painter that he could never be a camera.

James, ever the theorist, used the terminology of painting: "principle of composition" and "picture" became critical terms for the discussion of the novel, and "foreshortening" was derived directly from the lexicon of the painter. "The most fundamental and general sign of the novel, from one desperate experiment to another, is its being everywhere an effort at *representation*," wrote James, adding that this was "the beginning and the end of it." And again, "it is the art of the brush, I know, as opposed to the art of the slate-pencil; but to the art of the brush the novel must return." He would probably have to amend this today. He would substitute "camera" for "slate-pencil" and would perhaps argue that the novelist had to turn back to the art of the word. James believed in the future of the novel because he felt that it was the most elastic of the literary forms, and that among the baubles of art which man has a way of using up and then discarding, the novel could least be discarded, since it embraces man's fundamental need to go on telling stories. The stories, however, were to be stories in words; and one remembers how jealous James was of illustration, how he held an illustrated story to be an affront to the artistic imagination. We also remember his short story "The Real Thing," a veritable parable for the art—in which the illustrator, confronted with models who are *real,* cannot paint them; there is nothing left for the imagination. But models emulating the real could be rendered with a bold and free use of the impressionism and symbolism of art.

Henry James was writing at the threshold of the cinema. He went to see the primitive bioscopic inventions, yet it never occurred to him that they might involve any threat to the verbal art—so safe did the Edwardians feel in their citadel of words, so authoritative, so ensconced for the future. James did recognize the appeal of cinema technique; he described one such image in his late tale "Crapy Cornelia," where at a given moment the character White-Mason looks at a woman's head "crowned with a little sparsely feathered black hat," and it "grew and grew, came nearer and nearer while it met his eyes, after the manner of images in the cinematograph." Joyce would not only describe this kind of camera technique; he would imitate it. He wanted to found a movie-house in Dublin; and *Ulysses,* as we have noted, in its adherence to angles of vision and its constructed scenes, is almost wholly cinema. So Dorothy Richardson, working at the same time as Joyce, learned to move toward or away from a camera, while keeping us within the intense subjectivity of her heroine. One recalls how, in her pioneering way, she carefully pictured London buildings moving toward the riders on the top of a bus; or our glimpse of her heroine after boarding the German train, seeing the platform flow away from her—as we have seen in countless movies. Miss Richardson acknowledged in her novel, without naming it, her indebtedness to the method of *The Ambassadors,* but presently she became herself a film critic, and moved from the early "cinema," devised in fiction, to the actual experience of photographic vision. Soon enough there would be the "camera-eye" of the surrealists and Dos Passos.

In the years since we have moved from camera devices, anticipated or imitated, to the camera itself, to the direct exploitation by novelists of the camera-visual. A novelist addicted to his word-world might wonder how the two can be integrated—novel and camera—beyond the ways in which they have used one another. With the talking pictures—that is, the use simultaneously of sight and sound—and with the third dimensionality to come, the verbal forms cannot compete. Fable-telling becomes picture-sequence, and the novel is often set aside for the picture. The novel, I believe, is in a bad way, not because we do not have fine craftsmen in our time, but because it has been shoved aside by technology, just as music—played music in salon and hall—has given way to the tape recorder and stereo, and printing is beginning to feel the effect of xerox and computer and other photo-reproducing processes. (pp. 177-82)

The visuality of our time can be, of itself, a virtue. We are endowed with two magnificent organs with which to take in the world and assimilate it to all our senses. Is it not therefore understandable that novelists should want to render this visuality in words, even as the camera has recorded it with its magical substitute for the human eye, by a means that gives permanence to life's pictures? The answer is obviously in the affirmative; and all our great novelists have been exceptionally "visual" in their use of words. The camera is a part of modern civilization. Sometimes tourists are so busy taking pictures that they have no time to enjoy sensually the landscape before them. They have time merely to peek at it through one eye. And however much some of us may feel that an hour spent looking at one landscape is better than a camera record of a dozen landscapes, framed in so small an area or rendered close up, we must recognize that the sensual endowment of the individual varies, and that not everyone has the capacity to contemplate and meditate and feel a landscape—or even read a book. However, this is not the issue here. I do not urge camera-smashing, Luddite fashion. The

issue is that the novel, in trying so desperately to become a camera, has ceased to be on the whole anything else, has ceased to be itself. It has stopped dead—and no longer knows that man not only acts, but thinks, that he has visions and fantasies, that he is the only reflective animal in existence, and that when a novel gives us the thinking man as well as the acting man, it makes possible an extraordinary enlargement of life. We know only our own thoughts, never the thoughts of others. Fiction, by invoking the use of the verbal imagination—that is, by making us active and imaginative readers, rather than inert picture-watchers—gives us the magical sense of being in relation with the world and with our fellow men and in ways that we can only rarely be, even though we are alone in a room with a book. (pp. 187-88)

Leon Edel, "Novel and Camera," in The Theory of the Novel: New Essays, *edited by John Halperin, Oxford University Press, 1974, pp. 177-88.*

Stanley Kubrick

[*An American director and screenwriter, Kubrick is considered one of the most ambitious and original filmmakers of the past four decades. A controversial director noted for his unconventional subjects and idiosyncratic cinematic style, his films include* Lolita (1955); Dr. Strangelove; or, How I Learned to Stop Worrying and Love the Bomb (1964); 2001: A Space Odyssey (1968); and A Clockwork Orange (1971). *In the following essay, Kubrick explains his method and philosophy of adapting a novel for film.*]

The perfect novel from which to make a movie is, I think, not the novel of action but, on the contrary, the novel which is mainly concerned with the inner life of its characters. It will give the adaptor an absolute compass bearing, as it were, on what a character is thinking or feeling at any given moment of the story. And from this he can invent action which will be an objective correlative of the book's psychological content, will accurately dramatise this in an implicit, off-the-nose way without resorting to having the actors deliver literal statements of meaning.

I think that for a movie or a play to say anything really truthful about life, it has to do so very obliquely, so as to avoid all pat conclusions and neatly tied-up ideas. The point of view it is conveying has to be completely entwined with a sense of life as it is, and has to be got across through a subtle injection into the audience's consciousness. Ideas which are valid and truthful are so multi-faceted that they don't yield themselves to frontal assault. The ideas have to be discovered by the audience, and their thrill in making the discovery makes those ideas all the more powerful. You use the audience's thrill of surprise and discovery to reinforce your ideas, rather than reinforce them artificially through plot points or phoney drama or phoney stage dynamics put in to power them across.

It's sometimes said that a great novel makes a less promising basis for a film than a novel which is merely good. I don't think that adapting great novels presents any special problems which are not involved in adapting good novels or mediocre novels; except that you will be more heavily criticised if the film is bad, and you may be even if it's

Stanley Kubrick in the 1950s.

good. I think almost any novel can be successfully adapted, provided it is not one whose aesthetic integrity is lost along with its length. For example, the kind of novel in which a great deal and variety of action is absolutely essential to the story, so that it loses much of its point when you subtract heavily from the number of events or their development.

People have asked me how it is possible to make a film out of *Lolita* when so much of the quality of the book depends on Nabokov's prose style. But to take the prose style as any more than just a part of a great book is simply misunderstanding just what a great book is. Of course, the quality of the writing is one of the elements that make a novel great. But this quality is a result of the quality of the writer's obsession with his subject, with a theme and a concept and a view of life and an understanding of character. Style is what an artist uses to fascinate the beholder in order to convey to him his feelings and emotions and thoughts. These are what have to be dramatised, not the style. The dramatising has to find a style of its own, as it will do if it really grasps the content. And in doing this it will bring out another side of that structure which has gone into the novel. It may or may not be as good as the novel; sometimes it may in certain ways be even better.

Oddly enough, acting comes into the picture somewhere here. At its best, realistic drama consists of a progression of moods and feelings that play upon the audience's feelings and transform the author's meaning into an emotional experience. This means that the author must not think of paper and ink and words as being his writing tools, but rather that he works in flesh and feeling. And in this sense

I feel that too few writers seem to understand what an actor can communicate emotionally and what he cannot. Often, at one point, the writer expects a silent look to get across what it would take a rebus puzzle to explain, and in the next moment the actor is given a long speech to convey something that is quite apparent in the situation and for which a brief look would be sufficient. Writers tend to approach the creation of drama too much in terms of words, failing to realise that the greatest force they have is the mood and feeling they can produce in the audience through the actor. They tend to see the actor grudgingly, as someone likely to ruin what they have written, rather than seeing that the actor is in every sense their medium.

You might wonder, as a result of this, whether directing was anything more or less than a continuation of the writing. I think that is precisely what directing should be. It would follow, then, that a writer-director is really the perfect dramatic instrument; and the few examples we have where these two peculiar techniques have been properly mastered by one man have, I believe, produced the most consistently fine work.

When the director is not his own author, I think it is his duty to be one hundred per cent faithful to the author's meaning and to sacrifice none of it for the sake of climax or effect. This seems a fairly obvious notion, yet how many plays and films have you seen where the experience was exciting and arresting but when it was over you felt there was less there than met the eye? And this is usually due to artificial stimulation of the senses by technique which disregards the inner design of the play. It is here that we see the cult of the director at its worst.

On the other hand, I don't want to imply rigidity. Nothing in making movies gives a greater sense of elation than participation in a process of allowing the work to grow, through vital collaboration between script, director and actors, as it goes along. Any art form properly practised involves a to and fro between conception and execution, the original intention being constantly modified as one tries to give it objective realisation. In painting a picture this goes on between the artist and his canvas; in making a movie it goes on between people.

> *Stanley Kubrick, "Words and Movies," in* Sight and Sound, *Vol. 30, No. 1, Winter, 1960-61, p. 14.*

Bruce Morrissette

[*Morrissette is an American educator and critic whose work often focuses on French authors. In the following excerpt, he discusses the French "cinema novel," a published work adapted from a film scenario and designed to serve as its literary counterpart.*]

Novel and film not only have been studied in their formal interrelationships, they have also raised the question of amalgamation into the genre of the cinema novel, as opposed to the novelistic scenario of many traditional films. What is the cinema novel? From the outset the question runs the risk of being confused in the tangle of arguments surrounding the general links between novel and cinema: reciprocal influences, parallel techniques, transpositions, convergencies, and correspondences. (p. 28)

My object here is to examine—particularly but not exclusively—a precise group of works, namely the contemporary cinema novels (which the French call *ciné-romans*) and published scenarios designed to be read by readers who have not necessarily seen the film in question, who are primarily readers of fiction and not spectators watching a film. It will doubtless come as no surprise to find that this rather limited group of works constitutes a microcosm of the wider area of cinema and novel in general, or that it sheds light on a "unified field" approach to the fictional structures and perspectives to be found in both novel and film. Naturally, any such research must admit certain fundamental, specific formal identifies that to a greater or lesser degree separate the two arts (images and sounds in the cinema, words and phrases in the novel), and it must avoid the trap of total assimilation of the two genres.

The early period of the silent film was marked by the priority of written sources for scenarios; and even the few films not drawn from existing novels made extensive use of forms borrowed from the novel. D. W. Griffith himself attributed his "cinematic" close-ups to models found in Dickens and Eisenstein credited Flaubert with Griffith's parallel montages. At that stage the film drew attention to fictional or dramatic forms not previously recognized or identified, so that literary critics like Jacques Scherer could speak of the "découpage" or scene cutting of Molière or Racine plays, while Paul Léglise . . . called the *Aeneid* a "precinematic work." Once such resemblances were identified, some critics began to view novels as essentially cinematic: George Bluestone, for example, complains frequently in his excellent *Novels into Film* that Hollywood has failed to transfer into the script or the shooting all the "cinematic" effects present in a given novel by Steinbeck or Flaubert. The number of scripts of value written expressly for the screen had never been large, and when they did develop (as with *Citizen Kane*) they were structured like the novels that had already influenced the cinema.

Gradually, scenarios were composed specifically for films, especially for the avant-garde silent film. Some of these scenarios were published. They were silent film scripts with a few subtitles but without dialogues, as, for example, the text of *Un chien andalou* by Dali and Buñuel. This scenario is a good example of the earliest attempts to use verbal descriptions to suggest to a reader the visual images of the screen. Had the sound film not come into existence at about this time, no doubt a considerable development of silent film scripts would have occurred; those that do exist in magazines of the era remain largely unstudied. The "pure" silent film, so regretted when it disappeared, was followed, as is well known, by over a decade of shallow "talkies" based largely on noncinematic popular plays with rigid decors and a plethora of wordy dialogue. Eventually, with the contemporary cinema novel, the novelized script made its appearance, and once more sound and image were mixed in written form.

An associated phenomenon has been the most parenthetical but instructive development of a new subgenre, novels created from films, "le roman tiré du film." This inversion of the traditional order, in which adaptations always went from novel into film, demonstrates the conscious or unconscious domination of the literary over the filmic, since the writers who take on the textualizing of these books

from films (which are neither scenarios, cinema novels, nor genuine novels) feel it essential to restore to the narrative all the "literary" elements whose absence from the film itself may constitute its chief value. These writers invent for their readers all sorts of novelistic insertions found in the actual film only, if at all, by suggestion or implication: interior monologues, psychological analysis, even sociological commentaries. A good example is found in the novelized version of Godard's *A bout de souffle* (*Breathless*). The protagonist, played by Belmondo, stands for a long time in silence before a large photographic poster of Humphrey Bogart; the wordless effect is powerful. This scene of the inexpressive and silent Belmondo becomes in the "roman tiré du film" several pages of conventional interior monologue, beginning "Well, Bogey, old pal." Similarly, the famous final betrayal of the hero by the heroine, deliberately left ambiguous in the film, is explicated at length in the book in an archconventional passage of popular psychological analysis. Traditional novelistic forms and structures invade the film, revealing an absence of understanding of the new artistic and filmic values created by the screen genre.

One of the earliest works that may be called a true cinema novel, the deliberate creation of an author who composed his text originally to be filmed, is *Les jeux son faits* of Jean-Paul Sartre. Despite the absence in this "novelized scenario" of any cinematic vocabulary (close-up, panoramic shot, and the like), Sartre nevertheless retains and describes a large number of scenic effects (the sun's rays falling on a hand, for example), even if he does not specify the camera angle or movement involved. (In fact, the camera moves about little in this not very cinematic film.) What makes the written narrative most similar to a film is the rhythm of the *découpage* or scene cutting, especially in the sequences of increasingly rapid alternating scenes of decreasing duration depicting the parallel stories of the hero and heroine at the beginning of the film. Here again we note that this parallel montage is only the prolongation and acceleration of a novelistic procedure pointed out by Eisenstein in the nineteenth-century novel such as *David Copperfield*, which films appropriated as particularly effective. To Sartre the film, like the novel and the drama, is only partially an artistic genre, finding its chief role as a vehicle of moral, philosophical, or political messages. Although Sartre criticizes the logical structures of conventional narrative genres, he freely violates his theoretical pronouncements in *Les Jeux sont faits*. In his famous attack on François Mauriac, whom he denounces for adopting a godlike point of view that focuses on both the exterior and the interior of successive characters, Sartre argues that in the post-Eisensteinian world the only logical or acceptable point of view must be a relative one anchored in the consciousness of an individual observer. But the Sartrian strictures of "François Mauriac et la liberté" are largely ignored in Sartre's own film (and in many of his novels as well). Far from trying to "justify" the various camera viewpoints of his film, and of his cinema novel, Sartre leaves them indefinite and arbitrary. Not only is the position of the camera not identified, its choice of visual subject or object seems to depend on no basic existential observational viewpoint. The result is a visual fiction subject to no relativistic controls, and about as godlike as that Sartre denounced in the case of Mauriac.

The question of justified viewpoints (that is, their correspondence to the perceptions of specific characters in the narrative or film) was destined to become a major concern in novelistic and filmic criticism. The great debates over "subjective camera," inspired by the well-known film *The Lady in the Lake,* shot by the actor-director Robert Montgomery with a camera attached to his breast, underline the importance of the use of the "first-person" film narrative, with most if not all of the visual angles justified through the implied eye of an observer-protagonist. At the height of the justified viewpoint movement, Robbe-Grillet published his "Notes on the Localization and Displacement of Viewpoint in Novelistic Description," not only attacking traditional Balzacian descriptive techniques (especially the use of an omniscient viewpoint that could see into closed drawers as well as into the minds of characters), but also praising the cinema as always showing its scenes "from a human viewpoint" of an active or passive observer. The novel itself, as well as the cinema novel, began to follow the principle of the "ciné-oeil," or observing eye. A few dissenters disagreed: Robert Champigny, for example, alleged curiously, in his theoretical study *Le genre romanesque* (1963), that while the novel *must* practice the principle of justified viewpoint, the cinema does not do so. The [following] statement by Claude Simon . . . best illustrates the insistence on justification of point of view in the *nouveau roman*: "I cannot write my novels other than by constantly defining . . . camera angle, close up, medium shot, panoramic shot, motionless shot, etc."

Thus, for the typical author of the *nouveau roman* the novelistic narrative should emanate only from one or a series of individual consciousness, whose perceptions or images of the outside world are visually stylized in the manner of a film. According to one strict theory, there should be, in both novel and cinema, only "subjective" scenes. But both novel and film failed to adhere to these restrictions, and a number of principles of neojustification developed. Instead of purely subjective shots in which the camera, as in *The Lady in the Lake,* is substituted for the eye of a narrative protagonist, the cinema quickly showed a preference for scenes in which the camera is only *associated* with a character's viewpoint. This association can be of many kinds. A scene may be a short but fairly exact take of what a character would see through his eyes, as happens in each of the presumed observer's viewpoints in the kind of conversational exchange called in French *point-contre-point*: B as seen by A listening or speaking, and vice versa, from B's angle. Often the camera associates itself with a protagonist or other character by shooting his "view" from just behind his head, or off to one side, so that the viewer feels or understands that the camera is "looking" for the particular character. Total subjectivity becomes more and more restricted to scenes of memory (like the first quick flash scenes of the German soldier's hand in *Hiroshima mon amour*) or of hallucinatory pseudorecall (like many of the scenes in *L'année dernière à Marienbad*). In the novel proper, the single fictional masterpiece to employ total perspective subjectivity, without the intervention of thoughts, speeches, or even pronouns referring to the narrator, was Robbe-Grillet's *La jalousie.*

The written expression of visual or sensorial subjectivity has raised some vexing problems for the writers of scenarios and cinema novels. On the page, the printed text is called upon to describe or explicate what is only implied on the screen. If, for example, Marguerite Duras *writes* that suddenly the hand of a Japanese in a bed in Hiroshima is replaced by a flash shot of the clenched hand of a German soldier who died at Nevers during the war, the shock of the intuitive recognition of this as yet undefined *visual* memory by the spectator watching the film virtually disappears. A similar problem arises in the case of scene transitions involving *fondus* or fade-outs and fade-ins, in which an object or a decor is replaced abruptly or gradually by another, related to the first by a form, a psychological association, or some other diegetic linkage. Can descriptive prose create such an effect? A sort of flash shot may occur in prose when the text undergoes a sudden break in continuity; but is there, or can there be, a true written equivalent of the cinematic fade-out/fade-in?

I think that close equivalents do exist, but that they are of a somewhat different kind. The terms fade-out/fade-in or *fondu* may still be applied. Examples would include those passages in *La jalousie* by Robbe-Grillet wherein a transitional phrase or word is inserted between two quite different scenes: when the text suddenly veers from a description of the heroine and her lover in a hotel-room bed as imagined by the jealous husband to the scene in which the lover Franck's car explodes in a flaming crash as it strikes a tree, the two separate incidents are linked by a phrase whose main element, "accélère," applies equally to the erotic acceleration of the first image and the acceleration of Franck's car in the second. The critic Arnaldo Pizzorusso points out other transitions of this kind, which he terms "fondus"—citing the passage from a text describing a photograph on the husband's desk to one depicting a similar scene on the veranda, using vocabulary elements applicable to either or both scenes. . . . [In] a discussion of the possibility of textual *fondus* published in *Les cahiers du cinéma* (1961), the filmmaker Alain Resnais categorically denies the existence of literary *fondus,* while the novelist Robbe-Grillet vigorously affirms their existence.

The two films already mentioned, *Hiroshima mon amour* and *Marienbad,* are typical examples of the French cinema novel (in their printed forms). Both make considerable use of sudden flashbacks, false or imaginary scenes, even hallucinations. As cinema novels or scenarios, they illustrate several problems characteristic of the genre. For the filming of *Hiroshima* (directed by the same filmmaker as *Marienbad,* Alain Resnais), the author, Marguerite Duras, furnished a rather lyrical textual scenario, in a sometimes grandiloquent poetic style, with annotations of brief indications of the associated visual images and of accompanying, often in counterpoint, dialogues or sounds. The entire technical aspect (camera angles, distance of the framing, lighting, etc.), developed and added by Resnais, is absent from the printed script. If the greatest part of what could properly be called filmic is therefore lost in the book, we find on the other hand a whole file of accessory information completely lacking in the film itself. These are documents that served to impregnate Resnais and his actors with the atmosphere and tone of the story or diegesis, before and during the camera work, and that are retained in the text as if to produce in the reader a feeling of the "reality" of the film, in a sort of cinematic equivalent of the convention of older novels (including some as recent as Sartre's *La nausée*) presented as faithful transcripts of manuscripts found in a trunk, for example. This kind of scaffolding erected outside the film appears characteristic of the work of Resnais (who set up an elaborate chronological schema of *Marienbad* to guide his filming), and we find it in other scenarios used in his films, like his *Muriel*, with a text by Jean Cayrol. The published form of *Muriel* also illustrates what was at the time a relatively new technique in presenting the visual images seen on the screen: the edge of each printed page contains a series of photographs of the scenes covered in the adjacent text. Such a procedure also permits the author to reduce to a minimum the verbal descriptions of images. But the result no longer gives the impression of a real cinema novel and instead appears as an illustrated text, in the style of the Italian "photo novels."

If the printed texts of *Hiroshima* and *Muriel* are filled with such paranovelistic and nonfilmic accessories aimed at presenting the "depth" of character psychology and plot motivation, the published version of *Marienbad* represents, by comparison, a very different model of the cinema novel, one closer to the structures we associate with the *nouveau roman*. The emergence of the printed scenario from the script prepared by Robbe-Grillet is instructive. Alain Resnais, while making the film, stated that Robbe-Grillet had furnished a script so complete in every detail of dialogue and visual images that it could have been turned over to an "electronic robot" for the actual filming. The original script was typed (as was customary at the time) on facing pages, one containing the dialogue and sound effects, the other the visual angles, lighting, actor's movements, and the like. To compose the printed cinema novel, Robbe-Grillet took the two sets of pages, sounds and images, and melded them much as one might shuffle a deck of cards. Concerning the nondialogue parts of the final text, some critics observed that the language was "nonnovelistic," or nonliterary. Claude Ollier, himself one of the *nouveau roman* group, expressed his reaction as follows:

> Pour *Marienbad* . . . les textes en question ne sont pas organisés autour des mots et des descriptions, mais autour des sons et des images. Nul doute que si Robbe-Grillet avait commencé d'écrire non pas un film, mais un roman sur le même ciné-schéma, il aurait été amené bien vite à construire différemment ses phrases, et même probablement à concevoir autrement l'enchaînement des épisodes.

> In *Marienbad* . . . the texts in question are organized not around words and descriptions, but around sounds and images. There can be no doubt that if Robbe-Grillet had set out to write not a film but a novel using the same scenario, he would quickly have been impelled to construct his phrases differently, and even probably to conceive differently the arrangement of the episodes.

But is the text of *Marienbad*, as Ollier states, indeed nonliterary? A close study of the style of the descriptions of scenes and camera movements shows not only the "literary" quality of the texts, but also a close similarity between these passages and the descriptive passages of the author's previous novelistic works, such as *Le voyeur* and *La jalousie*. Also, it is difficult to give much weight to an argument based on a comparison between an existing film/novel and a hypothetical "novel" the author never imagined or planned. If we look instead at Robbe-Grillet's established techniques of scene linking in his actual novels, we find . . . "liaisons de scènes," subjective associations, psychological deformations projected against a

pseudorealistic decor, and the like. If strictly speaking *Marienbad* is a cinema novel rather than a novel *tout court*, one must nevertheless admit that it is closer, in its published form, to the domain of the Robbe-Grilletian novel than to that of an "unprocessed" scenario.

The printed scenario of *L'immortelle*, though it is designated by Robbe-Grillet as a "ciné-roman," seems, by comparison with *Marienbad*, something of a formal retreat, a return to an earlier format in which the genre made use of brief summaries of successive scenes. The scenes are spatially divided on the pages, and each bears a large numeral. These some three hundred identified parts or shots add to the nonliterary effect, as does the absence of the descriptive passages organized around sounds and images that characterize *Marienbad*. If the reading of *L'immortelle* is simplified, it is not made more cinematic, since the reader is deprived of the mental operation required by the text of *Marienbad*, which creates in that reader the impression that he is following the scenes in a film in quasi-visual fashion. In this sense *Marienbad* represents an unparalleled mixture of the two genres, film and novel.

Robbe-Grillet's difficulties in finding a suitable form for the publication of the scenario of his next film, *Trans-Europ-Express*, illustrate the problems of an evolving genre. For both *Marienbad* and *L'immortelle* there existed before the filming a more or less complete descriptive script, with sounds and images, that could be transformed with comparative ease to the written page. What procedures should apply, then, when the author-filmmaker, as was the case for *Trans-Europ-Express*, used for the filming only a sort of *récit*, or narrative version, composed in a written style of almost schematized simplicity, mixed with fragmentary and approximate dialogue, all of which underwent constant modification and improvisation during the actual shooting, along with the insertion of new scenes and the reversal of the order of others? What could be the modalities of the novelistic form of such a film? The author, going over his notes and his primitive scenario, which may no longer correspond to the actual film scenes, is forced to return almost to zero; he could find it difficult if not impossible, even looking at this film on a Movieola viewer, to give *his* form and style to a valid text for his proposed cinema novel. The author indeed finally abandoned the problem, and it was not until many films later that he was able to construct the new scenario form used in the published version of *Glissements progressifs du plaisir*. . . . *Intervening films, such as L'homme qui ment*, were made using the same sketchy, improvised shooting notes as *Trans-Europ-Express*, couched in a sort of utilitarian language directed at the actors and cameramen, at times using commonplace expressions and anthropocentric non-Robbe-Grilletian metaphors that the author would never tolerate in his *writings* (like "un soleil gai, sans souci," "a gay, carefree sunshine"). The conclusion is that if a film, at least in the case of a stylizing author like Robbe-Grillet, is not made with a scenario that already has a form permitting its adaptation in terms of the writer's own characteristic style, the cinema novel will fail to materialize, since writing it would constitute all the difficulties of composing an entirely new work, which not only would deform the existing film, but could also fail as a novel.

An important aspect of the cinema novels as well as those films themselves that deal with subjective and imaginary reality or truth, and in which memory and interior time come into play (an aspect closely linked to the writing or description of filmed scenes), is the controversial question of cinematic time as compared with novelistic time, and that of the tenses of verbs in written or spoken language. Does the film contain (apart from dialogue) the equivalent of the tenses of verbs? Since Béla Balázs, it has been customary to state that "films have no tenses" and to claim, perhaps too hastily, that a filmed scene always takes place in an eternal present, or perhaps in Alain Resnais's "zone atemporelle ou de tous les temps." Robbe-Grillet, in his preface to *Marienbad,* upholds the thesis that the film, existing physically (at least when projected) only in the present, is particularly suitable for expressing psychological reality, which always exists in a perpetual present. But cannot films also express, depict, or imply their own kind of past? After all, even a regular novel is always *read* in the present, and its "past," to which the film is accused of having no equivalent, is usually contained in a system involving the tenses of verbs. In reading a scene of the past, do we not mentally "see" it in the present? If we consider the simple flashback, inserted into the film to fill a gap in the narrative or to provide information about a certain character, it is perhaps true that the flashback scene appears to be taking place in the present. Suppose such a scene in a novel were written with verbs in the present tense (a style increasingly employed in the *nouveau roman* and elsewhere). Would it not also seem to occur in the present? And if the filmed scene evokes the past in relation to the present, as done first perhaps in the famous memory scenes of the film *Brief Encounter,* with fade-outs in the present (in the train) leading to recent events that only gradually "take over" the present? Does the film not thus acquire its own type of cinematic past? This effect is especially felt in those films in which the past is presented as an aspect of the present, in the "present" memory of a character or in a dynamic conflict between past and present, as in *Hiroshima* or *Marienbad*. A strong cinematic feeling of the past emerges from the confrontation, on the screen, of present and past. Even in the literary narrative, the tone of the tenses used (like the well-known present and *passé simple* of Camus's *L'etranger*) is quickly converted by the reader into a conventional modality by which, as with a film, he "sees" in the present tense, except when the contrast between present and past gives rise to a true temporal feeling.

Authors of novels taken from films and the writers of film reviews and summaries in popular magazines such as *Midi-Minuit* and *Ciné-Revue* "narrate" the films, interestingly, more often in the past tense than the present; as disconcerting as this practice seems, it shows to what extent the conditioned mentality of certain would-be authors prevents them from truly grasping narrative time, almost automatically transforming filmic images from their cinematic present, or timelessness, into the kind of frozen *récit* of dead characters and complete events expressed, in French, by the *passé simple* or literary past tense. If the deepest feeling of the past always arises from a confrontation of two times, the film should no doubt be more successful than the novel in this respect, especially when it makes use of the two stereo channels available to it, image and sound, to create counterpoint effects such as past image against present sound, or vice versa. The innovative films of Robbe-Grillet and others continue to progress in this research for new forms. (pp. 28-37)

Bruce Morrissette, "The Cinema Novel," in his Novel and Film: Essays in Two Genres, *The University of Chicago Press, 1985, pp. 28-39.*

THE ART OF THE SCREENPLAY

John Gassner

[*Gassner, a Hungarian-born American scholar, was a great promoter of American theater, particularly the work of Tennessee Williams and Arthur Miller. He edited numerous collections of modern drama and wrote two important dramatic surveys,* Masters of the Drama *(1940) and* Theater in Our Times *(1954). In the following excerpt from the introduction to* Twenty Best Film Plays, *Gassner asserts the validity of the screenplay as a literary form.*]

There is now a literature of the screen—the screenplay. If this fact has not been widely recognized, it is only because screenplays have not been properly accorded the dignity of print, a situation that is being corrected to some degree by [*Twenty Best Film Plays*]. Naturally, not everything that is set down on paper is worth publishing, but it will be found on very little investigation that film writing already has substantial claims to literary recognition. Anyone who proclaims that the American film has been growing up would do well, indeed, to pay close attention to the written film. Too often his eulogies sound hollow because he can appeal only to the movie public's rather fleeting impression at a movie theatre, where the noteworthy motion picture is sandwiched in between a Grade B picture for the younger generation and a newsreel or a Donald Duck cartoon and flash intimations of the melodramatic or sentimental marvels with which the patrons will be edified next week. Too often, therefore, he can only deliver his panegyric in generalities, as if a string of superlatives constituted an argument. On this matter our native humorist George Ade has some sound advice fetched straight out of his cracker-barrel: "In uplifting, get underneath." And it stands to reason that one way of getting underneath, as well as having some evidence to provide in black and white, is to turn to the screenplays. Most of the talking pictures that have given the American film its claim to distinction have been fashioned out of a body of writing that commands respect as writing: that is, as theme, story, style, and drama. Its form has been shaped by the requirements of cinematic art, which makes it somewhat unique among the forms of writing hitherto familiar to the reader, but it is nonetheless literature that can stand scrutiny. (p. vii)

Anyone familiar with the many radically differing forms of writing for the stage during the past twenty-five centuries—anyone acquainted with the scenarios of the *commedia dell' arte,* the dance recitatives of the oriental Noh plays, the choral drama of the Greeks, and the multi-scened, continually-flowing dramas of Shakespeare and his contemporaries—cannot snobbishly exclude the screenplay as dramatic literature.

To say that the screenplay is only a verbal record of enacted events does not vitiate the argument, as the same point may be pressed, to a degree, against a play by Sophocles or Shakespeare, to which the status of literature has never been denied. The real question is whether the dramaturgy, dialogue, and meaning of a particular film are worthy and pleasurable.

The argument that the scenario requires mechanical means of projection cannot be admitted, because the staging of a play by Shakespeare or Ibsen also involves mechanical devices; even the ever-so-literary Greek tragedies called for mechanics, as when the actor impersonating some god was lowered to the top of the scene building by means of a crane, creating the illusion of his coming from the sky. It is true of course that the screenplay, as written today, embodies ever so many more technical directions than any other piece of creative literature, and these affect the quality of the writing. Reiteration of stock terms—"dissolve," "pan," "long shot," etc.—becomes more tiresome, because more frequent, than the often equally stereotyped directions written for the stage. But this is the machine age and some mechanical terms are its legitimate property; and besides, many of these terms can be translated into better usage. This is also an age of rapid movement—different in this respect from previous centuries as the speed of a Flying Fortress differs from the pace of a horse-drawn chariot; words conveying movement are therefore part of our linguistic equipment and cannot be fastidiously banished as "unliterary."

The difference in speed is particularly apparent in the number of scenes to be found in a screenplay. There may be only one in many stage plays, but a full-length film play uses more than a hundred and fifty scenes; the text of *The Grapes of Wrath* consists of 265 "shots." But if this were to be charged up as a demerit, by the same token we should have to declare the artistic form of Shakespeare's *Antony and Cleopatra,* which has 42 scenes, inferior to that of *Abie's Irish Rose.* In all periods of genuine creativity, dramatic form has taken its cue from prevailing mechanical facilities. What really matters in art is the transfiguration of reality into the manifestation of essential truth, spirit, and vision.

Even more specious, of course, would be the argument that screenplays are inferior as literature because they are based on "original" material bought from novelists, story writers, biographers and historians. The same reasoning would dismiss the great Attic tragedians as hacks because they helped themselves generously to what the first of them called "slices from Homer's banquet," as well as to the floating literature of legend and tradition. And Shakespeare would then be placed at the foot of the class because he reworked other men's plays and took his plots from such sources as Bandello's short stories and Holinshed's *Chronicles.* All life and all literature consist of borrowings, some conscious, others unconscious; some avowed, some unavowed—and in our day of plagiarism suits and copyright laws they had better be avowed. The entire question of "originality" is, in fact, largely predicated on social attitudes toward literature as a commodity on the market, having a market value. Neither the Greeks nor the Elizabethans were seriously concerned with the question.

What matters ultimately is the use we make of what we borrow: Not merely what we add or subtract, not merely even what individual interpretation we provide, but also how well we shape the material to the unique demands of different forms of art. A completely gratifying movie can never be a mere transcript of a good book, even when the plots are nearly identical. *The Informer* was a creative work as a novel. It was a freshly creative—basically original—work as a screenplay. It is one thing to criticize adaptations when they cheapen or distort a novel or story; and incompetence, commercialism, official and pressure-group censorship, and timidity have often invited such charges quite legitimately. It is another thing to press a case against the creativeness of the filmwriter because his work is based on material in books or plays. Actually, the shoe fits on the other foot, since there is reason for complaining that writers in other fields cheapen their work by trying to trim it for sale to the films—whereas the cinema has raised its standards by resorting to published and stage material. Hollywood's output was greatly improved when it began to pay careful attention to good literature, new and old, instead of relying solely on plots originated by people segregated in a Los Angeles suburb and notoriously disposed toward intellectual interbreeding. This trend may have discouraged the creation of original stories by writers in the studios, but it has been far from catastrophic, and there has even been notable work written directly for films in both story and scenario forms, as evidenced . . . by Norman Krasna's original story for *Fury* and Dudley Nichols' *This Land Is Mine.*

It is true that often too many writers work on the same script, and as a rule the impress of a single creative or recreative personality is to be preferred in a work of art. But the fact is that many a distinguished screenplay is the solo work of some screenwriter. Among such solo efforts we may single out Sidney Buchman's *Mr. Smith Goes to Washington,* Nunnally Johnson's script of *The Grapes of Wrath,* Philip Dunne's *How Green Was My Valley,* and Dudley Nichols' *The Informer.* Recently some writers have even begun to function as producers and directors of their screenplays. In other instances, authors like Ben Hecht and Charles MacArthur have long worked as a team both for the stage and the screen. In other collaborations where two or more authors are credited with a script, the impress of a dominant personality is sometimes evident to one who is familiar with the work of the writers. Besides, there has been no dearth of acknowledged and unacknowledged collaboration for the stage. We have reason to wonder about how many hands shaped the beautiful religious plays of the medieval communion, and collaboration was frequent in Shakespeare's time. (In 1602 that enterprising Elizabethan "angel" Philip Henslowe lent a certain company five pounds with which to pay "Anthony Munday, Thomas Middleton, Michael Drayton, John Webster, and the rest, for a play entitled *Caesar's Fall.*") Certainly the script of *Mrs. Miniver,* credited to four writers, reveals more distinction and unity of style than many another work for screen or stage credited to a single author. In one way or another the dramatic arts have always involved collaboration; if not between writers, certainly between the writer and those who staged his work. Of course, these remarks are not intended as justification or apology for arbitrary interference with the writers' creative job, but in such instances the results usually expose the misdemeanor. (pp. x-xii)

Strictly considered, a shooting script is a swiftly moving drama consisting of dialogue, descriptions, and narrative sections, presented in many scenes—some as short as a flash, others lasting considerably longer, though they are much shorter than scenes in all but the most expressionistic stage plays.

That the dialogue is usually more meagre than in a play or, as a rule, in a novel, is a condition of the film medium, in which visual movement is paramount. The abbreviation of dialogue is a trend of the times—the eighteenth century art of conversation has regrettably diminished over the years; and, of course, even abbreviated dialogue can be superb, just fair, or downright bad. The descriptions in screenplays are generally brief or even stenographic, because the background of the various scenes will be set up and photographed at the discretion of the director, the costumes will be designed by other artists, the physical appearance of the characters will be fully realized only through the actors in the cast. This is also true of that superb form of literature, the stage play—as perusal of the text of a Greek tragedy or of a Shakespeare quarto or folio will disclose. The practice of writing elaborate descriptions in plays first arose toward the end of the past century, long after the composition of most of the theatre's masterpieces. Nor is there anything except economy of time and paper to prevent a screenplay from having detailed descriptions, and the reader will, as a matter of fact, find them in abundance in such screenplays as *The Good Earth* and *Mrs. Miniver.* (Though, as in the case of stage plays, these are often changed by the director of the production, and by that part of the actor's personality and physical appearance which is more or less immutable!) But drama has never rested its claims on description. Representation of character engaged in action and in reaction; of tensions, crises and climaxes in individual and collective experience; of ideas and meaning rising out of the projected experiences—that is the essence of dramatic literature.

The narrative in a film play is, as a rule, extensive. But it is brisk and is predominantly a record of movement, since film is movement. It reflects the modern age of activity and of constantly stepped up tempo. Moralists and philosophers may regret this state of affairs as much as they please, and they may be justified. But the form of the screenplay stems from modern consciousness, as well as from the nature of *motion* pictures, and it is the business of any vital art to employ the idiom and resources of its time. The plays of Shakespeare and his fellow-dramatists, composed in the vigorous and expanding age of Queen Bess, are replete with swiftly moving action in numerous scenes widely separated in time and space, much to the discomfort of purists, as well as with impassioned rhetoric and brisk low comedy. They seemed painfully barbaric to the courtiers of the Bourbons in the seventeenth and eighteenth century who favored the work of Jean Racine and preferred a restraint in art that paralleled the political aims of autocracy. But it would be inept for anyone to regret that Shakespeare did not write *Hamlet* in the leisurely style of Racine. And it would have spelled artistic suicide for an English dramatist to dam the tide of Elizabethan energy on the dynamic stage of The Globe. We do not of course prescribe the speed of the cinema for other forms of art—for the theatre, for instance, but we cannot proscribe the literature of the films, because it possesses such tempo. The narrative portions of a screenplay when not too carelessly written are, in short, artistically right for the medium, and can provide legitimate gratifications.

Needless to say, there is vast room for improvement in the literary composition of a screenplay apart from content. But the improvement is possible, and in some respects is already on the way. Although the length of dialogue in an effective film will always have to be kept within strict bounds, room may be found for those outbursts of passion and thought that form purple patches in the world's great plays. A place may even be found for poetry, for the spare modern kind of poetry written by Robert Frost, and by T. S. Eliot and Archibald MacLeish in their later phases. The excellent screenplay *All That Money Can Buy* . . . would have achieved even greater literary distinction if the late Stephen Vincent Benet had been called upon to put some of its longer passages into the kind of poetry he wrote so well. Already notable are the colloquial vigor and color of such film plays as *The Grapes of Wrath, How Green Was My Valley,* and *Mr. Smith Goes to Washington;* the hortatory eloquence of climactic scenes in *This Land Is Mine, The Life of Emile Zola, Fury,* and *Mr. Smith Goes to Washington;* the poetry of the interne's soliloquy in Pare Lorentz' *The Fight for Life,* as well as the narrative poetry of his other documentary film, *The River,* which recalls Walt Whitman's sweeping lines. (pp. xiv-xv)

There are, in addition, unique possibilities of fluidity, suggestiveness, and emotional scoring in the screenplay—all related of course to the demands of motion pictures. The presence of many scenes is, as previously noted, not a special attribute, as there have been many multi-scened plays (even modern ones, like *Faust* and *Peer Gynt*), and actually the film play merely avails itself of the novel's freely shifting background. What is unique is the flexible alternation of scenes of varying duration, of contrasting shortness and length for emphasis, of suggestion and symbolization. Objects extrapolated from their surroundings can be used with tremendous effect, and a part can speak eloquently for the whole, while routine exposition can be reduced to a flash. A separate "shot" of a pen moving on a piece of paper or of a foot pushing against a door can create an instant sense of expectancy and suspense. A crumpled piece of paper clinging to a man who has sold his friend's life for a small reward may suggest the informer's troublesome conscience more eloquently than an extended verbal analysis. Seemingly unrelated "shots" of objects in quick succession, superimposed on each other or dissolving into each other, may establish a situation, enforce a comment, or convey the essence of an emotion in fresh and startling ways. A poetry of sensations or relations is often achieved by this kind of composition, for which the technical word is "montage." Speech can be shuttled back and forth, or can be supplemented and counterpointed by picturized events, as well as alternated with effective silence while pantomime and visual backgrounds carry on the dialogue's content. The screenwriter knows that he can rely on the new technical resources of sound recording, described by Lewis Jacobs:

> An art of sound devices now parallels the art of camera devices: the elimination of all but one voice or sound on the sound track parallels the camera close-up; the mingling of voices or noises corresponds to the double exposure; the traveling of sound is like the panning or dollying of the camera; the elongation of sound beyond normal parallels a

lengthy still shot. The dissolve and the fade, the stop-voice and the play-back—these are other sound devices which approximate devices of the camera.

One written "shot" (the equivalent of a scene in a play) can follow another without preparation and intermission for a change of scene, as in a play; without delaying explanation of the transition, as in a novel. One accepts the convention as natural because films habituate us to freedom of movement in time and space. The viewpoint can also be tellingly differentiated for emphasis. The view can be expressively panoramic, distant and fully inclusive ("full shot"), fairly close and partially revealing ("medium shot"), or close and right on top of us (in a "close-up"). The view can also move to and fro, and up and down; it can expand or contract for revelation or emphasis; it can move with a character ("the camera pans with him" is the usual phrase) or precede him. The scene can "fade in" (generally conveying the start of a "sequence," a segment of the story), by the gradual materialization of a scene. It can "fade out," the gradual disappearance of the scene creating a sense of pause or of finality, generally suggesting the end of a sequence. It can dissolve quickly or lingeringly into another image, suggesting not merely a lapse of time but a special relationship with the image that follows. (A man's face is seen scowling and as it "dissolves out" a picture of his being beaten as a child "dissolves in" simultaneously, creating an impression of psychological continuity and relationship.) The shot can "wipe off"—as though a tissue were being peeled off, giving place to another picture, like another, deeper layer of tissue. The scene can be "cut"—that is, concluded abruptly, changed before its logical termination to achieve some staccato effect. Scenes, moreover, can be presented from the viewpoint of different characters, enabling us to see an object or some transpiring action as some character—personally involved or affected—views it, objectively or subjectively.

The viewpoint of the camera excels that of the static spectator or reader, for it is all-seeing and omniscient. The composition of a screenplay is predicated on the fact that the camera can be moved in all directions and that the view on the screen is in continuous movement. The screenplay, too, is movement, of varying speed and duration. The actors are moving, the background is moving, objects are moving, symbols are moving, the angles of vision are moving.

The resources of the motion picture are virtually inexhaustible, and the form and the detail of the screenplay correspond to them. Since the camera that takes the photographs corresponds to the eye of the observer, the "shooting script" visualizes the film for the reader. The directions intended for those who make the film in the studios or "on location" become, in the reading of the script, "seeing" directions. They tell the reader what to see and imagine, or—if he has already seen the film—what to "resee."

The famous Russian film director Eisenstein scores a fundamental point when he maintains in his book, *The Film Sense,* that many masters of literature expressed themselves in the cinematic manner long before the advent of the film, citing Milton's battle scenes in *Paradise Lost* and Pushkin's narrative poem *Poltava.* In the latter, an episode is given in terse one-line scenes such as

"Too late," someone then said to them,
And pointed finger to the field.
Then the fatal scaffold was dismantled,
A priest in cassock black was praying,
And onto a wagon was being lifted
By two cossacks an oaken coffin.

Examples from many other masterpieces of poetry and prose (Eisenstein also alludes to Maupassant's work) all the way down to Homer could be cited just as easily. In short, there is no intrinsic reason why the film form cannot provide notable literature. (pp. xv-xvii)

> *John Gassner, "The Screenplay as Literature," in* Twenty Best Film Plays, *edited by John Gassner and Dudley Nichols, Crown Publishers, 1943, pp. vii-xxx.*

Dudley Nichols

[Nichols was among the most successful and accomplished Hollywood screenwriters during the 1930s and 1940s. His screenplay for The Informer, *directed by John Ford and based on a novel by Liam O'Flaherty, won an Academy Award in 1935. Other films on which Nichols worked as a screenwriter include* Stagecoach *(1929) and* The Bells of St. Mary's *(1945). In the following excerpt, he discusses his screenplays for* The Informer *and* This Land Is Mine *(1943).]*

[Almost] everyone who is seriously interested in the cinema has seen *The Informer* on the screen, and as the film projects the screenplay with great fidelity I am prompted . . . to explain the method by which I translated Mr. O'Flaherty's novel into the language of film. In 1935 this was in a certain sense an experimental film; some new method had to be found by which to make the psychological action photographic. At that time I had not yet clarified and formulated for myself the principles of screenwriting, and many of my ideas were arrived at instinctively. I had an able mentor as well as collaborator in the person of John Ford and I had begun to catch his instinctive feeling about film. I can see now that I sought and found a series of symbols to make visual the tragic psychology of the informer, in this case a primitive man of powerful hungers. The whole action was to be played out in one foggy night, for the fog was symbolic of the groping primitive mind: it is really a mental fog in which he moves and dies. A poster offering a reward for information concerning Gypo's friend became the symbol of the evil idea of betrayal, and it blows along the street, following Gypo; it will not leave him alone. It catches on his leg and he kicks it off. But still it follows him and he sees it like a phantom in the air when he unexpectedly comes upon his fugitive friend.

So it goes all through the script; some of the symbolism is obvious, much of it concealed except from the close observer. The officer uses a stick when he pushes the blood-money to Gypo at headquarters, symbolic of contempt. The informer encounters a blind man in the dark fog outside and grips his throat in sudden guilt. The blind man is a symbol of the brute conscience, and Gypo releases him when he discovers the man cannot see. But as Gypo goes on to drown his conscience in drink, the tapping of the blind man's stick follows him; we hear it without seeing the blind man as Gypo hears his guilt pursuing him in his own soul. Later when he comes face to face with his conscience for a terrifying moment he tries to buy it off—by giving the blind man a couple of pounds, a lordly sum. . . . Sufficient to say that the method of adaptation in this instance was by a cumulative symbolism, to the very last scene where Gypo addresses the carven Christ, by which the psychology of a man could be made manifest in photographic terms. In this case I believe the method was successful.—I might add that I transferred the action of the drama from its original, rather special setting to a larger and more dramatic conflict which had national connotations. Whether that was any gain I do not know. Size of conflict in itself I hold to be unimportant. It is the size of characters within a conflict and how deeply they are probed that matters.

So much for the adaptation. (pp. xxxvi-xxxvii)

[The] serious film-writer cannot resign himself to Hollywood's barriers against original work designed for the screen. The average Hollywood entrepreneur is an intelligent man, and it is up to writers and directors to prove to him that films which probe into the chaos of life can be successful. John Ford made *The Informer* in spite of studio resistance; even after its completion it was held to be a failure and a waste of money by certain entrepreneurs. But the film did go out and make a profit. There *was* an audience for the realistic film. In spite of this and other instances I will say in all fairness that usually the studio heads have been right and the film-makers wrong: because usually the film-makers have not measured up to their task and their responsibilities when granted freedom. They have not measured up or they have wanted both money

Dudley Nichols

and freedom, which are incompatible. It is an axiom that no one will pay you to be a free artist. You are hired for profit—that is common sense. Very well, then, you must stop working for salary, you must devote yourself to the task in hand as do the novelist and dramatist, and only be recompensed if the film makes a profit. Economically I believe the writer and director will fare even better with this arrangement than under the salary system. Spiritually they will become whole men and work with integrity.

I have gone into this divagation to illuminate the fact that *This Land Is Mine* was originated and made into film under just such circumstances: Jean Renoir and I had gained the respect and confidence of an unusually intelligent studio head and he gave us complete freedom to make a film, without any other impediment than our own shortcomings.

There are a thousand ways to initiate a film but it may be worth while to set down our process in this instance. We both wished to lift entertainment to a higher level. We believed that a film should say something as well as hold attention. There are many themes knocking about within the head of every writer. Jean Renoir had lately come from Europe and was a volcano of feeling as a result of what he had seen and experienced. We were dissatisfied with the films against Fascism we had seen, because they all seemed distortions which dealt only with the surface of evil. A good film against Fascism ought to seem shocking even to the German and Italian peoples, and we were convinced that the sensational films on this theme made in Hollywood would only be laughed at, as we in America laugh at the Nazi film *Oom Kruger*. Exaggeration misses the point and becomes risible. Only the truth is shocking.

But to accomplish our purpose we knew we had to deal in ideas, to attempt to penetrate to the core of what had happened in Europe, and that was not easy; because ideas need words for their expression and an excess of words is a stumbling-block to good cinema technique. Words are not entertaining to the mass, who need simpler images.

All this while our imaginations were at work, simply because we had addressed ourselves to the task. Finally we began to clothe our ideas in characters. At first the characters had little life, and the film seemed like a morality play (which even the final film is in its essence). But gradually as the people of our imagination began to grow, they took on more human traits and eccentricities, and the ideas which had begotten them began to sink out of sight into their hearts, where the motivating ideas of every one of us lie hidden. Once the work had progressed this far the drama began to create itself—that is the only way one may describe it. You may stare at white paper, you may walk the floor, but you are obsessed finally and driven on to a conclusion, digging deep or following the contours of your people, according to your capacity. For myself I must say that I discovered many truths about one modern aspect of good and evil by wrestling with the lives of these characters. I discovered how plausible and attractive Fascism can appear to some people, and if we do not face that truth we can never triumph over it. I saw how much of it there was around me, how much of it perhaps in my own heart. That too must be faced if we are to win over evil.

There was no villain in the drama. We had ruled him out at the outset, for, there are no villains in life but only human beings embodying elements of good and evil. I should like to be more explicit about the writing of this screenplay, for the guidance of those who may be interested in this form of writing, but I cannot. We did not say, *Now we make this move to bring about that situation, Now we have that action to heighten suspense.* Instinctively the writer who deals with dramatic forms knows how to create character, situation and suspense; but if this is not done almost unconsciously then you are guilty of mere fabrication. . . . (pp. xxxviii-xxxix)

In any case, proceeding as I have lightly sketched above, we finally arrived at the screenplay. . . . It does not contain the voluminous notes we made on sets, music and a score of other things. It contains the flaws we had foreseen from the start, a talkativeness that is contrary to my own instinctive sense of cinema. But the ideas had been embodied within characters, their actions and reactions; a conflict of ideas had become a conflict of human beings; it had become a simple drama of good and evil, the conflict of two contradictory drives in the hearts of men—for power and for freedom. Its form had become that of the mystery play—in a sense, the medieval mystery play as well as the modern: men and women, their lives woven together by fate and circumstance, committed certain seemingly inevitable acts which we do not quite fathom or understand; then in the final act the mystery of a man's life is solved by the protagonist and we suddenly understand everything.

It may be interesting to compare this screenplay with the finished film. You will notice many alterations and elisions, which only prove that a screenplay is not a completed thing in itself but only the first (though most important) stage in the creation of a film. We found, for example, that we had to pare down dialogue still further. Not only because the screen is a laconic medium, but because the film had turned out to be a sort of mystery play and we found that here and there the characters told too much about their lives; some things had to be held back to hold attention more tightly. Whole sequences had to be dropped out in the cutting room, because they extended the film beyond its correct artistic length. There is no absolute rule for length—a film determines its own length finally in the cutting room. Our first assembled print was more than fourteen thousand feet in length; our final cut was around 9300 feet, about an hour and forty minutes of running time, an average length for "feature films" nowadays.

This, then, is the genesis of an original film. Each writer and director will originate a story in a different way, but the process described is typical. If there is one grave fault in the approach of Hollywood to a story, it is the tendency to regard a story as an invention, as something cleverly contrived, with the accent on a novel arrangement of actions rather than on characters. A story is always characters, imagined people who take on a life of their own, plus what is in the back of the mind of the author. As the cinema becomes more concerned with human character we shall have better films. . . . (pp. xxxix-xi)

Dudley Nichols, "The Writer and the Film," in Twenty Best Film Plays, *edited by John Gassner and Dudley Nichols, Crown Publishers, 1943, pp. xxxi-xl.*

Martin S. Dworkin

[*In the following excerpt, Dworkin considers the changing role of the screenwriter in the evolution of cinema.*]

"The movie writer does not need to know how to write; he does need a talent for plot contrivance and a sense of colloquial dialogue. This has been true of the movies since the beginning." So saith Leo Rosten, in his *Hollywood: The Movie Colony; The Movie Makers,* a work applying methods of sociology where "possible," in an attempt to make " . . . the difference between social science and gossip, between systematic analysis and casual journalism," in studying what was the world center of film production at its height of power and glory. Rosten later shows sufficient respect for screenwriters, even quoting Samuel Goldwyn on the "author" as the "indispensable requirement" of a good film, as " . . . a picture can't rise higher than its story." The implied denigration nevertheless remains, as Rosten stresses the limitations of the writer's role, and his inevitable frustration and bitterness, in what is essentially and traditionally a collaborative process, producing salable merchandise for the entertainment market place.

Whether or not it has been "true . . . from the beginning," the notion itself is a persistent one, since the earliest efforts to do more in films than record action for its own sake. And it was surely more "true" in the years before the addition of simultaneous sound reproduction to the images on screen, when it was the function of the director that was established as principal in the reality of film making—and in its mythology. Writers provided story outlines or scenarios, then continuities for directors to bring to cinematic life. The writing had no being, as matter to be read, apart from what was there to cue or inspire the director's imagination. Only in the usually separate craft of doing titles to accompany the pictures on screen did writing convey meaning directly to audiences. The rest was silence, if almost always with musical accompaniment, and often with sound effects. The public saw what the director created for the screen, even the new gods and goddesses of movie stardom seeming to have burst from his forehead in a cinematic cataclysm.

This view, putting the writer in his place, is purveyed, for but one appropriately curious example, in a popular detective novel of the early 1920s, one of an already sizable genre of books and stories inventing a brash new world of miraculous movie making and magical movie people. *The Film Mystery,* by Arthur B. Reeve, in a series featuring "Craig Kennedy," redoubtable practitioner of crime detection as exact science, has to do with a couple of suitably ingenious murders, via envenomed pins and botulin toxin, during the shooting of *The Black Terror,* being made, significantly, at a mansion at Tarrytown, near New York City, then still in the running with Hollywood as a production center. At one point, the producer scoffs at a question as to the whereabouts of the script writer:

An author on the lot at the filming of his picture, to bother the director and to change everything? Out! When the scenario's done he's through. He's lucky to get his name on the screen. It's not the story but the direction which counts, except that you've got to have a good idea to start with, and halfway decent script to make your lay-outs from.

The narrator, a character in the story, vaunts his movie

knowledge in remarking that the producer may have known he was exaggerating, "going counter to the tendency to have the author on the lot." But the decisive commentary may be in the *dénouement* itself (there being no mystery that books are written by writers). It is the screenwriter, after all, who is discovered to be the murderer, having done in . . . yes, the star actress *and* the director!

To run down the writer in film making, of course, is to raise up the director, first and most of all, leading to what looks to some, notably writers, as an "extravagant critical cult of the director," in the phrase of Terence Rattigan. This cult, "a legacy, and a bad legacy, of the days of silent film," he has said, is perpetuated by "responsible film critics," who persist in giving the public "the impression that it is the director and not the screenwriter who writes the script." This may have been true before sound, when "the status of the pre-Jolsonian screenwriter was often merely that of translator, stenographer, and general hack." But it is time for the screenwriter to

> . . . throw off the shackles of the director (and the camera) and remember that the screenplay is the child not only of its mother, the silent film, but also of its father, the Drama; that it has affinities not only with Griffith, De Mille and Ingram, but also with Sophocles, Shakespeare, and Ibsen.
> ["A Magnificent Pity for Camels," in *Diversion: Twenty-two Authors on the Lively Arts,* edited by John Sutro, 1950]

Reeves's fictional producer disdains the "story" in film making as but a step on the way to the images conceived by the director, prepared for and captured by the camera, and selected and joined in the editing process. Rattigan raises a working writer's banner on behalf of a dramatic and literary integrity of the written script, at once independent of the intended filmic outcome, yet ineluctably vital to it. Both positions are overstated, the former, perhaps, only slightly more than the latter. But both continue to be maintained, with appropriate exaggerations, in arguments among film industry people, critics, and audiences—as is surely evident in the often savage snarling over the *auteur* theory of film "authorship," that began in Paris in the 1950s and '60s. Future scholars may in puzzlement ascribe the confused bickerings of critics and packs of critics there, and later in Britain and the U. S., as much to contending political ideologies, or to opportunism of rival self-publicists bidding for some new kind of movie stardom, as to any differences over film theory and practice. The forces of ambient politics, and the drive of individual motivations aside, however, what made the controversy possible, and probably inevitable, was a convergence of two complex factors: the one, a rediscovery of the history of motion pictures; and the other, a renewed urgency to establish the credentials of cinema as "art" among the traditionally accepted arts.

The new awareness of film history had much to do with the growth of serious study of popular culture in general, but it was especially invigorated and informed by a new and increasing availability of the ancient movie artifacts. These, although once and for so long treated as ephemera by the film makers themselves, were now lovingly pursued, collected, and belatedly preserved, with all the furious dedication of Poggio Bracciolini and the Humanist scholar-sleuths, searching out the manuscript remnants of classical culture. Not only an affection for silent films, but a veritable mystique of their "purity" as cinema and as folk culture, became essential elements of intellectual apparatus after the turn of mid-century. Not least affected were new waves of film makers, nostalgic for a halcyon era of the movies before most of them were born.

Notions of the nature of film creation idealizing silent film techniques were renovated, often subordinating or even eliminating the scriptwriting function, going so far as to permit—nay, to *demand*—spontaneous conception on the part of the director, and improvised action and dialogue by actors. And, it was no mere coincidence that there were available new, highly portable cameras, sound recorders, and lighting equipment, as well as hypersensitive film materials, that allowed not only a release from dependence on studios, with their elaborate installations, but also a kind of careful, sophisticated imitation of what were seen as unencumbered techniques of early cinematography.

All this was happening, to be sure, at a time of general upheaval in the motion picture industry. The great complexes, after being forced under anti-monopoly regulations to disengage their radiating chains of theatres, were being disintegrated, or transformed into manufactories for television. Film production could now be "independent" of studio control and the programming requirements of established networks of distribution and exhibition. That this industrial system had usually worked to restrict film makers, including scriptwriters, was an old and real complaint among those who look first to the artistic and informational potentialities of the screen. However true this may be, there ought to be puzzlement, if not embarrassment, for the more doctrinaire of these critics in the current rediscovery of so many of those slick products of the high days of the movie studio system as works of authentic cinematic style and preeminently popular entertainment.

In any event, the more the movies are taken seriously, the greater the tensions between what must be regarded as individual and creative, and what is inescapably collaborative, technical, and industrial, in their production and provision for audience participation. The opposing forces, exhibiting a Heraclitean dynamic in balance, affect interpretations of the history of motion pictures, as well as judgments of particular films, and inevitably come to issue in all the arguments over "authorship," the role of writers, and what screenwriting in general has to do with writing, an established "art," and with cinema, a parvenu of uncertain pedigree.

A good case can be made for screenwriting as a special, privileged function in film making, with unique problems and relationships to all other operations involved. But in the contentions over the importance of writers there are elements of what are in some ways periodic urges to assert the distinctive contribution of one role or another in the complex of crafts and activities having to do with making films and bringing them to audiences. These claims for recognition, at the very least, have their own justification, but are also clearly punctual in a time of heightening disaffection with depersonalized processes of mass production and anonymous services, and of radical ventures to assert a sense of participation in the making of things of value. In this case, questions of worth of contributions have the more power to raise banners of passionate advocacy, as the making of films implicates so many essential functions in all its stages. There can be talk of what is done by directors, producers, actors, cameramen, editors, composers, designers, and a score of others, as well as of writers, that could not go on in discussions of any other medium—saving, of course, television, which, for all its many differences, is near enough in nature to cinema: nearer, say, than is live-performance theatre.

Even those working in the logistical and commercial phases of motion pictures may claim some creative involvement in what happens in the theatrical transaction that is vital to the realization of a film before audiences. And the assertions are made not only by trade groups, or orators at conventions of industry people, celebrating the indisputable leadership of this or that part of the movie business. In fact, it was an artist, a maker of highly subjective, abstract expressionist films, who made the point most clearly and forcefully, without pretension, in an interview some years ago.

He had come to films from painting, which had already gained him recognition by museums and collectors, in order, he told this writer, to fulfill the latent cinematic implications of his graphic art. But, while persisting in working alone or in close direction of others, trying for as much control over techniques and outcomes in his films as he had sought in his painting, it was not he who completed his work, he insisted, but his distributor: the agent-entrepreneur—albeit one plainly concerned with more than commerce—who took his films, sought out their potential audiences, and arranged for them to be *seen,* to come alive as cinema in theaters, auditoriums, and classrooms. What was on the reels, he implied, had only potential reality, and this far less than, and far different from that of a painting in a closet, say, or on an easel in an empty room; or of a book on a shelf; or even of a musical score awaiting performance.

The argument is not at all new, to any who have thought seriously about the special nature of this quintessentially modern *techné,* in which all individuality must be mediated by an intricate technology and an immense industry, functioning to create experiences for audiences of multitudes at once—so that still pictures appear to move, figures of light and shadow seem to speak and sing, and distances of time and space to be bridged in an absolute velocity of illusion. The lesson, however, always needs renewal, and never more urgently than when defenders of cinema as "art" misappropriate criteria of creativity from the established aesthetics of older media, themselves often more conventional and historically variable than philosophically coherent.

In the belated eagerness of intellectuals to recognize the qualities and powers of the cinema, as, indeed, of modern "popular art" in general, many curiously misunderstand and diminish the essential differences that make simple identification with traditional "fine arts" misleading. Past and present are thereby falsified, in forgetting that, as in the wise observation of the eminent historian of ideas Paul Oskar Kristeller:

> . . . the various arts (in the course of history) change not only their content and style, but also their relations to each other, and their place in the general system of culture, as do religion, philosophy, or science. . . .

and, further to the point being made here,

> . . . the moving picture is a good example of how new techniques may lead to modes of artistic expression for which the aestheticians of the eighteenth and nineteenth century (*sic*) had no place in their systems.
> ["The Modern System of the Arts: A Study in the History of Aesthetics," in the *Journal of the History of Ideas*, 1952]

This is by no means to support the aggressive naiveté of know-nothings, including fanatic audio-visualists as well as miners of "underground" ideologies, who disconnect cinema from all antecedent culture, talking as if seeing is somehow opposed to thinking, and there is possible a critical, yet somehow non-intellectual rhetoric that is valid only for judging films. As was said by no less a prophet of the visual in cinema than Sergei Eisenstein—while asseverating the fundamentally intellectual nature of *viewing:*

> . . . our cinema is not altogether without parents and without pedigree, without a past, without the traditions and rich cultural heritage of the past epochs. It is only very thoughtless and presumptuous people who can erect laws and an esthetic for cinema, proceeding from the premises of some incredible virgin-birth of this art!
> ["Dickens, Griffith, and the Film Today," in *Film Form: Essays in Film Theory,* edited and translated by Jay Leyda, 1949]

What *is* argued is, or ought to be, a commonplace: that the "art" of cinema may not be reasonably considered as prior to or separate from its *techné,* involving the essential industrial technology, collaborative creativity, complex logistics, and social transformations that are the very stuff of the "dreams that money (*must*) buy;" that what makes cinema new and unique among the arts is precisely what must be always recognized, in order to discuss films meaningfully in ways that are coherent with our critical understandings of all other aspects, media, and individual creations of culture.

In this light, it becomes possible to regard as archaic and irrelevant, as well as exaggerated, both Rosten's view (whether this be "social science" or "gossip") of the screenwriter as a kind of skilled illiterate, and Rattigan's idealization of him as an embattled *litterateur.* To begin with, writing as *writing* is not one, but many, many things—and long may they flourish, in all conceivable diversity of mode and manner! But writing for filming is something else again, for reasons good, bad, and worse, that writers, first of all people, have argued "from the beginning" to explain, or explain away, what they were doing.

Almost to a man (and woman!), writers who have worked for the screen, whether preparing original scripts or adapting existing books, plays, stories, and other materials, have made much of the distinctive nature of their task, both in praise or, commonly enough, in disparagement. The latter attitude, in fact, became quite fasionable among writers in Hollywood, as is testified to in innumerable memoirs, exposés, *romans à clef,* and even films—as well as in more-or-less disciplined studies of the place and industry, led in seriousness and merit by Rosten's and Powdermaker's [Hortense Powdermaker, *Hollywood, the Dream Factory: An Anthropologist Looks at the Movie Makers,* 1950]. Writers for filming elsewhere have shown more of the same mixture of outraged intelligence, self-destructive cynicism, and resigned opportunism—perhaps because the emoluments for screenwriting in other countries notoriously have been so much smaller.

The attitude has sufficient justification, as thousands upon thousands of films sadly attest. For themselves, writers have given the blackest accounts of menial labors on motion picture assembly lines, chronicling violated literary integrity, enforced anonymity, collective rape of individual creation, ideological repression, total, demeaning domination by corrupt authority—and, as may be surprising, usually precarious livelihood. But there have always persisted the straight questions as to why the writers have gone on with it all; and whether there may not have been, and may yet be, despite any limiations and attendant evils, some realistically worthy opportunities in screenwriting, that may attract the best people, with some hope of honorable fulfillment. The answers given by writers to both questions are predictably various, and there are good writers who have had good reasons for both quitting screen work or staying with it. But there must be a case, after all, for what is surely a sensible professional attitude, and there has been quite enough good writing for films to bear witness. Moreover, there are good writers for the screen, Graham Greene for one, who are careful to preach what they practice, especially inveighing against the self-fulfilling denigration of screenwriting so often played-at by the mediocre, or by those good writers who let themselves do less than they can do. Nigel Balchin, for another, has spoken of what he regards as

> . . . the greatest pitfall of the novelist-turned-screenwriter; the pitfall of thinking of the job as highly paid hackwork in an inferior medium. It is true that a large number of bad films are made. But for that matter a large number of bad novels are written and so is a large quantity of bad verse. There are no bad media; there are only bad performances in a medium. It is fatal to start a script from the attitude that however good it is, the resulting film will be bad. Bad films are sometimes made from good scripts. But in nine cases out of ten bad films originate from bad scripts; and one of the most fruitful sources of bad scripts is the author who thinks the job too crude and simple for him. I cannot think of any novelist now writing whose most subtle ideas are too subtle for film treatment—if he learns how to handle the medium as carefully as he has learnt to write his books.
>
> ["Writing in Pictures," in *Diversion: Twenty-two Authors on the Lively Arts,* edited by John Sutro, 1950]

Balchin's argument (which can draw support from the statements of Greene, as well as from the example of his screenwriting), must not be taken to intend that books may simply and fully be translated into films. The key word and issue here is the "ideas" contained, and the point is that the two media are distinct, methodologically, for all that a "scene" on a page may be transmogrified to one on screen that is instantly recognizable. And, the old truism means, too, for only one more thing, that the scene on the page remains, its potentiality for the imagination at least provisionally unchanged, even if a filmed version appears utterly different. It is this consideration, of a sustained life for a literary work despite what happens in a movie adaptation, that has comforted so many writers in allowing their books to be made into films, or in participating in the transformation themselves.

Here, it is Greene who may be the most notable, perhaps unique example, having had, it is likely, more to do with screen work, directly and indirectly, than any major literary figure, so far in the century. Indeed, significant revelation of the Reverend Gene D. Phillips' book, *Graham Greene: The Films of His Fiction,* is that Greene's admiration for the motion picture medium, and his mixed feelings about the film versions of his own work, may finally be based on his certainty that his writing will survive whatever filmic transliteration, good or bad. As to the latter, he told Phillips, " . . . I can only repeat what I have said before: In the long run the smile will be on the author's face. For the book has the longer life." Father Phillips does not concur, arguing that the good films made from Greene's work "will last as long as anything he has written." But this disagreement, if there is any, in no way weakens the insistence of the good screenwriters, such as Balchin and Greene, on the essentiality of good screen writing for good films—which Phillips in fact corroborates in comparing the film versions of Greene's fiction prepared by other screenwriters with those he did himself.

In any case, it would be foolish to fault Greene for having faith in his literary work, even if it may be too soon—the survival of something cultural being always problematical, and of anything photographic being hardly predictable—to talk of altering Ovid's famous paean to the permanence of writing, *Scripta . . . ,* to *Cinema ferunt annos.* As to this, it may be worth noting that there is an extra-added attraction today, for writers turning from print to cinema, an outcome of the change in public attitude discussed earlier, that has encouraged study of films as serious works, and has elevated erstwhile merely popular movies to cultural respectability.

In the event, there has grown a new regard for film scripts—with which writers, after all, have something to do, for all the frequently decisive reshaping by directors and others. Whether or not they may be "read" as are books or plays, film scripts are now published frequently, in what is an established genre of the enormous contemporary production of printed works on cinema. While still fundamentally related to what is realized on screen, the published scripts nevertheless present screenwriting to audiences in ways hardly possible before, with inevitable consequences for the writers' own notion of themselves and what they are doing.

And what they are doing, in fact, may not be so clear as is the easy distinction of printed words and images on screen, that is so decisive and fundamental, but that can be carried to fearsome oversimplifications, as in contrasting, usually in polemic, what is given as "purely verbal" discourse with something called "pure cinema." Even to say, "to write a film," or "to film a story," implies such integration of media in the imagination, if not in the tactics of production, as to call for some revision, at the least, of conventional separations of the arts—exemplifying once again the natural dynamism of cultural activity, that has been remarked before. Printed words, indeed, are involved with filmed images in ways that, as this writer has [argued in "The Printed Screen," *Educational Forum XXXIII,* November, 1968], "may be the best example for our time of a practical, if not essential interdependence of the arts—or, at the least, of an integral relationship among media of mass communications."

The arts once were not separated from each other, or from either the paramount or the least concerns and activities of the people who created them and lived their meaning. Even now, their distinctiveness, as creative media and as experiences to have and to share, may be more truly a matter of conventional attitudes, or of limited abstraction for philosophical analysis, than of essential differentiation. We may observe this integration, surely, in considering the bearing of music, and its orchestrated silences, on the whole experience of motion pictures. And, returning to the matter of writing and what it has to do with film, we may wonder whether what is happening, when verbal ideas and narratives become particular images and sequences of thought and action on screen, may not be a reassertion of the very nature of writing, rather than evidence of its passing potency.

This, or something not unrelated, may have been in Federico Fellini's mind when he said to me, during a talk in 1957, that he had come to making films precisely because he is a *writer*. Well, precisely what he meant at that moment he could not clarify; it sounded good to him, and somehow right, and maybe, as is the way of the arts, it is a matter of becoming: clearer, for one thing, but truer, for all the rest. (pp. 75-87)

> *Martin S. Dworkin, "The Writing on the Screen," in* The Antigonish Review, *Vol. V, No. 24, Winter, 1975, pp. 75-88.*

John Huston   (interview with Gideon Bachmann)

[*An American director, screenwriter, and actor, Huston was one of the most prominent figures in world cinema. During his long career he made a variety of films, including many successful adaptations from works of literature, among them* The Maltese Falcon *(1941), based on a novel by Dashiell Hammett;* The Treasure of the Sierra Madre *(1949), based on a novel by B. Traven; and* Night of the Iguana *(1964), from the play by Tennessee Williams. In the following excerpt from an interview, Huston offers his ideas on the process of screenwriting and discusses the relation between his work as a screenwriter and as a director.*]

BACHMANN: Could you put into words some principles you employ in order to put ideas into film form? Do you feel there are any rules a writer for the cinema must follow?

HUSTON: Each idea calls for a different treatment, really. I am not aware of any ready formula, except the obvious one that films fall into a certain number of scenes, and that you have to pay attention to certain limitations that have to do with time, according to subject. Depending on what you are writing about, you have to decide the time balance between words and action. It seems to me, for example, that the word contains as much action as a purely visual scene, and that dialogue should have as much action in it as physical motion. The sense of activity that your audience gets is derived equally from what they see and from what they hear. The fascination, the attention of the man who looks at what you have put together, must be for the thoughts as much as for the happenings in your film. In

fact, when I write I can't really separate the words from the actions. The final action—the combined activity of the film, the sum of the words and the visuals—is really going on only in the mind of the beholder. So in writing I have to convey a sense of overall progression with all the means at my command: words and images and sounds and everything else that makes film.

BACHMANN: This brings up one of the basic questions about films that adapt literary works: in a book there are many things that you can't see or hear, but which in reading you translate directly into your own interior images and feelings. Emotions that are created in you neither through dialogue nor action. How do you get these into film? The monologues from *Moby Dick,* for example?

HUSTON: Well, first of all, I try to beware of literal transfers to film of what a writer has created initially for a different form. Instead I try to penetrate first to the basic idea of the book or the play, and then work with those ideas in cinematic terms. For example, to see what Melville wanted to say in the dialogue, what emotions he wanted to convey. I always thought *Moby Dick* was a great blasphemy. Here was a man who shook his fist at God. The thematic line in *Moby Dick* seemed to me, always, to have been: who's to judge when the judge himself is dragged before the bar? Who's to condemn, but he, Ahab! This was, to me, the point at which I tried to aim the whole picture, because I think that's what Melville was essentially concerned with, and this is, at the same time, the point that makes *Moby Dick* so extremely timely in our age. And if I may be allowed the side-observation: I don't think any

John Huston

of the critics who wrote about the film ever mentioned this.

BACHMANN: I suppose you are speaking about the problem of taking personal responsibility in an age where the group has largely attempted to make decisions for the individual. This is an interpretation of Melville, or perhaps I should say one interpretation of Melville. And so in the attempt to understand the basic idea of a work (in order to translate those ideas into film) you are really doing more than that: you add your own interpretation, you don't just put into images what the original author wanted to say.

HUSTON: I don't think we can avoid interpretation. Even just pointing a camera at a certain reality means an interpretation of that reality. By the same token, I don't *seek* to interpret, to put my own stamp on the material. I try to be as faithful to the original material as I can. This applies equally to Melville as it applies to the Bible, for example. In fact, it's the fascination that I feel for the original that makes me want to make it into a film.

BACHMANN: What about original material, where you are not adapting a play or a book? Are there any ideas of yours, basic ideas, which you try to express in your work? Do you feel that there is a continuity in your work in terms of a consistent ideology? In short, do you feel you are trying to say something coherent to mankind?

HUSTON: There probably is. I am not consciously aware of anything. But even the choice of material indicates a preference, a turn of mind. You could draw a portrait of a mind through that mind's preferences.

BACHMANN: Well, let me do that for a minute, and see if what I see as a unifying idea in your work is indeed a coherent feeling on your part. I see that in your films there is always a man pitched against odds, an individual who seeks to retain a sense of his own individuality in the face of a culture that surrounds and tends to submerge him. I would call the style of your films the style of the frontier, or what the frontier has come to symbolize in American culture: a sense of rebellion against being put into a system, into a form of life and into a mode of thinking rigidly decided by others.

HUSTON: Yes, I think there is something there. I do come from a frontier background. My people were that. And I always feel constrained in the presence of too many rules, severe rules; they distress me. I like the sense of freedom. I don't particularly seek that ultimate freedom of the anarchist, but I'm impatient of rules that result from prejudice.

BACHMANN: In any case, you believe that at the basis of every film of yours there is a basic idea, whether an idea of yours or one of another author. But how do you proceed to put that idea into film form? In writing, what do you do first, for example?

HUSTON: I don't envisage the whole thing at the beginning. I go a little bit at a time, always asking myself whether I am on the track of the basic thought. Within that, I try to make each scene as good as I can. This applies both to the writing and to the directing—to the whole process of preparation and production, in fact—which are only extensions of the process of writing. It's hard to break down into details. (pp. 100-01, 104)

BACHMANN: What is the technical process of your script-writing?

HUSTON: Usually I write in longhand first, and then dictate a later version. I use a standard script form: action on the left and dialogue on the right. When it's finished it's mimeographed and distributed to the people who need to see it. I often change again later. Sometimes I finish the final version on the set itself, or change again something I've written as a final version the day before. Mostly these changes come to me when I hear the words first spoken by an actor. It's always different once it comes out of a living person's mouth. By this I do not mean that I try to adjust to an actor's personality—I try to do that as little as possible. When I write, I don't have in mind an actor, but a character. I don't conceive this character with a specific star in my mind. I guess what I am trying to do with this constant changing, is to try to put to work more than my own imagination, or at least allow my imagination the liberty of play, the liberty of coming out of its cage—which is me, my body, when I am alone and writing—and in this way it begins to live and to flower and gives me better service than when I put it to work abstractly, alone, in a room with paper and pencil, without the living presence of the material. Then, when the character has been born out of this extended imagination, I have to look for someone to play the role, and this someone isn't always necessarily the person whom I thought could play it originally, because often it no longer is the same character. In fact, I've often—at least, sometimes—delayed the making of a film because I couldn't find anybody to play the new and adjusted character that I had finally arrived at construing. Although in my experience you usually find someone; there are enough good actors if you are willing to wait a little. (p. 105)

BACHMANN: Let's see if we can follow your film-making method through logically and go on to a description of the process of turning the script into film.

HUSTON: Actually I don't separate the elements of film-making in such an abstract manner. For example, the directing of a film, to me, is simply an extension of the process of writing. It's the process of rendering the thing you have written. You're still writing when you're directing. Of course you're not composing words, but a gesture, the way you make somebody raise his eyes or shake his head is also writing for films. Nor can I answer precisely what the relative importance, to me, of the various aspects of film-making is, I mean, whether I pay more attention to writing, directing, editing, or what-have-you. The most important element to me is always the idea that I'm trying to express, and everything technical is only a method to make the idea into clear form. I'm always working on the idea: whether I am writing, directing, choosing music or cutting. Everything must revert back to the idea; when it gets away from the idea it becomes a labyrinth of rococo. Occasionally one tends to forget the idea, but I have always had reason to regret this whenever it happened. Sometimes you fall in love with a shot, for example. Maybe it is a *tour de force* as a shot. This is one of the great dangers of directing: to let the camera take over. Audiences very often do not understand this danger, and it is not unusual that camera-work is appreciated in cases where it really has no business in the film, simply because it is decorative or in itself exhibitionistic. I would say that there are maybe half a dozen directors who really know their camera—how to move their camera. It's a pity that critics often do not appreciate this. On the other hand I think it's OK that audiences should not be aware of this. In fact, when the camera is in motion, in the best-directed scenes, the audiences should not be aware of what the camera is doing. They should be following the action and the road of the idea so closely that they shouldn't be aware of what's going on technically.

BACHMANN: Am I right in assuming, then, that you do not share the modern view that the form of a film can be as important as its content? I take it, from what you say, that you are interested more in what is being said than in how it is being said.

HUSTON: When you become aware of *how* things are being said, you get separated from the idea. This doesn't mean that an original rendering isn't to be sought after, but that rendering must be so close to the idea itself that you aren't aware of it.

BACHMANN: If the optimum is to stay close to the original idea without imposing one's individuality upon it, then the old Thalberg-Ince system of having a script written by one man and then farming it out to another to shoot, wouldn't appear to be so bad.

HUSTON: That's carrying a principle to an extreme. Let's be sure to have enough regard for *style.* I am not saying that the director who is carrying on to film the idea created by another man should obliterate his individuality. After all, there are many ways—as many as there are people—to do any one thing, including the direction of a film. One sticks to an idea within one's own ability and with the means that are native to oneself, and not through employing means that are so commonplace that anybody could use them. What goes for film also goes for literature, for any form of art; the originality of Joyce is in no way to be divorced from what he was saying. There's no separation between style and subject matter, between style and intention, between style and—again—the idea. I do not mean to indicate, in anything I say, that the work of a man shouldn't bear witness to the personality of that man, beyond the fact that he expresses a specific idea in that work. It's the combination of his personality and the idea he expresses which creates his style. (pp. 109-10)

BACHMANN: Do you think the fewer words spoken in a film, the better film it is?

HUSTON: Depends on the film. Some films depend on words. Take *Night of the Iguana.* Take the spoken words out of that, and you won't have very much.

BACHMANN: Is that only because that particular script was based on a play? Or do you feel that scripts that are very word-oriented could also be read as literature as a play can?

HUSTON: I don't think you can make rules. In the case of *Iguana* the words were important because they carried Tennessee Williams's thoughts. But I think a good screenplay could be read as literature, too. It simply depends on the particular material.

BACHMANN: You are not taking sides, then, in the perennial controversy over what's more important in film, the word or the image?

HUSTON: I don't see that they are in conflict. Depending on what is being said, they complement each other in the hands of a good craftsman. (p. 114)

> *John Huston and Gideon Bachmann, in an interview in* Hollywood Voices: Interviews with Film Directors, *edited by Andrew Saris, The Bobbs-Merrill Company, Inc., 1971, pp. 97-119.*

Ernest Lehman   (interview with John Brady)

[*Lehman is an American screenwriter who is best known for his original screenplay for* North by Northwest *(1959), directed by Alfred Hitchcock. He has also written adaptations for* West Side Story *(1961),* The Sound of Music *(1965),* Who's Afraid of Virginia Woolf? *1966), and numerous other notable films. In the following excerpt from an interview, Lehman comments on his career as a screenwriter.*]

BRADY: Do you think that most bad films can be traced to a bad script?

LEHMAN: I just happen to be one of those irrational persons who think that a film cannot be any good if it isn't well written. It just *can't* be. And in all likelihood, if it's bad, it was badly written. Most, but not all bad movies, can be traced to a bad script. (p. 179)

BRADY: In the scripts you did with Hitchcock, I sensed that you really underplayed the exposition because you felt that the viewer knows that in a Hitchcock film, every little detail somehow or other adds up.

LEHMAN: Right. You got a lot more attention paid to every little thing you did and said in a Hitchcock picture. It's amazing, you know, how he could manipulate an audience. Take *North by Northwest,* for example: the beginning of the crop-duster sequence, in particular, when Cary Grant is standing alone by the roadside waiting for a man he has not met (but has been mistaken for) to show up. Most directors would have had maybe one or two cars whiz by, and figure that that was about all an audience could tolerate. But Hitchcock knew better than that. He had a car come from one direction, zoom by and disappear in the distance; then he held on a long interval in which nothing was happening; then he had a car come from the *other* direction, and zoom by and disappear in the distance; and then *another* long interval of silence with nothing happening; and then a truck came by and merely blew dust all over Cary Grant and disappeared in the distance. And still nothing had really happened. Hitch knew how to milk that sequence in a way that no other director would have known how to do, or would have had the guts to do. There was an awful lot of ominous *nothing* going on for a long time before the stranger appeared on the other side of the road. That was just one aspect of Hitchcock's unique style.

BRADY: What other earmarks would there be in that style? *North by Northwest* struck me as being a highly readable script, lively and filled with delightful lines.

LEHMAN: If you didn't try for that, you weren't writing a Hitchcock picture. There had to be a certain amount of wit, or an *attempt* at wit. No matter how melodramatic the

Humphrey Bogart, Peter Lorre, Mary Astor, and Sidney Greenstreet in The Maltese Falcon, *John Huston's first film as screenwriter and director.*

goings-on were, the characters had to have a sense of humor. They could not take themselves too seriously. And they had to speak in circumlocutions—those were the rules. The James Mason character in *North by Northwest* is typical of a Hitchcock heavy. They never talk "nasty" talk; they talk silken, suave, professorial talk while they tell you they are going to have to kill you. The vocabulary of a Hitchcock villain contains many expressions like "I'm afraid that," or "Unfortunately, my dear fellow," or "I regret to tell you"—you know, do away with him but be a gentleman about it.

BRADY: There's a great line by Cary Grant in the film when he says that the girl uses sex the way some people use a flyswatter.

LEHMAN: You liked that, huh?

BRADY: Do you work hard at developing such one-liners?

LEHMAN: I must say I find writing that kind of dialogue a little less than difficult. If I have a style, it tends to have people, maybe to their detriment, display a predilection for the wisecrack, repartee, the flip manner. And I myself tend to be a little bit like my characters when I'm writing—not a tongue-in-cheek attitude exactly, but I don't

seem to take writing as seriously as some writers would, or should.

BRADY: Could that perhaps explain why your successes for the most part have been what might be called entertainments?

LEHMAN: I think calling my films "entertainments" might be too much of a generalization, and perhaps very slightly unflattering. Part of *Somebody Up There Likes Me* was entertainment, and part of it wasn't; very little of *From the Terrace* was an entertainment; *Executive Suite* was not an entertainment. And what about *West Side Story,* and *Who's Afraid of Virginia Woolf?,* not to mention *Black Sunday* and suchlike? I'm trying to think of what your definition of the word "entertainment" would be.

BRADY: I'm speaking of *tone,* perhaps. You took a rather entertaining approach to *The Prize,* I thought, given the rather somber, almost heavy-handed nature of the book.

LEHMAN: I would say that the book was serious, and quite properly took itself seriously. It was my own choice, right or wrong, that the serious subject and serious approach would not be viable film fare. Maybe I didn't know how to do it as a serious film. Maybe I felt people would not go to see it as such. I wanted it to be a success as a film, and I felt that in order to make it work (we use words like that: "How do we make this work?"), it would have to be made into a *movie* movie—amusing and nonserious. I made the Paul Newman character pretty flip. I think I was stealing from myself, sort of road company Hitchcock. *Very* road company, I'd say. (pp. 183-85)

BRADY: You strike me as being an extremely sensitive human being in a business that requires the insensitivity and the thickness of . . .

LEHMAN: An elephant's hide. How many writers have you met who could just bull their way through all this? I have never met one. In my day I did some pretty wild things, starting with the very first picture I wrote. By then I had written for publication. I was used to seeing my by-line in national magazines—*Collier's, Cosmopolitan, Esquire*—and my attitude was: That's *my* story. Nobody was talking about who the editor was, or the publisher. Then came Hollywood. I write my first movie, *Executive Suite,* and I see a cover story on the film in *Newsweek*—a five-page takeout inside with a big glowing review, and everybody is mentioned—the head of the studio, the name of the dog in the picture, *everyone.* Except me. Nowhere is there the word "screenplay." Nowhere is my name. I was new. I didn't realize that it was par for the course. And I was furious. I fired off a telegram to the editor of *Newsweek.* He not only printed my wire, he printed a box in a subsequent issue apologizing to me for not having included my name in the review. That was just the beginning.

I used to phone film critics. I'd get their home telephone numbers. One poor lady who used to review for a local evening paper in L. A. wrote this great review for *North by Northwest.* Not a mention of me. I called her at home. She started *weeping* on the telephone. "What can I do? You're so right. Let me write something immediately."

Ernest Lehman

No. I said I didn't want her to write something immediately, but to remember, the next time she reviewed a picture, that pictures are *written* as well as acted and directed and photographed and edited and scored and all that. The screenwriter determines what scenes are in and what scenes are out; decides whether that bit of information is dramatized or just referred to; whether it takes place on or off screen. There are a million decisions made by the screenwriter. When he's adapting someone else's work, he's the one who looks at a sequence in the book or play and decides: "It won't work in the movie. We'll just have to forget it. Or change it from a ship to a plane." The director doesn't say, "I've got an idea. Let's shoot the scene in a plane instead of a boat." No, it's written. It's *written.*

I remember the *Newsweek* review said, "Director Robert Wise then moves his drama to the boardroom for the final sequence," and I said to myself: "No. The director doesn't move the drama to the boardroom; the screenwriter moves it to the boardroom because that's where he and/or the novelist thinks it should be." All those decisions are screenplay decisions, and those reviewers simply don't know it. Some of them still don't even know how pictures are made.

BRADY: The situation seems to be changing for the better today.

LEHMAN: Yes. I think so. Screenwriters like Bill Goldman certainly have become very well known. Paul Schrader with a slew of startling pictures also got to be well known. But still, largely only in the industry. They still are probably Bill Who and Paul Who to the public at large. Me? I have *two* names—Ernie Who and Ernest Who.

The public knows more about the director than anyone else because film critics, in order to be able to write reviews, apparently have to personalize and channel the creative forces into one persona. It's just too difficult for them, or too much work for them, to review a film and find out who did what to whom. They make it easier for themselves by unconsciously falling into the *auteur* theory, and that perpetuates the *auteur* theory, and it then becomes an untrue fact of life. So when films are listed in various magazines, it's Robert Altman's So-and-So and John Huston's So-and-So and George Roy Hill's So-and-So—insert the title. The magazines don't say So-and-So, directed by Hal Ashby, written by So-and-So and produced by So-and-So. It's the director's film. Magazines use the directorial possessive almost exclusively.

I used to play a little trick on interviewers. I would say: There was this writer and he read a novel which he thought lent itself very well to the medium and he decided to take an option on it and went to a producer and the producer was enthusiastic, too. And they got a director who was interested. So the writer took a ream of paper and a typewriter and locked himself in his study for three or four months and wrote a first draft—and the producer and director were *very* enthusiastic. Anyway, to make a long story short, the script was produced and, oh, they got this star and they got that star, and it was a smash hit. Then I'd say to the interviewer: What am I talking about now? Am I talking about a *movie?* Or am I talking about *Teahouse of the August Moon* on the *stage?* Or am I talking about Goodrich and Hackett's stage adaptation of *The Diary of Anne Frank?* Or am I talking about the musical play that was done, based on the novel *7½ Cents* and called *Pajama Game?* I had made the interviewer think I was talking about a movie. See, I was trying to show him there really is not all that much difference between writing a movie and writing a play, because in both cases you wind up with a dramatic manuscript which is then *produced*—the difference being that in movies it is photographed and edited and scored. But the *writing* process is very much the same. Now, I wasn't even talking about *original* screenplays, because with them it's even *more* similar to writing a play.

BRADY: Isn't it true, though, that in the theater the playwright has approval of script changes that a screenwriter would not have?

LEHMAN: That's true. Also, the playwright can't be replaced or rewritten without this approval. And the actors can't change their lines without his approval. But I was just trying to convince this journalist that there isn't that much difference in the *creative process* of writing the two forms of drama, except that one of them is to be put on the screen.

BRADY: Though you have produced and directed films, do you take yourself by and large as a *writer*?

LEHMAN: Yes, of course. (pp. 187-90)

BRADY: You've done some landmark films. Which one gave you the most satisfaction as a script and as a film?

LEHMAN: *Somebody Up There Likes Me* with *North by Northwest* a strong second.

BRADY: Why would *Somebody* share honors with *North by Northwest?* Is a good adaptation of a book as rewarding to do as an original?

LEHMAN: Well, you'd have to read Rocky Graziano's book before you'd know whether I had done a *good* adaptation. But I liked the screenplay because I had done research and felt I had found the *real* story of Rocky, which I didn't feel was totally revealed in his autobiography. Nevertheless, some of my screenplay was fiction, you know. I just had to make some of it up in order to make the drama work, because the district attorney of New York City didn't want to cooperate with me. A couple of assistant DA's threatened to sue me *and* MGM if we tried to portray them in any way. And the whole third act depended upon Rocky losing his boxing license. I still see it on TV and still think it's a good picture and a good script.

BRADY: What sort of research did you do for *Somebody Up There Likes Me?* Did you know much about boxing previous to that screenplay?

LEHMAN: I had never seen a professional fight before I started on that film. I had listened to them on the radio, but I had never seen one. I went to Stillman's Gym in New York and hung around. Rocky took me to all the places he had lived in, and the places he had robbed. I went to his local police station and had long sessions with DA Frank Hogan, and with the very people who had tried to prosecute Rocky, including the assistant DA. I talked to Rocky's wife, because I wanted to find out what his relationship had been with his father, which I had suspected was at the root of his delinquent criminal life. That's the

kind of research I did. Oh yes, I went to a couple of professional fights, too. And hated them.

BRADY: From what you . . . are saying now about *Somebody Up There Likes Me,* it sounds as if you take the title and use it as an umbrella when adapting, but that one is not likely to find too many lines from the original property in the script.

LEHMAN: That's accurate only if the property I'm working on doesn't have the kind of material that, in my opinion, would make for a good film. It wasn't true of *West Side Story,* and it wasn't true of *Who's Afraid of Virginia Woolf?* There was an awful lot in those two plays that was brilliant on stage and equally brilliant when used for the screen version. I always regard myself as a person who stands guard over the original work: "No, I'm not going to take that out. It's *good.*" It was one of the reasons that Bob Wise was eager to have me do *West Side Story.* He felt that I wasn't going to throw anything out just to prove how good I was, that I had enough confidence in myself not to have to *prove* anything.

It's quite difficult when you adapt a famous work. There is a tendency to say, "I have to justify my existence," a tendency to say, "Look at what *I* did." Still and all, I do think I did my share to improve on the original works. Things I did with *West Side Story* people don't even know about. To me the picture is infinitely better-structured as a film drama from beginning to end, with proper places for the music, and things like that. *The Sound of Music* was a famous musical play, but its success in the theater was far more commerical than artistic, and I had to take drastic liberties with it to make it a movie. It's much better as a movie than it is on stage—in *my* opinion, of course.

Albee's work is unusual in that there are places where he departed from the dramatic line completely; yet his verbal music was so dazzling that it worked on the stage. But I felt you couldn't always get away with that in a film. I would take those detours out, or they would appear in another scene instead of where he had placed them. But people are not aware of those things, fortunately. The less the seams show, the better.

BRADY: What do you mean by verbal music?

LEHMAN: Dazzling language, dazzling ideas, very esoteric at times. Something brilliant, affecting an audience's subconscious. Sometimes they didn't even know why they were feeling the emotions that were overwhelming them. (pp. 195-97)

BRADY: As an adapter, do you experience any creative surges, or do you view what you do as a craftsmanlike job?

LEHMAN: No, I don't regard it as only a craftsmanlike job. I definitely wind up feeling that I am involved in as much of a creative endeavor as though I were writing something totally original. It gets to be the same kind of writing experience to me. Whether it is or isn't, that's the way it feels. In other words, if there happens to be a ten-page scene in a novel and I am writing it as a two-page scene for a script and I like only two lines of dialogue in the entire novel scene, I don't stop to say, "Oh, yeah, that line I'm putting down was written by John O'Hara." In fact, one of the tricks is to be able to use things from the source material and create new material and not show the seams—so that

Richard Burton and Elizabeth Taylor in the film version of Edward Albee's play Who's Afraid of Virginia Woolf?

you don't know where the novelist ends and the screen-writer begins. (pp. 216-17)

> *Ernest Lehman and John Brady, in an interview from* The Craft of the Screenwriter: Interviews with Six Celebrated Screenwriters *by John Brady, Simon and Schuster, 1981, pp. 177-247.*

Neil Simon   (Interview with John Brady)

[*Simon is one of the most popular playwrights in the modern American theater. His plays, many of which he has adapted for film, include* Barefoot in the Park *(1963),* The Odd Couple *(1963), and* The Sunshine Boys *(1972). He has also written a number of original screenplays. In the following excerpt from an interview, Simon discusses his alternating careers as playwright and screenwriter.*]

BRADY: What were your early screenwriting days like after all that early success on Broadway?

SIMON: Well, I made my reputation as a playwright, so it wasn't a matter of life or death to me with the movies, whether I made it or not, in the beginning. It was another outlet for me. I had already done *Barefoot in the Park* and

The Odd Couple as plays, so I was established. Still, I went through some depression. I was depressed when I saw *Come Blow Your Horn* as a movie, even though I didn't write it, because it was still part of my output. And I was depressed about some movies I did in the early days that I learned a great deal from.

I learned that I had better speak up and not turn over so much power to the director, which is a very difficult thing because in this town if you don't have any personal clout, that's what's going to happen to you. Writers are treated really as the low men on the totem pole. Not me, because I had a reputation that preceded me—but in the beginning it was still difficult. The studios had a lot more to say about the casting and the interpretation of a property, and I was also disappointed in my own work as a screenwriter. So I had to go through some apprenticeship years writing movies that I wasn't very happy with until I learned to do it right, just as I had spent all those years writing special material in nightclubs, working in television—making a living, but still learning my craft—so that by the time I got to Broadway, I knew a lot about writing for the stage. Not so with the movies.

I just sort of plunged in, and when I wrote that first movie, *After the Fox,* I thought I had a very funny, satirical, contemporary script. It got in the hands of Vittorio De Sica, though—whom I idolized and was so in awe of that I wouldn't dare say a word about what he was doing to the script—and I didn't understand what he was doing. It just seemed all wrong to me. I watched it and said, "This is a fiasco. This picture is never going to work." I used the experience as a learning device, and one of the things I learned is never do a movie with a man who doesn't speak English very well.

BRADY: I should think that some of the humor would be lost in translation.

SIMON: All of it. All of it.

BRADY: What happened?

SIMON: Well, I just rewrote the script completely. I rewrote it with De Sica's writer Cesare Zavattini, who wrote *The Bicycle Thief, Miracle in Milan* and many other brilliant films. Zavattini is a great social writer, a great social commentator. But I was not writing great social commentary. I was writing a contemporary farce with some satirical overtones about the making of foreign movies at the time. Zavattini and I literally collaborated on the screenplay, but neither of us spoke the other's language—so we had an interpreter in the room. The interpreter was a writer himself, so he didn't really interpret what we said; he just put down what he felt like writing.

The script became a mishmash, and Peter Sellers and I both wanted to get out in the middle of it. We both asked United Artists to let us out, and we would give them a movie free; but they said, "No, we think that between De Sica and you all, you can pull it out." Well, none of us did. But I learned from that one, and I learned from some of the others.

I learned from *Plaza Suite,* for example. I was very obstinate—because I consider myself essentially a playwright, I think. I thought I could take my plays and translate them to the screen with very few changes. What I got with *Plaza Suite* was a film version of the play, which is not as good as the play and not as good as most movies. I did that pretty much with *Last of the Red Hot Lovers,* too—left it so you're spending an hour and a half virtually in one room, and it becomes claustrophobic. I didn't open it up, and I was not being fair to myself about learning the craft of screenwriting. I think it's only been in the last six or seven years that I learned how to write a good screenplay.

BRADY: Are you now reevaluating some of your early work? When you were doing *Plaza Suite,* you must have had a pretty good measure of confidence.

SIMON: Well, obviously you don't sit down and write something and say, "I know this is bad, and I will learn from it years later." At the time I thought, "Yes, this is the right way to do it." What I disagreed with the studio on was having Walter Matthau play all three roles in that film. I said that won't work. You need three separate actors to give it some new input at least every thirty-five minutes. But Walter was adamant. That's the only way he would do the film, and the studio said Walter was the star. So they did it.

That's why I like the theater a lot better. One never has to make those kinds of compromises. I could do a play starring an unknown actor, unknown actresses, and have a big hit. That's almost impossible to do in films; at least

it was in those days. One can do it a little bit today; audiences are willing to accept it more.

BRADY: Yet *Plaza Suite* had the same actor in all three segments on stage. Why doesn't it work in film?

SIMON: As consummate an actor as Walter is, I don't think his judgment is always accurate. I think he cannot play the part that George C. Scott played on stage in the first act. I think that George is just better at it, whereas I think Walter is wonderful at farce. When I gave him *The Odd Couple,* Walter wanted to play the role of Felix (which Jack Lemmon eventually played). He said, "Oscar is too easy for me." I said, "If you want to act, act in somebody else's movie. I just want you to do what I think is the right character for you."

I think that the idea of one person playing six or seven roles in a film really went out years ago with Alec Guinness and Peter Sellers, too. It's just a gimmick that doesn't work and doesn't interest me. For example, in the play *California Suite* we used four actors to play all the various roles—four separate roles apiece in that play. But in the movie we used all new actors, and it was the right thing to do. I didn't keep it in one room. I opened it up all over Los Angeles, all over the Beverly Hills Hotel and its environs. It was an infinitely more successful movie.

BRADY: Did your personal involvement in *Chapter Two* make it difficult to "open up" the script for the movie version? Isn't that a bit like tampering with a precious memory?

SIMON: I no longer say, as I did earlier on, "How do I film this play?" I say, "I'm going to write a film. Now, what material from this play can I use to help tell the story of the movie that I am about to write?" I think of it in cinematic terms completely—going to various places and following the story. It was a lot easier with *Chapter Two,* actually, than with, say, *Plaza Suite,* because all the action in *Plaza Suite* takes place in one apartment. Same for *Red Hot Lovers.* The action in *Chapter Two,* though, occurs in various places offstage as a play: They come home from their honeymoon; he just gets picked up at the airport; they were playing softball in the park. These things are mentioned on the stage, so it was infinitely easier to do the screenplay because I could just go to those places. And it's strange, because the movie is forty minutes shorter than the play; yet I think there is more material in it. I was able to get more information in it because the stage often creates obligations you have to fulfill. For example, while two actors are off changing costumes for the next scene, you've got to do a scene waiting for them. I can't have a bare stage. Well, I don't have that problem in the movies. There were sections of material that I did not need from the play, so I just got rid of them. Many scenes with the secondary couple in *Chapter Two,* for example, were tossed. I just used them for key moments and for pushing the story and the main point ahead.

In the play, of course, the actual honeymoon occurs between acts. It's not seen on stage; yet it's a peak of interest. In the movie the honeymoon is one of the vital parts. I think it takes about twelve minutes of screen time in various stages, from the time they arrive for the honeymoon, then how well it's all going, then George's first encounter with someone who reminds him of the past, the haunting feeling of the past—to his first bit of antagonism and his guilt feelings about starting a new life while his wife is now deceased. All of this is graphically shown in the movie, which I couldn't do in the play. The play worked despite it, but I wish I'd had that opportunity.

BRADY: Why didn't you write it as a movie from the start?

SIMON: There is no way I would write that movie as an original script. I have to write the play first to get deeply into the characters. It's like making a big sketch of this canvas you are about to paint on later—and I don't mean that the play is really a test for a movie; to me the play is an entity in its own, and it's still what I prefer to do more than anything, because a play is so verbal. I can spend a lot of time learning about the characters. It's very hard to do that in a movie. That's why I've done few original screenplays: *The Goodbye Girl, The Heartbreak Kid, After the Fox, The Out-of-Towners, Murder by Death, The Cheap Detective;* and those last two are different—I almost had a form to copy. They were satires of other forms of moviemaking, and that's not as difficult. And *The Out-of-Towners* was really elongating an episode, though it was partly successful, I think. (pp. 320-24)

BRADY: What is the percentage of change in a play script . . . from first version to final performance?

SIMON: It depends on the specific play. I have changed anywhere from ten percent to sixty or seventy percent. For *Come Blow Your Horn* I went through twenty drafts, word for word; things were thrown out the window. Others I've had not an awful lot to do . . . three or four drafts, then rehearsal changes.

BRADY: Are start-up problems similar for writing a stage script and a screenplay?

SIMON: You have the same problems. You have to have a beginning, middle and end. The blueprint is always in my mind. It's a feeling. It's instinct. You just get a glimpse of something that's almost subliminal. It flashes by in your mind somewhere. I hear one sentence in my mind: *The Sunshine Boys*—the story of two old men who get into terrible battles trying to have a reunion to do their old act, and they eventually end up in the Old Actors Home. That's about as much as I know, and I start to write it. I know vaguely where I'm going, but I let the incidents unfold for themselves.

The only good piece of advice that I ever read about playwriting was from John Van Druten, who said, "Don't outline everything, because it makes the writing of the play a chore." In other words, the fun and discovery are already gone . . . and now you've just got to write it out. Some writers *must* blueprint, but I would find it a chore to do that and then just try to dialogue it. I'm in the middle of a new play now—got about two-thirds of it done— and I don't know *exactly* how it's going to end, but I know I'll get it, and if one ending doesn't work, I'll just keep writing until I get it. They're all like big jigsaw puzzles, and that's what the fun of it is. You just keep looking around for the pieces. And I am not afraid of the innumerable amounts of rewriting that one has to do. It's the process I grew up on. It's the only way I know how to do it.

I don't like working with other writers. I could not collaborate. I don't even like collaborating with the director. If a director says to me, "I really don't think this scene works," and if I see his point, I don't need any more discussion with him. I'll say, "I'll see you next week," and come back with another version. Sometimes that version is the right one, or the fifth version is the right one; but I don't like to collaborate with a director, because then it means seeing the play from his point of view, and I don't want it from his point of view. Almost all of my works are highly personal, and I want them from *my* point of view. What I want him to do is to tell me whether he believes it or not. If he says to me, "I don't believe this. It doesn't smack of the truth. It sounds like something you wrote rather than really experienced"—and I don't mean *lived,* but something that comes from the place inside us that is a common truth, which is what we all respond to when we see something good—then I say, "That's OK with me," and I have to go back and work on it. It's like getting to a funny line. If he says, "This is not funny to me," I can't keep knocking him over the head, saying, "I'm telling you it's funny." That's petty, because you find out soon enough when you get in front of an audience with a play. They tell you if it's funny or not.

The advantage of all of this for my screenplays is that I will often be able to explore a character much more in depth for the movie version. By being able to rework the play script, by evaluating all of what I've seen on the stage over, say, a two-year period, I can often say more with fewer words for the screenplay. And a camera going up close can reveal something in a character's face infinitely more than seven lines of stage dialogue, too. So you change the approach. (pp. 343-45)

BRADY: Do you consider your work on musicals as worthy a task as writing your other scripts?

SIMON: Not really, although I think that the work I did in *Promises* and *Little Me* and, particularly, *They're Playing Our Song* is good work. I don't put it on a par with *Chapter Two* or *The Odd Couple,* because you don't have as much time. You have, say, seventy pages of dialogue as opposed to a hundred and twenty pages; so, missing fifty pages, I'm not going to really tell the story as I want to. It's a craft more than anything else, and it's one of the hardest crafts. It is *much* harder than any play, *much* harder than any movie. I spent a year and a half writing a musical, and it was complete collaboration—numerous conferences with the songwriters, the director, the choreographer. It goes on and on. That's why I don't do them very often; and I will probably never do another one again. *They're Playing Our Song* was very gratifying, great fun. I enjoyed it. But it was a break between doing what I consider more personal projects.

BRADY: You once wrote a film for Marsha Mason and Burt Reynolds that was scratched, didn't you?

SIMON: That became *Seems Like Old Times,* with Chevy Chase, Goldie Hawn and Charles Grodin.

BRADY: When the casting changes, does that mean a heavy rewrite?

SIMON: I did a rewrite. Marsha wasn't right for it, in my opinion. I didn't think Marsha had the qualities that were needed for this girl. I think Marsha is best at things that require complete honesty of character. This was a farce. It needed somebody immediately identifiable with something that's funny. That's why I think Goldie Hawn was righter for it than Marsha.

BRADY: Is it true that you check your film casts with pre-rehearsal script readings?

SIMON: Yeah, it's been the case since I've been personally involved in my movies—about five years. I'm a great fan of Billy Wilder. We had lunch one day, and I mentioned to him that I was going to have a reading for this movie that I was about to go into rehearsal with. It was unheard of to Billy—to have a reading prior to the first day of rehearsal. I said it's something I discovered in playwriting about ten years ago. Why wait until the very first day of rehearsal to find out I'm going to be in trouble?

All I do is get the actors together and say, "You want to come over to my house Sunday? Let's just sit around and read it." This occurs three months before rehearsal, if I can get them that soon. We just sit around and read the script, and I say, "Thank you very much," and then I re-write it. I did that with *Goodbye Girl* three times before we ever started the movie, and by the time we got to rehearsal I was no longer in major trouble; most of the re-writing was done. But if we went into rehearsal or started to shoot the picture with the first script of *Goodbye Girl*, no way could I have saved it—because I did a month's re-writing on that film before it even began.

BRADY: What goes on during a reading? Do you sit there scribbling notes?

SIMON: I don't take a note. I just hear it. It's like I have a tape-recording machine in my head. I will be able to go over every single line of the script and tell you what works for me and what doesn't. Not only the lines, but entire sections—if they seem wrong, I throw them out, don't even listen to the lines there. A reading is like the first night with an audience when I do a play. I sit down with a pad and pencil and say I'm going to take notes on all the things that I like and don't, and I end up without a single note—because I've recorded it in my mind, and generally I can jump on it next day and improve the script.

I think that's a block a lot of writers have: They get no help from hearing their work read. They listen to it and say, "Well, we'll see when it gets in front of an audience." As for me, I like to anticipate all of that stuff. I rewrite a lot sooner. (pp. 349-51)

BRADY: Have any of your films been shot in chronological sequence? (p. 364)

SIMON: *The Goodbye Girl* was shot fairly much in continuity. I liked what I saw every day. I just thought we were making this tiny little movie.

BRADY: The characters are incredibly rich, though.

SIMON: Yes, but as you do just little bits and pieces, you don't see that richness. It takes development. I watch it now, and I say to myself, "That's really good," and even get a little awed by it. "That's hard work," I say to myself. "I don't think I could do that again." That's when you get scared—when you sit back at the typewriter and say, "My God, all of those *details* that I've got to try to get into something again."

Nobody—the best—Woody [Allen], anybody, ever really knows, ever is that positive. I am speaking for all of the good writers, all of the good directors, all of the good actors. You *should* have great self-doubt, because if you don't you become pompous, rigid, and you do not improve on the work. I know people like that. There was a writer friend of mine many, many years ago whose one piece of advice was, "Don't let the producer or the director change anything. You just tell them to go screw themselves. They don't know what they're talking about." It seemed a very rigid way of working. I said to myself, "It seems wrong to me. I want the input of everybody. I don't have to accept it, but I want to hear it." His attitude was no, his was the final authority and he was going to control everything. Well, that guy barely works today, and he was once extremely talented.

BRADY: You have to be a team player.

SIMON: Because it is a collaborative medium—both films and plays, as opposed to doing novels.

BRADY: And ultimately, how would you like to be remembered?

SIMON: As a good playwright. (p. 365)

Neil Simon and John Brady, in an interview from The Craft of the Screenwriter: Interviews with Six Celebrated Screenwriters *by John Brady, Simon and Schuster, 1981, pp. 312-65.*

Raymond Federman

[*Federman is an American fiction writer and critic. In the following essay, he analyzes Samuel Beckett's* Film *(1964), finding that this screenplay, like Beckett's work as a dramatist and prose writer, is to a significant extent concerned with the essential nature of an artistic form, in this instance cinematic form, and exemplifies an increasing artistic alliance between literature and film.*]

Having led the novel form into an inextricable impasse whereby language itself is totally disrupted, having stripped the theater of its most essential elements to the point of literally burying the characters in the ground or in giant urns, having even experimented with the obsolete form of the radio play in an effort to silence sound, it was inevitable that Samuel Beckett should turn to the cinema, and eventually, as he did more recently, to television.

If Beckett's last novel, *How It Is*, can be read as an ultimate indictment of fiction in its failure to communicate reality with words, and his most recent play (appropriately entitled *Play*, and just made into a film under the direction of Rumanian-born Mariu Karmitz) can be interpreted as a statement of the theater's failure to create illusion through gestures and speech, then Beckett's first scenario, *Film*, consistent with the Beckettian aesthetic system of destruction and purification, represents an attempt to expose one of the cinema's most flagrant failings today: the exploitation of sound, action, plot, and message to the detriment of the visual image.

Though Beckett may stand here in opposition to the avant-garde cinema whose main tendency is, in fact, to achieve a confusion of the multiple elements of the film, his attempt, as with his theater and fiction, is to return to the essence of the medium. This in itself represents an avant-garde effort. For as Beckett himself has expressed it in one of the few striking statements he has made about the creative process: "A step forward is, by definition, a step backward." Therefore, in this first cinematographic venture, Beckett incorporates all the themes and devices he has been exploiting over and over again for more than thirty years, and by simply transposing these to a new medium arrives at a critical judgment of the cinema.

Film, a 24-minute piece, featuring "the funnyman who never smiled," Buster Keaton, is a dialogueless experiment whose main theme is the picture itself, that is to say, vision within vision. Expretly directed by Alan Schneider, who is responsible for some of the best Beckett productions staged in this country, the film was the first production of Evergreen Theater, a subsidiary of Grove Press, whose entry into the motion picture field is, according to Barney Rosset (chief editor of Grove Press and head of Evergreen Theater) "a logical extension of our activity as publisher of many of the leading contemporary playwrights and novelists." It coincides with two important developments in the world of literature and film which tend to bring the two closer together: the growing interest among many important writers in the film as a means of artistic expression, and a growing world-wide audience for creative films which emphasizes the shift of the creative role toward the writer. *Film* will eventually form part of a trilogy, with the other scenarios by Eugene Ionesco and Harold Pinter.

Though eagerly awaited by Beckett's admirers, *Film* received a rather cold and negative reception at the Third New York Film Festival both from audience and reviewers. In general, it was found "vacuous and pretentious," too simple, too obvious in its symbolism. One critic went so far as to say that it was "a miserable and morbid exercise"—though the film received several awards at European film festivals. Nevertheless, it is true that anyone even vaguely familiar with Beckett's work in the novel or in the drama might expect a deeper, less naïve, and above all less *obvious* piece of work, simply because Samuel Beckett has acquired the false reputation of being a complex writer; but it is also true that by demanding depth, sophistication, obscure meaning, and intellectual complexity from him we are failing to recognize the basic purpose of his art. For what most people still refuse to accept in all of Beckett's work, and perhaps failed to grasp in this film, is the fact that his entire artistic production is based on the exploitation of the commonplace, the banal, the cliché, in other words, the obvious, or in Beckett's own terms: "The nothing new."

In 1949, in a series of dialogues on painting with art critic Georges Duthuit (published in *Transition*), Beckett made some revealing statements about the dilemma of the artist and art in modern society. Emphasizing that there is nothing new to paint or to say, he defends in a subtle dialectical argument the position of the artist who, even though aware that there is "nothing to express, nothing with which to express, nothing from which to express, no power to express, no desire to express, together with the obligation to express," nonetheless continues to create an art " . . . weary of its puny exploits, weary of pretending to be able, of doing a little better than the same old thing, of going a little further along the same dreary road."

Only if one accepts this paradoxical condition can one understand Beckett's aesthetic position, and more particularly the purpose of the present film. It is by returning to the most basic forms of expression, to the primary sources of any artistic medium (in the case of the cinema to the moving image itself and its silent origin), Beckett seems to suggest, that art can be renewed. Thus, in reference to his own work, to the futility of his own creative efforts, he stated in a recent interview: "I am working with *impotence* and *ignorance.*" This agony of artistic expression is the theme Beckett has reiterated throughout his work. Why then should we expect from his first film more than what has enabled him to achieve greatness and originality in his novels and plays—basically, the stubborn exploitation of impotence and ignorance, and consequently of artistic failure?

We the quasi-sophisticated theater-going audience, the faithfuls of art films, too often expect from writers such as Beckett messages of deep philosophic meaning, even if we must ourselves impose these values on the work. We are no longer satisfied with the obvious, and yet what seemed so "obvious" in this film is, in fact, its main theme: the simple reaffirmation of the essence of cinema, that is to say, visual expression of life and movement through photographic manipulation. If we accept this as the basic theme, we can then accept *Film* as a work of art which exploits its own substance so as to reveal its own limitation and failure. Therein lies the originality and meaning of Beckett's scenario.

Essentially, all of Beckett's work, in the novel as well as in the drama, exploits its own medium, its own creative elements, as its central subject. The novels of Beckett are all stories of a writer (narrator-hero) who struggles helplessly with the process of putting words together in order to fabricate a fraudulent reality, that of his own fictitious existence within a make-believe world. The theater of Beckett, almost always in the form of a play within a play, reveals in tragicomic terms the *play*-ful and futile process of improvising with words and gestures a theatrical illusion. It is, therefore, logical that Beckett's first film should use as its subject its own essence: visual perception. In other words, if Beckett's concern in the novel is to expose the agony of linguistic expression, and in the theater to reveal the agony of verbal and gestic expression, then, turning to motion pictures, the message he wants to impart is what he himself defines in the screenplay as "the agony of perceivedness."

The theme of *Film,* visual perception, is explicitly sustained throughout by three striking devices: the absence of sound, the obsessive presence of eyes (human, animal, and symbolic), and a limited viewing-angle for the camera-eye which cannot exceed a 45° angle of vision—and for the greater part of the film sees the protagonist strictly from the back. This perceptual limitation is exploited even further by the use of different degrees of luminosity in some images, as well as an increasing blurriness intended to reveal the gradual blindness of the protagonist. Thus Beckett emphasizes that the cinema should primarily appeal to the sense of sight, and only secondarily to the sense of hearing or even to the intellect. For this reason, not only does he eliminate sound in favor of visual images, but he renders the meaning of his script so simple, so apparent that the story itself becomes trivial, almost irrelevant.

This over-simplification of the plot's meaning was obvious

to everyone who saw the film, and was summed up by *Time* in these words:

> It is a stark, black-and-white portrait of an old man who awaits death in a small, lonely room. Seeking absolute solitude, he turns out his cat and dog, closes the curtains, covers the parrot cage and gold-fish bowl with his coat, and blacks out the room's only mirror. Finally, he destroys the last reference to the world in which he has lived, a packet of old photographs. But he cannot escape himself, and as he lifts his eyes to the barren wall before him, he comes face to face with the image of his own dead-pan likeness, with a patch over one blind eye.

Indeed, a very banal, commonplace story whose symbolic meaning is self-evident, a story which Beckett has been telling and retelling with comic stubbornness in his novels, in his plays, and now in this film. In fact, *Film* is so reminiscent of *Krapp's Last Tape* that one cannot fail to relate the two works. But the interest here does not lie in the story, nor does it lie in the obvious symbolism or the pathetic condition of the protagonist. It rests essentially on what the *Time* reviewer seems to have failed to *see*, even though inadvertently he stresses it in his summary: Beckett's obsessive use of the eye as the symbol of perception.

This emphasis on visual perception is clearly established at the beginning of the film by a close-up of a withered human eye which stares grotesquely toward the audience. This enormous eye announces the theme. As it picks up the action, it functions both as the perception of the camera-spectator in pursuit of the protagonist, and as the perception of the protagonist in pursuit of himself. This eye follows the main character, Buster Keaton, as he moves clumsily with his back to the camera through three different settings: a street scene, a staircase, and a room. Only at the end of the last sequence does his face come in full view of the camera, in that moment of revelation when he encounters his own self—that tortured image against the wall, with a patch over one blind eye.

From the start of the film, then, an angle of vision ("angle of immunity" Beckett calls it in the script) is established which does not permit the audience a full view of the protagonist. Consequently, he cannot become the "perceiver" but must remain the "perceived object" viewed only from behind at an angle never exceeding 45°. Conventionally, the viewer of a film sees more than the characters in the film. One might say that the spectator has a total perception of the action whereas the characters have a partial perception. In *Film*, however, since the field of vision of the camera-eye never exceeds that of the protagonist, the viewer is denied total perception. It is this restricted "angle of immunity" which creates the "agony of perceivedness."

One of the main objections to this film, however, may result from the fact that the two different perceptions are not clearly established, or too late in the last sequence. Beckett was aware of the difficulty involved here when he specified in his script that

> throughout first two parts all perception is E's. E is the camera. But in third part there is O's perception (O being the protagonist) of the room and contents and at the same time E's continued perception of O. This poses a problem of images which I cannot solve without technical help.

Alan Schneider and Boris Kaufman tried to resolve this difficulty by following Beckett's own suggestion that "this difference of quality might perhaps be sought in different degrees of development, the passage from the one to the other being from greater to lesser and lesser to greater definition of luminosity." Technically this was not totally successful because the dual perception was never clearly drawn at the beginning of the film. Though the "agony of perceivedness" as expressed by Buster Keaton and as felt by the viewer represents two separate entities which converge toward a unified anguish, it remains somewhat gratuitous. Beckett anticipated this when he stated: "I feel that any attempt to express them [the two separate perceptions] in simultaneity (composite images, double frame, superimposition, etc.) must prove unsatisfactory."

Unable to gain a total view of the character, the spectator is placed in a strained perspective which he cannot exceed either visually or mentally. Similarly, the actor himself is restricted both in his movements and actions as he is forced to remain within the angle of immunity. The dual perception contained in the eye viewing the object in flight, and in the object seeking to affirm its own perception of the self, is a limited and anguished vision which cannot fully apprehend what it sees and what it seeks. Though Buster Keaton excels in this performance, particularly since he can only express his perceptual anguish through the motions of his half-hidden body, his attempt (and of course that of the director) to have both visions coincide remains ambiguous. Beckett understood the problem when he explained in the script that the protago-

Buster Keaton and Samuel Beckett on the set of Beckett's Film.

nist is in flight while the viewer is in pursuit, and that "it will not be clear until the end of the film that the pursuing perceiver is not extraneous but the self." For the viewer to grasp this requires on his part an unusual effort of acceptance of the camera-eye with the vision of the protagonist seen objectively and separately by the same camera-eye. But this is in fact the main point of this film, or for that matter of all Beckett's work: to develop in the reader or spectator an extra sense of perception.

While the man rushes through the first two sequences of the film (the street and the staircase that lead to the room) he encounters three other human beings. In the street he stumbles into an old couple who, upon viewing his face, react with a fearful expression toward the camera. A similar reaction of anguish occurs when an old flower-seller in the staircase sees the protagonist from the front. It seems then that what the spectator is not permitted to view causes visual agony for those facing the other side.

In the room, the protagonist is no longer subjected to human sight (except of course for the eye of the camera which, as suggested by the opening shot, is human). He now enters the field of vision of animals and symbolic eyes. He is seen by the eyes of a cat, a dog, a parrot, a gold fish, and symbolically by the eyes of a deity in a picture on the wall, by the reflection of a mirror, by the light of the window, and even by two carved holes in the back of a rocking-chair, which suggest two eyes. Obviously disturbed by these animal and inanimate perceivers, he feverishly eliminates them one by one. In a stylized sequence typical of Beckettian comedy, he puts out the cat and dog, covers the parrot and goldfish with his coat, closes the curtains, places a blanket over the mirror, tears the picture on the wall, and then sits down in the chair thus covering with his back the two eye-like holes.

All this he performs with his back to the camera. However, there remains one last set of eyes which stare at him from his past, those of the people and of himself at various stages of life in the old photographs he now examines. These relics of his past existence represent another perceptual dimension in the film, a kind of play within the play, or in this case pictures within the picture. In great distress he destroys the photographs, and seemingly out of sight now of all extraneous perception, he leans back in the chair to be confronted with his own inner self, his own inner vision. Projected on the wall before him appears his own image, seen for the first time from the front, thus revealing his half-blindness.

The various perceptions which have been established throughout the film as distinct perspectives are now gathered into one and interiorized into the protagonist. This new and concentrated vision results, however, in a series of blurred images which contrast sharply with the clarity of the viewer's perception. While the camera and the spectator have a clear and distinct view, though limited by its angle, the total inner vision of the protagonist is blurred and unprecise. What Beckett suggests here, and what Boris Kaufman achieves through his excellent photography, is a visual ambivalence which stresses and exposes the tragic limitations of external and internal vision, or as Beckett explains in the introduction of his script: "It is a search of non-being in flight from extraneous perception breaking down in inescapability of self-perception."

By exposing the imperfection of the eye, and by reducing the meaning of his plot to self-evidence, Beckett forces the viewer to concentrate on the images themselves, however restricted these may be. But he also uses another device to reinforce his purpose: the absence of sound. The film is silent except for one startling sound which, paradoxically, accentuates the silence. It is a soft "sssh" spoken in the first sequence by the woman in the couple as she silences her male companion who was about to speak (or scream) when the half-blind protagonist stumbles into them. Forbidden to express his inner reaction in words he stares agonizingly, mouth gaping, into the camera. The same expression appears on the face of the flower-girl, when, unable to express her terror verbally, she transfers this fear to her eyes. The silent spectator in his seat, involved with the images on the screen, is also made to endure the uneasiness and frustration of the situation as he is repeatedly deprived of a clear and full view of the protagonist.

One can conclude, therefore, that the film's purpose is to show the ambiguity of perception, which is shared both by the perceiver and that which is perceived. The perceiver is first represented by the camera-eye and the audience, shifts momentarily to the other three characters in the film, then to the animals, and so on, to become finally the inner vision of the protagonist. Beckett implies by this technique that the "agony of perceivedness" results from the fact of being seen and yet not being able to apprehend that vision, and, moreover, from seeing and not being able to communicate what is seen. In other words, as with all his other works, Beckett once again exposes not only the limitations of the art form he uses, but also the human limitations.

The novel cannot truly pass for reality, the theater is unable to create believable illusion, and the cinema, which essentially should communicate with the viewer simply through a series of moving images, must rely on sound or other devices to achieve its primary goal. Though it is true that for more than thirty years the cinema did communicate meaning solely through images, and that it is generally agreed that the most powerful and truly cinematic moments are not reliant upon dialogue or sound, nonetheless, most film-makers today ignore the basic communicative power of the image. Too often, in fact, as is the case in experimental films which emphasize photographic manipulation, the images are gratuitous and irrelevant to the whole film. Visual perception alone (as exemplified in *Film*) results in frustration and failure. This is indeed a paradoxical process of creation, but a process to which Beckett has remained stubbornly faithful in his effort to create works of art which contain their own critical and analytical judgment. As one of Beckett's own creator-heroes proclaims: to make of failure "a howling success." (pp. 275-83)

Raymond Federman, in an extract in Samuel Beckett: The Critical Heritage, *edited by Lawrence Graver and Raymond Federman, Routledge & Kegan Paul, 1979, pp. 275-83.*

GENRE LITERATURE/GENRE FILM

Edward D. Hoch

[*Hoch is an American writer of detective fiction. In the following excerpt, he surveys film adaptations of works of mystery and detective fiction.*]

I've learned a great deal about television and movie adaptations since my first short story was dramatized on the old *Alfred Hitchcock Show* back in 1965. My stories have been done well and done poorly, rendered faithfully and twisted completely out of shape. Television and the movies are like that.

Perhaps the first mystery writer to suffer indignities at the hands of the film adapters was Sir Arthur Conan Doyle, whose Sherlock Holmes was portrayed in a short film as early as 1903, the same year as that pioneering narrative film *The Great Train Robbery*. Movies in those days generally ran ten minutes or less, and it's unfair to begin a critical review of screen adaptations with such a preliminary period.

But by the following decade, at least one of the pet peeves of mystery writers and readers alike had surfaced for the first time on screen. The film version of a classic detective novel had omitted the author's detective! A silent 1915 version of *The Moonstone* by Wilkie Collins eliminated Sergeant Cuff. In the years that followed, this sort of tampering with an author's creation was to become all too commonplace. To cite just two of many examples, the Sam Spade character was called Ted Shayne in a 1936 version of Dashiell Hammett's *The Maltese Falcon,* which we'll discuss later, and Ellery Queen is absent from an otherwise reasonably faithful adaptation of Queen's *Ten Days' Wonder,* released in 1972.

Happily, no one has yet attempted a film version of *The Hound of the Baskervilles* without Sherlock Holmes, but how is it that such classic detective characters as Sam Spade and Ellery Queen can be so easily omitted? The answer lies in the fact that the screen and the printed page are two different media. In adapting a published short story or novel for the screen, certain liberties must necessarily be taken. For one thing, the average mystery novel contains many more pages than the average feature-length film script.

In deciding what stays and what goes in an adaptation, the screenwriter must be granted a certain amount of leeway. The budget of the film, the director's needs, and even the star's wishes are factors to be considered. It's not surprising, therefore, that the standard contract for a film or television sale grants the producer the right to make any necessary changes in the author's creation. It's extremely rare for an author to have any control whatsoever over the final screen version of his or her book—even when that book has been a bestseller—unless the author has an actual financial interest in the production.

In fact, even the screenwriter loses control once the script of the adaptation leaves the typewriter. It may be altered or completely rewritten by others, whole pages or scenes may be scrapped by the director during filming, and the final cut of the film—often dictated by the distributor—may not please the director. The original author, at the start of a long chain of creative decisions, is forgotten. (Cornell Woolrich was not even invited to the opening of the popular film version of *Rear Window.*)

But this brings us to another question. If the original author seems so expendable in the scheme of things, why is he or she necessary at all? Why purchase a property that is to be changed and rewritten, often to the point where it bears little or no resemblance to the original? Take the case of Dashiell Hammett's first novel, *Red Harvest* (1929). The book is a hard, tough private eye novel in which the nameless Continental Op cleans up a corrupt town after more than a score of murders. It was filmed by Paramount within a year after publication, but this 1930 movie version, *Roadhouse Nights,* was a comedy-melodrama with Charles Ruggles, Helen Morgan, and Jimmy Durante that bore no resemblance to the original source.

Obviously, a film company does not pay relatively large sums of money for a book it has no intention of using, but as was pointed out earlier, a great many things can change along the way. In this instance, perhaps it was the casting that played a large part in the direction taken by the final story line.

Hammett's second novel, *The Dain Curse* (1929), fared much better when it was finally filmed as a television mini-series in 1978. The poorest of the author's five novels and the only one not previously filmed, it had the advantage of nearly five hours of running time to help make sense out of a complicated plot line. Some critics thought this was far too long for the material, but at least the finished product was reasonably faithful to its source.

The mini-series, a relatively recent development during television's past decade, has provided an effective solution to the problem of translating the countless characters and events of a long novel to the screen. Especially in the hands of British producers, with their large pools of fine acting talent, adaptations of classic novels—both mystery and mainstream—were able to win both ratings and awards during the 1970s. From Collins's *The Moonstone* through the novels of Dorothy L. Sayers and up to John Le Carré's highly contemporary *Tinker, Tailor, Soldier, Spy,* the British mini-series did very well by the classic mystery.

But to return to the films of the pre-World War II years, it is with the three versions of Hammett's *The Maltese Falcon* that both the problems and the possibilities of screen adaptation can be most fully studied. After publication of the novel in book form during 1930, it quickly sold to Warner Brothers for a 1931 film starring Ricardo Cortez and Bebe Daniels. This first version of *The Maltese Falcon* was a reasonably straightforward rendition of the book, although it lacked any great distinction in directing or acting.

When Warner decided to remake the film five years later, they naturally needed a different title and certain superficial plot and character changes. The 1936 film was called *Satan Met a Lady* and starred Warren William as a more debonair detective named Ted Shayne. Bette Davis costarred in the role later made famous by Mary Astor. The falcon statue became a horn filled with jewels, and the menacing "fat man" became a hulking old woman.

This film version met with little more success than the first, and five years later Warner tried it once more. This time, with John Huston directing Humphrey Bogart and Mary Astor in the lead roles and with fine support from Sydney Greenstreet, Peter Lorre, and Elisha Cook, Jr., a film classic was born. A close comparison of Hammett's novel with the film or with Richard J. Anobile's book reconstruction by means of fourteen hundred frame blow-ups (*The Maltese Falcon,* Film Classics Library, Avon/Flare Books, 1974) shows how closely Huston followed the source both in the writing and the direction. (Huston wrote his own screenplay for the film.)

Compare, for example, the end of chapter 4 and chapter 5 in the book with the film scene in which Joel Cairo (Lorre) comes to Spade's office for the first time and pulls a gun on him twice. The dialogue and movements of the characters are almost identical, and even the contents of Cairo's pockets are exactly as described by Hammett. Again and again the film echoes the novel, down to the smallest detail. This is a faithfulness of adaptation rarely seen today, and it played no small part in the lasting fame of Huston's film. Even today *The Maltese Falcon* remains one of the best adaptations of a classic mystery novel to be put on the screen.

One minor change does come at the very end of the film. The police indicate to Spade that they have arrested Gutman—the "fat man"—and the others. In the book, they report that Gutman has been killed by Wilmer, the young hood he tried to double-cross.

Continuing with Dashiell Hammett's novels for the moment, we find two versions of *The Glass Key* (1935 and 1942) and, more significantly, the first of the Thin Man series. MGM's 1934 production of *The Thin Man* warrants our attention for a number of reasons. It is perhaps the best example of Hollywood's taking a detective character—or team, in this case—that appeared in a single book and creating a series from it.

As most mystery readers know, the title *The Thin Man* is not a reference to detective Nick Charles but to the murder victim, an inventor who is missing as the book and film open. The film proved such an instant success with the public that five more adventures of Nick and Nora followed: *After the Thin Man* (1936), *Another Thin Man* (1939), *Shadow of the Thin Man* (1941), *The Thin Man Goes Home* (1944), and finally *Son of the Thin Man* (1947). "The Thin Man" had come to mean Nick Charles in the public mind, even though actor William Powell was not particularly slim.

But more interesting for this study is the fact that the films continued on from the single original work. Hammett contributed the original story idea for the second film, and the third one was a reworking of one of his pulp tales about the Continental Op ("The Farewell Murder"), but he took no part at all in the three films that followed. In this era of the 1930s and 1940s, when urban film palaces generally opened a new double bill each week, Hollywood produced far more movies than at present. At least half of them were so-called B pictures, running a little over an hour and generally having mystery or Western plots. Although the Thin Man series were all A films, playing at the top of the bill, most other mystery series of the period were second features. In an effort to fill this spot on the bill with a cons-tant stream of new pictures, studios naturally turned to series, just as television was to do a decade later.

Nick and Nora Charles were not the only characters stretched far beyond their creator's single work. A lengthy Boston Blackie series grew from one book of connected short stories by an ex-convict, Jack Boyle. Some sixteen films about the Falcon originated in a single Michael Arlen short story, "Gay Falcon," in a 1940 issue of *Town & Country* magazine. And series about reformed crook Jimmy Valentine and Western outlaw the Cisco Kid each had their origins in a single short story by O. Henry. It's interesting to note that in all four of these cases the screen presentation of the character is softened from the hard-boiled original.

Not only was a character softened and made more likable for a series run, when circumstances demanded, he could even be killed off. The Falcon became the only American series detective ever to die on screen when actor George Sanders relinquished the role to his real-life brother Tom Conway in a film titled, appropriately enough, *The Falcon's Brother.*

It would be easy to say that the contortions suffered by mystery plots and characters in this period were the result of inept screenplays turned out by Hollywood hacks. But as we have seen, one of the best of them, *The Maltese Falcon,* was the work of John Huston. And many lesser films were often the work of well-known mystery writers. Stuart Palmer and Craig Rice wrote some of the Falcon screenplays, and Dashiell Hammett and Raymond Chandler both worked in Hollywood on various projects.

Chandler's second novel, *Farewell, My Lovely* (1940), became in fact the basis for the third Falcon movie, *The Falcon Takes Over,* two years before the definitive screen version with Dick Powell as Philip Marlowe in *Murder My Sweet* (1944). Chandler's third novel, *The High Window* (1942), was likewise used as the plot for a Michael Shayne movie, *Time to Kill,* five years before George Montgomery starred as Marlowe in *The Brasher Doubloon* (1947).

The Marlowe films made in the 1940s from Chandler's first four novels generally treated their source material well, allowing for the quirks of individual directors, such as the "subjective camera" technique of Robert Montgomery in *Lady in the Lake* (1946). Two later remakes in the 1970s starred Robert Mitchum as Marlowe. *Farewell, My Lovely* was carefully set in 1940s Los Angeles, but *The Big Sleep* transported Marlowe to modern England, where the story suffered in spite of liberal use of Chandler's dialogue.

Another writer of the period much favored by Hollywood was James M. Cain. His short novel *Double Indemnity* was successfully filmed in 1944 with a screenplay by director Billy Wilder and Raymond Chandler that brought them an Academy Award nomination. This was quickly followed by a filming of Cain's novel *Mildred Pierce* (1941), its drama enhanced for the screen by a climatic murder that does not appear in the book.

Cain's best-known novel, *The Postman Always Rings Twice* (1934), was filmed in 1946 and again in 1981. Although the later version was able to be much more explicit sexually, it unaccountably ended with the accidental death of Cora, completely eliminating the final chapter of the novel and the ironic point of the movie's title.

The mid-1940s also saw the first and best of three film versions of Agatha Christie's classic novel *And Then There Were None*. Although the ending of the film is quite different from the book's conclusion, there is a very good reason. The book was first published in England in 1939 with the unfortunate title *Ten Little Niggers*. It proved so popular that Christie quickly converted it to an equally popular play, but for the stage a new ending was needed. The book's finale, with everyone on the island found murdered and a later letter from the killer explaining everything including his own suicide, did not make for good stage drama. The play ended, instead, with the lovers left alive, facing the murderer and outwitting him. The film *And Then There Were None,* although it used the book title of the American edition, was really a film version of the play. This play, also called *Ten Little Niggers* in London, was titled *Ten Little Indians* in its American version, a title which served for the two later film versions and for some later American editions of the novel.

Different as they are, both versions of the ending are excellent. It's a rare example of one ending working best in print while another works best on stage and screen. The main difference among the three film versions of the book and play is in the setting. Originally set on an isolated island, as it is in the 1945 film, the action moves to a snowbound castle in the Alps for the 1965 version and to a luxury hotel in the Iranian desert for the 1975 film.

The stage and film versions (1957) of Christie's excellent short story "Witness for the Prosecution" also differ from the printed version by continuing on for an extra page-and-a-half of dialogue and a dramatic final murder. The killer, who escapes punishment at the end of the short story, receives justice of a sort. Both versions work well, with the film version adding a final ironic bit of dialogue. (pp. 104-10)

We have seen how some mystery plots suffered at the hands of filmmakers, and perhaps this is the best place to treat the movies of Alfred Hitchcock, whose career spanned six decades and whose techniques often enhanced the books he chose to film.

One of the most famous spy novels of all time is John Buchan's *The Thirty-Nine Steps* (1915), a portrait of pre-World War I espionage that became Hitchcock's first undoubted masterpiece when he updated and filmed it in 1935. Yet the ending of the movie, in which the cryptic meaning of the title is revealed in a theater during Mr. Memory's act, does not appear in the book at all. The steps of the title, originally stairs down a Kentish cliffside by which spies could escape to a waiting submarine, are transformed into the name of a secret spy organization. Hitchcock and his screenwriter, Charles Bennett, also added a love story to accommodate Robert Donat's co-star, Madeleine Carroll. Despite the grumblings of British critics at such liberties, there can be little doubt that Buchan's fine novel was actually strengthened by Hitchcock's treatment. The plot is remembered today mainly in its popular film version, and first-time readers of the book are often surprised to find their favorite scenes missing.

Hitchcock's *The Lady Vanishes* (1938) was another that improved on the source material, a good but hardly outstanding novel by Ethel Lina White called *The Wheel Spins.* The fame of the movie caused the book to be retitled in most of its subsequent reprintings. But the director's habit of changing plot lines and altering endings was not always for the better. *Suspicion* (1941), which brought an Academy Award to actress Joan Fontaine, suffers from an ending which is a complete reversal of the book's conclusion. It must be said in Hitchcock's defense that he wanted to use the book's ending but was forced to bow to studio pressure. RKO was not about to let Cary Grant be portrayed as a wife murderer. (Some years earlier MGM did cast James Stewart as the killer in one of the Thin Man movies, but this was before his on-screen personality as a slow-speaking, honest hero had been firmly established.)

In 1951, Hitchcock took an excellent novel by Patricia Highsmith, *Strangers on a Train,* published the previous year, and transformed it into a masterpiece. By changing the protagonist's occupation from architect to tennis pro, the director was able to include a memorable suspense scene at a tennis match. True, the film ending is different from the book's and much more upbeat, but both versions satisfy.

Cornell Woolrich's fine novelette *Rear Window* became the basis for a 1954 Hitchcock film of the same title. Once again, love interest was added, this time in the person of Grace Kelly, and other characters like Thelma Ritter in the role of a visiting nurse helped to relieve the somewhat claustrophobic qualities of the original plot. But James Stewart as the protagonist confined to his room with a broken leg, who sees evidence of a murder through his rear window, is quite faithful to the spirit of the Woolrich original.

During the 1950s, the French mystery-writing team of Pierre Boileau and Thomas Narcejac produced two novels—*The Woman Who Was* (1954) and *The Living and the Dead* (1956)—which might have escaped notice in this country had it not been for a pair of remarkable screen adaptations. Both mysteries revolve around characters who may or may not be dead, and the film versions were eerie masterpieces of the director's art. The first became the classic 1954 French film *Diabolique,* directed by Henri-Georges Clouzot, and the second became the 1958 Hitchcock film *Vertigo.* For the mystery reader, the Hitchcock film contained a number of disappointments, mainly in the fact that the surprise solution is revealed too early, unlike *Diabolique,* which saves some of its shocks for the end. But there can be no faulting Hitchcock's technique, and some critics believe *Vertigo* to be his most fully realized masterpiece.

The most popular of Hitchcock's films was *Psycho* (1960), based on Robert Bloch's novel of the same title. Although the film sale earned Bloch very little money, it brought him lasting fame and proved to be a cinematic milestone, unleashing a decade of psychopathic horror films. The film is generally faithful to the book, although the book opens from the viewpoint of Norman Bates rather than Mary Crane, the girl who becomes the first victim. And the murder in the shower features a beheading that Hitchcock wisely omitted.

The next film from Hitchcock, and the last of his big successes, was *The Birds* (1963). Based on a short story by Daphne du Maurier that furnished little more than the general idea and ending, the film must really be viewed as the work of screenwriter Evan Hunter, with liberal doses of Hitchcockian technique.

As a general rule, in these films and all his others, Hitchcock took more liberties with his source material than most other directors. But the liberties were almost always concerned with technique or with the necessities of the marketplace. Although authors might complain about their treatment by Hollywood or the amount of money they were paid, it's doubtful that many of them were dissatisfied with the end result of a Hitchcock adaptation. In most cases he produced a film that was equal or superior to the story on which it was based.

The 1940s saw a number of other fine mystery films that helped establish the fame of the novels on which they were based. Vera Caspery's *Laura* was filmed in 1944 by Otto Preminger. While remaining faithful to the book, Preminger improved on it in several small ways—the hiding place of the murder weapon, for instance. The book, good as it is, suffers somewhat from an awkward use of shifting first-person narration, with first Waldo, then Lieutenant McPherson, and then Laura herself taking up the story. Such a technique was automatically eliminated from a film version, and the main plot line flowed more smoothly, helped immeasurably by fine background music.

Likewise, the 1944 film version of Eric Ambler's *The Mask of Dimitrios,* with a screenplay by American mystery writer Frank Gruber, helped establish Ambler as a master of international intrigue. It was especially remarkable for its time in that no romance was added to the plot to fit popular stars. The cast was composed mainly of character actors who carried the action very well. It was a faithful rendering that showed romance was not an essential element of the mystery-intrigue film.

Before we leave the 1940s, something should be said about the series detectives who occupied the bottom half of double bills. They all but disappeared in the 1950s with the coming of television, but in the postwar years they were still around. Some have been mentioned earlier in comments about series which grew from single stories, but there were others whose creators turned out a large body of adventures for them. Often they did not fare well on film. The movie Nick Carter, for instance, was an updated detective who bore not the slightest resemblance to the dime-novel sleuth of the same name. Basil Rathbone and Nigel Bruce made their first appearances as Sherlock Holmes and Dr. Watson in a fine 1939 version of *The Hound of the Baskervilles,* moodily faithful to the flavor if not the letter of Conan Doyle's text. But after one more period piece, *The Adventures of Sherlock Holmes,* the series was modernized, no doubt for budget reasons, and relegated to the bottom half of double bills. Although some of the resulting films were enjoyable enough, they weren't really about the Holmes and Watson we'd come to love through the books.

Charlie Chan fared somewhat better in the long series of films based on Earl Derr Biggers's character. Oddly enough, the early silent films taken from the first three novels altered and minimized Chan's role. He is listed twelfth in the cast of *The House without a Key,* a 1926 serial, and makes only a token appearance at the end of *Behind That Curtain* (1929). Even in *Charlie Chan Carries On,* the first Chan talking film and a close adaptation of the book, Warner Oland's Chan appears only in the final portion of the plot. This was, of course, true of most of Biggers's books, which usually opened with other characters carrying the action until Chan appeared. Only in the last of Biggers's six Chan novels, *Keeper of the Keys* (1932), does Charlie himself appear in the opening scene, although *Charlie Chan Carries On* opens with a Scotland Yard inspector receiving a letter from him. Thus, movie audiences usually saw more of the famed detective in the string of second features using the character—more, perhaps, than his creator had intended.

A full decade passed after the first of Leslie Charteris's books about the Saint before the character was translated to the screen in *The Saint in New York* (1938), but a string of generally successful films followed. A few were based on the Charteris books, but more used the character in new adventures in typical B picture fashion. (pp. 110-14)

The only mystery film with a series detective ever to win an Academy Award for best picture of the year was *In the Heat of the Night* (1967). (Other winners with more than a touch of mystery included *Rebecca, The Godfather,* and *The Sting.*) This first adventure of John Ball's black detective Virgil Tibbs made a compelling motion picture, even though some slight changes were made in the plot. Tibbs, a Pasadena homicide detective in the book, becomes a Philadelphia detective in the film. Since both book and movie are set in a small Southern town, Tibbs's home hardly seems that important, and one wonders why the change was made. Two later Tibbs films were not based on Ball's books and were less successful.

The Godfather was perhaps the best example during the 1970s of how a bestselling crime novel could be faithfully and powerfully adapted for the screen. If some incidents, flashbacks, and subplots had to be trimmed from the lengthy novel, these were mostly covered in the sequel to the film, and both films were combined for television as a mini-series. The author, Mario Puzo, and the viewers were well served by director Francis Ford Coppola, and one reason for this successful adaptation must surely lie in the fact that the original author and the director collaborated on the screenplay.

The spy film, which has had its ups and downs in Hollywood, always seems to be better made in England, just as the best espionage novelists are, almost without exception, British. Graham Greene fared especially well in adaptations of his work, possibly because he was often involved as screenwriter. Even since the filming of *Orient Express* in 1934, Greene's work has been turned into a series of evocative films. *This Gun For Hire* (1942), *The Ministry of Fear* (1943), *Confidential Agent* (1945), and *Brighton Rock* (1946) all captured the mood of the books admirably while sometimes deviating from individual plot points. Greene's own willingness to recognize the differences between books and films can be seen in comparing the printed and movie versions of *The Third Man,* Greene's 1949 masterpiece of intrigue in postwar Vienna. Greene wrote the short novel only as a preliminary step to the screenplay, without any intention of publishing it. Although he has written that the novelist "cannot help resenting many of the changes necessary for turning [his book] into a film play," Greene admits to making changes in *The Third Man* himself to better adapt it to the screen. And he credits Carol Reed, the director, with suggesting the proper downbeat ending to the film's romantic subplot.

But in one area the films of Greene's work have almost completely ignored their source material. The religious aspect of his characters, present even in books like *This Gun for Hire*, usually vanished from the film versions. Perhaps that is why a movie like *True Confessions* (1981), adapted by John Gregory Dunne and his wife Joan Didion from Dunne's novel, is so successful. It has the courage to mix religion and murder, a mixture that has frightened earlier generations of producers and editors.

If Greene's religious views frightened the filmmakers, so did his political views. The 1957 film version of *The Quiet American* had its ironic ending reemphasized in such a way that the film became anti-Communist while the book was anti-American, at least regarding America's role in the Far East. The latest Greene novel to be filmed, *The Human Factor,* follows its source exactly, although it is not as successful as the book.

But the spy films of the 1960s and 1970s were more likely to feature a James Bond sort of hero than the melancholy protagonists of Greene's books. As they increased in box-office popularity, the Bond films moved further away from Ian Fleming's novels into a world of stylized gimmickry where the goal seemed merely to top the sensations of the previous Bond film. Beginning with *Dr. No* in 1963, a faithful adaptation of the book, they progressed to *The Spy Who Loved Me, Moonraker,* and *For Your Eyes Only,* in which nothing of Fleming's books remained except the titles.

The harsh realism of *The Spy Who Came in from the Cold,* directed by Martin Ritt in 1965 from John Le Carré's best-selling novel, was a welcome relief from Bond. But although the well-acted film was faithful to its source, the harsh, grainy black-and-white photography added too much of a downbeat note to a story that hardly needed it. Le Carré was better served by the 1980 television mini-series of *Tinker, Tailor, Soldier, Spy.*

If the film versions of Fleming and Le Carré followed in the wake of their popular books, the movie adaptation of Len Deighton's *The Ipcress File* (1965) was so successful that it made Michael Caine a star and lifted the Deighton book from obscurity. Deighton's American publisher had bypassed his second novel, *Horse under Water,* and it remained unpublished in the United States for five years. But his third and fourth books, *Funeral in Berlin* (1964) and *The Billion Dollar Brain* (1966), proved popular here and were filmed as sequels to *The Ipcress File.* The main difference between the films and the books is that Deighton's nameless, reluctant spy became "Harry Palmer" on the screen. (p. 114-17)

It is a difficult thing for an author to see his or her work tampered with in another medium. Perhaps all of us share something of the resentment mentioned by Graham Greene [see excerpt below] when even necessary changes are made. We wish for a film as fine and as faithful to us as Huston's *Maltese Falcon* was to Hammett. More often, we end with something far removed from what we have written, and we watch the images on the screen as if they were the work of a stranger.

As indeed they are. (p. 117)

Edward D. Hoch, "Mystery Movies: Behind the Scenes," in The Murder Mystique: Crime Writers on Their Art, *edited by Lucy Freeman, 1982, pp. 104-17.*

S. S. Prawer

[*Prawer is a German-born English critic and educator specializing in German literature, particularly the work of Heinrich Heine. He is also the author of* Caligari's Children: The Film as Tale of Terror *(1980), which examines the masterpieces of Gothic cinema and theorizes on the function and significance of the artistic expression of horror. In the following excerpt from that study, Prawer explicates the interrelationship of films and literature devoted to horror, especially that provoked by what Sigmund Freud has termed* das Unheimliche *("the uncanny").*]

In October 1826, on a visit to London, the much-travelled Prince Hermann von Pückler-Muskau visited what he called "the English Opera." "The house," he reported in his anonymously published *Letters by a Dead Man* (1830),

> is neither elegant nor large, but the actors are not at all bad. There was no opera, however; instead, we had terrible melodramas. First *Frankenstein,* where a human being is made by magic, without female help—a manufacture that answers very ill; and then *The Vampire,* after the well-known tale falsely attributed to Lord Byron. The principal part in both was acted by Mr Cooke, who is distinguished by a handsome person, very skilful acting, and a remarkably distinguished and noble deportment. The playing was, indeed, admirable throughout, but the pieces were so stupid and nonsensical that it was impossible to sit out the performance. The heat, the exhalations, and the audience were not the most agreeable. Besides all this, the performance lasted from seven to half past twelve—too long for the best.

The double bill which Pückler-Muskau saw at the English Opera House on that October evening was to become, over a hundred years later, the most celebrated double bill in the history of the cinema: the reissue of James Whale's *Frankenstein* along with Tod Browning's *Dracula* (both originally shown separately in 1931). And as in the English theatre of the first half of the nineteenth so in the English-speaking cinema of the first half of the twentieth century: this double bill of man-made-monster- and vampire-tales marked the emergence of personable actors specializing in grotesque and macabre creations—though the task which Thomas Potter Cooke had shouldered by himself in the 1820s was divided between two players, Bela Lugosi and Boris Karloff, in the 1930s. That is not, however, what the promoters had originally envisaged: the role of Frankenstein's monster had been offered to Bela Lugosi after his triumph as Dracula; and when Lugosi refused it, the continuity between the two offerings which was brought to the theatrical double bill by T. P. Cooke was assured by giving key parts in both the films to Dwight Frye and Edward Van Sloan. The fact that both these actors had appeared with Lugosi in a celebrated Broadway production of *Dracula* may serve to remind us that there is a strong link between tales of terror on the stage and on the screen; that the American terror-film of the early thirties was preceded, and plainly influenced, by a spate of Broadway plays in which fantasy and terror were principal ingredients.

Both the melodramas which Pückler-Muskau saw were, of course, adaptations of prose-fictions published some years before: Mary Shelley's *Frankenstein: or, The Modern Prometheus* (1818) and Dr. John Polidori's *The Vampyre* (1819). The creation of these prose-fictions goes back to an evening in the Villa Deodati near Lake Geneva, where Byron, Shelley, Mary Shelley, and Polidori had stimulated their imagination by reading a volume of ghost-stories translated from the German, and had then competed with one another in inventing spooky tales of their own which embodied—in ways whose analysis is not our present concern—their own emotional and intellectual problems. Mary Shelley, indeed, when visiting London in 1823, had seen T. P. Cooke perform in the theatrical adaptation of her novel in the same English Opera House in which Pückler-Muskau saw those two "hideous melodramas" three years later. Her account of this experience presents further remarkable parallels with the experience she could have had, with the aid of Wells's time-machine, some one hundred and ten years later in the cinema. The list of dramatis personae included the entry "———, by Mr. T. Cooke"; the opening credits of Whale's film were to play a variation on that with the billing: "The Monster . . . ?" Frankenstein had acquired a servant, who rushes from the room when his master exclaims "it lives"; a first sketch, it would seem, for the part assumed in the film by Dwight Frye. The laboratory in which the monster is created was reached by a staircase leading off from the stage—and the great staircase leading to Frankenstein's tower laboratory was to be one of the most impressive features of the film's studio-built sets. Last but not least, Mary Shelley's description of Cooke's performance suggests some likeness to that of Boris Karloff: "his seeking, as it were, for support; his trying to grasp at the sounds he heard; all, indeed, he does was well imagined and executed." Cooke, however, does not seem to have hidden his "handsome person" and "distinguished and noble deportment" under as striking a make-up as his cinematic successor. Mary Shelley professed herself "much amused" by it all, and reports (as she might have reported of the film too) that "it appeared to excite a breathless eagerness in the audience."

These reports by Pückler-Muskau and Mary Shelley of their experiences in London theatres of the early nineteenth century are instructive on many counts. They show, first of all, that the urge to see "the film of the book," whose satisfaction then reacts back on to the sales of "the book of the film," is not a specifically twentieth-century phenomenon. Not content with reading *Frankenstein* in print, the nineteenth-century audience demanded, and received, several dramatic reworkings of its thrilling story. Indeed, among the most important sources of the *Dracula* and *Frankenstein* films of the early 1930s were theatrical adaptations by Hamilton Deane and Peggy Webling.

Novel, theatrical performance, and film are three very different media; and so much energy has been expended, in recent years, on working out the distinctions between them that our generation is less likely than any previous one to underestimate the part which the special possibilities and limitations of each medium plays in the shaping and reception of works of art. At the same time, however, it would be absurd to deny the continuities and links between the media. To say, for instance, as Julia Briggs does in *Night Visitors,* that the English ghost-story has been dead since 1914, without taking into account its remarkable transmigration into the cinema—think of *Thunder Rock, A Place of One's Own, The Halfway House, Dead of Night, The Queen of Spades, The Uninvited, The Haunting,* and *The Plague of the Zombies!*— is to court a charge of premature burial. The term "ghost-story," Julia Briggs pertinently reminds us, denotes in common usage "not only stories about ghosts, but about possession and demonic bargains, spirits other than those of the dead, including ghouls, vampires, werewolves, the 'swarths' of living men and the 'ghost-soul' or 'Doppelgänger'." One only has to look at this list to realize how many variations the film has played on each of its items, especially since the pioneering efforts of Paul Wegener, Stellan Rye, and Henrik Galeen in *The Student of Prague* (1913) and *The Golem* (1914). If these are indeed the subjects of the ghost-story, then that genre is alive and well and living in the cinema.

In speaking of the film as a "tale" of terror, I want to draw attention to its links with Hoffmann, Poe, and other purveyors of literary "tales" of this nature. . . . [However,] we must be ever mindful of the *dramatic* impact of films seen in the cinema; of the audience's sense, to use a formulation by Frank M. Fowler, that something "is *happening now,* something that cannot be stopped or accelerated [by the individual viewer], something with an assertive rhythm and dynamic of its own, something that normally demands to be experienced whole, well-nigh uninterrupted, commanding undivided attention from a body of people temporarily freed from . . . distraction."

Pückler-Muskau's and Mary Shelley's reports have served to alert us to the interaction between various media. That by no means exhausts their usefulness, however; they may also serve to illustrate three kinds of reaction which the terror-*film* was no less likely to elicit than the terror-*play.* One of these is the "breathless eagerness" Mary Shelley noticed in the audience—the unsophisticated response of seekers after theatrical thrills on which the adaptors and exhibitors speculated, and from which they reaped handsome dividends. Mary Shelley's own response, in contrast to this, is one of amused detachment—the detachment of the intellectual observer, piquantly complicated by the fact that Mary Shelley could rightly see herself as the ultimate begetter of these thrills and could therefore feel gratified by the power her imaginings had over the assembled multitudes. Pückler-Muskau's attitude is different again. He is clearly a connoisseur, whose varied experience enabled him to appreciate to the full the skill shown by the British actors he had paid to see, but who dismissed the plays they performed as unworthy of such a sophisticated theatre-goer as he deemed himself. The audience and its "exhalations" were as disagreeable to him as the entertainment which had brought him into their presence; such "stupid and nonsensical" stuff, he felt, attracted the wrong people into the theatre and pandered to a taste that lacked the refinement necessary to appreciate what is good and great.

All three of these attitudes could be observed again when the tale of terror invaded the cinema: the audience's "breathless eagerness"; the detached amusement of intellectuals (many of whom had a hand in providing thrills for the multitude and could occasionally be seen winking over the heads of the "hicks" they thus served); and the indignant rejection of the aristocratic connoisseur, whose appreciation of the skill involved in such entertainments only increased his scorn of their intellectual and moral content. There are, however, many other ways of responding to tales of terror on the big screen. The Surrealists' admiration of popular "horror-movies" comes immediately to mind, with its loudly proclaimed approbation of their involuntary poetry, their unexpected visual juxtapositions, their disorientating power *(pouvoir de dépaysement),* their dream-quality, their celebration of *amour fou* and everything that is *délirant* and *convulsif.* This Surrealist response enters as an element into another attitude commonly adopted by admirers of the cinematic tale of terror: that of exalting such works as the genuine art of our time, as models of meaningful film-making much to be preferred to the more sophisticated works of a Kubrick, a Polanski, or a Fellini. Such critics, more common in France than elsewhere, will cheerfully dismiss much of the work of Ingmar Bergman while exalting Terence Fisher as a great *auteur.* Attitudes of this kind contrast with another, frequently taken up by horror-movie enthusiasts in Britain and the United States, who are aware of what is naïve and crude and banal in the films they like to see, but who find a perverse sort of delight in that very crudity and banality—a kind of appreciation to which our time has given the name "camp." In France too a phrase like "un splendide film kitsch" will be taken as a commendation by experienced film-buffs. A truly unsophisticated, direct response to such movies, corresponding to the eager breathlessness of the nineteenth-century audience at a *Frankenstein* play, still occurs, but is becoming increasingly rare in these days of ubiquitous television—except, of course, with children. Many members of cinema audiences today will look to the horror-movie for violent shock-images, for titillations of sexual and aggressive instincts which have to take more indirect forms in the entertainments television companies beam into our homes. (pp. 1-5)

Writing in 1913, after seeing a number of trick-films in which objects appeared to assume a life of their own and actions took place in reverse order or upside down, seeming to defy the laws of causality and gravity. Georg Lukács was struck by the suitability of the cinema for the presentation of meaningful fantasy—a fantasy, he stressed, that did not stand in contrast to life as actually lived but represented another aspect of it.

> These are images and scenes of a world like that of
> E. T. A. Hoffmann or Poe, Arnim or Barbey
> d'Aurevilly—but the great poet who interprets and
> orders them, who uses the fantastic quality which
> merely derives from adventitious technical factors
> for meaningful metaphysical and stylistic purposes,
> has not yet appeared. What we have had so far
> came into being naively, simply out of the spirit of
> cinematic technology and technique; an Arnim or
> a Poe of our day, however, would here find an in-
> strument for the fulfilment of his yearning to dram-
> atize—an instrument as rich and intrinsically ade-
> quate as (say) the Greek stage was for Sophocles.

But just as we cannot adequately discuss Sophocles without some reference to the use he made of the Greek stage, so we cannot discuss the terror- or fantasy-film without

looking at its use of the opportunities offered by the cinema-medium at a definite stage of its historic development. We must constantly ask ourselves, as R. V. Perkins does in his significantly titled book *Film as Film,* how imaginatively, how meaningfully, the complex sign-system, the language, of the film or of a specific genre has been used in individual instances. We must ask ourselves what difference framing-devices like those in *Caligari* and Lang's *Woman in the Window,* shifts of perspective like those in Mamoulian's *Jekyll and Hyde* (or, *a fortiori,* those in *Rashomon* and *Citizen Kane)* can make to the true and total meaning of a film; and ask, too, where we can detect signs of a personal vision, and where signs of cynical exploitation of proven effects or commercially dictated efforts to "go one better." What happens to the terror-genre when wisecracking reporters are deliberately introduced as "distancing" agents, or when Abbott and Costello "Meet the Killer, Boris Karloff," Old Mother Riley "Meets the Vampire," and the *Carry On* gang "Carry on Screaming"? The makers of the macabre film like to play all sorts of games with their audiences; games of allusion, as when Gloria Holden, in *Dracula's Daughter,* repeats a line spoken by Bela Lugosi in the original *Dracula* of 1931; or "double-take" games, as when the hero-villain of Karl Freund's *Mad Love* is shown as the assiduous patron of a *Grand Guignol* show, nudging the audience into awareness that they too have come to watch Grand Guignol—a theme struck in more serious vein by Michael Powell in *Peeping Tom,* whose central protagonist photographs the agony of women he kills with the pointed stand of his camera; or film-within-film, world-within-world games: as when the vampire-count Yorga, played by Robert Quarry, watches one of the sexier Hammer vampire-films on television in *The Return of Count Yorga.* But literature is older than the film; we should therefore constantly ask ourselves what the film has in fact derived from literature, what images and devices and story-lines it has taken over and what it has done with its borrowings. . . . Beyond that we may also, of course, enquire into what modern literature has learnt from the film and is learning from the film's successor and rival, television: an enquiry which might fruitfully begin with Dos Passos, and take in the significance of optical imagery in Proust, and Kafka's apparent emulation of scenes from grotesque American film-comedy, on its way.

As Theodore Ziolkowski has convincingly demonstrated [in *Disenchanted Images: A Literary Iconography*], attempts to understand the "truth-value" of uncanny iconography, in literature and in the film, may benefit by a glance across from literary and cinematic criticism proper to such fields as anthropology, philosophy of religion, and history. I propose to confine our brief attention to the last three.

It is, in fact, the father of modern psycho-analysis to whom we owe the fullest and the best-known monograph on the uncanny. In 1919 Freud published in *Imago* the first version of his paper 'Das Unheimliche" ["The Uncanny"] whose centre piece is an interesting analysis of a story by E. T. A. Hoffmann. This story is "The Sandman," which contains the episode (well known to all who frequent the opera and the ballet) of the ingenious mechanical doll with whom a highly strung young man falls in love. Freud draws parallels between events in this story and cases that have come under clinical observation and suggests that what Hoffmann has here given his readers is an enactment of the fears and fantasies of a man rendered incapable of normal love by traumatic childhood experiences—and that the tale in fact embodies, in an extreme and disguised form, tendencies present in even its most sane and "normal" readers. His knowledge of such fears and fantasies a writer draws to some extent, in Freud's opinion, from observation of his fellow-men, but more from introspection, from following a deep tap-root into his own unconscious mind. Feelings of the uncanny arise, in this view, from our penetration into hidden areas of the author's psyche which we recognize as akin to hidden areas of our own; they are at once familiar and strange, *heimlich* and *unheimlich.* The artist who explores them is brother to both patient and analyst; he drags to light what is hidden in the individual mind, thereby purging himself of the poison of the repressed and helping others to know truths of feeling—helping others, moreover, to face their own fears in the distanced and comparatively non-committal world of art. "Reading," Simon Lesser has said [in *Fiction and the Unconscious*], "is a means of dealing with our most urgent problems, even those we ordinarily shun . . . [Fiction] gives form to our most fleeting impulses and fully discloses their consequences and ramifications." Here too the fiction-film may be seen as a continuation of literary fiction by different means. These means include the characteristic suspensions of judgement, hesitations, doubts as to whether a given phenomenon is psychological or supernatural, which characterize such works as *Cat People* and *The Other* (1972); mysterious images like the huge wall in Lang's *Tired Death* or *Destiny* which fills the screen so completely that we imagine its infinite extension upwards and sideways—a wall in which a dream opens a breach that allows us to penetrate to the cave of Death; and irruptions of the archaic into the modern, as when in Wegener's first *Golem* film we see the ancient clay statue come to light, and ultimately to life, in a more recent Prague than that of its medieval maker and controller.

Five years before Freud's paper one of his disciples, Otto Rank, had published a study from which the master was able to draw some of his material—an essay called "Der Doppelgänger" ("The Phantom Double") which examined a motif used for different purposes by writers that range from Hoffmann and Jean Paul Richter to Stevenson and Oscar Wilde. Significantly, Rank begins his examination with an analysis of a German film, *The Student of Prague;* and he finds in its course yet another psychological spring of the uncanny: regression to the primitive, the return of fears common in primitive societies, apparently left behind in more enlightened ages but living a shadow life even among us. Might they not, after all, have some foundation? Might not magical thinking, animism, belief in the power of the mind to affect the material world directly—might not these correspond to something in reality? The figure of the phantom double owes its perennial fascination to doubts such as this, doubts whose causes Freud and Rank attribute to 'a return of the repressed', *Wiederkehr des Verdrängten.* A *Doppelgänger* represents, in the first instance, the hidden part of our self, whether super-ego (as in Poe's "*William Wilson*") or id (as in Hoffmann's *The Devil Elixir* and Stevenson's *Dr. Jekyll and Mr. Hyde*); but it also revives primitive beliefs in the independent, almost bodily, existence of our soul, mirror and puppet magic, demons or gods that amuse themselves by taking on our shapes—and all these combine to produce

a shudder that is full of dim memories. A study of psychoanalytic writers thus confirms a belief to which many aestheticians now subscribe: that even the most sophisticated writer retains (to follow Wayne Shumaker's formulation in *Literature and the Irrational*) contact with more instinctive, less intellectualized processes than our own; that he retains control of the 'forgotten language' of presentational symbols, the language of ritual, myth, and dreams. The film-makers too, we may now say without fear of contradiction, have often used their mysterious, multivalent, disturbing, stimulating images as pathways to a deeper darkness than the chiaroscuro so characteristic of the cinematic tale of terror.

Freud confesses, in the course of his paper on "Das Unheimliche," that he was not himself sensitive to feelings of the uncanny, though he did not consider this a reason for barring such well-attested phenomena from his notice. It is far different with C. G. Jung, as several passages from his autobiography—notably those dealing with his attitude to his mother—make abundantly clear. Among Jung's earliest experiences, it seems, was that of his mother's dual personality, "one innocuous and human, the other uncanny," and of his own ambivalent feelings: "By day she was a loving mother, but at night, in dreams, she seemed uncanny." It is this, perhaps, which has led him to take what some of us might feel to be an inordinate interest (shared by the film-makers of many countries) in Rider Haggard's *She,* and to pay particular attention, in literature, to the figure of the nixie or mermaid, alluring and perilous beings which play a prominent part in the writings of the German Romantics. In the nixie Jung sees "an early stage . . . of a magical feminine being that I call the anima, the woman in man." Such images he feels to be at once uncanny and numinous, to hold at once a threat and a promise; "It is tragic," he says in one place, "that the demon of the inner voice should spell greatest danger and indispensable help at the same time." Their power lies in their ability to dredge slime out of the depths, slime which contains not only unpleasant or dangerous matter, but also the germs of new life—in their ability, above all, to reach a deeper region than that of the personal unconscious. "The anima," he declares, in *The Integration of the Personality,* "is not always merely the feminine aspect of the individual man. It has an archetypal aspect—"the eternal feminine", *das Ewigweibliche*—which embodies an experience . . . far older than that of the individual. This anima is reflected, of course, in mythology and legend. It can be Siren or wood-nymph, Grace or Erl-King's daughter, lamia or succubus. . . . " Feelings of the uncanny would seem to indicate, in Jung's view, that we are nearing that dark, transpersonal realm of the collective unconscious, that realm of mythological forms where things and persons become magical, taboo, dangerous, and yet full of the promise of enrichment and salvation. It is surely no accident that so many of the illustrations of a key work like *Man and his Symbols,* written by Jung and his pupils and published in 1964, should turn out to be stills from films of the most varied kinds. These include, on page 92, a picture of Godzilla which is adorned with the caption: "Perhaps the monsters of modern 'horror' films are distorted versions of archetypes that will no longer be repressed."

Jung's fears of his uncanny mother find a remarkable parallel in the life of one of the greatest figures in the cinema:

S. M. Eisenstein. [In *Eisenstein: The Growth of a Cinematic Genius*] Yon Barna quotes his account of an incident in which Eisenstein's mother terrified her young son by denying that she *was* his mother. "As she said it, her face became set, her eyes glassy and staring. Then she came slowly towards me. There you have all the characteristic elements: a fixed, stony expression; a mask with ice-cold eyes; a face devoid of life." These "characteristic elements" Eisenstein later transmuted in his films. Greater historical events in which Eisenstein was caught up along with his generation also played their part, of course, in evoking that "ocean of cruelty" which is so characteristic of his films, shaping those terrible incidents which Barna lists again and again:

> In *Strike* workers are killed off like oxen in a slaughterhouse and children hurled from the rooftops; in *Potemkin* the crowd is massacred wholesale and children trampled underfoot on the steps; men and children are thrown to the flames in *Nevsky,* poisoned or stabbed to death in *Ivan the Terrible . . .*

—but we cannot ignore Eisenstein's own sense that his obsession with such cruelties had deep roots in his childhood; in childhood incidents which Jung would certainly have seen as the repetition of archetypal ones, and therefore apt to stir up archetypal memories when transmuted in works of cinematic art. In considering the effect of Eisenstein's work on the terror-film proper, we would do well to keep in mind David O. Selznick's advice, in a letter written late in 1926, that American directors and studio-technicians should pore over *Battleship Potemkin* "in the same way that a group of artists might view and study a Rubens or a Raphael."

Students of the uncanny, in film as well as in literature, have recently paid a good deal of attention to the work of Jacques Lacan, with its conjunction of neo-Freudianism, structural linguistics, and structural anthropology. Lacan's analysis of the "disjunction" between lived experience and the sign which replaces it, his stress on the Freudian concept of *Spaltung* (a kind of psychic and social alienation easily symbolized by the *Doppelgänger*), his "undermining of the notion of a unified and consistent subject" (R. Coward and J. Ellis), his treatment of visual images as forms of metaphor and metonymy, his demonstration of how the "imaginary" metamorphoses into the "symbolic," his views on the coexistence and intersection of the Symbolic, the Imaginary, and the Real, his notion of "suturing functions"—all these have profoundly influenced the way recent critics have looked at tales of terror and talked about them. When Paul Willemen, in an Edinburgh Festival pamphlet written in 1975, showed how Jacques Tourneur's films dramatize the barrier between the "space" of the viewer and that of the story unfolding on the screen, how Tourneur makes the image on the screen suggest that it is "a deceptive text to be deciphered," a text that requires a "secondary" reading, and how all this can be seen as "a dramatization of the structure of phantasy itself," then we cannot but realize that present-day discourse about fantastic and uncanny films has been powerfully affected by recent conjunctions of structuralism and psycho-analysis. The leading exponent of this conjunction is, in many observer's eyes, Jacques Lacan who, in his *Four Fundamental Concepts of Psycho-*

analysis (1973), revived Freud's notion of *eine andere Lokalität,* another locality, another space, another scene, between perception and consciousness; who talked, in this same collection of lectures, of "a split between the eye and the gaze" and ventured an aphorism that will find a special resonance in the minds of those who occupy themselves with the uncanny, the fantastic, and the terrible in the cinema: "In this matter of the visible, everything is a trap." He has impelled his disciples to look for Freudian elements in the structure as well as the content of a literary or cinematic work. I must admit that I myself have not found Lacan's writings helpful, and that I doubt whether his influence—so strong at the time of writing—will long outlast him.

"Psychology," of course, is not simply a synonym of "psycho-analysis"; and while no student of the uncanny in literature and the film can afford to spurn such help as psycho-analysts, from Freud and Jung to Harry Stack Sullivan, R. D. Laing, and possibly Jacques Lacan, can give him, he will also find that many earlier writers have successfully attempted to uncover the psychological springs of uncanny feelings. We need think only of Schopenhauer's celebrated analysis of the terror we feel when some apparent exception to the law of causality makes us doubt the principle of individuation; of Kierkegaard's description of our common dread "of something unknown, something on which one dare not look, a dread of the possibilities of one's own being, a dread of oneself "; of Nietzsche's comments on the moral suppression of sex that leads to its return in "hideous disguises" and "uncanny vampire forms," and his constatation of a "German soul" that has "paths and corridors . . . caves, hiding places and dungeons," that knows about "secret ways towards chaos." Heidegger also has some memorable pages on the way the uncanny can act as an impulsion towards authenticity of living and thinking. A judicious study of writers outside the psycho-analytic orbit, a sound dose of common sense, and training in aesthetic analysis (which includes training in exact observation and logical thinking)—these should enable us to avoid most of the perils that attend psycho-analytic ventures into literary criticism, and criticism of the film: the danger of making no distinction, like Stekel in *Dreams of the Poets* or Rank in *The Incest Theme in Poetry and Legend,* between the work of fifth-rate scribblers and that of great poets; the danger of bizarre distortions—like those of Marie Bonaparte in her book on Poe—which have the aim of reducing everything to the same infantile fantasy. Psycho-analysis tends itself to form the notions which it then "discovers"; and nothing can be more ridiculous than a criticism of literature and the film that relies on unexamined and archaic psycho-analytic concepts. "As an area of applied psychoanalysis," an editorial in *Screen* (xvi. summer 1976) rightly insisted:

> psychoanalytic studies of film will remain tributary to psychoanalysis in two respects: any knowledge will remain dependent for its authority on a practice outside film study itself, i.e. on clinical analysis; and that knowledge will be of more value as corroboration of the theses of psychoanalytic theory than for its contribution to any understanding of the cinema.

Warnings such as these should encourage us to cultivate a degree of healthy scepticism that will help us resist a temptation to which even Jung seems on occasions to succumb: the temptation to build airy constructions which have insufficient base in observed or experienced reality. To say this is not, of course, to belittle the very real insights Jung has been able to give to sensitive critics like Maud Bodkin, Anniela Jaffé, and C. F. Keppler.

Keppler, in *The Literature of the Second Self,* used Jung's concepts of Shadow, Anima, Animus, Wise Old Man, and Chthonic Mother to illuminate the "double" figure that confronts us so often in literature and the cinema. He showed convincingly how many different things may be meant by those who speak of doubles, *Doppelgänger,* or second selves: "an objective second self, a case of mistaken identity"; or "a subjective second self, a mental content mistaken for external fact"; or what he calls "the genuine second self, always simultaneously both objective and subjective, and never explainable as a mistake." Such "second selves" figure in legend, literature, and film, as twin brother, pursuer, tempter, "vision of horror," saviour, beloved, or visitor from another point in the time-sequence; they bring suffering and death, but they also bring fulfilment, for they complete the "partial" personalities as which we must all take our place in the social world.

> It is this end which is the goal of the adventure of self-meeting. If we ask why it should be sought, when the seeking is so often unpleasant and even fatal, we can only answer that there appears to be in living creatures generally the urge to do a thing which can never be justified in practical terms: to see the unseen, to sail beyond the sunset, to cross the mountains of the moon. And when the un-crossed mountains are within as well as without (for . . . one's relationship with oneself is not wholly distinguishable from one's relationship with other selves)—when this is the case there seems to be a special urgency, arising out of a sense of incompleteness, even of self-deception and self-deprivation. For to live as only half oneself is to live a kind of lie, and to live a kind of lie is to live a kind of death.

The urge of which this passage so eloquently speaks is one that also helps to account for the impetus to make, and the impetus to see, . . . terror-films. . . .

From Pabst's (technically superb) *Secrets of a Soul* to Hitchcock's *Spellbound* (1945) and Wise's *The Haunting,* films have seldom benefited from an unironic use of textbook psycho-analysis; oversimplification could never be avoided. At the same time the makers of terror-films could not help being influenced, from the first, by what they had absorbed of Freud, Jung, Melanie Klein, and the rest. Writing in a German film-magazine in 1929, Henrik Galeen, who helped to script *The Golem, Nosferatu, Waxworks,* and *The Student of Prague,* spelt out why he and his colleagues felt obliged to delve, deliberately, into the unconscious when they took over motifs from fairy-tales, Romantic literature, and the subliterary *Schauerroman* ["horror novel"]:

> What does the old "fantastic" fairytale world of the Brothers Grimm and Wilhelm Hauff, of E. T. A. Hoffmann and even, perhaps, of Edgar Allan Poe, mean to us and our children today? Let us look at it through today's spectacles. It is a stimulus to us, a stimulus of genius, but no more than that; for what we see around us today is more fantastic than anything even a Jules Verne could conceive. Today's reality has become the equivalent of yesterday's fantasy. In our films, therefore, we had to look for new problems in this field.
>
> What can we still call "fantastic" today? Everything that seems possible in our unconscious, although it is not to be found in our common, everyday reality.

It would have been surprising if film-makers in search of fantastic *frissons* had neglected the help which they felt Freudians could given them in their exploration of the personal, and Jungians in their exploration of the "collective," unconscious.

Jung admits to having learnt a great deal from Rudolf Otto's book *The Idea of the Holy,* from which he borrowed one, at least, of his key terms, and he may therefore serve as a convenient stepping-stone to the second of the three disciplines I am calling to the aid of the critic in evaluating the phenomena of the uncanny: that of religious philosophy. In *The Idea of the Holy,* first published in 1917, Otto speaks of a feeling of the "numinous" which he sees as the prerequisite of all religious feeling. This sense of the numinous has many constituents; but one of the most important of these is what Otto calls an apprehension of "awe-inspiring mystery," the *mysterium tremendum* of the divine. Such religious "dread" or "awe" has, as an antecedent stage,

> daemonic dread . . . with its queer perversion, a sort of abortive off-shoot, the dread of ghosts. It first begins to stir in the feeling of something "uncanny" *unheimlich* is the term Otto uses. It is this feeling which, emerging in the mind of primeval man, forms the starting point for the entire religious development in history. "Demons" and "gods" alike spring from this root and all the products of "mythological apperception" or "fantasy" are nothing but different modes in which it has been objectified.

Otto's contention, here and elsewhere, that the numinous is an essential constituent of *all* religious experience has rightly been challenged, notably by Karl Kerenyi and Father Victor White: but no one, I think, will sever again the connection he has made between the numinous and the uncanny. It is behind Martin Buber's description, for instance, in *The Eclipse of God,* of the uncanny as a "dark gate" through which we must pass to reach the love of God—though Buber reminds us forcibly that it is "only a gate and not, as some theologians believe, a dwelling." For Buber, the uncanny is something that helps to pierce the protective armour assumed by modern man in his endeavours to shut out the call of a beyond. We may remember, too, Paul Tillich's repeated assertion that the demonic belongs into the sphere of the holy, and that, wherever the demonic appears, there the question of its correlate, the divine, will also be raised. But one cannot, I think, proceed very far in the study of modern literature and film without reaching the conclusion that much of their uncanny quality is due to secularization, to a recession of a sense of the divine, to a drying-up of metaphysical aspirations to a loss of faith.

In Poe's "The Pit and the Pendulum" with its talk of "demons," "fiends," "angels" turning to "meaningless spectres," and so on, and in Mamoulian's *Jekyll and Hyde,* where Ivy speaks of Jekyll as "her angel" and of Hyde as "the devil," metaphysical imagery seems to have lost its moorings, and what is left may perhaps best be described in Sartre's phrase as "a ghost of transcendence floating about in immanence." But we would do well to heed the claim made by many masters of uncanny effects that they were the guardians of a metaphysical outlook in a mechanistic and positivist world—from Poe, who declared that his stories penetrated, "however rudderless or compassless, into the vast ocean of the 'light ineffable'," to Georg Heym, who saw in his own work, "the best proof of a metaphysical land that stretches its black peninsulas far into our fleeting days." And I think that the works so far discussed will tend to confirm the view, advanced by Mircea Eliade, of the "real spiritual function" of the nineteenth-century novel: that it constitutes "despite all scientific realistic or social 'formulas' . . . the great repository of degraded myth."

That the same can be said for the film, with even greater justification, should be obvious from any reflection on the motifs and themes of the terror-movie. Even if we confine our attention to Greek myths alone, we can soon recognize such myths as those of Prometheus, Hephaestus, the Sirens, the Harpies, Circe, the Medusa, Oedipus, Electra, and Procrustes determining the plot-patterns and images of such films; to say nothing of the conscious and explicit use of Greek myths announced by the very titles of *Dr. Cyclops* and *The Gorgon.* This whole subject—the existence, provenance, evolution, and decline of myth in the cinematic tale of terror—has been intelligently discussed by Gérard Lenne in *Le Cinéma fantastique et ses mythes* (1970). Alas, the book was written too early to include Harry Kümel's *Malpertuis* (1973), a strange and complex tale adapted from a book by Jean Ray which takes as one of its subjects that degradation of the classical gods in the modern world which had so fascinated Heine a century before.

The conflict between a social order ostensibly based on Christian values and long-suppressed pagan cults that yet survive—a conflict which the later Heine so often made his theme—has been given frightening shape by one of the most memorable British terror-films of recent years: *The Wicker Man* (1973), written by Anthony Shaffer, directed by Robin Hardy, and acted, subtly and sympathetically, by Edward Woodward, as the representative of our established order, and Christopher Lee, as the leader of the ancient cult. The thrilling impact of this film was undoubtedly due, not only to its literate dialogue and imaginative camera-work, but also to the powerful image announced by its title: the image of a harvest-god, the Wicker Man, to whom human sacrifices are, once again, offered up.

In considering the uncanny in a religious context, we must guard against two particularly insidious dangers. One of these is the temptation to equate the uncanny too readily with the demonic, and thus treat all its manifestations as belonging, positively or negatively, into the sphere of the holy. But it needs only a glance at any anthology of ghost-stories, or at films like Lang's *Dr. Mabuse the Gambler,*

to see that many *unheimlich* phenomena take us to the realm of table-tapping and mediumistic effects—and most religious thinkers will agree with Paul Tillich that such things, however inexplicable, however mysterious, belong to the sphere of nature and not to a true beyond. The second danger is that of treating the uncanny as a timeless absolute, of forgetting that it confronts us in history. Yet in fact one of the most fascinating of all the tasks that face us when we study this phenomenon is to estimate the degree to which authors and film-makers have found it possible, at various times and in various places, to assimilate their sense of the uncanny into an over-all, historically conditioned world-view. The early Gothic novel still operates with either a broadly Christian scheme, or at least an ethical scheme of right and wrong; these are both called in question in the subtler and darker novels of the nineteenth century (English readers will at once remember *Wuthering Heights*), until in the works of Kafka the uncanny stands naked, as it were, unassimilated into any recognizable transcendent or ethical scheme. Much of the effort of the terror-film, in recent years, seems to have gone into attempts to reverse this history; but even in films with less theologically bleak endings than *Rosemary's Baby, The Omen* and *Carrie,* it would seem to be Satan rather than God who remains lord of the world.

In the detailed analysis of four representative works which makes up the bulk of his book on *Horror Films,* R. H. W. Dillard has pointed to their "parabolic intensity," and to the "metaphysical" response these films invite:

> If a viewer chooses *Frankenstein* (1931) as an example of a valid and significant esthetic expression of experience, then he has chosen an understanding of the nature of life which is light-centered, progressive, open and ongoing—a life in which moral freedom is the natural human condition. If he chooses *The Wolf Man* (1941), he has chosen a life which is fate-centered, static, closed and circular—a life in which moral limitation is the natural human condition. If he chooses *Night of the Living Dead* (1968) he has chosen a life in which moral failure is the natural human condition. If he chooses Fellini's *Satyricon* (1969) he has chosen a life which is life-centered, moving, dangerous but opening out—a life in which moral striving is the natural human condition.

Not everyone will be as ready as Professor Dillard to accept Fellini's *Satyricon* as a horror-film rather than one that makes occasional use of the imagery characteristic of that genre—in many ways, *The Exorcist* would have been a more appropriate film to conclude the series; but he has seen, clearly and truly, the "metaphysical" dimension of our response to such works, and the historically conditioned nature of the world-view they present.

We have now turned to the third and last of the contextual fields within which the uncanny should, indeed must, be analysed. Is it not shaped by historical as well as by timeless and absolute forces? Does it not sublimate—to use a term that Karl Mannheim took over from Freud—the psychic forces of the society within which it is produced as well as those of the individual that produced it?

From what has already been said it will have become clear that an analysis of the uncanny in literature and the film must take into account the historical processes generally grouped as "secularization"; and that implies recourse to the work of sociologists and historians like Alfred Weber and R. H. Tawney. But there is another, related concept (a much abused one!) that will be found indispensable: the concept of *Entfremdung* or alienation. Hegel first spoke of this, in his *Philosophy of History,* as a necessary process through which the Absolute realized its purposes—the Idea, *Geist,* must be alienated in order to become embodied in nature, man must alienate himself in order to confront himself in his own handiwork; but Feuerbach, and more forcibly Marx, soon converted Hegel's positive into a negative, deploring religious alienation (through which man projected what is best and noblest in himself into a beyond) and social alienation (which deprived man of the control of his own handiwork). A man's labour, writes Marx in 1844, "takes on its own existence . . . it exists outside him, independently, and alien to him . . . it stands opposed to him as an autonomous power. The life which he has given to the object sets itself against him as an alien and hostile force." In the very attempt to gain greater and greater control of natural forces man feels himself losing that control, and turning the world against himself—that is the theme which occurred to Hawthorne, for instance, when he sketched an uncanny story in one of the notebooks he kept between 1835 and 1853. "A steam engine in a factory to be supposed to possess a malignant spirit; it catches one man's arm, and pulls it off; seizes another by the coat-tails and almost grapples him bodily, catches a girl by the hair, and scalps her; and finally draws a man and crushes him to death." The "possessed" machine has in fact become a favourite motif in recent films, from *2001* to the TV movie *Killdozer* (1974), in which bulldozers escape human control and go on a murderous rampage. The sinister truck of Steven Spielberg's *Duel,* which would seem to have served *Killdozer* as a model, is controlled by a human driver; but since we are never shown that driver's face we come to have the feeling that here too a machine is possessed by a destructive impulse of its own. All this is clearly related to that classic of the uncanny . . . : Mary Shelley's *Frankenstein,* a work that can be seen, at one of its many levels, as a symptom of a cultural neurosis, a fear of science, fear of the control of natural forces, without adequate corresponding control of the soul and psyche. It is also behind the feeling, so common in twentieth-century literature, that there is something inherently uncanny in *things.* One remembers how Törless, the hero of an early novel by Robert Musil, felt things, as well as events and people, "as something which, through the power of some inventor, had been tied to a harmless explanatory word, and then again as something quite alien, which threatened to break loose at any moment." It may also be relevant to recall at this point the *tropismes* of Nathalie Sarraute, described (by Sartre) as "a protoplasmic vision of our interior universe: roll away the stone of the commonplace and find running discharges, slobberings, mucus . . . " *Unheimlich* in fact: you start with the commonplace and find yourself suddenly confronted with something that gives you the shivers.

As for alienation in the film—we have only to close our eyes for the images to come rolling up on our interior screens. Images from the German films of Fritz Lang, for instance: the machines that enslave men in *Metropolis,* and are, at one delirious moment, seen as Moloch; the cold indifference of the empty stairwell in *M* that betokens the death of a child as surely as the abandoned balloon in the same film; or, still in *M,* the heap of lumber amidst which the terrified murderer hides, himself a reject, in a dreary attic; the printing-presses at the beginning of *The Testament of Dr. Mabuse* (1932-3), chug-chugging away while a man is hounded into madness. Nor did the American cinema need German directors to teach it the meaning of urban alienation. The very title of John Huston's *The Asphalt Jungle* (1950) indicates a constant theme of the *film noir:* the "mean streets" through which characters invented by Chandler and Hammett must walk; the actual settings in Las Vegas and Seattle which Dan Curtis's TV terror-films, scripted by Richard Matheson, have memorably used as the scene of vampirism and fantastic rejuvenation. And what could be more alienating than the New York of Depression days, shown to us in the *King Kong* of 1933, which can find no use for Ann Darrow at the beginning, and which imprisons, and ultimately defeats, a free son of the woods seized by an *amour fou?* That the Kong we see is in fact himself only the iconic image of a man-made object, the image of an articulated machine disguised as an ape projected by another machine, the unseen cinema-projector, is one of the many delicious ironies of this imaginative movie. In his British as well as his American thrillers Alfred Hitchcock has demonstrated, from the first, a disconcerting capacity for turning objects of our ordinary world and everyday use into agents of threat and betrayal: from the bread-knife in *Blackmail* and the coffee-cup (huge in the foreground) of *Notorious* to the Statue of Liberty itself in *Saboteur.* In this as in so many other respects he has shown himself an apt pupil of Fritz Lang.

If, in one way, terror-films convey experiences of alienation, they can also, in another, provide reassurance. This point has been convincingly made by Denis Gifford [in *A Pictorial History of Horror Movies*] when he characterized the studio-built sets and stereotyped plots in the Universal movies of the thirties:

> The settings were interchangeable, the ambience unchangeable. This was the secret of the Universal universe. It gave the great films a continuity that was comforting to come back to, whatever the horror that walked abroad. Familiar faces, familiar places: a sort of security in a world of fear. . . . The impossible took place in a tight false world of studio-built landscape, where every tree was carefully gnarled in expressionistic fright, every house cunningly gabled in Gothic mystery, every shadow beautifully lit into lurking terror; and where every actor was caught in the closing ring of horrors, untouched by the possibility of a normal world beyond.

The provision of an alternative world, an imaginative widening of the horizon of common experience, is not the least of the pleasures that audiences look for in a terror-film; and having once experienced that alternative world, related to yet different from their own, they long to recapture the pleasure they felt in new variations and intensifications. The pleasure of widening experience can even be derived from being precipitated for a time, in the safety of the cinema, into the radical alienation of a world distorted by drugs or madness: the distorted drawings and flats of *Caligari;* the fish-eye lens view of Frankenheimer's *Seconds* (1966); and the ever more menacing perspectives of Polanski's *Repulsion,* which reverse the vampire-film's contention that sexuality leads to aggression by showing murderous impulses triggered off by disgust at physical, sexual contact.

An awareness of historical and social processes will illuminate at every turn the form in which the uncanny confronts us in a given period of literature or of the film. Let us go back to literature for a moment, to look at a motif which has played a significant part in the terror-film too, from *Dr. Mabuse the Gambler* to *The Devil Rides Out* (1967) and *Rosemary's Baby:* the motif, so ubiquitous in the eighteenth-century *Schauerroman,* of the secret society and its sinister emissaries. We can, we must, refer that to common paranoiac fantasies; we can, we must, see in it also a characteristic perversion of the lost faith in providence. In eighteenth-century German literature it takes the specific form it does, however, only because of the powerful part that Illuminatism, Freemasonry, and Rosicrucianism played in eighteenth-century German life, and because of widespread feelings of political and social powerlessness of which we have other historical and literary evidence. A work like Grosse's *Der Genius* (one of the most widely read of all eighteenth-century fear-jerkers, both in Germany and, under its title *Horrid Mysteries,* in England) shows highly complicated feelings towards an authority that controlled even one's private actions—the shudder of almost religious awe mingles with revolted fear. In the course of the nineteenth century the fear of higher masters is supplemented by that of invaders from below: an old theological opposition, of course, but one that now assumes a new social significance. Lord Ruthven, the aristocratic vampire, is joined in popular mythology by the demon-barber of Fleet Street, by Sweeney Todd and his pie-woman, and the menace of dark forces from the social underworld extends from Sue's *Mysteries of Paris* to the Morlocks that threaten and sustain the graceful world of the Elois in H. G. Wells's *The Time Machine.* It is not, perhaps, irrelevant to recall in this connection that the *Communist Manifesto* of 1848 begins with a recognizably uncanny image: "Ein Gespenst geht um in Europa"—a spectre walks in Europe; the spectre of Communism. One recalls, here, the speech Val Lewton and his team gave to Boris Karloff in *The Body Snatcher,* a film adapted from a story by Robert Louis Stevenson in 1945:

> I'm a small man, a humble man, and being poor,
> I've had to do so much that I did not want to do.
> But so long as the great Dr MacFarlane jumps at
> my whistle, that long am I a man—and if I have not
> that, I have nothing. Then I am only a cabman and
> a grave-robber.

Shades of Uriah Heep! And between these social extremes, between the threat of unseen masters above and menacing proletarians below, stands the *bon bourgeois* whom E. T. A. Hoffmann, and those followers of his who created the world of the silent German film, found perhaps the most uncanny of all: that Coppelius who seemed a solid if eccentric citizen, an *Advokat* with a firm place in society, but who turns out, if you look at him more closely, to be a demonic being that brings, wherever it appears, "lamentation—anguish—and perdition to body and soul."

Each age, each nation, incarnates the uncanny in a different way. It is fed by, and may be made to nourish, popular prejudices: sinister monks and nuns invade the Gothic novel in the wake of the Gordon Riots, sinister scientists appear in greater and greater numbers in the course of the nineteenth century, and the use made of grotesque Jewish figures in the consciously uncanny works of such writers

as Meyrink, Ewers, Panizza, and Strobl should have given the wise food for thought.

The same might be said of the use of actors with pronounced Jewish features, or made up to simulate such features, in German films made during the Weimar Republic. There was rarely any conscious anti-Semitic intent in this. Fritz Lang was genuinely indignant when critics charged him with furthering anti-Jewish resentments by giving the wealthy, avaricious, and treacherous Alberich of *Die Nibelungen* (1923-4) what contemporaries would see as "Jewish" traits: beard, hooked nose, thick lower lip, small stature . . . There was quite a simple explanation, Lang replied; he and his make-up artist were influenced by the grotesque character make-up used by the Habimah, the Russian-Jewish ensemble whose performances of *The Dybbuk* and other plays had excited the admiration of Berlin theatre-goers in the early twenties. But this, of course, does not explain why it was the wretched Alberich who was modelled on the Habimah players, while the make-up of the hero of the tale, Alberich's Nordic adversary Siegfried, resplendent in a blond wig that was made to shine like a halo by means of blue streaks added to the straw-coloured hair, remained quite untouched by any such influence. The film-makers were usually oblivious of what they were doing; but the subliminal influence of their work was none the less powerful for that.

When we notice, as we must, how strong a strain of the uncanny there has been in the literature of the United States, from Charles Brockden Brown to William Faulkner, and how readily the American cinema of the thirties assimilated the pioneer efforts of the German terror-films, we shall do well to remain aware of the complementary American dream of innocence and rationality (how could we appreciate a film like Richard Mulligan's *The Other* without that?); of the "power of blackness" brought into New England life by Puritanism; and especially (for the strain is particularly strong in Southern writers) of the facts of which we are reminded in C. Vann Woodward's *The Burden of Southern History:* "The experience of evil and the experience of tragedy are parts of the Southern heritage that are as difficult to reconcile with the American legend of innocence and felicity as the experience of poverty and defeat are to reconcile with the legends of abundance and success." In Europe as in America the uncanny film and the uncanny tale are part of a great historical dialogue between Enlightenment and Irrationalism or Occultism. (pp. 115-33)

> *S. S. Prawer, "The Uncanny," and in an introduction to his* Caligari's Children: The Film as Tale of Terror, *Oxford University Press, Oxford, 1980, pp. 1-7, 108-37.*

THE WRITER AND THE FILM INDUSTRY

Bertolt Brecht

[Brecht was a German dramatist whose imagination, artistic genius, and profound grasp of the nature of drama

made him a chief innovator of modern theatrical techniques. Brecht effectively exploited an exquisite stage-sense to promote his political and humanistic concerns for the improvement of society, using theater to arouse the social conscience of his audience. Brecht's "epic" style of drama is, according to his own definition, intended to appeal "less to the feelings than to the spectator's reason." This is achieved through various "alienation effects" which undermine the life-like illusion of traditional theater and demand that the audience consider the intellectual issues presented by the play rather than becoming emotionally engaged by its characters. In the following excerpt from his account of a lawsuit against German director G. W. Pabst over the film adaptation of Die Dreigroschenoper (The Threepenny Opera), *Brecht discusses the social and artistic possibilities of filmmaking versus the often "vulgar" realities of the medium.]*

We have often been told (and the court expressed the same opinion) that when we sold our work to the film industry we gave up all our rights; the buyers even purchased the right to destroy what they had bought; all further claim was covered by the money. These people felt that in agreeing to deal with the film industry we put ourselves in the position of a man who lets his laundry be washed in a dirty gutter and then complains that it has been ruined. Anybody who advises us not to make use of such new apparatus just confirms the apparatus's right to do bad work; he forgets himself out of sheer open-mindedness, for he is thus proclaiming his willingness to have nothing but dirt produced for him. At the same time he deprives us in advance of the apparatus which we need in order to produce, since this way of producing is likely more and more to supersede the present one, forcing us to speak through increasingly complex media and to express what we have to say by increasingly inadequate means. For the old forms of communication are not unaffected by the development of new ones, nor do they survive alongside them. The filmgoer develops a different way of reading stories. But the man who writes the stories is a filmgoer too. The mechanization of literary production cannot be thrown into reverse. Once instruments are used even the novelist who makes no use of them is led to wish that he could do what the instruments can: to include what they show (or could show) as part of that reality which constitutes his subject-matter; and above all, when he writes, to assume the attitude of somebody using an instrument.

For instance it makes a great difference whether the writer approaches things as if using instruments, or produces them "from within himself." What the film itself does, that is to say how far it makes its individuality prevail against "art," is not unimportant in this connection. It is conceivable that other kinds of writer, such as playwrights or novelists, may for the moment be able to work in a more cinematic way than the film people. Up to a point they depend less on means of production. But they still depend on the film, its progress or regress; and the film's means of production are wholly capitalist. Today the bourgeois novel still depicts "a world." It does so in a purely idealistic way from within a given *Weltanschauung:* the more or less private, but in any case personal outlook of its "creator." Inside this world every detail of course fits exactly, though if it were taken out of its context it would not seem authentic for a minute by comparison with the "details"

of reality. What we find out about the real world is just as much as we find out about the author responsible for the unreal one; in other words we find out something about the author and nothing about the world.

The film cannot depict any world (the "setting" in which it deals is something quite different) and lets nobody express himself (and nothing else) in a work, and no work express any person. What it provides (or could provide) is applicable conclusions about human actions in detail. Its splendid inductive method, which at any rate it facilitates, could be of infinite significance to the novel, in so far as novels still signify anything. To the playwright what is interesting is its attitude to the person performing the action. It gives life to its people, whom it classes purely according to function, simply using available types that occur in given situations and are able to adopt given attitudes in them. Character is never used as a source of motivation; these people's inner life is never the principal cause of the action and seldom its principal result; the individual is seen from outside. Literature needs the film not only indirectly but also directly. That decisive extension of its social duties which follows from the transformation of art into a paedagogical discipline entails the multiplying or the repeated changing of the means of representation. . . . This apparatus can be used better than almost anything else to supersede the old kind of untechnical, anti-technical "glowing" art, with its religious links. The socialization of these means of production is vital for art. . . .

To understand the position we must get away from the common idea that these battles for the new institutions and apparatus only have to do with one part of art. In this view there is a part of art, its central part, which remains wholly untouched by the new possibilities of communication (radio, film, book clubs, etc.) and goes on using the old ones (printed books, freely marketed; the stage, etc.). Quite different from the other, technically-influenced part where it is a matter of creation by the apparatus itself: a wholly new business, owing its existence in the first place to certain financial calculations and thereby bound to them for ever. If works of the former sort are handed over to the apparatus they are turned into goods without further ado. This idea, leading as it does to utter fatalism, is wrong because it shuts off so-called "sacrosanct works of art" from every process and influence of our time, treating them as sacrosanct purely because they are impervious to any development in communication. In fact, of course, the whole of art without any exception is placed in this new situation; it is as a whole, not split into parts, that it has to cope with it; it is as a whole that it turns into goods or not. The changes wrought by time leave nothing untouched, but always embrace the whole. In short, the common preconception discussed here is pernicious.

This preconception is equivalent to the notion that films have got to be vulgar. Such an eminently rational view (rational because nobody is going to make any other kind of film, or look at it once made) owes its relevance to the inexorable way in which the metaphysicians of the press, with their insistence on "art," call for profundity. It is they who want to see the "element of fate" emphasized in all dealings between people. Fate, which used (once) to be among the great concepts, has long since become a vulgar one, where the desired "transfiguration" and "illumination" are achieved by reconciling oneself to circumstances—and a purely class-warfare one, where one class fixes the fate of another. As usual, our metaphysicians' demands are not hard to fulfil. It is simple to imagine everything that they reject presented in such a way that they would accept it with enthusiasm. Obviously if one were to trace certain love stories back to Romeo and Juliet, or crime stories to Macbeth, in other words to famous plays that need contain nothing else (need show no other kind of human behaviour, use no other kind of energy to govern the world's movements), then they would at once exclaim that vulgarity is determined by How and not What. But this "it all depends how" is itself vulgar.

This beloved "human interest" of theirs, this How (usually qualified by the word "eternal," like some indelible dye) as applied to Othello (my wife is my property), Hamlet (better sleep on it), Macbeth (I'm destined for higher things) and co., now seems like vulgarity and nothing more when measured on a massive scale. If one insists on having it, this is the only form in which it can be had; simply to insist is vulgar. What once determined the grandeur of such passions, their non-vulgarity, was the part they had to play in society, which was a revolutionary one. Even the impact which *Potemkin* made on such people springs from the sense of outrage which they would feel if their wives were to try to serve bad meat to them (I won't stand it, I tell you!), while Chaplin is perfectly aware that he must be "human," i.e. vulgar, if he is to achieve anything more, and to this end will alter his style in a pretty unscrupulous way (viz. the famous close-up of the doggy look which concludes *City Lights).*

What the film really demands is external action and not introspective psychology. Capitalism operates in this way by taking given needs on a massive scale, exorcizing them, organizing them and mechanizing them so as to revolutionize everything. Great areas of ideology are destroyed when capitalism concentrates on external action, dissolves everything into processes, abandons the hero as the vehicle for everything and mankind as the measure, and thereby smashes the introspective psychology of the bourgeois novel. The external viewpoint suits the film and gives it importance. For the film the principles of non-aristotelian drama (a type of drama not depending on empathy, mimesis) are immediately acceptable. Non-aristotelian effects can be seen in the Russian film *The Road to Life,* above all because the theme (re education of neglected children by specific socialist methods) leads the spectator to establish causal relationships between the teacher's attitude and that of his pupils. Thanks to the key scenes this analysis of origins comes so to grip the spectator's interest that he "instinctively" dismisses any motives for the children's neglect borrowed from the old empathy type of drama (unhappiness at home plus psychic trauma, rather than war or civil war). Even the use of work as a method of education arouses the spectator's scepticism, for the simple reason that it is never made clear that in the Soviet Union, in total contrast to all other countries, morality is in fact determined by work. As soon as the human being appears as an object the causal connections become decisive. Similarly in the great American comedies the human being is presented as an object, so that their audience could as well be entirely made up of Pavlovians. Behaviourism is a school of psychology that is based on the industrial producer's need to acquire means of influencing the customer;

an active psychology therefore, progressive and revolutionary. Its limits are those proper to its function under capitalism (the reflexes are biological; only in certain of Chaplin's films are they social). Here again the road leads over capitalism's dead body; but here again this road is a good one. (pp. 47-50)

> *Bertolt Brecht, "The Film, the Novel and Epic Theatre," in his* Brecht on Theatre: The Development of an Aesthetic, *edited and translated by John Willett, Hill and Wang, 1964, pp. 47-51.*

Graham Greene

[*Greene is considered one of the most important novelists in modern English literature. In his major works, he explores the problems of spiritually and socially alienated individuals living in the corrupt and corrupting societies of the twentieth century. Greene is also esteemed as a film critic and biographer, as well as a literary critic with a taste for the works of undeservedly neglected authors. In the following excerpt, he discusses his experiences with the film industry, both as a screenwriter and as a novelist whose works have been adapted for the screen.*]

[When] you sell a book to Hollywood you sell it outright. The long Hollywood contracts—sheet after closely printed sheet as long as the first treatment of the novel which is for sale—ensure that you have no "author's rights." The film producer can alter anything. He can turn your tragedy of East End Jewry into a musical comedy at Palm Springs if he wishes. He need not even retain your title, though that is usually almost the only thing he wishes to retain. *The Power and the Glory,* a story I wrote in 1938 of a drunken Mexican priest with an illegitimate child who carries on his vocation stumblingly, sometimes with cowardice, during the religious persecution of the early 30's, became, as *The Fugitive,* the story of a pious and heroic priest: the drunkenness had been drained away and the illegitimate child (I believe this is so, for I never saw Mr. John Ford's film) became the bastard of the police-officer who pursued the priest. One gets used to these things (like the strange intrusion of a girl conjuror into *This Gun for Hire* [a novel bought from Greene by Paramount in 1934]) and it is a waste of time to resent them. You take the money, you can go on writing for another year or two, you have no just ground of complaint. And the smile in the long run will be on your face. For the book has the longer life.

The most extreme changes I have seen in any book of mine were in *The Quiet American;* one could almost believe that the film was made deliberately to attack the book and the author, but the book was based on a closer knowledge of the Indo-China war than the American director possessed and I am vain enough to believe that the book will survive a few years longer than Mr. Mankiewicz's incoherent picture. Again, why should one complain? He has enabled one to go on writing. (p. 55)

I am grateful to the cinema. It made twenty years of life easier and now, if the inferior medium of television kills it, I wonder whether television will do as much for the author. At least the cinema, like a psychiatrist, has enabled one to do without it.

But that last sentence which slipped unthinkingly off the pen has a certain sadness. Am I the same character who in the 1920's read *Close-Up* and the latest book on montage by Pudovkin with so much enthusiasm, who felt in *Mother, The Gold Rush,* in *Rein que les heures, Souvenirs d' automne, Warning Shadows,* even in such popular Hollywood films as *Hotel Imperial* and *Foolish Wives,* the possibility of a new kind of art? of a picture as formal in design as a painting, but a design which moved? The "talkies" were a set-back, but a temporary one. Quite quickly—even in so early a film as *The Perfect Alibi,* they too began to show here and there, in isolated scenes more often than in complete films, a selectivity of sound which promised to become as formal as the warning shadow—and they had a special interest to the writer. He was no longer merely the spectator or the critic of the screen. Suddenly the cinema needed him: pictures required words as well as images. (p. 56)

This was more dangerous to him, for a writer should not be employed by anyone but himself. If you are using words in one craft, it is impossible not to corrupt them by employing them in another medium under direction. (Proust found even conversation dangerous—the more intelligent the more dangerous, "since it falsifies the life of the mind by getting mixed up in it.") This is the side of my association with films that I most regret and would most like to avoid in future if taxation allows me to.

My first script—about 1937—was a terrible affair and typical in one way of the cinema-world. I had to adapt a story of John Galsworthy—a sensational tale of a murderer who killed himself and an innocent man who was hanged for the suicide's crime. If the story had any force at all it lay in its extreme sensationalism, but as the sensation was impossible under the rules of the British Board of Film Censors, who forbade suicide and forbade a failure of English justice, there was little of Galsworthy's plot left when I had finished. This unfortunate first effort was suffered with good-humoured nonchalance by Laurence Olivier and Vivien Leigh. I decided after that never to adapt another man's work and I have only broken that rule once in the case of *Saint Joan*—the critics will say another deplorable adaptation, though I would myself defend the script for retaining, however rearranged, Shaw's epilogue and for keeping a sense of responsibility to the author while reducing a play of three-and-a-half hours to a film of less than two hours.

I have a more deplorable confession—a film story directed by Mr. William Cameron Menzies called *The Green Cockatoo* starring Mr. John Mills—perhaps it preceded the Galsworthy (the Freudian Censor is at work here). The script of *Brighton Rock* I am ready to defend. There were good scenes, but the Boulting Brothers were too generous in giving an apprentice his rope, and the film-censor as usual was absurd—the script was slashed to pieces by the Mr. Watkyn of his day. There followed two halcyon years with Carol Reed, and I began to believe that I was learning the craft with *The Fallen Idol* and *The Third Man,* but it was an illusion. No craft had been learnt, there had only been the luck of working with a fine director who could control his actors and his production.

If you sell a novel outright you accept no responsibility; but write your own script and you will observe what can happen on the floor to your words, your continuity, your idea, the extra dialogue inserted during production (for which you bear the critics' blame), the influence of an actor who is only concerned with the appearance he wants to create before his fans. . . . Perhaps, you will come to think, there may be a solution if the author takes a hand in the production.

I thought that myself, and I do retain the happy memory of one unsuccessful film, *The Stranger's Hand:* days at Venice drinking grappa with Mario Soldati, running races down the Giudecca with Trevor Howard, the friendliness of the Italian unit. It encouraged me to go further along this road in a film which shall be nameless. To be a co-producer is no job for a writer. One becomes involved with the producer's monetary troubles: one has to accept actors who are miscast because another man's money is involved. As a writer one hasn't the blind optimism of the filmmaker who believes against all evidence that somehow the wrong actors, the wrong director, the wrong cameraman, the wrong art-director, the wrong colour-process, will all come together and produce a lucky accident.

It isn't the way that books are made. We have to learn our craft more painfully, more meticulously, than these actors, directors and cameramen who are paid, and paid handsomely, whatever the result. They can always put the blame for a disaster elsewhere which no novelist can. So the author—turned co-producer—shrugs his shoulders and gives up while the game is only half through. He knows what the result will be. Why go through the unpopular motions of fighting every battle lost at the start? He knows that even if a script be followed word by word there are those gaps of silence which can be filled with the banal embrace, irony can be turned into sentiment by some romantic boob of an actor. . . . No, it is better to sell outright and not to connive any further than you have to at a massacre. Selling outright you have at least saved yourself that ambiguous toil of using words for a cause you don't believe in—words which should be respected, for they are your livelihood, perhaps they are even your main motive for living at all. (pp. 56-61)

Graham Greene, "The Novelist and the Cinema—A Personal Experience," in International Film Annual, *No. 2, 1958, pp. 54-61.*

Ben Hecht

[*An American fiction writer, dramatist, and screenwriter, Hecht was one of the most prolific and successful writers in Hollywood from the 1920s to the 1940s. Among his original screenplays are the Academy Award-winning* Underworld (1927), *directed by Josef von Sternberg, and* Scarface (1932), *directed by Howard Hawks. In the following excerpt from his autobiography, Hecht looks back on his career as a Hollywood screenwriter.*]

For many years I looked on movie writing as an amiable chore. It was a source of easy money and pleasant friendships. There was small responsibility. Your name as writer was buried in a flock of "credits." Your literary pride was never involved. What critics said about the movie you had written never bothered you. They were usually criticizing something you couldn't remember. Once when I was a guest on a radio quiz show called "Information Please," the plot of a movie I had written a year before and that was playing on Broadway then was recited to me in full. I was unable to identify it.

For many years Hollywood held this double lure for me, tremendous sums of money for work that required no more effort than a game of pinochle. (pp. 466-67)

The movies are one of the bad habits that corrupted our century. Of their many sins, I offer as the worst their effect on the intellectual side of the nation. It is chiefly from that viewpoint I write of them—as an eruption of trash that has lamed the American mind and retarded Americans from becoming a cultured people.

The American of 1953 is a cliché-strangled citizen whose like was never before in the Republic. Compared to the pre-movieized American of 1910-1920, he is an enfeebled intellect. I concede the movies alone did not undo the American mind. A number of forces worked away at that project. But always, well up in front and never faltering at their frowsy task, were the movies.

In pre-movie days, the business of peddling lies about life was spotty and unorganized. It was carried on by the cheaper magazines, dime novels, the hinterland preachers and whooping politicians. These combined to unload a rash of infantile parables on the land. A goodly part of the population was infected, but there remained large healthy areas in the Republic's thought. There remained, in fact, an intellectual class of sorts—a tribe of citizens who never read dime novels, cheap magazines or submitted themselves to political and religious howlers.

Ben Hecht

It was this tribe that the movies scalped. Cultured people who would have blushed with shame to be found with a dime novel in their hands took to flocking shamelessly to watch the picturization of such tripe on the screen.

For forty years the movies have drummed away on the American character. They have fed it naïveté and buncombe in doses never before administered to any people. They have slapped into the American mind more human misinformation in one evening than the Dark Ages could muster in a decade. One basic plot only has appeared daily in their fifteen thousand theaters—the triumph of virtue and the overthrow of wickedness.

Two generations of Americans have been informed nightly that a woman who betrayed her husband (or a husband his wife) could never find happiness; that sex was no fun without a mother-in-law and a rubber plant around; that women who fornicated just for pleasure ended up as harlots or washerwomen; that any man who was sexually active in his youth, later lost the one girl he truly loved; that a man who indulged in sharp practices to get ahead in the world ended in poverty and with even his own children turning on him; that any man who broke the laws, man's or God's, must always die, or go to jail, or become a monk, or restore the money he stole before wandering off into the desert; that anyone who didn't believe in God (and said so out loud) was set right by seeing either an angel or witnessing some feat of levitation by one of the characters; that an honest heart must always recover from a train wreck or a score of bullets and win the girl it loved; that the most potent and brilliant of villains are powerless before little children, parish priests or young virgins with large boobies; that injustice could cause a heap of trouble but it must always slink out of town in Reel Nine; that there are no problems of labor, politics, domestic life or sexual abnormality but can be solved happily by a simple Christian phrase or a fine American motto.

Not only was the plot the same, but the characters in it never varied. These characters must always be good or bad (and never human) in order not to confuse the plot of Virtue Triumphing. This denouement could be best achieved by stereotypes a fraction removed from those in the comic strips.

The effect on the American mind of this forty-year barrage of Mother Goose platitudes and primitive valentines is proved by the fact that the movies became for a generation the favorite entertainment of all American classes.

There are millions of Americans who belong by nature in movie theaters as they belong at political rallies or in fortuneteller parlors and on the shoot-the-chutes. To these millions the movies are a sort of boon—a gaudier version of religion. All the parables of right living are paraded before them tricked out in gang feuds, earthquakes and a thousand and one near rapes. The move from cheap books to cheap movie seats has not affected them for the worse.

But beside these grass-root fans of platitude sit the once intellectual members of the community. They are the citizens whose good taste and criticism of claptrap were once a large part of our nation's superiority. There is little more in them today than the giggle of the movie fan. Watching the movies, they forget that they have taste, that their intelligence is being violated, that they are being booted back into the nursery. They forget even that they are bored.

In the movie theaters, all fifteen thousand of them, the U.S.A. presents a single backward front. (pp. 468-70)

As a writer in Hollywood, I spent more time arguing than writing—until the last four years when the British boycott left me without much bargaining power. My chief memory of movieland is one of asking in the producer's office why I must change the script, eviscerate it, cripple and hamstring it? Why must I strip the hero of his few semi-intelligent remarks and why must I tack on a corny ending that makes the stomach shudder? Half of all the movie writers argue in this fashion. The other half writhe in silence, and the psychoanalyst's couch or the liquor bottle claim them both.

Before it might seem that I am writing about a tribe of Shelleys in chains, I should make it clear that the movie writers "ruined" by the movies are for the most part a run of greedy hacks and incompetent thickheads. Out of the thousand writers huffing and puffing through movieland there are scarcely fifty men and women of wit or talent. The rest of the fraternity is deadwood. Yet, in a curious way, there is not much difference between the product of a good writer and a bad one. They both have to toe the same mark.

Nor are the bad writers better off spiritually. Their way is just as thorny. Minus talent or competence, the need for self-expression churns foolishly in them and their hearts throw themselves in a wild pitch for fame. And no less than the literary elite of Hollywood they feel the sting of its knout. However cynical, overpaid or inept you are, it is impossible to create entertainment without feeling the urges that haunt creative work. The artist's ego, even the ego of the Hollywood hack, must always jerk around a bit under restraint.

The studio bosses are not too inconvenienced by this bit of struggle. Experience has proved that the Hollywood artist in revolt is usually to be brought to heel by a raise in salary. My own discontent with what I was asked to do in Hollywood was so loud that I finally received a hundred and twenty-five thousand dollars for four weeks of script writing.

I have taken part in at least a thousand story conferences. I was present always as the writer. Others present were the "producer," the director and sometimes the head of the studio and a small tense group of his admirers.

The producer's place in movie making is a matter that, in Hollywood, has not yet been cleared up. (pp. 473-74)

There are different kinds of producers in the studios, ranging from out-and-out illiterates to philosophers and aesthetes. But all of them have the same function. Their task is to guard against the unusual. They are the trusted loyalists of cliché. Writers and directors can be carried away by a "strange" characterization or a new point of view; a producer, never. The producer is the shadow cast by the studio's Owner. It falls across the entire studio product.

I discovered early in my movie work that a movie is never any better than the stupidest man connected with it. There are times when this distinction may be given to the writer or director. Most often it belongs to the producer.

The job of turning good writers into movie hacks is the producer's chief task. These sinister fellows were always my bosses. Though I was paid often five and ten times more money than they for my working time, they were my judges. It was their minds I had to please.

I can recall a few bright ones among them, and fifty nitwits. The pain of having to collaborate with such dullards and to submit myself to their approvals was always acute. Years of experience failed to help. I never became reconciled to taking literary orders from them. I often prepared myself for a producer conference by swallowing two sleeping pills in advance.

I have always considered that half of the large sum paid me for writing a movie script was in payment for listening to the producer and obeying him. I am not being facetious. The movies pay as much for obedience as for creative work. An able writer is paid a larger sum than a man of small talent. But he is paid this added money not to use his superior talents.

I often won my battle with producers. I was able to convince them that their suggestions were too stale or too infantile. But I won such battles only as long as I remained on the grounds. The minute I left the studio my victory vanished. Every sour syllable of producer invention went back into the script and every limping foot of it appeared on the screen.

Months later, watching "my" movie in a theater, I realized that not much damage actually had been done. A movie is basically so trite and glib that the addition of a half dozen miserable inanities does not cripple it. It blares along barking out its inevitable clichés, and only its writer can know that it is a shade worse than it had to be. (pp. 475-76)

> Ben Hecht, "Artist, Friend, and Moneymaker," in his A Child of the Century, *Simon and Schuster, 1954, pp. 357-514.*

Raymond Chandler

[*Along with Dashiell Hammett, Chandler elevated the genre known as the hard-boiled detective story into an American art form. His novels describe luridly realistic action in a sophisticated literary style uncommon to pulp mystery fiction. For many readers Chandler's books represent the essence of southern California: the superficialities of Hollywood, crime and vice glossed over with wealth, the cult of glamor, and a certain enduring mystery which eludes precise definition. A number of Chandler's novels were adapted for film—including* The Big Sleep; Farewell, My Lovely; *and* The Long Goodbye—*and for a time Chandler worked as a screenwriter. His screenplay credits include* Double Indemnity (1944), *directed by William Wyler and based on the novel by James M. Cain, and* Strangers on a Train (1951), *directed by Alfred Hitchcock. In the following excerpt, Chandler describes the function and status of writers in Hollywood during the 1940s.*]

I hold no brief for Hollywood. I have worked there a little over two years, which is far from enough to make me an authority, but more than enough to make me feel pretty thoroughly bored. That should not be so. An industry with such vast resources and such magic techniques should not become dull so soon. An art which is capable of making all but the very best plays look trivial and contrived, all but the very best novels verbose and imitative, should not so quickly become wearisome to those who attempt to practise it with something else in mind than the cash drawer. The making of a picture ought surely to be a rather fascinating adventure. It is not; it is an endless contention of tawdry egos, some of them powerful, almost all of them vociferous, and almost none of them capable of anything much more creative than credit-stealing and self-promotion.

Hollywood is a showman's paradise. Showmen make nothing; they exploit what someone else has made. But the showmen of Hollywood control the making—and thereby degrade it. For the basic art of motion pictures is the screenplay; it is fundamental, without it there is nothing . . . But in Hollywood the screenplay is written by a salaried writer under the supervision of a producer—that is to say, by an employee without power or decision over the uses of his own craft, without ownership of it, and, however extravagantly paid, almost without honor for it . . .

I am not interested in why the Hollywood system exists or persists, nor in learning out of what bitter struggles for prestige it arose, nor in how much money it succeeds in making out of bad pictures. I am interested only in the fact that as a result of it there is no such thing as an art of the screenplay, and there never will be as long as the system lasts, for it is the essence of this system that it seeks to exploit a talent without permitting it the right to be a talent. It cannot be done; you can only destroy the talent, which is exactly what happens—when there is any to destroy.

Granted that there isn't much. Some chatty publisher (probably Bennett Cerf) remarked once that there are writers in Hollywood making two thousand dollars a week who haven't had an idea in ten years. He exaggerated—backwards: there are writers in Hollywood making two thousand a week who never had an idea in their lives, who have never written a photographable scene, who could not make two cents a word in the pulp market if their lives depended on it. Hollywood is full of such writers, although there are few at such high salaries. They are, to put it bluntly, a pretty dreary lot of hacks, and most of them know it, and they take their kicks and their salaries and try to be reasonably grateful to an industry which permits them to live much more opulently than they could live anywhere else.

And I have no doubt that most of them would like to be much better writers than they are, would like to have force and integrity and imagination—enough of these to earn a decent living at some art of literature that has the dignity of a free profession. It will not happen to them, and there is not much reason why it should. If it ever could have happened, it will not happen now. For even the best of them (with a few rare exceptions) devote their entire time to work which has no more possibility of distinction than a Pekinese has of becoming a Great Dane: to asinine musicals about technicolor legs and the yowling of nightclub singers; to "psychological" dramas with wooden plots, stock characters, and that persistent note of fuzzy earnestness which suggests the conversation of schoolgirls in puberty; to sprightly and sophisticated comedies (we hope) in which the gags are as stale as the attitudes, in which there is always a drink in every hand, a butler in every doorway, and a telephone on the edge of every bathtub; to historical epics in which the male actors look like female impersonators, and the lovely feminine star looks just a little too starry-eyed for a babe who has spent half her life swapping husbands; and last but not least, to those pictures of deep social import in which everybody is thoughtful and grown-up and sincere and the more difficult problems of life are wordily resolved into a unanimous vote of confidence in the inviolability of the Constitution, the sanctity of the home, and the paramount importance of the streamlined kitchen.

And these, dear readers, are the million-dollar babies—the cream of the crop. Most of the boys and girls who write for the screen never get anywhere near this far. They devote their sparkling lines and their structural finesse to horse operas, cheap gun-in-the-kidney melodramas, horror items about mad scientists and cliff hangers concerned with screaming blondes and circular saws. The writers of this tripe are licked before they start. Even in a purely technical sense their work is doomed for lack of the time to do it properly. The challenge of screenwriting is to say much in little and then take half of that little out and still preserve an effect of leisure and natural movement. Such a technique requires experiment and elimination. The cheap pictures simply cannot afford it.

Let me not imply that there are no writers of authentic ability in Hollywood. There are not many, but there are not many anywhere. The creative gift is a scarce commodity, and patience and imitation have always done most of its work. There is no reason to expect from the anonymous toilers of the screen a quality which we are very obviously not getting from the publicized litterateurs of the bestseller list, from the compilers of fourth-rate historical novels which sell half a million copies, from the Broadway candy butchers known as playwrights, or from the sulky maestri of the little magazines.

To me the interesting point about Hollywood writers of talent is not how few or how many they are, but how little of worth their talent is allowed to achieve. Interesting—but hardly unexpected, once you accept the premise that writers are employed to write screenplays on the theory that, being writers, they have a particular gift and training for the job, and are then prevented from doing it with any independence or finality whatsoever, on the theory that, being merely writers, they know nothing about making pictures; and of course if they don't know how to make pictures, they couldn't possibly know how to write them. It takes a producer to tell them that.

I do not wish to become unduly vitriolic on the subject of producers. My own experience does not justify it, and after all, producers too are slaves of the system. Also, the term "producer" is of very vague definition. Some producers are powerful in their own right, and some are little more than legmen for the front office; some—few, I trust—receive less money than some of the writers who work for them.

For my thesis the personal qualities of a producer are rather beside the point. Some are able and humane men and some are low-grade individuals with the morals of a goat, the artistic integrity of a slot machine, and the manners of a floorwalker with delusions of grandeur. In so far as the writing of the screenplay is concerned, however, the producer is the boss; the writer either gets along with him and his ideas (if he has any) or gets out. This means both personal and artistic subordination, and no writer of quality, will long accept either without surrendering that which made him a writer of quality, without dulling the fine edge of his mind, without becoming little by little a conniver rather than a creator, a supple and facile journeyman rather than a craftsman of original thought.

It makes very little difference how a writer feels towards his producer as a man: the fact that the producer can change and destroy and disregard his work can only operate to diminish that work in its conception and to make it mechanical and indifferent in execution. The impulse to perfection cannot exist where the definition of perfection is the arbitrary decision of authority. That which is born in loneliness and from the heart cannot be defended against the judgment of a committee of sycophants. The volatile essences which make literature cannot survive the clichés of a long series of story conferences. There is little magic of word or emotion or situation which can remain alive after the incessant bone-scraping revisions imposed on the Hollywood writer by the process of rule by decree. That these magics do somehow, here and there, by another and even rarer magic, survive and reach the screen more or less intact is the infrequent miracle which keeps Hollywood's handful of fine writers from cutting their throats.

Hollywood has no right to expect such miracles, and it does not deserve the men who bring them to pass. Its conception of what makes a good picture is still as juvenile as its treatment of writing talent is insulting and degrading. Its idea of 'production value' is spending a million dollars dressing up a story that any good writer would throw away. Its vision of the rewarding movie is a vehicle for some glamor-puss with two expressions and eighteen changes of costume, or for some male idol of the muddled millions with a permanent hangover, six worn-out acting tricks, the build of a lifeguard, and the mentality of a chicken-strangler. Pictures for such purposes as these, Hollywood lovingly and carefully makes. The good ones smack it in the rear when it isn't looking. (pp. 117-21)

Raymond Chandler, "Writers in Hollywood," in his Raymond Chandler Speaking, *edited by Dorothy Gardiner and Kathrine Sorley Walker, Houghton Mifflin Company, 1977, pp. 116-25.*

Daniel Fuchs

[*An American novelist and screenwriter, Fuchs is best known for* The Williamsburg Trilogy (1934-37), *which has been praised for its vivid depiction of Jewish life in a New York ghetto. He also wrote several original screenplays and adaptations, including the Academy Award-winning* Love Me or Leave Me (1955). *In the following piece entitled "A Hollywood Diary," written in 1938, Fuchs recounts a phase of his career as a screenwriter.*]

April 26—For ten days I have been sitting around in my two-room office, waiting for some producer on the lot to call me up and put me to work on a script. Every morning

I walk the distance from my apartment on Orchid Avenue and appear at the studio promptly at nine. The other writers pass my window an hour or so later, see me ready for work in my shirt sleeves and suspenders, and yell jovially "Scab!" But I don't want to miss that phone call.

I sent my secretary back to the stenographic department and told her I'd call her when I needed her. It was embarrassing with the two of us just sitting there and waiting.

Naturally, I can't expect an organization of this size to stop everything until I'm properly placed, but they pay me two hundred dollars a week and I do nothing to earn it. Himmer, my agent, tells me I'm getting "beans" and have no reason to think of the waste of money.

The main thing is not to grow demoralized and cynical.

A letter from home: "Hollywood must be different and exciting. Which actress are you bringing East for a wife?"

In the evening I walk down Hollywood Boulevard with all the other tourists, hoping for a glimpse of Carole Lombard and Adolphe Menjou. And after I get tired of walking I drop into a drugstore, where, with the lonely ladies from Iowa, I secretly drink a thick strawberry soda.

April 27—The telephone rang today but it was only the parking-lot attendant across the street. He wanted to know why I hadn't been using the parking space the studio assigned to me. I explained I had no car, which left him bewildered.

The truth is I can't buy one. When I left New York I owned a five-dollar bill and had to borrow six hundred dollars from my agent to pay my debts and get out here respectably.

My agent is collecting his six hundred dollars in weekly installments of fifty dollars. Also taking nips out of my check are his twenty-dollar weekly commisssion, the California unemployment tax, the federal old-age relief tax, and the Motion Picture Relief Fund, so that what actually comes to me isn't two hundred dollars at all, and it would take some time to get enough money together for a car.

With all these cuts I'm still making more money than I ever earned per week. Just the same, I'm kicking. The trouble is, I suppose, that it's misleading to think of salary in weekly figures when you work for the movies. Hardly anyone works fifty-two weeks a year; my own contract lasts thirteen weeks.

Still no telephone call from any producer.

April 28—Himmer, my agent, dropped in. He doesn't seem worried by my inactivity. "The check comes every week, doesn't it?" he asks. "It's good money, isn't it?"

April 29—I was put to work this morning. Mara, a sad-looking man who produces B pictures for the studio, asked me to do a "treatment" of a story called "No Bread to Butter." This is an "original"—a twenty-page synopsis of a picture for which the studio paid fifteen hundred dollars. Mara had put some other writers to work on treatments, but hadn't liked what they'd done any better than he liked the original. I didn't understand at all. Why had he bought "No Bread to Butter" if it was no good, I asked him. Mara smoked his cigar patiently for a while. "Listen," he said, "do I ask you personal questions?"

Daniel Fuchs

He wouldn't tell me what was wrong with the original or what he wanted. "The whole intention in the matter is to bring on a writer with a fresh approach. If I talk, you'll go to work with preconceived notions in your head. Tell the story as you see it and we'll see what comes out."

I went back to my office. "No Bread to Butter" seems to be a baldly manufactured story, but I'm anxious to see what I can do with it. I feel good, a regular writer now, with an assignment. It appears to worry the other writers that I have found something to do at last. They seemed fonder of me when I was just hanging around.

I phoned Himmer to tell him the good news. "See?" he said. "Didn't I tell you I'd take care of it? You let me handle everything and don't worry." He talked with no great enthusiasm.

May 5—The boys tell me I'm a fool to hand in my treatment so soon. Two or three weeks are the minimum time, they say, but I was anxious to get the work done to show Mara what I could do. Mara's secretary said I should hear from him in the morning.

May 6—Mara did not phone.

May 10—No phone.

May 11—No phone.

May 12—Mr. Barry phoned. He's assistant to the vice-president in charge of production and represents the front office. He called me at my apartment last night, after work. "Listen here, kid," he said, "I've been trying to reach you at your home all day. You've been out on the Coast a month now. Don't you think it's time you showed up at the lot?"

I protested, almost tearfully.

Seems that the administration building checked up on the absences of writers by the report sent in by the parking-lot attendant. Since I had no car, I hadn't been checked in. I explained, but Barry hung up, sounding unconvinced.

May 13—Nothing.

The malted milks in this town are made with three full scoops of ice cream. Opulence.

May 14—Mara finally called me in today, rubbed his nose for a few minutes, and then told me my treatment was altogether too good. "You come in with a script," he explained. "It's fine, it's subtle and serious. It's perfect—for Gary Cooper, not for my kind of talent."

I tried to get Mara to make a stab at the script anyhow, but nothing doing. Naturally, I'm not especially depressed.

May 17—Barry, front-office man, called me up again, this time at my office. He told me Mara had sent in an enthusiastic report on me. I was a fine writer—"serious"—and fit only for the A producers. Barry, who is taking "personal charge" of me, told me to see St. John, one of the company's best producers.

St. John's secretary made an appointment for me for the morning. She seemed to know who I was.

May 18—St. John gave me a cordial welcome and told me he's been wanting to do a historical frontier picture but has been held up because he can't find the right character. He's been hunting for three years now and asked me to get to work on the research.

I told him frankly I didn't imagine I'd be very successful with this, but he brushed my objections aside.

I'm back at the office and don't know exactly what to do. I don't want to spend time on anything as flimsy as this assignment. Nevertheless, I phoned the research department and asked them to send me everything they had on the early West. This turns out to be several very old books on Texas. I go through them with no great interest.

May 19—Still Texas. Sometimes, when I stop to see myself sitting in a room and reading books on Texas, I get a weird, dreamlike feeling.

Frank Coleman, one of the writers I've come to know, dropped in and asked me to play a little casino with him, five cents a hand. We played for about a half-hour.

May 21—Inter-office memo from St. John: "The front office tells me their program for the year is full and they have no room for an expensive frontier picture. Sorry."

I was struck again with the dream-like quality of my work here.

Frank Coleman, who dropped in for some casino, explained St. John's note. When a writer goes to work for a producer, the writer's salary is immediately attached to the producer's budget. St. John simply didn't want to be responsible for my salary.

At any rate I'm glad to be free of the Texas research.

May 24—Barry, front-office man, sent me to another producer, Marc Wilde, who gave me the full shooting script of *Dark Island*, which was made in 1926 as a silent picture. "My thought," said Wilde, "is to shoot the story in a talking version. However, before I put you to work on it, I want to find out what you think of it, whether you care to work on it, et cetera. So read it."

May 25—I didn't like *Dark Island* at all, but I didn't want to antagonize Wilde by being too outspoken. I asked him what *he* thought of it. "Me?" Wilde asked. "Why ask me? I haven't read the script."

Coleman and I play casino every afternoon now.

May 26—I've been coming to work at nine-thirty lately and today I walked in at ten. All the boys seem to like me now, and it is well-intentioned friendship, too. They pick me up at twelve for lunch at the commissary, where we all eat at the "round table." That is, the lesser writers ($100-$500) eat at a large round table. The intermediates ($500-$750) eat privately or off the lot. The big shots eat at the executives' table along with top-flight stars and producers. They shoot crap with their meals.

We're at lunch from twelve to two. Afterward we tour the lot for an hour or so in the sunshine, just walking around and looking at the sets in the different barns. Then it takes us a half-hour to break up at the doorway to the writers' building. When we finally go to our separate offices the boys generally take a nap. I took one, too, today. Coleman comes in at four for a half-hour's play at the cards and then we meet the other boys again at the commissary for afternoon tea, which amounts to a carbonated drink called 7 up. This leaves me a few minutes for these notes; I put on my hat and go home.

May 28—My fingernails seem to grow very rapidly. It may be the climate or simply because I have more time to notice them.

June 1—Very lazy. I read picture magazines from 10:30 until 12. After that the day goes fast enough.

June 3—The story editor called me up today and said Kolb wants to see me. Kolb is second- or third-ranking producer on the lot; when I mentioned the news to the boys, they all grew silent and ill at ease with me. No casino, no tour, no tea.

Appointment with Kolb in the morning. Himmer, who dropped in, seemed impressed. "Kid," he said, "this is your big chance."

June 4—Kolb strikes me as a man who knows what he wants and how to get it. He is a short man, conscious of his shortness. He stands on his toes when he talks, for the sake of the height, and punches out his words.

It seems I have to take a special course of instruction with him before he will put me to work. We spent an hour today in friendly conversation, mainly an autobiographical sketch of Kolb, together with lessons drawn therefrom

for my own advantage. I'm to return to his office after the weekend.

Coleman passed me and didn't speak.

June 6—Today Kolb described his system to me. You start off with a premise.

"Just for the sake of example," he said, "you take a girl who always screams when she sees a milkman. See, she's got a grudge against the milkman because a dearly beloved pet dog was once run over by a milk truck." Something like that—good comedy situation. Only, you must first invent a springboard. This is the scene which starts the picture, and Kolb wants it intriguing, even mystifying. "I'm not afraid of any man, big or small," he said, "but I shake in my boots when that skinny little guy in the movie theatre begins to reach under his seat for his hat." The function of the springboard is to hold the skinny man in his seat. "For example, purely for example, suppose we show the boy when the picture opens. See, he's walking into the Automat. He goes to the cake slot. He puts in two nickels or three nickels, as the case may be. The slot opens and out comes—the girl! Is that interesting? Will the skinny guy take his hat? No, he wants to know how that girl got there and what's going to happen now."

Kolb started to continue with the complications his springboard made possible, but was still fascinated by the Automat girl. He considered for a while and then said, "What the hell. It's nuts!" Then he seemed to lose interest in the lesson. "Listen," he finally said, "the best way to know what I want is to see the actual products. You go down and see the stuff I've made." He told his secretary to make arrangements.

June 7—Kolb's secretary sent me to a projection room, where I was shown three of his pictures. I understand what Kolb means by springboards. His pictures all begin very well, sometimes with shock, but the rest of the plot is a mess because it has to justify the outrageous beginning.

June 8—Kolb's secretary phoned and told me I was to see three more Kolb *opera*. I sit all by myself in a projection room, thinking of Ludwig of Bavaria in his exclusive theatre, and feeling grand too.

What impresses me is the extent to which these pictures duplicate themselves, not only in the essential material, but in many details of character, gags, plot, etc.

June 9—Three more pictures today.

June 10—More Kolb masterpieces. He has been in movies for twenty years and must have made a hundred pictures.

June 14—Today I was rescued from the projection room and was put to work. Kolb really shone with enthusiasm for the assignment he was giving me.

His idea was to rewrite a picture he did two years ago called *Dreams at Twilight*. If it pulled them in once, he said, then it would pull them in again. *Dreams at Twilight* involved a dashing, light-hearted hero who was constantly being chased by a flippant-minded girl. The hero deeply loved the girl, but avoided her because he was prejudiced against matrimony. "Sweet premise," Kolb said. "It's got charm, see what I mean?"

In addition to outwitting the heroine, the hero is fully occupied in the course of the picture: he is a detective and has a murder to solve.

"Now," Kolb said, "we remake the picture. *But*—instead of having the dashing boy detective, we make it a dashing girl this time. In other words, we make the picture in reverse. How's that for a new twist?"

He stood back in triumph and regarded my face for shock.

"Know why I'm changing the rôles?" he whispered. His whole manner suddenly became wickedly secretive. "This picture is for Francine Waldron!"

I began to tremble gently, not because Waldron was one of three most important actresses in Hollywood but because Kolb's mood was contagious and I had to respond as a matter of common politeness. When he saw the flush of excitement deepen on my face, he sent me off to work. He told his secretary to put me on his budget.

June 15—I finished a rough outline of the Waldron script, working hard on it—nine to five, and no drifting about the lot. It's a bare sketch but I'd like to get Kolb's reaction to it before going ahead. His secretary, however, told me Mr. Kolb was all tied up at the moment.

I'm going ahead, filling in the outline rather than waste the time.

June 18—Phoned Kolb's secretary, but he's still busy.

That peculiar feeling of dreamy suspension is very strong with me lately.

June 20—*Hollywood Reporter* notes that Kolb has bought a property called "Nothing for a Dime." It is described as a story in which a girl plays the part of a debonair detective, usually assigned to a man.

What's going on?

June 21—Finished a forty-page treatment of the Waldron script and asked Kolb's secretary to show this to him, since he couldn't see me. She said he would get it immediately and would let me know very shortly.

June 22—Begins nothing again.

June 23—Nothing.

June 24—Frank Coleman dropped in for casino—a depressing sign.

June 25—Barry, of the front office, called me in for a long personal interview. He told me that I was respected as a fine, serious writer, held in high regard. Was everything—office accommodations—suitable in every way? Then he said that the studio was putting me entirely on my own, allowing me to work without restrictions or supervision. The point was, I was an artist and could work without shackles.

At this point I interrupted and told him about the script I had written for Kolb.

"Kolb?" Barry asked. "Who says you're working for Kolb? He hasn't got you listed as one of his writers. You've been marked 'available' for twenty-four days now."

Nevertheless, I insisted that the story editor had sent me to Kolb, I had worked for him, and was waiting to see what he thought of my story. Barry didn't understand it. "O.K.," he said uncertainly. "I'll see Kolb at once and clear this all up."

More and more confusing. What impresses me, though, is that I don't feel bewildered or affected in any way. It's as though I'm not the one who's concerned here. Other days, other places, I should have been, to put it mildly, raving. However, I did phone Himmer, my agent. He heard me out and said he would scout around and that I was not to worry.

June 29—Barry phoned. He had seen Kolb and Kolb didn't like my script. Would I please get to work on my unrestricted, unsupervised assignment?

I didn't know quite how to begin on a thing like that and so I decided to make a beginning after the weekend. Went to the commissary for a soda and bumped into Kolb himself, coming out. He beamed kindly at me. "Kid, I know what it is to wait around," he said. "I'm awfully busy at the moment but sooner or later I'll get around to reading your script." He patted my shoulder and left.

June 30—Himmer dropped in. "About that Kolb," he said. "I picked up the inside story. See, what it was was this: when Kolb came to put you on his budget he called up to find out what your salary was. That's how he found out you get two hundred."

"So?"

So. Kolb figures he deserves the best writers on the lot. He told them he wouldn't put up with any two-hundred-dollar trash. It's a natural reaction."

We both sat there a while, passing time and talking about the administration in Washington.

"By the way," Himmer asked, "what kind of a story did Kolb have you work on?"

"A business for Francine Waldron."

Himmer laughed genially. "Waldron has no commitments on this lot. She doesn't work here, you know."

We both laughed pleasantly at the strange mind Kolb had and what went on in it.

July 1 Nothing worth noting.

July 12—I asked Coleman over casino how the front office told you that you were fired. "They don't tell you," Coleman said. "They're supposed to pick up options two weeks before the contract expires. If they don't, they don't. That's all."

The two-week period with me began some days ago.

July 14—I keep coming to work, although I understand this isn't really necessary. But it's pleasant to see the boys, who are touching in their solicitude for me.

July 15—I came to work at ten-thirty this morning and found a genial, eager chap sitting at my desk in his shirt sleeves. "There must be some mistake," he stammered. "I'm new here. They told me to take this office."

I assured him there was no mistake. He seemed to be a fine

fellow, sincere and impatient to start work. We sat around and chatted for an hour or so. While I cleaned up my desk, he had the embarrassed tact to leave me alone. (pp. 22-4, 26)

> *Daniel Fuchs, "A Hollywood Diary," in* The New Yorker, *Vol. XIV, No. 25, August 6, 1938, pp. 22-4, 26.*

AUTHORS ON FILM ADAPTATIONS OF THEIR WORKS

James R. Messenger

[*In the following excerpt, Messenger reports the comments of nineteen novelists regarding film adaptations of their works.*]

Surely everybody—at least once—has gone to the movies and seen a film based on some book they've read and remarked, "That wasn't *anything* like the book!" Many times there's a second statement attached to the first: "I think I liked the book better."

As a practical matter, there are many reasons for the discrepancies between what appears on the printed page and what one sees on a motion picture screen. *Literature/Film Quarterly* deals with this matter on a regular basis. (p. 125)

But one thing has been noticeably missing from so much of the discussion about making movies from books and plays: The author's opinion of the screen version of his or her work. For every novelist . . . who speaks on the issue, there are many more who remain part of the literary "silent majority."

As amateur critics, we all make our declarations on the appropriateness of a novel in screen form. But what about the authors? Have they been consistently satisfied with what they saw or has there been more often than not a large measure of disappointment for them in terms of final result?

During my graduate school days a few years ago, I took it upon myself to look into the matter. I sent a questionnaire to as many authors as I could find addresses for. My only criterion was that the authors had had one or more of their novels made into motion pictures. Nineteen authors were kind enough to reply. They are, in alphabetical order:

> William Armstrong
> James Leo Herlihy
> John Hersey
> Evan Hunter
> James Jones
> Bel Kaufman
> Sue Kaufman
> Ken Kesey
> Daniel Keyes
> John Knowles
> Helen MacInnes
> Bernard Malamud

> Irving Stone
> Robert Penn Warren
> Morris West
> Thornton Wilder
> Kathleen Winsor
> Herman Wouk
> Frank Yerby

My survey consisted of four questions:

1. Do you feel changes made in translating your work to the screen ultimately violated the thesis of your book?

2. Do you agree or disagree with the characters and/or segments eliminated? Is there an example of a character or segment you feel important to the development of your story which is missing?

3. Do you feel filmmakers should be obliged to adhere strictly to a literary piece when adapting for the screen in view of the differences between the medium of the novel and the medium of the film?

4. Were you consulted during the adaptation process?

Each questionnaire addressed itself specifically to one or two of the author's novels. Question #1 was intended to gather an assessment of the novel as a movie according to the author. This was the essential issue. Did the book make it to the screen or not?

Question #2 was a refinement of the first question. It attempts to move the author at least one step away from a "gut level" reaction, and to objectify what has caused the distortion of the author's work on the screen, if he or she sees it as such.

Question #3 probes an author's awareness of the process of adaptation. Does he have any comprehension of the problems involved in going from words to celluloid? Does he, in fact, understand the basic "differences" between the two media? This question also was intended to reveal something of the degree of antipathy or acceptance on the part of the author to film form.

Question #4 was designed to establish the author's role in the adaptation process. Was the author "left out" of the adaptation process? If so, would this perhaps be evidence of a source of negative feelings towards filmmakers and/or screen adaptation of novels?

Now that all sounds nice and neat and objective. So why don't I open the door to our Pandora's box and see what comes out?

> *Do you feel changes made in translating your work to the screen ultimately violated the thesis of your book?*

Twelve writers felt the basic thesis of their novel (or novels) had been violated by the filmmakers in bringing their work to the screen. Two writers, James Jones and Helen MacInnes were split on their decision. James Jones, for instance, while " . . . relatively disappointed in the screen adaptation of both *From Here to Eternity* and *Some Came Running,*" nevertheless felt that "*From Here to Eternity* was remarkably well translated into film," while the script of *Some Came Running,* "was a mis-managed butchery of the entire book."

Helen MacInnes felt that to make the screen version of her novel *Above Suspicion,* "there were some changes but perhaps necessary for film purposes." But in contrast to that, "in *The Venetian Affair,* even the background scenes in Venice were altered. Ridiculous!"

Thornton Wilder, whose response is not included in the tabulation, was either being serious or kind when commenting about the screen versions of his novel *The Bridge of San Luis Rey:* "There were two movies made from that book. I've forgotten them both."

> *Do you agree or disagree with the characters and/or segments eliminated?*
>
> *Is there an example of a character or segment you feel is important to the development of your story which is missing?*

Condensation of novels when they go to film form is a necessary evil. (This may be changing now that television is producing expanded mini-series based on best sellers.) A long, rambling novel simply will not fit into ninety minutes of film time, which is more or less the norm for feature films these days. This is one fact of life a novelist must cope with if he or she sells their work to the movie people.

The survey found that even for those authors who basically agreed with changes made in their story, there still proved to be changes that irritated. William Armstrong, the author of *Sounder,* was one of those who agreed with changes made to his story. Yet he says: "Except the change of teacher weakened the story."

Likewise, Bel Kaufman, author of *Up the Down Staircase,* wrote:

> Many scenes were deleted which read very well but possibly may not have played as well. I had but one objection to—not a deletion, but an inclusion: the character of Mr. Barringer was totally and completely changed in the writing and a gratuitous scene was added for him to play, which struck a false note both in the character of the man and in the concept of the book.

And John Knowles: "The film version of *A Separate Peace* was extremely faithful to the novel as far as the film was able to go. It was unable to convey a sort of redemption to Gene's experience at the end of the novel."

Evan Hunter provided one of the two affirmative responses which had no misgivings (the other was James Leo Herlihy): "We're looking for the spirit of the work, and not the letter. *The Blackboard Jungle,* for example, retained hardly a word of the book on the screen. And yet the film was faithful to the novel."

The comments of those who disagreed with changes to their works ranged in tone from passive acceptance to mild outrage:

James Jones on *Some Came Running*

> I would say that just about only the character of 'Bama, played by Dean Martin, had any bearing on the book at all.

Sue Kaufman on *Diary of a Mad Housewife*

I feel the character of Jonathan, the husband, was made too much of a caricature—and I felt that they did not do enough with the setting, the Madness of New York, an important part of the book.

Ken Kesey on *Sometimes a Great Notion*

> The whole pivot between Viv and Lee [was missing].

Daniel Keyes on *Flowers for Algernon ("Charly")*

> I think the filmmakers lost a lot when they avoided the dénouement, and made a quick jump from Charly's discovery of what was going to happen to him, to a sudden end. They felt that the audience couldn't stand the agony of the downward curve. But this is the major power and structure of the book. Charly should have been shown, at least to some degree, going down as well as up.

Helen MacInnes on *The Venetian Affair*

> *All* the characters were changed and emphasis shifted. Heroine of book became minor part; and secondary part of dedicated communist ex-wife was promoted to heroine of the film.

Irving Stone on *Lust for Life*

> I was unhappy that they left out the complete opening chapter in England, because that explained what transformed Vincent's life.

Kathleen Winsor on *Forever Amber*

> As for the characters: I could not recognize them, except when they were given names in the script. Otherwise I should [have] had no faintest clue as to who those people were up there simpering and strutting. No acquaintances of mine, certainly.

Herman Wouk on *Youngblood Hawke*

> As clear an example as I can think of is the traducing of *Youngblood Hawke.* Hawke lives at the end. This alone destroys the novel's theme and story structure.

Frank Yerby on *The Foxes of Harrow*

> In the first film, *The Foxes of Harrow,* at least *five* characters, and twenty scenes are missing.

Bernard Malamud gracefully handled the question with an "I don't remember," and Thornton Wilder replied: "The one thing that the movies can't do in 1-2 hours: grip one's attention on four simultaneous plots."

> *Do you feel filmmakers should be obliged to adhere strictly to a literary piece when adapting for the screen in view of the differences between the medium of the novel and the medium of the film?*

This question was designed to probe an author's understanding of the film medium as well as hopefully to provide a less emotional and more objective evaluation by authors of the novel to movie process.

Interestingly enough, fifteen authors were in favor of giving filmmakers a free hand in adapting for the screen. However, it should be added that carte blanche destruction of a literary work was not advocated by anyone. Replies were more along the line that the resultant film should at least hold to the spirit of the book:

Daniel Keyes

I don't think filmmakers can or should be obliged to adhere to a literary piece, but I do think that changes should be made only to intensify and to translate, maintaining the integrity of the work rather than to modify for commercial reasons.

Helen MacInnes

Necessary changes; but [the film] should remain within the spirit of the book.

The Venetian Affair was a best seller here and in Europe for many months. The film was a flop. Doesn't this teach the revisionists, when they put their theories into scripts, something to remember? What are these people on—ego trips? In contrast to all this, the scriptwriter was faithful to the story of Forsyth's *Day of the Jackal,* so that it was as successful, as a film, as it had been as a novel.

Frank Yerby

The media are too different, but the author should be consulted.

Bel Kaufman

As for adapting a novel to the screen, the same rules should apply as to a translation from a foreign language. Instead of a literal rendition, some approximation of the spirit of the work, some idiom indigenous to the screen that would correspond to the written word.

A book is a book. A film is a film—and seldom the twain do meet.

Evan Hunter

I don't believe there is *any* excuse for not being able to translate a literary work effectively to the screen. (Please note that I use the word "translate." Making a movie from a book is in every way a "translation.")

It's impossible to adhere strictly to the work when translating it to film.

But then Hunter, like several other respondents, goes on to weigh some of the problems stemming from the differences in the two forms:

The two experiences are essentially different. A person reads *alone;* the communication between author and reader is entirely private. A film is viewed in public, and the reaction to the film is certainly affected by the reactions of those sitting around you as well. A film is created by a large group of people and seen by a large group of people. A novel or short story is created by one person (usually) and read by one person. The escalation in numbers alone would make it necessary for the original work to be substantially changed in translation. Add to that the visual advantage of film and the change becomes necessary.

James Jones, Irving Stone and Herman Wouk all pointed out that the usually necessary problem of compressing a novel into approximately ninety minutes of film often makes it impossible to adhere strictly in adaptation:

Irving Stone

The medium of the printed word and film are quite

different. The filmmaker is obliged to get the essence of a novel; there is almost no way for him to get the bulk.

Herman Wouk

Your question is, I fear, naive. How do you propose to "oblige" film makers to adhere strictly to a literary piece? In large-scale novels such as I write, there must be severe cinematic condensation. Results are sometimes fortunate: I think of *Dr. Zhivago* and *From Here to Eternity.* Smaller books can be screened with fidelity, if the producer, director, and writer have the sense to do it. Here I think of *To Kill a Mockingbird* and *The Bridge over the River Quai.* But no contractual controls make any difference, if film makers are determined to rewrite a book. An author cannot engage in a legal struggle with a film corporation.

James Jones

. . . I don't see how film makers can possibly be obliged to adhere strictly to a book they are adapting. The two media are simply just too different. To adapt *Some Came Running* faithfully would have required some ten hours of film. Obviously this would be impossible. And, since some wording and changing is [sic] required, it is next to impossible to make a producer keep within the spirit of a book.

I know from the experience of other writers that insisting on a script approval does not work. Even if you have approved a script, the director can, and generally does, change it all around from the written script during the actual shooting.

James Jones, Irving Stone and Kathleen Winsor pointed out how business and social decisions tend to interfere with the adaptation process:

James Jones

There are also "business" and "social" restrictions applied to film which do not apply to the novel. Getting a proper star, for example. Keeping in step with current social censorship.

Irving Stone

I thought characters were sometimes miscast for what they called "box-office insurance."

Kathleen Winsor

I cannot blame the company which made the picture entirely, for the code in those days determined that they show a "fallen woman" by having her put rouge on her cheeks—whereas nowadays it has apparently (I stay away from pornography of all kinds) gone to the opposite extreme, or worse.

Four respondents had extremely liberal attitudes towards adapting for the screen. Thornton Wilder felt filmmakers should be given a generous leeway in bringing literary works to the screen, but he also has high expectations of the practitioners of the craft:

I believe that cinema in important hands is another way of telling a story and should be permitted large liberty in adapting a novel to the form.

Later [after *Bridge of San Luis Rey*] a movie was made of my play *Our Town.* That play is rendered partly abstract, partly universal (in the sense of meaning: the events could happen anywhere, which has proved so because it has found attentive audiences in Chile and Turkey and many other places.) To my great disappointment the movie director did not find a *cinemagraphic* way of restoring that quality: he photographed solid houses, churches, and so on.

Robert Penn Warren sees nothing wrong with using one creative work as the roots of another:

> It seems to me that a film maker has to start from scratch, in the new medium, and that there is no necessary obligation to make the film a transcription of the book. For example, the film of AKM [*All the King's Men*] had a very different meaning from that of the novel, but it was, in its own terms, a very fine film.

James Leo Herlihy also agrees with this vein of thinking. His answer to whether or not filmmakers should be obliged to follow a book closely was: "No. Not at all. They are making films; have no 'literary' debts."

John Knowles's reason for allowing filmmakers a free hand in adapting for the motion pictures is that "if they did that [it] would make for a great many tedious movies."

Ken Kesey was the sole voter in favor of forcing filmmakers to adhere closely to an original work. At the time Kesey received his questionnaire, which referred to the adaptation of his book *Sometimes a Great Notion,* the film of his novel *One Flew Over the Cuckoo's Nest* was in production. About this he says: "The same thing altho worse is happening right now to *Cuckoo's Nest.* A most depressing situation—like finding out you signed something long ago permitting your child to be raped."

Morris West, while basically agreeing that "the grammar of film is different," nevertheless suggests that: "The argument must remain pure. . . . In European Law, the artist's work is protected by 'droit moral' which even he cannot abrogate legally. American contracts abrogate 'droit moral' and try to allow unlimited change by producers."

Kathleen Winsor's and John Hersey's votes on this question went unrecorded because both had serious doubts about whether movies should be made from novels anyway:

Kathleen Winsor

> As to your question about whether or not filmmakers should adhere to the original story or novel, I do not know. In many—most—instances, I should think that a direct translation from the printed page to the screen would be impossible. In fact, I have always wondered why they continue to try doing it, since it is always ridiculous in the final result. It would seem to me that scripts written directly for the screen have a much better chance of adapting to the screen than something written in a medium so different as the novel.

John Hersey

> I'm not sure I think novels ought to be made into films at all. These are two very different art forms. To my mind the only *really* successful translation from one form to the other was *Gone With the Wind.*

Were you consulted during the adaptation process?

This question proved far larger in scope than anticipated. For instance, of the twelve writers who answered "No," four of these writers, John Hersey, Robert Penn Warren, Thornton Wilder and Kathleen Winsor, said they *did not* want to be consulted.

John Hersey

> I was not consulted during the adaptation process. This was by my own choice. I had seen too many novelists struggle to maintain the integrity of their books as they went to film—and fail. I took the attitude that the income from films would subsidize my proper work, the writing of more novels; and that I would just turn my back on the process, and if a good film came along that would be good luck.

Kathleen Winsor

> . . . I thought the screen production of *Forever Amber* was absurd, and I am exceedingly happy to say that I had nothing whatever to do with it—as a result of my agent's foresightedness, who advised me that they would pretend I was a "technical assistant"—or whatever they called it—and proceed without reference to the suggestions for historical, or other accuracy, but I would be blamed for it later.

Bel Kaufman corroborated this approach to the author as technical advisor:

> Although I was what's known as a technical consultant, I did not get much of an opportunity to be consulted. I hung around the set, which was fun—but I had no voice in casting or the ultimate decisions, some of which were contrary to my own personal knowledge of schools.

This state of affairs was also verified by Ken Kesey, Morris West, and James Leo Herlihy:

Ken Kesey

> Yes, consulted and Jacked-off.

Morris West

> Yes, but advice rejected.

James Leo Herlihy

> Yes, but not listened to. Which is OK by me.

Bernard Malamud started off as a consultant then backed out: "I read Dalton Trumbo's first draft [of *The Fixer*] and asked not to see more."

Only three authors seemed to feel any sense of achievement in having worked on the production side of the adaptation process, John Knowles, James Jones, and Herman Wouk. Even then, only John Knowles was apparently really satisfied: "I was consulted during the adaptation process [of his novel *A Separate Peace*] and made a number of suggestions about changing the screen play, almost all of which were followed."

James Jones's and Herman Wouk's comments took this form:

James Jones

> Overall, I feel that *From Here to Eternity* was remarkably well translated into film.

With regard to *Some Came Running,* I was less happy. I had nothing to do with the script of that, whereas I did have some influence with *Eternity.*

Herman Wouk

On some occasions I have been consulted in the adaptation process; on others, not. The films have been a little better when I have been consulted. Ultimately, however, it's a matter of luck. If the director grasps the vision of the work, it has a chance of arriving on the screen with its essence preserved. I have not had that good fortune, in the five films that have been made of my works.

Of those who were excluded from the adaptation process, the additional comments ranged from wounded pride to a measure of understanding:

Sue Kaufman

No, alas.

Irving Stone

I was not consulted in any way during the adaptation of *Lust for Life, The Agony and the Ecstasy,* and *The President's Lady* for the screen. No author is, unless he is hired to write his own screenplay as Leon Uris did with *Battle Cry.* The studios seem to feel that the author will only confuse them, and they would: "Why have you left out these master scenes?" "What is that new scene you have put in that is not in my book?"

Evan Hunter

I have never been consulted by a screenwriter or a director when one of my own novels was being translated to film by another writer. Nor have I been asked to consult with the original author when translating someone else's work. It's an old Hollywood custom to consider the original work, however marvelous it might be, as only the blueprint or the outline for the film. Hollywood, I firmly believe, hates writers anyway, be they novelists or screenwriters. I'm sure they would shoot movies *without* a script, if they could possibly get away with it.

A Sort of Conclusion

Remember that nobody can compel an author to sell his works to films. Necessity, however, can. So can greed. So can inexperience. If one takes the film maker's money, one must abide the results. It is a mistake to expect artistic fidelity, though it can happen.

                                 Herman Wouk

As it seems clear by this point, most of the authors felt their novels failed to reach the screen. And as we also saw, many of the authors were able to be quite specific as to what they felt prevented their book from reaching the screen. This high degree of objectivity demonstrated on the part of the majority of the authors is certainly at odds with the stereotyped view of the novelist as "ungrateful complainer."

But if the novelists as a whole were unsatisfied with the results, what do they expect? Obviously more than they're getting. However, John Hersey suggests that there's really not much chance for authors to ever be completely satisfied with the films made from their novels:

There's a basic conflict of visions here—and I do mean, exactly, visions. The author of the novel has seen in his mind's eye for many months, or for years, the faces, the gestures, the mannerisms of his characters. Then on the screen appear total strangers displacing those images, asserting new characteristics, outward and inward. The writer almost can't help being outraged.

George Bernard Shaw suggested long ago that the answer may be for writers to make the film version of their own work, or, at least, as Bel Kaufman says, of any future go around with the cinema: "I should want to—insist on—doing my own screenplay adaptation!"

When it comes to motion picture adaptations of novels, French critic André Bazin doesn't think there is anything for an author to worry about except his pride anyway. Sales of a novel, he tells us in his book *What Is Cinema?,* almost invariably go up following the release of an adaptation. If the adaptation turns out to be a bad film, those who know the book will disregard the film. And a book's life, he also says, surely is longer than a film's, at least judging by current film distribution practices.

For the dedicated novelist, there could be worse things than a bad adaptation—like not having time to write, as Katherine Anne Porter complained on James Day's PBS interview program "Day at Night." The money for the screen rights to *Ship of Fools* finally gave Porter the freedom and independence to spend her primary efforts on her writing. Unfortunately, she was 72 years of age at the time. . . .

In truth, there is probably no "ultimate" solution to the author's dilemma. Once a novelist's book leaves his or her hands, as Herman Wouk says, "it's a matter of luck." The variables of motion picture production are so great, and an author's vision of his work is so precise, that a clash between the two is inevitable. Besides, as Robert Senglaub, a very wise film director, once told me: "There are very few writers. But *everybody* can rewrite." (pp. 125-34)

> *James R. Messenger, " 'I Think I Liked the Book Better': Nineteen Novelists Look at the Film Version of Their Work," in* Literature/Film Quarterly, *Vol. VI, No. 2, Spring, 1978, pp. 125-34.*

Heinrich Mann

[*A German fiction writer, dramatist, and critic, Mann is considered the father of the German intellectual Left. Both in his fiction and nonfiction he criticized the authoritarian mentality and examined its social and psychological effects. He is best known for his novel* Professor Unrat, *a satire about the abuse of power which was popularized in Josef von Sternberg's film version,* The Blue Angel. *In the following excerpt, Mann recalls the genesis of* Professor Unrat *and discusses Sternberg's film.*]

The events which unfold [in the film *The Blue Angel*] came first to my attention while I was watching a play in Florence. During the intermission, a newspaper was sold in the theater which reported from Berlin the story of a professor whose relations with a cabaret singer had caused him to commit a crime. I had barely finished reading the few lines when the figure of Professor Unrat, that of his seductress, and even the place of her activities, the Blue Angel, arose in my mind's eye.

At that time, I was young enough for the experiences of my boyhood still to be close and at instant recall. As a child, one does not yet know a host of people; they do not crowd each other out, and each one appears as soon as his tone is sounded. Professor, for me, meant simply high school teacher. The unusual linking of a professor with a *chanteuse* immediately suggested to me a stern but inexperienced man who, usually lording it over his students, now becomes less than a student, a mere toy in the hands of a girl. Once and for all, the girl looked as she would have had to look in order to make an aging man forget all his principles. As for the joint, it was always called the Blue Angel, was located in a side street near the harbor and suffused with the odor of tar, beer, and powder. The hearts of the boys who secretly sneaked there had beaten violently. Accordingly, the professor I envisaged during that intermission possessed a number of boyish traits.

From the very start, I knew him inside out. He and his fate had only to be elaborated and put down on paper. They had made their appearance without my having to invent them. A chance report had summoned them, and a vision had introduced them to me.

A few days later, by the way, the Italian newspapers rounded out the story. The *chanteuse*'s friend was actually a journalist covering the stock market and calling himself professor. He probably was the very opposite of my fictitious character who had gained so firm a foothold on my imagination.

The figure of Professor Unrat and the novel by that name are pretty old hat by now. The novel has been read by numerous generations of readers, and for many the figure has become one of those close acquaintances one frequently thinks of. For among the people we know intimately there are, upon careful reflection, more imaginary than real ones.

A novel is a world in itself, for it does not count in vain on man's greatest and most fatal gift, his imagination. We build a city, a house, a room and fill the latter with people. We place other people in other rooms, lead the ones to the others, and, while they move, their fate is decided. Our fellow beings are in a dither because an unusual event and an extraordinary character have come to the fore. We stage these events, although only verbally. Still, they are made visible to the imagination. Our work is that of an extremely independent and ingenious stage director, and viewed from this angle, writing a novel is equivalent to putting on a play.

Is that the reason why, from the start, I felt sympathetic toward the film *The Blue Angel?* A film is no novel; its action cannot unfold exactly as it does in literature, for the streets, as well as human lives, require different perspectives. Like the other collaborators on the film, I, too, endeavored to effect the transition from one medium to the other. The director (Sternberg) and the actor Jannings had to have clear sailing when their work began.

Finally, the strange moment arrived when, together with Jannings (who wore the mask of Professor Unrat), I found myself in the professor's messy bedroom. Jannings sat on the bed, with shelves full of dusty books above him. Dusty books everywhere, and a stove pipe ran right through the room. The technicians were working on their cameras, and we had to wait until they were ready. Then I recalled the first appearance of this "Unrat": Florence, the intermission—a long time ago. Here he was and he had not changed a bit.

He had gone through many experiences in the meantime and had passed through different times and heads. But he still loved the same kind of women, was as ponderous and innocent as before, and was headed for exactly the same fate. A great actor, Emil Jannings, had borrowed his shape and was now displaying it to me. He had enlarged on the figure, following its innermost nature, for in the novel Unrat does not die; but Jannings knew and realized the manner of his death.

The director, Sternberg, knew every step which this and the other figures were to take through the little town. He knew exactly what gestures, sounds, noises, songs and screams were in store for it. The corners and nooks of the plastically reconstructed city and street came to life for him even before the actors made them lively. I, for my part, remembered all these corners from the past. Not only Professor Unrat's messy bedroom but the entire Blue Angel from top to bottom had been revived in the studios of Neubabelsberg. I passed through the hall and climbed the winding stairs, as I might have done previously. Everything seemed to have returned uncannily out of the blue. In Neubabelsberg, there were two steps at the entrance to the Blue Angel, and I was immediately convinced that the same was true of its model. The rather shady lane passing by the cabaret was certain to lead into the once familiar city. At any rate, it led to the downfall of the figure that was still close to me.

Later on, I repeatedly watched the shooting and felt sympathetic toward the work of the actors, as I always do. I was unable to see the completed film in Berlin. The producer, Erich Pommer, had to go to Paris and was kind enough to bring the film to Nice, where I was then dwelling. Here he showed it to me.

This happened in a large and empty theater at the beach, in the morning and while the cleaning ladies were at work. The operator had some trouble with the reels since the sound track system was technically rather advanced. Even the French exclamations which resounded through the building made me feel how long a road the Blue Angel and its protagonist had travelled—from the port city in the North, where they acted out their story with me as their only witness, to the beach in the South where they were now shown to me.

There were only three spectators in the large French theater; and we saw the admirable Jannings smile—the gentle, childlike smile of a late and dangerous happiness breaking forth and shining through an unhappy face. Many people in several continents will soon have occasion to see it, too. While they look at these gaudy pictures and this gaudy world, they ought to sense the terror of a fate lived to its bitter end. (pp. 125-28)

Heinrich Mann, " 'The Blue Angel' is Shown to Me," translated by Ulrich Weisstein, in Authors on Film, *edited by Harry M. Geduld, Indiana University Press, 1972, pp. 125-28.*

T. S. Eliot

[*Perhaps the most influential poet and critic to write in the English language during the first half of the twentieth century, Eliot is closely identified with many of the qualities denoted by the term Modernism: experimentation, formal complexity, artistic and intellectual eclecticism, and a classicist's view of the artist working at an emotional distance from his or her creation. He introduced a number of terms and concepts that strongly affected critical thought in his lifetime, among them the idea that poets must be conscious of the living tradition of literature in order for their work to have artistic and spiritual validity. In general, Eliot upheld values of traditionalism and discipline, and in 1928 he annexed Christian theology to his overall conservative worldview. In the following excerpt, Eliot comments on the adaptation of his verse drama* Murder in the Cathedral *as a film directed by George Hoellering.*]

Murder in the Cathedral is, I believe, the first contemporary verse play to be adapted to the screen. That is in itself a justification for publishing this film script, apart from the value and interest of the illustrative matter. It is certainly the only excuse for a preface by the author of the play.

I should like, first of all, to make clear the limits of my collaboration. At the beginning, Mr. Hoellering asked me to make a film recording of the entire play in my own voice. This recording (which was only completed after a number of sessions) was to serve as a guide, for himself and for the actors, to the rhythms and emphases of the verse as I heard it myself. He tells me that he found this recording very useful: I only know that it suggested to him the possibility of using my voice for the words of the Fourth Tempter—after he had had the happy idea of presenting the Fourth Temptation merely as a voice preceeding from an invisible actor. (He did wisely in demanding of me another recording of this voice, made later after the filming of the scene: for no one—certainly not the author—can throw himself completely into any one part, when he is reading all the parts in succession.)

After making this first recording, I wrote the preliminary scenes which he told me would be needed to turn the play into an intelligible film. He gave me the subject–matter of these scenes; and I had only to provide the words. Of the necessity of these additional scenes I shall have something to say presently. As to the quality of the verse, I should like to say this: that if it seems inferior to that of the original play, I must ask the critic to observe that I had to imitate a style which I had abandoned as unsuitable for other purposes than that of this one play; and that to compose a pastiche of one's own work some years later is almost as difficult as to imitate the work of another writer. If the new lines are judged to be as good as the old ones, that may call into question the value of the play itself as a contribution to poetry; but I shall nevertheless conclude that the additions constitute a successful *tour de force*.

Beyond the execution of these two definite tasks, my collaboration in the making of the film seems to have been limited to frequent discussions with the producer, in which I accepted nearly all of his suggestions, to frequent visits to the workshop and the studio, and one or two lengthy arguments where differences of opinion arose. Such occasions were rare. I learned something about film technique. And, just as, in learning a foreign language, we learn more about the resources and limitations of our own, so I think that I learned something more about the theatre, in discovering the different resources and limitations of the screen.

The first and most obvious difference, I found, was that the cinema (even where fantasy is introduced) is much more realistic than the stage. Especially in an historical picture, the setting, the costume, and the way of life represented have to be accurate. Even a minor anachronism is intolerable. On the stage much can be overlooked or forgiven; and indeed, an excessive care for accuracy of historical detail can become burdensome and distracting. In watching a stage performance, the member of the audience is in direct contact with the actor, is always conscious that he is looking at a stage and listening to an actor playing a part. In looking at a film, we are much more passive; as audience, we contribute less. We are seized with the illusion that we are observing the actual event, or at least a series of photographs of the actual event; and nothing must be allowed to break this illusion. Hence the precise attention to detail given by Mr. Hoellering, an attention which at first seemed to me excessive. In the theatre, the first problem to present itself is likely to be that of casting. For the film of *Murder in the Cathedral,* Mr. Hoellering's first care was that the materials for the costumes should be woven in exactly the same way, from exactly the same materials, as they would have been in the twelfth century. I came to appreciate the importance of texture of material, and the kinds of folds into which the material falls, when fashioned into garments and worn by the actors, after I had seen the first photographing.

The difference between stage and screen in respect of realism is so great, I think, as to be a difference of kind rather than degree. It does not indicate any superiority of either medium over the other: it is merely a difference. It has further consequences. The film, standing in a different relation to reality from that of the stage, demands rather different treatment of *plot*. An intricate plot, intelligible on the stage, might be completely mystifying on the screen. The audience has no time to think back, to establish relations between early hints and subsequent discoveries. The picture passes before the eyes too quickly; and there are no intervals in which to take stock of what has happened, and make conjectures of what is going to happen. The observer is, as I have said, in a more passive state. The film seems to me to be nearer to narrative and to depend much more upon the episodic. And, as the observer is in a more passive state of mind than if he were watching a stage play, so he has to have more explained to him. When Mr. Hoellering pointed out to me that the situation at the beginning of the play of *Murder in the Cathedral* needed some preliminary matter to make it intelligible, I at first supposed that what he had in mind was that a film was aimed at a much larger, and therefore less well informed audience, ignorant of English history, than that which goes to see a stage play. I very soon became aware that it was not a difference between one type of audience and another, but between two different dramatic forms. The additional scenes, to explain the background of events, are essential for *any* audience, including even those persons already familiar with the play. On the other hand, I hope that no amateur stage producer will ever be so ill-advised as to add these scenes to his production. They are right for the film;

they would ruin the shape of the play. In the play, there is not room, beside Thomas Becket, for another dominating character such as Henry II; but in the film, he is not only admissible, but necessary.

I then discovered another interesting and important difference. The speeches of my Four Knights, which in the play are addressed directly to the audience, had to be completely revised. (Mr. Hoellering himself is responsible for the ingenious rearrangement and abbreviation; and I am responsible only for the words of the new ending of the scene.) This also is a consequence of the *realism* of film: the *Stilbruch*—as such an abrupt change is aptly called in German—would be intolerable. (It took me some time, and much persuasion, to understand the difference, and accept it.) For one thing, the camera *must never stand still.* An audience can give their attention to four men actually speaking to them; but to look at the picture of the same four men for that length of time would be an intolerable strain. Furthermore, having once got away from the scene of the murder, it would be impossible to get back to it. Therefore the speeches have to be adapted so as to be spoken to the crowd assembled at the cathedral; and when the third knight turns at last to address the audience, he must make his point very quickly and clearly, so that his hearers may return at once to the illusion of being eye-witnesses of an event which took place nearly eight hundred years ago.

In looking at a film we are always under *direction of the eye*. It is part of the problem of the producer, to decide to what point on the screen, at every moment, the eyes of the audience are to be directed. You are, in fact, looking at the picture, though you do not realise it, through the eyes of the producer. What you see is what he makes the camera see. The fact that the audience's vision is directed by the producer of the film has special consequences for a verse play. It is important, first, that what you see should never distract your attention from what you hear. I believe this presented Mr. Hoellering with some of his most difficult problems. No one perhaps but I, who followed the creation of the film from beginning to end, can appreciate these difficulties, and Mr. Hoellering's success in solving them. Several visual effects, magnificent in themselves, were sacrificed because he was convinced that the audience in watching them would cease to attend to the words. Second, the fact that the illustration of the words by the scene is, so much more positively than on the stage, an interpretation of the meaning of the words, means that only a producer who understands poetry, and has taken a good deal of trouble to grasp the value of every line, is competent to deal with such a play at all. If the production of this film of *Murder in the Cathedral* leads—as I hope it may—to further experiment in the cinema with verse by living poets (and with plays written by poets *for* the cinema, not merely adaptations from the stage) the results can only be successful where there has been close co-operation and understanding between author and producer.

The play was originally written to be performed under the special conditions of the Chapter House at Canterbury, accepting the limitations and exploiting the special advantages of such a setting. Allowing for the great differences of aim and technique between stage and screen, I think that in some respects—notably in the treatment of the choral passages—this film version makes the meaning

clearer, and in that way is nearer to what the play would have been, had it been written for the London theatre and by a dramatist of greater experience. (pp. v-ix)

> *T. S. Eliot, in a preface to* The Film of "Murder in the Cathedral" *by T. S. Eliot and George Hoellering, Harcourt Brace Jovanovich, 1952, pp. v-ix.*

James M. Cain (interview with Peter Brunette and Gerald Peary)

[*An American fiction writer, Cain is the author of* The Postman Always Rings Twice *(1934),* Double Indemnity *(1943), and other novels which explore the American obsession with sex, violence, and money. This subject matter, along with a direct prose style and relentless action, have led to Cain's reputation as a leading figure in the hard-boiled school of writers that includes Dashiell Hammett and Raymond Chandler. In the following excerpt from an interview, Cain comments on film adaptations of his fiction.*]

BRUNETTE AND PEARY: We would like to know about your various writings turned into films. Could you begin with *When Tomorrow Comes* (1939) from a Cain short story?

CAIN: Much earlier, an editor at *Collier's* almost curdled my blood the first interview I had with him. He told me that he wanted "a Cinderella story with a modern twist," and I thought, "Oh Christ, what a formula." Then I thought: "Why don't you write a story that tells what really happens when the waitress marries the Harvard man?" Ten years later, I wrote the story, and then *Collier's* didn't buy it. I wrote about this Harvard guy who falls for this girl and marries her and about how his sisters treated her.

It was a fairly good story, I have to say. It finally published as "The Root of His Evil," though its working title was "The Modern Cinderella." It was put out by Avon and sold by my agent to Universal for a nice price. They cast the Harvard man with the guy in Hollywood who could not play a Harvard man, Charles Boyer, and the girl was Irene Dunne, who had it in her contract that she had to sing at least one number. *When Tomorrow Comes* had a waitress who sings as good as Irene Dunne sings, and they made *him* a French pianist. This movie bore no relation to the original story. That's how they mangle things up. (p. 54)

BRUNETTE AND PEARY: What of *Wife, Husband, and Friend* (1939) from your novel, *Career In C Major?*

CAIN: There were two movies from that book. *Wife, Husband, and Friend* was the first version. Nunnally Johnson did the script. In 1949, Twentieth was looking for some place to put this actor, Paul Douglas, because he had just made a big hit on Broadway and was a hot property. Nunnally Johnson used the same script for *Everybody Does It.*

I can't remember if I saw the second version. I didn't much care for *Wife, Husband, and Friend.* I was rather bored by it, though it didn't make much difference to me. My friend Vincent Lawrence was very bitter about the movie and he was savagely annoyed that I wan't getting worked up over it.

Zanuck had put in some sure-fire laughs about this fellow trying to be an opera singer who does all this slapstick. I said, "Well, what the hell, they're laughing." "Yes," said Lawrence, "and *every* one of these laughs was at the expense of the character. They made a clown out of him." That's what Lawrence had to say: never make a clown out of your leading man.

BRUNETTE AND PEARY: Do you have a stronger affection for *Double Indemnity* (1944)?

CAIN: I had to see *Double Indemnity* probably half a dozen times in various connections, and I was never bored. I must say Billy Wilder did a terrific job. It's the only picture I ever saw made from my books that had things in it I wish I had thought of. Wilder's ending was much better than my ending, and his device for letting the guy tell the story by taking out the office dictating machine—I would have done it if I had thought of it.

There are situations in the movie that can make your hands get wet, you get so nervous, like the place where Eddie Robinson comes in to talk to Fred MacMurray. Robinson is working close to what the murder explanation is—to connecting MacMurray and Barbara Stanwyck. And *she* comes and is about to rap on MacMurray's door when she hears something and pulls back and the door opens and Eddie Robinson comes out with MacMurray

and she's hiding behind the door. I tell you, there for a minute, it is just beautiful. I wish I had thought of something like it. (p. 55)

BRUNETTE AND PEARY: In the novel Phyllis is fixated on a "death trip," but that is not translated to the movie.

CAIN: No, they didn't make any effort to. I don't know whether it *can* be translated. In any case Barbara Stanwyck was about as good as they come as an actress and at the same time she was reasonably young and appetizing. Stanwyck is also a very wonderful and likable person. We had an easy, informal acquaintanceship.

BRUNETTE AND PEARY: There seems to be a father-son relationship between Robinson and MacMurray in the movie.

CAIN: I think there's a hint of that in the book, isn't there? But it was extended in the movie. When Eddie is told at the end that all the time the killer was right across the desk from him, Eddie says, "Closer than that, Walter." It was a nice moment, right at the end where you want a nice moment.

BRUNETTE AND PEARY: Why did Raymond Chandler co-author the script and not you?

CAIN: They didn't ask me to write the script. I don't

Barbara Stanwyck and Fred MacMurray in Double Indemnity, *directed by William Wilder.*

know. I never met Chandler until the day we had a story conference. Wilder wanted to explain to me why they weren't using more of my "deathless dialogue." He fell for the dialogue in my book and he was annoyed that Chandler wasn't putting more of it in the script. To try and prove his point, he got three contract people up and they ran through these scenes with my dialogue. But to Wilder's astonishment, he found out it *wouldn't* play. Chandler said, "I tried to tell him, Jim," with that easy familiarity they have out in Hollywood; even first meeting me, he calls me by my first name. "Jim, that dialogue of yours is to the *eye*." I said I knew my book is to the eye, although I *could* write to the ear. Chandler said, "I tried to explain it to Billy."

A thing was said at this story conference—and not by Chandler—that made even more of an impression on me. A young guy named Joe Sistrom was Paramount's producer on the picture. He was bothered that in the script and to some extent in the book this guy hit on the scheme for the perfect murder much too quick and easy. I said that it was implied that he had been subconsciously meditating this for years.

Well, this didn't satisfy Joe Sistrom. He sat there unhappily in a sulk and then suddenly said, "All characters in B pictures are too smart." I never forgot it. It was a curious observation, putting into words—vivid, rememberable words—a principle that when a character is too smart, convenient to the author's purposes, everything begins getting awfully slack in the story, and slick. Slack is one fault and slick is another. Both are bad faults in a story.

BRUNETTE AND PEARY: Why did it take so long to film *Double Indemnity,* after it was written in the mid-Thirties?

CAIN: Because of the Hays Office, which cost me hundreds of thousands of dollars. When I originally wrote that story, I had it mimeographed, then sent over to my agent. The next day I was lunching with him in the Vine Street Derby and he seemed gloomy. He was afraid he had priced my book too low. "I did a real snow job on it yesterday. I've already had five calls on it this morning. I've never had such a reaction to a story before." He had priced it at $25,000 and he would have to let it go there or be out of business. I told him that $25,000 wasn't hay.

That afternoon the Hays Office report came in and it started off, "Under no circumstances" and ended up, "Way, shape, or form." My agent asked if I wanted to hear what was in between, and I told him I could guess.

Now skip ten years. *Double Indemnity* was to come out in *Three of a Kind,* along with *The Embezzler* and *Career in C Major,* both of which already had sold to pictures. My new agent, H. N. Swanson, sent it again to eight studios. Well, one day Billy Wilder couldn't find his secretary. The relief girl said, "Well, Mr. Wilder, I think she's still in the Ladies' Room reading that story." Wilder said, "What story?" About this time she came out with *Double Indemnity* pressed to her bosom—she'd just finished it and had this ga-ga look on her face—and Wilder snatched the book from her and took it home and read it.

The next day I had an offer. $15,000. Now there's $10,000 the Hays Office cost me on one book. Wilder made a perfectly decent picture with no trouble about it. Well there was a little trouble caused by this fat girl, Kate Smith, who

carried on propaganda asking people to stay away from this picture. Her advertisement probably put a million dollars on its gross.

BRUNETTE AND PEARY: What are the events behind *Mildred Pierce?*

CAIN: Jim McGinnis, my old producer friend at Columbia, once made a remark that led to *Mildred Pierce.* Out in Hollywood all they talk about is *story*—secretaries, everybody—*story.* Well, one day we were going to lunch, talking about stories, and he said, "There's one that's never failed yet, and that's the story of a woman who uses men to gain her ends." I thought, well, if it's never failed yet, that sounds like a pretty good story to me.

Secretly then I began to try to adjust this formula. For a while I had the woman as an airline stewardess. Then she was a girl who won a beauty contest and came to Hollywood. Neither of these came to life, so I thought, maybe it makes some difference *what* ends. I suddenly thought it might help if her children were the ends she used men for, and naturally it would be better if it focused on one child. But I had to have another child in there so it wouldn't seem so pat and easy.

Then I made her not a femme fatale at all, just a housewife, but she had that instinct to use men. Every time I had trouble with that book I thought, "My friend, you've forgotten what your story is about. This is not the story of a woman who is devoted to her daughter and is nuts about her; it's a story about a woman who uses men to gain her ends." Every time I'd remember that and reinstate that theme in the book, it would go.

No reviewer or anybody who read it ever detected that's what the book is about. I didn't highlight it enough. I don't take much pride in *Mildred Pierce,* I have to confess to you. It's not my kind of book. I made some egregious mistakes in it, especailly right at the end, which is a very costly place to make mistakes.

BRUNETTE AND PEARY: And the movie?

CAIN: *Mildred Pierce* was loused up by the idea that Monty had died. Mark Hellinger, the first to get interested in *Mildred,* proclaimed that they would have this melodrama. Veda would be held for murdering Monty, the guy that Mildred, her mother, was sleeping with. Jesus Christ! What kind of a fantastic superimposition that had no bearing whatsoever on the theme! It made no sense to me, so I was never really able to praise *Mildred Pierce.* (p. 56)

BRUNETTE AND PEARY: Was *The Postman Always Rings Twice* your most successful book?

CAIN: It was not the most successful of my books in hardcover. That was *Past All Dishonor.* But in total sales, yes, it's this *Postman.* As far as Hollywood, the same thing happened with *Postman* as to *Double Indemnity.* Metro bought it and the Hays Office turned it down. After *Double Indemnity* was made, Breen at the Hays Office—it was now technically the Breen Office—finally okayed the script.

BRUNETTE AND PEARY: Is it true that you never saw the film *Postman* until recently—thirty years after?

CAIN: One of my friends took me to see it the other night. I was surprised that it was no worse than it was. It was a passably viewable picture, the first time I ever actually saw the release form. After the "sneak" in Glendale in 1946, I went up the aisle on my hands and knees for fear I would run into Carey Wilson, the producer. The rough-cut they showed at this preview was just so utterly ghastly. I thought, "Jesus Christ." But when I saw it the other night, the stuff that made my blood curdle out in Glendale had been cut out.

There's a place in the book where he runs off with a girl who had a cat act, and he takes her somewhere to Mexico. Well, in the first version I saw, they had this girl's cat act in the picture—leopards and pumas and lions and everything rolling around with each other—and it had no more relationship with the story than the man in the moon.

Shortly after the picture was released, I was having dinner alone in Murphy's, a corned beef and cabbage kind of place with wonderful food, and I looked up and saw Harry Ruskin standing in front of me, the guy who did the script. He was standing with his hands on his hips in a very belligerent way, and he said, "Well, why don't you say it? It *stinks.*"

I told him I didn't think it stunk any worse than most of them do. I was moderately friendly, though not exactly praising the picture. He told me that he had Lana Turner dressed in white so that the public understood that the girl's pure. She may be playing around with the guy, but she's not taking her pants off for him.

Ruskin had asked Carey Wilson, "Is this girl shacking this guy into bed? I know we don't put it on the screen, but *I* have to know." But Wilson couldn't make up his mind whether Lana was screwing Garfield. "Jim," Ruskin said, "He didn't know then and he doesn't know *now.* That's why the central part of the thing is so fuzzy and shaky and squashy."

I thought of that while looking at the movie the other night. It didn't seem to make much of a difference. . . .

BRUNETTE AND PEARY: You have stated elsewhere that the first time you went to see a film you really couldn't believe that people were entertained.

CAIN: When we were boys, a friend and I walked downtown to this nickelodeon. On his way to buy tickets, my friend said, "I don't say it's good entertainment. It's the best entertainment the town affords." Inside, we laughed ourselves into stitches, not at how good the jokes were but at how awful they were. John Bunny was one of the comedians. The feature was *The Great Train Robbery.* I had no idea that this was moving picture history. To us it was utterly beyond belief, it was so lousy. We came out agreeing it was *not* good entertainment, but it passed the time. Movies pretty much affect me this way now.

Recently I did see a revival of the Harold Lloyd picture, *Girl Shy.* I have to confess this one picture out of hundreds of pictures I've seen did entertain me. It was very adroitly done, this silent picture. The audience was in the aisles.

The next week I went down to see Harold Lloyd again in another picture. It was talking and it was just Christawful. This time the audience sat there in glum, bitter silence. Only when Lloyd began hanging by his fingernails over the street twenty stories below did they come to life a little, but never as they had the other night.

BRUNETTE AND PEARY: What is the last movie you saw at the time it was released?

CAIN: *The Exorcist.* The picture interested me in one respect: it was the most beautifully lit thing I ever saw. The story itself was nauseating. They overtold it. The place where the ghost was supposed to shake the girl in bed—God, they had to make the bed dance up and down and do tricks and all but turn over on her. But I expected the story to stink. I didn't mind that, but the lighting was incomparable.

BRUNETTE AND PEARY: Have you seen other pictures in recent years?

CAIN: I can tell you all the movies I've seen since coming back East in 1947. I saw *High Noon, Come Back Little Sheba, Kontiki,* two others I can't remember. I don't even look at them on TV for free. Most pictures aren't worth seeing. Let's face it, the moving picture never did lick reality. Pictures don't go deep. If a girl has a pretty face, that's as far as the camera can look. (p. 57)

James M. Cain, "Tough Guy," in an interview with Peter Brunette and Gerald Peary in Film Comment, *Vol. 12, No. 3, May-June, 1976, pp. 50-7.*

FICTION INTO FILM: COMPARATIVE ESSAYS

Roger Shatzkin

[In the following essay, Shatzkin describes the artistic and legal obstacles to the adaptation of Raymond Chandler's 1939 novel The Big Sleep *for Howard Hawk's 1946 film of the same name, explaining how the film version ultimately remained faithful to its source.]*

Raymond Chandler's *The Big Sleep* appears to fit that category of novel critic Edmund Wilson identified as capable of being "poured . . . on to the screen as easily as if it had been written in the studios . . . " ("The Boys in the Back Room" [1940]). In many respects, director Howard Hawks and his collaborators did succeed in pouring the essence of Chandler into their 1946 film. Most notably, they recreated the novel's atmosphere of evanescent corruption and emphasized character at the expense of formal considerations of plot. Nevertheless, the glibness of Wilson's metaphor disguises the "filtering" process operant in any transfer of narrative from one medium to another: Chandler's story of his hero's failed individualistic and Romantic quest became on screen a dark romantic comedy that explores the feasibility of human and sexual commitment between a man and a woman, in this case the film's stars and real-life lovers, Humphrey Bogart and Lauren Bacall. (In practical terms, Hawks was making a sequel to *To Have and Have Not* [1944], which first starred the pair.)

For *The Big Sleep,* there are added problems with Wilson's simple-minded notion of adaptation: Chandler's rather loosely plotted and crowded narrative (synthesized ingeniously out of four pulp magazine stories) became even more complex on screen. The reason for this was a seemingly straightforward filtering mechanism: the Hollywood Production Code's objection to "censorable" aspects of the novel. "Much of the illogic of the film," James Monaco has written, "is simply due to cuts which were made to conform to the Code." But let us take a closer look at some of the misconceptions surrounding the novel and the film, and the apparently intertwined issues of incomprehensibility and censorship.

The first misconception: *The Big Sleep,* both as novel and film, defies comprehension. True, Raymond Chandler confessed to suffering "plot-constipation," wished to possess "one of these facile plotting brains, like Erle [Stanley] Gardner or somebody," and admitted that *The Big Sleep* "happens to be more interested in people than in plot. . . ." And granted, director Hawks persisted in glorifying the illogic of his adaptation: in interview after interview he insisted that he "never could figure the story out, . . . " that he "can't follow it," and so on. What is more, one of the oft-repeated anecdotes about a film's production links author and *auteur* in mutual confusion: during the filming, Bogart, the picture's Philip Marlowe, apparently asked Hawks just who killed one of the minor characters, a chauffeur named Owen Taylor. (Taylor turns up in his employer's Buick, awash in the Pacific.) Since neither Hawks nor his screenwriters William Faulkner and Leigh Brackett knew, they cabled Chandler. And Chandler wired back: "I don't know."

For the record: with a little effort, novel and film *can* be comprehended, if what is meant by that is that their plots can be linearized, sorted out. (Paul Jensen deserves credit for mentioning this in his article on Chandler in *Film Comment,* November-December, 1974.) But to shift perspective, the popular myths about *The Big Sleep* are important. Though their events and characterizations may be ultimately deciphered, novel and film are texts *about* confusion; impenetrability, if not their final result, is at their core. So the question becomes, not "who killed Owen Taylor?" but, more properly (to echo Edmund Wilson's skepticism about detective fiction), "who *cares* who killed Owen Taylor?"

Neither Chandler, nor Marlowe, the novel's detective-narrator, seems to have cared. Hired by the elderly, infirm General Sternwood to investigate some gambling debts his younger daughter, Carmen, has incurred, debts which in turn may become the basis for blackmail, Marlowe plunges into intrigue more complex than circumstances would seem to warrant. For one thing, the General's son-in-law, "Rusty" Regan is missing, and his older daughter, Regan's wife Vivian, suspects that Marlowe has been engaged to find him. As is clear in Chandler: Carmen's ostensible blackmailer, Arthur Geiger, runs a pornographic lending library; Geiger is murdered at his home in the presence of a stupefied Carmen; he has provided drugs and photographed her nude for future extortion schemes. Marlowe rescues Carmen, entering Geiger's place after hearing shots and observing two men leaving in quick succession. The first man turns out to be Taylor, who drives off to his mysterious death.

Marlowe (and Chandler) forget about Taylor. Attention shifts instead to the second man out of the house, Joe Brody, who, like Taylor, is an ex-boyfriend of Carmen's.

Brody somehow obtains the negatives of Carmen and proceeds to blackmail her. Marlowe goes to Brody's apartment to recover the negatives and pictures; he first disarms Brody and then Carmen, who has come to retrieve the blackmail materials herself. After Carmen leaves, Carol Lundgren, Geiger's valet and lover shoots Brody, mistakenly thinking that Brody has killed Geiger. As Marlowe later explains, Taylor, chivalrously defending his old flame Carmen, had actually done the deed.

Either William Faulkner or Leigh Brackett (Hawks's original screenwriters) was the person concerned about what happened to Taylor. One of them wrote some dialogue for a scene, patterned after one in the novel (but cut from the final film), that sums up, more neatly than Chandler, what happened. In this scene, mid-way through the novel and screenplay, Marlowe is explaining his involvement in the affair to the district attorney. In the novel, Marlowe merely alludes to the events that have transpired and then responds to the D.A.'s queries. In the screenplay, the D.A., in dialogue never filmed, adds his own summation:

> So Taylor killed Geiger because he was in love with the Sternwood girl. And Brody followed Taylor, sapped him and took the photographs and pushed Taylor into the ocean. And the punk [Lundgren] killed Brody because the punk thought he should have inherited Geiger's business and Brody was throwing him out.

Although no one involved with the production seems to recall this unshot speech, the screenwriters' D.A. would have settled the question of Taylor's demise once and for all, tying up a "loose end" over which Chandler himself apparently never fretted.

Faulkner or Brackett's dialogue here strives for order (despite Hawks's recollection that "there was no sense in making [the story] logical. So we didn't"). And the dialogue, in changing Lundgren's motivation from a lover's revenge also manifests another tendency toward "logic." And this brings us to the second misconception about the film: how it censored the novel.

Throughout the two drafts of the script, the screenwriters anticipated that many sections of the novel might offend the Production Code—matters of sexual conduct, police misconduct, Marlowe's final decision to let a murderer go free—and they took steps to circumvent possible problems. Many of the novel's "objectionable" aspects did have to be cut from the final film. Geiger's pornography racket is nowhere mentioned (we just see some posh clients skulking about his "bookstore"), nor is the homosexual relationship between Geiger and Lundgren. Both of these omissions cause confusions (as does the film's ending to a degree, but for reasons other than censorship). But other changes, such as presenting a clothed Carmen at Geiger's and later at Marlowe's apartment, do not alter the final quality of the film. A recent assessment, such as Gavin Lambert's that the movie "seems badly hobbled by censorship" (*The Dangerous Edge,* 1975), hardly seems appropriate.

Prior censorship was the rule in the screenplays. The screenwriters transformed Geiger's business from pornography and extortion to the vaguer endeavor of blackmail alone (late in the second script draft Marlowe actually finds packing cases of "manilla filing envelopes, ledgers,

Lauren Bacall and Humphrey Bogart in The Big Sleep, *directed by Howard Hawks.*

etc."). Lundgren's relationship to Geiger becomes all business. Even Carmen Sternwood's nymphomania is desexed (though one wonders how Martha Vickers sultry performance in the film could have possibly jibed with the script's conception). Carmen's psychotic and homicidal behavior is brought on by jealousy. She murders Regan and attempts to murder Marlowe, according to Faulkner and Brackett, because she has lost the affections of both of them (at least in her mind) to her sister Vivian, and *not* because they are the only two men who refuse to sleep with her. And though Hawks has credited the Production Code office with rejecting the novel's ending and, when prodded, providing their own, Faulkner and Brackett had already altered Chandler's denouement in their first script. (In letting Carmen go free to be "cured" in the book, Marlowe violates the Code's provision against unpunished crimes. The film's ending is actually a *third* script revision of the novel's ending.)

But Faulkner and Brackett's careful anticipation of the Code and their finely wrought "logic" were to no avail. Hawks excised a number of scenes from their screenplay as he shot. And the filming, done from the second draft or Temporary script, had run too long. So "Jules Furthman was called in," according to Leigh Brackett, "for a rewrite to cut the remaining or unshot portion [of the

script] into a manageable length. . . . " Whatever coherence the original screenwriters had concocted (or preserved from Chandler) was eradicated in shortening an overlong screenplay; it was not the direct evisceration of the novel for the censors, as Monaco and other critics have averred, that cause the movie's notorious incomprehensibility.

But the film, in its final and less "coherent" form, becomes—in the best Hawks tradition—a type of Rorschach test in which the elipses can be filled in by the audience. And, paradoxically, it moves closer to the novel as a result. In the minds of viewers imbued with the requisite imagination, the spirit of the book's censorable content remains, albeit sometimes between the lines. As Charles Gregory has written, despite the fact that the movie had to avoid "explicit references to sex, dope and pornography that are woven into the novel . . . somehow the film reflects all this to the sophisticated viewer without ever drawing the ire of the censors or even the notice of the prudes."

Typical of the cuts made to shorten the script was the removal of a shot in the first scene showing Owen Taylor washing the Sternwood Buick as Marlowe passes from the General's mansion to his hothouse (a direct transposition from the novel intended to identify the chauffeur and fore-shadow his complicity in Geiger's murder). In the film, Marlowe simply walks from the mansion's hallway into the greenhouse—the magic of film editing has connected the two edifices. And Taylor gets whisked away to the limbo of legend.

But as Leigh Brackett observed: "Audiences came away feeling that they had seen the hell and all of a film even if they didn't rightly know what it was all about. Again, who cared? It was grand fun, with sex and danger and a lot of laughs. . . ." Again, who cared? Let us turn to the novel and film in more detail to see if we can decipher what they are all about—and if it matters if they are *about* anything.

For that matter, what *is* Raymond Chandler's *The Big Sleep* about? The novel functions as an entertainment, a sometimes self-satiric, self-contained world of double-cross, moral and political corruption in which our confusion as readers helps engender our involvement and our identification with the hero, Philip Marlowe. The central movement of the novel, though, focuses on its protagonist's quest, not for the solution to a puzzle or a mystery (though that is necessarily accomplished), but primarily for his double, his *doppelganger*. It is this covert quest—which informs the bulk of Chandler's novels but is most prominent in *The Big Sleep* and *The Long Goodbye* (1954)—and its requisite failure that create many of the novel's strong, if fugitive, resonances.

Marlowe's search for Terence "Rusty" Regan is the hidden energizing force of the novel (hidden, in some ways, from Chandler himself). It is also the genesis of the novel's seeming confusion and impenetrability. But the pattern of Marlowe's search for Regan does not emerge readily from the narrative. Throughout roughly the first half of the novel, questions about Regan, Vivian Sternwood's missing husband, keep surfacing, but Marlowe's chief preoccupation lies with keeping Carmen safe and the Sternwood's family name unbesmirched through the three deaths that touch on them (i.e., Geiger's, Taylor's, and Brody's). Marlowe's identification with Regan is established at his initial visit to the General (where he replaces Regan as the old man's sensual surrogate—drinking and smoking for Sternwood's vicarious enjoyment—and is hired for a job that Regan, the General's confidant as well as son-in-law, would probably have undertaken). But Marlowe does not turn his attention to the missing man until the mystery that propels the beginning half of the action, concerning Carmen's blackmail, has ostensibly been resolved. And all along, he denies various allegations that he *is* looking for Regan, even though, ironically, they are true.

At this point, to better understand Regan's place in the novel, it will help to clarify the structure of *The Big Sleep.* Writing on the film, James Monaco has offered a helpful description that applies equally well to the novel. He notes in the movie's construction a "dual structure: a 'surface' mystery (usually the client's) and a 'deep' mystery (the metaphysical or political problem which presents itself to the detective)." Fredric Jameson views Chandler's dual structure slightly differently, noting a tendency for the novels to mislead readers because a Chandler work "passes itself off as a murder mystery." Jameson points out that "In fact Chandler's stories are first and foremost descrip-

tions of searches. . . ." Here the "murder mystery" corresponds to Monaco's "surface" enigma, the "search" to the "deep" structure. Jameson later expresses the double nature of the narrative in terms of time:

> The final element in Chandler's characteristic form is that the underlying crime is always old, lying half-forgotten in the pasts of the characters before the book begins. This is the principal reason why the readers attention is diverted from [the underlying crime]; he assumes it to be a part of the dimension of the present. . . .

Relating this to *The Big Sleep* then, this is what happens: the crime in the past that generates the whole novel, yet which is unknown to Marlowe or the reader at the outset of the book, is the murder of Regan by Carmen Sternwood. Regan, like some entombed character in Poe, lies mouldering in a sump in the oilfield below the Sternwood mansion while four more deaths result from the unrecognized cover-up of his demise. And Marlowe spends all his initial energy treating the symptoms of the case, the surface of the present, before turning to their cause in the past.

I do not believe that Chandler was in complete touch with the metaphysical significance of Regan for his protagonist. Chandler, as is most clearly exemplified in his *Atlantic* essay, "The Simple Art of Murder," written five years after *The Big Sleep,* tended to conceive of his hero in extremely idealized terms:

> . . . Down these mean streets a man must go who is not himself mean, who is neither tarnished nor afraid. . . . He must be the best man in his world and a good enough man for any world!

Despite Chandler's notion of the hero as knight in a corrupt world (a conception taken up too uncritically by many who have written about him), Marlowe is a far from simplistic character. In the beginning of *The Big Sleep,* he does literally project himself into a tableau on a stained-glass panel in the Sternwood home, depicting "a knight in dark armor rescuing a lady . . . [who] didn't have any clothes on. . . . " "I would have to climb up there and help him," Marlowe says to himself. "He didn't seem to be really trying." However, later in the novel, when a naked Carmen invades his bedroom, he looks down at his chessboard and concludes that "Knights had no meaning in this game. It wasn't a game for knights." The thought is reemphasized when he enters the Sternwood house for the last time and observes the knight, who "still wasn't getting anywhere. . . . "

In short, a dialectic exists within the novel: Marlowe begins as knight, but is forced to cope in a sordid world: to do so he must be willing to summon a darker side of himself. Chandler's idealization represses this darker side. This is where Regan as "double" comes in: Chandler fractionalizes his hero into two characters. Regan, missing and dead (ultimately repressed!) throughout the entire novel represents the potentially corruptible side of his protagonist which Chandler cannot brook. Regan has crossed the line. He is beyond the law all the way—a successful gangster-bootlegger. He commits himself sexually to women: he marries Vivian Sternwood; he (probably) has an affair with Mona Mars, before and after she is married. He commits himself to public social causes: he fought for the I.R.A. in 1922. He commits himself to having (if not coveting) money: he carries fifteen thousand dollars in bills at all times. In fact, the D.A. surmises that the real reason Sternwood hired Marlowe in the first place was to find out if Regan had betrayed his trust by being the real force behind the blackmail instigated by Geiger (ironically, he is). In sum, Regan is Marlowe's alter ego, an adult version of the detective's adolescent, solipsistic Romantic, who in "growing up" has taken the fall.

Throughout the novel we are given hints of the Marlowe-Regan bond. Marlowe resembles Regan: the D.A.'s man Bernie Ohls describes Regan as a "big guy as tall as you and a shade heavier." Both men are in their thirties. Their relationships to women intersect completely. Vivian Sternwood and Mona Mars are both attracted to Marlowe as they were to Regan, and Carmen tries to shoot Marlowe, as she did Regan, because he too would not sleep with her. (The link of the two men through the women is possibly covert evidence of Marlowe's repressed homoerotic attraction to Regan.) General Sternwood's butler explicitly compares the two men, and the General takes a paternal (and perhaps homosexual) interest in both. And when Marlowe confronts a photograph of Regan, the detective describes his impressions in terms he might as easily use for himself. It was "Not the face of a tough guy and not the face of a man who could be pushed around much by anybody. . . . [It was] a face that looked a little taut, the face of a man who would move fast and play for keeps. . . ." Marlowe concludes portentously, "I would know that face if I saw it."

So Marlowe's search for Regan represents maximally an investigation into his own identity, into his own soul's potential weaknesses and arrested tendencies. In his final soliloquy Marlowe intones the following famous lines in speaking of his entombed "brother" Regan:

> Where did it matter where you lay once you were dead? In a dirty sump or in a marble tower on top of a high hill? You were dead, you were sleeping the big sleep, you were not bothered by things like that. Oil and water were the same as wind and air to you. You just slept the big sleep, not caring about the nastiness of how you died or where you fell. Me, I was part of the nastiness now. Far more a part of it than Rusty Regan was. . . .

Marlowe, who when captive at one point made macabre jokes about his choice of casket and about Eddie Mars's henchman digging *him* a grave, finally comes face to face with his own mortality only through Regan. In so doing, he begins to understand his corruptibility, as well (on the ethical level as "knight" he has let murderess Carmen go unpunished). He is "part of the nastiness now . . . " and that is the full import of his search. For the reader, as Fredric Jameson has put it, the end of the novel "is able to bring us up short, without warning, against the reality of death itself, stale death, reaching out to remind the living of its own mouldering resting place." [Shatzkin adds in a footnote: "Only one scene in Hawks's movie comes near the evocative power of Marlowe's speech (which strongly recalls Hamlet's oration over Yorick). When Marlowe first enters Geiger's house in the film, he finds Geiger dead and Carmen giddy and intoxicated. He puts Carmen to sleep on a couch, and at one point later in his investigation, glances from the supine dead man to the drugged

woman. Only in that fleeting instant, does the mutability of life into death loom as large as in Chandler."]

Paradoxically, Faulkner, Brackett, and Hawks's screen version immediately makes the Marlowe-Regan connection much more explicit than in the novel. In the Hawksian tradition of professional equals, Marlowe's first dialogue with the General reveals that he and Regan have been respectful opponents during prohibition, each on a different side of the law ("We used to swap shots between drinks, or drinks between shots—whichever you like."). But if anything, Regan (mysteriously now named "Shawn") is invoked quickly only to be exorcised. Though the surface mystery in the film remains the same, still concerning Carmen's blackmail, the deep mystery will ultimately concern, as Monaco has pointed out, what gambler Eddie Mars "has" on Vivian Sternwood Rutledge (Lauren Bacall), here a divorcee. (In the novel, Mars is blackmailing Vivian over Carmen's murder of Regan; he has helped her dispose of Regan's body.) The question of what Mars "has" on Vivian masks the real thrust of Hawks's film, which is to determine with whom Vivian will ultimately side, and as in his best comedies whether or not she and Marlowe will realize their mutual romantic attraction.

To emphasize leading lady Bacall as Vivian, Hawks and his writers placed her in three scenes in which she does not appear in the novel (Marlowe returning Carmen to her home, his visit to Brody's apartment, his incarceration in Realito at the hands of Mars's man Canino); they lengthened one encounter from the book (Vivian's visit to Marlowe's office), and added one long scene that appears only in the film. This scene, the famous Cafe/Horserace double entendre sequence (mandated by Warners' front office a full year after the rest of the movie was in the can, to give the stars yet more exposure together) is indicative of a pattern of attraction-repulsion between Vivian and Marlowe that firmly establishes as the center of the film the question of their eventual fate together.

In almost every scene in which they appear together, up until the penultimate one, Marlowe and Vivian begin a wary, but cordial verbal sparring. But each encounter ends in witty vitriol ("Kissing is nice, but your father didn't hire me to sleep with you."). The first mode of verbal skirmishing is the substitute for and correlative of a romantic language founded on emotion that Hawks employs throughout his romantic "screwball" comedies. Though Hawks took this convention from his comedies, in *The Big Sleep* he left its significance open ended. The dialogue between Marlowe and Vivian can end in romance or—in keeping with Chandler, the tradition of the *femme fatale* in general and of *film noir* in particular—in betrayal.

Near the end of the film, an obligatory "lay off the case" scene with Bernie Ohls (Regis Toomey) was written into the film; it confirms that Marlowe's vacillating relationship with Vivian has become the film's deep structure and raison d'être. After Ohls has conveyed his message instructing Marlowe to desist, the detective recapitulates the case so far and indicates why he must go on:

> "Bernie, put yourself in my shoes for a minute. A nice old guy has two daughters. One of them is, well, wonderful. And the other is not so wonderful. As a result somebody gets something on her. The father hires me to pay off. Before I can get to the guy, the family chauffeur kills him! But that didn't

stop things. It just starts them. And two murders later I find out somebody's got something on wonderful."

So the film comes down to Marlowe's endeavors to "clear" and win "wonderful."

When the ending does come, it makes little plot sense. Marlowe and Vivian are united after the detective forces Mars, his only serious "rival," out of a door into a hail of machine-gun fire. In Jules Furthman's reworking of the conclusion, the only logical extra-textual explanation for Mars's death is that he, not Carmen, killed Regan, and that he is blackmailing Vivian by making her think Carmen did it.

If the narrative logic is flawed, the emotional logic is not. We care about Marlowe/Bogart and Vivian/Bacall; they have earned our respect through their mutual (and mostly verbal) abilities to cope with a hostile environment. And it is satisfying to see their compatibility, which we have sensed all along, romantically vindicated. Likewise, in the novel, despite his limitations, we care about Marlowe. His voice unifies the quicksilver and chaotic world in which he operates, a world in which almost all events can never be known but only hypothesized about. And that extends to one misplaced chauffeur, at sea in the depths of illogic, about whom one ultimately need not care. Peace to you, Owen Taylor. (pp. 80-94)

> Roger Shatzkin, "Who Cares Who Killed Owen Taylor?" in The Modern American Novel and the Movies, edited by Gerald Peary and Roger Shatzkin, Frederick Ungar Publishing Co., 1978, pp. 80-94.

Sidney Gottlieb

[*In the following essay, Gottlieb compares the film* The Day of the Locust, *directed by John Schlesinger, with Nathanael West's novel, a work which is widely considered the best and most bitter fictional treatment of Hollywood.*]

When Nathanael West was finishing work on *The Day of the Locust* (1939), he was concerned that it be read as he intended it. Fearing that his novel might be taken too superficially, he urged his publisher to design and promote it in a way that would make clear that "the book isn't another 'Boy Meets Girl,' 'Once in a Lifetime,' or 'Queer People,' but that it has a real and even 'serious' theme." John Schlesinger and Waldo Salt, the director and scriptwriter of the film version of *The Day of the Locust* (1975) are clearly aware that they have sacrificed more than a bit of West's "seriousness" in their work. Schlesinger and Salt have extracted what is essentially a love story with an hysterical climax from a novel that plots out deeper things: the disintegration of American society and the threat of class warfare in the precarious days before World War II.

I was tempted to say "only" a love story, but that would slight the achievement of the film. As a love story, the film focuses much more intently than the novel on characterization, and its greatest success is surely its presentation of the major figures and their odd relationships. The casting—William Atherton as Tod, Karen Black as Faye Greener, Donald Sutherland as Homer Simpson, Burgess

Meredith as Harry Greener—is excellent, and the actors ably bring to light aspects of the characters that are purposefully underdeveloped in the novel.

Tod Hackett is the most important figure in the story, and West barely evades making him too likable. Early on, West makes sure to point out Tod's "large sprawling body, his slow blue eyes and sloppy grin," his "doltish" appearance, and comments that "he was lazy and didn't like to walk." West also takes great pains to show the violent underside of Tod, that his "love" for Faye is largely based on his terrible desire to crush "her egglike self-sufficiency." Tod has recurring rape fantasies and once even attacks Faye, although somewhat half-heartedly. West says of Tod that "he was really a very complicated young man with a whole set of personalities, one inside the other like a nest of Chinese boxes." This can be taken to mean that Tod has a certain "depth" which distinguishes him from the others in the novel; but it also may indicate what he shares with them: multiple cracks in his psychology, a personality ranging from passive and perceptive to suspicious and highly dangerous.

William Atherton's Tod in the movie is normally so amiable and untroubled that, unlike West's enigmatic creation, we are rarely out of sympathy with him. Yet even here, Tod is no stalwart Olympian observer; his unfettered outside betrays a core of irrationality and violence. In the film Tod seriously tries to rape Faye when they visit Miguel's camp in the woods; and although some critics felt this scene uncalled for, it is quite in line with Tod's character and West's message: like everybody else, Tod is teased and cheated and messed over, and his response is sometimes no less pathological.

But in spite of Atherton's sharp characterization, the film runs into problems precisely because Tod's key role as an observer is not exploited as it might be. Ultimately we should sympathize with Tod *not* because of his actions—he is a compromised character involved with, even in love with, the decaying world around him—but because he alone has some perspective on what he sees. We watch as Tod pieces together his most important work of art, "The Burning of Los Angeles," and we are well aware that he is the only character able to register something beyond a personal feeling of frustration and disappointment. But we simply do not get enough of his vision of the world. We see him looking past Faye occasionally, but for the most part he only looks at her, and this limits the scope of the film.

Faye is a fascinating character and Karen Black's performance brings her to life. She is the embodiment of sexuality as dry heat, as friction, as an emptiness which is sometimes entered but never filled. Faye is rarely tender and never fragile, but she is always alluring, and West spends much of his time trying to articulate her appeal:

> Her invitation wasn't to pleasure, but to struggle, hard and sharp, closer to murder than to love. If you threw yourself on her, it would be like throwing yourself from the parapet of a skyscraper. You would do it with a scream. You couldn't expect to rise again. Your teeth would be driven into your skull like nails into a pine board and your back would be broken. You wouldn't even have time to sweat or close your eyes.

Perhaps even more than the novel, the film explores the brutality that is never far from Faye's love. We see not only Tod driven to violence by his feelings for Faye, but Faye's other lovers as well; they become the real victims. When Miguel is attracted to her at the campsite, he is smashed on the head with a stick by Earle. When Earle tries to dance with her at the party, he is rammed in the groin by Abe Kusich, the midget. When Abe goes for her, he is thrown head first across the room onto a table by Miguel. And Homer Simpson, who wants only to love and care for Faye, is her most pathetic victim. His death is a stark enactment of the fate prophesized in the passage quoted above: he is literally broken and torn apart.

Still, we never completely abandon our sympathy for Faye. Just as we must not like Tod too much in West's novel, it is important that we not hate Faye too much. The film of *Day of the Locust* follows West's presentation in carefully placing Faye beyond our reproach. Although incredibly vain, shallow, self-involved, and shrill, she somehow manages to come out looking fresh, newborn, and pure. When Karen Black sits down in front of a makeup mirror reflecting three views of her face and sings "Jeepers, Creepers, / Where'd ya get those peepers?" to herself, we have a perfect image of Faye's triumphant narcissism.

Perhaps it is this desire to emphasize Faye's absolute purity and self-sufficiency—West's own description of her—that leads Schlesinger and Salt to end the movie by focusing on Faye. In his uncomplimentary review of the film, Stanley Kauffmann questioned the wisdom of this choice:

> Why should it be Faye who comes back one day to look at Tod's now-empty apartment in the building where once they both lived? Surely, if the film is to have a shred of esthetic and psychological consistency, it ought to close with Tod. Why couldn't he have come back to look at *her* empty apartment?

The film could have ended with the riot at the Hollywood movie premiere, but perhaps Schlesinger and Salt are pursuing the implications of this essential passage about Faye from the novel:

> Nothing could hurt her. She was like a cork. No matter how rough the sea got, she would go dancing over the same waves that sank iron ships and tore away piers of reinforced concrete. [Tod] pictured her riding a tremendous sea. Wave after wave reared its ton on ton of solid water and crashed down only to have her spin gaily away.

The film may be perfectly right in deciding that Tod leaves but Faye remains. More than a survivor, she surfaces virtually untouched.

Homer Simpson is the last of the major characters, and he is obviously more troubled and grotesque than Tod or Faye. Tod's first view of Homer in the novel is right to the point: "He didn't mean to be rude but at first glance this man seemed an exact model for the kind of person who comes to California to die, perfect in every detail down to fever eyes and unruly hands." Donald Sutherland follows West's clues closely in creating this man who is a pathetic study in repression. Unlike Faye, who is completely buoyant and untouchable, and Tod, who is able to alternate between involvement and detachment, Homer is a constant prisoner of emotions which can never be expressed or sat-

isfied. According to the ancient definition of the word, he is an idiot, an absolutely private man. Much like the characters in William Gass's story "In the Heart of the Heart of the Country" (1967), Homer "lives alone—how alone it is impossible to fathom."

Sutherland's physical appearance and mannerisms perfectly convey Homer's clumsiness and vulnerability. His stare is vacant and only his hands speak truly for him; they are always rubbing together, wandering, nearly out of control. His belly sticks out, almost inviting a punch, and nearly everyone takes an opportunity to abuse him.

Beyond following Nathanael West's hints in picturing Homer, John Schlesinger decided to add a religious dimension to his characterization, and this is not always successful or appropriate. It is absurd for Homer to be a religious fanatic, to be the one who brings the Greeners to the revivalist church meeting. In the novel he has nothing at all: no illusions and no solace. He simply coils tighter and tighter. In the film, after the cockfight and the party where he is terribly humiliated, Homer is moved to a kind of biblical wrath. In a voice that is uncharacteristically threatening, he says "O Lord, forgive me . . . but sometimes I wish I could tear it all down." This forced glimpse into Homer's psyche undercuts the power of his sudden turn to violence at the end. When Adore Loomis, that hideous little androgyne, hits him in the face with a rock, we should be totally surprised by Homer's murderous response.

More strangely, Schlesinger suddenly sees Homer as an unlikely Christ, enraged at Adore, he who casts the first stone. As Homer is tossed by the mob at the end of the film, his arms are flung outward, as though on a cross. West does not entertain this kind of religious parody except for his title of *The Day of the Locust* (perhaps he had exhausted this vein in his earlier novel, *Miss Lonelyhearts* [1933]). Yet, Schlesinger and Salt use this form of burlesque elsewhere quite effectively, not only to characterize Homer's situation, but also to remind us that the film is set deep in a fallen world.

There are several striking sequences set in Homer's backyard, which is meant as a kind of primordial garden turned to seed. In the first of these scenes, Homer sits alone. Fruit drops around him, but there is no sense of lushness; the garden is overgrown with weeds and there is only a lizard to stare at. Everything is quiet and Homer is, as always, restless. His hands move aimlessly until they seize on a child's game to play; "Here is the church, here is the steeple" is a neurotic ritual for Homer, repeated constantly as in the novel, but the claustrophobic film setting manifests that this is the only kind of church he can build there, in this post-Edenic wasteland. In a later scene in the backyard, Faye joins Homer in a depressing tableau: they stand in this ruined garden as overweight Adam and eternally tempted Eve.

Now, given that the film of *The Day of the Locust* is filled with generally excellent characterization, and given that it is not "merely" a love story, what exactly is the film missing? First of all, the film is lacking the philosophical insights—most often conveyed third person, through Tod's observations—which give meaning to many incidents in the novel. Secondly, characterization is developed in a void. The characters form too exclusive a society, whereas West carefully placed them in a much broader social context. Until the end, the film virtually avoids the most potent force in the novel, the mob of people who are never even named, except in one of West's original titles for this story: "The Cheated."

There are three major scenes in which Schlesinger and Salt apparently try to go beyond the individual characters to more general and significant points but none succeeds fully. The collapse of the set during the filming of the Battle of Waterloo, the visit to the revivalist church meeting, and, of course, the riot at the Hollywood premiere are all extremely important to the story, and it is worth analyzing how the film and the novel differ in these parts to see why the film falls short.

In the film, while searching for Faye, Tod walks onto the set where the Battle of Waterloo is being reenacted. The director is not at all pleased with the action and, to Tod's amusement, he orders the extras to be killed again and again. While this goes on, though, Tod notices something more serious: the carpenters have not finished building the supports for part of the set and signs warning everyone off are hidden from sight. As the battle continues, the actors advance onto the unfinished hill and it falls apart, injuring many of them. This is visually a spectacular scene, but hardly any real meaning is squeezed out of it. It serves only two limited purposes. First, it brings Tod and Faye together for one tender, loving moment. They embrace outside the set and confess how worried they were about each other when the hill collapsed. (Needless to say, there is no such "tender moment" in the novel.) Secondly, we get a fleeting view of how the Hollywood tycoons respond to the near tragedy: they insist that the signs were properly posted and that in any event the insurance companies will take care of the damages. (Film historians may look back on this as another of the obligatory "cover-up" scenes that dot so many American films of the Watergate 1970s.)

When we inspect this scene in the novel we become aware of how much the film has cut out and how it has trivialized what remains. Here more than in any other place in *The Day of the Locust* West expresses what he feels the Hollywood movie-making enterprise is all about. In his walk across the movie sets in search of Faye, Tod enters into an "Unreal City." West's description comes directly from his own experience of Hollywood studios and it is worthy of Eliot and Baudelaire:

> He pushed his way through a tangle of briars, old flats and iron junk, skirting the skeleton of a Zeppelin, a bamboo stockade, an adobe fort, the wooden horse of Troy, a flight of baroque palace stairs that started in a bed of weeds and ended against the branches of an oak, part of the Fourteenth Street elevated station, a Dutch windmill, the bones of a dinosaur, the upper half of the Merrimac, a corner of a Mayan temple, until he finally reached the road.

The rapid shift from one scene to another to make a striking association is an important part of film art, but the above is not montage: it is madness. As West goes on to show, Hollywood is a "dream dump" where entropy and disorder rule. Yet this walk through the movie sets, so important as a prelude to the chaos to follow on the Waterloo set, is missing from the film.

In the novel, the section in which the set collapses is meant to do considerably more than dramatize the irresponsibility of Hollywood producers. West is trying to work out something much deeper. Whether consciously or not, he is giving dramatic form to two ominous observations on human history. The first is philosopher George Santayana's well-known statement that those who do not learn from the errors of the past are doomed to repeat them. West points out clearly that the mistake on the movie set is the same that Napoleon actually made at Waterloo. The mistake is not quite as devastating here, of course, but it connects well with the second idea of history that may also have been in West's mind: Marx's notion that events occur first as tragedy, then recur as farce. Here is West's description of the battle:

> The French killed General Picton with a ball through the head and he returned to his dressing room. Alten was put to the sword and also retired. The colors of the Lunenberg battalion, borne by a prince of the family of Deux-Ponts, were captured by a famous child star in the uniform of a Parisian drummer boy. The Scotch Grays were destroyed and went to change into another uniform. Ponsonby's heavy dragoons were also cut to ribbons. Mr. Grotenstein would have a large bill to pay at the Western Costume Company.

West seems to suggest that we are in an age of diminution, and that this is an irreversible process. We can never again reach the heights of tragedy; and as we see when the set collapses, the inevitable next stage after farce is chaos.

The scenes in the film of the gigantic revival meeting are further indications that Schlesinger and Salt are quite willing to be satirical and spectacular but that they generally hold back from more serious analyses. Harry Greener (Burgess Meredith) is quite sick and Homer and daughter Faye escort him to a church service where he may be "cured." As we might expect, this service is done Hollywood style: it is an extravaganza. There is quick cutting to help raise the emotional pitch and, for the first time in the film, we see a great mass of people getting worked up about something. The music is loud and insistent, and a neon cross urges everyone "to give" in the most meaningful way—by sending in money. In front of a large broadcast microphone stands a woman who is both preacher and M.C., but her pleas and prayers contain more than a trace of bullying and her "miracles" are most unseemly. It is not enough to make the lame walk, to the roars of the crowd, she insists that an old woman run back and forth across the stage.

Harry Greener is placed in a wheelchair, wheeled to the front, and then, to the astonishment of all, miraculously brought back to his feet. He swoons for a moment, but, once on stage, Harry literally does come to life. The gospel music slowly blends into a ragtime tune until finally we are in the middle of a Hollywood production number. It is all splendidly ludicrous. Harry conspicuously winks at us as he begins his old soft show routine to pleasantly usher out the scene. We are meant to smile and shrug our shoulders with Harry. After all, religion is just another kind of show biz, so dance along.

To point out that religion is a racket, and a show business racket at that, is hardly sufficient for West, though, and his description of Tod's wandering among the new churches springing up is anything but charmingly cynical:

> He visited the "Church of Christ, Physical" where holiness was attained through the constant use of chestweights and spring grips; the "Church Invisible" where fortunes were told and the dead made to find lost objects; the "Tabernacle of the Third Coming" where a woman in male clothing preached the "Crusade Against Salt"; and the "Temple Moderne" under whose glass and chromium roof "Brain-Breathing, the Secret of the Aztecs" was taught.

This is certainly ridiculous, but not easily laughed away. And the crowds of worshipers who attend these churches are not at all comical:

> He would not satirize them as Hogarth or Daumier might, nor would he pity them. He would paint their fury with respect, appreciating its awful, anarchic power and aware that they had it in them to destroy civilization.

This section on the weird churches is only one of the many crowd scenes throughout the novel. As noted, the mob is never far from West's mind; and rather than being merely the background for the action, their existence is really the main subject of the book. Like many other writers and political thinkers of the late 1930s, West was preoccupied with the question of whether the lower-middle classes of America would turn toward Fascism as their counterparts in Italy and Germany had already done. Perhaps at another time in history West might have had the luxury to pick out the comedy in the crazy behavior of the crowds, but at this time he was rightly more sensitive to the threatening and brutal side of all instances of irrationality. By 1938, when he was rewriting and completing the novel, West saw only locusts, not comedians, in the mob.

The film seems hardly interested in the masses of people at all; they become a concern only at the very end, in the scenes of the riot at the Hollywood premiere. Where have they been all this time? For a while the crowd is only mildly intimidating, unconscious of its own power and thus able to be held back by the comparatively weak barriers set up by the police. But when Homer Simpson, the most repressed character of all, springs to action, it is a signal for everyone to crash through the barriers. Homer stomps child star Adore Loomis to death and he is almost immediately seized by the crowd and brutally executed. Once begun, the violence can hardly stop here. Cars are overturned, the movie stars are attacked, windows are smashed, and soon everything is in flames. Tod's leg has been crushed somehow and he cannot flee. Instead he is forced to watch and scream in horror as his collage, "The Burning of Los Angeles," comes to life.

One cannot fault John Schlesinger on his presentation of the riot. It is quite lengthy and appropriately overexaggerated. The visual effects are sometimes excruciatingly painful and this is as it should be in a scene that attempts to envision the apocalypse. There are fine touches of nightmare here: the crowd swarms eerily, some frighteningly masked—locusts, glimpsed in full riot regalia. Even the screen we are watching seems to burn through, the film becoming, at least for that brief illumination, a self-consuming artifact, victimized by the disorderly throng it presents and warns against.

Ironically, though, the intensity of the climax reminds us of how superficial and tangential much of the earlier part of the film has been. The riot, though well done, is virtually unsupported by all that precedes it, and its impact is undercut by its abruptness. We are shocked by the sudden violence, but we are never given any real clues as to why these people act as they do. Throughout the novel, on the other hand, West not only keeps the mob before our eyes but also explains why they are so dangerous and how they got that way:

> It was a mistake to think them harmless curiosity seekers. They were savage and bitter, especially the middle-aged and the old, and had been made so by boredom and disappointment. . . . They realize that they've been tricked and burn with resentment. Every day of their lives they read the newspapers and went to the movies. Both fed them on lynchings, murder, sex crimes, explosions, wrecks, love nests, fires, miracles, revolutions, wars. This daily diet made sophisticates of them. The sun is a joke. Oranges can't titillate their jaded palates. Nothing can ever be violent enough to make taut their slack minds and bodies. They have been cheated and betrayed. They have slaved and saved for nothing.

For the film to have been so broadly perceptive as West's analysis, for it to have underscored and understood the role of the crowd, it would have had to have been as continually intense and disquieting as the novel. Although we are often given quite vivid images of a whole landscape and its inhabitants literally coming apart, *The Day of the Locust* remains a shy and uneven film, clear in portraying the disintegrating relationships of its main characters, but unclear about the context within which these breakups and breakdowns occur—or even why they are so frightening. (pp. 95-106)

> *Sidney Gottlieb, "The Madding Crowd in the Movies," in* The Modern American Novel and the Movies, *edited by Gerald Peary and Roger Shatzkin, Frederick Ungar Publishing Co., 1978, pp. 95-106.*

Gerald Peary

[In the following essay, Peary discusses W. R. Burnett's 1929 novel Little Caesar *and its screen adaptation in the context of American culture during the 1920s and 1930s, as well as in relation to other gangster films of that era.]*

Little Caesar was the first novel of W. R. Burnett, who was later to write *High Sierra* (1940), *The Asphalt Jungle* (1949), and other gangland classics during a prolific career. The book was researched and written in the harsh and snowy winter of 1928 in Chicago, where Burnett had migrated from his native Ohio—also the fictional birthplace of his protagonist, Rico Bandello. At the time, as Burnett explained in his preface to the novel, "Capone was King. Corruption was rampant. Big Bill Thompson, the mayor, was threatening to punch King George of England in the 'snoot.' Gangsters were shooting each other all over town."

Burnett began to read articles on crime for his book, including a volume of sociology from the University of Chicago Press. "In this coldly factual survey, I came across an account of the rise and fall of the Sam Cardinelli gang. This account served as the nucleus for the novel that was originally called *The Furies.*" The temporary title, far too literary, was replaced by another in a mystical moment reminiscent of that dreary November night described in Mary Shelley's *Frankenstein.* "Rico, the leading figure, began to take on nightmare proportions. . . . I was afraid I was giving birth to a monster. But then a consoling thought came to me. . . . [M]y leading figure, Rico Bandello, killer and gangleader, was no monster at all, but merely a little Napoleon, a little Caesar."

The movie of *Little Caesar* was, at its release by Warner Brothers in 1930, an instant popular success. "Doors Are Smashed at Strand in Rush to See Gang Film" headlined a story in the New York *Daily Mirror,* which explained how "Police reserves were summoned last night when a crowd of 3,000 persons stormed the doors of the Warner Brothers Strand Theater." *Little Caesar* surpassed the previously record financial fortunes of Warner Brothers' 1928 *The Lights of New York* and Paramount's 1927 *Underworld* and every other gangster movie produced to that time. Surely the first reason for its contemporary popularity was that audiences in 1930 attended the picture with Al Capone in mind. Edward G. Robinson had reached fame by playing a thinly disguised version of Capone in the 1928 Broadway play *The Racket.* According to Chicago Judge John Lyle in *The Dry and Lawless Years* (1960), "Scarface was . . . 5 feet 8 inches, 190 pounds. He had a large flabby face with thick lips and coarse features. His nose was flat; his brows dark and shaggy, and a bullet-shaped head was supported by a short thick neck." All in all, a passable description of Robinson.

Yet Burnett had *not* based his primary story of Rico Bandello on Capone but on the exploits of the obscure Cardinelli gang. Still, Capone's dynamic presence crossed into the novel through Burnett's characterization of the Big Boy. For Burnett, his crude, unnamed Big Boy is an oversized animal, a bull in the china shop, who has held to his lower-class crudities while moving up to take over Chicago. In the novel: "The Big Boy sat opposite . . . his derby on the side of his head, and his huge fists which had swung a pick in a section gang, lying before him . . . " "The Big Boy . . . stood leaning his huge hairy paws on the table." "The Big Boy put his head back and brayed." Burnett's Big Boy is a parvenu, a pretender to culture. " 'See that picture over there?' He pointed to an imitation Velasquez. 'That baby set me back one hundred and fifty berries.' "

In the movie *Little Caesar,* a major switch occurs. The Big Boy is turned into a refined upper class gangleader, with the uncouth qualities all pushed over to Rico. Big Boy is played by poised and polished Sidney Blackmer, a gentleman all the way. When he transports Rico to his mansion for one tiny scene (Rico's sole glimpse of the "power elite"!), he also points to a fancy painting on the wall. "That cost me $15,000," he says. The price of the painting is much higher than in the novel, the vulgar talk about "berries" is eliminated, and there is no indication that the painting is fake. The movie Big Boy possesses refined artistic taste, and his talk of prices is only to bedazzle the gloating, ever-materialistic Rico.

The Blackmer character never needs to struggle the way Rico (or the novel's Big Boy) had to. In social status, he begins at the top. Explains William K. Everson in *The Bad Guys* (1964):

> The "higher-ups" were, by the very nature of things, rarely seen—and then only briefly. They represented the omnipotence of power above the law; they had a culture and veneer . . . that the self-made Robinson type of gangster could only admire and never dream of duplicating. . . .

So although the film Big Boy does represent Capone in his stranglehold over the city of Chicago, his personality does not match up with "Scarface" Al's. Nor do any specific actions assigned to him in the narrative. Rather, it is around Rico that Capone analogies are woven, beginning with the lower-class Italian origins of both and their initial professions as rabidly ambitious gunmen. Perhaps the best way to view the movie is to understand that the Al Capone personage is split between Rico on the rise and the Big Boy at the top. Rico's feverish objective is to make himself and the Big Boy one and the same—a fusion which he never reaches before his Fall.

Warners went far beyond Robinson's physical resemblance to Al Capone to emphasize the fastidious and narcissistic elements in Rico's character (already noted in Burnett) that matched the sartorial Capone, typically described by *Time* as "Sleek, porcine, bejeweled and spatted . . . " And from Judge Lyle: "Capone's bedroom was elaborate with fine furniture and oriental rugs. The bed was turned down. The sheets and pillow cases were silk and monogrammed 'A.C.' Silk pajamas on the bed had the same handworked initials." In the movie of *Little Caesar,* Rico ostentatiously combs his black locks, buys fancy suits, jewelry, spats, acquires a grand apartment bedecked in splendorous imitation of the domiciles of both the fictional Big Boy and the real-life Capone.

The decision of the filmmakers to emphasize Rico's resemblances to Capone are symptomatic of the *roman à clef* strategy chosen by Warners to sell their project. In fact, *Little Caesar* is certainly one of the few movies ever where the film story strives to be *closer* to real events than the novel. Here are three examples from the movie:

> (1) When Rico arrives in Chicago, the city is controlled in part by "Diamond Pete" Montana, clearly meant to recall "Big Jim" or "Diamond Jim" Colosimo, the Boss of Chicago when Capone arrived there from New York. Colosimo's propensity for jewels was the stuff of legend. "He acquired his name . . . by arraying his huge check-suited body with diamonds, diamonds on fingers, clothes and accessories, and diamonds carried in leather bags in his pockets, through which he delved as he talked, like a child with a heap of coloured beads" (Kenneth Allsop's 1961 *The Bootleggers*).

> In Burnett, the character is simply called Pete Montana. "He was dressed very quietly, wore no jewelry. . . . " He bears no correspondence to a real person.

> (2) In both novel and film, Tony is placed "on the spot" by Rico, who machine guns him as he stands on the steps of a Catholic church. In 1926 Hymie Weiss, rosary around his neck, had been executed in these circumstances by Capone's henchmen, as "more than fifty bullets flew across the street and spattered the stonework of the Holy Name Cathedral" (Allsop).

In Burnett, the historical analogies end here. In the movie version of *Little Caesar*, Tony is given a huge funeral parade in the streets, with sanctimonious gangsters (including his killers) united to pay last respects. This motor caravan seems meant to recall the notorious processional in memory of Dion O'Banion in 1924, which brought Capone and gang, his alleged assassins, into Chicago's Loop for the ostentatious wake.

(3) Rico shoots and kills the new Crime Commissioner, McClure. This incident of violence in the movie has its recognizable basis in the famous unsolved 1926 death of William McSwiggin, Assistant State's Attorney of Cook County, while he allegedly was conducting investigations into Capone's crime capitol of Cairo, Illinois. Capone had denied any involvement with the murder by issuing a statement of classical cynicism: "Of course I didn't kill him. Why should I? I liked the kid. Only the day before he got killed he was up to my place and when he went home I gave him a bottle of Scotch. . . . I paid McSwiggin and I paid him plenty, and I got what I was paying for." Charges were levied at Capone for a time, but then he was exonerated of any complicity in the murder. Still, memories of this incident persisted—and were incorporated into the film.

In the novel, Rico murders a character referred to as "Courtney, the bull." That is all the information offered, so again Burnett refers to no specific historical individual.

When Jack Warner read *Little Caesar* in 1929, he was attracted to the project because he thought that "the book was a thinly disguised portrait of Al Capone. . . ." The concern with maintaining Capone's presence in the Warners' film was in order to take advantage of public curiosity about the life of the racketeer. This interest could be translated into profits for the film studio. But there was more: the life of Capone was also borrowed by the filmmakers for its rich metaphoric possibilities.

Warner Brothers' earlier 1930 film, *The Doorway to Hell,* had utilized Capone as the deflated and failed symbol of the Depression age—reduced, in the enervated figure of Louis Ricarno (Lew Ayres), to a state of complete stagnation at the end of a futile quest for family happiness and domestic tranquility. *Little Caesar* also examines this theme, but in a totally different and indirect manner. Whereas Ricarno talks obsessively about his family, miming Capone's own public utterances ("I could bear it all if it weren't for the hurt it brings my mother and my family"), Rico Bandello never mentions his family at all, nor does bachelor Rico have any love interests.

Rico's alienation from the opposite sex can be traced to Burnett's novel:

> Rico had very little to do with women. He regarded them with a sort of contempt; they seemed so silly, reckless and purposeless. . . . What he feared most in women . . . was . . . their ability to relax a man, to make him soft and slack. . . . He was given to short bursts of lust, and this lust once satisfied, he looked at women impersonally . . . as one looks at inanimate objects.

By the First Script, scenarist Robert N. Lee had removed *all* heterosexual interests. For instance, Rico attended his testimonial banquet in Burnett's novel with Blondy Belle, the ex-girlfriend of Little Arnie Lorch. In the movie banquet, however, when Rico comments, "I'm glad you guys brought your molls with you," he himself is flanked conspicuously by two men.

Thematically, what is the meaning of a Rico without a female lover? A simple Freudian reading of the above quote makes Rico a repressed homosexual whose hostility toward women is combined with fear of impotence. But this interpretation, however evocative, seems inadequate to explain his familial isolation also. Lacking any loved ones, he is better understood as a perfect emblem of the Depression times, a person completely dislocated, solitary, forlorn.

In the film version, there is no past for Rico, only the dim knowledge that he has come from elsewhere than the big city. (He arrives from Youngstown, Ohio, in the novel, but references to this specific birthplace were eliminated in an earlier script.) So when he finds that his criminal career has ebbed, he cannot even attempt a return to his roots. He is condemned to wander the belly of the city until he meets his doom. In a scene invented for the movies, Rico lies around a fifteen-cents-a-night flophouse, a disheveled, alcoholic and unemployed tramp. Blatant Depression settings are thus fused onto the already basic *angst* of the gangster story.

Rico is alone, alone. Where is the traditional immigrant mother who represents some semblance of moral order in the gangster's otherwise murky life? Tom Powers in *The Public Enemy* (1931) has a kind mother who cares for him as does Tony Camonte in *Scarface* (1932). (There is one mother in *Little Caesar,* novel and film, but she is Tony's, not Rico's.)

Hardly noticed in *Little Caesar* is perhaps a greater irony: that Rico is rewarded with a "surrogate mother," a nightmare version of maternity. This is the filthy, witchlike hag "Ma" Magdalena, who hides Rico from the police—for a price. She is a "fence"—greedy, untrustworthy, different from the normal Madonna-like mothers of other gangster movies. If these others withdraw from the Depression morality, "Ma" thrives in the shyster, "dog-eat-dog" environment, where everyone scraps for a living.

When Rico is pursued, he runs, in both novel and film, to his "Ma." A *real* mother in such stories takes in her son, no questions asked, no matter what his crime. Family always comes first. But "Ma" Magdalena cares only for Rico's money. With $150 in her hand, "Ma" takes Rico behind her fruit store through a labyrinth of walkways into a clandestine, tiny back room. Mervyn LeRoy based his movie set on this description from Burnett's novel: "She led him through a dark tunnel and back into the hide-out. A small, round opening just large enough to admit one person had been pierced in the wall." The symbolism is evident—Rico's flight back to the womb, even a surrogate womb, a temporary respite before being thrust back out onto the streets.

Little Caesar's concentration on Rico's familial dissociation seems partly borrowed from the publicized domestic turmoils of Capone. But the movie of *Little Caesar* uses the Capone legend metaphorically in another way, foreign to gangster films up to this time. The auspicious rise of Rico Bandello proves the most dynamic point of Capone's life—that crime can pay, and handsomely. A young thug like Capone—or Rico—with the right temperament and plenty of "drive," can rise high, much as a young businessman with the right blend of personality credentials. As Burnett described his protagonist, "Rico's great strength lay in his single-mindedness, his energy and his self-discipline." And later, "Rico made decisions quickly, seldom asked for advice, and was nearly always right. . . . Rico had been in the game long enough to know that to make money you've got to spend money."

Like his prototype Capone, Rico climbs to wealth and power within the gangland hierarchy. How does Rico differ from previous film gangsters who began low in the criminal organizations? Most had turned virtuous and quit racketeering. James Cagney in *Sinners Holiday* (1930) was the first to murder his boss. But Rico is the first to step on his bosses—Vittori, Arnie Lorch, "Diamond Pete" Montana—and over them, on the way to the top, until he has earned the title of Boss himself. "The illicitness of his incontrovertible power corresponds to the illicitness of the employee who would like to tell his boss to go to hell," theorized Parker Tyler in *The Hollywood Hallucination* (1944).

For film director Mervyn LeRoy, Rico's obsessive drive to get higher and higher was his dominant theme for the movie:

> Rico . . . was a man with a driving ambition to be on top. . . . He always tried to copy the man higher up, in hopes that he would thus assume the characteristics and eventually the job of that man.—(*Take One,* 1974)

In almost all previous movies (except a 1928 Raoul Walsh film *Me, Gangster*), the gangster's rise to the top would be nonexistent or very brief. But *Little Caesar* concentrates the prime time of its story on carefully plotting Rico's advancement, dwelling on his acquisition of fine clothes and a fancy suite of rooms. His fall is only in the last minutes, a total reversal of fortune, a shock to Rico and maybe to viewers as well. *Time* described these final moments: "[II]is luck changes. He loses his power, his money, becomes a flop-house derelict, and finally dies behind a billboard chewed by bullets from a machine-gun."

What went wrong? Certainly there was no precedent in the Horatio Alger story, which held only the prospect for even greater success for a hero who has followed the rules of conduct correct in his milieu. "Ragged Dick," for instance, finishes as "Richard Hunter, Esq, . . . a young gentleman on the way to fame and fortune. . . ."

Why did the real-life gangster Al Capone fall? Many have theorized that he was too devoted to the limelight. He was the last major figure of organized crime to seek celebrity and he probably paid for insisting that the world know his name. Said social historian Andrew Sinclair: "His successors are harder fish to net. They have heeded Brecht's rhetorical question, 'What is robbing a bank compared with founding a bank?' And they have been rewarded with both the millions and the ease and the semirespectability that Alphonse Capone wanted all his life and never found. . . ." (*Era of Excess,* 1964).

Rico Bandello likewise was finished because he *had* to respond to the insults to his name, planted in the newspaper by Flaherty the policeman. Defending his wilted honor, a ragged and derelict Rico returns to the open, where he is shot and killed. As he dies, his magnificent creation dies with him. "Mother of Grace, is this the end of Rico?" His name is his last word.

What does death mean for Rico? In the standard twenties gangster movie, *Underworld* for example, a gangleader who commited terrible deeds, including murder, was allowed to absolve himself gracefully of his sins through heroic sacrifice, often to save the sacred love of a young and innocent couple. By giving up his life for this moral cause, he would instantly bring meaning to his existence by showing knowledge of his sins and a desire for reformation. As Parker Tyler talks of the prototype crime story, *Crime and Punishment,* "Raskolnikoff's behavior . . . is a *moral* suicide, a true expiation, an exchange of a sense of Hell for a sense of Purgatory, and therefore not self-extinction. . . ."

But Rico Bandello reaches no moral understanding. Despite his murders and unmitigated brutality, he is shocked when mortally wounded and cannot understand why he has been robbed of his life. He cannot be expected to reach the articulation of a Robert Warshow, who noted accurately that

> Every attempt to succeed is an act of aggression leaving one alone and guilty and defenseless among enemies: one is *punished* for success. This is our intolerable dilemma: that failure is a kind of death and success is evil and dangerous and—ultimately—impossible ("The Gangster as Tragic Hero," 1948).

While this message applies both to Al Capone and Rico Bandello, finally there is a point where the two part company. Capone, for all his complaints, had it infinitely better. In October, 1930, W. R. Burnett himself offered this exalted view of Capone for *The Saturday Review:* "Capone is immune. He has a villa in Florida; he is a millionaire; his name has become a household word. The old pre-Prohibition slogan, 'you can't win,' is shown to be pure nonsense." But this slogan is the very essence of *Little Caesar,* the cinema's ultimate antisuccess story. As film critic Creighton Peet described the opening night for the readers of *Outlook and Independent:*

> (T)his film seems to bring out the sturdier and more aggressive members of the community who have come to see a story about the Boy Who Made Good. And let me tell you that when Sergeant Flaherty's machine guns cut him down at the end, the audience goes home mighty quiet and depressed.

Little Caesar's last question, "Is this the end of Rico?" is addressed desperately to "the Mother of Grace"—perhaps because he hasn't an earthly mother. He receives no answer, but succumbs in cosmic silence, as cruel and potent as the indifferent world of the naturalistic novel. (pp. 286-96)

> *Gerald Peary, "Rico Rising: Little Caesar Takes Over the Screen," in* The Classic American Novel and the Movies, *edited by Gerald Peary and Roger Shatzkin, Frederick Ungar Publishing Co., 1977, pp. 286-96.*

Jorge Luis Borges

[*Borges was an Argentine short story writer, poet, and essayist. His writing is often used by critics to illustrate the modern view of literature as a highly sophisticated game. Justifying this interpretation of Borges's works are his admitted respect for stories that are artificial inventions of art rather than realistic representations of life, his use of philosophical conceptions as a means of achieving literary effects, and his frequent variations on the writings of other authors. Such characteristic stories as "The Aleph," "The Circular Ruins," and "Pierre Menard, Author of the Quixote" are demonstrations of the subjective, the infinitely various, and the ultimately indeterminate nature of life and literature. Accompanying the literary puzzles and the manipulations of variant models of reality, there is a somber, fatalistic quality in Borges's work which has led critics to locate his fictional universe in close proximity to the nightmarish world of Franz Kafka and the philosophical wasteland of Samuel Beckett. In his literary criticism, Borges is noted for his insight into the manner in which an author both represents and creates a reality with words, and the way in which those words are variously interpreted by readers. With his fiction and poetry, Borges's critical writing shares the perspective that literary creation of imaginary worlds and philosophical speculation on the world itself are parallel or identical activities. In the following excerpt, Borges criticizes film adaptations of Robert Louis Stevenson's novel* Strange Case of Dr. Jekyll and Mr. Hyde *(1886).*]

Hollywood has, for the third time, defamed Robert Louis Stevenson. This defamation is entitled *Dr. Jekyll and Mr. Hyde* and it was perpetrated by Victor Fleming who repeats the esthetic and moral errors of Mamoulian's version (or perversion) with unfortunate fidelity. In the 1886 novel, Dr. Jekyll is morally dual, as are all men, while his hypostasis—Edward Hyde—is wicked through and through. In the 1941 film, Dr. Jekyll is a young pathologist who practices chastity, while his hypostasis—Hyde—is a rake with sadistic and acrobatic tendencies. The Good, for Hollywood thinkers, is betrothal to the well-bred, well-heeled Miss Lana Turner; Evil (which so preoccupied David Hume and the heresiarchs of Alexandria) is illicit cohabitation with Fröken Ingrid Bergman or Miriam Hopkins. It is useless to observe that Stevenson is wholly innocent of this limitation or deformation of the problem. In the final chapter of the work he states Jekyll's defects: sensuality and hypocrisy. In 1888, in one of the *Ethical Studies,* he attempts to enumerate "all the manifestations of the truly diabolic" and proposes this list: "envy, malice, lies, mean silence, libellous truths, the slanderer, the petty tyrant, the querulous poisoner of domestic life." (I would contend that ethics do not encompass sexual matters unless they are contaminated by treason, covetousness, or vanity.)

The structure of the film is even more rudimentary than its theology. In the book, the identity of Jekyll and Hyde is a surprise; the author saves it for the end of the ninth chapter. The allegorical narration feigns to be a detective story. No reader guesses that Hyde and Jekyll are the same person; even the title makes us postulate that they are two. Nothing would be easier than transferring this approach to the cinema. Let us imagine a case for the police:

two actors, recognizable to the public, will figure in the plot (let us say, George Raft and Spencer Tracy). They can use analogous words; they can mention facts that presuppose a common past; when the problem becomes undecipherable, one of them imbibes the magic drug and changes into the other. (Of course, the satisfactory execution of this plan would involve two or three phonetic readjustments: the modification of the names of the protagonists.) More civilized than I, Victor Fleming manages to avoid all surprise and all mystery. In the opening scenes of the film, Spencer Tracy fearlessly downs the versatile potion and is transformed into Spencer Tracy with a different wig and negroid features.

Going beyond Stevenson's dualistic parable and approaching *The Colloquy of the Birds,* which was composed (in the twelfth century of our age) by Farid ud-din Attar, we can conceive of a pantheistic film whose numerous characters are resolved finally in the One, which is everlasting.

Jorge Luis Borges, "Dr. Jekyll and Edward Hyde, Transformed," in Borges: A Reader, edited by Emir Rodriguez Monegal and Alastair Reid, E. P. Dutton, 1981, p. 140.

Geoffrey Wagner

[*Wagner is an American novelist, poet, translator, and critic. In the following excerpt, he compares Thomas Mann's 1913 novella* Death in Venice *with the 1971 film version directed by Luchino Visconti.*]

As a fiction, *Death in Venice* is obviously many things. It is at times an application of Nietzsche's *The Birth of Tragedy* and *The Genealogy of Morals* (some of whose *Abhandlungen,* indeed, are given us almost verbatim by Tonio Kröger). The Marxist Georg Lukács saw it as a predictive statement of the barbarous underworld of the German psyche, a *Geistesgeschichte,* as it were, or what Albert Thibaudet formulated as the "roman brut." In correspondence Mann said that it also originated in an interest in Goethe's elderly passion for Ulrike Levetzow; certainly, Aschenbach's moderation is destroyed as was Goethe's Eduard of *The Elective Affinities.* The upright, disciplined author of a work on Frederick the Great, whose life is symbolised by a fisted hand and whose favourite motto is *Durchhalten,* has become altogether too Apollonian, it is plain; together with Heinrich Mann's Professor Unrat, he has grown over-stiff a *persona* and fails to recognise his irrational instincts. Venice, which Nietzsche equated with the musical, "this most improbable of cities"—art built on the unconscious sea itself—"relaxed his will." Licence overtakes discipline. Aschenbach rises each morning "as early as though he had a painting press of work" and yet the only writing he does on the Lido would seem to be a Dionysiac or frankly pornographic eulogy of Tadzio that leaves him spent and exhausted "as it were after a debauch" (the orgasmic suggestion is also given, though at a different point, by Visconti). *"Death in Venice,"* Mann has written, in a necessary over-simplification, "portrays the fascination of the death idea, the triumph of drunken disorder over the forces of a life consecrated to rule and discipline."

Clearly, Visconti was forced to concentrate on one aspect

Ingrid Bergman, Spencer Tracy, and Lana Turner in a publicity photograph for the 1941 film adaptation of Dr. Jekyll and Mr. Hyde, *directed by Rouben Mamoulian.*

of this extraordinary *Liebestod,* of what Heller calls "invalid love rising from the invalidity of life." He did so by seeking into another Gustav's life, that of Mahler, who is said to have met Mann in a railway carriage utterly broken by a similar infatuation. Writing prior to the best of Proust and Gide, Mann suggested that *Death in Venice's* "musical affinities may have been what endeared it." Whether Mahler did, in fact, transvalue an erotic entanglement of the sort into great art or not (he died in the same year that Mann's story was published), Visconti's response to it seems, at first sight, legitimate enough.

It has often struck me also that something of the horror with which the European intelligentsia watched the collapse of Oscar Wilde—Gide's Ménalque—before a similarly worthless symbol of Eros-Thanatos may lie in the mists behind Mann's masterpiece. Wilde indulged at the end in that rouging and powdering which was for Aschenbach a mock-Faustian rejuvenation; we remember Wilde's allusions to the natural corruption of Venice, while Sebastian (though not explicitly Sebastian Melmoth) is once cited by Mann, in *Death in Venice,* as "the most beautiful symbol, if not of art as a whole, yet certainly of the art we speak of here." Visconti therefore took Mahler as an anagram of Aschenbach (=stream of ashes) beset by his

Dionysos (=Tadzio). He drenched his images in a soundtrack of, largely, the plaintive *adagietto* of Mahler's Fifth Symphony, made Dirk Bogarde look like the composer, and gave him via flashbacks an associate called Alfred, a young man with curly hair. This automatically invited certain reactions. To start off, scholarly purists pointed out that for the Mann of this moment music—as in *Tristan*—is used for the Dionysiac and, if not the disordered, at least the suspiciously non-verbal. As in *The Magic Mountain* (its title taken from *The Birth of Tragedy*) words are associated with control, music with rapture. In that charming depiction of *fin-de-siècle* dilettantism mentioned, the *Tristan* of 1902, it is Gabriele Eckhof's expressly forbidden playing of Wagner that brings on her death. You can say that she woos death through art, but it is *this sort of* beauty that causes her to die—"death and beauty had claimed her for their own."

Visconti replies to and organises this sense of desperate and ecstatic pessimism with considerable integrity. It is true that he starts his story with Aschenbach on the steamer arriving at Venice, rather than introduces the (fictionally important) first death figure, that of the wanderer with his rucksack by the cemetery who so irrationally arouses Aschenbach's latent unrest. He makes an effort, however, to interlink this new beginning with his general theme. In his film the visit is evidently motivated, we later learn, by the composer's collapse at a concert, and the ship is called *Esmeralda,* which is the name of the innocent-looking, almost boyish prostitute Visconti has Aschenbach take, to his own disgust, in a brothel (this flashback is initiated from a moment in the present when Tadzio is playing on a piano). The first abortive visit Mann has his protagonist make to an Adriatic island is omitted; in the original it is not Dionysiac enough for Aschenbach's mood—"it annoyed him not to be able to get at the sea." Yet the episode is not all that important. The real difficulty is the appearance of Bogarde, looking like an absent-minded professor who is in reality a lecherous fag. Vincent Canby aptly described him here as "a fussy old man who develops a crush on a beautiful youth." This happens because Visconti has no time to insinuate Tadzio into Aschenbach's consciousness as gently and delicately as does the original author. He has to throw the image at us, via the handsome Björn Andresen, and make what story he has at his disposal move. Tadzio's glances, which Mann only lets us notice through the filter of Aschenbach's point-of-view, now seem explicit, the boy almost propositioning Aschenbach. As Paul Zimmerman put it, "He and the boy exchange lengthy glances, whose sexual explicitness turns Aschenbach into a foolish dirty old man, and the boy into a pretty little tease."

Visconti's original intentions seem to have been far from this. In an early interview with Guy Flatley he declared that he was making a story about "love without eroticism, without sexuality." One of the errands of Mann's work, which came out before Freud's Leonardo essay, seems to have been to emphasise the nature of love rather than the love object as primary—hence the Platonic references in the text. He at one point mentions Aschenbach's "paternal affection" for Tadzio. But images are not implicit; and they led Visconti into certain contradictions which he tried to resolve through the extraneous matter thrown in. Thus, Stuart Byron saw in Aschenbach and his associate Alfred that relationship between men which society condones; we move from Alfred's encomium of the senses to an image of Tadzio, in the present, lifting an orange and smelling it—and the suggestion is that society still deems any other relationship between two males illegitimate.

One further cover-up Visconti indulges in is to expand Aschenbach's fear of old age. In Mann's text we read: "The presence of the youthful beauty that had bewitched him filled him with disgust of his own ageing body." This longing for youth is enlarged by the film's imagery. In the first flashback there is an important speech when Aschenbach mentions the hour-glass in his father's house (an hour-glass is seen on a table by the couch), and how one does not notice the sand trickling away until it runs out: then all the questions that one has not asked spring suddenly to mind. Visconti maintains the vanishing sand metaphor right through Aschenbach's death on the beach at the end. Unfortunately, Bogarde is too young to need the barber's rejuvenation, it merely feminises him. After this he has a journey through the underworld following Tadzio, as a beckoning figure of youth and beauty. Disinfectant is seen squirted like semen, fires burn in the streets, and there is one emphatic background of balustrades that repeats the hour-glass shape. Here Aschenbach has a greenish pallor similar to the later face of the mountebank, one of Mann's

many death figures. Behind a rank of candles in a church there is a twisted Byzantine column to the right of the frame (showing Tadzio's praying face) whose glittering greenish bands suggest the serpentine nature of the voyeur's passion.

The sense of the ominous, narcissistic and corrupt is what needs to be conveyed, the lulling of a great critical and creative faculty by fascination with the "abyss." The susurration and overlapping of voices at the table of Tadzio's mother (played by Silvana Mangano) is almost flattering to Mann's uni-referential ascription of Dionysiac qualities to Polish or generally Slavic characters (cp. Clavdia Chauchat of *The Magic Mountain*). Visconti gains a good deal of analogical power here by the lovely music: for, as Stanley J. Solomon noted, "What Visconti tries to achieve here is an emotional response to the total impact of the narrative that in some way resembles what readers derive from the Mann text."

The narrative of the original is so undramatic that all these auditory additions seem quite justified and, indeed, one blenches a bit when Visconti encroaches on his stylisation by the over-dramatic flashbacks to Aschenbach's past, notably that involving the prostitute—which I can only find suggested in the text by the words, "He had been young and crude with the times and by them badly counselled." For some reason, also, the Visconti re-telling has Aschenbach's daughter die rather than his wife (the death of youth?).

All this is needlessly distracting to a genuinely "felt" texture. The film is so strongly expressive in its own right that when Bogarde sits at table, at the Hôtel des Bains, looks over the menu and says to the waiter, "Soup, fish, that's all," one is suddenly brought down to earth, as one is when he breathes out, much to our discomfort, "I love you." There has been an interference with, a reduction of, the obtaining stylisation. When an objective reality interferes by itself like this, we realise what a remarkable feat it is for any film-maker to preserve surface order for a long time, as does Bergman, in the absence of overt narrative action.

A cinematic analogy like Visconti's cannot be a treachery since it does not presume to be the original. We have by now broken away from the book-illustration approach, the xerography, of early transposition, studied above. Whether or not Visconti's assault on *Death in Venice* is a great film is open to opinion; but it surely succeeds in complementing its wonderful original, in the manner of some richly visual footnote.

Art is seen to heighten life: Tadzio is first glimpsed by Aschenbach as the sole object of beauty in a gloriously vulgar *fin-de-siècle* hotel gathering punctuated by fantastic female hats, a masterpiece of set decoration. And yet, this passion is "like crime." The man's love-role quickly declines. He is identified by the knowing governesses. He eats the over-ripe strawberries and becomes the true author of *The Abject,* in fact his own subject. Visconti handles the difficult point-of-view well. Since Tadzio is never seen except by Aschenbach "for us," as it were, he may never exist; all Tadzio's actions are, within the Mann text, intensional, a result of compulsions and passions inside the viewer himself. The refraction, that of the reader being psychologically a step ahead of the main character, is fictionally gripping and has been often copied (as in *Lolita*). Visconti has to stabilise the boy beyond the narrator's vision, yet he does so fairly tactfully, and indeed faithfully. A passage in which Aschenbach walks to the beach is cleverly threaded with some semi-balletic movements by Tadzio, nearly touching him, which one soon realises are imaginative. The more common entry of reality into this film is what really disturbs it, rather than any departure from its original. The overlong, almost tedious scene of the entertainers at the hotel is one such example: here Mann's fourth death figure, who receives the overlarge payment due to the illegal gondolier representing Charon earlier, is exaggerated and over-insistent. The trickles of black dye down Dirk Bogarde's face at his deck-chair death are also uncomfortably extraneous.

All in all, however, this analogy has to be respected. It struggles inside a work of great original vigour and resonance. As Aschenbach is lured towards the subconscious ocean at the end, in front of which the sturdy youth Jaschiu performs a surrogate homosexual act on Tadzio (more explicit in Mann than in Visconti), "a camera on a tripod stood at the edge of the water, apparently abandoned." This literal image, entirely natural in its surroundings, stands in for the tripod before the Delphic oracle, and makes a perfect synonym with that helplessness life feels in front of cinema, without the controlling transmutation of Apollo. (pp. 340-47)

Geoffrey Wagner, " 'Death in Venice' (1971)," in his The Novel and the Cinema, *Fairleigh Dickinson University Press, 1975, pp. 338-47.*

Diane Jacobs

[*Jacobs is an American writer specializing in film criticism. In the following essay, she discusses* Apocalypse Now, *directed by Francis Ford Coppola, in relation to the work from which it was adapted, Joseph Conrad's novella* Heart of Darkness.]

Critics have traditionally felt uneasy with anything that might be construed as intellectualism in the American cinema. So it is no surprise that even as astute a critic as Michael Wood should chortle a bit at Francis Ford Coppola's bald allusions to "The Hollow Men" in Colonel Kurtz's weird Cambodian haven in the final scenes of *Apocalypse Now* (1979). (T. S. Eliot himself is rarely chided for excerpting Conrad's "Mistah Kurtz—he dead" for his poem's epigraph.) "I would like to think Kurtz is drawn to this poem by Coppola's sense of humor," writes Wood in the *New York Review of Books.* ". . . But I am afraid the attraction is purely pedantry."

There *is* a touch of not unpleasing pedantry and seductive virtuosity to *Apocalypse Now,* as there is to its uncredited source, Joseph Conrad's *Heart of Darkness* (1902). Still, the issue is not Coppola's literariness, but whether his borrowing from Eliot and more especially from Conrad are decorative or organic. What relevance has Conrad's Victorian allegory to Coppola's contemporary vision of soldiers water-skiing through combat zones, of sailors shooting heroin, of officers sniffing napalm for the scent of victory, and of the sort of gnarled genius who would think to sever the recently innoculated arms of enemy children?

Coppola himself broached this issue of decoration versus substance when discussing his more abstracted film *The Conversation* (1974). Because he could not identify with his protagonist, Coppola told Brian De Palma, he decided to "enrich" him: to embellish the wiretapper Harry Caul with his own childhood polio, his love for music, his Catholicism, etc. Unfortunately, that "enrichment" shows, and despite a nuanced performance by Gene Hackman, Harry remains a skein of quirks and obsessions. He plays the saxophone, suffers a pesky guilt, and clings tenaciously to his privacy. These details add up to a fascinating concept, but the character and ultimately the film itself lack sinew.

A number of critics insist that a similar esthetic decoration is at work in *Apocalypse Now,* that *Heart of Darkness* is little more than "enrichment," neatly appended to John Milius's genre script and no more essential to the film than polio is to Harry. To my mind, this is not the case: *Heart of Darkness* is the spine of *Apocalypse Now.* The film succeeds as an updated interpretation of Conrad because author and filmmaker share uncannily similar goals; because Coppola's thoughts on American involvement in Vietnam and on power and the compulsion to vanquish the enemy are compatible with Conrad's thoughts on avarice and colonialism, with its "strange commingling of desire and hate"; because Marlow's up-river journey, in the novel, to the "horror" of colonial Africa is a fittingly ironic paradigm for Captain Willard's (Martin Sheen's) penetration of Asia; because Mr. Kurtz's lust for something beyond ivory is a fitting correlative for Colonel Kurtz's yen for the ineffable beyond victory; and, finally, because Marlon Brando's murky, corpulent, "unsound" Kurtz is very much Conrad's Kurtz: a superior individual "on the threshold of great things," "exalted," and not just "hollow at the core" but unreal and sometimes unbelievable. There is a crucial difference between the novel and the film, but more on this later.

Like the novel, the film opens with its narrator anxiously awaiting a mission. Captain Willard prowls his Saigon hotel room, gulping booze, muttering about how uncomfortable he felt on his leave at home, and finally splintering a mirror with his fist and bloodying himself. When two men usher him off to receive orders for a top-secret mission, Willard's reaction could be summed up in Marlow's pre-existential musing: "I don't like work,—no man does—but I like what is in the work—the chance to find yourself. Your own reality—for yourself, not for others. . . ."

Marlow is a seaman, Willard an intelligence officer. Marlow, in the employ of a Belgian trading company in colonial Africa, sets off up the Congo to discover what has happened to one of his predecessors, the legendarily successful ivory trader, Mr. Kurtz. Willard, in the employ of the government, sets off not only to find but to kill his Kurtz, the Army's erstwhile favorite son Colonel Kurtz, who has taken the war effort into his own hands. Against orders, Kurtz has crossed the Cambodian border and (like his Congo counterpart) has set himself up as a god/king to the willing natives. As a commanding officer points out to Willard, "what Lincoln calls 'the better angel of our nature' " has lost out in the battle for Kurtz's soul.

Like *Heart of Darkness, Apocalypse Now* is on one level an adventure tale. Conrad sends Marlow off to do battle with inclement weather, unfriendly geography, cannibals, inef-

Dennis Hopper, Martin Sheen, and Frederic Forrest in Apocalypse Now, *directed by Francis Ford Coppola.*

ficient Europeans, and unsympathetic natives with deadly weapons. Coppola dispatches Willard on a mission that will pit him against the NLF, tigers, and routine carnage as well as his "choice of nightmares."

Yet very little actually happens, either to Marlow or to Willard. They wait, and they watch. Marlow waits for a mission, and, once he has it, observes the coast of Africa ("smiling, frowning, inviting, grand, mean, insipid or savage and always mute with an air of whispering, come and find out") from the deck of a French steamer. Arriving at his company's Central Station, he discovers his boat sunk and wrecked and waits for the rivets with which to mend it. By the time he encounters Kurtz, the novel is nearly two-thirds finished: Marlow's intellect has digested the quiddities of Africa and the human soul, and he has done almost nothing.

Similarly, Willard anticipates and endures and, most importantly, scrutinizes: a helicopter attack, the ravaging of a village, playboy bunnies teasing the sex-starved troops, a bridge reconstructed every day to be demolished nightly. He observes carefully, but only rarely—when he shoots a Vietnamese woman, for instance—is he called upon to participate or to make decisions.

Coppola's "heart of darkness," like Conrad's, is a triumph

of style over story. Or rather, the description—words for Conrad, *mise-en-scène* for Coppola—is the story's *raison d'être*. Marlow confronts the particulars of Africa in order to expatiate on the "flabby, pretending, weak-eyed devil of a rapacious and pitiless folly," or to explore "the fascination of the abomination." Marlow is not really concerned with rivets. The rivets are so diaphanously a pretext for him to ruminate on man's relation to work that he never bothers to inform us where the rivets ultimately came from. One moment he is struck, the next he is on his way, with no explanations offered.

The day-to-day, arduous reality of combat is equally irrelevant to Coppola, who is no more concerned with the little man in the trench than Conrad is with rivets. He is out to forge a vision of War, of the Vietnam War, and—less convincingly—of related horrors through dense, multilayered cinematography (by Vittorio Stovaro) and sound (by Walter Munch).

Neither Conrad nor Coppola really succeeds in fathoming "the horror" because neither succeeds in rendering Kurtz palpable. Conrad describes him as "very little more than a voice" and his "horror" as "the strange commingling of desire and hate." But what, after all, is this? For Coppola, "the horror" is a similarly elliptical distance between superiority and madness. Like Conrad, Coppola is at his best when circling that horror, when presenting it a few rungs down on a recognizable, pedestrian level. Thus, *Apocalypse Now* is most effective when describing not Kurtz himself but the world surrounding him.

Like Conrad's language, Coppola's *mise-en-scène* at once batters and soothes. While the Dolby sound whooshes at us from myriad speakers, the limpid images attract us with their sensual beauty and repel us with their content. Similarly, the cinematography renders us both victim and perpetrator of numerous horrors. In the film's most spectacular scene, for instance, we watch Lieutenant Colonel Kilgore (Robert DuVall) and his fire-spitting helicopters swoop down from the skies as if we were the bewildered Vietnamese on the ground. Kilgore has ordered that his tapes of *The Ride of the Valkyries* be played, and the Wagner meshing with the helicopter descent and the splaying of bomb fire is at once terrifying and absurd—clearly a lesser Conradian "nightmare." But in the next shot, the tables are suddenly turned. Now, the camera places us in the plane with Kilgore and directly behind the helicopter controls, thus affording us the arrogant, shameful exhilaration of power—yet another "nightmare."

Contrary to much critical opinion, *Apocalypse Now* gets into trouble not in its allegiance to Conrad, but when it veers away from the book's assumptions. Indeed, the one serious problem with this often brilliant film is the character of Willard. Like Harry Caul and unlike Marlow, Willard is too idiosyncratic, too much the unknown variable to sustain the complexities of the work we perceive through his eyes. He is not an Everyman to *Apocalypse Now* the way that Marlow is to *Heart of Darkness*.

We can identify with many of Willard's traits and impulses. He is an efficient officer, for instance, and his judgments on such matters as Kilgore's bizarre helicopter descent—"If that's how Kilgore fought the war, I began to wonder what they had against Kurtz"—would surely be ours and Marlow's. But in other respects, Willard is inscrutable and perhaps malevolent, for example when he abruptly kills a Vietnamese woman in order to get on with his up-river journey. Willard's companion has capriciously wounded the woman for the sin of harboring a small dog in her boat. She is badly injured and in pain, and she will almost certainly die; yet, if given proper medical care, she might possibly live. To his credit, Willard will not have the woman suffer, but neither will he deflect his mission in order to find her a proper doctor. Shooting her is a half-merciful, half-murderous compromise.

It is useful to compare Willard's reaction to the woman with Marlow's response to the "too fleshy" man with the "exasperating habit of fainting" who accompanies him on a two-hundred-mile hike through thickets and ravines. Clearly, he is a bungling albatross, and Marlow admits as much: "Annoying, you know, to hold your coat like a parasol over a man's head while he is coming-to." Still, hold that coat he does. Marlow is a moral quantity we know; Willard is an enigma.

As a rule, there is no reason to cavil about the idiosyncratic protagonist, but *Apocalypse Now*, like *Heart of Darkness*, demands a narrator we can trust. Coppola is flirting with myth, not debunking it (as Altman was, for instance, in his irreverent adaptation of Chandler's *The Long Good-*

bye). He is dealing with characters who are larger and situations that are, on the whole, more sweeping and less delineated than life. To lead us through this mythic world and, more importantly, to render that world credible, he needs a guide whose quirks we recognize and understand. We need someone to make sense of bridges that are destroyed every night and rebuilt each dawn to keep up the *appearance* of an open waterway. We need a sensibility capable of observing the particular lunacy of soldiers ordered to surf while a town explodes around them and to take that lunacy a step further. Willard is not quite that man. He is too shifty, too reticent with his ideas. Thus the horror he glimpses not only in Kurtz, but in himself, is not as universal as Marlow's, and the film is not as powerful as it might have been.

Despite this weakness, *Apocalypse Now* is the most successful interpretation of Conrad to date. While its flaws are numerous, Coppola has achieved a felicitous welding of literary structure and genre subject: no mean accomplishment. (pp. 211-17)

Diane Jacobs, "Coppola Films Conrad in Vietnam," in The English Novel and the Movies, *edited by Michael Klein and Gillian Parker, Frederick Ungar Publishing Co., 1981, pp. 211-17.*

Stuart Y. McDougal

[*McDougal is an American educator and critic. In the following excerpt, he presents an analysis of Ambrose Bierce's short story "An Occurrence at Owl Creek Bridge" and of the adaptation of this work for a film by Robert Enrico.*]

Ambrose Bierce carefully chose the title for his short story to emphasize the insignificance and obscurity of his subject. The outlines of the story are quite simple: During the Civil War, a Southerner is caught trying to sabotage a remote bridge and is hanged for punishment. However, the event is considerably less important than the thought processes it occasions, for at the moment of his death the convicted man experiences an extended sense of time, during which he imagines himself escaping to his wife and home. So skillfully does Bierce blend his protagonist's fantasies with the actual events of the story that the absorbed reader can easily confuse the two.

The plot of Bierce's tale is much more complex than the simple story outlined above. The author has divided the story into three sections and rearranged the chronology of events in order to produce a powerful effect on the reader. Bierce employs an omniscient third-person narrator throughout, but the narrator is sometimes quite impersonal, at other times rather intrusive. These shifts from objectivity to subjectivity are often subtle; they indicate the transition from reality to fantasy in the mind of the protagonist.

The story begins in an impersonal fashion, almost like a piece of military reportage. Although details are described thoroughly, important information is deliberately withheld (such as the protagonist's name) in order to create more interest in him, to heighten our sense of detachment, and to make the presentation more objective. The scene is nearly static.

The first break in the objective presentation occurs in the second paragraph, with the personification of death. In the third paragraph the protagonist's physical appearance is described, and here too we become aware of the presence of a narrator as he creates a favorable picture of the protagonist: The protagonist has "good" features and a "kindly expression." "Evidently this was no vulgar assassin," he notes. We are gradually moving away from the objectivity of the opening.

Action is described for the first time in the next paragraph, as the final arrangements for the hanging are completed. Then, suddenly, we enter the consciousness of the protagonist: Bierce writes, "The arrangement commended itself to his judgment as simple and effective." As we continue reading, we realize that we are sharing the protagonist's perceptions. In the opening sentence of the story, the protagonist looked down into "the swift water twenty feet below"; now he lets "his gaze wander to the swirling water of the stream racing madly beneath his feet." Bierce's choice of language here reflects the shift from objective to subjective presentation. As the protagonist stares downward, a strange thing happens: His sense of time begins to change. He watches a piece of driftwood in the stream, and instead of going quickly it appears to move slowly, despite the "racing" movement of the water. He closes his eyes to think and is disturbed by a regular ticking that grows slower and slower as it increases in volume. While this occurs, he opens his eyes, looks down at the water, and then fantasizes about escaping. The reader can easily share and sympathize with his fantasy. Finally, we are told. "The Sergeant stepped aside." No more is said, but we know the results: The noose tightens as the Southern planter plunges downward.

The first part of the story raises more questions than it answers. We learn the fate of the protagonist (hanging), and we know in considerable detail how and where this occurs. But we do not know specifically who he is or why he is there. These questions are answered only in the second section of the story: We discover the protagonist's name and more details about his occupation and background. The point of view here is objective, but the diction reflects the attitudes of Peyton Farquhar: The Southern army is "gallant," they had fought a "disastrous" campaign, Farquhar "chafed under the inglorious restraint." Every attempt is made to have us identify more closely with Farquhar. Although this section does not present Farquhar's thoughts, it prepares us for the conclusion of Bierce's tale in another way: It has a surprise ending. Now we begin to understand the organization of Bierce's plot: If we reverse the first two sections (and place them in their proper chronological order), the ending ceases to be a surprise and the descriptive passages in the first part appear labored. In their present order, they engage the reader's interest and prefigure the development of the story as a whole.

Thus, the attentive reader should begin the third part prepared for the possibilities the story holds. The section takes up where the first part ended, with Farquhar's fall through the bridge. The rope tightens on his neck, and he swings "through unthinkable arcs of oscillation, like a vast pendulum." The prevalence of verbs of uncertainty in this paragraph (*seem* and *appear*), as well as the significantly large number of tropes, signal the shift to a totally subjective vision.

The subjective vision is, of course, Farquhar's fantasy of escape. Farquhar stands outside himself and observes his actions, as in a dream; he lunges up out of the water like a newborn child, his senses "preternaturally keen and alert." By the end of this section, as he wanders homeward "through so wild a region," there can be little doubt that he is living in a purely illusory world.

But Bierce gives us one final, unavoidable clue: in the penultimate paragraph, he shifts to the use of the historical present:

> He [Farquhar] stands at the gate of his own home . . . As he pushes open the gate and passes up the wide white walk, he sees a flutter of female garments . . .

Here, Farquhar's fantasy is nearly realized: His wife approaches him, and he reaches out for the safety of her arms. But darkness and silence suddenly engulf him, and the story ends with a return to the terse, objective style of the opening section.

The conclusion of Bierce's tale comes as a surprise only to the inattentive reader, for through structural and verbal means Bierce has prepared the reader for the shift from reality to illusion and back to reality. The story provides a challenge to the filmmaker, who must find visual equivalents for these clues as well as a satisfactory way of depicting Farquhar's vision.

Instead of expanding Bierce's story to the length of a feature film, Robert Enrico preserved the limitations of his source in a short film, which has been widely acclaimed. The film begins in an objective manner, which captures the tone of Bierce's opening. The first shot is of a sign, nailed on an old tree:

> ORDER. Any Civilian caught interfering with the railroad bridges, tunnels, or trains will be SUMMARILY HANGED. April 4, 1862.

This is all that Enrico has retained of part two of Bierce's story: the explanation of the crime and an identification of the time period. Then Enrico cuts to a high-angle long establishing shot of the bridge and moves toward the civilian about to be hanged. By the time we see the condemned man, we know his crime and his punishment but not who he is. In fact, his name is mentioned only once during the film—by the soldier whose voice and movements have been slowed down.

A number of things distinguish the realistic opening scenes of Enrico's film from the later scenes of the imagined escape: the lighting, the sound, the background, and the absence of visual and aural distortions. Like Bierce, Enrico gives his viewers ample, though subtle, indications of how to evaluate what they are viewing. The opening scenes are shot in the light of dawn, so that the bridge, setting, and soldiers appear in sharp clarity. Sounds are entirely natural but are magnified considerably to indicate the subjective (and already heightened) sense of hearing of the protagonist. There is an absence of music. The viewer is struck by the mechanical nature of the ceremony, where the "code of military etiquette" clearly prevails. As Enrico noted in an interview:

. . . I purposefully shot all the frames in this section in a very stylized way, to be in keeping with the style of the bridge itself. The people move about on it almost like puppets. The entire hanging proceeds in the fashion of an inexorable machine impossible to deter. The passage of time is expressed solely in gestures, in the deployment of officers and soldiers, up to the moment when the order is given and the plank passes dizzyingly out of the frame into the void. All this had to be expressed mathematically and not lyrically or poetically. Poetry and lyricism were to be used in the portion of the film which followed.

The bleakness of the setting is due in part to the fact that this portion of the film was shot at the end of winter. The fantasy portions were shot two weeks later, when leaves and buds had begun to appear.

Although the hanging sequence is primarily objective, there are some moments of subjectivity that prepare us for the fantasy to follow. The exaggerated natural sounds are clearly subjective. There is also some use of subjective camera (as when the protagonist views the piece of driftwood) as well as the short fantasy in which he sees his wife and home. Here, as in the story, the condemned man is disturbed by the insistent ticking of his watch. Enrico has added an effective bit of action: The protagonist's vision of wife and home is interrupted by the strident tones of the captain's voice, ordering one of the soldiers to take his watch. As the gold watch and chain are removed, the doomed man is literally and figuratively deprived of time. The viewer is also prepared for the temporal distortions that follow.

The rope breaks and the man falls into the river. His time under water seems excessively long, so that virtually all spectators are gasping for breath before he surfaces. He then stares in amazement at the forest, whose most minute details appear in great clarity, down to the veins on a blade of grass. The first music in the film, the song "A Livin' Man," expresses his joy at being alive. The sequence closes ominously, with an extreme close-up of a fly caught in the web of a spider. Then the man turns and views the bridge. The soldiers move in slow motion across the bridge (as had his wife in his earlier vision). Sound, too, is initially slowed down, and then both the commands and the movements come up to normal speed. The men prepare to fire, and his flight begins.

Although the internal rhythm is rapid during the shots of the final flight, Enrico successfully conveys the feeling that his protagonist is going nowhere. He is shown swimming first in one direction, then another. At one point, Enrico employs a circular pan shot, filmed by having the man run in a circle around the panning camera. Although he appears to be moving forward, we sense that he is not. A similar effect is achieved at the conclusion, when he runs to embrace his wife. Enrico uses a telephoto lens, which compresses the space and conveys the impression that the man is running on a treadmill.

The song, "A Livin' Man," with which the fantasy sequence began, recurs at the end of the film, as the man reaches home and approaches his wife. Here, as one critic has observed, Enrico uses "the rhythm of his music to create an editing pattern for the sequence." The rhythms make a hypnotic vision of repeated actions, which mo-

mentarily lull the viewer. Then, as Farquhar calls his wife's name, the music stops. The sudden shock of the hanging is abrupt. Enrico follows it with a recapitulation in reverse order, of the opening shots of the film. The hanged man and his setting are shown with objectivity. Time has returned to normal.

Enrico succeeds in convincingly portraying the final instant of a man's life, an instant in which he seems to live out his fantasy of flight. So strongly do most viewers share the desire of the condemned man to escape that they overlook all evidence pointing to the subjective nature of this vision. The concluding shock brings us back to reality and underscores the impermanence of life and the evanescence of dreams. (pp. 329-33)

> *Stuart Y. McDougal, "Time: 'An Occurence at Owl Creek Bridge'," in his* Made into Movies: From Literature to Film, *Holt, Rinehart and Winston, 1985, pp. 329-33.*

Eric R. Birdsall and Fred H. Marcus

[*Marcus is an American educator and critic who has served as the literary supervisor of several films and is the author of* Short Story/Short Film *(1971). In the following essay, Marcus and Birdsall consider the film* Midnight Cowboy, *directed by John Schlesinger and based on the novel by James Leo Herlihy, as an example of a cinematic adaptation that as an artistic achievement surpasses its literary source.*]

John Schlesinger's film *Midnight Cowboy* captured the 1969 Academy Award for best motion picture of the year. In this instance, popular acclaim and artistic achievement meshed appropriately. The award was justified.

It seems unlikely that many of the film's viewers noted or cared that *Midnight Cowboy* had been adapted from a novel. In 1965 James Leo Herlihy's book attracted little critical or popular attention. Anyone reading the novel and seeing the movie would recognize a family resemblance. But Schlesinger's transformation of novel to film underscores a crucial point: the film medium differs radically from the literary medium.

Herlihy's novel tells the three-part story of Joe Buck, a sturdy and very naive Texan, who dreams of making his fortune serving as a stud to rich New York women. The opening section of the novel explores Joe's life prior to the moment he boards a Greyhound bus bound for New York. In part two, he arrives in the city, where he is victimized by several of its predatory denizens. The final section begins with Joe attending a Warholish party, where he encounters the first woman willing to pay for his services; the novel ends with another bus journey, this time culminating in Miami.

Through his use of compression, expansion, and imaginative visual invention, Schlesinger reshapes the novel. Using the language of film, he alters the structure of the book and creates a film of great beauty, insight, and emotional feeling. The movie concentrates on the last two sections of the novel. Only fifteen minutes of the 110-minute film have elapsed when Joe arrives in New York. Schlesinger reveals important background details in Joe's life by using relevant flashbacks from part one of Herlihy's novel.

By cutting and compressing the first two-fifths of the novel, Schlesinger shifts the central focus of the story. The novel belongs to Joe, whose naive dreams are crushed by harsh reality. But the film is more tender—without sentimentality—and emphasizes the human relationship between Joe and Ratso; it focuses upon a fragile but growing friendship in a hostile environment.

In Herlihy's novel, Joe's radio plays a symbolic role. In much the same way that romantic novels supplied world views to the innocent Americans of Henry James, Joe's radio supplies his view of reality. When he arrives in New York, he promptly unpacks his radio, "hoping its sounds would give him the feeling of having truly arrived in this new place." The radio links Joe with the world; it filters and translates reality into something he can understand. In New York, the first thing he hears is a woman's cure for insomnia: to get up and stay awake. Joe reacts significantly: he "felt sorry for the lady but at the same time he was delighted by what he'd heard. For it seemed to bear out all those rumors about Eastern women." Joe hears and believes. He assumes that his radio reveals reality.

Schlesinger recognizes the utility of the radio symbol; he also expands it and adds television touches (which Herlihy suggests but develops less fully). Joe's bus trip from Texas to New York shows Joe's dependence on his ever-present eight-transistor radio. This sequence of shots illustrates how a movie director can convert a concept into the visual, concrete language of film. Quick cuts depict the passage of time and individual shots characterize Joe Buck as well as his surroundings. The sequence begins with the bus in Texas. Joe and his radio. The countryside in bright daylight. Inside the bus with Joe, radio tuned to another station. Faces (close-ups) on the bus. Different countryside. A small town. A long shot of the bus moving down the highway at night. Morning in a new town. Different people. Another station on the radio glued to Joe's ear. Change in countryside. Joe walking through the bus, radio to his ear. More quick cuts—with the radio on the film's sound track punctuating the journey.

The film director supplements novelistic details with small, nicely ironic touches. It is the radio which announces the arrival of the bus in New York. In a second, more significant addition, Schlesinger foreshadows Joe's future relationship with the city. Arriving in his hotel room, resplendent in a cowboy shirt and movie cowboy boots, Joe turns on the television. It doesn't work. He thumps it with his hand; it still doesn't work. Finally, Joe realizes he will have to pay—it takes a quarter to operate the television set. Schlesinger visually says: nothing is free, not even "free" TV. Joe will pay, and pay again, for everything he gets in the city.

Schlesinger communicates his view of the city through a series of short visuals, invented entirely for the film. For example, Joe goes looking for his first "customer." In a series of quick cuts, we watch him following first one woman, then another. Cut to a jewelry store; close-up of a huge gem in the window of the store. Cut back to Joe, following another woman, looking delighted. A bank with the vault open; huge piles of cash seen through the window. Another woman. Quick cut to a long shot of a man passed out on the sidewalk (in front of Tiffany's!). Passersby scarcely glance at him. Joe walks into view, one of many pedestrians. He alone stops, looks down. His face shows concern. Joe's stop contrasts with the rapid, unchanging pace of the city. He looks up at the people passing; he looks down again. Confusion replaces concern on his face. Hesitantly, he moves off, glancing back at the still figure. Joe has encountered his initial example of the inhumanity of the city; his reluctant retreat is his first defeat.

Joe Buck's optimistic and simplistic approach to his "career" begins with a calculated walk along Park Avenue. His ingenuous "line" about being new in the city and looking for the Statue of Liberty produces two responses. One, almost a motherly rebuke, declares he ought to be ashamed of himself. The second brings us closer to the ugly reality of the city. Joe's "rich New York lady" is walking her French poodle. Joe's Statue of Liberty gambit is almost beyond belief, but her harsh, "It's up in Central Park taking a leak" retort, taken from the novel, succeeds in establishing the vast gulf between Joe, the ingenuous would-be hustler, and this professional city-dweller. The second "rich lady" leads; Joe merely follows. The sexual sequence which follows underscores the pattern of exploitation; Joe is hustled, not hustler. Indeed, the lady's ardor evaporates rapidly into viciousness when Joe hints delicately that he receive his "stud fee." Violent reaction and phony weeping reduce Joe to an abject state. Ironically, his first hustling "success" costs him twenty dollars. His next experience, encountering Enrico (Ratso) Rizzo, continues the irony of the hustled hustler, but leads the film into a new and major dimension.

Schlesinger's characterization of Ratso demonstrates the ability of film to translate verbal symbols into concrete images which enable the viewer to "see, feelingly." The novel describes Ratso as a "skinny, child-sized man of about twenty-one or twenty-two," with "big brown eyes" and "big ears that [stick] straight out. . . . " He is a cripple, his left leg "small and misshapen." As he walks, "his entire body [dips] to the side so that his walk [has] a kind of rolling motion to it like the progress of a lopsided wheel." Much of Herlihy's description is concrete, but words are, inevitably, more abstract than film particulars. (What, for example, does twenty-one or twenty-two really *show?*) In the film, Schlesinger's direction and Dustin Hoffman's superlative acting transform Herlihy's words into a character so specific and immediate that the viewer physically experiences his presence and character long after the movie ends. He wears a slightly soiled white suit, a marvellously ironic contrast to his venal character. Physically, Ratso has dirty, stringy hair, yellow-green slime on his teeth, and a three-day beard compounded equally of whiskers and city grime. When he walks, his crazy, rolling gait makes his whole body seem deformed. In Dustin Hoffman's portrayal, a reader/watcher perceives a twentieth-century Dickensian figure whose exterior reflects the interior man.

Since film must *show* character, Schlesinger visualizes Ratso in actions. Herlihy's novel tells us that Ratso is a creature of the city who knows its ways intimately, that he has a shrewd resourceful mind, and that he is quick to exploit any available opportunity. Schlesinger uses incidents to show us such characterization. Shortly after Joe and Ratso meet, they cross a busy street. A taxi bears down on them, braking just in time. Ratso knows his rights. He hammers on the hood of the taxi; he snarls at the driver, "I'm walkin' here. Ya hear dat? I'm walkin'

Dustin Hoffman and Jon Voight in Midnight Cowboy, *directed by John Schlesinger.*

here!" As he continues across the street, the driver mutters something. Ratso immediately executes a nice pirouette on his good leg, throws his arm in the air in a classic Italian gesture of contempt, and at the top of his lungs cries, "Up yours, ya son-of-a-bitch!" The incident takes place in the center of a busy street, in less time than it takes to describe. Ratso continues on as though nothing untoward had occurred; for him, it is commonplace action. This richly comic scene does not occur in the novel, but it is superb visual characterization.

An earlier scene also *pictures* Ratso's fine scheming mind. The plot details approximate Herlihy's narration. Ratso meets Joe in a bar (where Joe is recovering from the "lady with the French poodle" sequence). Ratso learns that Joe perceives himself as a hustler, a stud in the service of rich ladies. Schlesinger and Herlihy both utilize the irony of the hustler hustled. Ratso encourages Joe's fantasy; all Joe needs is proper "management," which, for a small fee, Ratso will provide. He tells Joe how he set up a similar fellow "just the other day," and adds that the other fellow really isn't much of a stud. Off they go to see Mr. O'Daniel, who will manage Joe. In a visual addition not in the Herlihy novel, Ratso waves toward a couple at a table, a man and a wealthy looking woman, and calls out, "Hiya Bernie, how ya doin', kid?" The implication is

clear; Joe assumes that this is one of the men Ratso has set up in business. The audience can see, if Joe cannot, that "Bernie" is a complete stranger to Ratso.

In another scene created visually by the film director, Ratso and Joe walk past a telephone booth. Without interrupting his conversation, almost without missing a step, Ratso automatically slides into the booth and rattles the coin return, checking for forgotten dimes. Finding nothing, he swivels back out and continues along with Joe. The purely automatic action by Ratso is perfect cinematic characterization. Ratso is so well schooled in the minutiae of his daily grubbing that his routine scavenging is almost unconscious.

But Ratso is also complex. While both novel and film emphasize his ratlike ability to survive, both also recognize that the death of his father has left him desperately lonely. Nor is successful scavenging likely to ease his special need. In Herlihy's book, we learn about his father when Ratso speaks about him, a man who died as unimpressively as he lived, but who left at least one void. Schlesinger must modify the *telling;* the quicker pace of the film requires showing. So he invents a brilliant short sequence. The scene: a small cemetery in the city where Ratso takes Joe to visit the grave of his father. The sky is gray behind a small marble headstone. While Joe looks both uncomfortable and sympathetic, Ratso's words and appearance reveal him in a new light. In a close-up, the director demonstrates Ratso's strong and sincere emotion. But Schlesinger avoids a sentimentality that could destroy the film's credibility. In a master stroke, he has Ratso nab a floral offering from a nearby grave and place it on his father's. The gesture defines the character: emotional and exploitive. It also foreshadows the ironic film ending. Joe's loneliness has led him through suspicion of Ratso to concern, and finally, real affection. When Joe arrives at the readiness for a meaningful friendship, Ratso dies. When Ratso finds someone to give to and lean on, it is too late.

By expanding the role of Ratso and using quick intercut flashbacks to suggest much of Herlihy's first section on Joe's background, Schlesinger maintains the theme of loneliness—and even expands it—but changes the focus from Joe's story to an exploration of the relationships between Joe and Ratso and the city. The themes are universal; the plot and visual characterization are unique. A film must necessarily be concrete and individual. But extension of the unique to universality explains the richness of the film experience.

Technically, Schlesinger achieves his creation through several necessary transformations from the novel. In Herlihy's *Midnight Cowboy* Ratso first appears in chapter 6 of part two, almost midway through the novel. In the film, he appears in all but some twenty-five minutes of the 110-minute film. The director compresses and eliminates many of the particulars in part one, the section which explains *why* Joe is lonely and hungry for friendship. Yet Schlesinger retains essential clues. He shows, through quick flashbacks, Joe's fatherless boyhood and his sexual relationship with Annie, an illusion-ridden relationship that Herlihy describes didactically. Joe is illusion-prone and the novelist tells us so—literally. In one two-sentence paragraph, Herlihy completes a piece of narration with, "That was the way Joe imagined it. This is what actually took place."

Schlesinger's compression gives the film a kind of tightly knit unity the book doesn't achieve. Necessary background is woven into the main stream of the plot through judicious juxtaposition. Herlihy's authorial intrusions, particularly on the subject of Joe's daydreaming and illusions, are replaced by sequences which create the fantasies visually.

Twice, in the short space of two pages, Herlihy suggests that the city is a force acting upon Joe and debilitating him, but he tends more often to use New York merely as the place in which his characters move. Using invented concrete examples, Schlesinger amplifies the concept of the city as an evil and destructive force. While Joe's innocence and naivete are apparent prior to his arrival in New York, the most destructive brutality and the most heinous experiences occur in the city itself. Indeed, it is the ever-colder city that has reduced Ratso to the dying parasitic exploiter we see and experience.

In the film, we twice see that Joe is capable of brutality. In each case, Schlesinger alters Herlihy's material. In the first instance, Joe allows a young homosexual to perform fellatio on him—for a price. The economic realities of the city already have begun to take their toll. When he finds that the young man has no money to pay him, Joe begins to rough him up. He quickly softens, though, recognizing that the boy is in terror, and allows him to leave. Through foreshadowing, Schlesinger demonstrates Joe's potential brutality. But in the novel, there is no violence; Joe never touches the boy. Herlihy makes a point of it: "Joe looked at him hard, restraining an impulse to hit him across the face." Joe is angry, of course, and his impulse is to strike out, but he can still restrain himself.

In the second instance, Joe is consciously brutal, even sadistic, in his treatment of Towny. Joe allows Towny, a well-to-do homosexual, to lure him up to his hotel room. Joe's purpose—possibly a mitigating reason—is to get enough money to take the critically-ill Ratso to Florida. Towny resists giving him the money he needs, and Joe, desperate, decides to take it. He uses more force than necessary to take the money. At the end of the scene, Joe snatches the telephone from Towny and brutally jams the receiver into his mouth, hurting him badly, perhaps killing him.

In the novel, the scene plays differently. Joe (as in the film) is desperate for the money. But this time Towny encourages brutality; he is a masochist. The film hints at masochism only at the end of the sequence. In the novel, when Joe hits him, Towny is ecstatic: "I'm bleeding! Oh, thank God, I'm bleeding! I deserve to bleed!" When Joe realizes that Towny solicits and enjoys violence, it sickens him. Even the telephone is used differently; Herlihy explains that when Joe becomes brutal, it stems from fear and confusion. In the novel, as Joe begins to leave, Towny tries to use the telephone to call for help. Joe reacts by pulling the telephone out of the wall. In the meantime, Towny begins to run toward the door to call for help. Joe throws the receiver at him to stop him. Finally, when Joe stuffs the receiver into Towny's mouth, it is because:

> Joe still held in his mind the image of the man and the telephone, the telephone and the man, and in his confusion he still felt it necessary to subdue the two of them. He therefore pushed [Towny] to the floor, sat astride his chest, and shoved the telephone's receiver into the toothless mouth.

Schlesinger's portrait of Joe's capacity for brutality is not the only change he makes in Joe. He also supplies a significant addition which makes Joe seem more selfless than in the novel. After he successfully sells himself to Sylvia following the party, Sylvia calls a friend and recommends Joe to her. She agrees to sample his particular brand of service, and makes an appointment for later in the week. (Joe's "success" as a stud does *not* occur in the Herlihy novel.) Joe seems, finally, to be on his way to realizing his dream. He has been a success, and there is the promise, now, of a brighter future. Immediately after this scene, which Schlesinger added, Joe returns elated only to find Ratso ill, and decides to take him to Florida immediately. The function of this addition, then, is to underscore Joe's self-sacrifice, for, in a crucially ironic decision, he gives up precisely what he had sought in order to help a friend—his only friend.

Both Herlihy and Schlesinger envision individual humanity as a forceful agent for change. When Joe optimistically vows to earn enough money to take both Ratso and himself to Florida, Ratso's first response is one of incredulity. Does Joe really intend to take him along? Assured, he worries about Joe's actions. Not quite out of character, he warns Joe not to run foolish risks. Schlesinger enlarges upon Herlihy's brief indication in Ratso. His faltering invitation to Joe to share lodgings, his stealing a coat too large for himself, exposing his sentiment for his father: these all prepare the viewer for the change in Ratso.

If human caring for other human beings represents earthly salvation, Schlesinger presents the decadence of the city as antagonistic to such human trust and involvement. Schlesinger fills *Midnight Cowboy* with visions of decadence. In one scene, Ratso, cold and lonely, appears in front of a display window filled with elegant furs. Joe and Ratso share an unspeakable condemned tenement flat, without gas or electricity. Ratso's progressive illness accelerates with the oncoming of winter. Indeed, an icebox graces the apartment, not to keep food cold, but to keep the cockroaches out. To Schlesinger, the city is both degrading and vulgar. Before Joe loses his room and prized horsehide suitcase, the most dramatic image he sees from the window of his cheap hotel is a sign advertising Mutual of New York—M.O.N.Y.—which is how Joe thinks "money" is spelled. It is the city which strips Joe of his illusions, forcing him to sell himself to homosexuals, and to become increasingly brutal. The viewer experiences the degrading force of the city because the film's visual images are specific, powerful, and immediate.

The closing film sequences maintain Schlesinger's dark view of the city's corrupting power. On the bus to Florida, Joe discards his gaudy cowboy shirt symbolic of his earlier "stud" ambitions; he and Ratso wear new clothes bought by Joe. Ratso's shirt with palm trees symbolizes the final break from the bondage of New York. But Ratso dies on the bus—and the difference in emphasis between Schlesinger's film and Herlihy's novel becomes apparent. The closing lines of the book read:

> He [Joe] put his arm around him to hold him for a while, for these last few miles anyway. He knew this comforting wasn't doing Ratso any good. It was for himself. Because of course he was scared now, scared to death.

Herlihy has come full circle. The story is still Joe's and the didactic tendency of the novelist persists. But Schlesinger expands Herlihy's verbal suggestions to close his film with a series of superb visual shots: a close-up of Joe that takes the viewer into the guts of his feeling; other passengers gawking at the specter of death; an unconcerned woman powdering her nose (recalling the experience of the stricken man ignored by New York's hurrying throng). The final shot is from outside the bus, looking in at Joe and Ratso's body; the camera reveals Joe's pain. Reflected in the bus window we visualize the Miami (big city) skyline.

Are all dreams so ephemeral, so without hope of realization as Joe's? Schlesinger's final ambiguity—humanity coexistent with man's inhumanity—seems to tip in the direction of tentative hope for the human spirit. Joe Buck, despite the Miami skyline and his New York experiences, has come a long and human way since leaving Houston, Texas. In the film, his pain is not self-centered; love, not loneliness, symbolizes the human condition. (pp. 178-89)

> *Eric R. Birdsall and Fred H. Marcus, "Schlesinger's 'Midnight Cowboy': Creating a Classic," in* Film and Literature: Contrasts in

Media, *edited by Fred H. Marcus, Chandler Publishing Company, 1971, pp. 178-89.*

FURTHER READING

Abel, Richard. "The Contribution of the French Literary Avant-Garde to Film Theory and Criticism (1907-1924)." *Cinema Journal* XIV, No. 3 (Spring 1975): 18-40.
Demonstrates that "the cinema—especially the American cinema—had a tremendous impact on the two generations of the Parisian literary avant-garde during the early decades of this century," and that the writings of early twentieth-century French poets, primarily those associated with the Surrealist movement, were instrumental in the development of serious film criticism.

Barnes, Walter. *The Photoplay as Literary Art.* Newark, N.J.: Educational and Recreational Guides, 1936, 40 p.
Study of the practical and theoretical principles of the screenplay.

Bluestone, George. *Novels into Film.* Berkeley and Los Angeles: University of California Press, 1966, 237 p.
Theoretical study of the nature and development of novels and films, followed by an analysis of six films adapted from novels.

Cawelti, John G. *The Six-Gun Mystique.* Bowling Green: Bowling Green University Popular Press, n.d., 138 p.
Includes an examination of the structural and thematic formulas of the "Western," while discussing this popular form as developed in works of fiction and film.

Clair, René. "Theater and Cinema." In his *Cinema Yesterday and Today,* edited by R. C. Dale, translated by Stanley Appelbaum, pp. 159-69. New York: Dover Publications, 1972.
Considers the cultural, artistic, and economic effects of cinema on the theater from the 1920s through the 1960s.

Coates, Paul. "Cinema, Symbolism and the *Gesamtkunstwerk*." In *Comparative Criticism: A Yearbook,* edited by E. S. Shaffer, pp. 213-29. Cambridge: Cambridge University Press, 1982.
Demonstrates that "In many significant respects Symbolist poetry and cinema intersect; that their common moment of birth stamps them with a similar passion for multiplicity, which in Symbolist verse takes the form of the variety of meanings extricable from a sliding mass of syntactic and semantic ambiguities, and which in the cinema is represented by the multiple personality inscribed in the gaps and inconsistencies within the work; and that in both cases the result is an art without a receiver, or rather, an art whose receiver is negativity, 'the absent one,' who can repeat after Corbière, 'je suis là, mais comme une rature' ['I am there, but only like an erasure']."

Cohen, Keith. *Film and Fiction: The Dynamics of Exchange.* New Haven: Yale University Press, 1979, 216 p.
Focuses on the reciprocal influence of film and literature between 1895 and 1925.

Corliss, Richard. *Talking Pictures: Screenwriters in the American Cinema.* New York: Penguin Books, 1974, 398 p.
   Examines the most important works of thirty-five American screenwriters.

Dardis, Tom. *Some Time in the Sun.* New York: Penguin Books, 1976, 297 p.
   Traces the screenwriting careers of F. Scott Fitzgerald, William Faulkner, Nathanael West, Aldous Huxley, and James Agee.

Darlington, W. A. "Stage and Film Technique." In his *Through the Fourth Wall,* pp. 110-14. London: Chapman & Hall, 1922.
   Contrasts dramatic and cinematic techniques, concluding that the presentation of drama is more difficult and ultimately more artistic.

Durgnat, Raymond. "Caligari Is Dead—Long Live Caligari." In his *Films and Feelings,* pp. 87-98. Cambridge, Mass.: M.I.T. Press, 1967.
   Chronicles the influence of German Expressionism on filmmaking, particularly as the thematic and stylistic traits of this movement were integrated with the predominant realism of the cinema.

Eidsvik, Charles. *Cineliteracy: Film among the Arts.* New York: Horizon Press, 1978, 303 p.
   Contains discussion of film adaptations from fiction and drama.

Eikhenbaum, Boris. "Literature and Cinema (1926)." In *Russian Formalism: A Collection of Articles and Texts in Translation,* edited by Stephen Bann and John E. Bowlt, pp. 122-27. Edinburgh: Scottish Academic Press, 1973.
   Discusses the sequence of images in film as comprising a "language" into which works of literature may be translated.

Farrell, James T. "The Language of Hollywood." In his *The League of Frightened Philistines, and Other Papers,* pp. 164-83. New York: Vanguard Press, 1945.
   Condemns the influence of Hollywood films on American literature and culture.

Fiedler, Leslie A. "The End of the Thirties: Artificial Paradises and Real Hells." In his *Waiting for the End,* pp. 51-64. New York: Stein and Day, 1964.
   Details the influence of Hollywood on American fiction writers from the 1920s to the 1960s.

Fine, Richard. *Hollywood and the Profession of Authorship, 1928-1940.* Ann Arbor, Mich.: UMI Research Press, 1985, 206 p.
   Historical and cultural study of Hollywood's reputation as a "destroyer" of the literary talent and careers of American authors.

Griffith, D. W. "Moving Pictures Can Get Nothing from the Stage," "Some Prophecies: Film and Theatre, Screenwriting, Education," and "The New Stage Supplants the Old." In *Focus on D. W. Griffith,* edited by Harry M. Geduld, pp. 32, 34-5, 48-9. Englewood Cliffs, N.J.: Prentice-Hall, 1971.
   Reflections on the independence of film from the traditions and techniques of the theater.

Hammond, Paul. *The Shadow and Its Shadow: Surrealist Writings on Cinema.* London: British Film Institute, 1978, 133 p.
   Collection of essays by major and minor poets, critics, and filmmakers associated with the Surrealist movement.

Hannon, William Morgan. *The Photodrama: Its Place among the Fine Arts.* New Orleans: Ruskin Press, 1915, 68 p.
   Considers the artistic advantages and disadvantages of silent film scenarios as contrasted with novels and dramas.

Horton, Andrew, and Margretta, Joan, eds. *Modern European Filmmakers and the Art of Adaptation.* New York: Frederick Ungar, 1981, 383 p.
   Twenty-three essays comparing film adaptations by European directors with their original literary sources.

Hurt, James, ed. *Focus on Film and Theatre.* Englewood Cliffs, N.J.: Prentice-Hall, 1974, 188 p.
   Collection of seminal essays by critics, playwrights, actors, and filmmakers.

Kovács, Steven. *From Rage to Enchantment: The Story of Surrealist Cinema.* London: Associated University Presses, 1980, 297 p.
   Divided into chapters on the work of Robert Desnos, Francis Picabia and René Clair, Man Ray, Antonin Artaud, and Salvador Dalí and Luis Buñuel.

Kuenzli, Rudolf E., ed. *Dada and Surrealist Film.* New York: Willis Locker & Owens, 1987, 255 p.
   Collection of essays on Dada and Surrealist films and film scenarios, focusing on works by Luis Buñuel.

Lillard, Richard G. "Movies Aren't Literary." *The English Journal* XXIX, No. 9 (November 1940): 735-43.
   Emphasizes the differences between literature and film as artistic forms. Lillard concludes: "No successful playwrights, no great authors, no writers of best sellers are necessary in the studios. Only great preparers of scenarios are needed—researchers, technicians, and directors who think in visual terms and work from the ground up to create the likes of *Intolerance, The Gold Rush, Pasteur, Zola,* and *Juarez.* These motion-picture classics stand as independent works of art. They aren't literary."

Lindsay, Vachel. "Thirty Differences between the Photoplays and the Stage." In his *The Art of the Moving Picture,* pp. 179-98. 1922. Reprint. New York: Liveright, 1970.
   Isolates qualities that distinguish film from theater in order to facilitate appreciation of both artistic media.

MacGowan, Kenneth. "The Movies—The Curtain Becomes the Stage." In his *The Theatre of Tomorrow,* pp. 178-85. New York: Boni and Liveright, 1921.
   Concludes that cinema is limited by the realism of its images and its "second-hand" representation of life, whereas the theater offers greater possibilities for symbolism and is able to present life directly.

Magny, Claude-Edmonde. *The Age of the American Novel: The Film Aesthetic of Fiction between the Two Wars.* Translated by Eleanor Hochman. New York: Frederick Ungar Publishing Co., 1972, 239 p.
   Compares narrative techniques in fiction and film, focusing on the works of John Dos Passos, Ernest Hemingway, John Steinbeck, and William Faulkner.

Mailer, Norman. "A Course in Filmmaking." In his *Maidstone: A Mystery,* pp. 137-80. New York: New American Library, 1971.

Reflections on filmmaking in general and the making of the film *Maidstone* in particular.

Mamoulian, Rouben. "Stage and Screen." *The Screen Writer* II, No. 10 (March 1947): 1-15.
Contrasts drama and film as artistic forms, concluding that both are in a state of creative decline.

Manvell, Roger. *Theater and Film: A Comparative Study of the Two Forms of Dramatic Art, and of the Problems of Adaptation of Stage Plays into Films.* London: Associated University Presses, 1979, 303 p.
Devoted for the most part to analyses of film adaptations of dramatic works from those of Euripides to Edward Albee.

Marcus, Fred H. *Short Story/Short Film.* Englewood Cliffs, N.J.: Prentice-Hall, 1977, 447 p.
Reprints ten short stories along with the screenplays of their film adaptations and provides comparative criticism of the two forms.

Mast, Gerald, and Cohen, Marshall, eds. "Film, Theater, and Literature." In their *Film Theory and Criticism: Introductory Readings,* pp. 233-351. London: Oxford University Press, 1974.
Reprints commentary by Hugo Munsterberg, Susan Sontag, Béla Balázs, André Bazin, George Bluestone, and Sergei Eisenstein, with a subsection of essays devoted to "Shakespeare and Film."

Michalczyk, John J. *The French Literary Filmmakers.* London: Associated University Presses, 1980, 187 p.
Studies the work of seven French authors who are also notable filmmakers: Jean Cocteau, Sacha Guitry, Marcel Pagnol, Jean Giono, André Malraux, Alain Robbe-Grillet, and Marguerite Duras.

Miller, Gabriel. *Screening the Novel: Rediscovered American Fiction in Film.* New York: Frederick Ungar Publishing Co., 1980, 208 p.
Comparative studies of eight novels and their film adaptations, including *The Postman Always Rings Twice, They Shoot Horses, Don't They?,* and *The Treasure of the Sierra Madre.*

Moeller, Hans-Bernhard. "Literature in the Vicinity of the Film: On German and *Nouveau Roman* Authors." *Symposium* XXVIII, No. 4 (Winter 1974): 315-35.
Examines the role of cinema in the careers of several German and French authors, including Bertolt Brecht, Peter Weiss, Phillip Sollers, and Alain Robbe-Grillet.

Morris, C. B. *This Loving Darkness: The Cinema and Spanish Writers, 1920-1936.* Hull, England: University of Hull Publications, 1980, 196 p.
Describes the influence of the cinema on such leading Spanish writers as Rafael Alberti, Luis Cernuda, and Federico García Lorca.

Morsberger, Robert E., and Morsberger, Katharine M. "Screenplays as Literature: Bibliography and Criticism." *Literature/Film Quarterly* 3, No. 1 (Winter 1975): 45-59.
Critical survey and bibliography of published screenplays.

Murray, Edward. *The Cinematic Imagination: Writers and the Motion Pictures.* New York: Frederick Ungar Publishing Co., 1972, 330 p.

Discusses the work of a variety of American and European dramatists and novelists in relation to film.

Nathan, George Jean. "The Movies versus the Stage." *The American Mercury* 58, No. 246 (June 1944): 682-86.
Humorous dialogue with film director Rouben Mamoulian in which Nathan argues for the technical and artistic superiority of theater over cinema.

Nathan, Robert. "A Novelist Looks at Hollywood." *Hollywood Quarterly* I, No. 2 (January 1946): 146-47.
Finds that screenplays share more characteristics with the novel than with drama.

Ortman, Marguerite. *Fiction and the Screen.* Boston: Marshall Jones Co., 1935, 148 p.
Discusses a scattered range of subjects but primarily focuses on the history of drama, film adaptations of novels, and an analysis of the screen version of *David Copperfield.*

Poague, Leland A. "Literature vs. Cinema: The Politics of Aesthetic Definition." *Journal of Aesthetic Education* 10, No. 1 (1976): 75-91.
Contends that film and literature are essentially identical as forms of artistic expression.

Read, Herbert. "The Poet and the Film." In his *A Coat of Many Colours,* pp. 225-31. London: George Routledge & Sons, 1945.
Finds that film and literature are equally dependent on images to achieve their artistic purposes.

Reynolds, Lessie M. "Film as a Poetic Art and Contemporary Epic." *South Atlantic Bulletin* XXXVIII, No. 2 (May 1973): 8-14.
Asserts that "film can . . . be shown to have an inherent epic nature because of its spatial and temporal scope, which causes many films to embody other characteristics remarkably similar to those of the conventional epic. And since film is still a new and immature art, it generally seems most analogous to epics of a pre-literate age."

Ross, Harris. *Film as Literature, Literature as Film: An Introduction to and Bibliography of Film's Relationship to Literature.* New York: Greenwood Press, 1987, 346 p.
Most comprehensive bibliography of writings on this subject.

Ruhe, Edward. "Film: The 'Literary' Approach." *Literature/Film Quarterly* 1, No. 1 (January 1973): 76-83.
Compares the literary and cinematic approaches to film criticism.

Ruppert, Peter, ed. *Ideas of Order in Literature & Film: Selected Papers from the 4th Annual Florida State University Conference on Literature and Film.* Tallahassee: University Presses of Florida, 1980, 136 p.
Collection of essays, many of which are concerned with the relationship between literature and film as narrative forms.

Schmidt, Nancy J. "African Literature on Film." *Research in African Literatures* 13, No. 4 (Winter 1982): 518-31.
Discussion of eight films adapted from works by such major African authors as Athol Fugard and Wole Soyinka.

Scholes, Robert. "Narration and Narrativity in Film." *Quarterly Review of Film Studies* 1, No. 3 (August 1976): 283-96.
Contrasts the techniques used by fiction and film to nar-

rate a story and examines the effect of these differing approaches on the experience and interpretation of literary and cinematic works.

Seldes, Gilbert. "The Cinema Novel." In his *The Seven Lively Arts,* pp. 383-90. New York: Harper & Brothers Publishers, 1924.
 Outlines cinematic structures used in novels by Blaise Cendrars and Jules Romain.

Self, Robert T. "Film & Literature: Parameters of a Discipline." *Literature/Film Quarterly* 15, No. 1 (1987): 15-21.
 Assessment of the various approaches to the interdisciplinary study of film and literature.

Sontag, Susan. "Theatre and Film." In her *Styles of Radical Will,* pp. 99-122. New York: Farrar, Straus and Giroux, 1969.
 Analysis of the artistic and technical differences between theater and cinema.

Spatz, Jonas. *Hollywood in Fiction: Some Versions of the American Myth.* The Hague: Mouton, 1969, 148 p.
 Study of American fiction and drama in which "Hollywood or Southern California is more than a background; it is an important cultural phenomenon, an active and influential force in the imaginations and moral lives of its inhabitants."

Spiegel, Alan. *Fiction and the Camera Eye: Visual Consciousness in Film and the Modern Novel.* Charlottesville: University Press of Virginia, 1976, 203 p.
 Attributes the increasing emphasis on visual imagery in the modern novel to the influence of film.

Stam, Robert. *Reflexivity in Film and Literature from Don Quixote to Jean-Luc Godard.* Ann Arbor, Mich.: UMI Research Press, 1985, 285 p.
 Study of "what might be termed 'the other tradition' in literature and cinema: the tradition of reflexivity as embodied in novels, plays, and films which break with art as enchantment and point to their own factitiousness as textual constructs."

Stromgren, Richard L., and Norden, Martin F. "Film and Literature" and "Film and Theater." In their *Movies: A Language in Light,* pp. 167-82, 183-99. Englewood Cliffs, N.J.: Prentice-Hall, 1984.
 Overview of the relationship between film and literature in general and film and theater in particular.

Taylor, John Russell. *Strangers in Paradise: The Hollywood Émigrés, 1933-1950.* London: Faber and Faber, 1983, 256 p.
 Cultural history of European artists and intellectuals who fled to Southern California during the rise of Adolf Hitler.

Van Nostrand, Albert. "Hollywood Payoff." In his *The Denatured Novel,* pp. 105-32. Indianapolis: Bobbs-Merrill Co., 1960.
 Argues that film adaptations and the economics of filmmaking "have eroded the novel form more than anything else in the novel's history."

Van Wert, William F. *The Theory and Practice of the Ciné-Roman.* New York: Arno Press, 1978, 382 p.
 Comprehensive study relating the "cinema novel," a published work adapted from a film scenario and designed to serve as its literary counterpart, to the French New Novel and New Wave films of the 1950s.

Waller, Gregory A. *The Stage/Screen Debate: A Study in Popular Aesthetics.* New York: Garland Publishing, 1983, 424 p.
 Critical history of issues, viewpoints, and controversies involving the relationship between theater and cinema.

Weinberg, Herman G. "Novel into Film." *Literature/Film Quarterly* 1, No. 2 (April 1973): 99-102.
 Survey of successful and unsuccessful film adaptations of classic novels.

Wilbur, Richard. "A Poet and the Movies." In *Film and the Liberal Arts,* edited by T. J. Ross, pp. 167-71. New York: Holt, Rinehart and Winston, 1970.
 Wilbur comments on the influence of film on his poetry.

Williams, Linda. *Figures of Desire: A Theory and Analysis of Surrealist Film.* Urbana: University of Illinois Press, 1981, 229 p.
 Focuses on the films of Luis Buñuel.

Winston, Douglas Garrett. *The Screenplay as Literature.* Rutherford, N.J.: Fairleigh Dickinson University Press, 1973, 240 p.
 Studies the nature and techniques of the screenplay and examines adaptations and original scripts for films by American and European directors.

Psychoanalysis and Literature

INTRODUCTION

Since the formulation of psychoanalysis by Sigmund Freud at the turn of the twentieth century, many commentators have maintained that a significant relationship exists between psychoanalysis and literature in that they are both concerned with emotions, thought processes, and behavior, as well as social and moral questions resulting from human relationships. Freud commented that poets had discovered the unconscious long before he did, and he found precedents and corroboration for many of his theories—the Oedipus complex, for example—in mythology and literature. In turn, psychoanalysis has influenced literary works, resulting in such innovations as the stream-of-consciousness narrative technique, and has served as a theoretical foundation for interpretations of literature. Early psychoanalytic critics often attempted to psychoanalyze authors based on their works and to apply psychoanalytic concepts to literary characters in the same way they would to living people. This approach has generally been condemned as reductive, and more recent psychoanalytic criticism tends to focus on other matters: the nature of artistic creativity, reader response to literature, and the similarities between accounts of psychoanalytic treatment and literary texts. While some psychoanalysts and literary critics resent attempts to relate their respective disciplines, many common issues and concerns ensure that psychoanalysis and literature will continue to be closely allied fields, each of which can benefit from insights provided by the other.

OVERVIEWS

William Phillips

[An American man of letters, Williams is a founding editor of Partisan Review and has edited numerous collections of modern literature. In the following excerpt, he surveys the development of the relationship between psychoanalysis and literature and suggests ways in which psychoanalysis can aid in understanding literature.]

The coupling of literature and psychoanalysis goes back to Freud himself. A new world of research and speculation began when he observed that the creative faculty draws on drives and fantasies buried in the unconscious, and that they provide the clue to understanding the imaginative mind as well as individual works. Freud also noted the parallels between literary composition and such common activities as children's play and daydreaming, and between literature and myths, which reveal the fantasies of entire communities and nations and even of the whole of early humanity.

Originally Freud thought that the force of such works as Oedipus Rex and Hamlet derived from the fact that their central themes touched on the psychic experience of modern man. He also believed that the unconscious of the writer was connected to that of the reader by the neuroses they shared. Later he placed more emphasis on literary talent and skill, though he felt that its secrets could not be explained by psychoanalysis. Freud's greatest contribution, however, was probably in the subtle application of his theories and discoveries to individual writers and artists, in the course of which he modified some of his earlier views.

Since then, Freud's original remarks have been expanded, developed, modified, and transformed, in an enormous mass of writing, turned out by psychoanalysts of various schools and by very different kinds of critics, coming from every conceivable position, and going in all directions. The diversity of themes and approaches has been so great that we can scarcely speak of a single subject—or a single question. What we have is a bewildering variety of subjects, methods, and assumptions. Countless books and essays have dealt with the creative process, the relation of literature to psychoanalytic theory, the links between writers' neuroses and their work, the neurotic elements of writers' lives, the connection between literature and health, and between literature and neurosis, the psychic content of specific works, the parallels between popular myths and unconscious motives. More recently, under the influence of the new theories of structuralism and deconstruction, there have been many attempts at a kind of psychoanalytic, free-wheeling reconstruction of the literary text. Also with the new idea of the reader as an accomplice of the author, some analysts and critics have tried to assimilate literary works to the psychic make-up of the ideal, or imaginary, reader.

The common denominator of all these studies is that there is no common denominator. And, unlike work in some more scientific disciplines, each new essay, while making a token bow to the seminal figure of Freud and to earlier writings in the field, actually ignores the findings of other analysts and critics. Rarely does a new study build on an old one. So great is the diversity that one suspects it might be due less to natural differences of opinion than to the fact that the subject itself, that is, the relation of psychoanalysis to literature, is one that makes for unbridled speculation and idiosyncratic approaches. Undoubtedly this laissez-faire state of thinking is encouraged by the fact that there are no accepted definitions of literature, or of the creative mind, or of the way psychic forces mesh with presumably more objective ideas and perceptions about the world.

One says "presumably," because we have learned both epistemologically and clinically that all views are colored by psychology and by personal history. In fact, one of the premises of modern philosophy, from Nietzsche through the later existentialists, has been that existence determines thinking. Clinically too, it has been found that there are no fixed, clearly defined connections between subjective and objective attitudes. And this is also true particularly in the area of literature, where the imagination plays games with observed reality. If indeed a good part of literature is a reconstruction, if not an invention, of actuality, then it is not always easy to find the dividing line between the so-called objective world and the subjective world of the writer.

The most striking thing about the writings on psychoanalysis and literature is that so many theories have been constructed on so few solid definitions and common assumptions. But perhaps some of the invisible logic of this seemingly disorganized field might be seen if we look back briefly at the stages in the literature on the subject. The early entries, by Freud and others, were attempts to relate the creative act to psychoanalytic theory, and to probe the life and work of famous artists whose known neuroses might lend themselves to generalizations about their psychic make-up, and its manifestation in their work. Thus Freud found that such spontaneous activities as daydreaming and play drew on hidden images much in the same way that writing or painting did. In later studies, such as those on Leonardo and Michelangelo, he drew parallels between artists' psychic lives and their careers. In neither case, however, was Freud able to show a connection between the artists' actual work and their neurotic dispositions, beyond their treatment of subject matter. The actual texture and quality of their work seemed to lie outside even Freud's analytic powers. The closest Freud came to dealing with all aspects of a work was in his brilliant essay on Dostoevsky, but here, too, only some components of Dostoevsky's fiction were illuminated. Psychoanalysis was not yet an instrument for dealing with the complex of meanings, ideas, and language that constitutes a work of fiction. Other figures, like Rank and Jung, without the perceptiveness of genius and Freud's uncanny sense of the appropriate, tackled the mysteries of creation and the secrets of individual works, usually focusing on special problems and themes. But the impression remained that the essence of art eluded—perhaps was bound to elude—the kind of analysis that psychology was able so far to bring to it. The fact remains that a psychoanalytic approach to literature is not necessarily literary criticism, though it may provide many useful insights.

A stream of essays by analysts and psychiatrists followed, mostly on individual writers. Among the better-known practitioners were C. G. Jung, Marie Bonaparte, Phyllis Greenacre, Erich Fromm, Henry Rosenzweig, Henry Murray, Selma Freiberg, Ernst Kris, Ernest Jones, Theodore Reik. They had an eye for the more neurotic writers, and they wrote what might be described as literary case studies, or, rather, case studies of literature, dealing with those creative figures who qualified as members of the neurotic but gifted tribe in our culture, from Swift to Kafka. These books and essays contained many remarkable insights into the lives and works of their subjects, and they added substantially to that store of information and perception that lies behind all good critical writing. But, again, something seemed to be missing. These studies were not based on any idea of literature, beyond the popular and conventional reduction of fiction and poetry to their manifest content. And most of them emphasized such analytic themes as the Oedipus complex, anality, schizoid tendencies, latent or expressed homosexuality, guilt, etc., pointing out the roles they played in the works of the writers under discussion. What was lacking was a sense of the relation of these factors to the impact or the quality of the work as a whole, and the relation of psychic elements to those meanings and that mastery of the medium that makes a work of literature.

Consider, for example, one of the best exercises in psychoanalytic interpretation, Ernest Jones' very impressive essay on Hamlet. Taking his cue from Freud's observation that Hamlet's indecision was rooted in his Oedipal entanglements with his father and mother (the King and the Queen), Jones, with an irresistible psychological logic, ascribes every failure of Hamlet to act to his suppressed feelings of hate and love and his consequent paralyzing guilt. So far, so good. But to the question of the power of the play, rhetorical as well as thematic, Jones can only reply that Shakespeare, like Sophocles, engaged the deepest and most tortured conflicts in all men. Unfortunately this ignores the history and the special appeals of the medium. It fails to take into account Shakespeare's seductive and overpowering rhetoric, and his uncanny ability to lift a homely observation into a transcendent perception. Besides, only a few novels and plays have dealt with such basic ideas as the Oedipus complex. What do we do with all those fictions that make only marginal use of the main themes of psychoanalytic theory?

Another of the pioneers was Marie Bonaparte, whose massive study of Poe drew heavily on Freud's interpretation of dreams. Through detailed analyses of such stories as "The Black Cat," "Murders in the Rue Morgue," "The Purloined Letter," "The Gold Bug," "The Tell-Tale Heart," "The Fall of the House of Usher," Bonaparte indicated their similarity to the structure of dreams. Poe's fiction, according to Bonaparte, displayed the dream-like mechanisms of displacement, condensation, substitution, splitting of characters, and secondary elaboration. She argued that Poe's stories and poems are filled with infantile attachments, and with references to the basic symbolization of father, mother, and the genitalia. All of Poe's work, wrote Bonaparte, was charged with anxiety, and its power came from the resulting affects "which have reemerged from deep and hidden sources in the unconscious."

Also among the early contributions was Phyllis Greenacre's exhaustive work on Swift, which traced the neurotic components in his life and his writing. Greenacre's portrait of Swift is that of a witty, charming, tortured man with magnified oedipal problems, given to hypochondria, fear of death, masturbatory fantasies, homosexual inclinations, sexual fears, anal tendencies, and scatological fixations—the full load of neurotic possibilities. She makes a striking connection between the oversized and undersized people in Gulliver and Swift's own morbid concern with body parts and functions, following observations on this subject by Ferenczi. A central theme in Swift's life work, maintains Greenacre, was his distaste for women's bodies and his urge to neuter their femininity. The following passage, concisely summarizing Swift's psychic history, is typical of the psychoanalytic thinking of the time:

> This study of Swift was stimulated by an interest in fetishism and the part played in its development by

sensations of instability of body size. It is pertinent then to make some brief further references to these questions here. There is no indication that Swift was an overt fetishist, although he shares much in the structure of his personality with those who develop the manifest symptom. The anal fixation was intense and binding, and the genital response so impaired and limited at best, that he was predisposed to later weakness. A retreat from genital sexuality did actually occur in his early adult life, probably beginning with the unhappy relationship to Jane Waring, the first of the goddesses. After this he never again seemed willingly to consider marriage, while his expressed demands were that women who were closest to him should be as much like boys as possible. His genital demands were probably partly sublimated through his creative writings, but even these showed the stamp of his strong anal character. He did not need a fetish because he resigned from physical genitality. In a sense, his converting of the women of his choice into boys fulfilled a fetishistic need. Especially Stella was to be the faithful, dependable, unchanging bisexualized object, a cornerstone for his life. With her death he began to go to pieces.

Lemuel Gulliver went a step further than his creator in that he was a married man, who was however continually escaping from his marriage which was so predominantly disgusting to him, though his periodic sojourns at home sufficed sometimes for the depositing of a child with his wife. . . . The Travels appear as the acting out of Lemuel's masturbatory fantasies which, like the character of Swift, are closely interwoven with anal preoccupations and ambitions rather than with genital ones.

(Phyllis Greenacre, *Jonathan Swift.* In *Art and Psychoanalysis,* ed. William Phillips.)

Among those who added to the earlier thinking on literature and psychoanalysis, some of the more prominent were Theodore Reik, Fritz Wittels, and Franz Alexander. Reik's best-known study is of Offenbach's *The Tales of Hoffman,* which recounted the life of E. T. A. Hoffman and his three loves. Reik uncovers the sources of the three in Hoffman's unconscious. The seductress, says Reik, belonged to Hoffman's mature years; the doll was a reversal of Hoffman's own infantile dependencies as a child; and the third, the artist, is "the figure of death . . . the last image of woman as she appears to the old man."

Wittels wrote a suggestive analysis of the life and work of Heinrich von Kleist, the great German author who produced all his writing in only eight years, and committed suicide at the age of thirty-four. Wittels finds the core of Kleist's existence in his struggle against homosexuality, from which he could escape only through death. He fell in love with a sick and disfigured woman, who represented, according to Wittels, a denial of life and a door to death, and he acted out a double suicide pact with her. Kleist's plays and stories, argues Wittels, represented the masculine inversion in Kleist; hence they are full of torture, atrocities, and cruelty, approaching the horrors of the Nazi mind.

One of the more significant general statements about art was made by Franz Alexander in an essay on contemporary art. Alexander characterized the anti-rational and non-representative components of modern painting as a reaction against the orderly, optimistic views of an earlier epoch and a return to the unconscious mind. Though he saw this phenomenon as both a manifestation of disorder and an attempt to superimpose a sense of order, Alexander essentially disapproved of the new trends as reinforcements of the chaos of modern life. To be sure, one's perspective in these matters is decisive. Alexander's attitude is consistent with the rational and therapeutic side of analysis, as opposed to the more literary view of early modernist art as an exploitation of the medium and as a reaction against the commercial uses of representation.

Clearly one of the limitations of this early stage of psychoanalytic writing has been that it was done mostly by analysts, not by literary critics. The next stage—the chronology is impure—saw the entrance of professional critics into the enterprise. As might be expected, the level of literary sophistication rose perceptibly, as literary figures like Thomas Mann, W. H. Auden, Lionel Trilling, William Empson, Alfred Kazin, E. H. Gombrich, Meyer Schapiro, Geoffrey Hartman, William Barrett, began to address the subject. No longer was esthetic quality taken for granted, and formal questions as well as those broader ones involving literary tradition and social history were now being taken into consideration.

After all, writing about literature tends to be remote and scholastic when it is not infused with literary sensibility and a sense of the quality of the work one is talking about. With the entrance of professional critics into the psychoanalytic arena, there was less of the feeling that people from Mars were studying people from Venus. Thomas Mann was one of the earliest writers to relate literature to psychoanalysis formally rather than methodologically, but as belonging to the same ambiance. Mann not only concluded, he actually assumed that Freud was a leading exponent of the same mind that produced our novelists and poets. Auden, Trilling, Kazin, and other critics aware of the cultural meaning of Freud's daring speculations also took for granted that psychoanalysis and literature were part of a single imaginative enterprise. These modern critics addressed themselves to special literary and psychological problems more in the spirit of recent literary criticism, with its emphasis both on close reading and on the kind of analysis that derives from a historical sense.

Both Alfred Kazin and Erich Heller wrote about the psychic forces at play in modern literature. Heller focused on the special relation of the basic themes of modernism to psychoanalytic theory. Meyer Schapiro introduced another dimension by stressing the importance of scholarship, questioning some of Freud's facts in his famous essay on Leonardo, and indicating that many elements in Leonardo's painting attributed by Freud to the artist's psyche were actually accounted for in the history of the medium. E. H. Gombrich, in a remarkably original essay, was one of the first to connect psychoanalytic observations with the actual language of literature, by applying some of Freud's ideas about the linguistic aspects of wit to literary composition. Steven Marcus demonstrated further literary sophistication in his examination of the case history of Dora as a literary document—a work of fiction. He not only noted in Dora the kind of transformations and imaginative shifts one finds in novels and stories, but he posed the idea, for the first time, of countertransference as a literary as well as a psychological force.

Lionel Trilling and William Barrett raised one of the central questions concerning the sources of creative inspiration: the relation of neurosis to art. While this question frequently had been touched on before, it had never been resolved, and indeed often contradictory views had been entertained. On the one hand, art was associated with madness; on the other, with prophetic wisdom. When madness was dealt with specifically and clinically by psychoanalysis, art was connected with neurosis-psychosis, though more often by way of illustration than theoretically. Of course, the question remained: if art drew its content as well as its strength from madness, how did it make its appeal to a varied, if not universal, audience? Was it a collective madness, as Laing and Szasz—in their different ways—appeared to believe, that united literature with its readers? Or was it something else, the catharsis of madness, that created the bond between writer and reader? In the eighteenth century, under the impetus of rationalism, the normal and healthy aspects of art were favored. Charles Lamb, for example, was the first to advance the view that art represented the victory of man's healthy faculties. For Lamb, the very act of creation was the assertion of one's rationality, which, almost by definition, was healthy. The nineteenth century began to probe abnormal psychology and the pendulum swung to the celebration of the neurotic artist. Freud, so far as we know, side-stepped the issue by emphasizing the common elements in the psyche of literature and the psyche of humanity, although he recognized the skill and esthetic power that separated the writer from the ordinary neurotic.

In the twentieth century, the debate was pursued by Trilling and Barrett, with Trilling leaning toward the healthy side of the equation, and Barrett toward the neurotic one. To be sure, neither side can be demonstrated either theoretically or clinically. It is largely a matter of persuasion, of an appeal to shared beliefs—in the end, perhaps, to common sense. But the issue is also fraught with semantic confusion, and with honorific arguments, often concealed by arbitrary definitions. Basically, when we speak of *neurosis* or *health* as the energy that produces art and shapes its content, we are employing vague, rhetorical concepts, neither of which are creators or organizers of the formal and intellectual elements of literature, not, at least, in an exact or concrete sense. However, the proponents of neurosis have this at least in their favor: most writers have been quite neurotic, if not mad, and neurosis is a force that takes possession of a person. Broadly defined, neurosis is the warp in a person's psyche stemming from some unresolved inner conflict. It is admittedly difficult to see how an unresolved conflict can produce that masterful combination of form and content that we think of as literature. Nevertheless, we have noted that neurotics, at least gifted ones, do seem to be propelled in certain significant directions in their thinking and their sensibility. It is not difficult to think of this propulsion—sometimes amounting to a compulsion—as the mainspring of literature. The idea of health in relation to literature is even vaguer and more hortatory than is that of neurosis. There is no accepted definition of a healthy mind, at least no definition that is ideological rather than clinical, nor is there a common idea of the kind of rational, healthy vision of man and society that can be counterposed to a neurotic vision. Unfortunately, there are no simple formulas in the area of thought of health and sickness, truth and neurotic distortion. Where do we put Nietzsche, Kafka, Dostoevsky, Beckett? It begins to appear that the entire argument has been couched in false terms and in oppositions that reflect ideological biases.

For those who view literature as an expression of the sunlit side of existence, of man's progress toward light and truth, the idea of writing drawing on man's "healthy" rather than his "sick" propensities will seem to be more attractive—and sounder. On the other hand, those who see literature, particularly modern literature, as a reflection of man's more morbid and perverse tendencies are likely to stress the neurotic components of the creative mind. Behind these stances, there is in addition the question haunting critical and esthetic inquiry of whether the aim of literature is to reveal some "truth," if not *the* "truth," about ourselves and the world we inhabit. This is of course a philosophical question, again one that cannot be empirically determined, and it has never been settled. For, as with so many other philosophical issues, the stand one takes depends on one's entire outlook. Plato, it will be recalled, regarded art as a source of false emotions and ideas, while Aristotle took the opposite position. Through the middle ages and up to the nineteenth century, mostly under the influence of Christian doctrine, art without uplift—form without content—was considered frivolous. It was only later in the nineteenth century, after Nietzsche had challenged the old idols of belief, that writers began to think of literature not as the expression of our moral and philosophical ideals, but as the mirror of the underside of life. Oscar Wilde described art as an elaborate lie—and not only to exercise his perverse wit. More recently, the modernist esthetic has tended to define art in adversary terms, understanding it not as the bearer of a common truth, but as the lens by means of which an alienated and subversive group reinterpreted "reality." The possible contradiction between this view of literature and the assumption that psychoanalysis deals with general psychic truths presents a further difficulty. How do these general "truths" pervade works that question the idea of general truth, that present biased, perhaps warped, versions of the human condition? Perhaps different orders of experience are involved, and what has been called the adversary strain does not necessarily come into conflict with deeper layers of human conduct. But yet another difficulty presents itself: are these problems more pertinent to literature than to the other arts, if only because they entail an old-fashioned idea of content not readily applicable to plastic art and music? The "content" of these other arts is in no way comparable to that of literature. It is not easily identifiable, perhaps non-existent in the sense that the term is commonly used.

Ironically, it would appear that as the approaches to psychoanalysis and literature became more sophisticated, they solved fewer old problems and raised more new ones. They also brought the thinking on the subject into distant reaches from which there seemed to be no return, and they introduced complexities of formulation and speculation that sometimes left one helplessly nostalgic for Freud's own simpler observations. This seems true of the latest stage, which might be characterized as the French appropriation of Freud and its application to the domain of literature. Two currents came together on the French scene. As latecomers to the recognition of Freud, the French were determined to outdo psychoanalysts in other countries in bringing Freud up to date. Parallel to this discovery and revision of Freud, structuralism and its offspring, deconstruction, were born, and soon took over much of French philosophy and criticism. These trends have dominated the French discussion of psychoanalysis and literature and have had considerable influence on American criticism, particularly in some academic circles.

It is difficult to pin down the meaning of this new ideological enterprise. For, in addition to the revision of Freud and the use of structuralism and deconstruction for literary criticism, the new approaches are steeped in the Saussurean school of linguistics, in Derrida's and Lacan's open-ended idea of all meanings, historical and textual, and in formalist theories of literature. Furthermore, certain Marxist attitudes have been absorbed into French criticism, such as an adversary position in relation to bourgeois culture and a belief in the necessity of its demystification, a view of history as relative and changing, and a generally radical stance on political and cultural questions. But if one were to try to distill the essence of these various strains, it is the notion that everything can be interpreted as a text. Meanings, events, ideas, theories, literary works—all are texts. In a sense, all life is a text. Thus, for example, Freud's and Marx's writings are texts to be reinterpreted so freely as to amount to revision. In this respect, the new French criticism and its American counterpart go beyond the ordinary textual analysis of the formalists. A new component has been added: the free exercise of the imagination on the part of the interpreter. And this depends on extending the old principle that readings of texts vary with new historical situations—extending it to the point where it is completely transformed, since in the past it was assumed that new readings could produce only small variations in a relatively fixed core of meanings. The premise behind what might be called a permanent revision of meanings is that each reader creates a new text out of the old one. Initially this seemed to sanction an interpretive free-for-all, particularly chaotic and meaningless since it ignored the competence of the reader-reinterpreter. The problem was soon resolved, however, by narrowing the idea of the reader to the ideally competent one, and by Stanley Fish's ingenious notion of the revamping of texts by a community of presumably informed readers. Fish's contribution did not really differ much from the view of literary history held by critics who are not structuralists or deconstructionists. As to the ideal readers, they turned out to be, for the most part, Derrida, Lacan, Barthes, Girard, Todorov, Genette, and their students.

These then are the ideological sources of a good deal of recent writing about psychoanalysis and literature. Lacan, of course, is central. His writings on literature reflect not only his revision of Freud in theory and in clinical practice, but also express his generally free-wheeling and cavalier attitude to Freud and Freudian analytic thinking. Lacan's much publicized piece on Poe's "Purloined Letter" utilizes his favorite concepts of phallic symbolism, the Other, the mirror image, and the linguistic structure of the unconscious. However it is a very narrow and one-sided reading of the story. Similarly, Lacan's discussion of Hamlet uses many of Freud's and Jones' observations, but it also focuses on the presumed phallic meaning of Hamlet's role in the play, and on the significance of word-play, another of Lacan's private notions. But most important in these and Lacan's other ventures into literary interpretation is what might be characterized as a free-associational form of thinking set up by the work under examination.

Lacan spins ideological fantasies as he reinterprets and co-authors the text. As in actual analysis, anything goes. An ideological version of what the patient does in analysis is applied to the study of literature. What Lacan contributes as an analyst stems from his linguistic analysis of the unconscious of the leading characters.

Lacan's disciples in the analysis of literature are mainly critics, not analysts. And their method is more esoteric and even more idiosyncratic than his own. Many of them are to be found in seminars and publications associated with Yale and Johns Hopkins Universities, which have become intellectual centers in this country for structuralists and deconstructionists. Taking their cue from Lacan, they explore a text as though they were intellectual pioneers entering virgin territory. Even more than Lacan, their approach employs a combination of revisionist psychoanalytic theory and French linguistics. Hence their writing emphasizes the representation of signifiers and signified elements in literary works, and the language of texts. Needless to say, most analysts and non-academic critics, particularly in the United States and England, have not been persuaded by the Lacanian version of psychoanalytic criticism, and having been trained in Anglo-American traditions of criticism and psychoanalysis, they often find it incomprehensible.

But aside from the question of its validity, Lacanian criticism has brought the examination of psychoanalysis and literature full circle, to a point which is almost a reversal of the intentions of Freud and the early analysts. Freud, and those who followed his lead, assumed that the discoveries of psychoanalysis about human drives and motives threw some light on the lives of writers and the psychic mechanisms of their characters. They did not see psychoanalysis as an instrument for deconstructing, that is, for taking apart and recreating philosophical ideas, literary works, and historical events. To accomplish the latter, psychoanalysis itself had to be deconstructed, which meant it had not only to be textually revised, but had to be open to constant reinterpretation. Psychoanalysis, like a literary text, is now seen by the French and their American disciples as so much grist for the analysts' and the critics' creative mill.

With so many unforeseen and bewildering developments in psychoanalysis and in criticism, it would seem time to take stock and to reexamine the contributions that psychoanalysis can make to the understanding of literature. Obviously, the original aims have been sidetracked, when not completely transformed. It is doubtful that either literature or psychoanalysis has been advanced or illuminated in the process. What critics like Hartman, Doubrovsky, Girard, Genette, Todorov, and others coming out of the French school have produced are brilliant *tours de force*—captious, idiosyncratic, scattershot, with no effort at consistency or roundedness; and their connections with other writings on the subject are sporadic and highly personal. One is tempted to conclude that some very intelligent critics have become the exponents of a theory that gives free rein to all the creative and speculative impulses previously held in check by a sense of the limits of the subject. The theory that all of human culture is made up of texts, and that language is the common element in all these texts, diminishes the number of fixed—or relatively fixed—meanings, and vastly increases the possibilities of new meanings. Furthermore, the number of novel interpretations becomes endless if the reaction of the reader is legitimized as part of the text. Essentially, this has been accomplished by the elimination of history, thus making all texts contemporary—and eliminating traditional meanings.

In its more extreme forms, as in Lacan, we can see the danger of interpretation running wild. But the original difficulty, it would seem, comes from conceiving of criticism—and therefore psychoanalytic criticism—principally as interpretation. In fact, both the French and American approaches often appear to assume that criticism and psychoanalysis have similar functions, the former interpreting literature, the latter interpreting the psyche. The problem with such a parallel is that interpretation is only one of the functions of criticism, particularly when it leads to over-interpretation. And, generally, a certain amount of distortion is bound to result from the use of a single discipline or theory to analyze or interpret literature. We have seen the reductive and distorting effects of an exclusively social, or historical, or Marxist view of literature, and an attempt to fit literature into a psychoanalytic mold can be equally misleading.

In short, it should be clear that criticism is not a branch of psychoanalysis any more than psychoanalysis is a branch of criticism, and neither is a section of linguistics. It is not easy to define so complex and protean an activity as literary criticism, but if its nature is to be found in its history, then it has to be seen as combining many perspectives and aims—formal, historical, traditional, and textual. It tends to emphasize matters pertaining to craft and to literary tradition. But its main function is the exercise of taste and judgment. The best contemporary critics, such as Trilling, Empson, Howe, Kazin, Rahv, Heller, have taken advantage of the insights of analysis to add to the arsenal of criticism, instead of inventing a new linguistic-psychoanalytic method and terminology that often complicates simple questions and creates an aura of discovery around things that are known.

But whatever critical or analytic approach one takes to literature, there remain two major questions to be faced: a theoretical one concerning the relation of literature to neurosis, and the practical one of applying analytic knowledge to a given writer. If we take these questions out of the conceptual stratosphere of the new psycho-criticism, it may be possible to find some more mundane answers. If literature is taken to be the sum of its psychological components or as a variety of dream or fantasy, then we have no literary criteria for judging it, nor any way of distinguishing it from other kinds of dream or fantasy. If we attribute the power or significance of a work to the neurosis of the author, we have to assume that its meaning lies wholly in its psychological content, which, in turn, corresponds to the reader's. We would then have to read *The Possessed,* for example, as a story of the criminal mind, and we could not account for its stature as a political novel. Or, to take a different example, characterizing Rilke's spurts of activity between long fallow periods as signs of health would simply be to define the act of writing as a manifestation of health. One might just as well call it neurotic, since Rilke's process of composition was obsessive and dreamlike. Certainly writing often resembles compulsive acts and states of hallucination, and all we gain by calling it healthy rather than neurotic is the reas-

surance that we are not revelling in disease—a reassurance, incidentally, that Thomas Mann certainly did not require.

Ironically, a way out of the dilemma might be made possible by using the terms *neurosis* and *psychosis* more loosely. Viewed non-clinically, these disorders often involve a distortion of experience whereby certain human events are given an undue, even obsessive, emphasis. In those who are not writers, a distorted view of reality is simply part of illness and inability to adjust, and may be of no intellectual interest. In someone like Kafka, however, the paranoid picture of the world in both his life and his writing was coupled with a gift of a higher order and a mind capable of original and striking observation. The paranoia became plausible, if not "true." Similarly, D. H. Lawrence's sexual dreams would have had only a clinical interest without his literary powers.

To generalize further, much modern writing is centered in some obsessive theme or some biased image of human affairs, growing out of the fixations of the author. This seems true of even so carefully constructed a work as *The Waste Land,* whose meanings appear mainly cultural and religious. But Eliot's concern, in our culture and religion, as well as in our personal lives, is that we no longer know who we are, and the image of this failure is provided by the sexual ambiguity of Tiresias, the psychological core of the poem. The homosexual theme crops up constantly, often in an explicit way, but it is also expressed symbolically in the perversion of feelings and the spiritual impotence running through *The Waste Land.* One would have to know more about Eliot's private preoccupations to speculate further about the effect of his psychic makeup on his wasteland vision, but it is reasonable to assume that this vision reflects to some extent the more personal elements in his life.

What then does it mean to say that the work of writers like Swift, or Kafka, or Eliot contained some distortion of experience traceable in part to their own psychic history? From everything we know about writing, it would seem reasonable to assume that neurotic images of the world coincided with impressions which were not neurotic, and that they energized and organized each other.

Kafka is, of course, the classic example of this process, for his psychic disorders have been most visible and they have been integrated most clearly in all his writing. The merging in Kafka of neurotic and objective vision is perhaps clearer than in any other writer. It is probably for this reason that Kafka has been a favorite subject for psychological probing. His strange fictional world, in which dreams and realities, symbols and objects, fantasies and facts, are indistinguishable from each other, cannot be understood in the ordinary terms of fictional and literary criticism. Kafka might serve as an illustration of how psychoanalytic insights could enlarge the scope of a more traditional criticism. The paranoia, for example, which colored his social and sexual relations, became in his fiction a psychological focus for a world in which the characters are the victims of organized ignorance and authority. The living Kafka's search for psychological solutions merged in his writing with a search for religious and metaphysical solutions.

Kafka's novels and stories would seem to have many apparently distinct aspects: moral, religious, political, and psychological. Attempts have been made to read Kafka from each of these viewpoints—not only reducing Kafka's writing to one of its components but also reducing his stature as a writer. Other views of Kafka aside, the limitations of a psychological exegesis should be noted. There have been many such informed interpretations of Kafka's fiction . . . , and they have conscientiously probed the secrets of Kafka's inner life. By now we are familiar with his paranoia, his hypochondria, his insomnia, his awkward, inhibited relations with women, his inability until the end of his life to marry, his overpowering feelings of anxiety and guilt, his resentment and fear of his father. We also know of his compulsive, largely nocturnal writing habits and accompanying feverish and hallucinatory states. We can discern the representations, sometimes literal, often veiled, of these morbid, self-destructive elements in his fiction and his diaries. But unless we can see how these neurotic—or psychotic?—tendencies are merged with more objective attitudes and ideas, and made into a highly crafted whole, we are dealing with a disturbed patient, not a major writer. Some process, not yet known to psychology, fused the different parts of Kafka's unconscious and conscious mind into a unified vision. Even this more integrated approach is not enough, for Kafka's fiction would not have its uncanny, seductive, and unnerving effect if his sense of the world were not encased in a controlled, almost matter-of-fact prose, at once precise and full of nightmarish associations. Psychology cannot be separated from the history and use of the medium of fiction.

Kafka's paranoia and his feelings about arbitrary parental authority were translated in *The Trial* and other works into a sense of authority both suffocating and reassuring and at once political, religious, and metaphysical. So, too, his fear of women and his dependence on them, based to some extent on his family history, emerged in the soft, shadowy, ultimately unreliable accomplices of authority in his fiction. His story "The Burrow" is a fantastic projection into the underground existence of a burrow that affords an escape from the outside world but is full of its own dangers. Here, too, by means of a prose that creates a totally natural and exact description of the activities of the burrow, the world of the story takes on the menacing qualities of the human world where, for Kafka, the dangers one constantly faces were part of one's fate. The anxiety this evokes is given a biological cast when it is incorporated into the bodily sensations of the burrow. Perhaps most striking in Kafka is the conversion of personal guilt into the pervasive moral, psychological, and political guilt stemming not from specific transgression but rather from the accusatory power of all higher authorities. Again it must be emphasized that we are dealing here not only with a psychological but also a literary act, and if one might generalize further about the literary uses of psychology, one can see a suggestive link from Kafka to the subversive imagination of Dostoevsky. In *Notes from the Underground,* the self-lacerating "anti-hero" of the story says repeatedly that he feels like an insect, diminished and worthless. In *The Metamorphosis,* Gregor Samsa takes the logical and psychological next step. He becomes an insect.

Dostoevsky is another dramatic example of a major figure in whom conscious and unconscious components are both distinct and merged, and who requires, therefore, a combination of traditional criticism and psychoanalytic awareness. (pp. 1-17)

In novels like *The Possessed* and *Crime and Punishment,* the blending of ideological motifs with morbid psychology is even more apparent. Both elements are essential not only in the workings of Dostoevsky's mind, but to the fictional power of the two books. Dostoevsky had strong convictions about the moral arrogance and intellectual emptiness of those personal or political ideas that led to the taking of lives. He viewed killing in the name of the revolution and murder in the name of some transcendent idea as parts of the same evil, rooted in atheism, divorce from the people, and the celebration of "Western" progressive ideas. A passionate Slavophile and a Christian, he believed that salvation could come only through confession and expiation of one's sins. Thus, criminality was identified with political hubris and Godlessness in the character of Raskolnikov, and in the revolutionists of *The Possessed.* The revolutionaries considered everything possible because they did not believe in God; Raskolnikov and Stavrogin could follow their evil impulses because of their criminal psychology. Raskolnikov had the dreams of a superman, Stavrogin the personality of one. Stavrogin was probably the most complete projection of Dostoevsky's dual nature, of his own destructive drives and of the elaborate structure he created to contain them; perhaps this is why Stavrogin is an unfinished character, one whom Dostoevsky could not develop fully without tearing himself apart. Without psychology, Dostoevsky would be another conservative, though one with prophetic vision; without ideology, Dostoevsky would be a novelist of the psychic underground; without literary genius he would be a writer of sensational stories.

The unique combination of neurotic experience with some apparently objective or plausible view of the world, such as we find in Kafka, or Proust, or Mann, seems to be characteristic of much modern literature. Indeed, it is this experience that we designate as the modern experience. Although this experience seems to be shared by a sufficient number of writers and readers to make up a tradition, it has at the same time certain affinities with neurotic experience. Themes such as loneliness, self-doubt, hypersensitivity, perversities of all kinds, estrangement from the community all have their counterparts among the common neuroses, and the two modes of experience, normal and abnormal, often have been joined in such a way that it becomes difficult to separate them.

What we have been describing is the literature of *modernism.* But it has been argued that the modernist movement is dead, and that we are in a post-modernist phase whose qualities and contours still have not been satisfactorily defined. The debate has not been resolved. However it is clear that most contemporary writing lacks the mythic force, the adversary posture, and the complicated sensibility associated with modernism. Fiction today is quieter, more modest, more naturalistic, less symbolic. It is sexually freer and more explicitly perverse, but in a way that would seem to reflect contemporary experience rather than private inclinations. A good deal of recent fiction is also concerned with social causes and liberating values. It is on the whole more open, and less layered; and its deeper psychological meanings are mostly on the surface, just as psychoanalysis itself is on the tips of all tongues. One wonders whether psychoanalytically oriented criticism will find contemporary fiction a fertile field to plow, and whether the highly theoretical and esoteric turn of the new psycho-criticism is not to some extent a reaction to a new fiction with fewer hidden psychological meanings, whether the complexities of criticism are compensating for the simpler experience of literature.

Perhaps these dilemmas will serve as a reminder that what Mann called "the psychology of the unconscious" cannot be equated with the history of consciousness, of which literature is a major part. (pp. 17-18)

> *William Phillips, in an introduction to* Literature and Psychoanalysis, *edited by Edith Kurzweil and William Phillips, Columbia University Press, 1983, pp. 1-18.*

Lionel Trilling

[*Trilling was one of the twentieth century's most significant and influential American literary and social critics, and he is often called the single most important American critic to apply Freudian theories to literature. In the following essay, he explores what he calls the "reciprocal relationship" between Freud's ideas and literature.*]

The Freudian psychology is the only systematic account of the human mind which, in point of subtlety and complexity, of interest and tragic power, deserves to stand beside the chaotic mass of psychological insights which literature has accumulated through the centuries. To pass from the reading of a great literary work to a treatise of academic psychology is to pass from the reading of a great literary work to a treatise of academic psychology is to pass from one order of perception to another, but the human nature of the Freudian psychology is exactly the stuff upon which the poet has always exercised his art. It is therefore not surprising that the psychoanalytical theory has had a great effect upon literature. Yet the relationship is reciprocal, and the effect of Freud upon literature has been no greater than the effect of literature upon Freud. When, on the occasion of the celebration of his seventieth birthday, Freud was greeted as the "discoverer of the unconscious," he corrected the speaker and disclaimed the title. "The poets and philosophers before me discovered the unconscious," he said. "What I discovered was the scientific method by which the unconscious can be studied."

A lack of specific evidence prevents us from considering the particular literary "influences" upon the founder of psychoanalysis; and, besides, when we think of the men who so clearly anticipated many of Freud's own ideas—Schopenhauer and Nietzsche, for example—and then learn that he did not read their works until after he had formulated his own theories, we must see that particular influences cannot be in question here but that what we must deal with is nothing less than a whole *Zeitgeist,* a direction of thought. For psychoanalysis is one of the culminations of the Romanticist literature of the nineteenth century. If there is perhaps a contradiction in the idea of a science standing upon the shoulders of a literature which avows itself inimical to science in so many ways, the contradiction will be resolved if we remember that this literature, despite its avowals, was itself scientific in at least the

sense of being passionately devoted to a research into the self.

In showing the connection between Freud and this Romanticist tradition, it is difficult to know where to begin, but there might be a certain aptness in starting even back of the tradition, as far back as 1762 with Diderot's *Rameau's Nephew.* At any rate, certain men at the heart of nineteenth-century thought were agreed in finding a peculiar importance in this brilliant little work: Goethe translated it, Marx admired it, Hegel—as Marx reminded Engels in the letter which announced that he was sending the book as a gift—praised and expounded it at length, Shaw was impressed by it, and Freud himself, as we know from a quotation in his *Introductory Lectures,* read it with the pleasure of agreement.

The dialogue takes place between Diderot himself and a nephew of the famous composer. The protagonist, the younger Rameau, is a despised, outcast, shameless fellow; Hegel calls him the "disintegrated consciousness" and credits him with great wit, for it is he who breaks down all the normal social values and makes new combinations with the pieces. As for Diderot, the deuteragonist, he is what Hegel calls the "honest consciousness," and Hegel considers him reasonable, decent, and dull. It is quite clear that the author does not despise his Rameau and does not mean us to. Rameau is lustful and greedy, arrogant yet self-abasing, perceptive yet "wrong," like a child. Still, Diderot seems actually to be giving the fellow a kind of superiority over himself, as though Rameau represents the elements which, dangerous but wholly necessary, lie beneath the reasonable decorum of social life. It would perhaps be pressing too far to find in Rameau Freud's id and in Diderot Freud's ego; yet the connection does suggest itself; and at least we have here the perception which is to be the common characteristic of both Freud and Romanticism, the perception of the hidden element of human nature and of the opposition between the hidden and the visible. We have too the bold perception of just what lies hidden: "If the little savage [i.e., the child] were left to himself, if he preserved all his foolishness and combined the violent passions of a man of thirty with the lack of reason of a child in the cradle, he'd wring his father's neck and go to bed with his mother."

From the self-exposure of Rameau to Rousseau's account of his own childhood is no great step; society might ignore or reject the idea of the "immorality" which lies concealed in the beginning of the career of the "good" man, just as it might turn away from Blake struggling to expound a psychology which would include the forces beneath the propriety of social man in general, but the idea of the hidden thing went forward to become one of the dominant notions of the age. The hidden element takes many forms and it is not necessarily "dark" and "bad"; for Blake the "bad" was the good, while for Wordsworth and Burke what was hidden and unconscious was wisdom and power, which work in despite of the conscious intellect.

The mind has become far less simple; the devotion to the various forms of autobiography—itself an important fact in the tradition—provides abundant examples of the change that has taken place. Poets, making poetry by what seems to them almost a freshly discovered faculty, find that this new power may be conspired against by other agencies of the mind and even deprived of its freedom; the names of Wordsworth, Coleridge, and Arnold at once occur to us again, and Freud quotes Schiller on the danger to the poet that lies in the merely analytical reason. And it is not only the poets who are threatened; educated and sensitive people throughout Europe become aware of the depredations that reason might make upon the affective life, as in the classic instance of John Stuart Mill.

We must also take into account the preoccupation—it began in the eighteenth century, or even in the seventeenth—with children, women, peasants, and savages, whose mental life, it is felt, is less overlaid than that of the educated adult male by the proprieties of social habit. With this preoccupation goes a concern with education and personal development, so consonant with the historical and evolutionary bias of the time. And we must certainly note the revolution in morals which took place at the instance (we might almost say) of the *Bildungsroman,* for in the novels fathered by *Wilhelm Meister* we get the almost complete identification of author and hero and of the reader with both, and this identification almost inevitably suggests a leniency of moral judgment. The autobiographical novel has a further influence upon the moral sensibility by its exploitation of all the modulations of motive and by its hinting that we may not judge a man by any single moment in his life without taking into account the determining past and the expiating and fulfilling future.

It is difficult to know how to go on, for the further we look the more literary affinities to Freud we find, and even if we limit ourselves to bibliography we can at best be incomplete. Yet we must mention the sexual revolution that was being demanded—by Shelley, for example, by the Schlegel of *Lucinde,* by George Sand, and later and more critically by Ibsen; the belief in the sexual origin of art, baldly stated by Tieck, more subtly by Schopenhauer; the investigation of sexual maladjustment by Stendhal, whose observations on erotic feeling seem to us distinctly Freudian. Again and again we see the effective, utilitarian ego being relegated to an inferior position and a plea being made on behalf of the anarchic and self-indulgent id. We find the energetic exploitation of the idea of the mind as a divisible thing, one part of which can contemplate and mock the other. It is not a far remove from this to Dostoevski's brilliant instances of ambivalent feeling. Novalis brings in the preoccupation with the death wish, and this is linked on the one hand with sleep and on the other hand with the perception of the perverse, self-destroying impulses, which in turn leads us to that fascination with the horrible which we find in Shelley, Poe, and Baudelaire. And always there is the profound interest in the dream—"Our dreams," said Gerard de Nerval, "are a second life"—and in the nature of metaphor, which reaches its climax in Rimbaud and the later Symbolists, metaphor becoming less and less communicative as it approaches the relative autonomy of the dream life.

But perhaps we must stop to ask, since these are the components of the *Zeitgeist* from which Freud himself developed, whether it can be said that Freud did indeed produce a wide literary effect. What is it that Freud added that the tendency of literature itself would not have developed without him? If we were looking for a writer who showed the Freudian influence, Proust would perhaps come to mind as readily as anyone else; the very title of his novel, in French more than in English, suggests an en-

terprise of psychoanalysis and scarcely less so does his method—the investigation of sleep, of sexual deviation, of the way of association, the almost obsessive interest in metaphor; at these and at many other points the "influence" might be shown. Yet I believe it is true that Proust did not read Freud. Or again, exegesis of *The Waste Land* often reads remarkably like the psychoanalytic interpretation of a dream, yet we know that Eliot's methods were prepared for him not by Freud but by other poets.

Nevertheless, it is of course true that Freud's influence on literature has been very great. Much of it is so pervasive that its extent is scarcely to be determined; in one form or another, frequently in perversions or absurd simplifications, it has been infused into our life and become a component of our culture of which it is now hard to be specifically aware. In biography its first effect was sensational but not fortunate. The early Freudian biographers were for the most part Guildensterns who seemed to know the pipes but could not pluck out the heart of the mystery, and the same condemnation applies to the early Freudian critics. But in recent years, with the acclimatization of psychoanalysis and the increased sense of its refinements and complexity, criticism has derived from the Freudian system much that is of great value, most notable the license and the injunction to read the work of literature with a lively sense of its latent and ambiguous meanings, as if it were, as indeed it is, a being no less alive and contradictory than the man who created it. And this new response to the literary work has had a corrective effect upon our conception of literary biography. The literary critic or biographer who makes use of the Freudian theory is no less threatened by the dangers of theoretical systematization than he was in the early days, but he is likely to be more aware of these dangers; and I think it is true to say that now the motive of his interpretation is not that of exposing the secret shame of the writer and limiting the meaning of his work, but, on the contrary, that of finding grounds for sympathy with the writer and for increasing the possible significances of the work.

The names of the creative writers who have been more or less Freudian in tone or assumption would of course be legion. Only a relatively small number, however, have made serious use of the Freudian ideas. Freud himself seems to have thought this was as it should be: he is said to have expected very little of the works that were sent to him by writers with inscriptions of gratitude for all they had learned from him. The Surrealists have, with a certain inconsistency, depended upon Freud for the "scientific" sanction of their program. Kafka, with an apparent awareness of what he was doing, has explored the Freudian conceptions of guilt and punishment, of the dream, and of the fear of the father. Thomas Mann, whose tendency, as he himself says, was always in the direction of Freud's interests, has been most susceptible to the Freudian anthropology, finding a special charm in the theories of myths and magical practices. James Joyce, with his interest in the numerous states of receding consciousness, with his use of words as things and of words which point to more than one thing, with his pervading sense of the interrelation and interpenetration of all things, and, not least important, his treatment of familial themes, has perhaps most thoroughly and consciously exploited Freud's idea.

It will be clear enough how much of Freud's thought has

significant affinity with the anti-rationalist element of the Romanticist tradition. But we must see with no less distinctness how much of his system is militantly rationalistic. Thomas Mann is at fault when, in his first essay on Freud, he makes it seem that the "Apollonian," the rationalistic, side of psychoanalysis is, while certainly important and wholly admirable, somehow secondary and even accidental. He gives us a Freud who is committed to the "night side" of life. Not at all: the rationalistic element of Freud is foremost; before everything else he is positivistic. If the interpreter of dreams came to medical science through Goethe, as he tells us he did, he entered not by way of the *Walpurgisnacht* but by the essay which played so important a part in the lives of so many scientists of the nineteenth century, the famous disquisition on Nature.

This correction is needed not only for accuracy but also for any understanding of Freud's attitude to art. And for that understanding we must see how intense is the passion with which Freud believes that positivistic rationalism, in its golden-age pre-Revolutionary purity, is the very form and pattern of intellectual virtue. The aim of psychoanalysis, he says, is the control of the night side of life. It is "to strengthen the ego, to make it more independent of the super-ego, to widen its field of vision, and so to extend the organization of the id." "Where id was,"—that is, where all the irrational, non-logical, pleasure-seeking dark forces were—"there shall ego be,"—that is, intelligence and control. "It is," he concludes, with a reminiscence of Faust, "reclamation work, like the draining of the Zuyder Zee." This passage is quoted by Mann when, in taking up the subject of Freud a second time, he does indeed speak of Freud's positivistic program; but even here the bias induced by Mann's artistic interest in the "night side" prevents him from giving the other aspect of Freud its due emphasis. Freud would never have accepted the role which Mann seems to give him as the legitimizer of the myth and the dark irrational ways of the mind. If Freud discovered the darkness for science he never endorsed it. On the contrary, his rationalism supports all the ideas of the Enlightenment that deny validity to myth or religion; he holds to a simple materialism, to a simple determinism, to a rather limited sort of epistemology. No great scientist of our day has thundered so articulately and so fiercely against all those who would sophisticate with metaphysics the scientific principles that were good enough for the nineteenth century. Conceptualism or pragmatism is anathema to him through the greater part of his intellectual career, and this, when we consider the nature of his own brilliant scientific methods, has surely an element of paradox in it.

From his rationalistic positivism comes much of Freud's strength and what weakness he has. The strength is the fine, clear tenacity of his positive aims, the goal of therapy, the desire to bring to men a decent measure of earthly happiness. But upon the rationalism must also be placed the blame for the often naïve scientific principles which characterize his early thought—they are later much modified—and which consist largely of claiming for his theories a perfect correspondence with an external reality, a position which, for those who admire Freud and especially for those who take seriously his views on art, is troublesome in the extreme.

Now Freud has, I believe, much to tell us about art, but whatever is suggestive in him is not likely to be found in those of his works in which he deals expressly with art itself. Freud is not insensitive to art—on the contrary—nor does he ever intend to speak of it with contempt. Indeed, he speaks of it with a real tenderness and counts it one of the true charms of the good life. Of artists, especially of writers, he speaks with admiration and even a kind of awe, though perhaps what he most appreciates in literature are specific emotional insights and observations; as we have noted, he speaks of literary men, because they have understood the part played in life by the hidden motives, as the precursors and coadjutors of his own science.

And yet eventually Freud speaks of art with what we must indeed call contempt. Art, he tells us, is a "substitute gratification," and as such is "an illusion in contrast to reality." Unlike most illusions, however, art is "almost always harmless and beneficent" for the reason that "it does not seek to be anything but an illusion. Save in the case of a few people who are, one might say, obsessed by Art, it never dares make any attack on the realm of reality." One of its chief functions is to serve as a "narcotic." It shares the characteristics of the dream, whose element of distortion Freud calls a "sort of inner dishonesty." As for the artist, he is virtually in the same category with the neurotic. "By such separation of imagination and intellectual capacity," Freud says of the hero of a novel, "he is destined to be a poet or a neurotic, and he belongs to that race of beings whose realm is not of this world."

Now there is nothing in the logic of psychoanalytical thought which requires Freud to have these opinions. But there is a great deal in the practice of the psychoanalytical therapy which makes it understandable that Freud, unprotected by an adequate philosophy, should be tempted to take the line he does. The analytical therapy deals with illusion. The patient comes to the physician to be cured, let us say, of a fear of walking in the street. The fear is real enough, there is no illusion on that score, and it produces all the physical symptoms of a more rational fear, the sweating palms, pounding heart, and shortened breath. But the patient knows that there is no cause for the fear, or rather that there is, as he says, no "real cause": there are no machine guns, man traps, or tigers in the street. The physician knows, however, that there is indeed a "real" cause for the fear, though it has nothing at all to do with what is or is not in the street; the cause is within the patient, and the process of the therapy will be to discover, by gradual steps, what this real cause is and so free the patient from its effects.

Now the patient in coming to the physician, and the physician in accepting the patient, make a tacit compact about reality; for their purpose they agree to the limited reality by which we get our living, win our loves, catch our trains and our colds. The therapist will undertake to train the patient in proper ways of coping with this reality. The patient, of course, has been dealing with this reality all along, but in the wrong way. For Freud there are two ways of dealing with external reality. One is practical, effective, positive; this is the way of the conscious self, of the ego which must be made independent of the super-ego and extend its organization over the id, and it is the right way. The antithetical way may be called, for our purpose now, the "fictional" way. Instead of doing something about, or to, external reality, the individual who uses this way does something to, or about, his affective states. The most common and "normal" example of this is daydreaming, in which we give ourselves a certain pleasure by imagining our difficulties solved or our desires gratified. Then, too, as Freud discovered, sleeping dreams are, in much more complicated ways, and even though quite unpleasant, at the service of this same "fictional" activity. And in ways yet more complicated and yet more unpleasant, the actual neurosis from which our patient suffers deals with an external reality which the mind considers still more unpleasant than the painful neurosis itself.

For Freud as psychoanalytic practitioner there are, we may say, the polar extremes of reality and illusion. Reality is an honorific word, and it means what is *there;* illusion is a pejorative word, and it means a response to what is *not there*. The didactic nature of a course of psychoanalysis no doubt requires a certain firm crudeness in making the distinction; it is after all aimed not at theoretical refinement but at practical effectiveness. The polar extremes are practical reality and neurotic illusion, the latter judged by the former. This, no doubt, is as it should be; the patient is not being trained in metaphysics and epistemology.

This practical assumption is not Freud's only view of the mind in its relation to reality. Indeed, what may be called the essentially Freudian view assumes that the mind, for good as well as bad, helps create its reality by selection and evaluation. In this view, reality is malleable and subject to creation; it is not static but is rather a series of situations which are dealt with in their own terms. But beside this conception of the mind stands the conception which arises from Freud's therapeutic-practical assumptions; in this view, the mind deals with a reality which is quite fixed and static, a reality that is wholly "given" and not (to use a phrase of Dewey's) "taken." In his epistemological utterances, Freud insists on this second view, although it is not easy to see why he should do so. For the reality to which he wishes to reconcile the neurotic patient is, after all, a "taken" and not a "given" reality. It is the reality of social life and of value, conceived and maintained by the human mind and will. Love, morality, honor, esteem—these are the components of a created reality. If we are to call art an illusion then we must call most of the activities and satisfactions of the ego illusions; Freud, of course, has no desire to call them that.

What, then, is the difference between, on the one hand, the dream and the neurosis, and, on the other hand, art? That they have certain common elements is of course clear; that unconscious processes are at work in both would be denied by no poet or critic; they share too, though in different degrees, the element of fantasy. But there is a vital difference between them which Charles Lamb saw so clearly in his defense of the sanity of true genius: "The . . . poet dreams being awake. He is not possessed by his subject but he has dominion over it."

That is the whole difference: the poet is in command of his fantasy, while it is exactly the mark of the neurotic that he is possessed by his fantasy. And there is a further difference which Lamb states; speaking of the poet's relation to reality (he calls it Nature), he says, "He is beautifully loyal to that sovereign directress, even when he appears most to betray her"; the illusions of art are made to serve the purpose of a closer and truer relation with reality. Jacques Barzun, in an acute and sympathetic discussion of Freud,

puts the matter well: "A good analogy between art and *dreaming* has led him to a false one between art and *sleeping*. But the difference between a work of art and a dream is precisely this, that the work of art *leads us back to the outer reality by taking account of it.*" Freud's assumption of the almost exclusively hedonistic nature and purpose of art bars him from the perception of this.

Of the distinction that must be made between the artist and the neurotic Freud is of course aware; he tells us that the artist is not like the neurotic in that he knows how to find a way back from the world of imagination and "once more get a firm foothold in reality." This however seems to mean no more than that reality is to be dealt with when the artist suspends the practice of his art; and at least once when Freud speaks of art dealing with reality he actually means the rewards that a successful artist can win. He does not deny to art its function and its usefulness; it has a therapeutic effect in releasing mental tension; it serves the cultural purpose of acting as a "substitute gratification" to reconcile men to the sacrifices they have made for culture's sake; it promotes the social sharing of highly valued emotional experiences; and it recalls men to their cultural ideals. This is not everything that some of us would find that art does, yet even this is a good deal for a "narcotic" to do.

I started by saying that Freud's ideas could tell us something about art, but so far I have done little more than try to show that Freud's very conception of art is inadequate. Perhaps, then, the suggestiveness lies in the application of the analytic method to specific works of art or to the artist himself? I do not think so, and it is only fair to say that Freud himself was aware both of the limits and the limitations of psychoanalysis in art, even though he does not always in practice submit to the former or admit the latter.

Freud has, for example, no desire to encroach upon the artist's autonomy; he does not wish us to read his monograph on Leonardo and then say of the "Madonna of the Rocks" that it is a fine example of homosexual, autoerotic painting. If he asserts that in investigation the "psychiatrist cannot yield to the author," he immediately insists that the "author cannot yield to the psychiatrist," and he warns the latter not to "coarsen everything" by using for all human manifestations the "substantially useless and awkward terms" of clinical procedure. He admits, even while asserting that the sense of beauty probably derives from sexual feelings, that psychoanalysis "has less to say about beauty than about most other things." He confesses to a theoretical indifference to the form of art and restricts himself to its content. Tone, feeling, style, and the modification that part makes upon part he does not consider. "The layman," he says, "may expect perhaps too much from analysis . . . for it must be admitted that it throws no light upon the two problems which probably interest him the most. It can do nothing toward elucidating the nature of the artistic gift, nor can it explain the means by which the artist works—artistic technique."

What, then, does Freud believe that the analytical method can do? Two things: explain the "inner meanings" of the work of art and explain the temperament of the artist as man.

A famous example of the method is the attempt to solve the "problem" of *Hamlet* as suggested by Freud and as carried out by Dr. Ernest Jones, his early and distinguished follower. Dr. Jones's monograph is a work of painstaking scholarship and of really masterly ingenuity. The research undertakes not only the clearing up of the mystery of Hamlet's character, but also the discovery of "the clue to much of the deeper workings of Shakespeare's mind." Part of the mystery in question is of course why Hamlet, after he had so definitely resolved to do so, did not avenge upon his hated uncle his father's death. But there is another mystery to the play—what Freud calls "the mystery of its effect," its magical appeal that draws so much interest toward it. Recalling the many failures to solve the riddle of the play's charm, he wonders if we are to be driven to the conclusion "that its magical appeal rests solely upon the impressive thoughts in it and the splendor of its language." Freud believes that we can find a source of power beyond this.

We remember that Freud has told us that the meaning of a dream is its intention, and we may assume that the meaning of a drama is its intention, too. The Jones research undertakes to discover what it was that Shakespeare intended to say about Hamlet. It finds that the intention was wrapped by the author in a dreamlike obscurity because it touched so deeply both his personal life and the moral life of the world; what Shakespeare intended to say is that Hamlet cannot act because he is incapacitated by the guilt he feels at his unconscious attachment to his mother. There is, I think, nothing to be quarreled with in the statement that there is an Oedipus situation in *Hamlet;* and if psychoanalysis has indeed added a new point of interest to the play, that is to its credit. And, just so, there is no reason to quarrel with Freud's conclusion when he undertakes to give us the meaning of *King Lear* by a tortuous tracing of the mythological implications of the theme of the three caskets, of the relation of the caskets to the Norns, the Fates, and the Graces, of the connection of these triadic females with Lear's daughters, of the transmogrification of the death goddess into the love goddess and the identification of Cordelia with both, all to the conclusion that the meaning of *King Lear* is to be found in the tragic refusal of an old man to "renounce love, choose death, and make friends with the necessity of dying." There is something both beautiful and suggestive in this, but it is not *the* meaning of *King Lear* any more than the Oedipus motive is *the* meaning of *Hamlet.*

It is not here a question of the validity of the evidence, though that is of course important. We must rather object to the conclusions of Freud and Dr. Jones on the ground that their proponents do not have an adequate conception of what an artistic meaning is. There is no single meaning to any work of art; this is true not merely because it is better that it should be true, that is, because it makes art a richer thing, but because historical and personal experience show it to be true. Changes in historical context and in personal mood change the meaning of a work and indicate to us that artistic understanding is not a question of fact but of value. Even if the author's intention were, as it cannot be, precisely determinable, the meaning of a work cannot lie in the author's intention alone. It must also lie in its effect. We can say of a volcanic eruption on an inhabited island that it "means terrible suffering," but if the island is uninhabited or easily evacuated it means something else. In short, the audience partly determines the meaning of the work. But although Freud sees something of this when he says that in addition to the author's intention we must take into account the mystery of *Hamlet's* effect, he nevertheless goes on to speak as if, historically, *Hamlet's* effect had been single and brought about solely by the "magical" power of the Oedipus motive to which, unconsciously, we so violently respond. Yet there was, we know, a period when *Hamlet* was relatively in eclipse, and it has always been scandalously true of the French, a people not without filial feeling, that they have been somewhat indifferent to the "magical appeal" of *Hamlet.*

I do not think that anything I have said about the inadequacies of the Freudian method of interpretation limits the number of ways we can deal with a work of art. Bacon remarked that experiment may twist nature on the rack to wring out its secrets, and criticism may use any instruments upon a work of art to find its meanings. The elements of art are not limited to the world of art. They reach into life, and whatever extraneous knowledge of them we gain—for example, by research into the historical context of the work—may quicken our feelings for the work itself and even enter legitimately into those feelings. Then, too, anything we may learn about the artist himself may be enriching and legitimate. But one research into the mind of the artist is simply not practicable, however legitimate it may theoretically be. That is, the investigation of his unconscious intention as it exists apart from the work itself. Criticism understands that the artist's statement of his conscious intention, though it is sometimes useful, cannot finally determine meaning. How much less can we know of his unconscious intention considered as something apart from the whole work? Surely very little that can be called conclusive or scientific. For, as Freud himself points out, we are not in a position to question the artist; we must apply the technique of dream analysis to his symbols, but, as Freud says with some heat, those people do not understand his theory who think that a dream may be interpreted without the dreamer's free association with the multitudinous details of his dream.

We have so far ignored the aspect of the method which finds the solution to the "mystery" of such a play as *Hamlet* in the temperament of Shakespeare himself and then illuminates the mystery of Shakespeare's temperament by means of the solved mystery of the play. Here it will be amusing to remember that by 1935 Freud had become converted to the theory that it was not Shakespeare of Stratford but the Earl of Oxford who wrote the plays, thus invalidating the important bit of evidence that Shakespeare's father died shortly before the composition of *Hamlet.* This is destructive enough to Dr. Jones's argument, but the evidence from which Dr. Jones draws conclusions about literature fails on grounds more relevant to literature itself. For when Dr. Jones, by means of his analysis of *Hamlet,* takes us into "the deeper workings of Shakespeare's mind," he does so with a perfect confidence that he knows what *Hamlet* is and what its relation to Shakespeare is. It is, he tells us, Shakespeare's "chief masterpiece," so far superior to all his other works that it may be placed on "an entirely separate level." And then, having established his ground on an entirely subjective literary judgment, Dr. Jones goes on to tell us that *Hamlet* "probably expresses the core of Shakespeare's philosophy and outlook as no other work of his does." That is, all the contradictory or complicating or modifying testimony of the other plays is dismissed on the basis of Dr. Jones's acceptance of the peculiar position which, he believes, *Hamlet* occupies in the Shakespeare canon. And it is upon this quite inadmissible judgment that Dr. Jones bases his argument: "It may be expected *therefore* that anything which will give us the key to the inner meaning of the play will *necessarily* give us the clue to much of the deeper workings of Shakespeare's mind." (The italics are mine.)

I should be sorry if it appeared that I am trying to say that psychoanalysis can have nothing to do with literature. I am sure that the opposite is so. For example, the whole notion of rich ambiguity in literature, of the interplay between the apparent meaning and the latent—not "hidden"—meaning, has been reinforced by the Freudian concepts, perhaps even received its first impetus from them. Of late years, the more perceptive psychoanalysts have surrendered the early pretensions of their teachers to deal "scientifically" with literature. That is all to the good, and when a study as modest and precise as Dr. Franz Alexander's essay on *Henry IV* comes along, an essay which pretends not to "solve" but only to illuminate the subject, we have something worth having. Dr. Alexander undertakes nothing more than to say that in the development of Prince Hal we see the classic struggle of the ego to come to normal adjustment, beginning with the rebellion against the father, going on to the conquest of the super-ego (Hotspur, with his rigid notions of honor and glory), then to the conquest of the id (Falstaff, with his anarchic self-indulgence), then to the identification with the father (the crown scene) and the assumption of mature responsibility. An analysis of this sort is not momentous and not exclusive of other meanings; perhaps it does no more than point up and formulate what we all have already seen. It has the tact to *accept* the play and does not, like Dr. Jones's study of *Hamlet,* search for a "hidden motive" and a "deeper working," which implies that there is a reality to which the play stands in the relation that a dream stands to the wish that generates it and from which it is separable; it is this reality, this "deeper working," which, according to Dr. Jones, produced the play. But *Hamlet* is not merely the product of Shakespeare's thought, it is the very instrument of his thought, and if meaning is intention, Shakespeare did not intend the Oedipus motive or anything less than *Hamlet;* if meaning is effect then it is *Hamlet* which affects us, not the Oedipus motive. *Coriolanus* also deals, and very terribly, with the Oedipus motive, but the effect of the one drama is very different from the effect of the other.

If, then, we can accept neither Freud's conception of the place of art in life nor his application of the analytical method, what is it that he contributes to our understanding of art or to its practice? In my opinion, what he contributes outweighs his errors; it is of the greatest importance, and it lies in no specific statement that he makes about art but is, rather, implicit in his whole conception of the mind.

For, of all mental systems, the Freudian psychology is the one which makes poetry indigenous to the very constitution of the mind. Indeed, the mind, as Freud sees it, is in the greater part of its tendency exactly a poetry-making organ. This puts the case too strongly, no doubt, for it seems to make the working of the unconscious mind equivalent to poetry itself, forgetting that between the un-

conscious mind and the finished poem there supervene the social intention and the formal control of the conscious mind. Yet the statement has at least the virtue of counterbalancing the belief, so commonly expressed or implied, that the very opposite is true, and that poetry is a kind of beneficent aberration of the mind's right course.

Freud has not merely naturalized poetry; he has discovered its status as a pioneer settler, and he sees it as a method of thought. Often enough he tries to show how, as a method of thought, it is unreliable and ineffective for conquering reality; yet he himself is forced to use it in the very shaping of his own science, as when he speaks of the topography of the mind and tells us with a kind of defiant apology that the metaphors of space relationship which he is using are really most inexact since the mind is not a thing of space at all, but that there is no other way of conceiving the difficult idea except by metaphor. In the eighteenth century Vico spoke of the metaphorical, imagistic language of the early stages of culture; it was left to Freud to discover how, in a scientific age, we still feel and think in figurative formations, and to create, what psychoanalysis is, a science of tropes, of metaphor and its variants, synecdoche and metonymy.

Freud showed, too, how the mind, in one of its parts, could work without logic, yet not without that directing purpose, that control of intent from which, perhaps it might be said, logic springs. For the unconscious mind works without the syntactical conjunctions which are logic's essence. It recognizes no *because,* no *therefore,* no *but;* such ideas as similarity, agreement, and community are expressed in dreams imagistically by compressing the elements into a unity. The unconscious mind in its struggle with the conscious always turns from the general to the concrete and finds the tangible trifle more congenial than the large abstraction. Freud discovered in the very organization of the mind those mechanisms by which art makes its effects, such devices as the condensation of meanings and the displacement of accent.

All this is perhaps obvious enough and, though I should like to develop it in proportion both to its importance and to the space I have given to disagreement with Freud, I will not press it further. For there are two other elements in Freud's thought which, in conclusion, I should like to introduce as of great weight in their bearing on art.

Of these, one is a specific idea which, in the middle of his career (1920), Freud put forward in his essay *Beyond the Pleasure Principle.* The essay itself is a speculative attempt to solve a perplexing problem in clinical analysis, but its relevance to literature is inescapable, as Freud sees well enough, even though his perception of its critical importance is not sufficiently strong to make him revise his earlier views of the nature and function of art. The idea is one which stands beside Aristotle's notion of the catharsis, in part to supplement, in part to modify it.

Freud has come upon certain facts which are not to be reconciled with his earlier theory of the dream. According to this theory, all dreams, even the unpleasant ones, could be understood upon analysis to have the intention of fulfilling the dreamer's wishes. They are in the service of what Freud calls the pleasure principle, which is opposed to the reality principle. It is, of course, this explanation of the dream which had so largely conditioned Freud's theory of art. But now there is thrust upon him the necessity for reconsidering the theory of the dream, for it was found that in cases of war neurosis—what we once called shellshock—the patient, with the utmost anguish, recurred in his dreams to the very situation, distressing as it was, which had precipitated his neurosis. It seemed impossible to interpret these dreams by any assumption of a hedonistic intent. Nor did there seem to be the usual amount of distortion in them: the patient recurred to the terrible initiatory situation with great literalness. And the same pattern of psychic behavior could be observed in the play of children; there were some games which, far from fulfilling wishes, seemed to concentrate upon the representation of those aspects of the child's life which were most unpleasant and threatening to his happiness.

To explain such mental activities Freud evolved a theory for which he at first refused to claim much but to which, with the years, he attached an increasing importance. He first makes the assumption that there is indeed in the psychic life a repetition-compulsion which goes beyond the pleasure principle. Such a compulsion cannot be meaningless, it must have an intent. And that intent, Freud comes to believe, is exactly and literally the developing of fear. "These dreams," he says, "are attempts at restoring control of the stimuli by developing apprehension, the pretermission of which caused the traumatic neurosis." The dream, that is, is the effort to reconstruct the bad situation in order that the failure to meet it may be recouped; in these dreams there is no obscured intent to evade but only an attempt to meet the situation, to make a new effort of control. And in the play of children it seems to be that "the child repeats even the unpleasant experiences because through his own activity he gains a far more thorough mastery of the strong impression than was possible by mere passive experience."

Freud, at this point, can scarcely help being put in mind of tragic drama; nevertheless, he does not wish to believe that this effort to come to mental grips with a situation is involved in the attraction of tragedy. He is, we might say, under the influence of the Aristotelian tragic theory which emphasizes a qualified hedonism through suffering. But the pleasure involved in tragedy is perhaps an ambiguous one; and sometimes we must feel that the famous sense of cathartic resolution is perhaps the result of glossing over terror with beautiful language rather than an evacuation of it. And sometimes the terror even bursts through the language to stand stark and isolated from the play, as does Oedipus's sightless and bleeding face. At any rate, the Aristotelian theory does not deny another function for tragedy (and for comedy, too) which is suggested by Freud's theory of the traumatic neurosis—what might be called the mithridatic function, by which tragedy is used as the homeopathic administration of pain to inure ourselves to the greater pain which life will force upon us. There is in the cathartic theory of tragedy, as it is usually understood, a conception of tragedy's function which is too negative and which inadequately suggests the sense of active mastery which tragedy can give.

In the same essay in which he sets forth the conception of the mind embracing its own pain for some vital purpose, Freud also expresses a provisional assent to the idea (earlier stated, as he reminds us, by Schopenhauer) that there is perhaps a human drive which makes of death the final

and desired goal. The death instinct is a conception that is rejected by many of even the most thoroughgoing Freudian theorists (as, in his last book, Freud mildly noted); the late Otto Fenichel in his authoritative work on the neurosis argues cogently against it. Yet even if we reject the theory as not fitting the facts in any operatively useful way, we still cannot miss its grandeur, its ultimate tragic courage in acquiescence to fate. The idea of the reality principle and the idea of the death instinct form the crown of Freud's broader speculation on the life of man. Their quality of grim poetry is characteristic of Freud's system and the ideas it generates for him.

And as much as anything else that Freud gives to literature, this quality of his thought is important. Although the artist is never finally determined in his work by the intellectual systems about him, he cannot avoid their influence; and it can be said of various competing systems that some hold more promise for the artist than others. When, for example, we think of the simple humanitarian optimism which, for two decades, has been so pervasive, we must see that not only has it been politically and philosophically inadequate, but also that it implies, by the smallness of its view of the varieties of human possibility, a kind of check on the creative faculties. In Freud's view of life no such limitation is implied. To be sure, certain elements of his system seem hostile to the usual notions of man's dignity. Like every great critic of human nature—and Freud is that—he finds in human pride the ultimate cause of human wretchedness, and he takes pleasure in knowing that his ideas stand with those of Copernicus and Darwin in making pride more difficult to maintain. Yet the Freudian man is, I venture to think, a creature of far more dignity and far more interest than the man which any other modern psychological system has been able to conceive. Despite popular belief to the contrary, man, as Freud conceives him, is not to be understood by any simple formula (such as sex) but is rather an inextricable tangle of culture and biology. And not being simple, he is not simply good; he has, as Freud says somewhere, a kind of hell within him from which rise everlastingly the impulses which threaten his civilization. He has the faculty of imagining for himself more in the way of pleasure and satisfaction than he can possibly achieve. Everything that he gains he pays for in more than equal coin; compromise and the compounding with defeat constitute his best way of getting through the world. His best qualities are the result of a struggle whose outcome is tragic. Yet he is a creature of love; it is Freud's sharpest criticism of the Adlerian psychology that to aggression it gives everything and to love nothing at all.

One is always aware in reading Freud how little cynicism there is in his thought. His desire for man is only that he should be human, and to this end his science is devoted. No view of life to which the artist responds can insure the quality of his work, but the poetic qualities of Freud's own principles, which are so clearly in the line of the classic tragic realism, suggest that this is a view which does not narrow and simplify the human world for the artist but on the contrary opens and complicates it. (pp. 33-55)

Lionel Trilling, "Freud and Literature," in his The Liberal Imagination: Essays on Literature and Society, *1950. Reprint by Harcourt Brace Jovanovich, 1979, pp. 33-55.*

Marshall Edelson

[*Edelson is an American psychiatrist, author, and educator. In the following essay, he considers several aspects of the relationship between psychoanalysis and poetry.*]

My first question is: Why should the psychoanalyst qua psychoanalyst pay any special attention to poetry?

First, because language is the source of the primary data of psychoanalysis. The psychoanalyst may turn to poetry, as I have [in *Language and Interpretation in Psychoanalysis*], for examples of an intensely concentrated exploitation of the many resources of language. In poetry, the psychoanalyst becomes aware of hypersemanticity, of the way in which different but related meanings intersect or converge upon a word or phrase. In poetry, he discovers patterns of sounds supporting semantic structures as a chordal progression underlies a melody or a tone of voice illuminates a discourse. These patterns, together with syntactic forms, provide emphasis, create tension, and arouse anticipations and expectations. Sounds by their own qualities, and in the context of the semantic structures in which they are embedded, symbolize conceptions of affect and attitude. Syntactic forms, similarly, present rather than represent meanings by exemplifying and thereby alluding to the very properties of a syntactic form itself. The probability is that each use of language the psychoanalyst encounters in poetry has found or will find its way into the psychoanalytic situation. Theoretical and research interests aside, it is always possible that by reading poetry with pleasure and care the psychoanalyst enhances his readiness to hear and respond to such uses of language in his clinical work.

Second, because poetry is a product of the mind, the same mind that produces to some extent in much the same way dreams, symptoms, and parapraxes. Poetry constrains the psychoanalyst to construct a theory of the mind that is consistent with the mind's production of the former as well as the latter. Poetry informs the psychoanalyst that operations such as condensation and displacement are involved in the most disciplined and integrated, as well as in the most wayward and pathological, creations of man.

Third, because poetry instigates acts of interpretation by literary critics, as the verbal productions of the analysand instigate acts of interpretation by the psychoanalyst. There are questions here worth investigating. In what ways are the "acts of interpretation" carried out by one importantly alike and in what ways importantly unlike the "acts of interpretation" carried out by the other? What is the difference between understanding a poem and interpreting it, between understanding what the analysand says and interpreting it? What is the difference between explaining a poem and interpreting it, between explaining what the analysand says and interpreting it? What are the events that provide occasions for or instigate acts of interpretation, and to what extent are they similar or dissimilar in the two cases? Such events may include apparent senselessness when one expects or assumes sense; ambiguities—syntactic, semantic, phonological, and logical; deviance; disjunctions, sudden changes in content or style, abrupt breaks in continuity, a felt lack of relatedness; tropes or figures of speech. To what extent are the aims and the context of acts of interpretation by literary critic and psychoanalyst congruent?

With regard to the last question, a few comments are in order. The psychoanalyst's principal skill lies not in making interpretations but in creating a situation in which his acts of interpretation are mutative (that is, affect the analysand). Interpretation in psychoanalysis is a three-termed predicate; it is a relation requiring three terms for its expression. It involves a joint effort by psychoanalyst and analysand to enable the analysand to make sense out of what appears senseless—a dream, a neurotic symptom, a parapraxis. However, interpretation as it is carried out by the literary critic is often discussed as if it were a two-termed predicate. What is emphasized is interpretation of a text and the difficulties in the relationship between interpreter and text—rather than interpretation of a text for someone else (a reader, an audience) to whom the text is problematic and whose relation to the text may be affected by the interpretation. Little is said about the vicissitudes of the relationship between interpreter and reader, and usually interest in this relationship is aroused only when the literary critic is also a teacher.

There is a major flaw here in the application of psychoanalysis. For either the writer of the text is regarded as a patient, although he cannot join the literary critic in, or contribute to, the effort to interpret the text—a crucial part of any process we call psychoanalytic—or the literary critic is regarded as a patient conducting a self-analysis, whose unconscious mental processes, reactions to the text, and attitudes toward the writer of the text, constitute both an obstacle to interpretation and the means that make interpretation possible. Surely, however, if there is an analogy to psychoanalytic interpretation, then the relation between a text that is apparently senseless and someone else—a reader—for whom it should make sense and who is to be altered by interpretation is also important. The literary critic somehow has to find ways to affect some reader. The literary critic's skill is ultimately to be evaluated in terms of some change brought about in at least one reader's capacity to comprehend, appreciate, or respond to a poem. One could, of course, respond to the last three sentences: (1) by denying that there is an analogy between psychoanalytic interpretation (as defined in the previous paragraph) and literary interpretation of a text; or (2) by rejecting one or another aspect of the definition of psychoanalytic interpretation here given (for example, that psychoanalytic interpretation always involves an effort to make sense out of what appears to be senseless).

Fourth, the psychoanalyst qua psychoanalyst should pay special attention to poetry, because the reader's response to poetry is a phenomenon which, like many another, calls for psychoanalytic investigation. I. A. Richards [in his *Practical Criticism*] once reported a study of the obstacles within readers that led to their misreading poetry. Certainly, his list of obstacles would be enriched if the psychoanalyst were to bring to bear upon such a problem the psychoanalytic theory of the mind and its account of primary and secondary mental processes; a consideration of the difference between motivated disguises and the apparent senselessness brought about by a particular mode of representation of meaning; and the study of defenses against impulses and affects and resistance to the apprehension of images or ideas that will unleash or arouse these. A psychoanalyst who focused upon this one problem might shed a good deal of additional light on the interaction between modes of representation, motivational structures, and cognitive functioning.

Not only the creation of poetry, but also the satisfaction it brings, are as much mysteries of the mind as the creation of music and the satisfaction it brings. Stone [in his *Psychoanalytic Situation*] writes of the mother-of-separation, the mother who is in contact not physically but through acts of speech, as the primal transference figure in psychoanalysis. Surely, the intense response to voice alone, regardless of content, to patterns of sound, to linkages between sound and sense, has something to do in both the reader of poetry and the analysand with the relation to the mother-of-separation and her quintessentially linguistic presence. Here, poetry and psychoanalysis may share a common foundation, and the connection between the response to poetry and the response to the psychoanalyst's voice cries for psychoanalytic investigation.

Similarly, the intense response to condensations and verbal communications in poetry may have its source in a recognition and enjoyment of a mode of mental functioning. This phenomenon is also observed in the psychoanalytic situation. Here, the analysand may, for example, fear, but often as well delight and take pride in, the dreams he creates and the operations he discovers which have entered into his construction of his dreams. Psychoanalytic investigation of the connection between these phenomena should yield important information about the human capacity for observing and taking pleasure in one's own modes of mental functioning.

My second question is: what assumptions are made in some uses of psychoanalysis in literary criticism, which call for examination by the psychoanalyst? The ones that come to mind especially are assumptions about the relation between tropes or figures of speech and mechanisms of defense.

First, the assumption may be made that literal language is not possible, that language is ineluctably figurative, and that in a fundamental (that is, literal!) sense, any use of language is, in part at least, tropological. (I have discussed this assumption in passing in ["What Is the Psychoanalyst Talking About?"]) This assumption requires examination in the light of psychoanalytic theorems about different modes of ego functioning; the relation between language and cognition; and the extent to which and the circumstances in which uses of language can be purely cognitive and, therefore, at least relatively drive-autonomous and affect-autonomous.

Second, the assumption may be made that all figurative language (and, therefore, under the previous assumption, any use of language) is always, in part at least, defensive; that is, whatever functions it serves, it serves defense as well. Defense is regarded as a ubiquitous aspect of human action. This assumption requires examination in the light of psychoanalytic theorems about ego-autonomous functions, which are presumed to have origins neither in drive nor in defense.

Third, the assumption may be made that each trope or figure of speech expresses, serves, or is connected with a specific mechanism of defense. This assumption requires examination in the light of psychoanalytic theorems about the nature of defense. To what extent is it useful to conceive of defenses as abstract mechanisms and to what extent as, rather, kinds of fantasies (for example, of turning away or shutting one's eyes, of swallowing or taking in an object, of changing the image of one's self)? Are defenses essentially linguistic? Can they be defined solely in terms of linguistic operations? Are specific defenses and tropes regularly associated or correlated? Are defenses and specific figurative ways of using language connected by virtue of the relation of each to some third factor such as innate style of cognition?

I have no comment to make about these assumptions here. They do require further discussion but, even more important, they are suitable for empirical study by the psychoanalyst in the psychoanalytic situation itself. (pp. 113-18)

Marshall Edelson, "Two Questions about Psychoanalysis and Poetry," in The Literary Freud: Mechanisms of Defense and the Poetic Will, *edited by Joseph H. Smith, Yale University Press, 1980, pp. 113-18.*

Robert Coles

[*Coles is an American psychiatrist and author best known for his five-volume* Children of Crisis *(1967-78), in which he documents the psychological effects of poverty and racial discrimination on children. He has also written on literary figures, including George Eliot and Elizabeth Barrett Browning. In the following essay, he questions the value of a psychoanalytic approach to literature.*]

I don't think it is melodramatic to suggest that literary talent, in its inspired forms, has obsessed if not haunted psychoanalytic psychology. Freud's well-known remark on creativity, set down in an essay (1928) on Dostoevsky ("Before the problem of the creative artist, analysis must, alas, lay down its arms"), indicates the frustrated combativeness of a man himself exceptionally talented. The psychoanalyst who thought of himself as a conquistador had a canny sense of when to abstain from a battle. Nevertheless, all of Freud's followers by no means followed his lead. In the 1930s Edmund Bergler, a New York City analyst, turned out a succession of books and articles meant to show how "sick," how "neurotic" writers are. (In that regard, the irony of his own writing campaign never seemed to strike him as odd or amusing.) When I got to know William Carlos Williams fairly well (I wrote my college "major paper" on his poetry), I was warned several times in letters about a trend he considered dangerous indeed: "I'm tired of seeing writers singled out for these blasts. If I read doctor Freud right, he's telling us that we're all full of conflicts—the way it goes for the human mind. So what's new! Oh, I pull back: what's new is that he's probed our mental affairs—whereas Sophocles or Shakespeare brought them to life. The probe is for doctors! When you leave the theatre and go to your office you need a probe! But some of these psychoanalytic literary critics have created a new medical specialty: the artist or writer as victim! You remember my dogs, 'sniffing' in *Paterson*? Some of the psychology I read, about writers and their writing, makes me think of 'sniffing'—that 'I smell shit look' people sometimes get."

In his paper on Heinz Kohut's interesting and important work, Dr. Ernest Wolf suggests early on that psychoanalysts have been wrongly charged with "besmirching and degrading" their various "betters," who have given us what gets called in the essay "sublime inspirations." Such a charge, we are told, is incorrect: "This distorted view of the psychoanalysis of literature surely does not fit Freud nor most psychoanalytic commentators." Yet later on the same author quotes Heinz Kohut himself as feeling it necessary to take issue with a good number of his colleagues: "He sharply criticizes the amateurishness and reductionism of some psychoanalytic critics." Needless to say, the issue is not percentages. Many, maybe most, psychoanalysts have all they can do to deal with the challenges of their everyday clinical work. But from those who have chosen to pursue "applied psychoanalysis," there have been plenty of logical lapses, not to mention abusive sprees, as Kohut seems to imply when he hesitates long and hard about the very point of using psychoanalytic ideas in a nonclinical intellectual setting.

Maybe Anna Freud had it right, so far as some psychoanalytic criticism of artists and writers goes, when she referred to "the universally envied gift of creative energy." Envy can take many forms, one of which is condescension—the astonishing acknowledgment in Marie-Louise von Franz's paper that "psychology . . . can even learn from it [literature]." Why the author felt it necessary to use the word "even" is, of course, her own business, but one is struck at the gratuitous presence of such an adverb. Nor is the following remark anything but a reminder of the kind of self-serving arrogance one not rarely encounters in supposedly "friendly" comments from analytic psychologists of the Jungian persuasion: "But more frequently the artist just simply has no idea himself of what has been said through him and is relieved and impressed if one can show it to him." A bit further on we are told that "all truly creative people know [this]: the woundedness of their soul through the creative impulse." No wonder Flannery O'Connor, in her letters (*The Habit of Being*), observes that "to religion I think he [Freud] is much less dangerous than Jung." Maybe the same holds for literary criticism—because an apparent friendliness can mask a brutal *hauteur*. Nor do murky pieties about "archetypes" bring us all that closer to the contours of psychological reality, be it a patient's or that offered us on a canvas, or in the words of a poet, a novelist.

I refer to the above references . . . because I believe they indicate, yet again, some of the difficulties that plague a kind of psychological literary criticism. Nor is the issue only a matter of arrogance, or single-minded (and self-serving) professional simplification of exceedingly complex issues. I wonder whether, finally, we are not confronted with a question of sensibility—that of the social scientist as against that of the humanist. "It is the business of fiction to embody mystery through manners," said Flannery O'Connor—and then she added this: "mystery is a great embarrassment to the modern mind." For her, such mystery was not to be "resolved," that cool, slippery word that so many of us use today. If anything, stories and poems aim, unashamedly, to deepen mystery. To quote from another letter of Dr. Williams: "Some want to analyze the air—and tell us how much oxygen and hydrogen are around. Others want to enjoy the air, and mix things up—mist, fog, rain, blinding sun."

But even if we take social science logic on its own conceptual merits, we are in trouble when we come across a statement such as this: "An essay on Sylvia Plath by Weisblatt

delineated the narcissistic elements in certain of her poems." Dr. Wolf admittedly has no time to tell us more about those "elements," but surely he ought to stop and remind us that there are "narcissistic elements" in *all* writing—all poems, all critiques of poems, and yes, all essays written on narcissism, or on other essays concerned with narcissism, not to mention comments such as these with respect to sentences that appear in that last-mentioned category. The issue is not narcissism—in Shakespeare's sonnets or Yeats or Keats or for that matter Heinz Kohut's writing. (The two leading theorists of narcissism, Kohut and Otto Kernberg, have proved their humanity by the way they have narcissistically argued with each other.) The issue is language—the uses to which it is put. There are "narcissistic elements" in all language, of course—that of the suicidally disturbed and that of the normal, that of smart critics and that of ordinary working people with no pretension to learned thinking, and not least, that of psychoanalysts and psychoanalysands, as well as that of men and women who write poems or who criticize the content of those poems, evaluate their words.

To tell us that Sylvia Plath shows to a reader "narcissistic elements in certain of her poems" is to tell us that Sylvia Plath was, finally, a human being. Sylvia Plath's narcissism was easily matched, if not exceeded, by the narcissism of thousands and thousands of other human beings. We remember her for her words, their arrangement. Her narcissism did not generate those words. What did? The mystery of the origins of language persists: neurophysiological and biochemical processes, speech centers in the brain—and on and on. As for the cognitive gifts that enable a Sylvia Plath to see so much, understand so much—is biology to be denied a significant causative role? But geneticists and neurochemists or neuroanatomists or linguistic scholars or cognitive psychologists are not the ones who keep trying to "explain" talent, or "delineate" this or that "element" in one or another poet's work.

Are we really helped to understand Shakespeare or Goethe, Tolstoy or Joyce (I disagree with, and resent, the characterization of *Ulysses* as a work flawed by "nihilistic bias" in the von Franz paper), by the statement of Freud's that "the creative writer does the same as the child at play"? The creative writer does quite something else. He doesn't "create a world of fantasy which he takes seriously." He creates a work of art. Sometimes, as we strain for resemblances (in pursuit of what—an explanation of someone else's enviable achievements?), we forget the most obvious distinctions in the world. Millions of children play, millions of adults create their worlds of fantasies, and God knows (as in mental hospital patients!) take their fantasies all too seriously. A few (James Joyce, for instance) come up with the astonishing subtleties and nuances of word and meaning, the triumph of scholarship and imagination, the bravura performance of a *Ulysses*.

What any number of us psychiatrists fail to perceive (and not only in connection with writers and artists) is that psychopathology or even normal emotional development are but one part of mental life. Language itself is, after all, what distinguishes us from all other creatures—the ability to gain distance on ourselves and our situation through words. We are the ones who ask why and how. We are the ones who come into "consciousness" through the strange phenomenon that still eludes us: the baby speaks—and thereafter, a new being, so to speak, has emerged. To paraphrase John of the New Testament: in the beginning, man's beginning, was the Word, and then "the Word became Flesh." For all Noam Chomsky's brilliance, or that of any other student of linguistics, semiotics, or whatever, we are yet left with cortical "areas," with inherited capacities, potentialities, mechanisms. Granted, one day we'll know more about the mechanistic details of this most basic aspect of ourselves—but is there *any* reason why our emotional development need be so decisively and insistently brought into the matter? If both Chomsky and Piaget shrink from trying to explain to us the "origins" of literary accomplishment, if they refuse to tackle our Sylvia Plaths, whose cognitive and linguistic attainments are the reasons we attend them, then why are our experts in psychopathology so eager, on such scant evidence, to be so consistently interpretive, if not outright convinced of their speculative accuracy?

Why, moreover, these days, do literary critics, never mind historians, embrace so willingly these psychological ruminations? Is Jung doing religious thinking, not to mention ordinary, faithful worshipers of God Almighty, any favor when he tells us that we have a "religious need"? A *noblesse oblige* slap on the back, perhaps! A twentieth-century sanctioning nod to those who might otherwise worry all too much that they'll be considered naive, superstitious! Or a tautological banality: the observer who watches some of us praying quite hard, or struggling long and painfully to figure out the meaning of this life, and concludes thereafter that—we are doing, we are impelled to do, just that! Similarly with art and artists, literature and writers: they have graced us over and over again with their sketches and paintings, their statements, epic or epigrammatic, their chronicles, brief or ever so extended—and in this century some of us say yes, they are sick, this way or that, or yes, they would be sick, one way or another, if they weren't writing, or yes, it is a particular vulnerability, a certain reparative tendency, that accounts for *Middlemarch* and *War and Peace* and *Lear* and *Hamlet* and all the other plays, novels, stories, poems. Maybe some of us are born (Nature's gift) with linguistic excellence. Maybe some of us have God-given visual or linguistic capacities—brains a touch more able to use words, or visualize and reproduce externally what is visualized. I don't know. No one does. Geneticists keep their silence and investigate. Neurobiologists do likewise. As do those psychologists who pursue the paths of our intellectual growth. I think that psychiatrists and psychoanalysts, some already struggling bravely . . . to straighten out their own house, ought for a good while to stop poking into homes next door, if not those located on an entirely different street. (pp. 207-11)

> *Robert Coles, "Commentary on 'Psychology and Literature'," in New Literary History, Vol. XII, No. 1, Autumn, 1980, pp. 207-11.*

Shoshana Felman

[*In the following excerpt, Felman comments on the relationship between psychoanalysis and literature.*]

"Love," says Rimbaud, "has to be reinvented." It is in much the same spirit that we would like here to reinvent the seemingly self-evident question of the mutual relationship between literature and psychoanalysis. We mean indeed to suggest that not only the approach to the question, but also, the very relationship between literature and psychoanalysis—the way in which they inform each other—has in itself to be reinvented.

Let us outline this suggestion in a series of programmatic remarks, the purpose of which would be to analyze and to put in question the apparently neutral connective word, the misleadingly innocent, colorless, meaningless copulative conjunction: *and,* in the title: "Literature and Psychoanalysis." What does the *and* really mean? What is its conventional sense, its traditional function, in the usual approach to the subject? In what way would we like to *displace* this function (to reinvent the "and"),—what would we like it to mean, how would we like it to *work,* in this issue?

Although "and" is grammatically defined as a "coordinate conjunction," in the context of the relationship between "literature and psychoanalysis" it is usually interpreted, paradoxically enough, as implying not so much a relation of coordination as one of *subordination,* a relation in which literature is submitted to the authority, to the prestige of psychoanalysis. While literature is considered as a body of *language*—to *be interpreted*—psychoanalysis is considered as a body of *knowledge,* whose competence is called upon *to interpret.* Psychoanalysis, in other words, occupies the place of a *subject,* literature that of an *object;* the relation of interpretation is structured as a relation of master to slave, according to the Hegelian definition: the dynamic encounter between the two areas is in effect, in Hegel's terms, a "fight for recognition," whose outcome is the sole recognition of the master—of (the truth of) psychoanalytical theory; literature's function, like that of the slave, is to *serve* precisely the *desire* of psychoanalytical theory—its desire for recognition; exercising its authority and *power* over the literary field, holding a discourse of masterly competence, psychoanalysis, in literature, thus seems to seek above all its own *satisfaction.*

Although such a relationship may indeed be satisfying to psychoanalytical theory, it often leaves dissatisfied the literary critic, the reader of a text, who feels that, in this frame of relationship, literature is in effect *not recognized* as such by psychoanalysis; that the psychoanalytical reading of literary texts precisely *misrecognizes* (overlooks, leaves out) their literary specificity; that literature could perhaps even be defined as that which remains in a text precisely *unaccounted for* by the traditional psychoanalytical approach to literature. In the literary critic's perspective, literature is a subject, not an object; it is therefore not simply a body of language to interpret, nor is psychoanalysis simply a body of knowledge, with which to interpret, since psychoanalysis itself is equally a body of language, and literature also a body of knowledge, even though the mode of that knowledge may be different from that of psychoanalysis. What the literary critic might thus wish, is to initiate a real exchange, to engage in a real *dialogue* between literature and psychoanalysis, as between two different bodies of language and between two different modes of knowledge. Such a dialogue has to take place outside of the master-slave pattern, which does not allow for true dialogue, being, under the banner of competence, a unilateral monologue of psychoanalysis *about* literature.

In an attempt to disrupt this monologue, master-slave structure, we would like to reverse the usual perspective, and to consider the relationship between psychoanalysis and literature *from the literary point of view*. We would not presuppose, as is often done, that the business of defining, of distinguishing and of relating literature and psychoanalysis belongs, as such, to psychoanalysis. We would like to suggest . . . that in much the same way as literature falls within the realm of psychoanalysis (within its competence and its knowledge), psychoanalysis itself falls within the realm of literature, and its specific logic and rhetoric. It is usually felt that psychoanalysis has much or all to teach us about literature, whereas literature has little or nothing to teach us about psychoanalysis. If only as a working hypothesis, we will discard this presupposition. Instead of literature being, as is usually the case, submitted to the authority and to the knowledge of psychoanalysis, psychoanalysis itself would then here be submitted to the literary perspective. This reversal of the perspective, however, does not intend to simply reverse the positions of master and slave in such a way that literature now would *take over* the place of the master, but rather its intention is to disrupt altogether the position of mastery as such, to try to avoid *both* terms of the alternative, to deconstruct the very structure of the *opposition*, mastery/slavery.

The odd status of what is called a "literary critic" indeed suffices to mix and shuffle the terms of the alternative. It could be argued that people who choose to analyze literature as a profession do so because they are unwilling or unable to choose between the role of the psychoanalyst (he or she who analyzes) and the role of the patient (that which is being analyzed). Literature enables them not to choose because of the following paradox: 1) the work of literary analysis resembles the work of the psychoanalyst; 2) the status of what is analyzed—the text—is, however, not that of a patient, but rather that of a master: we say of the author that he is a master; the text has for us authority—the very type of authority by which Jacques Lacan indeed defines the role of the psychoanalyst in the structure of transference. Like the psychoanalyst viewed by the patient, the text is viewed by us as "a subject presumed to know"—as the very place where meaning, and *knowledge* of meaning, reside. With respect to the text, the literary critic occupies thus at once the place of the psychoanalyst (in the relation of interpretation) *and* the place of the patient (in the relation of transference). Therefore, submitting psychoanalysis to the *literary* perspective would necessarily have a subversive effect on the clear-cut polarity through which psychoanalysis handles literature as its other, as the mere object of interpretation.

There is another point on which literature can inform psychoanalytical discourse in such a way as to deconstruct the temptation of the master's position and the master-slave pattern. There is one crucial feature which is constitutive of literature but is essentially lacking in psychoanalytical theory, and indeed in theory as such: irony. Since irony precisely consists in dragging authority as such into a scene which it cannot master, of which it is *not aware* and which, for that very reason, is the scene of its own self-destruction, literature, by virtue of its ironic force, fundamentally deconstructs the fantasy of authority in the same way, and for the same reasons, that psychoanalysis deconstructs the authority of the fantasy—its claim to belief and

to power as the sole window through which we behold and perceive reality, as the sole window through which reality can indeed reach our grasp, enter into our consciousness. Psychoanalysis tells us that the fantasy is a fiction, and that consciousness is itself, in a sense, a fantasy-effect. In the same way, literature tells us that authority is a *language effect,* the product or the creation of its own *rhetorical* power: that authority is the *power of fiction;* that authority, therefore, is likewise a fiction.

The primacy granted here to the literary point of view would therefore not simply mean that literature, in its turn, would claim—as has been done—priority and authority over psychoanalysis as its influential *historical source,* as its ancestor or its predecessor in the discovery of the unconscious; but rather, the reversal of the usual perspective is here intended to displace the whole pattern of the relationship between literature and psychoanalysis from a structure of rival claims to authority and to priority to the scene of this structure's deconstruction.

In view of this shift of emphasis, the traditional method of *application* of psychoanalysis to literature would here be in principle ruled out. The notion of *application* would be replaced by the radically different notion of *implication:* bringing analytical questions to bear upon literary questions, *involving* psychoanalysis in the scene of literary analysis, the interpreter's role would here be, not to *apply* to the text an acquired science, a preconceived knowledge, but to act as a go-between, to *generate implications* between literature and psychoanalysis—to explore, bring to light and articulate the various (indirect) ways in which the two domains do indeed *implicate each other,* each one finding itself enlightened, informed, but also affected, displaced, by the other.

In its etymological sense, "implication" means "being folded within" (Latin: im-plicare = in + fold): it indicates, between two terms, a spatial relation of *interiority.* Application, on the other hand, is based on the presumption of a relation of exteriority; a presumption that, in the case of literature and psychoanalysis, can be shown to be a deceptive one. From the very beginning, indeed, literature has been for psychoanalysis not only a contiguous field of external verification in which to test its hypotheses and to confirm its findings, but also the constitutive texture of its *conceptual* framework, of its theoretical body. The key concepts of psychoanalysis are references to literature, using literary *"proper"* names—names of fictional characters (Oedipus complex, Narcissism) or of historical authors (masochism, sadism). Literature, in other words, is the language which psychoanalysis uses in order to *speak of itself,* in order to *name itself.* Literature is therefore not simply *outside* psychoanalysis, since it motivates and *inhabits* the very names of its concepts, since it is the *inherent reference* by which psychoanalysis names its findings.

However, the relation of *interiority* conveyed by the interimplication of literature and psychoanalysis is by no means a simple one. Since literature and psychoanalysis are *different* from each other, but, at the same time, they are also "enfolded within" each other, since they are, as it were, at the same time outside and inside each other, we might say that they compromise, each in its turn, the interiority of the other. The cultural division, in other words, of scholarly "disciplines" of research is by no means a natural geography: there are no *natural* boundaries between literature and psychoanalysis, which clearly define and distinguish them; the border between them is undecidable since they are really *traversed* by each other.

Each is thus a potential threat to the interiority of the other, since each is contained in the other as its *otherness-to-itself,* its *unconscious.* As the unconscious traverses consciousness, a theoretical body of thought always is traversed by its own unconscious, its own "unthought," of which it is not aware, but which it contains in itself as the very conditions of its disruption, as the possibility of its own self-subversion. We would like to suggest that, in the same way that psychoanalysis points to the unconscious of literature, *literature, in its turn, is the unconscious of psychoanalysis;* that the unthought-out shadow in psychoanalytical *theory* is precisely its own involvement with literature; that literature *in* psychoanalysis functions precisely as its *"unthought"*: as the condition of possibility *and* the self-subversive blind spot of psychoanalytical *thought.* (pp. 5-10)

Shoshana Felman, "To Open the Question," in Yale French Studies, *Nos. 55-56, 1977, pp. 1-10.*

FREUD ON LITERATURE

Sigmund Freud

[*An Austrian neurologist, Freud was the founder of psychoanalysis, which is both a comprehensive theory for explaining human development and behavior and a method for treating psychopathology. Freud believed that early experiences are critical in determining personality and that normal and abnormal behavior are parts of a continuum rather than qualitatively different. An extremely complex body of thought, psychoanalysis includes interrelated theories which define the unconscious (primitive impulses and repressed thoughts), sequential stages of human psychosexual development (oral, anal, phallic, and genital), and the structure of personality (id, ego, and superego). Freud was attacked by contemporaries for his insistence on infantile sexuality and has been criticized by modern commentators for being culturally and historically bound and for inadequately explaining women's development. Nevertheless, Freud's ideas revolutionized the theory and practice of psychology and significantly influenced other disciplines in both the humanities and social sciences. With Karl Marx, Friedrich Nietzsche, and Albert Einstein, Freud is one of the most important thinkers of modern times. A prolific author, Freud published works in which he outlined central concepts of his thought, presented case studies of individual patients, and applied his ideas to other fields, including art and literature. In the following essay, he compares the literary process with daydreaming and with children's play.*]

We laymen have always been intensely curious to know—like the Cardinal who put a similar question to Ariosto—from what sources that strange being, the creative writer, draws his material, and how he manages to make such an impression on us with it and to arouse in us emotions of which, perhaps, we had not even thought ourselves capable. Our interest is only heightened the more by the fact that, if we ask him, the writer himself gives us no explanation, or none that is satisfactory; and it is not at all weakened by our knowledge that not even the clearest insight into the determinants of his choice of material and into the nature of the art of creating imaginative form will ever help to make creative writers of *us.*

If we could at least discover in ourselves or in people like ourselves an activity which was in some way akin to creative writing! An examination of it would then give us a hope of obtaining the beginnings of an explanation of the creative work of writers. And, indeed, there is some prospect of this being possible. After all, creative writers themselves like to lessen the distance between their kind and the common run of humanity; they so often assure us that every man is a poet at heart and that the last poet will not perish till the last man does.

Should we not look for the first traces of imaginative activity as early as in childhood? The child's best-loved and most intense occupation is with his play or games. Might we not say that every child at play behaves like a creative writer, in that he creates a world of his own, or, rather, re-arranges the things of his world in a new way which pleases him? It would be wrong to think he does not take that world seriously; on the contrary, he takes his play very seriously and he expends large amounts of emotion on it. The opposite of play is not what is serious but what is real. In spite of all the emotion with which he cathects his world of play, the child distinguishes it quite well from reality; and he likes to link his imagined objects and situations to the tangible and visible things of the real world. This linking is all that differentiates the child's 'play' from 'phantasying'.

The creative writer does the same as the child at play. He creates a world of phantasy which he takes very seriously—that is, which he invests with large amounts of emotion—while separating it sharply from reality. Language has preserved this relationship between children's play and poetic creation. It gives [in German] the name of '*Spiel*' ('play') to those forms of imaginative writing which require to be linked to tangible objects and which are capable of representation. It speaks of a '*Lustspiel*' or '*Trauerspiel*' ('comedy' or 'tragedy': literally, 'pleasure play' or 'mourning play') and describes those who carry out the representation as '*Schauspieler*' ('players': literally 'show-players'). The unreality of the writer's imaginative world, however, has very important consequences for the technique of his art; for many things which, if they were real, could give no enjoyment, can do so in the play of phantasy, and many excitements which, in themselves, are actually distressing, can become a source of pleasure for the hearers and spectators at the performance of a writer's work.

There is another consideration for the sake of which we will dwell a moment longer on this contrast between reality and play. When the child has grown up and has ceased to play, and after he has been labouring for decades to envisage the realities of life with proper seriousness, he may one day find himself in a mental situation which once more undoes the contrast between play and reality. As an adult he can look back on the intense seriousness with which he once carried on his games in childhood; and, by equating his ostensibly serious occupations of to-day with his childhood games, he can throw off the too heavy burden imposed on him by life and win the high yield of pleasure afforded by *humour*.

As people grow up, then, they cease to play, and they seem to give up the yield of pleasure which they gained from playing. But whoever understands the human mind knows that hardly anything is harder for a man than to give up a pleasure which he has once experienced. Actually, we can never give anything up; we only exchange one thing for another. What appears to be a renunciation is really the formation of a substitute or surrogate. In the same way, the growing child, when he stops playing, gives up nothing but the link with real objects; instead of *playing,* he now *phantasies*. He builds castles in the air and creates what are called *daydreams*. I believe that most people construct phantasies at times in their lives. This is a fact which has long been overlooked and whose importance has therefore not been sufficiently appreciated.

People's phantasies are less easy to observe than the play of children. The child, it is true, plays by himself or forms a closed psychical system with other children for the purposes of a game; but even though he may not play his game in front of the grown-ups, he does not, on the other hand, conceal it from them. The adult, on the contrary, is ashamed of his phantasies and hides them from other people. He cherishes his phantasies as his most intimate possessions, and as a rule he would rather confess his misdeeds than tell anyone his phantasies. It may come about that for that reason he believes he is the only person who invents such phantasies and has no idea that creations of this kind are widespread among other people. This difference in the behaviour of a person who plays and a person who phantasies is accounted for by the motives of these two activities, which are nevertheless adjuncts to each other.

A child's play is determined by wishes: in point of fact by a single wish—one that helps in his upbringing—the wish to be big and grown up. He is always playing at being 'grown up', and in his games he imitates what he knows about the lives of his elders. He has no reason to conceal this wish. With the adult, the case is different. On the one hand, he knows that he is expected not to go on playing or phantasying any longer, but to act in the real world; on the other hand, some of the wishes which give rise to his phantasies are of a kind which it is essential to conceal. Thus he is ashamed of his phantasies as being childish and as being unpermissible.

But, you will ask, if people make such a mystery of their phantasying, how is it that we know such a lot about it? Well, there is a class of human beings upon whom, not a god, indeed, but a stern goddess—Necessity—has allotted the task of telling what they suffer and what things give them happiness. These are the victims of nervous illness, who are obliged to tell their phantasies, among other things, to the doctor by whom they expect to be cured by mental treatment. This is our best source of knowledge, and we have since found good reason to suppose that our patients tell us nothing that we might not also hear from healthy people.

Let us now make ourselves acquainted with a few of the characteristics of phantasying. We may lay it down that a happy person never phantasies, only an unsatisfied one. The motive forces of phantasies are unsatisfied wishes, and every single phantasy is the fulfilment of a wish, a correction of unsatisfying reality. These motivating wishes vary according to the sex, character and circumstances of the person who is having the phantasy; but they fall naturally into two main groups. They are either ambitious wishes, which serve to elevate the subject's personality; or they are erotic ones. In young women the erotic wishes predominate almost exclusively, for their ambition is as a rule absorbed by erotic trends. In young men egoistic and ambitious wishes come to the fore clearly enough alongside of erotic ones. But we will not lay stress on the opposition between the two trends; we would rather emphasize the fact that they are often united. Just as, in many altarpieces, the portrait of the donor is to be seen in a corner of the picture, so, in the majority of ambitious phantasies, we can discover in some corner or other the lady for whom the creator of the phantasy performs all his heroic deeds and at whose feet all his triumphs are laid. Here, as you see, there are strong enough motives for concealment; the well-brought-up young woman is only allowed a minimum of erotic desire, and the young man has to learn to suppress the excess of self-regard which he brings with him from the spoilt days of his childhood, so that he may find his place in a society which is full of other individuals making equally strong demands.

We must not suppose that the products of this imaginative activity—the various phantasies, castles in the air and daydreams—are stereotyped or unalterable. On the contrary, they fit themselves in to the subject's shifting impressions of life, change with every change in his situation, and receive from every fresh active impression what might be called a 'date-mark'. The relation of a phantasy to time is in general very important. We may say that it hovers, as it were, between three times—the three moments of time which our ideation involves. Mental work is linked to some current impression, some provoking occasion in the present which has been able to arouse one of the subject's major wishes. From there it harks back to a memory of an earlier experience (usually an infantile one) in which this wish was fulfilled; and it now creates a situation relating to the future which represents a fulfilment of the wish. What it thus creates is a day-dream or phantasy, which carries about it traces of its origin from the occasion which provoked it and from the memory. Thus past, present and future are strung together, as it were, on the thread of the wish that runs through them.

A very ordinary example may serve to make what I have said clear. Let us take the case of a poor orphan boy to whom you have given the address of some employer where he may perhaps find a job. On his way there he may indulge in a day-dream appropriate to the situation from which it arises. The content of his phantasy will perhaps be something like this. He is given a job, finds favour with his new employer, makes himself indispensable in the business, is taken into his employer's family, marries the charming young daughter of the house, and then himself becomes a director of the business, first as his employer's partner and then as his successor. In this phantasy, the dreamer has regained what he possessed in his happy childhood—the protecting house, the loving parents and the first objects of his affectionate feelings. You will see from this example the way in which the wish makes use of an occasion in the present to construct, on the pattern of the past, a picture of the future.

There is a great deal more that could be said about phantasies; but I will only allude as briefly as possible to certain points. If phantasies become over-luxuriant and over-powerful, the conditions are laid for an onset of neurosis or psychosis. Phantasies, moreover, are the immediate mental precursors of the distressing symptoms complained of by our patients. Here a broad by-path branches off into pathology.

I cannot pass over the relation of phantasies to dreams. Our dreams at night are nothing else than phantasies like these, as we can demonstrate from the interpretation of dreams. Language, in its unrivalled wisdom, long ago decided the question of the essential nature of dreams by giving the name of 'day-dreams' to the airy creations of phantasy. If the meaning of our dreams usually remains obscure to us in spite of this pointer, it is because of the circumstance that at night there also arise in us wishes of which we are ashamed; these we must conceal from ourselves, and they have consequently been repressed, pushed into the unconscious. Repressed wishes of this sort and their derivatives are only allowed to come to expression in a very distorted form. When scientific work had succeeded in elucidating this factor of *dream-distortion,* it was no longer difficult to recognize that night-dreams are wish-fulfilments in just the same way as day-dreams—the phantasies which we all know so well.

So much for phantasies. And now for the creative writer. May we really attempt to compare the imaginative writer with the 'dreamer in broad daylight', and his creations with day-dreams? Here we must begin by making an initial distinction. We must separate writers who, like the ancient authors of epics and tragedies, take over their material ready-made, from writers who seem to originate their own material. We will keep to the latter kind, and, for the purposes of our comparison, we will choose not the writers most highly esteemed by the critics, but the less pretentious authors of novels, romances and short stories, who nevertheless have the widest and most eager circle of readers of both sexes. One feature above all cannot fail to strike us about the creations of these story-writers: each of them has a hero who is the centre of interest, for whom the writer tries to win our sympathy by every possible means and whom he seems to place under the protection of a special Providence. If, at the end of one chapter of my story, I leave the hero unconscious and bleeding from severe wounds, I am sure to find him at the beginning of the next being carefully nursed and on the way to recovery; and if the first volume closes with the ship he is in going down in a storm at sea, I am certain, at the opening of the second volume, to read of his miraculous rescue—a rescue without which the story could not proceed. The feeling of security with which I follow the hero through his perilous adventures is the same as the feeling with which a hero in real life throws himself into the water to save a drowning man or exposes himself to the enemy's fire in order to storm a battery. It is the true heroic feeling, which one of our best writers has expressed in an inimitable phrase: 'Nothing can happen to *me*!' It seems to me, however, that through this revealing characteristic of invulnerability we can immediately recognize His Majesty the Ego, the hero alike of every day-dream and of every story.

Other typical features of these egocentric stories point to the same kinship. The fact that all the women in the novel invariably fall in love with the hero can hardly be looked on as a portrayal of reality, but it is easily understood as a necessary constituent of a day-dream. The same is true of the fact that the other characters in the story are sharply divided into good and bad, in defiance of the variety of human characters that are to be observed in real life. The 'good' ones are the helpers, while the 'bad' ones are the enemies and rivals, of the ego which has become the hero of the story.

We are perfectly aware that very many imaginative writings are far removed from the model of the naïve day-dream; and yet I cannot suppress the suspicion that even the most extreme deviations from that model could be linked with it through an uninterrupted series of transitional cases. It has struck me that in many of what are known as 'psychological' novels only one person—once again the hero—is described from within. The author sits inside his mind, as it were, and looks at the other characters from outside. The psychological novel in general no doubt owes its special nature to the inclination of the modern writer to split up his ego, by self-observation, into many part-egos, and, in consequence, to personify the conflicting currents of his own mental life in several heroes. Certain novels, which might be described as 'eccentric', seem to stand in quite special contrast to the type of the day-dream. In these, the person who is introduced as the hero plays only a very small active part; he sees the actions and sufferings of other people pass before him like a spectator. Many of Zola's later works belong to this category. But I must point out that the psychological analysis of individuals who are not creative writers, and who diverge in some respects from the so-called norm, has shown us analogous variations of the day-dream, in which the ego contents itself with the role of spectator.

If our comparison of the imaginative writer with the day-dreamer, and of poetical creation with the day-dream, is to be of any value, it must, above all, show itself in some way or other fruitful. Let us, for instance, try to apply to these authors' works the thesis we laid down earlier concerning the relation between phantasy and the three periods of time and the wish which runs through them; and, with its help, let us try to study the connections that exist between the life of the writer and his works. No one has known, as a rule, what expectations to frame in approaching this problem; and often the connection has been thought of in much too simple terms. In the light of the insight we have gained from phantasies, we ought to expect the following state of affairs. A strong experience in the present awakens in the creative writer a memory of an earlier experience (usually belonging to his childhood) from which there now proceeds a wish which finds its fulfilment in the creative work. The work itself exhibits elements of the recent provoking occasion as well as of the old memory.

Do not be alarmed at the complexity of this formula. I suspect that in fact it will prove to be too exiguous a pattern. Nevertheless, it may contain a first approach to the true state of affairs; and, from some experiments I have made, I am inclined to think that this way of looking at creative writings may turn out not unfruitful. You will not forget that the stress it lays on childhood memories in the writer's life—a stress which may perhaps seem puzzling—is ultimately derived from the assumption that a piece of creative writing, like a day-dream, is a continuation of, and a substitute for, what was once the play of childhood.

We must not neglect, however, to go back to the kind of imaginative works which we have to recognize, not as original creations, but as the re-fashioning of ready-made and familiar material. Even here, the writer keeps a certain amount of independence, which can express itself in the choice of material and in changes in it which are often quite extensive. In so far as the material is already at hand, however, it is derived from the popular treasure-house of myths, legends and fairy tales. The study of constructions of folk-psychology such as these is far from being complete, but it is extremely probable that myths, for instance, are distorted vestiges of the wishful phantasies of whole nations, the *secular dreams* of youthful humanity.

You will say that, although I have put the creative writer first in the title of my paper, I have told you far less about him than about phantasies. I am aware of that, and I must try to excuse it by pointing to the present state of our knowledge. All I have been able to do is to throw out some encouragements and suggestions which, starting from the study of phantasies, lead on to the problem of the writer's choice of his literary material. As for the other problem— by what means the creative writer achieves the emotional effects in us that are aroused by his creations—we have as yet not touched on it at all. But I should like at least to

point out to you the path that leads from our discussion of phantasies to the problems of poetical effects.

You will remember how I have said that the day-dreamer carefully conceals his phantasies from other people because he feels he has reasons for being ashamed of them. I should now add that even if he were to communicate them to us he could give us no pleasure by his disclosures. Such phantasies, when we learn them, repel us or at least leave us cold. But when a creative writer presents his plays to us or tells us what we are inclined to take to be his personal day-dreams, we experience a great pleasure, and one which probably arises from the confluence of many sources. How the writer accomplishes this is his innermost secret; the essential *ars poetica* lies in the technique of overcoming the feeling of repulsion in us which is undoubtedly connected with the barriers that rise between each single ego and the others. We can guess two of the methods used by this technique. The writer softens the character of his egoistic day-dreams by altering and disguising it, and he bribes us by the purely formal—that is, aesthetic—yield of pleasure which he offers us in the presentation of his phantasies. We give the name of an *incentive bonus,* or a *fore-pleasure,* to a yield of pleasure such as this, which is offered to us so as to make possible the release of still greater pleasure arising from deeper psychical sources. In my opinion, all the aesthetic pleasure which a creative writer affords us has the character of a fore-pleasure of this kind, and our actual enjoyment of an imaginative work proceeds from a liberation of tensions in our minds. It may even be that not a little of this effect is due to the writer's enabling us thenceforward to enjoy our own day-dreams without self-reproach or shame. This brings us to the threshold of new, interesting and complicated enquiries; but also, at least for the moment, to the end of our discussion. (pp. 143-53)

Sigmund Freud, "Creative Writers and Day-Dreaming," in The Standard Edition of the Complete Psychological Works of Sigmund Freud: Jensen's "Gradiva" and Other Works, Vol. IX, *edited and translated by James Strachey, in collaboration with Anna Freud, assisted by Alix Strachey and Alan Tyson, The Hogarth Press, 1959, pp. 141-153.*

Sigmund Freud

[*In the following excerpt, Freud offers psychoanalytical interpretations of Sophocles's* Oedipus Rex *and Shakespeare's* Hamlet.]

If the *Oedipus Rex* is capable of moving a modern reader or playgoer no less powerfully than it moved the contemporary Greeks, the only possible explanation is that the effect of the Greek tragedy does not depend upon the conflict between fate and human will, but upon the peculiar nature of the material by which this conflict is revealed. There must be a voice within us which is prepared to acknowledge the compelling power of fate in the *Oedipus,* while we are able to condemn the situations occurring in *Die Ahnfrau* or other tragedies of fate as arbitrary inventions. And there actually is a motive in the story of King Oedipus which explains the verdict of this inner voice. His fate moves us only because it might have been our own, because the oracle laid upon us before our birth the very

Sigmund Freud in middle age.

curse which rested upon him. It may be that we were all destined to direct our first sexual impulses toward our mothers, and our first impulses of hatred and violence toward our fathers; our dreams convince us that we were. King Oedipus, who slew his father Laius and wedded his mother Jocasta, is nothing more or less than a wish-fulfilment—the fulfilment of the wish of our childhood. But we, more fortunate than he, in so far as we have not become psychoneurotics, have since our childhood succeeded in withdrawing our sexual impulses from our mothers, and in forgetting our jealousy of our fathers. We recoil from the person for whom this primitive wish of our childhood has been fulfilled with all the force of the repression which these wishes have undergone in our minds since childhood. As the poet brings the guilt of Oedipus to light by his investigation, he forces us to become aware of our own inner selves, in which the same impulses are still extant, even though they are suppressed. The antithesis with which the chorus departs:—

> . . . Behold, this is Oedipus,
> Who unravelled the great riddle, and was first in power,
> Whose fortune all the townsmen praised and envied;
> See in what dread adversity he sank!

—this admonition touches us and our own pride, us who since the years of our childhood have grown so wise and so powerful in our own estimation. Like Oedipus, we live in ignorance of the desires that offend morality, the desires that nature has forced upon us and after their unveiling we may well prefer to avert our gaze from the scenes of our childhood.

In the very text of Sophocles' tragedy there is an unmistakable reference to the fact that the Oedipus legend had its source in dream-material of immemorial antiquity, the content of which was the painful disturbance of the child's relations to its parents caused by the first impulses of sexuality. Jocasta comforts Oedipus—who is not yet enlightened, but is troubled by the recollection of the oracle—by an allusion to a dream which is often dreamed, though it cannot, in her opinion, mean anything:—

> For many a man hath seen himself in dreams
> His mother's mate, but he who gives no heed
> To suchlike matters bears the easier life.

The dream of having sexual intercourse with one's mother was as common then as it is to-day with many people, who tell it with indignation and astonishment. As may well be imagined, it is the key to the tragedy and the complement to the dream of the death of the father. The Oedipus fable is the reaction of fantasy to these two typical dreams, and just as such a dream, when occurring to an adult, is experienced with feelings of aversion, so the content of the fable must include terror and self-chastisement. The form which it subsequently assumed was the result of an uncomprehending secondary elaboration of the material, which sought to make it serve a theological intention. The attempt to reconcile divine omnipotence with human responsibility must, of course, fail with this material as with any other.

Another of the great poetic tragedies, Shakespeare's *Hamlet,* is rooted in the same soil as *Oedipus Rex.* But the whole difference in the psychic life of the two widely separated periods of civilization, and the progress, during the course of time, of repression in the emotional life of hu-

manity, is manifested in the differing treatment of the same material. In *Oedipus Rex* the basic wish-phantasy of the child is brought to light and realized as it is in dreams; in *Hamlet* it remains repressed, and we learn of its existence—as we discover the relevant facts in a neurosis—only through the inhibitory effects which proceed from it. In the more modern drama, the curious fact that it is possible to remain in complete uncertainty as to the character of the hero has proved to be quite consistent with the overpowering effect of the tragedy. The play is based upon Hamlet's hesitation in accomplishing the task of revenge assigned to him; the text does not give the cause or the motive of this hesitation, nor have the manifold attempts at interpretation succeeded in doing so. According to the still prevailing conception, a conception for which Goethe was first responsible, Hamlet represents the type of man whose active energy is paralysed by excessive intellectual activity: "Sicklied o'er with the pale cast of thought." According to another conception, the poet has endeavoured to portray a morbid, irresolute character, on the verge of neurasthenia. The plot of the drama, however, shows us that Hamlet is by no means intended to appear as a character wholly incapable of action. On two separate occasions we see him assert himself: once in a sudden outburst of rage, when he stabs the eavesdropper behind the arras, and on the other occasion when he deliberately, and even craftily, with the complete unscrupulousness of a prince of the Renaissance, sends the two courtiers to the death which was intended for himself. What is it, then, that inhibits him in accomplishing the task which his father's ghost has laid upon him? Here the explanation offers itself that it is the peculiar nature of this task. Hamlet is able to do anything but take vengeance upon the man who did away with his father and has taken his father's place with his mother—the man who shows him in realization the repressed desires of his own childhood. The loathing which should have driven him to revenge is thus replaced by self-reproach, by conscientious scruples, which tell him that he himself is no better than the murderer whom he is required to punish. I have here translated into consciousness what had to remain unconscious in the mind of the hero; if anyone wishes to call Hamlet an hysterical subject I cannot but admit that this is the deduction to be drawn from my interpretation. The sexual aversion which Hamlet expresses in conversation with Ophelia is perfectly consistent with this deduction—the same sexual aversion which during the next few years was increasingly to take possession of the poet's soul, until it found its supreme utterance in *Timon of Athens.* It can, of course, be only the poet's own psychology with which we are confronted in *Hamlet;* and in a work on Shakespeare by Georg Brandes (1896) I find the statement that the drama was composed immediately after the death of Shakespeare's father (1601)—that is to say, when he was still mourning his loss, and during a revival, as we may fairly assume, of his own childish feelings in respect of his father. It is known, too, that Shakespeare's son, who died in childhood, bore the name of Hamnet (identical with Hamlet). Just as *Hamlet* treats of the relation of the son to his parents, so *Macbeth,* which was written about the same period, is based upon the theme of childlessness. Just as all neurotic symptoms, like dreams themselves, are capable of hyper-interpretation, and even require such hyper-interpretation before they become perfectly intelligible, so every genuine poetical creation must have proceeded from more than one motive, more than one impulse in the mind of the poet, and must admit of more than one interpretation. I have here attempted to interpret only the deepest stratum of impulses in the mind of the creative poet. (pp. 308-11)

> Sigmund Freud, "The Material and Sources of Dreams," in The Basic Writings of Sigmund Freud, edited and translated by A. A. Brill, The Modern Library, 1938, pp. 238-318.

PSYCHOANALYTIC VIEWS OF THE LITERARY PROCESS

Hanna Segal

[*Born in Poland, Segal is an English psychoanalyst who has written numerous articles and several books on Melanie Klein, a prominent theorist of the object-relations school of psychoanalysis. In the following excerpt, Segal uses psychoanalytic concepts to differentiate successful from unsuccessful artists.*]

The task of the artist lies in the creation of a world of his own.

In his introduction to the second Post-Impressionist Exhibition, Roger Fry writes: "Now these artists do not seek to give what can, after all, be but a pale reflex of actual appearance, but to arouse a conviction of a new and different reality. They do not seek to imitate life but to find an equivalent for life." What Roger Fry says of post-impressionists undoubtedly applies to all genuine art. One of the great differences between art and imitation or a superficial "pretty" achievement is that neither the imitation nor the "pretty" production ever achieves this creation of an entirely new reality.

Every creative artist produces a world of his own. Even when he believes himself to be a complete realist and sets himself the task of faithfully reproducing the external world, he, in fact, only uses elements of the existing external world to create with them a reality of his own. When, for instance, two realistic writers like Zola and Flaubert try to portray life in the same country, and very nearly at the same time, the two worlds they show us differ from each other as widely as if they were the most phantastic creations of surrealist poets. If two great painters paint the same landscape we have two different worlds.

> . . . . and dream
> Of waves, flowers, clouds, woods,
> Rocks, and all that we
> Read in their smiles
> And call reality.
>
> (Shelley)

How does this creation come about? Of all artists the one who gives us the fullest description of the creative process is Marcel Proust: a description based on years of self-observation and the fruit of an amazing insight. According to Proust, an artist is compelled to create by his need to recover his lost past. But a purely intellectual memory of the past, even when it is available, is emotionally valueless and dead. A real remembrance sometimes comes about unexpectedly by chance association. The flavour of a cake brings back to his mind a fragment of his childhood with full emotional vividness. Stumbling over a stone revives a recollection of a holiday in Venice which before he had vainly tried to recapture. For years he tries in vain to remember and re-create in his mind a living picture of his beloved grandmother. But only a chance association revives her picture and at last enables him to remember her, and to experience his loss and mourn her. He calls these fleeting associations: "intermittences du cœur" ["intermittences of the heart"], but he says that such memories come and then disappear again, so that the past remains elusive. To capture them, to give them permanent life, to integrate them with the rest of his life, he must create a work of art. "Il fallait . . . faire sortir de la pénombre ce que j'avais senti, de le reconvertir en un équivalent spirituel. Or ce moyen qui me paraissait le seul, qu'était-ce autre chose que de créer une œuvre d'art?" ("I had to recapture from the shade that which I had felt, to reconvert it into its psychic equivalent. But the way to do it, the only one I could see, what was it—but to create a work of art?")

Through the many volumes of his work the past is being recaptured; all his lost, destroyed, and loved objects are being brought back to life: his parents, his grandmother, his beloved Albertine. "Et certes il n'y aurait pas qu'Albertine, que ma grandmère, mais bien d'autres encore dont j'aurais pu assimiler une parole, un regard, mais en tant que créatures individuelles je ne m'en rappellais plus; un livre est un grand cimetière où sur la plupart des tombes on ne peut plus lire les noms effacés." ("And indeed it was not only Albertine, not only my grandmother, but many others still from whom I might well have assimilated a gesture or a world, but whom I could not even remember as distinct persons. A book is a vast graveyard where on most of the tombstones one can read no more the faded names.")

And, according to Proust, it is only the lost past and the lost or dead object that can be made into a work of art. He makes the painter, Elstir, say: "On ne peut récréer ce qu'on aime qu'en le renonçant." ("It is only by renouncing that one can re-create what one loves.") It is only when the loss has been acknowledged and the mourning experienced that re-creation can take place.

In the last volume of his work Proust describes how at last he decided to sacrifice the rest of his life to writing. He came back after a long absence to seek his old friends at a party, and all of them appeared to him as ruins of the real people he knew—useless, ridiculous, ill, on the threshold of death. Others, he found, had died long ago. And on realizing the destruction of a whole world that had been his he decides to write, to sacrifice himself to the re-creation of the dying and the dead. By virtue of his art he can give his objects an eternal life in his work. And since they represent his internal world too, if he can do that, he himself will no longer be afraid of death.

What Proust describes corresponds to a situation of mourning: he sees that his loved objects are dying or dead. Writing a book is for him like the work of mourning in that gradually the external objects are given up, they are reinstated in the ego, and re-created in the book. In her paper "Mourning and its Relation to Manic-Depressive

States", Melanie Klein has shown how mourning in grown-up life is a re-living of the early depressive anxieties; not only is the present object in the external world felt to be lost, but also the early objects, the parents; and they are lost as internal objects as well as in the external world. In the process of mourning it is these earliest objects which are lost again, and then re-created. Proust describes how this mourning leads to a wish to re-create the lost world.

I have quoted Proust at length because he reveals such an acute awareness of what I believe is present in the unconscious of all artists: namely, that all creation is really a re-creation of a once loved and once whole, but now lost and ruined object, a ruined internal world and self. It is when the world within us is destroyed, when it is dead and loveless, when our loved ones are in fragments, and we ourselves in helpless despair—it is then that we must re-create our world anew, reassemble the pieces, infuse life into dead fragments, re-create life.

If the wish to create is rooted in the depressive position and the capacity to create depends on a successful working through it, it would follow that the inability to acknowledge and overcome depressive anxiety must lead to inhibitions in artistic expression.

I should now like to give a few clinical examples from artists who have been inhibited in their creative activities by neurosis, and I shall try to show that in them it was the inability to work through their depressive anxieties which led to inhibitions of artistic activity, or to the production of an unsuccessful artistic product.

Case A is a young girl with a definite gift for painting. An acute rivalry with her mother made her give up painting in her early teens. After some analysis she started to paint again and was working as a decorative artist. She did decorative handicraft work in preference to what she sometimes called "real painting", and this was because she knew that, though correct, neat, and pretty, her work failed to be moving and æsthetically significant. In her manic way she usually denied that this caused her any concern. At the time when I was trying to interpret her unconscious sadistic attacks on her father, the internalization of her mutilated and destroyed father and the resulting depression, she told me the following dream: "She saw a picture in a shop which represented a wounded man lying alone and desolate in a dark forest. She felt quite overwhelmed with emotion and admiration for this picture; she thought it represented the actual essence of life; if she could only paint like that she would be a really great painter."

It soon appeared that the meaning of the dream was that if she could only acknowledge her depression about the wounding and destruction of her father, she would then be able to express it in her painting and would achieve real art. In fact, however, it was impossible for her to do this, since the unusual strength of her sadism and her resulting despair, and her small capacity to tolerate depression, led to its manic denial and to a constant make-believe that all was well with the world. In her dream she confirmed my interpretation about the attack on her father, but she did more than this. Her dream showed something that had not been in any way interpreted or indicated by me: namely, the effect on her painting of her persistent denial of depres-

sion. In relation to her painting the denial of the depth and seriousness of her depressive feelings produced the effect of superficiality and prettiness in whatever she chose to do—the dead father is completely denied and no ugliness or conflict is ever allowed to disturb the neat and correct form of her work.

Case B is that of a journalist aged a little over thirty, whose ambition was to be a writer, and who suffered, among other symptoms, from an ever-increasing inhibition in creative writing. An important feature of his character was a tendency to regress from the depressive to the paranoid position. The following dream illustrates his problem: "He found himself in a room with Goebbels, Goering, and some other Nazis. He was aware that these men were completely amoral. He knew that they were going to poison him and therefore he tried to make a bargain with them; he suggested that it would be a good thing for them to let him live, since he was a journalist and could write about them and make them live for a time after their death. But this stratagem failed and he knew that he would finally be poisoned."

An important factor in this patient's psychology was his introjection of an extremely bad father-figure who was then blamed for all that the patient did. And one of the results was an unbearable feeling of being internally persecuted by this bad internal father-figure, which was sometimes expressed in hypochondriacal symptoms. He tried to defend himself against it by placating and serving this bad internal figure. He was often driven to do things that he disapproved of and disliked. In the dream he showed how it interfered with his writing: to avoid death at the hands of internal persecutors he has to write for them to keep them immortal; but there is, of course, no real wish to keep such bad figures alive, and consequently he was inhibited in his capacity for writing. He often complained, too, that he had no style of his own; in his associations to the dream it became clear that he had to write not only for the benefit of the poisoners, and to serve their purposes, but also at their command. Thus the style of his writing belonged to the internal paternal figure. The case, I think, resembles one described by Paula Heimann [in "A Contribution to the Problem of Sublimation and its Relation to Process of Internalization", *International Journal of Psychoanalysis,* Vol. XXIII, Part I, 1942]. A patient of hers drew a sketch with which she was very displeased; the style was not her own, it was Victorian. It appeared clearly during the session that it was the result of a quarrel with another woman who stood for her mother. After the quarrel the painter had introjected her as a bad and revengeful mother, and, through guilt and fear, she had to submit to this bad internal figure; it was really the Victorian mother who had dictated the painting.

Paula Heimann described this example of an acute impairment of an already established sublimation. In my patient his submission to a very bad internal figure was a chronic situation preventing him from achieving any internal freedom to create. Moreover, although he was trying to appease his persecutors, as a secondary defence against them, he was basically fixed in the paranoid position and returned to it whenever depressive feelings were aroused, so that his love and reparative impulses could not become fully active.

All the patients mentioned suffered from sexual maladjustments as well as creative inhibitions. There is clearly a genital aspect of artistic creation which is of paramount importance. Creating a work of art is a psychic equivalent of procreation. It is a genital bisexual activity necessitating a good identification with the father who gives, and the mother who receives and bears, the child. The ability to deal with the depressive position, however, is the precondition of both genital and artistic maturity. If the parents are felt to be so completely destroyed that there is no hope of ever re-creating them, a successful identification is not possible, and neither can the genital position be maintained nor the sublimation in art develop.

This relation between feelings of depression and genital and artistic problems is clearly shown by another patient of mine. C, a man of thirty-five, was a really gifted artist, but at the same time a very ill person. Since the age of eighteen he had suffered from depression, from a variety of conversion symptoms of great intensity, and from what he described as "a complete lack of freedom and spontaneity". This lack of spontaneity interfered considerably with his work, and, though he was physically potent, it also deprived him of all the enjoyment of sexual intercourse. A feeling of impending failure, worthlessness and hopelessness, marred all his efforts. He came to analysis at the age of thirty-five because of a conversion symptom: he suffered from a constant pain in the small of his back and the lower abdomen, which was aggravated by frequent spasms. He described it as "a constant state of childbirth". It appeared in his analysis that the pain started soon after he learned that the wife of his twin brother was pregnant, and he actually came to me for treatment a week before her confinement. He felt that if I could only liberate him from the spasm he would do marvellous things. In his case identification with the pregnant woman, representing the mother, was very obvious, but it was not a happy identification. He felt his mother and the babies inside her had been so completely destroyed by his sadism, and his hope of re-creating them was so slight, that the identification with the pregnant mother meant to him a state of anguish, ruin, and abortive pregnancy. Instead of producing the baby, he, like the mother, was destroyed. Feeling destroyed inside and unable to restore the mother, he felt persecuted by her; the internal attacked mother attacked him in turn and robbed him of his babies. Unlike the other three patients described, this one recognized his depression and his reparative drive was therefore very much stronger. The inhibition both in his sexual and artistic achievements was due mainly to a feeling of the inadequacy of his reparative capacity in comparison with the devastation that he felt he had brought about. This feeling of inadequacy made him regress to a paranoid position whenver his anxiety was aroused. (pp. 388-93)

I should now like to attempt to formulate an answer to the question whether there is a specific factor in the psychology of the successful artist which would differentiate him from the unsuccessful one. In Freud's words: "What distinguishes the poet, the artist, from the neurotic daydreamer?" In his paper "Formulations Regarding the Two Principles in Mental Functioning", Freud says: "The artist finds a way of returning from the world of phantasy back to reality, with his special gifts he moulds his phantasies into a new kind of reality." Indeed, one could say that the artist has an acute reality sense. He is often neurotic and in many situations may show a complete lack of objectivity, but in two respects, at least, he shows an extremely high reality sense. One is in relation to his own internal reality, and the other in relation to the material of his art. However neurotic Proust was in his attachment to his mother, his homosexuality, his asthma, etc., he had a real insight into the phantastic world of the people inside him, and he knew it was internal, and he knew it was phantasy. He showed an awareness that does not exist in a neurotic who splits off, represses, denies, or acts out his phantasy. The second, the reality sense of the artist in relation to his material, is a highly specialized reality assessment of the nature, needs, possibilities, and limitations of his material, be it words, sounds, paints, or clay. The neurotic uses his material in a magic way, and so does the bad artist. The real artist, being aware of his internal world which he must express, and of the external materials with which he works, can in all consciousness use the material to express the phantasy. He shares with the neurotic all the difficulties of unresolved depression, the constant threat of the collapse of his internal world; but he differs from the neurotic in that he has a greater capacity for tolerating anxiety and depression. The patients I described could not tolerate depressive phantasies and anxieties; they all made use of manic defences leading to a denial of psychic reality. Patient A denied both the loss of her father and his importance to her: Patient B projected his impulses on to an internal bad object, with the result that his ego was split and that he was internally persecuted: Patient C did the same, though to a lesser extent. . . . (pp. 397-98)

In contrast to that, Proust could fully experience depressive mourning. This gave him the possibility of insight into himself, and with it a sense of internal and external reality. Further, this reality sense enabled him to have and to maintain a relationship with other people through the medium of his art. The neurotic's phantasy interferes with his relationships in which he acts it out. The artist withdraws into a world of phantasy, but he can communicate his phantasies and share them. In that way he makes reparation, not only to his own internal objects, but to the external world as well. (p. 398)

Hanna Segal, "A Psycho-Analytical Approach to Aesthetics," in New Directions in Psycho-Analysis: The Significance of Infant Conflict in the Pattern of Adult Behavior, *Melanie Klein, Paula Heimann, R. E. Money-Kyrle, eds., Tavistock Publications Limited, 1955, pp. 384-405.*

Leo Schneiderman

[*In the following excerpt, Schneiderman asserts that an author's life and work are closely related and that psychopathology plays an important role in literary creation.*]

[It] is difficult to avoid the conclusion that pathology is inseparable from the production of great works of fiction, drama, and poetry. Nor is the role of pathology confined to providing the motivation for literary creativity. The choice of themes, delineation of character, and development of crystallized literary styles cannot be separated from pathology. By *pathology* I mean severe emotional disturbance or profound characterological defects—and not merely anxieties and insecurities of mild or moderate severity. I realize that these conclusions, which I have accepted reluctantly, will be most unwelcome to all those who regard literary creativity as the outcome of productive thinking: a blend of imagination, cognitive restructuring, and controlled affect that has only an incidental relationship to the psychic conflicts of the author. But I find it impossible to separate the life of an author from his or her work.

It could be argued, of course, that great writing transcends the sufferings and confusions of the author and represents the achievement of new heights, where craftsmanship and inspiration overshadow the personal factor. In the same vein, it could be said that great writing replaces the personal and idiosyncratic with universal symbols and meanings. Inferior writing, in turn, could be characterized as showing all the seams that went into its composition, including the psychic scars of the author. But these arguments in favor of the essential normality of great writing are the result of wishful thinking, rather than being based on a careful study of the relationship between biography and literary creativity. Such a study reveals that great literary art is a synthesis of technical skill with tremendous fear, rage, or other powerful emotions, and that the fundamental character of great writers reveals significant failure along developmental lines, that is, a basic lack of maturity.

Whether there is a connection between certain kinds of pathology and the ability to produce literary works of distinction is a question that must await more systematic study. It is conceivable, for example, that writers whose psychological problems are of preoedipal origin produce literature that is fundamentally different from that of writers who are more mature. For example, writers such as Byron, J. M. Barrie, D. H. Lawrence, Faulkner, W. H. Auden, Tennessee Williams, and Beckett, who failed to achieve separation from the mother in early childhood, or were traumatized in the separation process, seem to be preoccupied with problems of self-preservation in their writings. Their fictional protagonists are vulnerable children menaced by the bad mother, or, in Barrie's case, lost boys in search of an elusive, idealized good mother who exists only as a ghost out of the past. In a more general sense, these fictional figures are overwhelmed by life's demands. By contrast, Hawthorne, William Carlos Williams, Hermann Hesse, Hemingway, Nabokov, and Eugène Ionesco have produced characters and situations that approximate the classical norm of oedipal rebellion and fear of retaliation by the father.

These are only hypotheses, of course, and it must be admitted that oedipal motifs are by no means absent in the writings, say, of E. T. A. Hoffmann, D. H. Lawrence, Sartre, and Georges Simenon. The precise balance between ego-preservative and oedipal motifs in the writings of a particular author has to be worked out. I suspect that most writers will show a predominance of one set of motifs over the other, but this supposition is not well grounded at the present time. Freud's discussion of "danger-situations" in "Inhibitions, Symptoms and Anxiety" (1926) drew attention to the role of signal anxiety as an anticipatory response to the threat of being rendered helpless through separation from the mother. Although signal anxiety in relation to the mother comes into play before castration anxiety, which belongs to the phallic stage, the

two dangers constitute a similar, though not identical challenge to the self-preservative functions of the ego.

If separation anxiety refers to the dread of losing a narcissistically valued love object in the form of the mother, castration anxiety, broadly conceived, denotes something in addition to fear of losing a narcissistically valued organ. The threat of castration is simultaneously a threat that the phallic son will never be united with the mother, and that his ties with the father will be sundered, as well. Viewed in this way, it becomes possible to understand oedipal rivalry, including the Electra complex, as an extension of the fear of losing the love of one or both parents. At the preoedipal level, where the danger consists of the fear of losing the object itself, the child is faced with the prospect of being thrust into a state of "psychical helplessness," as Freud puts it. At the phallic level, when the ego is stronger, the danger consists of losing the object's love, rather than the object itself—a less devastating possibility, but one that does not remove the danger to the ego. Unlike the preoedipal child, the phallic child has at his disposal a variety of ego defenses against anxiety, including sublimation upon the resolution of the oedipal crisis. Although the preoedipal and oedipal child are alike dependent on the mother, it is consistent with the main line of Freud's thinking to conclude that the child who is traumatized at the preoedipal level is placed in a more precarious situation. The fantasies that might arise from fear of object loss would, of necessity, be different from those occasioned by fear of losing the love of a permanent object, and would involve different coping strategies based on different levels of ego organization.

If we think of literature as resulting from—among other things—the effort to evolve ego-preservative strategies in fantasy or on the symbolic level, it follows that the solutions will vary along several dimensions, reflecting different degrees of ego strength. An overview of Thomas Hardy's novels, for example, shows a transition from purely ego-preservative, externally produced solutions based on accident, to self-initiated oedipal victories by the male protagonist, to a final relapse into psychical helplessness reflected in pessimism and defeat. In *Desperate Remedies* (1871), Hardy's first published novel, Manston, the evil oedipal rival of the young protagonist Springlove, conveniently commits suicide in prison after having murdered his wife. The young suitor, Dick Dewy, in Hardy's second novel, *Under the Greenwood Tree* (1872), does not have to exert himself any more than does Springlove in order to win the hand of the pretty ingenue Fancy Day. It is the female protagonist who chooses Dick Dewy in preference to an older rival, the Reverend Maybold. These effortless oedipal victories by the good son come to an end with Hardy's third novel, *A Pair of Blue Eyes* (1873), in which the female protagonist comes close to marrying her young suitor, Stephen Smith, but ultimately marries Lord Luxellian, a man of much higher status. As if to punish the heroine, Elfride, for marrying Lord Luxellian, an older man and a widower—hence a father figure—Hardy causes her to die of a miscarriage. Although the oedipal son, Stephen, was clearly defeated, the oedipal father won only a hollow victory. Elfride's father, the Reverend Swancourt, also won an empty victory over young Stephen by blocking his marriage to Elfride on the grounds that Stephen was of humble origin. Parenthetically, Hardy had been courting his first wife, Emma Gifford, at this time, and had been rejected by her father as an unsuitable choice for his daughter, primarily because the father was a snob.

Far From the Madding Crowd (1874), composed during the final months of Hardy's four-year courtship of Emma, still features a male protagonist who is destined for oedipal defeat, but who triumphs by accident. The victory of Gabriel Oak over his two rivals in love, Farmer Boldwood and the malevolent Sergeant Troy, was not the result of his own strength. If Farmer Boldwood had not shot Troy in a psychotic rage (thereby eliminating himself as well as Troy from competition for the hand of Bathsheba Everdene), Gabriel would have remained an oedipal loser. Gabriel is depicted as being inherently a victim who succeeds against all expectations because his rivals stumble. Four years later, Hardy, now married to Emma, who collaborated closely with him on most of his literary work, was still unable to produce a resourceful male protagonist in *The Return of the Native* (1878). Although the female protagonist, Eustacia Vye, is a passionate, restless woman, and a rebellious spirit, her husband, the idealistic Clym Yeobright, is a guilt-ridden, mother-fixated man who cannot cope with life. In the end, Hardy frees Clym from the unfaithful Eustacia by the expedient of drowning her and her lover. It is possible that Eustacia's fate represented a wish fulfillment by Hardy in relation to Emma, but there is nothing in his autobiography or in her published recollections to indicate that the marriage had begun to go bad at this point.

Hardy's method of resolving conflict between his characters in *The Return of the Native* was arbitrary and magical, because the defeated characters did not fall of their own weight, that is, by virtue of their flawed character. There is a strong resemblance between Hardy's solution and Nathaniel Hawthorne's gratuitous destruction of the bad father, Pyncheon, in *The House of Seven Gables.* In both instances, the reader is provided with good protagonists who are too weak and dependent to deal resourcefully with their powerful, manipulative adversaries. It remains for the author to rescue his fictional creations from psychical helplessness. In this context, an external, potentially devastating threat is confronted with a magical, preoedipal solution, the effect of which is to relieve pressure on an ego that is too weak to act in its own behalf. In this regard, S. S. Furst has linked psychic trauma with overstimulation of the ego, resulting in the replacement of ego functions by more primitive mechanisms of adaptation ["Psychic Trauma: A Survey," in S. S. Furst, ed., *Psychic Trauma*]. Hardy's good characters are traumatized by his bad ones because of the great disparity in their strength. The bad characters, embodiments of cruel and destructive id impulses, overwhelm the good characters, mobilizing their guilt and forcing them into childlike passivity. No doubt part of the appeal of *The Return of the Native* resides in the destructive vitality of Eustacia and her lover, Wildeve, who overshadow the lesser characters in the same degree that Milton's Satan outshines the other angels by his malign brilliance.

The Mayor of Casterbridge (1886), Hardy's next major novel, at last reveals an author who is strong enough, at least in fantasy, to attempt to resolve a fictional conflict by creating a self-reliant protagonist who triumphs over a seemingly formidable oedipal rival. I refer, of course, to Farfrae's humiliation of the bad father, Henchard, the mayor of Casterbridge. Farfrae's victory, and his marriage, first to Henchard's erstwhile mistress Lucetta, and then to Henchard's step-daughter, Elizabeth Jane, represent the mastery of an external menace in the form of a powerful oedipal rival. For this reason, the climax of *The Mayor of Casterbridge* belongs psychologically to a stage midway between *The Return of the Native*—with its helpless oedipal "sons," Clym and Diggory, and its vulnerable ingenue, Thomasin (as in Thomas Hardy?)—and Hardy's last important work, *The Dynasts,* completed in 1908. *The Dynasts,* with its thoroughgoing sense of life's futility, projected Hardy's depressive thoughts onto a world-historical dramatic stage. In *Tess of the D'Urbervilles* (1891), Hardy has begun to move away from self-assertion through his fictional characters, and to emphasize the motif of victimization. Although Tess is victimized by Alec, her seducer, she nevertheless has the power to destroy her nemesis by stabbing him to death. Hardy has once again provided an arbitrary solution, but it is less gratuitous than the accidental drowning of Eustacia and her lover in *The Return of the Native.* In contrast to Tess, who struggles against her harsh fate, her husband Angel Clare, like Clym in *The Return of the Native,* is a passive, masochistic individual—a true oedipal loser.

Jude the Obscure (1894), Hardy's last novel, was also his most pessimistic. To an even greater extent than *Tess of the D'Urbervilles,* it is a story of victimization and helplessness. At age fifty-four, Hardy had ceased to be on good terms with Emma. He was now a literary lion, wealthy, and inclined to reciprocate the affection bestowed upon him by a series of attractive young women with literary aspirations. Perhaps his guilt feelings toward Emma, who had remained entirely devoted to him, and whom he was to praise repeatedly in his poems after her death in 1912, contributed to the depressive tone of *Jude the Obscure.* The protagonist is a Job like character who is abandoned by the two women he loves, bereft of his children, and left to die in misery. Jude is the quintessential victim of forces beyond his control. From this story of pathetic failure to the depiction of the equally meaningless failure of collective human experience was but a short step for Hardy. Hence the production of the long epic poem, *The Dynasts,* with its Olympian view of the madness of the Napoleonic wars. Hardy had experimented with conflict resolution based on the strength or weakness of his characters, as well as with solutions based on the force of circumstance. Hardy's tendency to blame social forces and other situational factors for the failure of his protagonists makes it difficult to recognize the inherent weaknesses of these characters, especially the long list of antiheroes. *Jude the Obscure* went as far as Hardy could go in writing novels about failure and defeat. In the end, Hardy had to return to desperate remedies of ego preservation although he was capable, for a brief moment in his literary career, of creating characters who were not afraid of life.

In comparison with such later writers as Kafka, Beckett, or Ionesco, Hardy was far from being a thoroughgoing pessimist, if for no other reason than his belief that an imperfect society could somehow be redeemed by reform measures. But Hardy's characters already carry the seeds of their own destruction within them in the form of characterological defects, masochism, dependency, and helplessness. He is a transition figure on the road to twentieth-century fiction. The outlook of twentieth-century authors is indeed different from that of the most despairing of nineteenth-century writers, including Dostoevsky, who held out some glimmer of hope for human redemption through the self-sacrifice of such noble souls as Sonia in *Crime and Punishment* or Alyosha in *The Brothers Karamazov.* By contrast, a sense of irredeemable loss permeates the imaginative writing of our time. Is it despair resulting from the loss of traditional values and familiar sources of security grounded in unexamined assumptions or ancient folkways? Perhaps the problem is compounded by new modes of perception created by the breakdown of traditional aesthetic conventions. The restless aesthetic experiments of twentieth-century literature from Joyce onward reflect altered ways of looking at the world, but they are emblematic of a wider crisis of modernism. I speak, above all, of the loss of cherished objects of devotion.

What is missing in twentieth-century literature of the first rank is the ability to idealize love objects. The fictional characters of the nineteenth century can still experience unconflicted love for their fellow creatures, even if it is tinged with pity or inspired by a sense of duty. Writers such as E. T. A. Hoffmann, Gustave Flaubert, Tolstoy, and George Eliot, like Hardy, could still imagine wholehearted human relationships, but even their most integral characters show signs of unraveling, of drawing into themselves, and of becoming destructive. Twentieth-century fiction can provide us only with split-off atoms, or fictional characters whose central cores are gone, and who, moreover, cannot form real love relationships. To describe these fictional creations as alienated is to leave them unexplained. Similarly, to say that characters in modern fiction are more complex than their nineteenth-century predecessors is not entirely satisfactory. Instead, it is necessary to search out the causes of alienation in the lives of modern writers, and to trace their gift for complexity to their inner conflicts.

Hardy anticipates these developments without acknowledging that his protagonists are in the process of losing their ideals. Like Hardy, the atheist who could still participate in the religious life of his community, and who still had a strong emotional attachment to the liturgical, architectural, and atmospheric features of the Church of England, his characters still have one foot in the world of tradition. Their lack of conviction, however, adds to their vulnerability. They are aware, like Clym, of the existence of a world of unattainable ideals, but they gaze out at a remote, deterministic universe with the knowledge that their roots in the earth and in a special place have been partly severed.

Hardy's nineteenth-century protagonists (unlike his fictional chorus of peasants) are alienated from a changing and increasingly unfamiliar world. But the existence of this new universe does not invalidate their ideals, it merely emphasizes the difficulty of fulfilling them. By contrast, Joseph Conrad's fictional creations tell us that the meliorative goals that still meant something to an idealist like Clym Yeobright, or to a man of reason like Angel Clare, have all but lost their meaning by the start of the twentieth century. Conrad's antiheroes are destined not only to lose love, nurturance, and loyalty, but also the very objects of their devotion—swept away from them by death or by the force of circumstance. Conrad's novels are much closer in spirit to *Jude the Obscure* than to Hardy's earlier works

because they take place in a world in which the protagonists are profoundly insecure, lost, and without roots. Conrad's Lord Jim or Axel Heyst are men who value truth, goodness, courage, and honor in a world that has abandoned all absolute values and is as likely to reward good as evil. It is a world in which evil can turn into good and in which good can turn into evil. Society itself is powerless to separate the forces of good and evil, so they penetrate each other and traditional decencies are corrupted by the evils of opportunism. We are no longer among Hardy's hills of Wessex, where an intact folk culture still exists side by side with a corrosive outer world. Conrad's universe of seas and ships and remote islands is an uncharted hell in which a few good men wander about aimlessly, barely sustained by an innate sense of decency that cannot preserve them from destruction. Evil men are all around them and treachery is a way of life.

Conrad's tragic heroes and heroines are forerunners, as we will see, of Hemingway's code hero, and are motivated by similar though not identical compulsions. Conrad's protagonists, for example, still believe in altruism and feel pity for those who suffer from injustice. For Hemingway's code hero, the noble act is also a gratuitous and useless gesture and is not intended to help anyone, its nobility consisting only of stoical courage. In his autobiography, *A Personal Record,* Conrad professed to believe that the universe is not an ethical universe at all, but is rather a "spectacular universe" in which it is man's duty to use his senses and imagination to the fullest, and not to despair, because life itself is precious. This contradiction may be at the bottom of the discrepancy noted by Christopher Cooper [in his *Conrad and the Human Dilemma*], between the morality of Conrad's major protagonists and the overall morality of his books. Conrad's tales unfold in an amoral world where men normally can be expected to behave selfishly, but where a few men and women take it upon themselves to live up to a higher standard of conduct, usually with disastrous consequences.

Winnie Verloc, for example, the female protagonist of *The Secret Agent,* demonstrates by her love for her retarded brother Stevie that she is a caring, devoted person. She is otherwise relatively indifferent to moral considerations, and helps her husband in his pornography business, a front for his activities as a spy—indeed, a triple agent. Like Stevie, Winnie is not guided by formal moral principles as much as by an instinctive need to alleviate suffering. Although she ultimately kills her unscrupulous husband in revenge for his having caused Stevie's death, her violent act is the result of her outraged sense of justice. Winnie's suicide is representative of the fate of Conrad's protagonists. They do not meet Heinz Hartmann's criteria of successful adaptation to the external world [presented in his *Essays in Ego Psychology*], because the ego, in their cases, does not serve their long-range goals of survival. The failure of Conrad's protagonists is not caused by the pressure of overpowering id impulses, but by pressures exerted on them by unexpected environmental demands. This failure often takes the form of flight from society and avoidance of close human relationships by escape into a hermitlike existence. Hartmann's concept of *regressive adaptation* is useful in suggesting that such escapism is not pathological in itself, or a sign of pregenital fixation. It is the failure to use "regression in the service of the ego" to achieve a higher level of adaptation, or, to use Hartmann's terminology, to attain "secondary ego autonomy," that is, sublimation, that results in the eventual victimization of Conrad's protagonists. His implicit formula is: To be good is to be destroyed. Hence, the impulse toward altruism is dangerous, and flight from the risks of intimate involvement is to be preferred to pursuing a relationship to its possibly fatal conclusion.

Intimacy also poses the danger to Conrad's characters of losing the love object, the way Conrad lost his tubercular mother when he was seven years old and his father at eleven. He had been brought up in exile, almost completely bereft of the companionship of other children, and in a household clouded by his mother's lingering illness and his father's helplessness and grief. After his father's death, Conrad was raised by his relatives, but by the age of fifteen, inspired by adventure stories he had read, he resolved to go to sea. His guardians protested vigorously, and his tutor called him "an incorrigible, hopeless Don Quixote." Within a short time, Conrad made his way to England and began his career as a merchant mariner, eventually becoming a sea captain distinguished by his high standards of craftsmanship. Until his marriage at the age of thirty-nine, he led a wandering existence, corresponding with relatives but otherwise careful to avoid emotional entanglements for over twenty years. There was one exception, a brief but intense love affair that culminated in Conrad's apparent suicide attempt in 1878, when he was 21. Several of Conrad's protagonists commit suicide. In addition to Winnie Verloc, as I have mentioned, Captain Whalley, the planter of Malata, Martin Decoud in *Nostromo*, and Axel Heyst in *Victory* take their own lives.

Conrad gave up his career as a sea captain abruptly in 1894, only a few months after the death of his uncle and guardian, Thaddeus Bobroski, whom Conrad had loved and respected, according to his letters. He had been unable to find a new assignment at sea and decided to finish *Almayer's Folly*, his first novel, which he had started in 1889. The novel was finally published in 1895 and Conrad commenced a second career as a writer. A year later, he married Jessie George, a twenty-one year-old Englishwoman whom he had met six months earlier. The wording of his marriage proposal, which Conrad made while the couple were taking shelter from bad weather in the National Gallery, was as follows: "Look here, my dear, we had better get married and out of this. Look at the weather. We will get married at once and get over to France. How soon can you be ready? In a week—a fortnight?" The proposal captures something of the impersonal tone of Conrad's interactions with the people who knew him in England, and suggests as well a degree of inequality between the thirty-nine-year-old aristocrat and the young secretary, one of nine children and the product of a more humble background.

Conrad was to endure eighteen years of financial failure and literary obscurity in his career as a writer. Works such as *The Nigger of the Narcissus* (1898), *Lord Jim* (1900), *Heart of Darkness* (1902), *Nostromo* (1904), *The Secret Agent* (1907), and *Under Western Eyes* (1911)—Conrad's best novels—brought him scant recognition. It was not until the publication of *Chance* in 1913 that Conrad achieved popular success and financial security, but by then his literary powers had begun to wane. This decline reflected an intensification of earlier psychological de-

fenses, the tendency to "shrink from actualities when it came to face suffering," as his wife expressed it in her memoir [*Joseph Conrad as I Knew Him*]. Conrad's best work included fictional characters, such as Lord Jim, who suffered precisely because they could not blind themselves to the discrepancy between their lofty ideals and the actuality of their conduct. In such later works as *Chance, Victory, The Shadow Line,* and *The Rescue,* the protagonists have lost their capacity for feeling guilt or self-doubt, and have ceased to be complex. They have even lost their horror of death, and, like Renouard in "The Planter of Malata," prefer suicide to living without a love object. Conrad's later antiheroes no longer suffer from the terror of life, but surrender to their own passivity, like Lingard in *The Rescue,* who dreams only of spending his life at the feet of his beloved, soothed into a "World-embracing reverie." There is a marked loss of intensity in these characterizations, as if Conrad had come to terms with himself. All along, Conrad had combined naturalism with an aestheticism that was highly subjective and had also probed the motives of his protagonists, pitting them against their own weaknesses. Captain Giles in *The Shadow Line* continues to express this philosophy: "A man should stand up to his bad luck, to his mistakes, to his conscience, and all that sort of thing. Why—what else would you have to fight against?" But the narrator, to whom Giles has directed his remarks, has no answer, having already declared that he feels old and tired, even though, in comparison to his earlier mood of emptiness and despair, he is on the road to recovering his spirits.

The loss of dramatic tension in Conrad's later works is more than a reflection of the author's growing complacency, but is nevertheless related to the enervating effect of success. Conrad's deficiencies are associated with an increased use of the defense of splitting, as well. Now his characters begin to be divided into those who are absolutely good—Conrad *tells* us that they are honorable and courageous, like old Peyrol in *The Rover,* rather than showing us their inner qualities—and those who are absolutely bad. Hitherto, self-doubt had generated the dynamism in Conrad's best work, the anguish of his protagonists reflecting the insecurity of the neglected author. Once Conrad's characters are deprived of their capacity for unconscious duplicity, all that remains is the unequal struggle between a virtuous protagonist and the destructive people who surround him, such as Mrs. Fyne, the caricature of a power-seeking feminist in *Chance.* Even the sea recedes in Conrad's later works, taking with it much that is elemental and moving in Conrad's earlier productions.

These deficiencies are bound up, of course, with Conrad's aging process. They are also reminders of the psychological distance that Conrad had always maintained from his created characters and situations. Conrad's narrators who report events they have learned about second-hand, and his fictional love relationships, vapid and impersonal, such as that between Lingard and Mrs. Travers in *The Rescue,* are indicative of Conrad's difficulty with fictional object relations. Conrad was more successful in cathecting his fictional characters and describing them in depth when he was hard-pressed and almost despairing of popular and critical recognition. He was at his best under stress, when his imagination was fueled by frustration and the fear of failure. Success weakened Conrad's creative powers by making it unnecessary for him to identify himself with his antiheroes. In this sense, whatever had been pathogenic in his early life combined with the desperation of his apparently failed literary career (until the success of *Chance* in 1913) to produce a gallery of sympathetic and believable victims. Financial security, prestige, critical acclaim, a happy family life—all the ingredients of a normal, fulfilled existence—conspired to defeat Conrad as a writer.

If we use a developmental frame of reference, it can be argued that Conrad, at the peak of his creative ability, had to cope with two kinds of threat. On the one hand, he was faced with the task of neutralizing instinctual pressures of a sexual and aggressive type. These pressures, shaped by unfulfilled and apparently repressed dependency needs in Conrad the orphaned child, led to their neutralization and their effective use in the development of ego functions, including those of problem solving in reality and fantasy. The process of sublimation involved Conrad in a series of defensive adaptations consistent with his history of traumatic object loss. This process entailed distancing himself from people, first through his career as a seaman who held himself aloof from his fellow officers, and later, through his writing, in which he characteristically tried to hold his characters at arm's length. Paradoxically, the result of these ego-defensive strategies, particularly when Conrad dealt with his own frustration and despair through his fictional characters, was the production of powerful works of fiction.

The second source of threat to Conrad emanated from the external world, or what Hartmann labels the *conflict-free sphere,* as distinguished from intrapsychic conflict. Conrad's environment posed a series of difficult challenges to him. As the child of exiled, defeated parents who were visibly wasting away from tuberculosis, and who did not conceal their deep depression from their only child, Conrad started life with few emotional supports. Later, as the orphaned dependent of his extended family, Conrad lacked a secure home base, and had already begun to cut himself adrift emotionally from the people around him. As a sailor, he suffered from loneliness and "lived like a hermit with my passion" (for the sea), as he expresses it in his Author's Note to *The Mirror of the Sea.* As a British subject, he had to cope with an unfamiliar culture in which he never felt fully at home. As an impoverished and unsuccessful writer for most of his literary career, Conrad had to struggle with a language he never learned to speak with perfect fluency, without a marked foreign accent. Even his health, seriously impaired by his hardships as a seaman, added to his problems. Thus, the real world of object relations was hardly free of stress for Conrad, and continued to the end to make demands on him that exhausted him. But the true source of exhaustion was not hardship, illness, or old age. Conrad's depletion as a creative artist is traceable to his victory over poverty and neglect; the tightly coiled spring relaxed and lost its tension, and Conrad ended his career as a writer who was satisfied with himself.

I have described Hardy as a nineteenth-century writer who still believed in life-affirming ideals. At the same time, his deep insight into man's self-destructive drives made him pessimistic about the future of mankind. Hardy can be described as a naturalist with modern psychological insights resembling Hawthorne's guilt-consciousness. Nevertheless, he does not belong in the ranks of twentieth-century postsymbolists such as Joyce or Proust. The latter

had placed themselves at a distance from their characters even while dwelling in detail on their most minute perceptions and reflections. The moral perspective is still too strong in Hardy to classify him as a true modern.

Conrad, too, stands at the threshold of the modern age in literature because his fictional antiheroes are still aristocratic in their rectitude and bourgeois in their moral earnestness. They live and die, however, in a world that resembles the anomic landscape of twentieth-century fiction. Like Hardy's fictional idealists, they know they are on the side of virtue, but they have begun to doubt their ability to be true to themselves. Thus, Hardy is a modern insofar as he creates weak but noble men who are easily destroyed by deterministic forces operating in a still-familiar rural landscape. Conrad, by comparison, is a modern because he sketches a world that is far more amoral and primitive than the traditional folk culture that forms the backdrop for Hardy's fiction. In this semibarbarous universe, with the heartless and mindless sea as a constant reminder of man's smallness and vulnerability, Conrad's protagonists are doomed to sink to the bottom. Strangely enough, they still believe in a type of brave code hero not unlike Dominic Cervoni, Conrad's real-life mentor in the ways of the sea.

What really gives Hardy and Conrad their modern tone, even though they are not quite twentieth-century in their persistent attachment to positive values, is that they have all but given up on the objective world. Their protagonists cannot fulfill their ideals in this world. In fact, they can barely survive in this world, let alone salvage their self-respect as they are buffeted about by external forces or betrayed by inner weaknesses. The stage is set for Edmund Wilson's cast of twentieth-century newcomers, namely, William Butler Yeats, Paul Valery, T. S. Eliot, Proust, Joyce, and Gertrude Stein. As we shall see, Hemingway, as well, belongs with this cast of characters by virtue of his pessimism and his compensatory preoccupation with style. These writers not only have much in common, as Wilson makes clear in *Axel's Castle,* but are the ideological forerunners of Nabokov, Beckett, and Ionesco.

Hemingway's bleak view of society, like that of Yeats or T. S. Eliot, or any of the others, is the reciprocal of their emphasis on stylistic innovation. The greater the disenchantment with the manmade world, the greater the corresponding emphasis on *form*—sometimes, as in Gertrude Stein's case, at the expense of content. Yeats was not only concerned with form, but he even tried to substitute the landscape of a fairyland for the gritty contents of the real world, at least in his early writings. His heroes, for example, find the real world a depressing place and try to escape to an ideal realm of imagination, complete with its own magical people. These fictional characters—Oisin, Red Hanrahan and others—resemble Conrad's antiheroes who abandon the land for the sea, where they can be alone with their thoughts and safe from society's corruption.

The cultivation of subjective experience is based on the assumption that the objective world has nothing left to give but sensory impressions, which can serve as raw materials for reflection. As seen through the eyes of Proust or Joyce, the old ideals that inspired men to try to change the conditions of life are dead. In their place, the senses awaken to a life of their own. The life of the senses has nothing to do with solving problems or reforming the world, but is valid in its own right. For these writers and kindred spirits, the senses are the gates of imagination, and everything outside these gates is the world of inert matter. In fact, when we turn our attention to Hemingway, we see that the imagination has been all but eclipsed by the senses, which are linked not only with literal description, but with a self-validating hedonism as well.

With Hemingway, modern literature takes another step toward the depiction of an existential universe in which there is nothing of substance that an honest person can believe in. All that remains, once the senses have been given their due, is the bitter satisfaction that one has tried to live one's life with style, that is, so as not to offend the senses by a false or clumsy gesture. Hemingway even went so far as to try to discipline himself to write only about immediate experience, in the belief that it was a valid substitute for reflection. In so doing, he sought to evade the broad implications of his radical skepticism. As interpreted by Hemingway, Conrad's gentlemanly virtues of courage and dignity are translated into the compulsion to maintain good form, or grace under pressure. The same tendency pervades his strategy of literary composition, with its emphasis on absolute fidelity to sensory impressions and avoidance of "unmanly" elaboration or reflection.

In a universe without apparent meaning, Hemingway followed Conrad's lead in singling out the man whose essential decency consists of his stylistic integrity. Such men are not guided by substantive values, such as belief in justice or human freedom, but by the imperative to meet life-threatening challenges with grace and determination, and to endure pain without whimpering. Although Hemingway's code hero appears to be capable of idealizing love objects, he is fundamentally narcissistic and unconcerned with the fate of others. Instead of pursuing ethical goals, Hemingway's code-hero concentrates on style, on the perfection of method, on fighting or hunting or dying gracefully and in accordance with a set of aesthetic norms. When Hemingway's code hero is drawn into conflict with forces in the external world, his adversaries are hardly more than projections of id impulses in the form of wild animals, bulls, enormous fish, and an occasional gangster. I am not forgetting the fascists in *For Whom the Bell Tolls,* but then, by the time Hemingway was through with this novel, he had done a much better job of damning the Loyalists and their partisan allies.

As was true of the symbolists and their twentieth-century succesors generally, Hemingway's main concern was aesthetic. He was aware that his fictional heroes were without a cause, and were mere ritualists hunting, boxing, and soldiering for no other reason than to maintain their stylistic purity and to keep in shape. It did not concern him that his heroes were out of touch with social and political realities, nor did he try to convince his readers that his heroes risked their lives for high stakes. The essential quality of Hemingway's heroes is their ability to *endure,* but to endure the way an artist handles the frustrations associated with the practice of his craft, conscious of his need to strive for the perfection of form. Ironically, Hemingway's manly heroes, projections of his inordinate need to be strong and unsentimental, are engaged in a graceful dance of life. They endure, conscious that they are striking a pose, and knowing that it is absurd to endure. It is the gratuitous act par excellence to appear to remain unmoved

in extreme situations, knowing that the outcome makes no difference in a world in which all values can be summed up by the word *nada*—nothing, zero, emptiness. Hemingway's strategy as a writer is to try to replace lost illusions with a defensive posture, which he shares with his fictional protagonists. This posture reflects the "separate peace" that Hemingway made with his conscience, namely, to look at life egocentrically as a series of dangers to be met by cultivating a particular frame of mind in which the best defense is the aesthetically perfect mortal wound to the adversary.

Hemingway's self-centeredness made his writing an exercise in subjectivism disguised as the objective reporting of sensory impressions and the faithful recording of dialogue. His fears, hatreds, enormous vanity, and defensiveness— as well as his enthusiasms—colored everything he wrote. Always selective in his perceptions, Hemingway saw and felt only what was relevant to his defensive needs. The result was that his imagination was constricted, and his invented characters, such as the protagonists of *The Sun Also Rises,* are in many ways less interesting and less complex than their real-life prototypes. Hemingway's celebrated apprenticeship to Gertrude Stein and Ezra Pound, which sensitized him to the problems of form, merely confirmed his egocentricity and made it more difficult for him to free himself from the constricting influence of his destructive needs.

This criticism applies not only to Hemingway, but also to many writers of our time. Although Hemingway's defects as a writer were exaggerated by his egocentricity, they were the product of his cynicism as well. The collapse of traditional values and beliefs has made it difficult for creative artists to interpret human experience as if it had any significance. Hemingway's concern for purity of form, in this connection, has much in common with Pablo Picasso's search for new and distinctive art forms. In both cases there is a break with convention and an implied criticism of society, accompanied by an affirmation of life on the experiential level. This affirmation, which is playful at its best, makes no moral judgment, and lapses into self-indulgence at its worst. Similarly, Hemingway's commitment to form-in-lieu-of-faith resembles Joyce's need to effect an oceanic elaboration of form, in the absence of a coherent philosophy of life. D. H. Lawrence mingled the sex drive with the will to power to produce his own alternative to a life of meaning and purpose. Kafka, that master of the futile gesture, elevated suffering and isolation to the status of an art form, as in "The Hunger Artist," and consoled himself with the reflection that if life is devoid of human significance, perhaps it all adds up to something in the opaque mind of God.

Like a poor motherless child, the best writers and artists of our time cry out in their several ways, or turn their love inward, or hallucinate a reality of their own. It is no wonder that their antiheroes are destroyed from within and from without. It is a truism to say that modern society provides little nurturance for the life of the mind or the spirit, but we are dealing with more than the indifference of popular culture to serious art. Democratic and totalitarian societies alike are in the process of contracting the life space of writers and artists, and eventually ending their independent existence. If this prognosis seems alarmist it is only because we have assumed all along that serious fiction, poetry, and drama are perceived as performing a valuable and unassailable function in society. But these cultural activities are coming under increasing pressure under the conditions of mass society. In response to these conditions, art ceases to be a sublimated act based on the neutralized energy of instinctual drives. Instead, it becomes a compulsion that employs a set of symbolic defenses erected by the beleaguered ego in the face of a hostile cultural environment. The ideal of beauty, however defined, has no necessary place among these strategies of ego-preservation. The hostile conditions of which I speak are all the more threatening because they are not based exclusively on the exploitation of man by man, or by the state, but involve something new, namely, the growing irrelevance of the aesthetic side of life.

There is no evidence, of course, that beauty is a necessary condition of life, or even of civilization. The ability to create beauty, however, reflects the wish to transcend the limitations of everyday life, or at least to enhance objects of everyday use by imbuing them with some special distinction. Even the condemned of Terezin in the midst of the Holocaust continued to write poems, make drawings, and stage musical performances while awaiting deportation to the death camps. Were they conscious that their efforts were an affirmation of life? Surely they were aware of the irrelevance of their artistic productions to the designs of their executioners, or to the concerns of the embattled world around them. Yet there is a similarity between this art produced under the threat of extinction and modern art in general. The similarity consists of the artist's finding himself in an extreme situation, life-threatening in the first instance, and soul-crushing in the second. Under these conditions, art ceases to be a sublimation of sexual or aggressive drives. The prisoner who is being systematically starved to death has no need to neutralize his nonexistent libido; the modern artist who lives in a sexually permissive society is under no compulsion to redirect his sexual energies to sublimated activities. If they choose to create art, it can only be to signify their attachment to life or to express their resistance to the inhumanity of the world around them. When the aggressive drive cannot be expressed through open defiance, the artist is compelled to resort to indirection. The danger that blocked aggression will be turned against the self is very great. If humor, wit, satire, or parody are sublimated forms of aggression, as Freud maintained, then compulsive self-maceration, including self-ridicule, is also displaced hostility, but without sublimation. In the absence of neutralization of affect, the full force of the artist's bitterness makes itself felt through the metaphors and images of art.

I believe that aggression that is compulsively turned against the self underlies much of the best writing of the nineteenth and twentieth centuries. It is a dominant strategy of creation in such chroniclers of victimization and self-destruction as Dostoevsky, Hawthorne, Melville, Hardy, Henry James, D. H. Lawrence, Kafka, Faulkner, F. Scott Fitzgerald, Hesse, Tennessee Williams, Nabokov, Beckett, Ionesco, Simenon, and many other writers of the modern era.

These writers are caught in an inner struggle between the forces of life and death. Often, their life-affirming impulses are obscured and even hidden from themselves by their sense of decay and corruption. They provide catharsis neither for themselves nor for their readers. They can resolve neither the conflict between dependency and separation vis-à-vis their love objects, nor the conflict with the oedipal father. The playfulness of Barrie or H. H. Munro or Ionesco is less an expression of the pleasure principle than it is a cry of pain. Although Freud has made the search for sublimated sexual pleasure a basis for object cathexis and aesthetic achievement, it is evident that the most important writers of the modern period are motivated neither by the pleasure principle nor the quest for beauty. Their object choices in life as in art are narcissistic and their egocentricity drives them to create fictional protagonists in their own image. In addition, their expenditure of psychic energy in defense of the vulnerable ego fails to produce equilibrium either for the writer or his reader. Instead of tension reduction, something else takes place, namely, the reactivation of obsessive concerns reflecting excessive inner stimulation.

I agree with the formulation presented by Jack Spector in *The Aesthetics of Freud* when he states, "A major problem of arriving at a workable psychoanalytic aesthetics comes from its undue weighting of pleasure in its implied definition of beauty" [see Further Reading]. Freud's idea of beauty, as Spector notes, is also tied up with the concept of psychic integration, in which the ego achieves a balance between conscious and unconscious processes in the creation of a work of art. The literature of our time—leaving to one side the literature of popular culture—does not yield pleasure, and its implicit definition of beauty is as far removed from sublime tragedy as it is from the contemplation of the harmony of the cosmic spheres. [Many modern] literary works . . . convey pathos and lay bare the ugliness of the human comedy as perceived by contemporary writers. Nor is the ego always able to impose coherent artistic form on the emotions churned up out of the writer's unconscious. The reader of fiction or poetry and the play-viewer have accepted a new set of aesthetic conventions that makes room for unpleasure—disgust, despair, unrelieved fear, unredeemed failure, helplessness, loneliness, and lovelessness. Thus, the writer and his audience have come to share a common set of expectations about the function of art. If art, then, ever had a healing function, or provided people with a sense of harmony and beauty, this is no longer the case.

What is the function of modern art? It provides no haven from the everyday world, makes no effort to inspire people, provides no role models with whom the young can identify themselves in a life-affirming way, and does not permit catharsis. But it seeks out the truth intuitively and on the basis of empiricism, and therefore occupies a position somewhere between science and religion. Should we condemn the best writers of our time if they present us with unpleasant truths, and if these truth possess neither the rational properties of scientific thought nor the uplifting beauty of religious ritual? There is such a thing as the aesthetics of truth, in which beauty consists of the conquest of illusion, no less than in the creation of illusion that bespeaks an underlying truth. Modern literature has freed itself of the false idealism praised by Frederick Schlegel in his *History of Literature Ancient and Modern,* in which he speaks of idealism as "the system of those who recognize ideas as superior to sensation." The importance of Beckett or Kafka or even Hemingway is that, in the absence of certainty, they start at the beginning, with sensations, with the flux of mental images, with the sound of waves. The reader is entirely free to draw his own conclusions, although they can hardly be very consoling. The aesthetics of truth can move us, nevertheless, by presenting us with those facts of life we have repressed in order to maintain a counterfeit serenity. Art-based-on-truth will not allow us to steal away from the world or to hide from ourselves. If psychoanalysis as a theoretical system has failed to convince some people of the duplicity of the human heart, the best literature of our time cannot be brushed aside as easily. Its truths, which have been shaped by art, strike us with a powerful impact. We try vainly to evade the force of these unwelcome insights, and clap our hands as if to summon the reassuring gods of textual criticism or some other mode of exegesis. But the gods of reason, order, romantic idealism, social criticism—or of any of the other intellectual traditions—do not respond. Instead, demons appear and knock on the door with the haft of a knife, like the old man described by Laurence Sterne in *A Sentimental Journey Through France and Italy,* who banged on the table to summon the members of his family to dance after supper. They are the demons of truth, flushed out by Freud and other demon hunters. They summon us to the dance of life, but we must not be afraid to move in rhythm with the music, even when it is jarring, or so soft that all we can hear is our own ominous heartbeat. (pp. 206-27)

> *Leo Schneiderman, "The Eloquence of Pain,"
> in his* The Literary Mind: Portraits in Pain
> and Creativity, *Human Sciences Press, 1988,
> pp. 206-27.*

PSYCHOANALYTIC THEORIES OF RESPONSE TO LITERATURE

Norman N. Holland

[*An American critic who has received psychoanalytic training, Holland is one of the most prominent psychoanalytic critics in the United States. A prolific author, he is best known for his contribution to reader-response theory, outlined in such works as* The Dynamics of Literary Response *and* 5 Readers Reading *(1975). In the following excerpt from the first-named work, Holland proposes a model of literary response.*]

What should a "theory of literary response" do? It should, I take it, explain why we respond to literary works as we do. "Explain" is, of course, a philosophically tricky word, but, for our purposes, we can say, simply, to explain a phenomenon is to relate it to principles more general than itself. For example, to explain why a magnet attracts a bar of iron, we say the molecules in the magnet are all lined up one way, appealing to more general notions of molecular structures and the electrical forces associated with them. Similarly, we explain the "willing suspension of disbelief" by saying we introject literary works, because the word "introject" draws on general psychological princi-

ples about our relations to people and things. . . . But to say one can analyze literary experiences by principles applicable to all human experience is simply to say one can "explain" literary experiences. (p. 309)

Given this assumption [that literary experiences can be explained] I have developed a theory—or model—of literary response. The basic datum is the organic unity of the literary work: poems, plays, and stories are series of words; but in each of these series there are implicit groupings into themes and meanings. As readers, we make these implicit groupings more or less explicit, possibly along themes that are of particular concern to us, Marxist, Christian, social, moral, and so on. Among these possible groupings of the elements of the text, there is one with a special status: a psychoanalytic reading will arrive at a central or nuclear fantasy, known from clinical evidence, in which all the separate elements of the text play a role. Because we know these fantasies clinically, because they have to do with the primitive, unconscious part of our mental life, we can safely say they are what give literature its astonishing power over us. Literature transforms these nuclear fantasies toward meaningfulness and thereby allows them to elude the censoring part of our minds and achieve an oblique expression and gratification. In effect, a literary text has implicit in it two dimensions: one reaches "up," toward the world of social, intellectual, moral, and religious concerns; the other reaches "down," to the dark, chthonic, primitive, bodily part of our mental life.

The text itself is only a series of words—it is we who stretch it in these two directions. Unconsciously or half-consciously, we introject it, taking it into us as, at the most primitive level of our being, we long to incorporate any source of gratification. Consciously, however, we perceive the text as separate, think about it, judge it, and, most important, supply coherence if it is not built in. Thus, either the literary work itself embodies, or we supply, a transformation of fantasy toward meaning. It is this transformational process, this management of fantasy, that we take into ourselves, feeling it as though it were our own mental activity—which, indeed, it in part is. Further, we not only contribute meaning, we analogize, enriching the central fantasy with our own associations and experiences that relate to it. Thus, the text transforms not only its fantasy but ours as well.

Within the literary work itself, what establishes the central fantasy is plot in the very broadest sense: the sequence and significance of images or events portrayed. The author's hand shapes this plot toward meaningfulness; we experience his shaping and ordering as the transformation of our own fantasy. We can distinguish two other important agents of transformation. The first is structure or form (in a large sense), that which determines what we are aware of at any given moment as we are seeing the text. Form acts to manage the underlying fantasy in a way that, if it happened in a person rather than on a page, would look very like a defense mechanism. Form in this larger sense tends to operate like denial or regression or splitting or condensation or displacement or isolation.

A second agent of transformation is what we have called "the displacement to language." Present to some extent in any literary text, it becomes particularly important when a text calls attention to its own language, as, for example, poetry does. The displacement to language handles the fantasy content by transferring our involvement with the text (in technical terms, shifting our cathexis) from the fantasy to the language in which the fantasy is expressed. The language then seems to manage the fantasy content—partly by a kind of pseudo-logic that gives the illusion of mastery; partly by enlisting us kinesthetically in muscular actions that seem to manage the fantasy; partly by gratifying or violating our formal expectations about the language. Gratifying our formal expectations about language gives us a satisfying sense of mastery. Violating our expectations binds our attention (or cathexis) still more tightly to the verbal texture.

Put in its very briefest form, the theory says that literature is an introjected transformation. The literary text provides us with a fantasy which we introject, experiencing it as though it were our own, supplying our own associations to it. The literary work manages this fantasy in two broad ways: by shaping it with formal devices which operate roughly like defenses; by transforming the fantasy toward ego-acceptable meanings—something like sublimation. The pleasure we experience is the feeling of having a fantasy of our own and our own associations to it managed and controlled but at the same time allowed a limited expression and gratification.

Given such a model, what can we explain with it? . . . [It] tells us something about our value judgments of literature. We get the feeling "this is good," when a literary work successfully balances fantasy and its handling of the fantasy, neither over-managing nor under-managing it. Such a model supplies reasons for our evaluations of literary works in terms of specific properties of the work—the presence or absence of transformation toward meaning . . . ; the acceptability or unacceptability of the defensive maneuvers built into its formal structure. . . . It asks us to look specifically at all the factors in the dynamic balance of forces which is our experience of any given literary work. In a larger sense, such a model enables us to compare quite disparate experiences of literature in a way which I think is not possible without some such explanatory or generalizing system.

The notion of literature as a balance of fantasy and management of fantasy relates literary works to the psychoanalytic concept of character: libidinal level and habitual patterns of defense. Thus, the model enables us to relate the style (in both a broad and a narrow sense) to the man. One can see connections between a man's life and his work and between his various different works, even those which seem as special as *The Secret Agent* does in Conrad's total *œuvre.* The model also enables us to explain the somewhat puzzling role of myth in literature. Where we are aware of a mythic substructure in a literary work and where the work plays into its myth, it strengthens our introjection of the transformational process because the myth feels like a nurturing other both within and in addition to the text itself. Where the literary work plays against its myth, we feel the opposite—a sense of distance and parody, a weakening of our introjection.

Similarly, the model enables us to see what is meant by "identification" with a literary character. It is not exactly identification but rather an introjection, just one part of our introjection of the whole work. The work itself is a total economy of drive and management of drive. Some characters, like Romeo, we introject as vicarious satisfiers

of drives. Others, like Mercutio or the Nurse, we introject because they embody defensive maneuvers for dealing with the anxiety-arousing aspects of the central fantasy. In short, we do not identify with *a* character so much as with a total interaction of characters in which some satisfy needs for pleasure and others satisfy our need to avoid anxiety. Further, our concept of literature as a balance of fantasy and management of fantasy leads us to at least a tentative understanding of the sources of the affects we experience, not only in books but perhaps in life as well. That is, the literary work transforms a fantasy which has both drive-satisfying and anxiety-arousing aspects. If not much in the fantasy arouses anxiety, we feel the affects appropriate to drive-satisfaction if the fantasy is not over-managed; we feel the affects appropriate to lack of satisfaction or even frustration if the fantasy is heavily managed. If the fantasy has a good deal of anxiety implicit in it, we feel that anxiety if the fantasy is weakly controlled. But if an anxiety-arousing fantasy is strongly managed, the defensive operation of literary form operates selectively against the anxiety, leaving the drive-gratifying side of the fantasy relatively uncontrolled. We feel the affects appropriate to drive-satisfaction, not because anxiety has been transformed into other affects, but because anxiety has been subtracted out, leaving affects it would otherwise have masked.

Evaluation, the links between a man and his style, the role of myth, the nature of our relation to literary characters, the sources of affect—these are some of the specific questions about literature to which this model suggests answers. There are, of course, larger issues which any theory of literary response ought to at least clarify and preferably settle. One is the complex role of meaning in literary response. This theory, by saying literature is a transformation, gives meaning a central role. The pleasure we seek in literary experience is feeling our fantasies managed and controlled so they become acceptable to our conscious ego. Form is one way literature does this, but the act or process of meaning is at least as important. Confronted by works that seem to lack this transformation to meaning, audiences search almost frantically for it. In the lobby of a theater where the latest Antonioni or Bergman is showing, there is almost a chorus of "What does it mean?" "What is it all about?" Evidently, meaning is central to our experience, for we demand it and feel frustrated if we cannot find it. Meaning must therefore be an essential ingredient in our pleasure, whether it be readily available in the work or whether we have to work to find it. This model accounts for both possibilities.

The model also suggests a relationship between form and meaning as the two major modes of managing fantasy content. Meaning works somewhat like a sublimation—it allows disguised and partial satisfaction of the fantasy. The process of meaning works in the same direction as the push for expression. By contrast, form tends to work against the fantasy, omitting, splitting, reversing. A small change in the phrasing of a joke or a lyric without altering the meaning nevertheless makes a big change in the effect—why? Because, in our minds as we introject the work, form balances off pressures from the fantasy. As in any other balance of forces, a slight change on one side produces a much bigger change in the final position of the balance. Thus, form must be much more precise than meaning. We need meaning, but we can accept a wide variety of possible meanings to achieve literary pleasure. Almost any kind of interpretation we derive from a text will get it past the censor and permit our egos to enjoy the fantasy content. Form, however, must be more artfully chosen, as beginning poets to their sorrow find.

In general, any literary theory ought to account for the presence and function of different literary forms. This theory explains form as a quasi-defensive management of the fantasy content. Form can control what we are aware of at any given moment; it can split the psychological issues involved, omit (or repress) them, displace our involvement from the fantasy to a purely verbal resolution of it, and so on. Thus, our model can account for the differences between prose literature and verse: in one, the displacement to language is an important part of the defensive handling of the fantasy; in the other, it is not.

Similarly, our model accounts for the existence and relation of genres by considering them as different defensive modes. For example, Swift's "A Modest Proposal" represents a distinctive type of satire, one which advocates one proposition by reducing its opposite to absurdity. Having realistically explored the possibility of treating the Irish like cattle, we come away from the satire convinced that we should treat them like human beings and identify with them in some way other than eating them. Psychologically, Swift uses a reaction-formation that already exists in his reader, the horror and revulsion we feel at the idea of eating babies. One could define this kind of satire psychologically, then, as presenting a highly unpleasant fantasy and using, to manage it, a reaction-formation the reader already has.

One could define allegory as a genre that handles fantasies by making the transformation into meaning quite explicit. [In his *Allegory: The Theory of a Symbolic Mode*], Angus Fletcher has suggested allegory resembles obsessional or compulsive behavior. Tragedy, I have suggested [in *Psychoanalysis and Shakespeare*], involves the failure of a defense (the death of Mercutio, for example), leading to punishment for an impulse toward pleasure. Comedy builds up a defense, leading to gratification of an impulse toward pleasure without punishment. And so on. It seems unlikely that these psychological definitions could ever be phrased as exactly as definitions based on the formal properties of the various genres. Nevertheless, these psychological definitions do suggest the reason different genres exist: they represent different ways of managing fantasy materials. We seek out different genres because they supply a variety in the psychological experiences we get from literature. The different genres are related, then, as different defensive patterns—one could have a comedy, a tragedy, a satire, each a different way of managing the same core fantasy, and they would each feel like a quite different experience.

In short, our model supplies answers for a variety of fundamental questions about literature. Whether those answers are correct or, indeed, whether the model itself is, are matters for—ultimately—experimentation. The model does, however, gain some confirmation in that it returns us finally to the very things literary critics have always talked about—though with a difference. Form, language, character, plot, genre, sound—these are all important, but we can only talk intelligently about them if we recognize that they shape and balance a core of fantasy material.

Many statements about literature seem dogmatic or impressionistic because they deal only with one end of a total process of transformation and balance. it is as if literary critics have been looking at a group of children on one half of a somewhat mysterious see-saw, the other half being screened by a wall. They have been trying to explain why this board should rise or fall or stand out horizontally from the wall by examining only the weights and positions of the children on the end they can see. Similarly, one can analyze very, very precisely the sound of a line of poetry, but that analysis only makes sense when we understand the sound as a way of transforming and managing the fantasy content of the line.

Correct or not, the model does at least meet some of Robert E. Lane's rather telling objections to the usual statements about literature: that they lack classification, theory, methodology, or test procedure; that they are as unverifiable and poetic as the very texts they seek to explain [*The Liberties of Wit: Humanism, Criticism, and the Civic Mind*]. Whatever other virtues this model may have, it is at least testable. For example, the model says, when we willingly suspend disbelief, we are introjecting the literary text as a child (orally) fuses with a source of passive gratification of his oral needs. Similarly, Brenman and Gill found that easily hypnotizable people had more than their share of oral conflict and fixation. If the model is correct, one should be able to establish the same thing for the "willing suspension of disbelief": people who easily become absorbed in reading or play- or movie-watching should show more orality than those who don't. One should be able to correlate oral issues, discovered by projective tests or interviews, with literary absorption, observed directly or by interview.

Similarly, the model suggests that a reader will respond "I like it" to literary works whose formal or defensive techniques match his own. One should, then, be able to correlate different readers' preferences among a collection of more or less equally good short stories with the different readers' characteristic patterns of fantasy and defense, discovered by interview or projective test. One could use two versions of a given story or a line of poetry to explore the balance between form and fantasy content the model points to. One could, for example, ask readers to explain their preference for one of two versions of the same line of poetry to get at the way the sound of the line manages the fantasy. We have already seen something of this kind of test in the chapter on myth: texts in which we strongly sense mythic resonance have images of oral fusion; texts which are based on a myth, but in which we do not get a sense of resonance, lack images of oral fusion. One could test the role of meaning in the same way, by using different versions of a story in which the plot is made more or less meaningful and listening to the responses of readers.

That is, ultimately, what the model tells us: the things to tune into in the responses of readers. If one listens with the analyst's "third ear," one should be able to hear free associations to the fantasy content of, say, a story and perhaps also some indication of the defensive management. Thus, a particularly powerful way to test what the model tells us about any given fiction would be to ask a reader or readers to retell the story in their own words. Here is a free retelling by a freshman:

> Why and how can a book (the words) be more real

than the actual experience? Because . . . for me sometimes the words bring the experience closer—it makes you aware of things you wouldn't have noticed—perhaps for me this is because I don't have a very critical eye, and many times words describe something & make it more *real* for me. . . . My most favorite passage that I've ever read is in *One Flew Over the Cuckoo's Nest,* when the guy in the asylum is looking out the window and sees a dog playing and jumping in the moonlight—then the dog gets run-over by a car as he chases some geese high in the air. This is more *real* to me than *reality* because when I read it I feel like the dog, the grass, the dew, the moon, the geese, and the car. If I just saw this, I probably wouldn't see anything but the dog getting hit—I would have missed the dog's life and action and his (for me) joy at just being outside and free to jump and bay at the moon and chase the geese and the beauty of the moon and the wetness of the dew beneath him. The words bring all the little pieces of the larger reality to me magnified, and the total experience, although I only read it, is closer and more real and more meaningful to me than it would have been if I had *only* seen it.

Beginning student he may be, but his remarks make a handsome instance of the introjection process our model posits, particularly the introjection of a total economy of several elements interacting in different psychological ways ("I feel like the dog, the grass, the dew, the moon, the geese, and the car").

On the other hand, "My most favorite passage that I've ever read" is being rather dimly recollected. If one turns to the Kesey novel itself, one finds that the dog does not bay at the moon and does not chase the geese. "He was still standing with his paw up; he hadn't moved or barked when they flew over." Moreover, the novel only implies the dog is hit by the car; it does not show the event which, indeed, may not have happened at all. "I watched the dog and the car making for the same spot of pavement. The dog was almost to the rail fence at the edge of the grounds when I felt somebody slip up behind me," and that is the last we hear of either dog or car.

If we listen to the student's comments for the psychological issues involved, we hear him contrast the weakness of his "critical eye" with the way words make things realer than reality: "makes you aware of things you wouldn't have noticed." "If I just saw this, I probably wouldn't see anything but the dog getting hit." "The words bring all the little pieces of the larger reality to me magnified." He is expressing both a wish to see the event and a wish not to see but to be told about it instead. We can guess what it is he wishes to see and not see from some remarks I omitted in quoting him earlier:

> . . . many times words describe something & make it more *real* for me. Like at the first chapter, he is lonely at night and *hears sounds that a ghost who couldn't communicate would say*—this brings another dimension, another type of definition that I never would have thought of but will think of again. Maybe the next time I'm alone at night a noise will become more than a noise for me. My most favorite passage . . .

One can guess that what this student wishes to be told about has to do with sights and noises at night—certainly his "most favorite passage" does.

Curiously, though—or not so curiously—he omits from his recollection of the passage precisely the part that has most to do with investigating nighttime activities:

> I saw it was a dog, a young, gangly mongrel slipped off from home to find out about things went on after dark. He was sniffing digger squirrel holes, not with a notion to go digging after one but just to get an idea what they were up to at this hour. He'd run his muzzle down a hole, butt up in the air and tail going, then dash off to another. . . . Galloping from one particularly interesting hole to the next, he became so took with what was coming off—the moon up there, the night, the breeze full of smells so wild makes a young dog drunk—that he had to lie down on his back and roll. He twisted and thrashed around like a fish, back bowed and belly up, and when he got to his feet and shook himself a spray came off him in the moon like silver scales.
>
> He sniffed all the holes over again one quick one, to get the smells down good, then suddenly froze still with one paw lifted and his head tilted, listening.

The passage contains much genital symbolism: the dog poking his nose down holes; his phallic body, ultimately fish-like; the smells; phrases like, "Things went on after dark," "what were they up to at this hour," "what was coming off," or "a spray came off him." All this presented as a sight seen suggests that we are confronting a primal scene fantasy, most of which the student omits or blurs in remembering the passage.

The flight of the geese continues the primal scene symbolism, now, though, in as eerie a fashion as the silent, motionless wolves in Wolf-Man's primal scene dream [as described in Freud's "From the History of an Infantile Neurosis" (1918)]. "Then they crossed the moon—a black, weaving necklace, drawn into a V by that lead goose. For an instant that lead goose was right in the center of that circle, bigger than the others, a black cross opening and closing, then he pulled his V out of sight into the sky once more." During this flight, the dog stands motionless and silent. Then, "he commenced to lope off in the direction they had gone, toward the highway, loping steady and solemn like he had an appointment." The novel continues to a third version of primal scene material, the implicit collision of the dog and the car.

If we look at this section of the novel as a transformation, it is reworking the primal scene fantasy at its core into a meaningful theme: the inevitable spoiling of—everything. The dog's innocent curiosity about the squirrels becomes his wonder at the geese and his apparent wish to join them and is ended by the danger that he will be struck by a car when he tries to. Kesey's novel deals throughout with the issue of contact and contact observed: here, dog-squirrel, dog-grass, dog-geese, dog-car, and finally the attendants who grab the narrator from behind. Contact destroys in this novel. Here, so long as the dog does not actually touch a squirrel or a goose, all is well. Trouble comes when the dog tries to contact the geese or when the car nears the dog or the men grab the speaker. Kesey handles the primal scene fantasy at the core by disguising it symbolically and splitting it into three distinct episodes, each with a different tone representing different possible responses to the primal scene: curiosity, awe and wonder, fear.

The student responded to the passage by omitting (repressing?) the first, most explicit statement of the fantasy and coalescing the second and third into a noisier, boisterous image with something of the security of a cliché. Further, he makes the dog, not a silent watcher of the goose opening and closing in the circle of the moon, but an active, phallic dog "outside and free," jumping and baying at objects impossibly distant. So far from the words bringing him "all the little pieces of the larger reality . . . magnified," he has converted the words back into a picture that leaves out the little holes and changes the fear of passively experiencing a primal scene into solitary, phallic activity followed by punishment. Or so we can surmise. Actually to know what was going on in his mind, we would have to talk it over with him.

Even so, the model tells us what to listen for, both in the novel and in the student's response to it. Understanding literature as a transformational process leads us to the fantasy material and the relation between the novel's way of handling it and the reader's. Here, we can guess that the fantasy material and the symbolic disguise of it matched something in the reader; it is his "most favorite passage." But we can also surmise that the first statement of the primal scene fantasy was insufficiently disguised for him and the second and third unsatisfyingly so, for he omits the one and supplies noise, violent activity, and disastrous contact to the others. We can also guess that no small part of his pleasure in the passage comes from his own mastery of the threatening material, not the novel's. (pp. 310-21)

[The] possibilities for both critics and teachers to change a reader's pattern of responses are quite limited. Much the greater part of response depends on the reader's own character, which only a therapist—at best—can alter. One's whole ability to become engrossed, for example, depends on the capacity to regress and be passively receptive; one of the deepest of human traits, no pedagogy can touch it. Most teachers, I think, believe they can "improve" their students' tastes. As we have seen, though, preferences depend on character; a reader will respond "I like it" to those literary works that match his own patterns of fantasy and, particularly, defense. What a teacher may be able to do is get his student to accept more complex or exotic works within his established pattern of preferences. It seems very doubtful that he can change a characterological preference for one kind of defense or adaptation over another. Ultimately, the model insists, response depends on us, not our critics or teachers.

The teaching of literature thus inevitably raises another, more profound question: Does literature have any moral effect? Plato first raised the issue, banning poetry that would consist of untruths over-stimulating the emotions. Aristotle, supposedly, laid the issue to rest with his statement that catharsis or purgation of the emotions is healthy. Literature has a moral effect, but it is a good one. Thus, Northrop Frye writes [in his *Anatomy of Criticism*]: "There is no reason why a great poet should be a wise and good man, or even a tolerable human being, but there is every reason why his reader should be improved in his humanity as a result of reading him." Yet, if this were true, English departments would be filled with saintly men, whereas, in fact, English departments are widely thought to be the most cantankerous of all.

To be sure, a literary work can implant an idea in us. Just as the television commercial offers a product as a solution to the psychological issue it raises, so other kinds of literary work can provide an idea or an attitude as a solution to fantasy content. Satire typically does or, as we have seen, propaganda, such as the muckraking novels or the films of World War II in which nasty Nipponese menaced blond American nurses. The films offered combat—activity—as the way to erase the passive primal scene threat. But those who claim a moral effect for literature usually imply something more than the moral effect of a newspaper editorial—some kind of deeper change in character, an improvement in a man's humanity, to use Frye's phrase. Does literature "improve" a man "in his humanity"? That would seem to be a psychological question, but, as Robert E. Lane drily remarks [in his *Liberties of Wit*], "I am not aware of great attention by any of these [psychiatric] authors or by the psychotherapeutic profession to the role of literary study in the development of conscience—most of their attention is to a pre-literate period of life, or, for the theologians of course, to the influence of religion." Frye is only the latest in the long tradition of critics who have put aside psychological evidence to claim a moral value for literature.

Our model suggests an explanation at least for the subjective feeling that many readers have that they have been improved in their humanity by literature. . . . [In] introjecting the literary work, we partially regress. The work thus evokes in us a larger, deeper, richer self than the one we bring to everyday life. Moreover, within that larger self, the literary work embeds a fantasy or impulse which it—and we—then transform toward social, moral, or intellectual meaning. Transformed along with it are our own associations and analogizings to that fantasy. The condensations and displacements, both large and small, both in linguistic details and large segments of action, give us a feeling that we have mastered something—the fantasy content and our associations to it—which would ordinarily be repulsive to our egos. Literature has something in it of the saturnalia: the superego permits the ego to transgress all kinds of taboos for a limited time, then re-establishes control; and the re-establishment of control itself comes as a kind of relief and mastery.

This, however, is a subjective feeling of moral mastery that comes during and after the reading of some particular work. Do these short-term effects result in a permanent change in character, an improvement in our humanity? From a purely psychological point of view, it seems highly unlikely, for we know that character is formed largely in the oedipal and pre-oedipal stages. By the time we get round to reading books, we bring to them a rather firmly structured personality. On the other hand, we have all seen adolescents become, for a month or two, Hamlet or Raskolnikov or Julien Sorel under the influence of some reading experience. In effect, there is a change of character for a period much longer than just the reading itself. But this is precisely the task of adolescence in human development: to achieve an identity separate from the family unit by trying out a variety of identities. The adolescent can just as well imitate a teacher or a peer or a movie star as a literary character. In other words, the possible character changes a particular book might evoke in an adolescent have more to do with his adolescence than the nature of the literary experience.

Nevertheless, adolescence provides a clue to the changes in character literary experiences might cause. For all of us, not just adolescents, literature lets us try on a different identity. That is, with literature, we introject an experience of fantasy and (more important, morally) defensive modes we would not ordinarily have, namely those the writer has embodied in the text. For the long moment of the work of art, we experience his character-traits as our own, especially his defenses and adaptations.

Thus, the writer becomes willy-nilly a transmitter of cultural values, for he has been shaped, as all men have, by the culture in which he matured. . . . [I have] been relatively silent about the role of culture in an individual's literary response. My reason has been that the individual's own psychic structures make much more of a difference in response. A reader may adopt totally or totally reverse and reject the values embodied in a given writing, depending on his own character-traits, his attitudes toward authority, for example, or his sexuality or aggression. Nevertheless, culture has an effect and there is a kind of feedback loop: culture shapes the writer's character, his patterns of fantasy and defense; the reader introjects the writer's character for the time he is absorbed in the writer's writing; the reader may then modify the culture around him as a result of his literary experience. The human links in this feedback are quite unpredictable, however. The writer may radically modify the defenses or adaptations he has absorbed from his culture. The reader may change or reject the defenses and adaptations he takes in from the writer. And, of course, the motor inhibition of the aesthetic experience makes it quite problematic whether or not he will act on his culture as a result of his reading.

Even so, we can distinguish two opposite situations: where a writing closely conforms to cultural values; where it directly challenges them. Totalitarian governments, as Plato himself prescribed, have insisted their citizens get a steady diet of literature confirming the values of the state. It seems unlikely, however, that, say, the socialist realism of the Stalinist era and after played much part in brainwashing the Russian citizen. After all, the entire social and informational apparatus was engaged in this effort—art and literature can have been only a few among a great many experiences shaping the citizen's character toward a proper socialist state of mind. A much more likely effect of political censorship, it seems to me, is the elimination of literary experiences that might possibly loosen the rigidity with which the citizen applies culturally sanctioned patterns of defense and adaptation. Totalitarianism controls literary response not so much to teach as to avoid unteaching.

The pithy remarks of Marshall McLuhan, however, suggest a more accidental totalitarianism in art. The medium is the message: that is, in our terms, television, film, radio, books—any medium, "hot" or "cool"—gets us to introject and experience as our own the defenses and adaptations appropriate to that medium. McLuhan seems to be saying that sheer force of habit inculcates these defensive modes in us. A society in which all literature is in books will necessarily embody in its citizens linear, sequential modes of thought; the members of a television-oriented society will be more adept at projection and regression.

McLuhan may be right—I think he is—but it is well to recognize the limitations of what he says. If the medium is the message, then all works in that medium transmit the same message. All the books ever written encourage only one value: linear, sequential thought. Clearly, McLuhan is using the word "message" to mean something radically different from the "message" conveyed by particular poems, stories, or plays, which may enact pros and cons on a great variety of psychosocial issues. What McLuhan describes as "the message" is a pervasive structure (or, more fashionably, infrastructure) of the kind anthropologists like Kluckhohn or Lévi-Strauss discover. Such a structure all aspects of a society—especially all the technological aspects—tend to reinforce. The artistic totalitarianism McLuhan implies is no more than the tyranny of history.

The polar opposite of totalitarianism in art is the dissenting writer in a free society. Yet here, too, one can wonder if he works deep changes in those who read him, whether his "No! in Thunder" is really loud enough to muffle all the other cultural voices in the mind of his audience. Deep in the American grain is the defensive use of phallic activity as an escape from, or pseudo-solution of, needs for dependency—this is our Puritan and revolutionary heritage; it has been called "the American neurosis." Reading Leonard Cohen or any of the other good writers currently expounding a "love ethic" with its emphasis on giving in to dependency needs seems hardly likely to overcome the older adaptation in any given reader. One in whose character the Protestant work-ethic is deeply engrained may toss aside *Beautiful Losers* in outrage and disgust. Another reader, in whom the phallic solution has failed, may embrace the gospel. But such a "conversion" comes not so much from the novel itself as from the character the reader brings to the novel. The best a writer like Cohen can hope for from a reader with "the American neurosis" is that he will loosen the rigidity with which he applies his typical defense. In short, a free literature seems not so much to teach for or against a given set of cultural values as to keep open, at least for the time of reading, the possibility of change. Like the adolescent, we try on roles.

So, at least, say a group of psychological writers [including Marion Milner and Heinz Hartmann]. . . . [The] "willing suspension of disbelief," that partial, encapsulated regression, creates a richer, longer kind of self than our ordinary one. We become a "rind" of higher ego functions around a "core" regressed to the very deep, primary atoneness with a nurturing other—the text. As a result, we respond to literature in more complex, larger ways than we can to reality. According to Marion Milner, illusions such as art and play let us relax those early established boundaries between self and not-self. We regress preparatory to future growth, taking one step backward to gain two forward. "Regressive adaptation," Heinz Hartmann calls it, "precisely because of the detour through the archaic."

Literature, these writers suggest, may have two adaptive modes: it opens up possibilities of fuller response to the text itself; perhaps it also opens up possibilities of growth once we have put the text aside. Whether growth will in fact come is questionable—unless we make the quite unwarranted assumption that a momentary loosening of boundaries during reading will carry over to other activities. And even if growth comes, it will very likely come from quite unliterary experiences. The moral effect of literature, then, is really to create not long-term change in itself, but a possibility of change. Art, in Mrs. Milner's more optimistic phrasing [in her *On Not Being Able to Paint*], "is a making of new bottles for the continually distilled new wine of developing experience."

Mrs. Milner, however, goes further, suggesting that art may specifically break down in us the primal aggression from the frustrations inherent in the infant's early total dependence on a nurturing other: "this hate that is inherent in the fact that we do have to make the distinction between subject and object," "the primitive hating that results from the inescapable discrepancy between subjective and objective, between the unlimited possibilities of one's dreams and what the real world actually offers us."

> It is surely through the arts that we deliberately restore the split and bring subject and object together into a particular kind of new unity. What I had not seen clearly before was that in the arts, although a bit of the outside world is altered, distorted from its "natural" shape, to fit the inner experience, it is still a bit of the outside world, it is still paint or stone or spoken or written words or movements of bodies or sounds of instruments. It is still a bit of the outside world, but the difference is that work has been done, there has been a labour to make it nearer one's inner conception, not in the way of the practical work of the world, but in an 'as if' way. Thus it seemed that the experience of outer and inner coinciding, which we blindly undergo when we fall in love, is consciously brought about in the arts, through the conscious acceptance of the as-if-ness of the experience and the conscious manipulation of a malleable material. So surely it comes about that in the experience which we call the aesthetic one the cause of the primary hate is temporarily transcended.

She is reaching the same conclusion that the courtesy-books of the Renaissance did: art ennobles in the same way that being in love does. She, however, takes still another step:

> Not only is it [the primary hate] temporarily transcended, surely also it is permanently lessened. For in the satisfying experience of embodying the illusion there has in fact been an interchange. Since the object is thereafter endowed with a bit of the "me," one can no longer see it in quite the same way as before; and since the "me," the inner experience, has become enriched with a bit more of external reality, there is now a closer relation between wishes and what can really exist and so less cause for hate, less despair of ever finding anything that satisfies.

She states, in effect, that affection for works of art one has created or experienced persists, but whether this relation to certain bits of the outer world carries over to all the not-self—I wonder.

Either mode, though, seems worth encouraging, either permanent or temporary transcending of primal hate, toward particular objects or more generally. But "our whole traditional educational procedure tends to perpetuate this hate, by concentrating so much on only one half of our relation to the world, the part of it to do with intellectual knowing, the part in which subject and object have perforce to be kept separate."

Observations of problems to do with painting had

all led up to the idea that awareness of the external world is itself a creative process, an immensely complex creative interchange between what comes from inside and what comes from outside, a complex alternation of fusing and separating. But since the fusing stage is, to the intellectual mind, a stage of illusion, intoxication, transfiguration, it is one that is not so easily allowed for in an age and civilisation where matter-of-factness, the keeping of oneself apart from what one looks at, has become all-important. And this fact surely has wide implications for education. For it surely means that education for a democracy, if it is to foster that true sanity which is necessary in citizens of a democracy, foster the capacity to see the facts for oneself, rather than seeing only what one is told to see, must also fully understand the stages by which such objectivity is reached. In fact, it must understand subjectivity otherwise the objectivity it aims at will be in danger of fatal distortion.

Mrs. Milner's "surely's" suggest a certainty about the possibility of reducing man's primal aggression or of educating for democracy that I share only partly, at best. But I can surely agree that almost all education as we know it does far too little to nourish and understand subjectivity. Education in art and literature should seek to encourage the fusion of self and object in aesthetic experience, even though, as our model suggests, the ability to fuse stems from deep traits of character and there may be severe limits on what a teacher in a classroom can do. It is still undeniably worth a try.

In sum, literature seems to have two, in a way opposite, possibilities for moral effect. First, literature may reinforce or counter the defenses and adaptations our culture builds into us. Second, literature lets us experience those and other values in a more open, "as if" way; it breaks down—for a time—the boundaries between self and other, inner and outer, past and future, and it may neutralize the primal aggression bound up in those separations. Yet, given the firmness of cultural structures and individual character, it is very hard to see how the effects of literature can be more than small, local, and transient. All our inferences about the dynamics of literary response suggest that the experience of literature is but one experience among many to which we react, that other cultural and familial forces shape us much earlier and much more forcefully, to say nothing of our own heredity. Without experimental evidence, the best information we have suggests that we should make no claim of a long-term moral effect for literature. At most, literature may open for us some flexibility of mind so that growth from it and other kinds of experience remains possible.

A free literature makes for free men and an open society—that statement is perhaps true, perhaps only a little bit true, or, as seems most likely, it states a wish and illusion. What is not illusory is the especially deep psychic pleasure literature offers us. Having understood that pleasure somewhat, having through psychoanalysis seen its dark origins and its moral and social limitations, we need now the courage to accept literature, not for what we wish it were but for the one thing we can be certain it is—a source of rich and special pleasures, good in themselves, needing and perhaps having no further justification. In the deepest sense, to accept, understand, and enjoy literature for what it is, we must also accept, understand, and enjoy ourselves for what we are. Whatever psychoanalysis says about literature, it shows us how irreducibly human it is. As we respond, its glories become ours. As for its limitations, they have always been our own. (pp. 332-41)

Norman N. Holland, "The Model Moralized," in his The Dynamics of Literary Response, *Oxford University Press, Inc., 1968, pp. 308-41.*

Simon O. Lesser

[*Lesser is an American critic whose influential study* Fiction and the Unconscious *has been praised for its accessibility to readers not trained in psychoanalysis and for its lucid style. In the following excerpt from that work, Lesser analyzes conscious and unconscious processes involved in reader response to fiction.*]

We read [fiction] . . . to satisfy needs of which we are largely unaware—and of which in many cases we must remain unaware if reading is to give us pleasure. We know at least some of the reasons why such a make-believe activity as reading can provide compensation for the limitations, deprivations and discontents of our actual experience, and we know with what discretion fiction fulfils the service for which we turn to it.

The discretion is the more extraordinary because great fiction is far more intrepid in its approach to life than we ordinarily are ourselves. It resolutely probes conflicts we hesitate to examine, seeking to uncover all the factors involved in them and the exact influence of each. As in that chapter of *The Scarlet Letter* called "A Flood of Sunshine," it shows the virtue and perhaps the beauty of impulses we either deny or gratify in a shamefaced way which robs them of dignity. At the same time, and with equal strictness, it shows us the results of our misdeeds and our mistakes, whether these take the form of yielding to our impulses, denying them, or satisfying them in covert or neurotic fashion: it forces us to see consequences to which we would prefer to close our eyes or which we believe by some magic can be averted. And it arranges, it almost points, to make us see that certain happenings *are* consequences. Unlike life, it has no use for irrelevant developments which obscure connections or accidents which thwart the natural development of a given set of forces.

As we know, fiction contrives to give us these uncompromising images of our nature and our fate without permitting us to become aware of their personal relevance. It pretends, and we accept the pretense, that the characters whose affairs it chronicles are strangers in whom we have no reason to take a special interest. There is also a certain duplicity in the way it sets their affairs before us. Its light is like that furnished by those torches Hawthorne describes in "My Kinsman, Major Molineux," which conceal by their glare the very objects they illuminate. The light enables us to see without always being able to say precisely what it is we see, to understand without formulating our understanding.

Fiction accomplishes something more miraculous than this. It *involves* us in the events it puts before us, without permitting us to become aware of the nature and extent, or usually even the fact, of our involvement. The emotions fiction arouses in us are evidence of this: they are too pow-erful to be explained solely on the basis of our cognitive reactions, conscious and even unconscious. Normally, to be sure, even the emotions remain unnoticed, but sometimes they force themselves on our attention, occasionally by some visible sign, such as weeping. (pp. 188-89)

Let us attempt to reconstruct the entire process [of response]—its unconscious as well as its conscious components.

The difficulties of such an endeavor are apparent. In a way it is comparable to the attempt to reconstruct the dreamwork—the activity involved in transforming latent dream thoughts into a dream we may remember. In one way our endeavor is perhaps more difficult: at least after the latent dream thoughts have been reconstructed, it is only necessary to ask, "Why and how were they metamorphosed into the manifest dream?" One is working between two relatively fixed points. In our endeavor, only the story is fixed, and not all observers will agree about its meaning and objective qualities. Response to the story radiates centrifugally, is in part unconscious and, if not inexhaustible, is likely to be so copious that it is impossible to recapture *in toto*. Furthermore, as we know, response varies widely from individual to individual.

But these difficulties are less formidable than they appear. It does not really matter either that there are individual variations in response or that one cannot recapture all the reactions of a single reader. All we are after is knowledge of the *kinds* of reactions which occur; from such knowledge, without too much difficulty, we can identify at least some of the processes of response. And, fortunately, we sometimes have direct access to reactions of which we are normally unaware and even to the unconscious processes of response. As a result of the mechanism Freud described as flexibility of the repressions, we can occasionally catch a glimpse of reactions which usually take place below the threshold of awareness. This may occur during reading or perhaps during a second or third, and unusually analytic, reading of a given work. Far more frequently, according to my experience, it occurs *after* reading, as one mulls over the effect a story has had upon one. Sometimes a stray thought which crosses one's mind weeks or months after reading a story makes one aware of a reaction to it one was unaware until then of having had. Such glimpses, whenever they occur, will make most fair-minded people willing to admit that when they read fiction they may have many reactions of which they are usually oblivious.

Empirical studies of response to fiction provide evidence of unconscious response and a great deal of information—though not, of course, necessarily complete information—about its nature. Reports supplied to me by psychoanalysts who have cooperated with this study also show that reactions to fiction are by no means entirely conscious, as is sometimes assumed.

Of the reality of unconscious response to fiction, therefore, I believe there is no basis for reasonable doubt. The evidence also permits us to identify some of the processes which take place below the threshold of awareness, and to describe them with a fair degree of assurance. When we go beyond this and try to reconstruct the entire process of response, it is necessary to depend to some extent on reasoning and conjecture. In the theory to be offered here there are possibilities for error which I do not wish to minimize. It is possible that mechanisms as important as any of those we know about have eluded identification. Since the mechanisms to be dealt with cannot be seen steadily and clearly, I may make mistakes in describing them. Mistakes are still more likely to occur when we try to trace the connections among the mechanisms and to surmise the contribution each makes to the total impact of fiction. The present attempt to reconstruct the process of response to fiction is likely to resemble one of those crude early maps which exaggerate the dimensions of certain territories, underestimate others, describe some geographic features mistakenly and omit others of considerable significance. However, even a map which shows what is now known, or can be conjectured, is not to be despised. If it is accurate in broad outline, it may be helpful to later explorers.

Let us begin with a kind of rough sketch which will orient us to the more significant features of the experience we are going to consider.

To facilitate matters let us leave to one side response to books which do not attempt to involve us in the events they relate or do not succeed in doing so. Most comedies belong in the former class. Like works of fiction in any other genre, they move us emotionally as well as intellectually, but they do so almost entirely by appealing to us as spectators; they seldom seek to entangle us in the events they put before us. Books may also fail to involve us because we do not permit ourselves to become immersed in them. We approach certain books in an attitude of "adult discount," with a resolute coolness and detachment. For example, stories of whose suitability for our children we want to make sure might be read in this spirit, or favorites of our youth to which we return with feelings of amused superiority. Far more frequently, we remain detached despite a willingness and desire to immerse ourselves in what we are reading. We find a book we had expected to enjoy contrived or juvenile—exaggeratedly and conscientiously lurid, let us say—and while we read on, perhaps with a certain fascinated horror at its badness, we remain on the outside, aloof and critical.

Our first concern must be to ascertain what occurs in us when a story ensnares us and transports us to the special world it has created. The indispensable condition of such an experience, and the first stage of the experience itself, is a relaxation of the vigilance usually exercised by the ego. A willing suspension of disbelief, a receptive attitude, is essential not only to the enjoyment but even to the understanding of fiction. Since when we read or go to the theater it is because we are in search of the satisfactions fiction offers, it might be thought that the ego might be quite willing to relax, and no questions asked. And, indeed, there is ordinarily a certain willingness to let go, an impulse to loosen the reins somewhat. Actual reduction of control does not always follow immediately and automatically, however, any more than it does when we visit friends or engage in some other activity which promises to give us pleasure. Certain people simply cannot relax. Some basic personality difficulty, such as a weak ego organization and a consequent dread of fantasy, prevents it. Since the fantasies embedded in fiction often involve a potential threat to the ego's authority, even people with a trustworthy ego organization usually demand that a story satisfy certain conditions before they surrender themselves to it.

These conditions are variable rather than fixed. Because of differences in personality structure, some people—let us say compulsives, used to screening any experience carefully—are much stricter in their demands than others. A given person will scrutinize fiction more carefully at one time than another. Even one's preconceptions about the potential dangerousness of various genres, or individual works, may affect one's willingness to let go: standards are probably relatively high for tragedy, relatively low for musical comedy.

Because there are so many variables, it is difficult to make generalizations about the conditions governing relaxation. It appears, however, that the standards the average discriminating adult reader applies to serious fiction have to be characterized as rigorous rather than lax. While such a reader usually accepts, and even seems to welcome, departures from the literal facts about experience, he insists that the most airy fantasy, no less than a naturalistic novel, have some valid reference to psychological realities. As though distrustful of a work unwilling to abide by its own terms, he also insists that a work progress with a scrupulous regard for internal consistency. Finally, not only the discriminating reader but almost every reader tries to make sure that dangerous material is not handled in a way which is offensive. Though the judging activity of the ego becomes more automatic once its confidence has been won, it never ceases, and the ego will resume a vigilant attitude, and withdraw the trust it has provisionally granted, if a story transgresses against its standards. The conscious intelligence is not displaced in response to fiction because intense unconscious activity is also involved; there is work aplenty for all parts of the psychic apparatus.

It follows, incidentally, that there is no necessary quarrel between effortless, intuitive enjoyment of fiction and the close, careful reading for which some kinds of literary study equip one. There *may* be a quarrel, for the attempt to discover all the features and tendencies to which a student's attention has been directed may require him to read with a strained alertness, which is inimical to enjoyment. If in addition the student is under pressure to read at an unnaturally fast rate of speed, his reading is not likely to give him a great deal of pleasure. Fortunately, as it seems to me, pressures must be heavy and persistent to induce anyone to read fiction too alertly or too fast. To some extent at least the desire for pleasure may be counted upon to counteract the pressures, so that sooner or later, against one's resolve, one is likely to revert to a pace and a way of reading which are not incompatible with enjoyment.

Relaxation and enjoyment are impossible when a student, or anyone else, reads fiction which is really beyond him. But, again fortunately, only exceptional pressures, inner or outer, can induce one to do much reading of this character. Respectable motives, such as self-improvement, or less respectable ones, such as the desire to impress others, may make us ambitious to read certain works—usually "classics"—which we expect to find difficult, but we do not always "get around" to reading these works, nor finish them even if they are begun. . . . [We] tend to search for fiction which is on our own plane of intellectual and emotional sensibility. Our distaste for books which we would have to tax ourselves to follow should not be attributed to mere laziness. It perhaps indicates an intuitive awareness of how much a relaxed attitude contributes to the enjoyment and understanding of fiction. It may also be an expression of a desire to conserve energy for the very intensive unconscious psychic activity involved in response.

A final condition of reduction of control by the ego is that the reading experience should not threaten to lead to immediate physical action. The ego will not stand idly by while decisions affecting conduct are being reached. The dangerous fantasies embodied in fiction are tolerated only on condition that, and only so long as, they are taken as fantasies.

As in dreaming and daydreaming, the immobility of the body provides a certain amount of reassurance. But the ego demands additional safeguards as well. It requires that fiction be approached with a certain detachment—more technically, with instinctual energy sufficiently neutralized so that what we read is disassociated from our experience, from either gratifying needs in actuality or laying plans to gratify them. It requires that fiction be approached with a certain detachment—more technically, with instinctual energy sufficiently neutralized so that what we read is disassociated from our experience, from either gratifying needs in actuality or laying plans to gratify them. It requires that one part of us remain aware of the make-believe character of the reading experience. The importance of the resources available to fiction for reminding us of this—for differentiating and distancing its events from the world of our experience—is apparent. A work which eschews these resources and incites us to some action, disregarding or even attempting to obliterate the division between fiction and reality, labors under grave and perhaps insuperable handicaps. Because it keeps us on guard, it cannot engage our emotions and accomplish its practical objective. It cannot give us pleasure. To some extent even fiction which seeks to foster a particular attitude shares these handicaps. It arouses resistance. It may open our eyes to an aspect of a situation to which we have been blind, and this must be regarded as a valuable service. But unless it transcends its own purpose, it cannot touch our hearts. It cannot promote that rounded, compassionate seeing which is possible only when we are not too close to a situation, and not too partisan in our view of it.

Though even some of the "conscious" activities involved in response to fiction are sometimes quasi-automatic, they can be identified and described without too much difficulty. Basically the mind is occupied in following a story as it develops and in grasping its manifest meaning. Secondarily—incidentally rather than systematically—it is engaged in appraising: in judging such things as the honesty of a story, its relevance for the reader, the skill with which it is worked out. Both activities may involve "placing" a story—in terms of its period, tradition or genre, the previous work of the same author, or any other point of reference which facilitates understanding and judgment.

These activities can keep the conscious mind very busily employed. Even the task of following and interpreting the surface significance of a story often involves a great deal more than it may appear to. We feel impelled to read fiction at a fairly rapid speed. The events of a single story may be numerous, complex and intricately interrelated. Furthermore, they are not developed continuously; and certain things are left unexplained or are only partially explained. The storyteller requires the reader to make inter-

polations and draw inferences, to participate actively in the task of understanding his tale.

We could, of course, read only fiction which we can understand with an absolute minimum of effort. But we seem to avoid such fiction as instinctively as we avoid that which we would have to exert ourselves to understand. There is more than one reason . . . but the immediately relevant consideration is that it seems essential for the enjoyment of fiction that the mind should be rather fully occupied. If it is not, it is likely to penetrate to meanings and appeals which would arouse disquiet, or even revulsion, if brought to light. The engagement of the conscious intelligence seems a necessary condition and cover for the unconscious activity involved in response.

Of one or two of the characteristics of unconscious response we can also speak with reasonable assurance. If only from glimpses we occasionally catch of the unconscious in operation, we know that it often works at lightning speed. We know, too, that it is unbelievably perceptive, and prodigal in supplying us with impressions and associations. Certain peculiarities of the unconscious processes facilitate speed and prodigality. The unconscious does not have to work out anything in detail either to reach or express understanding. Unconscious understanding is immediate, intuitive. In expressing understanding, the unconscious employs either words or images, whichever are most suitable for its purpose, without regard for consistency. Sometimes it eschews both, so that the only trace of its activity lies in the alteration of our feelings. Unburdened by the need to be coherent or consistent, employing the most slapdash kind of shorthand, the unconscious can easily outspeed and outproduce the painstaking conscious intelligence. Thus a few unconnected words which come to our lips unbidden may bespeak an understanding of some buried, abstruse meaning of a story to which our intellect could penetrate only with the utmost difficulty and express with tiresome effort.

In writing about unconscious responses, incidentally, it is almost impossible to do justice to their darting speed and largely non-verbal character. To make their nature and influence clear one is almost compelled to use terms which suggest that they are more carefully and coherently worked out than in fact they are; indeed, one tends inevitably to describe them on the analogy of conscious mental operations. To take a simple example, a mother's acceptance of her son's relationship with a married woman (or some similar permissive plot element) might contribute to reader acceptance of the affair. In the reading experience a readier acceptance of the illicit relationship might be the only indication that the unconscious had been at work. A report of the experience, on the other hand, could hardly avoid suggesting that the mother's attitude had been singled out for special attention and its permissive influence verbalized. In reading this . . . it is necessary to allow for communication difficulties of this kind.

Three unconscious processes can be distinguished in response to fiction. Of course, they do not occur in isolation, but in admixture with one another and with conscious psychic operations.

The first process is a part of our "spectator" reaction to fiction. It is basically concerned with perception and understanding. "The heart has its reasons which the reason knows not," and the unconscious can immediately and effortlessly understand certain things which our conscious intelligence would find puzzling and even inexplicable.

What kinds of things are likely to be unconsciously rather than consciously apprehended? In answering, we should be careful to exclude things which though ostensibly hidden are really meant to be grasped by the intellect—for example, the real motives for a certain action as contrasted with the explanation offered by a character blind to the forces driving him, or dishonest reasons advanced to deceive someone. In such cases as these, fiction writers want us to be aware of the truth. The things which are meant to be apprehended unconsciously they are usually unaware of themselves—or, to be more accurate, they are unaware of their unconscious significance. Increasingly, however, now that knowledge of depth psychology is spreading, writers may consciously weave into their fiction things which they intend to be unconsciously understood. It seems safer to develop a definition in terms of the reader.

In general, it is things which would arouse anxiety, directly or indirectly, if consciously perceived which are likely to be apprehended unconsciously. It is not possible to specify the exact things, because these vary reader by reader. People differ widely in their ability to tolerate anxiety and in the things which cause them anxiety, and any given person may change in both respects at different times. "Economic" considerations complicate matters: isolated instances in which warded-off impulses secure gratification might be consciously observed, and accepted, because they mobilized relatively small amounts of anxiety. Yet these very things would be more likely to be unconsciously apprehended if they threatened to fit into an over-all interpretation which was inacceptable to the ego and a potential source of serious anxiety. A selective principle influences our understanding: we try to "repress," to keep from awareness, those perceptions which might cause us appreciable discomfort or pain. Of course, we are not always successful in doing so. An inexpert writer may compel us to take conscious note of things we would prefer to understand unconsciously.

Events or other aspects of fiction which have deep roots in the unconscious are especially likely to be unconsciously apprehended. In fiction, as in life, almost everything which happens is unconsciously determined to some extent. What is astonishing is the preoccupation of fiction with actions which are *decisively* determined by unconscious factors. The major actions . . . of a large proportion of all the world's fiction are so determined. Of course, unconscious springs of action are not always so hidden or so objectionable that they cannot be consciously apprehended; and in the relatively small body of fiction which appeals to us primarily as spectators even the perception of the ignoble motives animating the characters, from whom we feel disassociated, is ordinarily a source of pleasure. When we identify with the characters of a story, on the other hand, we are usually no more willing to acknowledge such motives than they are themselves.

Episodes which remind us of painful experiences or of aspects of our present situation about which we feel anxiety are also likely to be understood unconsciously. Empirical evidence indicates that such episodes also tend to be "forgotten" with comparative rapidity; in some cases, doubt-less, they have not so much been thrust from the mind as denied the opportunity to register upon it. Story elements which come too close to some psychic sore spot may seem incomprehensible, or be distorted, by readers who intellectually are quite capable of understanding them. Dr. Martha Wolfenstein's study of reactions of four-, five- and six-year-old children and their mothers to a story called "Sally and the Baby and the Rampatan" illustrates this dramatically ["The Impact of a Children's Story on Mothers and Children," *Monographs of the Society for Research in Child Development*, No. 42, XI, 1946]. The children, for whom the story provided a covert and acceptable way of expressing and working through hostility toward an expected second child, understood the story's central fantasy better than their mothers, who, identifying with the pregnant fictional mother, felt threatened by the very emotions the story was intended to arouse. Clearly, we are willing to go to great lengths *not* to become consciously aware of meanings which would cause us pain. But the storyteller must cooperate: when he deals with potentially upsetting material, he must keep part of our minds in darkness of what he is about.

Frequently the connections among various actions and meanings which run through an entire story would also arouse anxiety if brought to awareness, and are left to the unconscious to apprehend. There can be no question that in response to fiction the unconscious engages in a kind of activity which we may think of as a prerogative of consciousness: it ferrets out connections, draws inferences and establishes connections; *it synthesizes its observations.* When we read *Hamlet,* for example, it is the unconscious which is likely to take note of the contrast between the speed and sureness with which Hamlet acts on a half-dozen occasions and his powerlessness to proceed with that one action he has pledged himself to perform; the contrast between his dilatoriness and the speed with which Laertes acts in a similar situation; and countless other things which betray the secret sources of Hamlet's inability to carry out his mission. By piecing together and interpreting such observations the unconscious may penetrate to an entire level of meaning—or to numerous levels of meaning—to which, during reading at least, the conscious mind is blind.

In our response to a story as a unified whole, no less than in our understanding of many of its component parts, unconscious perception plays an indispensable role. The things the unconscious perceives have to be communicated, or we miss the deepest sources of pleasure procurable through reading fiction. They have to be communicated unconsciously, or they will backfire and arouse painful anxiety.

The second and third kinds of unconscious response to fiction constitute a kind of activity, though, of course, the activity is psychic, not actual, and tolerated by the ego on that account. They are forms of response in which we are actors and not merely spectators. In the first of these "active" forms of response, we unconsciously participate in the stories we read; in the second, we compose stories structured upon the ones we read (or upon parts of them) which give us an opportunity to relive or alter our actual experience or act out dramas revolving around our wishes and fears. The last-mentioned kind of response, the creation of stories parallel to the ones we read in which we play a part, I call analogizing.

Whereas unconscious perception supplements the cognitive activity of consciousness, unconscious participation and analogizing may be said to comprise our "action" response to fiction. We are almost never conscious of becoming involved in the fiction we read. We maintain the illusion that we are simply watching a story unfold itself.

Sometimes, of course, we are doing no more than that. The storyteller may skillfully compel us to take a spectator role, or we may be too detached in our attitude toward a story to become involved in it. As has been said, however, the most frequent cause of our remaining outside the fiction we read is the failure of the storyteller to engage our interests deeply, despite his endeavor to do so and our willingness to be absorbed. Try as we may, we do not always succeed in finding fiction in which, as we sometimes put it, we can "lose ourselves." Some stories revolve around situations which do not interest us, or have characters who impress us as being precious or crude or in some other way are so foreign to us that we cannot identify with them. Even when we finish stories to which we have such negative reactions, we seldom become sufficiently engrossed in them for the participation responses to occur.

When we are engrossed, a great deal of evidence indicates, *we imaginatively experience the entire action, ourselves act out every role.* The experience is, of course, imaginary; it is elliptical in the extreme; it utilizes energy which is at least partly neutralized. Despite all of these provisos, the experience is "real" and, in view of its speed, astonishingly complete; it includes, for example, an understanding of the unconscious significance of the acts we perform.

We do not, of course, ordinarily experience all parts of the action of a given story with the same degree of intensity. As we would expect, there are differences, in accordance with our individual nature and needs, in the completeness with which we identify with different characters and the abandon with which we participate in different episodes. What is startling, however, is how encompassing our experience usually is when we are engrossed. Edith Buxbaum's analysis of a twelve-year-old addict of detective stories ["The Role of Detective Stories in a Child's Analysis," *Psychoanalytic Quarterly,* X, 1941], shows that the boy identified not only, as we would expect, with the invincible and invulnerable heroes of the stories, but, as well, with the unsympathetically presented villains, and even with the victims in their terror, suffering and death. The boy secured the full measure of gratification, open or covert, which each of these roles afforded. Besides binding the anxiety the stories themselves aroused, the identification with the detectives served to make him more secure in the face of the terror his real-life situation inspired and to protect him against some of his own impulses. The identification with the villains satisfied his repressed but powerful hostile feelings toward his uncle, his mother and others; that with the victims, an even more deeply repressed wish to be overcome by the uncle and be the passive victim of love-making conceived as a sadistic assault.

Other studies of response to fiction also indicate that if we can understand and empathize with some of the characters in a story, with varying degrees of candor and completeness we can usually identify with them all. A superfi-

cial explanation is that the writer who possesses the magic to bring some of his characters to light can usually animate all of them. A more basic explanation is that all the characters are so many aspects, acknowledged or unacknowledged, lived-out or repressed, of the writer—and, if we respond to the writer, of ourselves. We know how many roles besides the one we play in life possess recognized attraction. Unconsciously, we may be sure, we desire to be many people besides that paltry thing we call our "self"; we long for many of the qualities we have crushed out in shaping that self.

In the fiction which engages us, characters who have the qualities we have stunted as well as those we have cultivated are both likely to be present. Indeed, many famous pairs of fictional characters are so closely linked that, like Dr. Jekyll and Mr. Hyde, they can be regarded as component parts of one person. They represent dominant and recessive, supplementary, conflicting, or conscious and unconscious aspects of one role. Myshkin and Rogozhin can be regarded in this way, as can Don Quixote and Sancho Panza, Lear and the Fool, possibly Macbeth and his Lady, and, as Dr. Mark Kanzer has observed, the pursuer and the pursued in any number of stories from *Les Misérables* and *Crime and Punishment* to the tales of Sherlock Holmes. If we can understand and identify with any one member of these pairs, we can scarcely fail to identify with the other. However, one identification may be almost conscious, the other deeply buried.

All the empirical evidence I have been able to gather indicates that most people have a wide capacity for identification. Correspondence between a reader and a fictional character facilitates identification, but differences in situation, age and sex do not preclude it. Nor do differences in personality structure, unless they are so pronounced that a reader finds the motivations and thought processes of a character incomprehensible.

In addition to participating vicariously in the stories in which we become absorbed, we frequently create and imaginatively act out stories structured upon them. We analogize. The stories we spin are, of course, highly elliptical. There is neither time nor need to develop them systematically.

Analogizing may involve nothing more than the recognition of a similarity between a fictional event and something which has happened to us, and a rapid reliving of the experience. Or it may involve some welcome alteration of past experience: as the long-suffering Dobbin tells off Amelia we may imagine ourselves speaking in like vein to someone who, we feel, has not sufficiently appreciated our merit and our love. Still more frequently, in all probability, analogizing takes the form of composing fantasies based upon our wishes and fears rather than upon our experience. (pp. 191-203)

Perhaps because [analogizing] is so closely akin to daydreaming, of which we feel vaguely ashamed, it is rarely mentioned in reports of response to fiction. Yet few will doubt that such an activity takes place: almost every reader of fiction has probably caught himself engaging in it at one time or another. Again because of the association with daydreaming, analogizing may not be regarded as a legitimate part of the reading experience. But analogizing should be distinguished from daydreaming. Whereas the latter uses a story only as a point of departure and gets farther and farther away from it, analogizing remains closely bound by the particular events which instigate it. It neither distracts our attention from what we read nor, so far as I have been able to ascertain, conflicts with any other form of response. Analogizing supplies additional evidence of the power of fiction to affect us simultaneously in many ways, and to engage us personally.

Although it will necessarily involve some repetition, it seems desirable to analyze response also from the point of view of the factors responsible for our reactions, conscious and unconscious. Such an analysis will help us to dovetail our knowledge of the processes of response with some of the things we know about fiction itself.

It is already evident that response to fiction is influenced, if not entirely determined, by three things—subject matter, form, and a third factor, as yet unnamed, the amount of difficulty a story offers, its plane of intellectual and emotional sensibility. Our choice of reading fare, which reflects our expectations of what will give us pleasure, is also influenced, though in somewhat different fashion, by the same three factors. Let us see the part each factor plays in selection and response.

Subject matter as it might be described in a book review, the manifest content of fiction, nearly always exerts a great deal of influence upon our decision of what we shall read. For example, we may decide to read a novel because it deals with some milieu which interests us—perhaps the community, or even the very neighborhood, in which we grew up, or some field in which we have worked or dreamed of working: the theater, let us say, or government, or journalism. Often, according to my experience and that of friends, we are disappointed in novels selected on such a basis. The milieux they describe, we find, are not the ones we knew, nor do the characters face the problems with which we expected them to be concerned.

The truth is that from one point of view our interests are so particular that only one novel—the one we intend to write ourselves but lazily seek in bookstores—will altogether satisfy it. From another point of view our interests are so broad that situation and setting tend to wash out as determinants of response. We want to know all places—the ones we have never visited as well as the ones we know. We want to know what it is like to be richer than we are and poorer: to know the world where people, we think, are more powerful and assured than we are and the world where they are more miserable and more desperate but have, we may suspect, certain secret and prized compensations. When we do become interested in the manifest content of a story, it may be for reasons quite different from those which prompted us to read it.

No matter what the source of our interest, it is essential, as we know, that we *be* interested. The waking intelligence must be pleasantly absorbed in order that still more important negotiations may go forward in the deeper chambers of the mind. Moreover, the intelligence must be satisfied with the internal consistency with which a story is worked out and the honesty and understanding with which it mirrors reality. It must be convinced that, in general, its values are being respected. Far from being unimportant, the characteristics of the manifest content have a significant influence upon response.

As we know, however, we turn to fiction primarily to satisfy desires inadequately gratified through our experience, desires which in most cases we do not acknowledge and are unaware we entertain. These desires are satisfied to a large extent through the latent content of fiction, the buried levels of meaning regularly found to be present in great narrative art. It would be difficult, I believe, to exaggerate the contribution the latent content makes to our enjoyment. To be sure, the gratifications it offers us must be firmly controlled, and harmonized with the demands of the regulating components of the psyche; they would be inacceptable if they were not. The essential point, however, is that the gratification of our most urgent strivings is a component of the experience great fiction offers us. Life itself involves the adjustment and reconciliation of various of our claims, but the adjustment arrived at is usually wasteful; it is achieved at the price of renunciations which may be unnecessary and to which we remain stubbornly unreconciled. Fiction strives for an equilibrium based upon maximum fulfilment.

As a rule, needs we would have no reason to disavow are satisfied through the manifest content of fiction, which is understood by the conscious mind; repudiated needs are satisfied through the latent levels of meaning, which are apprehended by the unconscious. But the relationships are not always as regular as this. Inacceptable needs are sometimes openly gratified. In at least incidental ways, the unconscious may participate in the assimilation of the manifest content, and the conscious mind is occasionally vouchsafed glimpses of buried levels of meaning.

If only because the reports from which we learn about books seldom tell us much about their formal qualities, considerations revolving around form do not often significantly influence our selection of books. The decision to read, however, is quite frequently influenced by the desire to secure certain satisfactions which are provided chiefly by form, above all by the desire to reduce feelings of anxiety and guilt and to escape to a more comprehensible world. Often the search for such satisfactions is of no more than supplementary importance, but at times it may be the decisive factor in impelling us to read.

In *response* to fiction there is no reason to suppose that form plays a role any less important than subject matter. Its role is, in part, auxiliary. One of the functions of form is to communicate a story's expressive content to us with the right degree of clarity. But if it does not achieve this right degree, and simultaneously solve a number of other problems which require consummate skill, we cannot enjoy a story, no matter how much we may be interested in its material.

Our apprehension of the formal qualities of fiction is probably unconscious to an even greater degree than our apprehension of content. We, of course, become aware of certain—usually rather external—formal features. We may be meant to become aware of them, as we are meant to focus our attention upon a story's manifest content. But by and large form strives to efface itself. It tries to give us direct access to the matter it puts before us. Form is abetted in making itself inconspicuous by the fact that many of its chief resources are not well known and are difficult to describe.

We are most likely to become aware of form when the storyteller is guilty of some failure, some deficiency of *expertise.* Even then we do not usually identify the formal problem which has been mishandled, unless it is one which is relatively superficial and specific, such as the management of chronology or point of view. We are aware of our dissatisfaction rather than the exact cause of it. Perhaps nothing is so likely to cause dissatisfaction as a disproportion of some kind between content and form. We are displeased if the expressive content is too laxly or too firmly controlled, if offensive elements are permitted to emerge too openly or innocuous ones are pointlessly concealed. A baldly told story may make us squirm with anxiety. A stylized, contrived story leaves us feeling frustrated and let down. In at least a general way we know what such a story withholds from us: libidinal content, passion, excitement—happenings that will satisfy our needs or purge us of our fears.

The third factor which influences our selection of fiction and our response to it could, strictly speaking, be regarded as in part an aspect of content, in part an aspect of form. But it deserves separate attention: it functions somewhat differently from the attributes of subject matter and form we have considered and cuts across the division between them. It refers to one specific thing: the crudity or subtlety with which a work is developed in all of its aspects, its general plane of intellectual and emotional sensibility. For want of a better word, let us designate this factor as *texture.*

Texture is of decisive importance in both our selection of books and response to them. If its influence receives little attention, it is because texture itself receives little. In the average book review, for example, the texture of the work discussed is even less likely to excite comment than its form. Texture is, of course, a difficult subject to say much about.

The influence expectations about texture exert upon selection can be inferred from our reactions to the appraisal of books made by others. No matter how highly a book is praised, and how much interest its subject matter appears to hold, we are not likely to want to read it if we feel that the taste, the general level of sensibility, of the person who recommends it is inferior to our own. In contrast, we may be willing to accept the recommendation of an admired friend even when he tells us very little about a story he has enjoyed. In part, of course, this is because we know his interests, but in larger part, I believe, it is because we know the texture of his mind. Whatever he likes, we unconsciously reason, will probably appeal to us also.

The influence of texture upon response is very easy to discern when we read fiction which is *not* on our own level of sensibility. Fortunately, that "level" covers a wide range of material; it should not be conceived as a particular point on a dial. A person may like Proust and Dashiell Hammett, Shakespeare and William Inge. Furthermore, the various factors involved in response interact upon one another, and we may be willing to read a subtler or simpler story than we normally enjoy if we feel it has something especially significant to say to us. But while the boundaries of our band of sensibility are fluid, we know very well when we have gone outside them. We are incapable of enjoying books above or below the band, and very often have strong negative feelings about them.

We may be aware of at least some of the factors responsible for those feelings. If we live in a world where good and evil seem intermixed, where we cannot even identify all the forces playing upon us, much less know which to trust and which to regard as suspect, we feel at once that a story which presents issues in black-and-white terms is false and worthless. Such a story may outrage our sensibilities to such an extent that we feel a need to disassociate ourselves from it. We are less likely to acknowledge that some works present a more complex vision of experience than we can readily understand and respond to, but we make accusations which suggest the source of our feelings: we call such works precious, or oversubtle, or overanalytical. There seems to be a certain correspondence between our attitude to books and to people we are considering as friends. Though we may admire people whose intelligence and emotional sensibility, we feel, exceeds our own, we may decide that friendship with them would involve too much effort and strain, or learn from experience that this is the case. On the other hand, people we do not respect will not do as friends. We do not feel that they understand us or our predicament. Sometimes our own words seem vulgarized and degraded in their mouths. We seek as friends people whose minds are textured as our own, who, whether or not they agree with us, or even share our particular interests, understand issues as we pose them; people, too, who, we believe, respond to things with as much feeling as we do ourselves.

Our analysis has already suggested one or two of the ways in which texture affects the unconscious processes of response. We know that the relaxation of control by the ego upon which everything else depends cannot occur when we read a story we must labor to understand or a story we find too simple. A story we find oversimple is likely to yield its secrets too easily to the conscious mind, or even permit unconscious processes of response to come to light. A story we find difficult and rarefied is unlikely to stimulate much pleasurable perception, conscious or unconscious. It would be an error to suppose that the unconscious mind would come to the aid of the intellect in achieving an understanding of a story beyond its particular range. The unconscious may perceive things hidden from consciousness for emotional reasons, but in no other respects are its powers of comprehension superior to those of the mind of which it is a part.

Texture plays a particularly important role in connection with the "active" unconscious processes of response. It is doubtful if we participate at all in the action of stories which impress us as being too simple or too complex: their characters and situations are likely to seem irrelevant, if not unreal. Texture may do more than either subject matter or form to foster participation. It is certain, in any case, that we can become deeply engrossed in stories which are on our plane of sensibility, even when our interest in their theme is remote or contingent. Of course, our participation is likely to be most complete and intense when a story appeals to us because of its content, texture and form.

Most evidently through the way it supplements the influence of subject matter, texture also helps to determine whether we will analogize on the basis of what we read, create fantasies related to our own experience, desires and fears. The content of an archetypal drama, such as *Macbeth,* is of potential interest to everyone. The play provides a frame for the enactment of almost any conflict in which the anarchistic part of the self wars with the forces, inner and outer, which seek to chasten it. But the play will actually instigate fantasies only if it is also on the reader's plane of sensibility.

Though here I am admittedly less sure of my ground, I believe that analogizing may also be stimulated by the very structure and texture of the events of a story, without regard to their content, except as that content, reduced to its most general and abstract terms (e.g., rise/fall), becomes indistinguishable from structure itself. In such cases, the fantasy activity should perhaps not be called analogizing, since it is not directed to the creation of some parallel legend. Rather, it is creating a legend which conforms to the formal and textural structure, flowing, as it were, where certain indentations have been made to facilitate its progress.

Behind everything which has been said about the effect of texture upon our selection of reading matter, an economic principle is clearly discernible. In accordance with a tendency which is pervasive in our psychic life, we seek to secure the satisfactions obtainable from fiction as effortlessly as possible. This does not mean, of course, that we search out the simplest fiction to be found; such fiction would not give us pleasure. It may be, however, that, rather than selecting only "what we have to stand on tiptoe to read," as Thoreau advised, we tend to read toward the bottom rather than toward the top of our particular band of interest, even though this entails the sacrifice of the richer satisfaction we could secure from somewhat more complex books. If this is the case, it suggests that education has an immediate as well as a long-range opportunity to improve reading taste. It can do everything possible to make students sensible of the pleasure they can obtain from fiction somewhat more complex than that which they normally tend to read, and make books which meet this description more readily available. If not carried to self-defeating lengths, such a measure can also make a contribution to a more gradual attempt to raise students' level of sensibility, so that they will develop an appetite for more mature and more rewarding fiction. (pp. 203-11)

*Simon O. Lesser, "The Processes of Response,"
in his* Fiction and the Unconscious, *1957. Reprint by Vintage Books, 1962, pp. 188-211.*

Robert N. Mollinger

[*Mollinger is an American psychoanalyst and critic. In the following excerpt, he discusses ways in which psychological factors determine what a person chooses to read.*]

The exploration of the reader's response to literature begins with Freud who stated that literature allows the reader to enjoy forbidden fantasies ["Creative Writers and Day-Dreaming"; see essay above]. Developing Freud's idea, Kris [in his *Psychoanalytic Explorations in Art;* see Further Reading] holds that the reader also attempts to control these fantasies so that reading involves an interchange between writer's and reader's fantasies and their modes of control. Drawing on Kris, Holland dwells more exclusively on what the reader brings to the literary text and how he recreates that text ["Unity Identity Text Self"; see Further Reading]. Holland finds that the reader

reads according to his identity. He finds his own fantasies in the text and transforms them to more intellectually significant meanings. Taking the final subjectivist step, Bleich states that the reader creates meaning as if the text did not exist ["The Subjective Paradigm in Science, Psychology, and Criticism," *New Literary History,* 7 (1975-76)]. In an attempt to be more encompassing and more objective, S. Mollinger [in an unpublished dissertation] explores the interrelations between the literary text, its author and his culture, and the reader. All these critics approach the problem of how readers find meaning in literature.

I shall look at a closely related, but possibly preceding, step: how a reader chooses what to read. Whereas much of the exploration of the reader's response has used for data psychological test results of the reader, I shall use the discoveries of the psychoanalytic therapeutic situation of three patients. I shall suggest "who these patients are," that is, those elements of their identities which influence their selection of reading matter and illuminate their perspective on what they read.

A., a young artist, is generally sociable and pleasant with her friends. Despite having little money—she lives financially from day to day—she serves them expensive dinners. Buying only the best ingredients, she works for days preparing numerous courses—quiches, soups, lamb, mousse, and pies. What concerns her most at these dinners is the ambience of the setting and the feeling that she is entertaining her friends lavishly. Creating a myth of not being poor, she spends money as if she does not need it. She buys herself expensive clothes and sends her daughter to an excellent, but costly, private school. Although poor in reality, in fantasy she is rich.

This mode of behavior is expressed in relation to me as well. She fantasizes about having tea with me in the therapy sessions, of entertaining me with stories, and of having me tell her stories as well. Once she brought me flowers. Particularly liking the fact that I am interested in the poetry of Wallace Stevens, she feels that it shows that I have "taste." She also enjoys socializing with another psychologist and his wife, particularly because they often have musical recitals in their home.

A. was reared by second-generation Americans with an Eastern European background. From her mother's point of view, her father and his family were lower-class brutes: they wore undershirts around the house, ate like pigs, and were generally slobs. In contrast, A.'s mother was interested in music, ballet, and "culture" and saw herself as a person of "higher quality." In A.'s estimation, her mother had aristocratic pretensions, even though it was her mother who introduced A. to all these cultural aspects of life. A. now has similar attitudes. Imitating her mother, A. views most of the men she dates as "brutes" and feels herself to be much above them, especially culturally.

A. tries to actualize the myth of wealth and culture in order to obtain approval and love from others. She romanticizes herself and others to protect herself from the realization of her feelings of unworthiness and of her fear of rejection because of this unworthiness. She serves her friends lavish dinners to obtain their approval; she brings me flowers so I will like her. In a dream, she dresses in a gray suit and stockings, as a "lady," for me, while at the same time she hopes I would dress better, more like a "gentleman." Another dream further illustrates her reason for carrying her "cultural baggage." In it, her former husband was going to take her away from her parents; meanwhile, she looked frantically for her books and paintings. Discussing the dream, she said that without these, she might not be good enough to be accepted by someone. She thinks that her husband would only love her if she has cultural interests. In addition, from A.'s perspective, her mother could only accept her, and she could only accept herself, if she was "highly cultured."

A.'s fantasy of herself is, then, of a young wealthy hostess who lavishly entertains her friends, who socializes with the culturally superior who enjoy music and art, and who at times must be victimized by the company of those beneath her, the brutes of the world. In her own eyes, she is a young, intelligent *bon vivant.*

It is suggestive that her favorite author is Henry James. Though she appreciates the complex psychological explorations in his works, they do not interest her. Though she is well travelled, the international plots and the contrast between America and Europe do not fascinate her. Though she loves to curl up with detective novels, the Jamesian mystery and ghost stories do not intrigue her. Though she is sensitive to her own psychic dynamics, James's focus on the self and "selfishness," does not strike her. What draws her primarily to the novels of Henry James is the ambience of "ladies" and "gentlemen." The afternoon teas, the social dinners, the distinctive "manners," the politeness, the ever presence of wealth and leisure, these are the aspects of James's work which particularly entrance A.

The opening of *The Portrait of a Lady* (1881) illustrates this kind of ambience: "Under certain circumstances there are few hours in life more agreeable than the hour dedicated to the ceremony known as afternoon tea." Present in the scene of the novel are, among others, an American banker, an expatriate and an English gentleman with "the air of a happy temperament fertilized by a high civilization—which would have made almost any observer envy him at a venture. . . . " The conversation turns to leisured comfort:

> "The fact is I've been comfortable so many years that I suppose I've got so used to it I don't know it."

> "Yes, that's the bore of comfort," said Lord Warburton. "We only know when we're uncomfortable."

The talk then turns to wealth: "You think too much of your pleasure. You're too fastidious, and too indolent, and too rich."

The elements in this scene are typically Jamesian, wealth, leisure, comfort, all symbolized by the taking of tea. Whenever A. is in distress, she loves to treat herself to a "calming cup of tea." It composes her, especially by stimulating her fantasy of herself in such a Jamesian scene: not poor but rich, not chaotic but calm, not lower middle class but aristocratic. Besides having tea to calm herself, she retreats to bed to read James, particularly after a narcissistic injury (either a social or professional rejection). She has said, "I'm like a lower-class English person who

likes to read of nobility. I identify with people who have grace, money, a library, a comfortable chair by the window, success." Though she sometimes reads detective novels, she worries that others, particularly me, will think that she has "bad" taste in literature. Of course, reading these "lesser works" also dents her fantasy of being "cultured."

I am suggesting that A.'s fantasy of herself—a restorative fantasy for her injured self-esteem, one which makes her feel more worthwhile after a rejection—influences her choice of James's works, especially since she reads him after being rejected or slighted. This relationship can also be understood by Holland's thesis that the reader finds his own defenses in the literary text. We have something additional here, the active seeking of reading material which buttresses a restorative, defensive fantasy. Reading James's scenes of manners, A. becomes a part of them, and acceptable to herself and to (imagined) others, such as her mother and me.

B., a creative young college student who composes and sings his own songs, also has a special interest in literature. When young, he was generally ignored or beaten. Sent away to a special school when he was two years old, he later attended a prep school far from home. Even at home, his parents were self-involved and paid little attention to him. One way B. handled this deprivation and rejection was to withdraw into his own fantasies. He constructed a huge model city and gave it his own name, spelled backward. He imagined himself a king of England with a castle and pictured himself on Mount Olympus. Now, he fantasizes himself as a famous entertainer surrounded by other "deities" of the entertainment world. One of his dreams shows his fortressed position:

> I'm in a castle. I was near the top.
> President Ford fell out of the window
> and got killed. I was offered the Presidency.

There is, of course, aggression and grandiosity here, but in addition there is a separateness, in the castle, and an immersion in the fantasy itself. B. feels as if there is a barrier between himself and others. Whereas A. used her fantasy at particular times, B. lives in his fantasy world most of the time. The actualization of this fantasy of grandiose success guides most of what he does: his writing, reading, and sexual behavior. Totally involved in these fantasies, he experiences them as a major element in his personality.

It is suggestive that what he reads and writes captures the ambience of his fantasies. He writes romantic, fantastical songs which have nothing to do with contemporary life or contemporary problems. He succeeds in putting himself at a distance from the life around him by going back toward the past. In reading literature, he chooses medieval works, like *Beowulf,* or science fiction (again far removed from the present), or literature that creates its own strange world, such as works by H. P. Lovecraft or Edgar Allan Poe:

> I entered the Gothic archway of the hall. . . .
> While the objects around me—while the carvings
> of the ceilings, the somber tapestries of the walls,
> the ebon blackness on the floors, and the phantas-
> magoric armorial trophies which rattled as I
> strode, were but matters to which, or to such as
> which, I had been accustomed from my infancy—

while I hesitated not to acknowledge how familiar was all this—I still wondered to find how unfamiliar were the fancies which ordinary images were stirring up.

("The Fall of the House of Usher")

Although the narrator hesitates to enter this other-worldly gothic environment, B. has no hesitancy. This is just the kind of world he loves to enter, one cut off from everyday reality and everyday concerns. In his sexual behavior, he is particularly drawn to the "mysterious" and grotesque back rooms and bathhouses of the homosexual world.

In B. we again see the influence of a psychic dynamic on the choice of reading matter. B. has been constructing such fantastical worlds since childhood, the city of his own name, his kingdom on Mount Olympus, his kingdom in England. His immersion in those earlier, created fantasies is now paralleled by his immersion in literature which presents worlds far removed from the ordinary—other planets (science fiction), other historical periods (*Beowulf*), and other atmospheres (gothic). Having originally withdrawn from his childhood reality, he now withdraws from contemporary life and from a literature involved with contemporary reality. He summed this up by saying, "I write escapist lyrics and poems and they come from when I was young and living in a world of magic and marvels."

C., a graduate student in literature who had a rigid Catholic upbringing, fears authority figures and dreads being abandoned by his lovers. To handle these fears he attempts to please others, but at times he is compelled to defy them. This increases his anxious expectation of punishment and abandonment. Overwhelmed by anxiety and rage, C. attempts to control these emotions by the use of his mind. In therapy he continually looks for patterns and connections to what he is saying, while in his everyday life, he attempts to make the "perfect decision." As he puts it, "If I'm rational, I won't crap up."

One of his dreams shows the necessity for control and the danger of loss of control. In the dream he was committing hari kari, but he had the thought that it would be too messy. So, not wanting anyone to know, he stopped. In associating to the dream, he said that during the day he felt he had to clean some messy spots off his suit jacket before seeing his departmental chairman. He said that his former wife and his mother, who were continually cleaning their respective houses, would always criticize him for spilling milk. This criticism caused him to feel that he had to hide his mess from them to avoid their anger. In thinking of hari kari, he stated that the Japanese believe the stomach is the seat of the emotions. He believed that he had to protect himself from the reaction of others to his "messiness," a messiness caused by opening himself up and showing his emotions.

Stressing his need to control, to intellectualize, and to use his rational powers continually, he often noted the appropriateness of his choices in literature. His major is eighteenth-century literature. Alexander Pope's "Essay on Man" (1733-1734), a representative eighteenth-century work, strikingly displays similar emphases. For Pope, the world is orderly: "throughout the whole visible world, an universal order . . . is observed." Poetically put, "Order

is Heaven's first law. . . . " For C., order is his "first law," what he needs and what he seeks for protection against all the minor disruptions and irregularities disturbing him.

Pope recommends that man submit to the order of the Universe: "Heaven bestows on thee. / Submit." If one submits, one will be rewarded: "Who sees and follows that great scheme the best, / Best knows the blessing, and will be most blessed." To defy the order is to commit a sin: "And who but wishes to invert the laws / Of order, sins against th' Eternal Cause." In similar case, C. feels he must submit to others, their demands, their "orders," their authority. If he does, he will be rewarded—by being liked, by not being abandoned, by being considered "good." In youth, he submitted to the Church; now he submits to more mundane authority figures. Even though defiance is "bad," he commits acts of defiance by "sinfully" living with a woman to whom he is not married, by not paying me for his therapy sessions, a defiance which to his mind might lead to my "cancelling him out," thereby both abandoning and destroying him.

For Pope, the way to submission to order is through reason, "to reason right is to submit." Reason is man's finest capacity, "reason alone countervails all other faculties." For C., also, it is reason which will save him from his own messy emotions, from the messiness which might result from conflicts with other people. He feels pressure to make "perfect" decisions, to say the "right" thing to me and other authority figures, and to find his psychological patterns "healthy." To achieve these goals, he is constantly thinking, reasoning, and mulling things over. He feels that if he thinks enough, he will find the right solutions, however long it may take.

In summary, we see how readers respond to literature in terms of their own fantasies and defenses. Fantasizing herself as culturally and aristocratically superior, A. concentrates on the leisured aristocratic aspects of James's works. Defending himself by constructing his own fantasy world, B. creates in his own works fantastical worlds and seeks the same in literature: historical, science fiction, or gothic. Defending himself against his messy emotions, C. uses his rationality to create order in his world, even if it means submitting to some ultimate authoritative order. He seeks such a reasoned, ordered world in his professional commitment to literature.

These readers not only find themselves in what they read, but they actively seek out themselves in literature. They use their literary interests to strengthen their defenses against what upsets them—recognition of unworthiness in A., contact with others in B., and emotionality in C. (pp. 153-61)

Robert N. Mollinger, in his Psychoanalysis and Literature: An Introduction, *Nelson-Hall, 1981, 178 p.*

Joseph Westlund

[*Westlund is an American educator and critic with a special interest in psychoanalytic readings of Shakespeare. In the following excerpt, he examines the psychological function of Shakespeare's comedies for the audience.*]

Psychoanalytic interpretation based on Freudian theory concerns itself mostly with sexuality, aggression, and conflict. The interpretation of Shakespeare's comedies resists such an approach and points up some limitations in psychoanalytic theory and its uses. With the exception of those plays termed "problematic"—and of the temporary jealousy of Posthumus and Leontes—Shakespeare underplays the role of sexuality. He focuses upon aggression, conflict, and sexuality only in the late comedies, and only to transcend them.

The comedies present a wide variety of ways in which the characters—and with them the audience—can move beyond conflict. We need a clearer theoretical basis for discussing the psychological implications of these and other works of literature. In the instance of the comedies, how do characters appear to deal with conflict—or, a question rarely asked—their self-doubt? How can members of an audience find these plays "comic" in their effect? And exactly what is this effect? We all bring with us to the experience of these plays our own actual or potential anger and guilt, and need to be encouraged by the comedy to transcend it for the moment—to feel richer, happier, more reconciled to life. The plays can be thought to assist in viewers' everyday "working through" of a wide range of hidden, conflicted, distorted feelings: in part simply by encouraging them to be admitted rather than defended against. Recently I discussed the "reparative" effects of Shakespeare's middle comedies and emphasized Melanie Klein's theory of how people can admit guilt for the real or imagined damage they have done and attempt to repair it [Joseph Westlund, *Shakespeare's Reparative Comedies: A Psychoanalytic View of the Middle Plays*]. I find, however, that Klein's approach needs to be augmented for reasons that go the the heart of psychoanalytic theory.

Psychoanalysis and psychoanalytic literary theory rarely discuss the nature of love, as distinct from sexuality; this curious silence has contributed to the difficulty of psychoanalytic critics in trying to account for the effect of these plays—and of many other works. A theory of reparation is essentially a theory about love—about love of others, love in an object-relational sense. In addition to focusing upon love as an object-relation, we need to consider another sort of love that is narcissistic: a healthy love of self, self-esteem. *Reparation* in the wide sense—a sense derived from but not quite the same as Klein's—is essentially the way in which we regain and preserve an idealized sense of self and of others.

The preoccupations of the psychoanalytic interpretation of literature derive from those of psychoanalytic theory. As the instance of Shakespeare's comedies reminds us, there are other dimensions to life and to art than those most often addressed by psychoanalytic thinkers. Other feelings are also crucial, such as love and self-esteem. We need to account for how a wide range of feelings are addressed in Shakespeare's comedies. The effect of one of these plays is in its own way roughly analogous—but certainly not identical—to that of psychoanalytic therapy. Literature is of course not therapy; we attend a play for enjoyment, not for treatment; our expectations are different and the outcome more modest and shortlived. Nevertheless, the desired results are rather similar: alleviation of anxiety and pain, of hopelessness and helplessness; and more positively, the gain of an enhanced sense of value in

self and others. The analogy seems worth pursuing since theorists find it so difficult to describe the effects of literature upon people. One reason for this difficulty is that the psychoanalytic theory upon which critics base their understanding of human nature has great trouble defining the effects of therapy upon people. Theorists describe the experience of the psychoanalytic process in terms that seem overly technical and rather remote from actual human feelings. I want to examine a central theoretical point about the potentially revitalizing effects of therapy before turning to literature. In both cases my concern is with reparation in the wide sense: the way in which people regain and strengthen an idealized sense of self and of others.

Theorists describe the process of transcending conflicted inner states and modifying habits of a lifetime as *working through*. It is very difficult to know quite how this process occurs, and theorists seem reluctant to pursue the issue. Freud states [in "Remembering, Repeating, and Working Through"] that "the doctor has nothing else to do" after working with the patient in uncovering resistances "than to wait and let things take their course, a course which cannot be avoided nor always hastened." This is brief indeed as an account of what Freud describes as "a part of the work which effects the greatest changes in the patient and which distinguishes analytic treatment from any kind of treatment by suggestion." Recently, Gottesman ["Working Through: A Process of Restitution," *Psychoanalytic Review*, 62 (1975)] surveyed a number of attempts to define the process of working through; the process frustrates therapists who assume that by bringing the unconscious to consciousness and connecting affect to insight, "through some magical reaction the patient will then change his patterns of behavior." It is this "magical reaction" that sorely needs clarification. To do so Gottesman introduces the term *restitution:* "the means by which the patient can relinquish his infantile wishes of the past for more adaptive and appropriate rewards in the present." The patient is led to "see in present reality a chance to make restitution for what he believes the past has failed to provide and for his own failures."

Melanie Klein describes a roughly similar process in far greater detail [in "Love, Guilt, and Reparation"]. Klein places the sort of restitution that Gottesman postulates in the widest human context by showing the need for it among us all and not just as part of the process of working through (which she seems not to connect to it). The great value of her concept of reparation is its relationship to so many aspects of life and its attempt at precision. Klein describes people as being from infancy onward intensely ambivalent: loving because of an awareness of benefit from others and hating out of unavoidable frustration. She assumes object-relations from birth; from them we establish a "relation to ourselves" in our inner world that consists of a relation to all that we love, a wealth accumulated through our relations to external people, and internalized. We also create harsh representations of others within ourselves—largely the result of destructive aggression—which results in a malign circle she calls the "paranoid-schizoid" position. Here, hatred of our own destructiveness and the fear that we will destroy the good within us leads to splitting feelings into exaggerations of either all-bad or all-good; we project the bad outside us to preserve the good, with the result that we then feel persecuted by these exaggerations. The result is inner turmoil, conflict, and misery. She heightens the difference between the state of loving with its positive tendency to idealize and the state of hating with its tendency to degrade and destroy.

Klein's most worthwhile innovation is her postulate of a "depressive" position wherein we can feel guilt for our destructiveness when and *if* we can see a way of repairing the real or fantasized damage. Winnicott describes the value of this theory: "arrival at this stage is associated with ideas of restitution and reparation, and indeed the human individual cannot accept the destructive and aggressive ideas in his or her own nature without experience of reparation, and for this reason the continued presence of the love object [that is, a representation of a person or an aspect of one] is necessary at this stage since only in this way is there opportunity for reparation" [D. W. Winnicott, "On the Kleinian Contribution"]. I see two distinct points. First, Klein's emphasis upon our constructive tendencies as a way of dealing with unconscious fears; we repair the destruction and alleviate guilt. Second, Klein's and Winnicott's emphasis on the crucial need for the continued presence of the love object—or, as Klein puts it, one's belief in one's own goodness.

Klein emphasizes guilt and the necessity of preserving our sense of goodness through reparation; this can help to clarify the mysterious process of working through. The process would seem to require a strong sense of our own destructiveness, and at the same time a strong sense of our own goodness—our ability to do good, to be constructive and reparative. These paradoxical requirements help to illuminate the potential difficulties a patient encounters: an inadequate, confused sense of guilt, or an overwhelming sense of guilt. In addition, these apparently conflicting requirements can easily undermine one's sense of self-esteem—belief in own's own goodness, strength, and ability to be constructive. As far as I can see, precarious self-esteem often proves to be a major cause of unresolved ambivalence, interminable conflict, and unsuccessful therapy.

Shakespeare's comedies can be seen as a literary version in miniature of a process analogous to working through: they have a reparative effect upon a viewer. The plays can awaken potential fears and consequent destructive impulses—for instance, with regard to manipulation in *Much Ado about Nothing*—and then reveal ways in which they can be resolved, as they are for characters such as Beatrice and Benedick. When the lords and ladies trick Beatrice and Benedick, they accuse each of them of pride and destructiveness in their fear that allowing themselves to love will mean loss of autonomy. At the same time, the tricksters convince each of them that he or she has the opportunity and strength to save the other from pining away for want of love. Viewers who identify with Beatrice and Benedick can feel a reparative effect: sense the lovers' fear of manipulation and yet see how it can be transcended in a manner that retains a degree of control and yields a heightened sense of self-esteem. In this small but readily accessible way, *Much Ado* offers the potential of making viewers feel happier about themselves and about those they love—or would love if they dared. The result may be that viewers feel, however briefly, happier, richer, and strengthened in their sense of self and others.

Therapy bogs down because patients feel powerless and hopeless; thus, an account of working through should include a discussion of its narcissistic dimension. Theorists who deal with this issue often distinguish between "self-esteem" grounded in realistic self-assessment and "narcissism" as a pathological defense. Grunberger [in his *Narcissism: Psychoanalytic Essays*], Kohut [in his *Restoration of the Self*], and others see a narcissistic component in all of us: a basic, vital sense of our potential for greatness and perfection. We idealize ourselves and others in an attempt, never to be achieved, to recapture an Edenic world that we either vaguely remember from the womb or have a strong sense of experiencing during infancy and childhood.

The need to believe in the existence of something extremely good lies at the heart of working through and of reparation. And yet, this belief is always at risk. How do people survive the hostile attacks from without and within? We seem to do so through a process similar to mourning at its most benign and effective.

In order to understand the vicissitudes of working through and its potentially good outcome, let us look at Gorkin's attempt to synthesize two conflicting theories and their resulting suggestions for treatment ["Narcissistic Personality Disorder and Pathological Mourning," *Contemporary Psychoanalysis,* 20 (1984)]. To Kernberg the narcissistic personality is a pathological, defensive state of someone who could not endure the depressive position (Klein's term), largely because his or her excessive aggression threatens to overwhelm the good object [*Borderline Conditions and Pathological Narcissism*]. To Kohut, the narcissistic personality is arrested at a primitive stage of normal development, unable to relinquish grandiose self and grandiose idealized objects, and perpetually in need of something or someone to mirror and confirm these exaggerations. Kernberg emphasizes—and interprets to the patient in therapy—anger and aggression. On the other hand, Kohut emphasizes—and provides the means to reestablish through the transference—the patient's need for an idealizing relationship. Gorkin suggests that *both* sets of feelings need to be addressed: sad longing for the ideal, and anger and aggression because it seems destroyed. They are part of a "mourning process which the narcissistic personality has avoided. The analytic working through does provide an opportunity for this mourning to take place."

What seems required in each instance is a sense of the potential for something extremely good in self and others: for Kohut, the idealizing transference, for Kernberg, the transference made possible by confrontation. Narcissistic disorders are a special case, but if the narcissistic component is present in all of us—as Kohut, Grunberger, and others argue—perhaps we can learn from this discussion something about working through in general. The process involves a sense of idealized self and others, and, just as important, mourning for their loss. A paradoxical state exists in mourning, in working through, and in reparation: to be able to feel guilt for what is bad in ourself, we need to feel secure in our sense of inner goodness. This means that idealization, which is usually seen as pathologically defensive, can in other ways be vitally necessary.

We can now begin to speculate about how Shakespeare's comedies produce their revitalizing effect. In all his works, but especially in his comedies, he proceeds upon the assumption that something exists that is extremely good.

Even in *The Comedy of Errors,* based on a hard-headed Roman farce, we find idealized love in the romance between Luciana and Antipholus of Syracuse, and even in Adriana, the shrewish wife. The father, Egeon, persists in a self-sacrificing search for his lost son, and both sets of twins become models of brotherly love at the end of the play. In *Twelfth Night,* Orsino's unrealistic sense of perfect love seems destined never to be fulfilled, but Viola actually gives him the extraordinary love and fidelity he thought he could only dream about. Even the problem comedies preserve this sense of some extremely good object. Helena idealizes herself as Bertram's wife; the play frustrates her longing, but no one within its confines ever denies her goals or her own intrinsic value. In *Measure for Measure* the Duke only partially attains his idealized conception of himself as a perfect ruler, but his goal remains tantalizingly alive to him—and to critics who praise or damn him according to whether or not they think he fulfills it. The husbands in *Cymbeline* and *The Winter's Tale* reveal grandiose selves at the outset, but despite their hostile, murderous devaluation of their wives, Posthumus and Leontes reform into near-perfect mates. Our sense of Prospero as a benign ruler endures despite his omnipotent tone toward others. Shakespeare's comedies persistently resort to idealization and present us with lovers and spouses, children and parents, brothers and sisters who are exemplary. They are indeed quite unrealistically good—or, if bad at the start, they prove to be exceptionally good at the end.

Because of this idealization, not despite it, these comedies can effect reparation for the characters and for members of the audience. In many instances, but not all of them, the characters acknowledge their destructiveness, admit guilt, and through constructive action make reparation. As far as literary figures can, they enter into a benign circle; giving love to others in the outside world and therefore being able to take love back into themselves from that world. Beatrice and Benedick, for instance, immediately devote themselves to the plight of their slandered friend, Hero, as soon as they admit their love. Rosalind in *As You Like It*—in a different version of this process—gives the impression that she has made reparation a way of life.

Shakespeare introduces dark, "tragic" aspects to his comedies, and the result is to add a sense of loss that instills in the characters—and can instill in the viewer—a sense of sad longing. This can be seen as part of the normal, healthy mourning process. Theorists describe this mourning process in various ways, but as Gorkin notes, it seems to be one that people normally repeat many times, even continuously, throughout life. This state of feeling—sad longing—is also accompanied by anger and aggression, which can thwart the mourning process by creating so much guilt that one cannot imagine the possibility of being constructive. This is the case, apparently, in the pathological mourning process of narcissistic disorders. The extent of the guilt depends upon the degree of aggression and anger toward what is lost; the more ambivalent one is, the more potential destructiveness and the more guilt. Again, I add that such states are probably more often present in normal people than we like to think—although observable only in certain areas of life.

By introducing loss and destructiveness Shakespeare's comedies may foster in the viewer mild states of sad longing and of aggression and anger that help to reactivate, along with the lighter, happier, more idealized states, a kind of mourning process. Such a process can lead to reparative attitudes in the characters—such as Beatrice and Benedick, Vincentio, and Leontes—and also in viewers who identify with them. Viola mourns in her own mild and sane way the kind of loss that we can identify with: loss of her brother, plus, for most of the play, the loss of her beloved; both losses, although apparent, seem painfully real to Viola for most of the play. Mourning is an integral part of her character, as shown by her mention of her dead sister—herself, it seems—who "pin'd in thought. . . . She sat like Patience on a monument, / Smiling at grief." Viola's exemplary patience and fidelity may also be part of her benign effect upon us. Sad longing of a tolerable sort can serve as a model, can be one of the things that makes Viola, Helena, and the heroines of the romances so admirable. Shakespeare introduces death at the end of *Love's Labour's Lost* in order to make the characters—and viewers—take courtship more seriously: the Princess literally mourns for her dead father; her sense of loss tempers the lords' heady idealization of themselves, of love, and of the ladies. As a result, surprisingly, the notion of love as something extremely good—and attainable—flourishes.

When anger and aggression become a significant part of characters' responses to others, as in *Measure for Measure,* the guilt comes into the open, whereas it can only be postulated in the effect of other instances of loss—such as that felt by the lords and ladies in *Love's Labour's Lost.* Duke Vincentio confronts characters but in ways that specifically encourage their sense of personal strength and goodness. The Duke helps to bring about reparation by addressing the narcissistic component. For instance, when he interrupts Isabella's self-centered attack on her brother to introduce the bed trick, he begins with praise that seems extravagant given her savage outburst: "the hand that hath made you fair hath made you good."

To describe the effect of these plays in terms of mourning, guilt, and reparation seems rather odd unless we remind ourselves that Shakespeare's plays repeatedly provoke such feelings. He introduces the threat or presence of death in various ways in the majority of these plays; it becomes a central plot device in the romances. By doing so, and by having characters experience apparent loss of friendship and affection, he draws the romantic, festive, happy aspects of the plays closer to everyday life. Loss and mourning—and the anger, aggression, guilt, and need for reparation that they elicit—are part of daily life and thus an integral part of our inner worlds. They are, for instance, one reason why we feel a tinge of sadness in our longing for anything extremely good.

What makes Shakespeare's comedies so excellent, and what makes them so useful an example here, is that they air these vital, ever-present feelings and facilitate our dealing with them on some level of consciousness. As Miller so thoroughly demonstrates, the major cause of our psychological misery is that we are usually denied a full range of emotions, and as a result we grow impoverished and confused; the feelings, say of anger or of neediness, go underground and turn up in some strange and terrifying form. This is why I dwell upon the relevance to comedy of such feelings as sad longing, mourning, and reparation.

Shakespeare's comedies concern themselves with love and festivity, with reunion and wonder. And yet, these plays also have their sad, dark, even tragic moments. Such moments and the feelings they give rise to cannot be avoided given our short, conflicted—and also loving and aspiring—lives. Part of what makes these plays deeply moving is their vibrant sense of being in touch with more than happy thoughts; these plays differ from most comedies in our language by their extraordinary inclusiveness, by their broad spectrum of feelings. The plays mirror our need to idealize by presenting plots that turn out surprisingly well and characters who are often so admirable—but most of all by emphasizing love. Shakespeare's comedies speak with intensity to our deepest longings.

Psychoanalytic theory pays scandalously little attention to love as distinct from sexuality. This deficiency may well account for why literary criticism based on this view of human nature so rarely addresses love—and for why the comedies tend to elude such criticism. By giving aggression equal rank with sexuality as a basic human trait, Klein clarifies the role of hatred—anger, aggression, and destructiveness—but also, strangely, of love: not simply sexuality, but love of an idealized, romantic sort. In so doing Klein makes one of her most profound, least recognized contributions.

Freud's libido theory has a number of problems in explaining love. As Wisdom points out: "one could say that Freud's libido theory was a theory of sex and Melanie Klein's theory of the depressive position a theory of love" ["Freud and Melanie Klein: Psychology, Ontology, and *Weltanschauung*," in C. Hanley and M. Lazerowitz, eds., *Psycho-analysis and Philosophy*]. Love is paradoxical in its ability to be both self-concerned and self-demoting; the self-concerned aspect can be explained in terms of libido, but the self-demoting aspect cannot. The theory of the depressive position can account for "self-concern"—wherein the lover creates the fantasy of the object, dominates it in hate, and absorbs it in love. The depressive position can also account for "self-demotion" in that the lover's attacks on the prized object can instill a sense of guilt and yet the attacks can be repaired, neutralized by reparation, and thus preserve the good object's idealized state. This aspect is the central one for our purposes, for it suggests how the idealized object retains its perfection unblemished: "in the state of ambivalence, the desired object is attacked; this attack is not cancelled, but redressed by reparation." I suspect that the lover maintains and even increases self-esteem by this process, feeling elation at being able to preserve the love object unblemished despite the destructive attempts against it.

Wisdom's account reveals an aspect of love that above all else explains its centrality in psychic life. The presence of something idealized—the loved, good object; the loving and constructive self—lends stability to our emotional life. This idealization is inherently precarious, but can be maintained by the capacity to repair inevitable attacks on it. The prized sense of self and of others persists as the result of conquered ambivalence and has an air of reality, since it survives repeated attacks of anger and aggression. In this, the idealization avoids the pathological implications of "splitting"—of being the result of isolation from reality, from other feelings—and the bad effects that result, such as a loss of feelings, potential for reversal to the hated opposite, and consequent delusion of persecution. As Wisdom sums it up, "the neutralization by reparation . . . relieves the desired object of all diminution of good quality. This state, being without blemish . . . resembles the idealization of the paranoid-schizoid position. But it is not the same. . . . it is not kept good by a split but by neutralization of its bad part." Here, then, is a nice glimpse into the way in which reparation proceeds in the beneficent presence of idealizations and at the same time helps to secure and burnish them.

One rather simple but effective way in which Shakespeare's comedies confirm the good object within us is that they present benign, powerful mother figures; the plays present a variety of exceptionally good female characters. In their own way the male central characters also present an idealized figure, the good father. The powerful rulers in the comedies are arbitrary, but adaptable, and in the end benignly disposed; this is true even of Posthumus and Leontes. The male rulers, like the heroines, offer idealized parent figures who can encourage our sense that such figures exist within our inner worlds, our emotional lives.

Shakespeare's presentation of someone, or something, extremely good is more thoroughgoing than this suggests. He characterizes lovers in a way that continually implicates them in ideals outside themselves. This may account for why his comedies usually subordinate sexuality to loving feelings. He suffuses the relationship between lovers and spouses with courtesy and altruism as much as with sexuality. Shakespeare's lovers in comedy and romance may be sexually aware, but he underplays this dimension by giving heroines male disguises and by engaging them in witty battles that lack the strong sexuality of those between such lovers as Antony and Cleopatra. When pronounced sexual feelings enter these comedies in *All's Well That Ends Well* and *Measure for Measure* the plays grow problematic—or, in the case of *Troilus and Cressida*—cease to be a comedy. In the romances, sexual aggression is the hero's mode in his mad delusion, not in his reparative reconciliation. Shakespeare's comedies subordinate sexuality to idealization as a vital aspect of love. Indeed, the plays treat an unusually inclusive variety of loving feelings that are not overtly sexual: between master and servant, friends, siblings, children and parents—as well as mildly sexual and intensely loving relationships between lovers and between spouses.

A major reason why Shakespeare's comedies have proven so popular—so revitalizing for members of the audience—is the wide variety of the kinds of love that they treat: friendly, romantic, marital, and familial. We can find in these plays versions of the world as we wish to find it—as we need to find it—and with the sort of constancy that might not otherwise obtain. We experience this constancy in one of it most effective and persuasive forms in the love relationships in these plays. In part, this may be owing to the fact that sexual and aggressive components—which might otherwise result in conflict, as in other sorts of comedy—continually appear in the presence of idealizing, narcissistic tendencies.

In this way Shakespeare's comedies further reveal the revitalizing effect of idealization. A strong sense of goodness allows healthy mourning to take place—and it seems necessary that this be possible given the nature of our inner and outer worlds. This strong sense of goodness also facili-

Back row: A. A. Brill, Ernest Jones, and Sandor Ferenczi. Front row: Sigmund Freud, G. Stanley Hall, and Carl Gustave Jung.

tates reparation, a process of continual importance to our sense of well-being. Although normal development is said to involve "an integration of the good and bad imagos [representations] of self and objects, and the relinquishment of the wish for the ideal state," it might be more accurate to describe this process as "tempering"—not "relinquishment." The wish persists. As Gorkin remarks, even in normal individuals there remains to some degree "a longing for the state of symbiotic oneness, or a kind of Garden of Eden in human relations"—a longing that "provides, in part, an impetus to love, and especially falling in love, and it emerges in some of our moments of religious, aesthetic, and patriotic celebration."

This longing persists throughout life, is implicated in the process of "working through" in the broadest sense, and constitutes a central aspect of Shakespeare's comedies. Although this narcissistic component leads us away from reality—often with terrible effects that I do not wish to underestimate—it also helps to preserve us in ways that we should acknowledge and ponder. For instance, healthy narcissism is an essential part of romantic love, which is intensely—if covertly—self-concerned. By idealizing the beloved we also idealize ourselves: the more perfect and above us we imagine the beloved to be, the more we bask

in the narcissistic glow of this extraordinary being. As Grunberger points out: "love is a feeling of elation, which is elevating rather than abasing. Even 'the earthworm in love with a star' basks in the reflections of the star's brilliance. . . . the imagined distance between the worm and the star bears the stamp of megalomania, even though omnipotence is projected onto the object."

We share in the intense sense of value that the lovers in Shakespeare's comedies often feel. This is true, paradoxically, even though the plays also reveal the unrealistic nature of such elation. Critics often comment that the male characters are usually less worthy than the heroines who love them; this is true of virtually every pair of lovers in the comedies from *Love's Labour's Lost* through *The Tempest*. We could say that, except for Beatrice, the ladies find excellence where we find mere competence. Perhaps Shakespeare had some personal reason for this proclivity, but what is most important for our purposes is that the pattern reveals his insistence upon idealizing tendencies. Certainly the problem comedies bear this out. Helena, for instance, turns Bertram into someone admirable despite his embarrassing lack of such traits; he is of noble birth and handsome, but Helena, rather like Grunberger's star-enchanted lover, turns Bertram into someone far above her and basks in his brilliance. Many viewers find her idealization of him, and hence of herself, so compelling that they try to explain away his faults. That Helena strains against reality is seen by other viewers as a sign of her foolish willfulness. Others, with greater compassion, see her idealization of Bertram as an indication of a deeply human need to do so.

In Shakespeare's late comedies the tendency to idealize is the cause of almost tragic consequences. Posthumus and Leontes "idealize" in the bad sense by defending against their unacknowledged ambivalence, against the destructiveness that soon overwhelms them and almost destroys their loved ones. And yet the late comedies also more strongly reveal the vital, beneficent sort of idealization. Paulina—and Hermione, we assume—maintain a sense of Leontes as a potentially good husband. Despite his murderous attempts, Paulina gives every indication that he can redeem himself, and this helps her, it would seem, to guide him through his repentance and reparation. In *Cymbeline,* Posthumus surprises us by his ability to maintain a sense of Imogen's essential perfection despite her "wrying but a little." That Posthumus can forgive his wife of adultery is in the context of the sources a novel and momentous advance. Imogen, however, is the figure who can most astonish us by her ability to maintain an idealization; she loves and can see no essential evil in her husband despite his attempt to have her murdered. When she learns of what he suspects and what he wants his servant to do, she at once blames not Posthumus but "some jay of Italy." Imogen fully admits her husband's destructiveness only briefly and at the very end of the play when they are reunited. Here, in a gesture that demonstrates the vital interrelationship between idealization and reparation, she confronts him with his cruelty: "Why did you throw your wedded lady from you? / Think that you are upon a rock, and now / Throw me again." She confronts herself and him with feelings of anger and aggression: she reveals her pent-up anger at what he did, and makes him aware of it. At the very same moment she addresses the other crucial aspect of the mourning process that both of them need to resolve: sad longing for the lost loved one—the good object—by embracing him in a gesture that reaffirms her enduring affection. Imogen's ability to be in touch with such feelings—and Posthumus's ability to rise to the occasion—"Hang there like fruit, my soul, / Till the tree die!"—can cause a kind of elation in viewers that is difficult to describe. Moments like this in Shakespeare's comedies do more than provide us with happy endings and admirable characters. Such moments help to reassure us of the human potential for near-perfection.

Posthumus—and heroes as diverse as Bassanio, Orsino, and Leontes—seems not to deserve such love, such a high estimate of value. That this is so, however, may not be the flaw in Shakespeare's comedies it is often taken to be. That the lover ultimately may not be worthy of such affection can help to convince viewers both of the heroine's excellence—her lifesaving generosity—and of the hero's potential for goodness far beyond our ability to imagine. Even the straining against reality, against credulity, can contribute to the reparative effect of the comedies: it reveals how much we need to believe in what can never be quite there. (pp. 83-94)

Joseph Westlund, "What Comedy Can Do for

Us: Reparation and Idealization in Shakespeare's Comedies," in Psychoanalytic Approaches to Literature and Film, *edited by Maurice Charney and Joseph Reppen, Fairleigh Dickinson University Press, 1987, pp. 83-95.*

Richard Kuhns

[*Kuhns is an American critic and educator who has written on philosophy and aesthetics. In the following excerpt, he proposes a psychoanalytic model for understanding audience response to tragic drama.*]

Psychoanalytic interpretations often begin with the question What does x express? This locution is common in expression theories of art; it presupposes that the work of art presents itself in a language, some parts of which are symbols whose meanings remain hidden, even though there is an available manifest sense. Expression is established when the manifest sense provides the initial given from which the observer can go to a remote latent content. The latent, upon interpretation, will be found to be a kind of thought. Recall the statement in [Freud's] "The History of the Psychoanalytic Movement": "Dreams are merely *a form of thinking.*" This generalization was applied to the latent content of art, folktales, fairy stories, myths, and many other kinds of cultural objects.

A good example of the psychoanalytic use of expression can be found in Freud's essay "The Theme of the Three Caskets," which attempts to interpret a theme that appears in several different kinds of stories. Although the literary forms are diverse (fairy story, myth, and drama), the basic theme is always the same—i.e., a man must make a choice between one of three women. Sometimes, as in the myth of Paris, it is explicitly three women, sometimes, as in Shakespeare's *The Merchant of Venice,* the three women are symbolically represented by caskets; and sometimes, as in *King Lear,* they are daughters. Freud enjoyed, somewhat in the manner of Lévi-Strauss, tracing the various forms and manifestations of symbolic themes. In "The Theme of the Three Caskets" he asks, "What is expressed by the three women, and by the choice?" Freud answers that the choice of one of three women expresses a number of thoughts. (1) It expresses a common life situation in which a man must deal with three women in his life, the three to be interpreted as mother, wife, and death. (2) It also expresses the anxiety we all feel toward death, and attempts to cope with that anxiety by transforming (through negation) death into that which is most beautiful and therefore freely chosen. (3) It transforms the fearful, ugly death into the beautiful, desirable woman. (4) The story also expresses a fatefulness we all recognize in the passage through life toward death. (5) The version of the theme in *King Lear,* in its similarity to the other versions, allows us to interpret the character of Cordelia: "Cordelia is death," Freud asserts in an identity that is startling.

With that identification, through the use of the copula *is,* Freud sums up a great deal of the kinds of interpretations psychoanalytic theory makes when it is applied to art. Cordelia is perceived manifestly as a character with a set of qualities we can readily discover through observing her behavior. But to add to those the noun *death* appears farfetched indeed. What Freud assumes in making this identification is that the manifest content relates to a latent content, and that we are able to go from manifest to latent through a consideration of the total symbolic situation which is the drama *King Lear* in an expanded sense that we usually refer to as an "interpretation" of *King Lear*. The method of interpretation is in part a translation—i.e., we translate the figure Cordelia into the idea of death; partly an expansion—i.e., we add the idea of death to the other ideas we entertain about Cordelia; and partly a transformation—i.e., we now see the Lear-Cordelia relationship differently, from a new perspective, as it were.

To assert "Cordelia is death" joins the manifest element of the drama *King Lear* with a latent theme of the play whose manifest presentations are so numerous that we see them woven into every thought and assertion of the play. To say "Cordelia is death" not only constitutes an interpretation of the final scene of the play, but also asserts that the play is *truly* or *really* about death, and consistent in its preoccupation with the reality of death. This should alert us to the fact that psychoanalytic theory of art, in making the manifest-latent distinction, is introducing a distinction of a philosophical kind between appearance and reality. In psychoanalytic theory "reality" does not refer exclusively to the external world of "physical reality"; but rather it refers to the internal reality which Freud refers to as "psychological reality." From this point of view, manifest and latent constitutes a contrast between that given to perception in experience, and that revealed as the psychological reality through an interpretation on psychoanalytic principles.

Freud's discussion of *King Lear* is of course but a brief example in an essay devoted to a larger theme, but his observations here, as in other places, completely overlook the political themes so central to the work. This neglect gives me [an] opportunity to relate the psychosexual and the political as we ought to do if we are to develop a psychoanalytic philosophy of art.

In the play *King Lear* there is a close connection between Lear's psychological preoccupations and his efforts to be a good ruler. The opening scene of the drama displays the conflict, and in itself indicates a way to bring together Freud's cultural and aesthetic insights.

Lear has two purposes in his division of the kingdom, of one of which he is aware, and to which he has given much thought; the other of which he is unaware, and which has a profound influence on his actions. The first we can properly call conscious, the second unconscious, purpose. Consciously Lear attempts to fulfill his obligations as a ruler: to preserve peace in the kingdom, establish continuity of rule, and publish his purpose that all may know his plan for political organization after his death. At the same time he struggles with a real political problem that comes a bit closer to the unconscious purposes. That is the problem of inheritance when the next generation is all daughters. Since a first-born son would inherit were there sons, the problem Lear has to cope with is complicated by there being only daughters. As Freud points out, this has a mythic content and has been dealt with many times in myth; but Freud fails to see the practical problem in political terms. Both the psychological and the political here require resolution.

Finally, Lear's actions show us that he is moved by unconscious needs that are personal and in conflict with the political obligations of a ruler. He has three daughters; only one does he love, and only one can be trusted. She is the youngest and about to be married, provided a husband can be persuaded to accept her. It is Lear's intention that a particular suitor be chosen (Burgundy) and that another (France) be rejected. This has political implications that are far-reaching, for Burgundy is the most powerful continental ruler, and a liaison between Lear's daughter Cordelia and Burgundy would ally England's ruler with the most powerful ruler abroad. Such an alliance would also insure that the other daughters (Regan and Goneril) would never be able to overwhelm Cordelia, and thus the safety of the kingdom would be assured.

Yet in the creation of this alliance Lear does strange things. It has often been said that Lear demonstrates either bad judgment or senility by his demand that his three daughters declare their love for him. In psychoanalytic terms such a demand is "over-determined"; that is to say, Lear has many motives for his demand, and seeks several outcomes to the performances he wishes the courtiers to witness. Politically, a declaration of love in a public setting before all the ranks in rule would be understood as an expression of fealty. In declarations of love, the daughters express their acceptance of the division of the kingdom, and their dedication to their father's continued presence in the kingdom. For remember that Lear plans to live with Cordelia with one hundred knights, a formidable fighting force.

To live with Cordelia, to be king yet not king, to see his kingdom as it will be and as it is after his death, projects, as in a fantasy, an odd and really an impossible state of affairs. It is not only impossible to survive one's own death; it is politically most unusual to give away your kingdom before you are dead. This contradiction well expresses the contradictory state of mind and affect from which Lear suffers. It is a clue to the deeper conflicts that trouble him and in the end prevent him from being a successful ruler.

Thus when Lear demands that his daughters declare their love for him he is doing several things at once. Consciously he seeks a public expression of fealty, an acceptance of his power and his plan. Goneril and Regan and their husbands are supposed to accept thankfully a third of the kingdom. Yet he asks them to accept thirds that are in two ways less than the third for Cordelia. First, they are geographically separated, Cornwall's domain being in the south, Albany's being in the north; Cordelia's "third" is actually larger and is in the middle separating the less dependable sisters from one another. Second, not only is Cordelia's third greater, her marriage as planned by Lear will ally her to the greatest continental power. In all this then Lear is hardly treating the three daughters equally. Yet he has a real political problem to solve, and given the natures of the three his plan is canny and well thought out.

However, since the declaration of love has other motives and purposes, we can expect a conflict to develop, for the "darker purpose" is not what Lear thinks it is. The conflict comes about with Cordelia's refusal to declare her love as Lear wishes it; she understands that the request hides a purpose that would destroy her. From that perception and its dreadful rebuke to Lear the tragedy flows. He first would deny her marriage to Burgundy—or to any man—since he wants Cordelia for himself. He is again frustrated by France's willingness to have Cordelia, who accepts him. That this betrayal is an ultimate rejection to Lear becomes clear in his immediate political response, for he does the one thing his plan was calculated to avoid, thus contradicting both his obvious outer and his most hidden inner intentions; he divides the kingdom in two. By giving Goneril and Regan equal portions and setting them in a position he will supposedly control by living alternately with each accompanied by his one hundred knights, he makes inevitable a conflict between the two powers. Given Goneril's and Regan's temperaments, they cannot brook one another's presence. And therefore Lear's plan to preserve the peace is transformed into a plan to guarantee war.

Such a reversal, in miniature the very tragic reversal itself, shows how much deeper and psychologically how much more complex Lear's purposes were than we at first suspected. The play does its work with remarkable economy; within one scene of one act the whole political and affective orientation is reversed, the relationships of all the rulers and family turned upside down in the sense that manifest considerations become overwhelmed in latent considerations, and rational considerations drowned in instinctual demands.

The analysis of *King Lear* just presented illustrates the need . . . for an integration of Freud's clinical and cultural writing. Provided as we are with an interpretation of Lear's quest and his complex relationship to public obligation and private need, to rule and to love, we lack the political which seems submerged in the psychosexual. There are political concerns expressed by the character King Lear which we shall find discussed in *Civilization and Its Discontents.* Here then is a case of interpretation calling for an integration of two consistently elaborated themes in Freud's thought. The tragedy itself poses the question of Freud's essay. Part III of *Civilization and Its Discontents* in fact summarizes and states the themes of *King Lear:* "the superior power of nature, the feebleness of our own bodies and the inadequacy of the regulations which adjust the mutual relationships of human beings in the family, the state and society. . . . As regards the third source, the social source of suffering, our attitude is a different one. We do not admit it at all: we cannot see why the regulations made by ourselves should not . . . be a protection and a benefit for every one of us. And yet, when we consider how unsuccessful we have been in precisely the field of prevention of suffering, a suspicion dawns upon us that here, too, a piece of unconquerable nature may lie behind—this time a piece of our own psychical constitution."

This suspicion becomes a certainty as we watch *King Lear,* but an understanding of that revelation requires political as well as psychological insight. *Civilization and Its Discontents* goes on to deal with the political conflicts: "So . . . the two urges, the one towards personal happiness and the other towards union with other human beings, must struggle with each other in every individual; and so, also, the two processes of individual and of cultural development must stand in hostile opposition to each other and mutually dispute the ground."

The full extent and various manifestations of this dispute are not developed in Freud's own writing. One manifesta-

tion, as I have argued, is in the art we call "tragedy," and it may be that every tragic drama has at its heart the "hostile opposition" of which Freud speaks. Whether that is so or not, the contribution of *Civilization and Its Discontents* is broader and more interesting than that. Human beings have a basic need to represent, to externalize, to set before themselves in forms of art the divisions, conflicts, and contradictions they find in themselves, in their actual needs and in their wish-fulfilling efforts to cope with their needs. In that respect works of art do not result simply from the sorts of frustrations Freud described in his early essay on the artist and daydreaming. Freud's own thought penetrated to a deeper level of human need and means to satisfy that need. In its greatest achievements, art enables human beings to examine and work through the conflicts between individuals and society, between the self and the political reality each one of us inhabits. Looking at psychoanalytic theory in this broader context allows us to overcome its own tendency to trivializing reductionism. Art is not simply a working through of the artists' problems and conflicts; it is a representation of universal communal conflicts in which everyone is entangled.

Civilization and Its Discontents . . . does contribute to a general theory of the arts through its contribution to a theory of tragedy, and the study of tragedy helps to illuminate the conflicts *Civilization and Its Discontents* defines, and ultimately despairs of resolving. However, it seems to me that the arts themselves, when conceived of as a class of enactments, do contribute to a possible resolution of the problems psychoanalytic theory struggled to subdue. We can readily see that the conflicts represented in tragic drama are often the sort Freud described in *Civilization and Its Discontents.* All the plays we consider tragedies present a protagonist who seeks to make congruent and consistent inner wishes, needs, gratifications, desires with the public obligations to others—to society at large—that he sustains as a forceful presence in the community.

Put in this broader context, psychoanalytic theory must ask, What is the effect on an audience of seeing these conflicts that tragedy represents? Since civilization, Freud argued, rests upon repression, and the norms of conduct that presuppose repression, the "message" of tragedy could very well be destructive to social coherence. The very impossibility of accommodating private and public—one of the deep truths discovered by tragedy—could lead some members of the audience to severe depression, wanhope and, ultimately, indifference to political values. Plato saw this, and argued that tragedy ought not be allowed; Aristotle saw it too, and argued that the knowledge delivered by tragedy could be liberating and civilizing rather than anarchic. The bringing together of this classical debate with Freud's reflections in *Civilization and Its Discontents* can lead to a much more satisfactory theory of tragedy than those we have so far formulated.

While *Civilization and Its Discontents* asks if the price we pay for civilization may be too high, the nature of tragic drama as set forth in both classical and psychoanalytic sources suggests that art itself—and perhaps especially tragic drama—may be of use in resolving or at least coming to an understanding of the conflict between individuals and their cultural obligations. May it not be the case that art ameliorates the conflict that it itself depicts? A society that encourages the arts, especially the more serious arts such as tragedy, deals with the deepest psychic conflicts, and in so doing helps the individual cope with the conflicts of growing up as a member both of a family and of society.

This view, which I attribute to an imaginative reconstruction of *Civilization and Its Discontents,* was explored by Aristotle in the *Poetics,* where he declares that "one must not seek any and every kind of pleasure from tragedy, but only the one proper to it." To defend the view that there is a *pleasure* in witnessing dire, frightening, sometimes horrifying events places the *Poetics* in a tradition that psychoanalytic theory could easily accommodate. The position Aristotle was attacking was, of course, that maintained by Plato, and later by Augustine and Rousseau, that the representation of painful events, and the feelings of pleasure connected to witnessing them, was a sign of human depravity. If it could be demonstrated that there is a right kind of response to tragedy, then the attack mounted by a politically puritanical vision of communal life might be mitigated, and a way made for a kind of representational action that has positive political consequence.

That tragedy concerns itself with the political was recognized both by Plato and Aristotle, with different conclusions drawn as to the justifiability of a political content that saw deeply into the grave difficulty in achieving just rule. Plato thought it necessary to hide the pessimistic content of tragic action from the community; Aristotle argued that such content delivered a deep and politically strengthening vision. Tragedy, so it was understood in the tradition of classical philosophy, turns upon a deep, pervasive, ineradicable conflict, that between private need and public obligation. The first is sexual, the second moral and political. Its most obvious example is the history of Oedipus, but we see the same conflict in all the tragic heroes— e.g., Lear, Hamlet, Othello—in different forms, with different developmental histories. But in all tragedy, and in much serious drama, the conflict is clear: private sexual need and public political obligation inevitably come into conflict. Simply stated, the tragic plots gain inextinguishable energy and force from a conflict that is unresolvable, because each side of the need cannot be satisfied without violation of the other.

King Lear cannot both divide the kingdom and possess Cordelia. Oedipus cannot both rule as king and possess his mother as his wife. No resolution of these conflicts is possible; tragic suffering, as Aristotle pointed out, follows from these conflicts with inevitability. We might call the well-made plot a syllogism of suffering. Grasping such a structure of events in itself gives pleasure, the pleasure of recognition, but more than that, the inevitable and unresolvable conflict arouses a deeper pleasure in us, for we respond to it with recognition of a pervasive human prohibition, and with our own sense of god-like power. We survey the tragic plot as if it were ours to dominate and control; we achieve immortal prescience, and that permits us to celebrate suffering as evidence of our now transcendent (although woefully transitory) powers. We seek to resolve an inevitable conflict of our own nature with a fantasy of suprahuman omnipotence.

There remains, however, an unanswered question regarding our capacity to find pleasure in representations of the painful. Why is it that we respond with a truly aesthetic delight to something which in real life would be both mor-

ally and politically unacceptable? Psychoanalytic theory not only helps to define the nature of the tragic conflict; it also suggests ways in which the conflict is ameliorated and internalized, for the relationship of audience to drama is one that participates in the larger complex relationship of transference, already described. Participation in a dramatic presentation—one of a class of events I have analyzed in the previous chapter as "enactments"—confronts the audience with events and feelings that have locations in the experience, conscious and unconscious, of each observer. The plot, characters, thought, scenes of suffering in the play reproduce and represent in metaphoric form varieties of affects, beliefs, wishes, fears, anxieties, hopes, and fantasy entertainments whose interconnections establish a psychosexual history for each person. The dramatic presence, however, achieves more than a mere mirroring; it "works through" the events to a resolution and coerces the audience to accord acceptance to the manifestly unacceptable. In that resolution a "katharsis," not simply of feeling but of belief and of thought about persons and events, becomes established in the private and public obligations whose competing claims must be recognized. The conclusion of a well-made plot then allows the recognitions to occur as part of a process that has affinities to the process of therapy. Indeed, it was one of Aristotle's deepest insights to see that tragic drama is in some ways like, but in a most fundamental way unlike, the ecstatic postures and wish-fulfillments of the bacchantic celebrants. The difference lies in this: for the bacchantic celebrants the ecstatic state must be sought again and again, while the well-made tragic plot effected a more permanent recognition in a changed attitude toward the self and the state and the impossibility of satisfactorily adjudicating their competing claims.

In other contexts Freud would refer to that outcome as a form of sublimation (*Sublimierung*), the condition in which an instinct, sexual in nature, is realized in a goal that is nonsexual, at least manifestly. Thus, the tragic drama receives great energy from sexual sources, and realizes a redirection of their aim and goal in analyzing them in a thoroughly political set of events. But to make this comparison between an insight of a classical text and psychoanalytic theory is simply to reiterate an observation of Freud's, that psychoanalysis was by no means the first thinking to recognize the deeper interrelationships of the sexual and the political. Both Aristotle and Freud would agree that a high achievement of culture was to realize the sublimating power of serious artistic representations.

Psychoanalytic explanations can be joined to the classical speculations to account for the mysterious evocation tragedy brings about through which an audience enjoys painful affects. The force first manifests itself in the maturational project of the human being who as child moves from "the third area" to full cultural functioning. Here I once again draw upon the thought of D. W. Winnicott, as well as more traditional theory, to account for the developmental possibility of tragedy.

My elaboration of Winnicott's views suggests that an enactment, such as tragic drama, is one of the ways an individual has to move out from the immediacy of internal and family conflict to the realities that the familiar plots present. If we consider tragic plots in terms of their familiarity, their repetitions, their continuity with some of the first stories a child hears, the early transitional objects stand in a sequence in which the objects we think of as *art* relate developmentally to the childhood manipulation of objects in play with the parents. There, frightening accounts produce real terror which can be modified as the representational nature of narration becomes understood. As the transitional object becomes work of art, shared by the community as a whole, it retains in some respects the properties of the earlier objects, and relies upon psychological conditions laid down in early years, conditions that function in later years when the transitional object has been succeeded by things like tragic plots.

The earlier condition, however, remains in some respects present and operative, for tragic plots are surrounded by much the same risks as early transitional tales: the hearer feels anxiety and suffers the painful affects that Aristotle referred to as "pity" and "fear." Yet the overall experience possesses deep and abiding satisfactions that make taking the risks worthwhile.

In two late papers Freud speculated on the psychological process by which the ambivalences of our experience with tragedy may be understood, and our willingness to take the risk of tragedy accounted for. Introducing the terms "split" and "splitting," Freud suggested in the uncompleted "An Outline of Psychoanalysis," and in the fragment "Splitting of the Ego in the Process of Defense," that we possess and use "splitting" as a means to cope with fearful and threatening situations. "Two psychical attitudes," he writes, "have been formed instead of a single one—one, the normal one, which takes account of reality, and another which under the influences of the instincts detaches the ego from reality. The two exist alongside of each other." Splitting of the ego, Freud goes on to say, characterizes many psychological processes, and we often find, especially in psychosis and neurosis, that "two different attitudes, contrary to each other and independent of each other," are to be found in many interactions between the ego and external reality.

Developing these views in a posthumously published fragment, Freud points out that in children we see the capacity to tolerate "a conflict between the demand by the instinct and the prohibition by reality," by taking two positions simultaneously and therefore splitting the ego. The child both turns away from reality, and turns toward reality, thus resolving what appears to be a contradiction with simultaneous affirmations: experience countenances and finds room for both A and not A, or for the contraries A and B, through maintaining a fantasy construal alongside a realistic construal of the world.

Transitional objects . . . become the first cultural objects through splitting. The participants assume two positions simultaneously: they recognize the terror and the suffering of the action, as they also deny the reality of the presentation because it is a representation. Storytelling, whether in the simple mode of familial play or in the sophisticated mode of serious drama, relies upon the process of splitting for the special pleasure it engenders.

One way in which that pleasure is encouraged and allowed to manifest itself is through the very content and structure of the dramatic plots themselves, for they too employ the process of splitting. In tragic drama splitting of objects and of selves occurs in many fascinating ways; the conflict between private sexual need and public political obligation splits persons and actions into seemingly irreconcilable dualities that yet must find a possible coexistence in the plot, and in so doing call upon the audience to participate in the splitting and the reconciliation. As we witness the plot, we are ourselves brought into the various bifurcations which enable us to maintain a dual set of responses, holding at once the painful and the pleasurable in an unresolved tension which is also a coordination. The affective life of the audience now must arrange these dualities into an acceptable response. Just how is that brought about?

Acceptable response refers to the pleasure peculiar to scenes of suffering that conclude tragic narratives. This is a pleasure unlike the pleasure of revenge, unlike the pleasure of simple excitement, unlike the pleasure we take in the beautiful. For in all these respects, in terms of these values—values of seeing an enemy fall, of entertainment, of the aesthetic—the pleasure Aristotle referred to is distinct, it is the pleasure appropriate to tragedy: we seek not any and every kind of pleasure from tragedy, but only the one it demands.

Since tragic drama both elicits and directs powerful feelings that are in other contexts painful, to experience the pleasure appropriate to tragedy suggests that the feelings are manipulated in a special way peculiar to this kind of representation; and it is not satisfactory to say that the pleasure we experience derives from the representational as such, for there are many representational effects that are revolting and thoroughly unacceptable. There must be a way that the tragic representations work for us and in us that will help to explain the pleasure we take in scenes of suffering. I propose that the process of splitting, as sketched out in the above discussion, accounts for the pleasure appropriate to tragedy.

To be sure, we discover the pleasure appropriate to tragedy at a late stage in our cultural maturation; it succeeds a much more simplified and simplifying view of ourselves that begins to take shape in our commerce with transitional objects. Each of the events embodied in tragic plots occurs over and over again in the stories we hear as we grow up.

The central cultural conflict that energizes tragic plots, the irresolvability of private sexual need and public political obligation, drives the action forward to a disclosure of the full incongruity humans must forever struggle to resolve. In that lifelong, and indeed historically constant, effort, an internal bifurcation expresses itself in the splitting of persons and objects. In taking up splitting as a part of its own representational concerns, tragedy separates out the painful and the pleasurable in plots so that we witnesses are led to perform the same kathartic clarification in ourselves.

Through the psychoanalytic concept of splitting, the classical concept of *Katharsis* assumes a broader application as we endeavor to establish the implications of that seemingly simple phrase, "the pleasure appropriate to tragedy," that Aristotle formulated as partial answer to Plato. The developmental trajectory of our quest to achieve wholeness in ourselves as part of our participation in both historical tradition and present political life finds support in many different kinds of cultural undertakings.

It should follow from the psychoanalytic contribution to

an understanding of tragedy, that Freud's writings on culture covertly imply the importance to civilization of enlarging the influence and availability of serious art forms. It seems to me that the psychoanalytic reflections on art and culture imply a possible therapeutic force in some of the arts; but Freud did not explicitly consider the place of art in society in these terms.

To establish the relationship of art to the developmental sequence of growing up, we must avoid simple reductionism. Ultimately, what makes artists and their work important psychoanalytically is their contribution to and critique of culture. Therefore, in Freud's own terms, though he did not say this, it may be the case that the arts are the most important social instruments for achieving both individual and cultural maturation. . . . [The] analysis of cultural objects which followed upon Freud's speculations established the deep importance for cultural functioning of cultural objects such as the ones I have been discussing here. The importance of those objects to an understanding of the psychoanalytic theory of art and culture is to be found in their very substance, for the greatest of them represent the interrelationship of objects and culture. Thus the quest undertaken by the character Lear when *King Lear* opens is precisely the quest we, as witnesses, have been undertaking in our lives—whether consciously recognized or not—and a quest we enact within ourselves as we witness the enactment. The failure of Lear's quest does not imply the failure of our own in the development process, though indeed the drama may make a statement we accept as true about the possibility of success in the quest we all enter upon in our political and psychosexual lives. As witnesses to the enactment, we respond to and use the enactment in ways that are foreclosed to the characters enacting. That very difference between characters within the representation and witnesses outside it is one of the powers of the enactment to bring about a transitional move, conveying us from our self-enclosed consciousness to remote areas both within ourselves (the unconscious) and without ourselves (the reality of nature and the communal life). Transitional experience depends upon more than the single object and the single experience of a single performance. Witnesses differ from characters in this respect: witnesses possess not simply the one enactment, but many enactments within the tradition, and many instances of the particular drama *King Lear*. The characters within possess knowledge of some other objects in the tradition, and if they do, they express that knowledge in the words they utter and the situations they find themselves in. They may refer to, quote, represent, imitate other enactments. What the characters know enters into our response as witnesses; yet what we know as witnesses always surpasses the wide spectrum of affects and the details of knowledge delivered in the single case because we have access to other cases.

The single case yet performs the transitional function: it delivers us to the Lear-world and its allied objects; it returns us from the Lear-world with whatever fragment of that presence we have been able to break off. In time, with successive reflections and comparisons, the tradition we possess is reshaped by the succession of objects and insights we have been able to inform with the Lear-presence. Placing that successfully is the task of interpretation, and that task is accomplished through the help of various—perhaps many—theories. No one theory can be designated as the one to meet all the needs of the object and our experience as witnesses. Tradition lays an obligation upon us to master the theories the objects demand, the theories through which our tradition realizes itself. Among those, the psychoanalytic has its own guidance to give, its interpretations to make, its truths to serve. That interpretations serve truth is itself a belief of the tradition we possess. (pp. 96-113)

Richard Kuhns, "Psychoanalytic Theory at Work: Style, Expression, Truth," in his Psychoanalytic Theory of Art: A Philosophy of Art on Developmental Principles, *Columbia University Press, 1983, pp. 83-129.*

PSYCHOANALYSIS AND LITERARY CRITICISM

Frederick J. Hoffman

[*Hoffman is an American educator and critic whose* Freudianism and the Literary Mind *has been called the "first significant examination of the relationship between Freud's psychoanalytic theories and modern literature." In the following excerpt from that work, he discusses the contribution that psychoanalytic concepts can make to literary criticism.*]

So many attempts have been made to discuss precisely the relationship of psychology with literature or to suggest the usefulness of psychology to criticism that one needs first of all to see if a new perspective isn't somehow available. I believe we know both the advantage and the limitations of the biographical study of writers; and no one can escape these days the dark presence of Jung's "primordial images." Perhaps we may find our best access to the problem by looking once again at a structure and terminology contributed at the beginning of the century and before by Sigmund Freud and elaborated upon by him in subsequent years.

I refer of course to Freud's definition, description and analysis of the psychic economy. These involve a series of metaphors, as bold a series as was ever advanced by a cautious scientist. Beginning only with the facts of the unconscious and the conscious mind, Freud saw first of all, or suspected, both the tension between the two and what he called the constancy, or balance, of energy that invariably characterized this tension. From these simple beginnings came the terminology with which we are all now familiar: the id, ego, super-ego; the unconscious, preconscious, conscious; the pleasure principle and the reality principle, and so on.

Described in Freud's own words (*The Ego and the Id*), " . . . the ego is that part of the id which has been modified by the direct influence of the external world acting through the Perceptual-Conscious: in a sense it is an extension of the surface-differentiation. Moreover, the ego has the task of bringing the influence of the external world to bear upon the id and its tendencies, and endeavors to substitute the reality-principle for the pleasure-principle which reigns surpeme in the id. In the ego perception plays the part which in the id devolves upon instinct. The ego represents what we call reason and sanity, in contrast to the id which contains the passions."

These terms were in the nature of accessory metaphors, introduced as the original insight into psychic tensions required elaboration and its subtleties needed definition. I am aware of the fact that these formulations stem from a desire to assert and affirm the existence of what underlay the conscious, external world, of what we know from having seen or sensed. It is also true that they are the product of a desire to pay a discreet tribute to the language of orthodox science. There is nothing at all unusual or surprising in Freud's characterization of these phenomena; nor was Freud the first to emphasize the need to examine an "unconscious" life or mind. It is perhaps in his admirable and patient *consistency* of attention that the merit of his system lies—as well as in its availability to almost endless fruitful elaboration.

Once we have established that the unconscious is a positive entity, a specific and viable aspect of the psyche, then we may proceed to describe it. We continue to do so, however, by the ingenious method of analyzing causally the aberrancies and obliquities of the conscious mind; and our major instrument in such analysis is language. We must assume a language norm, a norm of linguistic behavior, linked to a kind of systematic logical or rational form. If there are such norms—if they may be maintained without one's retreating too far into abstractions—then it is possible to examine variants, deviations, subterfuges, psychic "jamming," and to explain them as a part of the strategy of the id, as a verbal consequence of the tension resulting from the flow and counterflow of psychic energy.

Freud's own description of these processes is both precise and illuminating: "By virtue of its relation to the perceptual system, [the ego] arranges the processes of the mind in a temporal order and tests their correspondence with reality. By interposing the process of thinking it secures a postponement of motor discharges and controls the avenues to motility. . . . All the experiences of life that originate from without enrich the ego; the id, however, is another outer world to it, which it strives to bring into subjection to itself. It withdraws libido from the id and transforms the object-cathexes of the id into object-constructions. With the aid of the super-ego, though in a manner that is still obscure to us [1927], it draws upon the experiences of past ages stored in the id." (*The Ego and the Id*)

This is what amounts to a psychological analysis of the basic constituents of a literature. In terms of it we may illuminate much of what we discuss in literary criticism as form, texture, metaphor, and symbol. I should like to suggest the following plan for a criticism based upon Freud's initial descriptions of the psychic order. Let us assume that our psychic life may be divided into primary and secondary processes; that these, since they are located differently and react to different kinds of exposure, are in conflict with each other, or more accurately that they cause conflict in the psyche; that basic energies (whether of wish or desire, as Freud maintained, or of some other incentive) are turned back upon themselves, or are permitted only partial expression, or express themselves fully only in extraordinary circumstances; that our understanding of

these energies comes from the fact of their being thwarted, controlled, suspended in a state of partial expression; and that, ultimately, the ideal psychic state results from a *balance* of tensions and a *conservation* of psychic energy. A number of important opportunities for the description of our psychic lives occur to us. While the energies are not specifically one thing or another, they may be characterized with a quite satisfactory and useful precision. The push, drive, energy of the id are desire, wish, for pleasure, for specific gratifications; the agency for thwarting the desire is exposed to the reality itself, the external world which indicates its prohibitions by inflicting pain or forcing retreat. An uninhibited drive toward satisfaction of unconscious wishes (or expenditure of libidinal energy) would lead to death. The wish needs instruction in the shock of reality; if the character of inhibition is moderate, the shock will lead to readjustment; if the reality is too suddenly and too brutally enforced, the effect will be a traumatic shock, leading to one of several forms of compulsive behavior. Freud assumes stability in the external world; Hemingway among others did not find it so. But this shock is not limited either to the accidents of uninhibited desire or to the catastrophes of an uncontrolled reality. Repression is in itself a cause of pain; it may, in the interests of protecting the psyche and prolonging life, cause violent dislocations of the psychic system.

However inadequate this may be as a sketch of Freud's superbly exact descriptions, I introduce it here as a preliminary to examining its usefulness as a perspective upon literature. The two have in common what we may call a necessary language—language as the instrument of description becomes in the course of my discussion language as a system of strategies. Language is necessary at first to label and define; next, to put phenomena in order; then to characterize the nature of incentives for labeling and ordering, finally, in the most remarkable of its ranges of use, to effect changes in meaning, to represent situations as more complex than they might be or are or ought to be. In the mind of a person endowed with every resource of language, the phenomena of psychic tension, conflict, drive, repression, are articulated and represented in a discourse at once psychologically just and remarkably subtle. I should like to suggest, therefore, that literature may be viewed and analyzed in terms of the verbal and metaphorical equivalents of the psyche and its behavior. Literature possesses a greater metaphoric freedom than psychology, or perhaps it has the license of its own audacity. But it is actively engaged in providing verbal and metaphoric equivalents of and elaborations upon the simply described behavior of the id, ego, and superego in their dynamic relationships. I can scarcely go on from here, to insist upon exact equivalents; it is perhaps as unwise to find iddities and egocentricities in literature as it is to accept literally biographical peculiarities as definitive explanations of achieved works of art. To locate an author's id, ego, superego, etc., in either characters or lines is to violate the subtlety of their necessary arrangements. My purpose is, instead, to explain the complexities of literary work as the results of symbolic actions which report and reflect on a high level of linguistic articulateness and subtlety the basic tensions, balances, imbalances, repressions, and compensations of psychic energies contained within a system such as Freud has described.

In any application of such a criticism, we can begin with

fairly simple definitions. The creative process begins with a relaxation of ego control. There are other examples of such relaxation: drunkenness, forms of schizophrenia, dreams. But the work of the artist differs usually from these in that the regression is deliberate and controlled. The creative artist is *aware* of the regression; one may almost say he *wills* it (there have been cases of poets who have tried to force it by artificial means). The creative mind suspends its work between inspiration and control, or criticism. The artist is aware first of all that he is in a state of suspension; deliberately he has allowed the ego to give in to the flow of energy from the id. As Ernst Kris has put it (*Psychoanalytic Explorations in Art;* see Further Reading): (with Abraham Kaplan)

> We may speak here of *a shift in psychic level,* consisting in the fluctuation of functional regression and control. When regression goes too far, the symbols become private, perhaps unintelligible even to the reflective self; when, at the other extreme, control is preponderant, the result is described as cold, mechanical, and uninspired.

As Freud has pointed out (in *The Interpretation of Dreams* and elsewhere), in the unconscious which has been affected by the ego's inhibitions reside the potential strategies for circumventing the ego. Such strategies as condensation, displacement, additive substitutes for negations or for the conditional mode are all a product of the id-ego tension. The verbalization of this tension is available in the preconscious. Of basic interest to literary criticism is the fact that impulse and inhibition are herein *mixed,* that multiple meanings and ambiguities are thus a *result* of the conflict between desire and inhibition. An ambiguity may be said to suggest in language the subtlety of an achieved balance. The *complexity* of the human state resides neither in the fully charged impact of desire upon the ego nor in the ego's use of societal prohibitions to stop the impact (each of these by itself is superficial)—but, rather, in the *product* of the conflict. The ego provides the language of discourse in its relationship with the preconscious (which is largely charged with the oughtness and counter-energy of conscience); the id determines the strategies used to mitigate, violate, or circumvent. In a remarkable range of meanings and metaphor, literature records the infinite variety of these exchanges and conflicts.

There are two major considerations relevant to literary criticism: they are the multiplicity of meanings in literature and the element of form. Form is largely a product of the ego; social and moral forms are related to aesthetic forms; or, rather, aesthetic form is an extension of the logic of social and moral forms. That literary forms have great variety is no more remarkable a fact than that form persists through such variety. Experiment in literary form probably comes from a distrust of traditional form; the container no longer satisfactorily orders the thing contained. Thus an attempt to introduce a "qualitative" form, or to insist upon symbolic as distinguished from rational progression comes at least in part from a dissatisfaction with form as not allowing sufficient texture or as overly inhibiting the opportunity of texture. Texture is itself a variant of form: rhythm both encourages and controls freedom of meaning; a rhyme pattern both enhances the quality of word sounds and sets a limit to their frequency.

More specifically, the forms are the special province of the ego; they are the means of inhibition, the ways of containing creative energy, of balancing its tensions and of securing a maximum of discernibility within the range of particulars. The only way of making oneself understood, in short, of communicating, is to contain the charge of psychic energy within a formal pattern that has initially and psychologically been introduced as a way of *preventing* an uninhibited charge of energy. This process may cost much. A slavish obedience to form for form's sake is of course debilitating and unrewarding. But the tension set up by form and texture leads to articulation and then to containment of the basic energy drives that have existed initially inarticulate and without form. Ernst Kris has given us a very interesting discussion of what he calls "stringencies," a term he uses to define external restraints put upon expression in art.

> The level of stringency in works of art—their degree of interpretability—varies markedly from period to period. In some cases ambiguity is fully exploited, and correspondingly great demands are made on the audience; in other cases, there is no more ambiguity than is involved in the work's being aesthetic at all; the demands on the audience are minimal; the interpretations called for are rigidly limited. We may suggest that art is likely to be characterized by low stringency (i.e., high ambiguity and interpretability) where systems of conduct or ideals are in doubt or social values are in process of transition.

This is true especially when those aspects of form which define the thing contained while in the act of containing it no longer serve the ego adequately, whether because they have weakened through an excess of abstraction (the definitions no longer define), or because they have become too arbitrarily fixed (the definitions are too remote from the particulars they are supposed to contain). We may say that any form is the result of a series of accidents. As in any situation where balance serves to make energy intelligible, form in literature is the consequence of the need to compromise with energy by limiting it and allowing it exercise in terms of particular tensions.

Our final discussion of form in literature is by way of transition to its relationship with language and meaning. The major instruments which the ego possesses for the purpose of containing energy are time, space, convention, and logic. The id possesses none of these. They are the means of locating psychic energy within the focus of reality. Each of them is both specific and ambiguous. In simplest terms each arrests energy by shaping it, or shapes it in the act of arresting it. If we could imagine the id with a time sense at all, it would be a future sense—that is, the drive toward total gratification is pure future, and leads, if not inhibited, to death. The ego's function is to arrest future by means of past, to make the present moment a unity of past and future. The result of this process is to slow down the drive toward death; and in consequence, moments are realized and both addition and formal patterns of time are constructed. Similarly, the ego gives spatial concepts to the energy discharge; in the matter of time and space both, the ego localizes, forces the psychic energy into an awareness of *milieu.* Milieu itself is a product of objective temporal and spatial situations. Freud's elaborate discussions of the familial origins and progress of societies should concern us here, but they will have only to be assumed. (See *Totem and Taboo, The Ego and the Id, Moses and Monotheism.*

See especially Herbert Marcuse, *Eros and Civilization*.) It may be of some interest here to point to the range of psychoanalytic evaluations of milieu. Freud's is hypothetical, but only in the sense of generalizing historically from proven recurrences; a family centered milieu is in Freud's case derived from clinical practices, the interpretation based upon inferences from personal cases. I think that here we may see the source of what we may call "family-centered literature," in which formal controls are defined in terms of manners (for instance, *Buddenbrooks* and *The Magic Mountain*). Jung's milieu, though also an inference from a kind of therapeutic procedure, is nevertheless extremely wide in its range of descriptive implication. Neither conception of milieu is especially noted for its relationship to contemporary social or societal fact, a fact that other analysts are eager to assert. The literary implications of both Freud's and Jung's views are allied with universals, but Freud's universals are at least easier to associate with the particulars at their source. To continue with the discussion of the four terms, convention is a form of the human history of time and space as inhibiting factors. It is the most flexible, the least firm of all the forms of awareness which the ego uses to arrest the progress toward uninhibited gratification. Nevertheless, it may achieve great significance in literature. There is often a close link of social and moral convention with literary form. Convention is the social logic of literary usage. Logic itself is the final restriction imposed upon the psychic energy expressed in the id. There are basic logical principles common to an external world from which the ego draws its reserves of inhibition. These principles are largely either negating or qualifying; that is, they exclude (if this, then not this), or negate (not this), or prescribe (this and not this). Every grammatical detail is an index, a sign, of the inhibition which anticipates form; but as such it may also be a clue to the aesthetic means of articulating psychic balance.

In so arbitrarily stating the formal conditions of inhibition, I have tried to set the stage for the final phase of my discussion. I should maintain that ambiguity, word-play, and what Philip Wheelwright has called "plurisignation" are primarily a part of the process constantly occurring in the psyche which seeks to achieve an articulate balance of tensions between desire and preservation. The id is neither logical nor illogical; it is prelogical until it comes in contact with the ego or the ego with it. After that it acquires the devices of logic but makes them serve its own purposes. The *balance* in literature between the logical and the contradictory, between single and multiple meanings, is the substance of the very lively tension existing and verbalized between energy and form. Freud's description of the dream work is now so well known that I don't need to give it in detail; chapter seven of *The Interpretation of Dreams* is its initial formulation, and there are many explanations of it, by Freud and by others. I should like to infer from them what seems to me a statement important to literary criticism: every ambiguity purposefully introduced into literature is in one way or another a compromise between uninhibited energy and extreme formal inhibition. It is impossible to decide the ideal degree of ambiguity, but one may, I think, assume that the forms of ambiguity reflect both degrees of tension and conditions of balance within the psyche. There are levels, of course, of sophistication. In children there is a fairly free play of wish and inhibition, contained within a limited number of metaphorical possibilities. Alice is after all Lewis Carroll's

Alice and not Alice's. James's Maisie assumes the complexities of adulthood by necessity. In a great majority of adults the containment of energy is achieved in a relatively small number of rather abstract, though sentimentally overcharged, figures. The kinds of paradox and irony achieved by Donne, Marvell, Herbert, and others represent a highly endowed sense of the ambiguities residing in such tensions. Indeed, in the case of Donne the figures employed to express them reach a very high level of complexity, the purpose of which is both to individualize desire and to give it a degree of sophistication. The ambiguities resulting may be said to come partly from a genuine appreciation of human corruptibility (both moral and physical), partly from a wish to defend desire by means of defying those who would cynically dismiss it, partly from contemporary religious and metaphysical resources for transcendence. Such paradox is a result of the need both to admit a truth and at the same time to use available forms of transcendence in order to deny it; the admission and the denial are fused. Corruption becomes death, but death is contained within forms so successful in negating physical death that it triumphs over cynicism ("Only our love hath no decay," "The Anniversarie"). Similarly, the paradox of time and eternity may function within a poem; necessities forced upon us by time are denied by transforming the temporal into aspects of eternity. Yet the limits set by time (by which we narrowly view the corruption of the body as it "matures") are in themselves contained within the image of eternity; indeed, were it not for time, we should not *have* eternity. The complex nature of much religious poetry probably results from the interrelationship in each of us between our sense of physical instability and our desire for immortality; as for the latter, each of us has his own variant of it. Immortality is the ultimate formalization of desire; we continue to desire but come to realize that if we persist we shall die. To wish immortality is to hope for a removal of the reality principle, with a considerable gain in refinement of the pleasure principle. In the poetry of Laforgue and Corbière there is occasionally an attempt to set up ideally foreshortened versions of the id and either to satirize them ("Epitaphe") or to use them ("Locutions des Pierrots") as a means of satirizing, not the fact of ego-control in itself, but the prevailing accepted forms of control. Satire usually protests against the contemporary ways used by the ego to inhibit. In surrealism, and occasionally in the work of Rimbaud, there is an attempt to represent the id pure—or at least to allow the manifest dream content a free display—with the result that the literature describes, not a balance of tension but merely the consequence of a superficial exposure of wish to the idiom of ego.

The greatest range and the finest subtlety of all language exchanges based upon this principle of energy conflict and conservation are found in those types of communication described so brilliantly by Philip Wheelwright, in *The Burning Fountain*, as forms of "expressive language." I should like to use one or two of these, with the apology that I shall shift their context, perhaps even radically, from that of his intention. Mr. Wheelwright defines what he calls the "principle of plurisignation" as meaning "that an expressive symbol tends, on any given occasion of its realization, to carry more than one legitimate reference, in such a way that its proper meaning is a tension between two or more directions of semantic stress." That is, in terms I have chosen to explain it, that the language of the symbol retains the charge and tension of its psychic origins, or of the dynamic shifts and exchanges of the energy which it was before the state was articulated. The many possibilities of stress, of direction, of painful thrust and arrest, are here echoed in the multiplications of meaning within a given image, metaphor, or cluster of images. This symbolic maneuver is accessible to a great variety of strategies: the poet may wish to exploit the irony he sees in his state of acceptance-rejection (that is, he may accept only ostensibly, or reject only ostensibly, but he ironically juxtaposes both acceptance and rejection in his language.) I believe we may say that Eliot both accepts and rejects. He sees as well the pathetic consequences of pure acceptance or of pure rejection. Herein lies the almost too easy irony of some of his poems. The polarities are perhaps too neatly obvious; and the deficiencies of both Prufrock and Sweeney are too much derived from circumstances that forbid transcendence. Eliot's great admiration of Dante seems to me to have come from his recognizing in Dante a means of escaping from the dead ends of Prufrock and Sweeney, as well as from the forbidding milieu responsible for them. The *Paradiso* is prefigured in the *Inferno;* a terrestrial inferno, such as Eliot describes in the early poems, can suggest a purgatory and a heaven only by an act of daring transcendence, an act which of course Eliot attempted. Or the poet may wish to express the tragedy of acceptance which lies in its inevitability (that is, acceptance of control is most unwished for but not in the least uncalled for); or he may extend the ambiguity to such an extent that it makes a virtue of transcendence (the effort to create a viable mystic exchange out of a condition of stasis, behavioral or mechanical).

Mr. Wheelwright speaks also of what he calls the "principle of paralogical dimensionality," by which he wishes to suggest "that there are other dimensions or *nodi* of meaning than those of logical universality and existential particularity. . . . " The logical dimension is presumably that which restricts and limits within the strict terms of discernible reality. But, as I see it, this dimension is indispensable as a beginning; one must see what a thing is before he determines the scope and degree of its not being or of its being more. The co-ordinates of reality and desire are first set up, with such dimensional angularity as we are prosaically accustomed to use. The "paralogical dimensionality" of expressive language, as Mr. Wheelwright puts it, is nourished by the dissatisfactions accumulating from this initial effort at compromise. As the dream work refuses to accept either-or, the language of the poet suggests a multiple of meanings from a state of tension. There are several ways in which such a state may be true (effectual, "healthful," conducive of peace), several in which it may be false. These variants are all contained within the single linguistic or metaphoric representation of a state of balanced tension.

Finally, one must consider the problem of associating the most intricate of literary expressions with Jung's archetypes. The access to myth in recent criticism is at least partly a product of research, or of a quest of mythical surrogates for displaced symbols. The elaborate structure provided by Jung for the purpose of linking individual present with collective past is useful only in that it suggests the extremes to which the imagination may go in generalizing immediate necessities and experiences. But archetypes, beyond the service they perform in cataloguing and

arranging, are actually the most inflexible of forms. They may, in fact, arrest the process of articulating psychic tensions and they may over-simplify the results. Whatever one may say by way of crediting Jung's ingenuity and the vigor of his imagination, the archetypal process, by enlarging and depersonalizing the expressive experience, threatens to destroy both its individuality and its complexity. The appeal to literature and to literary criticism of Jung's archaic forms and residues is, of course, phenomenally great; and it is necessary to explain just what the archetype does to the act of literary creation.

First, the process of verbalizing, of constructing linguistic expressions of any psycho-dynamic state follows along the lines of its own logic. This is not a transcendent logic; it is as complex as the circumstances require and permit. Within the limits seen and set by Freud, transcendence of the actual condition set up by psychic tensions and balances always remains closely associated with them and takes on their quality. Metaphors used to define such states are always individualized according to terms set down by the experiences determined by them.

It follows that the particularities of psychic experiences lend themselves to the act of universalizing. But the universals follow from a commonalty of basic experience, or of basic sources from which the secondary qualities of experience are drawn. To the degree that they may form clusters about a static symbol, they may be called archetypes. The danger is that one will abandon the particular for the archetypical. Once an experience is defined as "shared archetype," its particulars are threatened by dismissal. This indeed is often Jung's therapeutic aim, as I see it.

The advantages of Jung's archetypal portrayal of the collective psyche for literary criticism come primarily from its being available to an almost infinite range of spectacular inference. If poets unconsciously share archetypal interests, and if critics can bring themselves to commune with poets in the sharing, then the lines of tradition, of a discernible past discernibly associated with a felt present, are blurred. There is a great difference between a tradition of the ritual observance of a fixed symbolic and mythical pattern and the direct, knowledgeable, ingenious, overt *use* of myth in modern literature. To explain present literary circumstance by reference to archetypal patterns is to ignore the peculiarities of present practice and need. To say that basically we are linked to the past by archetypal means is to describe falsely the particular nature of our hunger for transcendence. The desire for credible and trustworthy universals is after all, and peculiarly, a feature of our contemporary behavior. It is not that the *desire* is unique, but that its special properties are. In rationally undermining the foundations of our past belief, we have put ourselves in an especially compromising position. We do not submit to any archetypes entirely, but we do love to entertain all of them, as poetic means and as mythical experiences that are half real and half merely "curious."

This peculiarity of our modern circumstance is especially well served by Jung, who serves artists by rescuing them from an unflattering Freudian diagnosis and giving them the role of seer, prophetic bard, guardian of the temple, neighbor of the mystic. Such a characterization makes any analysis of the literary process such as I have sketched impractical and unnecessary. Inspiration is no longer available to psychological explanation, or at least psychological or indeed any other kind of explanation is unnecessary to it. Jung's elaborate system has tried, therefore, to satisfy a great hunger for transcendence. Transcendence, however, is difficult. Jung has tried to make of it a therapeutic necessity, the extreme of psychiatric indulgence. The language of Jung's discourses moves further and further from Freud's cautions; the psychoanalyst becomes priest, "godlike demon," dispenser of positive power, caretaker of archetypes.

To conclude, Freud's meticulously correct choreography of the unconscious maintains the advantages of its discretion. Language in all of its scope of meanings and half-meanings and super-meanings may fit into his remarkable analysis of the psychic economy. The ambiguities of our language are the push-and-pull of our intelligence, alternating between residence in the id and regretful acceptance of the ego. While we may find types of identity with the past, we are not what we were some thousands of years ago; however tempting it is to suggest archetypal identifications, our psychic peculiarities are in the end available only to the sober testimony of systematic investigation. To say otherwise is to ignore both the dilemma and the specific intelligence of our times. (pp. 317-30)

> *Frederick J. Hoffman, "Psychology and Literature," in his* Freudianism and the Literary Mind, *second edition, Louisiana State University Press, 1957, pp. 317-30.*

Edward Wasiolek

[*Wasiolek is an American educator and critic who specializes in Russian literature and contemporary critical theory. In the following excerpt, he identifies strengths and weaknesses in psychoanalytic criticism.*]

Psychoanalytic criticism has not constituted a bright episode in the history of twentieth-century criticism. The methodology has often been sloppy, the claims have often been exaggerated, and the conclusions have sometimes been outrageous. We have been treated to paradings of technical jargon, often irrelevant and seldom illuminating, to simple schematisms based on Freud's topography of the psyche, and to arbitrary patterns of symbolism. When a distinguished critic of Faulkner's novels tells us that Benjy in *The Sound and the Fury* represents the "Id," Quentin the "Ego," and Jason the "Super-ego," we may either yawn or we may rage, but we do not learn. When another critic tells us that Raskolnikov is a latent homosexual aching for Razumikhin, Luzhin, Svidrigaylov, Porfiry, and virtually every male character in *Crime and Punishment,* a useful psychoanalytic concept has been driven past usefulness. And when a clinical analysis of Dostoevsky results in the following, Freud's provocative suggestions about Dostoevsky's character have been transplanted into unprofitable jargon. Dr. Paul C. Squires sums up his analysis of Dostoevsky's character in the following way:

> Our formal diagnosis runs as follows: Dostoevsky was an epileptic schizophrene, paranoid type, complicated by hysterical overlay, *the epilepsy being foundational;* all the available data, including pictures of the man, point to an endocrine abnormality of which the chief components are hyperthyroid, hyperpostpituitary, and hyperparathyroid. *Dos-*
> *toevsky was essentially a pituitary-centered individual. His alcoholic and epileptoid heredity is outstanding* ["Fyodor Dostoevsky: A Psychopatrological Sketch," *Psychoanalytic Review,* XXIV (October 1937)].

Dr. Squires's last comment is the following: "Unquestionably, Fyodor Dostoevsky takes first place among the 'higher degenerates' in the history of literature and art."

Nor is one encouraged by progress in psychoanalytic criticism. In a book published in 1968 [*The Dynamics of Literary Response;* see excerpt above], Norman Holland, one of our most prolific writers on the subject, provides us with a methodology of analyzing imagery in art from a psychoanalytic point of view. Such methodology would consist of looking for oral, anal, urethic, and phallic imagery. By anal imagery he means the following:

> As for imagery, one finds in anal writings a preoccupation with dirt, with smells, particularly those which evoke disgust, and then with their transformations: fog, mist, sweet smells, pure air, light, even, ultimately, *logos,* the word of God. By this mechanism of "displacement upwards," the ear may come to stand for the anus—sounds are common anal images. The child-in-us may consciously fantasize that insemination takes place by fluids or air or words entering the ear (as in various paintings of the Annunciation analyzed by Ernest Jones). Anal fantasies tend to stress laws and rules, particularly meticulous, precise, petty behavior, which deals especially with collecting or excessive cleanliness or rituals. Control, either by oneself or by another, is an important theme.

> Another theme of anality is doing things in time: thus, impatience, procrastination, or things running by fits and starts would suggest that we are dealing with an anal fantasy, as would a concern with precise timing.

These examples are not very special. They are almost the norm, and the norm has driven large portions of the academic and literary community to condemn psychoanalysis as a respectable literary procedure. And yet many of these same critics will acknowledge psychoanalysis as a revolution in our thinking about ourselves and an illumination of large areas of human behavior and motivation. The contradiction is tantalizing and bewildering.

As critics we cannot avoid talking about human behavior, feelings, motivations, and conceptualizations. Psychoanalysis has something to say about how we think, feel, generalize, and act; why we feel tired and how we handle anxieties; how we love and what happens to us when we stop loving. If we do not use the processes and conclusions of psychoanalysis in discussing these things, we run the risk of condemning ourselves to repeating the facile and erroneous generalizations of a pre-psychoanalytic age or run the greater risk of spinning out our own arbitrary psychologisms.

We can generalize about love in a facile and conventional manner, or we can use Freud's theory of narcissism and his explanation of how self-love is displaced but never replaced. We may have known before Freud that we do not love and hate with impunity, but it was Freud who traced out the mechanisms and logic by which the abandoned love object is reinstated in the self, there to suffer in self-punishment the aggressive component of every love relationship. Freud's comments on aggressiveness—which held equal status with the sexual drive in his later years—are brilliant in the number and sharpness of insights. It is from Freud that we have learned that one can commit suicide, not because the times are out of joint and not because one hates oneself, but because one hates someone else, that guilt can be the cause of crime as well as its consequence, that what we revere and what we abhor have the same source, that we can castigate ourselves when we lose someone in death not because of guilt, but from aggressiveness toward the departed, that saintliness may lead to self-aggression, and repression of aggressiveness to increase of self-aggression.

Freud has given us a new logic of behavior in which what we say may not be what we mean, and what we think may serve not elucidation but only defense. We have known for a long time that we will lie when our interests are threatened, that we give to others what we fear in ourselves, and that we defend ourselves when we are threatened. But never until Freud and psychoanalysis have we understood the extent and complexity of the individual's defenses against what is painful and what he thinks is painful. He has taught us that the past exists not only in memory but also presently in the body. We act out in pantomime what we do not understand, and psychological offshoots of repressed and painful materials reach out to move our gestures and bend our tongues. We live in private and public worlds. What is more important, Freud has done more than perceive paradoxes—literary men have done that before him—he has explained them. He has with care and clarity fitted concept to concept, adjusted cause to cause, and brought fact to theory and theory to fact. It would seem strange indeed that literary critics who are called upon to generalize about human motives, feelings, aggressions, persecutions, love, hate, self-love, and depressions can afford to ignore the enormous body of specific insight and explanation that Freud and his followers have left us.

Nor does the possible usefulness of psychoanalytic insight stop with the analysis and expression of the individual psyche. Much of what Freud wrote and thought has important implications for the nature and purpose of art. One of the oldest problems of literary theory stems from the fact that some forms of art transmute painful content into pleasurable expression. We are accustomed to explaining this mystery by the mitigating influence of form, by aesthetic distance, and by the consciousness on the part of the audience that the terrible facts are not real. For Freud's conception of the repetition compulsion may have something to offer to our vocabulary and our understanding. One of the basic impulses of the child is to master painful situations by recreating them over and over again, so that by such recreation he can understand and master what is painful and threatening, and by such mastering render the painful matter harmless and even pleasurable.

There is even a fruitful analogy to be pursued between Freud's therapeutic aim and the function of art for the artist. Whatever else he is doing, the artist is dredging up what is inside him, externalizing it, and formalizing it; he raises what is inside him to consciousness where he may contemplate and confront it. This is similar to Freud's therapeutic goal, in which in the process of transference during the latter stage of a cure the patient raises to con-

sciousness what he has resisted knowing. Transference is a kind of dramatization and contemplation of what has gone on inside oneself. What one was possessed by, one now possesses.

Dream work, too, is in many respects similar to the kind of logic that obtains in a literary work. In both dream and art the representation of the world is "picture," and in both logical relations become spatial, recalling perhaps the New Critical insistence on the iconic quality of poetry and perhaps even to the Jamesian insistence that picture and scene are the essence of dramatic and novelistic art. In dream work spatial relations like contiguity, succession, transformations, and order take the place of such logical relations as cause and effect, comparison and contrast, and either-or relations. Both dream and art seem to be a re-translation of a world sorted out by logic back into a more primitive mode of apprehension and perhaps a fuller apprehension of the world's body.

The use of dream symbolism or the interpretation of detail on the analogy of dream symbolism has been the most frequently criticized part of psychoanalytic criticism. The criticism has come from what seems to be the arbitrary and farfetched connections that psychoanalytic critics make between the literal detail and its symbolic significance. But what strikes us as farfetched in psychoanalytic symbolism is not farfetched if one understands psychoanalytic theory. The neurotic for Freud reveals his inner world in his gestures, words, actions, but the interpretation of these gestures is oblique, associative, and different from our ordinary way of interpreting. The interpretation of symbols, as usually conceived, is conceptualized so that we expect some logical, conventional, or material relationship between the symbol and the object symbolized: the symbol may be conventional like the cross or the rose; or it may be synecdochical like the square and hammer for a trade, or the symbol may partake of the nature of the thing symbolized. But psychoanalytic symbolism operates according to a different logic. The symptom or the substitute formation—in life and in dream—may be something remote in character from the thing it symbolizes; indeed by the very logic of psychoanalysis it would have to be remote and hidden, because the substitute formation is permitted expression precisely because it has been sufficiently displaced from what it has been substituted for. Something trivial may be important and something remote very near. The basis for such symbolic relationships lies in the fact that substitute formations and symptoms, which are our clinical analogy to symbolic detail, are screens for what is symbolized. Between them and what is symbolized may intervene layers of repressive psychic offshoots, so that the distance between the substitute formations and the symbolized material may be very great. The symbol, psychoanalytically speaking, does not willingly reveal what it points to. It conceals what is symbolized, and the path back to the symbolized matter may be very oblique and circuitous. When psychoanalytic criticism gives us the connection between the substitute formation and the symbolized material, it is likely to strike the reader as arbitrary and farfetched, because the intervening associative steps have not been revealed. The connections are not arbitrary because they are supported by clinical evidence and a coherent theoretical structure. But psychoanalytic critics have the obligation to spell out the methodology of interpretation in a refined way, to tell us by what methods and rules they derive their symbolizations.

The implications of psychoanalysis for literature even today seem immense, and yet it is clear that psychoanalytic criticism has failed to translate a vast body of specific clinical insight about human behavior into specific analytic tools for literary criticism. The reasons for the failure are many and complicated, but the reductive nature of much of psychoanalytic criticism has something to do with the failure. Psychoanalytic criticism seems to have condemned itself to tedious uncoverings of oedipal complexes, oral and anal fixations, and equally monotonous chartings of works according to Freud's psychic topographies. Preponderant attention has been paid to a few rather abstract and unitary concepts and too little to Freud's body of specific clinical data.

But reductionism can only be partly responsible for the failure. Reductionism is a hazard of any critical procedure, a fact that is often forgotten by the critics of psychoanalytic criticism. I doubt that we have had much more of it in psychoanalytic criticism that in certain forms of social, philosophical, and theological criticism. Even formalist modes of criticism can be reductive and indeed often are. The probability is that the tendency of psychoanalytic criticism to see all literature, no matter how different in form and nature, as uniform and invariable exemplifications of Freudian concepts has brought more discredit to psychoanalytic criticism than any other factor. We may be ready to admit that certain works or certain portions of works lend themselves to Freudian analysis, but psychoanalytic criticism seems to act at times—from arrogance to stupidity—with the view that all works must lend themselves to interpretation along these lines. It is the inflexibility and invariability of the procedure that many of us find offensive. It is the inability or unwillingness of psychoanalytic critics to find limits of application for their procedures that has alienated many potential sympathizers and has contributed more than anything else to the failures of psychoanalytic criticism.

The justification for the universal applicability of psychoanalytic principles is not hard to find. Psychoanalysis is a universal explanation of human behavior, and it defines a core of human nature that is beyond history and culture. If then—the argument runs—human motives and feelings in art are like those of life, then it must follow that psychoanalytic principles are at work in the feelings and actions that are portrayed and expressed in all works of art. However plausible the universal application of psychoanalytic principles may be in life, we feel instinctively that some distinction has to be made in art. Art is and it is not life. It is life selected, formed, and artificialized. Psychoanalysis may underlie all human behavior, but may not underlie a particular artistic representation of human behavior. The artist may be ignorant of the universal springs of human behavior; psychoanalysis may be wrong; the particular artistic representation may concern itself only with the symptoms and psychic offshoots of the deepest springs of human behavior; culture and history may so screen the deepest motives that the artist himself may consciously or unconsciously be capable of representing only remote substitute formations. In any event psychoanalytic critics have an obligation to concern themselves with what the artist has actually represented and not with what the psy-

choanalytic universals decree. We have no right to translate every representation of human behavior back into correct psychoanalytic theory.

The future of psychoanalytic criticism will be determined in part by the success or failure on the part of psychoanalytic critics in finding criteria of limitation of applicability of psychoanalytic principles. If we are to find such criteria, it would be good to find them in psychoanalysis itself. The oedipal complex, for example, is universal in the sense that every individual must pass through certain biologically determined stages, the most important of which is the phallic stage and along the path of which the individual may be "fixated," that is, may fail to develop normally to the next stage. The oedipal stage is the most important of childhood aetiology, the most difficult to pass through successfully, and, in Freud's opinion, very few of us pass through it with complete success. That is, the feelings of sensuous attraction for the parents, the ambivalence to the other, the feeling of fear and terror before the threat of castration, and the severe repression of what we fear is forbidden stays with us all our life and can be recathected in situations of stress and trauma. But it is not always recathected; it is not always manifest; it does not always have a decisive or even an important influence on an individual's behavior. The chances are that my oedipal complex lies quiescent when I'm playing tennis or watching a movie, or dining out, or engaging in numerous other situations. Or to put it more broadly, we may all be in some degree neurotics, since somewhere along our development, we have passed through the aetiology of childhood with some difficulty and hence retain some predisposition to fixation. But regressions to these points are not occurring all the time, but only in very specific circumstances.

There is a difference in psychoanalytic theory between an oedipal complex that is latent and one that is manifest. The distinction would seem to be simple, but it is seldom invoked in the application of psychoanalysis to literature. Psychoanalytic criticism, for instance, may look upon what a character says as not what he means; the expression may be any number of psychic defenses, projections, distortions of his real meaning. But, it need not be. What we say in life and in art may be what we mean. We defend ourselves against what is painful to our consciousness, and when we defend, we distort. But the unconscious and the conscious are not always in conflict. We cannot assume that there is always something hidden behind a character's words, that every generalization is intellectual projection, that every action is a gesture of defense against the pain of an inner world. Nor can we in psychoanalytic symbolizations assume that ladders are always indications of sexual intercourse; sometimes they are simply ladders. Ploughshares, hammers, guns, revolvers, daggers, and countless other pointed objects are not always penises. Freud himself warned against such indiscriminate symbolizings in psychoanalysis; the danger is even greater in literary criticism. One must distinguish between universal applicability, which may be true in theory, and specific circumstantial applicability, which must be true in practice.

I do not underestimate the difficulty of applying such a distinction to specific situations. How are we to know when an oedipal situation is manifestly present, and how are we to know that it is not? To make such a distinction, we will have to have what good critics must always have:

judgment, knowledge, sensitivity, and patient observation. We will have to know psychoanalytic theory very well, too. When certain details are sufficiently insistent in a work of art, when they cluster—to use Kenneth Burke's term—about a situation that is sufficiently analogous to a psychoneurosis in the clinical sense, then we will be encouraged to entertain a psychoanalytic hypothesis. We may be encouraged to entertain a psychoanalytic explanation in situations where the motives given for an action are contradictory and numerous, as in *Crime and Punishment;* situations in which the events are structured as a series of evasions, as in Conrad's *Lord Jim;* or situations in which sexuality is manifest and an insistent part of the content. A large part of Faulkner's *The Sound and the Fury* is occupied explicitly with Quentin Compson's desires and inability to commit incest with his sister, and such a situation, I must maintain, permits the critic to entertain the possibility that psychoanalysis may throw some illumination on the feelings, motivations, and psychic wounds of Quentin. Cleanth Brooks in his study of Faulkner and his discussion of this novel never entertains such a hypothesis, and his reading of the novel leaves large portions of the novel opaque. No one can read Act III, scene iv of *Hamlet,* where Hamlet confronts his mother in her bedroom, without noticing how compulsively Hamlet's mind attaches itself to one thing and to one thing alone: his mother's sexuality and his furious and frantic condemnation of her sexuality. No explanation of Elizabethan society, audience, or theater convention and no argument from Hamlet's general nature, no matter how refined, will help us explain the specific and manifest sexual relation between son and mother. Not even the murder of Polonius can divert him—except for a moment—from the flow of invective and sullied sexuality that he showers on his mother. He wants one thing and one thing alone and that is for his mother to desist from sleeping with his uncle and surrogate father. T. S. Eliot misread the play because he thought Gertrude was too trivial for the emotions she evoked in Hamlet. Psychoanalysis has taught us the obvious truth that no mother is trivial to her son.

But unless a manifest situation is present in the literary work itself, sufficiently similar to the clinical data which defines a psychoneurosis, I do not believe we have the right to translate the behavior into the data of psychoanalysis. Psychoanalytic criticism must find its methodology of limitation and boundaries of responsible application, or its future will be met with as much abuse as its past practice. At the same time even where it may be legitimately applied to specific works, it does not have the automatic license to usurp to itself the function of being the sole valid mode of interpretation. *Hamlet* and *Crime and Punishment* have social and cultural dimensions, and we gain very little by dismissing them as simple rationalizations of psychological motivations. Some things are beyond culture, but not everything, and the form of psychoanalytic principles, if not the truths, varies a great deal with the culture. Freud himself pointed out that the oedipal situation was openly expressed in *Oedipus Rex,* but was hidden and repressed in *Hamlet.*

There is nothing in the theory or practice of psychoanalytic criticism that militates, for example, against formalist or structural approaches to art. Russian formalism may have something to tell us about the "felt quality" of poetic language and the situational devices by which forms are deconventionalized and made poetic. The Chicago neo-Aristotelians may be able to tell us something about the emotional effect and the causative factors that bring about the effect; and various modes of New Critical contextualism may be able to tell us a great deal about how ordinary propositions may be nuclei of ambiguity, complexity, and paradox. And none of them—in doing these things—will be necessarily in conflict with psychoanalytic criticism. Ernest Jones's interpretation of *Hamlet* tells us something about Hamlet's relationship to his mother, father, and to Ophelia and his stepfather. But it doesn't tell us how the wrenching emotional effect of the play comes about; Chicago neo-Aristotelianism might be able to do that. And Jones's interpretation tells us very little about the inexhaustible well of linguistic expressiveness of the play; and New Criticism might tell us.

Psychoanalytic criticism is concerned primarily with what we ordinarily call "content," but analyses of content have implications for structure. How we read the motives of a Quentin Compson, a Hamlet, and a Raskolnikov changes numerous internal relationships in the work of art. What we see affects how we see. If a work of art consists of "formed content," and not just of form alone, and if a work of art takes its subject matter from life—and where else would it take it from—then psychological considerations, as well as social, religious, and philosophical considerations, are inevitably the concern of a critic. I cannot hazard what will be the concerns of criticism in the future, but I have an opinion about what needs revitalization in our critical lexicon. The content factor in our equation of "formed content" needs such revitalization. Considerations of "content" or "subject matter" have been rigorously and systematically reduced to irrelevance by the dominant formalist modes of reasoning for almost half a century. We have no vocabulary to deal with "content," but we are tired of having content defined as some abstract and unreal summary of content, and then on that basis being told that it has nothing to do with art. Content can be refined or abstract, just as formal properties can be refined or abstract. Content affects form as much as form affects content. They are not the same as the clichés of formalism seem at times to suggest. They are inseparable, but they are conceptually distinct. Psychoanalytic criticism has fought a rear-guard action for the defense of content, that is, for the relevance of life to art. If psychoanalytic criticism can live up to the promise of Freud's brilliance and can divest itself of its own defenses and enter the main stream of literary criticism, it may have an important part of play in the future of literary criticism.

But psychoanalytic criticism has to find its place in the spectrum of critical approaches before this can happen, and what is just as important, the spectrum has to permit it to find its place. There has been enough good psychoanalytic criticism to temper our despair before the avalanche of bad criticism, and to give us intimations, if not of immortality, at least of promise. Freud himself was always sensible and illuminating in his remarks on art; Jones's work on Hamlet has established itself as a convincing reading of at least one aspect of the play; William Snodgrass has given us one of our best explanations of Raskolnikov's motives; Simon Lesser has written a provocative and suggestive book on the relationship of fiction and the unconscious; Kenneth Burke has often mixed psychoanalysis, sociology, Marxism, and grammar in an idiosyncratic but fruitful way; and Lionel Trilling has read Freud with sensitivity and addressed himself intelligently to some of the speculative implications of Freud's comments on art.

It now appears that the long-range influence of psychoanalytic criticism may be greater than the various modes of formalist criticism that engaged so powerfully our attention during the last generation. The excitement and freshness New Criticism brought to the forties and fifties have faded away. We have been taught for a generation to read closely, and it may take another generation to teach us to read broadly. We continue to read closely, but we are less comfortable with the artificialities and limitations of contextualism. Myth, religion, biography, and social concerns are beginning to engage our attention and critical sensibility. What was "extrinsic" is now beginning to appear to be "intrinsic." The condemned intellectualist disciplines continue to press their relevance upon us. I. A. Richards and his New Critical followers attempted to save poetry from science, but it appears now that we will have to save criticism by bringing back the science and the intellectualist disciplines that were so energetically and consistently excluded. In this respect psychoanalytic criticism may have an important role to play, for theoretically, at least, psychoanalytic criticism is based on a rigorous and carefully defined discipline, supported by clinical evidence and a coherent theoretical structure.

During the last three or four years a "nouvelle critique" has been developing in France, and it may be that we will have to look there for a way in which the accomplishments of New Criticism may be integrated with the continuing promise of "intellectualist disciplines" like psychoanalytic criticism. French "New Criticism" does not see the literary artifact as an entity sealed off from the advances of intellectual and scientific knowledge, but as a point of convergence of various modes of knowing. This is a sane and fruitful conception of art, and a conception that history seems to be driving us toward, whatever our theoretical reservations. Psychoanalysis is participating in the development of French "New Criticism," and it should participate in the continuing development of contemporary American criticism. If psychoanalytic criticism can find its limits of applicability and find new modes of transporting the accumulated and accumulating body of specific insight of psychoanalysis to literature, it has important contributions to make to criticism, and criticism has an obligation to let it make them. (pp. 153-67)

Edward Wasiolek, "The Future of Psychoanalytic Criticism," in The Frontiers of Literary Criticism, *edited by David H. Malone, Hennessey & Ingalls, Inc., 1974, pp. 149-68.*

Frederick Crews

[*Crews is an American educator and critic whose writings include examples of applied psychoanalytic criticism and essays on the merits of a psychoanalytic approach to literature. In 1980 Crews repudiated Freudianism as a viable therapeutic and intellectual doctrine (see Further Reading). In the following excerpt, he discusses some of the risks and benefits in applying psychoanalytic criticism to literature.*]

Anyone who believes, as I do, that principles of Freudian psychoanalysis can be usefully applied to literary criticism must find himself repeatedly assailed by doubts: about the theory itself, about methodological pitfalls, above all about the weak and sometimes comical record of the Freudian critical tradition. The partisan of literary psychoanalysis is likely to be busier apologizing for that tradition than improving it with contributions of his own. And no matter how many scrupulous distinctions he may draw between responsible and "wild" uses of Freud, he can never quite dispel the suspicion that psychoanalysis is, as its opponents have always said, inherently reductionistic. The record all too clearly shows that a special danger of dogmatism, of clinical presumption, indeed of monomania, accompanies a method that purports to ferret out from literature a handful of previously known, perennially "deep" psychic concerns. It must be admitted that Freudian criticism too easily degenerates into a grotesque Easter-egg hunt: find the devouring mother, detect the inevitable castration anxiety, listen, between the syllables of verse, for the squeaking bedsprings of the primal scene. A critic who may have been drawn toward Freud by the promise of a heightened sensitivity to conflict in literature may, without ever knowing what has happened to him, become the purveyor of a peculiarly silly kind of allegory.

If some academic Freudians are slow to recognize the hazard of reductionism, it is not for lack of advice from their nonpsychoanalytic colleagues. On the contrary, a Freudian hears so much sermonizing against Freudian reductionism that he may come to regard that term as a provocation to battle. Secretly, in fact, he may even agree with his detractors that psychoanalysis "robs literature of its autonomy"—for that may be just what he wants it to do. Psychoanalytic criticism in its recent American phase has deliberately set itself apart from a certain mystique of literary autonomy, championed first in New-Critical formalism and later in the taxonomic theory of Northrop Frye. Rightly or wrongly, that theory has been attacked (by myself among others) as implicitly sponsoring an affect-stifling approach to literature. Insofar as the Freudian critic resents the "civilizing" claims that have been put forth in behalf of the academic literary curriculum, his worry about reductionism is going to be mitigated by a certain satisfaction he can take in brushing past formal or generic or ironic or (above all) morally uplifting aspects of literature and showing instead that even the sublimest masterpiece traffics in unconscious wishes. Though in practice most Freudian criticism is far from invigorating to read, its practitioner may feel that in writing it he is conjuring the Lawrentian dark gods and setting them loose on the "English" establishment.

Anyone who is not blinded by such vengeful intent, however, would have to grant that literature *is* autonomous in one important sense. However strenuous its birth pangs, a poem or novel exists independently of the emotions that went into it. Regarded autobiographically, it points back to those emotions; but in another light, the one cast by Eliot's notion of aesthetic impersonality, the work is what it is precisely by virtue of having put those emotions behind it. On temperamental grounds we may incline toward one critical attitude or the other, but on evidential grounds we have to acknowledge that a poem can mean many things besides the poet's psychomachia. A good part of its significance, furthermore, derives from its intricate relations with other poems—from its place in a tradition whose laws of development have very little to do with the psychic vicissitudes of individual poets.

Some guardians of literary autonomy would take this point as a repudiation of all Freudian criticism, which they regard as reductionistic in its very essence. Psychoanalysis, they would say, is exactly a technique for making reductions from verbal manifestations to the psychic factors that supposedly determined those manifestations. If art is not mere behavior, wholly explainable by reference to the troubled minds that made it, then psychoanalytic criticism is always bound to falsify both the ontology and the multivalence of literature. What we want from criticism is not reduction to causes, but recognition of the inexhaustible and *irreducible* vitality that somehow inheres in the works themselves.

Expressed in such seemingly open-minded terms, the proscription against Freudian discourse sounds quite different from what it is, a denial of our right to pursue a certain range of problems. That psychoanalysis tends to treat a manifest text as an embodiment of psychic conflict cannot be doubted. But is this always and necessarily an unfruitful attitude for a critic to adopt? Authors do assuredly reveal wishes and anxieties when they write, and the experience of reading does have something to do with conflict management, if only in a simulated mode. Using psychoanalytic assumptions, a critic can show how a writer's public intention was evidently deflected by a private obsession. He can deal with blatant or subtle appeals to fantasy, as in the habitual practice of a genre like science fiction or the Gothic novel. He can reveal a hidden consistency behind shifts of tone or characterization, or make a new approach to a puzzle that has resisted commonsense solutions. Or again, he can draw biographical inferences on the basis of certain recurrent themes that the author hadn't consciously meant to display. Whatever its risks and deficiencies, Freudian reasoning has shown itself well adapted to such undertakings, which, though sternly denounced by purists, are established and useful critical enterprises.

In order to meet the real issue of reductionism without dismissing legitimate applications of psychoanalysis, it is necessary to realize that the mere proposing of a reductive idea doesn't in itself constitute reduction*ism,* the effective denial or denigration of all meanings but the reductive one that is being revealed. Reductive inferences are normal, though not equally prominent, in many schools of criticism. A critic is reducing—that is, diverting attention from the text to something that purportedly lies behind the text and helps to explain it—whenever he asserts that a work can be understood in relation to its author's social background or didactic intent or cultural allegiance, or even his literary tradition. Reductionism proper is a certain bigoted way of advancing such points, with the result that the work in its singularity is sacrificed to the interpretive scheme instead of being illuminated by it.

Thus it is reductive, but possibly quite justifiable and helpful, to maintain that a common current of homosexual feeling for "the Handsome Sailor" runs between Claggart and Vere in *Billy Budd;* although the point might not originally occur to anyone but a Freudian, he could show other readers that his reduction makes sense of otherwise obscure features of the text. If the same critic were to say or imply that homosexuality is "the meaning" of *Billy*

Budd, he would be not only reductive but reductionistic as well. Or again, to cite a recent example, when Michael West argues a connection in Thoreau's writings between excremental imagery, punning, distaste for women, contempt for philanthropic sympathy, and fear of tuberculosis, he is making reductions that would have been unthinkable before Freud ["Scatology and Eschatology: The Heroic Dimensions of Thoreau's Wordplay," *PMLA* 89 (October 1974)]. Yet West's article is not in my opinion reductionistic, for *Walden* in his hands, instead of dwindling to an illustration of theory, becomes richer and stranger than ever.

The fact remains, however, that the greater part of Freudian criticism is not just reductive, as it is bound to be, but reductionistic as well, and to a degree unmatched in any other school. When we ask why this should be the case, we find the answer immediately in the root assumptions of Freudian metapsychology. I have in mind the axioms that all psychic events are determined; that the deterministic chain originates in biological drives whose frustration and deflection eventuate in mental structures, ideas, and sublimated aims; and that the infantile and the prior therefore explain the adult and the contemporary. These notions together yield a picture of man as a creature chiefly occupied with fending off disturbing stimuli, both from his own soma and from external sources of disequilibrium. Alienated from his instinctive needs, absorbed in trying to appease a superego which has been precipitated from parental taboos, this rather sneaky fellow is conceived as being always on the lookout for ways to bootleg a little gratification, to give sway to the eternal baby within. And this narcissistic project, however petty and ridiculous it may appear to the uninitiated, is considered the quintessentially human activity, for man is above all the animal who turns against himself and then chafes against his self-inflicted unhappiness. Thus, no matter what action or text is being examined, the essentials of metapsychology dictate a mode of analysis in which persistent infantile factors will be stressed at the expense of nonconflictual ones—cognitive, conventional, formal, or ethical.

When man creates art, psychoanalysis disposes us to view that art as the product of a provisional unburdening, and to regard a work's meaning as coextensive with the thoughts or fantasies that were discharged in the act of composition. Hence the inevitable biographical orientation of all Freudian critics who haven't explicitly pledged to leave authors' minds out of account. However variously they may draw up the ground rules of criticism, psychoanalytic commentators tend to agree in taking a poem to be a need-satisfying, as opposed to a meaning-generating, device. Their one concession to multivalence is the idea of overdetermination—a principle which, as the name implies, allows several needs to be met by a single expression but does not depart from the basic Freudian orientation to conflict settlement. Interpretation, in short, remains a question of building bridges between the poem and the psychic conditions from which it arose, and of which it must be a manifestation. The fact that other people besides the artist respond to the poem is taken to indicate, not that a symptomatic interpretation is uncalled for, but that it can be applied to both parties in the transaction: author and reader are thought to communicate only in the sense that they both take the same words as their pretext for assuaging the tension with which they must continually live.

The narrowness of vision resulting from such assumptions is apparent even in highly refined statements of Freudian literary theory, the most imposing of which remains Norman N. Holland's *The Dynamics of Literary Response* [see excerpt above]. No Freudian has taken greater pains to make psychoanalysis accountable for subtle differences of genre and effect, and none has shown greater diffidence about armchair diagnosis of authors. Yet the rules set forth in the *Dynamics,* if followed to the letter, could hardly fail to result in reductionist criticism. For Holland asserts, merely on the basis of an extrapolation from the Freudian approach to dreams and jokes, that one infantile fantasy lies at the origin and heart of each literary work. Although he makes gestures of coexistence toward many styles of criticism, Holland nevertheless declares that "the psychoanalytic meaning underlies all the others"—a fact which can be announced in advance of any given instance, since, in Holland's view, the true purpose of even the most artifice-laden work is to enable a "core fantasy" to manifest itself in a respectable disguise. Holland even provides us with a "dictionary" of such fantasies—each pertaining to one of the classic erogenous zones and modes of gratification—in the certainty that he is cataloguing the very wellsprings of literary expression.

Holland is correct in believing that no one but a Freudian critic will be able to arrive at a work's "underlying meaning" in his sense of the term. What he does not realize, or hadn't yet realized in 1968, is that this is a handicap rather than an advantage. The handicap is at once social and intellectual, for the critic following Holland's lead can have no hope of gaining wide agreement to his readings and no opportunity to be chastened by reasonable objections from the unanalyzed, whose resistance is predicted and discounted by the theory. Above all, the critic will have locked himself into a rigid set of procedures: stripping each work to its supposed core and then presenting its other thematic and formal aspects as so many defensive strategies, whether or not they are experienced as defensive in the act of reading. Such overcommitment to a method prior to examining a given work can only diminish the critic's receptiveness and adaptability, meanwhile leaving the disagreeable, and finally incredible, impression that great literature is merely a subterfuge for venting such forbidden thoughts as "if I am phallically aggressive and do not submit to my mother, she will castrate me."

Although Holland's theory of literature is not the only one that might be drawn up from Freudian premises, it is disturbingly loyal to those premises—so much so that we must ask whether a full-scale commitment to psychoanalysis can make a critic anything *but* a reductionist. Here, however, I must attend to a strong objection from advocates of modern psychoanalysis. They would remind me that Freud's narrow determinism, with its exclusively male perspective, its overrating of the Oedipus complex, its neglect of interpersonal as opposed to intrapsychic dynamics, and its billiard-ball notion of cause and effect, has long been superseded within the psychoanalytic tradition. (In fact, I have previously been taken to task in print for using the very adjective "Freudian," which is thought to lend the movement an unnecessarily quaint air.) It is the psychoanalysts themselves, after all, who now warn against reductionist interpretation in the form of "originology," the automatic ascribing of determinative significance to infantile factors. Can't we, instead of appealing to nebulous and suspect ideas of critical sensibility, find a remedy for reductionism *within* contemporary psychoanalysis?

The hope for such a remedy rests with what is loosely called ego psychology: the totality of post-Freudian developments stressing the adaptive and integrative capacities of the mind. I refer to such theorists as Anna Freud, Heinz Hartmann, Rudolf Loewenstein, Ernst Kris, Robert Waelder, David Rapaport, and Erik Erikson. In different degrees all these analysts recognize that Freud's psychic model exaggerates the individual's helplessness to govern his life. All seek to loosen the strict determinism of infantile trauma and to deny or mitigate Freud's antithesis between libidinal impulse and the forces of civilization. By and large, the ego psychologists retain Freud's interest in drives and their derivatives, but by invoking such concepts as identity, neutralized energy, multiple function, and the conflict-free sphere of the ego, they try to make room within the Freudian system for an acknowledgment that the mind is not exclusively concerned with combating anxiety.

These developments, however, though they have certainly rendered psychoanalysis less dogmatic, do not seem to me to constitute a reliable antidote to reductionism. Most ego psychologists, despite their awareness that all-purpose explanatory universals really explain nothing, are scarcely more prepared than Freud himself was to acknowledge the prospective (not regressive) and meaning-creating (not confessional) aspects of art. Indeed, it would not be altogether perverse to suggest that ego psychology makes the problem of reductionism harder to recognize and address. The very sophistication of recent doctrine may allow its spokesman to forget what Freud usually remembered, that the secret of artistic genius is beyond his science. A theory like Ernst Kris's, which depicts creativity as playfully controlled regression, comes just near enough to accommodating artistic freedom to convince the critic that he can put reductionism behind him and deal with art in all its fullness. In actuality he is still bound to a largely passive and defensive conception of mind—one that omits or minimizes exactly that drive toward perfection of form that distinguishes the artist from the ordinary neurotic.

The ego psychologists' regard for a wide variety of social and historical factors unquestionably marks an advance over Freud's unvarying emphasis on the universal Oedipus complex. Again, however, we must ask whether the multiplying of considered determinants overcomes, or merely complicates, the functionalistic habit of interpretation. Isn't literature still being treated as a vector of the influences that attended its composition? And aren't some influences still being given an arbitrary precedence over others? The recent scholarly fashion of psychohistory, which has not yet had much impact on literary studies, provides some distressing examples of what happens when a commentator increases the number of potential determinants without relinquishing the priority afforded to infantile ones: the result is simply to widen the range of phenomena he thinks he has accounted for in classic Freudian terms. Ego psychology as we see it in, say, Erikson's writings is profoundly ambiguous, pointing simultaneously toward and away from the early crises of libidinal life. Such ambiguity does afford the ego psychologist some room in which to follow the promptings of common sense. Too often, however, ego psychology amounts to little more than a shift of mood or ideology on the critic's part, enabling him to give a positive, upbeat emphasis to the same data that used to be taken as signs of neurosis.

This scarcity of firm propositional content may help to explain why, in literary studies, "ego psychology" has been frequently invoked but almost never satisfactorily illustrated. Psychoanalytic reviewers, finding that psychoanalytic critics are still unearthing "id-psychological" infantile fantasies, regularly accuse those critics of not having incorporated the insights of ego psychology into their method. The implication is that the reviewers themselves do better in their own criticism, but this—to judge from the daisy chain of chiding reviews—is rarely the case. Each critic apparently hopes that by analyzing fantasy content he will be manifesting the adaptive and integrative power of the authorial ego that managed to put all this primitive material to aesthetic use. But since psychoanalysis offers no means of studying the transcendence of conflict, there is no way the critic can discuss that power without interrupting himself. Even if he pauses to toss off some handsome compliments to the author's flexibility before returning to the nitty-gritty of unconscious themes, those themes in all their rawness will probably govern the tone of his criticism. And if they don't—if the critic successfully represents his author as having reconciled multiple pressures on his equanimity—he may still be writing reductionistically, for reductionism comes precisely from the illusion that one has said all that bears saying.

There are, to be sure, some currents within ego psychology that look exceptionally salutary for the psychoanalytic critic who is as mindful of fallacies as of phalluses. Thus the post-Kleinian British theorists of "object-relations," such as W. R. D. Fairbairn, Edith Jacobson, and D. W. Winnicott, have been deservedly cited as fostering a subtle and constructive view of literature. In studying childhood these writers depart from the standard account of incestuous and patricidal conflict and offer instead a detailed picture of the child's efforts to survive the loss of maternal symbiosis—a project that predates sexual roles and continues beyond the so-called passing of the Oedipus complex. By focusing less on drives and defenses than on ego-stabilizing feats of introjection, the post-Kleinians succeed in connecting the terms of Freud's intrapsychic model to the real human figures—parents and their surrogates—who impinge on a subject's formation of identity. In consequence, a critic following their lead can consider works of art, not as symptomatic expressions, but as "transitional objects"—that is, as productions that both reconstitute a destroyed inner world and enact a new competence and a new mode of relatedness to the forbidding outer world. And this view in turn restores to literature some of the dignity it lost when Freud conceived of the writer as escaping from reality to self-aggrandizing fantasy. Now the artistic process appears as a special version of the way "reality" is continually constituted by each mind as it attunes itself to objects of longing and rage.

These are welcome potentialities, but they leave the problem of reductionism unresolved. A post-Kleinian is as likely as a Freudian to see a literary work not as an independent aesthetic structure but as a product of the forces that happen to interest him. When art is analogized to the "transitional" teddy bear instead of to the dream, it is still being treated as something other than itself, and its biographical genesis is still favored over its public import. The shifting of explanatory focus to an earlier stage of childhood, and from mechanisms of repression and displacement to those of projection and introjection, makes for a new set of insights but not for relief from the translating of literature into the preexisting terms of a system. And the system, again, is one whose orientation to need fulfillment leaves little room for appreciating the abundance and extravagance, the sheer surplus of invention, to be found in, say, a Shakespeare or a Dickens. The essential fact is inescapable: methodological provisos alone cannot ensure that a reductive style of interpretation won't result in reductionistic criticism.

If, despite all recent complications, psychoanalytic hermeneutics still give greatest weight to infantile themes, we must recognize that the method itself blocks the path of a critic who would avoid reductionism. For that method is at once reductive in impulse and uniquely minute in focus, entangling its user in line-by-line decodings that other readers may regard as entirely mad. (Marxist criticism, for instance, is just as zealous for explanation, but having no fondness for infancy and no technique for breaking statements into their alleged hidden components, it tends to come up with global formulations that can be accepted or shrugged off without much violence to our sense of what a given poem or novel contains.) To be a nonreductionist Freudian requires an extraordinary detachment from the very assumptions that allow one to perceive unconscious themes in the first place.

It is little wonder that few psychoanalytic critics are willing to endure the vertigo that accompanies such self-division. The alternative, however, is not simply dogmatism but—if the critic has an inkling of his plight—a special bewilderment that stems from prolonged reductive practice. A conscientious Freudian is bound to begin wondering, sooner or later, whether his conclusions say more about the text under discussion or about his own temperament. Here he is ill served by the notoriously compliant rules of exegesis that psychoanalysis has provided him. The very ease with which one critic can diagnose Keats's orality, and another Ben Jonson's anality, must leave each of them with the haunting fear that he has been taking those authors' works as projective ink blots and composing, not literary criticism, but cryptic fragments of a libidinal autobiography. When the critic appeals to the guidance of ego psychology, he gets only further cause for worry: if that school tells him anything at all, it is that minds, including his own, necessarily indulge in just such imperious misapprehensions in the interest of imposing a bearable stamp upon experience. The farther he gets beyond the provincial this-equals-that symbology of early psychoanalysis, the more vulnerable the critic becomes to misgivings about the rationale of his work. Now he may suspect, not simply that he has been a reductionist, but that his reductionistic statements have had himself as their secret object.

Some such realization appears to have struck Norman Holland, whose most recent pronouncements shed a new and surprising light on the whole question of Freudian reductionism. Holland, tacitly abandoning the mechanical fantasy-defense model of mental activity that underlay *The Dynamics of Literary Response,* has simultaneously made his peace with ego psychology and tried to face up to the shaky philosophical status of psychoanalytic interpretations. The two developments are intimately bound together. As soon as Holland replaces the search for a work's "core fantasy" with an ego-psychological search for its "identity theme"—that is, for the unalterable style of being-in-the-world that characterizes the work's author—he finds himself paralyzed by the thought that he too, as a critic, has an identity theme which is warping all his perceptions. The old Freudian exercise of compensating for one's bias, Holland decides, is futile, for even the most skeptical critic is exercising his identity in the very act of trying to neutralize it. Which is to say, in my terms, that psychoanalytic critics along with all others have been reductionists in a hitherto unsuspected sense: they have reduced literature to the rigid and narrow outlines of their own personalities.

Less sanguine Freudians than Holland, arriving at this evident impasse, might infer that their method must have been faulty from the start, or perhaps that life is too short to be squandered on such a chancy vocation as literary criticism. But if all critics, and not just psychoanalytic ones, write projectively, perhaps a Freudian can use his special insight to mark the way toward a new candor. The proper subject matter of criticism, Holland now sees, is not literary works at all, but the critic's private digestion of those works, whose actual properties, if any, can never be grasped. Let us (says Holland) continue being critics and redouble our study of psychoanalysis, but let us also purify our discourse of old-fashioned predications about the content of books. We Freudians, specifically, should henceforth eschew such statements as "the poem transforms this fantasy into that meaning" and "The poem strikes a good balance between fantasy and defense" and confine ourselves instead to such statements as "Here are my associations to the poem" and "For me the poem seems to hang together." Although Holland doesn't offer this proposal as a retreat from reductionism—indeed, he doesn't grant that his earlier scheme raised that problem—we cannot fail to notice that the curse of reductionism is being summarily lifted here, along with every other liability that attends the making of definite statements about literature.

Whether or not Holland's new reasoning is sound, it does inspire a utilitarian question: who will want to read the confessional criticism he now advocates? Why, if we must forgo criticism's traditional goal of making empirically adequate remarks about texts, should we take an interest in one another's ruminations about "how it feels to me"? The doubt is made more urgent by Holland's way of expounding his position. In his . . . *Five Readers Reading* [see Further Reading], he exhaustively analyzes the responses to certain pieces of literature by anonymous college students known to us as Sandra, Seymour, Samantha, *et al.,* who are variously reminded, when they read a certain poem, of a telephone call from home, a case of sunburn, and a judgment that the Pacific Ocean is placid. Granted, these revelations are not offered for their intrinsic value but as proof that the student readers are in some sense not apprehending the same poem. Yet Sandra and Seymour cannot help but impress us as disquieting harbingers of the new personal criticism recommended by Holland.

I for one would expect Holland's meditation in the pres-

ence of a poem to be more enlightening than Seymour's. All the same, I might become fatigued after a while by Holland's protestations that I needn't suppose *his* thoughts to apply to *my* perceived poem, as if I couldn't notice the differences without his help. Furthermore, and more fundamentally, Holland seems to me to be forgetting the entire raison d'être of critical activity. We don't go to criticism to discover Seymour's identity theme, or Holland's, or Frank Kermode's, or anyone else's. We go to criticism because we hope to learn more about literature than we could have figured out for ourselves. A critic who rejects that hope on philosophical principle, while nevertheless urging us to adopt an interpretive apparatus which is now guaranteed to yield no results, can only be regarded as conducting a highly unusual going-out-of-business sale.

But what about Holland's epistemological challenge? Isn't it the case that we can only know our own subjective construction of the world? And if so, mustn't we literary critics admit that our only basis of communication is to take turns displaying how we have each assimilated a poem to our private needs? Perhaps we *are* all incurable reductionists who have no means of mediating the inconsistencies between our readings.

This pessimism indeed follows from the tradition of epistemology in which Freudianism squarely resides—the "school of suspicion," as Paul Ricoeur has aptly named it [in his *Freud and Philosophy*]—which mounts a merciless critique of other people's social or psychic bias while holding out the prospect that the individual demystifier, armed with a special technique of self-correction, can get at the truth on his own. When that individual eventually begins to doubt his own objectivity, he typically becomes stranded, as Holland now is, with the feeling that knowledge is altogether chimerical; and then his one solace is that he has dared to look farther into the abyss than those simple Cartesians who still think they can make statements about objects—for example, about poems. All this chagrin, however, rests on a fundamental mistake about the basis of knowledge. Knowledge is a social project, not a personal one. It has nothing to do with the individual investigator's efforts to purge himself of unconscious bias, and everything to do with shared principles of validation. In Karl Popper's philosophy of science, for example, adequate (though not provably true) statements are considered possible thanks to a friendly-hostile social effort to falsify those statements according to agreed-upon empirical criteria; and Popper, as it happens, devotes some scathing pages [in *The Logic of Scientific Discovery* and *The Open Society and Its Enemies*] to the claim of Freudians, among other self-analyzers, to possess unique insight and hence a special insurance against error. Although knowledge of a poem is admittedly more problematic than knowledge of, say, a molecule, in each instance the hope of approximating that knowledge rests with a community of people who can be counted on to reject patently wrong ideas and eventually to prefer relatively accurate and useful ones. They can be counted on, that is to say, provided their concern for distinguishing between plausible and frivolous statements hasn't been eroded by a commitment to subjectivism.

Subjectivism, however, is in the air, and not just among captive freshmen who want to escape judgment by declaring each reading to be as valid as every other. As I indicated at the outset, American psychoanalytic criticism has drawn some of its energy from a wish to rescue literature in all its affectual intensity from the classifying and formalizing academicians, the high priests of objectivity. In announcing that no reader perceives the poem except as an extension of his ego, Holland withdraws the much-resisted "elitist" implication that some people are more careful readers than others; and this remission then permits all readers to trade associations to the poem on a relaxed and equal basis. As one of Holland's supporters remarks of the new attitude, "This in-mixing of self and other makes interpretation a potentially private affair, but it also can lead to a more inclusive sharing of emotional as well as intellectual dynamics than is now available" [Murray M. Schwartz, "The Space of Psychological Criticism," *Hartford Studies in Literature* 5 (1973)]. Don't we have here the ethos of "encounter," with a trading of isolated acts of introspection ("shared dynamics") replacing a concern for the object under discussion?

I know from my own experience in psychoanalytic seminars that a poem or story can trigger highly intuitive responses of the sort that Holland wants to make central to criticism. Some of the most exhilarating moments in my teaching have come when, during a pooling of free speculations about unconscious themes in a piece of literature, a sentiment of adventure and catharsis has swept across the classroom without anyone's being able to state what the apparent consensus was. Of course there wasn't any consensus; we were merely allowing one another a license to fantasize aloud in the aftermath of reading. I myself have hoped, as Holland's school does, that some of that subliminal excitement, that sense of having one's feelings brought into sudden and total coherence, could be carried directly into critical discourse. The hope, however, is illusory. For shared dynamics, as Sandra and Seymour remind us, lose a good deal in transposition to print, and readers of criticism will not be persuaded to accept their remnants in lieu of reasonable statements about literature. Whatever excitement criticism can generate must rest with the force and justice of those statements—must rest, in other words, with a propositional risk-taking that Holland now explicitly abjures.

Holland's new position may stand as an extreme example of the attempt to keep following psychoanalytic procedures regardless of the cost—to solve the problem of reductionism, not by adopting a broader outlook than that of psychoanalytic functionalism, but by ceasing to claim that one's reductive ideas are valid for other readers. My own preference is the more ordinary one of assuming that critics and their readers are apprehending approximately the same poem; of trying to narrow the differences of perception that do exist; and of coping with reductionism by explicitly recognizing Freudian inferences *as* reductions that will have to justify themselves on evidential grounds. If a critic remembers that psychoanalysis reduces as a matter of course, he may contrive ways of either using the method sparingly for limited ends or, if more ambitiously, then at least with cognizance of the factors that are automatically being excluded from his argument.

A critic who wants to avail himself of psychoanalysis would be well advised not only to seek out the most defensible and unmechanistic concepts within the system but also to think unsparingly about what is provincial and in-

tolerant in that system. If he understands that Freudian reasoning ascribes key significance to its favorite themes, and that its supple rules of interpretation make the discovery of those themes a foregone conclusion; if he sees that the method tends to dichotomize between manifest and latent content even when the border between them is undiscernible; if he knows that psychoanalysis can say nothing substantial about considerations that fall outside an economics of desire and defense; and if he admits that it has a natural penchant for debunking—for sniffing out erotic and aggressive fantasies in the "purest" works and for mocking all pretensions to freedom from conflict—the critic may be able to borrow the clinical outlook without losing his intellectual independence and sense of proportion. He could hardly be blamed if, after weighing all these hazards, he decided to exchange Freud for, say, Fredson Bowers. But if not—if he recognized that Freud in his often questionable manner grasped some essential truths about motivation—he would at least see his rhetorical task in a clear light. He would realize, that is, that in order to communicate with other readers he must look past psychoanalysis and establish a common ground of literary perception.

This counsel, I know, downgrades Freudian criticism in the orthodox sense of rendering texts into psychoanalese, as if they were just so many illustrations of clinical patterns. But that criticism has always violated the spirit of Freud's writings, which, though sometimes reckless and confused, were never simply the consequence of "applying the method" to new materials. Freud was forever testing his ideas, looking for the edges of their scope and drawing back in deference to the unknown or the inexplicable. In a word, Freud was not a doctrinaire Freudian; he was a man provisionally taking a reductive posture toward phenomena in order to find whether anything plausible and important might be learned that way. The nearest equivalent in literary criticism wouldn't be a consistent psychoanalytic reading of an author's works, but a book like Harold Bloom's *The Anxiety of Influence,* which, for all its arch mannerisms, emulates Freud at his most inquisitive: the Freud, I mean, who set aside cultural piety in order to look for psychic lawfulness where people would least have expected to find it.

The fact that a critic's thesis is reductive—for example, Bloom's thesis that a poet's real business is to render his predecessors less intimidating by misrepresenting them as mere forerunners of himself—is no reason to reject it out of hand. The question must always be whether we are better or worse readers for having attended to the critic's argument. By that criterion even an argument that oversteps itself at certain points may earn the right to be remembered. We owe more, after all, to an Empson or a Burke—both of them indebted to Freud's example but unbound by his "methodology"—than to dozens of exegetes who have never once strayed onto the forbidden ground of the extra-literary. Though Empson and Burke and Bloom all make reductions, none of them is to a significant degree a reductionist. For their reductions, however startling and even outrageous, are put forward *as* reductions, as intellectual thrusts that needn't be confounded with the essence or value of the literature being scrutinized. These critics constantly imply a humility before the poems which, with seeming arrogance, they are temporarily turning inside out.

The present disarray of psychoanalytic criticism is no doubt a cause for satisfaction among people who never cared for "deep" interpretation and who now feel confirmed in their resolution to allow literature to speak for itself. The only way to do that, however, is to remain silent—a sacrifice beyond the saintliest critic's power. To be a critic is precisely to take a stance different from the author's and to pursue a thesis of one's own. Among the arguments it is possible to make, reductive ones are without doubt the trickiest, promising Faustian knowledge but often misrepresenting the object of inquiry and deluding the critic into thinking he has cracked the author's code. To forswear all reductions, however, is not the answer: that is the path of phobia. A critic can avoid reductionism, yet still give his intellect free rein, only by keeping his skepticism in working order. If psychoanalysis, originally the most distrustful of psychologies, has by its worldly success and conceptual elaboration become a positive impediment to skepticism, we need be no more surprised than Freud himself would have been at such all-too-human backsliding. A critic's sense of limits, like Freud's own, must come not from the fixed verities of a doctrine but from his awe at how little he can explain. And that awe in turn must derive from his openness to literature—from his sense that the reader in him, happily, will never be fully satisfied by what the critic in him has to say. (pp. 166-85)

> *Frederick Crews, "Reductionism and its Discontents," in his* Out of My System: Psychoanalysis, Ideology, and Critical Method, *Oxford University Press, 1975, pp. 165-85.*

Peter Brooks

[*Brooks is an American educator and critic whose writings reflect his interest in a psychoanalytic approach to literature. In the following essay, he asserts the value of psychoanalytic criticism despite its limitations.*]

Psychoanalytic literary criticism has always been something of an embarrassment. One resists labeling as a "psychoanalytic critic" because the kind of criticism evoked by the term mostly deserves the bad name it largely has made for itself. Thus I have been worrying about the status of some of my own uses of psychoanalysis in the study of narrative, in my attempt to find dynamic models that might move us beyond the static formalism of structuralist and semiotic narratology. And in general, I think we need to worry about the legitimacy and force that psychoanalysis may claim when imported into the study of literary texts. If versions of psychoanalytic criticism have been with us at least since 1908, when Freud published his essay on "Creative Writers and Day-dreaming" [see excerpt above], and if the enterprise has recently been renewed in subtle ways by post-structuralist versions of reading, a malaise persists, a sense that whatever the promises of their union, literature and psychoanalysis remain mismatched bedfellows—or perhaps I should say playmates.

The first problem, and the most basic, may be that psychoanalysis in literary study has over and over again mistaken the *object* of analysis, with the result that whatever insights it has produced tell us precious little about the structure and rhetoric of literary texts. Traditional psychoanalytic criticism tends to fall into three general cate-gories, depending on the object of analysis: the author, the reader, or the fictive persons of the text. The first of these constituted the classical locus of psychoanalytic interest. It is now apparently the most discredited, though also perhaps the most difficult to extirpate, since if the disappearance of the author has been repeatedly announced, authorial mutants ceaselessly reappear, as, for instance, in Harold Bloom's *psychomachia* of literary history. Like the author, the fictive character has been deconstructed into an effect of textual codes, a kind of thematic mirage, and the psychoanalytic study of the putative unconscious of characters in fiction has also fallen into disrepute. Here again, however, the impulse resurfaces, for instance in some of the moves of a feminist criticism that needs to show how the represented female psyche (particularly of course as created by women authors) refuses and problematizes the dominant concepts of male psychological doctrine. Feminist criticism has in fact largely contributed to a new variant of the psychoanalytic study of fictive characters, a variant one might label the "situational-thematic": studies of Oedipal triangles in fiction, their permutations and evolution, of the roles of mothers and daughters, of situations of nurture and bonding, and so forth. It is work often full of interest, but nonetheless methodologically disquieting in its use of Freudian analytic tools in a wholly thematic way, as if the identification and labeling of human relations in a psychoanalytic vocabulary were the task of criticism. The third traditional field of psychoanalytic literary study, the reader, continues to flourish in ever-renewed versions, since the role of the reader in the creation of textual meaning is very much on our minds at present, and since the psychoanalytic study of readers' responses willingly brackets the impossible notion of author in favor of the acceptable and also verifiable notion of reader. The psychoanalytic study of the reader may concern real readers (as in Norman Holland's *5 Readers Reading* [see Further Reading]) or the reader as psychological everyman (as in Simon O. Lesser's *Fiction and the Unconscious* [see excerpt above]). But like the other traditional psychoanalytic approaches, it displaces the object of analysis from the text to some person, some other psychodynamic structure—a displacement I wish to avoid since, as I hope to make clear as I go along, I think psychoanalytic criticism can and should be textual and rhetorical.

If the displacement of the object of analysis has been a major failing of psychoanalytic literary criticism, it has erred also in its inability to rid itself of the underlying conviction that it is inherently explanatory. The problem with "literature and psychoanalysis," as Shoshana Felman has pointed out more effectively than any other critic, lies in that "and" [see excerpt below]. The conjunction has almost always implied a relation of privilege of one term to the other, a use of psychoanalysis as a conceptual system in terms of which to analyze and explain literature, rather than an encounter and confrontation between the two. The reference to psychoanalysis has traditionally been used to close rather than open the argument, and the text. This is not surprising, since the recourse to psychoanalysis usually claims as its very *raison d'être* the capacity to explain and justify in the terms of a system and a discourse more penetrating and productive of insight than literary critical psychology as usual, which of course harbors its own, largely unanalyzed, assumptions. As Lesser states the case, "no 'common-sense' psychology yet employed in criticism has been helpful"; whereas psychoanalysis provides a way to explore "the deepest levels of meaning of the greatest fiction."

Why should we reject such a claim? Even if psychoanalysis is far from being a "science" with the formal power of linguistics, for instance, surely some of its hypotheses are so well established and so universally illustrated that we can use them with as much impunity as such linguistic concepts as "shifters" or "the double articulation." Yet the recourse to linguistic and to psychoanalytic concepts implies a false symmetry: linguistics may be universalistic, but its tools and concepts are "cool" and their overextension easily recognized as trivial, whereas psychoanalysis is imperialistic, almost of necessity. Freud works from the premise that all that appears is a sign, that all signs are subject to interpretation, and that they ultimately tell stories that contain the same dramatis personae and the same narrative functions for all of us. It is no wonder that Freud called himself a "conquistador": he extends remarkably the empire of signs and their significant decipherment, encompassing all of human behavior and symbolic action. Thus any "psychoanalytic explanation" in another discipline always runs the risk of appearing to claim the last word, the final hermeneutical power. If there is one thing that post-structuralist criticism has most usefully taught us, it is the suspicion of this last word in the interpretive process and history, the refusal of any privileged position in analysis.

But if we refuse to grant psychoanalysis any position of privilege in criticism, if we refuse to consider it to be explanatory, what do we have left? What is the status of a de-authorized psychoanalytic discourse within literary-critical discourse, and what is its object? If we don't accord explanatory force to psychoanalysis, what is the point of using it at all? Why do we continue to read so many critical essays laced with the conceptual vocabulary of psychoanalysis? What is *at stake* in the current uses of psychoanalysis?

I want to begin this inquiry with the flat-footed (and unfashionable) assertion that I believe that the persistence, against all the odds, of psychoanalytic perspectives in literary study must ultimately derive from our conviction that the materials on which psychoanalysts and literary critics exercise their powers of analysis are in some basic sense the same: that the structure of literature *is* in some sense the structure of mind—not a specific mind, but what the translators of the *Standard Edition* call "the mental apparatus," which is more accurately the dynamic organization of the psyche, a process of structuration. We continue to dream of a convergence of psychoanalysis and literary criticism because we sense that there ought to be, that there must be, some correspondence between literary and psychic process, that aesthetic structure and form, including literary tropes, must somehow coincide with the psychic structures and operations they both evoke and appeal to. Yet here we encounter the truth of the comment made by Jack Spector in his book, *The Aesthetics of Freud:* "Neither Freud nor his followers . . . have ever shown concretely how specific formal techniques correspond to the processes of the unconscious" [see Further Reading].

Part of the attraction of psychoanalytic criticism has always been its promise of a movement *beyond* formalism, to that desired place where literature and life converge,

and where literary criticism becomes the discourse of something anthropologically important. I very much subscribe to this urge, but I think that it is fair to say that in the case of psychoanalysis, paradoxically, we can go beyond formalism only by becoming more formalistic. Geoffrey Hartman wrote a number of years ago—in *Beyond Formalism,* in fact—that the trouble with Anglo-American formalism was that it wasn't formalist enough. One can in general indict Anglo-American New Criticism for being too quick to leap from the level of formal explication to that of moral and psychological interpretation, neglecting the trajectory through linguistics and poetics that needs to stand between. This has certainly been true in traditional psychoanalytic criticism, which has regularly short-circuited the difficult and necessary issues in poetics. The more recent—rhetorical and deconstructive—kind understands the formalist imperative, but I fear that it may too often remain content with formal operations, simply bracketing the human realm from which psychoanalysis derives. Given its project and its strategies, such rhetorical/deconstructive criticism usually stays within the linguistic realm. It is not willing to make the crossover between rhetoric and reference that interests me—and that ought to be the *raison d'être* for the recourse to psychoanalysis in the first place.

One way to try to move out from the impasse I discern— or have perhaps myself constructed—might be through a return to what Freud has to say about literary form, most notoriously in the brief essay, "Creative Writers and Daydreaming." We would probably all agree that Freud speaks most pertinently to literary critics when he is not explicitly addressing art: the most impressive essays in psychoanalytic criticism have drawn more on *The Interpretation of Dreams,* the metapsychological essays, and *Beyond the Pleasure Principle,* for example, than on *Delusions and Dreams,* "The Moses of Michelangelo," or the essays on Leonardo and Dostoyevski. "Creative Writers and Day-dreaming" in fact gives an excessively simplistic view of art, of the kind that allows Ernst Kris, in his well-known *Psychoanalytic Explorations in Art* [see Further Reading], to describe artistic activity as regression in the service of the ego. Yet the essay may be suggestive in other ways.

Freud sets out to look for some common human activity that is "akin to creative writing," and finds it in daydreaming, or the creation of fantasies. Freud then stresses the active, temporal structure of fantasy, which

> hovers, as it were, between three times—the three moments of time which our ideation involves. Mental work is linked to some current impression, some provoking occasion in the present which has been able to arouse one of the subject's major wishes. From there it harks back to the memory of an earlier experience (usually an infantile one) in which this wish was fulfilled; and it now creates a situation relating to the future which represents a fulfilment of the wish. What it thus creates is a day-dream or phantasy, which carries about it traces of its origin from the occasion which provoked it and from the memory. Thus past, present and future are strung together, as it were, on the thread of the wish that runs through them.

Freud will promptly commit the error of making the past evoked in the construction of fantasy that of the author, in order to study "the connections that exist between the life of the writer and his works"—an error in which most critics have followed his lead. For instance, it is this fantasy model, reworked in terms of D. W. Winnicott and object relations psychoanalysis, that essentially shapes the thesis of one of the most interesting recent studies in literature and psychoanalysis, Meredith Skura's *The Literary Use of the Psychoanalytic Process* [see excerpt below]; Skura, too, ultimately makes the past referred to in fantasy a personal past, that of author or reader, or both. Yet the fantasy model could instead be suggestive for talking about the relations of textual past, present, and projected future in the plot of a novel, for example, or in the rhyme scheme of a sonnet, or simply in the play of verb tenses in any text. I would want to extrapolate from this passage an understanding of how fantasy provides a dynamic model of intratextual temporal relations and of their organization according to the plot of wish, or desire. We might thus gain a certain understanding of the interplay of *form* and *desire*.

Freud is again of great interest in the final paragraph of the essay—one could make a fruitful study of Freud's final paragraphs, which so often produce a flood of new insights that can't quite be dealt with—where he asks how the writer creates pleasure through the communication of his fantasies, whereas those of most people would repel or bore us. Herein, says Freud, lies the poet's "innermost secret," his "essential *ars poetica.*" Freud sees two components of the artistic achievement here: "The writer softens the character of his egoistic day-dreams by altering and disguising it, and he bribes us by the purely formal—that is, aesthetic—yield of pleasure which he offers us in the presentation of his phantasies. We give the name of an *incentive bonus,* or a *fore-pleasure,* to a yield of pleasure such as this, which is offered to us so as to make possible the release of still greater pleasure arising from deeper psychical sources. In my opinion, all the aesthetic pleasure which a creative writer affords us has the character of a forepleasure of this kind." I am deliberately leaving aside the end of this paragraph, where Freud suggests that the writer in this manner enables us "thenceforward to enjoy our own day-dreams without self-reproach or shame," since this hypothesis brings us back to the *person* of the reader, whereas I wish to remain on the plane of form associated with "forepleasure."

The equation of the effects of literary form with forepleasure in this well-known passage is perhaps less trivial than it at first appears. If *Lust* and *Unlust* don't take us very far in the analysis of literary texture, *Vorlust*—forepleasure—tropes on pleasure and thus seems more promising. Forepleasure is indeed a curious concept, suggesting a whole rhetoric of advance toward and retreat from the goal or the end, a formal zone of play (I take it that forepleasure somehow implicates foreplay) that is both harnessed to the end and yet autonomous, capable of deviations and recursive movements. When we begin to unpack the components of forepleasure, we may find a whole erotics of form, which is perhaps what we most need if we are to make formalism serve an understanding of the human functions of literature. Forepleasure would include the notion of both delay and advance in the textual dynamic, the creation of that "dilatory space" which Roland Barthes, in *S/Z,* claimed to be the essence of the textual middle. We seek to advance through this space toward the discharge of the end, yet all the while we are perversely delaying, returning backward in order to put off the promised end and perhaps to assure its greater significance.

Forepleasure implies the possibility of fetishism, the interesting threat of being waylaid by some element along the way to the "proper" end, taking some displaced substitute or simulacrum for the thing itself—a mystification in which most literature deals, sometimes eventually to expose the displacement or substitution as a form of false consciousness, sometimes to expose the end itself as the false lure. It includes as well the possibilities of exhibitionism and voyeurism, which surely are central to literary texts and their reading. In the notion of forepleasure there lurks in fact all manner of perversity, and ultimately the possibility of the polymorphous perverse, the possibility of a text that would delay, displace, and deviate terminal discharge to an extent that it became nonexistent—as, perhaps, in the textual practice of the "writable text" (*texte scriptible*) prized by Barthes, in Samuel Beckett, for instance, or Philippe Sollers. But we find as good an illustration of effective perversity in the text of Henry James, and in the principle (well known to the New Critics) that the best poems accommodate a maximum of ironic texture within their frail structures, a postponement and ambiguation of overt statement. In fact, the work of textuality may insure that all literature is, by its very nature, essentially perverse.

What is most important to me is the sense that the notion of forepleasure as it is advanced by Freud implies the possibility of a formalist aesthetic—one that can be extended to the properly rhetorical field—that speaks to the erotic, which is to say the dynamic, dimensions of form: form as something that is not inert but part of a process that unfolds and develops as texts are activated through the reading process. A neoformalist psychoanalytic criticism could do worse than undertake the study of the various forms of the "fore" in forepleasure, developing a tropology of the perversities through which we turn back, turn around, the simple consumption of texts, making their reading a worthy object of analysis. Such a study would be, as Freud suggests, about "bribing," or perhaps about *teasing* in all its forms, from puns to metaphors, ultimately—given the basic temporal structure of fantasy and of the literary text—about what we might call "clock-teasing," which is perhaps the way we create the illusion of creating a space of meaning within the process of ongoing temporality.

A more formalist psychoanalytic criticism, then, would be attuned to form as our situation, our siting, within the symbolic order, the order within which we constitute meaning and ourselves as endowed with meaning. This kind of psychoanalytic criticism would, of course, pay the greatest attention to the rhetorical aspect of psychic operations as presented by psychoanalysis and would call upon the rhetorical and semiotic reinterpretation of Freud advanced by Emile Benveniste, Jacques Lacan, and others. Yet it might be objected that this more obviously rhetorical version does not automatically solve the problem of how to use the crossover between psychic operations and tropes. The status of the *and* linking psychoanalysis and literary text may still remain at issue: what does one want to *claim* in showing that the structure of a metaphor in

Victor Hugo is equivalent to the structure of a symptom? What is alleged to be the place and the force of the occulted name of the father that may be written in metaphor as symptom, symptom as metaphor? Is there, more subtly now, a claim of explanation advanced in the crossover? Or is an ingenious piece of intertextuality all that takes place?

Something, I think, that lies between the two. My views on these questions have been clarified by an acute and challenging review of my book, *Reading for the Plot,* that appeared in *TLS* [see Further Reading]. In it, Terence Cave asks what he calls "the embarrassing question . . . what is the Freudian model worth?" In his discussion of a possible answer to this question, Cave notes that "Brooks's argument for a Freudian poetics doesn't appear to depend on an imperialist move which would simply annex a would-be science of the psyche and release it from its claim to tell the truth. He talks repeatedly as if the value of the Freudian model is precisely that it does, in some sense, give access to the way human desires really operate." I think this is accurate, and I am happy to be exonerated from the charge of imperialism in the reverse—the imperialism that would come from the incursion of literary criticism into psychoanalysis in search of mere metaphors, which has sometimes been the case with post-structuralist annexations of psychoanalytic concepts. I certainly do want to grant at least a temporary privilege to psychoanalysis in literary study, in that the trajectory through psychoanalysis forces us to confront the human stakes of literary form, while I think also that these stakes need to be considered *in* the text, as activated in its reading. As I suggested earlier, I believe that we constitute ourselves as human subjects in part through our fictions and therefore that the study of human fiction-making and the study of psychic process are convergent activities and superimposable forms of analysis. To say more precisely in what sense psychoanalysis can lead us to models for literary study that generate new insight, we might best look toward a concept that lies at the very heart of Freudian analytic practice, the concept of the transference as it is constituted between analysand and analyst. Here we may find the most useful elaboration of the fantasy model of the text. Let me, then, briefly explore the transference, in order to indicate one possible way of conceiving the relations of psychoanalysis to literary discourse.

The transference, as I understand it, is a realm of the *as-if,* where affects from the past become invested in the present, notably in the dynamics of the analysand-analyst relation, and the neurosis under treatment becomes a transference-neurosis, a present representation of the past. As Freud puts it in the Dora case history, the transference gives us "new impressions or reprints" and "revised editions" of old texts. One can call the transference textual because it is a semiotic and fictional medium where the compulsions of unconscious desire and its scenarios of infantile fulfillment become symbolically present in the communicative situation of analysis. Within the transference, recall of the past most often takes place as its unconscious repetition, an acting out of past events as if they were present: repetition is a way of remembering brought into play when recollection in the intellectual sense is blocked by repression and resistance. Repetition is both an obstacle to analysis, since the analysand must eventually be led to renunciation of the attempt to reproduce the past, and the principal dynamic of the cure, since only by way of its symbolic enact-

ment in the present can the history of past desire, its objects and scenarios of fulfillment, be made known, become manifest in the present discourse. The analyst (I paraphrase Freud here) must treat the analysand's words and symbolic acts as an actual force, active in the present, while attempting to translate them back into the terms of the past. That is, the analyst must work with the analysand to fit their emotional impulses into their proper place in his life history, to restore the links between ideas and events that have fallen away, to reconnect isolated memories, and to draw conclusions from interconnections and patterns. The analyst must help the analysand construct a narrative discourse whose syntax and rhetoric are more plausible, more convincing, more adequate to give an account of the story of the past than those that are originally presented, in symptomatic form, by the analysand.

Freud writes in one of his key essays on the transference, "Remembering, Repeating and Working-Through":

> The transference thus creates an intermediate region [*Zwischenreich*] between illness and real life through which the transition from the one to the other is made. The new condition has taken over all the features of the illness; but it represents an artificial illness which is at every point accessible to our intervention. It is a piece of real experience, but one which has been made possible by especially favourable conditions, and it is of a provisional nature.

Freud's description of this intermediate region—this *Zwischenreich*—that is both artificial and a piece of real experience makes it sound very much like the literary text. He who intervenes in it is the analyst or reader, first of all in the sense that the simple presence of this other brings to the analysand's discourse what Lacan calls "the dimension of dialogue" ["Intervention sur le transfert," *Ecrits*]. Texts are always implicitly or even explicitly addressed to someone. The "I" that speaks in a lyric ever postulates a "thou." Indeed, as Benveniste has shown [in his "De la subjectivité dans le langage," *Problémes de linguistique générale*], "I" and "thou" are linguistically interdependent, both signifiers without signifieds, and with referents that constantly change as each speaker in turn assumes the "I" in relation to the interlocutor, who from "I" becomes "thou." This situation is frequently dramatized in narrative texts, in what we call "framed tales," which stage the presence of a listener or narratee whose reactions to what is told are often what is most important in the narrative. Such is the case of Balzac's *Sarrasine,* which has become a classic point of reference since Roland Barthes in *S/Z* made it a model for the workings of the "narrative contract," and also Mary Shelley's *Frankenstein,* where the narratee of each embedded narrative is supposed to act upon what he has been told. In other cases, the simple presence of the narratee, even when silent, "dialogizes" the speech of the narrator, as Mikhail Bakhtin has so thoroughly demonstrated in the case of the Dostoyevskian monologue. A good example of dialogized monologue is Albert Camus' *La Chute,* where Jean-Baptiste Clamence's abject confession includes within it the unnamed and silent narratee's responses, with the eventual result of implicating the narratee within a discourse he would no doubt rather not listen to. Even in texts which have no explicit narrator or narratee, where the narrative is apparently "impersonal," there is necessarily a discourse which solicits a response, be it only by the play of personal pronouns and the conjugation of verbs.

The narratee, the addressee, the "you" of these texts is always in some measure a surrogate for the reader, who must define his own interpretation in response to the implied judgment, and the discursive implication, of the explicit or implicit textual "you." Contemporary reader-response criticism has often made excessive claims for the role of the reader—to the point of abolishing the semiotic constraint that the text exercises upon reading—but it has usefully shown us that the reader necessarily collaborates and competes in the creation of textual meaning. To return to Freud's term, we "intervene" in a text by our very act of reading, in our (counter) transferential desire to master the text, as also in the desire to be mastered by it. When we are what we call literary critics, our interventions—our efforts to rewrite and retransmit—may closely resemble the psychoanalyst's, with all the attendant perils of transference and countertransference.

However self-absorbed and self-referential they may appear, lyric and narrative discourses are always proffered for a purpose: to establish a claim on the listener's attention, to make an appeal to complicity, perhaps to judgment, and inevitably to interpretation and retransmission. In the transferential situation of reading, as in the psychoanalytic transference, the reader must grasp not only what is said, but always what the discourse intends, its implications, how it would work on him. He must—in Lacanian terms—refuse the text's demand in order to listen to its desire. In narrative, for instance, the reader must reconstruct and understand not only story events but also the relation of this story to the narrative discourse that conveys it in a certain manner, discourse that itself constitutes an interpretation which demands further interpretation. As Freud writes in "Remembering, Repeating and Working-Through," it occurs that the analysand "does not listen to the precise wording of his obsessional ideas." Narrators may be similar to the analysand in this respect, most obviously in such modernist and postmodernist narratives as those of Conrad, Gide, Faulkner, and Sarraute, but also in many more traditional novels, especially in the eighteenth century—in the work of Diderot and Sterne, for instance—and even at the very origins of the genre, in the *Lazarillo de Tormes,* a novel which both reveals and conceals its story. A certain suspicion inhabits the relation of narrative discourse to its story, and our role as readers calls for a suspicious hearing, a rewriting of the narrative text in a sort of agonistic dialogue with the words we are given to work with. Freud repeatedly describes the relations of analyst and analysand in the transference as one of struggle—struggle for the mastery of resistances and the lifting of repressions—which continually evokes a realm of the demonic. With reader and text, the struggle must eventually put into question any assumed position of mastery or privilege, which is why we must reread, speak again, retransmit.

The advantage of such a transferential model, it seems to me, is that it illuminates the difficult and productive encounter of the speaker and the listener, the text and the reader, and how their exchange takes place in an "artificial" space—a symbolic and semiotic medium—that is nonetheless the place of real investments of desire from both sides of the dialogue. The transference actualizes the

past in symbolic form so that it can be repeated, replayed, worked through to another outcome. The result is, in the ideal case, to bring us back to actuality, that is, to a revised version of our stories. As Freud writes in the last sentence of another important essay, "The Dynamics of Transference": "For when all is said and done, it is impossible to destroy anyone *in absentia* or *in effigie.*" The statement appears paradoxical, in that it is precisely "in effigy"—in the symbolic mode—that the past and its ghosts may be destroyed, or laid to rest, in analysis. What Freud means, I think, is that the transference succeeds in making the past and its scenarios of desire live again through signs with such vivid reality that the reconstructions proposed by analytic work achieve the *effect* of the real. They do not change past history—they are powerless to do that—but they rewrite its present discourse. Disciplined and mastered, the transference ushers us forth into a changed reality. And such is no doubt the intention of any literary text.

In such a conception of the transference, we have a rhetorical elaboration of the fantasy model of the text adumbrated in "Creative Writers and Day-dreaming." The text is conceived as a semiotic and fictive medium constituted as the place of affective investments that represent a situation and a story as both symbolic (given the absence of situation and story except "in effigy") and "real" (given the making-present of situation and story through their repetition). The text conceived as transference should allow us to illuminate and work through that which is at issue in the situation of the speaker, or the story of the narrator, that is, what must be rethought, reordered, interpreted from his discourse. Transference and interpretation are in fact interdependent, and we cannot assign priority to one over the other. If it is evident that transference calls forth interpretation, it is equally true that it is the potential of interpretation on the part of "the subject supposed to know"—as Lacan characterizes the analyst—that sets the transference going.

When, as analysand or as text, you call for interpretation from the analyst/reader, you put yourself into the transference. Through the rethinkings, reorderings, reinterpretations of the reading process, the analyst/reader "intervenes" in the text, and these interventions must also be subject to his suspicious attention. A transferential model thus allows us to take as the object of analysis not author or reader, but reading, including, of course, the transferential-interpretive operations that belong to reading. Meaning in this view is not simply "in the text" nor wholly the fabrication of a reader (or a community of readers) but comes into being in the dialogic struggle and collaboration of the two, in the activation of textual possibilities in the process of reading. Such a view ultimately destabilizes the authority of reader/critic in relation to the text, since, caught up in the transference, he becomes analysand as well as analyst.

Yet here I once again encounter Cave, who finds my evocations of "transference" and "dialogue" in *Reading for the Plot* to be largely metaphorical. "It seems curious," writes Cave, "to speak of a once-and-for-all written narrative as the medium for transference for a reader who has not supplied its materials. . . . How can there be a transference where there is no means by which the reader's language may be rephrased in coherent and manageable form by the text-as-analyst?" Cave has reversed the basic model, which would see text as analysand and reader as analyst; but that is a reversal that can, I have suggested, take place in the process of reading and interpretation. What is more to the point, there happens to be an essay of Freud's that indirectly responds to some of Cave's questions: "Constructions in Analysis" (1937), an essay from late in Freud's career in which he explicitly addresses the roles played by analysand and analyst in the creation of a life story and its discursive meaning.

Near the start of this essay, Freud notes that since the analyst has neither experienced nor repressed any of the story in question, he cannot be called upon to remember it. "His task," writes Freud, "is to make out what has been forgotten from the traces which it has left behind or, more correctly, to *construct* it." As Freud's essay proceeds, this construction becomes a radical activity. The analyst constructs a hypothetical piece of narrative and, writes Freud, "communicates it to the subject of analysis so that it may work on him; he then constructs a further piece out of the fresh material pouring in on him, deals with it in the same way and proceeds in this alternating fashion until the end." Confirmation that these constructions are correct does not take the form of a simple assent: a "yes" from the analysand has little value, says Freud, "unless it is followed by indirect confirmations, unless the patient . . . produces new memories which complete and extend the construction." As in reading, hypotheses of construal prove to be strong and valuable when they produce more text, when they create in the text previously unperceived networks of relation and significance, finding confirmation in the extension of the narrative and semantic web. The analytic work, the process of finding and making meaning, is necessarily a factor of listening and reading as well as telling. Freud indeed goes on to concede that there are moments when the analyst's construction does not lead to the analysand's recollection of repressed elements of his story but nonetheless produces in him "an assured conviction of the truth of the construction which achieves the same therapeutic result as a recaptured memory." Parts of the story thus seem to belong to the interpreter rather than to the person whose story it is, or was.

"Constructions in Analysis" as a whole gives a view of psychoanalytic interpretation and construction that notably resembles the active role of the reader in making sense of a text, finding hypotheses of interpretation that open up ever wider and more forceful semantic patterns, attempting always to reach the totality of the supreme because necessary fiction. The reader may not have written the text, yet it does change and evolve as he works on it—as he rewrites it, as those readers we call literary critics necessarily do. And as the reader works on the text, it does "rephrase" his perceptions. I think any of us could find confirmation of such a truly transferential and dialogic relation of text and analysis in our own experience. And there are of course literary texts that inscribe and dramatize acts of reading, interpretation, and construction: for instance, Balzac's *Le Lys dans la vallée,* where Natalie de Manerville reads Félix de Vandenesse's long confession and tells him that he has misinterpreted his own desires. Benjamin Constant's *Adolphe* stages a similar case of retrospective reading that provokes an entire reconstruction of the story. The epistolary novel of course stages nothing else: *Les Liaisons dangereuses* is all about different models and levels of construction in the reading of messages, and the writing of messages with a view toward their interpretation. The novels of Conrad and Faulkner are similar to Laclos' masterpiece in that they offer multiple constructions of events that never are verifiable, that can be tested only by the force of conviction they produce for listeners and readers.

Interpretation and construction are themselves most often dramas of desire and power, both within literature and in the reading of literary texts. Hence I would claim that the model of the transference is a far more literal model of reading than Cave would allow. I find it significant that toward the end of "Constructions in Analysis," Freud turns to a discussion of delusions, similar to hallucinations, which are produced in the analysand by the analyst's constructions: delusions that evoke a "fragment of historical truth" that is out of place in the story. Freud writes at this point, in an astonishing sentence, "The delusions of patients appear to me to be the equivalents of the constructions which we build up in the course of an analytic treatment—attempts at explanation and cure." That is, not only does the patient, in any successful analysis, become his own analyst; the analyst also becomes the patient, espouses his delusional system, and works toward the construction of fictions that can never be verified other than by the force of the conviction that they convey. And this seems to me a fair representation of good criticism, which involves a willingness, a desire, to enter into the delusional systems of texts, to espouse their hallucinated vision, in an attempt to master and be mastered by their power of conviction.

One final point needs to be made, again in reference to Cave—a resourceful critic whom one can never finally lay to rest. It can be argued—and I have myself argued—that much of Freud's understanding of interpretation and the construction of meaning is grounded in literature, in those "poets and philosophers" he was the first to acknowledge as his precursors. "In which case" writes Cave, psychoanalysis "can't itself provide a grounding, since it is part of the system it attempts to master." Cave continues: "Its advantage (though a precious one) would only be that, in its doubling of narrative and analysis, story and plot, it provides a poetics appropriate to the history of modern fiction." Cave here reverses the more traditional charge that psychoanalysis imperialistically claims to explain literature in order to make the more subtle (and contemporary) charge that psychoanalysis may be nothing *but* literature, and the relations of the two nothing more than a play of intertextuality, or even a tautology.

I am unwilling to concede so much. One can resist the notion that psychoanalysis "explains" literature and yet insist that the kind of intertextual relation it holds to literature is quite different from the intertextuality that obtains between two poems or novels, and that it illuminates in quite other ways. For the psychoanalytic intertext obliges the critic to make a transit through a systematic discourse elaborated to describe the dynamics of psychic process. The similarities and differences, in object and in intention, of this discourse from literary analysis creates a tension which is productive of perspective, of stereoptical effect. Psychoanalysis is not an arbitrarily chosen intertext for literary analysis, but rather a particularly insistent and demanding intertext, in that crossing the boundaries from one territory to the other both confirms and complicates our understanding of how mind reformulates the real, how it constructs the necessary fictions by which we dream, desire, interpret, indeed by which we constitute ourselves as human subjects. The detour through psychoanalysis forces the critic to respond to the erotics of form, that is, to an engagement with the psychic investments of rhetoric, the dramas of desire played out in tropes. Psychoanalysis matters to us as literary critics because it stands as a constant reminder that the attention to form, properly conceived, is not a sterile formalism, but rather one more attempt to draw the symbolic and fictional map of our place in existence. (pp. 334-48)

Peter Brooks, "The Idea of a Psychoanalytic Literary Criticism," in Critical Inquiry, Vol. 13, No. 2, Winter, 1987, pp. 334-48.

Cary Nelson

[*Nelson is an American educator and critic. In the following excerpt, he argues for the application of the same analytic techniques used for fiction to critical writing.*]

The first thing to be said about this topic—the psychology of criticism—is that many people believe criticism *has* no psychology. As an essentially disinterested activity, they would argue, criticism is not significantly influenced either by the psychology of the critic or by the dynamics of critical writing. So one barrier to this discussion is the collective response that its topic is no topic at all. An opposed barrier derives from another collective reaction: that the topic is essentially unspeakable and its revelations are to be avoided.

An anecdote will illustrate my point. At a conference on literature and psychology in 1977, I suggested that psychoanalysis might profitably direct itself toward an analysis of complex critical prose. One of the participants countered by saying he would be offended by any attempt to psychoanalyze his scholarship. Several people quickly pointed out the obvious irony in his position: he was quite committed to psychoanalysis as a method for interpreting fiction and poetry but was unwilling to permit its application to criticism, and especially to his own criticism. This defensive outrage can serve to characterize the second collective reaction to my topic. Both reactions are so conventional as to be exemplary. They represent, in miniature, a potential for more elaborate ways of avoiding the issues I will introduce here. If one thinks of more extended versions of these reactions—not only those reactions in print and those encountered in conversations with colleagues but also those implicit in the ideologies of scholars who have not confronted the issues openly—then one can see that discussion of the psychology of criticism is fronted by two kinds of discourse: the nonsensical and the forbidden. In much practice, of course, these are not really varieties of discourse but varieties of silence, since relatively few people give voice to either position.

I want not so much to reject either of these positions as to use them, to let them reflect one another in a way that may assist the discussion to take place between them. Both positions reflect a reluctance, indeed a refusal that is collectively sanctioned, to consider the psychological dimensions of a particular human activity—the writing of criticism. This reluctance is at the core of a more general resis-

tance to thinking about the nature of the critical activity. Imagine for a moment the potential answers to the question "What is Literature?" Few of us would be unwilling to address the subject, however unsatisfactory we might find our own answers. The complementary question "What is Criticism?" would receive quite different responses: a few disingenuously minimalist definitions, defensively moralistic platitudes, and silence. These are not only three alternate ways to react; they are also a predictable sequence or closed cycle of stances. As one fails, the critic can have recourse to the next.

I suspect that such limited responses would be sufficiently widespread that we might reasonably describe the writing of criticism as "that thing we do that we cannot speak of directly." Even courses in critical theory tend to reduce the subject either to a version of the history of ideas or to a series of alternate methods for reading literary texts. Few such courses give primary attention to critical texts as texts in their own right—to their internal verbal structures, to the economics of their production, or to the atmosphere of individual uncertainty and vision in which they were composed. All this leads me back again to my main topic—the psychology of criticism. It may be useful to consider as self-defining the general absence of discourse about criticism. Part of the psychology of criticism is the very tendency to deny that its psychology exists.

We are all aware that this silence has been invaded repeatedly during the last few years, but it is important not to exaggerate the amount of attention critics have recently given to their enterprise. Serious analysis of the critical activity remains infrequent. Curiously enough, very few psychoanalytic critics have worked in this area, although their contribution could be considerable. In any case, anyone who writes about the practice of criticism will be unable to ignore the tradition of *omerta* that surrounds the topic.

Silence surrounds not only general attitudes toward criticism but also the individual sentences of critical essays. A significant part of academic literary criticism amounts to the careful translation of individual experience into language that can be communally credited by the profession. This is partly an instance of a larger psychological necessity, one that Kenneth Burke describes succinctly: "I worked out a way of getting along by dodges, the main one being a concern with tricks whereby I could translate my self-involvements into speculations about 'people' in general." In criticism, such translation is mediated not only through other texts but also by professional constraints that require verbal adaptations not always pleasurable to a writer. To turn these adaptations, as Burke does, into forms of play, is to succeed in mastering your discourse at the very moment you disavow it. For many critics, however, particularly inexperienced ones, these translations may feel more like repression and self-negation.

The sense of what is permissible, of what can be said, varies from field to field and from journal to journal. It undergoes constant change and is never wholly fixed in any case. Moreover, it depends in part upon who the person is, what his reputation is, and precisely what his previous work has led his audience to expect. Nonetheless, a rough consensus about the kind of discourse that is admissible does obtain at any moment in time. To violate these norms might seem to risk the standard kinds of professional excommunication. But genuine violation of these norms may be impossible, since what critics can know (and say) is a function of the critical languages available to them. These languages establish the terms of and the limits to any rupture that can take place within them, a constraint that must, of course, apply to the present topic as well.

An example from my own work may help to demonstrate how these pressures can function in a critical text. Several years ago I was writing about Milton's fascination with physical rigidity as a manifestation of a character's resistance to temptation. As my work progressed, I concentrated on *Paradise Regained,* keeping in mind the evidence for Milton's interest in inflexible physical postures at key points in his other works, but leaving it out of my essay. I wanted to end the essay with an epiphanic reading of Christ's posture at the conclusion of *Paradise Regained.* I wished to evoke the implicit sexuality of the scene and to connect that sexuality with the poem's religious vision. My final sentences read: "Christ's crucified body is the vehicle through which the seed of Eve will be planted in heaven. Symbolically the poem points the fallen reader in the direction of paradise. Its final posture: Christ standing at the still center of the turning world—a stone phallus in the womb of nature." This passage has served as a kind of red flag for its readers, several of whom have found it indecorous, irrational, or absurd. When Murray Schwartz reviewed the book of which the *Paradise Regained* essay is a chapter, he singled the passage out as a case when the author "seems so determined to find transcendent unity in the image of the body that he transforms his subject into the form of his desire."

I think it is fair to say that much of the paraphrasable content of my paragraph could have been rendered in a form more acceptable to members of the profession. My style would have to be more discursive, less aphoristic. I would need to distance myself from the sense of apocalyptic participation communicated by my rhetoric; there are other kinds of enraptured exemplification that can serve similar emotional functions for the critic, while his readers find them more tolerable. Then I would need to reintroduce reasonably elaborate substantiation through Milton's other poems. Finally, I might allude to Jacques Lacan's analyses of the symbolic primacy of the phallus, so as to give my observations an external theoretical ground.

This sanitized, argumentative version of my paragraph would hardly be the same as the original. Yet my essential point—that similar insights become acceptable or unacceptable according to the language in which they are couched—remains unchanged. Though it does not negate Schwartz's point about my psychological motivation, it complicates it. What I wrote is arguably linked to Milton's text. Yet it is entirely relevant to ask what needs were served by my writing about the text in this particular way. The passage is not an instance of sheer subjectivity—if indeed such a thing exists—and an account of its psychology needs to treat all its components—textual, professional, and personal. Finally, it might be most fruitful to use the passage as a way of beginning to talk about the psychology of more prosaic portions of the essay. We need, in short, to be careful about how we privilege what seem to be overt admissions of a critic's own presence.

At least some of what I am saying here is common knowledge, but it is also largely unspoken knowledge. We all, no doubt, have had practice in negotiating between our individual experience and the consensus language of our particular fields. We recognize, at least in reading our own work, that its sentences record that kind of continual mediation. We know that mediation to be part of the substance of the critical activity, yet we remain largely silent about its effect on our own work and on that of others. For me, the satisfaction of writing criticism grows partly out of feeling that I am working at the edge of the state of consensus in my field, at the boundary where self-expression is brought forward, qualified, and brought forward again.

Let me try to identify a reasonably clear case of this kind of consensus in progress. At the end of a recent essay titled "Literary Theory: A Compass for Critics," Paul Hernadi writes "Practically everything I have said about texts in the foregoing pages also applies to the present essay. This means that you may wish to challenge the perspective or attitude of its implied author or else psychoanalyze its actual author and even reveal the socioeconomic motivation of his approach to literary theory." One reason I was struck by this passage was that I had recently included a similar gesture in an essay titled "Reading Criticism." Hernadi and I acknowledged the self-relexive component of what we had written. Neither of us chose to go back and draw frequent attention to that level of our writing. Even as a gesture, however, it has its satisfactions. First, it is a form of decorous confession. Second, it provides at least some defense against just that objection's being raised against the essay. Yet it is not merely shyness or humility that limited how far either of us pursued the issue. One may counter that we rejected a continual and overt self-reflection because we knew our readers would find it intrusive or boring. That may be true, but their boredom would be both consensually determined and defensive. It cannot be the case that self-reflection is somehow ontologically boring; it is potentially as subject to rhetorical management and interest as any other form of discourse. Yet I would argue that as of 1976 such a brief comment was the permissible limit for acknowledged self-reflexive meditation in published critical theory. You will have no trouble finding other evidence to support this contention. Take, for example, Norman Holland's statement in *5 Readers Reading* [see Further Reading], "my interpretations must necessarily express my own identity theme," or Harold Bloom's admission [in *The Anxiety of Influence*] that his theory of influence is offered "in the context of his own anxieties of influence." Neither Holland nor Bloom deals very effectively with the implications of their observations, though Holland makes a more serious effort than almost anyone else. For Bloom, of course, it is one proclamation among many. That in itself, however, is significant. While most critics would draw special attention to such moments—placing them strategically, using the first person and altering their tone, or making the point with obvious nervousness—Bloom's uniformly intense rhetoric makes it very difficult to privilege explicit self-reflection.

Now that I have called your attention to this small feature of the rhetoric of recent criticism, you may be inclined to dismiss it as mere rhetoric. Actually, I do not think that can ever quite be the case. Even if a critic merely appends such a comment as an afterthought, it will still reveal an awareness of the self-reflexive quality of critical writing and perhaps suggest both pleasure and uneasiness in that awareness. Such self-recognition, even when it is belated, contributes to the psychology of critical writing. At the same time, only the surrounding critical climate makes such self-awareness possible, permissible, and even probable. The consensus about acknowledged self-awareness in criticism is presently a highly unstable one. The critics I have cited here are, in effect, testing that consensus at the same time as they are testing themselves against their own work. Moreover, the rough consensus within the field of critical theory about how much self-recognition is possible and what forms it should take does not at all apply to the reactions of the profession as a whole, which responds according to my earlier model: self-consciousness is "silenced" as the nonsensical or the forbidden. Recent comments by Gerald Graff and Donald Reiman, among others, give sufficient voice to how the silent majority feels.

Although these reactions are predictable, they are nonetheless helpful. As long as they actually appear in print, even if they are merely sarcastic or incensed, they create an atmosphere of debate and curiosity. The profession really has only two tactics it can use successfully against discourse that it rejects: not to publish it at all, or, having published it, to ignore it. Someone who feels compelled to deal with you has given you the only audience you need. Moreover, the presence of the nonsensical and the forbidden are always signs that the discourse between them can change. That is precisely the use that Bloom's criticism has for the profession. His theory of influence may never be widely adopted, but the reviews his books have received are changing the nature of what can be said. His publications have helped to open the discussion of literary critics to issues previously excluded.

None of this makes our questions about the psychology of criticism easier to resolve. My intention is rather to make a two-fold claim: first, for the necessity of considering the psychology of criticism, and second, for the necessity of considering its continual relativity. I can think of no better way to emphasize the second point than by examining for a moment the recent work of the critic who has argued perhaps most visibly that literary interpretation is shaped by our individual psychology, Norman Holland.

Holland's recent work regularly includes characterizations of his own identity theme, which he feels governs both his relations to literary texts and his habitual critical stances. "For me," he writes, "the need to see and understand is very strong." "I feel a real conflict in me between scientific impulses and literary ones." He has "a passionate desire to know about the insides of things with an equally strong feeling that one is, finally, safer on the outside." For that reason, he writes, "I *like* examining the verbal surface of a text, looking particularly for an 'organic unity' in the way the parts all come together." As I read Holland's list, I find myself somewhat alienated by his cheerful form of self-presentation; it is not my style. Except for that, however, I have little difficulty in reciting his personal characteristics in the first person. Indeed, it would be curious if I did have trouble doing so, for these qualities are commonplace features of virtually any critical writing. They are, in short, unrevealing and impersonal; in different ways we can all assent to them. Perhaps we are intended to, thereby congratulating ourselves at how harmless and unthreatening psychoanalysis has proven to be and, of course, accepting Holland's theory, since we can presumably credit these as our identity themes as well.

These decorous, sanitized statements of the will to power are designed, perhaps unconsciously, to offer only the most minimal challenge to the current consensus about the motives for interpretation. Compare another version: "My identity theme [has] to do with preserving a sense of self and securing self-esteem by gaining power over relations between things, in particular, mastering them by knowing or seeing them from outside rather than being actually in the relationships." The next sentence is the crucial one: "Not a bad hang-up, if you want to be a literary critic." These are, as I have argued, conventional critical "hang-ups."

The identity themes I have just cited could actually have been presented with double sets of quotation marks, since they are now so codified for Holland that he offers them as self-quotation from his previous work. This pattern of self-quotation has two interesting effects. First, it gives his original speculation about his identity theme a retroactive evidentiary status, although that status is unconvincing and thus slightly comic. Second, the quotation marks give the material a fixed and immutable status; it need not be confronted or considered any further. Holland tends to place this cluster of identity themes at the end of his essays. The reader encountering the list for the first time comes to it expecting Holland to conclude with dramatic self-revelation and thus feels rather cheated. Yet perhaps there *is* more than a consensual code here. The persona Holland most often puts forward in his criticism is convincingly open, generous, and even innocent. If Holland has a sense of self-exposure and cleansing confession when he writes about his desire for power, perhaps it is because such a motive, however commonplace, is so remote from the voice he has already established in his criticism. Nonetheless, these statements of his identity theme are so formulaic that they block any extended exploration of the guilt critics usually feel when they recognize, however obliquely, their wish to reconstruct a text and reorder it in their minds. There are hints of that in Holland's very enthusiasm. There are also suggestions, elsewhere in his work, of how his perspective does differ from that of the profession as a whole. Earlier in one of these essays he reports that he feels "punished" by the second stanza of Wordsworth's "A Slumber did my Spirit Seal." That is a more curious and indeed more intimate reaction than those he reports in his official identity themes, and it shows that Holland can, when he wants, risk himself in his writing in ways most critics still resist.

In this sketch of some of the tensions in Holland's criticism, we see how it is possible to talk about the psychology of a particular critic's writing by testing it against the general psychology of criticism. There is rarely need, I would argue, to resort to biographical information in order to write about the psychology of most critics' work. What is essential now is to begin looking at critical texts themselves with some sensitivity to the psychology of their rhetoric. The goal is to elucidate the psychology of what has been written and thereby to read critical texts in a more informed and humanly plausible way, not to use critical texts as a way of reconstructing personal histories. I make that point not only in order to reassure those who are concerned about standards for professional interaction but also to emphasize the centrality of the critical texts themselves, as opposed to any information we can bring to them. I am not offering this dictum so as to privilege these texts in the New Critical sense, but merely to draw attention to language that critics have so far not been reading and discussing with sufficient care. One does, however, need to know the intellectual and cultural milieu in which a critic worked. Such matters as a critic's terminology or the tone he takes toward his contemporaries may be inexplicable or misleading without that information. Where more personal biographical evidence seems relevant, its use should be governed by the same standards for the passage of time that apply in discussions of poetry or fiction.

Actually, an inquiry into the psychology of criticism is an almost inevitable outgrowth of any effort to read and reread criticism as thoroughly as poetry and fiction. A first reading of a critical text might at best be comparable to reading a novel with complete absorption in its plot. Since we are more resistant to the literary properties of critical essays, we are likely to read them with even less sensitivity than that. As we reread a critical essay, however, or as we read a series of essays in which the same critic treats different texts, we are more likely to recognize those recurring metaphors and controlling verbal structures that typify a particular critic's work. As soon as we recognize a critic's own intellectual interests and rhetorical styles, they will be foregrounded when we read his prose. At that point the critic becomes a writer and the need to attend to psychological effect and motivation is apparent. In arguing that changing our reading habits would change what we feel to be appropriate and necessary to say about critical languages, I am, of course, aware that our present reading habits reinforce (and perhaps grow out of) the disinclination to discuss criticism in more human and literary terms.

My own thinking about the usefulness of psychological and psychoanalytic readings of critical texts has changed over the past few years. I first argued that psychoanalytic categories would prove too reductive to account for complex critical prose. Then I decided that psychoanalysis would be useful in reading critical texts that displayed fantasy material substantially unrelated to the primary texts discussed. In the first case, I had in mind works like Northrop Frye's *Anatomy of Criticism.* Would it be useful, I wondered, when Frye writes that criticism can show that all literature coheres in a single body, to assert that this reconstituted body is the body of the mother? Would it be useful to say of all interpreted texts, all texts reconstructed through critical meditation, that such texts are always the reconstituted mother? I have since decided that such generalizations are useful, that they provide a reductive challenge that can help us to see how critics work to avoid those very recognitions as they write. Sophisticated critical language cannot be dismissed by tracing its psychological motivation or by establishing its connection with primary psychoanalytic metaphors, but its tensions can be illuminated in that way. Just as many critics fear the sentimental and romantic components of their intellection, so too do many critics struggle against the motivational core of their work. The interest of criticism's elaborate verbal strategies can actually be intensified by the very reductive force that psychoanalytic language can exercise on these motivations. Nonetheless, initial reactions to this reductive challenge will not be positive. Indeed, I am reminded of the history of reactions to Kenneth Burke's infamous suggestion that Keats's most well-known line can also be

read "Body is turd, turd body." Burke's later comment on his notion suggests as well how critics often deal with self-knowledge as they write: "Any such bathos," Burke writes, "lurking behind the poem's pathos, is so alien to the formal pretenses of the work, if such indecorous transliterating of the poem's decorum had occurred to Keats, in all likelihood he would have phrased his formula differently, to avoid this turn." This kind of disguise and sublimation is essential to the psychology of criticism, especially as that psychology reflects the profession's consensus about what can and cannot be said in critical writing.

In terms of its object relations, criticism as we have agreed to practice it in America is grounded in a communal sense of how readers may and may not internalize the texts they discuss. In psychoanalytic language, we can say that the standards for object relations in criticism demand a distinction between introjection and incorporation. These would not, of course, be terms many critics would use to describe their enterprise. They do, however, reflect one assumption to which many of us would assent, namely, that criticism is always constituted *as* a relationship, since neither reader nor text can literally be subsumed by the other. (pp. 45-57)

To seek the truth about the psychology of criticism is not to denigrate the field or to risk its losing ground in competition with other fields whose pretenses to objectivity are more secure. In a time when the humanities are notoriously in crisis, perhaps we have more to gain by exploiting the very vulnerability of literary criticism as a mode of inquiry. If criticism is distinguished among the humanities in no other way, it is at least distinguished by the very bulk of its output over the past thirty years. If we can consider this body of discourse—in its very disparate collectivity—as a representative form of human knowledge, then at least it will not appear from the outside as gratuitous accumulation. Yet we need to deal with our own resistance to the project and we cannot do that without beginning to read and write about criticism in such a way as to open discussion of its psychology. When we restore to criticism a sense of the doubt, ambition, and vision that its sentences record, we will not find its human features to be unique or destructive.

The polemical energy of this essay is directed, then, not at the psychology of critics but at the prohibition against discussing their psychology. I would urge toward the work of individual critics not greater aggression but a more meticulous empathy. To enter into a critic's works, attempting to live in that world, eliciting the motivation structured into and compromised by individual sentences, describing the satisfaction and deception in large verbal structures—all this requires the same intimacy we experience with novelists and poets. This seems to me to be the special contribution that psychology and psychoanalysis can now make to the study of criticism. Does criticism have a psychology? Yes. Let this be thought, let it be written. (pp. 59-60)

Cary Nelson, "The Psychology of Criticism, or What Can Be Said," in Psychoanalysis and the Question of the Text, *edited by Geoffrey H. Hartman, The Johns Hopkins University Press, 1978, pp. 45-61.*

PSYCHOANALYSIS AS LITERATURE/LITERATURE AS PSYCHOANALYSIS

Jeffrey Berman

[*In the following excerpt from the introduction to his study* The Talking Cure: Literary Representations of Psychoanalysis, *Berman examines the portrayal of the psychoanalytic process in Freud's case studies and in works of fiction.*]

It was Bertha Pappenheim, Josef Breuer's celebrated "Fräulein Anna O." of *Studies on Hysteria* (1893-1895), who coined the term "talking cure" to describe the magical power of language to relieve mental suffering. Described by her physician as possessing unusual poetic and imaginative gifts, the 21-year old woman entered therapy in 1880 shortly after falling ill. During the following months she developed severe hysterical symptoms that today might be diagnosed as schizophrenia: frightening hallucinations of black snakes, near-total physical paralysis of arms and legs, and major disturbances of speech and sight. Breuer was mystified by her mad jumble of syntax, fusion of four or five languages, and prolonged silences. Her personality alternated between two contrasting states of consciousness, a normal but melancholy state in which she recognized her surroundings, and an hallucinatory state in which she became abusive and "naughty." Intrigued by the case, Breuer began visiting his patient regularly and spending more and more time with her. Guessing that he had somehow offended her at one point—he never tells us why or how—the physician obliged the patient to talk about her feelings toward him. Soon her verbal inhibitions inexplicably began to disappear, along with a remission of her other symptoms. The situation worsened, however, after the death of her beloved father, whom she had been nursing during his convalescence.

Around this time, Breuer noticed a curious phenomenon. While she was in an altered personality state, she would mutter a few words to herself that seemed to be related to her bizarre illness. Suspecting that her language held a clue to her disease, Breuer hypnotized her and requested the patient to relate the hallucinations she had experienced during the day. After the narration, she would wake up with a calm and cheerful disposition. Sometimes she invented sad stories the starting point of which resembled her own situation—a girl or young woman anxiously sitting by a sickbed. If for any reason she was unable to narrate these stories to Breuer during the evening hypnosis, she would fail to achieve therapeutic relief, and the next day she was compelled to tell him two stories before the talking cure took effect. This "chimney-sweeping," as she jokingly referred to the novel treatment, allowed her to use the products of her imagination—art—to sweep clean the terrifying demons of her life.

It is an intriguing accident of history that the first patient of psychoanalysis was also a storyteller. And the motive that prompted her to enter therapy, escape from imaginative terrors, was also the impulse behind her fiction. It was as if the creative and therapeutic process were inseparably joined. Yet, the relief she experienced from the talking cure lasted only a couple of days, after which she would once again grow moody and irritable. Sometimes she re-

Bertha Pappenheim, the "founding patient" of psychoanalysis, who is known in case history documents as "Anna O."

fused to talk at all. Breuer, who was both her physician and audience, then had to search for the right formula to unlock her stories, as if the key to her art was the only escape from a baffling illness. Like Kafka's Hunger Artist, whose performances depended upon the entertainer's starvation, Anna O. created stories from the depths of suffering. Her artistic gifts to Breuer affirmed both the destructive and creative uses of the imagination. Without a sympathetic audience, the artist could not create nor the patient improve. Unfortunately, Bertha Pappenheim never wrote about her experiences with Breuer, and so we do not have an account of therapy written from the point of view of the patient who achieved such prominence in the psychoanalytic movement. But we do have Breuer's account of the case history, supplemented by various comments Freud later made about his former collaborator's treatment of Anna O. The emerging story is filled with the ironies and contradictions that inevitably characterize most fictional and nonfictional accounts of psychological breakdown and recovery—the literature of the talking cure. (pp. 1-2)

To this day, the veil of obscurity surrounds not only the final stage of Breuer's treatment of Anna O. but virtually all accounts of the talking cure. The difficulty of writing a psychiatric case study may be seen in the fact that Freud published only five major case histories (excluding the brief sketches in *Studies on Hysteria*), dating from 1905 through 1918. They are, in the order of publication: *Fragment of an Analysis of a Case of Hysteria* ("Dora") in 1905, *Analysis of a Phobia in a Five-Year-Old Boy* ("Little Hans") in 1909, *Notes Upon a Case of Obsessional Neurosis* ("The Rat Man") also in 1909, *Psycho-Analytic Notes on an Autobiographical Account of a Case of Paranoia* (Schreber) in 1911, and *From the History of an Infantile Neurosis* ("The Wolf Man") in 1918. Two of the case histories are based on patients Freud either did not see or treated indirectly. The case of Schreber was based on an autobiographical memoir Freud came across, while the study of Little Hans was written from the notes supplied by the boy's father, a former patient of the psychoanalyst. Freud's case studies have become enduring psychiatric and literary classics, but they also reveal the paradigmatic difficulties of the genre. The problems fall under three main categories: medical confidentiality; belief; and the clinical phenomena of transference, countertransference, and resistance. Freud's psychiatric case studies offer an insight into the predictable and unpredictable problems that have subsequently vexed the novelists and playwrights writing about the talking cure.

Although psychiatric case studies often read like fiction, they are based upon actual patients. This obviously poses a major problem for the author, who must strike a compromise between truth and disguise. How much biographical information can the analyst reveal without disclosing the patient's identity? In *Studies on Hysteria,* Breuer and Freud conceded the constraints under which they were writing. It would have been a grave breach of confidence, they admitted, to publish material touching upon their patients' intimate lives. Consequently, the authors deleted some of the most important observations. Breuer's deliberate suppression of crucial information in "Fräulein Anna O." weakened both its literary richness and scientific credibility. One need not accept Robert Langs's extreme conclusion that the psychotherapeutic movement has its roots in complicity, lies, and evasions to agree that psychiatric case study literature has failed to disclose significant details of the therapeutic process.

Freud's fullest account of the problem of confidentiality appears in *Dora.* Conceding that the vagueness of information in *Studies on Hysteria* deprived researchers of the opportunity to test the authors' theory of hysteria, Freud vows to err in the opposite direction. "Whereas before I was accused of giving *no* information about my patients, now I shall be accused of giving information about my patients which ought not to be given." Obliquely hinting at Breuer's timidity, Freud insists on the physician's "duty" to publish all the facts about hysterical illness. Anything less than complete disclosure, he says, is "disgraceful cowardice." He acknowledges, though, that the complete discussion of a case of hysteria is bound to result in the betrayal of the patient's identity. To safeguard Dora's privacy, Freud makes several fictional changes, such as altering her name, place of residence, and other external details. In addition, he delayed publication of the case study for four years until he was convinced she would not accidentally come across the work. Nevertheless, Freud admits she would be upset if a copy of the case study fell into her hands. Freud returns to the subject of confidentiality in the introductory remarks of the *Rat Man,* telling us that he cannot give a complete history of treatment because that would compromise the patient's identity. "The im-

portunate interest of a capital city, focussed with particular attention upon my medical activities, forbids my giving a faithful picture of the case." He concedes, however, that deliberate fabrications in a case study are often useless and objectionable. If the distortions are slight, they are ineffective; if they are major, they destroy the intelligibility of the material. His conclusion is that it is easier to divulge the patient's most intimate thoughts (which usually do not cast light on his identity anyway) than to convey biographical facts.

But ambiguities over confidentiality still exist. Must the patient grant the analyst permission to write about his or her life? Medical ethics are unclear about this. Breuer did not have Bertha Pappenheim's permission to publish the precedent-setting "Fräulein Anna O." Despite his efforts to disguise her life, certain details in the case history, such as the date of her father's death and the beginning of therapy, made it possible for readers to infer her identity. Moreover, the Pappenheim family was prominent in Vienna, and many people knew about the young woman's breakdown and prolonged treatment by the eminent Breuer. Given the highly sensitive material found in a psychiatric case study, the author's freedom of expression is limited by confidentiality, ethics, and discretion.

Freud secured permission from the Rat Man, the Wolf Man, and Little Hans's father, but not from Dora. In 1924, he mentions that when Dora visited another analyst in that year and confided that she had been treated by Freud many years earlier, the well-informed colleague immediately recognized her as the Dora of the famous case study. Nor did Freud have Schreber's permission to publish a case history of the former judge's *Memoirs of a Nerve Patient,* which appeared in 1903. Though Freud never treated him, there were still medical and legal uncertainties concerning the propriety of the publication of the book. In his *Memoirs,* Schreber declares his intention to publish the work even if his psychiatrist, Dr. Flechsig of Leipzig, brought a legal suit against him, presumably for defamation of character. "I trust," Schreber says, "that even in the case of Geheimrat Prof. Dr. Flechsig any personal susceptibilities that he may feel will be outweighed by a scientific interest in the subject-matter of my memoirs." Freud cites this passage and urges upon Schreber the same considerations the jurist requested of Flechsig. Freud did not know whether Schreber was still alive in 1911 when he was writing the case study (as it turned out, Schreber died a few months after Freud's monograph was published); but the analyst strongly believed that scientific knowledge took priority over personal issues.

The problem of confidentiality exists even when the author of a psychiatric case study is the patient. Just as the psychiatrist worries about preserving the patient's confidentiality, so does the patient feel obliged to respect the analyst's privacy and professional reputation. Freud's analysts in training, for instance, remained deferential toward him in their accounts of their experiences. Ironically, despite Freud's sallies into psycho-biography—a genre he created in his book on Leonardo da Vinci (1910)—he was uncompromising about his personal life, which he jealously guarded. Displeased by Fritz Wittels' biography of him, Freud expressed the opinion in a sternly worded letter that the biographer should wait until his "subject is dead, when he cannot do anything about it and fortunately no longer cares." When it came to his own life, then, Freud valued privacy over the dissemination of knowledge. The author of a psychiatric case study requires even more tact than the biographer. It is difficult for a patient to write openly and truthfully when he knows that other participants in the story will read the narration. Since psychological illness usually involves ambivalent feelings toward the closest members of one's family, the publication of a case history is bound to reopen painful family wounds. Both the analyst and his patient, then, must resort to fictional disguises, omissions, and evasions to protect the living protagonists and antagonists of the story. The question of sufficient disguise, moreover, may become problematic.

Another problem Freud confronted was over the nature of the psychiatric case study. Is it primarily a scientific treatise, designed to be read by other medical researchers, or a literary endeavor, written for a broader audience? The question reflects a fascinating division in Freud's character. He could never reconcile his scientific training with the artistic and philosophical elements of his personality. Nowhere is this conflict more evident than in his role as storyteller in the case studies. "It still strikes me myself as strange," he writes in *Studies on Hysteria,* "that the case histories I write should read like short stories and that, as one might say, they lack the serious stamp of science." Yet Freud is disingenuous here, attributing the literary quality of the case studies to the nature of the material rather than to his artistic temperament. To describe a patient's psychiatric disorder, he adds, it is necessary to imitate the imaginative writer, who intuitively knows how to capture the workings of the mind. Unfortunately, few psychiatrists have needed to worry about the literary quality of their case studies, and it is strange to hear Freud professing horror at the thought that some readers will approach his case studies with anything other than scientific curiosity. "I am aware that—in this city, at least—there are many physicians who (revolting though it may seem) choose to read a case history of this kind not as a contribution to the psychopathology of the neuroses, but as a *roman â clef* designed for their private delectation." In rejecting "impure" motives for reading the psychiatric case study, Freud affirms the high seriousness of science. Yet he seems unduly embarrassed by the high seriousness of art—the aesthetic pleasure of reading and the sympathetic involvement with characters not terribly unlike ourselves. Freud's case studies are filled with the stuff of high drama: protracted family wars, twisted love affairs, unfulfilled hopes, broken promises, insoluble moral dilemmas. Few creative stories contain the involuted plots, demonic characterization, and racy dialogue of the *Rat Man* or the *Wolf Man*—their names alone seize our imagination and take their place among the world's enduring literature. The self-inflicted tortures of Freud's patients and their nightmarish settings make the case studies read like Gothic fiction. Appropriately, when Freud's name was mentioned for the Nobel Prize, it was more often for literature than for medicine.

It was not enough, however, for Freud to stimulate a reader's curiosity or fulfill his desire for aesthetic pleasure. Freud sought scientific truth, not artistic beauty (he took offense when Havelock Ellis maintained he was not a scientist but an artist), and he was vexed by the problem of converting intellectual skepticism into belief. How does the author of a psychiatric case study suspend the reader's

disbelief? It is made difficult because psychoanalysis does not allow an audience to observe directly the unfolding drama of a patient's story. The talking cure remains enshrouded in mystery. "You cannot be present as an audience at a psychoanalytic treatment," Freud informs his audience of medical students in the *Introductory Lectures;* "You can only be told about it; and, in the strictest sense of the word, it is only by hearsay that you will get to know psychoanalysis." Yet hearsay is notoriously unreliable, as Freud well knew. Through the power of language the storyteller succeeds in spinning his web, and Freud never underestimated the ancient magical power of words to make one person blissfully happy and to drive another person to despair. Both the psychoanalyst and storyteller succeed or fail through their language. Freud remained pessimistic, though, about the power of language alone to create conviction in the disinterested reader, the "benevolent skeptic," as he wished his audience to be. In both *Little Hans* and the *Wolf Man* he remarks on the regrettable fact that no written account of psychotherapy can create the conviction achieved only through the actual experience of analysis. This, of course, creates a tautology. Why publish a case study if it cannot persuade the reader? The convert to psychoanalysis requires no further proof, while the cynic remains unconvinced. Is Freud's admission merely a defense against failure or an accurate statement about the unique validation required for psychoanalytic belief?

This question brings us to the unconscious projective tendencies unleashed by psychoanalysis and the interactional nature of the patient-analyst relationship. Any account of the talking cure must include the phenomenon of transference, one of the most central but misunderstood issues in therapy. Freud insisted that the recognition of transference is what distinguishes psychoanalysis from other forms of psychotherapy, including Breucr's early cathartic method, which sought symptom relief rather than an understanding of the underlying causes of mental illness. The patient sees in the analyst, Freud writes in *An Outline of Psycho-Analysis,* "the return, the reincarnation, of some important figure out of his childhood or past, and consequently transfers on to him feelings and reactions which undoubtedly applied to this prototype." The psychic mechanism behind transference is projection, in which a perception, fear, or drive is first denied and then displaced upon another person or object. Transference is usually ambivalent (a word coined by Freud's contemporary, the Swiss psychiatrist Eugene Bleuler), consisting of positive (affectionate) and negative (hostile) feelings toward the analyst, who generally occupies the role of a parental surrogate. Freud learned from experience that transference is a factor of undreamed-of importance, a source of grave danger and an instrument of irreplaceable value. The patient has both a real and an unreal or symbolic relationship to the analyst; the unreal relationship must be explored and traced back to its distant roots. The analyst in turn must guard against the tendency toward countertransference, which would hopelessly entrap the patient in the analyst's own confusion.

The narrative implications of transference and countertransference are far reaching. Both participants in therapy, the analyst and the patient, influence what is observed and felt. The observer's point of view always influences what is observed—a basic truth psychoanalysts have not easily conceded. The analyst's interpretation, for example, may be perceived as intrusive or aggressive and thus have undesirable consequences for the patient. The most important moments in therapy may remain unverbalized or concealed in an ambiguous silence. Freud himself remained contradictory on the analyst's proper stance, and many of his metaphors are profoundly misleading. In "Recommendations to Physicians Practicing Psycho-Analysis" (1912) he equates the analyst with the surgeon, "who puts aside all his feelings, even his human sympathy, and concentrates his mental forces on the single aim of performing the operation as skillfully as possible." He then uses an even more impersonal analogy, comparing the analyst to a telephone receiver, converting sound waves into electric oscillations. Not only are these bad analogies, evoking a mechanistic image of the analyst, Freud returns to them in his writings, as if he could not stress too strongly the analyst's objectivity and detachment. "The doctor should be opaque to his patients and, like a mirror, should show them nothing but what is shown to him." This is the same Freud whose discovery of unconscious projective mechanisms shattered the myth of human objectivity and its literary equivalent, the "ideal" reader.

Although many analysts still adhere to the blank-mirror image, more and more therapists are agreeing with Heinz Kohut's position that the analyst's introspective, empathic stance defines the psychological field. Earlier, Erik Erikson pointed out that Freud's discovery of transference leads to the conclusion that psychological investigation is always accompanied by a degree of irrational involvement on the part of the observer. Freud's case studies demonstrate how transference and countertransference play a crucial role both in psychotherapy and in the narrations of the talking cure. Many of Freud's seemingly innocuous comments had unexpected literary and psychological implications. Breuer was certainly not alone in being entrapped in the emotional interlockings of psychoanalysis. (pp. 5-11)

The case histories of Dora, the Rat Man, and the Wolf Man reveal transference and countertransference complexities that escaped Freud's attention. These complexities add a highly personal element to psychoanalysis, making it as much an art as a science, and requiring a narrative point of view that encompasses the real and symbolic figures in the analyst's office. Freud refers to transference as the "battleground" on which the patient's illness is exposed, fought, and won. But the battleground is usually omitted from psychiatric case studies and literary accounts of psychological breakdown and recovery. In fact, Freud rarely discussed countertransference, believing that publication on this subject would seriously impair his effectiveness with patients familiar with psychoanalytic writings. To know too much about the analyst's personality, Freud feared, would deflect attention from the proper subject of psychoanalysis, the patient. He may have been right, but there was also a defensive element in Freud's silence. He had, after all, revealed an enormous amount of autobiographical material in *The Interpretation of Dreams*. In the decoding of his own dreams he exposed himself to relentless public scrutiny—demonstrated by the numerous biographies of Freud and book-length studies of his dreams. There were times he must have felt more like a confessional poet than a detached scientist. Many of the dreams he narrated, such as Irma's injection and the botanical garden, dramatize Freud's grandiose ambitions,

bitter frustrations over lack of success, and self-justifications. There were limits, though, to his willingness to open up his life to the reading public. None of his later books, including the deceptively entitled *An Autobiographical Study* (1925), repeats the candid self-analysis of the great dream book. (pp. 17-18)

Transference and countertransference undercut the traditional distinction between the outer and inner world, objectivity and subjectivity. The external world can be seen only through the internal world, but this perception inevitably alters the object in the mind's eye. Building upon the theory of the British analyst D. W. Winnicott, psychoanalytic literary critics have defined the text as a "potential space" or a "transitional object," in which there is an active interplay between objectivity and subjectivity, the external world of objects and internal world of readers. The interactional nature of the patient-analyst relationship is analogous in some ways to the reader's reconstruction of the text in the literary process. The object is incorporated and transformed into a new creation consistent with the reader's unique identity theme. The difference is that the therapeutic process involves a double act of reading: the patient attempts to read the analyst as if he were a text ("reading" his mind, "interpreting" his motives, "locating" his authorial point of view), just as the analyst is seeking to decipher the patient's text. In one of the few articles published in a literary journal on the subject, Arthur Marotti has indicated how countertransference responses occur in literature, "especially in the critical interpreter who not only reacts immediately to literary works but also makes it his business to react to his reactions" ["Countertransference, the Communication Process, and the Dimensions of Psychoanalytic Criticism," *Critical Inquiry* 4, No. 3, (Spring 1978)]. Psychoanalytic thinkers have been struck by the connection between Heisenberg's principle of indeterminacy and Freud's theory of transference. Just as the physicist's observations of subatomic particles alter the data, so does the analyst's presence influence the patient's responses. To date, literary critics have not adequately explored the role of transference and countertransference in fictional accounts of the talking cure.

It is surprising that critics have not considered transference to any extent in light of the ubiquitous presence of the psychoanalyst in literature. Few twentieth-century figures have evoked more fascination than the mental healer, whose image "extends from the analyst's couch and from the meeting halls of modern faith healers and miracle men to the shrines of worship of ancient Greece and Judea, to the thatched-roof huts of the primitive shaman or witch doctor" [Jay Ehrenwald, *The History of Psychotherapy*]. For many people, the analyst has replaced the priest as the healer of the diseased spirit or lost soul, though along with this overestimation comes inevitable hostility. One analyst has compared the mythic structure of psychoanalysis to the "Virgil-leading-Dante" pattern, in which the heroic introspective journey takes place not after death but in the shadowy dream world of the unconscious self. The rich mythic symbolism of psychoanalysis undoubtedly owes its existence to Freud's imagination, which was stirred by the great mythic figures of antiquity. Despite his aversion to publicity and his unusually quiet personal life, he remained convinced of his mission as destroyer of the world's peace. He conceived of himself as Prometheus stealing fire from the gods, Faust selling his soul to the devil in exchange for knowledge and power, Moses demonstrating superhuman restraint amidst betrayal and dissension. He chose as the motto for *The Interpretation of Dreams* a quotation from *The Aeneid: "Flectere si nequeo superos, Acheronta movebo"* ("If I cannot bend the Higher Powers, I will move the Infernal Regions").

Indeed, Freud's epigraph accurately foreshadows the antithetical image of the psychoanalyst in literature. Liberator and enslaver, healer and quack, ego ideal and repressive superego, the analyst serves as the object of intense ambivalence. Alternately worshiped and reviled, deified and damned, he evokes simultaneously the artist's fascination and contempt. The difference between the therapist and the rapist, Vladimir Nabokov never lets his readers forget, is a matter of spacing. Of the hundreds of fictional psychoanalysts, nearly all have been rendered into stereotypes. There are the lecherous analysts, such as Palmer Anderson in Iris Murdoch's *A Severed Head* and Adrian Goodlove in Erica Jong's *Fear of Flying,* eager to entice their attractive patients to bed; the deeply neurotic and conflicted psychiatrists, like Martin Dysart in Peter Shaffer's *Equus,* who regard their professional work as equivalent to emasculation; and the fraudulent therapists, such as Dr. Tamkin in Saul Bellow's *Seize the Day* and the sinister doctor who practices mythotherapy in John Barth's *The End of the Road.* The therapist usually dispenses bad prescriptions, smug morality, and dangerous advice. Sir William Bradshaw, the psychiatrist in Virginia Woolf's *Mrs. Dalloway,* embodies the artist's condemnation of the therapist. "Worshipping proportion, Sir William not only prospered himself but made England prosper, secluded her lunatics, forbade childbirth, penalised despair, made it impossible for the unfit to propagate their views until they, too, shared his sense of proportion. . . . "

The bitterness in Woolf's tone reflects the dominant attitude among writers, who regard psychotherapy as a threat to free will, creativity, spiritual belief, and individuality. The "pecking party" in Ken Kesey's *One Flew Over the Cuckoo's Nest,* "release games" performed under the supervision of the diabolical Doktor Amalia von Wytwyl in Nabokov's *Bend Sinister,* and "Ludovico's Technique" in Anthony Burgess' *A Clockwork Orange* all equate psychotherapy with brutal mind control. Not all therapists, of course, are treated with unmirthful contempt. Philip Bummidge ("Bummy"), the comic-turned-psychoanalyst hero of Bellow's zany play *The Last Analysis,* is not only a spoof of Freudianism but a parody of the self-help books that proliferated in the 1960s and 1970s and the language of psychobabble that has infected our contemporary culture. If, as Freud argues in *Jokes and Their Relation to the Unconscious,* caricatures represent the degradation of persons who command respect, even the Viennese analyst would have been startled by the unrelenting artistic debasement of his own profession. Only a handful of sympathetic and authentic analysts have been portrayed in literature; significantly, most of them have been women, such as Dr. Johanna von Haller in Robertson Davies' *The Manticore.* The majority of fictional analysts remain stereotypes, however, and (to paraphrase Mark Twain) have as much relation to genuine psychotherapists as the lightning bug has to lightning.

The nicknames of three representative analysts in [literature] . . . evoke the spectrum of attitudes toward psychotherapy, ranging from total rejection, through conditional acceptance, to enthusiastic support. Sir Harcourt-Reilly, the mysterious "Uninvited Guest" in T. S. Eliot's *The Cocktail Party* (1950), offers unorthodox clinical advice to his spiritually lost patients. A priest disguised as a psychiatrist, Eliot's hero betrays unmistakable hostility toward therapy as he guides Celia Coplestone to an ecstatic religious crucifixion. The play dramatizes the conflict between secular and spiritual approaches to mental suffering, leaving little doubt in the end about Eliot's mistrust of psychiatry. For Eliot, psychiatry remains an uninvited guest whose point of view is inimical to Christian salvation. He takes the same position toward psychological approaches to literature, a violation of the purity of the text. Mrs. Marks, "Mother Sugar" in Doris Lessing's *The Golden Notebook* (1962), is the Jungian psychoanalyst who helps Anna Wulf overcome a severe case of writer's block. Although Lessing treats psychoanalysis more sympathetically in *The Golden Notebook* than in *The Four-Gated City* (1969), Mother Sugar seems more interested in an arcane mythology than in understanding her patient's personal history. Furthermore, she dispenses sugar-coated myths that seem strikingly irrelevant to a contemporary society in which women are struggling for political and sexual freedom. Dr. Clara Fried, "Dr. Furii" in Joanne Greenberg's *I Never Promised You a Rose Garden* (1964), is the magical fairy godmother whose psychiatric power appears as purgatorial or volcanic fire to the schizophrenic Deborah Blau. Despite the novelist's efforts to avoid mythologizing the fictional analyst, we see an idealized portrait, with little hint that the main battleground in psychoanalysis lies in the transference relationship.

Apart from focusing on the relationship between the patient and analyst and the value of psychotherapy, these three literary works have another important element in common. In each case the writer suffered a psychological breakdown, entered psychotherapy, and later wrote an account of the talking cure in which the fictional analyst was loosely or closely based on the artist's actual therapist. Sir Harcourt-Reilly is roughly modeled on Dr. Roger Vittoz, the Swiss psychiatrist who treated Eliot during his nervous breakdown in the early 1920s, when he was writing *The Waste Land.* Mrs. Marks owes her origin to the Jungian analyst who treated Doris Lessing in the 1950s. And Dr. Fried is closely based on the distinguished American psychoanalyst Dr. Frieda Fromm-Reichmann, who successfully treated Joanne Greenberg at Chestnut Lodge in Maryland. Despite fundamental differences in genre, literary technique, clinical authenticity, and point of view, these three works dramatize protagonists who fall ill, seek professional help, and work out individual solutions to psychic conflict. The type of psychotherapy the characters receive varies radically from work to work, as do the characters' fates at the close of the book.

This does not imply that the autobiographical element necessarily predominates in these works, or that they are literal depictions of the authors' spiritual or psychological odysseys. The degree of autobiographical truth and clinical authenticity varies from story to story, as does the degree of literary success. Sometimes the character's fate at the end of a story is the opposite of the artist's in real life, thus confounding any one-to-one relationship between author and fictional projection. Additionally, although literary representations of mental illness are often based on personal experiences, the artist invokes a literary tradition which separates art from life. In *Madness in Literature,* Lillian Feder observes that while the madman of literature may be to some extent modeled on an actual character, the differences are at least as important as the similarities. The fictional character "is rooted in a mythical or literary tradition in which distortion is a generally accepted mode of expression; furthermore, the inherent aesthetic order by which his existence is limited also gives his madness intrinsic value and meaning." It is admittedly risky, Feder cautions, to consider literary works as psychological autobiographies or to diagnose the psychic ills of fictive madmen. Without losing sight of these distinctions, we may note, as Feder does, that literary characters often reveal the artist's unconscious mental processes, in particular, attitudes toward psychological health and illness. A study of literary accounts of the talking cure can reveal much about the fascinating relationship between the creative and therapeutic process, and the crossfertilization of literature and psychoanalysis. (pp. 21-5)

[The] popular conception of psychotherapy has changed from its beginnings in the late nineteenth century. "The Yellow Wallpaper" (1892) is a chilling fictionalized account of Charlotte Perkins Gilman's breakdown in the 1880s and her harrowing experience with S. Weir Mitchell, the foremost American neurologist of his time and the originator of the well-known "rest cure." At the end of "The Yellow Wallpaper" the first-person narrator goes mad—unlike the author, who recovered from her devastating breakdown and went on to become a prolific author whose stories and outspoken feminist writings alerted other would-be patients to the evils of the Mitchell rest cure. F. Scott Fitzgerald acquired the clinical material for *Tender Is the Night* (1934) partly from his readings on psychiatry and also from his marriage to Zelda, whose incurable schizophrenia and repeated hospitalizations served as the background material for Nicole Warren. But Fitzgerald's psychiatrist-hero, Dr. Dick Diver, also embodies the novelist's own fears of dissipation and loss of creativity, themes he later wrote about in the autobiographical *The Crack-Up* (published posthumously in 1945).

The Bell Jar (1963) is Sylvia Plath's classic account of depression, suicidal breakdown, and electroshock therapy. The loving female psychiatrist who treats Esther Greenwood, Dr. Nolan, is based upon Plath's actual psychiatrist at McLean Hospital in Massachusetts, Dr. Ruth Beuscher. The recent publication of Plath's journals confirms the overwhelming importance of psychoanalysis to her life and art. Indeed, Plath's secret return to analysis in the late 1950s was partly responsible for the startling burst of creativity in her late poems. And the celebrated Dr. Otto-Spielvogel of *Portnoy's Complaint* (1969) and *My Life as a Man* (1974) is modeled on the psychoanalyst who treated Philip Roth for many years, Dr. Hans Kleinschmidt. Roth writes with a clinical expertise few creative writers can equal and, while his feelings toward psychoanalysis are typically equivocal, the therapeutic setting has given rise to many of his finest and most authentic stories. The remaining two creative writers, Vladimir Nabokov and D. M. Thomas, also figure prominently into any discussion of literary representations of psychoanalysis, though neither writer has undergone analysis. The lifelong enemy of the "Viennese witch doctor," Nabokov remains the supreme parodist of the psychiatric case study. On nearly every page of *Lolita* (1955), Humbert mocks the psychoanalytic approach to life and art; it is not Quilty who constitutes Humbert's secret adversary but Freud, whom the novelist obsessively slays in book after book. By contrast, Thomas' *The White Hotel* (1981) is an astonishing recreation of the Freudian case study, a novel that at once reconstructs the historical Freud and at the same time transcends purely psychological approaches to human suffering.

It seems particularly appropriate to begin and end a study of fictional accounts of psychotherapy with "The Yellow Wallpaper" and *The White Hotel,* respectively. Gilman was an exact contemporary of Bertha Pappenheim, and the two women led strikingly similar lives. Born a year apart, they suffered crippling breakdowns at the same time, were treated by eminent male physicians who failed them, and later became ardent feminists. . . . Gilman was one of the sharpest critics of Freud, who had, ironically—and unpredictably—warmly praised the Mitchell rest cure. Published three years before *Studies on Hysteria,* "The Yellow Wallpaper" brilliantly captures a young woman's irreversible descent into madness. Narrated with extraordinary restraint and clinical detachment, it succeeds where Breuer's "Fräulein Anna O." fails in dramatizing the oppressive social, political, and sexual forces responsible for the heroine's fatal entrapment in her Victorian ancestral house. And the stunning conclusion of Gilman's short story makes the ending of Breuer's medical treatise seem like a fairy tale, utterly divorced from reality. *The White Hotel* appeared exactly 100 years after Breuer's treatment of Anna O. In fact, the "Frau Anna G." section of Thomas' novel, written in the form of a Freudian case study, abounds in quotations from *Studies on Hysteria* and Freud's other writings, including his technical papers and massive correspondence. No novel better illustrates the symbiotic relationship between literature and psychoanalysis than *The White Hotel.* It is certainly not the last novel to employ an analytic apparatus to explore the depths of the human psyche, but it is hard to imagine a more profound example of the intricate art of those who practice Freud's "impossible profession." Thomas refers to the genuine Freudian case studies as "masterly works of literature"; in *The White Hotel* he has himself created one of the most remarkable novels in years.

As a genre, the literature involving psychiatric case studies raises questions that go beyond the territory of literary criticism: the definition of psychological health and illness, the relationship between suffering and creativity, adaptive versus pathological solutions to psychic conflict. Freud's equation of the artist with the neurotic has rightly angered writers. Psychoanalysts continue to make unproven assertions of the artist's "narcissism," thus further provoking the writer's counterattack. Freud's theory of the neurotic artist not only singles out one class of people but lumps disparate individuals into the same group. It seems true, however, that certain individuals from widely differing backgrounds and occupations are capable of converting neurotic suffering into creativity. George Pickering has coined the term "creative malady" to describe the role of illness in otherwise dissimilar figures as Charles Darwin, Florence Nightingale, Mary Baker Eddy, Marcel Proust, Elizabeth Barrett Browning, and Freud. "The illness was an essential part of the act of creation rather than a device to enable that act to take place." In many cases, the creative work and illness have a common source in mental torment. Psychological illness may promote scientific and artistic creativity by encouraging adaptive and integrative solutions to inner conflict. There are many reasons to write about mental breakdown, including the desire to exorcise old demons and ward off new ones. This does not imply, of course, that writing about breakdown guarantees protection against future illness, or that madness and creativity are interrelated, as many ancient (Plato) and contemporary (R. D. Laing) thinkers claim. [Plath] . . . is an example of a writer for whom "dying is an art"—and whose art could not prevent her from prematurely dying.

Ironically, Freud suffered no less than many writers whose breakdowns receive greater public attention. His letters insist on the link between suffering and creativity. It is arguable that the first patient of psychoanalysis was not Bertha Pappenheim but Freud himself. (pp. 25-7)

Freud's neurotic symptoms do not invalidate his psychological theories any more than a writer's breakdown invalidates (or conversely, authenticates) his or her literary achievements. It would be unnecessary to say this were it not for the tendency of clinicians to perpetuate Freud's myth of the neurotic artist—and to remain silent about the neurotic psychoanalyst. From the beginning of his career, Freud recognized that health and illness are highly subjective words. One of the themes of *The Interpretation of Dreams* is that neurotic characteristics appear in healthy people. "Psycho-analytic research finds no fundamental, but only quantitative, distinctions between normal and neurotic life; and indeed the analysis of dreams, in which repressed complexes are operative alike in the healthy and the sick, shows a complete identity both in their mechanisms and in their symbolism." He repeats this point in *Little Hans,* saying that no sharp line can be drawn between normal and neurotic people. Individuals are constantly passing from the group of healthy people to that of the sick, while a smaller number make the journey in the opposite direction. And in "Analysis Terminable and Interminable," one of Freud's last essays, he asserts that normalcy is a fiction. "Every normal person, in fact, is only normal on the average."

If normalcy is a fiction, who is better able to explore the workings of the mind than the fiction writer? Not only did Freud generously pay tribute to the poets and playwrights who long ago discovered the unconscious self, he viewed the creative writer as the psychoanalyst's natural ally. Nowhere is he more eloquent in his praise for literature than in "Delusions and Dreams in Jensen's *Gradiva*" (1907), his first extended published analysis of a literary work. He ingeniously demonstrates that in *Gradiva* the nineteenth-century North German novelist has presented a powerful and unerring psychiatric case study of a young man's delusional love for a woman who died during the destruction of Pompeii in the year 79. Rejecting the belief that writers should leave the description of pathological states to physicians, Freud insists that "no truly creative writer has ever obeyed this injunction." The analysis of the human mind is the creative writer's domain, Freud says, and from time immemorial the artist has been the precursor to the scientist. Creative writers are valuable allies and their evidence is to be prized highly, "for they are apt to know a whole host of things between heaven and earth of which

our philosophy has not yet let us dream." The allusion to *Hamlet* reminds us that Freud's most famous discovery, the Oedipus complex, was first revealed in a letter in which, in the same breath he postulates the idea of a son's love of the mother and jealousy of the father, he applies the insight to the plays of Sophocles and Shakespeare. The birth of psychoanalysis, then, is inseparable from the birth of psychoanalytic literary criticism; for all of their differences, the analyst and artist look to each other for confirmation. Freud's conclusion in his essay on Jensen's *Gradiva* is that the "creative writer cannot evade the psychiatrist nor the psychiatrist the creative writer, and the poetic treatment of a psychiatric theme can turn out to be correct without any sacrifice of its beauty."

Elsewhere, it is true, Freud retreated from this position, and some of his statements are distinctly patronizing to the artist. In "Psychopathic Characters on the Stage," written a year or two before "Jensen's *Gradiva*," he frets over "sick art," fearing that the inept treatment of mental illness in literature may actually increase neurotic suffering. He implies that pathological characters should remain on the analytic couch, not on the theatre stage. (Outraged readers of "The Yellow Wallpaper" had the same reaction). He even seems ready to dismiss Hamlet as diseased. Freud's disturbing conclusion is that "If we are faced by an unfamiliar and fully established neurosis, we shall be inclined to send for the doctor (just as we do in real life) and pronounce the character inadmissible to the stage." Despite this contradiction, however, Freud envisioned the creative writer and analyst as collaborators, and he predicted a happy marriage between fiction and the psychiatric arts.

Thomas Mann also believed that the creative writer and the psychoanalyst are particularly well suited to explore the mysterious recesses of the mind. His observation about Hans Castorp in *The Magic Mountain* applies to all the writers in the following chapters, who regard illness not as an end in itself but as a means toward a higher goal. "What he comes to understand is that one must go through the deep experience of sickness and death to arrive at a higher sanity and health; in just the same way that one must have a knowledge of sin in order to find redemption." Disease is thus a necessary precondition to knowledge and health. To the extent that the creative writer succeeds in portraying the fluctuating borders between normal and abnormal states of mind, the artist may even be considered a healer. This is close to Edmund Wilson's view of the artist in his influential essay "Philoctetes: The Wound and the Bow." Wilson interprets Sophocles' play as a parable of human character and the paradoxical fusion of sickness and health within the artist. Wilson regards the artist as both "the victim of a malodorous disease which renders him abhorrent to society" and the "master of a superhuman art which everybody has to respect and which the normal man finds he needs." Like Mann, Wilson affirms the idea that "genius and disease, like strength and mutilation, may be inextricably bound up together." To write about illness in an illuminating and aesthetically pleasing manner is to transmute suffering into higher creativity. There are, of course, numerous qualifications to this view of art. The vast majority of people who suffer psychological breakdowns do not eventually write about their experiences. Suffering is rarely ennobling. Moreover, only a small number of literary narrations of the talking cure are sufficiently complex to warrant rereading.

Nevertheless, the creative writers who have experienced mental illness and undergone psychotherapy are often in a unique position to arrive at higher sanity and health. The catalyst for Mann's initiation into knowledge was, not surprisingly, Freud. In the Apollonian essay "Freud's Position in the History of Modern Thought," published in 1933 in T. S. Eliot's *The Criterion,* Mann argues that psychoanalysis has ceased to be merely a therapeutic movement and instead grown into a world view. In light of the catastrophic world events Mann could not foresee, and the gradual decline of psychoanalysis because of its failure to live up to the promises of its early enthusiasts, the novelist's optimism seem excessive. Yet Mann's affirmation of the ideal to which psychoanalysis remains committed still holds true half a century later:

> Its profoundest expertise in morbid states is unmistakably at work not ultimately for the sake of disease and the depths, not, that is, with an interest hostile to reason; but first and last, armed with all the advantages that have accrued from exploring the dark abysses, in the interest of healing and redemption, of "enlightenment" in the most humane sense of the word.

It is in the spirit of Mann's insight that we apply psychoanalytic theory to literature of the talking cure, always remembering, as the distinguished psychoanalytic theoretician Heinz Kohut observed shortly before his recent death, that "Freud's writings are not a kind of Bible but great works belonging to a particular moment in the history of science—great not because of their unchanging relevance but, on the contrary, because they contain the seeds of endless possibilities for further growth." Beset by controversies both within and outside the profession—Kohut's emerging self-psychology, for instance, has triggered off fierce debate in clinical circles—psychoanalysis remains, despite its imperfections, the most psychologically sophisticated explanatory system available, and indispensable for an understanding of literary representations of psychoanalysis. The warfare between the analyst and artist continues unabated, notwithstanding *The White Hotel:* Psychiatric journals still publish articles on neurotic or narcissistic artists, and novelists still portray rigid, repressive, or reductive analysts. Anna O.'s turbulent relationship to Breuer set a pattern that has been repeated countless times in life and literature. "Psycho-analysis brings out the worst in everyone," Freud sardonically declares in *On the History of the Psycho-Analytic Movement,* with more prophecy than he intends. But psychoanalysis can also bring out the best in everyone, and Freud continues to occupy a central position in contemporary literature. "No doubt fate would find it easier than I do to relieve you of your illness," D. M. Thomas' fictional Freud remarks to Lisa Erdman, echoing word for word the historical Freud's conclusion of *Studies on Hysteria,* "But much will be gained if we succeed in turning your hysterical misery into common unhappiness." Paradoxically, out of this hysterical misery and common unhappiness have come some of the most significant stories of our age. For a century now, Anna O.'s talking cure has seized the imagination of artists and analysts alike, and not even Freud could have foreseen the literary interest in the unending stream of characters narrating their adventures of lying on the couch. (pp. 28-32)

Jeffrey Berman, in his The Talking Cure: Literary Representations of Psychoanalysis, *New York University Press, 1985, pp. 1-32.*

Steven Marcus

[*Marcus is an American educator and critic. With Lionel Trilling and Ernest Jones, he edited* The Life and Works of Sigmund Freud *(1961). In the following excerpt, Marcus considers Freud's* "Fragment of an Analysis of a Case of Hysteria," *more popularly known as the case of Dora, as a literary work.*]

It is generally agreed that Freud's case histories are unique. Today, more than half a century after they were written, they are still widely read. Even more, they are still widely used for instruction and training in psychoanalytic institutes. One of the inferences that such a vigorous condition of survival prompts is that these writings have not yet been superseded. Like other masterpieces of literature or the arts, these works seem to possess certain transhistorical qualities—although it may by no means be easy to specify what those qualities are. The implacable "march of science" has not—or has not yet—consigned them to "mere" history. Their singular and mysterious complexity, density, and richness have thus far prevented such a transformation and demotion.

This state of affairs has received less attention than it merits. Freud's case histories—and his works in general—are unique as pieces or kinds of writing, and it may be useful to examine one of Freud's case histories from the point of view of literary criticism, to analyze it as a piece of writing, and to determine whether this method of proceeding may yield results that other means have not. My assumption—and conclusion—is that Freud is a great writer and that one of his major case histories is a great work of literature—that is to say, it is both an outstanding creative and imaginative performance and an intellectual and cognitive achievement of the highest order. And yet this triumphant greatness is in part connected with the circumstance that it is about a kind of failure, and that part of the failure remains in fact unacknowledged and unconscious.

"Fragment of an Analysis of a Case of Hysteria," better known as the case of Dora, is Freud's first great case history—oddly enough he was to write only four others. (pp. 153-54)

If we turn . . . to the Prefatory Remarks it may be illuminating to regard them as a kind of novelistic framing action, as in these few opening pages Freud rehearses his motives, reasons, and intentions and begins at the same time to work his insidious devices upon the reader. First, exactly like a novelist, he remarks that what he is about to let us in on is positively scandalous, for "the complete elucidation of a case of hysteria is bound to involve the revelation of intimacies and the betrayal of . . . secrets." Second, again like a writer of fiction, he has deliberately chosen persons, places, and circumstances that will remain obscure; the scene is laid not in metropolitan Vienna but "in a remote provincial town." He has from the beginning kept the circumstance that Dora was his patient such a close secret that only one other physician—"in whose discretion I have complete confidence"—knows about it. He has "postponed publication" of this essay for "four whole years," also in the cause of discretion, and in the same cause has "allowed no name to stand which could put a non-medical reader on the scent." Finally he has buried the case even deeper by publishing it "in a purely scientific and technical periodical" in order to secure yet another "guarantee against unauthorized readers." He has in short made his own mystery within a mystery, and one of the effects of such obscure preliminary goings-on is to create a kind of Nabokovian frame—what we have here is a history framed by an explanation which is itself slightly out of focus.

Third, he roundly declares, this case history is science and not literature: "I am aware that—in this city, at least—there are many physicians who (revolting though it may seem) choose to read a case history of this kind not as a contribution to the psychopathology of neuroses, but as a *roman à clef* designed for their private delectation." This may indeed be true; but it is equally true that nothing is more literary—and more modern—than the disavowal of all literary intentions. And when Freud does this again later on toward the end of "The Clinical Picture," the situation becomes even less credible.

Freud then goes on to describe other difficulties, constraints, and problematical circumstances attaching to the situation in which he finds himself. Among them is the problem of "how to record for publication" even such a short case—the long ones are as yet altogether impossible. Moreover, since the material that critically illuminated this case was grouped about two dreams, their analysis formed a secure point of departure for the writing. (Freud is of course at home with dreams, being the unchallenged master in the reading of them.) Yet this tactical solution pushes the *entire problematic* book only another step further, since Freud at once goes on to his additional presupposition, that only those who are already familiar with "the interpretation of dreams"—that is, *The Interpretation of Dreams* (1900), whose readership in 1901 must have amounted to a little platoon indeed—are likely to be satisfied at all with the present account. Any other reader "will find only bewilderment in these pages." As much as it is like anything else, this is like Borges—as well as Nabokov. This off-putting and disconcerting quality, it should be without saying, is characteristically modern; the writer succumbs to no impulse to make it easy for the reader; on the contrary, he is by preference rather forbidding and does not extend a cordial welcome. The reader has been, as it were, "softened up" by his first encounter with this unique expository and narrative authority; he is thoroughly off balance and is as a consequence ready to be "educated," by Freud. By the same token, however, if he has followed these opening few pages carefully, he is certainly no longer as prepared as he was to assert the primacy and priority of his own critical sense of things. He is precisely where Freud—and any writer—wants him to be.

Freud proceeds to specify what it is that is wrong with the stories his patients tell him. The difficulties are in the first instance formal shortcomings of *narrative:* the connections, "even the ostensible ones—are for the most part incoherent," obscured and unclear; "and the sequence of different events is uncertain." In short these narratives are disorganized, and the patients are unable to tell a coherent story of their lives. What is more, he states, "the patients' inability to give an ordered history of their life in so far as it coincides with the history of their illness is not merely characteristic of the neurosis. It also possesses great theoretical significance." What we are led at this juncture to conclude is that Freud is implying that a coherent story is in some manner connected with mental health (at the very least with the absence of hysteria), and this in turn implies assumptions of the broadest and deepest kind about both the nature of coherence and the form and structure of human life. On this reading, human life is, ideally, a connected and coherent story, with all the details in explanatory place, and with everything (or as close to everything as is practically possible) accounted for, in its proper causal or other sequence. And inversely illness amounts at least in part to suffering from an incoherent story or an inadequate narrative account of oneself.

Freud then describes in technical detail the various types and orders of narrative insufficiency that he commonly finds; they range from disingenuousness, both conscious and unconscious, to amnesias and paramnesias of several kinds and various other means of severing connections and altering chronologies. In addition, he maintains, this discomposed memory applies with particular force and virulence to "the history of the illness" for which the patient has come for treatment. In the course of a successful treatment, this incoherence, incompleteness, and fragmentariness are progressively transmuted, as facts, events, and memories are brought forward into the forefront of the patient's mind. And he adds as a conclusion that these two aims "are coincident"—they are reached simultaneously and by the same path. Some of the consequences that can be derived from these extraordinary observations are as follows. The history of any patient's illness is itself only a substory (or a subplot), although it is at the same time a vital part of a larger structure. Furthermore, in the course of psychoanalytic treatment, nothing less than "reality" itself is made, constructed, or reconstructed. A complete story—"intelligible, consistent, and unbroken"—is the theoretical, created end story. It is a story, or a fiction, not only because it has a narrative structure but also because the narrative account has been rendered in language, in conscious speech, and no longer exists in the deformed language of symptoms, the untranslated speech of the body. At the end—at the successful end—one has come into possession of one's own story. It is a final act of self-appropriation, the appropriation by oneself of one's own history. This is in part so because one's own story is in so large a measure a phenomenon of language, as psychoanalysis is in turn a demonstration of the degree to which language can go in the reading of all experience. What we end with, then, is a fictional construction which is at the same time satisfactory to us in the form of the truth, and as the form of the truth.

No larger tribute has ever been paid to a culture in which the various narrative and fictional forms had exerted for centuries both moral and philosophical authority and which had produced as one of its chief climaxes the great bourgeois novels of the nineteenth century. Indeed we must see Freud's writings—and method—as themselves part of this culmination, and at the same moment, along with the great modernist novels of the first half of the twentieth century, as the beginning of the end of that tradition and its authority. . . .

The historical difficulties are compounded by several sequential networks that are mentioned at the outset and that figure discernibly throughout the writing. First there is the virtual Proustian complexity of Freud's interweaving of the various strands of time in the actual account; or, to change the figure, his geological fusing of various time strata—strata which are themselves at the same time fluid and shifting. We observe this most strikingly in the palimpsest-like quality of the writing itself, which refers back to *Studies on Hysteria* of 1895; which records a treatment that took place at the end of 1900 (although it mistakes the date by a year); which then was written up in first form during the early weeks of 1901; which was then exhumed in 1905, and was revised and rewritten to an indeterminable extent before publication in that year; and to which additional critical comments in the form of footnotes were finally appended in 1923. All of these are of course held together in vital connection and interanimation by nothing else than Freud's consciousness. But we must take notice as well of the copresence of still further different time sequences in Freud's presentation—this copresence being itself a historical or novelistic circumstance of some magnitude. There is first the connection established by the periodically varied rehearsal throughout the account of Freud's own theory and theoretical notions as they had developed up to that point; this practice provides a kind of running applied history of psychoanalytic theory as its development is refracted through the embroiled medium of this particular case. Then there are the different time strata of Dora's own history, which Freud handles with confident and loving exactitude. Indeed he is never more of a historical virtuoso than when he reveals himself to us as moving with compelling ease back and forth between the complex group of sequential histories and narrative accounts, with divergent sets of diction and at different levels of explanation, that constitute the extraordinary fabric of this work. He does this most conspicuously in his analytic dealings with Dora's dreams, for every dream, he reminds us, sets up a connection between two "factors," an "event during childhood" and an "event of the present day—and it endeavors to reshape the present on the model of the remote past." The existence of recreation of the past in the present is in fact "history" in more than one of its manifold senses.

Just as Marx regards the history-makers of the past as sleepwalkers, "who required recollections of past world history in order to drug themselves concerning their own content," so Freud similarly regards the conditions of dream-formation, of neurosis itself, and even of the cure of neurosis, namely the analytic experience of transference. They are all of them species of living past history in the present. If the last of these works out satisfactorily, then a case history is at the end transfigured. It becomes an inseparable part of an integral life history. Freud is of course the master historian of those transfigurations.

At the very beginning, after he had listened to the father's account of "Dora's impossible behavior," Freud abstained from comment, for, he remarks, "I had resolved from the first to suspend my judgment of the true state of affairs till I had heard the other side as well." Such a suspension inevitably recalls an earlier revolutionary project. In describing the originating plan of *Lyrical Ballads,* Coleridge writes that it "was agreed that my endeavours should be directed to persons and characters supernatural, or at least romantic; yet so as to transfer from our inward nature a human interest and a semblance of truth sufficient to procure for these shadows of imagination that willing suspension of disbelief for the moment, which constitutes poetic faith." We know very well that Freud had a more than ordinary capacity in this direction, and that one of the most dramatic moments in the prehistory of psychoanalysis had to do precisely with his taking on faith facts that turned out to be fantasies. Yet Freud is not only the reader suspending judgment and disbelief until he has heard the other side of the story; and he is not only the poet or writer who must induce a similar process in himself if he is to elicit it in his audience. He is also concomitantly a principal, an actor, a living character in the drama that he is unfolding in print before us. Moreover, that suspension of disbelief is in no sense incompatible with a large body of assumptions, many of them definite, a number of them positively alarming.

They have to do largely with sexuality and in particular with female sexuality. They are brought to a focus in the central scene of Dora's life (and case), a scene that Freud orchestrates with inimitable richness and to which he recurs thematically at a number of junctures with the tact and sense of form that one associates with a classical composer of music (or with Proust, Mann, or Joyce). Dora told this episode to Freud toward the beginning of their relation, after "the first difficulties of the treatment had been overcome." It is the scene between her and Herr K. that took place when she was fourteen years old—that is, four years before the present tense of the case—and acted Freud said as a "sexual trauma." . . . [On] this occasion Herr K. contrived to get Dora alone "at his place of business" in the town of B——, and then without warning or preparation "suddenly clasped the girl to him and pressed a kiss upon her lips." Freud then asserts that "this was *surely* just the situation to call up a *distinct* feeling of sexual excitement in a *girl* of *fourteen* who had *never before* been approached. But Dora had at that moment a violent feeling of disgust, tore herself free from the man, and hurried past him to the staircase and from there to the street door" (all italics are mine). She avoided seeing the K.'s for a few days after this, but then relations returned to "normal"—if such a term survives with any permissible sense in the present context. She continued to meet Herr K., and neither of them ever mentioned "the little scene." Moreover, Freud adds, "according to her account Dora kept it a secret till her confession during the treatment," and he pretty clearly implies that he believes this.

This episode preceded by two years the scene at the lake that acted as the precipitating agent for the severe stage of Dora's illness; and it was this later episode and the entire structure that she and others had elaborated about it that she had first presented to Freud, who continues thus:

> In this scene—second in order of mention, but first in order of time—the behavior of this child of fourteen was already entirely and completely hysterical. I should without question consider a person hysterical in whom an occasion for sexual excitement elicited feelings that were preponderantly or exclusively unpleasurable; and I should do so whether or not

the person were capable of producing somatic symptoms.

Also, in Dora's feelings of disgust an obscure psychical mechanism called the "reversal of affect" was brought into play; but so was another process, and here Freud introduces—casually and almost as a throwaway—one more of his grand theoretical-clinical formulations, namely the idea of the "displacement of sensation," or as it has more commonly come to be referred to, the "displacement upward." "Instead of the genital sensation which would certainly have been felt by a healthy girl in such circumstances, Dora was overcome by the unpleasurable feeling which is proper to the tract of mucous membrane at the entrance to the alimentary canal—that is by disgust." Although the disgust did not persist as a permanent symptom but remained behind residually and potentially in a general distaste for food and poor appetite, a second displacement upward was the resultant of this scene "in the shape of a sensory hallucination which occurred from time to time and even made its appearance while she was telling me her story. She declared that she could still feel upon the upper part of her body the pressure of Herr K.'s embrace." Taking into account certain other of Dora's "inexplicable"—and hitherto unmentioned—"peculiarities" (such as her phobic reluctance to walk past any man she saw engaged in animated conversation with a woman), Freud "formed in my own mind the following reconstruction of the scene. I believe that during the man's passionate embrace she felt not merely his kiss upon her lips but also his erect member against her body. The perception was revolting to her; it was dismissed from her memory, repressed, and replaced by the innocent sensation of pressure upon her thorax, which in turn derived an excessive intensity from its repressed source." This repressed source was located in the erotogenic oral zone, which in Dora's case had undergone a developmental deformation from the period of infancy. And thus, Freud concludes, "the pressure of the erect member probably led to an analogous change in the corresponding female organ, the clitoris; and the excitation of this second erotogenic zone was referred by a process of displacement to the simultaneous pressure against the thorax and became fixed there."

The actual case of Dora was full of such literary and novelistic devices or conventions as thematic analogies, double plots, reversals, inversions, variations, betrayals, etc.—full of what the "sharp-sighted" Dora as well as the sharp-sighted Freud thought of as "hidden connections"—though it is important to add that Dora and her physician mean different things by the same phrase. And as the case proceeds Freud continues to confront Dora with such connections and tries to enlist her assistance in their construction. For example, one of the least pleasant characteristics in Dora's nature was her habitual reproachfulness—it was directed mostly toward her father but radiated out in all directions. Freud regarded this behavior in his own characteristic manner: "A string of reproaches against other people," he comments, "leads one to suspect the existence of a string of self-reproaches with the same content." Freud accordingly followed the procedure of turning back "each simple reproach on the speaker herself." When Dora reproached her father with malingering in order to keep himself in the company of Frau K., Freud felt "obliged to point out to the patient that her present ill-health was just as much actuated by motives and was just

as tendentious as had been Frau K.'s illness, which she had understood so well." At such moments Dora begins to mirror the other characters in the case, as they in differing degrees all mirror one another as well.

Part of that sense, we have come to understand, is that the writer is or ought to be conscious of the part that he—in whatever guise, voice, or persona he chooses—invariably and unavoidably plays in the world he represents. Oddly enough, although there is none of his writings in which Freud is more vigorously active than he is here, it is precisely this activity that he subjects to the least self-conscious scrutiny, that he almost appears to fend off. For example, I will not take my head in my hands and suggest that his extraordinary analysis of Dora's first dream is inadequate on just this count. He is only dimly and marginally aware of his central place in it (he is clearly incorporated into the figure of Dora's father), comments on it only as an addition to Dora's own addendum to the dream, and does nothing to exploit it. Instead of analyzing his own part in what he has done and what he is writing, Freud continues to behave like an unreliable narrator, treating the material about which he is writing as if it were literature but excluding himself from both that treatment and that material. At one moment he refers to himself as someone "who has learnt to appreciate the delicacy of the fabric of structures such as dreams," intimating what I surmise he incontestably believed, that dreams are natural works of art. And when, in the analysis of the second dream, we find ourselves back at the scene at the lake again; when Dora recalls that the only plea to her of Herr K. that she could remember is "You know I get nothing out of my wife"; when these were precisely the same words used by Dora's father in describing to Freud his relation to Dora's mother; and when Freud speculates that Dora may even "have heard her father make the same complaint . . . just as I myself did from his own lips"—when a conjunction such as this occurs, then we know we are in a novel, probably by Proust. Time has recurred, the repressed has returned, plot, double plot, and counterplot have all intersected, and "reality" turns out to be something that for all practical purposes is indistinguishable from a systematic fictional creation.

Finally when at the very end Freud turns to deal—rudimentarily as it happens—with the decisive issue of the case, the transferences, everything is transformed into literature, into reading and writing. Transferences, he writes, "are new editions or facsimiles" of tendencies, fantasies, and relations in which "the person of the physician" replaces some earlier person. When the substitution is a simple one, the transferences may be said to be "merely new impressions or reprints": Freud is explicit about the metaphor he is using. Others "more ingeniously constructed . . . will no longer be new impressions, but revised editions." And he goes on, quite carried away by these figures, to institute a comparison between dealing with the transference and other analytic procedures. "It is easy to learn how to interpret dreams," he remarks, "to extract from the patient's associations his unconscious thoughts and memories, and to practise similar explanatory arts: for these the patient himself will always provide the text." The startling group of suppositions contained in this sentence should not distract us from noting the submerged ambiguity in it. The patient does not merely provide the text; he also *is* the text, the writing to be read, the language to be interpreted. With the transference, however, we move to a different degree of difficulty and onto a different level of explanation. It is only after the transference has been resolved, Freud concludes, "that a patient arrives at a sense of conviction of the validity of the connections which have been constructed during the analysis." I will refrain from entering the veritable series of Chinese boxes opened up by that last statement, and will content myself by proposing that in this passage as a whole Freud is using literature and writing not only creatively and heuristically—as he so often does—but defensively as well.

The writer or novelist is not the only partial role taken up unconsciously or semiconsciously by Freud in the course of this work. He also figures prominently in the text in his capacity as a nineteenth-century man of science and as a representative Victorian critic—employing the seriousness, energy, and commitment of the Victorian ethos to deliver itself from its own excesses. We have already seen him affirming the positive nature of female sexuality, "the genital sensation which would certainly have been felt by a healthy girl in such circumstances," but which Dora did not feel. He goes a good deal further than this. At a fairly early moment in the analysis he faces Dora with the fact that she has "an aim in view which she hoped to gain by her illness. That aim could be none other than to detach her father from Frau K." Her prayers and arguments had not worked; her suicide letter and fainting fits had done no better. Dora knew quite well how much her father loved her, and, Freud continues to address her:

> I felt quite convinced that she would recover at once if only her father were to tell her that he had sacrificed Frau K. for the sake of her health. But, I added, I hoped he would not let himself be persuaded to do this, for then she would have learned what a powerful weapon she had in her hands, and she would certainly not fail on every future occasion to make use once more of her liability to ill-health. Yet if her father refused to give way to her, I was quite sure she would not let herself be deprived of her illness so easily.

This is pretty strong stuff, considering both the age and her age. I think, moreover, that we are justified in reading an overdetermination out of this utterance of Freud's and in suggesting that he had motives additional to strictly therapeutic ones in saying what he did.

How far he is willing to go begins to be visible as we observe him sliding almost imperceptibly from being the nineteenth-century man of science to being the remorseless "teller of truth," the character in a play by Ibsen who is not to be deterred from his "mission." In a historical sense the two roles are not adventitiously related, any more than it is adventitious that the "truth" that is told often has unforeseen and destructive consequences and that it can rebound upon the teller. But we see him most vividly at this implacable work in the two great dream interpretations, which are largely "phonographic" reproductions of dramatic discourse and dialogue. Very early on in the analysis of the first dream, Freud takes up the dream element of the "jewel-case" and makes the unavoidable symbolic interpretation of it.

As the case history advances it becomes increasingly clear to the careful reader that Freud and not Dora has become the central character in the action. Freud the narrator does in the writing what Freud the first psychoanalyst appears to have done in actuality. We begin to sense that it is his story that is being written and not hers that is being retold. Instead of letting Dora appropriate her own story, Freud became the appropriator of it. The case history belongs progressively less to her than it does to him. It may be that this was an inevitable development, that it is one of the typical outcomes of an analysis that fails, that Dora was under any circumstances unable to become the appropriator of her own history, the teller of her own story. Blame does not necessarily or automatically attach to Freud. Nevertheless, by the time he gets to the second dream he is able to write, "I shall present the material produced during the analysis of this dream in the somewhat haphazard order in which it recurs to my mind." He makes such a presentation for several reasons, most of which are legitimate. But one reason almost certainly is that by this juncture it is his *own* mind that chiefly matters to him, and it is *his* associations to her dream that are of principal importance.

At the same time, as the account progresses, Freud has never been more inspired, more creative, more inventive; as the reader sees Dora gradually slipping further and further away from Freud, the power and complexity of the writing reach dizzying proportions. At times they pass over into something else. Due allowance has always to be made for the absolutizing tendency of genius, especially when as in the case of Dora the genius is writing with license of a poet and the ambiguity of a seer. But Freud goes beyond this.

When Dora reports her second dream, Freud spends two hours of inspired insight in elucidating some of its meanings. "At the end of the second session," he writes, "I expressed my satisfaction at the results." The satisfaction in question is in large measure self-satisfaction, for Dora responded to Freud's expression of it with the following words uttered in "a depreciatory tone: 'Why, has anything so remarkable come out?' " That satisfaction was to be of short duration, for Dora opened the third session by telling Freud that this was the last time she would be there—it was December 31, 1900. Freud's remarks that "her breaking off so unexpectedly just when my hopes of a successful termination of the treatment were at their highest, and her thus bringing those hopes to nothing—this was an unmistakable act of vengeance on her part" are only partly warranted. There was, or should have been, nothing unexpected about Dora's decision to terminate; indeed Freud himself on the occasion of the first dream had already detected such a decision on Dora's part and had communicated this finding to her. Moreover, his "highest" hopes for a successful outcome of the treatment seem almost entirely without foundation. In such a context the hopes of success almost unavoidably become a matter of self-reference and point to the immense *intellectual* triumph that Freud was aware he was achieving with the material adduced by his patient. On the matter of "vengeance," however, Freud cannot be faulted; Dora was, among many other things, certainly getting her own back on Freud by refusing to allow him to bring her story to an end in the way he saw fit. And he in turn is quite candid about the injury he felt she had caused him. "No one who, like me," he writes, "conjures up the most evil of those half-tamed demons that inhabit the human breast, and seeks to wrestle with them, can expect to come through the struggle unscathed."

This admission of vulnerability, which Freud artfully manages to blend with the suggestion that he is a kind of modern combination of Jacob and Faust, is in keeping with the weirdness and wildness of the case as a whole and with this last hour. That hour recurs to the scene at the lake, two years before, and its aftermath. And Freud ends this final hour with the following final interpretation. He reminds Dora that she was in love with Herr K.; that she wanted him to divorce his wife; that even though she was quite young at the time she wanted " 'to wait for him, and you took it that he was only waiting till you were grown up enough to be his wife. I imagine that this was a perfectly serious plan for the future in your eyes.' " But Freud does not say this in order to contradict it or categorize it as a fantasy of the adolescent girl's unconscious imagination. On the contrary, he has very different ideas in view, for he goes on to tell her,

> "You have not even got the right to assert that it was out of the question for Herr K. to have had any such intention; you have told me enough about him that points directly towards his having such an intention. Nor does his behavior at L— contradict this view. After all, you did not let him finish his speech and do not know what he meant to say to you."

He has not done with her yet, for he then goes on to bring in the other relevant parties and offers her the following conclusion:

> "Incidentally, the scheme would by no means have been so impracticable. Your father's relation with Frau K. . . . made it certain that her consent to a divorce could be obtained; and you can get anything you like out of your father. Indeed, if your temptation at L—— had had a different upshot, this would have been *the only possible solution for all the parties concerned.*" (italics mine)

No one—at least no one in recent years—has accused Freud of being a swinger, but this is without question a swinging solution that is being offered. It is of course possible that he feels free to make such a proposal only because he knows that nothing in the way of action can come of it; but with him you never can tell—as I hope I have already demonstrated. One has only to imagine what in point of ego strength, balance, and self-acceptance would have been required of Dora alone in this arrangement of wife-and-daughter-swapping to recognize at once its extreme irresponsibility, to say the least. At the same time we must bear in mind that such a suggestion is not incongruent with the recently revealed circumstance that Freud analyzed his own daughter. Genius makes up its own rules as it goes along—and breaks them as well. This "only possible solution" was one of the endings that Freud wanted to write to Dora's story; he had others in mind besides, but none of them were to come about. Dora refused or was unable to let him do this; she refused to be a character in the story that Freud was composing for her, and wanted to finish it herself. As we now know, the ending she wrote was a very bad one indeed.

In this extraordinary work Freud and Dora often appear as unconscious, parodic refractions of each other. Both of them insist with implacable will upon the primacy of "re-ality," although the realities each has in mind differ radically. Both of them use reality, "the truth," as a weapon. Freud does so by forcing interpretations upon Dora before she is ready for them or can accept them. And this aggressive truth bounds back upon the teller, for Dora leaves him. Dora in turn uses her version of reality—it is "outer" reality that she insists upon—aggressively as well. She has used it from the outset against her father, and five months after she left Freud she had the opportunity to use it against the K.'s. In May of 1901 one of the K.'s children dies. Dora took the occasion to pay them a visit of condolence—

> She took her revenge on them. . . . To the wife she said: "I know you have an affair with my father"; and the other did not deny it. From the husband she drew an admission of the scene by the lake which he had disputed, and brought the news of her vindication home to her father.

She told this to Freud fifteen months after she had departed, when she returned one last time to visit him—to ask him, without sincerity, for further help, and "to finish her story." She finished her story, and as for the rest Freud remarks, "I do not know what kind of help she wanted from me, but I promised to forgive her for having deprived me of the satisfaction of affording her a far more radical cure for her troubles."

But the matter is not hopelessly obscure, as Freud himself has already confessed. What went wrong with the case, "its great defect, which led to its being broken off prematurely," was something that had to do with the transference; and Freud writes that "I did not succeed in mastering the transference in good time." He was in fact just beginning to learn about this therapeutic phenomenon, and the present passage is the first really important one about it to have been written. It is also in the nature of things heavily occluded. On Dora's side the transference went wrong in several senses. In the first place there was the failure on her part to establish an adequate positive transference to Freud. She was not free enough to respond to him erotically—in fantasy—or intellectually—by accepting his interpretations: both or either of these being prerequisites for the mysterious "talking cure" to begin to work. And in the second, halfway through the case a negative transference began to emerge, quite clearly in the first dream. Freud writes that he "was deaf to this first note of warning," and as a result this negative "transference took me unawares, and, because of the unknown quantity in me which reminded Dora of Herr K., she took her revenge on me as she wanted to take her revenge on him, and deserted me as she believed herself to have been deceived and deserted by him." This is, I believe, the first mention in print of the conception that is known as "acting out"—out of which, one may incidentally observe, considerable fortunes have been made.

We are, however, in a position to say something more than this. For there is a reciprocating process in the analyst known as the countertransference, and in the case of Dora this went wrong too. Although Freud describes Dora at the beginning of the account as being "in the first bloom of youth—a girl of intelligent and engaging looks," almost nothing attractive about her comes forth in the course of the writing. As it unwinds, and it becomes increasingly evident that Dora is not responding adequately to Freud, it also becomes clear that Freud is not responding favorably to this reponse, and that he doesn't in fact like Dora very much. He doesn't like her negative sexuality, her inability to surrender to her own erotic impulses. He doesn't like "her really remarkable achievements in the direction of intolerable behavior." He doesn't like her endless reproachfulness. Above all, he doesn't like her inability to surrender herself to him. For what Freud was as yet unprepared to face was not merely the transference, but the countertransference as well—in the case of Dora it was largely a negative countertransference—an unanalyzed part of himself. I should like to suggest that this cluster of unanalyzed impulses and ambivalences was in part responsible for Freud's writing of this great text immediately after Dora left him. It was his way—and one way—of dealing with, mastering, expressing, and neutralizing such material. Yet the neutralization was not complete; or we can put the matter in another way and state that Freud's creative honesty was such that it compelled him to write the case of Dora as he did, and that his writing has allowed us to make out in this remarkable fragment a still fuller picture. As I have said before, this fragment of Freud's is more complete and coherent than the fullest case studies of anyone else. Freud's case histories are a new form of literature—they are creative narratives that include their own analysis and interpretation. Nevertheless, like the living works of literature that they are, the material they contain is always richer than the original analysis and interpretation that accompany it; and this means that future generations will recur to these works and will find in them a language they are seeking and a story they need to be told. (pp. 160-74)

Steven Marcus, "Freud and Dora: Story, History, Case History," in Literature and Psychoanalysis, *edited by Edith Kurzweil and William Phillips, Columbia University Press, 1983, pp. 153-174.*

Meredith Anne Skura

[*An American educator and critic, Skura has written numerous essays on the relationship between psychoanalysis and literature. In the following excerpt, she compares the psychoanalytic process with literature.*]

Freud recommended that any young analyst include the study of literature as part of his training, and he himself drew on literary texts as illustration and inspiration for his "scientific" discipline. "The poets and philosophers discovered the unconscious before I did," he explained more than once. Probably very few literary critics, however, would advise their young colleagues to make such direct use of psychoanalysis in their discipline. The poets may indeed share with the analysts a knowledge of the unconscious depths which the rest of us had avoided, but it is the poets' conscious control when they write which interests the critics. It is not clear what literary critics can learn from a field which is devoted, if not to the study of unconscious illness, as we once thought, at least to the study of the unconscious, which is the lowest common denominator of the mind—a field devoted to everything that seems farthest from consciously shaped art. How can the study of our common primitive heritage reveal anything about

works whose very identity lies in their uncommon escape from mundane responses to experience?

One answer, of course, is that everything we understand about the way we think is helpful in understanding the way literature works. Every new discrimination we learn to make in observing our own thoughts or our exchanges with one another, every new alternative we become aware of as we study the given of what we have actually thought or said, makes us better and more responsive readers. And we can learn not only from the best and subtlest uses but from all uses of language; as we come to appreciate the variety of discourse, we better appreciate its excellences.

The most accurate reply, however, is that psychoanalysis is not merely the discovery of the unconscious. It is not dedicated solely to disease or symptoms or primitive experiences, but offers instead a theory and a method for studying how the whole mind works—for understanding another human being as he tries to describe his world in words and to draw on all his resources, both conscious and unconscious, in doing so. In fact the very identification of a so-called unconscious as a thing or a separate part of the mind existing unknown to us is misleading. It is the product of a falsely neat dichotomy between our rational, acceptable thinking (supposedly all conscious) and our irrational, primitive, and repressed thinking (supposedly all unconscious). Freud discovered that we are unaware of much that goes on in our minds and that indeed some of it has been willfully cast out of awareness, so that it does not easily return to consciousness, nor is it easily recognized when it does. Nonetheless, the quality of consciousness is not to be automatically assigned to a particular part of the mind or to a particular kind of thinking or even to a particular kind of thought. Freud himself later discarded the dichotomy of conscious and unconscious as an identification of parts of the mind and limited it to describing whether or not we are consciously aware of a particular thought, whatever that thought might be.

Even limited this way to its proper, descriptive function, however, the dichotomy has led to a good deal of fruitless debate about the relative value of conscious and unconscious meanings in applying psychoanalysis to literature. It has polarized critics and analysts, so that on the one hand the critic E. D. Hirsch declares [in his *Validity in Interpretation*] that "meaning is an affair of consciousness," and on the other, Sandor Ferenczi argues [in "The Psychoanalysis of Wit and the Comical"] that the conscious meaning can only be understood once we have plumbed the depths of the unconscious meaning. I . . . argue, however, that there is no single neatly definable meaning of which we are directly and all-encompassingly conscious in all it manifestations, nor is there any such thing as a meaning of which we are totally unconscious. There are, rather, different ways of being aware of things and different aspects of a text which compel a certain kind of awareness. Rather than looking only for unconscious or conscious meaning, the analyst describes a whole range of what has been called "modes of consciousness," or modes of representation. Rather than simply discovering the unconscious, Freud discovered the variety of ways in which we become aware of ourselves and our world and the means by which we represent both. (pp. 1-3)

The psychoanalytic process . . . begins with the assumption that communication has many facets, and the analyst must draw on "all the ways by which one human being understands another" as he tries to put his experience into words; the analyst is as interested in why and how something is said as he is in the words that are actually spoken. The psychoanalytic process provides no special or exotic means of reading the unconscious; its strength derives from two simple strategies: first, it insists on paying attention to everything, and second, it mistrusts the seemingly obvious implications of what it then observes. Freud prescribed "intense but uncritical attention," meaning *uncritical* in the sense of an editorial openness and a suspension of all conclusions. In each case the analytic listener tries to be open to the sudden switches and rearrangements that reveal alternate meanings and expose the dynamic play of meaning behind what may seem to be a simple surface. (pp. 200-01)

Reservations about using psychoanalytic models for literature usually come from a reluctance to reduce a complex literary text to the model of something much simpler, like a fantasy or a dream—efforts that, according to Paul de Man, "apply to less rigorous modes of consciousness than those at work in literary texts" [*Blindness and Insight*]. But the psychoanalytic process is designed to dismantle less rigorous modes of consciousness, to break up the defensively distorted versions of inner and outer reality that cramp a person's life and his language. The blindly symptomatic use of fantasy and dream may constitute a less rigorous mode of consciousness than the ordinary text, but when the psychoanalytic process is used correctly, its elements reflect on one another with the subtlety, rigor and self-consciousness of a literary text. Ernst Kris's description of "the good hour" in an analysis unwittingly comes closer to describing the way a poem works than anything he ever wrote about literature ["On Some Vicissitudes of Insight in Psychoanalysis," *International Journal of Psychoanalysis* 37 (1956)].

This resemblance implies that a study of the minute changes which take place during an analytic hour can not only suggest new meanings for texts but can also suggest how *any* meaning is created within and between people. We can thereby gain a renewed appreciation of the way language and literature work, not only in creating fictional scenes but in creating significance apart from any scene at all; in diverting, displacing, or elaborating meanings, expanding an image into a web of associations or condensing a flow of statements into a single focusing insight; in shifting meanings by shifting perspectives or changing the rules for interpretation. Many analysts themselves are coming to see the exchanges in the psychoanalytic process as the most important part of psychoanalysis, whether their interest is expressed in the continental philosophical terms of discourse with the "other" or in terms of the transference and countertransference that Freud first described. And it is in these exchanges, where analysis is most vital, that it is also most suggestive as a model for other disciplines. (pp. 201-02)

The connection between the psychoanalytic process and the aspect of poetry that makes it *poetry* (rather than paraphrasable statement) is even closer than the more immediately obvious connection between a dream and a "dreamlike" poem. To compare a work of literature to a fantasy is to isolate that aspect of the text which returns us to more primitive levels of experience. To compare it

to the psychoanalytic process is to discover those aspects that avoid such a return—but this can be accomplished only by exposing and taking account of the work's own fantasy and dreamlike elements.

The most obvious literary parallels to the reorganizations in analysis are found in relatively primitive works where the switch in how we see things is exaggerated, like the blatantly "surprising" jokes and the uncanny stories Freud studied, and these examples provide a good starting place for a closer look at the relation between the psychoanalytic process and literary texts. Jokes and uncanny stories depend on a single surprising moment of reorganization like the moment of insight in analysis, and they have a curiously similar emotional impact. As Freud suggests, for example, in the following joke, there is a switch in meaning, which makes us laugh:

First Jew: Have you taken a bath?

Second Jew: No, is one missing?

And in E. T. A. Hoffmann's uncanny tale "The Sand-Man," there is a switch that makes us shiver, when the nursery tale about a sandman coming to take out a boy's eyes suddenly seems to come true.

It is significant that jokes and the uncanny are the only genres Freud chose to write about at any length, because they provide the same kind of phenomena that his clinical experience provided. He never connected the two studies, of course; he would not have said that he was using the psychoanalytic process as a model, and he would not have agreed with my analysis of the switch that occurs in both genres. Instead, just as he had defined the goal of analysis as filling in the gaps in memory, he explained the "kinetic" effect of jokes and the uncanny by referring to the specific material which they revealed or "filled in." Freud attributed their power to the simple presence of specific "unconscious" or "wishful" ideas. The joke worked, according to Freud, by making it possible for unconscious material to escape the censor, and our response was not to the joke but to the unconscious material. Normally, we have to suppress the rebelliousness and perversity that makes the second Jew say, in effect, "I'm not listening to you about this civilized business of cleanliness; I'm so far from all of that, I don't even recognize the expression describing it." Similarly, the uncanny story worked, according to Freud, by making it possible for unconscious material—in this case, frightening infantile fantasies about oedipal wishes and the blinding ("castration") that follows as punishment—to escape the censor.

Freud denied that comic or uncanny effect could be explained by a conflict between ideas rather than by the presence of an inherently comic or uncanny idea. Theories defining jokes as the product of sense in conflict with nonsense, Freud said, described only an intellectual conflict, just as theories about the uncanny as the product of conflicting interpretations of events depended only on intellectual confusions. Merely intellectual conflicts, Freud insisted, could not produce the powerful effect a joke or an uncanny story has. These effects depend on the fact that a repressed idea from childhood has returned, only incidentally causing confusion.

With the more recent definition of the psychoanalytic process as a switching between two ways of seeing rather than between the absence and presence of a particular element, we can now take advantage of Freud's contribution to make a composite theory. As in the psychoanalytic process, it is not simply the visible presence or absence of some inherently powerful material that makes the joke, but the way the material makes its presence known. The joke depends not on the return of repressed material but on a change in relationship between manifest and latent significance of the same material: the joke begins when our ordinary interpretation gives way to an old, literal-minded one, and an absurd world emerges in the center of an ordinary landscape. Freud saw the innocent beginning of a joke as a mere disguise for or distraction from the really funny punch line; but without the beginning, the joke would not be funny. The humor lies in the movement from the innocent setup to the punch line. Jokes, at least the ones Freud cites, work by switching the grounds for interpretation. We think we are playing one game when we hear the first Jew ask, "Did you take a bath?" But we know we are playing another when the second answers, "No, is one missing?"

Even Freud, however, recognized implicitly that the joke depends on a general switch in our method of interpretation rather than on the introduction of a particular content. He claimed that what makes the audience laugh is the Jew's taboo motive for switching: the second Jew switches the meaning, not the joke. But even though he tried to locate the power of the joke solely in content and not in a general mode of representation or reading, Freud still felt that he had to take into account the joke's social context. Unlike other fiction, a joke needs an audience, Freud said, and it can only be understood in the rhetorical context of a purposeful exchange between teller and listener. Thus Freud implicitly recognized the joke's switch in narrative and linguistic conventions. Where he said the joke "needs an audience," we would say that it requires a set of conventional expectations to play with and against.

The same is true in the case of the uncanny. Here, too, Freud attributed a story's power to the mere presence of a forbidden idea, like the idea of castration in Hoffmann's "The Sand-Man"; or to the mere presence of a forbidden "way of thinking," like the fear of magical retaliation in the same story. But in both cases it is the play between two ways of thinking or seeing that causes the effect, as commentators have always noticed. What Freud has added to the understanding of the uncanny, as in the case of the joke, is that the necessary play must be between two different kinds of ideas or two different kinds of thinking, one of which is more primitive than the other. As he pointed out, this is what distinguishes the joke from the merely comic and the uncanny from the merely frightening.

Finally, with the more subtle model of the psychoanalytic process available, we can also use Freud's explanation as a starting point to discriminate between the joke and that which is uncanny. Working with his single-dimensional explanatory model of repression/openness, Freud wound up with the same explanation for both jokes and the uncanny: what makes a joke funny is the same "return of the repressed" that makes the uncanny story uncanny. We can now be more specific and say that each of these genres is defined by a switch in a different aspect of the material. The success of the joke depends on a switch in content or

reference, from "washing in a tub" to "stealing a tub." The uncanny, however, depends on a switch in what is accepted as truth. An old nanny's tale suddenly becomes real when the sandman comes after the grown-up Nathaniel's eyes. The uncanny and its related phenomena—*déjà vu, déjà raconté,* and *fausse reconaissance*—are more unsettling than jokes because they disrupt our sense of ourselves and our orientation in the world; these phenomena are what the analyst calls *ego disturbances.* The joke, on the other hand, merely distorts the message and does not affect us significantly.

The exceptions prove this rule that jokes switch content and the uncanny switches truth status; they illuminate material that falls between the categories of jokes and the uncanny. For example, in a now classic psychoanalytic essay on literature [*The Dynamics of Literary Response*], Norman Holland analyzes a *Playboy* joke that actually works like the uncanny in reverse and falls somewhere between the genres of the joke and the uncanny:

> A young executive had stolen company money and lost it on the stock market, and was about to jump off a bridge when an old crone appeared, said she was a witch, and promised to replace the money for a slight consideration—which turned out to be a night in a nearby motel. Though revolted, the man agreed. In the morning as he was about to escape, the crone asked how old he was. "Forty-two," he answered, "Why?" "Ain't you a little old to believe in witches?" she replied.

Holland explains the joke's effect in fairly strict Freudian terms: we are presented with the desired—but feared—threat of an oedipal encounter between the old hag and the young man, and our laughter follows when we learn, with relief, that we have been saved from it after all. But the joke's effect depends on more than an economy of wishes and fears. It depends on a switch in the joke's status as truth or fictional "truth." We think we are playing one game when the joke begins (a game in which we accept witches as realities), but we realize we are playing another at exactly the moment the executive realizes it. This is the same kind of switch that defines the uncanny. In that case, of course, the switch moves in the opposite direction: in "The Sand-Man," the fantasy sandman turns out to be real, but in the *Playboy* joke, the real witch turns out to be only a fantasy (which is probably why the joke amuses or annoys rather than frightens us). But it affects us in much the same way as the uncanny, challenging us on more levels than Freud's jokes do.

There are moments in his two essays when Freud seems to take all these factors into account and to come around to saying that a joke or an uncanny story is formed not simply by recalled material but also by the way in which this material is brought back. The uncanny, he says, can be generated by the return of even the least uncanny material; and jokes use material that was neither wish-fulfilling nor funny when it was first repressed. The mere resurrection of infantile memories is not enough to explain why we react as we do, even to these primitive forms of literature. One of the most poignant moments in Freud's book on jokes, in fact, is the closing statement, in which he moves away from seeing the joke as a simple return to earlier pleasure and comes closer than he does anywhere else to seeing jokes (and by implication, all the products of our discontented civilization) as something new, designed as a substitute for early experience, perhaps, but not as an imitation of it. Jokes, the comic, and humor, he says, attempt to regain from mental activity a pleasure that has been lost through the development of that activity—a euphoria which is "nothing other than the mood of a period of life . . . when we were ignorant of the comic, when we were incapable of jokes and when we had no need of humour to make us feel happy in life."

This is not the Freud who saw literature as only a simple escape to a mindlessly literal reproduction of our earliest fantasy worlds. Here Freud sees not simply a return of repressed material but a whole new world that takes account of it. He sees the indirections that move toward new forms of pleasure, the pleasure of insight, the Wordsworthian pleasures of consciousness, and the literary pleasures that escape any simple reflex explanation.

Obviously, the sudden shifts in jokes and uncanny stories move us more crudely than more sophisticated literature does, and their effect has less influence on the way we see the world after we have enjoyed them. The joke and the uncanny story lie at the borders of literature; they are examples of what Stephen Dedalus might call kinetic art, like pornography and propaganda, because, like these two pragmatic genres, they are meant to "move" us, though in a different way. They are in fact defined by the giggle and the *frisson*. Yet all literature moves us the same way these trivial texts do—by the way it presents material and not by its content alone. We recognize poetic touchstones by being "thoroughly penetrated by their power" [Matthew Arnold, "The Study of Poetry"], and though the punch in a joke's punchline may seem far removed from the finer touch of poetry Matthew Arnold was describing, it belongs in the same category.

The reorganization made suddenly explicit in a joke is related to that which we can find unfolding more slowly and less explosively in every aspect of literary texts—in their content, their function, their language and literary conventions, and their rhetorical dimension. The literary critics who most resemble psychoanalysts are not the ones who talk about fantasies but those who talk about ambiguity and who challenge the assumptions integral to ordinary reading processes, like William Empson, Kenneth Burke, and Sigurd Burckhardt. The alternative readings they point out are not always sexual (though Empson's and Burke's often are), but neither are the analyst's; what they share with the analyst is an eye for the tenuous as well as the tendentious and an appreciation of the way supposedly farfetched alternative readings may be much closer to the meaning of a text than we realize, in a context that shapes our final, "acceptable" reading.

In some cases the parallel between the psychoanalytic process and the text is easy to see; the reorganization is quite obviously part of the manifest text and is visible in many separate details. The study of such shifts is in fact one of the most traditional aspects of literary criticism. On the level of individual words and phrases these shifts have been studied as ambiguities of various kinds, the necessary wealth of alternatives that make poetic language. In broader, if vaguer, forms, they have been studied as the "irony" new critics believed to be the necessary condition for poetry. In a very different kind of criticism, Harold Bloom has examined not verbal but rhetorical switches—or "poetic crossings"—in which a poet changes from one

to another way of representing and coping with ideas. And more recently, we have begun to hear about a number of more subtly distinguished ways in which a text reveals an interaction between its simultaneous construction and deconstruction of meaning, or in which a text can destroy its own integrity if seen from another perspective.

On a larger scale, traditional critics have studied similar switches and reorganizations. In their studies, the model would no longer be the isolated moment of psychoanalytic insight, which parallels the simple joke or uncanny story; it is instead the entire "good hour" or "good analysis," as Kris has called it, which Cavell invoked. This larger unit provides a model for the kind of plot movement Aristotle described when he maintained that tragedy depended on a moment of recognition that reorganized an entire world. This model represents a movement toward revelation not only of a specific fact but of a fact that changes everything, that makes us give up one set of values and the belief that the world conforms to them, and shows us how to find another. This manifest movement toward reorganization can make any story resemble a stylized psychoanalysis, or at least the old-style traumatic revelation analysis.

Not surprisingly, nearly all the texts that Freud chose to analyze at length had this kind of plot. *Oedipus* is the most obvious example (its action "can be likened to the work of a psychoanalysis," Freud said), but Wilhelm Jensen's *Gradiva,* which inspired Freud's monograph on dreams and delusion, is another good example; it tells the story of a man who finds that his current love is a figure from his childhood. Even Hoffmann's "Sand-Man" takes the form of a psychological investigation; the author tries to find out what is the matter with Nathaniel, using outside diagnoses and clinical confession, and exploring the return to childhood. Today, of course, with a newer concept of a more subtle kind of revelation—as in Cavell's description which I have quoted—we might find literary analogues not in the plays about revelations but in the stories about failed revelation. Rather than looking for the caricatural "peak-experience" of old-style analysis, we would look to the analogy of the vision that disappears when Spenser's Calidore tries to capture it on Mount Acidale, or the vision that never materializes for Wordsworth in the Alps.

Whether the plot reorganization is sudden or more subtly interfused, however, the movement of thought in the psychoanalytic process takes more into account than that in the other models. It makes a more suggestive model for Shakespeare's plays, for example, than the static character analyses we discussed in chapter 2. What is interesting about Shakespeare's characters is not their diseases but their movement through disease to some kind of curative reorganization. Their proper parallel is not the neurotic but the neurotic in analysis. Freud's patients—neurotics, in general—are caught in stifling, reductive versions of reality, which permit only equally reductive behavior. For example, Frau Cäcilie . . . was caught in a cliché that was taken literally; she was so obsessed by her facial pains— the only way she acknowledged society's "slap in the face"—that she did not have to cope with anything else or confront any question about her relationships except "Does it make my face hurt or doesn't it?" Every neurotic is caught in a similarly reductive dichotomy, fixated on a question defined by its own terms. Analysis cures by releasing the patient so that he can see the world in new terms.

The parallel between the psychoanalytic process and Shakespeare's plays is easiest to see when a reductive dichotomy affects a character who is trapped in an almost pathologically defensive vision, and the most obvious examples are the several jealous husbands, trapped in obsessive dichotomies that *we* know are beside the point. Othello forgets everything he knows about Desdemona, once he begins his obsessive testing: "Did she or didn't she betray me?" Leontes, in *The Winter's Tale,* hardly bothers to consider the alternatives before he decides that Hermione has betrayed him; and Posthumus Leonatus, in *Cymbeline,* contaminates his marriage the moment he consents even to ask of his wife, "Will she or won't she betray me?" although at first he believes in her. Troilus, who has real cause to feel betrayed, watches Cressida with her new lover and, instead of reacting directly to the situation, is caught up in the terms of a dichotomy as he asks himself, "Is she or isn't she doing this—is this Cressida?" The movement of each of these plays, however, does not simply answer these obsessive questions but changes the terms in which each man sees his beloved. This redefinition of terms is characteristic of many other Shakespearean plays as well. What makes *Antony and Cleopatra* so strange a play, in fact, is the way in which Antony *starts out* by ignoring such reductive dichotomies, although they pose more appropriate questions for him than for the jealous husbands.

Less obvious but much more characteristic of Shakespeare's plays are the similar changes in characters who are not so blatantly disturbed but are nonetheless caught in their own reductive visions. The young aristocrats in *Love's Labour's Lost,* for example, have to be shaken out of their simplistic view of the world. The men have taken sides in the ancient war between discipline and pleasure, and from the moment they announce their withdrawal to a strict academe, they become caught up in a dichotomous view of the world as blinding as Othello's: "Should I devote myself to books or shouldn't I?"—or rather, "Can I devote myself to books or can't I?" Then the Princess arrives with her women, and the men of course all fall in love. But instead of escaping from their dichotomy, the men simply change it slightly and switch sides: the war becomes a struggle between study and love, and they dedicate themselves with equal extravagance to love. What we begin to see is that the categories have become irrelevant. What matters is neither study nor love, but the way in which the young men go about either one. They have rushed into both like brash, self-confident fools, out to conquer; the women are humbler, mellower, more receptive to what love brings and to forces beyond the control of their individual categorizing wills.

Not only characters but entire societies are sometimes caught up in paralyzing dichotomies. In *Romeo and Juliet,* the war between Montague and Capulet demonstrates such a dichotomy; we can see how irrelevant the categories are, how vital the stars that cut across, but the characters cannot see this until it is too late—and perhaps not even then. In *Troilus and Cressida,* we can at least tell the difference between Greeks and Trojans, but the stalemated war their dichotomous outlook generates is again beside the point. We do not care about their obsessive seven-year-old question as to "who will win, Greek or Trojan." What matters is a question that undermines both sides: what does it mean to win? And elsewhere in the plays we hardly have a chance to compare Roman and Goth, reason and love, Caesar and Brutus, before our comparison is out of date. Initially, we may get caught up in deciding who should be king, Richard or Henry, but before the end of the play we are always asking larger questions, like "What *is* a king?" and "Can there be a king?" The terms have changed, and the change is part of what the plays are about.

But in these cases, as the last examples show, the reorganization affects something more fundamental than the character's experience or the plot alone: it affects the audience as well. If Shakespeare's characters sometimes suffer from clichés, so do we as critics. We may avoid Othello's cage; we may escape the empty distinctions between Montagues and Capulets or Trojans and Greeks, which imprison an entire world. But we fall into other pits. We see beyond the distinction between Montague and Capulet, but elsewhere we find distinctions we think are the true ones. We find, for example, dichotomies between artificial and natural; restraint and freedom; wintry rigidity and spring release; and work world and holiday. These dichotomies have been described often, at least in the comedies, and seem to be embodied in the very geography of the plays: we see them in the contrasts between the city and the forest, the men's academy and the park around it where the women stay, the palace and the heath, Venice and Turkish outlands, and Venice and Belmont.

These dichotomies, however, are not the adequate measure of a play; they are the kind of thing cured by psychoanalysis—the wrong set of terms. And the cure is not simply a compromise between these dichotomous terms (Athenian rationality plus a healthy dose of the forest's irrationality), nor a Hegelian synthesis, nor a paradox beyond our common understanding. Rather, it is a complete reorganization, which shows dichotomy to be beside the point. The opening terms in a Shakespearean play slip away from us as the action moves toward a reorganization not only of characters and action but also of the very way in which we see both. The initial questions no longer remain, because the terms in which they have been defined are no longer relevant.

In Shakespearean criticism, the kind of movement characterizing the psychoanalytic process has also recently become the concern of traditional critics. Much of the Shakespearean criticism of the last ten years, though never mentioning psychoanalysis, has traced just such movements in individual plays, though usually implying that the given play is unique in its defiance of categories. It is not in Shakespeare's plays, however, that the literary parallel to psychoanalytic observation is most common. Critics have most often studied this kind of reorganization in works whose slowly elaborated and repetitive movement is even more like psychoanalysis than the swiftly streamlined movement in a Shakespearean play: a major field of study has been the highly self-conscious epic tradition, which culminates in Wordsworth's self-analysis in *The Prelude.* The readers' response, which Stanley Fish has described in Milton [*Surprised by Sin: The Reader in Paradise Lost*] and Paul Alpers has noted in Spenser [*The Poetry of "The Faerie Queene"*], is a movement from a cramped, constrictive view of the world to a more open and inclusive, if more confusing, one—just like the movement from symptom to insight. The symptom . . . is not a raw eruption of conflict but a rigid, unimaginative way of dealing with conflict by reducing it to a "pseudo-concreteness," such as a paralyzed arm, a horse phobia, or an obsession with clean hands.

At the beginning of his quest, Spenser's Red Cross Knight has a similarly unimaginative idea of holiness, as singly reductive as Frau Cäcilie's idea about human relationships and as closely tied to physical manifestations (such as his armor, for example). He thinks that his enemy is the "dragon" and does not realize that the real enemies in his world are not evils like Unholiness and Intemperance but rather the wrong ideas about holiness and temperance—and the lax attitudes that allow us to slip into them. He—and the reader—must slow down enough in the obsessive pursuit of dragons to be able to redefine the world in other terms. Only then can he escape his partial vision and achieve that wholeness which several critics have associated not only with holiness but with health.

This kind of criticism begins with a bias toward the sensitive but tentative reading necessary in a psychoanalysis. Not surprisingly, the starting point for all later Spenserian critics, William Empson's famous description of the Spenserian stanza [in *Seven Types of Ambiguity*], is really a description of the kind of attention needed to read it—the kind of "intense but uncritical" scrutiny Freud prescribed for the analyst's "evenly hovering attention."

> The size, the possible variety, and the fixity of this unit give something of the blankness that comes from fixing your eyes on a bright spot; *you have to yield yourself to it very completely* to take in the variety of its movement, *and, at the same time, there is no need to concentrate the elements of the situation into a judgment as if for action.* . . .
> [Emphasis added]

Paul Alpers elaborates on this description, suggesting that "the condition of Spenser's poetry is an abeyance of the will," which on Spenser's part amounts to a failure to maintain a dramatic identity in relation to his poem. But this is very much like the patient's failure—or, I should say, achievement—in the analytic situation. The failure to maintain a dramatic identity is an escape from the ordinary self that maintains a constant relation to what it sees and says and locates itself firmly in the narrative, whether directly, as opinionated narrator, or indirectly, in the person of a specific character. Whether on Spenser's part or on the reader's part, this "abeyance of the will" is one step further from ordinary reality than the "willing suspension of disbelief" we are familiar with. The latter requires only that we step into a new world, while the Spenserian—or psychoanalytic—stance requires that we give up the idea of any "world" at all, if by that we mean a physical place (however odd) with characters acting within the structure of a plot.

Both in reading and in the psychoanalytic process, the suspension of critical will opens one to moral and perceptual change—to the kind of change occurring in scientific revolutions and in great works of art, which break old schemata or change the way we see them and the way we see the world. Here, again, the analyst and the traditional critic have in common a search for texts that challenge the sche-mata and rework convention. In particular, they share a sensitivity to all the ways in which a conventional, naturalistic, literal-minded expectation about meaning is defeated; both have become wary of the "referential fallacy," and they look to other dimensions of a text besides the seemingly obvious literal meaning to which it refers.

Two of the most characteristic concerns of recent criticism, in fact, might be called the defining concerns of modern psychoanalysis: self-consciousness about artistic conventions and fictional status, and a related tendency to see these conventions as ends in themselves—to "find semantic value in formal qualities [Jonathan Culler, *Structuralist Poetics: Structuralism, Linguistics, and the Study of Literature*]. In the first case, the critic points to those moments of self-consciousness when we are reminded that "this is only a play"—moments paralleled in analysis by the analyst's habit of calling attention to the patient's defenses and making him self-conscious about them as defenses or fictions. In those moments we see with the eye of the creator, not the audience; means become ends. We experience what George Klein [in his *Perception, Motives and Personality*] has called a change in mode of consciousness, as we switch from seeing a three-dimensional world on a canvas to seeing a two-dimensional pattern. The power of this change depends of course not only on the way it makes us reexamine artistic conventions of realism (preventing us from accepting, for example, a bare wooden *O* as King Henry's England) but also on the way it calls into question those more insidiously hidden conventions that define "reality." This is precisely what the analyst does when he makes the patient conscious of the conventions he has begun to take for granted in his own role-playing. ("Of course I can't cry in front of my children," the patient may say—a revelation not only about the conventions he has accepted about playing parent but about the ones he may not know he has accepted to define his own feelings.)

In the second case, the critic calls attention to moments in literature that are even more like the reorganization deriving from the suspended will that characterizes analysis. These moments make us self-conscious about convention not simply by naming it but by switching conventions. Shakespeare may call attention to the wooden *O*, diverting us from the thing represented to the means of representation—not England but the barren, wooden boards of the stage. But Samuel Beckett unsettles us in another way when he switches the rules and makes us see the stage as the barren, wooden world. And in Racine's plays, the unities are not mere shapely containers; they become part of the characters' claustrophobic world. Even Shakespeare evokes this queasiness at times, making the audience uncertain about what is a means of representation and what is an end, about what the audience should see and what it is supposed to see through. *The Tempest* observes the unities but is *about* a playwright trying to observe the unities as he presents a drama that spans oceans and stretches from the dark "backward of time" to the future brave new world. And the rude mechanicals in *A Midsummer Night's Dream,* instead of asking that we take the wooden *O,* for a forest, enter a forest for their rehearsal and pretend that *it* is a wooden *O:* "This green plot shall be our stage. . . ."

These switches and their significance are part of what these texts are about, and much of the critical commentary has stressed what we can learn from becoming aware of them: the moral maturity not to be surprised by sin and the perceptual alertness not to be fooled by appearances. But besides instruction there is also delight. Poetry's oldest justifications, it turns out, apply to these switches in mode as well as to its content. The analyst sees in the moment of switching the giggle of insight or the more subtle pleasure and release resulting from cure. And like Aristotle, the critics have found this pleasure too—a delight not only in shapeliness but in a change of shape or a switch from chaos to shape. As Stephen Booth has suggested [in his *Essay on Shakespeare's Sonnets*], in explaining how Shakespeare's play of patterns in the sonnets affects us:

> Perhaps the happiest moment the human mind ever knows is the moment when it senses the presence of order and coherence—and before it realizes the particular nature (and so the particular limits) of the perception. At the moment of unparticularized perception the mind is unlimited. It seems capable of grasping and about to grasp a coherence beyond its capacity.

It is in texts where such self-conscious confrontations become part of the literary work, inseparable from the experience portrayed, that the psychoanalytic process finds its closest parallels. In fact, we can now see why *Oedipus Rex* and *Hamlet* have always been inseparable from conceptions of psychoanalysis. Freud said that this was because of their fantasy content—those secrets that he had just discovered but that the poets had apparently always known. But Freud had discovered the secrets partly by learning to read stories in new ways, and *Oedipus* and *Hamlet* are bound up with the process of discovery as much as with a presentation of facts about the Oedipus complex. They present the reorganizations necessary to incorporate the oedipal fantasy material in a meaningful world. The plays are based on suddenly shifting representations of experience—shifting relations between past and present, fact and fantasy, literal and figurative significance. As in the case of jokes and the uncanny, Freud stressed the importance of certain strong content in these plays, but their effect depends on the way in which that content is presented—on the kind of reorganization of experience that allowed Freud to see in it the secret wishes he was interested in.

The shifts in *Oedipus* in fact make it almost uncanny. Freud locates the play's power in the fact that two desires normally repressed are here presented openly—the wishes for murder and incest. But for anyone seeing the play, the power comes more immediately from the fact that on the literal level the impossible comes true and on another level something which was merely figurative becomes literal. What began as an oracle's pronouncement—which the critic can view as a mere manner of speaking symbolizing our general guilt—comes true. Any attempt to make sense of the events is even more unsettling, particularly if we have just seen Sophocles' play and not merely heard the myth. The play shows a self-confident, ambitious man ruling a city and solving its problems and, after the revelation about what he has done, desperately trying to punish Jocasta and himself. This man and these actions are what the play is about. Behind them we may possibly sense a symbolic murder and an incestuous rape, but only *as* symbols for the onstage drama. They are no more than a projection backward or a reconstruction from Oedipus's current situation, a useful fiction generated solely to explain what is happening on stage. But suddenly the virtual becomes actual, and it is no longer clear what is symbolizing what. The onstage events become symbols for the earlier offstage trespasses. Analysts look at Oedipus confronting the royal couple, Creon and Jocasta, or they look at him breaking into Jocasta's bedroom, waving his sword and crying out on her womb, and they see symbolic displacements of the offstage murder and incest. At first reading, it seems that Oedipus has merely murdered the idea of his father, as we all do; but the second reading shows that in his world the idea is real.

This seamless world generates a confusion that is unlike the simple one in which the past blends imperceptibly into the present (or fantasy blends into reality), as happens in some readings of fantasy material. This is rather a confusion in which the past sometimes seems as if it *were* the present reality; or rather, in which we cannot tell whether the past or the present has priority or whether the fact or the fantasy is "real." The result is a radical doubt about the world that goes beyond moral queasiness—like Hans Castorp's doubt when his doctor on the magic mountain lectures about "love," but uses

> the word love in a somewhat ambiguous sense, so that you were never quite sure where you were with it, or whether he had reference to its sacred or its passionate and fleshly aspect—and this doubt gave one a slightly seasick feeling. . . .

The uncomfortable reorganization in *Hamlet* works differently but has the same effect of challenging not only our images of ourselves but our ability to perceive and interpret the onstage experience. The play is unsettling on every level; the world of Hamlet is a world of unanswered questions and mystery and has lately been seen as one that upsets the audience with its questions as much as it upsets Hamlet. One critic has called this phenomenon "the tragedy of an audience that cannot make up its mind." We initially see the action the same way Hamlet sees it: he thinks he is a revenge play hero, and is caught in a conflict between what he believes he ought to do—murder Claudius—and his own inability to act. But Hamlet's feeling that "one must kill" is no more adequate to the play's world than was the young men's decision that "one must study" in the world of *Love's Labour's Lost,* and we, along with Hamlet, have to reorganize our conception of Hamlet's problem.

Even more unsettling, the simple events of *Hamlet* are hard to sort out. The content here seems to escape its presentation, almost as Tristram Shandy's subject matter escapes his efforts to set it down. We are accustomed to have the dramatist single out important events and devote time to them on stage; we relax in the expectation that he will allocate the scenes and lines in proportion to their importance and that what matters will take place on stage. But time passes unevenly, and events as important as Hamlet's farewell to Ophelia are almost tossed off as incidental reports, leaving us uncertain how to interpret them. Such confusions we are likely to attribute to our own failures rather than to the play, and so we are likely to ignore them as invalid or irrelevant responses. We feel we must have missed something. Still, such confusions leave a trace of Hans Castorp's seasickness.

Both Hamlet and Oedipus, of course, are dealing with material that is as emotionally explosive as Freud said it was, but their power comes as much from a literary and even a perceptual trespass as from a moral one: they violate our assumptions about what things mean as well as our assumptions about heroic natures. The confusion between latent oedipal fantasy and overt action is only one of several confusions; a play's more general instability is what allows the normally discarded fantasy to claim a place—especially in scenes that seem a little odd anyway, like the scene in which Hamlet speaks daggers to his mother in her closet or the one where Oedipus rushes into Jocasta's bedroom with his sword. But effective as this primitive material may be, it is not the sole challenge to our ordinary assumptions; these plays challenge us in *all* the ways that the tactless and suspicious psychoanalytic process does.

What is the difference, then, between the psychoanalytic process and literature—or between what the analyst sees and what the critic sees? The difference is in degree, not in kind, and amounts finally to a matter of tact. The analyst goes further and takes more risks. Even William Empson, despite his program of flouting tact, finally recognized it under another name: every poem has four thousand meanings, he said, but only the "relevant" ones are effective. He did not feel it necessary to explain what he meant by *relevant*. Although by now there are many critics who challenge the limitations of the term *relevant,* the analyst's chief difference from the critic is that he stretches its limits even further.

The critic is willing to question conventions if the text explicitly encourages such questions; but in the end he usually assumes that the governing conventions in the text and in his reading should coincide. The analyst, however, is more interested in the disjunction between the governing conventions and the ones he alternately entertains. He is always ready to see another meaning or a pattern latent in the whole text, which conflicts with the manifest one and which the literary critic would probably ignore because it is so fragile, peripheral, and unelaborated in the ordinary way. The critic filters out these alternative patterns on the basis of convention or on the basis of something like common sense, informed consensus, or an appeal to competence. The analyst trusts none of these.

The analyst is also more likely than the critic to look for primitive material—not only fantasies but primitive levels of organization. He is likely to question conventions on a much more basic level than the critic, suspending his belief not only in morality and decorum, not only in the obvious meaning of the plot, not only in conventions of genre, but also in conventions of representation and language. Because he is interested in the remnants of even the most primitive stages of thought, when the most basic conventions of thinking and representing experience were being internalized and were not yet taken for granted, the analyst does not automatically take them for granted. He looks not only for the neurotic patterns that may have developed later in life and affected a writer's sophisticated conventions and habits but also for the more fundamental patterns that, when they go wrong, make people psychotic. He examines not just certain private symbols but the more fundamental conventions of symbolism—the ones that the tactful critics, of necessity, agree to take as their starting point. No wonder the critics have mistrusted the analyst. It has taken them a long time to learn not to ask the "wrong" questions about literature, and they are understandably wary about anyone who systematically sets out to do so.

Two brief illustrations from the visual arts will serve as convenient models for the difference between critic and analyst and between the sort of analyses I looked at in the last section and the ones I now present for consideration. The first is Ernst Gombrich's example of misreading ["Reflections on the Greek Revolution," in *Art and Illusion: A Study in the Psychology of Pictorial Representation*]. He describes an Egyptian battle scene in which the figure of Pharaoh is represented much larger than the other figures, not to depict his actual size but to show his importance. When the Greeks copied the picture for their own purposes, however, the result was distorted by their misunderstanding: their version showed a gigantic Hercules at battle with Egyptians shown as pygmies, a literal translation of the Egyptian symbols. The Greeks, Gombrich concludes, misunderstood the picture because they used the wrong conventions to read it (they read visually instead of conceptually), and he implies that we should learn a lesson from their mistake. But his example is a specialized one because its two readings derive from different cultures, only one of which has shaped the text.

Walter J. Ong provides us with a second parallel to the difference between critic and analyst in his study of the title page for Thomas Hobbes's *Leviathan,* which he takes to be a typical product of the new *visual* mode of thinking fostered by the spread of printing ["From Allegory to Diagram in the Renaissance Mind: A Study in the Significance of the Allegorical Tableau," *Journal of Aesthetics and Art Criticism* 17 (1959)]. The title page consists of a leviathan man made up of tiny figures squeezed into his outlines. Ong laments the disappearance of conceptual realism here, but surely part of the power in this much reprinted emblem is the way it courts both a conceptual and a visual reading, both an "Egyptian" and a "Greek" reading, and plays them against one another. We may have to ignore the Greek reading to understand the first example, but we will miss the visual pun in the second unless we take the Greek reading into account.

The critic reads texts as if they were Egyptian paintings; the analyst, as if they were all emblems like the Leviathan. The question that must be answered is, How far should the analyst take his assumption? How far can he go in trying out new ways of reading? The answer, of course, is that there is no answer, because the question is not complete. It should be rephrased, How far can the analyst go for this particular purpose? The analyst's bias is to include as many purposes as possible within the central one of finding out what the text really means. He suggests that we open ourselves not only to the quite specialized task of "being objective" but also to the far more common state that comes before objectivity, before we perceive the pattern in the text and the coincidence between the text at hand and what we have learned about other texts. His method makes explicit the progress toward an "objective" reading. It makes explicit all the alternate readings discarded on the way and shows how any reading is the product of destruction and denial as well as creativity and perception. (This denial is not necessarily defensive; it is simply necessitated by the rules of this "objective" game.)

So at times the analyst sounds like the stereotypical naive

freshman, who regularly approaches highly conventional literature the way the Greeks approached the Egyptian painting, expecting obvious realism and criticizing Dickens's flat characters or insincere Elizabethan sonnets. The psychoanalytic critic acts as if he had never heard about literary conventions, so he approaches the text with the ragbag of literal-minded reading habits of childhood. He looks for naturalistic, literal mimesis where there is none, or he takes what other readers perceive as conventions and interprets them as literal facts about the fictional world. Thus Kenneth Muir takes Shakespeare's heroines for transvestites when they put on their masculine disguises [Kenneth Muir and Sean O'Loughlin, *The Voyage to Illyria: A New Study of Shakespeare*], and Harold Bloom sees homosexuality in the relation between Snow White and her mother ["Driving out Demons," review of Bruno Bettelheim's *The Uses of Enchantment, New York Review of Books,* 15 July 1976, pp. 10-12]. And Leo Bersani faults George Eliot's *Middlemarch* because the narrator claims to be describing a haphazard world without design yet does so by arranging neatly paralleled plots and revealing carefully designed coincidences [*A Future for Astyanax: Character and Desire in Fiction*]. Other readers would take Shakespeare's disguises to be externally motivated conventions, and they would interpret George Eliot's coincidences not as literal representations of simultaneous action but as conventional symbols that indicate more essential connections between events than those which are spatial and temporal.

Although we may with some reason feel that these interpretations distort the text, they are nonetheless true to it in a way. The analyst may sound like a freshman, but we are all naive freshmen, even if only for a moment, if only on first confrontation with a new text, in an initial response which we quickly dismiss. These are not just eccentric responses, either, but predictable ones, errors as traditionally associated with a text as the accepted reading is. The *Aeneid* is cumbersome after reading the *Odyssey;* there is too much coincidence in *Oedipus Rex;* and *Paradise Lost* is boring. Our final response may differ from these first reactions, but that response is partly defined by our original reactions. Even if we choose, as mature professional readers, to respect the customary conventions of the work as they were "intended," custom can be dangerous. It can dull the reader to his work as it dulls Elsinore's merry gravediggers to theirs, making it for them "a property of easiness" to sing as they dig (5.1.65-68). A periodic return to the chaos of possibilities emphasizes new details and fosters an openness to new patterns, tones, and nuances. It revitalizes the reader's perceptions of literature and gives him more to work with, even if he does not finally choose to use everything he finds.

The difference between a freshman's ignorance and the analyst's organized innocence—or "applied naiveté" as Brigid Brophy has called it—is important. It is one thing for Thomas Rymer to blunder past all dramatic conventions to support his famous complaint about how improbable *Othello* is. But Stanley Cavell makes a more sophisticated point when he persists, somewhat perversely, it is true, in asking why the audience does not rush onstage when Othello strangles Desdemona ["The Avoidance of Love: A Reading of *King Lear*," in *Must We Mean What We Say?*]. Cavell blames the audience's unfeeling acceptance of a customary distance between themselves and the ac-

tion onstage and likens this distance to the similar tragic distances that separate the characters on stage, each of which is maintained by convention as well. Why, for example, Cavell asks, does Edgar wait so long in *Lear* to reveal his true identity to his father? By the time he tells old Gloucester who he really is, it is too late, and the old man's heart cracks with the shock. For Cavell, this is an example of people's fear of confronting one another; for other critics, it is a matter of synchronizing plots or of making the physical revelation correspond to the more reluctant spiritual one it symbolizes. Cavell, in other words, has taken what other critics see as dramatic and symbolic conventions and has interpreted them as facts about a character's mind. We may object to his refusal to play the dramatic game; but in *Hamlet,* as we saw, this refusal is what the play is about. Hamlet's whole problem is that he cannot accept certain behavioral conventions; and by the end of Shakespeare's play, we have learned not to accept them either. The question that was "wrong" to ask in *Othello* is the one question we must ask in *Hamlet.*

Using the psychoanalytic process as a model for literary texts does not imply that all conventions, all literal meanings, or all ordinary functions in a text are there only to be questioned. But it does provide a reminder that the questions are always there and that the uncertainty they produce is part of what the text conveys, even if this uncertainty is slight and finally resolved. Texts are more unstable than we might think; they are less fixed than simpler models that merely look for "hidden" material might indicate. (pp. 216-42)

Meredith Anne Skura, in her The Literary Use of the Psychoanalytic Process, *Yale University Press, 1981, 280 p.*

FURTHER READING

Alcorn, Marshall W., and Bracher, Mark. "Literature, Psychoanalysis, and the Re-Formation of the Self: A New Direction for Reader-Response Theory." *PMLA* 100, No. 3 (May 1985): 342-54.
    Maintains that literature provides the reader with opportunities to redefine his or her identity.

Bann, Stephen. "Adrian Stokes: English Aesthetic Criticism under the Impact of Psychoanalysis." In *Freud in Exile: Psychoanalysis and Its Vicissitudes,* edited by Edward Timms and Naomi Segal, pp. 134-44. New Haven: Yale University Press, 1988.
    Traces the ways in which psychoanalysis influenced the aesthetic theory of Adrian Stokes, focusing particularly on the period between the First and Second World Wars.

Bergler, Edmund. "Psychoanalysis of Writers and of Literary Productivity." In *Psychoanalysis and the Social Sciences,* edited by Géza Róheim, pp. 247-96. New York: International Universities Press, 1947.
    Examines the nature of artistic creativity.

Bettelheim, Bruno. *The Uses of Enchantment: The Meaning*

and Importance of Fairy Tales. New York: Alfred A. Knopf, 1975, 328 p.

> Asserts that fairy tales have an important function in children's psychological development. Bettelheim states that "fairy stories represent in imaginative form what the process of healthy human development consists of, and . . . make such development attractive for the child to engage in."

Bloom, Clive. "The 'Humunculus.' " In his *The 'Occult' Experience and the New Criticism: Daemonism, Sexuality, and the Hidden in Literature,* pp. 27-55. Sussex: Harvester Press, 1986.

> Critique of Marie Bonaparte's *The Life and Work of Edgar Allan Poe,* an early psychobiography. Bloom notes: "Psychoanalytic practice, through its concepts, allows Marie Bonaparte to read Poe and us to read Bonaparte reading Poe."

Bracher, Mark. "Rouzing the Facilities: Lacanian Psychoanalysis and the Marriage of Heaven and Hell in the Reader." In *Critical Paths: Blake and the Argument of Method,* edited by Dan Miller, Mark Bracher, and Donald Ault, pp. 168-203. Durham, N.C.: Duke University Press, 1987.

> Uses a psychoanalytic model developed by Jacques Lacan to examine interaction between the reader and the text of William Blake's *The Marriage of Heaven and Hell.*

Brooks, Peter. *Reading for the Plot: Design and Intention in Narrative.* New York: Alfred A. Knopf, 1984, 363 p.

> Study of "plots and plotting, about how stories come to be ordered in significant form, and also about our desire and need for such orderings."

Bush, Marshall. "The Problem of Form in the Psychoanalytic Theory of Art." *The Psychoanalytic Review* 54, No. 1 (Spring 1967): 5-35.

> Attempts to reconcile a psychoanalytic understanding of the formal qualities of art with the traditional formalist aesthetics, concluding "it is the recognition of an ideal attainment in ego functioning which underlies the formal pleasure a work of art has to offer."

Cave, Terence. "The Prime and Precious Thing." *Times Literary Supplement* (4 January 1985): 14.

> Review of Peter Brooks's *Reading for the Plot: Design and Attention in Narrative.* Cave concludes that "in his insistence that we still *need* to read for the plot, Brooks offers us a fully articulate escape from a purely formalistic narratology."

Crews, Frederick, ed. *Psychoanalysis and the Literary Process.* Cambridge, Mass.: Winthrop Publishers, 1970.

> Essay collection intended "to demonstrate the range and potential usefulness of psychoanalytic criticism and to assist readers who are disposed to practice it themselves." The volume features a general essay in which Crews notes some of the limitations of psychoanalytic criticism and several examples of applied psychoanalytic criticism, including Albert D. Hutter on Charles Dickens's *Great Expectations* and David Leverenz on Herman Melville's *Moby-Dick.*

———. "The American Literary Critic Frederick Crews Explains Why He Has Rejected Freud." *London Review of Books* 23, No. 2 (4-17 December 1980): 3-4, 6.

> Interview in which Crews repudiates psychoanalysis as a theoretical and therapeutic doctrine. Crews explains:

"I found myself gradually obliged, by critiques I couldn't ignore, to shift the balance between the enticing features of psychoanalysis and unanswerable doubts about it."

Daiches, David. "Criticism and Psychology." In his *Critical Approaches to Literature,* rev. ed., pp. 329-49. London: Longman, 1981.

> Surveys various types of psychological criticism, such as the analysis of the author or a character, and the work of specific critics, including William Wordsworth, Edmund Wilson, and Northrop Frye.

Davis, Robert Con, ed. *Lacan and Narration: The Psychoanalytic Difference in Narrative Theory.* Baltimore: Johns Hopkins University Press, 1983, 223 p.

> Collection of essays which address "the question of the possibility of a narrative theory purloined from the linguistic model of Lacan's psychoanalytic theory." Contributors include Robert Con Davis, Jerry Aline Flieger, Shoshana Felman, and Richard Macksey.

———. "Error at Yale: Geoffrey Hartman, Psychoanalysis, and Deconstruction." In *Rhetoric and Form: Deconstruction at Yale,* edited by Robert Con Davis and Ronald Schleifer, pp. 135-56. Norman: University of Oklahoma Press, 1985.

> Critiques Geoffrey Hartman's essay "Psychoanalysis: The French Connection." Davis remarks that "Hartman is not the whole of American criticism, but his critical dilemmas—measured in self-awareness and performed in honest, broad gestures—assist us incalculably in reflecting on some of the dilemmas of American criticism in an increasingly theoretical and deconstructive age."

Eagleton, Terry. "Psychoanalysis." In his *Literary Theory: An Introduction,* pp. 151-93. Minneapolis: University of Minnesota Press, 1983.

> Explains basic concepts of psychoanalytic theory and examines the ideas of Jacques Lacan and other psychoanalytic theorists.

Felman, Shoshana. *Writing and Madness (Literature/Philosophy/Psychoanalysis).* Translated by Martha Noel Evans, Shoshana Felman, and Brian Massumi. Ithaca: Cornell University Press, 1985, 255 p.

> Discusses the relation between madness and literature, examining different theoretical approaches and a variety of literary works. Felman explains that she intends "to think about what 'speaking about madness' means by exploring the relationship between the texts of madness and the madness of texts."

Fish, Stanley. *Is There a Text in This Class? The Authority of Interpretive Communities.* Cambridge: Harvard University Press, 1980, 394 p.

> Series of essays which chronicle the evolution of Fish's model for understanding literature. Fish explains, "Whereas I had once agreed with my predecessors on the need to control interpretation lest it overwhelm and obscure texts, facts, authors, and intentions. I now believe that interpretation is the source of texts, facts, authors, and intentions."

Forrester, John. "Psychoanalysis or Literature?" *French Studies: A Quarterly Review* XXXV, No. 2 (April 1981): 170-79.

> Discusses issues raised in several books and essay collections on psychoanalysis and literature, such as differ-

ences in the approaches of American and French schools, language as it functions in poetry and psychoanalysis, and ways in which psychoanalysis can contribute to an understanding of reader response. The volumes examined include *Politique et Psychoanalyse* by Gilles Deleuze and Félix Guattari, *Psychoanalysis, Creativity, and Literature: A French-American Inquiry,* edited by Alan Noland, and *The Literary Freud: Mechanisms of Defense and the Poetic Will,* edited by Joseph H. Smith.

Freud, Sigmund. *The Standard Edition of the Complete Psychological Works of Sigmund Freud.* 24 vols. Translated by James Strachey with Anna Freud, Alix Strachey, and Alan Tyson. London: Hogarth Press, 1953-74.
    Contains all of Freud's major works, including pre-psychoanalytic writings and unpublished drafts.

Fuller, Peter. *Art and Psychoanalysis.* London: Writers and Readers Publishing Cooperative, 1980, 250 p.
    Four lectures relating aesthetic theories to post-Freudian psychoanalysis, particularly the ideas of the object-relations school in post-World War II Britain.

Funt, Karen Bryce. "From Memoir to Case History: Schreber, Freud, and Jung." *Mosaic* 20, No. 4 (Fall 1987): 97-115.
    Examines Freud's and Jung's conversion of the *Memoirs* of Daniel Paul Schreber into a case history as an example of the use of literary documents in the formation of psychological theory.

Gallop, Jane. "Reading the Mother Tongue: Psychoanalytic Feminist Criticism." *Critical Inquiry* 13, No. 2 (Winter 1987): 314-29.
    Provides a detailed reading of *The (M)other Tongue,* edited by Shirley Nelson Garner, Claire Kahane, and Madelon Sprengnether, the first anthology of psychoanalytic feminist criticism. Gallop asserts that "feminist criticism has, both directly and indirectly, given new viability to psychoanalytic criticism" and suggests that the combination "is clearly conducive to good reading, writing, and thinking."

Griffin, William J. "The Use and Abuse of Psychoanalysis in the Study of Literature." *Literature and Psychology* 1 (1951): 3-20.
    Assesses the strengths and weaknesses of a psychoanalytic approach to literature.

Grimaud, Michael. "Psychoanalysis, Contemporary Science, and the Quandaries of Psychocriticism." *Literature and Psychology* XXVII, No. 4 (1977): 183-89.
    Reviews two psychoanalytic journals, *Psychoanalysis and Contemporary Science* and *The Annual of Psychoanalysis,* and advocates interdisciplinary exchange, particularly between psychoanalysis and literary criticism.

Gunn, Daniel. *Psychoanalysis and Fiction: An Exploration of Literary and Psychoanalytic Borders.* Cambridge: Cambridge University Press, 1988, 251 p.
    Examines a variety of literary works and psychoanalytic theories to elucidate the relationship between psychoanalysis and literature.

Heller, Erich. "Observations on Psychoanalysis and Modern Literature." In his *In the Age of Prose: Literary and Philosophical Essays,* pp. 179-91. Cambridge: Cambridge University Press, 1984.
    Places Freud's ideas in the context of the literary and intellectual climate of the nineteenth and early twentieth centuries.

Hertz, Neil. "Freud and the Sandman." In *Textual Strategies: Perspectives in Post-Structuralist Criticism,* edited by Josué V. Harari, pp. 296-321. Ithaca: Cornell University Press, 1979.
    Analyzes Freud's reading of E. T. A. Hoffmann's "The Sandman," noting connections Freud made between the uncanny and his theory of repetition-compulsion and suggesting that the issues Freud explored in his essay "The Uncanny" were related to events in his personal life at the time.

Holland, Norman N. *Poems in Persons: An Introduction to the Psychoanalysis of Literature.* New York: Columbia University Press, 1973, 182 p.
    Uses the poetry of H. D. (Hilda Doolittle) to explore reader response, discussing the reactions of two students to H. D.'s "The Walls Do Not Fall" and other literary works and offering his own interpretations. Holland states, "It is not . . . the poem that embodies a mental process. It is the *reader.*"

———. *5 Readers Reading.* New Haven: Yale University Press, 1975, 418 p.
    Studies the responses of five subjects to the literary texts they read. Holland maintains that these readers "recreate the original literary creation in terms of their own personalities, themselves understood as a continuing process of transformation."

———. "Unity Identity Text Self." *PMLA* 90, No. 5 (October 1975): 813-22.
    Explores the relationship of the four concepts named in the title of the essay in order to establish "the creative and relational quality of all our experiences, not least the writing and reading of literature."

Huss, Roy. *The Mindscapes of Art: Dimensions of the Psyche in Fiction, Drama, and Film.* Rutherford, N.J.: Fairleigh Dickinson University Press, 1986, 225 p.
    Examines the treatment of psychoanalytic issues in selected works of literature, drama, and film. Huss states that he wishes to "redirect attention to the psychological interpretation of the *characters* of fiction, drama, and film, and to do so in such a way as to allow a whole new spectrum of psychological approaches to demonstrate their value."

Kaplan, Morton, and Kloss, Robert, eds. *The Unspoken Motive: A Guide to Psychoanalytic Literary Criticism.* New York: Free Press, 1973, 323 p.
    Collection comprising an introduction using examples from fiction to explain basic elements of psychoanalytic theory, applications of psychoanalytic criticism to a variety of literary works, a historical review of leading psychoanalytic critics, and an appendix which defines dissenting schools of psychoanalytic thought.

Kiell, Norman. *Psychoanalysis, Psychology, and Literature: A Bibliography.* 2 vols. Rev ed. Metuchen, N.J.: Scarecrow Press, 1982.
    Includes approximately 20,000 entries organized by topic with indexes to individual authors and subjects.

Kris, Ernst. *Psychoanalytic Explorations in Art.* New York: International Universities Press, 1952, 358 p.

Applies theories of "psychoanalytic ego psychology" to works of art and literature.

Kubie, Lawrence S. *Neurotic Distortions of the Creative Process.* Lawrence: University of Kansas Press, 1958, 152 p.
Explains ways in which preconscious, conscious, and unconscious processes produce both creativity and neurosis.

Lacan, Jacques. *Ecrits: A Selection.* Translated by Alan Sheridan. New York: W. W. Norton & Co., 1977, 338 p.
Collection of essays which demonstrate Lacan's version of psychoanalytic theory and its application to literature.

Mahoney, Patrick J. *Psychoanalysis and Discourse.* London: Tavistock, 1987, 259 p.
Collection of essays divided into two sections: "Discourse and the Clinical Context" and "Non-Clinical Discourse and Psychoanalysis." Topics include free association, Freud's interpretation of dreams, and examination of literary works such as Franz Kafka's "The Hunger Artist" and Shakespeare's Sonnet XX.

Nägele, Rainer. *Reading after Freud: Essays on Goethe, Hölderlin, Habermas, Nietzsche, Brecht, Celan, and Freud.* New York: Columbia University Press, 1987, 225 p.
Investigates Freud's influence on the interpretation of literature. Nägele notes: "Reading after Freud first means reading Freud, interpreting his texts; it also means reading Freud after Lacan, which in turn involves a reading of Lacan after Freud."

Natoli, Joseph, ed. *Psychological Perspectives on Literature: Freudian Dissidents and Non-Freudians.* Hamden, Conn.: Archon, 1984, 288 p.
Collection of essays that examine literary works using non-Freudian psychoanalytic theories and other psychological approaches. The essays include an application of Adlerian theory to *The Catcher in the Rye,* a consideration of *Wuthering Heights* using Reichian criticism, and a discussion of the ideas of R. D. Laing and the works of Edgar Allan Poe, Nathaniel Hawthorne, and Kate Chopin.

New Literary History. Psychology and Literature: Some Contemporary Directions XII, No. 1 (Autumn 1980): 1-218.
Essays considering the relationship between psychoanalysis and literature, including questions of language, narration, and interpretation. Among the contributors are André Green, Ernest S. Wolf, Roy Schafer, Marie-Louise von Franz, Phoebe C. Ellsworth, and William Kerrigan.

Orlando, Francesco. *Toward a Freudian Theory of Literature: With an Analysis of Racine's "Phèdre."* Translated by Charmaine Lee. Baltimore: Johns Hopkins University Press, 1978, 216 p.
Examines *Phèdre* using psychoanalytic concepts and then more fully develops a methodology for applying psychoanalytic concepts to literature, focusing especially on language.

Peel, Ellen. "Psychoanalysis and the Uncanny." *Comparative Literature Studies* XVII, No. 4 (December 1980): 410-17.
Examines Freud's essay "The Uncanny" and Tzvetan Todorov's *The Fantastic,* focusing on their views of the reader's response to the uncanny in literature.

Phillips, William, ed. *Art and Psychoanalysis.* New York: Criterion Books, 1957, 552 p.
Collection of essays including "studies of single works of art or creative artists, theoretical essays, and literary pieces." Contributors include Marie Bonaparte, William Empson, Sigmund Freud, Erich Fromm, Ernst Kris, Thomas Mann, Otto Rank, Theodore Reik, Lionel Trilling, and Edmund Wilson.

Punter, David. *The Hidden Script: Writing and the Unconscious.* London: Routledge & Kegan Paul, 1985, 193 p.
Examines evidence of the unconscious in the works of several modern writers, including Angela Carter, Doris Lessing, and Kurt Vonnegut.

Reppen, Joseph, and Charney, Maurice, eds. *The Psychoanalytic Study of Literature.* Hillsdale, N.J.: Analytic Press, 1985, 290 p.
Includes essays on Freudian concepts and the literary process; Freudian theory, philosophy, and linguistics; individual texts and authors from a psychocultural perspective; and Lacanian interpretation.

Roland, Alan, ed. *Psychoanalysis, Creativity, and Literature: A French-American Inquiry.* New York: Columbia University Press, 1978, 368 p.
Collection of essays intended to make French psychoanalytic ideas, including the work of Jacques Lacan, more accessible to Americans and to encourage dialogue between psychoanalysis and other disciplines. Contributors include Kenneth Burke, André Green, Norman N. Holland, Albert Rothenberg, and Ernest S. Wolf.

Rose, Gilbert J. *The Power of Form: A Psychoanalytic Approach to Aesthetic Form.* New York: International Universities Press, 1980, 234 p.
Explores the relationship between personality development and aesthetic form in art.

Schafer, Roy. *A New Language for Psychoanalysis.* New Haven: Yale University Press, 1976, 394 p.
Collection of essays in which Schafer develops "action language," a system of vocabulary and discourse which he contends should replace the terminology of Freud's psychoanalytic theories. Schafer views his work as "part of a new critical movement concerned with the logic, language, implications, and applications of Freudian psychoanalysis."

Shute, J. P. "Nabokov and Freud: The Play of Power." *Modern Fiction Studies* 30, No. 4 (Winter 1984): 637-50.
Studies Vladimir Nabokov's attitude toward Freud, remarking that "Nabokov's lifelong polemic against Freud has had the paradoxical effect of introducing him into his every text—but this is because, for the novelist, he is already there."

Simon-Miller, Françoise L. "Ambivalence and Identification: Freud on Literature." *Literature and Psychology,* XXVIII, No. 1 (1978): 23-40.
Explores possible reasons for Freud's ambivalence toward creative writers and literature and then discusses Freud's writings on literature and art.

Sitterson, Joseph C., Jr. "Psychoanalytic Models and Literary Theory." *University of Toronto Quarterly* 51, No. 1 (Fall 1981): 78-92.
Contends that much current psychoanalytic theory has little to add to an understanding of literature and urges

literary theorists to consider psychoanalytic ideas critically rather than assuming their value or lack of value.

Spector, Jack J. *The Aesthetics of Freud: A Study in Psychoanalysis and Art.* New York: Praeger Publishers, 1973, 242 p.

Attempts to "explore the subjective and personal aspects of Freud's apparently objective studies of art, and reveal the man beneath."

Tennenhouse, Leonard, ed. *The Practice of Psychoanalytic Criticism.* Detroit: Wayne State University Press, 1976, 279 p.

Collection of essays using psychoanalytic theory to examine individual literary works, including Thomas More's *Utopia,* Charles Dickens's *David Copperfield,* and John Steinbeck's "The Snake," as well as essays examining such topics as differences between the romance and the novel and the role of the ego in the creation of art. Contributors include Leonard Manheim, Charles E. May, Murray M. Schwartz, Edward Wasiolek, and Dianne Weisgram.

Weiss, Daniel. *The Critic Agonistes: Psychology, Myth, and the Art of Fiction,* edited by Eric Solomon and Stephen Arkin. Seattle: University of Washington Press, 1985, 270 p.

Contains two general essays on psychoanalysis and its relation to literature and one in which Weiss applies psychoanalytic criticism to two short stories by Frank O'Connor.

Wollheim, Richard. "Freud and the Understanding of Art." In his *On Art and the Mind,* pp. 202-19. Cambridge, Mass.: Harvard University Press, 1974.

Discusses Freud's views on art as presented in his essays on the *Moses* of Michelangelo, Leonardo da Vinci, and Wilhelm Jensen's novella *Gradiva.*

Wright, Elizabeth. "Modern Psychoanalytic Criticism." In *Modern Literary Theory: A Comparative Introduction,* edited by Ann Jefferson and David Robey, pp. 113-33. Totowa, N. J.: Barnes & Noble Books, 1982.

Surveys the development of psychoanalytic criticism, including the application of classical psychoanalytic theory to the author and character, the reader-response theory of Norman Holland, and the structural psychoanalysis of Jacques Lacan.

———. *Psychoanalytic Criticism: Theory in Practice.* London: Methuen, 1984, 208 p.

Surveys major schools of psychoanalytic criticism, including classical Freudian criticism, ego psychology, archetypal criticism, object relations, structural psychoanalysis, and post-structural psychoanalysis.

———. "Another Look at Lacan and Literary Criticism." *New Literary History* 19, No. 3 (Spring 1988): 617-27.

Examines Jacques Lacan's use of Freudian concepts and then discusses the work of Gilles Deleuze and Félix Guattari as an example of "post-Lacanian criticism."

Yale French Studies, Special Issue: French Freud: Structural Studies in Psychoanalysis, no. 48 (1972): 5-202.

Includes Jacques Lacan's "Seminar on 'The Purloined Letter,'" Jacques Derrida's "Freud and the Scene of Writing," and "The Unconscious: A Psychoanalytic Study," by Jean Laplanche and Serge Leclaire, with introductory notes to each essay written by Jeffrey Mehlman.

Yale French Studies, Special Issue: Literature and Psychoanalysis: The Question of Reading: Otherwise, no. 55/56 (1977): 2-507.

Essays include "Desire and the Interpretation of Desire in *Hamlet*" by Jacques Lacan, "Turning the Screw of Interpretation" by Shoshana Felman, "Freud's Writing on Writing" by Jean-Michel Rey, and "The Frame of Reference: Poe, Lacan, Derrida" by Barbara Johnson.

Theater of the Absurd

INTRODUCTION

"Theater of the Absurd" was established as a literary term by English critic Martin Esslin, whose 1960 essay and 1961 book of that title proposed that significant similarities could be observed in the works of a diverse group of dramatists writing in the 1950s and that these shared traits constituted a new and distinct type of theater. This new theater, Esslin argued, was epitomized by strikingly unrealistic characters and situations, a concern with the perennial ordeals of human existence rather than with ephemeral social and political issues, and a general sense that life is devoid of absolute meaning. As Esslin explains, the Theater of the Absurd "bravely faces up to the fact that for those to whom the world has lost its central explanation and meaning, it is no longer possible to accept art forms still based on the continuation of standards and concepts that have lost their validity; that is, the possibility of knowing the laws of conduct and ultimate values, as deductible from a firm foundation of revealed certainty about the purpose of man in the universe." Esslin found this absurdist world view embodied in the work of four principal dramatists: Samuel Beckett, Eugène Ionesco, Arthur Adamov, and Jean Genet. While these authors did not collaborate as a literary movement, Esslin contended that their plays, along with those of many other European and American writers, displayed a common artistic sensibility and philosophical attitude which have come to be denoted by the term "absurdist."

Esslin's grouping of works by several highly individual dramatists under the collective designation of the Theater of the Absurd has been a source of controversy. However, his central thesis that in the 1950s there arose a new style of theater, one that attempted to undermine earlier conceptions of both the modern stage and the human condition, has found wide acceptance among critics. Even Ionesco, who initially dismissed the idea of absurdist theater as itself an absurdity, can be seen in his recent essay "Theaters of the Absurd" to have largely adopted Esslin's perspective, stating of himself and his contemporaries in the theater: "We wanted to make evident to the spectators the existential condition of man even in his integrity, in his totality, in his deepest tragedy, his destiny—that is to say in the conscience of the absurdity of the world."

Like the philosophical movement of Existentialism to which it is often compared for its concern with the fundamental aspects of human life, the Theater of the Absurd was most conspicuous during the 1950s and early 1960s. With the possible exception of Ionesco, the dramatists associated with this term went on to pursue other styles of literary expression, some of which, like Adamov's dramas of political commitment, in direct opposition to the style and philosophy of absurdism. Nevertheless, the major works of the Theater of the Absurd, most prominently Beckett's *En attendant Godot* (*Waiting for Godot*) and Ionesco's *Les chaises* (*The Chairs*), retain a value apart from their influential role in theatrical history and are now considered classics of modern drama.

REPRESENTATIVE WORKS

Adamov, Arthur
  La grande et la petite manoeuvre (drama) 1950
  L'invasion (drama) 1950
    [*The Invasion*, 1968]
  La parodie (drama) 1952
  Le Professeur Taranne (drama) 1953
    [*Professor Taranne* published in *Four Modern French Comedies*, 1960]
  Le sens de la marche (drama) 1953
  Tous contre tous (drama) 1953
  Comme nous avons été (drama) 1954
    [*As We Were* published in journal *Evergreen Review*, 1957]
  Le ping-pong (drama) 1955
    [*Ping-Pong*, 1959]
  Paolo Paoli (drama) 1958
    [*Paolo Paoli*, 1959]
Albee, Edward
  The Zoo Story (drama) 1958
  The Sandbox (drama) 1959
  The American Dream (drama) 1961
Arrabal, Fernando
  Pique-nique en campagne (drama) [first publication] 1952
    [*Picnic on the Battlefield*, 1967]
  Le tricycle (drama) [first publication] 1953
    [*The Tricycle*, 1967]
  Cérémonie pour un noir assassiné (drama) [first publication] 1956
  Les deux bourreaux (drama) [first publication] 1956
    [*The Executioners* published in "*The Automobile Graveyard*" and "*The Executioners*," 1960; also published as *The Two Executioners*, 1962]
  Le labyrinthe (drama) [first publication] 1956
    [*The Labyrinth*, 1967]
  Cimetière des voitures (drama) [first publication] 1957
    [*The Automobile Graveyard* published in "*The Automobile Graveyard*" and "*The Executioners*," 1960; also published as *The Car Cemetery*, 1962]
  Fando et Lis (drama) 1958
    [*Fando and Lis*, 1962]
  Guernica (drama) 1959
    [*Guernica*, 1967]
  L'architecte et l'Empereur d'Assyrie (drama) [first publication] 1966

[*The Architect and the Emperor of Assyria,* 1969]
Le jardin des délices   (drama)   [first publication]
1969
[*The Garden of Earthly Delights,* 1974]
Beckett, Samuel
En attendant Godot   (drama)   1953
[*Waiting for Godot,* 1954]
Act sans paroles I   (drama)   1957
[*Act without Words I* published in *"Endgame"
followed by "Act without Words,"* 1958]
Fin de partie   (drama)   1957
[*Endgame,* 1958]
Krapp's Last Tape   (drama)   1958
Act sans paroles II   (drama)   1960
[*Act without Words II* published in *Krapp's Last
Tape, and Other Dramatic Pieces,* 1959]
Oh, les beaux jours!   (drama)   1961
[*Happy Days,* 1961]
Comédie   (drama)   1963
[*Play,* 1964]
Buzzati, Dino
Un caso clinico   (drama)   [first publication]   1953
Frisch, Max
Biedermann und die Brandstifter   (drama)   [first
publication]   1958
[*Biedermann and the Firebugs,* 1962]
Gelber, Jack
The Connection   (drama)   1959
Genet, Jean
Les bonnes   (drama)   1947
[*The Maids* published in *"The Maids" and
"Deathwatch,"* 1954]
Haute surveillance   (drama)   1949
[*Deathwatch* published in *"The Maids" and
"Deathwatch,"* 1954]
Le balcon   (drama)   1957
[*The Balcony,* 1957]
Les nègres   (drama)   1960
[*The Blacks,* 1960]
Les paravents   (drama)   1961
[*The Screens,* 1962]
Havel, Václav
Zahradní slavnost   (drama)   [first publication]
1963
[*The Garden Party,* 1969]
Vryozumění   (drama)   [first publication]   1965
[*The Memorandum,* 1967]
Ionesco, Eugène
La cantatrice chauve   (drama)   1950
[*The Bald Soprano* published in *Plays,* Vol. I, 1958;
also published as *The Bald Prima Donna,* 1958]
La leçon   (drama)   1951
[*The Lesson* published in *Plays,* Vol. I, 1958]
Le salon de l'automobile   (drama)   1951
[*The Motor Show* published in *Plays,* Vol. V, 1963]
Les chaises   (drama)   1952
[*The Chairs* published in *Plays,* Vol. I, 1958]
La jeune fille à marier   (drama)   1953
[*Maid to Marry* published in *Plays,* Vol. III, 1960]
Le maître   (drama)   1953
[*The Leader* published in *Plays,* Vol. IV, 1960]
Victimes du devoir   (drama)   1953
[*Victims of Duty* published in *Plays,* Vol. II, 1958]
Amédée ou comment s'en débarrasser   (drama)
1954

[*Amédée, or How to Get Rid of It* published in
Plays, Vol. II, 1958]
Jacques ou la soumission   (drama)   1955
[*Jack, or the Submission* published in Plays, Vol. I,
1958; also published as *Jacques, or Obedience,*
1958]
Le nouveau locataire   (drama)   1955
[*The New Tenant* published in *Plays,* Vol. II, 1958]
L'impromptu de l'Alma ou le caméléon du berger
(drama)   1956
[*Improvisation, or The Shepherd's Chameleon*
published in *Plays,* Vol. III, 1960]
*L'avenir est dans les oeufs ou il faut de tout pour faire
un monde*   (drama)   1957
[*The Future Is in Eggs, or It Takes All Sorts to
Make a World* published in *Plays,* Vol. IV, 1960]
Rhinocéros   (drama)   1959
[*Rhinoceros* published in *Plays,* Vol. IV, 1960]
Tueur sans gages   (drama)   1959
[*The Killer* published in *Plays,* Vol. III, 1960]
Délire à deux   (drama)   1962
[*Frenzy for Two* published in *Plays,* Vol. VI, 1965]
Le roi se meurt   (drama)   1962
[*Exit the King* published in *Plays,* Vol. V, 1963]
Le piéton de l'air   (drama)   1963
[*A Stroller in the Air* published in *Plays,* Vol. VI,
1965]
La soif et la faim   (drama)   1965
[*Hunger and Thirst* published in *Plays,* Vol. VII,
1968]
Kopit, Arthur
*Oh Dad, Poor Dad, Mamma's Hung You in the Closet
and I'm Feelin' So Sad*   (drama)   1960
Pinter, Harold
The Room   (drama)   1957
The Birthday Party   (drama)   1958
The Dumbwaiter   (drama)   1959
The Caretaker   (drama)   1960
A Slight Ache   (drama)   1961
The Collection   (drama)   1962
The Homecoming   (drama)   1965
Simpson, Norman Frederick
A Resounding Tinkle   (drama)   1957
The Hole   (drama)   1958
One Way Pendulum   (drama)   1959
The Form   (drama)   1961
Vian, Boris
L'équarrissage pour tous   (drama)   1950
[*The Knacker's ABC,* 1968]
Les bâtisseurs d'empire ou le schmürz   (drama)
1959
[*The Empire Builders,* 1967]

"THE THEATER OF THE ABSURD"

Martin Esslin

[*In the following essay, Esslin expounds the characteris-*

tics and discusses the leading playwrights of the Theater of the Absurd.]

The plays of Samuel Beckett, Arthur Adamov, and Eugène Ionesco have been performed with astonishing success in France, Germany, Scandinavia, and the English-speaking countries. This reception is all the more puzzling when one considers that the audiences concerned were amused by and applauded these plays fully aware that they could not understand what they meant or what their authors were driving at.

At first sight these plays do, indeed, confront their public with a bewildering experience, a veritable barrage of wildly irrational, often nonsensical goings-on that seem to go counter to all accepted standards of stage convention. In these plays, some of which are labeled "antiplays," neither the time nor the place of the action are ever clearly stated. (At the beginning of Ionesco's *The Bald Soprano* the clock strikes seventeen.) The characters hardly have any individuality and often even lack a name; moreover, halfway through the action they tend to change their nature completely. Pozzo and Lucky in Beckett's *Waiting for Godot,* for example, appear as master and slave at one moment only to return after a while with their respective positions mysteriously reversed. The laws of probability as well as those of physics are suspended when we meet young ladies with two or even three noses (Ionesco's *Jack or the Submission*), or a corpse that has been hidden in the next room that suddenly begins to grow to monstrous size until a giant foot crashes through the door onto the stage (Ionesco's *Amédée*). As a result, it is often unclear whether the action is meant to represent a dream world of nightmares or real happenings. Within the same scene the action may switch from the nightmarish poetry of high emotions to pure knock-about farce or cabaret, and above all, the dialogue tends to get out of hand so that at times the words seem to go counter to the actions of the characters on the stage, to degenerate into lists of words and phrases from a dictionary or traveler's conversation book, or to get bogged down in endless repetitions like a phonograph record stuck in one groove. Only in this kind of demented world can strangers meet and discover, after a long polite conversation and close cross-questioning, that, to their immense surprise, they must be man and wife as they are living on the same street, in the same house, apartment, room, and bed (Ionesco's *The Bald Soprano*). Only here can the whole life of a group of characters revolve around the passionate discussion of the aesthetics and economics of pinball machines (Adamov's *Ping-Pong*). Above all, everything that happens seems to be beyond rational motivation, happening at random or through the demented caprice of an unaccountable idiot fate. Yet, these wildly extravagant tragic farces and farcial tragedies, although they have suffered their share of protests and scandals, do arouse interest and are received with laughter and thoughtful respect. What is the explanation for this curious phenomenon?

The most obvious, but perhaps too facile answer that suggests itself is that these plays are prime examples of "pure theatre." They are living proof that the magic of the stage can persist even outside, and divorced from, any framework of conceptual rationality. They prove that exits and entrances, light and shadow, contrasts in costume, voice, gait and behavior, pratfalls and embraces, all the manifold mechanical interactions of human puppets in groupings that suggest tension, conflict, or the relaxation of tensions, can arouse laughter or gloom and conjure up an atmosphere of poetry even if devoid of logical motivation and unrelated to recognizable human characters, emotions, and objectives.

But this is only a partial explanation. While the element of "pure theatre" and abstract stagecraft is certainly at work in the plays concerned, they also have a much more substantial content and meaning. Not only *do* all these plays make sense, though perhaps not obvious or conventional sense, they also give expression to some of the basic issues and problems of our age, in a uniquely efficient and meaningful manner, so that they meet some of the deepest needs and unexpressed yearnings of their audience.

The three dramatists that have been grouped together here would probably most energetically deny that they form anything like a school or movement. Each of them, in fact, has his own roots and sources, his own very personal approach to both form and subject matter. Yet they also clearly have a good deal in common. This common denominator that characterizes their works might well be described as the element of *the absurd.* "Est absurde ce qui n'a pas de but . . ." ("Absurd is that which has no purpose, or goal, or objective"), the definition given by Ionesco in a note on Kafka, certainly applies to the plays of Beckett and Ionesco as well as those of Arthur Adamov up to his latest play, *Paolo Paoli,* when he returned to a more traditional form of social drama.

Each of these writers, however, has his own special type of absurdity: in Beckett it is melancholic, colored by a feeling of futility born from the disillusionment of old age and chronic hopelessness; Adamov's is more active, aggressive, earthy, and tinged with social and political overtones; while Ionesco's absurdity has its own fantastic knock-about flavor of tragical clowning. But they all share the same deep sense of human isolation and of the irremediable character of the human condition.

As Arthur Adamov put it in describing how he came to write his first play *La Parodie* (1947):

> I began to discover stage scenes in the most commonplace everyday events. [One day I saw] a blind man begging; two girls went by without seeing him, singing: "I closed my eyes; it was marvelous!" This gave me the idea of showing on stage, as crudely and as visibly as possible, the loneliness of man, the absence of communication among human beings.

Looking back at his earliest effort (which he now regards as unsuccessful) Adamov defines his basic idea in it, and a number of subsequent plays, as the idea "that the destinies of all human beings are of equal futility, that the refusal to live (of the character called N.) and the joyful acceptance of life (by the employee) both lead, by the same path, to inevitable failure, total destruction." It is the same futility and pointlessness of human effort, the same impossibility of human communication which Ionesco expresses in ever new and ingenious variations. The two old people making conversation with the empty air and living in the expectation of an orator who is to pronounce profound truths about life, but turns out to be deaf and dumb (*The Chairs*), are as sardonically cruel a symbol of this fundamentally tragic view of human existence as Jack (*Jack or the Submission*), who stubbornly resists the concerted urgings of his entire family to subscribe to the most sacred principle of his clan—which, when his resistance finally yields to their entreaties, turns out to be the profound truth: "I love potatoes with bacon" ("J'adore les pommes de terre au lard").

The Theatre of the Absurd shows the world as an incomprehensible place. The spectators see the happenings on the stage entirely from the outside, without ever understanding the full meaning of these strange patterns of events, as newly arrived visitors might watch life in a country of which they have not yet mastered the language. The confrontation of the audience with characters and happenings which they are not quite able to comprehend makes it impossible for them to share the aspirations and emotions depicted in the play. Brecht's famous "Verfremdungseffekt" (alienation effect), the inhibition of any identification between spectator and actor, which Brecht could never successfully achieve in his own highly rational theatre, really comes into its own in the Theatre of the Absurd. It is impossible to identify oneself with characters one does not understand or whose motives remain a closed book, and so the distance between the public and the happenings on the stage can be maintained. Emotional identification with the characters is replaced by a puzzled, critical attention. For while the happenings on the stage are absurd, they yet remain recognizable as somehow related to real life with *its* absurdity, so that eventually the spectators are brought face to face with the irrational side of their existence. Thus, the absurd and fantastic goings-on of the Theatre of the Absurd will, in the end, be found to reveal the irrationality of the human condition and the illusion of what we thought was its apparent logical structure.

If the dialogue in these plays consists of meaningless clichés and the mechanical, circular repetition of stereotyped phrases—how many meaningless clichés and stereotyped phrases do we use in our day-to-day conversation? If the characters change their personality halfway through the action, how consistent and truly integrated are the people we meet in our real life? And if people in these plays appear as mere marionettes, helpless puppets without any will of their own, passively at the mercy of blind fate and meaningless circumstance, do we, in fact, in our overorganized world, still possess any genuine initiative or power to decide our own destiny? The spectators of the Theatre of the Absurd are thus confronted with a grotesquely heightened picture of their own world: a world without faith, meaning, and genuine freedom of will. In this sense, the Theatre of the Absurd is the true theatre of our time.

The theatre of most previous epochs reflected an accepted moral order, a world whose aims and objectives were clearly present to the minds of all its public, whether it was the audience of the medieval mystery plays with their solidly accepted faith in the Christian world order or the audience of the drama of Ibsen, Shaw, or Hauptmann with their unquestioned belief in evolution and progress. To such audiences, right and wrong were never in doubt, nor did they question the then accepted goals of human endeavor. Our own time, at least in the Western world, wholly lacks such a generally accepted and completely integrated world picture. The decline of religious faith, the destruction of the belief in automatic social and biological

progress, the discovery of vast areas of irrational and unconscious forces within the human psyche, the loss of a sense of control over rational human development in an age of totalitarianism and weapons of mass destruction, have all contributed to the erosion of the basis for a dramatic convention in which the action proceeds within a fixed and self-evident framework of generally accepted values. Faced with the vacuum left by the destruction of a universally accepted and unified set of beliefs, most serious playwrights have felt the need to fit their work into the frame of values and objectives expressed in one of the contemporary ideologies: Marxism, psychoanalysis, aestheticism, or nature worship. But these, in the eyes of a writer like Adamov, are nothing but superficial rationalizations which try to hide the depth of man's predicament, his loneliness and his anxiety. Or, as Ionesco puts it:

> As far as I am concerned, I believe sincerely in the poverty of the poor, I deplore it; it is real; it can become a subject for the theatre; I also believe in the anxieties and serious troubles the rich may suffer from; but it is neither in the misery of the former nor in the melancholia of the latter, that I, for one, find my dramatic subject matter. Theatre is for me the outward projection onto the stage of an inner world; it is in my dreams, in my anxieties, in my obscure desires, in my internal contradictions that I, for one, reserve for myself the right of finding my dramatic subject matter. As I am not alone in the world, as each of us, in the depth of his being, is at the same time part and parcel of all others, my dreams, my desires, my anxieties, my obsessions do not belong to me alone. They form part of an ancestral heritage, a very ancient storehouse which is a portion of the common property of all mankind. It is this, which, transcending their outward diversity, reunites all human beings and constitutes our profound common patrimony, the universal language. . . .

In other words, the commonly acceptable framework of beliefs and values of former epochs which has now been shattered is to be replaced by the community of dreams and desires of a collective unconscious. And, to quote Ionesco again:

> . . . the new dramatist is one . . . who tries to link up with what is most ancient: new language and subject matter in a dramatic structure which aims at being clearer, more stripped of non-essentials and more purely theatrical; the rejection of traditionalism to rediscover tradition; a synthesis of knowledge and invention, of the real and imaginary, of the particular and the universal, or as they say now, of the individual and the collective . . . By expressing my deepest obsessions, I express my deepest humanity. I become one with all others, spontaneously, over and above all the barriers of caste and different psychologies. I express my solitude and become one with all other solitudes. . . .

What is the tradition with which the Theatre of the Absurd—at first sight the most revolutionary and radically new movement—is trying to link itself? It is in fact a very ancient and a very rich tradition, nourished from many and varied sources: the verbal exuberance and extravagant inventions of Rabelais, the age-old clowning of the Roman mimes and the Italian *Commedia dell'Arte,* the knockabout humor of circus clowns like Grock; the wild, archetypal symbolism of English nonsense verse, the baroque horror of Jacobean dramatists like Webster or Tourneur, the harsh, incisive and often brutal tones of the German drama of Grabbe, Büchner, Kleist, and Wedekind with its delirious language and grotesque inventiveness; and the Nordic paranoia of the dreams and persecution fantasies of Strindberg.

All these streams, however, first came together and crystallized in the more direct ancestors of the present Theatre of the Absurd. Of these, undoubtedly the first and foremost is Alfred Jarry (1873-1907), the creator of *Ubu Roi,* the first play which clearly belongs in the category of the Theatre of the Absurd. *Ubu Roi,* first performed in Paris on December 10, 1896, is a Rabelaisian nonsense drama about the fantastic adventures of a fat, cowardly, and brutal figure, *le père* Ubu, who makes himself King of Poland, fights a series of Falstaffian battles, and is finally routed. As if to challenge all accepted codes of propriety and thus to open a new era of irreverence, the play opens with the defiant expletive, *"Merde!"* which immediately provoked a scandal. This, of course, was what Jarry had intended. *Ubu,* in its rollicking Rabelaisian parody of a Shakespearean history play, was meant to confront the Parisian bourgeois with a monstrous portrait of his own greed, selfishness, and philistinism: "As the curtain went up I wanted to confront the public with a theatre in which, as in the magic mirror . . . of the fairy tales . . . the vicious man sees his reflection with bulls' horns and the body of a dragon, the projections of his viciousness. . . ." But Ubu is more than a mere monstrous exaggeration of the selfishness and crude sensuality of the French bourgeois. He is at the same time the personification of the grossness of human nature, an enormous belly walking on two legs. That is why Jarry put him on the stage as a monstrous potbellied figure in a highly stylized costume and mask—a mythical, archetypal externalization of human instincts of the lowest kind. Thus, Ubu, the false king of Poland, pretended doctor of the pseudoscience of Pataphysics, clearly anticipates one of the main characteristics of the Theatre of the Absurd, its tendency to externalize and project outwards what is happening in the deeper recesses of the mind. Examples of this tendency are: the disembodied voices of "monitors" shouting commands at the hero of Adamov's *La Grande et la petite manoeuvre* which concretizes his neurotic compulsions; the mutilated trunks of the parents in Beckett's *Endgame* emerging from ashcans— the ashcans of the main character's subconscious to which he has banished his past and his conscience; or the proliferations of fungi that invade the married couple's apartment in Ionesco's *Amédée* and express the rottenness and decay of their relationship. All these psychological factors are not only projected outwards, they are also, as in Jarry's *Ubu Roi,* grotesquely magnified and exaggerated. This scornful rejection of all subtleties is a reaction against the supposed *finesse* of the psychology of the naturalistic theatre in which everything was to be inferred between the lines. The Theatre of the Absurd, from Jarry onwards, stands for explicitness as against implicit psychology, and in this resembles the highly explicit theatre of the Expressionists or the political theatre of Piscator or Brecht.

To be larger and more real than life was also the aim of Guillaume Apollinaire (1880-1918), the great poet who was one of the seminal forces in the rise of Cubism and who had close personal artistic links with Jarry. If Apollinaire labeled his play *Les Mamelles de Tirésias* a *"drame surrealiste,"* he did not intend that term, of which he was one of the earliest users, in the sense in which it later became famous. He wanted it to describe a play in which everything was *larger than life,* for he believed in an art which was to be "modern, simple, rapid, with the shortcuts and enlargements that are needed to shock the spectator." In the prologue to *Les Mamelles de Tirésias,* a grotesque pamphlet purportedly advocating an immense rise in the French birthrate, Apollinaire makes the Director of the Company of Actors who perform the play, define his ideas:

> For the theatre should not be an imitation of reality
> It is right that the dramatist should use
> All the illusions at his disposal . . .
> It is right that he should let crowds speak, or inanimate objects
> If he so pleases
> And that he no longer has to reckon
> With time and space
> His universe is the play
> Within which he is God the Creator
> Who disposes at will
> Of sounds gestures movements masses colors
> Not merely in order
> To photograph what is called a slice of life
> But to bring forth life itself and all its truth . . .

Accordingly, in *Les Mamelles de Tirésias* the whole population of Zanzibar, where the scene is laid, is represented by a single actor; and the heroine, Thérèse, changes herself into a man by letting her breasts float upwards like a pair of toy balloons. Although *Les Mamelles de Tirésias* was not a surrealist work in the strictest sense of the term, it clearly foreshadowed the ideas of the movement led by André Breton. Surrealism in that narrower, technical sense found little expression in the theatre. But Antonin Artaud (1896-1948), another major influence in the development of the Theatre of the Absurd, did at one time belong to the Surrealist group, although his main activity in the theatre took place after he had broken with Breton. Artaud was one of the most unhappy men of genius of his age, an artist consumed by the most intense passions; poet, actor, director, designer, immensely fertile and original in his inventions and ideas, yet always living on the borders of sanity and never able to realize his ambitions, plans, and projects.

Artaud, who had been an actor in Charles Dullin's company at the Atelier, began his venture into the realm of experimental theatre in a series of productions characteristically sailing under the label *Théâtre Alfred Jarry* (1927-29). But his theories of a new and revolutionary theatre only crystallized after he had been deeply stirred by a performance of Balinese dancers at the Colonial Exhibition of 1931. He formulated his ideas in a series of impassioned manifestos later collected in the volume *The Theatre and Its Double* (1938), which continues to exercise an important influence on the contemporary French theatre. Artaud named the theatre of his dreams *Théâtre de la Cruauté,* a theatre of cruelty, which, he said, "means a theatre difficult and cruel above all for myself." "Everything that is really active is cruelty. It is around this idea of action carried to the extreme that the theatre must renew itself." Here too the idea of action larger and more real than life is the dominant theme. "Every performance will contain a physical and objective element that will be felt by all. Cries, Wails, Apparitions, Surprises, *Coups de Théâtre* of

Samuel Beckett

all kinds, the magical beauty of costumes inspired by the model of certain rituals. . . ." The language of the drama must also undergo a change: "It is not a matter of suppressing articulate speech but of giving to the words something like the importance they have in dreams." In Artaud's new theatre "not only the obverse side of man will appear but also the reverse side of the coin: the reality of imagination and of dreams will here be seen on an equal footing with everyday life."

Artaud's only attempt at putting these theories to the test on the stage took place on May 6, 1935 at the Folies-Wagram. Artaud had made his own adaptation ("after Shelley and Stendhal") of the story of the Cenci, that sombre Renaissance story of incest and patricide. It was in many ways a beautiful and memorable performance, but full of imperfections and a financial disaster which marked the beginning of Artaud's eventual descent into despair, insanity, and abject poverty. Jean-Louis Barrault had some small part in this venture and Roger Blin, the actor and director who later played an important part in bringing Adamov, Beckett, and Ionesco to the stage, appeared in the small role of one of the hired assassins.

Jean-Louis Barrault, one of the most creative figures in the theatre of our time, was in turn, responsible for another venture which played an important part in the development of the Theatre of the Absurd. He staged André Gide's adaptation of Franz Kafka's novel, *The Trial,* in 1947 and played the part of the hero K. himself. Undoubtedly this performance which brought the dreamworld of Kafka to a triumphant unfolding on the stage and demonstrated the effectiveness of this particular brand of fantasy in practical theatrical terms exercised a profound influ-

ence on the practitioners of the new movement. For here, too, they saw the externalization of mental processes, the acting out of nightmarish dreams by schematized figures in a world of torment and absurdity.

The dream element in the Theatre of the Absurd can also be traced, in the case of Adamov, to Strindberg, acknowledged by him as his inspiration at the time when he began to think of writing for the theatre. This is the Strindberg of *The Ghost Sonata, The Dream Play* and of *To Damascus.* (Adamov is the author of an excellent brief monograph on Strindberg.)

But if Jarry, Artaud, Kafka, and Strindberg can be regarded as the decisive influences in the development of the Theatre of the Absurd, there is another giant of European literature that must not be omitted from the list—James Joyce, for whom Beckett at one time is supposed to have acted as helper and secretary. Not only is the Nighttown episode of *Ulysses* one of the earliest examples of the Theatre of the Absurd—with its exuberant mingling of the real and the nightmarish, its wild fantasies and externalizations of subconscious yearnings and fears—but Joyce's experimentation with language, his attempt to smash the limitations of conventional vocabulary and syntax has probably exercised an even more powerful impact on all the writers concerned.

It is in its attitude to language that the Theatre of the Absurd is most revolutionary. It deliberately attempts to renew the language of drama and to expose the barrenness of conventional stage dialogue. Ionesco once described how he came to write his first play. . . . He had decided to take English lessons and began to study at the Berlitz school. When he read and repeated the sentences in his phrase book, those petrified corpses of once living speech, he was suddenly overcome by their tragic quality. From them he composed his first play, *The Bald Soprano.* The absurdity of its dialogue and its fantastic quality springs directly from its basic ordinariness. It exposes the emptiness of stereotyped language; "what is sometimes labeled the absurd," Ionesco says, "is only the denunciation of the ridiculous nature of a language which is empty of substance, made up of clichés and slogans. . . ." Such a language has atrophied; it has ceased to be the expression of anything alive or vital and has been degraded into a mere conventional token of human intercourse, a mask for genuine meaning and emotion. That is why so often in the Theatre of the Absurd the dialogue becomes divorced from the real happenings in the play and is even put into direct contradiction with the action. The Professor and the Pupil in Ionesco's *The Lesson* "seem" to be going through a repetition of conventional school book phrases, but behind this smoke screen of language the *real* action of the play pursues an entirely different course with the Professor, vampire-like, draining the vitality from the young girl up to the final moment when he plunges his knife into her body. In Beckett's *Waiting for Godot* Lucky's much vaunted philosophical wisdom is revealed to be a flood of completely meaningless gibberish that vaguely resembles the language of philosophical argument. And in Adamov's remarkable play, *Ping-Pong,* a good deal of the dramatic power lies in the contrapuntal contrast between the triviality of the theme—the improvement of pinball machines—and the almost religious fervor with which it is discussed. Here, in order to bring out the full meaning of the play, the actors have to act *against* the dialogue rather than with it, the fervor of the delivery must stand in a dialectical contrast to the pointlessness of the meaning of the lines. In the same way, the author implies that most of the fervent and passionate discussion of real life (of political controversy, to give but one example) also turns around empty and meaningless clichés. Or, as Ionesco says in an essay on Antonin Artaud:

> As our knowledge becomes increasingly divorced from real life, our culture no longer contains ourselves (or only contains an insignificant part of ourselves) and forms a "social" context in which we are not integrated. The problem thus becomes that of again reconciling our culture with our life by making our culture a living culture once more. But to achieve this end we shall first have to kill the "respect for that which is written" . . . it becomes necessary to break up our language so that it may become possible to put it together again and to re-establish contact with the absolute, or as I should prefer to call it, with multiple reality.

This quest for the multiple reality of the world which is real *because* it exists on many planes simultaneously and is more than a mere unidirectional abstraction is not only in itself a search for a re-established *poetical* reality (poetry in its essence expressing reality in its ambiguity and multi-dimensional depth); it is also in close accord with important movements of our age in what appear to be entirely different fields: psychology and philosophy. The dissolution, devaluation, and relativization of language is, after all, also the theme of much of present-day depth psychology, which has shown what in former times was regarded as a rational expression of logically arrived at conclusions to be the mere rationalization of subconscious emotional impulses. Not everything we say means what we intend it to mean. And likewise, in present-day Logical Positivism a large proportion of all statements is regarded as devoid of conceptual meaning and merely emotive. A philosopher like Ludwig Wittgenstein, in his later phases, even tried to break through what he regarded as the opacity, the misleading nature of language and grammar; for if all our thinking is in terms of language, and language obeys what after all are the arbitrary conventions of grammar, we must strive to penetrate to the real content of thought that is masked by grammatical rules and conventions. Here, too, then is a matter of getting behind the surface of linguistic clichés and of finding reality through the break-up of language.

In the Theatre of the Absurd, therefore, the real content of the play lies in the action. Language may be discarded altogether, as in Beckett's *Act without Words* or in Ionesco's *The New Tenant,* in which the whole sense of the play is contained in the incessant arrival of more and more furniture so that the occupant of the room is, in the end, literally drowned in it. Here the movement of objects alone carries the dramatic action, the language has become purely incidental, less important than the contribution of the property department. In this, the Theatre of the Absurd also reveals its anti-literary character, its endeavor to link up with the pre-literary strata of stage history: the circus, the performances of itinerant jugglers and mountebanks, the music hall, fairground barkers, acrobats, and also the robust world of the silent film. Ionesco, in particular, clearly owes a great deal to Chaplin, Buster Keaton, the Keystone Cops, Laurel and Hardy, and the Marx Brothers. And it is surely significant that so much of successful popular entertainment in our age shows affinities with the subject matter and preoccupation of the avantgarde Theatre of the Absurd. A sophisticated, but nevertheless highly popular, film comedian like Jacques Tati uses dialogue merely as a barely comprehensible babble of noises, and also dwells on the loneliness of man in our age, the horror of overmechanization and overorganization gone mad. Danny Kaye excels in streams of gibberish closely akin to Lucky's oration in *Waiting for Godot.* The brilliant and greatly liked team of British radio (and occasionally television) comedians, the Goons, have a sense of the absurd that resembles Kafka's or Ionesco's and a team of grotesque singers like "Les Frères Jacques" seems more closely in line with the Theatre of the Absurd than with the conventional cabaret.

Yet the defiant rejection of language as the main vehicle of the dramatic action, the onslaught on conventional logic and unilinear conceptual thinking in the Theatre of the Absurd is by no means equivalent to a total rejection of all meaning. On the contrary, it constitutes an earnest endeavor to penetrate to deeper layers of meaning and to give a truer, because more complex, picture of reality in avoiding the simplification which results from leaving out all the undertones, overtones, and inherent absurdities and contradictions of any human situation. In the conventional drama every word means what it says, the situations are clearcut, and at the end all conflicts are tidily resolved. But reality, as Ionesco points out in the passage we have quoted, is never like that; it is multiple, complex, many-dimensional and exists on a number of different levels at one and the same time. Language is far too straightforward an instrument to express all this by itself. Reality can only be conveyed by being *acted out* in all its complexity. Hence, it is the theatre, which is multidimensional and more than merely language or literature, which is the only instrument to express the bewildering complexity of the human condition. The human condition being what it is, with man small, helpless, insecure, and unable ever to fathom the world in all its hopelessness, death, and absurdity, the theatre has to confront him with the bitter truth that most human endeavor is irrational and senseless, that communication between human beings is well-nigh impossible, and that the world will forever remain an impenetrable mystery. At the same time, the recognition of all these bitter truths will have a liberating effect: if we realize the basic absurdity of most of our objectives we are freed from being obsessed with them and this release expresses itself in laughter.

Moreover, while the world is being shown as complex, harsh, and absurd and as difficult to interpret as reality itself, the audience is yet spurred on to attempt their own interpretation, to wonder what it is all about. In that sense they are being invited to school their critical faculties, to train themselves in adjusting to reality. As the world is being represented as highly complex and devoid of a clearcut purpose or design, there will always be an infinite number of possible interpretations. As Apollinaire points out in his Preface to *Les Mamelles de Tirésias:* "None of the symbols in my play is very clear, but one is at liberty to see in it all the symbols one desires and to find in it a thousand senses—as in the Sybilline oracles." Thus, it may be that the pinball machines in Adamov's *Ping-Pong* and the ideology which is developed around them stand for the futility of political or religious ideologies that are pursued with equal fervor and equal futility in the final result. Others have interpreted the play as a parable on the greed and sordidness of the profit motive. Others again may give it quite different meanings. The mysterious transformation of human beings into rhinos in Ionesco's latest play, *Rhinoceros,* was felt by the audience of its world premiere at Duesseldorf (November 6, 1959) to depict the transformation of human beings into Nazis. It is known that Ionesco himself intended the play to express his feelings at the time when more and more of his friends in Rumania joined the Fascist Iron Guard and, in effect, left the ranks of thin-skinned humans to turn themselves into moral pachyderms. But to spectators less intimately aware of the moral climate of such a situation than the German audience, other interpretations might impose themselves: if the hero, Bérenger, is at the end left alone as the only human being in his native town, now entirely inhabited by rhinos, they might regard this as a poetic symbol of the gradual isolation of man growing old and imprisoned in the strait jacket of his own habits and memories. Does Godot, so fervently and vainly awaited by Vladimir and Estragon, stand for God? Or does he merely represent the ever elusive tomorrow, man's hope that one day something will happen that will render his existence meaningful? The force and poetic power of the play lie precisely in the impossibility of ever reaching a conclusive answer to this question.

Here we touch the essential point of difference between the conventional theatre and the Theatre of the Absurd. The former, based as it is on a known framework of accepted values and a rational view of life, always starts out by indicating a fixed objective towards which the action will be moving or by posing a definite problem to which it will supply an answer. Will Hamlet revenge the murder of his father? Will Iago succeed in destroying Othello? Will Nora leave her husband? In the conventional theatre the action always proceeds toward a definable end. The spectators do not know whether that end will be reached and how it will be reached. Hence, they are in suspense, eager to find out *what* will happen. In the Theatre of the Absurd, on the other hand, the action does not proceed in the manner of a logical syllogism. It does not go from A to B but travels from an unknown premise X toward an unknowable conclusion Y. The spectators, not knowing what their author is driving at, cannot be in suspense as to how or whether an expected objective is going to be reached. They are not, therefore, so much in suspense as to *what* is going to happen *next* (although the most unexpected and unpredictable things do happen) as they are in suspense about what the next event to take place will add to their understanding of *what is happening*. The action supplies an increasing number of contradictory and bewildering clues on a number of different levels, but the final question is never wholly answered. Thus, instead of being in suspense as to what will happen next, the spectators are, in the Theatre of the Absurd, put into suspense as to *what* the play *may mean*. This suspense continues even after the curtain has come down. Here again the Theatre of the Absurd fulfills Brecht's postulate of a critical, detached audience, who will have to sharpen their wits on the play and be stimulated by it to think for themselves, far more effectively than Brecht's own theatre. Not only are the members of the audience unable to identify with the characters, they are compelled to puzzle out the meaning of what they have seen. Each of them will probably find his own, personal meaning, which will differ from the solution found by most others. But he will have been forced to make a mental effort and to evaluate an experience he has undergone. In this sense, the Theatre of the Absurd is the most demanding, the most intellectual theatre. It may be riotously funny, wildly exaggerated and oversimplified, vulgar and garish, but it will always confront the spectator with a genuine intellectual problem, a philosophical paradox, which he will have to try to solve even if he knows that it is most probably insoluble.

In this respect, the Theatre of the Absurd links up with an older tradition which has almost completely disappeared from Western culture: the tradition of allegory and the symbolical representation of abstract concepts personified by characters whose costumes and accoutrements subtly suggested whether they represented Time, Chastity, Winter, Fortune, the World, etc. This is the tradition which stretches from the Italian *Trionfo* of the Renaissance to the English Masque, the elaborate allegorical constructions of the Spanish *Auto sacramental* down to Goethe's allegorical processions and masques written for the court of Weimar at the turn of the eighteenth century. Although the living riddles the characters represented in these entertainments were by no means difficult to solve,

German production of Beckett's Waiting for Godot.

as everyone knew that a character with a scythe and an hourglass represented Time, and although the characters soon revealed their identity and explained their attributes, there was an element of intellectual challenge which stimulated the audience in the moments between the appearance of the riddle and its solution and which provided them with the pleasure of having solved a puzzle. And what is more, in the elaborate allegorical dramas like Calderón's *El Gran Teatro del Mundo* the subtle interplay of allegorical characters itself presented the audience with a great deal to think out for themselves. They had, as it were, to translate the abstractly presented action into terms of their everyday experience; they could ponder on the deeper meaning of such facts as death having taken the characters representing Riches or Poverty in a Dance of Death equally quickly and equally harshly, or that Mammon had deserted his master Everyman in the hour of death. The dramatic riddles of our time present no such clear-cut solutions. All they can show is that while the solutions have evaporated the riddle of our existence remains—complex, unfathomable, and paradoxical. (pp. 229-44)

> Martin Esslin, "The Theatre of the Absurd," in Theatre in the Twentieth Century, *edited by Robert W. Corrigan, Grove Press, Inc., 1963, pp. 229-44.*

MAJOR PLAYS AND PLAYWRIGHTS

Josephine Jacobsen and William R. Mueller

[*Jacobsen and Mueller are American critics who have collaborated on several critical studies of modern drama. In the following excerpt, they analyze exemplary works of the Theater of the Absurd by Beckett, Ionesco, and Jean Genet, distinguishing the approach of each dramatist to the philosophical concept of absurdity.*]

The most exciting theatre of our mid-century is that of the absurdists, particularly Samuel Beckett, Eugène Ionesco, and Jean Genet. They dazzle us, first, with a fine control of craft, with the precisely appropriate setting, stage dynamics, and language. Beckett's near-empty landscapes, his reduction of physical movement to a minimum, his sparse, austere, and wonderful poetry; Ionesco's multifarious and imaginative settings, his wild proliferation of persons and things in their snowballing confusion of ceaseless movement back and forth, up and down, around and around, his profusion of words regressing from nonsense to the no-words of syllables and letters; Genet's elaborate and eye-arresting sets, reaching four distinct levels in one of the scenes of *The Screens,* his shuttling between appearance and reality as props come and go, as characters shift roles, as play gives way to play-within-play, which in turn reverts to play, his poetry which sparkles on occasion with a sensuous, concrete richness—all these qualities make for the finest theatre of our day.

But Beckett, Ionesco, and Genet are more than masters of a craft: their artistry is equaled by their vision. From their plays we gain a perceptive composite portrait of the contemporary man for whom God is either dead or dying, of the man who sees himself in that strange twilight land between life and death. Beckett's *Waiting for Godot,* Ionesco's *The Killer,* and Genet's *The Balcony* form, in this respect, the perfect trilogy. Beckett's protagonists wait with the flicker of hope that approaches despair. Ionesco's Bérenger, first spun to ecstasy by his surface view of the Radiant City, then learns its utter, death-spawning rottenness, and finally can only surrender to the Killer with the "What can we do . . . What can we do" which paces the falling curtain. And Genet's players give Bérenger their heartening and victorious answer. The would-be Bishop speaks for many of them when, at the beginning of *The Balcony,* he describes his path as "a skillful, vigorous heading towards Absence. Towards Death." We *cannot,* as Bérenger learned, battle Death on equal terms, but we *can,* Genet affirms, beat Death at his own game, by seeking him out and gaining control over him through our very surrender to him. It is no rarity, in the history of political warfare, for conquered peoples to absorb and gain ascendancy over forces that in a frontal attack they never could have overcome. The three plays do give us a familiar portrait of the contemporary man who, first reduced to the faintest of hopes, asks the question of what he can do, and then resigns himself to the seeming inevitability of cosmic nothingness. Such is not the whole story, and not all men have laid down their arms before the forces, conscious or unconscious, which oppress them. But only the blind can deny that, in the thoughts of many men, it is the prevailing story. And though there are indeed those among us who are convinced that one's waiting for Godot will be crowned with success—through supernatural or human intervention, through a divine breakthrough or a reassertion of nobility, courage, and wisdom in man—the predominant disposition of our time is toward holocaust. It is this temperament which the theatre of the absurd has engraved with precision tooling. (pp. 1-2)

Initial productions of Beckett, Ionesco, and Genet came within six years of one another: Genet's *The Maids* in 1947, Ionesco's *The Bald Soprano* in 1950, Beckett's *Waiting for Godot* in 1953. The large majority of their plays were written during the 1950's. Their productivity has decreased during the 1960's and may be approaching its end. Perhaps Beckett has no more to say after *Happy Days* and *Play,* or Ionesco after the Bérenger plays, or Genet after *The Screens.* Even if this is true, their achievement of a decade and a half has been immense. No other twentieth-century "school" of playwrights has been more theatrically and philosophically effective; none has more vividly and deeply represented its age—an age conscious, perhaps above all else, of life's absurdity.

Albert Camus' "The Myth of Sisyphus" offers the most extended and precise definition of the word *absurd,* certainly as it applies to those dramatists so brilliantly analyzed in Martin Esslin's *The Theatre of the Absurd.* The sense of absurdity is born in a man, Camus affirms, when he no longer takes his habitual, mechanical, routine life (or death-in-life) for granted, when he begins to ask "why." Such thoughtfulness, introspection, and questioning give rise to a series of disquieting epiphanies. This startling awakening, which passes many men by, comes to the more sensitive, the *Myth* tells us, at the age of thirty—and so it does, in literature at least: Camus' "stranger," Meursault, is thirty at the time of his self-revealing trial; and Kafka's Joseph K. awakes to his trial on the morning of his thirtieth birthday. Man awakes, Camus tells us, to three potentially shattering discoveries.

First, a man comes to realize at thirty that *he* is going to die. He has long known that death *is,* that *one* dies, but he now recognizes that even he will be death's victim, that time, the *sine qua non* of mortality, is his fatal enemy. One of the most impressive literary expressions of this discovery is Tolstoy's "The Death of Ivan Ilyich," though Ivan is over thirty when he comes to his knowledge. And in Shakespeare's *Richard III* Ionesco finds that most profound truth before which all men must bow, a truth which "is simple and absolutely commonplace: I die, he dies, you die." Man's first step into consciousness of the absurd is the realization that he, who has taken life for granted and enjoyed some of its pleasures, will die.

If the sensitive man's first discovery is his true relationship to time, his second is his relationship to nature. The young are often Wordsworthians or Thoreauvians or Emersonians, feeling at home in the cosmic order, seeing in the natural world of earth and sea and sky, of grass and trees and flowers, of birds of the air and beasts of the field a personal kinship and compatibility. But they come to realize either, with Tennyson, that nature is "red in tooth and claw" (or, with Camus, plague-ridden), or that nature is indifferent, with neither care for nor consciousness of the descendants of Adam. The natural world comes to be viewed no longer as a home, but as a chilling, unfeeling complex oblivious to its human and transient dwellers.

Become aware of time's destructiveness and nature's indifference, man may turn with some hope to himself, only to find no solace there either. Formerly confident of his humanity, of his freedom to choose his way and guide gracefully his movements in a constant flux of activity, of his capacity to exercise that *élan vital* so dear to Henri Bergson, he now sees himself as a machine, bound to repetitive and fatuous gestures that deny his human beingness. Observe the unheard man in the telephone booth, turn off the sound but not the picture of the television, and, behold, the machine is at work. Etched in today's memory is the Charlie Chaplin of *Modern Times,* who, having spent his day tightening bolts on an assembly line, then walks home with his right arm still repeating the rigid movement of the day's unvarying labor.

To come to believe that time is his destroyer, that the natural world observes him not, and that he is brother to the machine—such is the way by which man arrives at a knowledge of the absurdity of this world, an absurdity born of the juxtaposition of all that he would wish life to be, with the way that life actually seems to be. Man yearns to defy time, to feel at home in the world, to rest confident of his humanity, but he comes to know his mortality, his loneliness, his machinelike rigidity. The absurd is, Camus writes, "that divorce between the mind that desires and the world that disappoints."

Camus presents an expository definition of absurdity. The playwrights of the absurd, as they speak to us across the footlights, transport us into the fabric of absurdity itself. They do not, as Mr. Esslin has remarked, tell us what the condition is—they enable us to experience it. And in most cases the experience into which we are drawn is that of the disparity between the life man hopes for and the life he endures. This observation, to be sure, is not so fully applicable to Genet as it is to Beckett and Ionesco.

Waiting for Godot, of all plays, perhaps best exemplifies "that divorce between the mind that desires and the world that disappoints." From their bleak and joyless world Vladimir and Estragon seek relief. They recall that, according to one of the gospels, one of the two thieves who flanked Jesus on the cross was saved. In Godot's promised arrival they place their hope for salvation. The first intruder upon their solitary and anxious waiting is the monstrous Pozzo, whom they initially mistake for Godot, but who, with his grotesque servant Lucky, is the epitome of all that is most vicious and degrading. Throughout the play the near-desperate waiting continues, in spite of all the frustrations and disappointments which the world heaps upon the protagonists. Despite their mutual impatience and offensiveness, they remain together, finding solace in each other's companionship and conversation, sparse and nagging as the latter frequently is. They are the perfect prototypes of Beckett's world, together comprising the Everyman sunk in the misery of this universe and, though seemingly powerless in themselves to amend their condition, awaiting a miraculous intervention of a supernatural force. They weather two ghastly meetings with Pozzo and Lucky, and two messages (there have been others antecedent to the play's action) from Godot that he will not appear on that evening, but certainly on the next. The last words of each

Eugene Ionesco

of the two acts, first spoken by Vladimir and next by Estragon, are "Yes, let's go," but the final stage direction of each act is *"They do not move."* The protagonists are remarkable for their tenacious clinging to a slim skein of hope, the threads of which seem difficult to weave in this world.

Other Beckett dramatic protagonists are less markedly waiting, but the juxtaposition of hope and disappointment, and, sometimes, of past joys and present miseries, is persistent. In *Endgame* the weary Hamm, miserably confined to his armchair, pathetically voices his hopes: "If I could sleep I might make love. I'd go into the woods. My eyes would see . . . the sky, the earth. I'd run, run, they wouldn't catch me." But he is sleepless, loveless, sightless to nature, and motionless. His servant Clov also has his vain dreams: "I love order. It's my dream. A world where all would be silent and still and each thing in its last place, under the last dust." Despite the seeming failure of all hopes, however, they share with Vladimir and Estragon a bold persistence to continue. Both Hamm and Clov, three-quarters of the way through the play, speak the same sentiment: "Keep going, can't you, keep going!" And certainly Winnie of *Happy Days,* finally buried up to her neck in the dirt, displays the most persevering quality of endurance, happy that her near-moribund husband Willie can respond to her conversation by so much as a wiggling of his fingers.

Other Beckett characters, mired in their wretchedness, can look back to better times when hopes were realized. Hamm's parents, Nagg and Nell, though trapped in their ash bins, remember happier days when, betrothed, they went rowing on Lake Como and capsized through their ecstatic motions. Krapp, who at seventy plays and replays those tapes which chronicle his earlier life, listens with particular fondness to the account of his one relationship approaching love, enjoyed three decades earlier and still his most precious memory: "I lay down across her with my face in her breasts and my hand on her. We lay there without moving. But under us all moved, and moved us, gently, up and down, and from side to side."

Ionesco, no less than Beckett, evokes from us that feeling of the wide gap between our hopes and our disappointments. *The Bald Soprano,* a "tragedy of language" as Ionesco calls it, strikes immediately a most unnerving truth for humanity, the truth that communication through language and feelings, the most basic necessity for human joy, simply does not exist—that persons impart nothing to each other because they no longer have anything to impart. And perhaps the most hilariously funny dialogue in the whole theatre of the absurd—the one spoken by Mr. and Mrs. Martin as they sit across from each other at the Smiths' and have the strange feeling they have met before—is also one of the most tragic. They recall in rigorous detail every material facet of their recent lives, every detail of their trip from Manchester to London, and every furnishing of their flat, but of each other neither spouse remembers anything. In what one would hope to be the most intimate of human relationships is found only the most profound ignorance and indifference.

Of all Ionesco's plays, perhaps *The Chairs* portrays most vividly the wide margin between human aspirations and the bitter truth of the way things are. The Old Man, in the leisurely seclusion of his lighthouse, has devoted most of his adult life to formulating and phrasing the message which will save the world. He would serve as the Godot for those millions who, he is convinced, would be lost without him: "I have a message, that's God's truth, I struggle, a mission, I have something to say, a message to communicate to humanity, to mankind." The message ready, he and his wife invite the citizens of the world to visit them and hear the saving words. No talented speaker, he has, as a last precaution to insure the success of his message, summoned the Orator to deliver the proclamation to the assembled guests. But when the curtain falls, we have beheld an orator who is mute and capable only of writing nonsense words and letters on the blackboard at his side. Nor can the Old Man try again. For made confident by the arrival of the Orator in whom he had such trust, he has happily leaped through the window to his death in the awaiting sea, mistakenly assured that the world would now be saved.

The Bérenger of *The Killer* is still another example of one whose highest hopes are completely negated. With wondrous memories of the joys of his youth, as well as more recent experiences of the bleakest and most depressing of worlds, he first sees in the Radiant City the epitome of all that life should be. But once he pierces the spurious decor of the city, penetrating deeper and deeper into its cancerous reality, he learns that death, not life, is dominant. Of the innumerable arguments he musters in trying to dissuade the Killer from his murderous ways, not one is sufficient either to convert the hideous adversary or to maintain his own faith in his ability to withstand the Killer's voiceless power. At the play's end, the helpless Bérenger can only stammer: "Oh God! There's nothing we can do. What can we do . . . What can we do." The final action shows the chuckling Killer moving toward his latest victim—most discouragingly, a victim whose resistance has been greater than that of many men

The plays of Beckett and Ionesco present vividly the disparity between the characters' yearnings and their accomplishments, yet with an important difference. The viewer or reader of a Beckett play feels little distance between himself and the protagonist. Vladimir and Estragon, Hamm and Clov, Krapp, Winnie—all of them may at first be viewed with some distaste or condescension, but not for long. For anyone who is moved to return to Beckett (and not everyone is) comes to suffer the most intensive empathy with his characters. Their longings, as well as their bitter disappointments, mirror our own hopes and responses to the daily round of life. More than this, the Beckett character is conscious of his predicament, much as we like to believe we are conscious of our own. There are, of course, various kinds of irony in Beckett's plays, but there is seldom the irony conveyed by the author's looking over the shoulder of his character, catching the eye of the reader, and entering into a tacit complicity, an unspoken "you and I, dear reader, are sufficiently intelligent, sophisticated, and sensitive to see what a fool I have created." Ring Lardner's "Haircut" is a fine example of this kind of irony; Gulliver's voyage to Brobdingnag, though more subtly and compassionately presented than "Haircut," has something of the same tone. The portraits of Lardner's monologist barber and Swift's Gulliver are ironic because the characters are ignorant, in different degree, of themselves. But Vladimir and Estragon and other Beckett protagonists know themselves as well as we know ourselves, which is not to say that they have all the answers to the ultimate problems of life but that they are aware of the highly problematic and mysterious condition of their lives.

Ionesco and his audience, however, usually stand above the characters, viewing them sometimes with Olympian detachment, frequently with condescension. The irony is greater, the sympathy less, than in Beckett. Bérenger comes closest to being the exception to the general rule, a fact which helps account for the power of *Rhinoceros* and the even greater power of *The Killer*. But the distance between the playgoer and, say, the Martins and the Smiths is immense. We hardly feel in empathy with the characters of *The Bald Soprano*. We find them funny and pathetic by turn (or simultaneously); we find some of our traits mirrored in them. But we view them more as caricatures than as human beings with whom we sense close kinship. We feel quite superior to them and, with Ionesco, look down upon them as we would upon dancing, erratic marionettes. But if we do not identify with Ionesco's characters, we do at least see them as he would have us see them. They succeed well in conveying to us his vision of the world, a vision set early in life, as Ionesco makes clear in recounting a memory of childhood:

> . . . when I was a child, I can still remember how my mother could not drag me away from the Punch and Judy show in the Luxembourg Gardens. I would go there day after day and could stay there, spellbound, all day long. But I did not laugh. That Punch and Judy show kept me there open-mouthed, watching those puppets talking, moving and cudgeling each other. It was the very image of the world that appeared to me, strange and improbable but truer than true, in the profoundly simplified form of caricature, as though to stress the grotesque and brutal nature of the truth.

Although Beckett and Ionesco do not stand in the same relationship to their respective characters, they share a wide area of agreement about the ways of the world and man's hopes and disappointments. They lament together the difficulties of human communication and the consequent terrible estrangement which separates man from his fellows and results in loneliness. They see man as a victim of circumstances, of the persistent assault of malign forces that seem beyond his control. And their areas of agreement are shared by many men who, with Beckett's characters in particular and certainly with the Bérenger of *Rhinoceros,* would resist the hovering presence of despair and continue to fight against the dark pressures which threaten every hope. Whatever the differences between Beckett's and Ionesco's interpretation of and response to life, they share far more in common than either has in common with Genet. Whereas they would, each in his own way, resist the demonic forces that plague humanity, Genet would join hands with the powers of darkness and set up his altar to them.

Genet's response to life's absurdity exhibits a most fascinating twist. He would stay "that divorce between the mind that desires and the world that disappoints" by changing man's desires. If communication is difficult, he would pride himself on the joy of noncommunication. If the mind finds its desire for honesty, fidelity, and heterosexual love difficult of attainment, he would direct the mind's desire toward the glories of theft, betrayal, and homosexuality. If Godot seems reticent, unseeing, and un-

Scene from Ionesco's The Bald Soprano.

hearing, Genet would remind us that Satan stands ready to receive the frustrated men-in-waiting. The gears must simply be reversed—love must give way to hate, creation to destruction, persuasion to power, God to Satan. In sum, if the juggernaut which is the world will not yield to man, then let man surrender to the world and, in the very process, gain power over what hitherto had been overpowering. Genet is the great accommodator.

Accordingly, the absurdist dimension of most of Genet's drama lies in the disparity between what the character holds as his ideal and what most of the theatre-goers see as their own. In terms of Camus' definition of absurdity, what distinguishes the Genet character most radically from that of Beckett or Ionesco is the nature of his desire. He desires what would, to say the least, bitterly disappoint a Vladimir or a Bérenger. It is difficult, for example, to conceive of Genet's writing a play which does not celebrate at least one murder. And whereas the Killer is one of the great antagonists of Ionesco's work, Genet's murderers are habitually the protagonists. Genet's love of death, preferably violently accomplished, is profound and passionate. Moreover, it is significant that, of all the murders committed in his plays, only one—Lefranc's strangling of Maurice—fails to bring a rich satisfaction to its perpetrator.

Among Genet's many protagonists, Lefranc of *Death-watch,* the first play composed though performed and published after *The Maids,* is the single unequivocal failure. His murder of Maurice is the only gratuitous one in

Genet's dramatic corpus. He commits the deed in emulation of his idol Green Eyes, whose wanton and seemingly unprovoked strangling of a girl had won him the plaudits of his prison community. Lefranc's violent act, on the other hand, reduces him to a cipher—and all because it was committed for the wrong reason. He is condemned to personal defeat not because of committing the act of murder *per se* but because of doing so without the vocation to murder, thus countering his destiny rather than bowing to it. But over *The Maids* and the suicide-murder involving Claire, Solange, and Madame hangs the aura of success. The maids were called to the deed, and the absurdity lies not in the disappointment of their desires, not in their being unwilling pawns, but in the disparity between their goals and the at least conscious goals of their audience. And Genet's most fully realized character, Saïd of *The Screens,* makes of his poverty, his wife's ugliness, his mother's offensiveness, and his fellows' violence and rapacity the steppingstones to his own long-sought and perfectly accomplished annihilation—by way of five revolver shots. Genet and his players join forces with the world's malignity and, in most cases, win the salvation and peace which, Genet insists, come with annihilation. The Genet formula, then, is the opposite of that of Beckett and Ionesco. (pp. 3-12)

Beckett would have us await, for a while longer at least, some superhuman intervention; Ionesco would have us continue to seek a way out of our labyrinth; Genet would pipe us to the void. (p. 24)

> *Josephine Jacobsen and William R. Mueller, "The Absurd Quest," in their* Ionesco and Genet: Playwrights of Silence, *Hill and Wang, 1968, pp. 1-24.*

Allan Lewis

[*Lewis is an American critic and educator who has written extensively on modern theater. In the following excerpt, he focuses on three seminal works of the Theater of the Absurd: Beckett's* Waiting for Godot, *Ionesco's* The Chairs, *and Genet's* The Balcony.]

The experimental theatre of Paris has provided the most devastating attack on traditional forms. Nothing has been sacred. To Beckett, Ionesco, Genet, Adamov, Vauthier, and Schehadé, the theatre of the past was false, anachronistic, dishonest, partial, and destructive, concerned with the personal pettiness of man. In an age where science seeks to control the universe and all life can be destroyed by pulling a switch, the individual is insignificant and his writhings inconsequential. And if the theatre reflects its age, then a century of rushing toward annihilation should have a theatre equally mad. (p. 259)

A consideration of Samuel Beckett's *Waiting for Godot,* the outstanding work of the theatre of the "absurd," offers detailed insight into the nature of the movement.

The sequence is extremely simple, as starkly naked as the set. Two tramps, Vladimir and Estragon, are waiting on a lonely road for Godot. Only a barren tree is visible on the empty plateau. They argue, take off their shoes, button their flies, discuss philosophy, embrace, attempt suicide, eat a carrot. Two other characters appear, Pozzo and Lucky, master and slave. Lucky, burdened down with a

heavy bag, a folding stool, a picnic basket, and a greatcoat, has a long rope tied around his neck. All four characters wear bowlers. Pozzo pulls the rope and snaps his whip. Lucky falls, gets up, does nothing until ordered to. When Pozzo commands him to think, he goes into a long verbal outburst, with his hat on, incoherent fragments of medieval scholarship and modern science. He is silenced only when all fall on him. Pozzo eats, tosses the chicken bones to Estragon, sprays his throat, discusses his pipe, the weather, time. Then the two go off, leaving Vladimir and Estragon alone, waiting for Godot. A boy appears to tell them that Godot will come tomorrow.

The second act takes place the next day. The only change in the scene is a few leaves that have sprouted on the tree. Nothing is finite. All is continuous with blurred edges, the shadows of existence. Time is elastic. It may be the next day, or any day, or another season, for waiting is all of life without beginning or end and the days matter little. As Estragon says, "There's no lack of void." They go through the same burlesque antics and comedy routines with hats and shoes, carrots and trousers and suicide. Pozzo and Lucky return. The rope is shorter now, the two tied together more closely, for Pozzo is blind. They leave, and the tramps go on waiting for Godot.

The play lends itself to innumerable interpretations. Beckett, unlike most contemporary playwrights, has refused to discuss the definition of his symbols. Perhaps he prefers the purposefully vague so that every member of the audience will supply his own meaning. Since no certainty exists, art cannot impose one. The play is unquestionably a morality play in which not faith but doubt binds man to God, if Godot stands for God—or a little God more intimate and clownish, like Pierrot for Pierre, or a combination of God and Charlot (the French for Charlie Chaplin). Names, like time, are elastic. Vladimir and Estragon are so called only in the listed cast of characters. Are they the split aspects of Everyman, reason and the senses, which would desert each other yet are bound together, or are they the divided world of East and West? In the play, these two characters use their childish nicknames of Didi and Gogo, two-syllable names with double repetition of vowel and consonant, but they are also referred to as Adam and Monsieur Albert. Pozzo becomes Bozzo or Gozzo, whose mother had the clap, or perhaps Godot, who passes by unrecognized, for he is evil and we seek the unknown, the unseen, the ineffable. Even Godot is called Godet, Godin. Neither man nor God completely possesses his own name; each may have many names like Shiva or Dionysus. Only Lucky remains so. Is he lucky because of his fixed and known relationship as slave? In any case, religious references run throughout the play: "hope deferred," "tree of life," "ye fools and blind," Christ and the two thieves. And the action is a series of separations and unions, of pilgrimage and appointment. Gogo and Didi twice attempt suicide; first they have no rope, and then the rope breaks, but there is hope that tomorrow they may have a stronger rope. At least there will be the sexual excitement that accompanies hanging, for "where the desire cometh, it is a tree of life." The tree becomes the Cross for their self-imposed crucifixion.

The movement of the play consists of conflict between the two pairs of characters and the conflict within each pair, intensified by successive symbols of duality. One couple is always on the move, the other stays and waits; one is tied together by necessity, the other by a rope. Pozzo and Lucky have distinct duties: one serves, the other consumes; the dominated and the dominating. They are closer to the real world, and undergo change. At the end they are tied closer together, the dumb leading the blind. Of Gogo and Didi, Didi is more rational, more compassionate; Gogo, more animal, more abused. He eats and sleeps and his shoes hurt. They are married to each other. Perhaps that is why there are no female characters—there is no need of birth and the continuity of the race if all is empty nothingness. For them, there is no change other than the festering of the sore and the leaves on the tree, the slim hope always deferred. Didi hopes for change, and Gogo answers, "It's never the same pus from one second to the next." For them there is no age, no time, their animal and intellectual longings competing with their spiritual salvation in the waiting for a Godot who will never come, whom they will never know, but for whom they must go on waiting. The parable is a bitter comment on existence. "What are we doing here?" asks Vladimir. "Are we needed?" They at least can find something to give them the impression that they do exist, and they can pass beyond "the danger of ever thinking any more." (pp. 261-63)

Eugene Ionesco, a Romanian by birth, who lives in Paris and writes in French, is, together with Samuel Beckett, the recognized leader of the theatre of negation. (p. 266)

He is like Beckett in rejecting established theatre conventions, but he differs in method. Both agree that since the world is absurd, its representation should be equally absurd. Science and reason, arising out of the Renaissance, have in four centuries distorted reality, confining it to demonstrable logic and eliminating the vaster areas of fancy, imagination, dreams. Artaud had called for a theatre that translates life into universal forms, and evokes hidden, primitivistic images. To Ionesco, mind has been free in only one direction, with the result that man is bereft of faith and freedom in others. Realism, which dominates the theatre:

> falls short of reality. . . . It does not take into account our basic truths and our fundamental obsessions: love, death, astonishment. It presents man in a reduced and strange perspective. Truth is in our dreams, in the imagination.

The middle-class world has become a victim of the rational universe decreed by the eighteenth century. Everything is confined to the narrow scope of proof by the laws of logic. Ibsen wanted to infuse that world with spiritual vitality. Ionesco would eliminate it entirely. (pp. 266-67)

Ionesco calls [his play *The Chairs*] a "tragic farce." . . . The place is a circular room atop a tower, surrounded by water, a setting for the wasted, isolated, mediocre lives of the Old Man, aged ninety-five, and the Old Woman, aged ninety-four, who are the only characters until the entrance of the Orator at the end. The opening lines are about the "bad smell from stagnant water," the world around them. The Old Woman wants to watch the boats in the sunlight and is told that it is nighttime. They review their past; childhood scenes merge with the present and the future. The Old Woman cradles her man in her lap, the return to the womb, and they play games, like imitating the months, the visual form of nonsense. The Old Man's words when he refers to Paris may even suggest Ionesco's prediction

that the world is threatened with atomic annihilation. "It was the city of light"—he uses the past tense—"but it has been extinguished for four hundred thousand years. . . . Nothing remains of it except a song."

> OLD WOMAN. What song?
>
> OLD MAN. A lullaby, an allegory. "Paris will always be Paris."

As they tell their past, the syncopated speech changes to a slow, dreamy rhythm. Words vanish into multiple meanings. The Old Man sits in her lap and wets, moaning: "I'm all spoiled . . . my career is spilled." Platitudes of success flow in and around their tale of failure. Many guests have been invited to hear the final message of the Old Man, his vindication. The couple speak to them as they arrive, arrange seats for them, interrupt conversations. The stage becomes full of chairs, until finally the Emperor enters. All the guests are imaginary and invisible, but idle chatter, flirtations, arguments with all of them, and the Old Man's hopes make them real. The scene rises to the animation of a ballet with the placing of the chairs, the music of doorbells, the sounds of the boats—all leading up to the great message of freedom from the misunderstood intellectual. So full of people is the imagined stage that the Old Man and Woman get lost in the crowd, and when the Old Man finds her, he says: "I am not myself. I am another. I am the one in the other"—an echo of Rimbaud's concept of the division of self, but here used also to show the sameness of all. The Old Man seeks certainty and truth in the midst of the absurd. Now that the Emperor is present, the Old Man can at last have the Orator deliver his message. His life "has been filled to overflowing." He will not have lived in vain. His words will be revealed to the world. Conscious that all has been arranged, or unable to undo the complications of their own plans, the Old Man and Woman leap out of the window to their death in the water below as the Orator moves to the dais. He, who is real, stands before the nonexistent assemblage and delivers to posterity the great message:

> He faces the rows of empty chairs; he makes the invisible crowd understand that he is deaf and dumb . . . he coughs, groans, utters the gutteral sounds of a mute, "He, mme, mm, mm. Ju, gou, hou, hou. Heu, heu, gu, gou, gueue."

Unable to speak, he writes on the blackboard: ANGEL-FOOD; then mutters more unintelligible sounds, erases what he has written, and replaces it with ADIEU.

The futility of life and the inability to communicate have rarely been dramatized so graphically. Ionesco wrote:

> In *The Chairs,* I have tried to deal with the themes that obsess me; with emptiness, with frustration, with this world, at once fleeting and crushing, with despair and death. The characters I have used are not fully conscious of their spiritual rootlessness, but they feel it instinctively and emotionally.
>
> (pp. 272-74)

Both Beckett and Ionesco herald the end of the conventional theatre. The difficulty in understanding their plays results from their complete departure from all that has been traditional, and their effort to pioneer a new tradition, discarding the myths of the past and, as the poet should, evolving new myths. Contradictory as their work

1952 production in Paris of Ionesco's The Chairs.

is, it is so because they themselves are involved in contradictions. Though they revolt against the rational world, they attempt to achieve the rigor and beauty of mathematics in rationalizing the irrational. To their credit lies the thoroughness with which they annihilate realism and introduce to the theatre the vast expanse of the impossible. Both are amazingly gifted in wit, mastery of language, knowledge of theatre, and ability to project freshness of vision. Freedom of speech acquires an internal meaning, for words are loosed from previous connotations. Though their laughter is acidic, it is man laughing at his own vacuity. (p. 276)

Genet does not truly belong to the theatre of the "absurd." Beckett and Ionesco present comic images of loneliness to emphasize the tragedy of man. But Genet glories in the triumph of evil with the religious intensity of a convert and the delirious delight of a criminal.

Strindberg, the source of the theatre of despair, felt surrounded by hate and corruption, but he did strive to discover a return to spiritual purity. Genet wallows in emptiness with sadistic pleasure, and exploits the horror of vice to give it prestige. Sartre, his enthusiastic admirer, wrote glowingly of Genet's plays:

Good is only an illusion. Evil is a Nothingness
which arises upon the ruins of Good.

He hailed Genet as the greatest of the "black magicians," a worthy heir to Villon, Sade, Rimbaud, and Baudelaire. Genet's characters are all angry outcasts from society because definition has made them so. The poet, also an outcast, is identical with the criminal, alone able to create a new beauty, uncontaminated by social decree. (p. 277)

The Balcony is Genet's most ambitious and complex play, his macabre imagination confining the world to a house of prostitution; . . . a portrayal of shadows within shadows, of shifting levels of appearance and reality. The Balcony is a brothel, run by Irma, wherein petty men are made bigger than life through re-enacting their fantasies. The clients impersonate their suppressed desires—to be a bishop, a general, a judge, a masochist defiling the Virgin. The brothel is the concentrated center of depravity, where men obtain momentary release in their dream world for a fee. Outside, a revolution is taking place. The gunfire increases in intensity as destruction in the real world threatens the House of Illusions. Chantal, who formerly worked for Irma, becomes the goddess of the people, the prostitute-saint. Roger, her lover and the leader of the revolt, will take over the city and destroy The Balcony. All the heads of government have disappeared. The clients who acted out their dreams now assume in real life the characters they imitated. Irma becomes the Queen, the symbol of order, to destroy Chantal, the symbol of freedom. Accompanied by the false Judge, General, and Bishop, she defeats the revolution. The Chief of Police, her accomplice and partner, lord of earthly power and vice, becomes the new Hero. The only obstacle in his path to perfection is his failure to have someone impersonate him—the proof that he belongs to the legendary myths of the people. In the final ironic touch, Roger, the revolutionary, enters the brothel to act the role of the Chief of Police. He ends by castrating himself. The symbolism implies that the revolution and the society it would overthrow are variations of the same sham and hypocrisy. A revolution from within the established order cannot effect change. Only evil, from without, deserves to triumph.

Each character sees a double who turns and mocks him. Each lie wears a mask, and men await its fall to return to reality, which is unendurable. The enjoyment of the heroic self remains a repeated but temporary vision that men prefer to pay for in private, while publicly they submit to servility. Genet's highly fantastic ceremonies are uncompromising desecrations, the destruction of all myths in order to elevate the criminal to sainthood. In [Genet's] *The Blacks,* Archibald addresses the audience, saying:

> . . . in order that you be assured that there is no danger of such a drama worming its way into your precious lives, we shall even have the decency, a decency learned from you, to make communication impossible. We shall increase the distance that separates us, a distance that is basic, by our pomp, our manners, our insolence.

If Artaud called for a "theatre of cruelty," and Ionesco is the "theatre of the absurd," Genet is the "theatre of insolence." Yet with all his theatricalism and richness of imagination, Genet does not attain dramatic power. His world is too personal, too distant, and too facilely repeated. Genet, the outcast, is too vindictive, too overwhelmed with hate to achieve communion. (pp. 280-81)

> *Allan Lewis, "The Theatre of the Absurd—Beckett, Ionesco, Genet," in his* The Contemporary Theatre: The Significant Playwrights of Our Time, *Crown Publishers, Inc., 1962, pp. 259-81.*

Jacques Guicharnaud and June Guicharnaud

[*In the following excerpt, the critics discuss the absurdist dramas of Boris Vian and Fernando Arrabal.*]

The awareness of an eminently dramatic situation—man confronted by the incomprehensible or unjustified aspect of his own condition—can be expressed in hundreds of ways. Whatever the solution (nihilistic acceptance, poetic transformation, or final confidence in a free will capable of overcoming that state of mind), the so-called absurd has in fact haunted playwrights of all times. Greek tragedy is based on it, as are Elizabethan theatre, Corneillian tragedy (with its values that result in a glorious nothingness), Racinian tragedy (where everything happens mechanically, in relation to a God—but a *hidden* God), and Romantic drama (in which the cry "fatalitas!" is no more than a rhetorical device). Without the absurd, taken in the broadest

sense, there would be no drama. When theatre becomes reasonable (as, for example, French eighteenth-century bourgeois theatre), it becomes drama repudiating drama, and one wonders why some writers have spent so much time writing plays only to say, in effect, that the drama of life can be resolved by reading three pages of rationalistic philosophy. André Malraux once commented that "reason cannot account for man." He may be wrong, but if one believes he is wrong, one denies the validity of theatre.

Much great literature is the expression of an impatience with the absurd. Playwrights of the past sometimes showed that impatience through a rational ordering, a presentation of perceived disorder in conflict with a style, a form, or even the structure of an anecdote that expressed either the poet's desire for harmony or what he believed to be a hidden intention of God. Today's theatre of the absurd is characterized by an emphasis on the inhuman or irrational pole of the conflict. (pp. 178-79)

These playwrights paint a direct portrait of agonized consciousness as an individual experiences it through the gestures and language of everyday life or in ordinary situations related to the customs of today (divorce, a *Reader's Digest* variety of psychoanalysis, modern war). Any metaphors involved are those of man at grips with his condition—not of a mystical or poetic beyond. Arrabal's virgins crowned with thorns are fantasies of an eternal child who was never able to dissociate his first Communion from his erotic discoveries—not images of the real presence of the Virgin and Christ in the world. . . . Ionesco's rhinoceroses are metaphors of an individual consciousness' horror of others—not the symbol of some "black beast" in the manner of Audiberti or the embodiment of a diabolical evil that existed *elsewhere* before subjugating the world.

Indeed, it is in relation to Ionesco and also to Beckett that this new group of writers must be considered. For their means are somewhat similar: verbal incantation, expressionistic tricks, what appear to be the most old-fashioned naturalistic details (reminiscent of Zola, Courteline, and Jean-Jacques Bernard), cabaret or vaudeville acts. By concentrating on the individual confronted by his absurd condition, even in the most personal or intimate situations, and with great freedom in their use of theatrical devices, these few playwrights have managed to create a kind of "chamber theatre." Even when they deal with collective adventures like the Spanish revolution or war in general, their theatre brings the spectator—whether through laughter or horror—back to that awkward and pathetic "self" whose sphere of action never exceeds the space of a small stage. Pascal described that self as "hateful," but Boris Vian [and Fernando Arrabal] . . . tell us it is all we have, absurd as it may be.

It took some time for the dramatic works of Boris Vian, who died in 1959, to finally be performed. A poet, novelist, trumpet player, and dramatist, Vian was a kind of new Jarry—but a melancholy and tender Jarry. His works convey a taste for life in all its forms and also—like those of Ionesco or Raymond Queneau—an obsession with death. Death is not the sumptuous horror of decaying flesh or the supernatural phenomenon that it was for Ghelderode, but extinction in itself, a nothingness in the face of which man's agitation has little value.

This attitude led Vian, in two of his plays (*L'Equarrissage pour tous* and *Le Goûter des généraux*), to poke fun at the ambitions and incoherencies displayed by mankind in performing the act it would seem to take most seriously: war. Greedy, opportunistic, or simply childish, Vian's characters—generals, politicians, soldiers, and civilians of all nationalities and all leanings—take part, with an almost Ubuesque lack of awareness, in what seem like cabaret acts. According to a tradition dear to French children, the generals, properly dressed in the uniforms of today's army, have a tea party, during which they take a few alcoholic drinks on the sly (out of fear of an overpowering mother) and organize a war in all its detail—until they realize that they have forgotten to choose an enemy (*Le Goûter des généraux*). Similarly, amid the ravages of a war involving the French, the Americans, and the Germans, a wedding is being prepared—that of a French girl to a German soldier, who is fighting a hundred yards away and is called to the wedding by telephone (*L'Equarrissage pour tous*). War being absurd, Vian improves on its absurdity; but his method consists essentially in treating it with nonchalance.

The spectator at such plays is, in a sense, struck by the horrors of massacre and the general incoherence, but far more by the absolute irreverence with which things are minimized—even those that in reality are the most shattering. In *L'Equarrissage,* for example, everything is set up for a torture scene, but the torture consists in tickling the victim. Vian's intention is to shock, but the shock comes less from aggressive provocation than from total disrespect in both form and substance. The tension in *Le Goûter* and *L'Equarrissage* is created by the enormous incongruity between bad jokes, intentionally superficial in nature, and the seriousness of the values involved. An antimilitarist and author of the well-known French song "Chanson du déserteur," Vian is subversive by way of frivolity. In the face of the universal phenomenon of death, the social and political problems melt away and are not even worthy of being attacked seriously.

As a final disrespectful and facile gesture, Vian does away with all his characters at the end of both plays. The generals and politicians of *Le Goûter* kill themselves one after another during a collective game of Russian roulette which they find highly amusing; the setting of *L'Equarrissage* having disappeared in an explosion, the few survivors kill each other to the sound of the "Marseillaise." Vian may well be saying that mankind, both military and civilian, entertains a death wish for collective annihilation, falsely glorified by big words and noble pretexts. But his burlesque and spectacular finales are also a sign that he is the last to take his own creations really seriously: his game is altogether subversive in that it itself is an object of subversion.

In a third play, *Les Bâtisseurs d'empire,* Vian presents the reality in relation to which all human values and ambitions become equalized in their indignity and comic absurdity: death. *Les Bâtisseurs* approaches allegory but, as in Beckett and most of Ionesco, stops short of it to the extent that the equation between what is seen or heard and the concepts suggested remains ambiguous, polyvalent, and thus not intellectually translatable. The play as a whole follows a rigorous movement from progressive suffocation and isolation to final and complete obscurity. Taken literally, it is a nightmare of invasion from the outside: as a

family flees from apartment to apartment, its members disappear one after another, until only the Father is left, and his last refuge is then invaded, in the dark, by the deadly enemies. Confronted by this mysterious destruction of the world, the characters try—very comically—to justify their existence or their achievements, using a language made up of clichés and paralogisms, and doing their best to ignore the invasion, the shrinking space of their successive lodgings, and the gradual disappearance of the members of the family.

With more obviously social and political implications, Georges Michel has recently picked up this theme in his *Promenade du Dimanche,* but Vian's play goes beyond that level of a "plague" à la Camus. It is also concerned with a metaphor of individual death and in this respect may be compared to one of Ionesco's later plays, *Le Roi se meurt.* While the family disappears and the living space gets progressively smaller and shabbier, one realizes that the Father's flight from room to room is illusory, for he is always accompanied by his Schmürz, an ignoble, bloody, and permanent witness-scapegoat. The Schmürz is sometimes ignored and sometimes—in fact, quite regularly—beaten up, but he is always there, silent. If he is meant to represent anything, it would be, in a very general way, an aggregate of outer and inner realities (evil, bad faith, sadistic impulses, and the desire to subject others, hence the shame and joy of being a master) which men sometimes recognize in distrust or hate and try to destroy or frequently prefer to ignore so that they may contrive to live with it in some measure of satisfaction. Scenically, the Schmürz is an embodiment of malaise—the malaise of reality, which is actually the unacknowledged awareness of future annihilation, of a death which keeps men from *really* living: a few seconds before the final obscurity, the Schmürz dies, but he does so just before the door is smashed in and the invaders at last make their entrance. The invaders are never seen, but they are "perhaps," says Boris Vian, "Schmürzes."

In fact, the Schmürz is the image that gives Vian's dramatic works their meaning. For the nightmare horror of *Les Bâtisseurs d'empire,* along with its implacable rigor, is what justifies the nonchalance and burlesque elements of his other two plays. None of this, however, excludes a touch of infinite tenderness, which is far more obvious in certain of Vian's poems or in a novel such as *L'Ecume des jours,* in which the heroine dies from a flower that grows in her chest, and the hero, in charge of "growing" guns, manages to produce them, but each with, at the end of its barrel, a rose.

In the nightmare that dominates the works of Fernando Arrabal, the fiend is not so much death as the powers of this world—judges, policemen, formidable mothers, torturers—who are always ready to detect the fateful flaw, punish it, or treacherously encourage it with an eye to even more severe punishment. Sometimes similar to Beckett's tramps, sometimes akin to the victims in Adamov's early plays, and colored by memories of Charlie Chaplin or the Marx Brothers, Arrabal's protagonists exist in a very special zone of their own: they have the mentality of children and the sexual prowess of adults—and hence a rather picturesque strangeness. The interests and somewhat perverse freshness of children are clearly shown, for example, in this dialogue between Climando and Mita in *Le Tricycle:*

> CLIMANDO. Listen, Mita, where will we pee in heaven?
>
> MITA. You don't pee in heaven.
>
> CLIMANDO. What a pity.
>
> MITA. You'll get used to it.
>
> CLIMANDO. (*Enthusiastically*) Mita, you're so intelligent, you know everything.

Being children, they are also, in a strangely innocent way, curious about gory or sexual acts. Above all, they have an intermittent sense of guilt and a fear of policemen, who are terrifying when they appear and just as quickly forgotten when their backs are turned. When these characters do something "bad," they are rarely conscience-stricken; rather, they consider it only a possible cause for punishment. Indeed, all the games they play are censured by the adult world, from the flagellation of dolls (*Le Grand Cérémonial*) to bloody murder (*Le Grand Cérémonial, Le Tricycle, Cérémonie pour un noir assassiné*).

In point of fact, however, the characters are adults. Although they commit their dread deeds while playing, they do commit them. Their sexual curiosity is actually voyeurism; they don't pretend to make love in coffins, they really do. And though they hide corpses as a child would hide broken toys, their corpses are real. Arrabal tries to portray sadism, masochism, necrophilia, and the taste for murder in all their horror but also in all their innocence.

The childishness of Arrabal's characters and their lack of any moral conscience evoke a kind of paradise lost forever. Responsibility for the fall is generally put on the mother image, which appears in many plays. Its cruel power is most clearly apparent in *Les Deux Bourreaux,* a play very similar in its rigor to certain of Adamov's early works. The mother is held responsible for the denunciation and torture of the father, whose screams are heard from behind the scenes, and whose corpse, hung on a stick like a dead animal, is carried across the stage by the two executioners; before the curtain falls, the two sons accept their mother's lies, give in to her, and ask her pardon. Here, added to the mother image, is that of police authority, the official executioners. In *Le Grand Cérémonial* the hero who whips dolls and murders a young girl is maintained in his psychotic state by the presence of an authoritarian and Machiavellian mother and her sentimental blackmail, while at given moments the sirens of police cars are heard offstage. This double prison of the protagonists—one deriving from Freud, the other from the police structure of the outside world—has its roots in Arrabal's private life and his memories of the Franco regime and its persecutions. His theatre is thus an extremely personal affair—the exploitation of an individual nightmare, which in itself is rich in possibilities.

On the other hand, Arrabal's presentation of nostalgia for a lost paradise is oversimplified, and the double game of innocence and guilt remains clinical. Throughout the show of generalized perversity an emphasis on horror and the whole baggage of devices that derive from the Grand Guignol or from a specialized brothel limit its scope to that of documents of pathological cases. The horror is too

often simply horror in itself, so that the spectacle of a hunchback named Cavanosa who achieves orgasm by whipping a doll remains a mere curiosity. Original goodness and the Passion it leads to are the subject matter of *Le Cimetière des voitures,* where, with great imagination, Arrabal peoples the stage with a miserable and actively sexual community lodged in the graveyard's heaps of disabled cars. In their pitiful and comic midst there appears a "good" trumpet player, accompanied by two other musicians. This hero is of course a slaughterer whenever he feels the urge, but he is called Emmanou, is eventually betrayed and beaten up, and at the end is carried across the stage tied to a bicycle, a woman wiping his face with a cloth. The transposition of the Passion of Jesus is far too obvious, and the naïveté of the symbol lessens the power of the play, which is otherwise rich in invention and meaning.

In the past few years Arrabal has added a new dimension to the performance of his fantasies: the theatrical notion of ceremony. The intentions behind the rites in which his characters try to transcend their ambiguous game are clear from the very titles of the plays (*Le Grand Cérémonial, Le Couronnement, Cérémonie pour un noir assassiné*) and from the stage directions in the published texts (a ceremonial kiss, a sacrificial gesture, and so on). Crowns of thorn or confirmation dresses and staging that is meant to transform the acts of torture, sadomasochism, or necrophilia into a kind of Mass or sacrament are used in an attempt to make the spectator feel that during the performance he is committing the sacrilege of those who do not bow their heads during the high moments of the Catholic liturgy. Arrabal thus seeks to transform simple voyeurism of the psychoanalyst's-couch variety into mystical blasphemy. Indeed, the ambitious goal of these works is to damn us along with themselves, and to create *panic*—that is to say, the sacred horror that springs from the black sanctification, through ritual, of the evil within us.

Despite the recognizable echoes of Ionesco, Beckett, and others, Arrabal's theatre does have its originality. It is full of striking effects: an automobile graveyard, corpse-conveying bicycles, adult-conveying baby carriages, life-size dolls, strong suggestions of torture, the double image—both hated and adored—of oppression and unhappiness, and the Grand Guignol pathology of sadomasochistic ceremonies. Yet, while Arrabal shows great promise, he still fails to attain poetry, to absorb the spectator into the ceremony, or to transfigure unhappiness and personal fantasies into contemporary and universal situations—all of which has finally been achieved by that other fallen angel, Jean Genet. (pp. 179-87)

Jacques Guicharnaud and June Guicharnaud, "The Absurd Has Many Faces: Vian, Arrabal, Duras, Dubillard," in their Modern French Theatre: From Giraudoux to Genet, *Yale University Press, 1967, pp. 178-95.*

J. L. Styan

[Styan is an English critic and educator who has written numerous studies of the theater, including the three-volume Modern Drama in Theory and Practice *(1981). In the following excerpt, Styan examines early plays by Arthur Adamov and Edward Albee.]*

Beginning as a highly subjective surrealistic poet, and influenced by an indigestible mixture of works by Strindberg, Kafka and Artaud, Arthur Adamov presented the unusual case of an absurdist playwright whose perspectives noticeably widened as his plays reached a bigger public. Adamov's early plays dramatized his personal despair, but before he committed suicide, he was writing in the more positive manner of Brechtian epic theatre, and was fully committed to the social realist cause. His first play, *La Parodie* (*The Parody*) was another early absurdist piece written in a surrealistic style before *Waiting for Godot* was known. Written in 1947, it was not produced until 1952. It was intended as a "parody" of life, in which one man, a nameless optimist, keeps a pointless rendezvous with a girl, Lili, who never meets him; meanwhile, another man, a pessimist, merely waits in despair for her to pass by, although she never does. As a result of their behaviour, the first man is sentenced to a term in prison, and the second is run over in the street and swept up in an ashcan. As in some Strindbergian dream play, the same characters appear in different guises, all to emphasize man's loneliness and the world's meaninglessness. *Le Professeur Taranne* (*Professor Taranne*), directed by Roger Planchon in 1953, was based upon an actual nightmare Adamov had had. In this play an elderly scholar and gentleman is accused, among other things, of the unlikely crime of indecent exposure. However, in the manner of Kafka's *The Trial*, the more poor Taranne denies the charges and defies his accusers, the more he appears to convict himself.

With *Le Ping-pong* (*Ping Pong*, 1955), it is possible to recognize Adamov's new interest in the stage as a medium for social criticism. This is a play of great wit, in which two young students devote their lives to the study and worship of pinball machines, which are presumably to symbolize the mechanical emptiness of modern society. They are still obsessed with the trivial intricacies of the machine when they are old men on the point of death. Social realism is even more explicit in Adamov's *Paolo Paoli*, directed by Planchon in 1957. This is a Marxist satire on capitalism in France just before the outbreak of the First World War. The play uses the informative and distancing device of news headlines projected on screens, a technique borrowed from the theatre of Piscator and Brecht, but its cleverest alienating effect is built into the subject itself. The chief objects of trade between Algeria and metropolitan France at that time, and the source of heated interest to the characters of the play, are nothing more than butterflies and ostrich feathers. However, implicit in such satire must be the desire to correct what is wrong with society, and once it is accepted that the wrongs of the world can be put right, then an absurdism that preaches the total irrationality of life is no more.

In America, Edward Albee was initially influenced enough by Ionesco to write surrealistic one-act plays in the absurdist manner. His brief allegory of modern society, *The Zoo Story*, was first produced in the Werkstatt of the Schiller Theater in Berlin in 1959, directed by Walter Henn. It was afterwards produced at the Provincetown Playhouse in New York by Milton Katselas in 1960, and then at the Arts Theatre, London, by Henry Kaplan. The play presents two men who meet on a bench in Central Park, New York. Peter is an older man and comes from the middle-classes; Jerry is a young working-class rebel. Speaking in quasi-realistic dialogue, they are unable to un-

Scene from Adamov's Paolo Paoli.

derstand each other: in the jargon of the day, they fail to communicate. Not only this, but violence is the only medium they have in common. So it is that Jerry provokes Peter to fight him, with Jerry finally impaling himself on the knife he had tossed to Peter.

Albee's *The Sandbox,* written in 1959 and directed by Lawrence Arrick at the Jazz Gallery, New York, in 1960 and *The American Dream,* written in 1960 and directed by Alan Schneider at the York Playhouse, New York, in 1961, are twin one-act plays, amusing but caustic, intended to satirize the hollow social values of contemporary America. In the latter play, American aspirations towards the good life are symbolized by the arrival of a handsome, but vacuous, young man. He is joyfully adopted by a stereotyped American family, with a domineering Mommy and an emasculated Daddy. Only Grandma, every moment expecting to be taken away by the removal van, speaks the truth. These sketches are strongly derivative from Ionesco, but were simple to stage, made their point immediately and were immensely popular on college campuses during the rebellious sixties. With their emblematic, two-dimensional, cardboard characters, they also seemed refreshing after so long a period of realism on the American stage.

In 1961, Albee's gift for fluent and incisive dialogue helped his first long play, *Who's Afraid of Virginia Woolf,* to immediate and international fame. It was directed by Alan Schneider with Uta Hagen and Arthur Hill in the leading parts at the Billy Rose Theatre, New York, and at the Piccadilly Theatre, London, in 1964. An idealistic and newly married couple are entertained by a disillusioned, older couple, and the conjunction of the two groups has the effect of throwing up a variety of ghosts and skeletons. In spite of its absurdist title, the play constituted a retreat to a naturalistic mode of accentuated, Strindbergian, psychological realism, with a liberal addition of symbolic suggestions about the futility of human illusions. Harold Clurman found Albee's next play, *A Delicate Balance* (1966), to be superior, but if it was more subtle, it was less popular, more absurdist and less verbally sensational. It was directed by Alan Schneider with Jessica Tandy and Hume Cronyn at the Martin Beck Theatre, New York, and afterwards by Peter Hall with Peggy Ashcroft and Michael Hordern at the Aldwych Theatre, London, in 1969. In this play, another family is catalysed, this time by a visit from friends who are trying to escape from a mysterious terror, and who insist on staying the night when they are not wanted. It is the task of the quiet but downtrodden head of the family, Tobias, to maintain a "balance" between family and friends. *All Over* (1971) has a famous man dying in his bed on the stage throughout the play while his wife and mistress, his family and friends, talk about him and each other. The play was not so well received as its predecessors, but in its experiments with forms of speech selected to lend a ritual tone to the scene, it was an interesting advance in absurdist technique. Nevertheless, Albee's strength lies in his cynical and seemingly realistic observation of people under stress, and "theatre of the absurd" is a term that can no longer be readily applied to his work. (pp. 141-44)

Pure absurdism was like private poetry: even when it had expressed itself as fully as it could, it had little future. In any case, Joseph Chiari asked tellingly in his *Landmarks of Contemporary Drama,* if there is no communication possible between people in an absurdist world, why try to write an absurdist play in the first place? (p. 145)

> J. L. Styan, *"Theatre of the Absurd: Ionesco and Others,"* in his Modern Drama in Theory and Practice: Symbolism, Surrealism and the Absurd, Vol. 2, *Cambridge University Press, 1981, pp. 137-45.*

THE THEATER OF THE ABSURD AND THE CONCEPT OF THE ABSURD

Martin Esslin

[*In the following excerpt, Esslin details the social, psychological, and religious significance of the Theater of the Absurd.*]

When Nietzsche's Zarathustra descended from his mountains to preach to mankind, he met a saintly hermit in the forest. This old man invited him to stay in the wilderness rather than go into the cities of men. When Zarathustra asked the hermit how he passed his time in his solitude, he replied: "I make up songs and sing them; and when I make up songs I laugh, I weep, and I growl; thus do I praise God." Zarathustra declined the old man's offer and continued on his journey. But when he was alone, he spoke thus to his heart: "Can it be possible! This old saint in the forest has not yet heard that God is dead!"

Zarathustra was first published in 1883. The number of people for whom God is dead has greatly increased since Nietzsche's day, and mankind has learned the bitter lesson of the falseness and evil nature of some of the cheap and vulgar substitutes that have been set up to take his place. And so, after two terrible wars, there are still many who are trying to come to terms with the implications of Zarathustra's message, searching for a way in which they can, with dignity, confront a universe deprived of what was once its centre and its living purpose, a world deprived of

a generally accepted integrating principle, which has become disjointed, purposeless—absurd.

The Theatre of the Absurd is one of the expressions of this search. It bravely faces up to the fact that for those to whom the world has lost its central explanation and meaning, it is no longer possible to accept art forms still based on the continuation of standards and concepts that have lost their validity; that is, the possibility of knowing the laws of conduct and ultimate values, as deducible from a firm foundation of revealed certainty about the purpose of man in the universe.

In expressing the tragic sense of loss at the disappearance of ultimate certainties the Theatre of the Absurd, by a strange paradox, is also a symptom of what probably comes nearest to being a genuine religious quest in our age: an effort, however timid and tentative, to sing, to laugh, to weep—and to growl—if not in praise of God (whose name, in Adamov's phrase, has for so long been degraded by usage that it has lost its meaning), at least in search of a dimension of the Ineffable; an effort to make man aware of the ultimate realities of his condition, to instil in him again the lost sense of cosmic wonder and primeval anguish, to shock him out of an existence that has become trite, mechanical, complacent, and deprived of the dignity that comes of awareness. For God is dead, above all, to the masses who live from day to day and have lost all contact with the basic facts—and mysteries—of the human condition with which, in former times, they were kept in touch through the living ritual of their religion, which made them parts of a real community and not just atoms in an atomized society.

The Theatre of the Absurd forms part of the unceasing endeavour of the true artists of our time to breach this dead wall of complacency and automatism and to re-establish an awareness of man's situation when confronted with the ultimate reality of his condition. As such, the Theatre of the Absurd fulfils a dual purpose and presents its audience with a two-fold absurdity.

In one of its aspects it castigates, satirically, the absurdity of lives lived unaware and unconscious of ultimate reality. This is the feeling of the deadness and mechanical senselessness of half-unconscious lives, the feeling of "human beings secreting inhumanity," which Camus describes in "The Myth of Sisyphus":

> In certain hours of lucidity, the mechanical aspect of their gestures, their senseless pantomine, makes stupid everything around them. A man speaking on the telephone behind a glass partition—one cannot hear him but observes his trivial gesturing. One asks oneself, why is he alive? This malaise in front of man's own inhumanity, this incalculable letdown when faced with the image of what we are, this "nausea," as a contemporary writer calls it, also is the Absurd.

This is the experience that Ionesco expresses in plays like *The Bald Soprano* or *The Chairs,* Adamov in *La Parodie,* or N. F. Simpson in *A Resounding Tinkle.* It represents the satirical, parodistic aspect of the Theatre of the Absurd, its social criticism, its pillorying of an inauthentic, petty society. This may be the most easily accessible, and therefore most widely recognized, message of the Theatre of the Absurd, but it is far from being its most essential or most significant feature.

In its second, more positive aspect, behind the satirical exposure of the absurdity of inauthentic ways of life, the Theatre of the Absurd is facing up to a deeper layer of absurdity—the absurdity of the human condition itself in a world where the decline of religious belief has deprived man of certainties. When it is no longer possible to accept complete closed systems of values and revelations of divine purpose, life must be faced in its ultimate, stark reality. (pp. 350-52)

Concerned as it is with the ultimate realities of the human condition, the relatively few fundamental problems of life and death, isolation and communication, the Theatre of the Absurd, however grotesque, frivolous, and irreverent it may appear, represents a return to the original, religious function of the theatre—the confrontation of man with the spheres of myth and religious reality. Like ancient Greek tragedy and the medieval mystery plays and baroque allegories, the Theatre of the Absurd is intent on making its audience aware of man's precarious and mysterious position in the universe.

The difference is merely that in ancient Greek tragedy—and comedy—as well as in the medieval mystery play and the baroque *auto sacramental,* the ultimate realities concerned were generally known and universally accepted metaphysical systems, while the Theatre of the Absurd expresses the absence of any such generally accepted cosmic system of values. Hence, much more modestly, the Theatre of the Absurd makes no pretence at explaining the ways of God to man. It can merely present, in anxiety or with derision, an individual human being's intuition of the ultimate realities as he experiences them; the fruits of one man's descent into the depths of his personality, his dreams, fantasies, and nightmares.

While former attempts at confronting man with the ultimate realities of his condition projected a coherent and generally recognized version of the truth, the Theatre of the Absurd merely communicates one poet's most intimate and personal intuition of the human situation, his own *sense of being,* his individual vision of the world. This is the *subject-matter* of the Theatre of the Absurd, and it determines its *form,* which must, of necessity, represent a convention of the stage basically different from the "realistic" theatre of our time.

As the Theatre of the Absurd is not concerned with conveying information or presenting the problems or destinies of characters that exist outside the author's inner world, as it does not expound a thesis or debate ideological propositions, it is not concerned with the representation of events, the narration of the fate or the adventures of characters, but instead with the presentation of one individual's basic situation. It is a theatre of situation as against a theatre of events in sequence, and therefore it uses a language based on patterns of concrete images rather than argument and discursive speech. And since it is trying to present a sense of being, it can neither investigate nor solve problems of conduct or morals.

Because the Theatre of the Absurd projects its author's personal world, it lacks objectively valid characters. It cannot show the clash of opposing temperaments or study human passions locked in conflict, and is therefore not dramatic in the accepted sense of the term. Nor is it concerned with telling a story in order to communicate some moral or social lesson, as is the aim of Brecht's narrative, "epic" theatre. The action in a play of the Theatre of the Absurd is not intended to tell a story but to communicate a pattern of poetic images. To give but one example: things happen in *Waiting for Godot,* but these happenings do not constitute a plot or story; they are an image of Beckett's intuition that *nothing really ever happens* in man's existence. The whole play is a complex poetic image made up of a complicated pattern of subsidiary images and themes, which are interwoven like the themes of a musical composition, not, as in most well-made plays, to present a line of development, but to make in the spectator's mind a total, complex impression of a basic, and static, situation. In this, the Theatre of the Absurd is analogous to a Symbolist or Imagist poem, which also presents a pattern of images and associations in a mutually interdependent structure.

While the Brechtian epic theatre tries to widen the range of drama by introducing narrative, epic elements, the Theatre of the Absurd aims at concentration and depth in an essentially lyrical, poetic pattern. Of course, dramatic, narrative, and lyrical elements are present in all drama. Brecht's own theatre, like Shakespeare's, contains lyrical inserts in the form of songs; even at their most didactic, Ibsen and Shaw are rich in purely poetic moments. The Theatre of the Absurd, however, in abandoning psychology, subtlety of characterization, and plot in the conventional sense, gives the poetical element an incomparably greater emphasis. While the play with a linear plot describes a development in time, in a dramatic form that presents a concretized poetic image the play's extension in time is purely incidental. Expressing an *intuition in depth,* it should ideally be apprehended *in a single moment,* and only because it is physically impossible to present so complex an image in an instant does it have to be spread over a period of time. The formal structure of such a play is, therefore, merely a device to express a complex total image by unfolding it in a sequence of interacting elements.

The endeavour to communicate a total sense of being is an attempt to present a truer picture of reality itself, reality as apprehended by an individual. The Theatre of the Absurd is the last link in a line of development that started with naturalism. The idealistic, Platonic belief in immutable essences—ideal forms that it was the artist's task to present in a purer state than they could ever be found in nature—foundered in the philosophy of Locke and Kant, which based reality on perception and the inner structure of the human mind. Art then became mere imitation of external nature. Yet the imitation of surfaces was bound to prove unsatisfying and this inevitably led to the next step—the exploration of the reality of the mind. Ibsen and Strindberg exemplified that development during the span of their own lifetimes' exploration of reality. James Joyce began with minutely realistic stories and ended up with the vast multiple structure of *Finnegans Wake.* The work of the dramatists of the Absurd continues the same development. Each of these plays is an answer to the questions "How does this individual feel when confronted with the human situation? What is the basic mood in which he faces the world? What does it feel like to be he?" And the answer is a single, total, but complex and contradictory poetic image—one play—or a succession of such images, complementing each other—the dramatist's *oeuvre*.

In apprehending the world at any one moment, we receive simultaneously a whole complex of different perceptions and feelings. We can only communicate this instantaneous vision by breaking it down into different elements which can then be built up into a sequence in time, in a sentence or series of sentences. To convert our perception into conceptual terms, into logical thought and language, we perform an operation analogous to that of the scanner that analyses the pictures in a television camera into rows of single impulses. The poetic image, with its ambiguity and its simultaneous evocation of multiple elements of sense association, is one of the methods by which we can, however imperfectly, communicate the reality of our intuition of the world. (pp. 353-56)

Here lies the chief difference between poetry and prose: poetry is ambiguous and associative, striving to approximate to the wholly unconceptual language of music. The Theatre of the Absurd, in carrying the same poetic endeavour into the concrete imagery of the stage, can go further than pure poetry in dispensing with logic, discursive thought, and language. The stage is a multidimensional medium; it allows the simultaneous use of visual elements, movement, light, and language. It is, therefore, particularly suited to the communication of complex images consisting of the contrapuntal interaction of all these elements.

In the "literary" theatre, language remains the predominant component. In the anti-literary theatre of the circus or the music hall, language is reduced to a very subordinate role. The Theatre of the Absurd has regained the freedom of using language as merely one—sometimes dominant, sometimes submerged—component of its multidimensional poetic imagery. By putting the language of a scene in contrast to the action, by reducing it to meaningless patter, or by abandoning discursive logic for the poetic logic of association or assonance, the Theatre of the Absurd has opened up a new dimension of the stage. (pp. 356-57)

[Communication] between human beings is . . . often shown in a state of breakdown in the Theatre of the Absurd. It is merely a satirical magnification of the existing state of affairs. Language has run riot in an age of mass communication. It must be reduced to its proper function—the expression of authentic content, rather than its concealment. But this will be possible only if man's reverence toward the spoken or written word as a means of communication is restored, and the ossified clichés that dominate thought (as they do in the limericks of Edward Lear or the world of Humpty Dumpty) are replaced by a living language that serves it. And this, in turn, can be achieved only if the limitations of logic and discursive language are recognized and respected, and the uses of poetic language acknowledged.

The means by which the dramatists of the Absurd express their critique—largely instinctive and unintended—of our disintegrating society are based on suddenly confronting their audiences with a grotesquely heightened and distorted picture of a world that has gone mad. This is a shock therapy that achieves what Brecht's doctrine of the "alienation effect" postulated in theory but failed to achieve in practice—the inhibition of the audience's identification

with the characters on the stage (which is the age-old and highly effective method of the traditional theatre) and its replacement by a detached, critical attitude.

If we identify ourselves with the main character in a play, we automatically accept his point of view, see the world in which he moves with *his* eyes, feel *his* emotions. From the standpoint of a didactic, Socialist theatre, Brecht argued that this time-honoured psychological link between the actor and the audience must be broken. How could an audience be made to see the actions of the characters in a play *critically* if they were made to adopt their points of view? Hence Brecht, in his Marxist period, tried to introduce a number of devices designed to break this spell. Yet he never completely succeeded in achieving his aim. The audience, in spite of the introduction of songs, slogans, nonrepresentational décor, and other inhibiting devices, continues to identify with Brecht's brilliantly drawn characters and therefore often tends to miss the critical attitude Brecht wanted it to assume toward them. The old magic of the theatre is too strong; the pull toward identification, which springs from a basic psychological characteristic of human nature, is overwhelming. If we see Mother Courage weep for her son, we cannot resist feeling her sorrow and therefore fail to condemn her for her acceptance of war as a business, which inevitably leads to the loss of her children. The finer the characterization of a human being on the stage, the more inevitable is this process of identification.

In the Theatre of the Absurd, on the other hand, the audience is confronted with characters whose motives and actions remain largely incomprehensible. With such characters it is almost impossible to identify; the more mysterious their action and their nature, the less human the characters become, the more difficult it is to be carried away into seeing the world from their point of view. Characters with whom the audience fails to identify are inevitably comic. If we identified with the figure of farce who loses his trousers, we should feel embarrassment and shame. If, however, our tendency to identify has been inhibited by making such a character grotesque, we laugh at his predicament. We see what happens to him from the outside, rather than from his own point of view. As the incomprehensibility of the motives, and the often unexplained and mysterious nature of the characters' actions in the Theatre of the Absurd effectively prevent identification, such theatre is a comic theatre in spite of the fact that its subject-matter is sombre, violent, and bitter. That is why the Theatre of the Absurd transcends the categories of comedy and tragedy and combines laughter with horror.

But, by its very nature, it cannot provoke the thoughtful attitude of detached social criticism that was Brecht's objective. It does not present its audience with sets of social facts and examples of political behaviour. It presents the audience with a picture of a disintegrating world that has lost its unifying principle, its meaning, and its purpose—an absurd universe. What is the audience to make of this bewildering confrontation with a truly alienated world that, having lost its rational principle, has in the true sense of the word gone mad?

Here we are face to face with the central problem of the effect, the aesthetic efficacy and validity, of the Theatre of the Absurd. It is an empirical fact that, in defiance of most of the accepted rules of drama, the best plays of this kind are effective as theatre—the convention of the Absurd *works.* But *why* does it work? To some extent, the answer has been given in the foregoing account of the nature of comic and farcical effects. The misfortunes of characters we view with a cold, critical, unidentified eye *are* funny. Stupid characters who act in mad ways have always been the butt of derisive laughter in the circus, the music hall, and the theatre. But such comic characters usually appeared in a rational framework, and were set off by positive characters with whom the audience could identify. In the Theatre of the Absurd, the whole of the action is mysterious, unmotivated, and at first sight nonsensical.

The alienation effect in the Brechtian theatre is intended to activate the audience's critical, intellectual attitude. The Theatre of the Absurd speaks to a deeper level of the audience's mind. It activates psychological forces, releases and liberates hidden fears and repressed aggressions, and, above all, by confronting the audience with a picture of disintegration, it sets in motion an active process of integrative forces in the mind of each individual spectator.

As Eva Metman says in her remarkable essay on Beckett ["Reflections on Samuel Beckett's Plays," *Journal of Analytical Psychology,* January 1960]:

> In times of religious containment, [dramatic art] has shown man as protected, guided, and sometimes punished by [archetypal] powers, but in other epochs it has shown the visible tangible world, in which man fulfils his destiny, as permeated by the demonic essences of his invisible and intangible being. In contemporary drama, a new, third orientation is crystallizing in which man is shown not in a world into which the divine or demonic powers are projected but alone with them. This new form of drama forces the audience out of its familiar orientation. It creates a vacuum between the play and the audience so that the latter is compelled to experience something itself, be it a reawakening of the awareness of archetypal powers or a reorientation of the ego, or both. . . .

One need not be a Jungian or use Jungian categories to see the force of this diagnosis. Human beings who in their daily lives confront a world that has split up into a series of disconnected fragments and lost its purpose, but who· are no longer aware of this state of affairs and its disintegrating effect on their personalities, are brought face to face with a heightened representation of this schizophrenic universe. "The vacuum between what is shown on the stage and the onlooker has become so unbearable that the latter has no alternative but either to reject and turn away or to be drawn into the enigma of the plays in which nothing reminds him of any of his purposes in and reactions to the world around him." Once drawn into the mystery of the play, the spectator is compelled to come to terms with his experience. The stage supplies him with a number of disjointed clues that he has to fit into a meaningful pattern. In this manner, he is forced to make a creative effort of his own, an effort at interpretation and integration. The time has been made to appear out of joint; the audience of the Theatre of the Absurd is being compelled to set it right, or, rather, by being made to see that the world has become absurd, in acknowledging that fact takes the first step in coming to terms with reality. (pp. 360-63)

In the Theatre of the Absurd, the spectator is confronted with the madness of the human condition, is enabled to see his situation in all its grimness and despair. Stripped of illusions and vaguely felt fears and anxieties, he can face this situation consciously, rather than feeling it vaguely below the surface of euphemisms and optimistic illusions. By seeing his anxieties formulated he can liberate himself from them. This is the nature of all the gallows humour and *humour noir* of world literature, of which the Theatre of the Absurd is the latest example. It is the unease caused by the presence of illusions that are obviously out of tune with reality that is dissolved and discharged through liberating laughter at the recognition of the fundamental absurdity of the universe. (p. 364)

In trying to deal with the ultimates of the human condition not in terms of intellectual understanding but in terms of communicating a metaphysical truth through a living experience, the Theatre of the Absurd touches the religious sphere. There is a vast difference between *knowing* something to be the case in the conceptual sphere and *experiencing* it as a living reality. It is the mark of all great religions that they not only possess a body of knowledge that can be taught in the form of cosmological information or ethical rules but that they also communicate the essence of this body of doctrine in the living, recurring poetic imagery of ritual. It is the loss of the latter sphere, which responds to a deep inner need in all human beings, that the decline of religion has left as a deeply felt deficiency in our civilization. We possess at least an approximation to a coherent philosophy in the scientific method, but we lack the means to make it a living reality, an experienced focus of men's lives. That is why the theatre, a place where men congregate to experience poetic or artistic insights, has in many ways assumed the function of a substitute church. Hence the immense importance placed upon the theatre by totalitarian creeds, which are fully aware of the need to make their doctrines a living, experienced reality to their followers.

The Theatre of the Absurd, paradoxical though this may appear at first sight, can be seen as an attempt to communicate the metaphysical experience behind the scientific attitude and, at the same time, to supplement it by rounding off the partial view of the world it presents, and integrating it in a wider vision of the world and its mystery.

For if the Theatre of the Absurd presents the world as senseless and lacking a unifying principle, it does so merely in the terms of those philosophies that start from the idea that human thought *can* reduce the totality of the universe to a complete, unified, coherent system. It is only from the point of view of those who cannot bear a world where it is impossible to know why it was created, what part man has been assigned in it, and what constitutes right actions and wrong actions, that a picture of the universe lacking all these clear-cut definitions appears deprived of sense and sanity, and tragically absurd. The modern scientific attitude, however, rejects the postulate of a wholly coherent and simplified explanation that must account for all the phenomena, purposes, and moral rules of the world. In concentrating on the slow, painstaking exploration of limited areas of reality by trial and error—by the construction, testing, and discarding of hypotheses—the scientific attitude cheerfully accepts the view that we must be able to live with the realization that large segments of knowledge and experience will remain for a long time, perhaps forever, outside our ken; that ultimate purposes cannot, and never will be, known; and that we must therefore be able to accept the fact that much that earlier metaphysical systems, mythical, religious, or philosophical, sought to explain must forever remain unexplained. From this point of view, any clinging to systems of thought that provide, or purport to provide, complete explanations of the world and man's place in it must appear childish and immature, a flight from reality into illusion and self-deception.

The Theatre of the Absurd expresses the anxiety and despair that spring from the recognition that man is surrounded by areas of impenetrable darkness, that he can never know his true nature and purpose, and that no one will provide him with ready-made rules of conduct. As Camus says in "The Myth of Sisyphus":

> The certainty of the existence of a God who would give meaning to life has a far greater attraction than the knowledge that without him one could do evil without being punished. The choice between these alternatives would not be difficult. But there is no choice, and that is where the bitterness begins.

But by facing up to anxiety and despair and the absence of divinely revealed alternatives, anxiety and despair can be overcome. The sense of loss at the disintegration of facile solutions and the disappearance of cherished illusions retains its sting only while the mind still clings to the illusions concerned. Once they are given up, we have to readjust ourselves to the new situation and face reality itself. And because the illusions we suffered from made it more difficult for us to deal with reality, their loss will ultimately be felt as exhilarating. In the words of Democritus that Beckett is fond of quoting, "Nothing is more real than Nothing."

To confront the limits of the human condition is not only equivalent to facing up to the philosophical basis of the scientific attitude, it is also a profound mystical experience. It is precisely this experience of the ineffability, the emptiness, the nothingness at the basis of the universe that forms the content of Eastern as well as Christian mystical experience. For if Lao-tzu says, "It was from the nameless that Heaven and Earth sprang, the named is but the mother that rears the ten thousand creatures, each after its kind," St. John of the Cross speaks of the soul's intuition "that it cannot comprehend God at all," and Meister Eckhart expresses the same experience in the words, "The Godhead is poor, naked, and empty, as though it were not; it has not, wills not, wants not, works not, gets not. . . . The Godhead is as void as though it were not." In other words, in facing man's inability ever to comprehend the meaning of the universe, in recognizing the Godhead's total transcendence, his total otherness from all we can understand with our senses, the great mystics experienced a sense of exhilaration and liberation. This exhilaration also springs from the recognition that the language and logic of cognitive thought cannot do justice to the ultimate nature of reality. Hence a profoundly mystical philosophy like Zen Buddhism bases itself on the rejection of conceptual thinking itself:

> The denying of reality is the asserting of it,
> And the asserting of emptiness is the denying of it.

The . . . rise of interest in Zen in Western countries is an expression of the same tendencies that explain the success of the Theatre of the Absurd—a preoccupation with ultimate realities and a recognition that they are not approachable through conceptual thought alone. Ionesco has been quoted as drawing a parallel between the method of the Zen Buddhists and the Theatre of the Absurd, and in fact the teaching methods of the Zen masters, their use of kicks and blows in reply to questions about the nature of enlightenment and their setting of nonsense problems, closely resemble some of the procedures of the Theatre of the Absurd.

Seen from this angle the dethronement of language and logic forms part of an essentially mystical attitude toward the basis of reality as being too complex and at the same time too unified, too much of one piece, to be validly expressed by the analytical means of orderly syntax and conceptual thought. As the mystics resort to poetic images, so does the Theatre of the Absurd. But if the Theatre of the Absurd presents analogies with the methods and imagery of mysticism, how can it, at the same time, be regarded as expressing the scepticism, the humble refusal to provide an explanation of absolutes, that characterize the scientific attitude?

The answer is simply that there is no contradiction between recognizing the limitations of man's ability to comprehend all of reality in a single system of values and recognizing the mysterious and ineffable oneness, beyond all rational comprehension, that, once experienced, gives serenity of mind and the strength to face the human condition. These are in fact two sides of the same medal—the mystical experience of the absolute otherness and ineffability of ultimate reality is the religious, poetic counterpart to the rational recognition of the limitation of man's senses and intellect, which reduces him to exploring the world slowly by trial and error. Both these attitudes are in basic contradiction to systems of thought, religious or ideological (e.g. Marxism), that claim to provide complete answers to all questions of ultimate purpose and day-to-day conduct.

The realization that thinking in poetic images has its validity side by side with conceptual thought and the insistence on a clear recognition of the function and possibilities of each mode does not amount to a return to irrationalism; on the contrary, it opens the way to a truly rational attitude.

Ultimately, a phenomenon like the Theatre of the Absurd does not reflect despair or a return to dark irrational forces but expresses modern man's endeavour to come to terms with the world in which he lives. It attempts to make him face up to the human condition as it really is, to free him from illusions that are bound to cause constant maladjustment and disappointment. There are enormous pressures in our world that seek to induce mankind to bear the loss of faith and moral certainties by being drugged into oblivion—by mass entertainments, shallow material satisfactions, pseudo-explanations of reality, and cheap ideologies. At the end of that road lies Huxley's Brave New World of senseless euphoric automata. Today, when death and old age are increasingly concealed behind euphemisms and comforting baby talk, and life is threatened with being smothered in the mass consumption of hypnotic mechanized vulgarity, the need to confront man with the reality of his situation is greater than ever. For the dignity of man lies in his ability to face reality in all its senselessness; to accept it freely, without fear, without illusions—and to laugh at it.

That is the cause to which, in their various individual, modest, and quixotic ways, the dramatists of the Absurd are dedicated. (pp. 373-77)

Martin Esslin, "The Significance of the Absurd," in his The Theatre of the Absurd, *revised edition, Anchor Books, 1969, pp. 350-77.*

Lionel Abel

[*In the following excerpt, Abel denies that a form of theater exists that may be called "absurd" in a literal sense.*]

Is the world we live in "absurd?" And has it become so recently? And does our world, newly "absurd," require a particular kind of theatrical art expressing "absurdity?" (p. 454)

The world can no more become "absurd" than it can sin, starve, or fall down. There are many absurdities in the world; most of them were always there.

But was there always a Theatre of the Absurd? I claim there was not and that there is no such thing now. Esslin claims that (1) there was a Theatre of the Absurd in the past and (2) the group of contemporary dramatists whom he has singled out write the kinds of plays they do in response to a particular crisis the world is going through at this time. But the two claims refute each other. Esslin maintains that there is a particular spiritual crisis, and that a certain kind of dramatic art has been produced in order to express it; but he cannot maintain, then, that forms of theatre like those being produced now long antedated the crisis. Yet in a chapter entitled "The Tradition of the Absurd," Esslin ranges through past history for prototypes of the new kinds of plays now being written. The mimes of the Middle Ages, the court jesters, the clowns of Shakespeare, the harlequinades which entered into the British music hall and American vaudeville, the Commedia dell'Arte, the nonsense verse of Lear and Lewis Carroll are all called on to account for the character of specifically modern works, which character, in turn, is supposed to be due to a special contemporary predicament. Esslin writes: "This is not the place for a detailed study of Shakespearean clowns, fools, and ruffians as forerunners of the Theatre of the Absurd." No, it is not.

But let us consider Esslin's main contention that there is a Theatre of the Absurd at this time, quite apart from his other contention that it pre-existed its own *raison d'etre.* Is it true that Beckett, Ionesco, Adamov, Genet, Albee, Arrabal, Grass, Pinter, and Simpson can be best understood if considered as instigators of a new theatrical art, the Theatre of the Absurd? Some of the playwrights listed above have, to be sure, written plays to Esslin's specifications, but only one of these, Ionesco, is really important. The three major figures, as I am sure Esslin himself would agree, are Ionesco, Beckett, and Genet. But of these three, only Ionesco fits Esslin's formula.

One individual, to be sure, if an artist of rank, has as much interest as a whole school. And Ionesco is a remarkable playwright with some five or six masterpieces to his credit.

He has great invention and an exuberant humor; unfortunately, his ideas are topical, adventitious: the last thing one could say about them is that they are "new." One typically "new" idea of Ionesco's is that there are no new ideas, even in the construction of plays. Here he is quite wrong. He has written some plays that are really novel as structures. It is the ideas expressed in them that are all too familiar and which spring from the prevailing climate of political and metaphysical pessimism.

What is objectionable in Ionesco's theatre is curiously akin to what is objectionable in Esslin's whole concept. Ionesco thinks "absurdity" is something new; Esslin wants to give us news of the "absurd."

Esslin talks a lot about Samuel Beckett and Jean Genet. But in the fairly detailed analyses he makes of their lives and work he is unable to illuminate much of their art or even to give us the feeling that he has judged it wisely.

Beckett he discusses under this rubric: "The Search for the Self." And Esslin searches accordingly in Richard Ellmann's biography of James Joyce (who knew Beckett) for such data as might throw light on *Waiting for Godot* and *Endgame.* Now Ellmann's book is valuable on Beckett as well as on Joyce. For instance, it appears that Beckett is given to long silences and when he visited Joyce they often stared at each other for hours without uttering a word. Now this certainly tells us something about the kind of dialogue we have come to expect from Beckett. But what has the personal data about Beckett to do with a general cultural crisis, or with any modern feeling for "absurdity?" Beckett is a very strange man, no question of that. Even his handwriting, of which I have seen one instance, is peculiar in the extreme.

Esslin finds fault with my own view, expressed in a piece I did on Beckett for *The New Leader:* "Samuel Beckett and James Joyce in *Endgame,*" and in which I attempted to explain Beckett's play in terms of his attitude to James Joyce. Esslin says that my theory "surely becomes untenable;" not because there may not be a certain amount of truth in it (every writer is bound to use elements of his own experience of life in his work) but because, far from illuminating the full content of a play like *Endgame,* such an interpretation reduces it to a trivial level." Did I reduce the relationship between Hamm and Clov to a trivial level? I made the point that the *value* of recognizing the autobiographical material in the play was that by so doing, it was possible to absolve the author of the charge of pessimism. But never mind my own interpretation of the play. Here is Esslin's: "The experience expressed in Beckett's plays (including *Endgame*) is of a far more profound and fundamental nature than mere autobiography. They reveal his experience of temporality and evanescence; his sense of the tragic difficulty of becoming aware of one's own self in the merciless process of renovation and destruction that occurs with change in time; of the difficulty of communication between human beings; of the unending quest for reality in a world in which everything is uncertain and the borderline between dream and reality is ever shifting: of the tragic nature of all love relationships and the self-deception of friendship . . . and so on." Are Beckett's plays about all that? From this list of abstractions one would think that Beckett's plays had been written in the German language and not, exquisitely, in the French. Besides, what have Esslin's list of abstractions to do with the life of Samuel Beckett? And what has that life to do with a general cultural crisis? These are the connections Esslin is obliged to establish, and he does not.

On the subject of Genet, too, Esslin's concept of the "absurd" is little help. He turns to the data about Genet's life which we have from the playwright himself. It seems that Genet was abandoned as a child, and when accused of stealing, resolved to become a thief. Between 1930 and 1940, as Esslin notes, Genet led the life of an itinerant delinquent, among beggars and pimps; he made acquaintance with the French jails. Fortunately for the theatre, he never quite became "the hardened jail-bird on whom the prison gates shut forever."

These facts show Genet to be a very strange person, too. Should not his personal strangeness be related to his plays? But Esslin, out to prove his theory, disregards the personal facts and concentrates on the "absurdity of our historical epoch." He derives Genet's plays from the modern feeling of helplessness in facing a mechanized world. Esslin writes: "A feeling of helplessness when confronted with the vast intricacy of the modern world, and the individual's impotence in making his own influence felt on that intricate and mysterious machinery, pervades the consciousness of Western man today. A world that functions mysteriously outside our conscious control must appear absurd." Once again Esslin has trotted out fashionable and very misleading clichés. The world Genet describes in his plays is the product of a virile imagination, almost Elizabethan in its force and fancy. Genet could be compared to Marlowe, never to Kafka.

Art, it must be admitted, is unable to occupy a central position in the modern world; thus, the artist cannot be in the very center of things. But Homer was certainly in the very center of things Greek when he wrote the *Iliad,* though he wrote it in Ionia; and Sophocles was in the center of the Greek world when he wrote plays for the Athenian public. In the modern world, of course, no such privileged position is open to art. To look at all, the artist is probably condemned not to look all around him. Can anyone be in the center of things in our age? This is not sure. But this is sure: anyone who is, will not be an artist. That is why a Homer is utterly inconceivable today. (Hegel notes that there was not a single tool made by the Greeks which went unremarked in Homer's *Iliad.* Is it conceivable that any modern poet could sum up in song all the instruments manufactured in our society? Besides, to carry Hegel's point further, every tool Homer described was already an art object.) Very probably art requires, if it is to be practiced at all today, that its creator contribute to it his own personal oddity. I suggest that this is a logical consequence of the marginal situation of art as such. Political criticism of art, even when sensitive and cultivated, has proved utterly sterile, and unable to instigate any sort of new creation. It was based on a fallacy: that politics was central (this is certainly to be questioned) and that being central, it had the right to insist that art be central, also; now two things cannot occupy the same place at the same time—perhaps they can if infinitely smaller than miniscule. But the political critics of modern art and literature were not thinking along the lines of quantum physics. They were thinking of the art produced in past epochs when art *was* central. In fact, the history of what we call modern art and modern literature has been the successive

imposition on the public of bizarre standpoints, unexpected attitudes, peculiar effects. This has gone on for a fairly long time but it has only recently become a general trend in the theatre. Of course, Strindberg was as peculiar as Beckett or Genet; but he was more exceptional in the early part of this century. It is now to be expected that personally peculiar people will create the art which persons of sensibility are able to enjoy. Does this mean that a theatre created by "peculiar" persons should be called the Theatre of the Absurd?

I think the important point to make here is that this development in the theatre is belated, and follows some fifty or seventy years after personal oddity had vindicated itself in other fields—painting, poetry, and the novel—as essential to the production of authentic art. In fact, I would suggest that one reason good art has for so long a time been "advanced" art is that artists relished the freakishness attendant on being "ahead" of others. One way of being peculiar is to be in advance like the crane which, Lautréamont says, flying first, forces all the others to look at its behind.

But for the theatre—and Esslin does not see this at all—the need to be a bizarre, eccentric individual involves the creator in a dialectic, as it perhaps does not involve any other type of creator—painter, poet, or novelist. Admitted that it is an advantage if you want to create to be personally strange: still, in the theatre your personal strangeness has to have an immediate effect on an audience composed of very different persons, who have to react to the play presented before they have had a chance to be converted to it by the intimidating force of cultural opinion. I do not think the dialectic I have indicated should come to an end. I think it is this dialectic which has made the plays of both Beckett and Genet more available to us than their novels were. If Beckett had not turned to the theatre, he would have remained the eccentric writer of morbid tales in monotonous, if good, prose. If Genet had not turned to the play form, he would have remained a writer of lyrical pornography. The dialectic imposed by the theatre has made it possible for these "strangers" to speak in a language pleasing both to them and to us. It is this dialectic which makes the new plays more interesting to me, at least, than the new poems or novels. Of all modern works it is the new theatre pieces which are, and have to be, I suggest, the least "absurd." (pp. 455-59)

Lionel Abel, "The Theatre and the 'Absurd'," in Partisan Review, *Vol. XXIX, No. 3, Summer, 1962, pp. 454-59.*

Richard Gilman

[*In the following essay, Gilman offers a defense of the Theater of the Absurd.*]

Time magazine recently had its say about the Theatre of the Absurd. The playwrights of the absurdist school, *Time*'s nameless writer said, after bestowing some faint left-handed praise (the key honorific was "theatricality"—a word used by critics who may not either enjoy or understand but are aware that something lively is going on), are ultimately failures because they do not do what playwrights are supposed to do. That is to say, they fail technically because they disobey the laws of drama and morally because they do not "ennoble" us.

There isn't much one can say about the first part of the indictment, except that the charge has been made against every original dramatist since the theatre began (its counterpart having perennially been used to try to put down new movements in all the other arts) and that people who insist on plays obeying the "laws of drama" are hopelessly unable to tell true drama when it appears. Actually, it isn't too much to claim that every significant play, as every significant painting, poem or piece of music, breaks "laws" as an essential aspect of its creation. But of course what it is breaking are not laws at all, but precedents.

The second accusation, that of the failure to ennoble man, is more difficult to combat, though no less pitiful a revelation of the bourgeois mind: in Berdyaev's sense, a mind encased in rules and materiality, with a skin of radical sentimentality. For what are we to say to people who crave *to be* ennobled, by art or anything else? Did the Greeks attend their tragedies in order to have nobility served up, for reassurance? Or did they attend as participants in a celebration and ritual unfolding of an action which was noble *in itself,* and precisely because it dealt courageously with ignoble matters, painful matters, terrifying and shameful ones?

What the anonymous *Time* writer and the millions he presumably speaks for really want is to be told that man is good, wise, enduring, loving, reliable, predictable, profound, clean and dignified, above all dignified. As though Oedipus was dignified, with his bloody eyesockets and his hideous memories!

> Positively abominable play . . . infecting the modern theatre with poison . . . a dirty act done publicly . . . Offensive cynicism . . . Melancholy and malodorous world . . . Mass of vulgarity, egotism, coarseness and absurdity . . . Unutterably offensive . . . Scandalous . . . Revoltingly suggestive and blasphemous . . . Morbid, unhealthy, unwholesome and disgusting . . . A piece to bring the stage into disrepute and dishonor . . . A wicked nightmare . . . As foul and filthy a concoction as has ever been allowed to disgrace the boards. . . .

The Balcony? Happy Days? The Connection? No, *Ghosts,* after its first London production in 1891. Doubtless a similar compilation could be made from the Paris newspapers of 1830, after Hugo's *Hernani,* or of 1896, when *Ubu Roi* made its devastating appearance. " 'Indecent' is too often a synonym for human," Mauriac has written; and the history of efforts to make the stage more human, to sweep away the platitudes, frozen responses and lifeless gestures of a theatre bent on repetition and the maintenance of self-satisfaction, is that of a series of outcries, predictable, instinctive, filled with that inverted shame and strange violence we see in men whose illusions have been threatened.

And always the chief illusion is that things are basically well, that the beast has been tamed and man is in the saddle, that we get what we deserve and deserve what we get, that reverses are reversible, that we understand (although better by and by), that virtue triumphs and love conquers all. But we're not sure, so tell us again.

A child being comforted against the dark. But it happens that we are right to be frightened of that darkness. Contemporary man has known almost no light at all, and if contemporary man, like man of any other era, is noble, it is to the extent to which he faces the darkness, moves into

it and keeps his eyes open. And this is true whether he is a religious man or not. What is true in any case is that if we are noble we do not need to be told about it, and if we aren't we cannot be made so by being told about it.

But of course the bourgeois theatre, the theatre of *Theatre Arts, Time* and Marya Mannes, the *serious* bourgeois theatre as distinct from all that crass commercialism, is not really interested in ennoblement, but in optimism. When Miss Mannes scolds Tennessee Williams for his sordidness, or when Howard Taubman hopes that Genet will someday write about blacks and whites who love one another, we are in the presence of those old balloons filled with the gas of middle-class propositions about life.

It simply can't be that difficult, irrational, bloody and opaque (it can't be that funny, either!). We have a vision of existence as moderately difficult, moderately irrational, moderately bloody and moderately opaque: we see, we see, oh noble crown of moderate apotheosis set on man's deserving brow, we see—*Gideon!*

One more word. If optimism is what's wanted (the modern equivalent of faith and hope), there's a chance that the playwrights of the so-called absurd can give us better grounds for entertaining it than Chayefsky or MacLeish. That is, if we can accept the notion that there is something encouraging in looking into the abyss and not flinching. If we can, then Beckett's tramps waiting in intolerable anguish are encouraging and so are the words of Bérenger at the end of Ionesco's *The Killer:* "Oh God! There's nothing we can do. What can we do . . . What can we do. . . ." The fact that there is no question mark is exactly why it is so encouraging: the statement, summing up and crystallizing the entire astonishing and valorous play, tells us what our condition is. The nobility may or may not follow. (pp. 27-9)

> *Richard Gilman, "A Note on Ennoblement," in his* Common and Uncommon Masks: Writings on Theatre 1961-1970, *Random House, 1971, pp. 27-9.*

J. S. Doubrovsky

[*In the following excerpt, Doubrovsky contrasts the absurd in Ionesco's dramas with the concept of absurdity in the works of Existentialist philosophers Albert Camus and Jean-Paul Sartre.*]

Ionesco's plays, which some commentators have tried to dismiss as mere extravaganzas born of the author's dreams and anxieties, are a response to the demands of a given personal situation in history. His feelings are those of a man of his time, plunged in the agony of his century. As he says in *The Alma Impromptu:* "The creator himself is the only valid witness to his own time, he discovers it in himself, he alone, mysteriously and freely, expresses it." We must therefore understand the very impulses, desires and nightmares which he projects on the stage as constituting his *testimony* on the present condition of man, in no way inferior to any moral or political preaching. In case we wonder what evidence he intends to give, Madeleine is most explicit in *Victims of Duty:* "There are always things to say. Since the modern world is in a state of decomposition, you can be a witness to decomposition." If Ionesco's works appear at first so strange and disconcerting and seem so fond of the weird and the monstrous, it is not because they are immured within the universe of dream or delirium, but precisely because they open out into our world.

The aim of a theater of decomposition will be the decomposition of the theater. If the central theme of literature during the last twenty years is the absurdity of a world where man is left alone to fill in the void of God, give a name and a meaning to things and freely, but unjustifiably, create his own values, literary expression, it must be admitted, up to Beckett and Ionesco, had trailed far behind philosophical intent. In the same manner as Pascal strove to ruin reason in the eyes of the libertine by virtue of a rational dialectics, Sartre and Camus, in the exploring of absurdity which they undertook in *Nausea* or "The Myth of Sisyphus," use an admirably logical language to express the illogical, the internal necessity of their sentences to convey the total contingency of the world, and resort to literature in order to negate literature. A genuine experience of the absurd, however, will invent its own language and create forms that are not those of rational discourse. "I dream of an irrationalist theater," says the Poet in *Victims of Duty*. "A non-Aristotelian theater?—Exactly." What must be carried onto the stage is the radical revolution which, in the twentieth century, substituted many-valued logics for the logic of the excluded middle and Einsteinian for Newtonian space. Therefore an irrationalist theater is not merely a theater that attacks the idols of rationalism, indefinite-progress-towards-happiness-through-science (although Ionesco makes no bones about tilting at them many times, from *Victims of Duty* to *The Unrewarded Killer*), it is, above all, a theater which is meant to be a genuine expression of the irrational. The traditional theater was coherent because the human beings it presented were coherent. In this respect, even writers of the absurd, like Sartre or Camus, remain, in their plays as well as in their style, very conservative. Sartre's plays especially are exemplars of the "well-made" play and *Les mains sales* is a masterpiece of what Ionesco would call the "police" type of drama. The reason for this is that man as the source of "Sinngebung," as a universal dispenser of meaning and the measure of all things, is intact. Although he is like a sickness of being, that sick man retains both his cohesion and his coherence. An authentic rendering of absurdity will demand a double disintegration, that of personality and that of language.

The already famous passage in which Ionesco has one of his characters declare: "We shall give up the principle of the identity and unity of character, to the benefit of motion and dynamic psychology . . ." is a highly significant text. But its interpretation remains a delicate affair and we must not be misled by the author's choice of terms. The words he uses are those of classical psychoanalysis ("dynamic psychology," "contradictory forces") and we might be tempted to construe the decomposition of personality we find in Ionesco's theater through analogy with dream manifestations. Some critics have even yielded to the temptation. But if it were only a matter of psychoanalysis, rationality would fare well. We must not forget that the play from which the quote is taken is meant to be a sharp satire on the claims of psychoanalysis, whose formulas the writer enjoys parodying. In *Victims of Duty* we see a policeman-psychoanalyst (with all the ratiocinative connotations of the word for Ionesco) ruthlessly pursuing "Mallot

with a t at the end" through the dreams and memories of another character called Choubert and asserting: "I don't believe in absurdity, everything is coherent, everything becomes understandable . . . thanks to the endeavors of human thought and science." This manifesto could have been signed by Freud himself and the whole play aims at ridiculing it. "Mallot with a t at the end" is nowhere to be discovered, for the good reason that he cannot be recovered: "You *cannot* retrieve Mallot," cries out the exasperated Policeman, "you have a hole in your memory. We shall *fill up* that hole in your memory." The final scene of the play, with its extraordinary crescendo of frantic chewing and eating on the part of Choubert, brings out one of Ionesco's central themes and illustrates the symbolism of the "hole," analysed by Sartre at the end of *Being and Nothingness*. What all that manducation is trying to achieve is to fill an absolute gap and give thought a substantial existence.

But Choubert gorges in vain and his thought really is an unfillable void. In that sense, one might say that Ionesco's is an ontological theater. He seems to be one of the first playwrights to have taken seriously the philosophical assertion that thought is not a region of being, but, on the contrary, a nothingness in the plenum of the world. (pp. 3-5)

The revelation of absurdity is usually accompanied by anguish, the anguish of man's dignity for Camus, that of man's responsibility for Sartre. But if one goes further in the experience of absurdity, man becomes suddenly so unimportant that tragedy turns into a farce, and an absurd laughter bursts forth. That kind of laughter had already been heard at the end of *The Wall* by Sartre and at the most humiliating point of the French defeat in *Roads to Liberty*. But this laughter is still inauthentic, it plays the part of a "safety valve," which André Breton assigned to grim humor; it is a type of human behavior which consists, once our projects have lost any possible transcendence into the future, in shifting the responsibility for an absurd situation onto the world and thus getting rid of it. In Sartre's eyes, as he wrote in *Nausea*, "nothing that exists can be comic." But let man cease to be a "humanist" and to view himself in a tragic light or even to take himself seriously, let him stand back at the theater and look at himself from the outside at last, let him see himself as the puppet he really is, and then, as Nicolas, in *Victims of Duty*, exclaims: "No more drama nor tragedy: the tragic becomes comic, the comic is tragic, and life becomes so gay . . . life becomes so gay. . . ." This determination to be gay in face of the utter confusion and final disappearance of all values offers no salvation, it does not conquer absurdity, it stresses it, it does not try to dodge it, it revels in it. It is an act of accusation against man much more than against the world. It is man throwing doubt on the possibility of being a man. In our awkward moments, Bergson saw what he called a mechanical something grafted upon life: in our best moments, we discover ourselves to be but a living something grafted upon mere mechanism. The "useless passion" which existentialists thought man to be now becomes eminently laughable. The laughter that suddenly rings out is Ionesco's. (p. 10)

J. S. Doubrovsky, "Ionesco and the Comic of Absurdity," in Yale French Studies, *No. 23, Summer, 1959, pp. 3-10.*

Kenneth Tynan

[A dramatist, screenwriter, and critic, Tynan was a prominent figure in the English theater during the 1950s and 1960s. In the following excerpt, he questions the artistic and ethical values of the Theater of the Absurd.]

Ever since the Fry-Eliot "poetic revival" caved in on them, the ostriches of our theatrical intelligentsia have been seeking another faith. Anything would do as long as it shook off what are known as "the fetters of realism." Now the broad definition of a realistic play is that its characters and events have traceable roots in life. Gorki and Chekhov, Arthur Miller and Tennessee Williams, Brecht and O'Casey, Osborne and Sartre have all written such plays. They express one man's view of the world in terms of people we can all recognize. Like all hard disciplines, realism can easily be corrupted. It can sink into sentimentality (N. C. Hunter), half-truth (Terence Rattigan), or mere photographic reproduction of the trivia of human behaviour. Even so, those who have mastered it have created the lasting body of twentieth-century drama: and I have been careful not to except Brecht, who employed stylised production techniques to set off essentially realistic characters.

That, for the ostriches, was what ruled him out of court. He was too real. Similarly, they preferred Beckett's *Fin de Partie,* in which the human element was minimal, to *Waiting for Godot,* which not only contained two tramps of mephitic reality but even seemed to regard them, as human beings, with love. Veiling their disapproval, the ostriches seized on Beckett's more blatant verbal caprices and called them "authentic images of a disintegrated society." But it was only when M. Ionesco arrived that they hailed a messiah. Here at last was a self-proclaimed advocate of *anti-théâtre:* explicitly anti-realist, and by implication anti-reality as well. Here was a writer ready to declare that words were meaningless and that all communication between human beings was impossible. The aged (as in *The Chairs*) are wrapped in an impenetrable cocoon of hallucinatory memories; they can speak intelligibly neither to each other nor to the world. The teacher in *The Lesson* can "get through" to his pupil only by means of sexual assault, followed by murder. Words, the magic innovation of our species, are dismissed as useless and fraudulent.

Ionesco's is a world of isolated robots conversing in cartoon-strip balloons of dialogue that are sometimes hilarious, sometimes evocative, and quite often neither, on which occasions they become profoundly tiresome. (As with shaggy-dog stories, few of M. Ionesco's plays survive a second hearing. I felt this particularly with *The Chairs.*) This world is not mine, but I recognise it to be a valid personal vision, presented with great imaginative aplomb and verbal audacity. The peril arises when it is held up for general emulation as the gateway to the theatre of the future, that bleak new world from which the humanist heresies of faith in logic and belief in man will for ever be banished.

M. Ionesco certainly offers an "escape from realism," but an escape into what? A blind alley, perhaps, adorned with *tachiste* murals. Or a self-imposed vacuum, wherein the author ominously bids us observe the absence of air. Or, best of all, a fun-fair ride on a ghost train, all skulls and hooting waxworks, from which we emerge into the far more intimidating clamour of diurnal reality. M. Ionesco's

theatre is pungent and exciting, but it remains a diversion. It is not on the main road: and we do him no good, nor the drama at large, to pretend that it is. (pp. 407-09)

> Kenneth Tynan, "The French Theatre," in his Curtains: Selections from the Drama Criticism and Related Writings, *Atheneum Publishers, 1961, pp. 407-09.*

John Killinger

[A Baptist minister, literary critic, and philosopher, Killinger has written several studies combining his dual expertise in the fields of theology and literature. In the following excerpt, he examines the philosophical foundations of the Theater of the Absurd.]

Man, who our Western religious traditions teach us was created "a little lower than the angels," is usually seen [in the Theater of the Absurd] as barely more than an animal, if indeed he possesses *that* much dignity. Ionesco in particular has blotted out the distinction between the animals and the human kingdom and has written plays in which human beings lay eggs (*Jack, or The Submission*) and become rhinoceroses (*Rhinoceros*). Beckett's characters are usually more cerebral, sometimes striking one as the dramatic extensions of Valéry's Monsieur Teste, but they appear to be merely highly developed creatures who have sexual memories and befoul themselves in their own ordure. Harold Pinter's authentically British characters, for all their realism, seem to be only subhuman, with a kind of speech that is amazingly opaque and noncommunicative. Language is in fact regarded as one of the central problems in most of the plays of the absurd: it is seen to be much less than the precise tool we had thought it to be. Ionesco's first play, *The Bald Soprano,* was constructed entirely out of the imbecilic non sequiturs people use in ordinary speech. He said he realized after he had completed it that he had written "the tragedy of language." N. F. Simpson's *A Resounding Tinkle* bears obvious resemblance to previous English nonsense literature like *Alice in Wonderland* and employs an urbane, sophisticated kind of jabberwocky throughout its ridiculous plot. One critic, studying particularly the works of Beckett, Ionesco, Adamov, and Vauthier, calls their drama "the theater of Babel."

If Babel is a reminder of the biblical symbol of human pride and the loss of God, there is no absence of religious reference in this theater. One of the most disturbing things about it is the inversion of the idea of *presence* in it, as of a vacuum from which God, Christ, and spirituality have withdrawn, leaving only an uncanny sense of isolation and alienation among men. Beckett's subtle and incessant use of religious allusions only underscores the taut and desperate situation of his characters: there is no longer any great overarching myth to impart life and meaning to their world; they live in the rubble and the wasteland of all past belief, with nothing capable of sustaining them in their own time. Arrabal, whose characters likewise live in this burned-over world of no meaning, is more youthful and Promethean; in the *Architect and the Emperor of Assyria* he represents the Emperor, the one who has been corrupted by society and civilization, as heaping blasphemous indignities on the very name of God. *"Merde pour Dieu"* ["As for God—shit"], he sings in an operatic voice.

"Merde à sa divine image. Merde à son omniprésence" ["Shit on his divine image. Shit on his omnipresence"].

With the displacement of God and the traditional kind of religious hope has come a consequent displacement of the meaning of time and ordinary reality; these are obviously inventions of the mind, contrivances for handling the world more easily, now rendered silly and meaningless. Time no longer moves in a rectilinear path—it spins and swerves and recrosses itself until the mind is a hopeless tangle attempting to follow it. This is one reason action is finally impossible in such a theater: everything has happened before. Didi and Gogo, the hapless bums of *Waiting for Godot,* must go on waiting; they are condemned to repeating what they have said before, what they have seen before, what they have done before. Reality, too, is curved. Who can say where it crosses and recrosses itself, producing only illusion? The theme that has haunted modern dramatists since Ibsen and Strindberg and Pirandello and O'Neill and Tennessee Williams, of what the real is and how one distinguishes it from the illusory, becomes constant in all absurd theater. One of its most objective statements is in Jean Genet's *The Balcony,* which opens with scenes of a bishop, a judge, and a general, who then turn out to be impostors in a brothel (which the French call *la maison d'illusion*), masquerading as the persons they would like to be; and from there on out the play is one

Michael O'Sullivan as the Emperor in Arrabal's The Architect and the Emperor of Assyria.

trick of the mind after another. As Sartre has said, Genet shows us the whirligig, and makes "the *nothing* shimmer at the surface of the all." All of the absurdists have this in common, that they make us see what was in the precipice to whose edge the existentialists brought us; and there is no holding back, once one has seen it. It has a compelling power to enter our thinking and disturb us—compelling because it is what we have all known in our subconscious and in our dreams.

It is for this reason that Martin Esslin has tried to find in the poetic image based on dreams the lowest common denominator among the plays of the absurd. There is an unreal quality about the world of such plays—unreal because it is irrational, nonobjective, and irreducible. Yet no one, since Freud, would dare to call dreams unreal. It is a matter of which reality is real. And the Theater of the Absurd puts us in doubt of the one that is ordinarily chosen, the reality of the waking, workaday world where most of us earn our daily bread and take aspirin for headaches that seem to us to be slightly less than metaphysical. It questions our willingness to live within such a carefully proscribed and narrow area of our real potential for consciousness, shutting out the visions that do not conform to what is in *Webster's Dictionary* or the catalogue from Sears or Harrods.

It is a bit presumptuous, of course, to speak of the Theater of the Absurd as if it were a precisely defined corpus in the history of the stage, with a clearly articulated credo and a fastidiously managed entry of the names of particular authors. Esslin made the image stick with the title of his extremely lucid and comprehensive study, *The Theatre of the Absurd,* despite the negative criticism the volume has received; possibly there was a precedent for such a name in the preface to Cocteau's *The Wedding on the Eiffel Tower,* where Cocteau called the action in his play "absurd" because, as he said, "instead of attempting to keep this side of the absurdity of life, to lessen it, to organize and arrange it as we organize and arrange the story of an incident in which we played an unfavorable part, I accentuate it, I emphasize it, I try to paint *more truly than the truth."* (pp. 10-14)

It was once easy to dismiss anything to which one could affix the label absurd; such was the fate of Jarry's *Ubu* when it was first staged in 1896 and was received, as Henri Ghéon recalled, "with a chorus of whistles, hisses, protests, and jeers." But this is no longer true. The ideas of Freud and the psychologists have thoroughly legitimized the notion that the irrational dimension of human existence is fully as important as the rational one. Camus, following Kierkegaard and Heidegger and Sartre in a philosophy of the irrational, defined the absurd as a mode of human perception, as a posture for living. "A world that can be explained even with bad reasons," he wrote, "is a familiar world. But, on the other hand, in a universe suddenly divested of illusions and lights, man feels an alien, a stranger. His exile is without remedy since he is deprived of the memory of a lost home or the hope of a promised land. This divorce between man and his life, the actor and his setting, is properly the feeling of absurdity."

It is this feeling, born of the divorce between man and his life and expressed in the symbol of the divorce between the actor and his setting, with which the plays that are generally classified in the Theater of the Absurd have tried to deal. They have brought within the theater of our minds, at least on some occasions, an awareness of that grotesque reality which the biblical writers thought of as the chaotic and still demonic elemental power of the world, the *Ur*-chaos that threatens our very being, and which most of us have trained ourselves, by long effort, to ignore and disbelieve.

If there is any question, then, of the worth and validity of this theater vis-à-vis the theater of Broadway or the boulevard, Edward Albee may well have raised it in its proper form when he asked, in the title of his *New York Times Magazine* article, "Which theater is the absurd one?" [see excerpt below]. Beside the plays of Beckett and Ionesco and Arrabal, any other kind of theater is a mere theater of manners; and that, in an age when men are thirsting and dying for relationship and meaning, is the most absurd occupation of all. (pp. 15-16)

If there is anything close to a philosophy of approach or statement of purpose common to the plays [of the Theater of the Absurd], it is the notion of Artaud that the playwright must bring "metaphysical ideas" directly onto the stage and create "temptations" and "indraughts of air" around these ideas. Artaud knew that we overdomesticate life—that we reduce it to such small dimensions and neat configurations that we tend to forget its essential wildness, its mystery and passion, its whirlwinds of body and spirit. He wanted to plunge theatergoers into these whirlwinds, to shake them loose from their limited view of things, to turn their ordinary world upside down so that all the furniture cascades around them. He spoke of presenting "ideas which touch on Creation, Becoming, and Chaos" and doing it in such a manner as to create "a kind of passionate equation between Man, Society, Nature, and Objects."

Such an intention is, of course, not basically and totally different from that of more traditional dramatists. As Christopher Fry once said in an essay on playwriting, "it is the business of the poet or dramaturgist in any age to surprise the audience by the fresh appearance of what had always been familiar to it, thus restoring the sensations which habit and familiarity had robbed it of."

But the Theater of the Absurd, following surrealism's proclivity to extreme and violent images, has greatly exaggerated this effect and has even succeeded in *disorienting* the audience from the familiar, tumbling it through a nongravitational field where none of the old values and landmarks persist. Where Fry was intent upon reinvesting the familiar with meaning by treating it sensitively, poetically, Ionesco and Arrabal have destroyed it by turning it into the unfamiliar or the grotesque, by posing it as a physical threat to human existence. Words become objects, grapeshot assailing the hearers; instead of evoking images they constitute realities in themselves, hard as nonmeaning can be. Action often seems spontaneous, *sui generis,* so that the old logic of cause and effect is abandoned. Theater of the Absurd, in other words, is *bare* drama, the drama behind drama, where the play is forgotten because the audience is fighting for survival in a real contest. It was this submergence of the audience into the struggle that led Artaud to speak of a Theater of Cruelty. He did not intend by the phrase to invoke a reinvestiture of Spanish tragedy or Senecan bloodbaths. He referred rather to the therapeutic cruelty of making people face their existential situation,

of making them realize how entirely tenuous is the world they have fabricated when it is seen vis-à-vis the untamed world out of which it was siphoned.

To accomplish their subdrama or *proto*drama, then, dramatists of the absurd have virtually upended the world view of Western tradition deriving from Hellenistic and Hebraic-Christian sources. The Creation, as we had conceived of it, has been reversed, and chaos threatens to retake the scene. Man, bereft of God and the traditional anthropology, has lost all certainty as to who he is, or, what is worse, as to whether he is finally distinct from the animal kingdom at all. His grand system of ethics and morality has collapsed into rubble; it had depended almost solely on the existence of God and the kind of anthropology and sociology belief in the deity had warranted. Communication has likewise disintegrated or else become impossibly burdensome, unable to withstand the scrutiny no longer diverted by the great unifying myths of religion and the state. Even more frightening, the disintegration has underlined the fact that communion itself is impossible, that individuals reach out to one another but cannot touch, cannot meet, cannot become one. The terror of Bartleby, Melville's silent scrivener, and of Gregor Samsa, Kafka's man who turned into a crustaceous insect, has settled on us all and muffles life in noiseless desperation.

This is not the world with which we are familiar. It bears only enough resemblance to that world to assure us that it is indeed the world we live in, that it is not just conjured out of the imagination, that it is something to be frightened about because in its reality it threatens to crush and destroy the world into which we have escaped. What we are confronted by, in effect, is the examination of Job in modern form—not the one MacLeish faced us with in *J. B.,* where the protagonist is separated from his wealth and children, any more than the one Job himself was faced with in the mere loss of his goods and family—but the one Job faced when this loss was combined with the vision of monsters, behemoths, wonders of the deep—all the *not-*Jobs—and was, in the best and primary sense of the word, humiliated. It was as though Creation yawned before him and he saw into the depths of void and chaos again. The effect upon us, as upon Job, is, to use Artaud's word, metaphysical, or essentially religious. We are effectually reminded of our finitude, our impotence, our isolation from greater segments of being, our cosmological and ontological blindness.

It is easy enough to label such theater nihilistic—it does, in fact, pose our encounter with *le néant,* with the nothingness the existentialists so frequently described. On the surface it appears to be often cynical and negative and to prompt remarks like Alfonso Sastre's that *Waiting for Godot* is "a death certificate for hope." The twin theme of illusion and reality, so central to the undertaking of the absurdists, is always a dangerous one to deal with, for it suggests the predicament to which Chuang Tzu alluded in his story . . . about the man who dreamed he was a butterfly and, when he awoke, didn't know whether he was a man dreaming he was a butterfly or a butterfly dreaming he was a man. Which, in the end, is illusion and which is reality? There seems to be something endemically nihilistic about the suggestion that the life we normally live is illusory and the other life, the one we merely guess at, real. It raises a threat against the established order and signalizes anarchy and destruction.

The absurdists certainly do not hesitate to raise such a threat. Genet practically makes it the entire basis of his theater, involving the audience in such deceptions that it soon believes in the unreal and disbelieves in the real or confuses the two so completely that it doesn't know what to believe. Ionesco and Arrabal do the same, only at a more fantastical level. When we get to the end of *The Killer,* therefore, we are ready to accept with Bérenger the total purposelessness and meaninglessness of life; this has become utterly credible, for we have gradually accepted the absurd world in which Bérenger exists and must follow him unswervingly to his conclusions.

It is also possible, however, if one takes a very long stride of the imagination, to believe that most of the dramatists of the absurd write as they do out of an underlying belief in the essential goodness of creation and in the innate power of their audiences eventually to respond in positive fashion to the terror of their visions. Artaud, for whom life and the theater struggled under a single skin, so that the agonies of the artist's commitment finally took their toll upon his body, said once, "If I commit suicide, it will not be to destroy myself but to put myself back together again."

It is the same with the plays and playwrights we are discussing. Theater of the Absurd is theatrical and philosophical suicide. Like some supermoth with an intellect to perceive what it is doing, it defies the flame and the holocaust. But with the intention of *living,* not of destroying itself! With the intention of putting theater and philosophy back together again! Its ultimate goal, perhaps never articulated because one does not speak of such things before they have been accomplished, any more than a writer who is worth his salt discusses his most important work before it is out and he can look at it to see what he has done, is the restoration of plausibility to theater and of wholeness to the philosophical enterprise.

There is something instinctual in human nature that will not let us leap casually to destruction; if we leap casually, it is because we know, perhaps only subconsciously, that there is a net waiting to catch us, that we cannot really reach the bottom. I believe there is this kind of faith in the absurdists, so that they take what appear to be daring risks at the same time that they are confident of reprisal. They knock the world to pieces because they know instinctively that it will not stay that way, that it is tough and resilient, that it is perhaps after all held together by something men could believe in, half-credulously, something like what the late Paul Tillich called "the God beyond God." Picasso once said that he never hesitated to paint out colors on his canvas because, if they were good, they would come back. The absurdists work upon the same premise. They can do whatever they like in the theater to startle, jolt, or dislocate an audience, for, even if they make a mistake and go too far, the world will survive.

Ionesco says that the world is full of illusion but that it is still the best one we have. He is right, of course, and in this he does not differ at all from a long line of idealists beginning with Socrates and Plato; and, like other idealists, he says that what matters in life is presence and fullness.

It is to this presence and fullness that the Theater of the Absurd bids us to return. If we are pushed, tormented, bombarded, battered, and half destroyed by its unpredictable antics, its satirization of all we hold dear, its orgy of antiphilosophy and antihumanism, its uproar of physical release, its parody of language, its destruction of theater in the attempt to be theater, then it may be accomplishing its purposes and returning us to a chastened view of the world, in which our senses are scrubbed clean for perceiving again and our minds cut loose from the prisons of pattern and prejudice and our souls readied to front reality in all their glorious nakedness and *live* again.

Although the Theater of the Absurd may often appear destructive and nihilistic, then, its end is the opposite. The antitheism, the antiworld, the antiplay, all return us at last to theism and the world and even the play, subdued and refreshed for appreciating their real value. If we have been faced, like Job, with chaos, it may be that our latter end will be better than our beginning. (pp. 160-66)

> *John Killinger, "Introduction" and "Indraughts and Temptations," in his* World in Collapse: The Vision of an Absurd Drama, *Dell Publishing Co., Inc., 1971, pp. 1-16, 159-71.*

Arnold P. Hinchliffe

[*Hinchliffe is an English critic and educator whose writings focus primarily on English dramatists. In the following excerpt, he articulates the view of those who consider the Theater of the Absurd artistically and ideologically limited and ultimately based on false assumptions about human existence.*]

Absurdity has its own built-in obsolescence. The thorough-going nature of its revolt (and it is much more thorough-going than previous revolutionary movements, such as those of Ibsen and Strindberg) ensures that it must be either a *terminus ad quem* ["finishing point"] or a *terminus ab quo* ["starting point"]. Robert Corrigan has pointed out that, if a logically motivated hero and well-knit plot give meaning—spurious, illusory, and distorted—to the act which *exists*—alone and absurd—and rob it of its elemental importance which is simply absurdity, such absurdity is ill-suited to the extensiveness of literature, be it novel or drama. Making *situation* into the source of Absurd drama is exciting because dramatic situation is the essence of theatre, but it is also seriously limiting, and it is no accident that most Absurd dramas tend to be written in one act. . . .

Nor can it be simply a matter of technique, since the technique is suited to the subject and . . . each has an air of finality about it. Descriptions of absurdity must lead, if mere repetition is to be avoided, to the questions "how" and "why" and even "whence." Adamov abandons it altogether, Genet's plays lengthen as commitment grows, Ionesco moves to a more human kind of drama; only Beckett (as we might expect) moves logically towards a silence that may ultimately be just that. Moreover, where theatre is concerned, some sort of plot is probably necessary. Obscurity in a poem is one thing (we can, after all, keep the poem and re-read it), but a single visit to the theatre must leave us with something to hold on to. In short, the theatre of Nothing, if it is to develop at all, will have to move to

Something—whether the conventions and subjects are artistic, political, social, or religious. (p. 81)

The limitations of Absurdity are, therefore, to a great extent inevitable. Once each artist has defined the condition, he must develop a response to the awareness, and once sufficient artists have done this the idea has passed into history. The usual progress is towards social criticism for, as Sartre recognized, his existential man is *in a situation*—and we usually call it society. And if the philosophical impetus weakens with time, it may also be true that it is characteristically French and, like good wine, does not travel well. If these are the practical limitations to Absurd art, can one produce objections to Absurdity as such? . . . Mr. Tynan's perfectly legitimate preference . . . [is] shared by Adamov and Sartre among others: it is more appropriate to concentrate on removing problems capable of solution to clear the decks for the great problems which are, possibly, insoluble. The distinction appears more clear in theory than it often is. We have so many labels and patterns that it is difficult to feel they are useful. Is Absurdity useful? We do not ask at this stage if it is true, merely useful. (p. 88)

While Einstein, Planck, and Bohr destroyed the comfortable notions of causation, drama ignored events. It took the Russian revolution to drive drama into realism, and Hiroshima—the abdication of reason—to bring Absurd Theatre to the fore and show that man and his fate were merely a process of ever-changing and purposeless patterns. Technically such a theatre has made little or no impact in the use of space in the theatre, and it has failed to absorb the work of painters and sculptors as well as the discoveries of science. Thus, when man looks towards his future in the stars, the Absurd Theatre gives its audiences tales in the tradition of the Grand Guignol. . . . (pp. 88-9)

Because such a theatre has no obvious message with which to agree (or disagree), nor characters to love (or hate) and, as often as not tries to be as shocking as Ubu's first word, it invites in some a more forceful response than that of Tynan or Tutaev which, sometimes, looks suspiciously like bad temper. Joseph McMahon, for example, in his study of Genet, *The Imagination of Jean Genet* seems oddly unsympathetic to his subject, and complains of the "assorted annoyances of the theatre of the absurd," the poverty of ideas and endless repetition hardly redeemed by the occasional dramatic invention which becomes self-destructive and, in its fascination with indecision, overlooks the large amount of decision-making necessary in the process of keeping body and soul together. . . . But no philosophy has ever insisted more than existentialism on the necessity for making decisions—existence is, after all, nothing else. It is possible that much of this argument springs from an unstated Christian point of view, which must feel objections to a body of ideas which assumes the death of God as one of its axioms. This kind of objection is not against the limiting nature of the art form or its conceptual basis but against Absurdity itself. . . . (p. 89)

We can summarize three possible objections to Absurdity:

> 1. It is simply not true. By this we mean not that the works of art fail to persuade us, but that we have a strong conviction that the world is not absurd. There is no reply to this; it is as much an act of faith as its opposite, and under these circumstances we are likely to treat Absurd plays like any other, preferring those from which virtues as we understand them can be drawn. Thus we shall be moved by compassion in *Waiting for Godot,* just as we admire Mother Courage—although in either case their creator might strongly disapprove.

> 2. Absurdity cannot at one and the same time be a tradition and a particular contemporary phenomenon. We feel uneasy that Esslin (and others) find Absurdity everywhere and yet claim for it a special contemporary importance. But this is an understandable, if confusing, critical procedure. Literature develops: something absolutely new does not happen, but parts of that development are more striking than others, and a latent sense of meaninglessness was given at a particular time a frightening relevance.

> 3. In spite of an honest conviction of Absurdity, plays and novels are written about it, and this in itself seems Bad Faith.

The importance of these objections must be left open. What has to be admitted (which is what Esslin in effect claims) is that a considerable body of literature exists which derives its inspiration from an existential view of life. Its aims are partly social, occasionally political, sometimes metaphysical, but at best always literary. If they work—in the theatre or the study—a beginning has been made, and such pragmatism will be helped by a sympathetic, but not necessarily convinced, understanding of what has been meant by Absurdity. (pp. 91-2)

> *Arnold P. Hinchliffe, "Limitations" and "Objections," in his* The Absurd, *Methuen & Co. Ltd., 1969, pp. 78-87, 88-92.*

J. Chiari

[In the following excerpt from a discussion of Ionesco's plays, Chiari finds the philosophical premise of absurdity to be in conflict with the nature of theater as a form of communication.]

Ionesco's theatre is the mirror of an incoherent meaningless world, which, indulging in the mimetic fallacy, is itself often incoherent and utterly boring. The attempt to convey boredom, incoherence and incommunicability, mimetically or in their conceptualised forms, rests upon a self-contradictory foundation. It is obvious that if life were as utterly boring and incoherent as Ionesco and those who label it absurd believe it to be, it could neither be transmuted into art, nor would it be worth while trying to do so. Anyone who truly believes in life's absurdity can only leave every man to his own impenetrable absurd world without attempting the impossible and at the same time contradicting his own beliefs. The logic of such beliefs would be silence and not loquacity and claims to public attention. It is therefore obvious that Ionesco's belief in the absurdity and incoherence of life are both circumscribed to certain sections of life and are in many cases the result of social conventions and beliefs, which if modified would shed their detrimental effects. It is also obvious that Ionesco himself does not look upon himself and his work as fragments of the absurd world to which he is supposed to belong. He places himself outside this absurd world in order to laugh at it, and he hopes to find enough non-absurd readers or listeners to laugh with him at the absurdities which he describes, and to benefit from the cathartic effect of these experiences. All this means that the so-called priests of the absurd, whoever they are, should cast off any pretences at being the discoverers of a new, self-contradictory cult and recognise the fact that their notion of human absurdity and incoherence is as much a dramatic device as Molière's laughter at the Marquis, the Précieuses, the Hypocrites or the obsessed, like Harpagon or Oronte.

The incommunicability which is so much talked about is not a revelation of the twentieth century which has merely tried to systematise it. Men obsessed by their preoccupations, like Harpagon or others, followed their own trends of thoughts impervious to what happened around them. The important thing is that they were not as self-conscious, as is the case now, about their isolation. Besides that, the vital point is that the notion of incommunicability rests upon words and gestures which prepare the communicability or incommunicability of silence. People can only show that they do not understand one another by their words and their behaviour; without that, they do not know whether they connect or live and move in isolation. Therefore words still remain the most important means through which men can expound the incoherence, incommunicability or absurdity of their lives. One can only convey the lack of meaning through some kind of meaning which may convey the meaninglessness of the characters involved. Ionesco and his followers disclaim any use of traditional psychology, plot, and character sequence. Such notions postulate indeed a logic and coherence which they profess not to find in human life. So non-sense, non sequitur in behaviour and conversation are the dramatic means by which, according to them, one can show men's incoherence and isolation. There is no possible justification for logical behaviour, because obviously there are no values to which human behaviour can finally be referred to. Bérenger in *Tueur sans Gages* sets about to convince the killer of the uselessness of murder and ends in being compelled to admit that there is no reason not to kill, and that in fact, there is no reason for anything. In a world without categorical imperatives, humanistic or transcendental beliefs, all absurdities are given the same lack of importance, and life becomes a mixture of surrealistic fantasies and reality. . . . (pp. 64-6)

> *J. Chiari, "Drama in France," in his* Landmarks of Contemporary Drama, *Herbert Jenkins, 1965, pp. 49-80.*

George E. Wellwarth

[*An Austrian-born American critic, translator, and educator, Wellwarth has written extensively on modern European theater. In the following excerpt, he comments on the relationship between absurdist drama and its sociological context.*]

To put it in the simplest terms possible, absurdism says that there is nothing beyond what we see—the shadow is unchangeably and eternally the limit of our vision—and what we see is not good. Man is and remains a pitiful and helpless incongruity within the setting of an impersonal and incomprehensible Nature. His life is a futile struggle against the cruelty of a setting that he has not chosen and cannot change—a cruelty that is at once inhuman and superhuman, omnipresent in the external and immanent in the individual's inner world, an almost tangible entity in itself and at the same time an emanation of a greater, instinctively malicious entity. Nothing has significance in his life except the inevitable, meaningless and reasonless death at the end, which represents the re-merging of the human with the greater impersonal controlling power. During their short and uncertain lives men move aimlessly in mutually exclusive spheres running on courses unfathomable to their occupants.

Such a philosophical attitude, valid though it may be, is a luxury. Paradoxically, despair is a function of freedom. One despairs when one has nothing more pressing to do. The cosmic despair that is at the root of absurdism may well be the only philosophical attitude that makes any sense since it is the first philosophical system that has attempted to explain the human condition without recourse to the vaporings of metaphysics and mysticism, but it is nevertheless an attitude only the inhabitants of a free society are psychologically able to adopt. Absurdism is the modern version of tragedy, which is no longer the contemplation of unconsciously self-willed misfortune, but the defeat of man at the hands of forces greater than himself, inimical to him and beyond his comprehension. Tragedy is possible as an art form only in a society that is basically free and affluent. In a society comparatively bare of other worries, men can afford time to worry about the cosmos. Indulgence in vicarious tragic feeling is an emotional luxury only the inhabitants of a free society can wallow in. In a totalitarian society such as Spain's this indulgence is a hollow joke, a masochistic rubbing of salt into an open wound, rather than the satisfying release of emotional tension or the arousal of righteous indignation it ideally is. Furthermore, in a totalitarian society pessimism is discouraged since the whole point of such a society is redemption through faith in the state. Totalitarianism is religion reduced from the cosmic to the temporal level—which is why a sense of the tragic is also incompatible with religious faith. The so-called tragedies that have been written within a context of religious belief all boil down to a fall resulting from disobedience. The distinction between the *Oresteia, Samson Agonistes* and socialist realism is stylistic, not philosophical—degree, not kind. In a totalitarian society we find surface literature, which is propagandistic when it is serious, quiescent and anesthetic when it is not; and underground literature, which is critical and essentially hopeful. The paradox of despair being a function of a free society is matched by the paradox of hope as a function of a repressed society. (pp. 380-81)

> *George E. Wellwarth, "Manuel de Pedrolo and Spanish Absurdism," in* Books Abroad, *Vol. 46, No. 3, Summer, 1972, pp. 380-87.*

R. B. Parker

[*In the following excerpt, Parker examines seminal works of the Theater of the Absurd in light of Albert Camus's definition of the absurd in his essay "The Myth of Sisyphus."*]

"What distinguishes modern sensibility from classical sensibility is that the latter thrives on moral problems and the former on metaphysical problems." The generalization is not my own. It comes from "The Myth of Sisyphus," Albert Camus' brilliant essay which first popularized the term "absurd"—a stone since tied around the neck of one of the most important movements in modern theatre.

The particular metaphysical problem which Camus thinks most urgent is man's sense of the split between existence and the human consciousness. This focuses painfully in the individual's awareness of his own limitation and mortality. The anxiety it engenders, says Camus, can not be called precisely a metaphysic, nor even a belief. It is rather an "intellectual malady." Nonetheless, it is a sickness we all have, and ultimately we must come to terms with it. Most of us shirk this problem, burying ourselves in practical minutiae, or elaborating patterns of purely academic consistency, or committing what Camus calls "philosophical suicide" by a jump from logic into transcendental faiths. The honest thinker, however, will not shirk it. He will not try to avoid the anxiety but, on the contrary, will make it the rooftree of his thought, striving constantly to keep aware of the contradiction between his self and his surroundings, yet remaining constantly in rebellion against that contradiction.

The forms such rebellion can take are twofold, according to Camus. There is first the negative rebellion of suicide. Camus rejects this as being a premature surrender to time. Positive rebellion, on the contrary, he argues, will try to reduce time to a procession of human "presents," living always in the self-conscious moment. Deprived of a future, each act then becomes its own justification and all acts are recognized as wholly contingent.

A person holding this attitude will therefore strive for *quantity,* not *quality* of experience. In love, the unsentimental sincerity of Don Juan will be the ideal; in action, the mixed involvement and aloofness of the play actor or the condottiere; and in art, the ideal will be a creation which recognizes that it is only *mimesis,* an ephemeral alternative to reality with no claim at all to Universal Truth. The function of such art will not be to console, still less to offer any form of escape, but instead to sharpen its audience's awareness of anxiety and self-reliance.

As an example, Camus gives his own interpretation of the myth of Sisyphus—the man who was condemned to roll a stone up hill forever because he informed on one of Jupiter's amours. The stone, says Camus, represents man's fate, the grief produced by his hunger for happiness which will never be fulfilled. But by recognizing this torment as something which is his alone, man can turn it to advantage. From this point of view, even eternal senseless rock-pushing can be seen as a confirmation of his unique existence. So, concludes Camus, "One must imagine Sisyphus happy."

As a philosophy this seems dubious—rather like an argument that one should beat one's head against a wall in order to confirm that it's there: a kind of intellectual masochism. But it is not our present purpose to attack or defend the *theory,* merely to determine its viability as a key to the avant garde theatre. Let us use Camus' analysis to examine some aspects of the work of Beckett, Ionesco, and Genet, with occasional references to Pinter and Albee thrown in, keeping to roughly the same format as "The Myth of Sisyphus." That is: beginning with a section on what Sartre has called "nausea," anxiety before the manifest "otherness" of existence; then a section examining the problem of consciousness itself, especially as it applies to art; and, finally, a consideration of the positives, if any, with which the absurdists conclude.

Of the three main causes, or symptoms, of existential nausea the simplest is what Camus calls "the primitive hostility of the world," when we realize "to what a degree a stone is foreign and irreducible to us, with what intensity nature or a landscape can negate us." This sense of hostile environment is reflected in the two favourite locales of absurdist theatre.

A few plays are specifically set in forbidding, empty landscapes which emphasize human isolation. The tramps in Beckett's *Waiting for Godot,* for instance, are condemned to a plain with a single tree, while Winnie, the heroine of his *Happy Days,* is buried to the waist in what appears to be a desert. More frequent, however, is a second locale, where claustrophobic encirclement is represented by a closed room, often accompanied by a suggestion of darkness or blindness. This has as its ancestor the den to which Dostoyevsky's hero withdrew in *Notes from Underground,* and like that prototype, its implications are ambiguous. It is partly a prison, environment's constraint on consciousness, but it is also partly a retreat, a deliberate withdrawal from environment into subjectivity. At its most extreme, the room is obviously a symbol of the solipsist mind itself—as in the circular room with two high windows in which Beckett's *Endgame* is set, where Hamm, the blind, withdrawn consciousness, tyrannizes over Clov, his flagging faculties, and memory represented by his parents, Nag and Nell, shut up in ashcans of the unconscious. Pinter's first play, *The Room,* showed the intrusion into such a solipsism of external threat, specifically the threat of death; and this other mood—the feeling of encroachment—can be further illustrated by Ionesco's *The New Tenant,* which is a parable of materialism: beginning with an empty room, the new tenant brings in from outside a grotesque amount of furniture and belongings till, alone and completely obscured in the centre, he reaches up and switches off the light.

The mad proliferation of furniture in this play also illustrates the absurdist nausea before individual *things.* There are similar proliferations in other plays by Ionesco, where the stage is gradually covered with chairs, eggs, coffee cups, mushrooms, and even a giant corpse which grows perceptibly onstage and gradually pushes its murderers from their flat. The human body, in fact, can be seen as just one more object nauseatingly distinct from mind yet threatening its existence with mortality. Beckett conveys this strikingly by having his characters already half buried or stuck in ashcans and funeral urns.

Most of the objects just mentioned as swamping Ionesco's plays are artifacts, man made, and this too is significant. Man has now largely mastered nature, but, strangely, the human environment is no less alien to consciousness than the natural. In fact, it often seems more alien! The second main cause of nausea suggested by Camus is, in fact, a sense of futility in the routines of civilized life, the pointlessness of habit in ourselves and other people. This mechanical triviality is the prime target for satire in the theatre of the absurd. Beckett and Pinter satirize it in the empty ceremoniousness of their derelicts and illiterates, Genet by his fake rituals of authority, and Ionesco and

Albee by monstrous parodies of bourgeois conformity. There are, in fact, two sorts of absurdity to be distinguished in the theatre of the absurd: on the one hand, the absurdity of people whom Ionesco calls the "petit bourgeoisie," who hide from the terrors of isolation and choice behind complacent routines; and, on the other hand, the *conscious* absurdity of men who have realized and accepted their inescapable autonomy. By combining the two kinds, the theatre of the absurd produces a sort of black farce—basically depressing yet often wildly funny.

Both kinds of absurdity are concentrated in the absurdist attack on habits of language. On one level this merely satirizes clichés of thought and expression, but on another it questions whether concepts are meaningful at all. Ionesco's *The Bald Soprano,* for instance, which is made up of banalities from a *Teach Yourself English* primer, is a pure—if savage—satire on bourgeois conformity, but depths of terror open up in *Waiting for Godot* when rationalism is shown *in extremis* in the speech of a dying philosopher forced to go on thinking. There is only space to quote a bit of it:

> LUCKY. Given the existence as uttered forth in the public works of Puncher and Wattmann of a personal God quaquaquaqua with a white beard quaquaquaqua outside time without extension who from the heights of divine apathia divine athambia divine aphasia loves us dearly with some exceptions for reasons unknown but time will tell and suffers like the divine Miranda with those who for reasons unknown but time will tell are plunged in torment plunged in fire whose fire flames if that continues and who can doubt it will fire the firmament that is to say blast hell to heaven so blue still and calm so calm with a calm which even though intermittent is better than nothing but not so fast and considering what is more that as a result of the labours left unfinished crowned by the Acacacacademy of Anthropopopometry of Essy-in-Possy of Testew and Cunard it is established beyond all doubt all other doubt than that which clings to the labours of men that as a result of the labours unfinished of Testew and Cunard it is established as hereinafter but not so fast for reasons unknown that as a result of the public works of Puncher and Wattmann it is established beyond all doubt . . . etc.

This hideous collapse of logic and philosophy is the verbal equivalent of the spastic dance of "The Net" which the philosopher also has to perform in that play, and reminds us that for many of the absurdists language is literally what Wittgenstein called it in part—a linguistic "game" obedient to its own internal rules, without necessary reference to meaning or external reality. So the tramps in *Waiting for Godot* use language merely to kill time, debasing it to a vaudeville turn on a par with their comic exchange of bowler hats.

Ionesco, in particular, likes to play tricks with language; Tynan called him a "logical negativist." He parodies both the logical positivist theory that language is an arbitrary construction and the gestalt theory that words depend wholly on context for their meaning. In *The Lesson,* for example, a maniacal professor claims that all languages are identical and must have the same word for the same concept but that the meaning will vary with context—so a Frenchman saying "La Patrie" will mean France but an Italian saying it will mean Italy. After some comparable

fun with mathematics, he ends the lesson by murdering his pupil with rapid repetitions of the *word* "couteau" ["knife"]. Similarly, in *Jack or the Submission* the hero and heroine make love by exchanging an orgy of words containing the syllable "chat" but otherwise unrelated. Words are always degenerating into mere sound for Ionesco ("The Pope's eloped! The Pope's no soap! Soap is dope!"), and when his unlucky translator asked him the meaning of certain passages in one of his plays, he is reported to have replied: "None at all. That *is* the point! Put anything you like." For the absurdists, then, words too are often merely part of meaningless environment.

This raises one of the central issues of the theatre of the absurd—the problem of communication. Camus does not discuss this, but it is an inevitable dilemma for a philosophy of isolated consciousness. Beckett and Ionesco have both said that they do not believe communication is really possible. Their characters consequently live in private fantasies and never seem to listen properly or remember what other people have said. In Pinter, too, conversation degenerates to parallel monologues, and this is elaborated by Ionesco into a crazy, crisscrossed counterpoint where several conversations are going on simultaneously with everyone answering remarks addressed to other people in other groups. In Beckett, on the other hand, noncommunication takes the form of a pull back to the stream-of-selfconsciousness in which his novels are written: *Krapp's Last Tape* and *Happy Days* are virtually solo plays, monodramas.

Like the claustrophobic room settings, this lack of communication is ambivalent: it is partly willful—Pinter says his characters use clichés in order *not* to communicate; on the other hand, it can also be a threat, since the absurdists emphasize that the sense of one's own identity depends on relationships: we only see ourselves reflected from others. And if words fail to do this, the only recourse becomes violence: for the absurdists, as for De Sade, cruelty is the ultimate way of making contact. In *Waiting for Godot,* for instance, there are two symbiotic relationships, relationships of interdependency: Vladimir and Estragon relate conventionally by kindliness and attempts to talk and share, but Pozzo and Lucky are just as mutually bound by physical and mental pain. The hero of Beckett's novel *How It Is,* dying in mud, can only make contact by jabbing a can-opener into his companion's rear. And a more mental cruelty can be seen in the constant quarrelings of Ionesco's married couples or the desperate, sadistic games of *Who's Afraid of Virginia Woolf?* Perhaps the ultimate rationale lies in Ionesco's assertion in *The Alma Impromptu* that at the bottom of every individual consciousness lie fear and pain, and only on this level can there be a full communion.

This leads us to the last group of reasons which Camus suggests as causing nausea. The fear at the bottom of every consciousness is the fear of one's own mortality, one's absurd enslavement to time. Ionesco claims to have been haunted by the knowledge of death since he was four. It is not just dying that he is afraid of, however, but the possible meaninglessness of death—the nothingness behind death which will negate consciousness. This is presented most clearly in his play *The Killer* where, even though a utopian "Radiant City" has been achieved, it is terrorized by an arbitrary assassin. The hero, Berenger, tracks this murderer down and argues eloquently with him at great length; without speaking, the killer knifes him. "We are all murdered by time," says Ionesco. (*Notes and Counternotes*)

Samuel Beckett's favourite saying is "Nothing is more real than Nothing," and his whole drama—indeed, his whole oeuvre—is concerned with waiting for death and trying to conceive in rational terms the irrationality of non-being. He is haunted by the medieval nightmare of conscious death. His miserable protagonists exist with the minimal of life compatible with consciousness. They long for death, but while they are conscious, of course, it cannot come: the tramps continue to wait for Godot without suicide; Hamm plays his "endgame" of dying but is still alive when the curtain goes down; the sandpile creeps up from Winnie's waist to her neck but, like Zeno's logical enigma of the heap of millet, it cannot be completed while she is conscious.

The obsession naturally extends into speculation about the concept of time—one of the trickiest areas of modern theory. Again Beckett is the deepest thinker, though Ionesco, too, likes cocking a snook with beserk clocks and contradictory time schemes within the same play. Beckett is fascinated by the concept of "durée"—psychological *relativity* of time—which Proust adopted from Bergson. Accordingly, his characters often confuse past and present, and their situation of waiting slows down time for them almost, but never quite, to a standstill. Beckett's favourite stage direction, "Pause," like the silences of serial music or the holes in a Henry Moore sculpture, only serves to evoke what it seems to negate. His characters never quite achieve the existentialist ideal of time reduced to a procession of subjective "presents," because against this relativism Beckett sets Fate—as both linear time, the slow but inevitable slide to death, and as circular repetition, Cocteau's *Infernal Machine,* the buddhist wheel of recurrence: the dreary sameness of waiting days. Man fights this spiral of Fate (circular yet progressive) not only with psychological durée but with his own *willed* circles of routine: so Winnie, condemned to endless lucidity and slowly encroaching sands of time, creates within them her own procession of "happy days" by carefully repeated routines. This attempt to conceive of relative time in terms of spatial patterns seems peculiarly modern—our intellectual equivalent of the nineteenth century's synaesthesia. Resnais' films *Hiroshima Mon Amour* and *Last Year at Marienbad* and Fellini's *8½* are fascinating large scale experiments in the same mode.

Beckett plays off the various concepts of time most brilliantly in *Krapp's Last Tape,* where the obvious senility of Krapp contrasts with both durée and circular habit as he plays over and over on *his* "infernal machine" (the tape recorder) snatches of his former self. Or, rather, former *selves,* because the play also illustrates the idea of personality as a flux subservient to time and will—another idea which Camus develops in "The Myth of Sisyphus." Since his early work on Proust, Beckett has been fascinated by the idea of individuality as something through which time passes (is "decanted," is his phrase), not as something which passes through time. Genet too is fascinated by this problem but works through Pirandello not Proust. For him, as for Camus' play actor, personality exists only as a succession of deliberately acted roles, and roles within roles, in a potentially endless series, like reflections in two facing mirrors. In Pinter and Ionesco the concern takes the form rather of a fascination with the processes of brainwashing, the most bizarre example of which is Ionesco's satire on detective stories called *Victims of Duty,* where pointless interrogation drives the hero back through successive stages of his development to the womb, till he finally disappears! Far from finding a residual soul, Ionesco's heart of darkness is a néant: for him, as for Sartre, individual man is a "hole in Being," ultimately unthinkable *except* in terms of consciousness.

It is this insistence on consciousness which distinguishes absurdism from the earlier movement of surréalism which was also concerned with fluctuating personality and relative time. André Breton, the founder of surréalism, described it as a technique for tapping the subconscious, *universal* processes of thought, at which level he supposed there was a link between man and nonhuman nature. In drama this took the form of the kind of stream-of-unconsciousness which Strindberg had pioneered in his last plays, and to this form the absurdists are undoubtedly indebted, particularly Ionesco. Moreover, Ionesco has made such statements as: "Truth lies in our dreams, in our imagination," "It is perhaps only through subjectivity that we become objective," "Self in the absolute is universal." His object in writing, he insists, is to project onto the stage "the world within," the "archetypes" which the "petit bourgeois" ignores in favour of "stereotypes." (*Notes and Counternotes*)

Such statements seem to contradict the idea of isolated consciousness which is a defining concept of the absurd. Camus, in fact, has specifically said that a "really absurd work is *not* universal," and elsewhere Ionesco does distinguish himself from the surréalists, not only because he is more pessimistic than they are, but also because his technique is always consciously controlled, not the surrender to subconscious impulse advocated by Breton.

Now, Ionesco is often contradictory in his theoretical statements—deliberately so—but this particular inconsistency is also in "The Myth of Sisyphus," and may be basic to absurdity. At one place Camus says that in absurd art the intelligence is limited merely to finding images for the irrational:

> The absurd work illustrates thought's renouncing of its prestige and its resignation to being no more than the intelligence that works up appearances and covers with images what has no reason.

Yet in his broader definition of the absurd he says it is precisely the intelligence's *refusal* to renounce its demand for clarity which creates absurdity:

> . . . the mind that aims to understand reality can consider itself satisfied only by reducing it to terms of thought. . . . I said that the world is absurd, but I was too hasty. This world of itself is not reasonable, that is all that can be said. But what is absurd is the confrontation of this irrational and the wild longing for clarity whose call echoes in the human heart. . . . The absurd effect is linked to an excess of logic.

This problem of the function of consciousness in absurdist art we must now turn to consider in the next section of our analysis.

Of recent years the traditional, commonsense, "scientific" view of the mind's relation to data has been challenged on all sides—by philosophical idealism; by depth psychology; and, most important of all, by science's discovery that its traditional techniques are limited in their very nature—by the empirical need to admit logical contradictions in microphysics, for example, by the quantum principle of indeterminacy, by illogical numbers (zero or recurring decimals), and so on—which has led a physicist like Werner Heisenberg to say, "We can no longer speak of the behaviour of the particle independently of the process of observation." The attitude of science, therefore, has swung to the belief that human knowledge and creation are relative, limited (of their nature) to a series of closed systems akin to the mathematical "General Number Theory" of *limited field*. A "field" is an area of thought containing a *limited* collection of materials plus a *limited* system of laws for dealing with them, its relation to reality being therefore strictly contingent, statistical not ideal. On this principle computers have been programmed which produce processes once thought exclusive to the human mind, and do this so well that philosophy is now exercised by the problem of whether machines can be said to "think." *The New Yorker* had a cartoon of a scientist reading the tape from a computer, with the caption: "I'll be damned. It says, *'Cogito, ergo sum.'* "

Not surprisingly, this theory of limited field has influenced both the theory and practice of the arts. Logical Positivism assumes all languages are such closed systems and aims merely to tighten up the internal rules; limited field theory is also behind Huizinga's idea that civilization is a form of "play" and, in a different form, behind Arthur Koestler's more recent argument in *The Act of Creation* (1964) that creativity depends on a matching of closed patterns not previously associated; or, to come closer home, it is the justification Professor Frye gives in the introduction to *The Anatomy of Criticism* for the circular, selfconsistent patterns of its analysis. Beckett, too, claims, "I am interested in the shape of ideas even if I do not believe in them. . . . It is the shape that matters." While Ionesco says, "A real play for me is more likely to be a formal shape than a story," and claims to be trying to "rediscover the rhythms of drama in their purest state," "to make the mechanics of drama function in a vacuum. [To] experiment in abstract drama." (*Notes and Counternotes*) The same attempt to cut down to an abstract structure of pure form led, in painting, to the mathematically based analysis of Cubism; and in the cinema has resulted in such "pure" films as Fellini's *8½* and Resnais' *Last Year at Marienbad,* the latter, you will remember, constructed around the central symbol of a permutation game played with matchsticks.

It is this theory of mental process which Miss Elizabeth Sewell uses in her clever book *The Field of Nonsense* to explain the importance of logical patterns, particularly those of card and chess games, in the dream world of Lewis Carroll. "Nonsense," she argues, "arises from a struggle between arbitrary logic and the free flux of dream." And Miss Sewell makes another observation very pertinent to our present analysis when she points out that, whereas in true dream or poetry the constituent images flow organically one into the other, in nonsense literature—or absurdist—what we get is a pattern imposed on elements of experience which are kept carefully discrete, so that they may

be *manipulated the more easily by the logic and thus controlled.* But the control is recognized as arbitrary. The effect is like mosaic.

Now, this careful isolation of individual elements within an imposed pattern recognized as arbitrary is related to another, at first sight contradictory, movement in epistemology and art—what the French call the new "chosism," which emphasizes the uniqueness, the *quidditas* of everything—particularly objects. This movement ranges widely in its implications, from mystic abnegation of self in beatnik Zen at one extreme, through the semi-idealist position of poets such as Rilke and G. M. Hopkins, Joyce's theories of claritas and (in some interpretations) epiphany, imagism, and phenomenology, to the other extreme of Alain Robbe-Grillet whose neo-realism, like Dr. Johnson kicking the stone, reasserts the commonsense theory that things just are, they exist, and we only need to worry about whether we can use them or not.

One of the extreme forms of "chosism," which concerns us because of its direct influence on the absurdists, particularly Ionesco, is the so-called "College of 'Pataphysics" founded by Alfred Jarry, the author of *Ubu Roi* and generally considered the prophet-founder of the absurdist avant garde. 'Pataphysics is chiefly concerned with undermining established standards in all fields by emphasizing their contingency, but, in so far as it *has* a positive position, this is expressed in contentions such as: "each phenomenon is a law unto itself," "every event determines a law, a *particular* law," "for 'Pataphysics, all things are equal." The important implication of this is that the concept of "thingness" is extended from the objective world to the work-of-art itself: it is not only "art-for-art's sake" but "*each* work-of-art for its *own* sake." "An absolutely free art," says André Malraux in *The Voices of Silence,* "does not lead to the picture or to statuary but to objects." They have no extractable content or even form: the medium is the message! This is the wing of epistemology on which Professor McLuhan works—concerned with the modern fracturing of sequential pattern into discrete parts, space replacing time as an organizing principle, and the deliberate blurring of traditional Western distinctions between messages and medium, art and life. Ionesco's *Salon de l'Automobile* whose hero is equally prepared to marry his car or the salewoman, might have come straight from McLuhan's *The Mechanical Bride.*

Now, drama, because it is already a highly intellectualized art yet, because of the audience, always concerned with basic and immediate communication, is peculiarly able to investigate these areas; and one important aspect of the theatre of the absurd is that it is a sort of experimental workshop for theories of communication. Far from despairing about *narrating* the sensation of nausea, it experiments with ways of presenting the sensation directly, of *being* the absurdity itself, yet within a form which is also conscious of the experience as only one more, limited, "closed field."

Let us examine the aspect of "thingness" first. In the theatre of the absurd "thingness" is not confined to a sense of the nauseating "otherness" of objects; it is expanded into a basic technique, described by Ionesco as follows:

> I have . . . tried to exteriorize the anxiety . . . of
> my characters through objects; to make the stage

settings speak; to translate the action into visual terms; to project visible images of fear, regret, remorse, alienation. . . . I have thus tried to extend the language of the theatre.

(Notes and Counternotes)

In pursuit of this aim, the absurdists have produced some hauntingly effective icons: Beckett's woman smothering in sand, or his waiting tramps; Genet's grotesquely masked blacks; Ionesco's growing corpse or, most remarkable of all perhaps, his *The Chairs,* when the "presence" of an audience is conjured up merely by filling the stage with empty chairs and having the two janitors welcome nonexistent guests, yet continuing the crowd noises *after* the janitors have gone and only the chairs are left on stage. By this image Ionesco achieves the logically impossible: he creates an icon of absence!

This emphasis on the visual, not verbal aspects of theatre stems directly from Antonin Artaud's theory of "poetry of space" and is part of a widespread *theatricalist* movement to restore what Cocteau cleverly distinguished as "poetry *of* the theatre not *in* the theatre." To do this the theatricalists, including the absurdists, have drawn heavily on the visual techniques of vaudeville, circus, ballet and mime (Ionesco wishes his actors to appear like marionettes, Beckett writes ballet mimes, as does Genet), and, especially, the visual selectivity and montage techniques of the cinema. If Resnais and Fellini are analogues of the absurdist closed field, Truffaut and Jean Luc Godard, with their lingering appraisals of processes and objects, particularly advertisements, and their deliberately ragged handheld camera technique, are analogues of absurdist "chosism." At the recent Venice Film Festival, for instance, Godard explained that he made no distinction between art and life and put into his films anything which struck his notice.

Besides the search for things as epiphanies of states of mind, the absurdists also put quite autonomous objects on stage, deliberately "displaced" from their surroundings so

Jean Genet

as to seem discrete. This occurs on a small scale in many plays but becomes a major technique in Genet's latest play *The Screens* where the scenery is mostly two dimensional drawings on movable screens, sometimes actually sketched in on stage, but always juxtaposed with real objects for the purpose of contrast. This, of course, is closely akin to the painting—or collage, whatever it should be called—of someone like Robert Rauschenberg in New York, who sticks real objects onto his paintings, including a full sized angora goat with a car tire round its middle painted white. Rauschenberg is in reaction against painters such as Jackson Pollack or DeKooning who relied solely on the medium itself, because, according to him, the aesthetics involved in their work are wholly abstract and therefore ultimately subjective. Rauschenberg claims:

> I don't want a picture to look like something it isn't. I want it to look like something it is. And I think a picture is more like the real world when it is made out of the real world.
>
> *(New Yorker,* 29 Feb. 1964, 40.)

His most extraordinary production to date is a mattress and pillow covered with red paint and titled "Bed." It sounds like something out of Book III of *Gulliver's Travels* but is a quite logical extension of the collage theory of Picasso and Braque. And if you then propose to include a human being as the "real" object of the collage, you enter an area which will be investigated at the 1967 Montreal Exposition, where I see that they are going to try the aesthetic effects of combining live actors with film.

Malraux in his *Voices of Silence* calls the technique of using discrete autonomous areas of painting the "patch" technique and notes that in someone like Picasso this technique extends to the whole work. In drama such a "patch" need not necessarily be an object, of course; it can equally well be a piece of gratuitous action—the Beckett clown routines, for instance, or the way a character endlessly tears up paper for no obvious reason in Pinter's *The Birthday Party.* Extend this attitude to a whole play and you get what Peter Brook calls theatre as "pure behaviour," the logical outcome of which is the "Happening"—a recent neo-Dada form of entertainment where performers and audience collaborate in an improvised debauch of meaningless, ephemeral action, mostly destructive.

The absurdists use this idea of action as pure "behaviour" but combine it with its opposite extreme of arbitrary control, the closed field. The "absurd" includes both extremes but accepts neither. The precise balance between them varies from play to play and seems to me to be controlled by the relationship which is set up with the audience—a dimension where drama has an advantage over other arts, though jazz poetry readings and kinetic and "op" art are trying to manoeuvre in it too. In Ionesco, possibly because of Dada influence, the relationship tends to be a form of direct *assault* on the audience. His first play, *The Bald Soprano,* for instance, had alternative endings, in one of which extras, "planted" in the audience, were to start booing and the manager would bring in "police" who would threaten to machine gun the audience; in the other, there was to be a shout of "Author" and Ionesco, coming down to the footlights as if to bow, was to raise his fists and shout at the audience, "You bunch of crooks! I'll get you!" This logically extends the theory of communication-only-through-pain to the audience-stage relationship, to produce what Antonin Artaud christened "the theatre of cruelty." In Ionesco the audience tends to be a victim.

This is an extreme, of course; but all the absurdists have experimented with what these days is called "alienation effect"—the trick of acknowledging the audience's presence and emphasizing that the play is only a play. The effect of such alienation is paradoxical: by reminding the audience that it is in a theatre, the theatrical illusion is not destroyed but deepened, because the theatre is revealed as a real-life experience, not a holiday from actuality. This can be manipulated two main ways: the playwright can try to produce the illusion that his "play" is actually happening in the theatre, as Jack Gelber does with *The Connection,* where the actors claim to be real drug addicts coopted to make a film, which the director and camera men can be seen shooting from among the audience. Or, more generally and subtly, it can involve the audience in a theatrical experience with the implication that all life is similarly theatrical—as Shakespeare does in *The Tempest.* In modern times this latter effect was developed into practically a new genre by Pirandello, and its great contemporary master is Jean Genet.

Genet's is a theatre of closed-field illusions, of roles within roles within roles: in *The Maids* he wants adolescent boys playing actresses playing maids playing their mistress who is herself playing a social role. His most comprehensive image of this illusionism so far is probably *The Balcony,* a "house of illusion" as the French call brothels, where perverts can act out their fantasies of sex and power and which, during the play, draws into itself and contaminates with its pretense both authority and rebellion in the world outside. In Genet's stage direction for the brothel-setting a mirror is suggested which appears to reflect an unmade bed standing where actually the audience is sitting. The audience is thus drawn directly into the brothel and implicated as a voyeur of its sado-masochism. However, the complex relation with the audience is most clearly spelled out in *The Blacks,* where the (presumably) white audience watches an onstage audience of negroes grotesquely masked as white representatives of power who, in turn, are watching a company of blacks put on a ritual re-enactment of the way whites think negro men feel about white women. Genet insists that this series of intersecting mirrors depends on a white audience to be shocked by, and thus implicated in, his savage caricature of race relations; and at the end the negroes suddenly reveal that the whole performance was put on merely to distract the audience's attention from the execution of a traitor to the black freedom movement offstage.

Yet even this is not the final level of illusion. The offstage execution is, after all, just as fictional as the ritual on stage, and Genet devalues his own demand for a real white audience when he suggests that an audience of negroes wearing white masks, or even a single white dummy, will do as well. The apparently savage plea for negro independence is thus undermined by the play's suggestion of an infinite series of unrealities, mask under mask, in which the audience is entangled as inextricably as the stage.

This, however, raises problems of ultimate meaning which we must turn to briefly in our last section, limiting ourselves to Genet, Beckett, and Ionesco because of space. Is W. I. Oliver right to complain:

> . . . a good number of these playwrights [fail] to extend their role of philosopher-playwright beyond the initial confrontation and definition of absurdity?
>
> (T. Bogard and W. I. Oliver, eds. *Modern Drama: Essays in Criticism*)

Is not this sufficient justification of itself for absurdist art anyway, since "Living is keeping the absurd alive [and] keeping it alive is, above all, contemplating it" (Camus)? Or is there something more to justify Camus' claim that "even within the limits of nihilism it is possible to find the means to proceed beyond nihilism"? What positives are there, if any, in the theatre of the absurd?

Of the three, Genet would seem the most likely to offer a positive, even if an inverted one. His drama consistently explains personality as an act of will, a deliberately chosen role. Moreover, the role he advocates is always the same—that of outcast and rebel: the criminal, the pervert, the negro assassin. This is seen at its most striking in *The Screens* where the Algerian rebels adopt as their ideal, their myth, a thief so utterly outcast that he has betrayed even them: the nihilism of pure revolt is seen better in the traitor than in the successful rebel. One root of this intransigent rebelliousness in Genet is his romantic belief that completely untrammelled instinct is more "real" and creative than any form of discipline. This aspect of his thought is not far removed from the belief of a Christian existentialist like Nicholas Berdyaev that all creation springs from, and is *dependent* on, "not-being"; so that Genet's utter, anguished devotion to nihilism can be seen as a form of "saintlinesss," as Sartre has in fact suggested in his book *Saint Genet.*

But there is another, more fascinating aspect to Genet's nihilism, a negation which undercuts his romantic cult of not-being. He is aware that deliberate, willed nihilism does *not* have the true Dionysiac splendour; the fact that it is willed limits it. This is most clearly demonstrated in his early play *Deathwatch,* where a convict deliberately kills his cell mate in order to share the glamour of a third convict who is a murderer, but is then rejected by the murderer because his act was not one of instinctive passion. In the later plays this undermining of romantic nihilism takes the form of Genet's persistent, and increasing, theatricalism, his insistence that everything is fake; illusion lies beneath illusion; so that even deliberate wickedness is shown to be merely a ritual, a form of play—another closed system of limited validity. His final position, therefore, devalues deliberate evil because, like Dostoyevski's "underground man," he believes that consciousness automatically negates consistency; consciousness is fated to limited, closed fields; but an *illusion* of unity can be attained if it always stands in opposition to existing standards. The unity comes from what is opposed, however, not from the will of the opposer. Genet, then, comes very close to Camus' idea of art as self-consciously sterile:

> [Creation is] the staggering evidence of man's sole dignity [writes Camus]: the dogged revolt against his condition, perseverance in an effort considered sterile.

There is, however, an important nuance of difference here. For Camus, the artist perseveres in an effort he *considers* sterile: Genet perseveres in an art which he seems deliberately to *render* sterile. In current parlance, his art is "camp." It is perhaps merely the difference between Don Juan and the homosexual. But the effect is to emphasize the contingency of Genet's own vision; and perhaps we may assume that this was his intention?

To date, Beckett's most positive seeming play is *Happy Days.* This can (and has) been interpreted as a demonstration that, recognizing his metaphysical plight, man—or in this case, perhaps significantly, woman—can nevertheless create "happy days" through *willing* human standards. In this light, Winnie is a tragic heroine, fitting Camus' formula for absurd tragedy:

> . . . [it] might be the work that, after all future hope is exiled, describes the life of a happy man.

Like Camus' Sisyphus, she can be said to make absurdity into an affirmation of her own humanity. Such a view of the play depends, of course, on Winnie being conscious all the time of the implications of her plight (buried to the neck in sand). A certain amount of awareness is certainly suggested by the long unsmiling gaze with which she ends the play and by her stoical, London-in-the-Blitz sort of remarks throughout. However, her obvious stupidity and sentimentality and her tendency to escape from the present into nostalgia remind us that Beckett has explicitly denounced what he calls "our pernicious and incurable optimism." It is not quite clear which category of the absurd Winnie belongs to—the conscious, heroic rebel, or Ionesco's "petit bourgeois," so defensively complacent that she refuses to recognize the horrors which stare her in the face. The latter interpretation gains in likelihood, perhaps, if we notice the resemblance of her self-assuring rituals to the pathetic routines of *Godot*'s clowns and compare her

Scene from Genet's The Maids.

tendency to dream nostalgically of the past to the senile escapism of Krapp or of Nag and Nell in the dustbins of *Endgame.*

Beckett's alternative to Winnie's optimism is the resignation of Hamm in *Endgame,* settling down in silence to wait for death: a conscious opting-out, a recognition of the worst and a refusal to "play" any more. The same attitude is shown in his mime *Act without Words* I, where, after a little man has been repeatedly teased by good things let down from the flies and withdrawn just as he was about to grasp them, he settles down with his head in his hands and refuses to be tempted further. This is far more negative than Camus' energetic counsel of effort even without hope. It seems, in fact, to be the equivalent of suicide, cleansed of the escapism to which Camus objected—a sort of *conscious suicide.* Beckett fights nothingness with conscious denial, as Genet fights illusion with conscious insincerity.

To find anything approaching Camus' positive heroism in Beckett, we have to move outside the plays and consider their relation to the audience and the author himself. In *The Courage to Be* Paul Tillich insists that we make a distinction between decay and the "creative expression of decay," and praises "the courage that takes non-being into itself" because being can only be *thought* of negatively—as "the negation of the negation of being." This is close to Camus' idea that "within the limits of nihilism it is possible to find the means to proceed beyond nihilism." In this focus Beckett can be praised for his courageous "creative expression" of the limits of mind, which also increases his audience's metaphysical lucidity by keeping an experience of absurdity constantly before them. But, surely, it goes further and also implies at least a limited validity for art itself? Like his own characters, Beckett sets up a barrier of words against despair whose frailty he acknowledges but still relies on. Art seems to have contingent value for him, if only as a means to kill time.

There is the same need to step outside the plays themselves to find a positive position in Ionesco. He himself offers two: in the tradition of Artaud, he tentatively believes his work may have an epistemological value:

> If [my work] has any value, it should assist in the destruction and renewal of modes of expression.
> (*Notes and Counternotes*)

and he claims that, metaphysically, his plays help to overcome the nausea of absurdity. Here are some quotes:

> To attack absurdity is a way of stating the possibility of non-absurdity. To feel the absurdity or improbability of every day life and language is already to have transcended it.
> (*Notes and Counternotes*)

> Logic is revealed by an awareness of the illogicality of the absurd.
> (*Notes and Counternotes*)

Within his drama, however, only *Rhinoceros* seems to hint at a possible positive; and, looked at more closely, even this disintegrates. At the end of that play it does seem as though the hero, Berenger, is maintaining his individual integrity when all about him have turned to rhinos; there is even a hint of active rebellion as he prepares a gun to fight them. Consequently, the play has most often been interpreted as an allegory of individual humanism versus the Nazi mass-mind. But actually Berenger's heroism is fortuitous, and thus still absurd: he *wants* to become a rhino like the others but finds he can not! His humanism is *faute-de-mieux* ["for want of something better"], or rather *faute-de-pire* ["for want of something worse"]: more of a surrender to circumstance than a courageous rebellion. As in Genet, there is a second level of absurdity beneath the main one, the absurdity of man beneath the absurdity of rhinoceri—like the mime of Marcel Marceau where the hero patiently worms his way out of an invisible cage and stands upright, only to find himself inside a larger cage of exactly the same kind.

Thus, the full assertion of Camus' Sisyphus does not seem to be found anywhere *within* the theatre of the absurd: its characters are victims, not heroes. The plays can be defended as acts of courage by the author himself, or as epiphanies which force the spectator to recognize and reject absurdity; but such external factors are hard to assess. For me, at least, absurdist plays never wholly "negate negation." At best, they can be said sometimes to limit it. And their most persuasive positive is not the power to provoke rebellion, but their intermittent hints that nausea is a state of mind as relative as any other. The "closed field" aspect of consciousness, which is the main cause of absurdist despair, is also the ultimate defence against it; since, by the same logic, "contingency," too, is merely a contingent, and absurdity itself absurd. (pp. 421-41)

R. B. Parker, "The Theory and Theatre of the Absurd," in Queen's Quarterly, *Vol. LXXIII, No. 3, Autumn, 1966, pp. 421-41.*

Edward Albee

[*Considered one of the leading figures in contemporary American theater, Albee was associated by critics with the Theater of the Absurd following the production of his early plays* The Zoo Story *and* The American Dream. *His works often address the problem of effective communication in a world of increasing personal remoteness and emotional callousness. In the following excerpt, Albee contrasts the Theater of the Absurd with commercial theater in the United States.*]

When I was told, about a year ago, that I was considered a member in good standing of The Theatre of the Absurd I was deeply offended. I was deeply offended because I had never heard the term before and I immediately assumed that it applied to the theatre uptown—Broadway.

What (I was reasoning to myself) could be more absurd than a theatre in which the esthetic criterion is something like this: A "good" play is one which makes money; a "bad" play (in the sense of "Naughty! Naughty!" I guess) is one which does not; a theatre in which performers have plays rewritten to correspond to the public relations image of themselves; a theatre in which playwrights are encouraged (what a funny word!) to think of themselves as little cogs in a great big wheel; a theatre in which imitation has given way to imitation of imitation; a theatre in which London "hits" are, willy-nilly, in a kind of reverse of chauvinism, greeted in a manner not unlike a colony's obeisance to the Crown; a theatre in which real estate owners and theatre party managements predetermine the success

of unknown quantities; a theatre in which everybody scratches and bites for billing as though it meant access to the last bomb shelter on earth; a theatre in which, in a given season, there was not a single performance of a play by Beckett, Brecht, Chekhov, Genet, Ibsen, O'Casey, Pirandello, Shaw, Strindberg—or Shakespeare? What, indeed, I thought, could be more absurd than that? (My conclusions . . . obviously.)

For it emerged that The Theatre of the Absurd, aside from being the title of an excellent book by Martin Esslin on what is loosely called the avant-garde theatre, was a somewhat less than fortunate catch-all phrase to describe the philosophical attitudes and theatre methods of a number of Europe's finest and most adventurous playwrights and their followers.

I was less offended, but still a little dubious. Simply: I don't like labels; they can be facile and can lead to nonthink on the part of the public. And unless it is understood that the playwrights of The Theatre of the Absurd represent a group only in the sense that they seem to be doing something of the same thing in vaguely similar ways at approximately the same time—unless this is understood, then the labeling itself will be more absurd than the label.

Playwrights, by nature, are grouchy, withdrawn, envious, greedy, suspicious and, in general, quite nice people—and the majority of them wouldn't be caught dead in a colloquy remotely resembling the following:

> IONESCO. (*At a Left Bank café table, spying Beckett and Genet strolling past in animated conversation*) Hey! Sam! Jean!
>
> GENET. Hey, it's Eugene! Sam, it's Eugene!
>
> BECKETT. Well, I'll be damned. Hi there, Eugene boy.
>
> IONESCO. Sit down, kids.
>
> GENET. Sure thing.
>
> IONESCO. (*Rubbing his hands together*). Well, what's new in The Theatre of the Absurd?
>
> BECKETT. Oh, less than a lot of people think. (*They all laugh.*)

Etc. No. Not very likely. Get a playwright alone sometime, get a few drinks in him, and maybe he'll be persuaded to sound off about his "intention" and the like—and hate himself for it the next day. But put a group of playwrights together in a room, and the conversation—if there is any—will, more likely than not, concern itself with sex, restaurants, and the movies.

Very briefly, then—and reluctantly, because I am a playwright and would much rather talk about sex, restaurants, and the movies—and stumblingly, because I do not pretend to understand it entirely, I will try to define The Theatre of the Absurd. As I get it, The Theatre of the Absurd is an absorption-in-art of certain existentialist and post-existentialist philosophical concepts having to do, in the main, with man's attempts to make sense for himself out of his senseless position in a world which makes no sense—which makes no sense because the moral, religious, political, and social structures man has erected to "illusion" himself have collapsed. (pp. 168-70)

So much for the attempt to define terms. Now, what of this theatre? What of this theatre in which, for example, a legless old couple live out their lives in twin ashcans, surfacing occasionally for food or conversation (Samuel Beckett's *Endgame*); in which a man is seduced, and rather easily, by a girl with three well-formed and functioning noses (Eugène Ionesco's *Jack, or The Submission*); in which, on the same stage, one group of Negro actors is playing at pretending to be Negro (Jean Genet's *The Blacks*)?

What of this theatre? Is it, as it has been accused of being, obscure, sordid, destructive, anti-theatre, perverse, and absurd (in the sense of foolish)? Or is it merely, as I have so often heard it put, that, "This sort of stuff is too depressing, too . . . too mixed-up; I go to the theatre to relax and have a good time."

I would submit that it is this latter attitude—that the theatre is a place to relax and have a good time—in conflict with the purpose of The Theatre of the Absurd—which is to make a man face up to the human condition as it really is—that has produced all the brouhaha and the dissent. I would submit that The Theatre of the Absurd, in the sense that it is truly the contemporary theatre, facing as it does man's condition as it is, is the Realistic theatre of our time; and that the supposed Realistic theatre—the term used here to mean most of what is done on Broadway—in the sense that it panders to the public need for self-congratulation and reassurance and presents a false picture of ourselves to ourselves, is, with an occasional very lovely exception, really and truly The Theatre of the Absurd.

And I would submit further that the health of a nation, a society, can be determined by the art it demands. We have insisted of television and our movies that they not have anything to do with anything, that they be our never-never land; and if we demand this same function of our live theatre, what will be left of the visual-auditory arts—save the dance (in which nobody talks) and music (to which nobody listens)?

It has been my fortune, the past two or three years, to travel around a good deal, in pursuit of my career—Berlin, London, Buenos Aires, for example; and I have discovered a couple of interesting things. I have discovered that audiences in these and other major cities demand of their commercial theatre—and get—a season of plays in which the froth and junk are the exception and not the rule. To take a case: in Berlin, in 1959, Adamov, Genet, Beckett, and Brecht (naturally) were playing the big houses; this past fall, Beckett again, Genet again, Pinter twice, etc. To take another case: in Buenos Aires there are over a hundred experimental theatres.

These plays cannot be put on in Berlin over the head of a protesting or an indifferent audience; these experimental theatres cannot exist in Buenos Aires without subscription. In the end—and it must always come down to this, no matter what other failings a theatre may have—in the end a public will get what it deserves, and no better.

I have also discovered, in my wanderings, that young people throng to what is new and fresh in the theatre. Happily, this holds true in the United States as well. At the various colleges I have gone to to speak I have found an eager, friendly, and knowledgeable audience, an audience which is as dismayed by the Broadway scene as any proselytizer

for the avant-garde. I have found among young people an audience which is not so preconditioned by pap as to have cut off half of its responses. (It is interesting to note, by the way, that if an off-Broadway play has a substantial run, its audiences will begin young and grow older; as the run goes on, cloth coats give way to furs, walkers and subway riders to taxi-takers. Exactly the opposite is true on Broadway.)

The young, of course, are always questioning values, knocking the status quo about, considering shibboleths to see if they are pronounceable. In time, it is to be regretted, most of them—the kids—will settle down to their own version of the easy, the standard; but in the meanwhile . . . in the meanwhile they are a wonderful, alert, alive, accepting audience.

And I would go so far as to say that it is the responsibility of everyone who pretends any interest at all in the theatre to get up off their six-ninety seats and find out what the theatre is *really* about. For it is a lazy public which produces a slothful and irresponsible theatre.

Now, I would suspect that . . . The Theatre of the Absurd (or the avant-garde theatre, or whatever you want to call it) as it now stands is on its way out. Or at least is undergoing change. All living organisms undergo constant change. And while it is certain that the nature of this theatre will remain constant, its forms, its methods—its devices, if you will—most necessarily will undergo mutation.

This theatre has no intention of running downhill; and the younger playwrights will make use of the immediate past and mold it to their own needs. (Harold Pinter, for example, could not have written *The Caretaker* had Samuel Beckett not existed, but Pinter is, nonetheless, moving in his own direction.) And it is my guess that the theatre in the United States will always hew more closely to the post-Ibsen/Chekhov tradition than does the theatre in France, let us say. It is our nature as a country, a society. But we will experiment, and we will expect your attention.

For just as it is true that our response to color and form was forever altered once the impressionist painters put their minds to canvas, it is just as true that the playwrights of The Theatre of the Absurd have forever altered our response to the theatre. (pp. 171-74)

Edward Albee, "Which Theatre Is the Absurd One?", in American Playwrights on Drama, *edited by Horst Frenz, Hill and Wang, 1965, pp. 168-74.*

Eugene Ionesco

[A Romanian-born French dramatist, Ionesco is a major exponent of the Theater of the Absurd. One of Ionesco's primary concerns is the impossibility of communication between human beings, and his plays often convey that idea through bizarre distortions of language, creating dialogue that is significant in its semantic vapidity. Incomprehensible on any superficial level, Ionesco's works create a darkly comic vision in which the grotesque and the mundane are both exaggerated to the point of surrealism to reveal the complacency with which human beings confront their absurd, collective situation. In the

following excerpt, Ionesco offers his most recent perspective on the Theater of the Absurd.]

"The theater of the absurd" names a certain number of theatrical works whose center of origin and creation was the Paris of the early 1950s. This theater was described as such by the well-known English critic Martin Esslin. Why did he call it "the theater of the absurd"? Maybe because one spoke a great deal of the absurd between 1945 and 1950, and Esslin had to consider that there was a rapport between our theater and thought, theories or obsessions made fashionable by Jean-Paul Sartre, Albert Camus, Georges Bataille, and a few others. It seemed to him that there was a rapport between this genre of theater and the way these writers saw the postwar world. Maybe he was right. As far as I'm concerned, I have had a certain amount of trouble accepting this definition. But now it has come to be called a certain genre of theater, and that definition applies to theatrical works in the current era. Since the definition and the theater belong to literary history, this has given me a reason to call the theater of the absurd "absurd." I would rather, like Emmanuel Jacquard, have called it "theater of derision." In effect, the characters of this theater, of my theater, are neither tragic nor comic but derisory. The characters are cut off from all transcendental and metaphysical roots. They cannot be but psychological puppets, or without psychology, as one used to say. Undoubtedly, they will continue to be symbolic characters, expressions of an era.

I had thought that half of the plays that had been written before us were absurd to the extent that they could be comical, for example, because the comic is absurd. I also thought that the ancestor of that theater, the great ancestor, could be Shakespeare, who has his hero say: "The world is a tale told by an idiot, full of sound and fury, signifying nothing." Perhaps one can say that this theater of the absurd goes back further and that Oedipus too was an absurd character, since what happened to him in effect was absurd. But with a difference: unconsciously, Oedipus broke the laws and was punished for having transgressed them. Nevertheless, there were laws and norms, even if he managed to violate them. In our theater, the characters don't seem to cling to anything, and if I may cite myself, the oldsters of my play *The Chairs* are lost in a world without laws, without rules, without transcendence. That is what I also wanted to show in a cheerful play like *The Bald Soprano*, for example: the characters without metaphysical roots, searching perhaps for a center they have lost, a point of support beyond them. Beckett wrote more coldly, maybe more lucidly, in the same sense.

But there already had been absurd theater that was neither comical nor happy, written in another style. I have the audacity to think that *The Bald Soprano, The Lesson, The Chairs,* and *Victims of Duty* are the plays that have given a novel impetus to an absurd "new style." The success of my early plays is incontestable. They have pleased the Germans, the English, the Americans, and men of the theater who have followed us with less talent, as much talent, or more talent. And I continue to maintain that the theater of the new absurd soared in the 1950s, more exactly, beginning with *The Bald Soprano* which played in 1950, *The Lesson* which was presented in 1951, *The Chairs,* which dates in 1952, and *Victims of Duty* from 1953. With much greater power than was generally realized, Beckett

arrived in the theater in 1953 with his unforgettable *Waiting for Godot.* I cannot affirm that what I wrote subsequently illustrates this style of theater. *Exit the King,* for instance, is probably too literary, except in the final scene which, however, is inspired by the Tibetan *Book of the Dead.*

I would also say that the word "absurd" is a bit forced, given that one cannot say of a thing that it is absurd without having a model of that which is not absurd. But I could say that the characters of *The Dead* were searching for a sense they didn't find, a law, supreme conduct, for what one cannot call anything other than divinity. For me, the theater of the absurd was also a theater of battle against the bourgeois theater it sometimes parodied and against realist theater. I held and I still hold that reality is not realistic, and it is realist theater, socialist realism, the Brechtian theater that I fought against and criticized. Realism is not reality; I said realism is a school of theater which has a certain way of envisaging the real, just as romanticism and surrealism do. What I disliked in bourgeois theater was that it was preoccupied with futilities: business, economy, politics, adultery, diversion in the Pascalian sense. One could even say the theater of adultery of the nineteenth century and the beginning of the twentieth century may have come down from Racine, with the enormous difference that adultery in Racine led to death. It was no more than a futile game for many of the post-Racinian writers. Another fault of realism is that it was an ideological theater, thus in some ways a theater of lies, a dishonest theater. It is so not only because one does not know what reality is and because no man of science can say what reality is, but also because the realist writer sullied himself to prove something, to engage the people, the spectators, the readers, in the name of an ideology of which the writer wanted to convince us but which was not legitimate for that reason. All realist theater is a theater of cheating, even, and especially, if the author is sincere. True sincerity comes from further away; it comes from the depths of the irrational, the unconscious. To speak of oneself is more convincing and more truthful than to speak of others, to engage people in an always debatable political cause.

I speak of myself in order to speak of everyone. The true poet does not lie, does not cheat, wants to engage no one, simply because the authentic poet does not lie, does not invent; he is totally different. In effect, imagination comes forth with images, with symbols that come from the depths, and it is for that reason that these images are significant and full of sense. Pirandello also had an ideology, psychological theories that, since the advent of depth psychology, no longer have truth or value: but the characters are alive, and one can always go to see Pirandello because his characters live with passion and live this passion dramatically.

To speak again of myself, and I excuse myself for it, I and some of the others among us wanted to show not only the condition of being in love, adulterous, even social. We wanted to make evident to the spectators the existential condition of man even in his integrity, in his totality, in his deepest tragedy, his destiny—that is to say in the conscience of the absurdity of the world. This is history "told by an idiot."

In this way we wanted to serve man's knowledge, if one

can use these words, through the most ingrained testimony of our being. I thought that the theater was in some sense useless but that one could live with the useless, that one needs the useless: what use are the vital football games and tennis matches and so many other contests? It is the useless that one cannot do without. But one can do without the so-called useless game of art, of contemplation, of prayer. Yes, art is useless, but its uselessness is indispensable. In the encyclopedias of the new China, the word "contemplation," it seems, has been suppressed. Contemplation is in a sense useless and at the same time essential, indispensable. People who have lost it and who are not astonished by their being, by existence, are spiritually infirm. Could I affirm that in our world art can replace religion? Since I questioned the utility of art, I could ask myself about the utility of the magnificent construction of the antique temples. Constructed to receive the faithful who would come to pray, today they are visited only by tourists, and no longer by believers, since these religions are dead; the best among them appreciate and admire the pure construction of the spirit, since an architectural construction is an idea, a construction of the spirit, an abstract structure.

I still don't know very well what the word "absurd" means unless it is the interrogation of the absurd, and I repeat that those who no longer are astonished that they exist, those who don't ask questions about being, who find that all is normal, natural now that the world is rejoining the supernatural, are infirm. I don't know if one is to feel sorry for them or to rejoice for them. But the wonderment will come; the question of the absurdity of this world cannot fail to be posed even if there is no possible response. All those who live in the immediately useful, in routine, in politics are to be pitied, whereas it is before the incomprehensible that we ought to kneel.

At least one should ask oneself about the existential problems the ecologists have posed. Soon the atmosphere's ozone may be missing. This will, for example, be the fault of the politicians, of the engineers and chemists who construct death engines instead of preoccupying themselves with the only important thing: the possible end of this world. But let us try to uplift ourselves at least by thinking about what is rot-proof, about the real, that is to say about the sacred, and about the ritual that expresses the sacred and cannot be found without the creation of great art.

I absolutely don't know whether the theater of the absurd has a future or not, whether the different realist theaters have a future or not. I can probably respond to this question by interrogating my fortune-teller. But those who ask about the vitality of this theater of the absurd are the enemies of the theater of the absurd and the partisans of one sort of political realism or another. There always will be one theater of the absurd or another, other numerous forms of the absurd—unless one were to find, tomorrow or the day after tomorrow, the key to the enigma.

Yet I think that in part all this preceding discourse is superfluous. I wanted to talk about the battles, the polemics we had during that period with certain active and virulent Brechtians, among them Kenneth Tynan. The texts of these polemics are historical. But the ideologies, we all know, are passé. The pure spectacles, the productions, provisionally replace them. Furthermore, the absurd has invaded the real in such a fashion that what one calls "re-

alist reality," the reality of realities and realisms, to us seems as real as the absurd; and the absurd appears to us as reality: let's look around us.

The incontestable Beckett, who came to the theater in 1953, with his admirable *Waiting for Godot,* is not simply an author of the so-called absurd drama because he is as much an absurdist as he is a realist. Beckett has brought us to the edge of the absurd in his drama and in his comedy which have become routine. It has surpassed the limits that go to the absurd and beyond, beyond the reality we now have reached. (pp. 45-9)

Eugène Ionesco, "Theatres of the Absurd," translated by Edith Kurzweil, in Partisan Review, *Vol. LVI, No. 1, 1989, pp. 45-9.*

Martin Esslin

[In the following essay, Esslin presents a reconsideration of the Theater of the Absurd.]

Having, to coin a phrase, "coined a phrase," I am in two minds about whether I should feel a thrill of pride every time I read a reference to the Theatre of the Absurd in a newspaper or a book, or whether I should not rather hide my head in shame; for what I intended as a generic concept, a working hypothesis for the understanding of a large number of extremely varied and elusive phenomena, has assumed for many people, including some drama critics, a reality as concrete and specific as a branded product of the detergent industry.

When I wrote my book I had been struck by the fact that the work of dramatists writing quite independently of one another in different countries had certain fundamental features in common. I was excited and moved by writers like Beckett, Ionesco, and Harold Pinter. So I thought it would be useful to isolate and describe what was the common factor that made their plays so difficult to follow. Shortly after the book was published, the very different and individual writers were immediately asked by officious journalists, "Do you agree with Martin Esslin that you belong to the school of the Theatre of the Absurd?" Which is an absurd question. You might as well ask an African tribesman who carves masks whether he agrees that he is a member of the cubist school. Neither the primitive sculptor nor the most sophisticated modern playwright is, in his creative activity, concerned with anything but his own vision, his own impulse.

A concept like the Theatre of the Absurd concentrates on certain important elements in individual works containing a multitude of other elements that make them, in other respects, quite different from one another. It is a basic mistake to assume that all the works that somehow come under this label are the same, or even very similar; and it is nonsense to try to attach a value judgment to the whole category. If the common factor among the absurdists were an ideology, then the category could be rejected en bloc. If one disagrees with Stalinism, one can reject all art that embodies strictly Stalinist precepts. But—and I thought I went to great lengths in my book to make this clear— what these writers express is not an ideological position but rather their bewilderment at the absence of a coherent and generally accepted integrating principle, ideology, ethical system, call it what you will, in our world. And the lack of such a unifying force, an individual's sense that it is lacking, is not an ideological position; it is a matter of fact. If Ionesco feels unsatisfied by Catholicism or Communism or any other ism, that is his own very personal affair which is not really susceptible to argument. As it happens, one writer covered in *The Theatre of the Absurd,* Adamov, in the course of his development has managed to find a firm ideological foundation for his work—and has therefore ceased to come under the heading of the Absurd.

What is far more important to the concept of the Theatre of the Absurd is the *form* in which this sense of bewilderment and mystery expresses itself: the devaluation or even downright dissolution of language, the disintegration of plot, characterization, and final solution which had hitherto been the hallmark of drama, and the substitution of new elements of form—concrete stage imagery, repetition or intensification, a whole new stage language.

Innovations in form can be judged only in particular contexts. It would be silly to say that the five-act play is a better form than the three- or one-act play, that the circle is a more satisfying shape than the square. The Theatre of the Absurd is above all a new form of the theatre that says some very important things about our time. And what it says is not necessarily, as is sometimes claimed, totally nihilistic, totally negative. As I have tried to point out in my book, the recognition that there is no simple explanation for all the mysteries of the world, that all previous systems have been oversimplified and therefore were bound to fail, will appear to be a source of despair only to those who still feel that such a simplified system *can* provide an answer. The moment we realize that we may have to live without any final truths the situation changes; we may have to readjust ourselves to living with less exalted aims and by doing so become more humble, more receptive, less exposed to violent disappointments and crises of conscience—and therefore in the last resort happier and better-adjusted people, simply because we then live in closer accord with reality.

This open world view, humble and without preconceived notions, is, as I tried to point out in the last chapter of my book [see excerpt above], complementary to the scientific attitude—science concentrates on the area of light about nature and the world, which it tries to extend by patient probing; the attitude of the artists of the Theatre of the Absurd concentrates on the area of darkness that surrounds the patch of light of science. To be well adjusted to reality we have to be as aware of the one as of the other.

I am often asked whether I agree with those who say that the Theatre of the Absurd has now said what it could say and that drama will henceforth develop in other directions. What I feel is that the writers I have grouped in that category have developed a whole new vocabulary of theatrical forms that has enriched the stage's possibilities of expression immensely and added a new dimension to the art of the theatre. The innovations and new devices introduced by the absurdists will, I am convinced, continue to be used and will eventually be absorbed into the mainstream of the tradition.

Which are the innovations of the absurdists, the new modes they have contributed to the vocabulary and syntax of the theatre? Above all they have demonstrated that poetry in the theatre is not merely a matter of language but that the theatre itself is a form of poetry: concretized metaphor, complex imagery on multiple planes of meaning and association, from the most earthily concrete to the most esoterically abstract.

To illustrate what I mean, in *The Theatre of the Absurd* I described the reaction of the convicts of San Quentin to a performance of *Waiting for Godot* by Herbert Blau's and Jules Irving's Theatre Workshop: they unhesitatingly interpreted Godot as the freedom they were waiting for. At a meeting of theatre personalities from east and west of the Iron Curtain held in Vienna in March 1965 Jean Duvignaud, the French critic who used to teach at Tunis, reported on a performance of *Waiting for Godot* in Algeria when that country was still a French possession: the audience of landless fellaheen had no doubt that Godot referred to the long-awaited but never forthcoming distribution of land to the peasants. A Polish delegate countered by pointing out that in Warsaw in 1956 the same play had been enthusiastically received as a parable of the ever promised but never forthcoming national independence of Poland from the Russians. Everyone knows the interpretation according to which Godot stands for salvation in a Christian sense. How can all these totally contradictory interpretations be true? asked some literal-minded participant in Vienna.

The answer, of course, is that the play is so powerful a poetic metaphor, so archetypal an image, that all these interpretations are not only equally acceptable, they all equally *impose* themselves; the play provides an existential reconstruction of one of the basic human emotions and situations—it is a poetic image of the *act of waiting* itself. No wonder everyone immediately thinks of whatever it is that he has been vainly waiting for in his own personal, spiritual, or political life. Of course, the theatre has always been able to provide such basic poetic archetypes: the encounter of Romeo and Juliet stands as an image of all nascent love, Lear's lonely ravings on the storm-tossed heath for all the loss of aging and death. It is the special achievement of the absurdists, however, to have demonstrated that such archetypal images need not be accidental by-products of conventional plot but are capable of being put on the stage as the very centre and essence of a play; that the poetic image is not just an illustration but the centre of the dramatic experience. In doing so they have liberated the stage from the tedious and long-winded necessities of conventional exposition and the even more tedious tying up of plots at the end of plays. Just as lyrical poetry is far more compressed and economical a form than the realistic novel, a poetic theatre of this kind is far more compressed and economical of time than a naturalistic theatre.

The absurdists have further demonstrated the theatre's ability to deal not only with external reality in providing a concrete and photographically correct reconstruction of real life but also, and much more interestingly, with the vast field of *internal* reality—the fantasies, dreams, hallucinations, secret longings, and fears of mankind. This too represents an eruption of the poetical into the theatre in both subject matter and technique: archetypal situations in associative sequence, rather than strictly photographic situations in rigidly chronological order. Here again the absurdists have merely enlarged a long-established practice: the ghosts of Hamlet's father, Banquo and Caesar, to name but the most obvious examples, also concretize inner visions of the Prince of Denmark, Macbeth, and Brutus. What the absurdists have done is liberate this kind of internal reality from the necessity of having to emerge from an external plot situation with neat transitions from reality to dream, from nature to hallucination.

The Theatre of the Absurd, having conditioned audiences to accept happenings on the stage as expressions of internal, psychic reality, has added an additional element of suspense to the theatre: the action can now often be seen *both* as reality and as dream, as natural and as hallucinatory at one and the same time, an ambivalence and ambiguity that is in itself of the essence of poetry. Hamm and Clov in *Endgame,* for example, are acceptable as human beings living in a kind of science-fiction reality of a post catastrophic age; they can at the same time be regarded as archetypes, components of a single dreamer's mind. In Harold Pinter's theatre the external reality of the characters in plays like *The Caretaker* and *The Homecoming* is completely convincing, their speech almost terrifyingly real. Yet at the same time *The Caretaker* works most forcefully as a dream, a myth of the expulsion of the Father by the Sons, while in *The Homecoming* the weird situation of a father and two younger brothers turning the elder brother's wife into a prostitute is presented in such a way that the play can be seen both as a completely realistic piece of near pornography and as a dramatization of the archetype of the sons' dream of taking over a mother image as an object of sexual enjoyment (the elder brother then appears as a reduplication of the father image, his wife as a reduplication of the mother—and here Pinter has brilliantly suggested that the dead mother in the play may also have been a prostitute, while the elder brother's wife, like the mother, is shown as having three sons, and the play ends with the old father begging the reincarnation of his wife for some scraps of her sexual favours now bestowed upon the two younger sons). In this kind of theatre reality co-exists with myth, the audience can experience the mythical character of reality as well as the reality of mythical situations.

Another important achievement of the absurdists has been the destruction of the concept of drama as no more than another literary form: they have re-emphasized the *physical* nature of the theatre, its intimate links with ballet, slapstick, acrobatics, and the magical physical actions of ritual. In some senses this has amounted to a *devaluation* of language; it has enabled the playwright to use inarticulate sounds, meaningless clichés, or language that is openly belied by the action. It can also be argued that this has made language more rather than less important in the theatre. After all in lyrical poetry, too, language is freed from the dry utilitarian function of merely conveying factual information. By placing the main burden of the action on the physical happenings on the stage, the absurdists have increased the *poetical* potential of language in the theatre; its rhythm, sound, tonal quality again become important autonomous elements.

Precisely because the action in *Waiting for Godot* consists in the absence of anything happening and because the dialogue has been freed from any storytelling function, we are enabled to see the language in Beckett's masterpiece as an infinitely rich symphony of poetic sound and subtly varied rhythmical patterns. Yet these poetic patterns and rhythms are not just arias or superimposed ornamenta-tion, they *are* the patterns and rhythms of the action of the play itself. The same applies, *mutatis mutandis,* to such poetic masterpieces as Genet's *The Blacks,* Ionesco's *The Chairs,* Pinter's *The Dumb Waiter,* or—to take an example from a completely different sphere—Tadeusz Rozewicz's brilliant play *The Witnesses,* in which the horror of our time is expressed by such devices as a dialogue between a married couple, in the whimsically bantering tones of cheap romantic love fiction, from which it gradually emerges that they are watching a kitten being brutally blinded and buried alive by children outside their window. Once again the language is not just a straight expression of the content it relates, it is in a dialectical relationship to that content and emphasizes its horror by seemingly denying it.

It may appear paradoxical but is nevertheless true that the absurdists have also greatly re-emphasized the *importance of form* in the theatre. One frequently finds the notion that the Theatre of the Absurd has made the craft of playwriting too easy by allowing anyone to turn the most spontaneous and formless whims of his imagination into drama. This conception is on a par with the idea that expressionist and abstract painting is on the level of the childish scribblings of infants and equally easy. On the contrary, the greater the fluidity of the subject matter, the more associative rather than chronological the sequence of events in a play, the *greater* becomes the need for formal control, for shape and structure. This is again analogous to the case of lyrical poetry where ideas and images are presented in a non-narrative, associative pattern and devices such as rhyme, rhythm, and fixed patterns of repetition impose themselves. In a novel or short story it is the chronology and logical sequence of events that enables the reader to keep pace with the contents; in a poem it is the formal pattern that serves this purpose by arranging the imagery in an aesthetically satisfying order. Exactly the same is the case in a theatre of concretized poetic images in associative sequence. An examination of any of the really successful works of the Theatre of the Absurd will confirm this rule: the symmetry of Acts I and II of *Waiting for Godot,* the rigid ritual structure of *The Blacks,* the movement from repose to paroxysm and back to repose in *The Bald Prima Donna,* the inexorable accumulation of empty chairs in *The Chairs,* the strophic form of the duologues in *The Dumb Waiter,* are cases in point. Each play of this type has to find its *own,* rigidly formal pattern, which must inevitably arise from and express the *basic conception* of the play. Much of the tension and suspense in this kind of drama lies in the gradual unfolding of its formal pattern. Hence its formal pattern must embody the very essence of the action. And so, in the Theatre of the Absurd, form and content not only match, they are inseparable from each other.

In its rebellion against the naturalistic convention the Theatre of the Absurd entered the consciousness of its audiences as an *anti*-theatre, a completely new beginning, a total breach with the conventions of the past. Now that the first and delicious shock effects have worn off, we can see that the absurdists merely emphasized hitherto neglected aspects, stressed some forgotten technical devices, and discarded some unduly inflated aspects of a long-existing tradition of drama. Far from being anti-theatre, they were in the very centre of the mainstream of its development, just as revolutionary movements of the past—

Ibsen, Strindberg, Shaw, or the Expressionists—that were regarded as the grave-diggers of tradition can now be seen as its main and decisive representatives. Indeed, seen from the vantage point of today, it is the brief episode of photographic realism in the theatre that stands out as a deviation from the mainstream of the development of drama. It is the achievement of the Absurdists together with the Brechtians to have brought the theatre back to the full richness of its traditional vocabulary, to have freed it from the narrow restrictionism of pretending to be reality observed through a missing fourth wall, which made it impossible for actors to be aware of and to address their audience, forbade them to reveal their inner lives directly through monologue, confined them in the strait-jacket of the actual time of action (with endless pouring out of coffee and lighting of cigarettes) and banished all the delicious world of the dreamlike, the supernatural, and its stage machinery from the theatre. (pp. 219-27)

> Martin Esslin, "The Theatre of the Absurd Reconsidered," in his Brief Chronicles: Essays on Modern Theatre, *Maurice Temple Smith Ltd., 1970, pp. 219-27.*

THEATRICAL TECHNIQUES

Roderick Robertson

[*In the following excerpt, Robertson examines the manner in which the stage sets and techniques of the Theater of the Absurd support its essential themes.*]

A stage is two things: an instrument for the presentation of theatrical events and, on another plane, a metaphor of some kind. Both concepts are familiar ones, the first particularly in light of the many experiments made upon stages in this century, and the second in light of the many insights given recently by scholars upon stages of the past. We can understand how Shakespeare's scaffold was a microcosm of the world as he and his contemporaries envisaged it. The Greek stage of a round, open space backed by a permanent structure suggests to us things about the Greek view of the world, and the italianate proscenium stage has associations which extend into art, architecture, philosophy, and even religion.

The Absurdists too write for a stage which is both instrument and metaphor, both of them already formed when they came to it and both capable of modification to suit their own particular ideas of theatre. It is perhaps easier to look at the stage as an instrument since all we have to do is make some objective observations of what it is and how it is used. But in actual practice we cannot completely separate the stage as instrument from the stage as metaphor. Here again, two concepts interpenetrate. But starting from the basis of the nineteenth century proscenium stage, we can easily observe several new lines of approach to the stage as instrument. Edward Gordon Craig, for example, called for a new unified control of the instrument through an all-powerful and all-creative being, the stage director. But the ends of his theatre were those not of truth

but of beauty: "It has never been the purpose of art to reflect and make uglier the ugliness of things, but to transform and make the already beautiful more beautiful, and, in following this purpose, art shields us with sweet influences from the dark sorrows of our weakness." Adolphe Appia, for all his splendid insights into the use of living light and his analysis of the stage instrument, remained rather too closely bound to the twilight romanticism of Wagner, but both Craig and Appia were stimulating influences on theatre.

Others could be mentioned: Copeau and his formalistic stage, a refreshing wind of change for both stage instrument and metaphor; Meyerhold and the other experimentalists of the Russian stage of the 1920's; and finally Piscator and Brecht, who exposed the stage instrument in a frank way so as fully to exploit its potential and its intrinsic qualities. These names by no means exhaust the list; there were all kinds of experiments being made upon the stage, some to chop away the proscenium arch, some to thrust the actors into the audience, others to thrust the audience into the play. What do these developments in lighting, stage machinery, and stage design mean for the theatre of the Absurd? They have provided it with a far freer and more flexible stage than existed sixty years ago. But at the same time, they seem to have had very little direct effect on the work of these dramatists. Their scripts ask for little or nothing that could not be provided by any minor repertory company of half a century ago, and they are quite content with an old-fashioned, picture-frame stage.

Take an example more or less at random. Ionesco's outrageous farce, *Amédée,* in which a corpse grows to amazing proportions before our eyes, is set in "an unpretentious dining-room, drawing-room, and office combined." While there is some trick in making a corpse grow in front of us, it is a familiar kind of stage sleight-of-hand, and one can easily imagine Sabbattini in the seventeenth century writing a chapter, "How to Make a Dead Body Appear to Grow to Monstrous Size." Ionesco's later play, *The Killer,* admittedly does call for in the first act for a familiar empty stage with all sense of decor conjured up by the lighting; he then cunningly contrasts this (defying all the rules of unity of style) with a heavily realistic second act. He has good reason for this contrast in the dramatic point he is trying to make; such manipulation shows that Ionesco is quite sophisticated about using the stage instrument, aware of its potentialities and willing to use the stage in any way that suits his purposes.

Pinter's scenes are invariably realistic rooms; Albee's *The American Dream* calls for an ordinary living room; even Arrabal's *The Automobile Graveyard,* though the setting is heavily symbolic, calls for a plainly recognizable automobile graveyard, well within the compass of any ordinary stage. (pp. 31-3)

Let us grant that the stage, in the most significant drama, is a metaphor of the world. What sort of world, then, does the stage of the Absurdists imply?

At one end of a continuum we encounter a metaphor which has occasional difficulty in distinguishing itself from reality, though usually for a conscious purpose. Pirandello (a kind of playwright of the Absurd, I suppose) delighted in the paradox of the stage itself; he enjoyed playing with the ideas of reality and illusion as they present themselves in the stage world of make-believe. His point in *Six Characters in Search of an Author* and *Tonight We Improvise* is that we cannot always tell for sure the difference between reality and illusion; life is perhaps all illusion, and all illusion is perhaps life. This familiar paradox, endlessly fascinating to Pirandello, does not attract the Absurdists. Illusion or reality, whatever it is we face is quite real enough as it is; the problem is not so much what it is as how to face it. Two Absurdists do touch on the illusion-reality question. In Genet's *The Maids,* for instance, Claire and Solange play an elaborate game of role-taking until at the climax Claire willingly drinks the poisoned tea while pretending to be Madame—somehow both aware and unaware of what she is doing. The make-believe quality is heightened if we take Genet's suggestion and have men play the women's roles. In *The Blacks,* the ritual is also a charade, with Negroes wearing white masks and acting out what turns out to be games within the stage frame. The edge of reality does occasionally become blurred, though there is little of the Pirandellian playfulness.

The point is carried to the extreme in Gelber's *The Connection,* in which the dramatist makes occasional efforts to get us to believe that the play is being improvised on the spot, that the actors are really junkies, and that things do not work out onstage at all in the way he planned them. The stage at times almost ceases to be a stage and becomes real life. The playwright later seems to abandon these devices, and he is well-advised in this, for the reality of the drama has nothing to do with the realism of its production. Fidelity to "the way things really are" is no indication that we are faced with theatrical truth—that is, truth in the theatre.

Since the drama of the Absurd is built in great part on situation rather than a linear sequence of action, it follows that the action is often restricted to a single location. Many of the plays are in one act, and even the longer ones such as *Rhinoceros, The Killer,* and *Ping Pong* (Adamov), while they may change the scene, do not much shift the perspective or alter the atmosphere. We remain always in the same rather static world, a world fairly constant, unified, and without levels of significance for the inhabitants. On the Shakespearean stage one could see an order before one's eyes from the subterranean passages of the devil up to the star-fretted canopy and the throne of God. One saw also a significant social range of characters from the rude mechanics up to the high majesty itself. Their places were set in the world before one, and their philosophies and attitudes reflected their given positions. In the Absurd drama, the characters are remarkably alike, regardless of their position in any worldly scheme. The bums in *Waiting for Godot* and *The Caretaker* are really not so different from the middle-class, solid citizens in *The Bald Soprano* and *One Way Pendulum.* One critic has complained that there is hardly a memorable character in the plays of the Absurd. As to the sameness of characters, those of Genet seem to stand at least a little apart. . . . In any event, the essential fact about all the characters in these works is not that they are enmeshed in their particular environment, whatever that may be, but that they are enmeshed in the absurdity of the human condition.

In *One Way Pendulum* and *The Bald Soprano* we can see a surface of familiar satire on the bourgeois mentality—but the satire does not remain comfortably on the surface, as it might in a more conventional comedy or thesis play. Particularly in *The Bald Soprano,* the clatter of futile clichés hits us not so much simply as an attack upon bourgeois mentality but rather as an indictment of language itself and of all human struggles to wring sense from words or inject sense into them, an exposition ultimately of the absurd horror of life itself.

It is interesting to see how often the extremely conventional bourgeois environment is taken for the setting. Any number of Ionesco's dramas start off with a comfortable picture of happy middle-class life into which some grotesquely comic horror or other inevitably intrudes or begins to emerge from the characters. Pinter and Simpson give us the familiar English living room—or the decaying remnants of it. Even in the plays of Beckett, the original startled reaction to the blasted heath or the "bare interior" gives way to the realization that the specific location is *our* world abstracted to its simplest form. Vladimir and Estragon happen to be on a country road, but they could as easily be in a bus station or a cheap rooming house. The stage is a place all right, but it is less a specific place than simply the *human* place. The world of the Absurd looks all too familiar. Even the brothel of *The Balcony* is not a brothel but a human place, not such a long way really from the rooms and places of more conventional experience. The Absurd is here, close at hand; the world before us on the stage is the room we live in or the place on which we are stranded waiting. In a poetic sense, the stage is the *living* room, the room we live in—at base the human place, where we all are.

Even the behavior in the living room or human place is all too familiar. In *Amédée,* for instance, there is that dreadful growing corpse with its attendant mushrooms sprouting up in a Paris apartment. Amédée and Madeleine take this rather calmly and try to deal with the extraordinary situation in precisely the way we might deal with a case of dry rot or a begonia that grows too fast. The comic device of the proper response to an insane stimulus is carried almost to the extreme, but we never lose sight of the fact that the response is proper. There is a familiar logic of behavior, the logic, no doubt, of Aristotle applied to a world in which strange and inexplicable mutations have taken place. In all the plays of the Absurd, the characters are firmly resolved to face up to the situation and deal with it as well as they can. Buried up to her neck, Winnie [in Beckett's *Happy Days*] never loses hope for long. She carries on. There is even a kind of bizarre but grave logic in the ritual of *The Blacks.* The people are totally involved; there is no detachment; they go about their jobs with a will—even in the face of perceived insanity and destruction. There is little defeatism in the world of the Absurd.

What kind of weird metaphor, then, does this add up to? . . . [The] stage of the Absurd is more illusionistic than conventional. The stage is, as in all profound drama, a microcosm of the world, but harking back to the best theatre of the past, the Absurdists have attempted to make their stage a universal metaphor—it stands directly for all the world. There is nothing beyond the stage; outside the door is the void; beyond our plot of heath, who knows what? But if the world has been reduced to a spot of ground or a grubby living room, it is our spot, our room;

the forces that exist outside it in the void threaten and must be dealt with, but they are mainly unknowable. The living room or space is presented in naturalistic terms, and thus we immediately recognize it. There is no obscurantism or deep abstraction, none of the misty romantic symbolism of Maeterlinck. Brothels, automobile graveyards, and middle-class flats are closer to our lives than any towering palace or enchanted wood. We are pushed face to face with the familiar world—but we are made to see the absurdity in it. The metaphor is a universal one, then: it is the world, all there is. And in this world we are alone. It makes little real difference if there are any social distinctions; the hierarchies of Shakespeare make no sense here. We are in the same boat together, and differences are insignificant. Even the two visitors from the outside, Goldberg and McCann, who come to brainwash and remove Stanley in *The Birthday Party,* have their private horrors and uncertainties. They have their job to do, but they do not really understand the situation any more than do the regular inhabitants of the room. Clowns and kings face equally the existential situation.

The living room or human space is both inhabitable (for the time being) and intolerable to those who recognize its absurdity. We must go away, but we don't go. We somehow or other ought to act, but if we act, our act is absurd. So we wait—and that isn't much better. It is a situation of unrelieved balance, tension, paradox, and, yes, absurdity. The future is as hopeless and nameless as the past and present. But despair is as absurd as hope. In the meanwhile we may struggle against the nameless horror, sometimes unaware of what we are doing, as in *The Bald Soprano,* and sometimes with glimmerings, as with the character of Bérenger in *The Killer* and *Rhinoceros.* The tramps waiting for Godot know the absurdity of their position; yet they cannot move. A little less aware are the junkies in *The Connection.* They at least know what they are waiting for and have therefore something concrete to live for, heroin. Because they think they can find some momentary satisfaction in life, they are more akin to the obtuse middle-class families in Ionesco than to the tramps of *Godot.* But at the same time, they see both the middle class and themselves as equally deluded; so they rest perhaps somewhere between the middle-class family and the tramps.

The final problem is that of the relationship of the audience to the stage metaphor. A metaphor is a link between two separate worlds which enables one world to be explored in terms of another. For all its universality, the metaphor of the Absurd, the living room or space, is akin more to the parlor metaphor of, for example, *Hedda Gabler* than to the ranging, kaleidoscopic images of *Peer Gynt.* It draws us to it easily by its familiarity either in setting or characters, then repels us when the nameless horror of absurdity appears, and what seemingly ought to have made sense now makes only nonsense—not the babbling nonsense of the non-objective dadaist but the meaningful nonsense of Ophelia, in which method is embedded in madness. Yet this world is often too horrible for us to be easily swept into it. If we do not achieve a Brechtian alienation effect, we are at least thrown back upon our own resources so that we cannot easily accept or reject but must *deal with* the experience: "The spectator is forced to make a creative effort of his own, an effort at interpretation and integration. The time has been made to appear out of joint; the audience of the Theatre of the Absurd is

being compelled to set it right or rather, by being made to see that the world has become absurd, in acknowledging that fact takes the first step in coming to terms with reality" [see Esslin excerpt above]. We are forced, dog-like, to stick our noses into our own mess and inhale the stench. Yet this goes far beyond the social theatre of muckraking. [Mordecai] Gorelik, in defining the theatre of revelation, said that the theatre must "see beyond the disharmonies of prosaic life into the world of eternal values." But the theatre of the Absurd sees that those very disharmonies of the prosaic are not necessarily the facade covering an inner truth but are themselves a part of the absurdity of existence, and in them are embedded inner as well as outer truths.

Even the supposedly familiar metaphors of the Absurdists can sometimes become maddeningly complex or maddeningly obscure. They appear familiar but lash us with their strangeness. This theatre, like a plague, "releases conflicts, disengages powers, liberates possibilities, and if these possibilities and these powers are dark, it is the fault not of the plague nor of the theatre, but of life" [Antonin Artaud, *The Theatre and Its Double*]. The conventions, these metaphors that release the dark powers, can be nearer to or farther from the surface of life. We have already said that the metaphors of the Absurd are more illusionistic than conventional. The stage is representational; there is little or no direct address to the audience and very little sense of immutable ritual. Things seem to be happening right now, as they perhaps ought on a stage. But the more we look at this familiar metaphor, the more we find our senses outrunning the illusion, which seems to lose itself in a greater convention without ceasing to lose its illusionistic quality. The metaphor is both conventional and illusionistic, which the best stage metaphors always are. This suggests a subtle use of the qualities of the stage to project a message that is both simple and complex: "The stage is a multi-dimensional medium; it allows the simultaneous use of visual elements, movement, light, and language. It is, therefore, particularly suited to the communication of complex images consisting of the contrapuntal interaction of all these elements" [Martin Esslin, *The Theatre of the Absurd*].

This complexity has correlates in the world of the dream, but plays of the Absurd are not at all dream plays. The situations in Ionesco, Beckett, and Pinter are not dream situations: they are not metaphors twice removed, that is removed first onto a stage and secondly into a dream. The plays present direct visions of life as it is in essence, and any dream-like quality they have is but an extension of the dream quality in life. Here again, Artaud has pointed the way: "The theatre will never find itself again—i.e. constitute a means of true illusion—except by furnishing the spectator with the truthful precipitates of dreams, in which his taste for crime, his erotic obsessions, his savagery, his chimeras, his utopian sense of life and matter, even his cannibalism, pour out, on a level not counterfeit and illusory, but interior." The key phrase here is "truthful precipitates of dreams," for this is precisely the kind of thing being attempted by the Absurdists. Life and dream blend into each other, and the old paradox of Pirandello is now developed beyond the Pirandellian game into an exploration of the very core and essence of human existence.

We meet absurdity in our daily lives whether we are profound artists or not. The absurdity of bureaucratic institutions in which rule triumphs over sense plagues us daily; we muddle along in the absurdity of the ritual games of social behavior; and above all we live in a world in which politics and absurdity have become almost synonymous. We have gained the means to destroy ourselves and our civilization. Our politicians tell us with straight faces that the only means of saving ourselves is to prepare to destroy ourselves. That they can keep straight faces is perhaps the ultimate absurdity of all. Confronted with such absurdity we can fight back with the inadequate means of a private citizen; we can dig our hole and crawl in; we can euphorically ignore the whole business; or we can laugh the mocking laugh of the Absurd. Laughter will not, of course, change the situation objectively; and the theatre of the Absurd is therefore not a didactic theatre, not a tribunal. It is, instead, a theatre of revelation. Gorelik was indeed correct in ending his study with such a theatre; he could not of course see what the nature of this revelation would be. But by plunging back into the most fundamental questions of all, the theatre of the Absurd is making an attempt to formulate a new aesthetic in terms of ultimate confrontation with reality. This aesthetic is by no means antithetical to that of the Brechtian theatre—which is the only other really significant theatre of our time. On the contrary, the Brechtian approach is simply another attack, more worldly and perhaps more practical, on the problem of absurdity. It is absurdity seen from mainly the social and economic points of view, and it attempts not only to present clear visions but to suggest avenues of action. In Brecht's own hand, this theatre is limited by its materialistic and Marxist bias, but the Brechtian theatre as an idea is capable of being used by men of other persuasions, even if it has not often been.

The theatre of the Absurd goes both farther and not so far. It goes farther in that it looks beyond the social and economic and at the naked face of absurdity itself. Yet it has not up to now really suggested any proper solution beyond espousal of resignation or at least persistence. The most hopeful of the new plays is *Rhinoceros* or perhaps even *Waiting for Godot.* In both plays the final note is one of persistence, of enduring in the face of unendurable situations. The later plays of Beckett put characters into less and less maneuverable situations until, in *Happy Days,* Winnie has only her head free. And what a witless head it is! It may be that the head will be covered up and that will be all—for drama as well as anything else. But as long as heads are uncovered there will be plays, and the extremities of mankind will still excite in playwrights the will to create. Ionesco is more hopeful, to be sure, and Pinter, while seemingly as desperate as Beckett, is working out his solutions in terms which suspend both hope and despair for a rather terrifying astonishment. These dramatists are not likely to fill us with cheer, but the battle still goes on somehow, and the war is not yet quite over.

In terms of theatre, the Absurdists have been using the stage instrument without much concern for the theorists. Ionesco is perhaps the most sophisticated of these writers with his delightful use of old farce techniques, but neither he nor the others seem to have read the fiery stage revolutionaries of the past half-century or given them much thought. They have been concerned not with thrusting the actor into the auditorium but with thrusting the play into the hearts and minds of the audience. Their main stage

metaphor is a simple one, their techniques straightforward, their effects highly provocative. They have been criticized for their attacks on language as if their contributions were primarily the development of non-verbal stage techniques. Actually, the non-verbal techniques they use are not new at all, and the attacks on language but a way of clearing out dead wood to reveal the truths which often lie behind words. They have launched a satirical attack not only on clichés but on a life that allows us to become as encumbered with language as the new tenant is with furniture. The theatre of the Absurd is not primarily non-verbal. Language is employed along with many other tools; in fact in the living room or human place of the Absurdists the language is not only superficially proper but also goes far beyond naturalistic tape-recorder dialogue to suggest a deeper reality in the manner of poetic stage language. In any case, the theatre will not be saved or even much improved by a return to poetic eloquence. What is more important is a presentation of the deepest truths with the power to penetrate an audience.

At this point in the game we must admire the Absurdists for their imaginative use of a new metaphor, for their determination to be cruel and face up squarely to the metaphysical implications of scientific thought, and for their attempt to create Artaud's "passionate equation between Man, Society, Nature and Objects." Their theatre is an attempt to search out precisely this equation between man and the world. To do this they have stripped down the stage metaphor to essentials and have attempted to place man squarely in his existential position at the center. This is surely a partial answer to the familiar complaint: "The actor no longer dominates the stage, because man is no longer seen as the measure of all things and the center of his universe" [Lee Simonson, *The Stage Is Set*]. In a sense, the characters in the Absurd have a central position, and if they do not exactly "dominate" the stage, they at least fill it up.

The metaphor of the living room or human space works on its own terms, but there is no denying that in practice it sometimes seems a bit limiting. There is eventually an end to satire; likewise there are perhaps limits to the possibilities of the existential man in his small plot of ground— at least in theatrical terms. Although the flexibility, the precision, and the intensity the Absurdists have been able to achieve are to be admired, one occasionally feels the need for a larger framework, for the vastness of Brecht's almost cinematic theatre. There is probably nothing inherent in the drama of the Absurd that makes the narrow perspective mandatory or the representational mode obligatory. Although the Absurdists have worked out a magnificent and profound style of theatre for themselves, there is no reason to think they should forever be bound by it. After *Happy Days,* there is hardly anywhere to go except toward silence or a more fluid stage. Genet seems to be exploring such new directions in *The Blacks,* albeit in his unique and perhaps inimitable style; one hopes he will continue such explorations and that other Absurdists will reach out as well. However, the use of the stage instrument and even the development of stage metaphors are secondary to the higher aim of reaching an audience with a significant vision. Gorelik's theatre of revelation has been partly realized in the theatre of the Absurd if for no other reason than that the Absurdists have looked hard at the profoundest realities, have found a means of communication, have communicated with vigor, and continue to work out that "passionate equation" which must be the heart of any significant theatre. (pp. 34-43)

Roderick Robertson, "A Theatre for the Absurd: The Passionate Equation," in Drama Survey, *Vol. 2, No. 1, June, 1962, pp. 24-43.*

Walter Kerr

[*Kerr is an American dramatist, director, and critic who won a Pulitzer Prize for drama criticism in 1978. A long-time drama critic for the* New York Times, *as well as the author of several book-length studies of modern drama, he has been one of the most important and influential figures in the American theater since the 1950s. In the following excerpt, Kerr denigrates playwrights associated with the Theater of the Absurd, focusing on what he considers the inferior use of ambiguity in their works compared with the way ambiguity is used by playwrights of traditional theater.*]

Oddly enough, ambiguity is a quality that has often been admired in the theater. It is not a quality anyone can let alone, even when he professes to admire it: confronted with it, the most understanding scholar and the least subtle member of the audience will instantly begin to wrestle with it in an effort to pull apart its superimposed uncertainties and reduce them to simple, separated propositions. The character of Hamlet, we say, is ambiguous. Is Hamlet a man of action or a man incapable of action? More than three hundred years of grappling have not resolved the issue; neither have they quieted the demon that keeps urging us to try to resolve it. The implications of *King Lear* are ambiguous: whose fault is it that Lear's children treat him as they do? Alceste, Molière's misanthrope, is ambiguous: in demanding that society behave more honorably than it does, is he right, is he ridiculous, or is he both right and ridiculous? Even the forthright Antigone, useful as she may have proved in our own time as a symbol of private conscience versus the totalitarian state, is not so uncompromisingly defined in her Greek beginnings; as Sophocles drew her, doesn't a shadow of intractable personal pride fall across, and faintly corrupt, her defiance of Creon, and isn't Creon's position in some degree defensible? We do probe as though it were essential to us to know the answers.

Yet even as we probe, and cannot stop probing, we recognize that the very mystery that bedevils us, and has so far defeated us, is in some measure responsible for the greatness of the play. We grasp what T. S. Eliot is saying when he suggests that Shakespeare was never able to discover an "objective correlative" for the emotions he felt about the Hamlet he was drawing, and we find the coined phrase useful to us in our other literary work. But insofar as Mr. Eliot's analysis suggests that *Hamlet* is, as a consequence, something less than a fully realized play, we will have none of his reasoning. We have an experience of *Hamlet* that tells us it is fully realized; even as we return to our habit of gnawing at the text to see whether or not we can dispel its apparent inconsistencies, we know ourselves to be fully satisfied. It is curious that so many of the plays we elevate to the very highest rank should have this eternal elusiveness about them, and more curious still that recognized masterpieces which speak their minds more openly—as *Macbeth* does, as *Tartuffe* does—should seem, in their clarity, less substantial. Clarity is, after all, a virtue. How do we dare, then, cling so passionately to, and reserve our deepest homage for, these several-faced conundrums from which an ultimate clarity is presumably absent?

We dare for several reasons, no doubt. One is that we sense an ultimate clarity in them, an intuited clarity of the core, that untouchable center—infinitesimal and red-hot—which sends its rays outward in intangible wave lengths to lave, with the same slant-of-light, a half-dozen surfaces which in themselves appear irreconcilable. This is a great deal like saying we "know" an intimate friend whose oddities of behavior baffle everyone else; our intimacy, so existential as to constitute a breathing in and out together, has enabled us to give assent to what we could not possibly have named. Another reason is that plays which can be known only as friends are known—by radar, through confusion compounded—seem to us closer to the conditions of life. Here we discover in the concrete what we could never have defined in the abstract; we stand face to face with a multidimensional reality across which a complex of veils is constantly playing, throwing now this side and now that into surprising relief. The dance of veils, with its illuminating relief work, implies a solid behind it; the combined sensations of evanescence and solidity correspond nicely to the yes-and-no, now-you-see-it-and-now-you-don't lives we lead. The degree to which a play is ambiguous, but knowable in and through its ambiguity, is often the measure of our affection and respect for it.

In what sense is this also true, or should it be true, of that most deliberately ambiguous of all theaters, the avant-garde form that has come to be called the Theater of the Absurd? Certainly the plays of Samuel Beckett, Eugene Ionesco, Harold Pinter, N. F. Simpson, and Arrabal have not at once capitalized upon our instinctive admiration for the indeterminate, though satisfying, image. Mr. Pinter's *The Caretaker* was given an impeccable production on Broadway, not off, and met with an enthusiasm in the press that ought to have guaranteed it substantial audiences for a lengthy run. The production did not find those audiences; the preinterested attended for a few moderately lively weeks, though never in sufficient numbers to fill the theater to capacity, and the houses dwindled thereafter as rapidly as though the work had been received as a near-failure. Such examples of the form as have achieved "long" runs—Jean Genet's *The Balcony,* and the double bill of Samuel Beckett's *Krapp's Last Tape* and Edward Albee's *The Zoo Story*—have generally done so in off-Broadway playhouses which restrict their capacities to 299 seats. Nor can the relative reluctance of audiences to expose themselves to a new ambiguity be attributed to the strangeness of being asked to accept a duality of meanings. *Hamlet* and *Antigone* were instantly successful; whatever was ambiguous about them did not operate as a barrier.

At the same time, and just as certainly, the form cannot be dismissed as a mere temporary aberration, irrelevant to the atmosphere in which audiences as well as playwrights live: it has already demonstrated too much fecundity for that. In a few years—ten at the most—it has not only captured the loyalty of talented writers during their most productive time of life, it has leapfrogged its way from country to country and from continent to continent so energetically as to suggest that a degree of universality is in it. It is apparently not to be shaken off as easily as German expressionism was shaken off, or as the theatrical explorations of an e. e. cummings were shaken off, forty years ago. It is a theater of ambiguity with the power to proliferate, though not with the power to compel the large-scale assent that has sometimes welcomed a degree of obscurity in the past. Allowing for the fact that genius commands where talent moves tentatively, and acknowledging the fact that Beckett makes no claim to be Sophocles, is there nevertheless some essential difference between the uncertainties we grant *The Misanthrope* and the uncertainties we resist in *The Caretaker*?

The Theater of the Absurd, which is likely to retain that generic label now that Martin Esslin has effectively formalized it in the first full-length study anyone has made of a fairly diversified school of playmaking, is so thoroughly soaked in ambiguity as to seem, upon acquaintance, composed of nothing else. The mathematical formulas upon which the universe may be thought to rest, numbers themselves, are ambiguous in Ionesco's *The Lesson*:

> ". . . Here are three matches. And here is another one, that makes four. Now watch carefully—we have four matches. I take one away, now how many are left?"
>
> "Five. If three and one make four, four and one make five."

The words with which we describe to one another our knowledge of the universe are ambiguous in nearly all such plays, as they are in this Joyce-inspired passage from Beckett's *Waiting for Godot*:

> ". . . the practise of sports such as tennis football running cycling swimming flying floating riding gliding conating camogie skating tennis of all kinds dying flying sports of all sorts autumn summer winter winter tennis of all kinds hockey of all sorts penicillin and succedanea in a word I resume . . ."

Whenever we wish to use words as tools of reason, as soldiers in a syllogism designed to prove one or another proposition about the universe, the proof also becomes ambiguous. Arrabal's *The Automobile Graveyard*:

> "What a brain! And you know how to prove things, like the big shots?"
>
> "Yeah, I have a special method for that. Ask me to prove something for you, something real hard."
>
> "All right, prove me that giraffes go up in elevators."
>
> "Let's see. Giraffes go up in elevators . . . because they go up in elevators."
>
> "God, that was great! . . . Suppose I asked you to prove giraffes *don't* go up in elevators."
>
> "That's easy. I just prove the same thing, but the other way around."

If the insubstantiality of digits, words, syntax, and logic tend to make all communication between people at the very least ambiguous, people are ambiguous as well. An old couple, married or not married, childless or parents of a son, speak constantly at cross-purposes in Ionesco's *The Chairs*:

> " . . . Where is my mamma? I don't have a mamma anymore."
>
> "I am your wife, I'm the one who is your mamma now."
>
> "That's not true, I'm an orphan, hi, hi."
>
> "My pet, my orphan, dworfan, worfan, morphan, orphan . . . We had one son . . . he's gone away . . . he was seven years old, the age of reason, I called after him: 'My son, my child, my son, my child.' . . . He didn't even look back . . ."
>
> "Alas, no . . . no, we've never had a child. . . . I'd hoped for a son . . ."

Critical actions performed by the characters may mean one thing or another. The climax of Beckett's *Happy Days* is reached when a husband, in frock coat and top hat, crawls on hands and knees to the foot of a mound of sand in which his wife is buried to her neck. A revolver is "conspicuous to her right on mound." With painful effort, the husband attempts to claw his way up the mound. "Oh I say, this is terrific!" cries the wife, certain he is coming to offer her one last kiss. During a pause, doubt crosses her mind. "Is it me you're after, Willie . . . or is it something else?" She does not look at the revolver; Willie does not reach the top of the mound; the play ends without our knowing whether Willie wished to kill himself or kiss his wife (or kill his wife).

The new play of ambiguity is apt to take place in "A bare interior" or on a stage possessing "No decor" during "A late evening in the future." The printed instructions to the stage director may be optional: "The clock strikes as much as it likes." There is ambiguity before the curtain has gone up, ambiguity in rehearsal: "He either kisses or does not kiss Mrs. Smith."

Now the open meanings, the choices among several or many possible meanings, we are cataloguing here are obviously different from the fluid ambiguities of character and narrative implication we so highly prize in certain plays of the past. At first sight the difference may seem a mere matter of quantity. Hamlet possesses a few ambiguities that are titillating in a world composed mainly of plain statement; here *everything* is unnamed, down to the last detail of stage management, and nothing is at any time defined, spelled out, clothed, made plain.

Curiously this is not so. While vast portions of the familiar world are being steadily atomized in the avant-garde play, and while the familiar tools that help us deal with it are being cumulatively mocked, certain aspects of our residence in the universe are being spelled out in such bold, crude lettering, are being cast in concrete in such a dense and literal way, as to make the dramatic statement seem close to simple-minded. For instance, environment may generally be left vague. But the effect which a given playwright thinks environment may have on us is not left vague at all. It is bill-posted. Suppose it is a playwright's intention to show us that, no matter how free the human animal thinks it is, the human animal is irretrievably earth-bound. Is there any ambiguity, or even any slight subtlety, in presenting us with a woman choked in sand up to the neck? It would be difficult to conceive a less elusive or more literal illustration of thought. Suppose one wishes to dwell upon the ruthless discard into which the aged or maimed are thrown. In *Endgame,* Beckett deposits an elderly couple in ash bins, downstage left. In *La Parodie,* Arthur Adamov causes street cleaners to sweep one of his principal figures, who has been run over, into the garbage. Plainness could not speak better for itself. Suppose a dramatist wishes to convey to us the notion that our once-efficient world has broken down. When he composes his stage of a disconnected stove, a frame without a picture in it, a rusty lawn mower, a collection of empty suitcases, a rolled-up rug, yesterday's yellowed newspapers, a toaster with a broken plug, and then covers the litter over with a noisily leaking roof—as Pinter has done in *The Caretaker*—he is leaving very, very little to chance.

Ironically, there is far less ambiguity—and, indeed, far less complexity—in each of these illustrations than there would have been if identical attitudes had been incorporated into much more conventional plays. It is possible to suggest that a woman is earth-bound even while she is moving rapidly and gracefully about an expansive living room; as it is possible to imply that the elderly are being discarded even when they are being coddled or that the world is showing a fissure although the kitchen sink is functioning. We should not see the "truth" as readily, of course; we should have to dig beneath the surface for what is not at all obvious; catching a hint of the interior content, we should have to be willing to continue to look at the play on two levels, although it is generally the Theater of the Absurd that asks for attention at two levels; from the dramatist's point of view, the play of concealed comment, of secret texture contradicted by surface texture, is much harder to bring off—its very activity is, in its nature and in the manner of nature, so ambiguous. By contrast, some aspects of avant-garde drama seem rigidly fixed, not fluid but frozen.

There are other things that might lead one to question the degree of ambiguity actually present in what is sometimes called antidrama. The length of the plays is one of them, the recurrence of themes another. Logically speaking, whatever is truly ambiguous ought to require a longer time for its development than whatever is truly plain. Either "yes" or "no" can be said more rapidly than "yes and no." The exploration of shifting colorations, of faces looked at now in this perspective and now in that, of meanings so chameleon-like that they can only be identified after they have been seen against every kind of foliage, should take longer to record than a snapshot does. Yet it is the avant-garde play that most often seems a snapshot. Some examples of the genre take as little as eight minutes to play. Though Beckett, Ionesco, Pinter, and Genet have all written full-length plays, only those of Genet seem to demand the running time allotted to a conventional evening in the theater. Most of the work of most practitioners of the Theater of the Absurd is either in the one-act form or otherwise marked by brevity; playwrights are notably slow, in some cases confessedly reluctant, to move beyond miniaturism. Urged on, they have developed a somewhat standard defense. "What *is* a full-length play?" becomes the riposte. "A play has achieved its full length when it has said what it has to say," even if it has said what it has to say in twenty or twenty-four minutes. Some of this clinging to the short form may be due to the newness of the genre and to an understandable fear that experimentation, in a too rapid advance, may betray itself by borrowing from conventional sources; some of it, though proba-

bly not much of it, may be due to a conviction that audiences are not yet supple enough to be able to endure prolonged exposure to persistent ambiguity.

What the tendency toward brevity cannot help but suggest, however, is that the premise upon which the play rests possesses neither the complexity nor the many-sidedness requiring an extended examination under a variety of lights and shadows. Prolonged investigation of the material, instead of thickening its substance by discovering fresh layers, would apparently lead only to dangerous repetition. (Thus Albee's longish *American Dream,* interesting as it is, is not more interesting than the very short *The Sandbox,* which it resembles; it runs the perfectly obvious risk of belaboring a theme that has earlier been delicately, and adequately, intimated.) Somehow the new ambiguity is an ambiguity that leaves relatively little room for maneuver; somewhere inside it is a knot that resists being unraveled.

Equally strange in a form professedly devoted to an infinity of meanings is the prevalence of a handful of repeated themes. The difficulty, or the impossibility, of communication between people is demonstrated so often—in *The Zoo Story,* in *The Caretaker,* in nearly any play by Ionesco—as to become a badge of the genre. The encrusting effect of conformity, of habitual response in thought and behavior, of automaton-like devotion to false ideals, is not the special insight of *Rhinoceros* and *The Apple;* it appears so frequently that it constitutes, in itself, a kind of conformity.

Closely related to the repeated theme of encrustation is the equally repeated theme of loss of identity. People make so many conventional gestures that they forget, or never have time to discover, what a truly personal gesture might be: "You don't know who you are until you're dead." And when the interior emptiness that is loss of identity is coupled with the exterior pressure of encrustation—when our habits and the universe harden about us—we find ourselves in the "zero" world that Samuel Beckett creates again and again (as do his imitators). Imprisonment in a chair, in a room, in a sandbank becomes the familiar point of departure; the act of waiting, for nothing that ever arrives or for something that proves not to have been worth waiting for when it does arrive, becomes the familiar line of tension; either gibberish or a view of the void becomes the not unexpected summation of the essentially static situation. Having seen Beckett's *Endgame,* and having watched an old man climb to a window, put a telescope to his eye, and report that he sees "Nothing . . . nothing," one is entirely prepared to follow a young man as he goes to a window, puts a telescope to his eye, and reports that "there's nothing out there to see" in the youthful Arthur L. Kopit's *Oh Dad, Poor Dad, Mamma's Hung You in the Closet and I'm Feelin' So Sad.* Echoes scamper from play to play, and sometimes coalesce to make a single play a kind of countinghouse of themes. But when one has counted off the problem of communication, the problem of encrustation, the problem of identity, and the problem of the surrounding void, one is surprised to discover he has more than five fingers left over. There are obvious reasons why these should be special themes for our time: what is puzzling is that there should be so few of them in a theater that has carefully arranged itself for a maximum flexibility, for an endless openness to overtone.

Perhaps it is the combination of these last two odd qualities—shortness of form and familiarity of point—that creates a further impression of essential literalness rather than far-ranging ambiguity in much of the work of the avant-garde. The Theater of the Absurd is generally theater in a state of shock; it also means, by its methods, to shock those who attend it. But there are occasions when its shock is not the bewilderment of the adult confronted by too much that is eluding him but the shock of a child who has just now noticed the obvious and is shrilly calling it to our attention in brief, agitated, reiterated rhythms. For example, the excited insistence that words lack absolute meaning takes on, after a while, just such a tantrum tone. When one is first exposed to a play in which the words slip and slide into one another, blurring their identities until they begin to lose touch with any possible referents, the verbal sleight-of-hand may provoke mild amusement. When one has been exposed to dozens of such plays, and heard the shocked discovery announced dozens of times in unabated wide-eyed clamor, a reaction may set in. "Yes, yes, of course," one is apt to respond, "it is true that words are arbitrary and artificial constructs, mere mechanical agreements, which do not in any absolute sense either contain or describe their referents. They are at best conventional, and, lacking an unbreakable link with the realities they are meant to signify, they are always unstable. But hasn't everyone always known that, and why so much fuss just now?" If the arbitrariness and instability of words had not always been perfectly evident, no one would ever have been tempted to make a pun. A pun, of course, is mankind's playful admission that the words he makes use of are notoriously slippery. It is doubtful, indeed, that without this awareness anyone could have conceived the possibility called poetry. For poetry makes its whole effect out of the absence of an absolute value in words: if the word "fire" signified only and absolutely the specific chemical activity of oxidation, Yeats could not so much as write "a fire was in my head." Puns and poetry are discoveries of the dawn, not of late last night, and they remind us that what many new plays trumpet in headlines is not in any real sense news.

As we begin to notice that the proposition is not altogether novel, we notice something else: the statement of the proposition is not really ambiguous. If a playwright were to write a sentence that seemed to mean one intelligible thing and actually meant another, *that* would be ambiguous. But if he writes an unintelligible sentence in order to say that words are unintelligible, he is being utterly straightforward. The line "such caca, such caca, such caca, such caca, such caca, such caca, such caca, such caca, such caca" does not give us a choice of meanings. It confines us to the single, simple, unsupple assertion that there is no meaning.

Thus, though we may feel the world slipping from beneath our feet as we first make acquaintance with the Theater of the Absurd, not everything in the form is fluid. What is being said and done is often being said and done absolutely: a woman is absolutely earth-bound (we are given no opportunity to believe otherwise), words are absolutely without meaningful content (we are not led from an illusion of content to a discovery of vacuousness but are handed the vacuousness right off). What is said and done absolutely can, as a rule, be said and done quickly: plays tend

to be short. And because absolute assertion tends to close in on itself, instead of putting out tentacles toward possible alternatives, it does not tend to mate with other subject matter but to repeat itself: a few propositions, close to geometrical postulates, are repeated from play to play.

What sort of theater is this that it should, in spite of what we feel to be intangible about it, insist upon a fixity, a precision that is almost bald, at certain of its extremities? It is, in essence, a philosopher's theater, rather than a poet's, for it is the philosopher who needs to make as rigid as possible the external terms in which he clothes his thought. Because the philosopher's thought is insubstantial—in the sense that it is an immaterial idea darting this way and that in his head—he is under great pressure to freeze the formulas in which he attempts to record his thought as absolutely, and as unambiguously, as possible. Each term in his hypothesis must mean one thing and no other; the center of his syllogism dare not be undistributed; he does not wish to be guilty of "loose thought." The philosopher deals in defined, and hence hardened, concepts.

The poet, historically, does not work in this way. He begins not with an immaterial concept but with a material fragment of nature, with something embodied in a ready-made musculature of its own. He starts with something concrete, however mysterious its inner sources of energy may be to him. Because it is concrete and has its own sources of energy he is able to throw over it a loose-fitting robe, a garment that partially conceals and partially reveals. The looseness will suggest something of the form beneath it; but it will not constrict it, not bind it, not keep it from moving under its own laws and displaying itself in its very freedom. (pp. 189-201)

Molière, the poet, keeps his character elusive at the surface: we watch Alceste behave now this way, now that, most contrarily. But the tension of his surface contrariness leads us to his identity. By the time he leaves us, we know that we know him; we know that the man moving away from us down the loneliest of roads, hurling imprecations over his shoulder as he abandons us forever, is a real man. The movement has been circuitous, but its path has been determined by a center. The antidramatist, philosophical precisionist that he is, restricts his terms at the surface as firmly as Beckett restricts his heroine to a home in the sand, or as Ionesco restricts his hero who does not become a rhinoceros (there is no choice here; the last man on earth yearns to become a rhinoceros and *cannot*). But as we mine the explicit surface to see where the mother lode is, we do not come closer to a subterranean reality, we become more and more aware that there may not be one. The philosopher has carved his road markers absolutely and then, in a coquettish gesture that may have been born of irresponsible prankishness and may have been born of real pain, refused to say what they mark the way to. There is, or is not, a reality at the end of the road. (p. 211)

Walter Kerr, "Antiform: The Ambiguity of the Theater of the Absurd," in his The Theater in Spite of Itself, *Simon and Schuster, 1963, pp. 189-211.*

PREDECESSORS OF THE THEATER OF THE ABSURD

Manuel L. Grossman

[*Grossman is an American critic and educator. In the following excerpt, he focuses on the influence of Alfred Jarry on the Theater of the Absurd.*]

During the last fifteen years the advent of the theatre of the absurd has brought Alfred Jarry into prominence. Various contemporary critics have noted his importance. Martin Esslin in his book *The Theatre of the Absurd* states that " . . . Jarry left an oeuvre that has been exerting a growing influence ever since he died and that still continues to increase." Esslin goes on to say that *Ubu Roi*, "a play that had only two performances in its first run and evoked a torrent of abuse, appears in the light of subsequent developments as a landmark and a forerunner." Leonard Pronko, an authority on French experimental theatre, tries to be even more specific. He draws a clear parallel between Jarry and the theatre of the absurd. " . . . the *Ubu* plays point straight forward to the works of today's avant-garde in France, and particularly to the theater of Ionesco. . . . The apprehensive laughter which Ubu elicits is the same laughter which explodes today in the theaters where *Waiting for Godot* and *The Lesson* are performed."

Still another authority George Wellwarth, author of *The Theater of Protest and Paradox,* underscores this view of Alfred Jarry as the forerunner of the new form. "The theatre of the absurd began, I believe, abruptly and suddenly on the evening of December 10, 1896 with the first performance of Alfred Jarry's *Ubu Roi.*"

Although critics have pointed to the significance of Alfred Jarry in the development of the theatre of the absurd, they have not provided a detailed account of the relationship between Jarry's ideas and the tenets of the newer form. This study, by concentrating on Jarry's philosophy of pataphysics and his attempts to break down the distinction between tragedy and comedy, examines two important aspects of this relationship.

According to Martin Esslin, the man who first coined the phrase, the theatre of the absurd is based upon a highly specialized definition of the word "absurd."

> Absurd originally means "out of harmony," in a musical context. Hence its dictionary definition: "out of harmony with reason or propriety; incongruous, unreasonable, illogical." In common usage in the English-speaking world, "absurd" may simply mean "ridiculous." But this is not the sense in which it is used when we speak of the Theatre of the Absurd. In an essay on Kafka, Ionesco defined his understanding of the term as follows: "Absurd is that which is devoid of purpose . . . cut off from his religious, metaphysical, and transcendental roots, man is lost; all his actions become senseless, absurd, useless."

Esslin distinguishes between dramatists such as Anouilh, Giraudoux, Salacrou, Sartre, and Camus and those of the absurd theatre. Although these playwrights also express "the senselessness of life," they do so in such a way as to "present their sense of the irrationality of the human condition in the form of highly lucid and logically constructed reasoning. . . ." With the absurdists it is an entirely different story. "The Theatre of the Absurd strives to express its sense of the senselessness of the human condition and the inadequacy of the rational approach by the open abandonment of rational devices and discursive thought . . . it merely *presents* it in being—that is, in terms of concrete stage images of the absurdity of existence."

Esslin's comments convey something of the sense of kinship which exists between the world created by Jarry's theatre and the world of the absurdists. The idea of "concrete stage images of the absurdity of existence" is reminiscent of Jarry's theatre. This is particularly true in the case of the *Ubu* cycle which contains such elements as a mass slaughter of the so-called pillars of society (*Ubu Roi*), a scientist who treats his instruments as if they were living beings (*Ubu cocu*), a disobedience drill in which the soldier who is least obedient to orders is given the most praise, and a dictator who when finally brought to trial gloriously confesses to all of his bloody crimes (*Ubu enchaîné*). Jarry may have himself thrown down the banner which the absurdists chose to follow when he stated that "relating comprehensible things only serves to deaden the spirit and falsify the memory, whereas the absurd exercises the spirit and makes the memory work."

Moreover, Jarry's philosophy of pataphysics served to underscore many of the principles of absurdity. The tenets of pataphysics were first advanced in the *Gestes et opinions du Docteur Faustroll, pataphysician,* a novel which was published after Jarry's death in 1911. As "the science of the particular," pataphysics questions some of the premises of the scientific method.

> Pataphysics . . . will examine the laws which govern exceptions, and will explain the universe supplementary to this one; or, less ambitiously, will describe a universe which can be—and should be—envisioned in the place of the traditional one, since the laws which are supposed to have been discovered in the traditional universe are also correlations of exceptions, albeit more frequent ones, but in any case accidental data which, reduced to the status of unexceptional exceptions, possess no longer even the virtue of originality.

The definition of pataphysics, as Jarry expressed it, is based on the idea of "imaginary solutions." "DEFINITION. *Pataphysics is the science of imaginary solutions which symbolically attributes the properties of objects, described by their virtuality, to their lineaments.*" In his essay "What is Pataphysics?" Roger Shattuck offers a detailed explanation of the concept of "imaginary solutions."

> In the realm of the particular, every event arises from an infinite number of causes. All solutions, therefore, to particular problems, all attributions of cause and effect, are based on arbitrary choice, another term for scientific imagination. Gravity as curvature of space or as electro-magnetic attraction—does it make any difference which solution we accept? Understanding either of them entails a large exercise of scientific imagination. Science must elect the solution that fits the facts—travel of light or fall of an apple.

Richard Coe connected pataphysics with the idea underlying the philosophy of the absurd. "For Pataphysics," claimed Coe, "all things are equal. The 'scientific' and the 'nonsensical' weigh alike in the scale of eternity, since both are arbitrary, both are absurd." "Above all," he continues, "Pataphysics incarnates, through its very absurdity, the practical philosophy of the absurd." After defining pataphysics, Martin Esslin concurs as to its instrumental role in the development of the absurdist philosophy.

> In effect, [pataphysics is] the definition of a subjectivist and expressionist approach that exactly anticipates the tendency of the Theatre of the Absurd to express psychological states by objectifying them on the stage. And so Jarry . . . must be regarded as one of the originators of the concepts on which a good deal of contemporary art, and not only in [*sic*] literature and the theatre is based.

Perhaps even more revealing, the world created in Eugene Ionesco's plays closely parallels Jarry's concept of pataphysics. Jacques Guicharnaud, the author of *Modern French Theatre,* has pointed out many of the similarities.

> The revolutionary aspect of his plays [Ionesco's], denying the traditional flow of action and traditional concept of characters, plus the often incoherent or disconnected appearance that results makes them seem like parodies of the real world. Here fantasy is not a door opened onto a beyond; it is the source of a farcical universe parallel to traditional reality.

Guicharnaud used the very language of Jarry's pataphysics to describe Ionesco's theatre. "Ionesco creates a universe parallel to ours which, presented with the greatest objectivity and in terms of realism, enjoys the same right to exist as our world."

Ionesco's personal life has also reinforced his connection with Jarry. He has been a member of the erstwhile College of Pataphysics. In this capacity he recently gave a talk on a B.B.C. program in which he examined "The Pataphysics of the Theatre." He began this curious talk with a characteristically Jarryesque line, "Reality is the only unreality."

Another way in which Jarry's theatre may have anticipated the theatre of the absurd was in its tendency to break down the distinction between comedy and tragedy. According to Robert W. Corrigan, editor of *Comedy: Meaning and Form,* this tendency has become increasingly dominant among contemporary exponents of the theatre of the absurd.

> We see it in the plays of such different writers as Beckett, Ionesco, Pinter, and Albee, all of whom use what were once considered comic techniques to serve serious aims. It is a view of life and drama which employs the comic to make its point, a point that is comic only in the sense that Baudelaire found life comic. In the work of all these playwrights the lines of the comic mask have become those of the tragic; in them we find that the relationship of means to ends is a paradox. Whereas in the comedy of earlier times, comic means were used to comic ends, in the modern theatre comic means are employed to serious ends.

Although *Ubu Roi* was presented in 1896 as a "comedie dramatique," Jarry was particularly disturbed when he realized that the audience had interpreted it strictly as a comedy. After the performance, he lectured the audience who had found *Ubu Roi* a droll play. He proposed that the masks alone should have been enough of an indication that this was a comedy only in the same sense that the "macabre English clown or the dance of death" is a comedy. He went on to mock those who found Père Ubu's dialogue humorous. According to Jarry, Père Ubu's vicious remarks should not have been interpreted as "des mots d'esprit" ["witticisms"], as various "ubucules" had interpreted them, but rather as "stupid phrases" which justifiably evoked the retorts "Quel sot homme! . . . quel triste imbecile" ["What a stupid man! . . . What a pathetic imbecile"] and other suitable epithets from Mére Ubu.

Moreover, Jarry informed the audience that he and Lugné-Poe, the director of the production, had at first seriously considered performing *Ubu Roi* "en tragique" ["as a tragedy"]. This decision had been made when both the playwright and the director had assumed that Lugné-Poe would play the part of Ubu. When Firmin Gémier, an actor with the Comédie Française, consented to do the role, the original conception of the character was modified.

In a recent book entitled *La Comédie,* Pierre Voltz sums up the form of comedy which is expressed in Jarry's theatre. Referring to it as the "comedy of the absurd," he proposes that this type of comedy arises from the absurdity of Ubu's behavior, which is "cruelly and irrefutably logical" while at the same time the actions of a purely instinctual being. It is a variation on this type of comedy which the exponents of the theatre of the absurd have perfected. This is particularly true of Eugene Ionesco and Samuel Beckett, the two principal spokesmen of the movement.

Ionesco and Beckett, like Jarry before them, have attempted to evoke an atmosphere of the absurd through the comic techniques of the popular theatre. Although Beckett explores the images of the circus and the music hall, and Ionesco is more preoccupied with the conventions of the Punch and Judy theatre, both playwrights, following Jarry's lead, make use of the "comedy of the absurd." In pointing out the basic distinction between Beckett and Ionesco, Ruby Cohn, in her book *Samuel Beckett: The Comic Gamut,* made clear the debt that both owe to Jarry and his flamboyant disciple Antonin Artaud. "Although Beckett and Ionesco both have learned from Artaud and Jarry to express serious theatrical concerns in spectacular terms, it is Beckett for whom theater is the more immediate metaphor of the world. The worn-out acts of vaudeville and the thread-bare devices of drama emphasize our presence at a spectacle, and symbolize our lives."

Guicharnaud provides a philosophical rationale for Beckett's use of the "comedy of the absurd."

> Life is no more than the comedy of life, no more than an attempt to play at living, no more than an embryonic farce. The often childish or capricious "games" that represent life on stage must necessarily be borrowed from genres in which failure, stumbling, and the resistance of objects make up the spectacles: circus and vaudeville sketches and their out-growth, the motion picture.

By his own testimony, Ionesco also stresses the "comedy of the absurd." He has commented on the idea that the previously distinct forms of tragedy and comedy are becoming more and more blurred. "It all comes to the same thing anyway; comic and tragic are merely two aspects of the same situation, and I have now reached the stage when

I find it hard to distinguish one from the other." (pp. 473-77)

Manuel L. Grossman, "Alfred Jarry and the Theatre of the Absurd," in Educational Theatre Journal, *Vol. XIX, No. 4, December, 1967, pp. 473-77.*

Bettina L. Knapp

[*Knapp is an American critic specializing in modern French literature. In the following excerpt, she elaborates on the influence of the dramatic theories of Antonin Artaud on the Theater of the Absurd.*]

Artaud was like a torrent that burst forth upon a Paris already replete with currents and cross-currents: Symbolism, Dadaism, Surrealism, etc. The impact of Artaud's ideas upon the already virile artistic forces generated a whole new series of thought-waves which, in turn, gathered momentum, slowly at first then with volcanic power, culminating in the works of another generation of writers: Genet, Beckett, Ionesco, et al.

Although influenced by the Greeks, Romans and Orientals; by such thinkers as Nietzsche, Wagner, Jarry, Appia, and Strindberg, Artaud's *unique* theatrical invention was a direct result of his malady. His physical and mental torment was so acute as to make it impossible for him to see the world except through the dark prism of his tortured *Self*. Unable to master his titanic inner force he became its slave. His dramatic aesthetics not only reflect an awareness of this state of affairs, but also a painfully urgent need to restore harmony and balance to a discordant and unsteady personality.

Artaud's theatrical concepts were in many ways similar to that of the ancients, looking upon the dramatic spectacle as a ritual, a Myth, capable of evoking a numinous or religious experience within the spectators. Just as collective Myths (that is, man's living religion) had been dramatized by Aeschylus, Sophocles, Seneca, and others, so must modern authors, he felt, write from their own numinous experiences to create new myths. To make the spectators' theatrical experience meaningful, these up-to-date myths must be enacted on stage in modern terms to suit man's present day needs.

The religious (enactment of a Myth) or metaphysical drama advocated by Artaud would deal with the eternal conflict between man and natural forces. Artaud rejected the occidental theater's stress on intellectual understanding, on psychology (character study), on didacticism. He looked to the oriental theater for guidance. To evoke that which is profoundest within man and endemic to him, the Orientals combined formalized gestures, evocative sound effects, rhythmic movements, physical attitudes, words used as symbols and a whole metaphysical breathing technique. Artaud wished to use the same elements to express the contents of modern man's unconscious.

The Theater of Cruelty which Artaud invented sought visceral reactions from the audience through the use of a new theatrical language. This language would be capable of expressing aurally and plastically the equivalent of the inner non-material world of man and the cosmos. Artaud conceived of a concrete theatrical language that would appeal to the senses rather than to the intellect; for he did not believe that the rational approach was the most effective way to reach into man's being. After all, Artaud wrote, a serpent does not react to music because of the "intellectual" notion he brings to it. As it slithers along the ground, it comes into contact with the musical vibrations which act upon the serpent like a "subtle massage." So the theater must act upon the spectators and "charm the viewers through their organism" or shock them into a more profound state of awareness. With this deepened insight, audiences would be able to project their own torments on to the stage happenings and by means of such objectification, hopefully, become aware of their problem, making catharsis possible.

Artaud's ideas may be outlined very briefly in the following manner:

1. Rejection of psychological, literary, and didactic theater:

2. Return to a theater of myth (a metaphysical theater) as known to the ancients and to the Orientals;

3. Founding of a Theater of Cruelty (action), in order to create a new optic;

4. The invention of a new theatrical spatial language (the importance accorded to gesture, movements, masks, etc.)

5. The pre-eminence of the dream world or of the unconscious which explains the archetypal nature of the characters in Artaudian theater;

6. The intent to touch, stir, shock the spectator for *therapeutic* reasons by eliciting sharp visceral effects;

7. The use of new breathing techniques by actors as a basis for their portrayals;

8. Each theatrical performance should be a fresh experience for the participants;

9. The role played by the audience as a contributing factor to the dynamism of the spectacle;

10. Theatrical performance as a microcosm in the cosmic whole.

(pp. 220-22)

Artaud was a seminal force: a man who helped create an intellectual climate. One may talk of Artaud's direct or indirect influence upon writers, directors, actors and spectators, but more important than this is the role he played in setting the stage for an entirely different point of view: namely, a therapeutic theater that is the meeting ground for visceral and spiritual actions and reactions. His work has achieved acceptance because it answers a *need* in man today.

It is difficult to define the *precise* influence Artaud had on modern authors and directors (whether acknowledged or not). The following paragraphs will make the attempt, but only in the briefest manner and on the most superficial levels.

In Jean Genet's theater, for example (*The Blacks, The Balcony*), religious atmosphere and ritual are of primary importance. In Beckett's drama (*Waiting for Godot, Endgame*) archetypal characters use the densest language and all action is symbolic. Eugène Ionesco's plays (*The Bald Soprano, The Chairs*) are, for the most part, allegories in which a shattering of language patterns gives words the force and presence of concrete objects: the words become characters in themselves. Fernando Arrabal's spectacles (*Fando and Lis, The Automobile Graveyard*) reveal the most secret fantasies as a series of grotesque creatures emerge full grown from his dream world or from his unconscious. Jean Vauthier uses (*Captain Bada, The Character against Himself*) a spatial language very similar to what Artaud had advocated: sound effects, objects, accessories, and lighting are given volatile personalities of their own, in order to arouse and disturb the spectator. Harold Pinter (*The Homecoming, The Birthday Party*) pays particular attention to verbal patterns which he uses to intensify the tensions of his instinctual fractured characters. Arnold Wesker (*The Kitchen*), drawn to fables, employs Artaud-like sound effects extensively. Edward Albee (*The Zoo Story, Who's Afraid of Virginia Woolf?*) has a penchant for shocking language and situations as advocated by Artaud. The more socially oriented Günter Grass (*The Tin Drum, The Wicked Cooks*) is drawn to elliptical stage happenings, jarring sounds and bizarre visual patterns to shake the spectators' complacency as does Peter Weiss (*Marat/Sade, The Investigation*). Peter Schaffer's *The Royal Hunt of the Sun* is, in my opinion, a virtual transposition of Artaud's metaphysical drama *The Conquest of Mexico.*

Directors also have been affected by Artaud's aura—directly and indirectly. Roger Blin, for example, who directed plays by Genet and Beckett, is prone to emphasize sets, lights, gestures as well as the metaphysical aspects of a work. Michael Cacoyannis (*Iphigenia* and the opera *Mourning Becomes Electra*) accords extreme importance to stylized acting, choreography and sound effects. When Peter Hall directed *The Homecoming* he underscored the mystery and horror of the drama by creating a series of mobile stage images, by using gestures and words as the repositories of arcane contents. *Marat/Sade* as directed by Peter Brook, became a horrendous drama—a dance—in which all theatrical forces (visual, aural, intellectual) were mustered in order to arouse a visceral reaction in the spectator. In fact, Peter Brook and Charles Marowitz founded a Theater of Cruelty (1963), an experimental group affiliated with the Royal Shakespeare Company which produced works by Artaud, Robbe-Grillet, Brook, Genet, Arden, etc. Realistic, naturalistic, psychological approaches to the theater were banished, as the twelve actors and actresses chosen to participate in this adventure, were plunged "into the swirling waters of Artaudian theory." (pp. 223-25)

Artaud knew, prophetically, that the world would adopt his optic eventually. Though the Theater of Cruelty remained only a vision during his lifetime, the seed he perceived and planted took root in the creative arts with the passage of time. Today, in the theater, in music, the pictorial arts—*cruelty,* as envisioned by Artaud has become a living reality, part of everyday jargon. The theater of the Absurd and the theater of happenings, op, pop, and psychedelic art, electronic, serial and *musique concrète* are all designed to arouse, disturb, and evoke bizarre and powerful sensations within man, visceral reactions capable of transforming or distorting man's conceptions of the world and himself. (p. 225)

Bettina L. Knapp, in a conclusion to Antonin Artaud: Man of Vision, *Avon Books, 1969, pp. 220-25.*

Beatrice Corrigan

[*In the following excerpt, Corrigan observes how the dramas of Luigi Pirandello anticipate those of the Theater of the Absurd.*]

It is surprising that Martin Esslin in his *Theatre of the Absurd* refers only once to Pirandello, saying that Ionescu considers him outdated. Pirandello was one of the most widely known European dramatists of his generation, whose plays were performed in France and Germany as frequently as in Italy, and such a casual dismissal of his influence on the playwrights who succeeded him is open to challenge. Diego Fabbri, more justly, holds that all contemporary theatre, not that of Italy alone, owes him a debt. In both themes and techniques he prepared the way for writers whose work came to maturity after World War II, and it can be shown that the relations between their drama and Pirandello's are far less tenuous than the German critic would have us believe.

Esslin defines the Theatre of the Absurd as an attempt to express "a sense of the metaphysical anguish of the absurdity of the human condition," with "an open abandonment of rational devices and discursive thought." This philosophical sense of anguish is of course basic to Pirandello. Camus defined the absurd as "the stranger who at certain seconds comes to meet us in a mirror," and in Pirandello's plays it is always when man sees an unfamiliar image of himself in the mirror of other people's opinions that his tragedy begins. Pirandello himself uses the expression "farse transcendentali" for the plays of the *teatro grottesco* which supplied him with much of his dramatic idiom, and he speaks of the "goffe ombre d'ogni gesto tragico" which seem ironic mockery of man's deepest suffering.

Esslin ascribes much of this sense of absurdity to a loss of religion which became fully conscious only after 1945. But already in 1904, in *Il fu Mattia Pascal,* Pirandello had expressed his sense of the absurdity of man's life if it is thought to end in the grave with no further meaning than the temporal. (p. 3)

Pirandello's plays are of course much later than this novel, and it was in *Così è (se vi pare),* written in 1913 but not performed until 1916, that he first confronted dramatically the theme of *il nulla. . . .* From that date on his work is constantly concerned with the torment of man's existence in a universe without meaning but which suffering forces him to question.

For Pirandello and his successors alike, the cause for man's anguish is his isolation which is intensified—though not caused—by the increasing mechanization of the world. The tyranny of the machine interested Pirandello's contemporaries Bontempelli and Cavacchioli, as it was later to interest Simpson and Adamov, but it appears only in one play of Pirandello's, *Questa sera si recita a soggetto.* There the producer, a parody of the German Max Reinhardt, is more concerned with the lighting and stage-effects than with the play the actors are attempting to perform. Here the mechanics of the theatre threaten to destroy the dramatic performance for which the theatre was created, and it is not until the actors rebel against the producer and take matters into their own hands that they can present the work of art with sincerity and feeling.

For Pirandello man's isolation is fundamental and inescapable. "No man is an island," said John Donne, but to Pirandello every man is an island, and communication between the islands is impossible, though it is desperately desired. One character after another, Signora Frola and Signor Ponza in *Così è,* the Father and the Stepdaughter in *Sei personaggi,* Enrico IV within the prison of self-created madness, pours forth a lava torrent of words which convey to the listeners only a shadow of the passionate sense of injustice that inspires them, or which are actually rejected as the reverse of the truths to which the listeners hold fast. Two people may share the same experience, yet be separated in their reaction to it by the abyss of their different convictions and preoccupations. At the end of *Diana e la Tuda,* for instance, the old sculptor Giuncano and Tuda, the beautiful model for a statue of Diana, both lament over the body of Sirio Dossi, whom Giuncano had slain in a fit of jealousy. But Giuncano's lament is the litany of old age, realizing too late the blindness of human desire; Tuda's is the threnody of youth condemned to live on without love or hope.

Man's urgent need to communicate his anguish is seen in two plays which present some striking similarities, Pirandello's *L'uomo dal fiore in bocca* and Albee's *The Zoo Story.* In both, two men meet casually: in Pirandello's play at a small café, in Albee's on a park bench: and one of these men begins to pour forth his dilemma to the other's reluctant ears. In each play the principal character is doomed, and bitterly resents his fate. Pirandello's anonymous Man is dying of cancer, Albee's Jerry can win acceptance from no one, not even from his landlady's dog, and is resolved on suicide. Imminent death has made both men intensely conscious of the wonder of the common things of life. To Pirandello's Man the wrapping and tying of a parcel has become a miracle of skill which he describes in minute detail. To Jerry the purchase of some hamburger is a miniature drama, to be re-enacted with gusto and immediacy. Both men reject human sympathy because their fate is now too desperate to permit any alleviation, and each can voice his intolerable pain only to a stranger who cannot share it. Though still living, they have already entered into the awful isolation of death. But Pirandello's Man accepts his solitude as inescapable, whereas Jerry forces a dreadful intimacy on the stranger he has encountered by making him his involuntary murderer.

Accompanying this necessity for communication, and frequently its cause, is a sense of guilt, accepted or, more often, rejected. This again is a theme common both to Pirandello and to the Theatre of the Absurd; indeed it is a classical dramatic theme, but in modern times it has assumed a new form. No longer is man punished by his own pursuing conscience. He now attempts to transfer the responsibility for his acts to others, or to the convenient theory of multiple personality. The Father in *Sei personaggi* refuses blame for the sorrow he has caused his wife and her younger children. He maintains that his motives in sending her away from him and in separating her from her son were humanitarian. He is ashamed of the sensual needs which caused him to encounter his step-daughter in

the hat-shop of Madama Pace, but those needs were part of his common humanity, and again he must not be blamed for them.

Moreover, as man changes from one day to another, he cannot be held responsible today for the deeds of yesterday. Acts of murder and adultery committed by sudden impulse, as in a dream, have no coherence with the conscious life of Romeo in *Non si sa come;* and though he accepts his guilt and its punishment, as an intellectual concept they seem to him unjust. Indeed, who is to say whether any given action is virtuous or evil? In *Ciascuno a suo modo* an actress betrays her fiancé with another man. Was she trying to save the fiancé from an unsuitable marriage, was she trying to revenge herself on society, or was she simply overcome by a passion she was unwilling to acknowledge? She herself does not know, and accepts each motive in turn as it is set before her.

In the Theatre of the Absurd this denial of responsibility has been carried to its logical conclusion. No one is to blame for his actions, the murderer never will or should be punished, and though in Genet's *Les noirs* and *Les bonnes* a ritual of guilt is performed, the very performance brings its own absolution and slayer and victim continually exchange roles. Genet may be compared with Pirandello from another aspect. In *Le balcon* the characters who act out wish-fulfilment fantasies are reminiscent of Enrico IV, who can find security only in an historical masquerade. But again Genet has gone one step farther, and the creatures of fantasy eventually become substitutes for the real figures which they have mimicked.

The denial of moral consequences coupled with a conviction of the absurdity of life explains at least in part the strong vein of black humor which may be found in Pirandello and, even more darkly, in his successors. In the *Prefazione* to the *Sei personaggi* Pirandello tells us that the *Fantasia* who is the faithful servant of his art prefers to dress in black, yet at any moment she may pull from her pocket the jester's scarlet cap jingling with bells and set it on her head. The characters she creates endure ludicrous sufferings, are exposed to grotesque humiliations. A mother returns to her home after an absence of twenty years and finds that her daughter's love is all given to a dead mother who had never existed; this devotion to a ghost inspires cruelty to the living being who seems trying to usurp its place. A devoted upright father, in *Tutto per bene,* discovers that the girl he thinks is his daughter was fathered by another man, that the dead wife he reveres was false to him, and that everyone, including the girl herself, believes that he knows the truth and has for years been shamelessly blackmailing his betrayer. The tragic masquerade in which Enrico IV lives out his life is turned into buffoonery by his dyed hair and red-daubed cheeks. In play after play the human beetle is impaled on the pin of circumstance, and its anguished struggles are observed with an ambiguous mixture of derision and compassion.

Even the physical appearance of Pirandello's characters is described as though they were seen in the distorting mirrors of a fun-fair: awkward gestures, a bird-like head, both laughable and sinister; a Valkyrie's face elaborately constructed with cosmetics beneath artificially blonde hair. In the *Sagra del Signore della Nave,* Lavaccara and his family are almost indistinguishable from the favourite pig they have brought to be slaughtered, so that their subsequent feast of pork resembles a cannibal's banquet. But in the Theatre of the Absurd, with its increasing sensationalism, men and women are reduced to caricatures and its plays are often peopled with the refuse of humanity—tramps, derelicts, the senile, the maimed, and the blind. Here, however, physical deformity is often used to symbolize the psychic mutilations inflicted on the individual by society, as though Armageddon or a universal flood had left behind these sad dreadful remnants of mankind.

The intolerable cruelty of life forces escape through illusion, and here again Pirandello anticipated the Theatre of the Absurd. In his first metaphysical play, *Così è,* he portrayed Signora Frola as able to lead an otherwise normal life only if encouraged to believe that her dead daughter is still alive. Her son-in-law, Signor Ponza, on the other hand, must convince his associates that her daughter is dead, and that the lady living with him is his second wife. This self-created world of illusion which denies reality and rejects an unacceptable truth occurs in different forms in other plays: *Enrico IV,* for instance, *Vestire gli ignudi,* and *La vita che ti diedi.* It is interesting that in this last play, as well as in *Così è,* Pirandello portrays a mother refusing to accept the death of a child, for this also becomes a motif in Albee's plays. Indeed Albee goes farther, for his self-deluded women cling to belief in the existence of a child that has never been born, as in *Who's Afraid of Virginia Woolf,* or even, as in *The American Dream,* crave for a child that they themselves have helped to destroy. In this they become symbolical, as Pirandello's are not, of a protest against the sterility of the contemporary world.

All three characters of Pinter's *The Caretaker* can survive only through compulsive fantasies. The tramp, Davies, believes that when he recovers his identification papers from Sidcup he will be prosperous; Mick believes that he can transform the junk-room in which he lives into an elegant modern apartment; and Aston believes that he can repair what is hopelessly broken, including the tramp himself. The self-created illusion is, as we have seen, a theme in several of Genet's plays, and in Sartre's *Huis clos* the inability to escape from reality into illusion constitutes the cruelest punishment of hell.

Waiting for Godot, one of the best and most enduring plays in the Theatre of the Absurd, adds a different but still Pirandellian twist to the theme. The tramps who wait with their freakish mixture of impatience and resignation not only share a common illusion—if it is an illusion—but are upheld in it by the appearance of the child who assures them that Godot will indeed come to them. Pirandello too holds that the individual cannot feel secure in his illusion unless he can persuade others to share it. Enrico IV must be surrounded by counsellors who obey his commands, the *Sconosciuta* in *Come tu mi vuoi* can create the character of Lucia only as long as she thinks that those around her believe she is Lucia. When the illusion is challenged it is destroyed, for it, like everything else, is relative and the creation of the human mind.

The resemblances then between the Pirandellian themes and those of the Theatre of the Absurd are numerous, and the most obvious differences lie in a darkening of tone and in a new idiom. The casual violence of Pirandello's plays, nearly every one of which contains a suicide, a murder, or a duel, in the Theatre of the Absurd becomes more savage, just as the dark humor becomes more macabre. Indeed it

would not be unfair to say that the Theatre of the Absurd probably learned a good deal from the Grand Guignol. The horrors of the concentration camp too seem to have stimulated a pleased fascination with cruelty, so that the juxtaposition of *atroce* and *assurdo* assumes a new meaning, as for instance in Ionescu's *Jack.* The glitter of madness too spangles both the old dramas and the new.

The predominance of the irrational accompanies a strong Surrealist element in contemporary theatre which already existed to some extent in Pirandello's early work and became more pronounced as he grew older, particularly in *Quando si è qualcuno, Sogno (ma forse no),* and *I giganti della montagna.* But in most of his plays realism outweighed the fantastic, whereas the majority of the modern dramas discard realism almost entirely. Pirandello's character could never have appeared in ash cans or in piles of sand, as Beckett's do. They might appear pig-like but never, like Ionescu's, turn into rhinoceroses. Pirandello's dialogue, too, is realistic, and shows none of the apparently inconsequential dislocation which both Beckett and Ionescu learned from James Joyce. Again, Pirandello's symbols are usually the traditional ones of the mirror and the mask, but the modern play is likely to contain a multiplicity of arcane images to evoke man's problems in the universe. The decline in realism almost inevitably is accompanied by a decline in human interest: too many of the new plays seem mere tricks of construction, clever but without substance.

In his last play, *I giganti della montagna,* Pirandello composed a parable of the last and saddest isolation of all, the loss of communication between man and art. The poetic imagination has been exiled from society, and is exercised by vagabonds and derelicts, who anticipate the characters in Beckett's plays. The images they evoke through their magic are beautiful but meaningless, disconnected, each intelligible only to its own creator. The "giganti," who represent modern industrialized society, are too busy with their own affairs to listen to a dramatic fable. The working people whom they send as an audience in their stead want only buffoonery, and in their rage murder the actress who is dedicated to the work of a dead poet. The play they prevent her from reciting, *La favola del figlio cambiato,* is an allegory of Poetry's throne usurped by a mad buffoon, and of Poetry himself finding his rightful place among the humble people who can give him tranquility, love, and happiness.

In this prophetic play Pirandello seems to forecast the excesses of the Theatre of the Absurd. It is a school capable of wild flashes of poetry, and it occasionally produces a work of sustained dramatic power, but only too often the inspiration is intermittent and the images can be understood by the author alone. Technically one of Pirandello's most important gifts to the new theatre was the bare stage awaiting a performance. He himself could people it with the lasting creations of his dramatic genius, but the empty setting of the Theatre of the Absurd often remains untenanted by any but the most ephemeral of phantoms. (pp. 3-6)

Beatrice Corrigan, "Pirandello and the Theatre of the Absurd," in Cesare Barbieri Courier, *Vol. VIII, No. 1, Spring, 1966, pp. 3-6.*

Joyce Carol Oates

[*Oates is an American fiction writer and critic who is perhaps best known for her novel* them, *which won a National Book Award in 1970. Her fiction is noted for its exhaustive presentation of realistic detail as well as its striking imagination, especially in the evocation of abnormal psychological states. As a critic, Oates has written on a diversity of authors, including William Shakespeare, Herman Melville, and Samuel Beckett, and is appreciated for the individuality and erudition that characterize her critical work. In the following excerpt, she illuminates techniques and themes of Theater of the Absurd playwrights by comparing their works with those of Anton Chekhov.*]

The faithful rendering of life as it is truly lived, its tragedy always conditioned by the relentless banality of life and so transformed into something akin to comedy; the insistence upon the unheroic, the unmelodramatic, the self-deceiving, the futile; the paralysis of will that is at once a mark of the cultured and a sign of their decadence: these are the obvious characteristics of Chekhov's drama. The point at which Chekhov's meticulous symbolic naturalism touches the inexplicable, the ludicrous, and the paradoxical is the point at which his relationship to our contemporary theater of the absurd is most clear. Much of what seems stunning and *avant garde* in the last two decades of theater has been anticipated in both theory and practice by Chekhov. For instance, one has only to examine the central issues of *The Cherry Orchard* and *The Three Sisters*—the hopeless, comic-pathetic loss of a tradition and the futile longing for Moscow—to see how closely Chekhov is echoed in Beckett's *Waiting for Godot* and other works.

The concept of the "absurd" must be defined. It is a confusing term, for we are accustomed to equating the works of many modern writers with the existential concept of "absurdity." Sartre and Camus systematically examine the bases and the consequences of an absurd world, a world without meaning, but their works of literature, particularly their plays, are traditional in structure and language. However, when the playwright attempts to give expression to the absurd through both the structure and language of his work, he is then considered a playwright in the theater of the absurd (a term that could be set off by quotation marks, since its meaning is by no means simple). Chekhov's philosophical basis is clearly nineteenth-century naturalism, but his technique is only apparently naturalistic: it is fundamentally symbolic. What is absurd in Chekhov is the content of his works—what actually happens—and several of the devices he uses, particularly those dealing with language. Again and again we are confronted with intelligent people who have somehow lost their capacity for self-expression, whether wealthy landowners and their offspring, or working-class people, or the "emancipated." And with this capacity for self-expression they have also lost their ability to live.

All literature deals with contests of will, but drama makes most clear the spiritual struggles that life demands through its ritualistic enactment of the agon. Lifelong conflicts—conflicts of an abstract and spiritual nature—are given body, compressed, and played out before us on the stage. On the stage someone is either being born or dying; if his struggle is not with the resisting forces of other people (as in much of Shakespeare), it is with the forces of his unknown self, or, as in the Ionesco play *Exit the King,* with the force of death. Chekhov's works are tragedies of the impotence of will about to transform themselves into comedies, because their protagonists are diminished human beings; as Chekhov says, *The Cherry Orchard* is almost farcical in places, though it deals with the end of an entire social order and the splitting-up of a family. This kind of bitter comedy is, perhaps, tragedy that can no longer sustain faith in itself.

In his philosophical grasp of his material, as well as in a number of particular dramatic devices, Chekhov anticipates the contemporary theater of the absurd. (pp. 117-19)

In some ways the absurdist playwrights are more conventional than Chekhov. With the exception of Beckett, they provide situations of tension that build up to climaxes—a rhythm of movement any audience can feel though perhaps it cannot understand. Beckett's works, like Chekhov's, are dramas of the loss of will, in which the unattainable salvation is deliberately vague, as in a dream, and in which language is man's sole occupation. Since salvation is transcendent and exterior to man, action is certainly needless; one sits and talks. In Chekhov the actions that occur are irrelevant to the willed desires of the characters. What is scrupulously denied is a catharsis of any recognizable sort, even a true dramatic climax. When climaxes are provided they are always out of focus, for Chekhov's people cannot see clearly enough to do what might be expected of them by ordinary standards. Treplev in *The Sea Gull* has already tried to kill himself, and so his successful suicide is somehow anticlimactic; moreover, the audience is denied, like Treplev, the meaning this action will have to the others. So the action is simply an action, and as long as it is not interpreted within the context of the play, it never achieves meaning. The climax of *The Three Sisters*—Tuzenbach's death in a duel—affirms the sisters' loss rather than tying it together in a single, compact image, the death being denied sentimental value and even meaning, for Irina does not love Tuzenbach. The climax of *The Cherry Orchard*—the merchant Lopakhin's revelation that it is he who has bought the estate on which his father was once a serf ("I bought it," he announces with pride and awe)—initiates wrong reactions from everyone, for Lopakhin is the central character and had wanted in some confused way recognition for what he had done; this leads into the strange fourth act, an act of abandonment and leave-taking conducted with the most banal of conversations. Technically, a climax occurs in each play, but thematically, it is somehow not the right climax. The true issues are always avoided. Only in *Uncle Vanya* does the "hero" accurately sight his enemy, but of course he is unable to kill him and unable to commit suicide. If there is a catharsis in any acceptable sense in Chekhov, it must be through the accumulation of detail and the revelation of character, through the history of a given moment in terms of numbers of people and not simply, as in most drama, in terms of one or two people. The cathartic recognition of the relationship between the reality on stage and the reality it is meant to mirror in the real world makes the works art, but this art is difficult because it guides the emotional expectations of the audience up to a certain point and then baffles these expectations, allows a tragic situation to turn comic, denies its heroes or heroines the knowledge that would make them noble, and, strangest of all, deliberately scatters the audience's emotions among a group of people. If the audience could focus its sympathies upon one person, this person might achieve a kind of elevation; but in Chekhov it is rather the relationships between people and not the "realistics" of the people themselves that are of interest. Such art is difficult because no audience is prepared for it.

By contrast, such well-known absurdist plays as Ionesco's *The Bald Soprano, The Lesson,* and *The Chairs* are structured along lines that are almost anecdotal, in each case ending with a catharsis of violence in which the accumulated tensions are exorcized by complete irrationality. *The Killer,* Ionesco's most interesting long play, ends with a final scene that is really an act in itself, in which a fairly ordinary, intelligent, pseudoheroic man confronts the mysterious killer, a deformed, giggling creature, and is finally overcome by his "infinitely stubborn will." Despite the metaphysical poetry of Ionesco's images—his "arbitrary issues" that remind us of the private, privately created world of Kafka—the accumulation and release of tension in these plays is actually classic. The audience's emotions are guided by an expert hand. Ionesco is concerned with *change,* and despite the difficulties one might have intellectually with this change, its emotional, visual reality is clear enough. He speaks of the two fundamental states of consciousness at the root of all his plays: feelings of evanescence and heaviness. Most often, "lightness changes to heaviness, transparence to thickness; the world weighs heavily; the universe crushes. . . . Matter fills everything, takes up all space, annihilates all liberty under its weight. . . . Speech crumbles." If it is not matter precisely that annihilates, it is the savagery that weighs down upon the spiritual—the metamorphoses of men into beasts, never subtle, or the actual killing of characters onstage. In Chekhov this demonstration of the play's structure is never clear; the audience's emotions are dissipated, go off in several directions, cannot focus upon any single conflict. The meaning of Ionesco may be baffling, but the dramatic focus of his art is not. In Chekhov the meaning is perhaps inexplicable apart from the actual terms of the plays themselves, but the concentration of dramatic action is in itself baffling. Hence the notorious problems of staging Chekhov. When the dying old servant, Firs, limps in at the end of *The Cherry Orchard,* having been left alone in the big house by the departing characters, one does not know whether to laugh or cry; the conclusion is brilliantly appropriate, and yet impossible to define. Surely this is the real end of the "old order"—a faithful servant who sentimentally recalls serfdom, abandoned by his former owners without a second thought. But in another sense, a more theatrical sense, it is simply absurd, gratuitous and unexpected, and distracts attention from what has been supposed the main action: the effects of selling the estate upon the main characters.

In Ionesco the play ends abruptly because the characters, who are soulless, have been accepted simply as theatrical approximations of life in its ludicrous or mysterious sense, and the meaning of the work is ultimately abstract and universal; in Chekhov the play ends technically, but the characters, given life so scrupulously, carry its meaning along with them and do not surrender it when the curtain falls. The absurdist theater has limited powers because its works are essentially parables whose success or failure depends entirely upon the ingenuity of the transformation of idea (for example, the idea that man waits endlessly for his true life, his real self, his salvation) into arresting images, and, as parables, they can evoke only an intellectual response in the audience. One can laugh at Beckett's people, since they deliberately invite laughter, but one cannot share their sorrow because it is not a human sorrow; it is a representation, at its most sterile an allegorical representation, of real sorrow that exists somewhere in the human world—a curious parallel to the assumptions of the medieval morality play. In Chekhov, even the most mysterious characters are made real for us by some abrupt switching of point of view, so that the character—Solyony or Charlotta—does not slip safely into caricature. Chekhov's stage "looks" real enough, and his characters speak a language that has the surface formlessness of that of real life, but in essence his conception of drama is more complex and more iconoclastic than that of the absurdists, whose revolt is chiefly in terms of a simplification of life and an attendant exaggeration of limited experiences. (pp. 119-23)

Most interesting of all the similarities between the Chekhovian and the *avant-garde* theater is the use of the "arbitrary issue" as poetic image. In absurdist theater the arbitrary issue is that which, despite its apparent inadequacy, is to carry the burden of the character's obsession. In Adamov's *Le Ping-Pong,* it is a pinball machine that captivates the imaginations of two men who grow old playing it, wasting their lives, transforming their natural human impulses toward transcendence into nonsensical trivialities about the machine itself. As Esslin notes in his excellent study of the play, the work is a powerful image of the "alienation of man through the worship of a false objective"—the machine itself an obvious metaphor for anything that captivates men's lives without being worth the sacrifice. In Ionesco as well the arbitrary issue is that which is "given" without explanation: one must find out whether Mallot spelled his name with a "t" or a "d," one must get the growing corpse out of the apartment, one must resist to the end the metamorphosis into a rhinoceros. The images are not significant in themselves (except as theater), but only in what they suggest. This conception of writing differs from, for instance, the very real and not at all arbitrary issues of Ibsen, attacking the hypocrisy of society in *Ghosts,* or of Strindberg, passionately attacking the vampirish female. As if the world no longer offered real issues, these several playwrights create grotesque and parodying issues that will dominate their characters' imaginations and, when the play is successful, the audience's imagination as well. Such theater is really poetry, as Kafka's works are poetry: the creation of a sustained image that is the vehicle for symbolic meaning, yet never glibly contained by this meaning. But because the image is necessarily private and not social, historical, or mythical, the meaning must be expanded by the audience, which as a kind of unified consciousness can no longer be content to know—as Picasso says of most people—only what they already know. The difficulty with absurdist theater is its deliberate refusal to tell us what we already know, its unheroic heroes and unvillainous villains, its mock plots, its insistence upon baffling expectation, its taking over the prat-falls and rapid dialogue of vaudeville entertainment while leaving behind the "honest" foolishness. But as poetry, its images are closer to Pound's definition of the image than are, perhaps, such readily acceptable images as the paper lantern in Williams' *A Streetcar Named Desire* and the doomed bird in *Miss Julie.* In 1913 Pound defined the "image" as "that which presents an intellectual and emotional complex in an instant of time. . . . It is the presentation of such a 'complex' instantaneously which gives that sense of sudden liberation; that sense of freedom from time limits and space limits; that sense of sudden growth, which we experience in the presence of the greatest works of art." The Imagists themselves created no images that broke so completely from the conventionally "poetic" as did the dramatists of the absurd.

In traditional theater the central issue is always acted upon; this is the only means of plot. One finally kills the king, though at great expense; one manages to marry the inevitable person; one breaks free from husband, children, and hypocritical society. Generally, in Chekhov and the absurd dramatists, the central issue is either not understood or not acted upon or both. The cherry orchard has all the makings of a symbol except—unlike the stuffed seagull in the earlier play—its symbolism points in several directions. It is various things to various people, and yet in itself it does not exist; it has no meaning. Never does anyone see the cherry orchard for what it is; they see wasted opportunities for making money, or they see ghostly faces in it, whether the student Trofimov's vision of the faces of serfs or Madame Ranevskaya's vision of her dead mother walking in it. They are capable of seeing only what they bring to it, of seeing only themselves. And when the orchard is finally sold, when the catastrophe happens, there is a queerly inappropriate relief; Gayev, though totally displaced by the change, says cheerfully:

> "Yes, indeed, everything is all right now. Before the cherry orchard was sold we were all worried and miserable, but afterward, when the question was finally settled once and for all, everybody calmed down and felt quite cheerful."

One is reminded of Mann's famous definition of irony in his essay, "Goethe and Tolstoy": a technique that glances at both sides, playing "slyly and irresponsibly among opposites." With such irony there is no possibility of sentimental excess, since the writer does not choose sides.

If this is so, the theatergoer wants to ask, then what is the play about? Why has it been written? That the apparent central issue of a work should be declared quite trivial and insignificant after all the words and tears exerted for it is an extraordinary event in literature. It is as if the conventional form of art were calling itself into question, calling its very reason for existence into question, or calling, at least, the conventional audience's expectations into question. If it is ever appropriate to talk of genres in close relationship to actual works of art, one might say that for the tragic vision, deadly seriousness must always surround this central issue, and what the play undertakes is of real concern not only within the context of the play, but symbolically for its audience. Tragedy is a sacred art form. When self-consciousness or doubt or an impulse toward self-parody enter, tragedy disintegrates. In Chekhov this is precisely the case.

As in Beckett, the less tangible the means of salvation, the greater the urgency for salvation becomes. The intelligent human beings of such drama, caught in the purgatorial present, can only *talk;* it is the stupid—Natasha, Solyony, Arkadina, the professor of *Uncle Vanya*—who live on some level of existence, forcing others to submit to their wills, the simple fact of their being able to live involving

a death for others. As one element gains strength, so another element loses strength. The ghostliness of the central issue or image in Chekhov gives way abruptly to the flagrant mystery of the central issue of a play like *Godot.* Godot as image approaches the unfathomable just as Melville's white whale does—the former by its very absence, the latter by its tremendously detailed presence. Chekhov's imagery is more conventional than that of the absurdists, of course, since he is committed to a naturalistic stage, but his use of the image is similar: the truly poetic image whose meaning, as Pound says, gives one a sense of liberation and sudden growth by refusing to confine itself—in other words, to the easily explicable.

If there is intellectual debate in the theater of the absurd it is, like the "intellectual" discussions in Chekhov, ironic, exaggerated, and foolish, coming as it does at the point in history at which philosophy is divorced from the transcendental values it once tried to discover or support. Hence debate, talk, and duets of dialogue become meaningless, and characters are their own chorus, speaking and commenting endlessly upon their own speech. Are there images behind this speech? Are there realities behind these images? The prevailing tone in existential literature is that of mystery. In this art a strange, dissipated action, or the memory or vague desire for action, has replaced the older, more vital, ritualistic concerns of the stage. Chekhov and the absurdists remain true to their subject—life—by refusing to reduce their art to a single emotion and idea. (pp. 132-37)

Joyce Carol Oates, "Chekhov and the Theater of the Absurd," in her The Edge of Impossibility: Tragic Forms in Literature, *Victor Gollancz Ltd, 1976, pp. 115-37.*

INFLUENCE OF THE THEATER OF THE ABSURD

Marketa Goetz Stankiewicz

[*In the following essay, Stankiewicz contrasts the social and political context of plays by eastern and western European dramatists associated with the Theater of the Absurd.*]

When in Shaw's Epilogue to *Saint Joan* his heroine returns after twenty-five years in order to see how things are going in the world, the Earl of Warwick greets her with reverence: "Madam: my congratulations on your rehabilitation. I feel I owe you an apology." The audiences of New York, London or Paris will be much more amused by Joan's polite answer, "Oh, please don't mention it," than by the Earl's comment on her rehabilitation. The laughter which the exchange is bound to arouse will stem from amusement about a situation in which a great moral wrong, involving the torture and execution of a human being is reduced to the level of social chit-chat in which one cliché is countered by another. The historical event of Joan of Arc's burning at the stake has thus been minimized to a trifling social faux pas or mistake. The automatic, polite response to an apology is to reject it as unnecessary and to assure the apologizer that nothing unpleasant happened. To apply the same automatic response in the case of a brutal execution produces a grotesque effect, or, as we choose to call it today, an absurd situation.

When the same play was staged in Prague in 1966 and the Earl of Warwick spoke his lines: "Madam: my congratulations on your rehabilitation," the audience did not wait for the "funny" response to follow but began to clap, cheer and stamp their feet so that the end of the play was drowned out by the noise. The audience had heard a highly topical line, the political meaning of which was crystal clear to the point that some members of the audience might actually have experienced the situation personally or in their immediate families. The word "rehabilitation" was charged with electrifying meaning. The Czech audience responded to the absurdity of the situation portrayed on stage because they recognized in it their own reality—a threatening, ever-present reality which had to be accepted as the normal course of events in their everyday lives and the absurdity of which, being officially carefully concealed, could be imparted off the record only to a trusted friend. After all, Rudolf Slansky who had been a top man in the Czechoslovak communist party, who had fallen into disgrace and been executed after a show trial in 1951, was declared innocent of all major crimes in 1962 and officially rehabilitated. Now the people of Prague who had witnessed all this at close hand suddenly saw a parallel situation displayed on the stage and felt free to show how acutely they recognized it. The playful dictum "Nothing is as exciting as the truth" could be considered the all but playful motto of absurd theatre in Eastern Europe.

What has happened here is the large scale, magnified illustration of an important ingredient of the joke, the way Freud sees it. In his treatise *Der Witz* he describes the workings of the unconscious joke, the effect of which he considers particularly strong. He illustrates it, as always, with an example from the life of one of his patients: Two children, a boy and a girl, entertain their relatives by giving a performance of a little play they thought up: the boy acts a husband returning from the wars after a long absence, and regales his wife (the girl) with tales about heroic deeds and victorious battles which were all fought for her sake. She counters this by informing him, that she too had not forgotten him and during the time he fought all those battles she had been preparing a surprise for his homecoming. Pointing to twelve dolls neatly lined up in the background, she tells him that she has made all these beautiful children for him to enjoy after his return. Freud tells us that, when the whole family burst out laughing, the children, confused and hurt, refused to continue with their play and withdrew, obviously disturbed by the strange reaction to their performance. The audience had seen a joke the "playwrights" had not intended. If Shaw had sat among the Prague audience during a performance of his *Saint Joan* he might have been similarly surprised.

The same could be said of more recent writers like, to mention just one example, Edward Albee, whose play *A Delicate Balance*—which was reviewed in New York as "dissecting the agony and fear of emptiness"—was withdrawn from performance in Prague in 1969 because of the political impact of one single sentence. The neighbourly couple that has dropped in to help ease various emotional

tensions answers the irritated daughter's question, "Have you come to stay forever?" with the words, "If need be." Surely Albee never dreamt of an audience both cheering and jeering at these words because they reminded them vividly of Party-line comments about the Russian troops who were to stay in Czechoslovakia as long as "need be" to repress undesirable developments and "normalize" the situation.

Playwrights in Eastern Europe who have had to cope with the monster of censorship for years, and for whom the truth is the sweetest of forbidden fruits, are, of course, acutely aware of this situation and have grasped the electrifying power of the *sub rosa* statement. When the Polish playwright Mrozek has one of his characters come to the conclusion that "true freedom exists only in the place where there is no ordinary freedom," he can foresee the effect of these words on the Polish audience which will perceive in them much more than an elegant twist of logic: namely a wry, ironic comment on the ways a totalitarian régime stifles freedom and simultaneously creates a phantom freedom officially invented and imposed on the imagination of the people.

Under the guise of nonsense—or absurdity—thus using the ancient prerogative of the fool to say what others must conceal, the best writers of Eastern Europe address themselves directly to their audiences, discussing with them the burning questions confronting men who have been denied the truth, whose minds have been choked with slogans, and who have to comply with absolute values which dictate their lives although they are beyond their comprehension. The Polish philosopher Leszek Kolakowski sees the writer in the role of the ancient jester whose task it is to formulate and express his mistrust of "the stabilized world," and whose contribution is "an always active imagination which thrives on the resistance it must overcome." This is the common ground on which the playwright and the audience meet in Eastern Europe—another level than that on which the play seems to take place, a level on which the clear air, if not of truth itself, at least of the honest search for truth, is recreated in the stuffy atmosphere of a crowded theatre. This, as the English critic Martin Esslin has repeatedly reminded us, is something that has not happened in the theatre for a long time, and that makes for an entirely different theatre atmosphere than we have in the West.

The Eastern European play performed in the West undergoes a less obvious but equally interesting change. Martin Esslin tells us that when visiting Poland he found his Polish friends very surprised that Slawomir Mrozek's *Tango* had a "message" for the Western world too. They had seen it exclusively in terms of the Communist domination of Poland. But they would have been even more surprised if they had read the English critic John Weightman's comments in *Encounter*. One character in the play is a proletarian thug who, having killed off the truth-seeking hero and subdued his half confused, half opportunistic family, emerges as the absolute victor when the curtain falls. To the Polish audience this is a clear comment on the Communist muzhik who seizes power at the opportune moment and subdues the idealist-intellectual with brute force. Mr. Weightman, who saw the play produced in London, interprets the same figure as "the pure exercise of Existentialist freedom in the form of destructive neo-

Nietzscheanism." Although he vaguely admits that the Polish language might give the play a different meaning, he is obviously blind to the highly charged political implications.

Scanning Western comments on East European plays one discovers that the political fable of East Europe has to pass the existentialist-absurd test before it becomes respectable in the West. Mrozek's *Tango* passed the test with high marks because it is so multilevelled a play that, like the best plays—at least from the short perspective of a contemporary—it radiates meanings which touch the deepest problems of man's life. But take another of Mrozek's works. The Western journal *East Europe,* when reprinting one of his best satirical one-act plays *At Sea,* introduced the play with the following comment: "Although superficially its targets seem to be the abuses of the Stalinist past—the principle of 'voluntariness,' the caste system based on 'proletarian origin,' the brainwashing techniques of self-criticism and public confession—it also reflects the contemporary Polish disgust with politics in general. Mrozek's comment on the human condition resembles that of Westerners such as Beckett and Ionesco." Here we have the play's "passport" to the West: reference to the human condition, a vague parallel to Beckett and Ionesco, only the "existential anguish" is missing. In another case we get even that. The young Czech writer Václav Havel's play *The Memorandum* is a highly committed brilliant social satire and neither contains existentialist anguish nor does the author here try, in Ionesco's words, to "discover the fundamental problem common to all men." Martin Esslin, who introduced the Penguin edition of *Three East European Plays,* which contains *The Memorandum,* writes that Václav Havel's work fuses two seemingly irreconcilable traditions of his own country: Jaroslav Hasek's "low-life clowning" on the one hand and Franz Kafka's "metaphysical anguish" on the other. Surely, it is true that the madhouse of bureaucracy for its own sake which Havel exposes in his play brings to mind the oppressive bureaucracy of Kafka's nightmarish world, but to stress the affinity to such a point that it is regarded as a key to Havel's work is misleading. Such a comment represents a—perhaps unconscious—attempt to provide Havel with a "passport" to the West, confirmed by one of the top critics of the absurd theatre.

Reversing the situation once again and looking at the reception of the Western absurd play by East European theatre critics we find what is to be expected, namely that their reaction has to be more socially "responsible" as well as more analytical than the impulsive response of an anonymous theatre audience. Apart from official Marxist critics who, for example, attack Ionesco for "understanding the human being only from the ideological point of view of his class," we find interesting assessments like the following: "Beckett has never written examples for the theses of the existentialist textbook. His writing is diametrically opposed to the writings of, say, Sartre. . . . Beckett is always only a dramatic poet." By stressing the aesthetic quality of Beckett's work, the Czech critic underplays its dark message and pessimism which, although apolitical, is contrary to Communist ideology with its grim optimism and stress on the paradise to come. Another case in point is the attitude of a Polish critic to Harold Pinter's *The Homecoming.* Comparing the latter play with Mrozek's *Tango,* the critic vaguely discusses differences between the

two plays and then proceeds to extract what he regards the message common to both, namely that "in each case the figure of the liberal, albeit it shows the sharpest perceptiveness, proves to be insufficient." The Czech critic has made the issue an aesthetic one, the Polish critic has made a statement of far-reaching ambiguity. Yet each has somehow—cautiously or shrewdly, as the case may be—adapted the play to his society by dodging aspects which might cause trouble among the powers that be, or by stressing areas which would make the play officially acceptable. Western plays, too, need "passports" to Eastern Europe. In fact they need them in order to be performed there at all, whereas the "passports" issued by Western critics to plays from Eastern Europe serve as guides to attractions rather than as sine qua non travel documents.

Out of all this two main questions arise: firstly, why have two so vastly different societies provided the soil for so similar an art form? Secondly, how does the strange metamorphosis come about when a play changes from one environment to the other?

In this connection it may be interesting to refer to an essay of Jan Grossman, a prominent Czech director and producer who worked closely with Václav Havel on the first staging of his plays. "Really great theatre" says Grossman, "fixes the attention of the audience . . . above all on what is going on between it and the stage. The source of such a theatre . . . is primarily subject matter which is capable of evoking direct speech and action between the stage and the audience." Stressing repeatedly the "dialog-like" quality (an inadequate translation of "dialogicnost") of a topic which a great dramatic writer is able to uncover, Grossman points directly at a basic and unique ingredient of the theatre of the absurd in the East—the immediate creation of a highly rational atmosphere in the theatre while the absurd action of the play is going on. Here, it seems to me, lies the basic distinction between the appeal of an absurd play in the West as opposed to that in the East. The Western absurd play is aimed at the audience's response to irrationality, the Eastern absurd play at its response to rationality.

With this in mind I would like to explore briefly one of the main themes of the theatre of the absurd. In the West and East alike the writer's imagination has been fired by the theme of the automatization of man, the condition of the human being who has lost his reasoning power through pressures of society, tradition, ideology or habit and whose reactions are merely conditioned, automatic responses. It is no over-statement to say that literally thousands of pages have been dedicated to critical discussion of this topic. Open any book or journal dealing with contemporary drama and you will find an essay or chapter dealing with it. The idea of man's non-rational responses fascinates the contemporary mind, which spends more time and energy on observing the behavior of apes than on studying the writings of its great philosophers. The theme of automatization is, of course, by no means new. It appears in many guises. When, in 1882, Ibsen's Peter Stockman informs his wayward brother that "as an officer under the Committee you have no right to any individual opinion," or when, in 1920, Karel Capek writes a play about man-made robots which fulfill their assigned tasks without understanding their nature, these authors are concerned with related problems. However, what had been on the periphery of the writer's vision of man and his world, has now moved into the centre of his attention. The puppet-like characters of Ionesco who go through a meaningless dialogue consisting of ready made phrases are close kin to one of Mrozek's characters whose wife discovers after several years of "happy" marriage that her husband is made of plasticine. In one of Arrabal's plays a soldier's mother automatically treats war the same way she would treat an inconvenient occurrence in everyday life, for example a rain-shower. When bombs start falling and interrupt her picnic she nonchalantly opens her umbrella and motions her husband to come underneath. Arrabal is obviously trying to express a similar awareness as the Slovak writer Peter Karvas whose play *The Great Wig* deals with a ruler who is convinced that he has found the subversive elements and reasons for the general disorder in the country and proceeds to eliminate them. With a striking twist of irony Karvas exposes the arbitrariness of the ruler's decision: the conviction that the bald members of society are the subversive ones. The persecution leads to endless complications—the whole nation ends up wearing wigs and no one knows what is underneath. Arrabal's middle-class lady had reasoned: if something falls from the sky it must be rain. Karvas' characters reasoned: if people are to be divided into good ones and bad ones and someone provides you with a way to distinguish them, use it.

Words and actions emptied of meaning, people with automatic reactions, speaking in slogans and phrases the actual meaning of which has escaped them, such are the targets of absurd writings of East and West alike. In both cases the characters are presented as having become prisoners of a social reality which has emptied them of all but irrational, automatic responses. Yet there is a difference. Ionesco defines such a purely social character as "impoverished, alienated, empty," because "the conformist, the petit bourgeois, the ideologist of no matter which 'society' . . . is lost and dehumanized." The very fact that Ionesco throws the relativistic petty bourgeois into one pot with the ideologist, shows that he is unaware of what certain social pressures can mean for the individual. Despite the fact that the statement contains a deep human truth, his belief that the "real society, the authentic human community, is extra social," can at best sound naive to East European writers.

Ionesco, as we can gather from his own ample explanatory commentary as well as the echoes of the critics, writes to point out the essential inadequacy of man's seemingly logical—but actually merely habitual and hence automatic—chain of reasoning. In *The Bald Soprano* two characters come to the conclusion that, since they live in the same house, sit at the same table, sleep in the same bed and have the same child, they must be man and wife. Whereupon the maid, the omniscient confidante of the audience, informs the latter that the couple's reasoning was fallacious, that they are not man and wife—in fact she can prove it. This "proof," however, is as absurd in its logic as the couple's arguments. The point at which the couple recognize man and wife in each other is the realization that each has a daughter with one white and one red eye. A physiological fact plus a name is their proof: the color of the girl's eyes and her name, Alice. Then, they conclude, "there can be no doubt about it, . . . you are my own wife . . . Elizabeth, I have found you again!" And the answer is: "Donald, it's you, darling!" Here the maid enters on tiptoe and,

her finger to her lips so as not to disturb the blissful couple in their illusion, lets the audience in "on a secret." The two were utterly wrong. Namely his child has a red left and a white right eye, whereas her child has a white left and a red right eye. So far so good. But then the maid follows up her information with a fallacious conclusion which invalidates her whole argument: "In spite of the extraordinary coincidences which seem to be definite proofs, Donald and Elizabeth, not being parents of the same child, are not Donald and Elizabeth." This is a case of *ignoratio elenchi,* one of the logical fallacies: proving the wrong point and reaching the wrong conclusion. The maid's argument to prove the fallacy of human logic is just as fallacious as the latter. Ionesco has thus revealed the weakness not only of reasoning but also of the logical critique of reason. This attack on human reasoning is at the basis of the problem of modern man's automatic responses.

Another case in point is the conversation in Beckett's *Waiting for Godot,* in which Vladimir and Estragon are debating the possibility of hanging themselves. Estragon, having warmed up to the idea, wants quick action:

> ESTRAGON. Let's hang ourselves immediately!
>
> VLADIMIR. From a bough? *(They go towards the tree.)* I wouldn't trust it.
>
> ESTRAGON. We can always try.
>
> VLADIMIR. Go ahead.
>
> ESTRAGON. After you.
>
> VLADIMIR. No, no, you first.
>
> ESTRAGON. Why me?
>
> VLADIMIR. You're lighter than I am.
>
> ESTRAGON. Just so!
>
> VLADIMIR. I don't understand.
>
> ESTRAGON. Use your intelligence, can't you? *(Vladimir uses his intelligence.)*
>
> VLADIMIR. *(Finally)* I remain in the dark.
>
> ESTRAGON. This is how it is. *(He reflects.)* The bough . . . the bough . . . *(Angrily)* Use your head, can't you?
>
> VLADIMIR. You're my only hope.
>
> ESTRAGON. *(With effort)* Gogo light—bough not break—Gogo dead. Didi heavy—bough break—Didi alone. Whereas—
>
> VLADIMIR. I hadn't thought of that.

Vladimir hoped to convince Estragon with a logical argument: Estragon was lighter. Estragon proceeds to reveal the fallaciousness of this reasoning by another type of logic. Each reasons according to his own advantage. It is the situation which dictates their reasoning. Vladimir's logic says, the lighter man should try first because the bough should undergo the easier test first and, having passed it, could be submitted to the more difficult test. Estragon's logic says, if the bough passed the difficult test first, it would logically also bear up under easier tests. Vladimir has based his logic on testing the branch as such, Estragon on its performing the required function. This double display of reasoning, however, is proved irrelevant a moment later when the two realize that actually they have no idea as to who is heavier. "There is an even chance. Or nearly." Estragon muses.

As in Ionesco's play, the chain of reasoning is proven useless because the premise is wrong or unknown. This deep mistrust of human reason permeates the theatre of the absurd of the West. It is equally obvious in Harold Pinter's work. The playwright of Eastern Europe is also deeply concerned with pat responses to a situation, tries to shed light on man's automatic reactions, and questions his reasoned behavior. However, he works on a different premise. He has not lost his trust in reason—neither the reason of his audience nor that of man in general. In his essay with the forbidding title *On the Dialectics of Metaphysics* Václav Havel speculates about the truth "always being an exciting thing" which sometimes emerges in opinions that seem to tackle a question from the wrong end and which may be the contrary of those "unquestionably correct" ideas which have been proven and organized. It is needless to point out to what extent a totalitarian régime relies on and cultivates certain unchangeable—automatic, we might say—responses to certain concepts. Here is ample work for Kolakowski's jester. From many examples that come to mind I will mention only Havel's play *The Garden Party* in which a group of characters conform with absolute logic to a theoretically logical but in practice totally absurd situation: the régime has decided to abolish the Office for Liquidation and the Office for Inauguration is charged with this task. But this, the Office for Liquidation insists with steadfast logic, is impossible because only the Office of Liquidation can liquidate. The young hero, Hugo Pludek, develops in the course of the action from an avid chess-player to an expert in another game, the career-game of bureaucracy. At the end of the play he has been thoroughly depersonalized, has shed the last despicable trace of reactionary individuality, and juggles the nonsensical phrases of his organization with automatic agility. Having been invested with the important task of liquidating the Office for Liquidation he has ceased to think of himself as "I." He has become Hugo Pludek, the Director of Liquidation and when upon his returning home and discussing his career in the third person he is asked by his bewildered father who on earth he is, if he isn't his son Hugo, he answers the simpleton with didactic assurance: "I? Who I am? Look here, I don't like such onesided questions, really I don't! How can you ask so simply?" and after a lengthy tirade on the complexity and multilevelledness of truth, Hugo makes his prize statement: "We always are a little bit and a little bit we are not . . . because a man who here and there is a little bit not, will never not be!" This is not only a take-off on the twisted logic of senseless rhetorics but can also be regarded as a parody on Engels' explanation of motion in terms of the dialectical law of contradiction—a body at the same moment of time being both in one place and another place.

In Mrozek's short play *The Police* the last political prisoner of a police state who has decided to become a loyal citizen and give up his bad revolutionary ways, brings about an embarrassing situation for the state police: with the loss of this last prisoner it is no longer needed. Finally the police are saved by the self-effacing loyalty of one of their members who takes it upon himself to "play" a political revolutionary and thus restore to the police force its rea-

son for being. This admirable deed is not without consequences for him. "Colonel, can you tell me, what am I?" he dejectedly asks the Chief of Police, "I just don't know what I am now, a policeman or a prisoner. And another thing, if I'm a policeman, am I myself, or if I'm a prisoner, am I myself, and since I must be myself, am I a policeman or a prisoner?"

Just as with Havel's Hugo Pludek the automatic reasoning of the character has led him to a question of identity. He no longer knows who he is, himself or merely a part of the mechanism to which he belongs. Ionesco, too, raised the problem of identity with the maid's comment in *The Bald Soprano*. Is Elizabeth Elizabeth? Is Donald Donald? But, having raised the question, he drops it without pursuing it any further. It was only a gesture, a brilliant stage trick perhaps, not integrated into his artistic view of the world. In the case of the Eastern European playwright the reasoning which has been proven fallacious with Beckett and Ionesco is applied to a premise so well-known to the audience that it immediately grasps the logic behind the fallacy. The problem remains clear, the lines where absurdity begins are clearly drawn. In the "dialogue" between the audience and stage the source of this absurdity is identified: it is the way in which the project in a man's mind—an idea—can create a mechanism which, once it begins to function, adapts people to its function and makes them part of the mechanism. The theme of automatization in the Eastern branch of the theatre of the absurd is a search for that concealed point at which logical reasoning becomes absurd. The same theme in the Western branch of the theatre of the absurd revolves around the claim that this point can never be found.

George Wellwarth introduces his book on contemporary drama, *The Theatre of Protest and Paradox,* with disturbing comments like "today's intellectuals [are] men without faith. They can no longer scream because they can no longer hope. They can no longer speak directly to their hearers because they can no longer believe that they are heard. They can only express themselves indirectly in sardonic paradoxes." If the author had decided to include a discussion of East European plays in his book, he would have to rewrite his introduction, although his title could stand. But as it is, his introduction still stands and its gloomy content can be found in a hundred variations in critical writings on the theatre of the absurd in the West. And so it remains for us to ask: Why this belief in the absence of faith and hope? Why this fascination with the work of Albert Camus who has made the elimination of hope the main prerequisite for the Western intellectual?

Let us recall Kolakowski's opposing figures of the Jester and the Priest. "The philosophy of the jester," he writes, "is a philosophy which in every epoch denounces as doubtful what appears as unshakeable; it points out the contradictions in what seems evident and incontestable; it ridicules common sense and reads sense into the absurd . . . ; the jester represents an "attitude of negative vigilance in the face of any absolute and of the non-intellectual values inherent in an attitude the perils and absurdities of which we know." It goes without saying that Kolakowski's essay on the jester—the artist, the writer—does not make a sociological comment. He develops a philosophical argument which goes far beyond the immediate social and political situation and could refer to Aristophanes as much as to Shakespeare, Molière or Chekhov. But if we apply his comments to the theatre of the absurd, we suddenly stop short. It works for the plays of Eastern Europe (in fact they are a perfect illustration for the provocative theory) but as for the Western countries, only one of Kolakowski's comments is applicable: namely that the jester "ridicules common sense and reads sense into the absurd." The rest simply does not apply. Why? Because in the Western world today the rarest of fabled beasts is the sacred cow. Is it not completely extinguished? The task of "negative vigilance" is no longer the artist's task. In a society where critical attack and revolution (if I may be permitted to use the maltreated word in the faded sense in which it is used today by everyone) has become common to the extent that it is practically a built-in convenience, the artist as the jester who harrasses the mind that holds unshakeable beliefs has become superfluous. In other words, in the West, the jester is depressingly out of a job. Unless, that is, he takes on a greater opponent than the man-made absolutes of the day, namely the nature of life itself, the nature of time and hope and faith. Whether it is a coincidence that the genius of the greatest poet of the West today, Samuel Beckett, finds its outlet precisely in this direction is a moot question.

To what extent writers in the West are aware of these problems is impossible to say. If they all think like the Swiss writer Max Frisch, they have failed to grasp the potential of the jester's "absurd" message. Max Frisch once said that if he were a dictator, he would permit only productions of Ionesco because "the more absurd the action on the stage becomes, the more natural and acceptable reality will seem to us." It is obvious that Frisch has failed to realize that absurdity on the stage may in some instances shed strong light on the absurdity of reality. Another Swiss writer, Friedrich Dürrenmatt, has a character in one of his plays explain to us that outside the king's palace there is a huge statue with an exchangeable head. After all, why go through the expense of putting up a new statue every time the power structure was changing? Simply stick a new head on your ruler's statue and you not only save big expense but also keep up with the times.

Above the old city of Prague there is an empty pedestal. It used to bear a huge statue of Stalin which was removed when Stalinism became officially downgraded. The statue had been expensive and its removal was equally costly. Dürrenmatt's exchangeable head would have served a useful purpose. Is it surprising that the play in which he conceived this "absurd" idea was never performed in Prague? (pp. 54-63)

Marketa Goetz Stankiewicz, "The Metamorphosis of the Theatre of the Absurd or the Jobless Jester," in Pacific Coast Philology, *Vol. VII, April, 1972, pp. 54-64.*

George W. Woodyard

[*In the following essay, Woodyard surveys dramas by Spanish-American playwrights that have affinities with the Theater of the Absurd.*]

The sophistication of the contemporary Spanish American theatre links it seriously with the world avant-garde movement. Following the break with the domination of the Spanish tradition which prevailed until the experimental period of the late 1920's and 30's, the Spanish American playwrights became more eclectic in their orientation, expanding their vision to include their European and North American precursors and contemporaries. The reality-illusion conflicts of Pirandello, the alienation techniques of Brecht, the existentialist preoccupations of Camus and Sartre, and more recently, the absurdist inclinations of Beckett and Ionesco provided models which have been incorporated within a Spanish American context. The stimulus to themes and techniques has resulted in a new wave of experimentation which has been widespread, making itself felt in all the major theatrical capitals of Spanish America.

The last fifteen years, especially, have been characterized by renewed vigor and activity. In the front rank are such contemporary dramatists as Argentina's Osvaldo Dragún, Puerto Rico's René Marqués, Guatemala's Carlos Solórzano, and Mexico's Emilio Carballido. These playwrights, and others with a similarly significant production, are the interpreters of a Spanish American reality. Their sociopsychological awareness has resulted in the creation of serious new plays commenting on particular aspects of the social and human condition. Their plays transcend national limitations and become significant commentaries on a universal scale. Much of the sensationalism, melodrama, and sentimentality associated with earlier plays has been suppressed through improved control over dramatic structure and technique. Complex lighting and sound effects intensify the total theatrical experience, as well as the new dimensions added through the use of spatial dislocations, constructed around a double or revolving stage, and temporal dislocations involving flashbacks or unexplained sequences of time. Their characters are vital, complex creations, multi-faceted, who function on different levels simultaneously.

While incorporating avant-garde devices and techniques acquired from the absurdists into their plays, these dramatists see the absurdity of life, not so much in terms of idealistic man in conflict with a chaotic world, but rather in the social conventions which impinge upon man's freedom and deprive him of the opportunity of self-expression and dignity. Society is insensitive to his needs; its effects are annihilating. Both internal and external conflicts alienate him from himself and his society. His search for identity, however, continues to take place on many levels, often overlapping—national, cultural, religious, social, psychological, and metaphysical. These conflicts are sometimes posited in terms of massive cultural confrontations, inspired by figures or episodes from the national past, such as that seen in Dragún's *Tupac Amarú,* in which the Incan chief's mission represents the eternal struggle for individual freedom against an antagonistic society. By distorting the historical reality, and by couching the struggle within an existential ethic, Dragún effectively bridges the time differential in terms meaningful to modern man. While Dragún's most recent production reflects a leftist political commitment which debilitates his artistic potential, his early work shows great talent, especially his *Historias para ser contadas.* These unconventional pieces, conceived in the "commedia dell'arte" tradition as vignettes with disproportionately long titles, exemplify the dehumanizing pressures of society.

The cultural conflict is also strong in many of René Marqués' works, as he decries the assimilation of Puerto Rico's Hispanic culture into that of her aggressive North American neighbor. *Los soles truncos,* based on his own earlier short story "Purificación en la calle del Cristo," recounts the tragedy of three sisters who withdraw into an artificial world in order to compensate for progressive cultural and economic losses and their inability to adjust to the changing times. A later Marqués play, *La casa sin reloj,* introduces the absurd through Marqués' interpretation of a Puerto Rican reality. Subtitled a "Comedia antipoética en dos absurdos y un final razonable," the setting is the "island of Puerto Rico, although it could be any other place where the absurd dwells." The protagonist Micaela denies the reality of measured time; she has no consciousness of the sterility of her own existence. Time enters into her world only when she makes the existential decision to murder her brother-in-law, a fugitive Nationalist. In doing so, she achieves, paradoxically, redemption through guilt. With subtle reminiscences of Camus' *Le malentendu,* the play is a personal view of a political absurdity based essentially on a Puerto Rican situation. By extension, however, it becomes any place where people exist without making commitments to life, free of any socio-political obligations in a timeless existence.

As well as the politico-economic forces which oppress man, the institution of the church, traditionally dominant in Spanish America, is used to establish an atmosphere of ignorance and fear which leaves man helpless against its intransigent authority. The need for personal freedom—in opposition to the influence of the state, religion, or traditions—is the underlying theme of Carlos Solórzano's theatre. The influence of Camus is evident in his *Las manos de Dios,* which denounces the oppression of the church and state, and develops an existential situation in which the protagonist Beatriz is challenged to act decisively in order to gain her brother's (i.e., mankind's) freedom and her own authenticity. This undercurrent of personal liberty which pervades Solórzano's literary production is lacking only in his *Cruce de vías.* In this Kafka-like one-act play, the setting and title constitute an ironic metaphor of a non-encounter between two people. A man and woman arrange by correspondence to meet in a railway station, but the woman is old and unattractive to the younger man, and he rejects her. Life has passed her by, leaving her afraid "of living, of being . . . as if all your life you had been waiting for something which never arrives." The absurd dialogue with the Switchman reminds us of Arreola's "Guardagujas" and sets the atmosphere for the subsequent lack of communication between the two principal characters, who talk but without achieving comprehension or the significance of existence. The anti-illusionist atmosphere produced by the stylized movements of the characters Solórzano attributes to the influence of the silent screen. Frank Dauster, who has already observed this effect, remarks about the play: "The relationship between the Man and Woman, then, rather than poignant, becomes very nearly pointless, and the entire work takes on an atmosphere of sheer absurdity, of hopeless loss."

Argentina's Augustín Cuzzani through his unique "farsátiras" laments the loss of individual liberty in *El centroforward murío al amanecer* and *Sempronio.* In the latter play, a philatelist who becomes radioactive by licking Japanese stamps loses his power supply when the state removes him from his home and loved ones in order to exploit his talents and resources. Certainly one of the hemisphere's most important young dramatists is Emilio Carballido of Mexico, who has been extremely successful in experimenting with fantastic and expressionistic techniques which border on the absurd. *La hebra de oro* presents provincial characters involved in complex psychological relationships within a framework of isolation, frustration, and lack of communication, with the resulting onus to see themselves as they really are. His recent satirical *Yo también hablo de la rosa* is a reinterpretation in terms of a symbolic rose (after Sor Juana Inés de la Cruz and Xavier Villaurrutia) of the many mysteries of man's existence and behavior which are subject to exterior analyses but which ultimately remain hidden in the human heart.

Sporadic instances of the absurd exist within the dramatic production of these writers. For the most part, however, the senselessness and chaos of life are related to man's inhumanity to his neighbor and the forces of the Establishment which deprive him of his rights and values. To convey this philosophy, these dramatists have generally employed logical and rational dramatic constructions. Their characters are challenged to recognize the faith of existential commitment and stubbornly to maintain their dedication to principles. Although a violent death (suicide or murder) may be the result, this is not necessarily tragic; the real tragedy is to live out a meaningless existence without goals or principles. Although the opposing forces may be insuperable, the character is redeemed if the cause championed carries a value worth defending. The determining factor is the search for an authentic existence, for personal liberty and for the dignity of the individual above the oppressive denigration and the anonymity produced by society.

The Theatre of the Absurd, therefore, which has been unfolding over the past ten years in Spanish America, does not appear unheralded. The turn from the social problems of a Spanish American reality to universal metaphysical preoccupations (not necessarily divorced from a Spanish American context) marks the direction of the new movement. The absurdist playwrights explore the anguish and the helplessness of modern man in attempting to impose a rational order upon an incomprehensible world. At odds with his fellow man and especially with himself, he thrashes about searching for understanding of the world and the human condition. In the process, he often invents and plays out games which substitute for the religious conventions or the traditions of another epoch. For greater intensity, the dramatists often limit themselves to two-character plays, a technique which permits closer examination, not of motivation and psychological development, but of the irrationality of the frustrated and desperate human animal—anti-heroes instead of the traditional heroic figures. Feelings of contempt, insult, and hatred lead to physical violence; interpersonal relationships are brutally shattered. Fragmentation occurs in many areas: the disintegration of the personality, with the same character assuming a new identity; the distortion of language so that rational, sequential dialogue frequently ceases to exist; distortion of time and space relationships; and the disintegration of traditional dramatic structure, so that short (one-act) plays are common, and act and scene divisions accommodate, in Brechtian fashion, the spirit of the work. This paper will focus on the outstanding Spanish American dramatists whose *Weltanschauung* and production for the stage are firmly established within the contemporary idiom of the Theatre of the Absurd.

The position of Mexico's Elena Garro within the absurdist movement has already been noted by both Ruth Lamb and Frank Dauster. The tone of her earlier plays, six of which are collected under the title *Un hogar sólido,* is retained in her recent *El árbol.* In this one-act play, the two characters are Marta and the old Indian woman who relates to her the story of a murder she has committed and the time spent in prison. To this point the history has remained a secret; the only exception was that the Indian woman poured out her confession to a tree, which soon withered up. Now that she has told her story to a person for the first time, the chilling suggestion that Marta will be affected like the tree reinforces the dominant note of terror. The suspense and mystery remain unbroken, even at the end, by what is left unsaid. The Indian woman may be crazy or obsessed by her conscience, but whether or not she poses a threat to Marta's safety is left unresolved. Miss Garro makes no attempt to provide logical motivations or solutions. We are unsure, in fact, about what question is being raised. We simply see two people, previously acquainted but long out of touch, interact in a terrifying way within a delimited space. Although Miss Garro denies any spiritual kinship with Ionesco and the vanguardists, claiming instead as the source of her inspiration the classic to modern Spanish prose writers and dramatists ("those incomparable and eternal Spanish vanguardists"), the format used suggests the absurdist technique of enclosing two people within a room to see what will develop.

In Cuba the Revolution has, among other things, produced a renewed interest in the theatre, although both Virgilio Piñera and Antón Arrufat were writing absurd theatre before the rise to power of Fidel Castro. Arrufat has maintained himself on an apolitical plane in spite of the Revolution, although he has been censured for writing theatre of the absurd in a socialist society where "the logical and rational procedure of things must be pointed out." His *La zona cero* combines Sartrian existentialism and the futility of Beckett into an effective commentary on the absurd condition. The principal characters arrive at a kind of hotel where they meet and play canasta, suggestive of the chess game in Beckett's *Endgame.* The game serves as a dramatic metaphor of their existence, a game they play out in which no right or wrong exists and for which the rules are constantly changing. The action of Scene I resumes in Scene III, indicating the timelessness of their situation and their eternal commitment to a kind of Hell. This effect is emphasized by the chronological displacement of Scene II, which takes place before Scene I. The starkness of the physical stage, punctuated by a clock with no hands and a mirror without a frame, underscores the emptiness of their lives. Raimundo, the owner of the hotel, symbolizes the other forces of life, both internal and external, which impinge with authority upon the individual, leaving him helpless. Teresa and Reinaldo propose to kill him in a search for freedom, but unable to make a commitment and carry out the task, they remain subject to his control. Gómez, the servant, finds a temporary and artificial escape through drugs, but he too ultimately returns to Raimundo's domination. The characters are miserable, suffering great spiritual and mental anguish; they are afraid of time and life and yet afraid of death. They search

for morality and order in the universe, but their life holds no such security: life is amoral, disordered, senseless and chaotic. Yet they insist on knowing. When their search for the truth eludes them, they invent their own truths and find an illusory security in their fabrication. Ineffective in their search for meaning, they are resigned, as Vladimir and Estragon, to waiting:

> TERESA. (To REINALDO) What shall we do now?
>
> REINALDO. Nothing.
>
> TERESA. Let's wait.
>
> REINALDO. Perhaps tomorrow . . .

Virgilio Piñera had previously established a reputation as an absurdist although in his own particular vein. Dauster attributes this to "his willingness to shock, and his insistence on startling the audience in the process of criticizing social conditions. . . . His plays have a grotesque quality, due largely to his personal vision of the Cuban sense of humor, which he believes to be a form of escape from an unacceptable reality." In his recent two-act *Dos viejos pánicos,* which won the Casa de las Américas Theatre Award for 1968, a sixty-year-old couple invents complex games to pass the time. The game consists of strangling one another, and "being dead." They stay alive in order to play dead, and playing dead enables them to stay alive. Fear pervades the play, although it is impossible to define whether it is the fear of senility (Tabo's burning paper cutouts), fear of the political system (the questionnaire), or simply fear itself, personified. In the dissociated state of the game, the characters torment their live counterparts and chastise them for their mistakes—principally for marrying each other. In "death" they experience the same emotions and the same contradictory relationships which exist in life. They congratulate each other on innovations in the game, but they recognize that it is a senseless exercise designed to pass the time, until tomorrow, when the regenerative cycle will be repeated. The elliptic dialogue conveys the tension through mystery, and the gross language coordinates well with the scenes of violence (strangulations and smotherings). The game in which they play God, controlling the rules, opens new dimensions of human experience that allows them to get through life by killing time until time kills them.

Griselda Gambaro of Argentina has established a reputation as one of her nation's foremost young dramatists. Her most recent play *El campo* was considered one of the best of the 1968 Buenos Aires season; her earlier *Los siameses* was equally successful the previous year. The latter play, which finds its roots in existentialism and Ionesco's *Jacques, ou La Soumission,* deals with the schizophrenia of the human personality, and the appropriation of the weaker by the stronger, or as Esslin says, "the stealing of one's identity as a form of rape." Virginia Ramos Foster has correctly identified Lorenzo and Ignacio, the two principal characters, as "the two poles of human existence, perhaps the total personality of man." The two brothers were Siamese twins, previously joined physically and still joined spiritually after their operation. Lorenzo explains: "What happens, in operations of this kind, is that they cannot save both; one is ruined. To leave one fellow in perfect condition, they have to ruin the other. Necessarily." Sometimes in harmonious union and ostensibly compatible, more often the brothers are in open contradiction because the devious Lorenzo connives to destroy the naive Ignacio. The tension of the play relies on the contrapuntal technique of alternating compassion and understanding with hostility and incomprehension. Lorenzo presages Ignacio's early death, which eventually occurs through his machinations with the two absurd policemen (El Sonriente and El Gangoso). The real power of the play lies in the highly symbolic simple actions, e.g., Lorenzo's packing Ignacio's valise with his old newspapers, or his fetish of wearing heavy wool gloves in the summer. Lorenzo, through the death of Ignacio, has usurped some of his qualities which he coveted in life, but this Pyrrhic victory produces greater anguish than their earlier confrontations. Using the familiar techniques of fragmented personality and black humor, Miss Gambaro provides a highly original interpretation of modern man's hostilities and frustrations in terms of the Biblical Cain and Abel episode.

One of the most accomplished of the young Spanish American writers in dealing with the idiom of the absurd, both technically and thematically, is the Chilean Jorge Díaz. His best plays to date have been the social absurd *Topografía de un desnudo* and *El cepillo de dientes*. The latter is a Pirandellian exercise in both verbal and physical non-communication in which the two characters, husband and wife, search out another reality. In their daily breakfast ritual, they participate in a game, also of killing time, until at the end of Act I He discovers that She has used his toothbrush in order to clean her shoes. Believing that She has thus deprived him of his last vestige of individuality, he "strangles" her, but She returns in Act II disguised as the cleaning woman. Despite elaborate pretenses, they change roles freely, assuming new identities which lead to absurd situations, such as *his* supposed pregnancy (which focuses on the sterility of their marriage). The roles are violent, often grotesque, and generally anonymous; He remains unnamed, and She acquires many names, all equally meaningless to him. They are "intolerables" who methodically annihilate one another because they are different but also, paradoxically, because they are very much alike. Enclosed in a room symbolic of life itself, and bombarded by commercial propaganda, they suffer the ennui of a stale existence. In Brechtian style they dissociate themselves from the game on stage to address the audience directly; the alienation effect is intensified at the end by the dismantling of the set. At the final curtain they congratulate each other on the success of the game, as in the Piñera play, and their "tremendous love" for one another. The humor is often black, the integration of Carlos Gardel tangos smacks of high camp, but the theatrical effect is undeniable. These "náufragos en un parque de atracciones" search for amusement to restore the magic of excitement to their senseless marriage relationship and lives. After the Madrid premiere of this play, Monleón commented in *Primer Acto* on Díaz' debt to Beckett (*Waiting for Godot*) and Genet (*The Balcony*), to which we would add Pinter and Albee. Díaz has drawn freely from the absurdists, but the final product is uniquely his own.

Why has so little Theatre of the Absurd been written in Spanish America? The movement stems from the feeling that life, after all, may not be worth the effort; Esslin has said "from a feeling of deep disillusionment, the draining away of the sense of meaning and purpose in life." Esslin explains that the reason the United States has produced

very little Theatre of the Absurd is that the American dream of the good life still exists. A similar situation has obtained in Spanish America, where in spite of whimsical politics, economic underdevelopment, and foreign exploitation, a generally optimistic attitude about progress and the chances for success has prevailed. The basic values that are deeply rooted in the close family relationships within a strong Catholic tradition are not easily dismissed. These countries have not been ravaged by the massive physical and moral destruction which Europe witnessed during World War II. But although the climate for great despair has never existed before, perhaps it does exist now. With the Gross National Product barely keeping pace with the population explosion, the differential between Latin America and other technologically-oriented countries grows wider each year. The impact of foreign values through the various mass media has eroded many of the traditional family ties; the church's role as the panacea for all problems has been increasingly challenged. Contemporary man in Spanish America is being asked to face up to life as it is by writers sensitive to this cultural evolution.

This brief study does not pretend to be an exhaustive treatment of the Theatre of the Absurd in Spanish America. It will, hopefully, suggest a framework within which the study of the movement can be approached. The current indications are that the movement is still gaining momentum, and the very recent production of such talented authors as Egon Wolff, Dalmiro Sáenz, Carlos Maggi, and Rafael Vázquez should possibly be examined closely to determine their position and contribution. I have dealt here with only five authors who have developed a harmonious and fairly consistent poetic version of the absurd. Although their plays may suggest to us in both thematic and technical ways the strong influence of the European absurdists, we are nonetheless aware of their originality in combining and in creating new forms which make this Spanish American theatre worthy of international recognition. (pp. 183-91)

> *George W. Woodyard, "The Theatre of the Absurd in Spanish America," in* Comparative Drama, *Vol. 3, No. 3, Fall, 1969, pp. 183-92.*

David Goodman

[*In the following excerpt, Goodman discusses the Theater of the Absurd from a Japanese perspective and examines the works of two Japanese playwrights representing a specifically Japanese form of the Theater of the Absurd.*]

Applying terms and categories derived from Western experience to non-Western civilizations creates a tenuous problem. Kunio Shimizu and Minoru Betsuyaku . . . may well be writers in the theater of the absurd. Their work can be compared with that of their European counterparts in the theater of the absurd, and the similarities are, in fact, frequently noted by Japanese commentators. Like their European counterparts, they mimic an absurd reality, but the quality of this reality is sufficiently different from that in Europe to suggest that the unconditional subjugation of their work to the rubric of the theater of the absurd might be detrimental to its understanding. This has led me to postulate what I shall call the Japanese absurd, by which I mean a certain culturally- (not nationally-) specific perception of reality.

The existence of the Japanese absurd affects the quality of productions of classic European works of the theater of the absurd. When the Seinenza Company recently produced Ionesco's *The Chairs,* for example, the play came across, not as the mad farce of wild proliferation it is in the West, but as a parody, a precise and hilarious critique of specific aspects of Japanese society. Toward the end of Ionesco's play, an invisible emperor arrives to hear the Old Man's message. In the Seinenza Company's production, this bit of European silliness was made to coincide in a unique fashion with a certain painfully absurd reality, for in Japan there really is an emperor, and it is quite conceivable, though no less absurd for that fact, that he should be considered present when he is not. The Japanese Emperor is and historically has been a nonentity in whose name wars have been fought and peoples subjugated but who has seldom wielded real political power; who has, to all intents and purposes, been absent and invisible. "Not being there," in fact, has been among the Emperor's most functional attributes, for it has been his business to rule what the noted political scientist, Masao Maruyama, has described as a "system of irresponsibility."

The existence of the Japanese absurd also affects the critical assessments of European works of the theater of the absurd. Kaitarō Tsuno opens his first book, *A Criticism of Tragedy (Higeki no Hihan)*, with an essay describing *Waiting for Godot* as a modern tragedy very much in the European tradition. Tsuno sees Pozo in the first and second acts as a tragic hero of the classical and romantic traditions, as a conquering hero in the first act, a failed hero in the second, and he compares the play to Tom Stoppard's *Rosencrantz & Guildenstern Are Dead*, in which Hamlet is but a minor figure passing through the wings, but which nonetheless maintains the tragic superstructure Shakespeare provided in his original work. The only essential difference between Stoppard's play, Beckett's play and more easily recognizable modern tragedies is that their major events take place off stage, not on. Furthermore, Tsuno contends, Vladimir and Estragon are saved in typically tragic fashion at the end of the play as the moon rises and the two vagabonds, standing motionlessly, seem reconciled to the rhythms of nature and the peace it promises in death.

It is not necessary to agree completely with Tsuno's analysis to understand that *Waiting for Godot* is a very European play and a skillful reworking of the tragic form. It is not difficult, that is, to see that what Tsuno is indicating is that, to borrow Francis Fergusson's terms, the action being imitated in *Waiting for Godot* is that of modern Western tragedy and, by extension, Western civilization. This point is by no means at odds with Esslin's concept of the theater of the absurd, for he stresses throughout his classic book on the subject that the theater of the absurd has made an important contribution in describing the plight of Western man since the death of God; and a careful reading of Esslin's last two chapters will reveal the place of the theater of the absurd as a legitimate heir to the romantic and avant-garde traditions.

But if the Japanese are not Western men, neither has the death of the Western God been of much concern to them. Obviously, to the extent that Japanese theater is "mod-ern" it shares Western traditions and conventions; but the action being imitated in truly original Japanese drama is specifically Japanese and non-Western. While it might be appropriate to view a play like Kobo Abe's *Friends (Tomodachi,* 1967) in the tradition of the theater of the absurd without special qualifications, it will not be so easy to dispense with other works without reference to the Japanese absurd.

Kunio Shimizu was born in 1936. He graduated from Waseda University in 1960 and is the author of many plays. . . . (pp. 366-69)

The critic Ryūkō Saeki has suggested that Shimizu shares the perspective of Ionesco in that both writers believe that what is important in playmaking is the combination of a single clear obsession with a meaningful, easily understood pattern of development. Shimizu's major plays concern families who play games, whose lives and relationships have all been turned into games. As Saeki points out, "These games are autogenous, multiplying of their own accord, and thus the relationships of which the games consist constantly force the participants back to the ritual reconstruction of the obsessions that *appear* to constitute their past. . . . They have the power to incorporate everything into their games but not the power to quit."

One such game-playing family appears in *Madmen Shall Be Saved (Kyōjin nao mote Ojō o Togu,* 1969). Izuru, the eldest son in the family, seems for all the world to be out of his mind. He imagines his home to be a brothel, his mother its madam, his sister a whore and his father and brother customers. The idea of the game is Izuru's rehabilitation, and the curtain opens on Zenichiro, his father, installing a disgusting pink light in order to give the house a more lurid appearance. Only Keiji, the younger son, plans to marry and escape the family, but even this exit is blocked when Megumi, his fiancée, becomes unsuccessfully involved in the family's game.

> IZURU. What shall we do then? What? Let's pretend? Not let's pretend, I don't want to play let's pretend. But then, we might play let's pretend. . . .

The character of the family's game is mimetic. Izuru, in his madness, tries desperately to escape this mimetic game, to extrapolate experience to a higher level of abstraction and freedom, but he is always dragged back by the game's innate gravity.

> IZURU. Are you going to give up?
>
> AIKO [his sister]. No.
>
> IZURU. What are you going to do then?
>
> AIKO. I don't know.
>
> IZURU. We can't just sit here twiddling our thumbs, though. We're wasting time.
>
> AIKO. And we haven't much time.
>
> IZURU. We have to hurry.
>
> AIKO. What shall we do?
>
> IZURU. We'll make new changes.
>
> AIKO. That's it, we'll make new changes.

It is the impossibility of change, however, that forces the game's participants back to their original mimetic patterns, a hopeless fate that has driven Izuru to madness and Zenichiro to drink, for although the game is mimetic its players have long since forgotten what they are mimicking. All that is left is what Saeki calls the "ritualization of obsession."

The appearance of Megumi, however, presents a new challenge to the organism of the family. She has come to meet her prospective in-laws, but instead of a warm family circle she finds the house drenched in pink light and her new family playing whores and whoremasters. She is finally driven from the house as Zenichiro crumbles into a drunken stupor and Izuru continues to insist that she too is a whore. Keiji, his last hope of escape shattered, his attempt at love failed, follows her in distraction. When he returns it is morning, Izuru and Aiko have been seen kissing in the dark and are now together in Izuru's attic hideaway. Megumi is dead, murdered by her irate fiancé.

> KEIJI. I told you she was a dangerous woman. It was that body of hers that was most dangerous of all. Did you see those hips? Her pelvis was enormous. I'll bet she'd have babies like crazy. I once saw a picture of a woman who'd had eleven kids. Megumi had the same damned hips! She'd have eleven children, too, no doubt about it. . . . She's dangerous. We'd be in real trouble if we let her kind run loose in this world. Just think of all that power for life and destruction. . . . I just strangled her, that's all. I put her to sleep. It's for the best. I used to love her. It's for the best that I should lay her to rest.

With Megumi's murder Keiji breaks his last ties with the world of direct experience, with the world of love and fertility and joins his sister and brother in an incestuous ménage à trois. All three of them leap through the window and into their own mad world, where the game is no longer mimetic but utterly sterile and free. Looking after them, their father cries, "But I tried so hard to play with you. I tried so hard!"

The sense that the Japanese are like "one big happy family," an idea encouraged by their almost unparalleled racial, linguistic, historical and cultural homogeneity, is far from alien to Japanese thought, and when Shimizu elects to employ family units in his work, his choice has special implications. Although Shimizu may be seen as an author in the theater of the absurd, it is the Japanese absurd with which he is concerned. His works imitate the action of Japanese civilization; they are concerned with the disintegration of the symbolic game that is Japanese culture, the evanescence of the memories that are its transmitting medium and the impossibility of escaping from it without the enormous sacrifices of life and/or sanity.

Shimizu's work imitates the action of an absurd world where all experience is futile to the extent that it is ultimately dependent upon evanescent memory. *Madmen Shall Be Saved* describes the impossibility of love and creation in a world where all relationships are ultimately reduced to ritualized obsessions. Minoru Betsuyaku has described the other end of the life cycle in this absurd world.

Minoru Betsuyaku was born in Manchuria in 1937. Unable to pay his fees, he dropped out of the politics and economics department of Waseda University in 1960 during his sophomore year. In 1969 he left his job as a clerk for a labor union and made public his intention to devote himself full-time to his theatrical endeavors. Betsuyaku is the author of nearly twenty plays. . . . (pp. 370-71)

The Elephant (*Zō*, 1962; rewritten in its present form in 1965) is Betsuyaku's masterpiece. It centers around a survivor of the atomic bomb, who rests in a hospital room with an enormous keloid scar spreading across his back, and his nephew, who slowly begins to show signs of a-bomb disease. The nephew speaks to a nurse toward the middle of the play's first act.

> MAN. When the sun sets I bolt the door. If someone came, there would surely be the sound of knocking. Knock, knock, knock. At first it would be very light, and for a while I'd keep perfectly still. Knock, knock, knock. It would grow a little louder. Knock, knock, knock. I would slowly get to my feet and open the door. "Good evening. Who are you? Where have you come from? Might you have some business with me?" And the man would laugh hollowly. Looking at my face, he'd laugh, hollowly. With his slender fingers he'd point at me and slowly his swallowed laughter would spill from his lips. But I would not know how to explain. You understand? I do not know how to explain.
>
> NURSE. First of all you begin to bleed from the nose. Everyone is that way. First of all, you begin to bleed from the nose. . . .
> *Blackout.*

The nephew has had an experience. He has been exposed to atomic radiation. We do not know how he was exposed, whether his eposure was direct or indirect as an unborn infant, but in any event the young man is in no way responsible for his experience, nor can he control it. He cannot explain it, and he is terrified of being called upon to do so. His uncle, on the other hand, relishes his experience of the bomb. He speaks relentlessly about the days immediately following the war when he would pull his wagon out into the sun-drenched, dusty streets of "that town" and strike poses, displaying his keloid to best advantage. He dreams of making a comeback.

> WIFE. Do you think people will really come to see?
>
> INVALID. Of course they'll come. I used to pull the old wagon round the corner, and they'd call from this direction and that about how here comes the naked keloid man, and everyone'd come running. Don't you remember?

While his nephew wishes only to be left in peace, the Invalid dreams of being murdered on the street as he tries to display his keloid.

> INVALID. I'll be standing there with my feet planted firmly on the ground, my hands on my hips, scowling at the sky. Then, out of nowhere this bad guy's gonna come carrying a knife, and he's gonna run right into me and drive the knife through my belly. Blood'll come gushing out. Everyone will gather round and they'll carry me in their arms, but by that time I'll already be dead. . . . After I'm gone they'll realize for the

first time. The fact that I suffered, I mean. They'll catch on then for the first time that every day I'd been throwing myself into my work body and soul for them. That's why they might lynch the guy that murdered me. . . .

But times have changed. "That town" is not the same anymore. The sun no longer shines on dusty, rubble-strewn streets, but on broad, modern thoroughfares. The Invalid is but one of the millions of victims of war who have been forgotten, swept off to the grave or some sanitary clearing house one step before. Even his keloid, the symbol of his great personal experience, has lost its luster and become covered with spots. His experience has become devalued to the extent that he is even to be denied a personal death. Though alive he has already been doomed to joining the millions of other charred carcasses. But it is not the fact that he was a victim of the atomic bomb that assigns him his fate; it is rather the character of our age, where unique, personal, redeeming "tragic" death, the ultimate experience, has been made impossible, and where, by virtue of this fact, we are doomed to futility.

> MAN. Uncle, get this through your head. Listen. We mustn't do anything anymore. Not anything. To do something is the worst thing of all. No matter how hard it is, we've got to lie here patiently and keep our mouths shut. It's not because we're sick. That's not it. I don't say that. I'm no doctor. It's just that we mustn't try to do things, that's all. We are incapable of doing anything except being persecuted, hated, and destroyed. We cannot even think about being loved. When we're not being murdered, hated, or tormented, we wait. There's nothing left for us but to wait. We rest quietly.

The playwright Makoto Satō has commented on the similarities between *The Elephant* and the Duras-Resnais film, *Hiroshima Mon Amour*. This comparison is invaluable in comprehending the genius of both works, but it is especially useful in this context for understanding the Japanese absurd. *Hiroshima Mon Amour* is a brilliant film. Naturally enough it is thoroughly French in its orientation. Its focus inevitably falls upon the French actress who falls in love with a Japanese architect while making a peace film in Hiroshima. It is she who comes to Hiroshima, creates the necessary conditions for the action of the film and then returns to France. She has the power to name, and her last words to the Japanese architect she has come to love are, "Hi-ro-shi-ma, that's your name." He can only confirm her realization, naming her in turn, "Nevers." The actress returns to France while the architect remains in Hiroshima. Each returns to his respective habitat, there to nurture the memory of their love, which is at once Hiroshima and Nevers. Betsuyaku's *The Elephant* picks up where the film leaves off, for the action that it imitates is the impossibility of keeping these memories alive, the absurd world in which we live where even an experience as devastating as the atomic bomb is powerless to make a lasting impression. For all of Duras's endearing humanism, the lovers do part. The Japanese is left in Hiroshima, symbol of forgetfulness, there to face the steady recession of experience into memory and memory into dream. It is this absurdity, which remains after all the Europeans have gone home, that forms the central theme of *The Elephant* and that comprises the Japanese absurd.

The repeated historical experience of this phenomenon of forgetfulness and the terrifying suspicion that experience may be little more substantial than a dream is an essential part of the Japanese absurd. In order to grasp the significance and thrust of contemporary Japanese drama it is necessary to consider, not the theater of the absurd in Japan, but the theater of the Japanese absurd. (pp. 371-73)

> *David Goodman, "The Japanese Absurd," in* Books Abroad, *Vol. 46, No. 3, Summer, 1972, pp. 366-73.*

FURTHER READING

I. Anthologies

Esslin, Martin, ed. *Absurd Drama.* Harmondsworth, England: Penguin Books, 1965, 184 p.
  Includes *Amédée, or How to Get Rid of It* by Eugène Ionesco, *Professor Taranne* by Arthur Adamov, *The Two Executioners* by Fernando Arrabal, and *The Zoo Story* by Edward Albee, with an introduction by Esslin.

II. Secondary Sources

Ashmore, Jerome. "Interdisciplinary Roots of the Absurd." *Modern Drama* 14, No. 1 (May 1971): 72-83.
  Discusses the philosophical sources for the concept of the absurd and examines the works of Ionesco, Beckett, Pinter, and Genet.

Banarjee, R. B. "The Theatre of the Absurd." *The Literary Criterion* 7, No. 1 (Winter 1965): 59-62.
  Summarizes the central points of Esslin's *The Theatre of the Absurd.*

Bermel, Albert. "Ionesco: Anything but Absurd." *Twentieth Century Literature* 21, No. 4 (December 1975): 411-20.
  Reacts to critics who consider Ionesco a nihilist with an examination of *The Chairs* that emphasizes the "positive artistry, liveliness, and humor" of this work.

"The Impact of the Theater of the Absurd on World Drama." *Books Abroad* 46, No. 3 (Summer 1972): 359-92.
  Section of this issue comprising five essays on the influence of the Theater of the Absurd in Yugoslavia, Japan, Finno-Baltic countries, Spain, and Poland and Czechoslovakia.

Bourque, Joseph. "Theatre of the Absurd: A New Approach to Audience Reaction." *Research Studies* 36, No. 4 (December 1968): 311-24.
  Argues that the popularity of absurdist plays is the result of the entertaining manner in which they are presented rather than in any universal truth they impart.

Brustein, Robert. "The Absurd and the Ridiculous." In his *Seasons of Discontent: Dramatic Opinions, 1959-1965,* pp. 60-3. New York: Simon and Schuster, 1965.
  Challenges Esslin's concept of a Theater of the Absurd. Brustein contends that "having theorized at length about this anti-theoretical drama, Mr. Esslin inadvertently reduces it to a formula—a manual of avant-garde dramaturgy, subject to imitation by every opportunistic

scribbler. And though he frequently cautions us to re-gard each playwright as an inspired individual rather than just a figure in a movement, the effect of his exertions is to make us overwhelmingly conscious of the fashion—and a good deal less aware of the art."

Carpenter, Charles A. " 'Victims of Duty'? The Critics, Absurdity, and *The Homecoming.*" *Modern Drama* 25, No. 4 (December 1982): 489-95.
  Argues that the enigmatic nature of Harold Pinter's *The Homecoming,* which is often considered an example of absurdist theater, is "the chief source of the play's power and of its richly deserved stature."

Den, Petr. "Notes on Czechoslovakia's Young Theater of the Absurd." *Books Abroad* 41, No. 2 (Spring 1987): 157-63.
  Considers the role of absurdist works by Czechoslovaki-an playwrights in revealing life under communist rule.

Elsom, John. "The End of the Absurd?" *Contemporary Review* 252, No. 1467 (April 1988): 198-201.
  Summary of the development of the philosophical concept of the absurd and its usefulness in present-day society.

Fischler, Alexander. "The Absurd Professor in the Theater of the Absurd." *Modern Drama* 21, No. 2 (June 1978): 137-52.
  Examines the stock theatrical character of the "absurd professor"—a figure whose most abiding trait is his "incongruity" with the other characters in the drama—as depicted in the Theater of the Absurd. Fischler concludes that the "Theater of the Absurd could not make the absurd professor seem logical any more than it could make him blend harmoniously with his surroundings. However, by accentuating and accelerating the disjointedness of character, setting and situation, . . . the Theater of the Absurd turned the professor into a central figure for the representation of man's condition in the modern world, in a way neither Mr. Chips nor his cousins, Molière's Docteurs, could have represented it."

Gilman, Richard. "The Absurd and the Foolish." *The Commonweal* 76, No. 2 (6 April 1962): 40-1.
  Provides a concise definition of the Theater of the Absurd, distinguishing between the representatives Gilman considers genuine, such as Beckett and Ionesco, and spurious ones, such as Jack Gelber and Arthur Kopit.

Gravitt, G. Jack. "The Modernity of *The Rehearsal:* Buckingham's Theatre of the Absurd." *College Literature* 9, No. 1 (Winter 1982): 30-8.
  Finds that the sixteenth-century drama *The Rehearsal* by George Villiers, second duke of Buckingham, anticipates dramatic devices of the Theater of the Absurd.

Huckabay, Keith. "Black Humor and Theatre of the Absurd." *Cimarron Review,* No. 20 (July 1972): 20-32.
  Observes parallels between the Theater of the Absurd and American "Black Humor" novels of the 1950s and 1960s, including Joseph Heller's *Catch-22* and John Barth's *Sot-Weed Factor,* stating that "primary to both genres is the assumption that existence is absurd. Both depict a world gone completely insane, a world where only the illogical is logical, where madness is the standard condition. The subject matter for both is usually the most hideous or pathetic imaginable. . . . Yet, paradoxically, the new genre treatment of this subject matter produces comedy. . . ."

Ionesco, Eugène. *Notes and Counter Notes: Writings on the Theatre.* Translated by Donald Watson. New York: Grove Press, 1964, 271 p.
  Includes interviews and Ionesco's commentary on his own plays, and reprints essays by Kenneth Tynan and others written in reaction to *The Chairs.*

Knight, Alan E. "The Medieval Theater of the Absurd." *PMLA* 86, No. 2 (March 1971): 183-89.
  Demonstrates resemblances between comic theater in late medieval France and the Theater of the Absurd, including the use of clowns and clowning techniques, a strong sense of the grotesque, and a satircal rendering of rigid conventions of society.

Orlich, Jessie Montejo de. "The Ultimate Purpose of the Theater of the Absurd." *Revista de la Universidad de Costa Rica,* No. 36 (December 1973): 101-03.
  Finds the ultimate purpose of the Theater of the Absurd to be highly affirmative rather than pessimistic, describing it as "an attempt to make man aware of his conditioning and a challenge to see fully the importance of self-realization before man can proceed to fulfill his destiny."

Palls, Terry L. "The Theatre of the Absurd in Cuba After 1959." *Latin American Literary Review* 4, No. 7 (Fall-Winter 1975): 67-72.
  Identifies dramas by Cuban playwrights that reflect elements of the absurd tradition and considers the relationship between these works and the Cuban revolution of 1959.

Pronko, Leonard Cabell. *Avant-Garde: The Experimental Theater in France.* Berkeley and Los Angeles: University of California Press, 225 p.
  Study largely devoted to playwrights associated with the Theater of the Absurd, including Beckett, Ionesco, Genet, and Adamov.

Quackenbush, L. H. "Theatre of the Absurd, Reality, and Carlos Maggi." *Journal of Spanish Studies* 3, No. 1 (Spring 1975): 61-72.
  Examines the combination of theatrical devices of the Theater of the Absurd with social issues in two plays by the Spanish American dramatist Carlos Maggi.

Sherzer, Dina. "Dialogic Incongruities in the Theater of the Absurd." *Semiotica* 22, Nos. 3-4 (1978): 269-85.
  Semiotic analysis of dialogue in plays by Beckett, Ionesco, Pinter, and Jorge Díaz. Observing that "one of the most innovative aspects of the Theater of the Absurd is that it plays down the referential aspect of language and focuses instead on the interactional patterns," Sherzer concludes that the "action in these static plays takes place *within* language rather than *with* language. Viewed in terms of verbal interactions, the *parlerie* of the Theater of the Absurd is an anamorphosis of both ordinary patterns of interaction and of traditional dialogues in the theater. It is a succession of implicit metacommunicative comments which make us aware both of the complexities of everyday interactions and of the conventions of the theater."

Singh, Ram Sewak. *Absurd Drama, 1945-1965.* Chandni Chowk, India: Nootan Press, 1973, 148 p.
  Introductory study with chapters devoted to Samuel Beckett, Eugène Ionesco, Jean Genet, and Harold Pinter.

Srivastava, Avadhesh K. "The Crooked Mirror: Notes on the Theatre of the Absurd." *The Literary Criterion* 11, No. 2 (Summer 1974): 58-62.

Describes the Theater of the Absurd as decadent because it "shares with the literature of decadence in other ages certain themes and tendencies such as extreme intellectualisation, forms of self-pity, and a romantic yearning unrelated to the rather plebeian aims of fulfillment or realisation." The critic also expands on Esslin's distinction between the absurd as a philosophical concept underlying the realistic dramas of Jean-Paul Sartre and Albert Camus and the absurd as a style of theater that is anti-realist.

Tolpin, Marian. "Eugene Ionesco's *The Chairs* and the Theater of the Absurd." *American Imago* 25, No. 2 (Summer 1968): 119-39.

Discusses *The Chairs* as an artistic manifestation of its author's "*psychic* reality which has been projected to stand for mankind's reality."

Venclova, Tomas. "Echoes of the Theater of the Absurd and of the 'Theater of Cruelty' in Contemporary Lithuania." In *Fiction and Drama in Eastern and Southeastern Europe: Evolution and Experiment in the Postwar Period,* edited by Henrik Birnbaum and Thomas Eekman, pp. 429-41. Columbus, Ohio: Slavica Publishers, 1980.

Establishes the influence of the Theater of the Absurd and Antonin Artaud's Theater of Cruelty on the Lithuanian playwrights K. Saja and J. Glinskis.

Wearing, J. P. "Two Early Absurd Plays in England." *Modern Drama* 16, Nos. 3-4 (December 1973): 259-64.

Examines two plays by Arthur Pinero, *Playgoers* and *A Seat in the Park,* as "remarkable for the traits they exhibit of what is now widely called the Theater of the Absurd."

Twentieth-Century
Literary Criticism

Cumulative Indexes
Volumes 1-38

This Index Includes References to Entries in These Gale Series

Contemporary Literary Criticism

Presents excerpts of criticism on the works of novelists, poets, dramatists, short story writers, scriptwriters, and other creative writers who are now living or who have died since 1960.

Twentieth-Century Literary Criticism

Contains critical excerpts by the most significant commentators on poets, novelists, short story writers, dramatists, and philosophers who died between 1900 and 1960.

Nineteenth-Century Literature Criticism

Offers significant passages from criticism on authors who died between 1800 and 1899.

Literature Criticism from 1400 to 1800

Compiles significant passages from the most noteworthy criticism on authors of the fifteenth through eighteenth centuries.

Classical and Medieval Literature Criticism

Offers excerpts of criticism on the works of world authors from classical antiquity through the fourteenth century.

Short Story Criticism

Compiles excerpts of criticism on short fiction by writers of all eras and nationalities.

Children's Literature Review

Includes excerpts from reviews, criticism, and commentary on works of authors and illustrators who create books for children.

Contemporary Authors Series

Encompasses five related series. *Contemporary Authors* provides biographical and bibliographical information on more than 95,000 writers of fiction, nonfiction, poetry, journalism, drama, motion pictures, and other fields. Each new volume contains sketches on authors not previously covered in the series. *Contemporary Authors New Revision Series* provides completely updated information on active authors covered in previously published volumes of *CA*. Only entries requiring significant change are revised for *CA New Revision Series. Contemporary Authors Permanent Series* consists of updated listings for deceased and inactive authors removed from the original volumes 9-36 when these volumes were revised. *Contemporary Authors Autobiography Series* presents specially commissioned autobiographies by leading contemporary writers. *Contemporary Authors Bibliographical Series* contains primary and secondary bibliographies as well as analytical bibliographical essays by authorities on major modern authors.

Dictionary of Literary Biography

Encompasses four related series. *Dictionary of Literary Biography* furnishes illustrated overviews of authors' lives and works and places them in the larger perspective of literary history. *Dictionary of Literary Biography Documentary Series* illuminates the careers of major figures through a selection of literary documents, including letters, notebook and diary entries, interviews, book reviews, and photographs. *Dictionary of Literary Biography Yearbook* summarizes the past year's literary activity with articles on genres, major prizes, conferences, and other timely subjects and includes updated and new entries on individual authors. *Concise Dictionary of American Literary Biography* comprises six volumes of revised and updated sketches on major American authors that were originally presented in *Dictionary of Literary Biography*.

Something about the Author Series

Encompasses three related series. *Something about the Author* contains heavily illustrated biographical sketches on juvenile and young adult authors and illustrators from all eras. *Something about the Author Autobiography Series* presents specially commissioned autobiographies by prominent authors and illustrators of books for children and young adults. *Authors & Artists for Young Adults* provides high school and junior high school students with profiles of their favorite creative artists in the mediums of print, film, television, drama, song lyrics, and cartoons.

Yesterday's Authors of Books for Children

Contains heavily illustrated entries on children's writers who died before 1961. Complete in two volumes.

Literary Criticism Series
Cumulative Author Index

This index lists all author entries in the Gale Literary Criticism Series and includes cross-references to other Gale sources. References in the index are identified as follows:

AAYA: *Authors & Artists for Young Adults,* Volumes 1-3
CAAS: *Contemporary Authors Autobiography Series,* Volumes 1-11
CA: *Contemporary Authors* (original series), Volumes 1-130
CABS: *Contemporary Authors Bibliographical Series,* Volumes 1-3
CANR: *Contemporary Authors New Revision Series,* Volumes 1-29
CAP: *Contemporary Authors Permanent Series,* Volumes 1-2
CA-R: *Contemporary Authors* (revised editions), Volumes 1-44
CDALB: *Concise Dictionary of American Literary Biography,* Volumes 1-6
CLC: *Contemporary Literary Criticism,* Volumes 1-61
CLR: *Children's Literature Review,* Volumes 1-21
CMLC: *Classical and Medieval Literature Criticism,* Volumes 1-5
DC: *Drama Criticism,* Volume 1
DLB: *Dictionary of Literary Biography,* Volumes 1-92
DLB-DS: *Dictionary of Literary Biography Documentary Series,* Volumes 1-7
DLB-Y: *Dictionary of Literary Biography Yearbook,* Volumes 1980-1988
LC: *Literature Criticism from 1400 to 1800,* Volumes 1-14
NCLC: *Nineteenth-Century Literature Criticism,* Volumes 1-28
PC: *Poetry Criticism,* Volume 1
SAAS: *Something about the Author Autobiography Series,* Volumes 1-9
SATA: *Something about the Author,* Volumes 1-59
SSC: *Short Story Criticism,* Volumes 1-6
TCLC: *Twentieth-Century Literary Criticism,* Volumes 1-37
YABC: *Yesterday's Authors of Books for Children,* Volumes 1-2

A. E. 1867-1935 .... TCLC 3, 10
See also Russell, George William
See also DLB 19

Abbey, Edward 1927-1989 ...... CLC 36, 59
See also CANR 2; CA 45-48;
obituary CA 128

Abbott, Lee K., Jr. 19?? .... CLC 48

Abe, Kobo 1924- .... CLC 8, 22, 53
See also CANR 24; CA 65-68

Abell, Kjeld 1901-1961........... CLC 15
See also obituary CA 111

Abish, Walter 1931- .... CLC 22
See also CA 101

Abrahams, Peter (Henry) 1919- ..... CLC 4
See also CA 57-60

Abrams, M(eyer) H(oward) 1912-... CLC 24
See also CANR 13; CA 57-60; DLB 67

Abse, Dannie 1923-............ CLC 7, 29
See also CAAS 1; CANR 4; CA 53-56;
DLB 27

Achebe, (Albert) Chinua(lumogu)
1930- .... CLC 1, 3, 5, 7, 11, 26, 51
See also CLR 20; CANR 6, 26; CA 1-4R;
SATA 38, 40

Acker, Kathy 1948- .... CLC 45
See also CA 117, 122

Ackroyd, Peter 1949-.......... CLC 34, 52
See also CA 123, 127

Acorn, Milton 1923-.............. CLC 15
See also CA 103; DLB 53

Adamov, Arthur 1908-1970 ...... CLC 4, 25
See also CAP 2; CA 17-18;
obituary CA 25-28R

Adams, Alice (Boyd) 1926- ... CLC 6, 13, 46
See also CANR 26; CA 81-84; DLB-Y 86

Adams, Douglas (Noel) 1952- ... CLC 27, 60
See also CA 106; DLB-Y 83

Adams, Henry (Brooks)
1838-1918 .... TCLC 4
See also CA 104; DLB 12, 47

Adams, Richard (George)
1920- .... CLC 4, 5, 18
See also CLR 20; CANR 3; CA 49-52;
SATA 7

Adamson, Joy(-Friederike Victoria)
1910-1980 .... CLC 17
See also CANR 22; CA 69-72;
obituary CA 93-96; SATA 11;
obituary SATA 22

Adcock, (Karen) Fleur 1934-...... CLC 41
See also CANR 11; CA 25-28R; DLB 40

Addams, Charles (Samuel)
1912-1988 .... CLC 30
See also CANR 12; CA 61-64;
obituary CA 126

Adler, C(arole) S(chwerdtfeger)
1932- .... CLC 35
See also CANR 19, CA 89-92; SATA 26

Adler, Renata 1938-............ CLC 8, 31
See also CANR 5, 22; CA 49-52

Ady, Endre 1877-1919 .... TCLC 11
See also CA 107

Agee, James 1909-1955 .... TCLC 1, 19
See also CA 108; DLB 2, 26;
CDALB 1941-1968

Agnon, S(hmuel) Y(osef Halevi)
1888-1970 .... CLC 4, 8, 14
See also CAP 2; CA 17-18;
obituary CA 25-28R

Ai 1947-...................... CLC 4, 14
See also CA 85-88

Aickman, Robert (Fordyce)
1914-1981 .... CLC 57
See also CANR 3; CA 7-8R

Aiken, Conrad (Potter)
1889-1973 . . . . **CLC 1, 3, 5, 10, 52**
See also CANR 4; CA 5-8R;
obituary CA 45-48; SATA 3, 30; DLB 9,
45

Aiken, Joan (Delano) 1924- . . . . **CLC 35**
See also CLR 1; CANR 4; CA 9-12R;
SAAS 1; SATA 2, 30

Ainsworth, William Harrison
1805-1882 . . . . **NCLC 13**
See also SATA 24; DLB 21

Ajar, Emile 1914-1980
See Gary, Romain

Akhmadulina, Bella (Akhatovna)
1937- . . . . **CLC 53**
See also CA 65-68

Akhmatova, Anna 1888-1966 . . . . **CLC 11, 25**
See also CAP 1; CA 19-20;
obituary CA 25-28R

Aksakov, Sergei Timofeyvich
1791-1859 . . . . **NCLC 2**

Aksenov, Vassily (Pavlovich) 1932-
See Aksyonov, Vasily (Pavlovich)

Aksyonov, Vasily (Pavlovich)
1932- . . . . **CLC 22, 37**
See also CANR 12; CA 53-56

Akutagawa Ryunosuke
1892-1927 . . . . **TCLC 16**
See also CA 117

Alain-Fournier 1886-1914 . . . . **TCLC 6**
See also Fournier, Henri Alban
See also DLB 65

Alarcon, Pedro Antonio de
1833-1891 . . . . **NCLC 1**

Alas (y Urena), Leopoldo (Enrique Garcia)
1852-1901 . . . . **TCLC 29**
See also CA 113

Albee, Edward (Franklin III)
1928- . . . **CLC 1, 2, 3, 5, 9, 11, 13, 25, 53**
See also CANR 8; CA 5-8R; DLB 7;
CDALB 1941-1968

Alberti, Rafael 1902- . . . . **CLC 7**
See also CA 85-88

Alcott, Amos Bronson 1799-1888 . . **NCLC 1**
See also DLB 1

Alcott, Louisa May 1832-1888 . . . . **NCLC 6**
See also CLR 1; YABC 1; DLB 1, 42;
CDALB 1865-1917

Aldanov, Mark 1887-1957 . . . . **TCLC 23**
See also CA 118

Aldington, Richard 1892-1962 . . . . . . **CLC 49**
See also CA 85-88; DLB 20, 36

Aldiss, Brian W(ilson)
1925- . . . . **CLC 5, 14, 40**
See also CAAS 2; CANR 5; CA 5-8R;
SATA 34; DLB 14

Alegria, Fernando 1918- . . . . **CLC 57**
See also CANR 5; CA 11-12R

Aleixandre, Vicente 1898-1984 . . . **CLC 9, 36**
See also CANR 26; CA 85-88;
obituary CA 114

Alepoudelis, Odysseus 1911-
See Elytis, Odysseus

Aleshkovsky, Yuz 1929- . . . . **CLC 44**
See also CA 121

Alexander, Lloyd (Chudley) 1924- . . **CLC 35**
See also CLR 1, 5; CANR 1; CA 1-4R;
SATA 3, 49; DLB 52

Alger, Horatio, Jr. 1832-1899 . . . . . **NCLC 8**
See also SATA 16; DLB 42

Algren, Nelson 1909-1981 . . . . **CLC 4, 10, 33**
See also CANR 20; CA 13-16R;
obituary CA 103; DLB 9; DLB-Y 81, 82;
CDALB 1941-1968

Alighieri, Dante 1265-1321 . . . . **CMLC 3**

Allard, Janet 1975- . . . . **CLC 59**

Allen, Edward 1948- . . . . **CLC 59**

Allen, Roland 1939-
See Ayckbourn, Alan

Allen, Woody 1935- . . . . **CLC 16, 52**
See also CANR 27; CA 33-36R; DLB 44

Allende, Isabel 1942- . . . . **CLC 39, 57**
See also CA 125

Allingham, Margery (Louise)
1904-1966 . . . . **CLC 19**
See also CANR 4; CA 5-8R;
obituary CA 25-28R

Allingham, William 1824-1889 . . . **NCLC 25**
See also DLB 35

Allston, Washington 1779-1843 . . . . **NCLC 2**
See also DLB 1

Almedingen, E. M. 1898-1971 . . . . . . **CLC 12**
See also Almedingen, Martha Edith von
See also SATA 3

Almedingen, Martha Edith von 1898-1971
See Almedingen, E. M.
See also CANR 1; CA 1-4R

Alonso, Damaso 1898- . . . . **CLC 14**
See also CA 110

Alta 1942- . . . . **CLC 19**
See also CA 57-60

Alter, Robert B(ernard) 1935- . . . . . . **CLC 34**
See also CANR 1; CA 49-52

Alther, Lisa 1944- . . . . **CLC 7, 41**
See also CANR 12; CA 65-68

Altman, Robert 1925- . . . . **CLC 16**
See also CA 73-76

Alvarez, A(lfred) 1929- . . . . **CLC 5, 13**
See also CANR 3; CA 1-4R; DLB 14, 40

Alvarez, Alejandro Rodriguez 1903-1965
See Casona, Alejandro
See also obituary CA 93-96

Amado, Jorge 1912- . . . . **CLC 13, 40**
See also CA 77-80

Ambler, Eric 1909- . . . . **CLC 4, 6, 9**
See also CANR 7; CA 9-12R

Amichai, Yehuda 1924- . . . . . . **CLC 9, 22, 57**
See also CA 85-88

Amiel, Henri Frederic 1821-1881 . . **NCLC 4**

Amis, Kingsley (William)
1922- . . . . . . **CLC 1, 2, 3, 5, 8, 13, 40, 44**
See also CANR 8; CA 9-12R; DLB 15, 27

Amis, Martin 1949- . . . . **CLC 4, 9, 38**
See also CANR 8; CA 65-68; DLB 14

Ammons, A(rchie) R(andolph)
1926- . . . . . . **CLC 2, 3, 5, 8, 9, 25, 57**
See also CANR 6; CA 9-12R; DLB 5

Anand, Mulk Raj 1905- . . . . **CLC 23**
See also CA 65-68

Anaya, Rudolfo A(lfonso) 1937- . . . . **CLC 23**
See also CAAS 4; CANR 1; CA 45-48

Andersen, Hans Christian
1805-1875 . . . . **NCLC 7; SSC 6**
See also CLR 6; YABC 1, 1

Anderson, Jessica (Margaret Queale)
19??- . . . . **CLC 37**
See also CANR 4; CA 9-12R

Anderson, Jon (Victor) 1940- . . . . **CLC 9**
See also CANR 20; CA 25-28R

Anderson, Lindsay 1923- . . . . **CLC 20**

Anderson, Maxwell 1888-1959 . . . . . **TCLC 2**
See also CA 105; DLB 7

Anderson, Poul (William) 1926- . . . . **CLC 15**
See also CAAS 2; CANR 2, 15; CA 1-4R;
SATA 39; DLB 8

Anderson, Robert (Woodruff)
1917- . . . . **CLC 23**
See also CA 21-24R; DLB 7

Anderson, Roberta Joan 1943-
See Mitchell, Joni

Anderson, Sherwood
1876-1941 . . . . . . **TCLC 1, 10, 24; SSC 1**
See also CAAS 3; CA 104, 121; DLB 4, 9;
DLB-DS 1

Andrade, Carlos Drummond de
1902-1987 . . . . **CLC 18**
See also CA 123

Andrewes, Lancelot 1555-1626 . . . . **LC 5**

Andrews, Cicily Fairfield 1892-1983
See West, Rebecca

Andreyev, Leonid (Nikolaevich)
1871-1919 . . . . **TCLC 3**
See also CA 104

Andrezel, Pierre 1885-1962
See Dinesen, Isak; Blixen, Karen
(Christentze Dinesen)

Andric, Ivo 1892-1975 . . . . **CLC 8**
See also CA 81-84; obituary CA 57-60

Angelique, Pierre 1897-1962
See Bataille, Georges

Angell, Roger 1920- . . . . **CLC 26**
See also CANR 13; CA 57-60

Angelou, Maya 1928- . . . . **CLC 12, 35**
See also CANR 19; CA 65-68; SATA 49;
DLB 38

Annensky, Innokenty 1856-1909 . . . **TCLC 14**
See also CA 110

Anouilh, Jean (Marie Lucien Pierre)
1910-1987 . . . . . . **CLC 1, 3, 8, 13, 40, 50**
See also CA 17-20R; obituary CA 123

Anthony, Florence 1947-
See Ai

Anthony (Jacob), Piers 1934- . . . . . . **CLC 35**
See also Jacob, Piers A(nthony)
D(illingham)
See also DLB 8

Antoninus, Brother 1912-
See Everson, William (Oliver)

Antonioni, Michelangelo 1912- . . . . . **CLC 20**
See also CA 73-76

Antschel, Paul 1920-1970
See Celan, Paul
See also CA 85-88

Anwar, Chairil 1922-1949 . . . . **TCLC 22**
See also CA 121

Apollinaire, Guillaume
1880-1918 . . . . **TCLC 3, 8**
See also Kostrowitzki, Wilhelm Apollinaris
de

Appelfeld, Aharon 1932- . . . . **CLC 23, 47**
See also CA 112

Apple, Max (Isaac) 1941-. . . . . **CLC 9, 33**
See also CANR 19; CA 81-84

Appleman, Philip (Dean) 1926- . . . **CLC 51**
See also CANR 6; CA 13-16R

Apuleius, (Lucius) (Madaurensis)
125?-175? . . . . **CMLC 1**

Aquin, Hubert 1929-1977. . . . . **CLC 15**
See also CA 105; DLB 53

Aragon, Louis 1897-1982. . . . . **CLC 3, 22**
See also CA 69-72; obituary CA 108;
DLB 72

Arbuthnot, John 1667-1735. . . . . **LC 1**

Archer, Jeffrey (Howard) 1940- . . . . **CLC 28**
See also CANR 22; CA 77-80

Archer, Jules 1915- . . . . **CLC 12**
See also CANR 6; CA 9-12R; SAAS 5;
SATA 4

Arden, John 1930- . . . . **CLC 6, 13, 15**
See also CAAS 4; CA 13-16R; DLB 13

Arenas, Reinaldo 1943- . . . . **CLC 41**

Aretino, Pietro 1492-1556. . . . . **LC 12**

Arguedas, Jose Maria
1911-1969 . . . . **CLC 10, 18**
See also CA 89-92

Argueta, Manlio 1936-. . . . . **CLC 31**

Ariosto, Ludovico 1474-1533. . . . . **LC 6**

Aristophanes
c. 450 B. C.-c. 385 B. C. . . . . . . **CMLC 4**

Arlt, Roberto 1900-1942 . . . . **TCLC 29**
See also CA 123

Armah, Ayi Kwei 1939-. . . . . **CLC 5, 33**
See also CANR 21; CA 61-64

Armatrading, Joan 1950-. . . . . **CLC 17**
See also CA 114

Arnim, Achim von (Ludwig Joachim von
Arnim) 1781-1831 . . . . **NCLC 5**

Arnold, Matthew 1822-1888 . . . . . . **NCLC 6**
See also DLB 32, 57

Arnold, Thomas 1795-1842 . . . . . . **NCLC 18**
See also DLB 55

Arnow, Harriette (Louisa Simpson)
1908-1986 . . . . **CLC 2, 7, 18**
See also CANR 14; CA 9-12R;
obituary CA 118; SATA 42, 47; DLB 6

Arp, Jean 1887-1966. . . . . **CLC 5**
See also CA 81-84; obituary CA 25-28R

Arquette, Lois S(teinmetz) 1934-
See Duncan (Steinmetz Arquette), Lois
See also SATA 1

Arrabal, Fernando 1932- . . . **CLC 2, 9, 18, 58**
See also CANR 15; CA 9-12R

Arrick, Fran 19??- . . . . **CLC 30**

Artaud, Antonin 1896-1948 . . . . . **TCLC 3, 36**
See also CA 104

Arthur, Ruth M(abel) 1905-1979. . . . **CLC 12**
See also CANR 4; CA 9-12R;
obituary CA 85-88; SATA 7;
obituary SATA 26

Artsybashev, Mikhail Petrarch
1878-1927 . . . . **TCLC 31**

Arundel, Honor (Morfydd)
1919-1973 . . . . **CLC 17**
See also CAP 2; CA 21-22;
obituary CA 41-44R; SATA 4;
obituary SATA 24

Asch, Sholem 1880-1957 . . . . **TCLC 3**
See also CA 105

Ashbery, John (Lawrence)
1927- . . . **CLC 2, 3, 4, 6, 9, 13, 15, 25, 41**
See also CANR 9; CA 5-8R; DLB 5;
DLB-Y 81

Ashton-Warner, Sylvia (Constance)
1908-1984 . . . . **CLC 19**
See also CA 69-72; obituary CA 112

Asimov, Isaac 1920-. . . . **CLC 1, 3, 9, 19, 26**
See also CLR 12; CANR 2, 19; CA 1-4R;
SATA 1, 26; DLB 8

Astley, Thea (Beatrice May)
1925- . . . . **CLC 41**
See also CANR 11; CA 65-68

Aston, James 1906-1964
See White, T(erence) H(anbury)

Asturias, Miguel Angel
1899-1974 . . . . **CLC 3, 8, 13**
See also CAP 2; CA 25-28;
obituary CA 49-52

Atheling, William, Jr. 1921-1975
See Blish, James (Benjamin)

Atherton, Gertrude (Franklin Horn)
1857-1948 . . . . **TCLC 2**
See also CA 104; DLB 9

Atwood, Margaret (Eleanor)
1939- . . . . **CLC 2, 3, 4, 8, 13, 15, 25, 44;**
SSC 2
See also CANR 3, 24; CA 49-52; SATA 50;
DLB 53

Aubin, Penelope 1685-1731? . . . . **LC 9**
See also DLB 39

Auchincloss, Louis (Stanton)
1917- . . . . **CLC 4, 6, 9, 18, 45**
See also CANR 6; CA 1-4R; DLB 2;
DLB-Y 80

Auden, W(ystan) H(ugh)
1907-1973 . . . . . **CLC 1, 2, 3, 4, 6, 9, 11,**
14, 43
See also CANR 5; CA 9-12R;
obituary CA 45-48; DLB 10, 20

Audiberti, Jacques 1899-1965 . . . . . . **CLC 38**
See also obituary CA 25-28R

Auel, Jean M(arie) 1936-. . . . . **CLC 31**
See also CANR 21; CA 103

Austen, Jane 1775-1817. . . . **NCLC 1, 13, 19**

Auster, Paul 1947-. . . . . **CLC 47**
See also CANR 23; CA 69-72

Austin, Mary (Hunter)
1868-1934 . . . . **TCLC 25**
See also CA 109; DLB 9

Avison, Margaret 1918-. . . . . **CLC 2, 4**
See also CA 17-20R; DLB 53

Ayckbourn, Alan 1939- . . . . **CLC 5, 8, 18, 33**
See also CA 21-24R; DLB 13

Aydy, Catherine 1937-
See Tennant, Emma

Ayme, Marcel (Andre) 1902-1967. . . **CLC 11**
See also CA 89-92; DLB 72

Ayrton, Michael 1921-1975. . . . . **CLC 7**
See also CANR 9, 21; CA 5-8R;
obituary CA 61-64

Azorin 1874-1967 . . . . **CLC 11**
See also Martinez Ruiz, Jose

Azuela, Mariano 1873-1952. . . . . . . **TCLC 3**
See also CA 104

"Bab" 1836-1911
See Gilbert, (Sir) W(illiam) S(chwenck)

Babel, Isaak (Emmanuilovich)
1894-1941 . . . . **TCLC 2, 13**
See also CA 104

Babits, Mihaly 1883-1941 . . . . **TCLC 14**
See also CA 114

Bacchelli, Riccardo 1891-1985 . . . . . **CLC 19**
See also CA 29-32R; obituary CA 117

Bach, Richard (David) 1936-. . . . . . . **CLC 14**
See also CANR 18; CA 9-12R; SATA 13

Bachman, Richard 1947-
See King, Stephen (Edwin)

Bacovia, George 1881-1957 . . . . **TCLC 24**

Bagehot, Walter 1826-1877 . . . . . . **NCLC 10**
See also DLB 55

Bagnold, Enid 1889-1981. . . . . **CLC 25**
See also CANR 5; CA 5-8R;
obituary CA 103; SATA 1, 25; DLB 13

Bagryana, Elisaveta 1893- . . . . . . **CLC 10**

Bailey, Paul 1937- . . . . **CLC 45**
See also CANR 16; CA 21-24R; DLB 14

Baillie, Joanna 1762-1851 . . . . **NCLC 2**

Bainbridge, Beryl
1933- . . . . **CLC 4, 5, 8, 10, 14, 18, 22**
See also CA 21-24R; DLB 14

Baker, Elliott 1922- . . . . **CLC 8, 61**
See also CANR 2; CA 45-48

Baker, Nicholson 1957-

Baker, Russell (Wayne) 1925-. . . . . . **CLC 31**
See also CANR 11; CA 57-60

Bakshi, Ralph 1938-. . . . . **CLC 26**
See also CA 112

Bakunin, Mikhail (Alexandrovich)
1814-1876 . . . . **NCLC 25**

Baldwin, James (Arthur)
1924-1987 . . . . . **CLC 1, 2, 3, 4, 5, 8, 13,**
15, 17, 42, 50
See also CANR 3; CA 1-4R;
obituary CA 124; CABS 1; SATA 9;
DLB 2, 7, 33; DLB-Y 87;
CDALB 1941-1968

Ballard, J(ames) G(raham)
1930- . . . . **CLC 3, 6, 14, 36; SSC 1**
See also CANR 15; CA 5-8R; DLB 14

Balmont, Konstantin Dmitriyevich
1867-1943 . . . . **TCLC 11**
See also CA 109

Balzac, Honore de
1799-1850 . . . . NCLC 5; SSC 5

Bambara, Toni Cade   1939- . . . . CLC 19
See also CA 29-32R; DLB 38

Bandanes, Jerome   1937- . . . . CLC 59, 59

Banim, John   1798-1842 . . . . NCLC 13

Banim, Michael   1796-1874 . . . . . . NCLC 13

Banks, Iain   1954- . . . . CLC 34
See also CA 123

Banks, Lynne Reid   1929- . . . . CLC 23
See also Reid Banks, Lynne

Banks, Russell   1940- . . . . CLC 37
See also CANR 19; CA 65-68

Banville, John   1945- . . . . CLC 46
See also CA 117; DLB 14

Banville, Theodore (Faullain) de
1832-1891 . . . . NCLC 9

Baraka, Imamu Amiri
1934- . . . . CLC 1, 2, 3, 5, 10, 14, 33
See also Jones, (Everett) LeRoi   ,
See also DLB 5, 7, 16, 38;
CDALB 1941-1968

Barbellion, W. N. P.   1889-1919 . . . TCLC 24

Barbera, Jack   1945- . . . . CLC 44
See also CA 110

Barbey d'Aurevilly, Jules Amedee
1808-1889 . . . . NCLC 1

Barbusse, Henri   1873-1935 . . . . TCLC 5
See also CA 105; DLB 65

Barea, Arturo   1897-1957 . . . . TCLC 14
See also CA 111

Barfoot, Joan   1946- . . . . CLC 18
See also CA 105

Baring, Maurice   1874-1945 . . . . TCLC 8
See also CA 105; DLB 34

Barker, Clive   1952- . . . . CLC 52
See also CA 121

Barker, George (Granville)
1913- . . . . CLC 8, 48
See also CANR 7; CA 9-12R; DLB 20

Barker, Howard   1946- . . . . CLC 37
See also CA 102; DLB 13

Barker, Pat   1943- . . . . CLC 32
See also CA 117, 122

Barlow, Joel   1754-1812 . . . . NCLC 23
See also DLB 37

Barnard, Mary (Ethel)   1909- . . . . . . CLC 48
See also CAP 2; CA 21-22

Barnes, Djuna (Chappell)
1892-1982 . . . CLC 3, 4, 8, 11, 29; SSC 3
See also CANR 16; CA 9-12R;
obituary CA 107; DLB 4, 9, 45

Barnes, Julian   1946- . . . . CLC 42
See also CANR 19; CA 102

Barnes, Peter   1931- . . . . CLC 5, 56
See also CA 65-68; DLB 13

Baroja (y Nessi), Pio   1872-1956 . . . . TCLC 8
See also CA 104

Barondess, Sue K(aufman)   1926-1977
See Kaufman, Sue
See also CANR 1; CA 1-4R;
obituary CA 69-72

Barrett, (Roger) Syd   1946-
See Pink Floyd

Barrett, William (Christopher)
1913- . . . . CLC 27
See also CANR 11; CA 13-16R

Barrie, (Sir) J(ames) M(atthew)
1860-1937 . . . . TCLC 2
See also CLR 16; YABC 1; CA 104;
DLB 10

Barrol, Grady   1953-
See Bograd, Larry

Barry, Philip (James Quinn)
1896-1949 . . . . TCLC 11
See also CA 109; DLB 7

Barth, John (Simmons)
1930- . . . . . . CLC 1, 2, 3, 5, 7, 9, 10, 14,
27, 51
See also CANR 5, 23; CA 1-4R; CABS 1;
DLB 2

Barthelme, Donald
1931-1989 . . . . . CLC 1, 2, 3, 5, 6, 8, 13,
23, 46, 59; SSC 2
See also CANR 20; CA 21-24R, 129;
SATA 7; DLB 2; DLB-Y 80

Barthelme, Frederick   1943- . . . . CLC 36
See also CA 114, 122; DLB-Y 85

Barthes, Roland   1915-1980 . . . . CLC 24
See also obituary CA 97-100

Barzun, Jacques (Martin)   1907- . . . . CLC 51
See also CANR 22; CA 61-64

Bashkirtseff, Marie   1859-1884 . . . NCLC 27

Bassani, Giorgio   1916- . . . . CLC 9
See also CA 65-68

Bataille, Georges   1897-1962 . . . . CLC 29
See also CA 101; obituary CA 89-92

Bates, H(erbert) E(rnest)
1905-1974 . . . . CLC 46
See also CA 93-96; obituary CA 45-48

Baudelaire, Charles   1821-1867 . . . . NCLC 6

Baudrillard, Jean   1929- . . . . CLC 60

Baum, L(yman) Frank   1856-1919 . . . TCLC 7
See also CLR 15; CA 108; SATA 18;
DLB 22

Baumbach, Jonathan   1933- . . . . . . CLC 6, 23
See also CAAS 5; CANR 12; CA 13-16R;
DLB-Y 80

Bausch, Richard (Carl)   1945- . . . . . . CLC 51
See also CA 101

Baxter, Charles   1947- . . . . CLC 45
See also CA 57-60

Baxter, James K(eir)   1926-1972 . . . . CLC 14
See also CA 77-80

Bayer, Sylvia   1909-1981
See Glassco, John

Beagle, Peter S(oyer)   1939- . . . . CLC 7
See also CANR 4; CA 9-12R; DLB-Y 80

Beard, Charles A(ustin)
1874-1948 . . . . TCLC 15
See also CA 115; SATA 18; DLB 17

Beardsley, Aubrey   1872-1898 . . . . . NCLC 6

Beattie, Ann   1947- . . . . CLC 8, 13, 18, 40
See also CA 81-84; DLB-Y 82

Beattie, James   1735-1803 . . . . NCLC 25

Beauvoir, Simone (Lucie Ernestine Marie
Bertrand) de
1908-1986 . . . CLC 1, 2, 4, 8, 14, 31, 44,
50
See also CA 9-12R; obituary CA 118;
DLB 72; DLB-Y 86

Becker, Jurek   1937- . . . . CLC 7, 19
See also CA 85-88

Becker, Walter   1950- . . . . CLC 26

Beckett, Samuel (Barclay)
1906-1989 . . . . . CLC 1, 2, 3, 4, 6, 9, 10,
11, 14, 18, 29, 57, 59
See also CA 5-8R; DLB 13, 15

Beckford, William   1760-1844 . . . . NCLC 16
See also DLB 39

Beckman, Gunnel   1910- . . . . CLC 26
See also CANR 15; CA 33-36R; SATA 6

Becque, Henri   1837-1899 . . . . NCLC 3

Beddoes, Thomas Lovell
1803-1849 . . . . NCLC 3

Beecher, John   1904-1980 . . . . CLC 6
See also CANR 8; CA 5-8R;
obituary CA 105

Beer, Johann   1655-1700 . . . . LC 5

Beer, Patricia   1919?- . . . . CLC 58
See also CANR 13; CA 61-64; DLB 40

Beerbohm, (Sir Henry) Max(imilian)
1872-1956 . . . . TCLC 1, 24
See also CA 104; DLB 34

Behan, Brendan
1923-1964 . . . . CLC 1, 8, 11, 15
See also CA 73-76; DLB 13

Behn, Aphra   1640?-1689 . . . . LC 1
See also DLB 39

Behrman, S(amuel) N(athaniel)
1893-1973 . . . . CLC 40
See also CAP 1; CA 15-16;
obituary CA 45-48; DLB 7, 44

Beiswanger, George Edwin   1931-
See Starbuck, George (Edwin)

Belasco, David   1853-1931 . . . . TCLC 3
See also CA 104; DLB 7

Belcheva, Elisaveta   1893-
See Bagryana, Elisaveta

Belinski, Vissarion Grigoryevich
1811-1848 . . . . NCLC 5

Belitt, Ben   1911- . . . . CLC 22
See also CAAS 4; CANR 7; CA 13-16R;
DLB 5

Bell, Acton   1820-1849
See Bronte, Anne

Bell, Currer   1816-1855
See Bronte, Charlotte

Bell, Madison Smartt   1957- . . . . CLC 41
See also CA 111

Bell, Marvin (Hartley)   1937- . . . . . CLC 8, 31
See also CA 21-24R; DLB 5

Bellamy, Edward   1850-1898 . . . . . . NCLC 4
See also DLB 12

Belloc, (Joseph) Hilaire (Pierre Sebastien
Rene Swanton)
1870-1953 . . . . TCLC 7, 18
See also YABC 1; CA 106; DLB 19

Bellow, Saul
1915- ..... **CLC 1, 2, 3, 6, 8, 10, 13, 15, 25, 33, 34**
See also CA 5-8R; CABS 1; DLB 2, 28;
DLB-Y 82; DLB-DS 3;
CDALB 1941-1968

Belser, Reimond Karel Maria de   1929-
See Ruyslinck, Ward

Bely, Andrey   1880-1934 ....**TCLC 7**
See also CA 104

Benary-Isbert, Margot   1889-1979 ...**CLC 12**
See also CLR 12; CANR 4; CA 5-8R;
obituary CA 89-92; SATA 2;
obituary SATA 21

Benavente (y Martinez), Jacinto
1866-1954 ....**TCLC 3**
See also CA 106

Benchley, Peter (Bradford)
1940- ....**CLC 4, 8**
See also CANR 12; CA 17-20R; SATA 3

Benchley, Robert   1889-1945 ....**TCLC 1**
See also CA 105; DLB 11

Benedikt, Michael   1935- ....**CLC 4, 14**
See also CANR 7; CA 13-16R; DLB 5

Benet, Juan   1927-.................**CLC 28**

Benet, Stephen Vincent
1898-1943 ....**TCLC 7**
See also YABC 1; CA 104; DLB 4, 48

Benet, William Rose   1886-1950 ...**TCLC 28**
See also CA 118; DLB 45

Benford, Gregory (Albert)   1941-....**CLC 52**
See also CANR 12, 24; CA 69-72;
DLB-Y 82

Benn, Gottfried   1886-1956.........**TCLC 3**
See also CA 106; DLB 56

Bennett, Alan   1934- ....**CLC 45**
See also CA 103

Bennett, (Enoch) Arnold
1867 1931 ....**TCLC 5, 20**
See also CA 106; DLB 10, 34

Bennett, George Harold   1930-
See Bennett, Hal
See also CA 97-100

Bennett, Hal   1930-................**CLC 5**
See also Bennett, George Harold
See also DLB 33

Bennett, Jay   1912-.................**CLC 35**
See also CANR 11; CA 69-72; SAAS 4;
SATA 27, 41

Bennett, Louise (Simone)   1919-.....**CLC 28**
See also Bennett-Coverly, Louise Simone

Bennett-Coverly, Louise Simone   1919-
See Bennett, Louise (Simone)
See also CA 97-100

Benson, E(dward) F(rederic)
1867-1940 ....**TCLC 27**
See also CA 114

Benson, Jackson J.   1930-.........**CLC 34**
See also CA 25-28R

Benson, Sally   1900-1972 ....**CLC 17**
See also CAP 1; CA 19-20;
obituary CA 37-40R; SATA 1, 35;
obituary SATA 27

Benson, Stella   1892-1933........**TCLC 17**
See also CA 117; DLB 36

Bentley, E(dmund) C(lerihew)
1875-1956 ....**TCLC 12**
See also CA 108; DLB 70

Bentley, Eric (Russell)   1916-......**CLC 24**
See also CANR 6; CA 5-8R

Berger, John (Peter)   1926- ......**CLC 2, 19**
See also CA 81-84; DLB 14

Berger, Melvin (H.)   1927-.........**CLC 12**
See also CANR 4; CA 5-8R; SAAS 2;
SATA 5

Berger, Thomas (Louis)
1924- ....**CLC 3, 5, 8, 11, 18, 38**
See also CANR 5; CA 1-4R; DLB 2;
DLB-Y 80

Bergman, (Ernst) Ingmar   1918-.....**CLC 16**
See also CA 81-84

Bergson, Henri   1859-1941 ....**TCLC 32**

Bergstein, Eleanor   1938- ....**CLC 4**
See also CANR 5; CA 53-56

Berkoff, Steven   1937-.............**CLC 56**
See also CA 104

Bermant, Chaim   1929- ....**CLC 40**
See also CANR 6; CA 57-60

Bernanos, (Paul Louis) Georges
1888-1948 ....**TCLC 3**
See also CA 104; DLB 72

Bernard, April   19??-..............**CLC 59**

Bernhard, Thomas
1931-1989 ....**CLC 3, 32, 61**
See also CA 85-88,; obituary CA 127;
DLB 85

Berriault, Gina   1926-.............**CLC 54**
See also CA 116

Berrigan, Daniel J.   1921-,,,,,,,,,,.**CLC 4**
See also CAAS 1; CANR 11; CA 33-36R;
DLB 5

Berrigan, Edmund Joseph Michael, Jr.
1934-1983
See Berrigan, Ted
See also CANR 14; CA 61-64;
obituary CA 110

Berrigan, Ted   1934-1983 ....**CLC 37**
See also Berrigan, Edmund Joseph Michael,
Jr.
See also DLB 5

Berry, Chuck   1926- ,,,,,,,,,,,,,..**CLC 17**

Berry, Wendell (Erdman)
1934- ....**CLC 4, 6, 8, 27, 46**
See also CA 73-76; DLB 5, 6

Berryman, John
1914-1972 .....**CLC 1, 2, 3, 4, 6, 8, 10, 13, 25**
See also CAP 1; CA 15-16;
obituary CA 33-36R; CABS 2; DLB 48;
CDALB 1941-1968

Bertolucci, Bernardo   1940- ....**CLC 16**
See also CA 106

Bertran de Born   c. 1140-1215 5 ...**CMLC 5**

Besant, Annie (Wood)   1847-1933 ...**TCLC 9**
See also CA 105

Bessie, Alvah   1904-1985..........**CLC 23**
See also CANR 2; CA 5-8R;
obituary CA 116; DLB 26

Beti, Mongo   1932- ....**CLC 27**
See also Beyidi, Alexandre

Betjeman, (Sir) John
1906-1984 ....**CLC 2, 6, 10, 34, 43**
See also CA 9-12R; obituary CA 112;
DLB 20; DLB-Y 84

Betti, Ugo   1892-1953 ....**TCLC 5**
See also CA 104

Betts, Doris (Waugh)   1932-....**CLC 3, 6, 28**
See also CANR 9; CA 13-16R; DLB-Y 82

Bialik, Chaim Nachman
1873-1934 ....**TCLC 25**

Bidart, Frank   19??-...............**CLC 33**

Bienek, Horst   1930-.............**CLC 7, 11**
See also CA 73-76; DLB 75

Bierce, Ambrose (Gwinett)
1842-1914? ....**TCLC 1, 7**
See also CA 104; DLB 11, 12, 23, 71, 74;
CDALB 1865-1917

Billington, Rachel   1942-...........**CLC 43**
See also CA 33-36R

Binyon, T(imothy) J(ohn)   1936- ....**CLC 34**
See also CA 111

Bioy Casares, Adolfo   1914-.....**CLC 4, 8, 13**
See also CANR 19; CA 29-32R

Bird, Robert Montgomery
1806-1854 ....**NCLC 1**

Birdwell, Cleo   1936-
See DeLillo, Don

Birney (Alfred) Earle
1904-....................**CLC 1, 4, 6, 11**
See also CANR 5, 20; CA 1-4R

Bishop, Elizabeth
1911-1979 ......**CLC 1, 4, 9, 13, 15, 32**
See also CANR 26; CA 5-8R;
obituary CA 89 92; CABS 2;
obituary SATA 24; DLB 5

Bishop, John   1935-................**CLC 10**
See also CA 105

Bissett, Bill   1939-................**CLC 18**
See also CANR 15; CA 69-72; DLB 53

Bitov, Andrei (Georgievich)   1937-...**CLC 57**

Biyidi, Alexandre   1932-
See Beti, Mongo
See also CA 114, 124

Bjornson, Bjornstjerne (Martinius)
1832-1910 ....**TCLC 7, 37**
See also CA 104

Blackburn, Paul   1926-1971 ......**CLC 9, 43**
See also CA 81-84; obituary CA 33-36R;
DLB 16; DLB-Y 81

Black Elk   1863-1950 ....**TCLC 33**

Blackmore, R(ichard) D(oddridge)
1825-1900 ....**TCLC 27**
See also CA 120; DLB 18

Blackmur, R(ichard) P(almer)
1904-1965 ....**CLC 2, 24**
See also CAP 1; CA 11-12;
obituary CA 25-28R; DLB 63

Blackwood, Algernon (Henry)
1869-1951 ....**TCLC 5**
See also CA 105

Blackwood, Caroline   1931- ....**CLC 6, 9**
See also CA 85-88; DLB 14

Blair, Eric Arthur 1903-1950
See Orwell, George
See also CA 104; SATA 29

Blais, Marie-Claire
1939- .... CLC 2, 4, 6, 13, 22
See also CAAS 4; CA 21-24R; DLB 53

Blaise, Clark 1940-.............. CLC 29
See also CAAS 3; CANR 5; CA 53-56R;
DLB 53

Blake, Nicholas 1904-1972
See Day Lewis, C(ecil)

Blake, William 1757-1827 .... NCLC 13
See also SATA 30

Blasco Ibanez, Vicente
1867-1928 .... TCLC 12
See also CA 110

Blatty, William Peter 1928-........ CLC 2
See also CANR 9; CA 5-8R

Blessing, Lee 1949-............... CLC 54

Blish, James (Benjamin)
1921-1975 .... CLC 14
See also CANR 3; CA 1-4R;
obituary CA 57-60; DLB 8

Blixen, Karen (Christentze Dinesen)
1885-1962
See Dinesen, Isak
See also CAP 2; CA 25-28; SATA 44

Bloch, Robert (Albert) 1917-....... CLC 33
See also CANR 5; CA 5-8R; SATA 12;
DLB 44

Blok, Aleksandr (Aleksandrovich)
1880-1921 .... TCLC 5
See also CA 104

Bloom, Harold 1930- .... CLC 24
See also CA 13-16R; DLB 67

Blount, Roy (Alton), Jr. 1941- ..... CLC 38
See also CANR 10; CA 53-56

Bloy, Leon 1846-1917............ TCLC 22
See also CA 121

Blume, Judy (Sussman Kitchens)
1938- .... CLC 12, 30
See also CLR 2, 15; CANR 13; CA 29-32R;
SATA 2, 31; DLB 52

Blunden, Edmund (Charles)
1896-1974 .... CLC 2, 56
See also CAP 2; CA 17-18;
obituary CA 45-48; DLB 20

Bly, Robert (Elwood)
1926- .... CLC 1, 2, 5, 10, 15, 38
See also CA 5-8R; DLB 5

Bochco, Steven 1944?-............ CLC 35

Bodker, Cecil 1927- .... CLC 21
See also CANR 13; CA 73-76; SATA 14

Boell, Heinrich (Theodor) 1917-1985
See Boll, Heinrich
See also CANR 24; CA 21-24R;
obituary CA 116

Bogan, Louise 1897-1970..... CLC 4, 39, 46
See also CA 73-76; obituary CA 25-28R;
DLB 45

Bogarde, Dirk 1921-.............. CLC 19
See also Van Den Bogarde, Derek (Jules
Gaspard Ulric) Niven
See also DLB 14

Bogosian, Eric 1953- .... CLC 45

Bograd, Larry 1953-............. CLC 35
See also CA 93-96; SATA 33

Bohl de Faber, Cecilia 1796-1877
See Caballero, Fernan

Boiardo, Matteo Maria 1441-1494 .... LC 6

Boileau-Despreaux, Nicolas
1636-1711 .... LC 3

Boland, Eavan (Aisling) 1944-...... CLC 40
See also DLB 40

Boll, Heinrich (Theodor)
1917-1985 ... CLC 2, 3, 6, 9, 11, 15, 27,
39
See also Boell, Heinrich (Theodor)
See also DLB 69; DLB-Y 85

Bolt, Robert (Oxton) 1924-........ CLC 14
See also CA 17-20R; DLB 13

Bond, Edward 1934-....... CLC 4, 6, 13, 23
See also CA 25-28R; DLB 13

Bonham, Frank 1914-............. CLC 12
See also CANR 4; CA 9-12R; SAAS 3;
SATA 1, 49

Bonnefoy, Yves 1923-........ CLC 9, 15, 58
See also CA 85-88

Bontemps, Arna (Wendell)
1902-1973 .... CLC 1, 18
See also CLR 6; CANR 4; CA 1-4R;
obituary CA 41-44R; SATA 2, 44;
obituary SATA 24; DLB 48, 51

Booth, Martin 1944-.............. CLC 13
See also CAAS 2; CA 93-96

Booth, Philip 1925-............... CLC 23
See also CANR 5; CA 5-8R; DLB-Y 82

Booth, Wayne C(layson) 1921- ..... CLC 24
See also CAAS 5; CANR 3; CA 1-4R;
DLB 67

Borchert, Wolfgang 1921-1947 ..... TCLC 5
See also CA 104; DLB 69

Borges, Jorge Luis
1899-1986 ... CLC 1, 2, 3, 4, 6, 8, 9, 10,
13, 19, 44, 48; SSC 4
See also CANR 19; CA 21-24R; DLB-Y 86

Borowski, Tadeusz 1922-1951...... TCLC 9
See also CA 106

Borrow, George (Henry)
1803-1881 .... NCLC 9
See also DLB 21, 55

Bosschere, Jean de 1878-1953..... TCLC 19
See also CA 115

Boswell, James 1740-1795.......... LC 4

Bottoms, David 1949-............. CLC 53
See also CANR 22; CA 105; DLB-Y 83

Boucolon, Maryse 1937-
See Conde, Maryse
See also CA 110

Bourget, Paul (Charles Joseph)
1852-1935 .... TCLC 12
See also CA 107

Bourjaily, Vance (Nye) 1922- .... CLC 8
See also CAAS 1; CANR 2; CA 1-4R;
DLB 2

Bourne, Randolph S(illiman)
1886-1918 .... TCLC 16
See also CA 117; DLB 63

Bova, Ben(jamin William) 1932-.... CLC 45
See also CLR 3; CANR 11; CA 5-8R;
SATA 6; DLB-Y 81

Bowen, Elizabeth (Dorothea Cole)
1899-1973 ..... CLC 1, 3, 6, 11, 15, 22;
SSC 3
See also CAP 2; CA 17-18;
obituary CA 41-44R; DLB 15

Bowering, George 1935-........ CLC 15, 47
See also CANR 10; CA 21-24R; DLB 53

Bowering, Marilyn R(uthe) 1949-... CLC 32
See also CA 101

Bowers, Edgar 1924- .... CLC 9
See also CANR 24; CA 5-8R; DLB 5

Bowie, David 1947- .... CLC 17
See also Jones, David Robert

Bowles, Jane (Sydney) 1917-1973.... CLC 3
See also CAP 2; CA 19-20;
obituary CA 41-44R

Bowles, Paul (Frederick)
1910- .... CLC 1, 2, 19, 53; SSC 3
See also CAAS 1; CANR 1, 19; CA 1-4R;
DLB 5, 6

Box, Edgar 1925-
See Vidal, Gore

Boyd, William 1952-.......... CLC 28, 53
See also CA 114, 120

Boyle, Kay 1903- .. CLC 1, 5, 19, 58; SSC 5
See also CAAS 1; CA 13-16R; DLB 4, 9, 48

Boyle, Patrick 19??-.............. CLC 19

Boyle, Thomas Coraghessan
1948- .... CLC 36, 55
See also CA 120; DLB-Y 86

Brackenridge, Hugh Henry
1748-1816 .... NCLC 7
See also DLB 11, 37

Bradbury, Edward P. 1939-
See Moorcock, Michael

Bradbury, Malcolm (Stanley)
1932- .... CLC 32, 61
See also CANR 1; CA 1-4R; DLB 14

Bradbury, Ray(mond Douglas)
1920- .... CLC 1, 3, 10, 15, 42
See also CANR 2; CA 1-4R; SATA 11;
DLB 2, 8

Bradford, Gamaliel 1863-1932..... TCLC 36
See also DLB 17

Bradley, David (Henry), Jr. 1950- .. CLC 23
See also CANR 26; CA 104; DLB 33

Bradley, John Ed 1959-........... CLC 55

Bradley, Marion Zimmer 1930-..... CLC 30
See also CANR 7; CA 57-60; DLB 8

Bradstreet, Anne 1612-1672......... LC 4
See also DLB 24; CDALB 1640-1865

Bragg, Melvyn 1939-............. CLC 10
See also CANR 10; CA 57-60; DLB 14

Braine, John (Gerard)
1922-1986 .... CLC 1, 3, 41
See also CANR 1; CA 1-4R;
obituary CA 120; DLB 15; DLB-Y 86

Brammer, Billy Lee 1930?-1978
See Brammer, William

Brammer, William 1930?-1978 ..... CLC 31
See also obituary CA 77-80

Brancati, Vitaliano 1907-1954 ..... **TCLC 12**
See also CA 109

Brancato, Robin F(idler) 1936- ..... **CLC 35**
See also CANR 11; CA 69-72; SATA 23

Brand, Millen 1906-1980 .... **CLC 7**
See also CA 21-24R; obituary CA 97-100

Branden, Barbara 19??- .... **CLC 44**

Brandes, Georg (Morris Cohen)
1842-1927 .... **TCLC 10**
See also CA 105

Branley, Franklyn M(ansfield)
1915- .... **CLC 21**
See also CLR 13; CANR 14; CA 33-36R;
SATA 4

Brathwaite, Edward 1930- .... **CLC 11**
See also CANR 11; CA 25-28R; DLB 53

Brautigan, Richard (Gary)
1935-1984 .... **CLC 1, 3, 5, 9, 12, 34, 42**
See also CA 53-56; obituary CA 113;
DLB 2, 5; DLB-Y 80, 84

Brecht, (Eugen) Bertolt (Friedrich)
1898-1956 .... **TCLC 1, 6, 13, 35**
See also CA 104; DLB 56

Bremer, Fredrika 1801-1865 ..... **NCLC 11**

Brennan, Christopher John
1870-1932 .... **TCLC 17**
See also CA 117

Brennan, Maeve 1917- .... **CLC 5**
See also CA 81-84

Brentano, Clemens (Maria)
1778-1842 .... **NCLC 1**

Brenton, Howard 1942- .... **CLC 31**
See also CA 69-72; DLB 13

Breslin, James 1930-
See Breslin, Jimmy
See also CA 73-76

Breslin, Jimmy 1930- .... **CLC 4, 43**
See also Breslin, James

Bresson, Robert 1907- ...., **CLC 16**
See also CA 110

Breton, Andre 1896-1966... **CLC 2, 9, 15, 54**
See also CAP 2; CA 19-20;
obituary CA 25-28R; DLB 65

Breytenbach, Breyten 1939-..... **CLC 23, 37**
See also CA 113

Bridgers, Sue Ellen 1942- .... **CLC 26**
See also CANR 11; CA 65-68; SAAS 1,
SATA 22; DLB 52

Bridges, Robert 1844-1930........ **TCLC 1**
See also CA 104; DLB 19

Bridie, James 1888-1951 .... **TCLC 3**
See also Mavor, Osborne Henry
See also DLB 10

Brin, David 1950-................. **CLC 34**
See also CANR 24; CA 102

Brink, Andre (Philippus)
1935- .... **CLC 18, 36**
See also CA 104

Brinsmead, H(esba) F(ay) 1922- .... **CLC 21**
See also CANR 10; CA 21-24R; SAAS 5;
SATA 18

Brittain, Vera (Mary) 1893?-1970... **CLC 23**
See also CAP 1; CA 15-16;
obituary CA 25-28R

Broch, Hermann 1886-1951....... **TCLC 20**
See also CA 117

Brock, Rose 1923-
See Hansen, Joseph

Brodkey, Harold 1930-........... **CLC 56**
See also CA 111

Brodsky, Iosif Alexandrovich 1940-
See Brodsky, Joseph (Alexandrovich)
See also CA 41-44R

Brodsky, Joseph (Alexandrovich)
1940- .... **CLC 4, 6, 13, 36, 50**
See also Brodsky, Iosif Alexandrovich

Brodsky, Michael (Mark) 1948- .... **CLC 19**
See also CANR 18; CA 102

Bromell, Henry 1947-............. **CLC 5**
See also CANR 9; CA 53-56

Bromfield, Louis (Brucker)
1896-1956 .... **TCLC 11**
See also CA 107; DLB 4, 9

Broner, E(sther) M(asserman)
1930- .... **CLC 19**
See also CANR 8, 25; CA 17-20R; DLB 28

Bronk, William 1918-............. **CLC 10**
See also CANR 23; CA 89-92

Bronte, Anne 1820-1849.......... **NCLC 4**
See also DLB 21

Bronte, Charlotte 1816-1855 .... **NCLC 3, 8**
See also DLB 21

Bronte, (Jane) Emily 1818-1848 .. **NCLC 16**
See also DLB 21, 32

Brooke, Frances 1724-1789 .... **LC 6**
See also DLB 39

Brooke, Henry 1703?-1783 .... **LC 1**
See also DLB 39

Brooke, Rupert (Chawner)
1887-1915 .... **TCLC 2, 7**
See also CA 104; DLB 19

Brooke-Rose, Christine 1926- ...... **CLC 40**
See also CA 13-16R; DLB 14

Brookner, Anita 1928-...... **CLC 32, 34, 51**
See also CA 114, 120; DLB-Y 87

Brooks, Cleanth 1906- .... **CLC 24**
See also CA 17-20R; DLB 63

Brooks, Gwendolyn
1917- .... **CLC 1, 2, 4, 5, 15, 49**
See also CANR 1; CA 1-4R; SATA 6;
DLB 5, 76; CDALB 1941-1968

Brooks, Mel 1926-............... **CLC 12**
See also Kaminsky, Melvin
See also CA 65-68; DLB 26

Brooks, Peter 1938-............. **CLC 34**
See also CANR 1; CA 45-48

Brooks, Van Wyck 1886-1963...... **CLC 29**
See also CANR 6; CA 1-4R; DLB 45, 63

Brophy, Brigid (Antonia)
1929- .... **CLC 6, 11, 29**
See also CAAS 4; CANR 25; CA 5-8R;
DLB 14

Brosman, Catharine Savage 1934-.... **CLC 9**
See also CANR 21; CA 61-64

Broughton, T(homas) Alan 1936- ... **CLC 19**
See also CANR 2, 23; CA 45-48

Broumas, Olga 1949- .... **CLC 10**
See also CANR 20; CA 85-88

Brown, Charles Brockden
1771-1810 .... **NCLC 22**
See also DLB 37, 59, 73;
CDALB 1640-1865

Brown, Claude 1937- .... **CLC 30**
See also CA 73-76

Brown, Dee (Alexander) 1908- .. **CLC 18, 47**
See also CAAS 6; CANR 11; CA 13-16R;
SATA 5; DLB-Y 80

Brown, George Douglas 1869-1902
See Douglas, George

Brown, George Mackay 1921-.... **CLC 5, 28**
See also CAAS 6; CANR 12; CA 21-24R;
SATA 35; DLB 14, 27

Brown, Rita Mae 1944-........ **CLC 18, 43**
See also CANR 2, 11; CA 45-48

Brown, Rosellen 1939-............ **CLC 32**
See also CANR 14; CA 77-80

Brown, Sterling A(llen)
1901-1989 .... **CLC 1, 23, 59**
See also CANR 26; CA 85-88;
obituary CA 27; DLB 48, 51, 63

Brown, William Wells
1816?-1884.................. **NCLC 2**
See also DLB 3, 50

Browne, Jackson 1950- .... **CLC 21**
See also CA 120

Browning, Elizabeth Barrett
1806-1861 .... **NCLC 1, 16**
See also DLB 32

Browning, Robert 1812-1889..... **NCLC 19**
See also YABC 1; DLB 32

Browning, Tod 1882-1962 .... **CLC 16**
See also obituary CA 117

Bruccoli, Matthew J(oseph) 1931- .. **CLC 34**
See also CANR 7; CA 9-12R

Bruce, Lenny 1925-1966 .... **CLC 21**
See also Schneider, Leonard Alfred

Brunner, John (Kilian Houston)
1934- .... **CLC 8, 10**
See also CANR 2; CA 1-4R

Brutus, Dennis 1924- .... **CLC 43**
See also CANR 2; CA 49-52

Bryan, C(ourtlandt) D(ixon) B(arnes)
1936- .... **CLC 29**
See also CANR 13; CA 73-76

Bryant, William Cullen
1794-1878 .... **NCLC 6**
See also DLB 3, 43, 59; CDALB 1640-1865

Bryusov, Valery (Yakovlevich)
1873-1924 .... **TCLC 10**
See also CA 107

Buchanan, George 1506-1582 .... **LC 4**

Buchheim, Lothar-Gunther 1918- .... **CLC 6**
See also CA 85-88

Buchner, (Karl) Georg
1813-1837 .... **NCLC 26**

Buchwald, Art(hur) 1925-.......... **CLC 33**
See also CANR 21; CA 5-8R; SATA 10

Buck, Pearl S(ydenstricker)
1892-1973 .... **CLC 7, 11, 18**
See also CANR 1; CA 1-4R;
obituary CA 41-44R; SATA 1, 25; DLB 9

Buckler, Ernest 1908-1984......... CLC 13
See also CAP 1; CA 11-12;
obituary CA 114; SATA 47

Buckley, Vincent (Thomas)
1925-1988 .... CLC 57
See also CA 101

Buckley, William F(rank), Jr.
1925- .... CLC 7, 18, 37
See also CANR 1, 24; CA 1-4R; DLB-Y 80

Buechner, (Carl) Frederick
1926- .... CLC 2, 4, 6, 9
See also CANR 11; CA 13-16R; DLB-Y 80

Buell, John (Edward) 1927-........ CLC 10
See also CA 1-4R; DLB 53

Buero Vallejo, Antonio 1916- ... CLC 15, 46
See also CANR 24; CA 106

Bukowski, Charles 1920-.... CLC 2, 5, 9, 41
See also CA 17-20R; DLB 5

Bulgakov, Mikhail (Afanas'evich)
1891-1940 .... TCLC 2, 16
See also CA 105

Bullins, Ed 1935- .... CLC 1, 5, 7
See also CANR 24; CA 49-52; DLB 7, 38

**Bulwer-Lytton, (Lord) Edward (George Earle
Lytton)** 1803-1873 .... NCLC 1
See also Lytton, Edward Bulwer
See also DLB 21

Bunin, Ivan (Alexeyevich)
1870-1953 .... TCLC 6; SSC 5
See also CA 104

Bunting, Basil 1900-1985.... CLC 10, 39, 47
See also CANR 7; CA 53-56;
obituary CA 115; DLB 20

Bunuel, Luis 1900-1983 .... CLC 16
See also CA 101; obituary CA 110

Bunyan, John 1628-1688 .... LC 4
See also DLB 39

Burgess (Wilson, John) Anthony
1917- ..... CLC 1, 2, 4, 5, 8, 10, 13, 15,
22, 40
See also Wilson, John (Anthony) Burgess
See also DLB 14

Burke, Edmund 1729-1797.......... LC 7

Burke, Kenneth (Duva) 1897- .... CLC 2, 24
See also CA 5-8R; DLB 45, 63

Burney, Fanny 1752-1840 .... NCLC 12
See also DLB 39

Burns, Robert 1759-1796............ LC 3

Burns, Tex 1908?-
See L'Amour, Louis (Dearborn)

Burnshaw, Stanley 1906-..... CLC 3, 13, 44
See also CA 9-12R; DLB 48

Burr, Anne 1937- .... CLC 6
See also CA 25-28R

Burroughs, Edgar Rice
1875-1950 ....TCLC 2, 32
See also CA 104; SATA 41; DLB 8

Burroughs, William S(eward)
1914- .... CLC 1, 2, 5, 15, 22, 42
See also CANR 20; CA 9-12R; DLB 2, 8,
16; DLB-Y 81

Busch, Frederick 1941- ... CLC 7, 10, 18, 47
See also CAAS 1; CA 33-36R; DLB 6

Bush, Ronald 19??-............... CLC 34

Butler, Octavia E(stelle) 1947- ..... CLC 38
See also CANR 12, 24; CA 73-76; DLB 33

Butler, Samuel 1835-1902 ...... TCLC 1, 33
See also CA 104; DLB 18, 57

Butor, Michel (Marie Francois)
1926- .... CLC 1, 3, 8, 11, 15
See also CA 9-12R

Buzo, Alexander 1916-............ CLC 61
See also CANR 17; CA 97-100

Buzzati, Dino 1906-1972 .... CLC 36
See also obituary CA 33-36R

Byars, Betsy 1928-................ CLC 35
See also CLR 1, 16; CANR 18; CA 33-36R;
SAAS 1; SATA 4, 46; DLB 52

Byatt, A(ntonia) S(usan Drabble)
1936- .... CLC 19
See also CANR 13; CA 13-16R; DLB 14

Byrne, David 1953?-.............. CLC 26

Byrne, John Keyes 1926-
See Leonard, Hugh
See also CA 102

Byron, George Gordon (Noel), Lord Byron
1788-1824 .... NCLC 2, 12

Caballero, Fernan 1796-1877..... NCLC 10

Cabell, James Branch 1879-1958 ... TCLC 6
See also CA 105; DLB 9

Cable, George Washington
1844-1925 .... TCLC 4; SSC 4
See also CA 104; DLB 12, 74

Cabrera Infante, G(uillermo)
1929- .... CLC 5, 25, 45
See also CA 85-88

Cage, John (Milton, Jr.) 1912- ..... CLC 41
See also CANR 9; CA 13-16R

Cain, G. 1929-
See Cabrera Infante, G(uillermo)

Cain, James M(allahan)
1892-1977 .... CLC 3, 11, 28
See also CANR 8; CA 17-20R;
obituary CA 73-76

Caldwell, Erskine (Preston)
1903-1987 .... CLC 1, 8, 14, 50, 60
See also CAAS 1; CANR 2; CA 1-4R;
obituary CA 121; DLB 9

Caldwell, (Janet Miriam) Taylor (Holland)
1900-1985 .... CLC 2, 28, 39
See also CANR 5; CA 5-8R;
obituary CA 116

Calhoun, John Caldwell
1782-1850 .... NCLC 15
See also DLB 3

Calisher, Hortense 1911-.... CLC 2, 4, 8, 38
See also CANR 1, 22; CA 1-4R; DLB 2

Callaghan, Morley (Edward)
1903- .... CLC 3, 14, 41
See also CA 9-12R; DLB 68

Calvino, Italo
1923-1985 .... CLC 5, 8, 11, 22, 33, 39;
SSC 3
See also CANR 23; CA 85-88;
obituary CA 116

Cameron, Carey 1952- .... CLC 59

Cameron, Peter 1959-............. CLC 44
See also CA 125

Campana, Dino 1885-1932....... TCLC 20
See also CA 117

Campbell, John W(ood), Jr.
1910-1971 .... CLC 32
See also CAP 2; CA 21-22;
obituary CA 29-32R; DLB 8

Campbell, (John) Ramsey 1946-.... CLC 42
See also CANR 7; CA 57-60

Campbell, (Ignatius) Roy (Dunnachie)
1901-1957 .... TCLC 5
See also CA 104; DLB 20

Campbell, Thomas 1777-1844 .... NCLC 19

Campbell, (William) Wilfred
1861-1918 .... TCLC 9
See also CA 106

Camus, Albert
1913-1960 .... CLC 1, 2, 4, 9, 11, 14, 32
See also CA 89-92; DLB 72

Canby, Vincent 1924-.............. CLC 13
See also CA 81-84

Canetti, Elias 1905- .... CLC 3, 14, 25
See also CANR 23; CA 21-24R

Canin, Ethan 1960-............... CLC 55

Cape, Judith 1916-
See Page, P(atricia) K(athleen)

Capek, Karel 1890-1938........ TCLC 6, 37
See also CA 104

Capote, Truman
1924-1984 ..... CLC 1, 3, 8, 13, 19, 34,
38, 58; SSC 2
See also CANR 18; CA 5-8R;
obituary CA 113; DLB 2; DLB-Y 80, 84;
CDALB 1941-1968

Capra, Frank 1897-............... CLC 16
See also CA 61-64

Caputo, Philip 1941-.............. CLC 32
See also CA 73-76

Card, Orson Scott 1951- .... CLC 44, 47, 50
See also CA 102

Cardenal, Ernesto 1925-........... CLC 31
See also CANR 2; CA 49-52

Carducci, Giosue 1835-1907....... TCLC 32

Carew, Thomas 1595?-1640 .... LC 13

Carey, Ernestine Gilbreth 1908-.... CLC 17
See also CA 5-8R; SATA 2

Carey, Peter 1943-............. CLC 40, 55
See also CA 123, 127

Carleton, William 1794-1869...... NCLC 3

Carlisle, Henry (Coffin) 1926-...... CLC 33
See also CANR 15; CA 13-16R

Carlson, Ron(ald F.) 1947-........ CLC 54
See also CA 105

Carlyle, Thomas 1795-1881 ...... NCLC 22
See also DLB 55

Carman, (William) Bliss
1861-1929 .... TCLC 7
See also CA 104

Carpenter, Don(ald Richard)
1931- .... CLC 41
See also CANR 1; CA 45-48

Carpentier (y Valmont), Alejo
    1904-1980 .... CLC 8, 11, 38
    See also CANR 11; CA 65-68;
        obituary CA 97-100

Carr, Emily 1871-1945............ TCLC 32
    See also DLB 68

Carr, John Dickson 1906-1977 ...... CLC 3
    See also CANR 3; CA 49-52;
        obituary CA 69-72

Carr, Virginia Spencer 1929-....... CLC 34
    See also CA 61-64

Carrier, Roch 1937- .... CLC 13
    See also DLB 53

Carroll, James (P.) 1943-.......... CLC 38
    See also CA 81-84

Carroll, Jim 1951- .... CLC 35
    See also CA 45-48

Carroll, Lewis 1832-1898......... NCLC 2
    See also Dodgson, Charles Lutwidge
    See also CLR 2; DLB 18

Carroll, Paul Vincent 1900-1968.... CLC 10
    See also CA 9-12R; obituary CA 25-28R;
        DLB 10

Carruth, Hayden 1921- .... CLC 4, 7, 10, 18
    See also CANR 4; CA 9-12R; SATA 47;
        DLB 5

Carter, Angela (Olive) 1940-..... CLC 5, 41
    See also CANR 12; CA 53-56; DLB 14

Carver, Raymond
    1938-1988 .... CLC 22, 36, 53, 55
    See also CANR 17; CA 33-36R;
        obituary CA 126; DLB-Y 84, 88

Cary, (Arthur) Joyce (Lunel)
    1888-1957 .... TCLC 1, 29
    See also CA 104; DLB 15

Casanova de Seingalt, Giovanni Jacopo
    1725-1798 .... LC 13

Casares, Adolfo Bioy 1914-
    See Bioy Casares, Adolfo

Casely-Hayford, J(oseph) E(phraim)
    1866-1930 .... TCLC 24
    See also CA 123

Casey, John 1880-1964
    See O'Casey, Sean

Casey, John 1939- .... CLC 59
    See also CANR 23; CA 69-72

Casey, Michael 1947-............... CLC 2
    See also CA 65-68; DLB 5

Casey, Warren 1935- .... CLC 12
    See also Jacobs, Jim and Casey, Warren
    See also CA 101

Casona, Alejandro 1903-1965 ...... CLC 49
    See also Alvarez, Alejandro Rodriguez

Cassavetes, John 1929-............ CLC 20
    See also CA 85-88

Cassill, R(onald) V(erlin) 1919-... CLC 4, 23
    See also CAAS 1; CANR 7; CA 9-12R;
        DLB 6

Cassity, (Allen) Turner 1929- .... CLC 6, 42
    See also CANR 11; CA 17-20R

Castaneda, Carlos 1935?-.......... CLC 12
    See also CA 25-28R

Castelvetro, Lodovico 1505-1571..... LC 12

Castiglione, Baldassare 1478-1529 ... LC 12

Castro, Rosalia de 1837-1885 ..... NCLC 3

Cather, Willa (Sibert)
    1873-1947 ...... TCLC 1, 11, 31; SSC 2
    See also CA 104; SATA 30; DLB 9, 54;
        DLB-DS 1; CDALB 1865-1917

Catton, (Charles) Bruce
    1899-1978 .... CLC 35
    See also CANR 7; CA 5-8R;
        obituary CA 81-84; SATA 2;
        obituary SATA 24; DLB 17

Cauldwell, Frank 1923-
    See King, Francis (Henry)

Caunitz, William 1935- .... CLC 34

Causley, Charles (Stanley) 1917-..... CLC 7
    See also CANR 5; CA 9-12R; SATA 3;
        DLB 27

Caute, (John) David 1936-......... CLC 29
    See also CAAS 4; CANR 1; CA 1-4R;
        DLB 14

Cavafy, C(onstantine) P(eter)
    1863-1933 .... TCLC 2, 7
    See also CA 104

Cavanna, Betty 1909-............. CLC 12
    See also CANR 6; CA 9-12R; SATA 1, 30

Cayrol, Jean 1911-............... CLC 11
    See also CA 89-92

Cela, Camilo Jose 1916-...... CLC 4, 13, 59
    See also CAAS 10; CANR 21; CA 21-24R

Celan, Paul 1920-1970...... CLC 10, 19, 53
    See also Antschel, Paul
    See also DLB 69

Celine, Louis-Ferdinand
    1894-1961 ..... CLC 1, 3, 4, 7, 9, 15, 47
    See also Destouches,
        Louis-Ferdinand-Auguste
    See also DLB 72

Cellini, Benvenuto 1500-1571 .... LC 7

Cendrars, Blaise 1887-1961........ CLC 18
    See also Sauser-Hall, Frederic

Cernuda, Luis (y Bidon)
    1902-1963 .... CLC 54
    See also CA 89-92

Cervantes (Saavedra), Miguel de
    1547-1616 .... LC 6

Cesaire, Aime (Fernand) 1913- .. CLC 19, 32
    See also CANR 24; CA 65-68

Chabon, Michael 1965?-........... CLC 55

Chabrol, Claude 1930-............ CLC 16
    See also CA 110

Challans, Mary 1905-1983
    See Renault, Mary
    See also CA 81-84; obituary CA 111;
        SATA 23; obituary SATA 36

Chambers, Aidan 1934- .... CLC 35
    See also CANR 12; CA 25-28R; SATA 1

Chambers, James 1948-
    See Cliff, Jimmy

Chandler, Raymond 1888-1959 ... TCLC 1, 7
    See also CA 104

Channing, William Ellery
    1780-1842 .... NCLC 17
    See also DLB 1, 59

Chaplin, Charles (Spencer)
    1889-1977 .... CLC 16
    See also CA 81-84; obituary CA 73-76;
        DLB 44

Chapman, Graham 1941?- .... CLC 21
    See also Monty Python
    See also CA 116

Chapman, John Jay 1862-1933 ..... TCLC 7
    See also CA 104

Chappell, Fred 1936- .... CLC 40
    See also CAAS 4; CANR 8; CA 5-8R;
        DLB 6

Char, Rene (Emile)
    1907-1988 .... CLC 9, 11, 14, 55
    See also CA 13-16R; obituary CA 124

Charles I 1600-1649............... LC 13

Charyn, Jerome 1937-...... CLC 5, 8, 18
    See also CAAS 1; CANR 7; CA 5-8R;
        DLB-Y 83

Chase, Mary Ellen 1887-1973....... CLC 2
    See also CAP 1; CA 15-16;
        obituary CA 41-44R; SATA 10

Chateaubriand, Francois Rene de
    1768-1848 .... NCLC 3

Chatterji, Bankim Chandra
    1838-1894 .... NCLC 19

Chatterji, Saratchandra
    1876-1938 .... TCLC 13
    See also CA 109

Chatterton, Thomas 1752-1770 .... LC 3

Chatwin, (Charles) Bruce
    1940-1989 .... CLC 28, 57, 59
    See also CA 85-88,; obituary CA 127

Chayefsky, Paddy 1923-1981....... CLC 23
    See also CA 9-12R; obituary CA 104;
        DLB 7, 44; DLB-Y 81

Chayefsky, Sidney 1923-1981
    See Chayefsky, Paddy
    See also CANR 18

Chedid, Andree 1920-............. CLC 47

Cheever, John
    1912-1982 ..... CLC 3, 7, 8, 11, 15, 25;
        SSC 1
    See also CANR 5; CA 5-8R;
        obituary CA 106; CABS 1; DLB 2;
        DLB-Y 80, 82; CDALB 1941-1968

Cheever, Susan 1943-......... CLC 18, 48
    See also CA 103; DLB-Y 82

Chekhov, Anton (Pavlovich)
    1860-1904 ...... TCLC 3, 10, 31; SSC 2
    See also CA 104, 124

Chernyshevsky, Nikolay Gavrilovich
    1828-1889 .... NCLC 1

Cherry, Caroline Janice 1942-
    See Cherryh, C. J.

Cherryh, C. J. 1942-.............. CLC 35
    See also CANR 10; CA 65-68; DLB-Y 80

Chesnutt, Charles Waddell
    1858-1932 .... TCLC 5
    See also CA 106, 125; DLB 12, 50

Chester, Alfred 1929?-1971 .... CLC 49
    See also obituary CA 33-36R

Chesterton, G(ilbert) K(eith)
1874-1936 . . . . TCLC 1, 6; SSC 1
See also CA 104; SATA 27; DLB 10, 19,
34, 70

Ch'ien Chung-shu 1910- . . . . CLC 22

Child, Lydia Maria 1802-1880 . . . . NCLC 6
See also DLB 1, 74

Child, Philip 1898-1978 . . . . CLC 19
See also CAP 1; CA 13-14; SATA 47

Childress, Alice 1920- . . . . CLC 12, 15
See also CLR 14; CANR 3; CA 45-48;
SATA 7, 48; DLB 7, 38

Chislett, (Margaret) Anne 1943?- . . . CLC 34

Chitty, (Sir) Thomas Willes 1926- . . CLC 11
See also Hinde, Thomas
See also CA 5-8R

Chomette, Rene 1898-1981
See Clair, Rene
See also obituary CA 103

Chopin, Kate (O'Flaherty)
1851-1904 . . . . TCLC 5, 14
See also CA 104, 122; DLB 12;
CDALB 1865-1917

Christie, (Dame) Agatha (Mary Clarissa)
1890-1976 . . . . . . CLC 1, 6, 8, 12, 39, 48
See also CANR 10; CA 17-20R;
obituary CA 61-64; SATA 36; DLB 13

Christie, (Ann) Philippa 1920-
See Pearce, (Ann) Philippa
See also CANR 4; CA 7-8

Christine de Pizan 1365?-1431? . . . . . . LC 9

Chulkov, Mikhail Dmitrievich
1743-1792 . . . . LC 2

Churchill, Caryl 1938- . . . . CLC 31, 55
See also CANR 22; CA 102; DLB 13

Churchill, Charles 1731?-1764 . . . . LC 3

Chute, Carolyn 1947- . . . . CLC 39
See also CA 123

Ciardi, John (Anthony)
1916-1986 . . . . CLC 10, 40, 44
See also CAAS 2; CANR 5; CA 5-8R;
obituary CA 118; SATA 1, 46; DLB 5;
DLB-Y 86

Cicero, Marcus Tullius
106 B.C.-43 B.C. . . . . CMLC 3

Cimino, Michael 1943?- . . . . CLC 16
See also CA 105

Clair, Rene 1898-1981 . . . . CLC 20
See also Chomette, Rene

Clampitt, Amy 19??- . . . . CLC 32
See also CA 110

Clancy, Tom 1947- . . . . CLC 45
See also CA 125

Clare, John 1793-1864 . . . . NCLC 9
See also DLB 55

Clark, (Robert) Brian 1932- . . . . CLC 29
See also CA 41-44R

Clark, Eleanor 1913- . . . . CLC 5, 19
See also CA 9-12R; DLB 6

Clark, John Pepper 1935- . . . . CLC 38
See also CANR 16; CA 65-68

Clark, Mavis Thorpe 1912?- . . . . CLC 12
See also CANR 8; CA 57-60; SAAS 5;
SATA 8

Clark, Walter Van Tilburg
1909-1971 . . . . CLC 28
See also CA 9-12R; obituary CA 33-36R;
SATA 8; DLB 9

Clarke, Arthur C(harles)
1917- . . . . . . CLC 1, 4, 13, 18, 35; SSC 3
See also CANR 2; CA 1-4R; SATA 13

Clarke, Austin 1896-1974 . . . . CLC 6, 9
See also CANR 14; CAP 2; CA 29-32;
obituary CA 49-52; DLB 10, 20, 53

Clarke, Austin (Ardinel) C(hesterfield)
1934- . . . . CLC 8, 53
See also CANR 14; CA 25-28R; DLB 53

Clarke, Gillian 1937- . . . . CLC 61
See also CA 106; DLB 40

Clarke, Marcus (Andrew Hislop)
1846-1881 . . . . NCLC 19

Clarke, Shirley 1925- . . . . CLC 16

Clash, The . . . . CLC 30

Claudel, Paul (Louis Charles Marie)
1868-1955 . . . . TCLC 2, 10
See also CA 104

Clavell, James (duMaresq)
1924- . . . . CLC 6, 25
See also CANR 26; CA 25-28R

Cleaver, (Leroy) Eldridge 1935- . . . . CLC 30
See also CANR 16; CA 21-24R

Cleese, John 1939- . . . . CLC 21
See also Monty Python
See also CA 112, 116

Cleland, John 1709-1789 . . . . LC 2
See also DLB 39

Clemens, Samuel Langhorne
1835-1910 . . . . . . TCLC 6, 12, 19; SSC 6
See also Twain, Mark
See also YABC 2; CA 104; DLB 11, 12, 23,
64, 74; CDALB 1865-1917

Cliff, Jimmy 1948- . . . . CLC 21

Clifton, Lucille 1936- . . . . CLC 19
See also CLR 5; CANR 2, 24; CA 49-52;
SATA 20; DLB 5, 41

Clough, Arthur Hugh 1819-1861 . . NCLC 27
See also DLB 32

Clutha, Janet Paterson Frame 1924-
See Frame (Clutha), Janet (Paterson)
See also CANR 2; CA 1-4R

Coburn, D(onald) L(ee) 1938- . . . . . . CLC 10
See also CA 89-92

Cocteau, Jean (Maurice Eugene Clement)
1889-1963 . . . . . . CLC 1, 8, 15, 16, 43
See also CAP 2; CA 25-28; DLB 65

Codrescu, Andrei 1946- . . . . CLC 46
See also CANR 13; CA 33-36R

Coetzee, J(ohn) M. 1940- . . . . CLC 23, 33
See also CA 77-80

Cohen, Arthur A(llen)
1928-1986 . . . . CLC 7, 31
See also CANR 1, 17; CA 1-4R;
obituary CA 120; DLB 28

Cohen, Leonard (Norman)
1934- . . . . CLC 3, 38
See also CANR 14; CA 21-24R; DLB 53

Cohen, Matt 1942- . . . . CLC 19
See also CA 61-64; DLB 53

Cohen-Solal, Annie 19??- . . . . CLC 50

Colegate, Isabel 1931- . . . . CLC 36
See also CANR 8, 22; CA 17-20R; DLB 14

Coleridge, Samuel Taylor
1772-1834 . . . . NCLC 9

Coles, Don 1928- . . . . CLC 46
See also CA 115

Colette (Sidonie-Gabrielle)
1873-1954 . . . . TCLC 1, 5, 16
See also CA 104; DLB 65

Collett, (Jacobine) Camilla (Wergeland)
1813-1895 . . . . NCLC 22

Collier, Christopher 1930- . . . . CLC 30
See also CANR 13; CA 33-36R; SATA 16

Collier, James L(incoln) 1928- . . . . . CLC 30
See also CLR 3; CANR 4; CA 9-12R;
SATA 8

Collier, Jeremy 1650-1726 . . . . LC 6

Collins, Hunt 1926-
See Hunter, Evan

Collins, Linda 19??- . . . . CLC 44
See also CA 125

Collins, Tom 1843-1912
See Furphy, Joseph

Collins, (William) Wilkie
1824-1889 . . . . NCLC 1, 18
See also DLB 18, 70

Collins, William 1721-1759 . . . . LC 4

Colman, George 1909-1981
See Glassco, John

Colter, Cyrus 1910- . . . . CLC 58
See also CANR 10; CA 65-68; DLB 33

Colton, James 1923-
See Hansen, Joseph

Colum, Padraic 1881-1972 . . . . CLC 28
See also CA 73-76; obituary CA 33-36R;
SATA 15; DLB 19

Colvin, James 1939-
See Moorcock, Michael

Colwin, Laurie 1945- . . . . CLC 5, 13, 23
See also CANR 20; CA 89-92; DLB-Y 80

Comfort, Alex(ander) 1920- . . . . CLC 7
See also CANR 1; CA 1-4R

Compton-Burnett, Ivy
1892-1969 . . . . CLC 1, 3, 10, 15, 34
See also CANR 4; CA 1-4R;
obituary CA 25-28R; DLB 36

Comstock, Anthony 1844-1915 . . . . TCLC 13
See also CA 110

Conde, Maryse 1937- . . . . CLC 52
See also Boucolon, Maryse

Condon, Richard (Thomas)
1915- . . . . CLC 4, 6, 8, 10, 45
See also CAAS 1; CANR 2, 23; CA 1-4R

Congreve, William 1670-1729 . . . . LC 5
See also DLB 39

Connell, Evan S(helby), Jr.
1924- . . . . CLC 4, 6, 45
See also CAAS 2; CANR 2; CA 1-4R;
DLB 2; DLB-Y 81

Connelly, Marc(us Cook)
    1890-1980 . . . . CLC 7
    See also CA 85-88; obituary CA 102;
    obituary SATA 25; DLB 7; DLB-Y 80

Conner, Ralph   1860-1937 . . . . TCLC 31

Conrad, Joseph
    1857-1924 . . . . TCLC 1, 6, 13, 25
    See also CA 104; SATA 27; DLB 10, 34

Conroy, Pat   1945- . . . . CLC 30
    See also CANR 24; CA 85-88; DLB 6

Constant (de Rebecque), (Henri) Benjamin
    1767-1830 . . . . NCLC 6

Cook, Michael   1933- . . . . CLC 58
    See also CA 93-96; DLB 53

Cook, Robin   1940- . . . . CLC 14
    See also CA 108, 111

Cooke, Elizabeth   1948- . . . . CLC 55

Cooke, John Esten   1830-1886 . . . . . NCLC 5
    See also DLB 3

Cooper, J. California   19??- . . . . CLC 56
    See also CA 125, 127

Cooper, James Fenimore
    1789-1851 . . . . NCLC 1, 27
    See also SATA 19; DLB 3;
    CDALB 1640-1865

Coover, Robert (Lowell)
    1932- . . . . CLC 3, 7, 15, 32, 46
    See also CANR 3; CA 45-48; DLB 2;
    DLB-Y 81

Copeland, Stewart (Armstrong)
    1952- . . . . CLC 26
    See also The Police

Coppard, A(lfred) E(dgar)
    1878-1957 . . . . TCLC 5
    See also YABC 1; CA 114

Coppee, Francois   1842-1908 . . . . . . TCLC 25

Coppola, Francis Ford   1939- . . . . CLC 16
    See also CA 77-80; DLB 44

Corcoran, Barbara   1911- . . . . CLC 17
    See also CAAS 2; CANR 11; CA 21-24R;
    SATA 3; DLB 52

Corman, Cid   1924- . . . . CLC 9
    See also Corman, Sidney
    See also CAAS 2; DLB 5

Corman, Sidney   1924-
    See Corman, Cid
    See also CA 85-88

Cormier, Robert (Edmund)
    1925- . . . . CLC 12, 30
    See also CLR 12; CANR 5, 23; CA 1-4R;
    SATA 10, 45; DLB 52

Corn, Alfred (Dewitt III)   1943- . . . . . CLC 33
    See also CA 104; DLB-Y 80

Cornwell, David (John Moore)
    1931- . . . . CLC 9, 15
    See also le Carre, John
    See also CANR 13; CA 5-8R

Corso, (Nunzio) Gregory   1930- . . . CLC 1, 11
    See also CA 5-8R; DLB 5, 16

Cortazar, Julio
    1914-1984 . . . . . CLC 2, 3, 5, 10, 13, 15,
                                                    33, 34
    See also CANR 12; CA 21-24R

Corvo, Baron   1860-1913
    See Rolfe, Frederick (William Serafino
    Austin Lewis Mary)

Cosic, Dobrica   1921- . . . . CLC 14
    See also CA 122

Costain, Thomas B(ertram)
    1885-1965 . . . . CLC 30
    See also CA 5-8R; obituary CA 25-28R;
    DLB 9

Costantini, Humberto   1924?-1987 . . . CLC 49
    See also obituary CA 122

Costello, Elvis   1955- . . . . CLC 21

Cotter, Joseph Seamon, Sr.
    1861-1949 . . . . TCLC 28
    See also DLB 50

Couperus, Louis (Marie Anne)
    1863-1923 . . . . TCLC 15
    See also CA 115

Courtenay, Bryce   1933- . . . . CLC 59

Cousteau, Jacques-Yves   1910- . . . . . . CLC 30
    See also CANR 15; CA 65-68; SATA 38

Coward, (Sir) Noel (Pierce)
    1899-1973 . . . . CLC 1, 9, 29, 51
    See also CAP 2; CA 17-18;
    obituary CA 41-44R; DLB 10

Cowley, Malcolm   1898-1989 . . . . CLC 39
    See also CANR 3; CA 5-6R; DLB 4, 48;
    DLB-Y 81

Cowper, William   1731-1800 . . . . NCLC 8

Cox, William Trevor   1928- . . . . . . CLC 9, 14
    See also Trevor, William
    See also CANR 4; CA 9-12R

Cozzens, James Gould
    1903-1978 . . . . CLC 1, 4, 11
    See also CANR 19; CA 9-12R;
    obituary CA 81-84; DLB 9; DLB-Y 84,
    DLB-DS 2; CDALB 1941-1968

Crabbe, George   1754-1832 . . . . NCLC 26

Grace, Douglas   1944- . . . . CLC 58

Crane, (Harold) Hart
    1899-1932 . . . . TCLC 2, 5
    See also CA 104; DLB 4, 48

Crane, R(onald) S(almon)
    1886-1967 . . . . CLC 27
    See also CA 85-88; DLB 63

Crane, Stephen
    1871-1900 . . . . TCLC 11, 17, 32
    See also YABC 2; CA 109; DLB 12, 54, 78;
    CDALB 1865-1917

Craven, Margaret   1901-1980 . . . . CLC 17
    See also CA 103

Crawford, F(rancis) Marion
    1854-1909 . . . . TCLC 10
    See also CA 107; DLB 71

Crawford, Isabella Valancy
    1850-1887 . . . . NCLC 12

Crayencour, Marguerite de   1903-1987
    See Yourcenar, Marguerite

Creasey, John   1908-1973 . . . . CLC 11
    See also CANR 8; CA 5-8R;
    obituary CA 41-44R

Crebillon, Claude Prosper Jolyot de (fils)
    1707-1777 . . . . LC 1

Creeley, Robert (White)
    1926- . . . . CLC 1, 2, 4, 8, 11, 15, 36
    See also CANR 23; CA 1-4R; DLB 5, 16

Crews, Harry (Eugene)
    1935- . . . . CLC 6, 23, 49
    See also CANR 20; CA 25-28R; DLB 6

Crichton, (John) Michael
    1942- . . . . CLC 2, 6, 54
    See also CANR 13; CA 25-28R; SATA 9;
    DLB-Y 81

Crispin, Edmund   1921-1978 . . . . CLC 22
    See also Montgomery, Robert Bruce

Cristofer, Michael   1946- . . . . CLC 28
    See also CA 110; DLB 7

Croce, Benedetto   1866-1952 . . . . . . TCLC 37
    See also CA 120

Crockett, David (Davy)
    1786-1836 . . . . NCLC 8
    See also DLB 3, 11

Croker, John Wilson   1780-1857 . . NCLC 10

Cronin, A(rchibald) J(oseph)
    1896-1981 . . . . CLC 32
    See also CANR 5; CA 1-4R;
    obituary CA 102; obituary SATA 25, 47

Cross, Amanda   1926-
    See Heilbrun, Carolyn G(old)

Crothers, Rachel   1878-1953 . . . . TCLC 19
    See also CA 113; DLB 7

Crowley, Aleister   1875-1947 . . . . TCLC 7
    See also CA 104

Crowley, John   1942-
    See also CA 61-64; DLB-Y 82

Crumb, Robert   1943- . . . . CLC 17
    See also CA 106

Cryer, Gretchen   1936?- . . . . CLC 21
    See also CA 114, 123

Csath, Geza   1887-1919 . . . . TCLC 13
    See also CA 111

Cudlip, David   1933- . . . . CLC 34

Cullen, Countee   1903-1946 . . . . . TCLC 4, 37
    See also CA 108, 124; SATA 18; DLB 4,
    48, 51; CDALB 1917-1929

Cummings, E(dward) E(stlin)
    1894-1962 . . . . CLC 1, 3, 8, 12, 15
    See also CA 73-76; DLB 4, 48

Cunha, Euclides (Rodrigues) da
    1866-1909 . . . . TCLC 24
    See also CA 123

Cunningham, J(ames) V(incent)
    1911-1985 . . . . CLC 3, 31
    See also CANR 1; CA 1-4R;
    obituary CA 115; DLB 5

Cunningham, Julia (Woolfolk)
    1916- . . . . CLC 12
    See also CANR 4, 19; CA 9-12R; SAAS 2;
    SATA 1, 26

Cunningham, Michael   1952- . . . . CLC 34

Currie, Ellen   19??- . . . . CLC 44

Dabrowska, Maria (Szumska)
    1889-1965 . . . . CLC 15
    See also CA 106

Dabydeen, David   1956?- . . . . CLC 34
    See also CA 106

Dacey, Philip 1939- . . . . CLC 51
See also CANR 14; CA 37-40R

Dagerman, Stig (Halvard)
1923-1954 . . . . TCLC 17
See also CA 117

Dahl, Roald 1916- . . . . CLC 1, 6, 18
See also CLR 1, 7; CANR 6; CA 1-4R;
SATA 1, 26

Dahlberg, Edward 1900-1977 . . . CLC 1, 7, 14
See also CA 9-12R; obituary CA 69-72;
DLB 48

Daly, Elizabeth 1878-1967 . . . . CLC 52
See also CAP 2; CA 23-24;
obituary CA 25-28R

Daly, Maureen 1921- . . . . CLC 17
See also McGivern, Maureen Daly
See also SAAS 1; SATA 2

Daniken, Erich von 1935-
See Von Daniken, Erich

Dannay, Frederic 1905-1982
See Queen, Ellery
See also CANR 1; CA 1-4R;
obituary CA 107

D'Annunzio, Gabriele 1863-1938 . . . . TCLC 6
See also CA 104

Dante (Alighieri)
See Alighieri, Dante

Danziger, Paula 1944- . . . . CLC 21
See also CLR 20; CA 112, 115; SATA 30,
36

Dario, Ruben 1867-1916 . . . . TCLC 4
See also Sarmiento, Felix Ruben Garcia
See also CA 104

Darley, George 1795-1846 . . . . NCLC 2

Daryush, Elizabeth 1887-1977 . . . . CLC 6, 19
See also CANR 3; CA 49-52; DLB 20

Daudet, (Louis Marie) Alphonse
1840-1897 . . . . NCLC 1

Daumal, Rene 1908-1944 . . . . TCLC 14
See also CA 114

Davenport, Guy (Mattison, Jr.)
1927- . . . . CLC 6, 14, 38
See also CANR 23; CA 33-36R

Davidson, Donald (Grady)
1893-1968 . . . . CLC 2, 13, 19
See also CANR 4; CA 5-8R;
obituary CA 25-28R; DLB 45

Davidson, John 1857-1909 . . . . TCLC 24
See also CA 118; DLB 19

Davidson, Sara 1943- . . . . CLC 9
See also CA 81-84

Davie, Donald (Alfred)
1922- . . . . CLC 5, 8, 10, 31
See also CAAS 3; CANR 1; CA 1-4R;
DLB 27

Davies, Ray(mond Douglas) 1944- . . CLC 21
See also CA 116

Davies, Rhys 1903-1978 . . . . CLC 23
See also CANR 4; CA 9-12R;
obituary CA 81-84

Davies, (William) Robertson
1913- . . . . CLC 2, 7, 13, 25, 42
See also CANR 17; CA 33-36R; DLB 68

Davies, W(illiam) H(enry)
1871-1940 . . . . TCLC 5
See also CA 104; DLB 19

Davis, H(arold) L(enoir)
1896-1960 . . . . CLC 49
See also obituary CA 89-92; DLB 9

Davis, Rebecca (Blaine) Harding
1831-1910 . . . . TCLC 6
See also CA 104; DLB 74

Davis, Richard Harding
1864-1916 . . . . TCLC 24
See also CA 114; DLB 12, 23

Davison, Frank Dalby 1893-1970 . . . CLC 15
See also obituary CA 116

Davison, Peter 1928- . . . . CLC 28
See also CAAS 4; CANR 3; CA 9-12R;
DLB 5

Davys, Mary 1674-1732 . . . . LC 1
See also DLB 39

Dawson, Fielding 1930- . . . . CLC 6
See also CA 85-88

Day, Clarence (Shepard, Jr.)
1874-1935 . . . . TCLC 25
See also CA 108; DLB 11

Day, Thomas 1748-1789 . . . . LC 1
See also YABC 1; DLB 39

Day Lewis, C(ecil)
1904-1972 . . . . CLC 1, 6, 10
See also CAP 1; CA 15-16;
obituary CA 33-36R; DLB 15, 20

Dazai Osamu 1909-1948 . . . . TCLC 11
See also Tsushima Shuji

De Crayencour, Marguerite 1903-1987
See Yourcenar, Marguerite

Deer, Sandra 1940- . . . . CLC 45

Defoe, Daniel 1660?-1731 . . . . LC 1
See also SATA 22; DLB 39

De Hartog, Jan 1914- . . . . CLC 19
See also CANR 1; CA 1-4R

Deighton, Len 1929- . . . . CLC 4, 7, 22, 46
See also Deighton, Leonard Cyril

Deighton, Leonard Cyril 1929-
See Deighton, Len
See also CANR 19; CA 9-12R

De la Mare, Walter (John)
1873-1956 . . . . TCLC 4
See also CA 110; SATA 16; DLB 19

Delaney, Shelagh 1939- . . . . CLC 29
See also CA 17-20R; DLB 13

Delany, Mary (Granville Pendarves)
1700-1788 . . . . LC 12

Delany, Samuel R(ay, Jr.)
1942- . . . . CLC 8, 14, 38
See also CA 81-84; DLB 8, 33

De la Roche, Mazo 1885-1961 . . . . . CLC 14
See also CA 85-88; DLB 68

Delbanco, Nicholas (Franklin)
1942- . . . . CLC 6, 13
See also CAAS 2; CA 17-20R; DLB 6

del Castillo, Michel 1933- . . . . CLC 38
See also CA 109

Deledda, Grazia 1871-1936 . . . . TCLC 23
See also CA 123

Delibes (Setien), Miguel 1920- . . . CLC 8, 18
See also CANR 1; CA 45-48

DeLillo, Don
1936- . . . . CLC 8, 10, 13, 27, 39, 54
See also CANR 21; CA 81-84; DLB 6

De Lisser, H(erbert) G(eorge)
1878-1944 . . . . TCLC 12
See also CA 109

Deloria, Vine (Victor), Jr. 1933- . . . . CLC 21
See also CANR 5, 20; CA 53-56; SATA 21

Del Vecchio, John M(ichael)
1947- . . . . CLC 29
See also CA 110

de Man, Paul 1919-1983 . . . . CLC 55
See also obituary CA 111; DLB 67

De Marinis, Rick 1934- . . . . CLC 54
See also CANR 9, 25; CA 57-60

Demby, William 1922- . . . . CLC 53
See also CA 81-84; DLB 33

Denby, Edwin (Orr) 1903-1983 . . . . . CLC 48
See also obituary CA 110

Dennis, John 1657-1734 . . . . LC 11

Dennis, Nigel (Forbes) 1912- . . . . CLC 8
See also CA 25-28R; DLB 13, 15

De Palma, Brian 1940- . . . . CLC 20
See also CA 109

De Quincey, Thomas 1785-1859 . . . NCLC 4

Deren, Eleanora 1908-1961
See Deren, Maya
See also obituary CA 111

Deren, Maya 1908-1961 . . . . CLC 16
See also Deren, Eleanora

Derleth, August (William)
1909-1971 . . . . CLC 31
See also CANR 4; CA 1-4R;
obituary CA 29-32R; SATA 5; DLB 9

Derrida, Jacques 1930- . . . . CLC 24
See also CA 124

Desai, Anita 1937- . . . . CLC 19, 37
See also CA 81-84

De Saint-Luc, Jean 1909-1981
See Glassco, John

De Sica, Vittorio 1902-1974 . . . . CLC 20
See also obituary CA 117

Desnos, Robert 1900-1945 . . . . TCLC 22
See also CA 121

Destouches, Louis-Ferdinand-Auguste
1894-1961
See Celine, Louis-Ferdinand
See also CA 85-88

Deutsch, Babette 1895-1982 . . . . CLC 18
See also CANR 4; CA 1-4R;
obituary CA 108; SATA 1;
obituary SATA 33; DLB 45

Devenant, William 1606-1649 . . . . LC 13

Devkota, Laxmiprasad
1909-1959 . . . . TCLC 23
See also CA 123

DeVoto, Bernard (Augustine)
1897-1955 . . . . TCLC 29
See also CA 113; DLB 9

De Vries, Peter
1910- . . . . CLC 1, 2, 3, 7, 10, 28, 46
See also CA 17-20R; DLB 6; DLB-Y 82

Dexter, Pete 1943-............ CLC 34, 55
  See also CA 127

Diamond, Neil (Leslie) 1941-....... CLC 30
  See also CA 108

Dick, Philip K(indred)
  1928-1982 .... CLC 10, 30
  See also CANR 2, 16; CA 49-52;
  obituary CA 106; DLB 8

Dickens, Charles
  1812-1870 .... NCLC 3, 8, 18, 26
  See also SATA 15; DLB 21, 55, 70

Dickey, James (Lafayette)
  1923- .... CLC 1, 2, 4, 7, 10, 15, 47
  See also CANR 10; CA 9-12R; CABS 2;
  DLB 5; DLB-Y 82

Dickey, William 1928-.......... CLC 3, 28
  See also CANR 24; CA 9-12R; DLB 5

Dickinson, Charles 1952-.......... CLC 49

Dickinson, Emily (Elizabeth)
  1830-1886 .... NCLC 21
  See also SATA 29; DLB 1;
  CDALB 1865-1917

Dickinson, Peter (Malcolm de Brissac)
  1927- .... CLC 12, 35
  See also CA 41-44R; SATA 5

Didion, Joan 1934-..... CLC 1, 3, 8, 14, 32
  See also CANR 14; CA 5-8R; DLB 2;
  DLB-Y 81, 86

Dillard, Annie 1945-............ CLC 9, 60
  See also CANR 3; CA 49-52; SATA 10;
  DLB-Y 80

Dillard, R(ichard) H(enry) W(ilde)
  1937- .... CLC 5
  See also CAAS 7; CANR 10; CA 21-24R;
  DLB 5

Dillon, Eilis 1920-................ CLC 17
  See also CAAS 3; CANR 4; CA 9-12R;
  SATA 2

Dinesen, Isak 1885-1962 .... CLC 10, 29
  See also Blixen, Karen (Christentze
  Dinesen)
  See also CANR 22

Disch, Thomas M(ichael) 1940-... CLC 7, 36
  See also CAAS 4; CANR 17; CA 21-24R;
  DLB 8

Disraeli, Benjamin 1804-1881 ..... NCLC 2
  See also DLB 21, 55

Dixon, Paige 1911-
  See Corcoran, Barbara

Dixon, Stephen 1936-............. CLC 52
  See also CANR 17; CA 89-92

Doblin, Alfred 1878-1957........ TCLC 13
  See also Doeblin, Alfred

Dobrolyubov, Nikolai Alexandrovich
  1836-1861 .... NCLC 5

Dobyns, Stephen 1941-............ CLC 37
  See also CANR 2, 18; CA 45-48

Doctorow, E(dgar) L(aurence)
  1931- ...... CLC 6, 11, 15, 18, 37, 44
  See also CANR 2; CA 45-48; DLB 2, 28;
  DLB-Y 80

Dodgson, Charles Lutwidge 1832-1898
  See Carroll, Lewis
  See also YABC 2

Doeblin, Alfred 1878-1957....... TCLC 13
  See also CA 110; DLB 66

Doerr, Harriet 1910- .... CLC 34
  See also CA 117, 122

Donaldson, Stephen R. 1947-....... CLC 46
  See also CANR 13; CA 89-92

Donleavy, J(ames) P(atrick)
  1926- .... CLC 1, 4, 6, 10, 45
  See also CANR 24; CA 9-12R; DLB 6

Donnadieu, Marguerite 1914-
  See Duras, Marguerite

Donne, John 1572?-1631 .... LC 10

Donnell, David 1939?-............ CLC 34

Donoso, Jose 1924-........ CLC 4, 8, 11, 32
  See also CA 81-84

Donovan, John 1928- .... CLC 35
  See also CLR 3; CA 97-100; SATA 29

Doolittle, Hilda 1886-1961
  See H(ilda) D(oolittle)
  See also CA 97-100; DLB 4, 45

Dorfman, Ariel 1942-............ CLC 48
  See also CA 124

Dorn, Ed(ward Merton) 1929-... CLC 10, 18
  See also CA 93-96; DLB 5

Dos Passos, John (Roderigo)
  1896-1970 ... CLC 1, 4, 8, 11, 15, 25, 34
  See also CANR 3; CA 1-4R;
  obituary CA 29-32R; DLB 4, 9;
  DLB-DS 1

Dostoevski, Fedor Mikhailovich
  1821-1881 .... NCLC 2, 7, 21; SSC 2

Doughty, Charles (Montagu)
  1843-1926 .... TCLC 27
  See also CA 115; DLB 19, 57

Douglas, George 1869-1902...... TCLC 28

Douglass, Frederick 1817-1895.... NCLC 7
  See also SATA 29; DLB 1, 43, 50;
  CDALB 1640-1865

Dourado, (Waldomiro Freitas) Autran
  1926- .... CLC 23, 60
  See also CA 25-28R

Dove, Rita 1952-................. CLC 50
  See also CA 109

Dowson, Ernest (Christopher)
  1867-1900 .... TCLC 4
  See also CA 105; DLB 19

Doyle, (Sir) Arthur Conan
  1859-1930 .... TCLC 7, 26
  See also CA 104, 122; SATA 24; DLB 18,
  70

Dr. A 1933-
  See Silverstein, Alvin and Virginia B(arbara
  Opshelor) Silverstein

Drabble, Margaret
  1939- .... CLC 2, 3, 5, 8, 10, 22, 53
  See also CANR 18; CA 13-16R; SATA 48;
  DLB 14

Drayton, Michael 1563-1631........ LC 8

Dreiser, Theodore (Herman Albert)
  1871-1945 .... TCLC 10, 18, 35
  See also CA 106; SATA 48; DLB 9, 12;
  DLB-DS 1; CDALB 1865-1917

Drexler, Rosalyn 1926- .... CLC 2, 6
  See also CA 81-84

Dreyer, Carl Theodor 1889-1968.... CLC 16
  See also obituary CA 116

Drieu La Rochelle, Pierre
  1893-1945 .... TCLC 21
  See also CA 117; DLB 72

Droste-Hulshoff, Annette Freiin von
  1797-1848 .... NCLC 3

Drummond, William Henry
  1854-1907 .... TCLC 25

Drummond de Andrade, Carlos 1902-1987
  See Andrade, Carlos Drummond de

Drury, Allen (Stuart) 1918-........ CLC 37
  See also CANR 18; CA 57-60

Dryden, John 1631-1700 .... LC 3

Duberman, Martin 1930-........... CLC 8
  See also CANR 2; CA 1-4R

Dubie, Norman (Evans, Jr.) 1945- .. CLC 36
  See also CANR 12; CA 69-72

Du Bois, W(illiam) E(dward) B(urghardt)
  1868-1963 .... CLC 1, 2, 13
  See also CA 85-88; SATA 42; DLB 47, 50;
  CDALB 1865-1917

Dubus, Andre 1936-........... CLC 13, 36
  See also CANR 17; CA 21-24R

Ducasse, Isidore Lucien 1846-1870
  See Lautreamont, Comte de

Duclos, Charles Pinot 1704-1772 ..... LC 1

Dudek, Louis 1918- .... CLC 11, 19
  See also CANR 1; CA 45-48

Dudevant, Amandine Aurore Lucile Dupin
  1804-1876
  See Sand, George

Duerrenmatt, Friedrich
  1921- .... CLC 1, 4, 8, 11, 15, 43
  See also CA 17-20R; DLB 69

Duffy, Bruce 19??-................ CLC 50

Duffy, Maureen 1933-............. CLC 37
  See also CA 25-28R; DLB 14

Dugan, Alan 1923-.............. CLC 2, 6
  See also CA 81-84; DLB 5

Duhamel, Georges 1884-1966 .... CLC 8
  See also CA 81-84; obituary CA 25-28R

Dujardin, Edouard (Emile Louis)
  1861-1949 .... TCLC 13
  See also CA 109

Duke, Raoul 1939-
  See Thompson, Hunter S(tockton)

Dumas, Alexandre (Davy de la Pailleterie)
  (pere) 1802-1870.......... NCLC 11
  See also SATA 18

Dumas, Alexandre (fils)
  1824-1895 .... NCLC 9

Dumas, Henry (L.) 1934-1968....... CLC 6
  See also CA 85-88; DLB 41

Du Maurier, Daphne 1907-... CLC 6, 11, 59
  See also CANR 6; CA 5-8R;
  obituary CA 128; SATA 27

Dunbar, Paul Laurence
  1872-1906 .... TCLC 2, 12
  See also CA 104, 124; SATA 34; DLB 50,
  54; CDALB 1865-1917

Duncan (Steinmetz Arquette), Lois
    1934- .... **CLC 26**
    See also Arquette, Lois S(teinmetz)
    See also CANR 2; CA 1-4R; SAAS 2;
    SATA 1, 36

Duncan, Robert (Edward)
    1919-1988 .... **CLC 1, 2, 4, 7, 15, 41, 55**
    See also CA 9-12R; obituary CA 124;
    DLB 5, 16

Dunlap, William 1766-1839 .... **NCLC 2**
    See also DLB 30, 37, 59

Dunn, Douglas (Eaglesham)
    1942- .... **CLC 6, 40**
    See also CANR 2; CA 45-48; DLB 40

Dunn, Elsie 1893-1963
    See Scott, Evelyn

Dunn, Stephen 1939- .... **CLC 36**
    See also CANR 12; CA 33-36R

Dunne, Finley Peter 1867-1936.... **TCLC 28**
    See also CA 108; DLB 11, 23

Dunne, John Gregory 1932-....... **CLC 28**
    See also CANR 14; CA 25-28R; DLB-Y 80

Dunsany, Lord (Edward John Moreton Drax
    Plunkett) 1878-1957......... **TCLC 2**
    See also CA 104; DLB 10

Durang, Christopher (Ferdinand)
    1949- .... **CLC 27, 38**
    See also CA 105

Duras, Marguerite
    1914- .... **CLC 3, 6, 11, 20, 34, 40**
    See also CA 25-28R

Durban, Pam 1947-............... **CLC 39**
    See also CA 123

Durcan, Paul 1944-............... **CLC 43**

Durrell, Lawrence (George)
    1912- .... **CLC 1, 4, 6, 8, 13, 27, 41**
    See also CA 9-12R; DLB 15, 27

Durrenmatt, Friedrich
    1921- .... **CLC 1, 4, 8, 11, 15, 43**
    See also Duerrenmatt, Friedrich
    See also DLB 69

Dwight, Timothy 1752-1817...... **NCLC 13**
    See also DLB 37

Dworkin, Andrea 1946- .... **CLC 43**
    See also CANR 16; CA 77-80

Dylan, Bob 1941-.......... **CLC 3, 4, 6, 12**
    See also CA 41-44R; DLB 16

East, Michael 1916-
    See West, Morris L.

Eastlake, William (Derry) 1917-..... **CLC 8**
    See also CAAS 1; CANR 5; CA 5-8R;
    DLB 6

Eberhart, Richard 1904-... **CLC 3, 11, 19, 56**
    See also CANR 2; CA 1-4R; DLB 48;
    CDALB 1941-1968

Eberstadt, Fernanda 1960-......... **CLC 39**

Echegaray (y Eizaguirre), Jose (Maria Waldo)
    1832-1916 .... **TCLC 4**
    See also CA 104

Echeverria, (Jose) Esteban (Antonino)
    1805-1851 .... **NCLC 18**

Eckert, Allan W. 1931- .... **CLC 17**
    See also CANR 14; CA 13-16R; SATA 27,
    29

Eco, Umberto 1932-........... **CLC 28, 60**
    See also CANR 12; CA 77-80

Eddison, E(ric) R(ucker)
    1882-1945 .... **TCLC 15**
    See also CA 109

Edel, Leon (Joseph) 1907-...... **CLC 29, 34**
    See also CANR 1, 22; CA 1-4R

Eden, Emily 1797-1869 .... **NCLC 10**

Edgar, David 1948-................ **CLC 42**
    See also CANR 12; CA 57-60; DLB 13

Edgerton, Clyde 1944- .... **CLC 39**
    See also CA 118

Edgeworth, Maria 1767-1849...... **NCLC 1**
    See also SATA 21

Edmonds, Helen (Woods) 1904-1968
    See Kavan, Anna
    See also CA 5-8R; obituary CA 25-28R

Edmonds, Walter D(umaux) 1903- .. **CLC 35**
    See also CANR 2; CA 5-8R; SAAS 4;
    SATA 1, 27; DLB 9

Edson, Russell 1905- .... **CLC 13**
    See also CA 33-36R

Edwards, G(erald) B(asil)
    1899-1976 .... **CLC 25**
    See also obituary CA 110

Edwards, Gus 1939-.............. **CLC 43**
    See also CA 108

Edwards, Jonathan 1703-1758........ **LC 7**
    See also DLB 24

Ehle, John (Marsden, Jr.) 1925-.... **CLC 27**
    See also CA 9-12R

Ehrenbourg, Ilya (Grigoryevich) 1891-1967
    See Ehrenburg, Ilya (Grigoryevich)

Ehrenburg, Ilya (Grigoryevich)
    1891-1967 .... **CLC 18, 34**
    See also CA 102; obituary CA 25-28R

Eich, Guenter 1907-1971
    See also CA 111; obituary CA 93-96

Eich, Gunter 1907-1971............ **CLC 15**
    See also Eich, Guenter
    See also DLB 69

Eichendorff, Joseph Freiherr von
    1788-1857 .... **NCLC 8**

Eigner, Larry 1927- .... **CLC 9**
    See also Eigner, Laurence (Joel)
    See also DLB 5

Eigner, Laurence (Joel) 1927-
    See Eigner, Larry
    See also CANR 6; CA 9-12R

Eiseley, Loren (Corey) 1907-1977.... **CLC 7**
    See also CANR 6; CA 1-4R;
    obituary CA 73-76

Eisenstadt, Jill 1963- .... **CLC 50**

Ekeloef, Gunnar (Bengt) 1907-1968
    See Ekelof, Gunnar (Bengt)
    See also obituary CA 25-28R

Ekelof, Gunnar (Bengt) 1907-1968 .. **CLC 27**
    See also Ekeloef, Gunnar (Bengt)

Ekwensi, Cyprian (Odiatu Duaka)
    1921- .... **CLC 4**
    See also CANR 18; CA 29-32R

Eliade, Mircea 1907-1986 .... **CLC 19**
    See also CA 65-68; obituary CA 119

Eliot, George 1819-1880.... **NCLC 4, 13, 23**
    See also DLB 21, 35, 55

Eliot, John 1604-1690 .... **LC 5**
    See also DLB 24

Eliot, T(homas) S(tearns)
    1888-1965 .... **CLC 1, 2, 3, 6, 9, 10, 13,**
        15, 24, 34, 41, 55, 57
    See also CA 5-8R; obituary CA 25-28R;
    DLB 7, 10, 45, 63; DLB-Y 88

Elkin, Stanley (Lawrence)
    1930- .... **CLC 4, 6, 9, 14, 27, 51**
    See also CANR 8; CA 9-12R; DLB 2, 28;
    DLB-Y 80

Elledge, Scott 19??- .... **CLC 34**

Elliott, George P(aul) 1918-1980..... **CLC 2**
    See also CANR 2; CA 1-4R;
    obituary CA 97-100

Elliott, Janice 1931-............... **CLC 47**
    See also CANR 8; CA 13-16R; DLB 14

Elliott, Sumner Locke 1917-....... **CLC 38**
    See also CANR 2, 21; CA 5-8R

Ellis, A. E. 19??-.................. **CLC 7**

Ellis, Alice Thomas 19??-.......... **CLC 40**

Ellis, Bret Easton 1964-........... **CLC 39**
    See also CA 118, 123

Ellis, (Henry) Havelock
    1859-1939 .... **TCLC 14**
    See also CA 109

Ellis, Trey 1964-.................. **CLC 55**

Ellison, Harlan (Jay) 1934-... **CLC 1, 13, 42**
    See also CANR 5; CA 5-8R; DLB 8

Ellison, Ralph (Waldo)
    1914- .... **CLC 1, 3, 11, 54**
    See also CANR 24; CA 9-12R; DLB 2;
    CDALB 1941-1968

Ellmann, Lucy 1956- .... **CLC 61**
    See also CA 128

Ellmann, Richard (David)
    1918-1987 .... **CLC 50**
    See also CANR 2; CA 1-4R;
    obituary CA 122; DLB-Y 87

Elman, Richard 1934-............. **CLC 19**
    See also CAAS 3; CA 17-20R

Eluard, Paul 1895-1952 .... **TCLC 7**
    See also Grindel, Eugene

Elyot, (Sir) James 1490?-1546....... **LC 11**

Elyot, (Sir) Thomas 1490?-1546 ..... **LC 11**

Elytis, Odysseus 1911-......... **CLC 15, 49**
    See also CA 102

Emecheta, (Florence Onye) Buchi
    1944- .... **CLC 14, 48**
    See also CA 81-84

Emerson, Ralph Waldo
    1803-1882 .... **NCLC 1**
    See also DLB 1, 59, 73; CDALB 1640-1865

Empson, William
    1906-1984 .... **CLC 3, 8, 19, 33, 34**
    See also CA 17-20R; obituary CA 112;
    DLB 20

Enchi, Fumiko (Veda) 1905-1986 ... **CLC 31**
    See also obituary CA 121

Ende, Michael 1930-.............. **CLC 31**
    See also CLR 14; CA 118, 124; SATA 42;
    DLB 75

Endo, Shusaku 1923- ..... CLC **7, 14, 19, 54**
  See also CANR 21; CA 29-32R

Engel, Marian 1933-1985 .... CLC **36**
  See also CANR 12; CA 25-28R; DLB 53

Engelhardt, Frederick 1911-1986
  See Hubbard, L(afayette) Ron(ald)

Enright, D(ennis) J(oseph)
    1920- .... CLC **4, 8, 31**
  See also CANR 1; CA 1-4R; SATA 25;
  DLB 27

Enzensberger, Hans Magnus
    1929- .... CLC **43**
  See also CA 116, 119

Ephron, Nora 1941- .... CLC **17, 31**
  See also CANR 12; CA 65-68

Epstein, Daniel Mark 1948- .... CLC **7**
  See also CANR 2; CA 49-52

Epstein, Jacob 1956- .... CLC **19**
  See also CA 114

Epstein, Joseph 1937- .... CLC **39**
  See also CA 112, 119

Epstein, Leslie 1938- .... CLC **27**
  See also CANR 23; CA 73-76

Erdman, Paul E(mil) 1932- .... CLC **25**
  See also CANR 13; CA 61-64

Erdrich, Louise 1954- .... CLC **39, 54**
  See also CA 114

Erenburg, Ilya (Grigoryevich) 1891-1967
  See Ehrenburg, Ilya (Grigoryevich)

Eseki, Bruno 1919-
  See Mphahlele, Ezekiel

Esenin, Sergei (Aleksandrovich)
    1895-1925 .... TCLC **4**
  See also CA 104

Eshleman, Clayton 1935- .... CLC **7**
  See also CAAS 6; CA 33-36R; DLB 5

Espriu, Salvador 1913-1985 .... CLC **9**
  See also obituary CA 115

Estleman, Loren D. 1952- .... CLC **48**
  See also CA 85-88

Evans, Marian 1819-1880
  See Eliot, George

Evans, Mary Ann 1819-1880
  See Eliot, George

Evarts, Esther 1900-1972
  See Benson, Sally

Everett, Percival L. 1957?- .... CLC **57**
  See also CA 129

Everson, Ronald G(ilmour) 1903- ... CLC **27**
  See also CA 17-20R

Everson, William (Oliver)
    1912- .... CLC **1, 5, 14**
  See also CANR 20; CA 9-12R; DLB 5, 16

Evtushenko, Evgenii (Aleksandrovich) 1933-
  See Yevtushenko, Yevgeny

Ewart, Gavin (Buchanan)
    1916- .... CLC **13, 46**
  See also CANR 17; CA 89-92; DLB 40

Ewers, Hanns Heinz 1871-1943 ... TCLC **12**
  See also CA 109

Ewing, Frederick R. 1918-
  See Sturgeon, Theodore (Hamilton)

Exley, Frederick (Earl) 1929- .... CLC **6, 11**
  See also CA 81-84; DLB-Y 81

Ezekiel, Nissim 1924- .... CLC **61**
  See also CA 61-64

Ezekiel, Tish O'Dowd 1943- .... CLC **34**

Fagen, Donald 1948- .... CLC **26**

Fair, Ronald L. 1932- .... CLC **18**
  See also CANR 25; CA 69-72; DLB 33

Fairbairns, Zoe (Ann) 1948- .... CLC **32**
  See also CANR 21; CA 103

Fairfield, Cicily Isabel 1892-1983
  See West, Rebecca

Fallaci, Oriana 1930- .... CLC **11**
  See also CANR 15; CA 77-80

Faludy, George 1913- .... CLC **42**
  See also CA 21-24R

Fante, John 1909-1983 .... CLC **60**
  See also CANR 23; CA 69-72;
  obituary CA 109; DLB-Y 83

Farah, Nuruddin 1945- .... CLC **53**
  See also CA 106

Fargue, Leon-Paul 1876-1947 ..... TCLC **11**
  See also CA 109

Farigoule, Louis 1885-1972
  See Romains, Jules

Farina, Richard 1937?-1966 .... CLC **9**
  See also CA 81-84; obituary CA 25-28R

Farley, Walter 1920- .... CLC **17**
  See also CANR 8; CA 17-20R; SATA 2, 43;
  DLB 22

Farmer, Philip Jose 1918- .... CLC **1, 19**
  See also CANR 4; CA 1-4R; DLB 8

Farrell, J(ames) G(ordon)
    1935-1979 .... CLC **6**
  See also CA 73-76; obituary CA 89-92;
  DLB 14

Farrell, James T(homas)
    1904-1979 .... CLC **1, 4, 8, 11**
  See also CANR 9; CA 5-8R;
  obituary CA 89-92; DLB 4, 9; DLB-DS 2

Farrell, M. J. 1904-
  See Keane, Molly

Fassbinder, Rainer Werner
    1946-1982 .... CLC **20**
  See also CA 93-96; obituary CA 106

Fast, Howard (Melvin) 1914- ...... CLC **23**
  See also CANR 1; CA 1-4R; SATA 7;
  DLB 9

Faulkner, William (Cuthbert)
    1897-1962 .... CLC **1, 3, 6, 8, 9, 11, 14,**
                18, 28, 52; SSC 1
  See also CA 81-84; DLB 9, 11, 44;
  DLB-Y 86; DLB-DS 2

Fauset, Jessie Redmon
    1884?-1961 .... CLC **19, 54**
  See also CA 109; DLB 51

Faust, Irvin 1924- .... CLC **8**
  See also CA 33-36R; DLB 2, 28; DLB-Y 80

Fearing, Kenneth (Flexner)
    1902-1961 .... CLC **51**
  See also CA 93-96; DLB 9

Federman, Raymond 1928- ...... CLC **6, 47**
  See also CANR 10; CA 17-20R; DLB-Y 80

Federspiel, J(urg) F. 1931- .... CLC **42**

Feiffer, Jules 1929- .... CLC **2, 8**
  See also CA 17-20R; SATA 8; DLB 7, 44

Feinberg, David B. 1956- .... CLC **59**

Feinstein, Elaine 1930- .... CLC **36**
  See also CAAS 1; CA 69-72; DLB 14, 40

Feldman, Irving (Mordecai) 1928- .... CLC **7**
  See also CANR 1; CA 1-4R

Fellini, Federico 1920- .... CLC **16**
  See also CA 65-68

Felsen, Gregor 1916-
  See Felsen, Henry Gregor

Felsen, Henry Gregor 1916- .... CLC **17**
  See also CANR 1; CA 1-4R; SAAS 2;
  SATA 1

Fenton, James (Martin) 1949- ...... CLC **32**
  See also CA 102; DLB 40

Ferber, Edna 1887-1968 .... CLC **18**
  See also CA 5-8R; obituary CA 25-28R;
  SATA 7; DLB 9, 28

Ferlinghetti, Lawrence (Monsanto)
    1919?- .... CLC **2, 6, 10, 27**
  See also CANR 3; CA 5-8R; DLB 5, 16;
  CDALB 1941-1968

Ferrier, Susan (Edmonstone)
    1782-1854 .... NCLC **8**

Feuchtwanger, Lion 1884-1958 ..... TCLC **3**
  See also CA 104; DLB 66

Feydeau, Georges 1862-1921 ...... TCLC **22**
  See also CA 113

Ficino, Marsilio 1433-1499 .... LC **12**

Fiedler, Leslie A(aron)
    1917- .... CLC **4, 13, 24**
  See also CANR 7; CA 9-12R; DLB 28, 67

Field, Andrew 1938- .... CLC **44**
  See also CANR 25; CA 97-100

Field, Eugene 1850-1895 .... NCLC **3**
  See also SATA 16; DLB 21, 23, 42

Fielding, Henry 1707-1754 .... LC **1**
  See also DLB 39

Fielding, Sarah 1710-1768 .... LC **1**
  See also DLB 39

Fierstein, Harvey 1954- .... CLC **33**
  See also CA 123

Figes, Eva 1932- .... CLC **31**
  See also CANR 4; CA 53-56; DLB 14

Finch, Robert (Duer Claydon)
    1900- .... CLC **18**
  See also CANR 9, 24; CA 57-60

Findley, Timothy 1930- .... CLC **27**
  See also CANR 12; CA 25-28R; DLB 53

Fink, Janis 1951-
  See Ian, Janis

Firbank, Louis 1944-
  See Reed, Lou
  See also CA 117

Firbank, (Arthur Annesley) Ronald
    1886-1926 .... TCLC **1**
  See also CA 104; DLB 36

Fisher, Roy 1930- .... CLC **25**
  See also CANR 16; CA 81-84; DLB 40

Fisher, Rudolph 1897-1934 .... TCLC **11**
  See also CA 107; DLB 51

Fisher, Vardis (Alvero) 1895-1968.... **CLC 7**
See also CA 5-8R; obituary CA 25-28R;
DLB 9

FitzGerald, Edward 1809-1883 .... **NCLC 9**
See also DLB 32

Fitzgerald, F(rancis) Scott (Key)
1896-1940 .... **TCLC 1, 6, 14, 28; SSC 6**
See also CA 110, 123; DLB 4, 9, 86;
DLB-Y 81; DLB-DS 1;
CDALB 1917-1929

Fitzgerald, Penelope 1916-... **CLC 19, 51, 61**
See also CAAS 10; CA 85-88,; DLB 14

FitzGerald, Robert D(avid) 1902-... **CLC 19**
See also CA 17-20R

Fitzgerald, Robert (Stuart)
1910-1985 .... **CLC 39**
See also CANR 1; CA 2R;
obituary CA 114; DLB-Y 80

Flanagan, Thomas (James Bonner)
1923- .... **CLC 25, 52**
See also CA 108; DLB-Y 80

Flaubert, Gustave
1821-1880 .... **NCLC 2, 10, 19**

Fleming, Ian (Lancaster)
1908-1964 .... **CLC 3, 30**
See also CA 5-8R; SATA 9

Fleming, Thomas J(ames) 1927- .... **CLC 37**
See also CANR 10; CA 5-8R; SATA 8

Fletcher, John Gould 1886-1950... **TCLC 35**
See also CA 107; DLB 4, 45

Flieg, Hellmuth
See Heym, Stefan

Flying Officer X 1905-1974
See Bates, H(erbert) E(rnest)

Fo, Dario 1929-.................. **CLC 32**
See also CA 116

Follett, Ken(neth Martin) 1949- .... **CLC 18**
See also CANR 13; CA 81-84; DLB-Y 81

Fontane, Theodor 1819-1898..... **NCLC 26**

Foote, Horton 1916-.............. **CLC 51**
See also CA 73-76; DLB 26

Forbes, Esther 1891-1967.......... **CLC 12**
See also CAP 1; CA 13-14;
obituary CA 25-28R; SATA 2; DLB 22

Forche, Carolyn 1950-............ **CLC 25**
See also CA 109, 117; DLB 5

Ford, Ford Madox 1873-1939... **TCLC 1, 15**
See also CA 104; DLB 34

Ford, John 1895-1973............. **CLC 16**
See also obituary CA 45-48

Ford, Richard 1944-............. **CLC 46**
See also CANR 11; CA 69-72

Foreman, Richard 1937-.......... **CLC 50**
See also CA 65-68

Fores, Maria Irene 1930-....... **CLC 39, 61**
See also CANR 28; CA 25-28R,; DLB 7,

Forester, C(ecil) S(cott)
1899-1966 .... **CLC 35**
See also CA 73-76; obituary CA 25-28R;
SATA 13

Forman, James D(ouglas) 1932- .... **CLC 21**
See also CANR 4, 19; CA 9-12R; SATA 8,
21

Forrest, Leon 1937- .... **CLC 4**
See also CAAS 7; CA 89-92; DLB 33

Forster, E(dward) M(organ)
1879-1970 .... **CLC 1, 2, 3, 4, 9, 10, 13,**
15, 22, 45
See also CAP 1; CA 13-14;
obituary CA 25-28R; DLB 34

Forster, John 1812-1876 .... **NCLC 11**

Forsyth, Frederick 1938-....... **CLC 2, 5, 36**
See also CA 85-88

Forten (Grimke), Charlotte L(ottie)
1837-1914 .... **TCLC 16**
See also Grimke, Charlotte L(ottie) Forten
See also DLB 50

Foscolo, Ugo 1778-1827.......... **NCLC 8**

Fosse, Bob 1925-1987............ **CLC 20**
See also Fosse, Robert Louis

Fosse, Robert Louis 1925-1987
See Bob Fosse
See also CA 110, 123

Foster, Stephen Collins
1826-1864 .... **NCLC 26**

Foucault, Michel 1926-1984 .... **CLC 31, 34**
See also CANR 23; CA 105;
obituary CA 113

Fouque, Friedrich (Heinrich Karl) de La
Motte 1777-1843 .... **NCLC 2**

Fournier, Henri Alban 1886-1914
See Alain-Fournier
See also CA 104

Fournier, Pierre 1916-............ **CLC 11**
See also Gascar, Pierre
See also CANR 16; CA 89-92

Fowles, John (Robert)
1926- .... **CLC 1, 2, 3, 4, 6, 9, 10, 15, 33**
See also CANR 25; CA 5-8R; SATA 22;
DLB 14

Fox, Paula 1923-................. **CLC 2, 8**
See also CLR 1; CANR 20; CA 73-76;
SATA 17; DLB 52

Fox, William Price (Jr.) 1926- ..... **CLC 22**
See also CANR 11; CA 17-20R; DLB 2;
DLB-Y 81

Foxe, John 1516?-1587............. **LC 14**

Frame (Clutha), Janet (Paterson)
1924- .... **CLC 2, 3, 6, 22**
See also Clutha, Janet Paterson Frame

France, Anatole 1844-1924 .... **TCLC 9**
See also Thibault, Jacques Anatole Francois

Francis, Claude 19??-............ **CLC 50**

Francis, Dick 1920- .... **CLC 2, 22, 42**
See also CANR 9; CA 5-8R

Francis, Robert (Churchill)
1901-1987 .... **CLC 15**
See also CANR 1; CA 1-4R;
obituary CA 123

Frank, Anne 1929-1945 .... **TCLC 17**
See also CA 113; SATA 42

Frank, Elizabeth 1945-............ **CLC 39**
See also CA 121, 126

Franklin, (Stella Maria Sarah) Miles
1879-1954 .... **TCLC 7**
See also CA 104

Fraser, Antonia (Pakenham)
1932- .... **CLC 32**
See also CA 85-88; SATA 32

Fraser, George MacDonald 1925-.... **CLC 7**
See also CANR 2; CA 45-48

Frayn, Michael 1933-...... **CLC 3, 7, 31, 47**
See also CA 5-8R; DLB 13, 14

Fraze, Candida 19??- .... **CLC 50**
See also CA 125

Frazer, Sir James George
1854-1941 .... **TCLC 32**
See also CA 118

Frazier, Ian 1951-................ **CLC 46**

Frederic, Harold 1856-1898...... **NCLC 10**
See also DLB 12, 23

Frederick the Great 1712-1786 ...... **LC 14**

Fredman, Russell (Bruce) 1929-
See also CLR 20

Fredro, Aleksander 1793-1876..... **NCLC 8**

Freeling, Nicolas 1927-........... **CLC 38**
See also CANR 1, 17; CA 49-52

Freeman, Douglas Southall
1886-1953 .... **TCLC 11**
See also CA 109; DLB 17

Freeman, Judith 1946-........... **CLC 55**

Freeman, Mary (Eleanor) Wilkins
1852-1930 .... **TCLC 9; SSC 1**
See also CA 106; DLB 12

Freeman, R(ichard) Austin
1862-1943 .... **TCLC 21**
See also CA 113; DLB 70

French, Marilyn 1929-...... **CLC 10, 18, 60**
See also CANR 3; CA 69-72

Freneau, Philip Morin 1752-1832.. **NCLC 1**
See also DLB 37, 43

Friedman, B(ernard) H(arper)
1926- .... **CLC 7**
See also CANR 3; CA 1-4R

Friedman, Bruce Jay 1930-.... **CLC 3, 5, 56**
See also CANR 25; CA 9-12R; DLB 2, 28

Friel, Brian 1929-........... **CLC 5, 42, 59**
See also CA 21-24R; DLB 13

Friis-Baastad, Babbis (Ellinor)
1921-1970 .... **CLC 12**
See also CA 17-20R; SATA 7

Frisch, Max (Rudolf)
1911- .... **CLC 3, 9, 14, 18, 32, 44**
See also CA 85-88; DLB 69

Fromentin, Eugene (Samuel Auguste)
1820-1876 .... **NCLC 10**

Frost, Robert (Lee)
1874-1963 ... **CLC 1, 3, 4, 9, 10, 13, 15,**
26, 34, 44
See also CA 89-92; SATA 14; DLB 54

Fry, Christopher 1907-....... **CLC 2, 10, 14**
See also CANR 9; CA 17-20R; DLB 13

Frye, (Herman) Northrop 1912- .... **CLC 24**
See also CANR 8; CA 5-8R

Fuchs, Daniel 1909-............ **CLC 8, 22**
See also CAAS 5; CA 81-84; DLB 9, 26, 28

Fuchs, Daniel 1934-.............. **CLC 34**
See also CANR 14; CA 37-40R

Fuentes, Carlos
   1928- . . . . . . **CLC 3, 8, 10, 13, 22, 41, 60**
   See also CANR 10; CA 69-72

Fugard, Athol 1932-. . . **CLC 5, 9, 14, 25, 40**
   See also CA 85-88

Fugard, Sheila 1932- . . . . **CLC 48**
   See also CA 125

Fuller, Charles (H., Jr.) 1939-. . . . . . **CLC 25**
   See also CA 108, 112; DLB 38

Fuller, (Sarah) Margaret
   1810-1850 . . . . **NCLC 5**
   See also Ossoli, Sarah Margaret (Fuller
      marchesa d')
   See also DLB 1, 59, 73; CDALB 1640-1865

Fuller, Roy (Broadbent) 1912-. . . . **CLC 4, 28**
   See also CA 5-8R; DLB 15, 20

Fulton, Alice 1952-. . . . . **CLC 52**
   See also CA 116

Furphy, Joseph 1843-1912. . . . . . . **TCLC 25**

Futrelle, Jacques 1875-1912 . . . . . . **TCLC 19**
   See also CA 113

Gaboriau, Emile 1835-1873 . . . . . . **NCLC 14**

Gadda, Carlo Emilio 1893-1973 . . . . **CLC 11**
   See also CA 89-92

Gaddis, William
   1922- . . . . **CLC 1, 3, 6, 8, 10, 19, 43**
   See also CAAS 4; CANR 21; CA 17-20R;
      DLB 2

Gaines, Ernest J. 1933- . . . . . . **CLC 3, 11, 18**
   See also CANR 6, 24; CA 9-12R; DLB 2,
      33; DLB-Y 80

Gale, Zona 1874-1938 . . . . **TCLC 7**
   See also CA 105; DLB 9

Gallagher, Tess 1943-. . . . . **CLC 18**
   See also CA 106

Gallant, Mavis
   1922- . . . . **CLC 7, 18, 38; SSC 5**
   See also CA 69-72; DLB 53

Gallant, Roy A(rthur) 1924- . . . . **CLC 17**
   See also CANR 4; CA 5-8R; SATA 4

Gallico, Paul (William) 1897-1976 . . . **CLC 2**
   See also CA 5-8R; obituary CA 69-72;
      SATA 13; DLB 9

Galsworthy, John 1867-1933. . . . . . . **TCLC 1**
   See also CA 104; DLB 10, 34

Galt, John 1779-1839. . . . . **NCLC 1**

Galvin, James 1951-. . . . . **CLC 38**
   See also CANR 26; CA 108

Gamboa, Frederico 1864-1939. . . . . **TCLC 36**

Gann, Ernest K(ellogg) 1910- . . . . . . **CLC 23**
   See also CANR 1; CA 1-4R

Garcia Lorca, Federico
   1899-1936 . . . . **TCLC 1, 7**
   See also CA 104

Garcia Marquez, Gabriel (Jose)
   1928- . . . . **CLC 2, 3, 8, 10, 15, 27, 47, 55**
   See also CANR 10; CA 33-36R

Gardam, Jane 1928-. . . . . **CLC 43**
   See also CLR 12; CANR 2, 18; CA 49-52;
      SATA 28, 39; DLB 14

Gardner, Herb 1934- . . . . **CLC 44**

Gardner, John (Champlin, Jr.)
   1933-1982 . . . . **CLC 2, 3, 5, 7, 8, 10, 18,
                                                      28, 34**
   See also CA 65-68; obituary CA 107;
      obituary SATA 31, 40; DLB 2; DLB-Y 82

Gardner, John (Edmund) 1926-. . . . . **CLC 30**
   See also CANR 15; CA 103

Garfield, Leon 1921-. . . . . **CLC 12**
   See also CA 17-20R; SATA 1, 32

Garland, (Hannibal) Hamlin
   1860-1940 . . . . **TCLC 3**
   See also CA 104; DLB 12, 71

Garneau, Hector (de) Saint Denys
   1912-1943 . . . . **TCLC 13**
   See also CA 111

Garner, Alan 1935-. . . . . **CLC 17**
   See also CLR 20; CANR 15; CA 73-76;
      SATA 18

Garner, Hugh 1913-1979 . . . . **CLC 13**
   See also CA 69-72; DLB 68

Garnett, David 1892-1981 . . . . **CLC 3**
   See also CANR 17; CA 5-8R;
      obituary CA 103; DLB 34

Garrett, George (Palmer, Jr.)
   1929- . . . . **CLC 3, 11, 51**
   See also CAAS 5; CANR 1; CA 1-4R;
      DLB 2, 5; DLB-Y 83

Garrigue, Jean 1914-1972 . . . . **CLC 2, 8**
   See also CANR 20; CA 5-8R;
      obituary CA 37-40R

Gary, Romain 1914-1980. . . . . **CLC 25**
   See also Kacew, Romain

Gascar, Pierre 1916-. . . . . **CLC 11**
   See also Fournier, Pierre

Gascoyne, David (Emery) 1916- . . . . **CLC 45**
   See also CANR 10; CA 65-68; DLB 20

Gaskell, Elizabeth Cleghorn
   1810-1865 . . . . **NCLC 5**
   See also DLB 21

Gass, William H(oward)
   1924- . . . . **CLC 1, 2, 8, 11, 15, 39**
   See also CA 17-20R; DLB 2

Gautier, Theophile 1811-1872 . . . . . **NCLC 1**

Gaye, Marvin (Pentz) 1939-1984 . . . **CLC 26**
   See also obituary CA 112

Gebler, Carlo (Ernest) 1954-. . . . . . . **CLC 39**
   See also CA 119

Gee, Maggie 19??- . . . . **CLC 57**

Gee, Maurice (Gough) 1931-. . . . . . . **CLC 29**
   See also CA 97-100; SATA 46

Gelbart, Larry 1923?-. . . . . **CLC 21, 61**
   See also CA 73-76

Gelber, Jack 1932-. . . . . **CLC 1, 6, 14, 60**
   See also CANR 2; CA 1-4R; DLB 7

Gellhorn, Martha (Ellis) 1908- . . **CLC 14, 60**
   See also CA 77-80; DLB-Y 82

Genet, Jean
   1910-1986 . . . **CLC 1, 2, 5, 10, 14, 44, 46**
   See also CANR 18; CA 13-16R; DLB 72;
      DLB-Y 86

Gent, Peter 1942-. . . . . **CLC 29**
   See also CA 89-92; DLB 72; DLB-Y 82

George, Jean Craighead 1919-. . . . . . **CLC 35**
   See also CLR 1; CA 5-8R; SATA 2;
      DLB 52

George, Stefan (Anton)
   1868-1933 . . . . **TCLC 2, 14**
   See also CA 104

Gerhardi, William (Alexander) 1895-1977
   See Gerhardie, William (Alexander)

Gerhardie, William (Alexander)
   1895-1977 . . . . **CLC 5**
   See also CANR 18; CA 25-28R;
      obituary CA 73-76; DLB 36

Gertler, T(rudy) 1946?- . . . . **CLC 34**
   See also CA 116

Gessner, Friedrike Victoria 1910-1980
   See Adamson, Joy(-Friederike Victoria)

Ghelderode, Michel de
   1898-1962 . . . . **CLC 6, 11**
   See also CA 85-88

Ghiselin, Brewster 1903- . . . . **CLC 23**
   See also CANR 13; CA 13-16R

Ghose, Zulfikar 1935-. . . . . **CLC 42**
   See also CA 65-68

Ghosh, Amitav 1943- . . . . **CLC 44**

Giacosa, Giuseppe 1847-1906 . . . . . . **TCLC 7**
   See also CA 104

Gibbon, Lewis Grassic 1901-1935. . . **TCLC 4**
   See also Mitchell, James Leslie

Gibbons, Kaye 1960- . . . . **CLC 50**

Gibran, (Gibran) Kahlil
   1883-1931 . . . . **TCLC 1, 9**
   See also CA 104

Gibson, William 1914-. . . . . **CLC 23**
   See also CANR 9; CA 9-12R; DLB 7

Gibson, William 1948-. . . . . **CLC 39**
   See also CA 126

Gide, Andre (Paul Guillaume)
   1869-1951 . . . . **TCLC 5, 12, 36**
   See also CA 104, 124; DLB 65

Gifford, Barry (Colby) 1946-. . . . . . . **CLC 34**
   See also CANR 9; CA 65-68

Gilbert, (Sir) W(illiam) S(chwenck)
   1836-1911 . . . . **TCLC 3**
   See also CA 104; SATA 36

Gilbreth, Ernestine 1908-
   See Carey, Ernestine Gilbreth

Gilbreth, Frank B(unker), Jr.
   1911- . . . . **CLC 17**
   See also CA 9-12R; SATA 2

Gilchrist, Ellen 1935-. . . . . **CLC 34, 48**
   See also CA 113, 116

Giles, Molly 1942- . . . . **CLC 39**
   See also CA 126

Gilliam, Terry (Vance) 1940-
   See Monty Python
   See also CA 108, 113

Gilliatt, Penelope (Ann Douglass)
   1932- . . . . **CLC 2, 10, 13, 53**
   See also CA 13-16R; DLB 14

Gilman, Charlotte (Anna) Perkins (Stetson)
   1860-1935 . . . . **TCLC 9, 37**
   See also CA 106

Gilmour, David 1944-
   See Pink Floyd

Gilroy, Frank D(aniel) 1925-........ **CLC 2**
See also CA 81-84; DLB 7

Ginsberg, Allen
1926-........... **CLC 1, 2, 3, 4, 6, 13, 36**
See also CANR 2; CA 1-4R; DLB 5, 16;
CDALB 1941-1968

Ginzburg, Natalia 1916-...... **CLC 5, 11, 54**
See also CA 85-88

Giono, Jean 1895-1970.......... **CLC 4, 11**
See also CANR 2; CA 45-48;
obituary CA 29-32R; DLB 72

Giovanni, Nikki 1943-........ **CLC 2, 4, 19**
See also CLR 6; CAAS 6; CANR 18;
CA 29-32R; SATA 24; DLB 5, 41

Giovene, Andrea 1904-............. **CLC 7**
See also CA 85-88

Gippius, Zinaida (Nikolayevna) 1869-1945
See Hippius, Zinaida
See also CA 106

Giraudoux, (Hippolyte) Jean
1882-1944 .... **TCLC 2, 7**
See also CA 104; DLB 65

Gironella, Jose Maria 1917-....... **CLC 11**
See also CA 101

Gissing, George (Robert)
1857-1903 .... **TCLC 3, 24**
See also CA 105; DLB 18

Gladkov, Fyodor (Vasilyevich)
1883-1958 .... **TCLC 27**

Glanville, Brian (Lester) 1931-...... **CLC 6**
See also CANR 3; CA 5-8R; SATA 42;
DLB 15

Glasgow, Ellen (Anderson Gholson)
1873?-1945................. **TCLC 2, 7**
See also CA 104; DLB 9, 12

Glassco, John 1909-1981 .... **CLC 9**
See also CANR 15; CA 13-16R;
obituary CA 102; DLB 68

Glasser, Ronald J. 1940?- .... **CLC 37**

Glendinning, Victoria 1937-........ **CLC 50**
See also CA 120

Glissant, Edouard 1928-........... **CLC 10**

Gloag, Julian 1930- .... **CLC 40**
See also CANR 10; CA 65-68

Gluck, Louise (Elisabeth)
1943- .... **CLC 7, 22, 44**
See also CA 33-36R; DLB 5

Gobineau, Joseph Arthur (Comte) de
1816-1882 .... **NCLC 17**

Godard, Jean-Luc 1930-........... **CLC 20**
See also CA 93-96

Godden, (Margaret) Rumer 1907-... **CLC 53**
See also CLR 20; CANR 4, 27; CA 7-8R;
SATA 3, 36

Godwin, Gail 1937-........ **CLC 5, 8, 22, 31**
See also CANR 15; CA 29-32R; DLB 6

Godwin, William 1756-1836...... **NCLC 14**
See also DLB 39

Goethe, Johann Wolfgang von
1749-1832 .... **NCLC 4, 22**

Gogarty, Oliver St. John
1878-1957 .... **TCLC 15**
See also CA 109; DLB 15, 19

Gogol, Nikolai (Vasilyevich)
1809-1852 .... **NCLC 5, 15; SSC 4**
See also CAAS 1, 4

Gokceli, Yasar Kemal 1923-
See Kemal, Yashar

Gold, Herbert 1924-....... **CLC 4, 7, 14, 42**
See also CANR 17; CA 9-12R; DLB 2;
DLB-Y 81

Goldbarth, Albert 1948-........ **CLC 5, 38**
See also CANR 6; CA 53-56

Goldberg, Anatol 1910-1982 .... **CLC 34**
See also obituary CA 117

Goldemberg, Isaac 1945- .... **CLC 52**
See also CANR 11; CA 69-72

Golding, William (Gerald)
1911- ..... **CLC 1, 2, 3, 8, 10, 17, 27, 58**
See also CANR 13; CA 5-8R; DLB 15

Goldman, Emma 1869-1940...... **TCLC 13**
See also CA 110

Goldman, William (W.) 1931-.... **CLC 1, 48**
See also CA 9-12R; DLB 44

Goldmann, Lucien 1913-1970 ...... **CLC 24**
See also CAP 2; CA 25-28

Goldoni, Carlo 1707-1793 .... **LC 4**

Goldsberry, Steven 1949-.......... **CLC 34**

Goldsmith, Oliver 1728?-1774....... **LC 2**
See also SATA 26; DLB 39

Gombrowicz, Witold
1904-1969 .... **CLC 4, 7, 11, 49**
See also CAP 2; CA 19-20;
obituary CA 25-28R

Gomez de la Serna, Ramon
1888-1963 .... **CLC 9**
See also obituary CA 116

Goncharov, Ivan Alexandrovich
1812-1891 .... **NCLC 1**

Goncourt, Edmond (Louis Antoine Huot) de
1822-1896 .... **NCLC 7**

Goncourt, Jules (Alfred Huot) de
1830-1870 .... **NCLC 7**

Gontier, Fernande 19??-........... **CLC 50**

Goodman, Paul 1911-1972.... **CLC 1, 2, 4, 7**
See also CAP 2; CA 19-20;
obituary CA 37-40R

Gordimer, Nadine
1923- ...... **CLC 3, 5, 7, 10, 18, 33, 51**
See also CANR 3; CA 5-8R

Gordon, Adam Lindsay
1833-1870 .... **NCLC 21**

Gordon, Caroline
1895-1981 .... **CLC 6, 13, 29**
See also CAP 1; CA 11-12;
obituary CA 103; DLB 4, 9; DLB-Y 81

Gordon, Charles William 1860-1937
See Conner, Ralph
See also CA 109

Gordon, Mary (Catherine)
1949- .... **CLC 13, 22**
See also CA 102; DLB 6; DLB-Y 81

Gordon, Sol 1923-................ **CLC 26**
See also CANR 4; CA 53-56; SATA 11

Gordone, Charles 1925-.......... **CLC 1, 4**
See also CA 93-96; DLB 7

Gorenko, Anna Andreyevna 1889?-1966
See Akhmatova, Anna

Gorky, Maxim 1868-1936 .... **TCLC 8**
See also Peshkov, Alexei Maximovich

Goryan, Sirak 1908-1981
See Saroyan, William

Gosse, Edmund (William)
1849-1928 .... **TCLC 28**
See also CA 117; DLB 57

Gotlieb, Phyllis (Fay Bloom)
1926- .... **CLC 18**
See also CANR 7; CA 13-16R

Gould, Lois 1938?-.............. **CLC 4, 10**
See also CA 77-80

Gourmont, Remy de 1858-1915.... **TCLC 17**
See also CA 109

Govier, Katherine 1948-........... **CLC 51**
See also CANR 18; CA 101

Goyen, (Charles) William
1915-1983 .... **CLC 5, 8, 14, 40**
See also CANR 6; CA 5-8R;
obituary CA 110; DLB 2; DLB-Y 83

Goytisolo, Juan 1931- .... **CLC 5, 10, 23**
See also CA 85-88

Gozzi, (Conte) Carlo 1720-1806 .. **NCLC 23**

Grabbe, Christian Dietrich
1801-1836 .... **NCLC 2**

Grace, Patricia 1937-............. **CLC 56**

Gracq, Julien 1910- .... **CLC 11, 48**
See also Poirier, Louis

Grade, Chaim 1910-1982 .... **CLC 10**
See also CA 93-96; obituary CA 107

Graham, Jorie 1951-.............. **CLC 48**
See also CA 111

Graham, R(obert) B(ontine) Cunninghame
1852-1936 .... **TCLC 19**

Graham, W(illiam) S(ydney)
1918-1986 .... **CLC 29**
See also CA 73-76; obituary CA 118;
DLB 20

Graham, Winston (Mawdsley)
1910- .... **CLC 23**
See also CANR 2, 22; CA 49-52;
obituary CA 118

Granville-Barker, Harley
1877-1946 .... **TCLC 2**
See also CA 104

Grass, Gunter (Wilhelm)
1927- .. **CLC 1, 2, 4, 6, 11, 15, 22, 32, 49**
See also CANR 20; CA 13-16R; DLB 75

Grau, Shirley Ann 1929-......... **CLC 4, 9**
See also CANR 22; CA 89-92; DLB 2

Graves, Richard Perceval 1945- .... **CLC 44**
See also CANR 9, 26; CA 65-68

Graves, Robert (von Ranke)
1895-1985 ... **CLC 1, 2, 6, 11, 39, 44, 45**
See also CANR 5; CA 5-8R;
obituary CA 117; SATA 45; DLB 20;
DLB-Y 85

Gray, Alasdair 1934-............. **CLC 41**
See also CA 123

Gray, Amlin 1946-............... **CLC 29**

Gray, Francine du Plessix 1930-.... **CLC 22**
See also CAAS 2; CANR 11; CA 61-64**

Gray, John (Henry)   1866-1934 .... TCLC 19
See also CA 119

Gray, Simon (James Holliday)
1936- .... CLC 9, 14, 36
See also CAAS 3; CA 21-24R; DLB 13

Gray, Spalding   1941- .... CLC 49

Gray, Thomas   1716-1771 .... LC 4

Grayson, Richard (A.)   1951- .... CLC 38
See also CANR 14; CA 85-88

Greeley, Andrew M(oran)   1928- .... CLC 28
See also CAAS 7; CANR 7; CA 5-8R

Green, Hannah   1932- .... CLC 3, 7, 30
See also Greenberg, Joanne
See also CA 73-76

Green, Henry   1905-1974 .... CLC 2, 13
See also Yorke, Henry Vincent
See also DLB 15

Green, Julien (Hartridge)   1900- .. CLC 3, 11
See also CA 21-24R; DLB 4, 72

Green, Paul (Eliot)   1894-1981...... CLC 25
See also CANR 3; CA 5-8R;
obituary CA 103; DLB 7, 9; DLB-Y 81

Greenberg, Ivan   1908-1973
See Rahv, Philip
See also CA 85-88

Greenberg, Joanne (Goldenberg)
1932- .... CLC 3, 7, 30
See also Green, Hannah
See also CANR 14; CA 5-8R; SATA 25

Greenberg, Richard   1959?- .... CLC 57

Greene, Bette   1934- .... CLC 30
See also CLR 2; CANR 4; CA 53-56;
SATA 8

Greene, Gael   19??- .... CLC 8
See also CANR 10; CA 13-16R

Greene, Graham (Henry)
1904- ..... CLC 1, 3, 6, 9, 14, 18, 27, 37
See also CA 13-16R; SATA 20; DLB 13, 15;
DLB-Y 85

Gregor, Arthur   1923- .... CLC 9
See also CANR 11; CA 25-28R; SATA 36

Gregory, Lady (Isabella Augusta Persse)
1852-1932 .... TCLC 1
See also CA 104; DLB 10

Grendon, Stephen   1909-1971
See Derleth, August (William)

Grenville, Kate   1950-............. CLC 61
See also CA 118

Greve, Felix Paul Berthold Friedrich
1879-1948
See Grove, Frederick Philip
See also CA 104

Grey, (Pearl) Zane   1872?-1939 ..... TCLC 6
See also CA 104; DLB 9

Grieg, (Johan) Nordahl (Brun)
1902-1943 .... TCLC 10
See also CA 107

Grieve, C(hristopher) M(urray)   1892-1978
See MacDiarmid, Hugh
See also CA 5-8R; obituary CA 85-88

Griffin, Gerald   1803-1840 .... NCLC 7

Griffin, Peter   1942- .... CLC 39

Griffiths, Trevor   1935- .... CLC 13, 52
See also CA 97-100; DLB 13

Grigson, Geoffrey (Edward Harvey)
1905-1985 .... CLC 7, 39
See also CANR 20; CA 25-28R;
obituary CA 118; DLB 27

Grillparzer, Franz   1791-1872...... NCLC 1

Grimke, Charlotte L(ottie) Forten   1837-1914
See Forten (Grimke), Charlotte L(ottie)
See also CA 117, 124

Grimm, Jakob (Ludwig) Karl
1785-1863 .... NCLC 3
See also SATA 22

Grimm, Wilhelm Karl   1786-1859 .. NCLC 3
See also SATA 22

Grimmelshausen, Johann Jakob Christoffel
von   1621-1676 .... LC 6

Grindel, Eugene   1895-1952
See also CA 104

Grossman, Vasily (Semenovich)
1905-1964 .... CLC 41
See also CA 124

Grove, Frederick Philip
1879-1948 .... TCLC 4
See also Greve, Felix Paul Berthold
Friedrich

Grumbach, Doris (Isaac)
1918- .... CLC 13, 22
See also CAAS 2; CANR 9; CA 5-8R

Grundtvig, Nicolai Frederik Severin
1783-1872 .... NCLC 1

Grunwald, Lisa   1959-............. CLC 44
See also CA 120

Guare, John   1938- .... CLC 8, 14, 29
See also CANR 21; CA 73-76; DLB 7

Gudjonsson, Halldor Kiljan   1902-
See Laxness, Halldor (Kiljan)
See also CA 103

Guest, Barbara   1920-............. CLC 34
See also CANR 11; CA 25-28R; DLB 5

Guest, Judith (Ann)   1936-....... CLC 8, 30
See also CANR 15; CA 77-80

Guild, Nicholas M.   1944-......... CLC 33
See also CA 93-96

Guillen, Jorge   1893-1984.......... CLC 11
See also CA 89-92; obituary CA 112

Guillen, Nicolas   1902-1989 .... CLC 48
See also CA 116, 125

Guillevic, (Eugene)   1907 .... CLC 33
See also CA 93-96

Gunn, Bill   1934-1989 .... CLC 5
See also Gunn, William Harrison
See also DLB 38

Gunn, Thom(son William)
1929- .... CLC 3, 6, 18, 32
See also CANR 9; CA 17-20R; DLB 27

Gunn, William Harrison   1934-1989
See Gunn, Bill
See also CANR 12, 25; CA 13-16R

Gurney, A(lbert) R(amsdell), Jr.
1930- .... CLC 32, 50, 54
See also CA 77-80

Gurney, Ivor (Bertie)   1890-1937 ... TCLC 33

Gustafson, Ralph (Barker)   1909-.... CLC 36
See also CANR 8; CA 21-24R

Guthrie, A(lfred) B(ertram), Jr.
1901- .... CLC 23
See also CA 57-60; DLB 6

Guthrie, Woodrow Wilson   1912-1967
See Guthrie, Woody
See also CA 113; obituary CA 93-96

Guthrie, Woody   1912-1967 .... CLC 35
See also Guthrie, Woodrow Wilson

Guy, Rosa (Cuthbert)   1928-..... CLC 26 13
See also CANR 14; CA 17-20R; SATA 14;
DLB 33

Haavikko, Paavo (Juhani)
1931- .... CLC 18, 34
See also CA 106

Hacker, Marilyn   1942- .... CLC 5, 9, 23
See also CA 77-80

Haggard, (Sir) H(enry) Rider
1856-1925 .... TCLC 11
See also CA 108; SATA 16; DLB 70

Haig-Brown, Roderick L(angmere)
1908-1976 .... CLC 21
See also CANR 4; CA 5-8R;
obituary CA 69-72; SATA 12

Hailey, Arthur   1920- .... CLC 5
See also CANR 2; CA 1-4R; DLB-Y 82

Hailey, Elizabeth Forsythe   1938-... CLC 40
See also CAAS 1; CANR 15; CA 93-96

Haines, John   1924-............... CLC 58
See also CANR 13; CA 19-20R; DLB 5

Haldeman, Joe   1943-............. CLC 61
See also CA 53-56; DLB 8

Haley, Alex (Palmer)   1921-...... CLC 8, 12
See also CA 77-80; DLB 38

Haliburton, Thomas Chandler
1796-1865 .... NCLC 15
See also DLB 11

Hall, Donald (Andrew, Jr.)
1928- ....CLC 1, 13, 37, 59
See also CAAS 7; CANR 2; CA 5-8R;
SATA 23; DLB 5

Hall, James Norman   1887-1951 ... TCLC 23
See also CA 123; SATA 21

Hall, (Marguerite) Radclyffe
1886-1943 .... TCLC 12
See also CA 110

Hall, Rodney   1935- .... CLC 51
See also CA 109

Halpern, Daniel   1945-............ CLC 14
See also CA 33-36R

Hamburger, Michael (Peter Leopold)
1924- .... CLC 5, 14
See also CAAS 4; CANR 2; CA 5-8R;
DLB 27

Hamill, Pete   1935-............... CLC 10
See also CANR 18; CA 25-28R

Hamilton, Edmond   1904-1977....... CLC 1
See also CANR 3; CA 1-4R; DLB 8

Hamilton, Gail   1911-
See Corcoran, Barbara

Hamilton, Ian   1938-.............. CLC 55
See also CA 106; DLB 40

Hamilton, Mollie   1909?-
See Kaye, M(ary) M(argaret)

Hamilton, (Anthony Walter) Patrick
 1904-1962 .... **CLC 51**
 See also obituary CA 113; DLB 10

Hamilton, Virginia (Esther) 1936-... **CLC 26**
 See also CLR 1, 11; CANR 20; CA 25-28R;
 SATA 4; DLB 33, 52

Hammett, (Samuel) Dashiell
 1894-1961 .... **CLC 3, 5, 10, 19, 47**
 See also CA 81-84

Hammon, Jupiter 1711?-1800? .... **NCLC 5**
 See also DLB 31, 50

Hamner, Earl (Henry), Jr. 1923- ... **CLC 12**
 See also CA 73-76; DLB 6

Hampton, Christopher (James)
 1946- .... **CLC 4**
 See also CA 25-28R; DLB 13

Hamsun, Knut 1859-1952....... **TCLC 2, 14**
 See also Pedersen, Knut

Handke, Peter 1942- .. **CLC 5, 8, 10, 15, 38**
 See also CA 77-80

Hanley, James 1901-1985 ... **CLC 3, 5, 8, 13**
 See also CA 73-76; obituary CA 117

Hannah, Barry 1942- .... **CLC 23, 38**
 See also CA 108, 110; DLB 6

Hansberry, Lorraine (Vivian)
 1930-1965 .... **CLC 17**
 See also CA 109; obituary CA 25-28R;
 DLB 7, 38; CDALB 1941-1968

Hansen, Joseph 1923-............. **CLC 38**
 See also CANR 16; CA 29-32R

Hansen, Martin 1909-1955 .... **TCLC 32**

Hanson, Kenneth O(stlin) 1922-.... **CLC 13**
 See also CANR 7; CA 53-56

Hardenberg, Friedrich (Leopold Freiherr) von
 1772-1801
 See Novalis

Hardwick, Elizabeth 1916- .... **CLC 13**
 See also CANR 3; CA 5-8R; DLB 6

Hardy, Thomas
 1840-1928 ... **TCLC 4, 10, 18, 32; SSC 2**
 See also CA 104, 123; SATA 25; DLB 18,
 19

Hare, David 1947- .... **CLC 29, 58**
 See also CA 97-100; DLB 13

Harlan, Louis R(udolph) 1922-..... **CLC 34**
 See also CANR 25; CA 21-24R

Harling, Robert 1951?-............ **CLC 53**

Harmon, William (Ruth) 1938- ..... **CLC 38**
 See also CANR 14; CA 33-36R

Harper, Frances Ellen Watkins
 1825-1911 .... **TCLC 14**
 See also CA 111, 125; DLB 50

Harper, Michael S(teven) 1938- .. **CLC 7, 22**
 See also CANR 24; CA 33-36R; DLB 41

Harris, Christie (Lucy Irwin)
 1907-....................... **CLC 12**
 See also CANR 6; CA 5-8R; SATA 6

Harris, Frank 1856-1931........ **TCLC 24**
 See also CAAS 1; CA 109

Harris, George Washington
 1814-1869 .... **NCLC 23**
 See also DLB 3, 11

Harris, Joel Chandler 1848-1908 ... **TCLC 2**
 See also YABC 1; CA 104; DLB 11, 23, 42

Harris, John (Wyndham Parkes Lucas)
 Beynon 1903-1969
 See Wyndham, John
 See also CA 102; obituary CA 89-92

Harris, MacDonald 1921- .... **CLC 9**
 See also Heiney, Donald (William)

Harris, Mark 1922- .... **CLC 19**
 See also CAAS 3; CANR 2; CA 5-8R;
 DLB 2; DLB-Y 80

Harris, (Theodore) Wilson 1921-.... **CLC 25**
 See also CANR 11; CA 65-68

Harrison, Harry (Max) 1925-...... **CLC 42**
 See also CANR 5, 21; CA 1-4R; SATA 4;
 DLB 8

Harrison, James (Thomas) 1937-
 See Harrison, Jim
 See also CANR 8; CA 13-16R

Harrison, Jim 1937-......... **CLC 6, 14, 33**
 See also Harrison, James (Thomas)
 See also DLB-Y 82

Harrison, Tony 1937-............. **CLC 43**
 See also CA 65-68; DLB 40

Harriss, Will(ard Irvin) 1922-...... **CLC 34**
 See also CA 111

Harte, (Francis) Bret(t)
 1836?-1902................. **TCLC 1, 25**
 See also CA 104; SATA 26; DLB 12, 64,
 74; CDALB 1865-1917

Hartley, L(eslie) P(oles)
 1895-1972 .... **CLC 2, 22**
 See also CA 45-48; obituary CA 37-40R;
 DLB 15

Hartman, Geoffrey H. 1929-....... **CLC 27**
 See also CA 117, 125; DLB 67

Haruf, Kent 19??-................ **CLC 34**

Harwood, Ronald 1934-........... **CLC 32**
 See also CANR 4; CA 1-4R; DLB 13

Hasek, Jaroslav (Matej Frantisek)
 1883-1923 .... **TCLC 4**
 See also CA 104

Hass, Robert 1941-............ **CLC 18, 39**
 See also CA 111

Hastings, Selina 19??- .... **CLC 44**

Hauptmann, Gerhart (Johann Robert)
 1862-1946 .... **TCLC 4**
 See also CA 104; DLB 66

Havel, Vaclav 1936-........... **CLC 25, 58**
 See also CA 104

Haviaras, Stratis 1935- .... **CLC 33**
 See also CA 105

Hawkes, John (Clendennin Burne, Jr.)
 1925- ...... **CLC 1, 2, 3, 4, 7, 9, 14, 15,
 27, 49**
 See also CANR 2; CA 1-4R; DLB 2, 7;
 DLB-Y 80

Hawthorne, Julian 1846-1934 ..... **TCLC 25**

Hawthorne, Nathaniel
 1804-1864 ... **NCLC 2, 10, 17, 23; SSC 3**
 See also YABC 2; DLB 1, 74;
 CDALB 1640-1865

Hayashi Fumiko 1904-1951...... **TCLC 27**

Haycraft, Anna 19??-
 See Ellis, Alice Thomas

Hayden, Robert (Earl)
 1913-1980 .... **CLC 5, 9, 14, 37**
 See also CANR 24; CA 69-72;
 obituary CA 97-100; CABS 2; SATA 19;
 obituary SATA 26; DLB 5, 76;
 CDALB 1941-1968

Hayman, Ronald 1932-............ **CLC 44**
 See also CANR 18; CA 25-28R

Haywood, Eliza (Fowler) 1693?-1756.. **LC 1**
 See also DLB 39

Hazzard, Shirley 1931- .... **CLC 18**
 See also CANR 4; CA 9-12R; DLB-Y 82

H(ilda) D(oolittle)
 1886-1961 .... **CLC 3, 8, 14, 31, 34**
 See also Doolittle, Hilda

Head, Bessie 1937-1986........... **CLC 25**
 See also CANR 25; CA 29-32R;
 obituary CA 109

Headon, (Nicky) Topper 1956?-
 See The Clash

Heaney, Seamus (Justin)
 1939-............ **CLC 5, 7, 14, 25, 37**
 See also CANR 25; CA 85-88; DLB 40

Hearn, (Patricio) Lafcadio (Tessima Carlos)
 1850-1904 .... **TCLC 9**
 See also CA 105; DLB 12

Hearne, Vicki 1946-.............. **CLC 56**

Heat Moon, William Least 1939-... **CLC 29**

Hebert, Anne 1916- .... **CLC 4, 13, 29**
 See also CA 85-88; DLB 68

Hecht, Anthony (Evan)
 1923-.................. **CLC 8, 13, 19**
 See also CANR 6; CA 9-12R; DLB 5

Hecht, Ben 1894-1964 .... **CLC 8**
 See also CA 85-88; DLB 7, 9, 25, 26, 28

Hedayat, Sadeq 1903-1951....... **TCLC 21**
 See also CA 120

Heidegger, Martin 1889-1976 ...... **CLC 24**
 See also CA 81-84; obituary CA 65-68

Heidenstam, (Karl Gustaf) Verner von
 1859-1940 .... **TCLC 5**
 See also CA 104

Heifner, Jack 1946-.............. **CLC 11**
 See also CA 105

Heijermans, Herman 1864-1924 ... **TCLC 24**
 See also CA 123

Heilbrun, Carolyn G(old) 1926-..... **CLC 25**
 See also CANR 1; CA 45-48

Heine, Harry 1797-1856
 See Heine, Heinrich

Heine, Heinrich 1797-1856 .... **NCLC 4**

Heinemann, Larry C(urtiss) 1944- .. **CLC 50**
 See also CA 110

Heiney, Donald (William) 1921-
 See Harris, MacDonald
 See also CANR 3; CA 1-4R

Heinlein, Robert A(nson)
 1907-1988 ...... **CLC 1, 3, 8, 14, 26, 55**
 See also CANR 1, 20; CA 1-4R;
 obituary CA 125; SATA 9; DLB 8

Heller, Joseph
 1923-........ **CLC 1, 3, 5, 8, 11, 36**
 See also CANR 8; CA 5-8R; CABS 1;
 DLB 2, 28; DLB-Y 80

Hellman, Lillian (Florence)
1905?-1984..... **CLC 2, 4, 8, 14, 18, 34, 44, 52**
See also CA 13-16R; obituary CA 112;
DLB 7; DLB-Y 84

Helprin, Mark 1947- ..... **CLC 7, 10, 22, 32**
See also CA 81-84; DLB-Y 85

Hemingway, Ernest (Miller)
1899-1961 ... **CLC 1, 3, 6, 8, 10, 13, 19, 30, 34, 39, 41, 44, 50, 61; SSC 1**
See also CA 77-80; DLB 4, 9; DLB-Y 81, 87; DLB-DS 1

Hempel, Amy 1951- .... **CLC 39**
See also CA 118

Henley, Beth 1952-................ **CLC 23**
See also Henley, Elizabeth Becker
See also DLB-Y 86

Henley, Elizabeth Becker 1952-
See Henley, Beth
See also CA 107

Henley, William Ernest
1849-1903 .... TCLC 8
See also CA 105; DLB 19

Hennissart, Martha
See Lathen, Emma
See also CA 85-88

Henry, O. 1862-1910 ... **TCLC 1, 19; SSC 5**
See also Porter, William Sydney
See also YABC 2; CA 104; DLB 12, 78, 79;
CDALB 1865-1917

Henry VIII 1491-1547............. **LC 10**

Hentoff, Nat(han Irving) 1925- ..... **CLC 26**
See also CLR 1; CAAS 6; CANR 5;
CA 1-4R; SATA 27, 42

Heppenstall, (John) Rayner
1911-1981 .... CLC 10
See also CA 1-4R; obituary CA 103

Herbert, Frank (Patrick)
1920-1986 .... **CLC 12, 23, 35, 44**
See also CANR 5; CA 53-56;
obituary CA 118; SATA 9, 37, 47; DLB 8

Herbert, Zbigniew 1924- .... **CLC 9, 43**
See also CA 89-92

Herbst, Josephine 1897-1969....... **CLC 34**
See also CA 5-8R; obituary CA 25-28R;
DLB 9

Herder, Johann Gottfried von
1744-1803 .... NCLC 8

Hergesheimer, Joseph
1880-1954 .... TCLC 11
See also CA 109; DLB 9

Herlagnez, Pablo de 1844-1896
See Verlaine, Paul (Marie)

Herlihy, James Leo 1927- .... **CLC 6**
See also CANR 2; CA 1-4R

Hernandez, Jose 1834-1886...... NCLC 17

Herrick, Robert 1591-1674 .... LC 13

Herriot, James 1916- .... **CLC 12**
See also Wight, James Alfred

Herrmann, Dorothy 1941-......... **CLC 44**
See also CA 107

Hersey, John (Richard)
1914- .... **CLC 1, 2, 7, 9, 40**
See also CA 17-20R; SATA 25; DLB 6

Herzen, Aleksandr Ivanovich
1812-1870 .... NCLC 10

Herzl, Theodor 1860-1904 .... TCLC 36

Herzog, Werner 1942- .... **CLC 16**
See also CA 89-92

Hesiod c. 8th Century B.C.- ...... CMLC 5

Hesse, Hermann
1877-1962 .... **CLC 1, 2, 3, 6, 11, 17, 25**
See also CAP 2; CA 17-18; SATA 50;
DLB 66

Heyen, William 1940- .... **CLC 13, 18**
See also CA 33-36R; DLB 5

Heyerdahl, Thor 1914-............ **CLC 26**
See also CANR 5, 22; CA 5-8R; SATA 2, 52

Heym, Georg (Theodor Franz Arthur)
1887-1912 .... TCLC 9
See also CA 106

Heym, Stefan 1913- .... **CLC 41**
See also CANR 4; CA 9-12R; DLB 69

Heyse, Paul (Johann Ludwig von)
1830-1914 .... TCLC 8
See also CA 104

Hibbert, Eleanor (Burford) 1906- .... **CLC 7**
See also CANR 9; CA 17-20R; SATA 2

Higgins, George V(incent)
1939- .... **CLC 4, 7, 10, 18**
See also CAAS 5; CANR 17; CA 77-80;
DLB 2; DLB-Y 81

Higginson, Thomas Wentworth
1823-1911 .... TCLC 36
See also DLB 1, 64

Highsmith, (Mary) Patricia
1921- .... **CLC 2, 4, 14, 42**
See also CANR 1, 20; CA 1-4R

Highwater, Jamake 1942- .... **CLC 12**
See also CAAS 7; CANR 10; CA 65-68;
SATA 30, 32; DLB 52; DLB-Y 85

Hikmet (Ran), Nazim 1902-1963.... **CLC 40**
See also obituary CA 93-96

Hildesheimer, Wolfgang 1916- ..... **CLC 49**
See also CA 101; DLB 69

Hill, Geoffrey (William)
1932- .... **CLC 5, 8, 18, 45**
See also CANR 21; CA 81-84; DLB 40

Hill, George Roy 1922- .... **CLC 26**
See also CA 110

Hill, Susan B. 1942-............... **CLC 4**
See also CA 33-36R; DLB 14

Hilliard, Noel (Harvey) 1929-...... **CLC 15**
See also CANR 7; CA 9-12R

Hilton, James 1900-1954........ TCLC 21
See also CA 108; SATA 34; DLB 34

Himes, Chester (Bomar)
1909-1984 .... **CLC 2, 4, 7, 18, 58**
See also CANR 22; CA 25-28R;
obituary CA 114; DLB 2, 76

Hinde, Thomas 1926-........... **CLC 6, 11**
See also Chitty, (Sir) Thomas Willes

Hine, (William) Daryl 1936-....... **CLC 15**
See also CANR 1, 20; CA 1-4R; DLB 60

Hinton, S(usan) E(loise) 1950- ..... **CLC 30**
See also CLR 3; CA 81-84; SATA 19

Hippius (Merezhkovsky), Zinaida
(Nikolayevna) 1869-1945...... TCLC 9
See also Gippius, Zinaida (Nikolayevna)

Hiraoka, Kimitake 1925-1970
See Mishima, Yukio
See also CA 97-100; obituary CA 29-32R

Hirsch, Edward (Mark) 1950-... **CLC 31, 50**
See also CANR 20; CA 104

Hitchcock, (Sir) Alfred (Joseph)
1899-1980 .... **CLC 16**
See also obituary CA 97-100; SATA 27;
obituary SATA 24

Hoagland, Edward 1932- .... **CLC 28**
See also CANR 2; CA 1-4R; SATA 51;
DLB 6

Hoban, Russell C(onwell) 1925- .. **CLC 7, 25**
See also CLR 3; CANR 23; CA 5-8R;
SATA 1, 40; DLB 52

Hobson, Laura Z(ametkin)
1900-1986 .... **CLC 7, 25**
See also CA 17-20R; obituary CA 118;
SATA 52; DLB 28

Hochhuth, Rolf 1931-........ **CLC 4, 11, 18**
See also CA 5-8R

Hochman, Sandra 1936-.......... **CLC 3, 8**
See also CA 5-8R; DLB 5

Hochwalder, Fritz 1911-1986 ...... **CLC 36**
See also CA 29-32R; obituary CA 120

Hocking, Mary (Eunice) 1921- ..... **CLC 13**
See also CANR 18; CA 101

Hodgins, Jack 1938-.............. **CLC 23**
See also CA 93-96; DLB 60

Hodgson, William Hope
1877-1918 .... TCLC 13
See also CA 111; DLB 70

Hoffman, Alice 1952-.............. **CLC 51**
See also CA 77-80

Hoffman, Daniel (Gerard)
1923- .... **CLC 6, 13, 23**
See also CANR 4; CA 1-4R; DLB 5

Hoffman, Stanley 1944-............ **CLC 5**
See also CA 77-80

Hoffman, William M(oses) 1939- ... **CLC 40**
See also CANR 11; CA 57-60

Hoffmann, Ernst Theodor Amadeus
1776-1822 .... NCLC 2
See also SATA 27

Hoffmann, Gert 1932- .... **CLC 54**

Hofmannsthal, Hugo (Laurenz August
Hofmann Edler) von
1874-1929 .... TCLC 11
See also CA 106

Hogg, James 1770-1835.......... NCLC 4

Holbach, Paul Henri Thiry, Baron d'
1723-1789 .... LC 14

Holberg, Ludvig 1684-1754.......... LC 6

Holden, Ursula 1921-............. **CLC 18**
See also CANR 22; CA 101

Holderlin, (Johann Christian) Friedrich
1770-1843 .... NCLC 16

Holdstock, Robert (P.) 1948-....... **CLC 39**

Holland, Isabelle 1920- .... **CLC 21**
See also CANR 10, 25; CA 21-24R;
SATA 8

Holland, Marcus 1900-1985
See Caldwell, (Janet Miriam) Taylor
(Holland)

Hollander, John 1929- ...... CLC 2, 5, 8, 14
See also CANR 1; CA 1-4R; SATA 13;
DLB 5

Holleran, Andrew 1943?- .... CLC 38

Hollinghurst, Alan 1954- .... CLC 55
See also CA 114

Hollis, Jim 1916-
See Summers, Hollis (Spurgeon, Jr.)

Holmes, John Clellon 1926-1988.... CLC 56
See also CANR 4; CA 9-10R;
obituary CA 125; DLB 16

Holmes, Oliver Wendell
1809-1894 .... NCLC 14
See also SATA 34; DLB 1;
CDALB 1640-1865

Holt, Victoria 1906-
See Hibbert, Eleanor (Burford)

Holub, Miroslav 1923- .... CLC 4
See also CANR 10; CA 21-24R

Homer c. 8th century B.C.- .... CMLC 1

Honig, Edwin 1919- .... CLC 33
See also CANR 4; CA 5-8R; DLB 5

Hood, Hugh (John Blagdon)
1928- .... CLC 15, 28
See also CANR 1; CA 49-52; DLB 53

Hood, Thomas 1799-1845....... NCLC 16

Hooker, (Peter) Jeremy 1941-...... CLC 43
See also CANR 22; CA 77-80; DLB 40

Hope, A(lec) D(erwent) 1907- .... CLC 3, 51
See also CA 21-24R

Hope, Christopher (David Tully)
1944- .... CLC 52
See also CA 106

Hopkins, Gerard Manley
1844-1889 .... NCLC 17
See also DLB 35, 57

Hopkins, John (Richard) 1931-...... CLC 4
See also CA 85-88

Hopkins, Pauline Elizabeth
1859-1930 .... TCLC 28
See also DLB 50

Horgan, Paul 1903- .... CLC 9, 53
See also CANR 9; CA 13-16R; SATA 13;
DLB-Y 85

Horovitz, Israel 1939- .... CLC 56
See also CA 33-36R; DLB 7

Horwitz, Julius 1920-1986........ CLC 14
See also CANR 12; CA 9-12R;
obituary CA 119

Hospital, Janette Turner 1942-..... CLC 42
See also CA 108

Hostos (y Bonilla), Eugenio Maria de
1893-1903 .... TCLC 24
See also CA 123

Hougan, Carolyn 19??-............ CLC 34

Household, Geoffrey (Edward West)
1900-1988 .... CLC 11
See also CA 77-80; obituary CA 126;
SATA 14

Housman, A(lfred) E(dward)
1859-1936 .... TCLC 1, 10
See also CA 104, 125; DLB 19

Housman, Laurence 1865-1959 ..... TCLC 7
See also CA 106; SATA 25; DLB 10

Howard, Elizabeth Jane 1923- ... CLC 7, 29
See also CANR 8; CA 5-8R

Howard, Maureen 1930- ..... CLC 5, 14, 46
See also CA 53-56; DLB-Y 83

Howard, Richard 1929- ...... CLC 7, 10, 47
See also CANR 25; CA 85-88; DLB 5

Howard, Robert E(rvin)
1906-1936 .... TCLC 8
See also CA 105

Howe, Fanny 1940- .... CLC 47
See also CA 117; SATA 52

Howe, Julia Ward 1819-1910 ..... TCLC 21
See also CA 117; DLB 1

Howe, Tina 1937-................ CLC 48
See also CA 109

Howell, James 1594?-1666.......... LC 13

Howells, William Dean
1837-1920 .... TCLC 7, 17
See also CA 104; DLB 12, 64, 74;
CDALB 1865-1917

Howes, Barbara 1914- .... CLC 15
See also CAAS 3; CA 9-12R; SATA 5

Hrabal, Bohumil 1914-............ CLC 13
See also CA 106

Hubbard, L(afayette) Ron(ald)
1911-1986 .... CLC 43
See also CANR 22; CA 77-80;
obituary CA 118

Huch, Ricarda (Octavia)
1864-1947 .... TCLC 13
See also CA 111; DLB 66

Huddle, David 1942- .... CLC 49
See also CA 57-60

Hudson, W(illiam) H(enry)
1841-1922 .... TCLC 29
See also CA 115; SATA 35

Hueffer, Ford Madox 1873-1939
See Ford, Ford Madox

Hughart, Barry 1934-............. CLC 39

Hughes, David (John) 1930- .... CLC 48
See also CA 116; DLB 14

Hughes, Edward James 1930-
See Hughes, Ted

Hughes, (James) Langston
1902-1967 .... CLC 1, 5, 10, 15, 35, 44;
SSC 6
See also CLR 17; CANR 1; CA 1-4R;
obituary CA 25-28R; SATA 4, 33;
DLB 4, 7, 48, 51, 86; CDALB 1929-1941

Hughes, Richard (Arthur Warren)
1900-1976 .... CLC 1, 11
See also CANR 4; CA 5-8R;
obituary CA 65-68; SATA 8;
obituary SATA 25; DLB 15

Hughes, Ted 1930- ..... CLC 2, 4, 9, 14, 37
See also CLR 3; CANR 1; CA 1-4R;
SATA 27, 49; DLB 40

Hugo, Richard F(ranklin)
1923-1982 .... CLC 6, 18, 32
See also CANR 3; CA 49-52;
obituary CA 108; DLB 5

Hugo, Victor Marie
1802-1885 .... NCLC 3, 10, 21
See also SATA 47

Huidobro, Vicente 1893-1948 ..... TCLC 31

Hulme, Keri 1947- .... CLC 39
See also CA 123

Hulme, T(homas) E(rnest)
1883-1917 .... TCLC 21
See also CA 117; DLB 19

Hume, David 1711-1776............. LC 7

Humphrey, William 1924-......... CLC 45
See also CA 77-80; DLB 6

Humphreys, Emyr (Owen) 1919-.... CLC 47
See also CANR 3, 24; CA 5-8R; DLB 15

Humphreys, Josephine 1945-.... CLC 34, 57
See also CA 121, 127

Hunt, E(verette) Howard (Jr.)
1918- .... CLC 3
See also CANR 2; CA 45-48

Hunt, (James Henry) Leigh
1784-1859 .... NCLC 1

Hunter, Evan 1926- .... CLC 11, 31
See also CANR 5; CA 5-8R; SATA 25;
DLB-Y 82

Hunter, Kristin (Eggleston) 1931-... CLC 35
See also CLR 3; CANR 13; CA 13-16R;
SATA 12; DLB 33

Hunter, Mollie (Maureen McIlwraith)
1922- .... CLC 21
See also McIlwraith, Maureen Mollie
Hunter

Hunter, Robert ?-1734.............. LC 7

Hurston, Zora Neale
1891-1960 .... CLC 7, 30, 61; SSC 4
See also CA 85-88; DLB 51, 86

Huston, John (Marcellus)
1906-1987 .... CLC 20
See also CA 73-76; obituary CA 123;
DLB 26

Huxley, Aldous (Leonard)
1894-1963 .. CLC 1, 3, 4, 5, 8, 11, 18, 35
See also CA 85-88; DLB 36

Huysmans, Charles Marie Georges
1848-1907
See Huysmans, Joris-Karl
See also CA 104

Huysmans, Joris-Karl 1848-1907 .. NCLC 7
See also Huysmans, Charles Marie Georges

Hwang, David Henry 1957-........ CLC 55
See also CA 127

Hyde, Anthony 1946?-............ CLC 42

Hyde, Margaret O(ldroyd) 1917- ... CLC 21
See also CANR 1; CA 1-4R; SATA 1, 42

Ian, Janis 1951- .... CLC 21
See also CA 105

Ibarguengoitia, Jorge 1928-1983.... CLC 37
See also obituary CA 113, 124

Ibsen, Henrik (Johan)
1828-1906 .... TCLC 2, 8, 16, 37
See also CA 104

Ibuse, Masuji 1898- .... CLC 22

Ichikawa, Kon 1915-.............. CLC 20
See also CA 121

Idle, Eric 1943-
See Monty Python
See also CA 116

Ignatow, David 1914-...... CLC 4, 7, 14, 40
See also CAAS 3; CA 9-12R; DLB 5

Ihimaera, Witi (Tame) 1944-....... CLC 46
See also CA 77-80

Ilf, Ilya 1897-1937 .... TCLC 21

Immermann, Karl (Lebrecht)
1796-1840 .... NCLC 4

Ingalls, Rachel 19??-.............. CLC 42
See also CA 123

Ingamells, Rex 1913-1955 .... TCLC 35

Inge, William (Motter)
1913-1973 .... CLC 1, 8, 19
See also CA 9-12R; DLB 7;
CDALB 1941-1968

Innaurato, Albert 1948-........ CLC 21, 60
See also CA 115, 122

Innes, Michael 1906-
See Stewart, J(ohn) I(nnes) M(ackintosh)

Ionesco, Eugene
1912- .... CLC 1, 4, 6, 9, 11, 15, 41
See also CA 9-12R; SATA 7

Iqbal, Muhammad 1877-1938 ..... TCLC 28

Irving, John (Winslow)
1942- .... CLC 13, 23, 38
See also CA 25-28R; DLB 6; DLB-Y 82

Irving, Washington
1783-1859 .... NCLC 2, 19; SSC 2
See also YABC 2; DLB 3, 11, 30, 59, 73,
74; CDALB 1640-1865

Isaacs, Susan 1943- .... CLC 32
See also CANR 20; CA 89-92

Isherwood, Christopher (William Bradshaw)
1904-1986 .... CLC 1, 9, 11, 14, 44
See also CA 13-16R; obituary CA 117;
DLB 15; DLB-Y 86

Ishiguro, Kazuo 1954- ...... CLC 27, 56, 59
See also CA 120

Ishikawa Takuboku 1885-1912 .... TCLC 15
See also CA 113

Iskander, Fazil (Abdulovich)
1929- .... CLC 47
See also CA 102

Ivanov, Vyacheslav (Ivanovich)
1866-1949 .... TCLC 33
See also CA 122

Ivask, Ivar (Vidrik) 1927- .... CLC 14
See also CANR 24; CA 37-40R

Jackson, Jesse 1908-1983 .... CLC 12
See also CA 25-28R; obituary CA 109;
SATA 2, 29, 48

Jackson, Laura (Riding) 1901-
See Riding, Laura
See also CA 65-68; DLB 48

Jackson, Shirley 1919-1965..... CLC 11, 60
See also CANR 4; CA 1-4R;
obituary CA 25-28R; SATA 2; DLB 6;
CDALB 1941-1968

Jacob, (Cyprien) Max 1876-1944 ... TCLC 6
See also CA 104

Jacob, Piers A(nthony) D(illingham) 1934-
See Anthony (Jacob), Piers
See also CA 21-24R

Jacobs, Jim 1942- and Casey, Warren
1942- .... CLC 12

Jacobs, Jim 1942-
See Jacobs, Jim and Casey, Warren
See also CA 97-100

Jacobs, W(illiam) W(ymark)
1863-1943 .... TCLC 22
See also CA 121

Jacobsen, Josephine 1908-......... CLC 48
See also CANR 23; CA 33-36R

Jacobson, Dan 1929- .... CLC 4, 14
See also CANR 2, 25; CA 1-4R; DLB 14

Jagger, Mick 1944-............... CLC 17

Jakes, John (William) 1932-....... CLC 29
See also CANR 10; CA 57-60; DLB-Y 83

James, C(yril) L(ionel) R(obert)
1901-1989 .... CLC 33
See also CA 117, 125

James, Daniel 1911-1988
See Santiago, Danny
See also obituary CA 125

James, Henry (Jr.)
1843-1916 .... TCLC 2, 11, 24
See also CA 104; DLB 12, 71, 74;
CDALB 1865-1917

James, M(ontague) R(hodes)
1862-1936 .... TCLC 6
See also CA 104

James, P(hyllis) D(orothy)
1920- .... CLC 18, 46
See also CANR 17; CA 21-24R

James, William 1842-1910..... TCLC 15, 32
See also CA 109

Jami, Nur al-Din 'Abd al-Rahman
1414-1492 .... LC 9

Jandl, Ernst 1925- .... CLC 34

Janowitz, Tama 1957- .... CLC 43
See also CA 106

Jarrell, Randall
1914-1965 .... CLC 1, 2, 6, 9, 13, 49
See also CLR 6, CANR 6; CA 5-8R;
obituary CA 25-28R; CABS 2; SATA 7;
DLB 48, 52; CDALB 1941-1968

Jarry, Alfred 1873-1907........ TCLC 2, 14
See also CA 104

Jeake, Samuel, Jr. 1889-1973
See Aiken, Conrad

Jean Paul 1763-1825 .... NCLC 7

Jeffers, (John) Robinson
1887-1962 .... CLC 2, 3, 11, 15, 54
See also CA 85-88; DLB 45

Jefferson, Thomas 1743-1826 .... NCLC 11
See also DLB 31; CDALB 1640-1865

Jellicoe, (Patricia) Ann 1927- ...... CLC 27
See also CA 85-88; DLB 13

Jenkins, (John) Robin 1912- .... CLC 52
See also CANR 1; CA 4Rk; DLB 14

Jennings, Elizabeth (Joan)
1926- .... CLC 5, 14
See also CAAS 5; CANR 8; CA 61-64;
DLB 27

Jennings, Waylon 1937-.......... CLC 21

Jensen, Laura (Linnea) 1948- ...... CLC 37
See also CA 103

Jerome, Jerome K. 1859-1927..... TCLC 23
See also CA 119; DLB 10, 34

Jerrold, Douglas William
1803-1857 .... NCLC 2

Jewett, (Theodora) Sarah Orne
1849-1909 .... TCLC 1, 22; SSC 6
See also CA 108, 127; SATA 15; DLB 12,
74

Jewsbury, Geraldine (Endsor)
1812-1880 .... NCLC 22
See also DLB 21

Jhabvala, Ruth Prawer
1927- .... CLC 4, 8, 29
See also CANR 2; CA 1-4R

Jiles, Paulette 1943-........... CLC 13, 58
See also CA 101

Jimenez (Mantecon), Juan Ramon
1881-1958 .... TCLC 4
See also CA 104

Joel, Billy 1949-................. CLC 26
See also Joel, William Martin

Joel, William Martin 1949-
See Joel, Billy
See also CA 108

Johnson, B(ryan) S(tanley William)
1933-1973 .... CLC 6, 9
See also CANR 9; CA 9-12R;
obituary CA 53-56; DLB 14, 40

Johnson, Charles (Richard)
1948- .... CLC 7, 51
See also CA 116; DLB 33

Johnson, Denis 1949-............. CLC 52
See also CA 117, 121

Johnson, Diane 1934-........ CLC 5, 13, 48
See also CANR 17; CA 41-44R; DLB-Y 80

Johnson, Eyvind (Olof Verner)
1900-1976 .... CLC 14
See also CA 73-76; obituary CA 69-72

Johnson, James Weldon
1871-1938 .... TCLC 3, 19
See also Johnson, James William
See also CA 104, 125; DLB 51

Johnson, James William 1871-1938
See Johnson, James Weldon
See also SATA 31

Johnson, Joyce 1935-............. CLC 58
See also CA 125

Johnson, Lionel (Pigot)
1867-1902 .... TCLC 19
See also CA 117; DLB 19

Johnson, Marguerita 1928-
See Angelou, Maya

Johnson, Pamela Hansford
1912-1981 .... CLC 1, 7, 27
See also CANR 2; CA 1-4R;
obituary CA 104; DLB 15

Johnson, Uwe
1934-1984 .... CLC **5, 10, 15, 40**
See also CANR 1; CA 1-4R;
obituary CA 112; DLB 75

Johnston, George (Benson) 1913- ... CLC **51**
See also CANR 5, 20; CA 1-4R

Johnston, Jennifer 1930- .... CLC **7**
See also CA 85-88; DLB 14

Jolley, Elizabeth 1923-............ CLC **46**

Jones, D(ouglas) G(ordon) 1929-.... CLC **10**
See also CANR 13; CA 113; DLB 53

Jones, David
1895-1974 .... CLC **2, 4, 7, 13, 42**
See also CA 9-12R; obituary CA 53-56;
DLB 20

Jones, David Robert 1947-
See Bowie, David
See also CA 103

Jones, Diana Wynne 1934- .... CLC **26**
See also CANR 4; CA 49-52; SATA 9

Jones, Gayl 1949-.............. CLC **6, 9**
See also CA 77-80; DLB 33

Jones, James 1921-1977.... CLC **1, 3, 10, 39**
See also CANR 6; CA 1-4R;
obituary CA 69-72; DLB 2

Jones, (Everett) LeRoi
1934- .... CLC **1, 2, 3, 5, 10, 14, 33**
See also Baraka, Amiri; Baraka, Imamu
Amiri
See also CA 21-24R

Jones, Madison (Percy, Jr.) 1925- ... CLC **4**
See also CANR 7; CA 13-16R

Jones, Mervyn 1922- .... CLC **10, 52**
See also CAAS 5; CANR 1; CA 45-48

Jones, Mick 1956?-
See The Clash

Jones, Nettie 19??-............... CLC **34**

Jones, Preston 1936-1979 .... CLC **10**
See also CA 73-76; obituary CA 89-92;
DLB 7

Jones, Robert F(rancis) 1934-....... CLC **7**
See also CANR 2; CA 49-52

Jones, Rod 1953- .... CLC **50**

Jones, Terry 1942?-
See Monty Python
See also CA 112, 116; SATA 51

Jong, Erica 1942-.......... CLC **4, 6, 8, 18**
See also CANR 26; CA 73-76; DLB 2, 5, 28

Jonson, Ben(jamin) 1572-1637....... LC **6**
See also DLB 62

Jordan, June 1936-.......... CLC **5, 11, 23**
See also CLR 10; CANR 25; CA 33-36R;
SATA 4; DLB 38

Jordan, Pat(rick M.) 1941- .... CLC **37**
See also CANR 25; CA 33-36R

Josipovici, Gabriel (David)
1940- .... CLC **6, 43**
See also CA 37-40R; DLB 14

Joubert, Joseph 1754-1824 .... NCLC **9**

Jouve, Pierre Jean 1887-1976...... CLC **47**
See also obituary CA 65-68

Joyce, James (Augustine Aloysius)
1882-1941 ...... TCLC **3, 8, 16, 26, 35;**
SSC **3**
See also CA 104, 126; DLB 10, 19, 36

Jozsef, Attila 1905-1937......... TCLC **22**
See also CA 116

Juana Ines de la Cruz 1651?-1695 .... LC **5**

Julian of Norwich 1342?-1416?....... LC **6**

Just, Ward S(wift) 1935-........ CLC **4, 27**
See also CA 25-28R

Justice, Donald (Rodney) 1925- .. CLC **6, 19**
See also CANR 26; CA 5-8R; DLB-Y 83

Kacew, Romain 1914-1980
See Gary, Romain
See also CA 108; obituary CA 102

Kacewgary, Romain 1914-1980
See Gary, Romain

Kadare, Ismail 1936- .... CLC **52**

Kadohata, Cynthia 19??- .... CLC **59**

Kafka, Franz
1883-1924 .... TCLC **2, 6, 13, 29;** SSC **5**
See also CA 105, 126; DLB 81

Kahn, Roger 1927-............... CLC **30**
See also CA 25-28R; SATA 37

Kaiser, (Friedrich Karl) Georg
1878-1945 .... TCLC **9**
See also CA 106

Kaletski, Alexander 1946-......... CLC **39**
See also CA 118

Kallman, Chester (Simon)
1921-1975 .... CLC **2**
See also CANR 3; CA 45-48;
obituary CA 53-56

Kaminsky, Melvin 1926-
See Brooks, Mel
See also CANR 16; CA 65-68

Kaminsky, Stuart 1934-........... CLC **59**
See also CA 73-76

Kane, Paul 1941-
See Simon, Paul

Kanin, Garson 1912-.............. CLC **22**
See also CANR 7; CA 5-8R; DLB 7

Kaniuk, Yoram 1930-............. CLC **19**

Kant, Immanuel 1724-1804 ...... NCLC **27**

Kantor, MacKinlay 1904-1977 ...... CLC **7**
See also CA 61-64; obituary CA 73-76;
DLB 9

Kaplan, David Michael 1946- ...... CLC **50**

Kaplan, James 19??-............. CLC **59**

Karamzin, Nikolai Mikhailovich
1766-1826 .... NCLC **3**

Karapanou, Margarita 1946-....... CLC **13**
See also CA 101

Karl, Frederick R(obert) 1927- ..... CLC **34**
See also CANR 3; CA 5-8R

Kassef, Romain 1914-1980
See Gary, Romain

Katz, Steve 1935-................ CLC **47**
See also CANR 12; CA 25-28R; DLB-Y 83

Kauffman, Janet 1945-............ CLC **42**
See also CA 117; DLB-Y 86

Kaufman, Bob (Garnell)
1925-1986 .... CLC **49**
See also CANR 22; CA 41-44R;
obituary CA 118; DLB 16, 41

Kaufman, George S(imon)
1889-1961 .... CLC **38**
See also CA 108; obituary CA 93-96; DLB 7

Kaufman, Sue 1926-1977 .... CLC **3, 8**
See also Barondess, Sue K(aufman)

Kavan, Anna 1904-1968........ CLC **5, 13**
See also Edmonds, Helen (Woods)
See also CANR 6; CA 5-8R

Kavanagh, Patrick (Joseph Gregory)
1905-1967 .... CLC **22**
See also CA 123; obituary CA 25-28R;
DLB 15, 20

Kawabata, Yasunari
1899-1972 .... CLC **2, 5, 9, 18**
See also CA 93-96; obituary CA 33-36R

Kaye, M(ary) M(argaret) 1909?-.... CLC **28**
See also CANR 24; CA 89-92

Kaye, Mollie 1909?-
See Kaye, M(ary) M(argaret)

Kaye-Smith, Sheila 1887-1956..... TCLC **20**
See also CA 118; DLB 36

Kazan, Elia 1909-.............. CLC **6, 16**
See also CA 21-24R

Kazantzakis, Nikos
1885?-1957............. TCLC **2, 5, 33**
See also CA 105

Kazin, Alfred 1915- .... CLC **34, 38**
See also CAAS 7; CANR 1; CA 1-4R

Keane, Mary Nesta (Skrine) 1904-
See Keane, Molly
See also CA 108, 114

Keane, Molly 1904- .... CLC **31**
See also Keane, Mary Nesta (Skrine)

Keates, Jonathan 19??-............ CLC **34**

Keaton, Buster 1895-1966 .... CLC **20**

Keaton, Joseph Francis 1895-1966
See Keaton, Buster

Keats, John 1795-1821........... NCLC **8**

Keene, Donald 1922- .... CLC **34**
See also CANR 5; CA 1-4R

Keillor, Garrison 1942- .... CLC **40**
See also Keillor, Gary (Edward)
See also CA 111; DLB 87

Keillor, Gary (Edward)
See Keillor, Garrison
See also CA 111, 117

Kell, Joseph 1917-
See Burgess (Wilson, John) Anthony

Keller, Gottfried 1819-1890....... NCLC **2**

Kellerman, Jonathan (S.) 1949-..... CLC **44**
See also CA 106

Kelley, William Melvin 1937-...... CLC **22**
See also CA 77-80; DLB 33

Kellogg, Marjorie 1922-............ CLC **2**
See also CA 81-84

Kelly, M. T. 1947-............... CLC **55**
See also CANR 19; CA 97-100

Kelman, James 1946-............. CLC **58**

Kemal, Yashar 1922- .... CLC 14, 29
  See also CA 89-92

Kemble, Fanny 1809-1893 .... NCLC 18
  See also DLB 32

Kemelman, Harry 1908-.......... CLC 2
  See also CANR 6; CA 9-12R; DLB 28

Kempe, Margery 1373?-1440? .... LC 6

Kempis, Thomas á 1380-1471 ...... LC 11

Kendall, Henry 1839-1882....... NCLC 12

Keneally, Thomas (Michael)
  1935- ...... CLC 5, 8, 10, 14, 19, 27, 43
  See also CANR 10; CA 85-88

Kennedy, John Pendleton
  1795-1870 .... NCLC 2
  See also DLB 3

Kennedy, Joseph Charles 1929-...... CLC 8
  See also Kennedy, X. J.
  See also CANR 4; CA 1-4R; SATA 14

Kennedy, William (Joseph)
  1928- .... CLC 6, 28, 34, 53
  See also CANR 14; CA 85-88; DLB-Y 85;
  AAYA 1

Kennedy, X. J. 1929- .... CLC 8, 42
  See also Kennedy, Joseph Charles
  See also DLB 5

Kerouac, Jack
  1922-1969 .... CLC 1, 2, 3, 5, 14, 29, 61
  See also Kerouac, Jean-Louis Lebrid de
  See also DLB 2, 16; DLB-DS 3;
  CDALB 1941-1968

Kerouac, Jean-Louis Lebrid de 1922-1969
  See Kerouac, Jack
  See also CA 5-8R; obituary CA 25-28R;
  CDALB 1941-1968

Kerr, Jean 1923-................. CLC 22
  See also CANR 7; CA 5-8R

Kerr, M. E. 1927-............. CLC 12, 35
  See also Meaker, Marijane
  See also SAAS 1

Kerr, Robert 1970?-........... CLC 55, 59

Kerrigan, (Thomas) Anthony
  1918- .... CLC 4, 6
  See also CANR 4; CA 49-52

Kesey, Ken (Elton)
  1935- .... CLC 1, 3, 6, 11, 46
  See also CANR 22; CA 1-4R; DLB 2, 16

Kesselring, Joseph (Otto)
  1902-1967 .... CLC 45

Kessler, Jascha (Frederick) 1929-.... CLC 4
  See also CANR 8; CA 17-20R

Kettelkamp, Larry 1933-.......... CLC 12
  See also CANR 16; CA 29-32R; SAAS 3;
  SATA 2

Kherdian, David 1931-.......... CLC 6, 9
  See also CAAS 2; CA 21-24R; SATA 16

Khlebnikov, Velimir (Vladimirovich)
  1885-1922 .... TCLC 20
  See also CA 117

Khodasevich, Vladislav (Felitsianovich)
  1886-1939 .... TCLC 15
  See also CA 115

Kielland, Alexander (Lange)
  1849-1906 .... TCLC 5
  See also CA 104

Kiely, Benedict 1919-.......... CLC 23, 43
  See also CANR 2; CA 1-4R; DLB 15

Kienzle, William X(avier) 1928- .... CLC 25
  See also CAAS 1; CANR 9; CA 93-96

Killens, John Oliver 1916-......... CLC 10
  See also CAAS 2; CANR 26; CA 77-80,
  123; DLB 33

Killigrew, Anne 1660-1685........... LC 4

Kincaid, Jamaica 1949?- .... CLC 43
  See also CA 125

King, Francis (Henry) 1923- ..... CLC 8, 53
  See also CANR 1; CA 1-4R; DLB 15

King, Stephen (Edwin)
  1947- .... CLC 12, 26, 37, 61
  See also CANR 1; CA 61-64; SATA 9, 55;
  DLB-Y 80

Kingman, (Mary) Lee 1919-........ CLC 17
  See also Natti, (Mary) Lee
  See also CA 5-8R; SAAS 3; SATA 1

Kingsley, Sidney 1906-........... CLC 44
  See also CA 85-88; DLB 7

Kingsolver, Barbara 1955-........ CLC 55

Kingston, Maxine Hong
  1940- .... CLC 12, 19, 58
  See also CANR 13; CA 69-72; SATA 53;
  DLB-Y 80

Kinnell, Galway
  1927- .... CLC 1, 2, 3, 5, 13, 29
  See also CANR 10; CA 9-12R; DLB 5;
  DLB-Y 87

Kinsella, Thomas 1928-...... CLC 4, 19, 43
  See also CANR 15; CA 17-20R; DLB 27

Kinsella, W(illiam) P(atrick)
  1935- .... CLC 27, 43
  See also CAAS 7; CANR 21; CA 97-100

Kipling, (Joseph) Rudyard
  1865-1936 .... TCLC 8, 17; SSC 5
  See also YABC 2; CA 105, 120; DLB 19, 34

Kirkup, James 1918- .... CLC 1
  See also CAAS 4; CANR 2; CA 1-4R;
  SATA 12; DLB 27

Kirkwood, James 1930-1989 .... CLC 9
  See also CANR 6; CA 1-4R

Kis, Danilo 1935-1989 .... CLC 57
  See also CA 118, 129; brief entry CA 109

Kizer, Carolyn (Ashley) 1925-... CLC 15, 39
  See also CAAS 5; CANR 24; CA 65-68;
  DLB 5

Klappert, Peter 1942-............. CLC 57
  See also CA 33-36R; DLB 5

Klausner, Amos 1939-
  See Oz, Amos

Klein, A(braham) M(oses)
  1909-1972 .... CLC 19
  See also CA 101; obituary CA 37-40R;
  DLB 68

Klein, Norma 1938-1989 .... CLC 30
  See also CLR 2; CANR 15; CA 41-44R;
  SAAS 1; SATA 7

Klein, T.E.D. 19??-............... CLC 34
  See also CA 119

Kleist, Heinrich von 1777-1811.... NCLC 2

Klima, Ivan 1931-................ CLC 56
  See also CANR 17; CA 25-28R

Klimentev, Andrei Platonovich 1899-1951
  See Platonov, Andrei (Platonovich)
  See also CA 108

Klinger, Friedrich Maximilian von
  1752-1831 .... NCLC 1

Klopstock, Friedrich Gottlieb
  1724-1803 .... NCLC 11

Knebel, Fletcher 1911-............ CLC 14
  See also CAAS 3; CANR 1; CA 1-4R;
  SATA 36

Knight, Etheridge 1931-........... CLC 40
  See also CANR 23; CA 21-24R; DLB 41

Knight, Sarah Kemble 1666-1727 ..... LC 7
  See also DLB 24

Knowles, John 1926- ...... CLC 1, 4, 10, 26
  See also CA 17-20R; SATA 8; DLB 6

Koch, C(hristopher) J(ohn) 1932- ... CLC 42

Koch, Kenneth 1925- .... CLC 5, 8, 44
  See also CANR 6; CA 1-4R; DLB 5

Kochanowski, Jan 1530-1584....... LC 10

Kock, Charles Paul de
  1794-1871 .... NCLC 16

Koestler, Arthur
  1905-1983 .... CLC 1, 3, 6, 8, 15, 33
  See also CANR 1; CA 1-4R;
  obituary CA 109; DLB-Y 83

Kohout, Pavel 1928-.............. CLC 13
  See also CANR 3; CA 45-48

Konigsberg, Allen Stewart 1935-
  See Allen, Woody

Konrad, Gyorgy 1933-........... CLC 4, 10
  See also CA 85-88

Konwicki, Tadeusz 1926-..... CLC 8, 28, 54
  See also CA 101

Kopit, Arthur (Lee) 1937- .... CLC 1, 18, 33
  See also CA 81-84; DLB 7

Kops, Bernard 1926-.............. CLC 4
  See also CA 5-8R; DLB 13

Kornbluth, C(yril) M. 1923-1958.... TCLC 8
  See also CA 105; DLB 8

Korolenko, Vladimir (Galaktionovich)
  1853-1921 .... TCLC 22
  See also CA 121

Kosinski, Jerzy (Nikodem)
  1933-........ CLC 1, 2, 3, 6, 10, 15, 53
  See also CANR 9; CA 17-20R; DLB 2;
  DLB-Y 82

Kostelanetz, Richard (Cory) 1940- .. CLC 28
  See also CA 13-16R

Kostrowitzki, Wilhelm Apollinaris de
  1880-1918
  See Apollinaire, Guillaume
  See also CA 104

Kotlowitz, Robert 1924-........... CLC 4
  See also CA 33-36R

Kotzebue, August (Friedrich Ferdinand) von
  1761-1819 .... NCLC 25

Kotzwinkle, William 1938- ... CLC 5, 14, 35
  See also CLR 6; CANR 3; CA 45-48;
  SATA 24

Kozol, Jonathan 1936-............ CLC 17
  See also CANR 16; CA 61-64

Kozoll, Michael 1940?-........... CLC 35

Author Index

Kramer, Kathryn 19??-............ CLC 34

Kramer, Larry 1935- .... CLC 42
See also CA 124, 126

Krasicki, Ignacy 1735-1801....... NCLC 8

Krasinski, Zygmunt 1812-1859 .... NCLC 4

Kraus, Karl 1874-1936............ TCLC 5
See also CA 104

Kreve, Vincas 1882-1954 .... TCLC 27

Kristofferson, Kris 1936- .... CLC 26
See also CA 104

Krizanc, John 1956-.............. CLC 57

Krleza, Miroslav 1893-1981........ CLC 8
See also CA 97-100; obituary CA 105

Kroetsch, Robert (Paul)
1927- .... CLC 5, 23,57
See also CANR 8; CA 17-20R; DLB 53

Kroetz, Franz Xaver 1946- .... CLC 41

Kropotkin, Peter 1842-1921...... TCLC 36
See also CA 119

Krotkov, Yuri 1917-.............. CLC 19
See also CA 102

Krumgold, Joseph (Quincy)
1908-1980 .... CLC 12
See also CANR 7; CA 9-12R;
obituary CA 101; SATA 48;
obituary SATA 23

Krutch, Joseph Wood 1893-1970.... CLC 24
See also CANR 4; CA 1-4R;
obituary CA 25-28R; DLB 63

Krylov, Ivan Andreevich
1768?-1844.................. NCLC 1

Kubin, Alfred 1877-1959 .... TCLC 23
See also CA 112

Kubrick, Stanley 1928-............ CLC 16
See also CA 81-84; DLB 26

Kumin, Maxine (Winokur)
1925- .... CLC 5, 13, 28
See also CANR 1, 21; CA 1-4R; SATA 12;
DLB 5

Kundera, Milan 1929- ..... CLC 4, 9, 19, 32
See also CANR 19; CA 85-88

Kunitz, Stanley J(asspon)
1905- .... CLC 6, 11, 14
See also CA 41-44R; DLB 48

Kunze, Reiner 1933-.............. CLC 10
See also CA 93-96; DLB 75

Kuprin, Aleksandr (Ivanovich)
1870-1938 .... TCLC 5
See also CA 104

Kurosawa, Akira 1910-............ CLC 16
See also CA 101

Kuttner, Henry 1915-1958........ TCLC 10
See also CA 107; DLB 8

Kuzma, Greg 1944-................ CLC 7
See also CA 33-36R

Labrunie, Gerard 1808-1855
See Nerval, Gerard de

Laclos, Pierre Ambroise Francois Choderlos
de 1741-1803 .... NCLC 4

La Fayette, Marie (Madelaine Pioche de la
Vergne, Comtesse) de
1634-1693 .... LC 2

Lafayette, Rene
See Hubbard, L(afayette) Ron(ald)

Laforgue, Jules 1860-1887....... NCLC 5

Lagerkvist, Par (Fabian)
1891-1974 .... CLC 7, 10, 13, 54
See also CA 85-88; obituary CA 49-52

Lagerlof, Selma (Ottiliana Lovisa)
1858-1940 ....TCLC 4, 36
See also CLR 7; CA 108; SATA 15

La Guma, (Justin) Alex(ander)
1925-1985 .... CLC 19
See also CA 49-52; obituary CA 118

Lamartine, Alphonse (Marie Louis Prat) de
1790-1869 .... NCLC 11

Lamb, Charles 1775-1834....... NCLC 10
See also SATA 17

Lamming, George (William)
1927- .... CLC 2, 4
See also CANR 26; CA 85-88

LaMoore, Louis Dearborn 1908?-
See L'Amour, Louis (Dearborn)

L'Amour, Louis (Dearborn)
1908-1988 .... CLC 25, 55
See also CANR 3; CA 1-4R;
obituary CA 125; DLB-Y 80

Lampedusa, (Prince) Giuseppe (Maria
Fabrizio) Tomasi di
1896-1957 .... TCLC 13
See also CA 111

Lampman, Archibald 1861-1899 .. NCLC 25

Lancaster, Bruce 1896-1963....... CLC 36
See also CAP 1; CA 9-12; SATA 9

Landis, John (David) 1950-........ CLC 26
See also CA 112

Landolfi, Tommaso 1908-1979... CLC 11, 49
See also obituary CA 117

Landon, Letitia Elizabeth
1802-1838 .... NCLC 15

Landor, Walter Savage
1775-1864 .... NCLC 14

Landwirth, Heinz 1927-
See Lind, Jakov
See also CANR 7; CA 11-12R

Lane, Patrick 1939-.............. CLC 25
See also CA 97-100; DLB 53

Lang, Andrew 1844-1912........ TCLC 16
See also CA 114; SATA 16

Lang, Fritz 1890-1976 .... CLC 20
See also CA 77-80; obituary CA 69-72

Langer, Elinor 1939- .... CLC 34
See also CA 121

Lanier, Sidney 1842-1881 .... NCLC 6
See also SATA 18; DLB 64

Lanyer, Aemilia 1569-1645 .... LC 10

Lapine, James 1949-.............. CLC 39

Larbaud, Valery 1881-1957....... TCLC 9
See also CA 106

Lardner, Ring(gold Wilmer)
1885-1933 ....TCLC 2, 14
See also CA 104; DLB 11, 25

Larkin, Philip (Arthur)
1922-1985 ... CLC 3, 5, 8, 9, 13, 18, 33,
39
See also CA 5-8R; obituary CA 117;
DLB 27

Larra (y Sanchez de Castro), Mariano Jose de
1809-1837 .... NCLC 17

Larsen, Eric 1941- .... CLC 55

Larsen, Nella 1891-1964 .... CLC 37
See also CA 125; DLB 51

Larson, Charles R(aymond) 1938-... CLC 31
See also CANR 4; CA 53-56

Latham, Jean Lee 1902-........... CLC 12
See also CANR 7; CA 5-8R; SATA 2

Lathen, Emma..................... CLC 2
See also Hennissart, Martha; Latsis, Mary
J(ane)

Latsis, Mary J(ane)
See Lathen, Emma
See also CA 85-88

Lattimore, Richmond (Alexander)
1906-1984 .... CLC 3
See also CANR 1; CA 1-4R;
obituary CA 112

Laughlin, James 1914-............ CLC 49
See also CANR 9; CA 21-24R; DLB 48

Laurence, (Jean) Margaret (Wemyss)
1926-1987 .... CLC 3, 6, 13, 50
See also CA 5-8R; obituary CA 121;
SATA 50; DLB 53

Laurent, Antoine 1952- .... CLC 50

Lautreamont, Comte de
1846-1870 .... NCLC 12

Lavin, Mary 1912-...... CLC 4, 18; SSC 4
See also CA 9-12R; DLB 15

Lawler, Raymond (Evenor) 1922- ... CLC 58
See also CA 103

Lawrence, D(avid) H(erbert)
1885-1930 .... TCLC 2, 9, 16, 33; SSC 4
See also CA 104, 121; DLB 10, 19, 36

Lawrence, T(homas) E(dward)
1888-1935 .... TCLC 18
See also CA 115

Lawson, Henry (Archibald Hertzberg)
1867-1922 .... TCLC 27
See also CA 120

Laxness, Halldor (Kiljan) 1902- .... CLC 25
See also Gudjonsson, Halldor Kiljan

Laye, Camara 1928-1980........ CLC 4, 38
See also CA 85-88; obituary CA 97-100

Layton, Irving (Peter) 1912- ..... CLC 2, 15
See also CANR 2; CA 1-4R

Lazarus, Emma 1849-1887....... NCLC 8

Leacock, Stephen (Butler)
1869-1944 .... TCLC 2
See also CA 104

Lear, Edward 1812-1888 .... NCLC 3
See also CLR 1; SATA 18; DLB 32

Lear, Norman (Milton) 1922-...... CLC 12
See also CA 73-76

Leavis, F(rank) R(aymond)
1895-1978 .... CLC 24
See also CA 21-24R; obituary CA 77-80

Leavitt, David 1961?-............. **CLC 34**
See also CA 116, 122

Lebowitz, Fran(ces Ann)
1951?-................... **CLC 11, 36**
See also CANR 14; CA 81-84

Le Carre, John 1931-... **CLC 3, 5, 9, 15, 28**
See also Cornwell, David (John Moore)

Le Clezio, J(ean) M(arie) G(ustave)
1940-..................... **CLC 31**
See also CA 116

Leduc, Violette 1907-1972......... **CLC 22**
See also CAP 1; CA 13-14;
obituary CA 33-36R

Ledwidge, Francis 1887-1917...... **TCLC 23**
See also CA 123; DLB 20

Lee, Andrea 1953- .... **CLC 36**
See also CA 125

Lee, Andrew 1917-
See Auchincloss, Louis (Stanton)

Lee, Don L. 1942-................ **CLC 2**
See also Madhubuti, Haki R.
See also CA 73-76

Lee, George Washington
1894-1976 .... **CLC 52**
See also CA 125; DLB 51

Lee, (Nelle) Harper 1926-...... **CLC 12, 60**
See also CA 13-16R; SATA 11; DLB 6;
CDALB 1941-1968

Lee, Lawrence 1903- .... **CLC 34**
See also CA 25-28R

Lee, Manfred B(ennington) 1905-1971
See Queen, Ellery
See also CANR 2; CA 1-4R, 11;
obituary CA 29-32R

Lee, Stan 1922-................. **CLC 17**
See also CA 108, 111

Lee, Tanith 1947-................ **CLC 46**
See also CA 37-40R; SATA 8

Lee, Vernon 1856-1935 .... **TCLC 5**
See also Paget, Violet
See also DLB 57

Lee-Hamilton, Eugene (Jacob)
1845-1907 .... **TCLC 22**

Leet, Judith 1935- .... **CLC 11**

Le Fanu, Joseph Sheridan
1814-1873 .... **NCLC 9**
See also DLB 21, 70

Leffland, Ella 1931- .... **CLC 19**
See also CA 29-32R; DLB-Y 84

Leger, (Marie-Rene) Alexis Saint-Leger
1887-1975
See Perse, St.-John
See also CA 13-16R; obituary CA 61-64

Le Guin, Ursula K(roeber)
1929-............... **CLC 8, 13, 22, 45**
See also CLR 3; CANR 9; CA 21-24R;
SATA 4, 52; DLB 8, 52

Lehmann, Rosamond (Nina) 1901- ... **CLC 5**
See also CANR 8; CA 77-80; DLB 15

Leiber, Fritz (Reuter, Jr.) 1910-.... **CLC 25**
See also CANR 2; CA 45-48; SATA 45;
DLB 8

Leino, Eino 1878-1926 .... **TCLC 24**

Leiris, Michel 1901-.............. **CLC 61**
See also CA 119, 128

Leithauser, Brad 1953-............ **CLC 27**
See also CA 107

Lelchuk, Alan 1938-.............. **CLC 5**
See also CANR 1; CA 45-48

Lem, Stanislaw 1921-........ **CLC 8, 15, 40**
See also CAAS 1; CA 105

Lemann, Nancy 1956-............. **CLC 39**
See also CA 118

Lemonnier, (Antoine Louis) Camille
1844-1913 .... **TCLC 22**

Lenau, Nikolaus 1802-1850 ...... **NCLC 16**

L'Engle, Madeleine 1918-......... **CLC 12**
See also CLR 1, 14; CANR 3, 21; CA 1-4R;
SATA 1, 27; DLB 52

Lengyel, Jozsef 1896-1975.......... **CLC 7**
See also CA 85-88; obituary CA 57-60

Lennon, John (Ono)
1940-1980 .... **CLC 12, 35**
See also CA 102

Lennon, John Winston 1940-1980
See Lennon, John (Ono)

Lennox, Charlotte Ramsay 1729 or
1730-1804 .... **NCLC 23**
See also DLB 39, 39

Lennox, Charlotte Ramsay
1729?-1804................. **NCLC 23**
See also DLB 39

Lentricchia, Frank (Jr.) 1940-...... **CLC 34**
See also CANR 19; CA 25-28R

Lenz, Siegfried 1926-............. **CLC 27**
See also CA 89-92; DLB 75

Leonard, Elmore 1925-........ **CLC 28, 34**
See also CANR 12; CA 81-84

Leonard, Hugh 1926-............. **CLC 19**
See also Byrne, John Keyes
See also DLB 13

**Leopardi, (Conte) Giacomo (Talegardo
Francesco di Sales Saverio Pietro)**
1798-1837 .... **NCLC 22**

Lerman, Eleanor 1952-............ **CLC 9**
See also CA 85-88

Lerman, Rhoda 1936-............. **CLC 56**
See also CA 49-52

Lermontov, Mikhail Yuryevich
1814-1841 .... **NCLC 5**

Leroux, Gaston 1868-1927....... **TCLC 25**
See also CA 108

Lesage, Alain-Rene 1668-1747....... **LC 2**

Leskov, Nikolai (Semyonovich)
1831-1895 .... **NCLC 25**

Lessing, Doris (May)
1919-.... **CLC 1, 2, 3, 6, 10, 15, 22, 40;
SSC 6**
See also CA 9-12R; DLB 15; DLB-Y 85

Lessing, Gotthold Ephraim
1729-1781 .... **LC 8**

Lester, Richard 1932-............. **CLC 20**

Lever, Charles (James)
1806-1872 .... **NCLC 23**
See also DLB 21

Leverson, Ada 1865-1936........ **TCLC 18**
See also CA 117

Levertov, Denise
1923- .... **CLC 1, 2, 3, 5, 8, 15, 28**
See also CANR 3; CA 1-4R; DLB 5

Levi, Peter (Chad Tiger) 1931-..... **CLC 41**
See also CA 5-8R; DLB 40

Levi, Primo 1919-1987........ **CLC 37, 50**
See also CANR 12; CA 13-16R;
obituary CA 122

Levin, Ira 1929- .... **CLC 3, 6**
See also CANR 17; CA 21-24R

Levin, Meyer 1905-1981 .... **CLC 7**
See also CANR 15; CA 9-12R;
obituary CA 104; SATA 21;
obituary SATA 27; DLB 9, 28; DLB-Y 81

Levine, Norman 1924-............. **CLC 54**
See also CANR 14; CA 73-76

Levine, Philip 1928-... **CLC 2, 4, 5, 9, 14, 33**
See also CANR 9; CA 9-12R; DLB 5

Levinson, Deirdre 1931-........... **CLC 49**
See also CA 73-76

Levi-Strauss, Claude 1908- .... **CLC 38**
See also CANR 6; CA 1-4R

Levitin, Sonia 1934-.............. **CLC 17**
See also CANR 14; CA 29-32R; SAAS 2;
SATA 4

Lewes, George Henry
1817-1878 .... **NCLC 25**
See also DLB 55

Lewis, Alun 1915-1944........... **TCLC 3**
See also CA 104; DLB 20

Lewis, C(ecil) Day 1904-1972
See Day Lewis, C(ecil)

Lewis, C(live) S(taples)
1898-1963 .... **CLC 1, 3, 6, 14, 27**
See also CLR 3; CA 81-84; SATA 13;
DLB 15

Lewis (Winters), Janet 1899-....... **CLC 41**
See also Winters, Janet Lewis
See also DLB-Y 87

Lewis, Matthew Gregory
1775-1818 .... **NCLC 11**
See also DLB 39

Lewis, (Harry) Sinclair
1885-1951 .... **TCLC 4, 13, 23**
See also CA 104; DLB 9; DLB-DS 1

Lewis, (Percy) Wyndham
1882?-1957................ **TCLC 2, 9**
See also CA 104; DLB 15

Lewisohn, Ludwig 1883-1955...... **TCLC 19**
See also CA 73-76, 107;
obituary CA 29-32R

L'Heureux, John (Clarke) 1934-.... **CLC 52**
See also CANR 23; CA 15-16R

Lieber, Stanley Martin 1922-
See Lee, Stan

Lieberman, Laurence (James)
1935-..................... **CLC 4, 36**
See also CANR 8; CA 17-20R

Li Fei-kan 1904-
See Pa Chin
See also CA 105

Lightfoot, Gordon (Meredith)
1938- .... CLC 26
See also CA 109

Ligotti, Thomas 1953- .... CLC 44
See also CA 123

Liliencron, Detlev von
1844-1909 .... TCLC 18
See also CA 117

Lima, Jose Lezama 1910-1976
See Lezama Lima, Jose

Lima Barreto, (Alfonso Henriques de)
1881-1922 .... TCLC 23
See also CA 117

Lincoln, Abraham 1809-1865..... NCLC 18

Lind, Jakov 1927-.......... CLC 1, 2, 4, 27
See also Landwirth, Heinz
See also CAAS 4; CA 9-12R

Lindsay, David 1876-1945........ TCLC 15
See also CA 113

Lindsay, (Nicholas) Vachel
1879-1931 .... TCLC 17
See also CA 114; SATA 40; DLB 54;
CDALB 1865-1917

Linney, Romulus 1930- .... CLC 51
See also CA 1-4R

Li Po 701-763................. CMLC 2

Lipsyte, Robert (Michael) 1938-.... CLC 21
See also CANR 8; CA 17-20R; SATA 5

Lish, Gordon (Jay) 1934-.......... CLC 45
See also CA 113, 117

Lispector, Clarice 1925-1977....... CLC 43
See also obituary CA 116

Littell, Robert 1935?-............. CLC 42
See also CA 109, 112

Liu E 1857-1909............... TCLC 15
See also CA 115

Lively, Penelope 1933-......... CLC 32, 50
See also CLR 7; CA 41-44R; SATA 7;
DLB 14

Livesay, Dorothy 1909-......... CLC 4, 15
See also CA 25-28R

Llewellyn, Richard 1906-1983....... CLC 7
See also Llewellyn Lloyd, Richard (Dafydd
Vyvyan)
See also DLB 15

Llewellyn Lloyd, Richard (Dafydd Vyvyan)
1906-1983
See Llewellyn, Richard
See also CANR 7; CA 53-56;
obituary CA 111; SATA 11, 37

Llosa, Mario Vargas 1936-
See Vargas Llosa, Mario

Lloyd, Richard Llewellyn 1906-
See Llewellyn, Richard

Locke, John 1632-1704 .... LC 7
See also DLB 31

Lockhart, John Gibson
1794-1854 .... NCLC 6

Lodge, David (John) 1935-......... CLC 36
See also CANR 19; CA 17-20R; DLB 14

Loewinsohn, Ron(ald William)
1937- .... CLC 52
See also CA 25-28R

Logan, John 1923- .... CLC 5
See also CA 77-80, 124; DLB 5

Lo Kuan-chung 1330?-1400? .... LC 12

Lombino, S. A. 1926-
See Hunter, Evan

London, Jack
1876-1916 .... TCLC 9, 15; SSC 4
See also London, John Griffith
See also SATA 18; DLB 8, 12;
CDALB 1865-1917

London, John Griffith 1876-1916
See London, Jack
See also CA 110, 119

Long, Emmett 1925-
See Leonard, Elmore

Longbaugh, Harry 1931-
See Goldman, William (W.)

Longfellow, Henry Wadsworth
1807-1882 .... NCLC 2
See also SATA 19; DLB 1, 59;
CDALB 1640-1865

Longley, Michael 1939-........... CLC 29
See also CA 102; DLB 40

Lopate, Phillip 1943-........... CLC 29
See also CA 97-100; DLB-Y 80

Lopez Portillo (y Pacheco), Jose
1920- .... CLC 46

Lopez y Fuentes, Gregorio
1897-1966 .... CLC 32

Lord, Bette Bao 1938-............ CLC 23
See also CA 107

Lorde, Audre (Geraldine) 1934-..... CLC 18
See also CANR 16, 26; CA 25-28R;
DLB 41

Loti, Pierre 1850-1923........... TCLC 11
See also Viaud, (Louis Marie) Julien

Lovecraft, H(oward) P(hillips)
1890-1937 .... TCLC 4, 22; SSC 3
See also CA 104

Lovelace, Earl 1935-.............. CLC 51
See also CA 77-80

Lowell, Amy 1874-1925........ TCLC 1, 8
See also CA 104; DLB 54

Lowell, James Russell 1819-1891 .. NCLC 2
See also DLB 1, 11, 64; CDALB 1640-1865

Lowell, Robert (Traill Spence, Jr.)
1917-1977 ... CLC 1, 2, 3, 4, 5, 8, 9, 11,
15, 37
See also CANR 26; CA 9-12R;
obituary CA 73-76; CABS 2; DLB 5

Lowndes, Marie (Adelaide) Belloc
1868-1947 .... TCLC 12
See also CA 107; DLB 70

Lowry, (Clarence) Malcolm
1909-1957 .... TCLC 6
See also CA 105; DLB 15

Loy, Mina 1882-1966............. CLC 28
See also CA 113; DLB 4, 54

Lucas, George 1944-............. CLC 16
See also CA 77-80

Lucas, Victoria 1932-1963
See Plath, Sylvia

Ludlam, Charles 1943-1987..... CLC 46, 50
See also CA 85-88; obituary CA 122

Ludlum, Robert 1927-......... CLC 22, 43
See also CANR 25; CA 33-36R; DLB-Y 82

Ludwig, Ken 19??- .... CLC 60

Ludwig, Otto 1813-1865......... NCLC 4

Lugones, Leopoldo 1874-1938..... TCLC 15
See also CA 116

Lu Hsun 1881-1936 .... TCLC 3

Lukacs, Georg 1885-1971......... CLC 24
See also Lukacs, Gyorgy

Lukacs, Gyorgy 1885-1971
See Lukacs, Georg
See also CA 101; obituary CA 29-32R

Luke, Peter (Ambrose Cyprian)
1919- .... CLC 38
See also CA 81-84; DLB 13

Lurie (Bishop), Alison
1926-............CLC 4, 5, 18, 39
See also CANR 2, 17; CA 1-4R; SATA 46;
DLB 2

Lustig, Arnost 1926-.............. CLC 56
See also CA 69-72; SATA 56

Luther, Martin 1483-1546........... LC 9

Luzi, Mario 1914-................ CLC 13
See also CANR 9; CA 61-64

Lynn, Kenneth S(chuyler) 1923-.... CLC 50
See also CANR 3; CA 1-4R

Lytle, Andrew (Nelson) 1902-...... CLC 22
See also CA 9-12R; DLB 6

Lyttelton, George 1709-1773........ LC 10

Lytton, Edward Bulwer 1803-1873
See Bulwer-Lytton, (Lord) Edward (George
Earle Lytton)
See also SATA 23

Maas, Peter 1929-............... CLC 29
See also CA 93-96

Macaulay, (Dame Emile) Rose
1881-1958 .... TCLC 7
See also CA 104; DLB 36

MacBeth, George (Mann)
1932- .... CLC 2, 5, 9
See also CA 25-28R; SATA 4; DLB 40

MacCaig, Norman (Alexander)
1910- .... CLC 36
See also CANR 3; CA 9-12R; DLB 27

MacCarthy, Desmond 1877-1952 .. TCLC 36

MacDermot, Thomas H. 1870-1933
See Redcam, Tom

MacDiarmid, Hugh
1892-1978 .... CLC 2, 4, 11, 19
See also Grieve, C(hristopher) M(urray)
See also DLB 20

Macdonald, Cynthia 1928-...... CLC 13, 19
See also CANR 4; CA 49-52

MacDonald, George 1824-1905..... TCLC 9
See also CA 106; SATA 33; DLB 18

MacDonald, John D(ann)
1916-1986 .... CLC 3, 27, 44
See also CANR 1, 19; CA 1-4R;
obituary CA 121; DLB 8; DLB-Y 86

Macdonald, (John) Ross
1915-1983 ...... CLC 1, 2, 3, 14, 34, 41
See also Millar, Kenneth

MacEwen, Gwendolyn (Margaret)
  1941-1987 .... **CLC 13, 55**
  See also CANR 7, 22; CA 9-12R;
  obituary CA 124; SATA 50; DLB 53

Machado (y Ruiz), Antonio
  1875-1939 .... **TCLC 3**
  See also CA 104

Machado de Assis, (Joaquim Maria)
  1839-1908 .... **TCLC 10**
  See also CA 107

Machen, Arthur (Llewellyn Jones)
  1863-1947 .... **TCLC 4**
  See also CA 104; DLB 36

Machiavelli, Niccolo 1469-1527 ...... **LC 8**

MacInnes, Colin 1914-1976 ...... **CLC 4, 23**
  See also CA 69-72; obituary CA 65-68;
  DLB 14

MacInnes, Helen (Clark)
  1907-1985 .... **CLC 27, 39**
  See also CANR 1; CA 1-4R;
  obituary CA 65-68, 117; SATA 22, 44

Macintosh, Elizabeth 1897-1952
  See Tey, Josephine
  See also CA 110

Mackenzie, (Edward Montague) Compton
  1883-1972 .... **CLC 18**
  See also CAP 2; CA 21-22;
  obituary CA 37-40R; DLB 34

Mac Laverty, Bernard 1942- .... **CLC 31**
  See also CA 116, 118

MacLean, Alistair (Stuart)
  1922-1987 .... **CLC 3, 13, 50**
  See also CA 57-60; obituary CA 121;
  SATA 23

MacLeish, Archibald
  1892-1982 .... **CLC 3, 8, 14**
  See also CA 9-12R; obituary CA 106;
  DLB 4, 7, 45; DLB-Y 82

MacLennan, (John) Hugh
  1907- .... **CLC 2, 14**
  See also CA 5-8R

MacLeod, Alistair 1936- .... **CLC 56**
  See also CA 123; DLB 60

MacNeice, (Frederick) Louis
  1907-1963 .... **CLC 1, 4, 10, 53**
  See also CA 85-88; DLB 10, 20

Macpherson, (Jean) Jay 1931- ...... **CLC 14**
  See also CA 5-8R; DLB 53

MacShane, Frank 1927- .... **CLC 39**
  See also CANR 3; CA 11-12R

Macumber, Mari 1896-1966
  See Sandoz, Mari (Susette)

Madach, Imre 1823-1864 .... **NCLC 19**

Madden, (Jerry) David 1933- .... **CLC 5, 15**
  See also CAAS 3; CANR 4; CA 1-4R;
  DLB 6

Madhubuti, Haki R. 1942- .... **CLC 6**
  See also Lee, Don L.
  See also CANR 24; CA 73-76; DLB 5, 41

Maeterlinck, Maurice 1862-1949 ... **TCLC 3**
  See also CA 104

Mafouz, Naguib 1912-
  See Mahfuz, Najib

Maginn, William 1794-1842 .... **NCLC 8**

Mahabharata
  c. 400 B.C.-c. 400 A.D. .... **CMLC 5**

Mahapatra, Jayanta 1928- .... **CLC 33**
  See also CANR 15; CA 73-76

Mahfuz Najib 1912- .... **CLC 52, 55**
  See also DLB-Y 88

Mahon, Derek 1941- .... **CLC 27**
  See also CA 113; DLB 40

Mailer, Norman
  1923- ...... **CLC 1, 2, 3, 4, 5, 8, 11, 14,
                                   28, 39**
  See also CA 9-12R; CABS 1; DLB 2, 16,
  28; DLB-Y 80, 83; DLB-DS 3

Maillet, Antonine 1929- .... **CLC 54**
  See also CA 115, 120; DLB 60

Mais, Roger 1905-1955 .... **TCLC 8**
  See also CA 105

Maitland, Sara (Louise) 1950- ...... **CLC 49**
  See also CANR 13; CA 69-72

Major, Clarence 1936- .... **CLC 3, 19, 48**
  See also CAAS 6; CANR 13; CA 21-24R;
  DLB 33

Major, Kevin 1949- .... **CLC 26**
  See also CLR 11; CANR 21; CA 97-100;
  SATA 32; DLB 60

Malamud, Bernard
  1914-1986 ..... **CLC 1, 2, 3, 5, 8, 9, 11,
                                   18, 27, 44**
  See also CA 5-8R; obituary CA 118;
  CABS 1; DLB 2, 28; DLB-Y 80, 86;
  CDALB 1941-1968

Malherbe, Francois de 1555-1628 ..... **LC 5**

Mallarme, Stephane 1842-1898 .... **NCLC 4**

Mallet-Joris, Francoise 1930- ...... **CLC 11**
  See also CANR 17; CA 65-68

Maloff, Saul 1922- .... **CLC 5**
  See also CA 33-36R

Malone, Louis 1907-1963
  See MacNeice, (Frederick) Louis

Malone, Michael (Christopher)
  1942- .... **CLC 43**
  See also CANR 14; CA 77-80

Malory, (Sir) Thomas ?-1471 .... **LC 11**
  See also SATA 33

Malouf, David 1934- .... **CLC 28**

Malraux, (Georges-) Andre
  1901-1976 ...... **CLC 1, 4, 9, 13, 15, 57**
  See also CAP 2, CA 21-24;
  obituary CA 69-72; DLB 72

Malzberg, Barry N. 1939- .... **CLC 7**
  See also CAAS 4; CANR 16; CA 61-64;
  DLB 8

Mamet, David (Alan)
  1947-1987 .... **CLC 9, 15, 34, 46**
  See also CANR 15; CA 81-84, 124; DLB 7

Mamoulian, Rouben 1898- .... **CLC 16**
  See also CA 25-28R

Mandelstam, Osip (Emilievich)
  1891?-1938? .... **TCLC 2, 6**
  See also CA 104

Mander, Jane 1877-1949 .... **TCLC 31**

Mandiargues, Andre Pieyre de
  1909- .... **CLC 41**
  See also CA 103

Mangan, James Clarence
  1803-1849 .... **NCLC 27**

Manley, (Mary) Delariviere
  1672?-1724 .... **LC 1**
  See also DLB 39

Mann, (Luiz) Heinrich 1871-1950 ... **TCLC 9**
  See also CA 106; DLB 66

Mann, Thomas
  1875-1955 ...... **TCLC 2, 8, 14, 21, 35;
                                   SSC 5**
  See also CA 104, 128; DLB 66

Manning, Frederic 1882-1935 ..... **TCLC 25**

Manning, Olivia 1915-1980 ...... **CLC 5, 19**
  See also CA 5-8R; obituary CA 101

Mano, D. Keith 1942- .... **CLC 2, 10**
  See also CAAS 6; CANR 26; CA 25-28R;
  DLB 6

Mansfield, Katherine
  1888-1923 .... **TCLC 2, 8**
  See also CA 104

Manso, Peter 1940- .... **CLC 39**
  See also CA 29-32R

Mapu, Abraham (ben Jekutiel)
  1808-1867 .... **NCLC 18**

Marat, Jean Paul 1743-1793 .... **LC 10**

Marcel, Gabriel (Honore)
  1889-1973 .... **CLC 15**
  See also CA 102; obituary CA 45-48

Marchbanks, Samuel 1913-
  See Davies, (William) Robertson

Marie de l'Incarnation 1599-1672 .... **LC 10**

Marinetti, F(ilippo) T(ommaso)
  1876-1944 .... **TCLC 10**
  See also CA 107

Marivaux, Pierre Carlot de Chamblain de
  (1688-1763) .... **LC 4**

Markandaya, Kamala 1924- ...... **CLC 8, 38**
  See also Taylor, Kamala (Purnaiya)

Markfield, Wallace (Arthur) 1926- ... **CLC 8**
  See also CAAS 3; CA 69-72; DLB 2, 28

Markham, Robert 1922-
  See Amis, Kingsley (William)

Marks, J. 1942-
  See Highwater, Jamake

Marley, Bob 1945-1981 .... **CLC 17**
  See also Marley, Robert Nesta

Marley, Robert Nesta 1945-1981
  See Marley, Bob
  See also CA 107; obituary CA 103

Marmontel, Jean-Francois
  1723-1799 .... **LC 2**

Marquand, John P(hillips)
  1893-1960 .... **CLC 2, 10**
  See also CA 85-88; DLB 9

Marquez, Gabriel Garcia 1928-
  See Garcia Marquez, Gabriel

Marquis, Don(ald Robert Perry)
  1878-1937 .... **TCLC 7**
  See also CA 104; DLB 11, 25

Marryat, Frederick 1792-1848 .... **NCLC 3**
  See also DLB 21

Marsh, (Dame Edith) Ngaio
1899-1982 .... CLC **7, 53**
See also CANR 6; CA 9-12R; DLB 77

Marshall, Garry 1935?- .... CLC **17**
See also CA 111

Marshall, Paule 1929- ..... CLC **27; SSC 3**
See also CANR 25; CA 77-80; DLB 33

Marsten, Richard 1926-
See Hunter, Evan

Martin, Steve 1945?- .... CLC **30**
See also CA 97-100

Martin du Gard, Roger
1881-1958 .... TCLC **24**
See also CA 118

Martineau, Harriet 1802-1876.... NCLC **26**
See also YABC 2; DLB 21, 55

Martinez Ruiz, Jose 1874-1967
See Azorin
See also CA 93-96

Martinez Sierra, Gregorio
1881-1947 .... TCLC **6**
See also CA 104, 115

Martinez Sierra, Maria (de la O'LeJarraga)
1880?-1974 .... TCLC **6**
See also obituary CA 115

Martinson, Harry (Edmund)
1904-1978 .... CLC **14**
See also CA 77-80

Marvell, Andrew 1621-1678......... LC **4**

Marx, Karl (Heinrich)
1818-1883 .... NCLC **17**

Masaoka Shiki 1867-1902 .... TCLC **18**

Masefield, John (Edward)
1878-1967 .... CLC **11, 47**
See also CAP 2; CA 19-20;
obituary CA 25-28R; SATA 19; DLB 10,
19

Maso, Carole 19??- .... CLC **44**

Mason, Bobbie Ann
1940- .... CLC **28, 43; SSC 4**
See also CANR 11; CA 53-56; SAAS 1;
DLB-Y 87

Mason, Nick 1945- .... CLC **35**
See also Pink Floyd

Mason, Tally 1909-1971
See Derleth, August (William)

Masters, Edgar Lee
1868?-1950 .... TCLC **2, 25**
See also CA 104; DLB 54;
CDALB 1865-1917

Masters, Hilary 1928- .... CLC **48**
See also CANR 13; CA 25-28R

Mastrosimone, William 19??- ...... CLC **36**

Matheson, Richard (Burton)
1926- .... CLC **37**
See also CA 97-100; DLB 8, 44

Mathews, Harry 1930-......... CLC **6, 52**
See also CAAS 6; CANR 18; CA 21-24R

Mathias, Roland (Glyn) 1915-...... CLC **45**
See also CANR 19; CA 97-100; DLB 27

Matthews, Greg 1949- .... CLC **45**

Matthews, William 1942-......... CLC **40**
See also CANR 12; CA 29-32R; DLB 5

Matthias, John (Edward) 1941-...... CLC **9**
See also CA 33-36R

Matthiessen, Peter 1927-... CLC **5, 7, 11, 32**
See also CANR 21; CA 9-12R; SATA 27;
DLB 6

Maturin, Charles Robert
1780?-1824................. NCLC **6**

Matute, Ana Maria 1925- .... CLC **11**
See also CA 89-92

Maugham, W(illiam) Somerset
1874-1965 .... CLC **1, 11, 15**
See also CA 5-8R; obituary CA 25-28R;
DLB 10, 36

Maupassant, (Henri Rene Albert) Guy de
1850-1893 .... NCLC **1; SSC 1**

Mauriac, Claude 1914-............. CLC **9**
See also CA 89-92

Mauriac, Francois (Charles)
1885-1970 .... CLC **4, 9, 56**
See also CAP 2; CA 25-28; DLB 65

Mavor, Osborne Henry 1888-1951
See Bridie, James
See also CA 104

Maxwell, William (Keepers, Jr.)
1908- .... CLC **19**
See also CA 93-96; DLB-Y 80

May, Elaine 1932- .... CLC **16**
See also CA 124; DLB 44

Mayakovsky, Vladimir (Vladimirovich)
1893-1930 .... TCLC **4, 18**
See also CA 104

Maynard, Joyce 1953-............. CLC **23**
See also CA 111

Mayne, William (James Carter)
1928- .... CLC **12**
See also CA 9-12R; SATA 6

Mayo, Jim 1908?-
See L'Amour, Louis (Dearborn)

Maysles, Albert 1926- and **Maysles, David**
1926- .... CLC **16**

Maysles, Albert 1926-
See Maysles, Albert and Maysles, David
See also CA 29-32R

Maysles, David 1932-
See Maysles, Albert and Maysles, David

Mazer, Norma Fox 1931- .... CLC **26**
See also CANR 12; CA 69-72; SAAS 1;
SATA 24

McAuley, James (Phillip)
1917-1976 .... CLC **45**
See also CA 97-100

McBain, Ed 1926-
See Hunter, Evan

McBrien, William 1930- .... CLC **44**
See also CA 107

McCaffrey, Anne 1926-........... CLC **17**
See also CANR 15; CA 25-28R; SATA 8;
DLB 8

McCarthy, Cormac 1933-........ CLC **4, 57**
See also CANR 10; CA 13-16R; DLB 6

McCarthy, Mary (Therese)
1912-1989-... CLC **1, 3, 5, 14, 24, 39, 59**
See also CANR 16; CA 5-8R; DLB 2;
DLB-Y 81

McCartney, (James) Paul
1942- .... CLC **12, 35**

McCauley, Stephen 19??-.......... CLC **50**

McClure, Michael 1932- .... CLC **6, 10**
See also CANR 17; CA 21-24R; DLB 16

McCorkle, Jill (Collins) 1958-...... CLC **51**
See also CA 121; DLB-Y 87

McCourt, James 1941-............. CLC **5**
See also CA 57-60

McCoy, Horace 1897-1955 .... TCLC **28**
See also CA 108; DLB 9

McCrae, John 1872-1918......... TCLC **12**
See also CA 109

McCullers, (Lula) Carson (Smith)
1917-1967 .... CLC **1, 4, 10, 12, 48**
See also CANR 18; CA 5-8R;
obituary CA 25-28R; CABS 1; SATA 27;
DLB 2, 7; CDALB 1941-1968

McCullough, Colleen 1938?- .... CLC **27**
See also CANR 17; CA 81-84

McElroy, Joseph (Prince)
1930- .... CLC **5, 47**
See also CA 17-20R

McEwan, Ian (Russell) 1948- ...... CLC **13**
See also CANR 14; CA 61-64; DLB 14

McFadden, David 1940-........... CLC **48**
See also CA 104; DLB 60

McGahern, John 1934-........ CLC **5, 9, 48**
See also CA 17-20R; DLB 14

McGinley, Patrick 1937-.......... CLC **41**
See also CA 120

McGinley, Phyllis 1905-1978 ...... CLC **14**
See also CANR 19; CA 9-12R;
obituary CA 77-80; SATA 2, 44;
obituary SATA 24; DLB 11, 48

McGinniss, Joe 1942-............. CLC **32**
See also CA 25-28R

McGivern, Maureen Daly 1921-
See Daly, Maureen
See also CA 9-12R

McGrath, Patrick 1950-........... CLC **55**

McGrath, Thomas 1916- .... CLC **28, 59**
See also CANR 6; CA 9-12R, 130;
SATA 41

McGuane, Thomas (Francis III)
1939- .... CLC **3, 7, 18**
See also CANR 5; CA 49-52; DLB 2;
DLB-Y 80

McGuckian, Medbh 1950-......... CLC **48**
See also DLB 40

McHale, Tom 1941-1982 .... CLC **3, 5**
See also CA 77-80; obituary CA 106

McIlvanney, William 1936-....... CLC **42**
See also CA 25-28R; DLB 14

McIlwraith, Maureen Mollie Hunter 1922-
See Hunter, Mollie
See also CA 29-32R; SATA 2

McInerney, Jay 1955- .... CLC **34**
See also CA 116, 123

McIntyre, Vonda N(eel) 1948- ..... CLC **18**
See also CANR 17; CA 81-84

McKay, Claude 1890-1948........ TCLC **7**
See also CA 104; DLB 4, 45

McKuen, Rod 1933- . . . . CLC 1, 3
See also CA 41-44R

McLuhan, (Herbert) Marshall
1911-1980 . . . . CLC 37
See also CANR 12; CA 9-12R;
obituary CA 102

McManus, Declan Patrick 1955-
See Costello, Elvis

McMillan, Terry 1951- . . . . CLC 50, 61

McMurtry, Larry (Jeff)
1936- . . . . CLC 2, 3, 7, 11, 27, 44
See also CANR 19; CA 5-8R; DLB 2;
DLB-Y 80, 87

McNally, Terrence 1939- . . . . . . CLC 4, 7, 41
See also CANR 2; CA 45-48; DLB 7

McPhee, John 1931- . . . . CLC 36
See also CANR 20; CA 65-68

McPherson, James Alan 1943- . . . . . CLC 19
See also CANR 24; CA 25-28R; DLB 38

McPherson, William 1939- . . . . CLC 34
See also CA 57-60

McSweeney, Kerry 19??- . . . . CLC 34

Mead, Margaret 1901-1978 . . . . CLC 37
See also CANR 4; CA 1-4R;
obituary CA 81-84; SATA 20

Meaker, M. J. 1927-
See Kerr, M. E.; Meaker, Marijane

Meaker, Marijane 1927-
See Kerr, M. E.
See also CA 107; SATA 20

Medoff, Mark (Howard) 1940- . . . CLC 6, 23
See also CANR 5; CA 53-56; DLB 7

Megged, Aharon 1920- . . . . CLC 9
See also CANR 1; CA 49-52

Mehta, Ved (Parkash) 1934- . . . . CLC 37
See also CANR 2, 23; CA 1-4R

Mellor, John 1953?-
See The Clash

Meltzer, Milton 1915- . . . . CLC 26 13
See also CA 13-16R; SAAS 1; SATA 1, 50;
DLB 61

Melville, Herman
1819-1891 . . . . NCLC 3, 12; SSC 1
See also DLB 3; CDALB 1640-1865

Membreno, Alejandro 1972- . . . . CLC 59

Mencken, H(enry) L(ouis)
1880-1956 . . . . TCLC 13
See also CA 105; DLB 11, 29, 63

Mercer, David 1928-1980 . . . . CLC 5
See also CA 9-12R; obituary CA 102;
DLB 13

Meredith, George 1828-1909 . . . . . . TCLC 17
See also CA 117; DLB 18, 35, 57

Meredith, William (Morris)
1919- . . . . CLC 4, 13, 22, 55
See also CANR 6; CA 9-12R; DLB 5

Merezhkovsky, Dmitri
1865-1941 . . . . TCLC 29

Merimee, Prosper 1803-1870 . . . . . . NCLC 6

Merkin, Daphne 1954- . . . . CLC 44
See also CANR 123

Merrill, James (Ingram)
1926- . . . . CLC 2, 3, 6, 8, 13, 18, 34
See also CANR 10; CA 13-16R; DLB 5;
DLB-Y 85

Merton, Thomas (James)
1915-1968 . . . . CLC 1, 3, 11, 34
See also CANR 22; CA 5-8R;
obituary CA 25-28R; DLB 48; DLB-Y 81

Merwin, W(illiam) S(tanley)
1927- . . . . . . CLC 1, 2, 3, 5, 8, 13, 18, 45
See also CANR 15; CA 13-16R; DLB 5

Metcalf, John 1938- . . . . CLC 37
See also CA 113; DLB 60

Mew, Charlotte (Mary)
1870-1928 . . . . TCLC 8
See also CA 105; DLB 19

Mewshaw, Michael 1943- . . . . CLC 9
See also CANR 7; CA 53-56; DLB-Y 80

Meyer-Meyrink, Gustav 1868-1932
See Meyrink, Gustav
See also CA 117

Meyers, Jeffrey 1939- . . . . CLC 39
See also CA 73-76

**Meynell, Alice (Christiana Gertrude
Thompson)** 1847-1922 . . . . TCLC 6
See also CA 104; DLB 19

Meyrink, Gustav 1868-1932 . . . . . . TCLC 21
See also Meyer-Meyrink, Gustav

Michaels, Leonard 1933- . . . . CLC 6, 25
See also CANR 21; CA 61-64

Michaux, Henri 1899-1984 . . . . . CLC 8, 19
See also CA 85-88; obituary CA 114

Michelangelo 1475-1564 . . . . LC 12

Michener, James A(lbert)
1907- . . . . CLC 1, 5, 11, 29, 60
See also CANR 21; CA 5-8R; DLB 6

Mickiewicz, Adam 1798-1855 . . . . . NCLC 3

Middleton, Christopher 1926- . . . . . . CLC 13
See also CA 13-16R; DLB 40

Middleton, Stanley 1919- . . . . CLC 7, 38
See also CANR 21; CA 25-28R; DLB 14

Migueis, Jose Rodrigues 1901- . . . . . CLC 10

Mikszath, Kalman 1847-1910 . . . . . TCLC 31

Miles, Josephine (Louise)
1911-1985 . . . . CLC 1, 2, 14, 34, 39
See also CANR 2; CA 1-4R;
obituary CA 116; DLB 48

Mill, John Stuart 1806-1873 . . . . . NCLC 11

Millar, Kenneth 1915-1983 . . . . CLC 14
See also Macdonald, Ross
See also CANR 16; CA 9-12R;
obituary CA 110; DLB 2; DLB-Y 83

Millay, Edna St. Vincent
1892-1950 . . . . TCLC 4
See also CA 104; DLB 45

Miller, Arthur
1915- . . . . CLC 1, 2, 6, 10, 15, 26, 47
See also CANR 2; CA 1-4R; DLB 7;
CDALB 1941-1968

Miller, Henry (Valentine)
1891-1980 . . . . . . CLC 1, 2, 4, 9, 14, 43
See also CA 9-12R; obituary CA 97-100;
DLB 4, 9; DLB-Y 80

Miller, Jason 1939?- . . . . CLC 2
See also CA 73-76; DLB 7

Miller, Sue 19??- . . . . CLC 44

Miller, Walter M(ichael), Jr.
1923- . . . . CLC 4, 30
See also CA 85-88; DLB 8

Millhauser, Steven 1943- . . . . CLC 21, 54
See also CA 108, 110, 111; DLB 2

Millin, Sarah Gertrude 1889-1968 . . CLC 49
See also CA 102; obituary CA 93-96

Milne, A(lan) A(lexander)
1882-1956 . . . . TCLC 6
See also CLR 1; YABC 1; CA 104; DLB 10

Milner, Ron(ald) 1938- . . . . CLC 56
See also CANR 24; CA 73-76; DLB 38

Milosz Czeslaw
1911- . . . . CLC 5, 11, 22, 31, 56
See also CANR 23; CA 81-84

Milton, John 1608-1674 . . . . LC 9

Miner, Valerie (Jane) 1947- . . . . CLC 40
See also CA 97-100

Minot, Susan 1956- . . . . CLC 44

Minus, Ed 1938- . . . . CLC 39

Miro (Ferrer), Gabriel (Francisco Victor)
1879-1930 . . . . TCLC 5
See also CA 104

Mishima, Yukio
1925-1970 . . . . CLC 2, 4, 6, 9, 27; SSC 4
See also Hiraoka, Kimitake

Mistral, Gabriela 1889-1957 . . . . TCLC 2
See also CA 104

Mitchell, James Leslie 1901-1935
See Gibbon, Lewis Grassic
See also CA 104; DLB 15

Mitchell, Joni 1943- . . . . CLC 12
See also CA 112

Mitchell (Marsh), Margaret (Munnerlyn)
1900-1949 . . . . TCLC 11
See also CA 109; DLB 9

Mitchell, S. Weir 1829-1914 . . . . . . TCLC 36

Mitchell, W(illiam) O(rmond)
1914- . . . . CLC 25
See also CANR 15; CA 77-80

Mitford, Mary Russell 1787-1855 . . NCLC 4

Mitford, Nancy 1904-1973 . . . . CLC 44
See also CA 9-12R

Miyamoto Yuriko 1899-1951 . . . . . . TCLC 37

Mo, Timothy 1950- . . . . CLC 46
See also CA 117

Modarressi, Taghi 1931- . . . . CLC 44
See also CA 121

Modiano, Patrick (Jean) 1945- . . . . . CLC 18
See also CANR 17; CA 85-88

Mofolo, Thomas (Mokopu)
1876-1948 . . . . TCLC 22
See also CA 121

Mohr, Nicholasa 1935- . . . . CLC 12
See also CANR 1; CA 49-52; SATA 8

Mojtabai, A(nn) G(race)
1938- . . . . CLC 5, 9, 15, 29
See also CA 85-88

Moliere 1622-1673 . . . . LC 10

Molnar, Ferenc 1878-1952........ TCLC 20
See also CA 109

Momaday, N(avarre) Scott
1934-...................... CLC 2, 19
See also CANR 14; CA 25-28R; SATA 30,
48

Monroe, Harriet 1860-1936....... TCLC 12
See also CA 109; DLB 54

Montagu, Elizabeth 1720-1800 .... NCLC 7

Montagu, Lady Mary (Pierrepont) Wortley
1689-1762 .... LC 9

Montague, John (Patrick)
1929-...................... CLC 13, 46
See also CANR 9; CA 9-12R; DLB 40

Montaigne, Michel (Eyquem) de
1533-1592 .... LC 8

Montale, Eugenio 1896-1981... CLC 7, 9, 18
See also CA 17-20R; obituary CA 104

Montgomery, Marion (H., Jr.)
1925-...................... CLC 7
See also CANR 3; CA 1-4R; DLB 6

Montgomery, Robert Bruce 1921-1978
See Crispin, Edmund
See also CA 104

Montherlant, Henri (Milon) de
1896-1972 .... CLC 8, 19
See also CA 85-88; obituary CA 37-40R;
DLB 72

Montisquieu, Charles-Louis de Secondat
1689-1755 .... LC 7

Monty Python.................... CLC 21

Moodie, Susanna (Strickland)
1803-1885 .... NCLC 14

Mooney, Ted 1951-............... CLC 25

Moorcock, Michael (John)
1939-.................... CLC 5, 27, 58
See also CAAS 5; CANR 2, 17; CA 45-48;
DLB 14

Moore, Brian
1921-......... CLC 1, 3, 5, 7, 8, 19, 32
See also CANR 1; CA 1-4R

Moore, George (Augustus)
1852-1933 .... TCLC 7
See also CA 104; DLB 10, 18, 57

Moore, Lorrie 1957-........... CLC 39, 45
See also Moore, Marie Lorena

Moore, Marianne (Craig)
1887-1972 ... CLC 1, 2, 4, 8, 10, 13, 19,
47
See also CANR 3; CA 1-4R;
obituary CA 33-36R; SATA 20; DLB 45

Moore, Marie Lorena 1957-
See Moore, Lorrie
See also CA 116

Moore, Thomas 1779-1852....... NCLC 6

Morand, Paul 1888-1976.......... CLC 41
See also obituary CA 69-72; DLB 65

Morante, Elsa 1918-1985........ CLC 8, 47
See also CA 85-88; obituary CA 117

Moravia, Alberto
1907-......... CLC 2, 7, 11, 18, 27, 46
See also Pincherle, Alberto

More, Hannah 1745-1833 .... NCLC 27

More, Henry 1614-1687............ LC 9

More, Thomas 1478-1573.......... LC 10

Moreas, Jean 1856-1910 .... TCLC 18

Morgan, Berry 1919-.............. CLC 6
See also CA 49-52; DLB 6

Morgan, Edwin (George) 1920-..... CLC 31
See also CANR 3; CA 7-8R; DLB 27

Morgan, (George) Frederick
1922-...................... CLC 23
See also CANR 21; CA 17-20R

Morgan, Janet 1945-............. CLC 39
See also CA 65-68

Morgan, Robin 1941-.............. CLC 2
See also CA 69-72

Morgenstern, Christian (Otto Josef Wolfgang)
1871-1914 .... TCLC 8
See also CA 105

Moricz, Zsigmond 1879-1942 ..... TCLC 33

Morike, Eduard (Friedrich)
1804-1875 .... NCLC 10

Mori Ogai 1862-1922............ TCLC 14
See also Mori Rintaro

Mori Rintaro 1862-1922
See Mori Ogai
See also CA 110

Moritz, Karl Philipp 1756-1793 ...... LC 2

Morris, Julian 1916-
See West, Morris L.

Morris, Steveland Judkins 1950-
See Wonder, Stevie
See also CA 111

Morris, William 1834-1896 .... NCLC 4
See also DLB 18, 35, 57

Morris, Wright (Marion)
1910-............. CLC 1, 3, 7, 18, 37
See also CA 9-12R; DLB 2; DLB-Y 81

Morrison, James Douglas 1943-1971
See Morrison, Jim
See also CA 73-76

Morrison, Jim 1943-1971......... CLC 17
See also Morrison, James Douglas

Morrison, Toni 1931-..... CLC 4, 10, 22, 55
See also CA 29-32R; DLB 6, 33; DLB-Y 81;
AAYA 1

Morrison, Van 1945- .... CLC 21
See also CA 116

Mortimer, John (Clifford)
1923-.................... CLC 28, 43
See also CANR 21; CA 13-16R; DLB 13

Mortimer, Penelope (Ruth) 1918-.... CLC 5
See also CA 57-60

Mosley, Nicholas 1923-........... CLC 43
See also CA 69-72; DLB 14

Moss, Howard
1922-1987 .... CLC 7, 14, 45, 50
See also CANR 1; CA 1-4R; DLB 5

Motion, Andrew (Peter) 1952-...... CLC 47
See also DLB 40

Motley, Willard (Francis)
1912-1965 .... CLC 18
See also CA 117; obituary CA 106

Mott, Michael (Charles Alston)
1930-.................... CLC 15, 34
See also CAAS 7; CANR 7; CA 5-8R

Mowat, Farley (McGill) 1921- ..... CLC 26
See also CLR 20; CANR 4; CA 1-4R;
SATA 3; DLB 68

Mphahlele, Es'kia 1919-
See Mphahlele, Ezekiel

Mphahlele, Ezekiel 1919-......... CLC 25
See also CA 81-84

Mqhayi, S(amuel) E(dward) K(rune Loliwe)
1875-1945 .... TCLC 25

Mrozek, Slawomir 1930-........ CLC 3, 13
See also CA 13-16R

Mtwa, Percy 19??-............... CLC 47

Mueller, Lisel 1924-........... CLC 13, 51
See also CA 93-96

Muir, Edwin 1887-1959........... TCLC 2
See also CA 104; DLB 20

Muir, John 1838-1914 .... TCLC 28

Mujica Lainez, Manuel
1910-1984 .... CLC 31
See also CA 81-84; obituary CA 112

Mukherjee, Bharati 1940-......... CLC 53
See also CA 107; DLB 60

Muldoon, Paul 1951-............. CLC 32
See also CA 113; DLB 40

Mulisch, Harry (Kurt Victor)
1927-...................... CLC 42
See also CANR 6; CA 9-12R

Mull, Martin 1943-.............. CLC 17
See also CA 105

Munford, Robert 1737?-1783........ LC 5
See also DLB 31

Munro, Alice (Laidlaw)
1931- .... CLC 6, 10, 19, 50; SSC 3
See also CA 33-36R; SATA 29; DLB 53

Munro, H(ector) H(ugh) 1870-1916
See Saki
See also CA 104; DLB 34

Murasaki, Lady c. 11th century-... CMLC 1

Murdoch, (Jean) Iris
1919- ...... CLC 1, 2, 3, 4, 6, 8, 11, 15,
22, 31, 51
See also CANR 8; CA 13-16R; DLB 14

Murphy, Richard 1927-........... CLC 41
See also CA 29-32R; DLB 40

Murphy, Sylvia 19??-............. CLC 34

Murphy, Thomas (Bernard) 1935-... CLC 51
See also CA 101

Murray, Les(lie) A(llan) 1938- ..... CLC 40
See also CANR 11; CA 21-24R

Murry, John Middleton
1889-1957 .... TCLC 16
See also CA 118

Musgrave, Susan 1951- .... CLC 13, 54
See also CA 69-72

Musil, Robert (Edler von)
1880-1942 .... TCLC 12
See also CA 109

Musset, (Louis Charles) Alfred de
1810-1857 .... NCLC 7

Myers, Walter Dean 1937- .... CLC 35
See also CLR 4, 16; CANR 20; CA 33-36R;
SAAS 2; SATA 27, 41; DLB 33

Nabokov, Vladimir (Vladimirovich)
1899-1977 .... CLC 1, 2, 3, 6, 8, 11, 15,
23, 44, 46
See also CANR 20; CA 5-8R;
obituary CA 69-72; DLB 2; DLB-Y 80;
DLB-DS 3; CDALB 1941-1968

Nagy, Laszlo 1925-1978............ CLC 7
See also obituary CA 112

Naipaul, Shiva(dhar Srinivasa)
1945-1985 .... CLC 32, 39
See also CA 110, 112; obituary CA 116;
DLB-Y 85

Naipaul, V(idiadhar) S(urajprasad)
1932- .... CLC 4, 7, 9, 13, 18, 37
See also CANR 1; CA 1-4R; DLB-Y 85

Nakos, Ioulia 1899?-
See Nakos, Lilika

Nakos, Lilika 1899?- .... CLC 29

Nakou, Lilika 1899?-
See Nakos, Lilika

Narayan, R(asipuram) K(rishnaswami)
1906- .... CLC 7, 28, 47
See also CA 81-84

Nash, (Frediric) Ogden 1902-1971 .. CLC 23
See also CAP 1; CA 13-14;
obituary CA 29-32R; SATA 2, 46;
DLB 11

Nathan, George Jean 1882-1958 ... TCLC 18
See also CA 114

Natsume, Kinnosuke 1867-1916
See Natsume, Soseki
See also CA 104

Natsume, Soseki 1867-1916..... TCLC 2, 10
See also Natsume, Kinnosuke

Natti, (Mary) Lee 1919-
See Kingman, (Mary) Lee
See also CANR 2; CA 7-8R

Naylor, Gloria 1950- .... CLC 28, 52
See also CANR 27; CA 107

Neff, Debra 1972-................ CLC 59

Neihardt, John G(neisenau)
1881-1973 .... CLC 32
See also CAP 1; CA 13-14; DLB 9, 54

Nekrasov, Nikolai Alekseevich
1821-1878 .... NCLC 11

Nelligan, Emile 1879-1941........ TCLC 14
See also CA 114

Nelson, Willie 1933-.............. CLC 17
See also CA 107

Nemerov, Howard 1920- .... CLC 2, 6, 9, 36
See also CANR 1; CA 1-4R; CABS 2;
DLB 5, 6; DLB-Y 83

Neruda, Pablo
1904-1973 .... CLC 1, 2, 5, 7, 9, 28
See also CAP 2; CA 19-20;
obituary CA 45-48

Nerval, Gerard de 1808-1855...... NCLC 1

Nervo, (Jose) Amado (Ruiz de)
1870-1919 .... TCLC 11
See also CA 109

Neufeld, John (Arthur) 1938- ...... CLC 17
See also CANR 11; CA 25-28R; SAAS 3;
SATA 6

Neville, Emily Cheney 1919-....... CLC 12
See also CANR 3; CA 5-8R; SAAS 2;
SATA 1

Newbound, Bernard Slade 1930-
See Slade, Bernard
See also CA 81-84

Newby, P(ercy) H(oward)
1918- .... CLC 2, 13
See also CA 5-8R; DLB 15

Newlove, Donald 1928- .... CLC 6
See also CANR 25; CA 29-32R

Newlove, John (Herbert) 1938-..... CLC 14
See also CANR 9, 25; CA 21-24R

Newman, Charles 1938-.......... CLC 2, 8
See also CA 21-24R

Newman, Edwin (Harold) 1919- .... CLC 14
See also CANR 5; CA 69-72

Newton, Suzanne 1936-.......... CLC 35
See also CANR 14; CA 41-44R; SATA 5

Ngema, Mbongeni 1955- .... CLC 57

Ngugi, James (Thiong'o)
1938- .... CLC 3, 7, 13, 36
See also Ngugi wa Thiong'o; Wa Thiong'o,
Ngugi
See also CA 81-84

Ngugi wa Thiong'o 1938-... CLC 3, 7, 13, 36
See also Ngugi, James (Thiong'o); Wa
Thiong'o, Ngugi

Nichol, B(arrie) P(hillip) 1944-..... CLC 18
See also CA 53-56; DLB 53

Nichols, John (Treadwell) 1940- .... CLC 38
See also CAAS 2; CANR 6; CA 9-12R;
DLB-Y 82

Nichols, Peter (Richard) 1927-... CLC 5, 36
See also CA 104; DLB 13

Nicolas, F.R.E. 1927-
See Freeling, Nicolas

Niedecker, Lorine 1903-1970.... CLC 10, 42
See also CAP 2; CA 25-28; DLB 48

Nietzsche, Friedrich (Wilhelm)
1844-1900 .... TCLC 10, 18
See also CA 107

Nievo, Ippolito 1831-1861 .... NCLC 22

Nightingale, Anne Redmon 1943-
See Redmon (Nightingale), Anne
See also CA 103

Nin, Anais
1903-1977 ...... CLC 1, 4, 8, 11, 14, 60
See also CANR 22; CA 13-16R;
obituary CA 69-72; DLB 2, 4

Nissenson, Hugh 1933-............ CLC 4, 9
See also CA 17-20R; DLB 28

Niven, Larry 1938-................ CLC 8
See also Niven, Laurence Van Cott
See also DLB 8

Niven, Laurence Van Cott 1938-
See Niven, Larry
See also CANR 14; CA 21-24R

Nixon, Agnes Eckhardt 1927-...... CLC 21
See also CA 110

Nkosi, Lewis 1936-.............. CLC 45
See also CA 65-68

Nodier, (Jean) Charles (Emmanuel)
1780-1844 .... NCLC 19

Nolan, Christopher 1965-.......... CLC 58
See also CA 111

Nordhoff, Charles 1887-1947...... TCLC 23
See also CA 108; SATA 23; DLB 9

Norman, Marsha 1947- .... CLC 28
See also CA 105; DLB-Y 84

Norris, (Benjamin) Frank(lin)
1870-1902 .... TCLC 24
See also CA 110; DLB 12, 71;
CDALB 1865-1917

Norris, Leslie 1921-.............. CLC 14
See also CANR 14; CAP 1; CA 11-12;
DLB 27

North, Andrew 1912-
See Norton, Andre

North, Christopher 1785-1854
See Wilson, John

Norton, Alice Mary 1912-
See Norton, Andre
See also CANR 2; CA 1-4R; SATA 1, 43

Norton, Andre 1912- .... CLC 12
See also Norton, Mary Alice
See also DLB 8, 52

Norway, Nevil Shute 1899-1960
See Shute (Norway), Nevil
See also CA 102; obituary CA 93-96

Norwid, Cyprian Kamil
1821-1883 .... NCLC 17

Nossack, Hans Erich 1901-1978..... CLC 6
See also CA 93-96; obituary CA 85-88;
DLB 69

Nova, Craig 1945-.............. CLC 7, 31
See also CANR 2; CA 45-48

Novak, Joseph 1933-
See Kosinski, Jerzy (Nikodem)

Novalis 1772-1801 .... NCLC 13

Nowlan, Alden (Albert) 1933-...... CLC 15
See also CANR 5; CA 9-12R; DLB 53

Noyes, Alfred 1880-1958 .... TCLC 7
See also CA 104; DLB 20

Nunn, Kem 19??-................ CLC 34

Nye, Robert 1939- .... CLC 13, 42
See also CA 33-36R; SATA 6; DLB 14

Nyro, Laura 1947- .... CLC 17

Oates, Joyce Carol
1938- ..... CLC 1, 2, 3, 6, 9, 11, 15, 19,
33, 52; SSC 6
See also CANR 25; CA 5-8R; DLB 2, 5,
DLB-Y 81; CDALB 1968-1987

O'Brien, Darcy 1939-............. CLC 11
See also CANR 8; CA 21-24R

O'Brien, Edna 1932-.... CLC 3, 5, 8, 13, 36
See also CANR 6; CA 1-4R; DLB 14

O'Brien, Fitz-James 1828?-1862.. NCLC 21
See also DLB 74

O'Brien, Flann
1911-1966 .... CLC 1, 4, 5, 7, 10, 47
See also O Nuallain, Brian

O'Brien, Richard 19??-............ CLC 17
See also CA 124

O'Brien, (William) Tim(othy)
1946- .... CLC 7, 19, 40
See also CA 85-88; DLB-Y 80

Obstfelder, Sigbjorn 1866-1900.... TCLC 23
See also CA 123

O'Casey, Sean
1880-1964 .... CLC 1, 5, 9, 11, 15
See also CA 89-92; DLB 10

Ochs, Phil 1940-1976............. CLC 17
See also obituary CA 65-68

O'Connor, Edwin (Greene)
1918-1968 .... CLC 14
See also CA 93-96; obituary CA 25-28R

O'Connor, (Mary) Flannery
1925-1964 ... CLC 1, 2, 3, 6, 10, 13, 15,
21; SSC 1
See also CANR 3; CA 1-4R; DLB 2;
DLB-Y 80; CDALB 1941-1968

O'Connor, Frank
1903-1966 .... CLC 14, 23; SSC 5
See also O'Donovan, Michael (John)
See also CA 93-96

O'Dell, Scott 1903-............... CLC 30
See also CLR 1, 16; CANR 12; CA 61-64;
SATA 12; DLB 52

Odets, Clifford 1906-1963 .... CLC 2, 28
See also CA 85-88; DLB 7, 26

O'Donovan, Michael (John) 1903-1966
See O'Connor, Frank
See also CA 93-96

Oe, Kenzaburo 1935-.......... CLC 10, 36
See also CA 97-100

O'Faolain, Julia 1932-....... CLC 6, 19, 47
See also CAAS 2; CANR 12; CA 81-84;
DLB 14

O'Faolain, Sean 1900- ..... CLC 1, 7, 14, 32
See also CANR 12; CA 61-64; DLB 15

O'Flaherty, Liam
1896-1984 .... CLC 5, 34; SSC 6
See also CA 101; obituary CA 113; DLB 36;
DLB-Y 84

O'Grady, Standish (James)
1846-1928 .... TCLC 5
See also CA 104

O'Grady, Timothy 1951- .... CLC 59

O'Hara, Frank 1926-1966 ..... CLC 2, 5, 13
See also CA 9-12R; obituary CA 25-28R;
DLB 5, 16

O'Hara, John (Henry)
1905-1970 .... CLC 1, 2, 3, 6, 11, 42
See also CA 5-8R; obituary CA 25-28R;
DLB 9; DLB-DS 2

O'Hara Family
See Banim, John and Banim, Michael

O'Hehir, Diana 1922-............. CLC 41
See also CA 93-96

Okigbo, Christopher (Ifenayichukwu)
1932-1967 .... CLC 25
See also CA 77-80

Olds, Sharon 1942-............ CLC 32, 39
See also CANR 18; CA 101

Olesha, Yuri (Karlovich)
1899-1960 .... CLC 8
See also CA 85-88

Oliphant, Margaret (Oliphant Wilson)
1828-1897 .... NCLC 11
See also DLB 18

Oliver, Mary 1935-............ CLC 19, 34
See also CANR 9; CA 21-24R; DLB 5

Olivier, (Baron) Laurence (Kerr)
1907- .... CLC 20
See also CA 111

Olsen, Tillie 1913-............. CLC 4, 13
See also CANR 1; CA 1-4R; DLB 28;
DLB-Y 80

Olson, Charles (John)
1910-1970 ..... CLC 1, 2, 5, 6, 9, 11, 29
See also CAP 1; CA 15-16;
obituary CA 25-28R; CABS 2; DLB 5, 16

Olson, Theodore 1937-
See Olson, Toby

Olson, Toby 1937- .... CLC 28
See also CANR 9; CA 65-68

Ondaatje, (Philip) Michael
1943- .... CLC 14, 29, 51
See also CA 77-80; DLB 60

Oneal, Elizabeth 1934-
See Oneal, Zibby
See also CA 106; SATA 30

Oneal, Zibby 1934-............... CLC 30
See also Oneal, Elizabeth

O'Neill, Eugene (Gladstone)
1888-1953 .... TCLC 1, 6, 27
See also CA 110; DLB 7

Onetti, Juan Carlos 1909-....... CLC 7, 10
See also CA 85-88

O'Nolan, Brian 1911-1966
See O'Brien, Flann

O Nuallain, Brian 1911-1966
See O'Brien, Flann
See also CAP 2; CA 21-22;
obituary CA 25-28R

Oppen, George 1908-1984 .... CLC 7, 13, 34
See also CANR 8; CA 13-16R;
obituary CA 113; DLB 5

Orlovitz, Gil 1918-1973 .... CLC 22
See also CA 77-80; obituary CA 45-48;
DLB 2, 5

Ortega y Gasset, Jose 1883-1955 ... TCLC 9
See also CA 106

Ortiz, Simon J. 1941-............. CLC 45

Orton, Joe 1933?-1967....... CLC 4, 13, 43
See also Orton, John Kingsley
See also DLB 13

Orton, John Kingsley 1933?-1967
See Orton, Joe
See also CA 85-88

Orwell, George
1903-1950 .... TCLC 2, 6, 15, 31
See also Blair, Eric Arthur
See also DLB 15

Osborne, John (James)
1929- .... CLC 1, 2, 5, 11, 45
See also CANR 21; CA 13-16R; DLB 13

Osborne, Lawrence 1958- .... CLC 50

Osceola 1885-1962
See Dinesen, Isak; Blixen, Karen
(Christentze Dinesen)

Oshima, Nagisa 1932- .... CLC 20
See also CA 116

Oskison, John M. 1874-1947...... TCLC 35

Ossoli, Sarah Margaret (Fuller marchesa d')
1810-1850
See Fuller, (Sarah) Margaret
See also SATA 25

Otero, Blas de 1916- .... CLC 11
See also CA 89-92

Owen, Wilfred (Edward Salter)
1893-1918 .... TCLC 5, 27
See also CA 104; DLB 20

Owens, Rochelle 1936-............. CLC 8
See also CAAS 2; CA 17-20R

Owl, Sebastian 1939-
See Thompson, Hunter S(tockton)

Oz, Amos 1939- ... CLC 5, 8, 11, 27, 33, 54
See also CA 53-56

Ozick, Cynthia 1928-........ CLC 3, 7, 28
See also CANR 23; CA 17-20R; DLB 28;
DLB-Y 82

Ozu, Yasujiro 1903-1963 .... CLC 16
See also CA 112

Pa Chin 1904-.................... CLC 18
See also Li Fei-kan

Pack, Robert 1929-................ CLC 13
See also CANR 3; CA 1-4R; DLB 5

Padgett, Lewis 1915-1958
See Kuttner, Henry

Padilla, Heberto 1932-............ CLC 38
See also CA 123

Page, Jimmy 1944-............... CLC 12

Page, Louise 1955-............... CLC 40

Page, P(atricia) K(athleen)
1916- .... CLC 7, 18
See also CANR 4, 22; CA 53-56; DLB 68

Paget, Violet 1856-1935
See Lee, Vernon
See also CA 104

Palamas, Kostes 1859-1943 .... TCLC 5
See also CA 105

Palazzeschi, Aldo 1885-1974....... CLC 11
See also CA 89-92; obituary CA 53-56

Paley, Grace 1922-........... CLC 4, 6, 37
See also CANR 13; CA 25-28R; DLB 28

Palin, Michael 1943- .... CLC 21
See also Monty Python
See also CA 107

Palma, Ricardo 1833-1919........ TCLC 29
See also CANR 123

Pancake, Breece Dexter 1952-1979
See Pancake, Breece D'J

Pancake, Breece D'J 1952-1979 .... CLC 29
See also obituary CA 109

Papadiamantis, Alexandros
1851-1911 .... TCLC 29

Papini, Giovanni 1881-1956....... TCLC 22
See also CA 121

Paracelsus 1493-1541............. LC 14

Parini, Jay (Lee) 1948- .... CLC 54
See also CA 97-100

Parker, Dorothy (Rothschild)
1893-1967 .... CLC 15; SSC 2
See also CAP 2; CA 19-20;
obituary CA 25-28R; DLB 11, 45

Parker, Robert B(rown) 1932- ...... CLC 27
See also CANR 1, 26; CA 49-52

Parkin, Frank 1940- .... CLC 43

Parkman, Francis 1823-1893 ..... NCLC 12
See also DLB 1, 30

Parks, Gordon (Alexander Buchanan)
1912- .... CLC 1, 16
See also CANR 26; CA 41-44R; SATA 8;
DLB 33

Parnell, Thomas 1679-1718 .... LC 3

Parra, Nicanor 1914- .... CLC 2
See also CA 85-88

Pasolini, Pier Paolo
1922-1975 .... CLC 20, 37
See also CA 93-96; obituary CA 61-64

Pastan, Linda (Olenik) 1932- ...... CLC 27
See also CANR 18; CA 61-64; DLB 5

Pasternak, Boris 1890-1960... CLC 7, 10, 18
See also obituary CA 116

Patchen, Kenneth 1911-1972... CLC 1, 2, 18
See also CANR 3; CA 1-4R;
obituary CA 33-36R; DLB 16, 48

Pater, Walter (Horatio)
1839-1894 .... NCLC 7
See also DLB 57

Paterson, Andrew Barton
1864-1941 .... TCLC 32

Paterson, Katherine (Womeldorf)
1932- .... CLC 12, 30
See also CLR 7; CA 21-24R; SATA 13, 53;
DLB 52

Patmore, Coventry Kersey Dighton
1823-1896 .... NCLC 9
See also DLB 35

Paton, Alan (Stewart)
1903-1988 .... CLC 4, 10, 25, 55
See also CANR 22; CAP 1; CA 15-16;
obituary CA 125; SATA 11

Paulding, James Kirke 1778-1860.. NCLC 2
See also DLB 3, 59, 74

Paulin, Tom 1949- .... CLC 37
See also CA 123; DLB 40

Paustovsky, Konstantin (Georgievich)
1892-1968 .... CLC 40
See also CA 93-96; obituary CA 25-28R

Paustowsky, Konstantin (Georgievich)
1892-1968
See Paustovsky, Konstantin (Georgievich)

Pavese, Cesare 1908-1950 .... TCLC 3
See also CA 104

Pavic, Milorad 1929- .... CLC 60

Payne, Alan 1932-
See Jakes, John (William)

Paz, Octavio 1914-.. CLC 3, 4, 6, 10, 19, 51
See also CA 73-76

Peacock, Molly 1947-............. CLC 60
See also CA 103

Peacock, Thomas Love
1785-1886 .... NCLC 22

Peake, Mervyn 1911-1968 .... CLC 7, 54
See also CANR 3; CA 5-8R;
obituary CA 25-28R; SATA 23; DLB 15

Pearce, (Ann) Philippa 1920-....... CLC 21
See also Christie, (Ann) Philippa
See also CLR 9; CA 5-8R; SATA 1

Pearl, Eric 1934-
See Elman, Richard

Pearson, T(homas) R(eid) 1956- .... CLC 39
See also CA 120

Peck, John 1941- .... CLC 3
See also CANR 3; CA 49-52

Peck, Richard 1934-............... CLC 21
See also CLR 15; CANR 19; CA 85-88;
SAAS 2; SATA 18

Peck, Robert Newton 1928-........ CLC 17
See also CA 81-84; SAAS 1; SATA 21

Peckinpah, (David) Sam(uel)
1925-1984 .... CLC 20
See also CA 109; obituary CA 114

Pedersen, Knut 1859-1952
See Hamsun, Knut
See also CA 104, 109

Peguy, Charles (Pierre)
1873-1914 .... TCLC 10
See also CA 107

Pepys, Samuel 1633-1703........... LC 11

Percy, Walker
1916- .... CLC 2, 3, 6, 8, 14, 18, 47
See also CANR 1; CA 1-4R; DLB 2;
DLB-Y 80

Perec, Georges 1936-1982 .... CLC 56

Pereda, Jose Maria de
1833-1906 .... TCLC 16

Perelman, S(idney) J(oseph)
1904-1979 ... CLC 3, 5, 9, 15, 23, 44, 49
See also CANR 18; CA 73-76;
obituary CA 89-92; DLB 11, 44

Peret, Benjamin 1899-1959 .... TCLC 20
See also CA 117

Peretz, Isaac Leib 1852?-1915..... TCLC 16
See also CA 109

Perez, Galdos Benito 1853-1920 ... TCLC 27
See also CA 125

Perrault, Charles 1628-1703 .... LC 2
See also SATA 25

Perse, St.-John 1887-1975.... CLC 4, 11, 46
See also Leger, (Marie-Rene) Alexis
Saint-Leger

Pesetsky, Bette 1932-............. CLC 28

Peshkov, Alexei Maximovich 1868-1936
See Gorky, Maxim
See also CA 105

Pessoa, Fernando (Antonio Nogueira)
1888-1935 .... TCLC 27
See also CA 125

Peterkin, Julia (Mood) 1880-1961... CLC 31
See also CA 102; DLB 9

Peters, Joan K. 1945-............. CLC 39

Peters, Robert L(ouis) 1924-........ CLC 7
See also CA 13-16R

Petofi, Sandor 1823-1849....... NCLC 21

Petrakis, Harry Mark 1923-........ CLC 3
See also CANR 4; CA 9-12R

Petrov, Evgeny 1902-1942 .... TCLC 21

Petry, Ann (Lane) 1908- ...... CLC 1, 7, 18
See also CLR 12; CAAS 6; CANR 4;
CA 5-8R; SATA 5

Petursson, Halligrimur 1614-1674 .... LC 8

Philipson, Morris (H.) 1926-....... CLC 53
See also CANR 4; CA 1-4R

Phillips, Jayne Anne 1952-..... CLC 15, 33
See also CANR 24; CA 101; DLB-Y 80

Phillips, Robert (Schaeffer) 1938-... CLC 28
See also CANR 8; CA 17-20R

Pica, Peter 1925-
See Aldiss, Brian W(ilson)

Piccolo, Lucio 1901-1969.......... CLC 13
See also CA 97-100

Pickthall, Marjorie (Lowry Christie)
1883-1922 .... TCLC 21
See also CA 107

Piercy, Marge 1936-... CLC 3, 6, 14, 18, 27
See also CAAS 1; CANR 13; CA 21-24R

Pilnyak, Boris 1894-1937?........ TCLC 23

Pincherle, Alberto 1907-
See Moravia, Alberto
See also CA 25-28R

Pineda, Cecile 1942-............. CLC 39
See also CA 118

Pinero, Miguel (Gomez)
1946-1988 .... CLC 4, 55
See also CA 61-64; obituary CA 125

Pinero, Sir Arthur Wing
1855-1934 .... TCLC 32
See also CA 110; DLB 10

Pinget, Robert 1919- .... CLC 7, 13, 37
See also CA 85-88

Pink Floyd.......... .... CLC 35

Pinkwater, D(aniel) M(anus)
1941- .... CLC 35
See also Pinkwater, Manus
See also CLR 4; CANR 12; CA 29-32R;
SAAS 3; SATA 46

Pinkwater, Manus 1941-
See Pinkwater, D(aniel) M(anus)
See also SATA 8

Pinsky, Robert 1940-........ CLC 9, 19, 38
See also CAAS 4; CA 29-32R; DLB-Y 82

Pinter, Harold
1930- ..... CLC 1, 3, 6, 9, 11, 15, 27, 58
See also CA 5-8R; DLB 13

Pirandello, Luigi 1867-1936..... TCLC 4, 29
See also CA 104

Pirsig, Robert M(aynard) 1928- ... CLC 4, 6
See also CA 53-56; SATA 39

Pisarev, Dmitry Ivanovich
1840-1868 .... NCLC 25

Pix, Mary (Griffith) 1666-1709....... LC 8

Plaidy, Jean 1906-
See Hibbert, Eleanor (Burford)

Plant, Robert 1948- .... CLC 12

Plante, David (Robert)
1940- .... CLC 7, 23, 38
See also CANR 12; CA 37-40R; DLB-Y 83

Plath, Sylvia
1932-1963 .... **CLC 1, 2, 3, 5, 9, 11, 14,
17, 50, 51**
See also CAP 2; CA 19-20; DLB 5, 6;
CDALB 1941-1968

Platonov, Andrei (Platonovich)
1899-1951 .... **TCLC 14**
See also Klimentov, Andrei Platonovich
See also CA 108

Platt, Kin 1911- .... **CLC 26**
See also CANR 11; CA 17-20R; SATA 21

Plimpton, George (Ames) 1927-..... **CLC 36**
See also CA 21-24R; SATA 10

Plomer, William (Charles Franklin)
1903-1973 .... **CLC 4, 8**
See also CAP 2; CA 21-22; SATA 24;
DLB 20

Plumly, Stanley (Ross) 1939- ...... **CLC 33**
See also CA 108, 110; DLB 5

Poe, Edgar Allan
1809-1849 .... **NCLC 1, 16; SSC 1**
See also SATA 23; DLB 3, 59, 73, 74;
CDALB 1640-1865

Pohl, Frederik 1919- .... **CLC 18**
See also CAAS 1; CANR 11; CA 61-64;
SATA 24; DLB 8

Poirier, Louis 1910-
See Gracq, Julien
See also CA 122, 126

Poitier, Sidney 1924?- .... **CLC 26**
See also CA 117

Polanski, Roman 1933- .... **CLC 16**
See also CA 77-80

Poliakoff, Stephen 1952- .... **CLC 38**
See also CA 106; DLB 13

Police, The .... **CLC 26**

Pollitt, Katha 1949- .... **CLC 28**
See also CA 120, 122

Pollock, Sharon 19??- .... **CLC 50**

Pomerance, Bernard 1940-......... **CLC 13**
See also CA 101

Ponge, Francis (Jean Gaston Alfred)
1899- .... **CLC 6, 18**
See also CA 85-88

Pontoppidan, Henrik 1857-1943 ... **TCLC 29**
See also obituary CA 126

Poole, Josephine 1933-............ **CLC 17**
See also CANR 10; CA 21-24R; SAAS 2;
SATA 5

Popa, Vasko 1922- .... **CLC 19**
See also CA 112

Pope, Alexander 1688-1744......... **LC 3**

Porter, Gene (va Grace) Stratton
1863-1924 .... **TCLC 21**
See also CA 112

Porter, Katherine Anne
1890-1980 ..... **CLC 1, 3, 7, 10, 13, 15,
27; SSC 4**
See also CANR 1; CA 1-4R;
obituary CA 101; obituary SATA 23, 39;
DLB 4, 9; DLB-Y 80

Porter, Peter (Neville Frederick)
1929- .... **CLC 5, 13, 33**
See also CA 85-88; DLB 40

Porter, William Sydney 1862-1910
See Henry, O.
See also YABC 2; CA 104; DLB 12;
CDALB 1865-1917

Potok, Chaim 1929- .... **CLC 2, 7, 14, 26**
See also CANR 19; CA 17-20R; SATA 33;
DLB 28

Potter, Dennis (Christopher George)
1935- .... **CLC 58**
See also CA 107

Pound, Ezra (Loomis)
1885-1972 ..... **CLC 1, 2, 3, 4, 5, 7, 10,
13, 18, 34, 48, 50**
See also CA 5-8R; obituary CA 37-40R;
DLB 4, 45, 63

Povod, Reinaldo 1959-............ **CLC 44**

Powell, Anthony (Dymoke)
1905- .... **CLC 1, 3, 7, 9, 10, 31**
See also CANR 1; CA 1-4R; DLB 15

Powell, Padgett 1952-............. **CLC 34**
See also CA 126

Powers, J(ames) F(arl)
1917- .... **CLC 1, 4, 8, 57; SSC 4**
See also CANR 2; CA 1-4R

Pownall, David 1938-............. **CLC 10**
See also CA 89-92; DLB 14

Powys, John Cowper
1872-1963 .... **CLC 7, 9, 15, 46**
See also CA 85-88; DLB 15

Powys, T(heodore) F(rancis)
1875-1953 .... **TCLC 9**
See also CA 106; DLB 36

Prager, Emily 1952-.............. **CLC 56**

Pratt, E(dwin) J(ohn) 1883-1964.... **CLC 19**
See also obituary CA 93-96

Premchand 1880-1936 .... **TCLC 21**

Preussler, Otfried 1923-........... **CLC 17**
See also CA 77-80; SATA 24

Prevert, Jacques (Henri Marie)
1900-1977 .... **CLC 15**
See also CA 77-80; obituary CA 69-72;
obituary SATA 30

Prevost, Abbe (Antoine Francois)
1697-1763 .... **LC 1**

Price, (Edward) Reynolds
1933- .... **CLC 3, 6, 13, 43, 50**
See also CANR 1; CA 1-4R; DLB 2

Price, Richard 1949- .... **CLC 6, 12**
See also CANR 3; CA 49-52; DLB-Y 81

Prichard, Katharine Susannah
1883-1969 .... **CLC 46**
See also CAP 1; CA 11-12

Priestley, J(ohn) B(oynton)
1894-1984 .... **CLC 2, 5, 9, 34**
See also CA 9-12R; obituary CA 113;
DLB 10, 34; DLB-Y 84

Prince (Rogers Nelson) 1958?- ..... **CLC 35**

Prince, F(rank) T(empleton) 1912- .. **CLC 22**
See also CA 101; DLB 20

Prior, Matthew 1664-1721.......... **LC 4**

Pritchard, William H(arrison)
1932- .... **CLC 34**
See also CANR 23; CA 65-68

Pritchett, V(ictor) S(awdon)
1900- .... **CLC 5, 13, 15, 41**
See also CA 61-64; DLB 15

Probst, Mark 1925- .... **CLC 59**
See also CA 130

Procaccino, Michael 1946-
See Cristofer, Michael

Prokosch, Frederic 1908-1989.... **CLC 4, 48**
See also CA 73-76; DLB 48

Prose, Francine 1947-............. **CLC 45**
See also CA 109, 112

Proust, Marcel 1871-1922 .. **TCLC 7, 13, 33**
See also CA 104, 120; DLB 65

Pryor, Richard 1940- .... **CLC 26**
See also CA 122

Przybyszewski, Stanislaw
1868-1927 .... **TCLC 36**
See also DLB 66

Puig, Manuel 1932- .... **CLC 3, 5, 10, 28**
See also CANR 2; CA 45-48

Purdy, A(lfred) W(ellington)
1918- .... **CLC 3, 6, 14, 50**
See also CA 81-84

Purdy, James (Amos)
1923- .... **CLC 2, 4, 10, 28, 52**
See also CAAS 1; CANR 19; CA 33-36R;
DLB 2

Pushkin, Alexander (Sergeyevich)
1799-1837 .... **NCLC 3, 27**

P'u Sung-ling 1640-1715 .... **LC 3**

Puzo, Mario 1920-......... **CLC 1, 2, 6, 36**
See also CANR 4; CA 65-68; DLB 6

Pym, Barbara (Mary Crampton)
1913-1980 .... **CLC 13, 19, 37**
See also CANR 13; CAP 1; CA 13-14;
obituary CA 97-100; DLB 14; DLB-Y 87

Pynchon, Thomas (Ruggles, Jr.)
1937- .... **CLC 2, 3, 6, 9, 11, 18, 33**
See also CANR 22; CA 17-20R; DLB 2

Quasimodo, Salvatore 1901-1968 ... **CLC 10**
See also CAP 1; CA 15-16;
obituary CA 25-28R

Queen, Ellery 1905-1982 .... **CLC 3, 11**
See also Dannay, Frederic; Lee, Manfred
B(ennington)

Queneau, Raymond
1903-1976 .... **CLC 2, 5, 10, 42**
See also CA 77-80; obituary CA 69-72;
DLB 72

Quin, Ann (Marie) 1936-1973 .... **CLC 6**
See also CA 9-12R; obituary CA 45-48;
DLB 14

Quinn, Simon 1942-
See Smith, Martin Cruz
See also CANR 6, 23; CA 85-88

Quiroga, Horacio (Sylvestre)
1878-1937 .... **TCLC 20**
See also CA 117

Quoirez, Francoise 1935-
See Sagan, Francoise
See also CANR 6; CA 49-52

Rabe, David (William) 1940-... **CLC 4, 8, 33**
See also CA 85-88; DLB 7

Rabelais, Francois 1494?-1553........ **LC 5**

Rabinovitch, Sholem 1859-1916
  See Aleichem, Sholom
  See also CA 104

Rachen, Kurt von 1911-1986
  See Hubbard, L(afayette) Ron(ald)

Radcliffe, Ann (Ward) 1764-1823 .. **NCLC 6**
  See also DLB 39

Radiguet, Raymond 1903-1923 .... **TCLC 29**

Radnoti, Miklos 1909-1944 ...... **TCLC 16**
  See also CA 118

Rado, James 1939-............... **CLC 17**
  See also CA 105

Radomski, James 1932-
  See Rado, James

Radvanyi, Netty Reiling 1900-1983
  See Seghers, Anna
  See also CA 85-88; obituary CA 110

Rae, Ben 1935-
  See Griffiths, Trevor

Raeburn, John 1941- .... **CLC 34**
  See also CA 57-60

Ragni, Gerome 1942-............. **CLC 17**
  See also CA 105

Rahv, Philip 1908-1973 .... **CLC 24**
  See also Greenberg, Ivan

Raine, Craig 1944-............... **CLC 32**
  See also CA 108; DLB 40

Raine, Kathleen (Jessie) 1908- ... **CLC 7, 45**
  See also CA 85-88; DLB 20

Rainis, Janis 1865-1929 .... **TCLC 29**

Rakosi, Carl 1903- .... **CLC 47**
  See also Rawley, Callman
  See also CAAS 5

Ramos, Graciliano 1892-1953 ..... **TCLC 32**

Rampersad, Arnold 19??-.......... **CLC 44**

Ramuz, Charles-Ferdinand
  1878-1947 .... **TCLC 33**

Rand, Ayn 1905-1982........ **CLC 3, 30, 44**
  See also CA 13-16R; obituary CA 105

Randall, Dudley (Felker) 1914-...... **CLC 1**
  See also CANR 23; CA 25-28R; DLB 41

Ransom, John Crowe
  1888-1974 .... **CLC 2, 4, 5, 11, 24**
  See also CANR 6; CA 5-8R;
    obituary CA 49-52; DLB 45, 63

Rao, Raja 1909- .... **CLC 25, 56**
  See also CA 73-76

Raphael, Frederic (Michael)
  1931-.................... **CLC 2, 14**
  See also CANR 1; CA 1-4R; DLB 14

Rathbone, Julian 1935- .... **CLC 41**
  See also CA 101

Rattigan, Terence (Mervyn)
  1911-1977 .... **CLC 7**
  See also CA 85-88; obituary CA 73-76;
    DLB 13

Ratushinskaya, Irina 1954- .... **CLC 54**

Raven, Simon (Arthur Noel)
  1927-...................... **CLC 14**
  See also CA 81-84

Rawley, Callman 1903-
  See Rakosi, Carl
  See also CANR 12; CA 21-24R

Rawlings, Marjorie Kinnan
  1896-1953 .... **TCLC 4**
  See also YABC 1; CA 104; DLB 9, 22

Ray, Satyajit 1921-............... **CLC 16**
  See also CA 114

Read, Herbert (Edward) 1893-1968 .. **CLC 4**
  See also CA 85-88; obituary CA 25-28R;
    DLB 20

Read, Piers Paul 1941- ...... **CLC 4, 10, 25**
  See also CA 21-24R; SATA 21; DLB 14

Reade, Charles 1814-1884 .... **NCLC 2**
  See also DLB 21

Reade, Hamish 1936-
  See Gray, Simon (James Holliday)

Reading, Peter 1946-.............. **CLC 47**
  See also CA 103; DLB 40

Reaney, James 1926-.............. **CLC 13**
  See also CA 41-44R; SATA 43; DLB 68

Rebreanu, Liviu 1885-1944 ...... **TCLC 28**

Rechy, John (Francisco)
  1934-................. **CLC 1, 7, 14, 18**
  See also CAAS 4; CANR 6; CA 5-8R;
    DLB-Y 82

Redcam, Tom 1870-1933 .... **TCLC 25**

Redgrove, Peter (William)
  1932-..................... **CLC 6, 41**
  See also CANR 3; CA 1-4R; DLB 40

Redmon (Nightingale), Anne
  1943-....................... **CLC 22**
  See also Nightingale, Anne Redmon
  See also DLB-Y 86

Reed, Ishmael
  1938-........ **CLC 2, 3, 5, 6, 13, 32, 60**
  See also CANR 25; CA 21-24R; DLB 2, 5,
    33

Reed, John (Silas) 1887-1920 ...... **TCLC 9**
  See also CA 106

Reed, Lou 1944-................. **CLC 21**

Reeve, Clara 1729-1807 .... **NCLC 19**
  See also DLB 39

Reid, Christopher 1949-........... **CLC 33**
  See also DLB 40

Reid Banks, Lynne 1929-
  See Banks, Lynne Reid
  See also CANR 6, 22; CA 1-4R; SATA 22

Reiner, Max 1900-
  See Caldwell, (Janet Miriam) Taylor
    (Holland)

Reizenstein, Elmer Leopold 1892-1967
  See Rice, Elmer

Remark, Erich Paul 1898-1970
  See Remarque, Erich Maria

Remarque, Erich Maria
  1898-1970 .... **CLC 21**
  See also CA 77-80; obituary CA 29-32R;
    DLB 56

Remizov, Alexey (Mikhailovich)
  1877-1957 .... **TCLC 27**
  See also CA 125

Renan, Joseph Ernest
  1823-1892 .... **NCLC 26**

Renard, Jules 1864-1910 .... **TCLC 17**
  See also CA 117

Renault, Mary 1905-1983 .... **CLC 3, 11, 17**
  See also Challans, Mary
  See also DLB-Y 83

Rendell, Ruth 1930-........... **CLC 28, 48**
  See also Vine, Barbara
  See also CA 109

Renoir, Jean 1894-1979 .... **CLC 20**
  See also obituary CA 85-88

Resnais, Alain 1922-.............. **CLC 16**

Reverdy, Pierre 1899-1960 .... **CLC 53**
  See also CA 97-100; obituary CA 89-92

Rexroth, Kenneth
  1905-1982 ...... **CLC 1, 2, 6, 11, 22, 49**
  See also CANR 14; CA 5-8R;
    obituary CA 107; DLB 16, 48; DLB-Y 82;
    CDALB 1941-1968

Reyes, Alfonso 1889-1959 .... **TCLC 33**

Reyes y Basoalto, Ricardo Eliecer Neftali
  1904-1973
  See Neruda, Pablo

Reymont, Wladyslaw Stanislaw
  1867-1925 .... **TCLC 5**
  See also CA 104

Reynolds, Jonathan 1942?- ...... **CLC 6, 38**
  See also CA 65-68

Reynolds, Michael (Shane) 1937-... **CLC 44**
  See also CANR 9; CA 65-68

Reznikoff, Charles 1894-1976 .... **CLC 9**
  See also CAP 2; CA 33-36;
    obituary CA 61-64; DLB 28, 45

Rezzori, Gregor von 1914-......... **CLC 25**
  See also CA 122

Rhys, Jean
  1890-1979 ...... **CLC 2, 4, 6, 14, 19, 51**
  See also CA 25-28R; obituary CA 85-88;
    DLB 36

Ribeiro, Darcy 1922-.............. **CLC 34**
  See also CA 33-36R

Ribeiro, Joao Ubaldo (Osorio Pimentel)
  1941-....................... **CLC 10**
  See also CA 81-84

Ribman, Ronald (Burt) 1932- .... **CLC 7**
  See also CA 21-24R

Rice, Anne 1941- .... **CLC 41**
  See also CANR 12; CA 65-68

Rice, Elmer 1892-1967.......... **CLC 7, 49**
  See also CAP 2; CA 21-22;
    obituary CA 25-28R; DLB 4, 7

Rice, Tim 1944- .... **CLC 21**
  See also CA 103

Rich, Adrienne (Cecile)
  1929- .... **CLC 3, 6, 7, 11, 18, 36**
  See also CANR 20; CA 9-12R; DLB 5, 67

Richard, Keith 1943- .... **CLC 17**
  See also CA 107

Richards, David Adam 1950-....... **CLC 59**
  See also CA 93-96; DLB 53

Richards, I(vor) A(rmstrong)
  1893-1979 .... **CLC 14, 24**
  See also CA 41-44R; obituary CA 89-92;
    DLB 27

Richards, Keith 1943-
  See Richard, Keith
  See also CA 107

Richardson, Dorothy (Miller)
      1873-1957 . . . . TCLC 3
   See also CA 104; DLB 36

Richardson, Ethel   1870-1946
   See Richardson, Henry Handel
   See also CA 105

Richardson, Henry Handel
      1870-1946 . . . . TCLC 4
   See also Richardson, Ethel

Richardson, Samuel   1689-1761 . . . . LC 1
   See also DLB 39

Richler, Mordecai
      1931- . . . . CLC 3, 5, 9, 13, 18, 46
   See also CA 65-68; SATA 27, 44; DLB 53

Richter, Conrad (Michael)
      1890-1968 . . . . CLC 30
   See also CA 5-8R; obituary CA 25-28R;
      SATA 3; DLB 9

Richter, Johann Paul Friedrich   1763-1825
   See Jean Paul

Riding, Laura   1901- . . . . CLC 3, 7
   See also Jackson, Laura (Riding)

Riefenstahl, Berta Helene Amalia
      1902- . . . . CLC 16
   See also Riefenstahl, Leni
   See also CA 108

Riefenstahl, Leni   1902- . . . . CLC 16
   See also Riefenstahl, Berta Helene Amalia
   See also CA 108

Rilke, Rainer Maria
      1875-1926 . . . . TCLC 1, 6, 19
   See also CA 104

Rimbaud, (Jean Nicolas) Arthur
      1854-1891 . . . . NCLC 4

Ringwood, Gwen(dolyn Margaret) Pharis
      1910-1984 . . . . CLC 48
   See also obituary CA 112

Rio, Michel   19??- . . . . CLC 43

Ritsos, Yannis   1909- . . . . CLC 6, 13, 31
   See also CA 77-80

Ritter, Erika   1948?- . . . . CLC 52

Rivera, Jose Eustasio   1889-1928 . . . TCLC 35

Rivers, Conrad Kent   1933-1968 . . . . . . CLC 1
   See also CA 85-88; DLB 41

Rizal, Jose   1861-1896 . . . . NCLC 27

Roa Bastos, Augusto   1917- . . . . CLC 45

Robbe-Grillet, Alain
      1922- . . . . . . CLC 1, 2, 4, 6, 8, 10, 14, 43
   See also CA 9-12R

Robbins, Harold   1916- . . . . CLC 5
   See also CANR 26; CA 73-76

Robbins, Thomas Eugene   1936-
   See Robbins, Tom
   See also CA 81-84

Robbins, Tom   1936- . . . . CLC 9, 32
   See also Robbins, Thomas Eugene
   See also DLB-Y 80

Robbins, Trina   1938- . . . . CLC 21

Roberts, (Sir) Charles G(eorge) D(ouglas)
      1860-1943 . . . . TCLC 8
   See also CA 105; SATA 29

Roberts, Kate   1891-1985 . . . . CLC 15
   See also CA 107; obituary CA 116

Roberts, Keith (John Kingston)
      1935- . . . . CLC 14
   See also CA 25-28R

Roberts, Kenneth   1885-1957 . . . . . . TCLC 23
   See also CA 109; DLB 9

Roberts, Michele (B.)   1949- . . . . CLC 48
   See also CA 115

Robinson, Edwin Arlington
      1869-1935 . . . . TCLC 5
   See also CA 104; DLB 54;
      CDALB 1865-1917

Robinson, Henry Crabb
      1775-1867 . . . . NCLC 15

Robinson, Jill   1936- . . . . CLC 10
   See also CA 102

Robinson, Kim Stanley   19??- . . . . CLC 34
   See also CA 126

Robinson, Marilynne   1944- . . . . CLC 25
   See also CA 116

Robinson, Smokey   1940- . . . . CLC 21

Robinson, William   1940-
   See Robinson, Smokey
   See also CA 116

Robison, Mary   1949- . . . . CLC 42
   See also CA 113, 116

Roddenberry, Gene   1921- . . . . CLC 17
   See also CANR 110

Rodgers, Mary   1931- . . . . CLC 12
   See also CLR 20; CANR 8; CA 49-52;
      SATA 8

Rodgers, W(illiam) R(obert)
      1909-1969 . . . . CLC 7
   See also CA 85-88; DLB 20

Rodriguez, Claudio   1934- . . . . CLC 10

Roethke, Theodore (Huebner)
      1908-1963 . . . . . . CLC 1, 3, 8, 11, 19, 46
   See also CA 81-84; CABS 2; SAAS 1;
      DLB 5; CDALB 1941-1968

Rogers, Sam   1943-
   See Shepard, Sam

Rogers, Thomas (Hunton)   1931- . . . . CLC 57
   See also CA 89-92

Rogers, Will(iam Penn Adair)
      1879-1935 . . . . TCLC 8
   See also CA 105; DLB 11

Rogin, Gilbert   1929- . . . . CLC 18
   See also CANR 15; CA 65-68

Rohan, Koda   1867-1947 . . . . TCLC 22
   See also CA 121

Rohmer, Eric   1920- . . . . CLC 16
   See also Scherer, Jean-Marie Maurice

Rohmer, Sax   1883-1959 . . . . TCLC 28
   See also Ward, Arthur Henry Sarsfield
   See also CA 108; DLB 70

Roiphe, Anne (Richardson)
      1935- . . . . CLC 3, 9
   See also CA 89-92; DLB-Y 80

Rolfe, Frederick (William Serafino Austin
      Lewis Mary)   1860-1913 . . . . . . TCLC 12
   See also CA 107; DLB 34

Rolland, Romain   1866-1944 . . . . . . TCLC 23
   See also CA 118

Rolvaag, O(le) E(dvart)
      1876-1931 . . . . TCLC 17
   See also CA 117; DLB 9

Romains, Jules   1885-1972 . . . . CLC 7
   See also CA 85-88

Romero, Jose Ruben   1890-1952 . . . TCLC 14
   See also CA 114

Ronsard, Pierre de   1524-1585 . . . . LC 6

Rooke, Leon   1934- . . . . CLC 25, 34
   See also CANR 23; CA 25-28R

Roper, William   1498-1578 . . . . LC 10

Rosa, Joao Guimaraes   1908-1967 . . . CLC 23
   See also obituary CA 89-92

Rosen, Richard (Dean)   1949- . . . . CLC 39
   See also CA 77-80

Rosenberg, Isaac   1890-1918 . . . . . . TCLC 12
   See also CA 107; DLB 20

Rosenblatt, Joe   1933- . . . . CLC 15
   See also Rosenblatt, Joseph

Rosenblatt, Joseph   1933-
   See Rosenblatt, Joe
   See also CA 89-92

Rosenfeld, Samuel   1896-1963
   See Tzara, Tristan
   See also obituary CA 89-92

Rosenthal, M(acha) L(ouis)   1917- . . . CLC 28
   See also CAAS 6; CANR 4; CA 1-4R;
      DLB 5

Ross, (James) Sinclair   1908- . . . . CLC 13
   See also CA 73-76

Rossetti, Christina Georgina
      1830-1894 . . . . NCLC 2
   See also SATA 20; DLB 35

Rossetti, Dante Gabriel
      1828-1882 . . . . NCLC 4
   See also DLB 35

Rossetti, Gabriel Charles Dante   1828-1882
   See Rossetti, Dante Gabriel

Rossner, Judith (Perelman)
      1935- . . . . CLC 6, 9, 29
   See also CANR 18; CA 17-20R; DLB 6

Rostand, Edmond (Eugene Alexis)
      1868-1918 . . . . TCLC 6, 37
   See also CA 104, 126

Roth, Henry   1906- . . . . CLC 2, 6, 11
   See also CAP 1; CA 11-12; DLB 28

Roth, Joseph   1894-1939 . . . . TCLC 33

Roth, Philip (Milton)
      1933- . . . . . . CLC 1, 2, 3, 4, 6, 9, 15, 22,
                                                   31, 47
   See also CANR 1, 22; CA 1-4R; DLB 2, 28;
      DLB-Y 82

Rothenberg, James   1931- . . . . CLC 57

Rothenberg, Jerome   1931- . . . . CLC 6
   See also CANR 1; CA 45-48; DLB 5

Roumain, Jacques   1907-1944 . . . . . . TCLC 19
   See also CA 117

Rourke, Constance (Mayfield)
      1885-1941 . . . . TCLC 12
   See also YABC 1; CA 107

Rousseau, Jean-Baptiste   1671-1741 . . . LC 9

Rousseau, Jean-Jacques   1712-1778 . . . LC 14

Roussel, Raymond 1877-1933 . . . . . **TCLC 20**
See also CA 117

Rovit, Earl (Herbert) 1927- . . . . **CLC 7**
See also CANR 12; CA 5-8R

Rowe, Nicholas 1674-1718 . . . . **LC 8**

Rowson, Susanna Haswell
1762-1824 . . . . **NCLC 5**
See also DLB 37

Roy, Gabrielle 1909-1983 . . . . . . **CLC 10, 14**
See also CANR 5; CA 53-56;
obituary CA 110; DLB 68

Rozewicz, Tadeusz 1921- . . . . **CLC 9, 23**
See also CA 108

Ruark, Gibbons 1941- . . . . **CLC 3**
See also CANR 14; CA 33-36R

Rubens, Bernice 192?- . . . . **CLC 19, 31**
See also CA 25-28R; DLB 14

Rudkin, (James) David 1936- . . . . . . **CLC 14**
See also CA 89-92; DLB 13

Rudnik, Raphael 1933- . . . . **CLC 7**
See also CA 29-32R

Ruiz, Jose Martinez 1874-1967
See Azorin

Rukeyser, Muriel
1913-1980 . . . . **CLC 6, 10, 15, 27**
See also CANR 26; CA 5-8R;
obituary CA 93-96; obituary SATA 22;
DLB 48

Rule, Jane (Vance) 1931- . . . . **CLC 27**
See also CANR 12; CA 25-28R; DLB 60

Rulfo, Juan 1918-1986 . . . . **CLC 8**
See also CANR 26; CA 85-88;
obituary CA 118

Runyon, (Alfred) Damon
1880-1946 . . . . **TCLC 10**
See also CA 107; DLB 11

Rush, Norman 1933-, ... **CLC 44**
See also CA 121, 126

Rushdie, (Ahmed) Salman
1947- . . . . **CLC 23, 31, 55, 59**
See also CA 108, 111

Rushforth, Peter (Scott) 1945- . . . . . **CLC 19**
See also CA 101

Ruskin, John 1819-1900 . . . . **TCLC 20**
See also CA 114; SATA 24; DLB 55

Russ, Joanna 1937- . . . . **CLC 15**
See also CANR 11; CA 25-28R; DLB 8

Russell, George William 1867-1935
See A. E.
See also CA 104

Russell, (Henry) Ken(neth Alfred)
1927- . . . . **CLC 16**
See also CA 105

Russell, Willy 1947- . . . . **CLC 60**

Rutherford, Mark 1831-1913 . . . . . . **TCLC 25**
See also CA 121; DLB 18

Ruyslinck, Ward 1929- . . . . **CLC 14**

Ryan, Cornelius (John) 1920-1974 . . . **CLC 7**
See also CA 69-72; obituary CA 53-56

Rybakov, Anatoli 1911?- . . . . **CLC 23, 53**
See also CA 126

Ryder, Jonathan 1927-
See Ludlum, Robert

Ryga, George 1932- . . . . **CLC 14**
See also CA 101; obituary CA 124; DLB 60

Séviné, Marquise de Marie de
Rabutin-Chantal 1626-1696 . . . . . **LC 11**

Saba, Umberto 1883-1957 . . . . **TCLC 33**

Sabato, Ernesto 1911- . . . . **CLC 10, 23**
See also CA 97-100

Sachs, Marilyn (Stickle) 1927- . . . . . **CLC 35**
See also CLR 2; CANR 13; CA 17-20R;
SAAS 2; SATA 3, 52

Sachs, Nelly 1891-1970 . . . . **CLC 14**
See also CAP 2; CA 17-18;
obituary CA 25-28R

Sackler, Howard (Oliver)
1929-1982 . . . . **CLC 14**
See also CA 61-64; obituary CA 108; DLB 7

Sade, Donatien Alphonse Francois, Comte de
1740-1814 . . . . **NCLC 3**

Sadoff, Ira 1945- . . . . **CLC 9**
See also CANR 5, 21; CA 53-56

Safire, William 1929- . . . . **CLC 10**
See also CA 17-20R

Sagan, Carl (Edward) 1934- . . . . **CLC 30**
See also CANR 11; CA 25-28R

Sagan, Francoise
1935- . . . . **CLC 3, 6, 9, 17, 36**
See also Quoirez, Francoise
See also CANR 6

Sahgal, Nayantara (Pandit) 1927- . . . **CLC 41**
See also CANR 11; CA 9-12R

Saint, H(arry) F. 1941- . . . . **CLC 50**

Sainte-Beuve, Charles Augustin
1804-1869 . . . . **NCLC 5**

Sainte-Marie, Beverly 1941-1972?
See Sainte-Marie, Buffy
See also CA 107

Sainte-Marie, Buffy 1941- . . . . **CLC 17**
See also Sainte-Marie, Beverly

Saint-Exupery, Antoine (Jean Baptiste Marie
Roger) de 1900-1944 . . . . **TCLC 2**
See also CLR 10; CA 108; SATA 20;
DLB 72

Saintsbury, George 1845-1933 . . . . . **TCLC 31**
See also DLB 57

Sait Faik (Abasiyanik)
1906-1954 . . . . **TCLC 23**

Saki 1870-1916 . . . . **TCLC 3**
See also Munro, H(ector) H(ugh)
See also CA 104

Salama, Hannu 1936- . . . . **CLC 18**

Salamanca, J(ack) R(ichard)
1922- . . . . **CLC 4, 15**
See also CA 25-28R

Salinas, Pedro 1891-1951 . . . . **TCLC 17**
See also CA 117

Salinger, J(erome) D(avid)
1919- . . . . **CLC 1, 3, 8, 12, 56; SSC 2**
See also CA 5-8R; DLB 2;
CDALB 1941-1968

Salter, James 1925- . . . . **CLC 7, 52, 59**
See also CA 73-76

Saltus, Edgar (Evertson)
1855-1921 . . . . **TCLC 8**
See also CA 105

Saltykov, Mikhail Evgrafovich
1826-1889 . . . . **NCLC 16**

Samarakis, Antonis 1919- . . . . **CLC 5**
See also CA 25-28R

Sanchez, Florencio 1875-1910 . . . . . **TCLC 37**

Sanchez, Luis Rafael 1936- . . . . **CLC 23**

Sanchez, Sonia 1934- . . . . **CLC 5**
See also CA 33-36R; SATA 22; DLB 41

Sand, George 1804-1876 . . . . **NCLC 2**

Sandburg, Carl (August)
1878-1967 . . . . **CLC 1, 4, 10, 15, 35**
See also CA 5-8R; obituary CA 25-28R;
SATA 8; DLB 17, 54; CDALB 1865-1917

Sandburg, Charles August 1878-1967
See Sandburg, Carl (August)

Sanders, (James) Ed(ward) 1939- . . . **CLC 53**
See also CANR 13; CA 15-16R, 103;
DLB 16

Sanders, Lawrence 1920- . . . . **CLC 41**
See also CA 81-84

Sandoz, Mari (Susette) 1896-1966 . . **CLC 28**
See also CANR 17; CA 1-4R;
obituary CA 25-28R; SATA 5; DLB 9

Saner, Reg(inald Anthony) 1931- . . . . **CLC 9**
See also CA 65-68

Sannazaro, Jacopo 1456?-1530 . . . . **LC 8**

Sansom, William 1912-1976 . . . . **CLC 2, 6**
See also CA 5-8R; obituary CA 65-68

Santiago, Danny 1911- . . . . **CLC 33**
See also CA 125

Santmyer, Helen Hooven
1895-1986 . . . . **CLC 33**
See also CANR 15; CA 1-4R;
obituary CA 118; DLB-Y 84

Santos, Bienvenido N(uqui) 1911- . . . **CLC 22**
See also CANR 19; CA 101

Sappho c. 6th-century B.C.- . . . . **CMLC 3**

Sarduy, Severo 1937- . . . . **CLC 6**
See also CA 89-92

Sargeson, Frank 1903-1982 . . . . **CLC 31**
See also CA 106, 25-28R; obituary CA 106

Sarmiento, Felix Ruben Garcia 1867-1916
See Dario, Ruben
See also CA 104

Saroyan, William
1908-1981 . . . . **CLC 1, 8, 10, 29, 34, 56**
See also CA 5-8R; obituary CA 103;
SATA 23; obituary SATA 24; DLB 7, 9;
DLB-Y 81

Sarraute, Nathalie
1902- . . . . **CLC 1, 2, 4, 8, 10, 31**
See also CANR 23; CA 9-12R

Sarton, Eleanore Marie 1912-
See Sarton, (Eleanor) May

Sarton, (Eleanor) May
1912- . . . . **CLC 4, 14, 49**
See also CANR 1; CA 1-4R; SATA 36;
DLB 48; DLB-Y 81

Sartre, Jean-Paul (Charles Aymard)
1905-1980 . . . **CLC 1, 4, 7, 9, 13, 18, 24,**
44, 50, 52
See also CANR 21; CA 9-12R;
obituary CA 97-100; DLB 72

Sassoon, Siegfried (Lorraine)
    1886-1967 .... CLC 36
    See also CA 104; obituary CA 25-28R;
    DLB 20

Saul, John (W. III) 1942- .... CLC 46
    See also CANR 16; CA 81-84

Saura, Carlos 1932- .... CLC 20
    See also CA 114

Sauser-Hall, Frederic-Louis 1887-1961
    See Cendrars, Blaise
    See also CA 102; obituary CA 93-96

Savage, Thomas 1915- .... CLC 40

Savan, Glenn 19??- .... CLC 50

Sayers, Dorothy L(eigh)
    1893-1957 .... TCLC 2, 15
    See also CA 104, 119; DLB 10, 36

Sayers, Valerie 19??- .... CLC 50

Sayles, John (Thomas)
    1950- .... CLC 7, 10, 14
    See also CA 57-60; DLB 44

Scammell, Michael 19??- .... CLC 34

Scannell, Vernon 1922- .... CLC 49
    See also CANR 8; CA 5-8R; DLB 27

Schaeffer, Susan Fromberg
    1941- .... CLC 6, 11, 22
    See also CANR 18; CA 49-52; SATA 22;
    DLB 28

Schell, Jonathan 1943- .... CLC 35
    See also CANR 12; CA 73-76

Scherer, Jean-Marie Maurice 1920-
    See Rohmer, Eric
    See also CA 110

Schevill, James (Erwin) 1920- ...... CLC 7
    See also CA 5-8R

Schisgal, Murray (Joseph) 1926- ..... CLC 6
    See also CA 21-24R

Schlee, Ann 1934- .... CLC 35
    See also CA 101; SATA 36, 44

Schlegel, August Wilhelm von
    1767-1845 .... NCLC 15

Schlegel, Johann Elias (von)
    1719?-1749.................... LC 5

Schmidt, Arno 1914-1979......... CLC 56
    See also obituary CA 109; DLB 69

Schmitz, Ettore 1861-1928
    See Svevo, Italo
    See also CA 104, 122

Schnackenberg, Gjertrud 1953- ..... CLC 40
    See also CA 116

Schneider, Leonard Alfred 1925-1966
    See Bruce, Lenny
    See also CA 89-92

Schnitzler, Arthur 1862-1931 ...... TCLC 4
    See also CA 104

Schorer, Mark 1908-1977 .... CLC 9
    See also CANR 7; CA 5-8R;
    obituary CA 73-76

Schrader, Paul (Joseph) 1946- ...... CLC 26
    See also CA 37-40R; DLB 44

Schreiner (Cronwright), Olive (Emilie
    Albertina) 1855-1920........ TCLC 9
    See also CA 105; DLB 18

Schulberg, Budd (Wilson)
    1914- .... CLC 7, 48
    See also CANR 19; CA 25-28R; DLB 6, 26,
    28; DLB-Y 81

Schulz, Bruno 1892-1942......... TCLC 5
    See also CA 115, 123

Schulz, Charles M(onroe) 1922- .... CLC 12
    See also CANR 6; CA 9-12R; SATA 10

Schuyler, James (Marcus)
    1923- .... CLC 5, 23
    See also CA 101; DLB 5

Schwartz, Delmore
    1913-1966 .... CLC 2, 4, 10, 45
    See also CAP 2; CA 17-18;
    obituary CA 25-28R; DLB 28, 48

Schwartz, John Burnham 1925- .... CLC 59

Schwartz, Lynne Sharon 1939- ..... CLC 31
    See also CA 103

Schwarz-Bart, Andre 1928- .... CLC 2, 4
    See also CA 89-92

Schwarz-Bart, Simone 1938- .... CLC 7
    See also CA 97-100

Schwob, (Mayer Andre) Marcel
    1867-1905 .... TCLC 20
    See also CA 117

Sciascia, Leonardo
    1921-1989 .... CLC 8, 9, 41
    See also CA 85-88

Scoppettone, Sandra 1936-........ CLC 26
    See also CA 5-8R; SATA 9

Scorsese, Martin 1942- .... CLC 20
    See also CA 110, 114

Scotland, Jay 1932-
    See Jakes, John (William)

Scott, Duncan Campbell
    1862-1947 .... TCLC 6
    See also CA 104

Scott, Evelyn 1893-1963........... CLC 43
    See also CA 104; obituary CA 112; DLB 9,
    48

Scott, F(rancis) R(eginald)
    1899-1985 .... CLC 22
    See also CA 101; obituary CA 114

Scott, Joanna 19??-.............. CLC 50
    See also CA 126

Scott, Paul (Mark) 1920-1978.... CLC 9, 60
    See also CA 81-84; obituary CA 77-80;
    DLB 14

Scott, Sir Walter 1771-1832 ..... NCLC 15
    See also YABC 2

Scribe, (Augustin) Eugene
    1791-1861 .... NCLC 16

Scudery, Madeleine de 1607-1701..... LC 2

Sealy, I. Allan 1951- .... CLC 55

Seare, Nicholas 1925-
    See Trevanian; Whitaker, Rodney

Sebestyen, Igen 1924-
    See Sebestyen, Ouida

Sebestyen, Ouida 1924- .... CLC 30
    See also CA 107; SATA 39

Sedgwick, Catharine Maria
    1789-1867 .... NCLC 19
    See also DLB 1

Seelye, John 1931-................ CLC 7
    See also CA 97-100

Seferiades, Giorgos Stylianou 1900-1971
    See Seferis, George
    See also CANR 5; CA 5-8R;
    obituary CA 33-36R

Seferis, George 1900-1971 .... CLC 5, 11
    See also Seferiades, Giorgos Stylianou

Segal, Erich (Wolf) 1937- .... CLC 3, 10
    See also CANR 20; CA 25-28R; DLB-Y 86

Seger, Bob 1945-................ CLC 35

Seger, Robert Clark 1945-
    See Seger, Bob

Seghers, Anna 1900-1983....... CLC 7, 110
    See also Radvanyi, Netty Reiling
    See also DLB 69

Seidel, Frederick (Lewis) 1936-..... CLC 18
    See also CANR 8; CA 13-16R; DLB-Y 84

Seifert, Jaroslav 1901-1986..... CLC 34, 44

Selby, Hubert, Jr. 1928- ..... CLC 1, 2, 4, 8
    See also CA 13-16R; DLB 2

Senacour, Etienne Pivert de
    1770-1846 .... NCLC 16

Sender, Ramon (Jose) 1902-1982 .... CLC 8
    See also CANR 8; CA 5-8R;
    obituary CA 105

Senghor, Léopold Sédar 1906-...... CLC 54
    See also CA 116

Serling, (Edward) Rod(man)
    1924-1975 .... CLC 30
    See also CA 65-68; obituary CA 57-60;
    DLB 26

Serpieres 1907-
    See Guillevic, (Eugene)

Service, Robert W(illiam)
    1874-1958 .... TCLC 15
    See also CA 115; SATA 20

Seth, Vikram 1952-.............. CLC 43
    See also CA 121

Seton, Cynthia Propper
    1926-1982 .... CLC 27
    See also CANR 7; CA 5-8R;
    obituary CA 108

Seton, Ernest (Evan) Thompson
    1860-1946 .... TCLC 31
    See also CA 109; SATA 18

Settle, Mary Lee 1918- .... CLC 19, 61
    See also CAAS 1; CA 89-92; DLB 6

Sevigne, Marquise de Marie de
    Rabutin-Chantal 1626-1696..... LC 11

Sexton, Anne (Harvey)
    1928-1974 .... CLC 2, 4, 6, 8, 10, 15, 53
    See also CANR 3; CA 1-4R;
    obituary CA 53-56; CABS 2; SATA 10;
    DLB 5; CDALB 1941-1968

Shaara, Michael (Joseph) 1929- .... CLC 15
    See also CA 102; obituary CA 125;
    DLB-Y 83

Shackleton, C. C. 1925-
    See Aldiss, Brian W(ilson)

Shacochis, Bob 1951-............ CLC 39
    See also CA 119, 124

Shaffer, Anthony 1926- .... CLC 19
    See also CA 110, 116; DLB 13

Shaffer, Peter (Levin)
1926- .... **CLC 5, 14, 18, 37, 60**
See also CANR 25; CA 25-28R; DLB 13

Shalamov, Varlam (Tikhonovich)
1907?-1982................... **CLC 18**
See also obituary CA 105

Shamlu, Ahmad 1925- .... **CLC 10**

Shammas, Anton 1951-........... **CLC 55**

Shange, Ntozake 1948-...... **CLC 8, 25, 38**
See also CA 85-88; DLB 38

Shapcott, Thomas W(illiam) 1935- .. **CLC 38**
See also CA 69-72

Shapiro, Karl (Jay) 1913- ...**CLC 4, 8, 15, 53**
See also CAAS 6; CANR 1; CA 1-4R;
DLB 48

Sharpe, Tom 1928-................ **CLC 36**
See also CA 114; DLB 14

Shaw, (George) Bernard
1856-1950 .... **TCLC 3, 9, 21**
See also CA 104, 109, 119; DLB 10, 57

Shaw, Henry Wheeler
1818-1885 .... **NCLC 15**
See also DLB 11

Shaw, Irwin 1913-1984....... **CLC 7, 23, 34**
See also CANR 21; CA 13-16R;
obituary CA 112; DLB 6; DLB-Y 84;
CDALB 1941-1968

Shaw, Robert 1927-1978 .... **CLC 5**
See also CANR 4; CA 1-4R;
obituary CA 81-84; DLB 13, 14

Shawn, Wallace 1943- .... **CLC 41**
See also CA 112

Sheed, Wilfrid (John Joseph)
1930- .... **CLC 2, 4, 10, 53**
See also CA 65-68; DLB 6

Sheffey, Asa 1913-1980
See Hayden, Robert (Earl)

Sheldon, Alice (Hastings) B(radley)
1915-1987
See Tiptree, James, Jr.
See also CA 108; obituary CA 122

Shelley, Mary Wollstonecraft Godwin
1797-1851 .... **NCLC 14**
See also SATA 29

Shelley, Percy Bysshe
1792-1822 .... **NCLC 18**

Shepard, Jim 19??-................ **CLC 36**

Shepard, Lucius 19??-............. **CLC 34**

Shepard, Sam
1943- .... **CLC 4, 6, 17, 34, 41, 44**
See also CANR 22; CA 69-72; DLB 7

Shepherd, Michael 1927-
See Ludlum, Robert

Sherburne, Zoa (Morin) 1912-...... **CLC 30**
See also CANR 3; CA 1-4R; SATA 3

Sheridan, Frances 1724-1766........ **LC 7**
See also DLB 39

Sheridan, Richard Brinsley
1751-1816 .... **NCLC 5**

Sherman, Jonathan Marc 1970?-.... **CLC 55**

Sherman, Martin 19??-............ **CLC 19**
See also CA 116

Sherwin, Judith Johnson 1936-... **CLC 7, 15**
See also CA 25-28R

Sherwood, Robert E(mmet)
1896-1955 .... **TCLC 3**
See also CA 104; DLB 7, 26

Shiel, M(atthew) P(hipps)
1865-1947 .... **TCLC 8**
See also CA 106

Shiga, Naoya 1883-1971.......... **CLC 33**
See also CA 101; obituary CA 33-36R

Shimazaki, Haruki 1872-1943
See Shimazaki, Toson
See also CA 105

Shimazaki, Toson 1872-1943...... **TCLC 5**
See also Shimazaki, Haruki

Sholokhov, Mikhail (Aleksandrovich)
1905-1984 .... **CLC 7, 15**
See also CA 101; obituary CA 112;
SATA 36

Sholom Aleichem 1859-1916 .... **TCLC 1, 35**
See also Rabinovitch, Sholem

Shreve, Susan Richards 1939-...... **CLC 23**
See also CAAS 5; CANR 5; CA 49-52;
SATA 41, 46

Shue, Larry 1946-1985........... **CLC 52**
See also obituary CA 117

Shulman, Alix Kates 1932- ...... **CLC 2, 10**
See also CA 29-32R; SATA 7

Shuster, Joe 1914- .... **CLC 21**

Shute (Norway), Nevil 1899-1960... **CLC 30**
See also Norway, Nevil Shute
See also CA 102; obituary CA 93-96

Shuttle, Penelope (Diane) 1947- ..... **CLC 7**
See also CA 93-96; DLB 14, 40

Siegel, Jerome 1914- .... **CLC 21**
See also CA 116

Sienkiewicz, Henryk (Adam Aleksander Pius)
1846-1916 .... **TCLC 3**
See also CA 104

Sigal, Clancy 1926-............... **CLC 7**
See also CA 1-4R

Sigourney, Lydia (Howard Huntley)
1791-1865 .... **NCLC 21**
See also DLB 1, 42, 73

Siguenza y Gongora, Carlos de
1645-1700 .... **LC 8**

Sigurjonsson, Johann 1880-1919... **TCLC 27**

Silkin, Jon 1930- .... **CLC 2, 6, 43**
See also CAAS 5; CA 5-8R; DLB 27

Silko, Leslie Marmon 1948- .... **CLC 23**
See also CA 115, 122

Sillanpaa, Franz Eemil 1888-1964... **CLC 19**
See also obituary CA 93-96

Sillitoe, Alan
1928- .... **CLC 1, 3, 6, 10, 19, 57**
See also CAAS 2; CANR 8, 26; CA 9-12R;
DLB 14

Silone, Ignazio 1900-1978 .... **CLC 4**
See also CAAS 2; CANR 26; CAP 2;
CA 25-28, 11-12R,; obituary CA 81-84

Silver, Joan Micklin 1935- .... **CLC 20**
See also CA 114, 121

Silverberg, Robert 1935- .... **CLC 7**
See also CAAS 3; CANR 1, 20; CA 1-4R;
SATA 13; DLB 8

Silverstein, Alvin 1933- .... **CLC 17**
See also CANR 2; CA 49-52; SATA 8

Silverstein, Virginia B(arbara Opshelor)
1937- .... **CLC 17**
See also CANR 2; CA 49-52; SATA 8

Simak, Clifford D(onald)
1904-1988 .... **CLC 1, 55**
See also CANR 1; CA 1-4R;
obituary CA 125; DLB 8

Simenon, Georges (Jacques Christian)
1903-1989 .... **CLC 1, 2, 3, 8, 18, 47**
See also CA 85-88; DLB 72

Simenon, Paul 1956?-
See The Clash

Simic, Charles 1938-....... **CLC 6, 9, 22, 49**
See also CAAS 4; CANR 12; CA 29-32R

Simmons, Charles (Paul) 1924-..... **CLC 57**
See also CA 89-92

Simmons, Dan 1948-.............. **CLC 44**

Simmons, James (Stewart Alexander)
1933- .... **CLC 43**
See also CA 105; DLB 40

Simms, William Gilmore
1806-1870 .... **NCLC 3**
See also DLB 3, 30

Simon, Carly 1945-............... **CLC 26**
See also CA 105

Simon, Claude (Henri Eugene)
1913- .... **CLC 4, 9, 15, 39**
See also CA 89-92

Simon, (Marvin) Neil
1927- .... **CLC 6, 11, 31, 39**
See also CA 21-24R; DLB 7

Simon, Paul 1941- .... **CLC 17**
See also CA 116

Simonon, Paul 1956?-
See The Clash

Simpson, Louis (Aston Marantz)
1923- .... **CLC 4, 7, 9, 32**
See also CAAS 4; CANR 1; CA 1-4R;
DLB 5

Simpson, Mona (Elizabeth) 1957-... **CLC 44**
See also CA 122

Simpson, N(orman) F(rederick)
1919- .... **CLC 29**
See also CA 11-14R; DLB 13

Sinclair, Andrew (Annandale)
1935- .... **CLC 2, 14**
See also CAAS 5; CANR 14; CA 9-12R;
DLB 14

Sinclair, Mary Amelia St. Clair 1865?-1946
See Sinclair, May
See also CA 104

Sinclair, May 1865?-1946 ...... **TCLC 3, 11**
See also Sinclair, Mary Amelia St. Clair
See also DLB 36

Sinclair, Upton (Beall)
1878-1968 .... **CLC 1, 11, 15**
See also CANR 7; CA 5-8R;
obituary CA 25-28R; SATA 9; DLB 9

Singer, Isaac Bashevis
1904- .... **CLC 1, 3, 6, 9, 11, 15, 23, 38;
SSC 3**
See also CLR 1; CANR 1; CA 1-4R;
SATA 3, 27; DLB 6, 28, 52;
CDALB 1941-1968

Singer, Israel Joshua 1893-1944 ... **TCLC 33**

Singh, Khushwant 1915-.......... **CLC 11**
See also CANR 6; CA 9-12R

Sinyavsky, Andrei (Donatevich)
1925-........................ **CLC 8**
See also CA 85-88

Sirin, V.
See Nabokov, Vladimir (Vladimirovich)

Sissman, L(ouis) E(dward)
1928-1976 .... **CLC 9, 18**
See also CANR 13; CA 21-24R;
obituary CA 65-68; DLB 5

Sisson, C(harles) H(ubert) 1914-..... **CLC 8**
See also CAAS 3; CANR 3; CA 1-4R;
DLB 27

Sitwell, (Dame) Edith 1887-1964... **CLC 2, 9**
See also CA 9-12R; DLB 20

Sjoewall, Maj 1935-
See Wahloo, Per
See also CA 61-64, 65-68

Sjowall, Maj 1935-
See Wahloo, Per

Skelton, Robin 1925- .... **CLC 13**
See also CAAS 5; CA 5-8R; DLB 27, 53

Skolimowski, Jerzy 1938- .... **CLC 20**

Skolimowski, Yurek 1938-
See Skolimowski, Jerzy

Skram, Amalie (Bertha)
1847-1905 .... **TCLC 25**

Skrine, Mary Nesta 1904-
See Keane, Molly

Skvorecky, Josef (Vaclav)
1924-..................... **CLC 15, 39**
See also CAAS 1; CANR 10; CA 61-64

Slade, Bernard 1930- .... **CLC 11, 46**
See also Newbound, Bernard Slade
See also DLB 53

Slaughter, Carolyn 1946-.......... **CLC 56**
See also CA 85-88

Slaughter, Frank G(ill) 1908- ...... **CLC 29**
See also CANR 5; CA 5-8R

Slavitt, David (R.) 1935- .... **CLC 5, 14**
See also CAAS 3; CA 21-24R; DLB 5, 6

Slesinger, Tess 1905-1945 .... **TCLC 10**
See also CA 107

Slessor, Kenneth 1901-1971........ **CLC 14**
See also CA 102; obituary CA 89-92

Slowacki, Juliusz 1809-1849 ..... **NCLC 15**

Smart, Christopher 1722-1771....... **LC 3**

Smart, Elizabeth 1913-1986........ **CLC 54**
See also CA 81-84; obituary CA 118

Smiley, Jane (Graves) 1949-....... **CLC 53**
See also CA 104

Smith, A(rthur) J(ames) M(arshall)
1902-1980 .... **CLC 15**
See also CANR 4; CA 1-4R;
obituary CA 102

Smith, Betty (Wehner) 1896-1972... **CLC 19**
See also CA 5-8R; obituary CA 33-36R;
SATA 6; DLB-Y 82

Smith, Cecil Lewis Troughton 1899-1966
See Forester, C(ecil) S(cott)

Smith, Charlotte (Turner)
1749-1806 .... **NCLC 23**
See also DLB 39

Smith, Clark Ashton 1893-1961 .... **CLC 43**

Smith, Dave 1942- .... **CLC 22, 42**
See also Smith, David (Jeddie)
See also CAAS 7; CANR 1; DLB 5

Smith, David (Jeddie) 1942-
See Smith, Dave
See also CANR 1; CA 49-52

Smith, Florence Margaret 1902-1971
See Smith, Stevie
See also CAP 2; CA 17-18;
obituary CA 29-32R

Smith, John 1580?-1631............. **LC 9**
See also DLB 24, 30

Smith, Lee 1944-................. **CLC 25**
See also CA 114, 119; DLB-Y 83

Smith, Martin Cruz 1942-......... **CLC 25**
See also CANR 6; CA 85-88

Smith, Martin William 1942-
See Smith, Martin Cruz

Smith, Mary-Ann Tirone 1944-..... **CLC 39**
See also CA 118

Smith, Patti 1946- .... **CLC 12**
See also CA 93-96

Smith, Pauline (Urmson)
1882-1959 .... **TCLC 25**
See also CA 29-32R; SATA 27

Smith, Rosamond 1938-
See Oates, Joyce Carol

Smith, Sara Mahala Redway 1900-1972
See Benson, Sally

Smith, Stevie 1902-1971.... **CLC 3, 8, 25, 44**
See also Smith, Florence Margaret
See also DLB 20

Smith, Wilbur (Addison) 1933-..... **CLC 33**
See also CANR 7; CA 13-16R

Smith, William Jay 1918- .... **CLC 6**
See also CA 5-8R; SATA 2; DLB 5

Smollett, Tobias (George) 1721-1771 .. **LC 2**
See also DLB 39

Snodgrass, W(illiam) D(e Witt)
1926-................. **CLC 2, 6, 10, 18**
See also CANR 6; CA 1-4R; DLB 5

Snow, C(harles) P(ercy)
1905-1980 .... **CLC 1, 4, 6, 9, 13, 19**
See also CA 5-8R; obituary CA 101;
DLB 15

Snyder, Gary (Sherman)
1930-............... **CLC 1, 2, 5, 9, 32**
See also CA 17-20R; DLB 5, 16

Snyder, Zilpha Keatley 1927-...... **CLC 17**
See also CA 9-12R; SAAS 2; SATA 1, 28

Sobol, Joshua 19??- .... **CLC 60**

Sodergran, Edith 1892-1923....... **TCLC 31**

Sokolov, Raymond 1941-.......... **CLC 7**
See also CA 85-88

Sologub, Fyodor 1863-1927........ **TCLC 9**
See also Teternikov, Fyodor Kuzmich
See also CA 104

Solomos, Dionysios 1798-1857 ... **NCLC 15**

Solwoska, Mara 1929-
See French, Marilyn
See also CANR 3; CA 69-72

Solzhenitsyn, Aleksandr I(sayevich)
1918- ... **CLC 1, 2, 4, 7, 9, 10, 18, 26, 34**
See also CA 69-72

Somers, Jane 1919-
See Lessing, Doris (May)

Sommer, Scott 1951- .... **CLC 25**
See also CA 106

Sondheim, Stephen (Joshua)
1930-.................... **CLC 30, 39**
See also CA 103

Sontag, Susan 1933-... **CLC 1, 2, 10, 13, 31**
See also CA 17-20R; DLB 2

Sophocles
c. 496? B.C.-c. 406? B.C...... **CMLC 2**

Sorrentino, Gilbert
1929-............ **CLC 3, 7, 14, 22, 40**
See also CANR 14; CA 77-80; DLB 5;
DLB-Y 80

Soto, Gary 1952-................. **CLC 32**
See also CA 119

Souster, (Holmes) Raymond
1921-..................... **CLC 5, 14**
See also CANR 13; CA 13-16R

Southern, Terry 1926- .... **CLC 7**
See also CANR 1; CA 1-4R; DLB 2

Southey, Robert 1774-1843 .... **NCLC 8**

Southworth, Emma Dorothy Eliza Nevitte
1819-1899 .... **NCLC 26**

Soyinka, Akinwande Oluwole 1934-
See Soyinka, Wole

Soyinka, Wole 1934- .. **CLC 3, 5, 14, 36, 44**
See also CA 13-16R; DLB-Y 86

Spackman, W(illiam) M(ode)
1905-.................... **CLC 46**
See also CA 81-84

Spacks, Barry 1931-.............. **CLC 14**
See also CA 29-32R

Spanidou, Irini 1946-............. **CLC 44**

Spark, Muriel (Sarah)
1918- .... **CLC 2, 3, 5, 8, 13, 18, 40**
See also CANR 12; CA 5-8R; DLB 15

Spencer, Elizabeth 1921-.......... **CLC 22**
See also CA 13-16R; SATA 14; DLB 6

Spencer, Scott 1945-............. **CLC 30**
See also CA 113; DLB-Y 86

Spender, Stephen (Harold)
1909-................ **CLC 1, 2, 5, 10, 41**
See also CA 9-12R; DLB 20

Spengler, Oswald 1880-1936 ...... **TCLC 25**
See also CA 118

Spenser, Edmund 1552?-1599 .... **LC 5**

Spicer, Jack 1925-1965 .... **CLC 8, 18**
See also CA 85-88; DLB 5, 16

Spielberg, Peter 1929- .... **CLC 6**
See also CANR 4; CA 5-8R; DLB-Y 81

Spielberg, Steven 1947- . . . . CLC 20
See also CA 77-80; SATA 32

Spillane, Frank Morrison 1918-
See Spillane, Mickey
See also CA 25-28R

Spillane, Mickey 1918- . . . . CLC 3, 13
See also Spillane, Frank Morrison

Spinoza, Benedictus de 1632-1677 . . . . LC 9

Spinrad, Norman (Richard) 1940-. . . CLC 46
See also CANR 20; CA 37-40R; DLB 8

Spitteler, Carl (Friedrich Georg)
1845-1924 . . . . TCLC 12
See also CA 109

Spivack, Kathleen (Romola Drucker)
1938- . . . . CLC 6
See also CA 49-52

Spoto, Donald 1941-. . . . . CLC 39
See also CANR 11; CA 65-68

Springsteen, Bruce 1949- . . . . CLC 17
See also CA 111

Spurling, Hilary 1940-. . . . . CLC 34
See also CANR 25; CA 104

Squires, (James) Radcliffe 1917-. . . . CLC 51
See also CANR 6, 21; CA 1-4R

Stael-Holstein, Anne Louise Germaine Necker,
Baronne de 1766-1817 . . . . . . NCLC 3

Stafford, Jean 1915-1979 . . . . . . CLC 4, 7, 19
See also CANR 3; CA 1-4R;
obituary CA 85-88; obituary SATA 22;
DLB 2

Stafford, William (Edgar)
1914- . . . . CLC 4, 7, 29
See also CAAS 3, CANR 5, 22; CA 5-8R;
DLB 5

Stannard, Martin 1947- . . . . CLC 44

Stanton, Maura 1946- . . . . CLC 9
See also CANR 15; CA 89-92

Stapledon, (William) Olaf
1886-1950 . . . . TCLC 22
See also CA 111; DLB 15

Starbuck, George (Edwin) 1931-. . . . CLC 53
See also CANR 23; CA 21-22R

Stark, Richard 1933-
See Westlake, Donald E(dwin)

Stead, Christina (Ellen)
1902-1983 . . . . CLC 2, 5, 8, 32
See also CA 13-16R; obituary CA 109

Steele, Timothy (Reid) 1948-. . . . . . . CLC 45
See also CANR 16; CA 93-96

Steffens, (Joseph) Lincoln
1866-1936 . . . . TCLC 20
See also CA 117; SAAS 1

Stegner, Wallace (Earle) 1909- . . . CLC 9, 49
See also CANR 1, 21; CA 1-4R; DLB 9

Stein, Gertrude 1874-1946 . . . TCLC 1, 6, 28
See also CA 104; DLB 4, 54

Steinbeck, John (Ernst)
1902-1968 . . . . . CLC 1, 5, 9, 13, 21, 34,
45, 59
See also CANR 1; CA 1-4R;
obituary CA 25-28R; SATA 9; DLB 7, 9;
DLB-DS 2

Steiner, George 1929-. . . . . CLC 24
See also CA 73-76

Steiner, Rudolf(us Josephus Laurentius)
1861-1925 . . . . TCLC 13
See also CA 107

Stendhal 1783-1842. . . . . NCLC 23

Stephen, Leslie 1832-1904 . . . . TCLC 23
See also CANR 9; CA 21-24R, 123;
DLB 57

Stephens, James 1882?-1950 . . . . . . TCLC 4
See also CA 104; DLB 19

Stephens, Reed
See Donaldson, Stephen R.

Steptoe, Lydia 1892-1982
See Barnes, Djuna

Sterling, George 1869-1926 . . . . . . TCLC 20
See also CA 117; DLB 54

Stern, Gerald 1925- . . . . CLC 40
See also CA 81-84

Stern, Richard G(ustave) 1928-. . . CLC 4, 39
See also CANR 1, 25; CA 1-4R

Sternberg, Jonas 1894-1969
See Sternberg, Josef von

Sternberg, Josef von 1894-1969 . . . . . CLC 20
See also CA 81-84

Sterne, Laurence 1713-1768. . . . . LC 2
See also DLB 39

Sternheim, (William Adolf) Carl
1878-1942 . . . . TCLC 8
See also CA 105

Stevens, Mark 19??- . . . . CLC 34

Stevens, Wallace 1879-1955. . . . . TCLC 3, 12
See also CA 104, 124; DLB 54

Stevenson, Anne (Katharine)
1933- . . . . CLC 7, 33
See also Elvin, Anne Katharine Stevenson
See also CANR 9; CA 17-18R; DLB 40

Stevenson, Robert Louis
1850-1894 . . . . NCLC 5, 14
See also CLR 10, 11; YABC 2; DLB 18, 57

Stewart, J(ohn) I(nnes) M(ackintosh)
1906- . . . . CLC 7, 14, 32
See also CAAS 3; CA 85-88

Stewart, Mary (Florence Elinor)
1916- . . . . CLC 7, 35
See also CANR 1; CA 1-4R; SATA 12

Stewart, Will 1908-
See Williamson, Jack
See also CANR 23; CA 17-18R

Still, James 1906-. . . . . CLC 49
See also CANR 10; CA 65-68; SATA 29;
DLB 9

Sting 1951-
See The Police

Stitt, Milan 1941-. . . . . CLC 29
See also CA 69-72

Stoker, Abraham
See Stoker, Bram
See also CA 105

Stoker, Bram 1847-1912 . . . . TCLC 8
See also Stoker, Abraham
See also SATA 29; DLB 36, 70

Stolz, Mary (Slattery) 1920-. . . . . . . CLC 12
See also CANR 13; CA 5-8R; SAAS 3;
SATA 10

Stone, Irving 1903-1989. . . . . CLC 7
See also CAAS 3; CANR 1; CA 1-4R;
SATA 3

Stone, Robert (Anthony)
1937?- . . . . CLC 5, 23, 42
See also CANR 23; CA 85-88

Stoppard, Tom
1937- . . . . . . CLC 1, 3, 4, 5, 8, 15, 29, 34
See also CA 81-84; DLB 13; DLB-Y 85

Storey, David (Malcolm)
1933- . . . . CLC 2, 4, 5, 8
See also CA 81-84; DLB 13, 14

Storm, Hyemeyohsts 1935- . . . . CLC 3
See also CA 81-84

Storm, (Hans) Theodor (Woldsen)
1817-1888 . . . . NCLC 1

Storni, Alfonsina 1892-1938 . . . . TCLC 5
See also CA 104

Stout, Rex (Todhunter) 1886-1975 . . . CLC 3
See also CA 61-64

Stow, (Julian) Randolph 1935- . . CLC 23, 48
See also CA 13-16R

Stowe, Harriet (Elizabeth) Beecher
1811-1896 . . . . NCLC 3
See also YABC 1; DLB 1, 12, 42;
CDALB 1865-1917

Strachey, (Giles) Lytton
1880-1932 . . . . TCLC 12
See also CA 110

Strand, Mark 1934- . . . . CLC 6, 18, 41
See also CA 21-24R; SATA 41; DLB 5

Straub, Peter (Francis) 1943- . . . . . . CLC 28
See also CA 85-88; DLB-Y 84

Strauss, Botho 1944- . . . . CLC 22

Straussler, Tomas 1937-
See Stoppard, Tom

Streatfeild, (Mary) Noel 1897- . . . . . CLC 21
See also CA 81-84; obituary CA 120;
SATA 20, 48

Stribling, T(homas) S(igismund)
1881-1965 . . . . CLC 23
See also obituary CA 107; DLB 9

Strindberg, (Johan) August
1849-1912 . . . . TCLC 1, 8, 21
See also CA 104

Stringer, Arthur 1874-1950 . . . . . . TCLC 37
See also DLB 92

Strugatskii, Arkadii (Natanovich)
1925- . . . . CLC 27
See also CA 106

Strugatskii, Boris (Natanovich)
1933- . . . . CLC 27
See also CA 106

Strummer, Joe 1953?-
See The Clash

Stuart, (Hilton) Jesse
1906-1984 . . . . CLC 1, 8, 11, 14, 34
See also CA 5-8R; obituary CA 112;
SATA 2; obituary SATA 36; DLB 9, 48;
DLB-Y 84

Sturgeon, Theodore (Hamilton)
1918-1985 . . . . CLC 22, 39
See also CA 81-84; obituary CA 116;
DLB 8; DLB-Y 85

Styron, William
1925- .... **CLC 1, 3, 5, 11, 15, 60**
See also CANR 6; CA 5-8R; DLB 2;
DLB-Y 80; CDALB 1968-1987

Sudermann, Hermann 1857-1928 .. **TCLC 15**
See also CA 107

Sue, Eugene 1804-1857 .... **NCLC 1**

Sukenick, Ronald 1932- ..... **CLC 3, 4, 6, 48**
See also CA 25-28R; DLB-Y 81

Suknaski, Andrew 1942- .... **CLC 19**
See also CA 101; DLB 53

Sully-Prudhomme, Rene
1839-1907 .... **TCLC 31**

Su Man-shu 1884-1918.......... **TCLC 24**
See also CA 123

Summers, Andrew James 1942-
See The Police

Summers, Andy 1942-
See The Police

Summers, Hollis (Spurgeon, Jr.)
1916- .... **CLC 10**
See also CANR 3; CA 5-8R; DLB 6

Summers, (Alphonsus Joseph-Mary Augustus)
Montague 1880-1948........ **TCLC 16**
See also CA 118

Sumner, Gordon Matthew 1951-
See The Police

Surtees, Robert Smith
1805-1864 .... **NCLC 14**
See also DLB 21

Susann, Jacqueline 1921-1974....... **CLC 3**
See also CA 65-68; obituary CA 53-56

Suskind, Patrick 1949-............ **CLC 44**

Sutcliff, Rosemary 1920- .... **CLC 26**
See also CLR 1; CA 5-8R; SATA 6, 44

Sutro, Alfred 1863-1933.......... **TCLC 6**
See also CA 105; DLB 10

Sutton, Henry 1935-
See Slavitt, David (R.)

Svevo, Italo 1861-1928........ **TCLC 2, 35**
See also Schmitz, Ettore

Swados, Elizabeth 1951- .... **CLC 12**
See also CA 97-100

Swados, Harvey 1920-1972 .... **CLC 5**
See also CANR 6; CA 5-8R;
obituary CA 37-40R; DLB 2

Swarthout, Glendon (Fred) 1918- ... **CLC 35**
See also CANR 1; CA 1-4R; SATA 26

Swenson, May 1919-1989..... **CLC 4, 14, 61**
See also CA 5-8R; SATA 15; DLB 5

Swift, Graham 1949- .... **CLC 41**
See also CA 117, 122

Swift, Jonathan 1667-1745.......... **LC 1**
See also SATA 19; DLB 39

Swinburne, Algernon Charles
1837-1909 .... **TCLC 8, 36**
See also CA 105; DLB 35, 57

Swinfen, Ann 19??-............... **CLC 34**

Swinnerton, Frank (Arthur)
1884-1982 .... **CLC 31**
See also obituary CA 108; DLB 34

Symons, Arthur (William)
1865-1945 .... **TCLC 11**
See also CA 107; DLB 19, 57

Symons, Julian (Gustave)
1912- .... **CLC 2, 14, 32**
See also CAAS 3; CANR 3; CA 49-52

Synge, (Edmund) John Millington
1871-1909 .... **TCLC 6, 37**
See also CA 104; DLB 10, 19

Syruc, J. 1911-
See Milosz, Czeslaw

Szirtes, George 1948-............. **CLC 46**
See also CA 109

Tabori, George 1914- .... **CLC 19**
See also CANR 4; CA 49-52

Tagore, (Sir) Rabindranath
1861-1941 .... **TCLC 3**
See also Thakura, Ravindranatha
See also CA 120

Taine, Hippolyte Adolphe
1828-1893 .... **NCLC 15**

Talese, Gaetano 1932-
See Talese, Gay

Talese, Gay 1932-................ **CLC 37**
See also CANR 9; CA 1-4R

Tallent, Elizabeth (Ann) 1954- ..... **CLC 45**
See also CA 117

Tally, Ted 1952-................. **CLC 42**
See also CA 120, 124

Tamayo y Baus, Manuel
1829-1898 .... **NCLC 1**

Tammsaare, A(nton) H(ansen)
1878-1940 .... **TCLC 27**

Tan, Amy 1952- .... **CLC 59**

Tanizaki, Jun'ichiro
1886-1965 .... **CLC 8, 14, 28**
See also CA 93-96; obituary CA 25-28R

Tarkington, (Newton) Booth
1869-1946 .... **TCLC 9**
See also CA 110; SATA 17; DLB 9

Tasso, Torquato 1544-1595 .... **LC 5**

Tate, (John Orley) Allen
1899-1979 .... **CLC 2, 4, 6, 9, 11, 14, 24**
See also CA 5-8R; obituary CA 85-88;
DLB 4, 45, 63

Tate, James 1943-............ **CLC 2, 6, 25**
See also CA 21-24R; DLB 5

Tavel, Ronald 1940-............... **CLC 6**
See also CA 21-24R

Taylor, C(ecil) P(hillip) 1929-1981 .. **CLC 27**
See also CA 25-28R; obituary CA 105

Taylor, Edward 1644?-1729........ **LC 11**
See also DLB 24

Taylor, Eleanor Ross 1920-......... **CLC 5**
See also CA 81-84

Taylor, Elizabeth 1912-1975 ... **CLC 2, 4, 29**
See also CANR 9; CA 13-16R; SATA 13

Taylor, Henry (Splawn) 1917-...... **CLC 44**
See also CAAS 7; CA 33-36R; DLB 5

Taylor, Kamala (Purnaiya) 1924-
See Markandaya, Kamala
See also CA 77-80

Taylor, Mildred D(elois) 1943- ..... **CLC 21**
See also CLR 9; CANR 25; CA 85-88;
SAAS 5; SATA 15; DLB 52

Taylor, Peter (Hillsman)
1917- .... **CLC 1, 4, 18, 37, 44, 50**
See also CANR 9; CA 13-16R; DLB-Y 81

Taylor, Robert Lewis 1912-........ **CLC 14**
See also CANR 3; CA 1-4R; SATA 10

Teasdale, Sara 1884-1933......... **TCLC 4**
See also CA 104; SATA 32; DLB 45

Tegner, Esaias 1782-1846........ **NCLC 2**

Teilhard de Chardin, (Marie Joseph) Pierre
1881-1955 .... **TCLC 9**
See also CA 105

Tennant, Emma 1937- .... **CLC 13, 52**
See also CAAS 9; CANR 10; CA 65-68;
DLB 14

Teran, Lisa St. Aubin de 19??- ..... **CLC 36**

Terkel, Louis 1912-
See Terkel, Studs
See also CANR 18; CA 57-60

Terkel, Studs 1912- .... **CLC 38**
See also Terkel, Louis

Terry, Megan 1932-............... **CLC 19**
See also CA 77-80; DLB 7

Tertz, Abram 1925-
See Sinyavsky, Andrei (Donatevich)

Tesich, Steve 1943?-.............. **CLC 40**
See also CA 105; DLB-Y 83

Tesich, Stoyan 1943?-
See Tesich, Steve

Teternikov, Fyodor Kuzmich 1863-1927
See Sologub, Fyodor
See also CA 104

Tevis, Walter 1928-1984 .... **CLC 42**
See also CA 113

Tey, Josephine 1897-1952 .... **TCLC 14**
See also Mackintosh, Elizabeth

Thackeray, William Makepeace
1811-1863 .... **NCLC 5, 14, 22**
See also SATA 23; DLB 21, 55

Thakura, Ravindranatha 1861-1941
See Tagore, (Sir) Rabindranath
See also CA 104

Thelwell, Michael (Miles) 1939- .... **CLC 22**
See also CA 101

Theroux, Alexander (Louis)
1939- .... **CLC 2, 25**
See also CANR 20; CA 85-88

Theroux, Paul
1941- .... **CLC 5, 8, 11, 15, 28, 46**
See also CANR 20; CA 33-36R; SATA 44;
DLB 2

Thesen, Sharon 1946-............. **CLC 56**

Thibault, Jacques Anatole Francois
1844-1924
See France, Anatole
See also CA 106

Thiele, Colin (Milton) 1920- .... **CLC 17**
See also CANR 12; CA 29-32R; SAAS 2;
SATA 14

Thomas, Audrey (Grace)
1935- .... **CLC 7, 13, 37**
See also CA 21-24R; DLB 60

Thomas, D(onald) M(ichael)
1935- . . . . CLC **13, 22, 31**
See also CANR 17; CA 61-64; DLB 40

Thomas, Dylan (Marlais)
1914-1953 . . . . TCLC **1, 8**; SSC **3**
See also CA 104, 120; DLB 13, 20

Thomas, Edward (Philip)
1878-1917 . . . . TCLC **10**
See also CA 106; DLB 19

Thomas, John Peter 1928-
See Thomas, Piri

Thomas, Joyce Carol 1938- . . . . CLC **35**
See also CA 113, 116; SATA 40; DLB 33

Thomas, Lewis 1913- . . . . CLC **35**
See also CA 85-88

Thomas, Piri 1928- . . . . CLC **17**
See also CA 73-76

Thomas, R(onald) S(tuart)
1913- . . . . CLC **6, 13, 48**
See also CAAS 4; CA 89-92; DLB 27

Thomas, Ross (Elmore) 1926- . . . . . . CLC **39**
See also CANR 22; CA 33-36R

Thompson, Ernest 1860-1946
See Seton, Ernest (Evan) Thompson

Thompson, Francis (Joseph)
1859-1907 . . . . TCLC **4**
See also CA 104; DLB 19

Thompson, Hunter S(tockton)
1939- . . . . CLC **9, 17, 40**
See also CANR 23; CA 17-20R

Thompson, Judith 1954- . . . . CLC **39**

Thomson, James 1834-1882 . . . . . . NCLC **18**
See also DLB 35

Thoreau, Henry David
1817-1862 . . . . NCLC **7, 21**
See also DLB 1; CDALB 1640-1865

Thurber, James (Grover)
1894-1961 . . . . CLC **5, 11, 25**; SSC **1**
See also CANR 17; CA 73-76; SATA 13;
DLB 4, 11, 22

Thurman, Wallace 1902-1934 . . . . . . TCLC **6**
See also CA 104, 124; DLB 51

Tieck, (Johann) Ludwig
1773-1853 . . . . NCLC **5**

Tillinghast, Richard 1940- . . . . CLC **29**
See also CANR 26; CA 29-32R

Timrod, Henry 1828-1867 . . . . NCLC **25**

Tindall, Gillian 1938- . . . . CLC **7**
See also CANR 11; CA 21-24R

Tiptree, James, Jr. 1915-1987 . . . CLC **48, 50**
See also Sheldon, Alice (Hastings) B(radley)
See also DLB 8

**Tocqueville, Alexis (Charles Henri Maurice
Clerel, Comte) de** 1805-1859 . . NCLC **7**

Tolkien, J(ohn) R(onald) R(euel)
1892-1973 . . . . CLC **1, 2, 3, 8, 12, 38**
See also CAP 2; CA 17-18;
obituary CA 45-48; SATA 2, 32;
obituary SATA 24; DLB 15

Toller, Ernst 1893-1939 . . . . TCLC **10**
See also CA 107

Tolson, Melvin B(eaunorus)
1900?-1966. . . . . CLC **36**
See also CA 124; obituary CA 89-92;
DLB 48, 124

Tolstoy, (Count) Alexey Nikolayevich
1883-1945 . . . . TCLC **18**
See also CA 107

Tolstoy, (Count) Leo (Lev Nikolaevich)
1828-1910 . . . . TCLC **4, 11, 17, 28**
See also CA 104, 123; SATA 26

Tomlin, Lily 1939- . . . . CLC **17**

Tomlin, Mary Jean 1939-
See Tomlin, Lily
See also CA 117

Tomlinson, (Alfred) Charles
1927- . . . . CLC **2, 4, 6, 13, 45**
See also CA 5-8R; DLB 40

Toole, John Kennedy 1937-1969 . . . . CLC **19**
See also CA 104; DLB-Y 81

Toomer, Jean
1894-1967 . . . . . CLC **1, 4, 13, 22**; SSC **1**
See also CA 85-88; DLB 45, 51

Torrey, E. Fuller 19??- . . . . CLC **34**
See also CA 119

Tournier, Michel 1924- . . . . . . CLC **6, 23, 36**
See also CANR 3; CA 49-52; SATA 23

Townsend, Sue 1946- . . . . CLC **61**
See also CA 119, 127; SATA 48, 55

Townshend, Peter (Dennis Blandford)
1945- . . . . CLC **17, 42**
See also CA 107

Tozzi, Federigo 1883-1920 . . . . TCLC **31**

Trakl, Georg 1887-1914 . . . . TCLC **5**
See also CA 104

Transtromer, Tomas (Gosta)
1931- . . . . CLC **52**
See also CA 117

Traven, B. 1890-1969 . . . . CLC **8, 11**
See also CAP 2; CA 19-20;
obituary CA 25-28R; DLB 9, 56

Tremain, Rose 1943- . . . . CLC **42**
See also CA 97-100; DLB 14

Tremblay, Michel 1942- . . . . CLC **29**
See also CA 116; DLB 60

Trevanian 1925- . . . . CLC **29**
See also CA 108

Trevor, William 1928- . . . . . CLC **7, 9, 14, 25**
See also Cox, William Trevor
See also DLB 14

Trifonov, Yuri (Valentinovich)
1925-1981 . . . . CLC **45**
See also obituary CA 103, 126

Trilling, Lionel 1905-1975 . . . . CLC **9, 11, 24**
See also CANR 10; CA 9-12R;
obituary CA 61-64; DLB 28, 63

Trogdon, William 1939-
See Heat Moon, William Least
See also CA 115, 119

Trollope, Anthony 1815-1882 . . . . . NCLC **6**
See also SATA 22; DLB 21, 57

Trotsky, Leon (Davidovich)
1879-1940 . . . . TCLC **22**
See also CA 118

Trotter (Cockburn), Catharine
1679-1749 . . . . LC **8**

Trow, George W. S. 1943- . . . . CLC **52**
See also CA 126

Troyat, Henri 1911- . . . . CLC **23**
See also CANR 2; CA 45-48

Trudeau, G(arretson) B(eekman) 1948-
See Trudeau, Garry
See also CA 81-84; SATA 35

Trudeau, Garry 1948- . . . . CLC **12**
See also Trudeau, G(arretson) B(eekman)

Truffaut, Francois 1932-1984 . . . . . . CLC **20**
See also CA 81-84; obituary CA 113

Trumbo, Dalton 1905-1976 . . . . CLC **19**
See also CANR 10; CA 21-24R;
obituary CA 69-72; DLB 26

Tryon, Thomas 1926- . . . . CLC **3, 11**
See also CA 29-32R

Ts'ao Hsueh-ch'in 1715?-1763 . . . . LC **1**

Tsushima Shuji 1909-1948
See Dazai Osamu
See also CA 107

Tsvetaeva (Efron), Marina (Ivanovna)
1892-1941 . . . . TCLC **7, 35**
See also CA 104, 128

Tunis, John R(oberts) 1889-1975 . . . CLC **12**
See also CA 61-64; SATA 30, 37; DLB 22

Tuohy, Frank 1925- . . . . CLC **37**
See also DLB 14

Tuohy, John Francis 1925-
See Tuohy, Frank
See also CANR 3; CA 5-8R

Turco, Lewis (Putnam) 1934- . . . . . . CLC **11**
See also CANR 24; CA 13-16R; DLB-Y 84

Turgenev, Ivan 1818-1883 . . . . NCLC **21**

Turner, Frederick 1943- . . . . CLC **48**
See also CANR 12; CA 73-76; DLB 40

Tutuola, Amos 1920- . . . . CLC **5, 14, 29**
See also CA 9-12R

Twain, Mark
1835-1910 . . . TCLC **6, 12, 19, 36**; SSC **6**
See also Clemens, Samuel Langhorne
See also YABC 2; DLB 11, 12, 23, 64, 74

Tyler, Anne
1941- . . . . CLC **7, 11, 18, 28, 44, 59**
See also CANR 11; CA 9-12R; SATA 7;
DLB 6; DLB-Y 82

Tyler, Royall 1757-1826 . . . . NCLC **3**
See also DLB 37

Tynan (Hinkson), Katharine
1861-1931 . . . . TCLC **3**
See also CA 104

Tytell, John 1939- . . . . CLC **50**
See also CA 29-32R

Tzara, Tristan 1896-1963 . . . . CLC **47**
See also Rosenfeld, Samuel

Uhry, Alfred 1947?- . . . . CLC **55**
See also CA 127

Unamuno (y Jugo), Miguel de
1864-1936 . . . . TCLC **2, 9**
See also CA 104

Underwood, Miles 1909-1981
See Glassco, John

Undset, Sigrid 1882-1949......... TCLC 3
See also CA 104

Ungaretti, Giuseppe
1888-1970............. CLC 7, 11, 15
See also CAP 2; CA 19-20;
obituary CA 25-28R

Unger, Douglas 1952-........... CLC 34

Unger, Eva 1932-
See Figes, Eva

Updike, John (Hoyer)
1932-...... CLC 1, 2, 3, 5, 7, 9, 13, 15,
23, 34, 43
See also CANR 4; CA 1-4R; CABS 2;
DLB 2, 5; DLB-Y 80, 82; DLB-DS 3

Urdang, Constance (Henriette)
1922-.................... CLC 47
See also CANR 9, 24; CA 21-24R

Uris, Leon (Marcus) 1924-....... CLC 7, 32
See also CANR 1; CA 1-4R; SATA 49

Ustinov, Peter (Alexander) 1921-.... CLC 1
See also CANR 25; CA 13-16R; DLB 13

Vaculik, Ludvik 1926-............. CLC 7
See also CA 53-56

Valenzuela, Luisa 1938-........... CLC 31
See also CA 101

Valera (y Acala-Galiano), Juan
1824-1905................. TCLC 10
See also CA 106

Valery, Paul (Ambroise Toussaint Jules)
1871-1945................ TCLC 4, 15
See also CA 104, 122

Valle-Inclan (y Montenegro), Ramon (Maria)
del 1866-1936............... TCLC 5
See also CA 106

Vallejo, Cesar (Abraham)
1892-1938.................. TCLC 3
See also CA 105

Van Ash, Cay 1918-.............. CLC 34

Vance, Jack 1916?-................ CLC 35
See also DLB 8

Vance, John Holbrook 1916?-
See Vance, Jack
See also CANR 17; CA 29-32R

**Van Den Bogarde, Derek (Jules Gaspard
Ulric) Niven** 1921-
See Bogarde, Dirk
See also CA 77-80

Vandenburgh, Jane 19??-.......... CLC 59

Vanderhaeghe, Guy 1951-.......... CLC 41
See also CA 113

Van der Post, Laurens (Jan) 1906-... CLC 5
See also CA 5-8R

Van de Wetering, Janwillem
1931-..................... CLC 47
See also CANR 4; CA 49-52

Van Dine, S. S. 1888-1939....... TCLC 23

Van Doren, Carl (Clinton)
1885-1950................. TCLC 18
See also CA 111

Van Doren, Mark 1894-1972..... CLC 6, 10
See also CANR 3; CA 1-4R;
obituary CA 37-40R; DLB 45

Van Druten, John (William)
1901-1957.................. TCLC 2
See also CA 104; DLB 10

Van Duyn, Mona 1921-.......... CLC 3, 7
See also CANR 7; CA 9-12R; DLB 5

Van Itallie, Jean-Claude 1936-...... CLC 3
See also CAAS 2; CANR 1; CA 45-48;
DLB 7

Van Ostaijen, Paul 1896-1928..... TCLC 33

Van Peebles, Melvin 1932-...... CLC 2, 20
See also CA 85-88

Vansittart, Peter 1920-............ CLC 42
See also CANR 3; CA 1-4R

Van Vechten, Carl 1880-1964 ...... CLC 33
See also obituary CA 89-92; DLB 4, 9, 51

Van Vogt, A(lfred) E(lton) 1912-..... CLC 1
See also CA 21-24R; SATA 14; DLB 8

Varda, Agnes 1928-.............. CLC 16
See also CA 116, 122

Vargas Llosa, (Jorge) Mario (Pedro)
1936-...... CLC 3, 6, 9, 10, 15, 31, 42
See also CANR 18; CA 73-76

Vassilikos, Vassilis 1933-........ CLC 4, 8
See also CA 81-84

Vazov, Ivan 1850-1921.......... TCLC 25
See also CA 121

Veblen, Thorstein Bunde
1857-1929................. TCLC 31
See also CA 115

Verga, Giovanni 1840-1922....... TCLC 3
See also CA 104, 123

Verhaeren, Emile (Adolphe Gustave)
1855-1916................. TCLC 12
See also CA 109

Verlaine, Paul (Marie) 1844-1896.. NCLC 2

Verne, Jules (Gabriel) 1828-1905 ... TCLC 6
See also CA 110; SATA 21

Very, Jones 1813-1880.......... NCLC 9
See also DLB 1

Vesaas, Tarjei 1897-1970......... CLC 48
See also obituary CA 29-32R

Vian, Boris 1920-1959 .... TCLC 9
See also CA 106; DLB 72

Viaud, (Louis Marie) Julien 1850-1923
See Loti, Pierre
See also CA 107

Vicker, Angus 1916-
See Felsen, Henry Gregor

Vidal, Eugene Luther, Jr. 1925-
See Vidal, Gore

Vidal, Gore
1925-........ CLC 2, 4, 6, 8, 10, 22, 33
See also CANR 13; CA 5-8R; DLB 6

Viereck, Peter (Robert Edwin)
1916-...................... CLC 4
See also CANR 1; CA 1-4R; DLB 5

Vigny, Alfred (Victor) de
1797-1863................. NCLC 7

Vilakazi, Benedict Wallet
1905-1947................ TCLC 37

**Villiers de l'Isle Adam, Jean Marie Mathias
Philippe Auguste, Comte de,**
1838-1889................ NCLC 3

Vinci, Leonardo da 1452-1519....... LC 12

Vine, Barbara 1930-............. CLC 50
See also Rendell, Ruth

Vinge, Joan (Carol) D(ennison)
1948-..................... CLC 30
See also CA 93-96; SATA 36

Visconti, Luchino 1906-1976....... CLC 16
See also CA 81-84; obituary CA 65-68

Vittorini, Elio 1908-1966...... CLC 6, 9, 14
See also obituary CA 25-28R

Vizinczey, Stephen 1933-......... CLC 40

Vliet, R(ussell) G(ordon)
1929-1984................. CLC 22
See also CANR 18; CA 37-40R;
obituary CA 112

Voight, Ellen Bryant 1943-....... CLC 54
See also CANR 11; CA 69-72

Voigt, Cynthia 1942-............ CLC 30
See also CANR 18; CA 106; SATA 33, 48

Voinovich, Vladimir (Nikolaevich)
1932-.................. CLC 10, 49
See also CA 81-84

Voltaire 1694-1778............... LC 14

Von Daeniken, Erich 1935-
See Von Daniken, Erich
See also CANR 17; CA 37-40R

Von Daniken, Erich 1935-......... CLC 30
See also Von Daeniken, Erich

Vonnegut, Kurt, Jr.
1922-...... CLC 1, 2, 3, 4, 5, 8, 12, 22,
40, 60
See also CANR 1; CA 1-4R; DLB 2, 8;
DLB-Y 80; DLB-DS 3;
CDALB 1968-1987

Vorster, Gordon 1924-............ CLC 34

Voznesensky, Andrei 1933-... CLC 1, 15, 57
See also CA 89-92

Waddington, Miriam 1917-........ CLC 28
See also CANR 12; CA 21-24R

Wagman, Fredrica 1937-........... CLC 7
See also CA 97-100

Wagner, Richard 1813-1883....... NCLC 9

Wagner-Martin, Linda 1936-...... CLC 50

Wagoner, David (Russell)
1926-................... CLC 3, 5, 15
See also CAAS 3; CANR 2; CA 1-4R;
SATA 14; DLB 5

Wah, Fred(erick James) 1939-...... CLC 44
See also CA 107; DLB 60

Wahloo, Per 1926-1975........... CLC 7
See also CA 61-64

Wahloo, Peter 1926-1975
See Wahloo, Per

Wain, John (Barrington)
1925-............CLC 2, 11, 15, 46
See also CAAS 4; CANR 23; CA 5-8R;
DLB 15, 27

Wajda, Andrzej 1926-............ CLC 16
See also CA 102

Wakefield, Dan 1932-............. CLC 7
See also CAAS 7; CA 21-24R

Wakoski, Diane
1937- .... CLC 2, 4, 7, 9, 11, 40
See also CAAS 1; CANR 9; CA 13-16R;
DLB 5

Walcott, Derek (Alton)
1930- .... CLC 2, 4, 9, 14, 25, 42
See also CANR 26; CA 89-92; DLB-Y 81

Waldman, Anne 1945- .... CLC 7
See also CA 37-40R; DLB 16

Waldo, Edward Hamilton 1918-
See Sturgeon, Theodore (Hamilton)

Walker, Alice
1944- ...... CLC 5, 6, 9, 19, 27, 46, 58;
SSC 5
See also CANR 9, 27; CA 37-40R;
SATA 31; DLB 6, 33; CDALB 1968-1988

Walker, David Harry 1911-........ CLC 14
See also CANR 1; CA 1-4R; SATA 8

Walker, Edward Joseph 1934-
See Walker, Ted
See also CANR 12; CA 21-24R

Walker, George F. 1947-....... CLC 44, 61
See also CANR 21; CA 103; DLB 60

Walker, Joseph A. 1935-.......... CLC 19
See also CANR 26; CA 89-92; DLB 38

Walker, Margaret (Abigail)
1915-....................... CLC 1, 6
See also CANR 26; CA 73-76; DLB 76

Walker, Ted 1934- .... CLC 13
See also Walker, Edward Joseph
See also DLB 40

Wallace, David Foster 1962-....... CLC 50

Wallace, Irving 1916-........... CLC 7, 13
See also CAAS 1; CANR 1; CA 1-4R

Wallant, Edward Lewis
1926-1962 .... CLC 5, 10
See also CANR 22; CA 1-4R; DLB 2, 28

Walpole, Horace 1717-1797.......... LC 2
See also DLB 39

Walpole, (Sir) Hugh (Seymour)
1884-1941 .... TCLC 5
See also CA 104; DLB 34

Walser, Martin 1927-............. CLC 27
See also CANR 8; CA 57-60; DLB 75

Walser, Robert 1878-1956....... TCLC 18
See also CA 118; DLB 66

Walsh, Gillian Paton 1939-
See Walsh, Jill Paton
See also CA 37-40R; SATA 4

Walsh, Jill Paton 1939-.......... CLC 35
See also CLR 2; SAAS 3

Wambaugh, Joseph (Aloysius, Jr.)
1937-..................... CLC 3, 18
See also CA 33-36R; DLB 6; DLB-Y 83

Ward, Arthur Henry Sarsfield 1883-1959
See Rohmer, Sax
See also CA 108

Ward, Douglas Turner 1930-....... CLC 19
See also CA 81-84; DLB 7, 38

Warhol, Andy 1928-1987.......... CLC 20
See also CA 89-92; obituary CA 121

Warner, Francis (Robert le Plastrier)
1937-..................... CLC 14
See also CANR 11; CA 53-56

Warner, Marina 1946-............ CLC 59
See also CANR 21; CA 65-68

Warner, Rex (Ernest) 1905-1986.... CLC 45
See also CA 89-92; obituary CA 119;
DLB 15

Warner, Sylvia Townsend
1893-1978 .... CLC 7, 19
See also CANR 16; CA 61-64;
obituary CA 77-80; DLB 34

Warren, Mercy Otis 1728-1814... NCLC 13
See also DLB 31

Warren, Robert Penn
1905-1989 ... CLC 1, 4, 6, 8, 10, 13, 18,
39, 53, 59; SSC 4
See also CANR 10; CA 13-16R. 129. 130;
SATA 46; DLB 2, 48; DLB-Y 80;
CDALB 1968-1987

Washington, Booker T(aliaferro)
1856-1915 .... TCLC 10
See also CA 114, 125; SATA 28

Wassermann, Jakob 1873-1934..... TCLC 6
See also CA 104; DLB 66

Wasserstein, Wendy 1950-...... CLC 32, 59
See also CA 121; CABS 3

Waterhouse, Keith (Spencer)
1929-...................... CLC 47
See also CA 5-8R; DLB 13, 15

Waters, Roger 1944-
See Pink Floyd

Wa Thiong'o, Ngugi
1938- .... CLC 3, 7, 13, 36
See also Ngugi, James (Thiong'o); Ngugi wa
Thiong'o

Watkins, Paul 1964-.............. CLC 55

Watkins, Vernon (Phillips)
1906-1967 .... CLC 43
See also CAP 1; CA 9-10;
obituary CA 25-28R; DLB 20

Waugh, Auberon (Alexander) 1939-.. CLC 7
See also CANR 6, 22; CA 45-48; DLB 14

Waugh, Evelyn (Arthur St. John)
1903-1966 ... CLC 1, 3, 8, 13, 19, 27, 44
See also CANR 22; CA 85-88;
obituary CA 25-28R; DLB 15

Waugh, Harriet 1944- .... CLC 6
See also CANR 22, CA 85-88

Webb, Beatrice (Potter)
1858-1943 .... TCLC 22
See also CA 117

Webb, Charles (Richard) 1939-...... CLC 7
See also CA 25-28R

Webb, James H(enry), Jr. 1946-.... CLC 22
See also CA 81-84

Webb, Mary (Gladys Meredith)
1881-1927 .... TCLC 24
See also CA 123; DLB 34

Webb, Phyllis 1927-.............. CLC 18
See also CANR 23; CA 104; DLB 53

Webb, Sidney (James)
1859-1947 .... TCLC 22
See also CA 117

Webber, Andrew Lloyd 1948-...... CLC 21

Weber, Lenora Mattingly
1895-1971 .... CLC 12
See also CAP 1; CA 19-20;
obituary CA 29-32R; SATA 2;
obituary SATA 26

Wedekind, (Benjamin) Frank(lin)
1864-1918 .... TCLC 7
See also CA 104

Weidman, Jerome 1913-............ CLC 7
See also CANR 1; CA 1-4R; DLB 28

Weil, Simone 1909-1943.......... TCLC 23
See also CA 117

Weinstein, Nathan Wallenstein 1903?-1940
See West, Nathanael
See also CA 104

Weir, Peter 1944-................ CLC 20
See also CA 113, 123

Weiss, Peter (Ulrich)
1916-1982 .... CLC 3, 15, 51
See also CANR 3; CA 45-48;
obituary CA 106; DLB 69

Weiss, Theodore (Russell)
1916-.................... CLC 3, 8, 14
See also CAAS 2; CA 9-12R; DLB 5

Welch, (Maurice) Denton
1915-1948 .... TCLC 22
See also CA 121

Welch, James 1940-......... CLC 6, 14, 52
See also CA 85-88

Weldon, Fay
1933- .... CLC 6, 9, 11, 19, 36, 59
See also CANR 16; CA 21-24R; DLB 14

Wellek, Rene 1903- .... CLC 28
See also CAAS 7; CANR 8; CA 5-8R;
DLB 63

Weller, Michael 1942-......... CLC 10, 53
See also CA 85-88

Weller, Paul 1958-................ CLC 26

Wellershoff, Dieter 1925-.......... CLC 46
See also CANR 16; CA 89-92

Welles, (George) Orson
1915-1985 .... CLC 20
See also CA 93-96; obituary CA 117

Wellman, Manly Wade 1903-1986 .. CLC 49
See also CANR 6, 16; CA 1-4R;
obituary CA 118; SATA 6, 47

Wells, Carolyn 1862-1942 .... TCLC 35
See also CA 113; DLB 11

Wells, H(erbert) G(eorge)
1866-1946 ...... TCLC 6, 12, 19; SSC 6
See also CA 110, 121; SATA 20; DLB 34,
70

Wells, Rosemary 1943-............ CLC 12
See also CLR 16; CA 85-88; SAAS 1;
SATA 18

Welty, Eudora (Alice)
1909- .... CLC 1, 2, 5, 14, 22, 33; SSC 1
See also CA 9-12R; CABS 1; DLB 2;
DLB-Y 87; CDALB 1941-1968

Wen I-to 1899-1946 .... TCLC 28

Werfel, Franz (V.) 1890-1945 ...... TCLC 8
See also CA 104

Wergeland, Henrik Arnold
1808-1845 .... NCLC 5

Wersba, Barbara 1932-........... **CLC 30**
See also CLR 3; CANR 16; CA 29-32R;
SAAS 2; SATA 1; DLB 52

Wertmuller, Lina 1928-.......... **CLC 16**
See also CA 97-100

Wescott, Glenway 1901-1987....... **CLC 13**
See also CANR 23; CA 13-16R;
obituary CA 121; DLB 4, 9

Wesker, Arnold 1932-........ **CLC 3, 5, 42**
See also CAAS 7; CANR 1; CA 1-4R;
DLB 13

Wesley, Richard (Errol) 1945-....... **CLC 7**
See also CA 57-60; DLB 38

Wessel, Johan Herman 1742-1785 .... **LC 7**

West, Anthony (Panther)
1914-1987 .... **CLC 50**
See also CANR 3, 19; CA 45-48; DLB 15

West, Jessamyn 1907-1984 ...... **CLC 7, 17**
See also CA 9-12R; obituary CA 112;
obituary SATA 37; DLB 6; DLB-Y 84

West, Morris L(anglo) 1916-..... **CLC 6, 33**
See also CA 5-8R; obituary CA 124

West, Nathanael 1903?-1940 .... **TCLC 1, 14**
See also Weinstein, Nathan Wallenstein
See also CA 125; DLB 4, 9, 28

West, Paul 1930- .... **CLC 7, 14**
See also CAAS 7; CANR 22; CA 13-16R;
DLB 14

West, Rebecca 1892-1983 .. **CLC 7, 9, 31, 50**
See also CANR 19; CA 5-8R;
obituary CA 109; DLB 36; DLB-Y 83

Westall, Robert (Atkinson) 1929-... **CLC 17**
See also CLR 13; CANR 18; CA 69-72;
SAAS 2; SATA 23

Westlake, Donald E(dwin)
1933-.................... **CLC 7, 33**
See also CANR 16; CA 17-20R

Westmacott, Mary 1890-1976
See Christie, (Dame) Agatha (Mary
Clarissa)

Whalen, Philip 1923-........... **CLC 6, 29**
See also CANR 5; CA 9-12R; DLB 16

Wharton, Edith (Newbold Jones)
1862-1937 .... **TCLC 3, 9, 27; SSC 6**
See also CA 104; DLB 4, 9, 12, 78;
CDALB 1865-1917

Wharton, William 1925-........ **CLC 18, 37**
See also CA 93-96; DLB-Y 80

Wheatley (Peters), Phillis
1753?-1784.................... **LC 3**
See also DLB 31, 50; CDALB 1640-1865

Wheelock, John Hall 1886-1978.... **CLC 14**
See also CANR 14; CA 13-16R;
obituary CA 77-80; DLB 45

Whelan, John 1900-
See O'Faolain, Sean

Whitaker, Rodney 1925-
See Trevanian

White, E(lwyn) B(rooks)
1899-1985 .... **CLC 10, 34, 39**
See also CLR 1; CANR 16; CA 13-16R;
obituary CA 116; SATA 2, 29;
obituary SATA 44; DLB 11, 22

White, Edmund III 1940-......... **CLC 27**
See also CANR 3, 19; CA 45-48

White, Patrick (Victor Martindale)
1912- .... **CLC 3, 4, 5, 7, 9, 18**
See also CA 81-84

White, T(erence) H(anbury)
1906-1964 .... **CLC 30**
See also CA 73-76; SATA 12

White, Terence de Vere 1912-...... **CLC 49**
See also CANR 3; CA 49-52

White, Walter (Francis)
1893-1955 .... **TCLC 15**
See also CA 115, 124; DLB 51

White, William Hale 1831-1913
See Rutherford, Mark
See also CA 121

Whitehead, E(dward) A(nthony)
1933- .... **CLC 5**
See also CA 65-68

Whitemore, Hugh 1936-.......... **CLC 37**

Whitman, Sarah Helen
1803-1878 .... **NCLC 19**
See also DLB 1

Whitman, Walt 1819-1892........ **NCLC 4**
See also SATA 20; DLB 3, 64;
CDALB 1640-1865

Whitney, Phyllis A(yame) 1903-.... **CLC 42**
See also CANR 3, 25; CA 1-4R; SATA 1,
30

Whittemore, (Edward) Reed (Jr.)
1919- .... **CLC 4**
See also CANR 4; CA 9-12R; DLB 5

Whittier, John Greenleaf
1807-1892 .... **NCLC 8**
See also DLB 1; CDALB 1640-1865

Wicker, Thomas Grey 1926-
See Wicker, Tom
See also CANR 21; CA 65-68

Wicker, Tom 1926-................ **CLC 7**
See also Wicker, Thomas Grey

Wideman, John Edgar
1941-................... **CLC 5, 34, 36**
See also CANR 14; CA 85-88; DLB 33

Wiebe, Rudy (H.) 1934-...... **CLC 6, 11, 14**
See also CA 37-40R; DLB 60

Wieland, Christoph Martin
1733-1813 .... **NCLC 17**

Wieners, John 1934-............... **CLC 7**
See also CA 13-16R; DLB 16

Wiesel, Elie(zer) 1928-..... **CLC 3, 5, 11, 37**
See also CAAS 4; CANR 8; CA 5-8R;
DLB-Y 87

Wiggins, Marianne 1948-.......... **CLC 57**

Wight, James Alfred 1916-
See Herriot, James
See also CA 77-80; SATA 44

Wilbur, Richard (Purdy)
1921- .... **CLC 3, 6, 9, 14, 53**
See also CANR 2; CA 1-4R; CABS 2;
SATA 9; DLB 5

Wild, Peter 1940-................ **CLC 14**
See also CA 37-40R; DLB 5

Wilde, Oscar (Fingal O'Flahertie Wills)
1854-1900 .... **TCLC 1, 8, 23**
See also CA 104; SATA 24; DLB 10, 19,
34, 57

Wilder, Billy 1906-............... **CLC 20**
See also Wilder, Samuel
See also DLB 26

Wilder, Samuel 1906-
See Wilder, Billy
See also CA 89-92

Wilder, Thornton (Niven)
1897-1975 ...... **CLC 1, 5, 6, 10, 15, 35**
See also CA 13-16R; obituary CA 61-64;
DLB 4, 7, 9

Wiley, Richard 1944-............. **CLC 44**
See also CA 121

Wilhelm, Kate 1928-............... **CLC 7**
See also CAAS 5; CANR 17; CA 37-40R;
DLB 8

Willard, Nancy 1936-.......... **CLC 7, 37**
See also CLR 5; CANR 10; CA 89-92;
SATA 30, 37; DLB 5, 52

Williams, C(harles) K(enneth)
1936-.................... **CLC 33, 56**
See also CA 37-40R; DLB 5

Williams, Charles (Walter Stansby)
1886-1945 ....**TCLC 1, 11**
See also CA 104

Williams, Ella Gwendolen Rees 1890-1979
See Rhys, Jean

Williams, (George) Emlyn
1905-1987 .... **CLC 15**
See also CA 104, 123; DLB 10

Williams, Hugo 1942-............. **CLC 42**
See also CA 17-20R; DLB 40

Williams, John A(lfred) 1925-.... **CLC 5, 13**
See also CAAS 3; CANR 6, 26; CA 53-56;
DLB 2, 33

Williams, Jonathan (Chamberlain)
1929- .... **CLC 13**
See also CANR 8; CA 9-12R; DLB 5

Williams, Joy 1944-.............. **CLC 31**
See also CANR 22; CA 41-44R

Williams, Norman 1952-.......... **CLC 39**
See also CA 118

Williams, Paulette 1948-
See Shange, Ntozake

Williams, Tennessee
1911-1983 .... **CLC 1, 2, 5, 7, 8, 11, 15,
19, 30, 39, 45**
See also CA 5-8R; obituary CA 108; DLB 7;
DLB-Y 83; DLB-DS 4;
CDALB 1941-1968

Williams, Thomas (Alonzo) 1926-... **CLC 14**
See also CANR 2; CA 1-4R

Williams, Thomas Lanier 1911-1983
See Williams, Tennessee

Williams, William Carlos
1883-1963 .... **CLC 1, 2, 5, 9, 13, 22, 42**
See also CA 89-92; DLB 4, 16, 54

Williamson, David 1932-.......... **CLC 56**

Williamson, Jack 1908-........... **CLC 29**
See also Williamson, John Stewart
See also DLB 8

Williamson, John Stewart 1908-
See Williamson, Jack
See also CANR 123; CA 17-20R

Willingham, Calder (Baynard, Jr.)
1922- . . . . CLC 5, 51
See also CANR 3; CA 5-8R; DLB 2, 44

Wilson, A(ndrew) N(orman) 1950- . . CLC 33
See also CA 112; DLB 14

Wilson, Andrew 1948-
See Wilson, Snoo

Wilson, Angus (Frank Johnstone)
1913- . . . . CLC 2, 3, 5, 25, 34
See also CANR 21; CA 5-8R; DLB 15

Wilson, August 1945- . . . . CLC 39, 50
See also CA 115, 122

Wilson, Brian 1942- . . . . CLC 12

Wilson, Colin 1931- . . . . CLC 3, 14
See also CAAS 5; CANR 1, 122; CA 1-4R;
DLB 14

Wilson, Edmund
1895-1972 . . . . CLC 1, 2, 3, 8, 24
See also CANR 1; CA 1-4R;
obituary CA 37-40R; DLB 63

Wilson, Ethel Davis (Bryant)
1888-1980 . . . . CLC 13
See also CA 102; DLB 68

Wilson, John 1785-1854 . . . . NCLC 5

Wilson, John (Anthony) Burgess 1917-
See Burgess, Anthony
See also CANR 2; CA 1-4R

Wilson, Lanford 1937- . . . . CLC 7, 14, 36
See also CA 17-20R; DLB 7

Wilson, Robert (M.) 1944- . . . . CLC 7, 9
See also CANR 2; CA 49-52

Wilson, Sloan 1920- . . . . CLC 32
See also CANR 1; CA 1-4R

Wilson, Snoo 1948- . . . . CLC 33
See also CA 69-72

Wilson, William S(mith) 1932- . . . . . CLC 49
See also CA 81-84

Winchilsea, Anne (Kingsmill) Finch, Countess
of 1661-1720 . . . . LC 3

Winters, Janet Lewis 1899-
See Lewis (Winters), Janet
See also CAP 1; CA 9-10

Winters, (Arthur) Yvor
1900-1968 . . . . CLC 4, 8, 32
See also CAP 1; CA 11-12;
obituary CA 25-28R; DLB 48

Wiseman, Frederick 1930- . . . . CLC 20

Wister, Owen 1860-1938 . . . . TCLC 21
See also CA 108; DLB 9

Witkiewicz, Stanislaw Ignacy
1885-1939 . . . . TCLC 8
See also CA 105

Wittig, Monique 1935?- . . . . CLC 22
See also CA 116

Wittlin, Joseph 1896-1976 . . . . CLC 25
See also Wittlin, Jozef

Wittlin, Jozef 1896-1976
See Wittlin, Joseph
See also CANR 3; CA 49-52;
obituary CA 65-68

Wodehouse, (Sir) P(elham) G(renville)
1881-1975 . . . CLC 1, 2, 5, 10, 22; SSC 2
See also CANR 3; CA 45-48;
obituary CA 57-60; SATA 22; DLB 34

Woiwode, Larry (Alfred) 1941- . . . CLC 6, 10
See also CANR 16; CA 73-76; DLB 6

Wojciechowska, Maia (Teresa)
1927- . . . . CLC 26
See also CLR 1; CANR 4; CA 9-12R;
SAAS 1; SATA 1, 28

Wolf, Christa 1929- . . . . CLC 14, 29, 58
See also CA 85-88

Wolfe, Gene (Rodman) 1931- . . . . . . CLC 25
See also CANR 6; CA 57-60; DLB 8

Wolfe, George C. 1954- . . . . CLC 49

Wolfe, Thomas (Clayton)
1900-1938 . . . . TCLC 4, 13, 29
See also CA 104; DLB 9; DLB-Y 85;
DLB-DS 2

Wolfe, Thomas Kennerly, Jr. 1931-
See Wolfe, Tom
See also CANR 9; CA 13-16R

Wolfe, Tom 1931- . . . CLC 1, 2, 9, 15, 35, 51
See also Wolfe, Thomas Kennerly, Jr.

Wolff, Geoffrey (Ansell) 1937- . . . . . CLC 41
See also CA 29-32R

Wolff, Tobias (Jonathan Ansell)
1945- . . . . CLC 39
See also CA 114, 117

Wolfram von Eschenbach
c. 1170-c. 1220 . . . . CMLC 5

Wolitzer, Hilma 1930- . . . . CLC 17
See also CANR 18; CA 65-68; SATA 31

Wollstonecraft (Godwin), Mary
1759-1797 . . . . LC 5
See also DLB 39

Wonder, Stevie 1950- . . . . CLC 12
See also Morris, Steveland Judkins

Wong, Jade Snow 1922- . . . . CLC 17
See also CA 109

Woodcott, Keith 1934-
See Brunner, John (Kilian Houston)

Woolf, (Adeline) Virginia
1882-1941 . . . . TCLC 1, 5, 20
See also CA 104; DLB 36

Woollcott, Alexander (Humphreys)
1887-1943 . . . . TCLC 5
See also CA 105; DLB 29

Wordsworth, Dorothy
1771-1855 . . . . NCLC 25

Wordsworth, William 1770-1850 . . NCLC 12

Wouk, Herman 1915- . . . . CLC 1, 9, 38
See also CANR 6; CA 5-8R; DLB-Y 82

Wright, Charles 1935- . . . . CLC 6, 13, 28
See also CAAS 7; CA 29-32R; DLB-Y 82

Wright, Charles (Stevenson) 1932- . . CLC 49
See also CA 9-12R; DLB 33

Wright, James (Arlington)
1927-1980 . . . . CLC 3, 5, 10, 28
See also CANR 4; CA 49-52;
obituary CA 97-100; DLB 5

Wright, Judith 1915- . . . . CLC 11, 53
See also CA 13-16R; SATA 14

Wright, L(aurali) R. 1939- . . . . CLC 44

Wright, Richard B(ruce) 1937- . . . . . . CLC 6
See also CA 85-88; DLB 53

Wright, Richard (Nathaniel)
1908-1960 . . . CLC 1, 3, 4, 9, 14, 21, 48;
SSC 2
See also CA 108; DLB-DS 2

Wright, Rick 1945-
See Pink Floyd

Wright, Stephen 1946- . . . . CLC 33

Wright, Willard Huntington 1888-1939
See Van Dine, S. S.
See also CA 115

Wright, William 1930- . . . . CLC 44
See also CANR 7, 23; CA 53-56

Wu Ch'eng-en 1500?-1582? . . . . LC 7

Wu Ching-tzu 1701-1754 . . . . LC 2

Wurlitzer, Rudolph 1938?- . . . . . CLC 2, 4, 15
See also CA 85-88

Wycherley, William 1640?-1716 . . . . . . LC 8

Wylie (Benet), Elinor (Morton Hoyt)
1885-1928 . . . . TCLC 8
See also CA 105; DLB 9, 45

Wylie, Philip (Gordon) 1902-1971 . . . CLC 43
See also CAP 2; CA 21-22;
obituary CA 33-36R; DLB 9

Wyndham, John 1903-1969 . . . . CLC 19
See also Harris, John (Wyndham Parkes
Lucas) Beynon

Wyss, Johann David 1743-1818 . . NCLC 10
See also SATA 27, 29

Yanovsky, Vassily S(emenovich)
1906-1989 . . . . CLC 2, 18
See also CA 97-100

Yates, Richard 1926- . . . . CLC 7, 8, 23
See also CANR 10; CA 5-8R; DLB 2;
DLB-Y 81

Yeats, William Butler
1865-1939 . . . . TCLC 1, 11, 18, 31
See also CANR 10; CA 104; DLB 10, 19

Yehoshua, A(braham) B.
1936- . . . . CLC 13, 31
See also CA 33-36R

Yep, Laurence (Michael) 1948- . . . . . CLC 35
See also CLR 3; CANR 1; CA 49-52;
SATA 7; DLB 52

Yerby, Frank G(arvin) 1916- . . . CLC 1, 7, 22
See also CANR 16; CA 9-12R; DLB 76

Yevtushenko, Yevgeny (Alexandrovich)
1933- . . . . CLC 1, 3, 13, 26, 51
See also CA 81-84

Yezierska, Anzia 1885?-1970 . . . . CLC 46
See also CA 126; obituary CA 89-92;
DLB 28

Yglesias, Helen 1915- . . . . CLC 7, 22
See also CANR 15; CA 37-40R

Yorke, Henry Vincent 1905-1974
See Green, Henry
See also CA 85-88; obituary CA 49-52

Young, Al 1939- . . . . CLC 19
See also CANR 26; CA 29-32R; DLB 33

Young, Andrew 1885-1971 . . . . CLC 5
See also CANR 7; CA 5-8R

Young, Edward 1683-1765 . . . . LC 3

Young, Neil 1945- . . . . CLC 17
See also CA 110

Yourcenar, Marguerite
1903-1987 . . . . CLC 19, 38, 50
See also CANR 23; CA 69-72; DLB 72

Yurick, Sol 1925- . . . . CLC 6
See also CANR 25; CA 13-16R

Zamyatin, Yevgeny Ivanovich
1884-1937 . . . . TCLC 8, 37
See also CA 105

Zangwill, Israel 1864-1926 . . . . TCLC 16
See also CA 109; DLB 10

Zappa, Francis Vincent, Jr. 1940-
See Zappa, Frank
See also CA 108

Zappa, Frank 1940- . . . . CLC 17
See also Zappa, Francis Vincent, Jr.

Zaturenska, Marya 1902-1982 . . . . CLC 6, 11
See also CANR 22; CA 13-16R;
obituary CA 105

Zelazny, Roger 1937- . . . . CLC 21
See also CANR 26; CA 21-24R; SATA 39;
DLB 8

Zhdanov, Andrei A(lexandrovich)
1896-1948 . . . . TCLC 18
See also CA 117

Ziegenhagen, Eric 1970- . . . . CLC 55

Zimmerman, Robert 1941-
See Dylan, Bob

Zindel, Paul 1936- . . . . CLC 6, 26
See also CLR 3; CA 73-76; SATA 16;
DLB 7, 52

Zinoviev, Alexander 1922- . . . . CLC 19
See also CA 116

Zola, Emile 1840-1902 . . . . . . TCLC 1, 6, 21
See also CA 104

Zorrilla y Moral, Jose 1817-1893 . . NCLC 6

Zoshchenko, Mikhail (Mikhailovich)
1895-1958 . . . . TCLC 15
See also CA 115

Zuckmayer, Carl 1896-1977 . . . . CLC 18
See also CA 69-72; DLB 56

Zukofsky, Louis
1904-1978 . . . . CLC 1, 2, 4, 7, 11, 18
See also CA 9-12R; obituary CA 77-80;
DLB 5

Zweig, Paul 1935-1984 . . . . CLC 34, 42
See also CA 85-88; obituary CA 113

Zweig, Stefan 1881-1942 . . . . TCLC 17
See also CA 112

Literary Criticism Series
Cumulative Topic Index

This index lists all topic entries in the Gale Literary Criticism Series *Contemporary Literary Criticism,*
Literature Criticism from 1400 to 1800, Nineteenth-Century Literature Criticism, and *Twentieth-Century Literary Criticism.*

The American Frontier in Literature NCLC
28: 1-103
    definitions, 2-12
    development, 12-17
    nonfiction writing about the frontier,
      17-30
    frontier fiction, 30-45
    frontier protagonists, 45-66
    portrayals of feminist readings, 86-98
    Native Americans, 66-86
    feminist readings, 86-98
    twentieth-century reaction against frontier
      literature, 98-100

***Bildungsroman* in Nineteenth-Century
Literature** NCLC 20: 92-168
    surveys, 93-113
    in Germany, 113-40
    in England, 140-56
    female *Bildungsroman*, 156-67

Bloomsbury Group TCLC 34: 1-73
    history and major figures, 2-13
    definitions, 13-17
    influences, 17-27
    thought, 27-40
    prose, 40-52
    and literary criticism, 52-4
    political ideals, 54-61
    response to, 61-71

Businessman in American Literature TCLC
26: 1-48
    portrayal of the businessman, 1-32
    themes and techniques in business fiction,
      32-47

Civic Critics, Russian NCLC 20: 402-46
    principal figures and background, 402-09
    and Russian Nihilism, 410-16
    aesthetic and critical views, 416-45

de Man, Paul, Wartime Journalism CLC
55: 382-424

Detective Fiction TCLC 38: 1-96
    genesis and history of the detective story,
      3-22
    defining detective fiction, 22-32
    evolution and varieties, 32-77
    the appeal of detective fiction, 77-90

Eliot, T. S., Centenary of Birth CLC 55:
345-75

English Caroline Literature LC 13: 221-307
    background, 222-41
    evolution and varieties, 241-62

    the Cavalier mode, 262-75
    court and society, 275-91
    politics and religion, 291-306

English Decadent Literature of the 1890s
NCLC 28: 104-200
    fin de siècle: the decadent period, 105-19
    definitions, 120-37
    major figures: "the tragic generation,"
      137-50
    French literature and English literary
      decadence, 150-57
    themes, 157-61
    poetry, 161-82
    periodicals, 182-96

English Romantic Poetry NCLC 28: 201-327
    overviews and reputation, 202-37
    major subjects and themes, 237-67
    forms of romantic poetry, 267-78
    politics, society, and romantic poetry,
      278-99
    philosophy, religion, and romantic
      poetry, 299-324

Film and Literature TCLC 38: 97-226
    overviews, 97-119
    film and theater, 119-34
    film and the novel, 134-45
    the art of the screenplay, 145-66
    genre literature / genre film, 167-79
    the writer and the film industry, 179-90
    authors on film adaptations of their
      works, 190-200
    fiction into film: comparative essays
      200-23

German Exile Literature TCLC 30: 1-58
    the writer and the Nazi state, 1-10
    definition of, 10-14
    life in exile, 14-32
    surveys, 32-50
    Austrian literature in exile, 50-2
    German publishing in the United States,
      52-7

German Expressionism TCLC 34: 74-160
    history and major figures, 76-85
    aesthetic theories, 85-109
    drama, 109-26
    poetry, 126-38
    film, 138-42
    painting, 142-47
    music, 147-53
    and politics, 153-58

**Glasnost and Contemporary Soviet
Literature** CLC 59: 355-97

The Gothic Novel NCLC 28: 328-402
    development and major works, 328-34
    definitions, 334-50
    themes and techniques, 350-78
    in America, 378-85
    in Scotland, 385-91
    influence and legacy, 391-400

Harlem Renaissance TCLC 26: 49-125
    principal issues and figures, 50-67
    the literature and its audience, 67-74
    theme and technique in poetry, fiction,
      and drama, 74-115
    and American society, 115-21
    achievement and influence, 121-22

**Hungarian Literature of the Twentieth
Century** TCLC 26: 126-88
    surveys of, 126-47
    Nyugat and early twentieth-century
      literature, 147-56
    mid-century literature, 156-68
    and politics, 168-78
    since the 1956 revolt, 178-87

Italian Humanism LC 12: 205-77
    origins and early development, 206-18
    revival of classical letters, 218-23
    humanism and other philosophies, 224-39
    humanisms and humanists, 239-46
    the plastic arts, 246-57
    achievement and significance, 258-76

**Muckraking Movement in American
Journalism** TCLC 34: 161-242
    development, principles, and major
      figures, 162-70
    publications, 170-79
    social and political ideas, 179-86
    targets, 186-208
    fiction, 208-19
    decline, 219-29
    impact and accomplishments, 229-40

Natural School, Russian NCLC 24: 205-40
    history and characteristics, 205-25
    contemporary criticism, 225-40

New Criticism TCLC 34: 243-318
    development and ideas, 244-70
    debate and defense, 270-99
    influence and legacy, 299-315

Newgate Novel NCLC 24: 166-204
    development of Newgate literature,
      166-73
    Newgate Calendar, 173-77
    Newgate fiction, 177-95
    Newgate drama, 195-204

New York Intellectuals and *Partisan Review*
TCLC 30: 117-98
  development and major figures, 118-28
  influence of Judaism, 128-39
  Partisan Review, 139-57
  literary philosophy and practice, 157-75
  political philosophy, 175-87
  achievement and significance, 187-97

**Nigerian Literature of the Twentieth
Century** TCLC 30: 199-265
  surveys of, 199-227
  English language and African life,
    227-45
  politics and the Nigerian writer, 245-54
  Nigerian writers and society, 255-62

**Opium and the Nineteenth-Century
Literary Imagination** NCLC 20: 250-301
  original sources, 250-62
  historical background, 262-71
  and literary society, 271-79
  and literary creativity, 279-300

Periodicals, Nineteenth-Century British
NCLC 24: 100-65
  overviews, 100-30
  in the Romantic Age, 130-41
  in the Victorian Era, 142-54
  and the reviewer, 154-64

Pre-Raphaelite Movement NCLC 20:
302-401
  overview, 302-04
  genesis, 304-12
  Germ and *Oxford and Cambridge
    Magazine*, 312-20
  Robert Buchanan and the "Fleshly
    School of Poetry," 320-31
  satires and parodies, 331-34
  surveys, 334-51
  aesthetics, 351-75
  sister arts of poetry and painting, 375-94
  influence, 394-99

Psychoanalysis and Literature TCLC 38:
227-338
  overviews, 227-46
  Freud on literature, 246-51
  psychoanalytic views of the literary
    process, 251-61
  psychoanalytic theories of response to
    literature, 261-88
  psychoanalysis and literary criticism,
    288-312
  psychoanalysis as literature / literature
    as psychoanalysis, 313-34

**Rushdie, Salman, *Satanic Verses*
Controversy** CLC 55: 214-63; 59: 404-56

Russian Nihilism, NCLC 28: 403-47
  definitions and overviews, 404-17
  women and Nihilism, 417-27
  literature as reform: the civic critics,
    427-33
  nihilism and the Russian novel:
    Turgenev and Dostoevsky, 433-47

Russian Thaw TCLC 26: 189-247
  literary history of the period, 190-206
  theoretical debate of socialist realism,
    206-11
  Novy Mir, 211-17
  Literary Moscow, 217-24
  Pasternak, *Zhivago*, and the Nobel
    Prize, 224-27

  poetry of liberation, 228-31
  Brodsky trial and the end of the Thaw,
    231-36
  achievement and influence, 236-46

**Salinger, J. D., Controversy Surrounding
*In Search of J. D. Salinger*** CLC 55:
325-44

Science Fiction, Nineteenth-Century
NCLC 24: 241-306
  background, 242-50
  definitions of the genre, 251-56
  representative works and writers, 256-75
  themes and conventions, 276-305

Sherlock Holmes Centenary TCLC 26:
248-310
  Doyle's life and the composition of the
    Holmes stories, 248-59
  life and character of Holmes, 259-78
  method, 278-79
  Holmes and the Victorian world, 279-92
  Sherlockian scholarship, 292-301
  Doyle and the development of the
    detective story, 301-07
  Holmes's continuing popularity, 307-09

Slave Narratives, American NCLC 20:
1-91
  background, 2-9
  overviews, 9-24
  contemporary responses, 24-7
  language, theme, technique, 27-70
  historical authenticity, 70-5
  antecedents, 75-83
  role in development of Black American
    literature, 83-8

Spanish Civil War Literature TCLC 26:
311-85
  topics in, 312-33
  British and American literature, 333-59
  French literature, 359-62
  Spanish literature, 362-73
  German literature, 373-75
  political idealism and war literature,
    375-83

Spasmodic School of Poetry NCLC 24:
307-52
  history and major figures, 307-21
  the Spasmodics on poetry, 321-27
  Firmilian and critical disfavor, 327-39
  theme and technique, 339-47
  influence, 347-51

**Steinbeck, John, Fiftieth Anniversary of
*The Grapes of Wrath*** CLC 59: 311-54

Supernatural Fiction, Modern TCLC 30:
59-116
  evolution and varieties, 60-74
  "decline" of the ghost story, 74-86
  as a literary genre, 86-92
  technique, 92-101
  nature and appeal, 101-15

Surrealism TCLC 30: 334-406
  history and formative influences, 335-43
  manifestos, 343-54
  philosophic, aesthetic, and political
    principles, 354-75
  poetry, 375-81
  novel, 381-86
  drama, 386-92
  film, 392-98

  painting and sculpture, 398-403
  achievement, 403-05

Symbolism, Russian TCLC 30: 266-333
  doctrines and major figures, 267-92
  theories, 293-98
  and French symbolism, 298-310
  themes in poetry, 310-14
  theater, 314-20
  and the fine arts, 320-32

Symbolist Movement, French NCLC 20:
169-249
  background and characteristics, 170-86
  principles, 186-91
  attacked and defended, 191-97
  influences and predecessors, 197-211
  and Decadence, 211-16
  theater, 216-26
  prose, 226-33
  decline and influence, 233-47

Theater of the Absurd TCLC 38: 339-415
  "The Theater of the Absurd," 340-47
  major plays and playwrights, 347-58
  the theater of the absurd and the
    concept of the absurd, 358-86
  theatrical techniques, 386-94
  predecessors of the theater of the
    absurd, 394-402
  influence of the theater of the absurd,
    402-13

Transcendentalism, American NCLC 24:
1-99
  overviews, 3-23
  contemporary documents, 23-41
  theological aspects of, 42-52
  and social issues, 52-74
  literature of, 74-96

**Travel Writing in the Twentieth
Century** TCLC 30: 407-56
  conventions and traditions, 407-27
  and fiction writing, 427-43
  comparative essays on travel writers,
    443-54

**Ulysses and the Process of Textual
Reconstruction** TCLC 26: 386-416
  evaluations of the new *Ulysses*, 386-94
  editorial principles and procedures,
    394-401
  theoretical issues, 401-16

Utopian Literature, Nineteenth-Century
NCLC 24: 353-473
  definitions, 354-74
  overviews, 374-88
  theory, 388-408
  communities, 409-26
  fiction, 426-53
  women and fiction, 454-71

World War I Literature TCLC 34:
392-486
  overview, 393-403
  English, 403-27
  German, 427-50
  American, 450-66
  French, 466-74
  and modern history, 474-82

Young Playwrights Festival, Eighth Annual
CLC 59: 398-403

**Young Playwrights Festival, Seventh
Annual** CLC 55: 376-81

TCLC Cumulative Nationality Index

AMERICAN

Adams, Henry **4**
Agee, James **1, 19**
Anderson, Maxwell **2**
Anderson, Sherwood **1, 10, 24**
Atherton, Gertrude **2**
Austin, Mary **25**
Barry, Philip **11**
Baum, L. Frank **7**
Beard, Charles A. **15**
Belasco, David **3**
Benchley, Robert **1**
Benét, Stephen Vincent **7**
Benét, William Rose **28**
Bierce, Ambrose **1, 7**
Black Elk **33**
Bourne, Randolph S. **16**
Bradford, Gamaliel **36**
Bromfield, Louis **11**
Burroughs, Edgar Rice **2, 32**
Cabell, James Branch **6**
Cable, George Washington **4**
Cather, Willa **1, 11, 31**
Chandler, Raymond **1, 7**
Chapman, John Jay **7**
Chesnutt, Charles Waddell **5**
Chopin, Kate **5, 14**
Comstock, Anthony **13**
Cotter, Joseph Seamon, Sr. **28**
Crane, Hart **2, 5**
Crane, Stephen **11, 17, 32**
Crawford, F. Marion **10**
Crothers, Rachel **19**
Cullen, Countee **4, 37**
Davis, Rebecca Harding **6**
Davis, Richard Harding **24**
Day, Clarence **25**
DeVoto, Bernard **29**
Dreiser, Theodore **10, 18, 35**

Dunbar, Paul Laurence **2, 12**
Dunne, Finley Peter **28**
Fisher, Rudolph **11**
Fitzgerald, F. Scott **1, 6, 14, 28**
Fletcher, John Gould **35**
Forten, Charlotte L. **16**
Freeman, Douglas Southall **11**
Freeman, Mary Wilkins **9**
Futrelle, Jacques **19**
Gale, Zona **7**
Garland, Hamlin **3**
Gilman, Charlotte Perkins **9, 37**
Glasgow, Ellen **2, 7**
Goldman, Emma **13**
Grey, Zane **6**
Hall, James Norman **23**
Harper, Frances Ellen Watkins **14**
Harris, Joel Chandler **2**
Harte, Bret **1, 25**
Hawthorne, Julian **25**
Hearn, Lafcadio **9**
Henry, O. **1, 19**
Hergesheimer, Joseph **11**
Higginson, Thomas Wentworth **36**
Hopkins, Pauline Elizabeth **28**
Howard, Robert E. **8**
Howe, Julia Ward **21**
Howells, William Dean **7, 17**
James, Henry **2, 11, 24**
James, William **15, 32**
Jewett, Sarah Orne **1, 22**
Johnson, James Weldon **3, 19**
Kornbluth, C. M. **8**
Kuttner, Henry **10**
Lardner, Ring **2, 14**
Lewis, Sinclair **4, 13, 23**
Lewisohn, Ludwig **19**
Lindsay, Vachel **17**
London, Jack **9, 15**

Lovecraft, H. P. **4, 22**
Lowell, Amy **1, 8**
Marquis, Don **7**
Masters, Edgar Lee **2, 25**
McCoy, Horace **28**
McKay, Claude **7**
Mencken, H. L. **13**
Millay, Edna St. Vincent **4**
Mitchell, Margaret **11**
Mitchell, S. Weir **36**
Monroe, Harriet **12**
Muir, John **28**
Nathan, George Jean **18**
Nordhoff, Charles **23**
Norris, Frank **24**
O'Neill, Eugene **1, 6, 27**
Oskison, John M. **35**
Porter, Gene Stratton **21**
Rawlings, Marjorie Kinnan **4**
Reed, John **9**
Roberts, Kenneth **23**
Robinson, Edwin Arlington **5**
Rogers, Will **8**
Rölvaag, O. E. **17**
Rourke, Constance **12**
Runyon, Damon **10**
Saltus, Edgar **8**
Sherwood, Robert E. **3**
Slesinger, Tess **10**
Steffens, Lincoln **20**
Stein, Gertrude **1, 6, 28**
Sterling, George **20**
Stevens, Wallace **3, 12**
Tarkington, Booth **9**
Teasdale, Sara **4**
Thurman, Wallace **6**
Twain, Mark **6, 12, 19, 36**
Van Dine, S. S. **23**
Van Doren, Carl **18**

Veblen, Thorstein 31
Washington, Booker T. 10
Wells, Carolyn 35
West, Nathanael 1, 14
Wharton, Edith 3, 9, 27
White, Walter 15
Wister, Owen 21
Wolfe, Thomas 4, 13, 29
Woollcott, Alexander 5
Wylie, Elinor 8

ARGENTINE
Arlt, Roberto 29
Lugones, Leopoldo 15
Storni, Alfonsina 5

AUSTRALIAN
Brennan, Christopher John 17
Franklin, Miles 7
Furphy, Joseph 25
Ingamells, Rex 35
Lawson, Henry 27
Paterson, A. B. 32
Richardson, Henry Handel 4

AUSTRIAN
Broch, Hermann 20
Hofmannsthal, Hugo von 11
Kafka, Franz 2, 6, 13, 29
Kraus, Karl 5
Kubin, Alfred 23
Meyrink, Gustav 21
Musil, Robert 12
Roth, Joseph 33
Schnitzler, Arthur 4
Steiner, Rudolf 13
Trakl, Georg 5
Werfel, Franz 8
Zweig, Stefan 17

BELGIAN
Bosschère, Jean de 19
Lemonnier, Camille 22
Maeterlinck, Maurice 3
Van Ostaijen, Paul 33
Verhaeren, Émile 12

BRAZILIAN
Cunha, Euclides da 24
Lima Barreto 23
Machado de Assis, Joaquim Maria 10
Ramos, Graciliano 32

BULGARIAN
Vazov, Ivan 25

CANADIAN
Campbell, Wilfred 9
Carman, Bliss 7
Carr, Emily 32
Connor, Ralph 31
Drummond, William Henry 25
Garneau, Hector Saint- Denys 13
Grove, Frederick Philip 4
Leacock, Stephen 2
McCrae, John 12
Nelligan, Emile 14
Pickthall, Marjorie 21
Roberts, Charles G. D. 8
Scott, Duncan Campbell 6
Service, Robert W. 15
Seton, Ernest Thompson 31

Stringer, Arthur 37

CHILEAN
Huidobro, Vicente 31
Mistral, Gabriela 2

CHINESE
Liu E 15
Lu Hsün 3
Su Man-shu 24
Wen I-to 28

COLOMBIAN
Rivera, Jose Eustasio 35

CZECHOSLOVAKIAN
Čapek, Karel 6, 37
Hašek, Jaroslav 4

DANISH
Brandes, Georg 10
Hansen, Martin A. 32
Pontopiddan, Henrik 29

DUTCH
Couperus, Louis 15
Frank, Anne 17
Heijermans, Herman 24

ENGLISH
Barbellion, W. N. P. 24
Baring, Maurice 8
Beerbohm, Max 1, 24
Belloc, Hilaire 7, 18
Bennett, Arnold 5, 20
Benson, E. F. 27
Benson, Stella 17
Bentley, E. C. 12
Besant, Annie 9
Blackmore, R. D. 27
Blackwood, Algernon 5
Bridges, Robert 1
Brooke, Rupert 2, 7
Butler, Samuel 1, 33
Chesterton, G. K. 1, 6
Conrad, Joseph 1, 6, 13, 25
Coppard, A. E. 5
Crowley, Aleister 7
De la Mare, Walter 4
Doughty, Charles 27
Dowson, Ernest 4
Doyle, Arthur Conan 7, 26
Eddison, E. R. 15
Ellis, Havelock 14
Firbank, Ronald 1
Ford, Ford Madox 1, 15
Freeman, R. Austin 21
Galsworthy, John 1
Gilbert, W. S. 3
Gissing, George 3
Gosse, Edmund 28
Granville-Barker, Harley 2
Gray, John 19
Gurney, Ivor 33
Haggard, H. Rider 11
Hall, Radclyffe 12
Hardy, Thomas 4, 10, 18, 32
Henley, William Ernest 8
Hilton, James 21
Hodgson, William Hope 13
Housman, A. E. 1, 10
Housman, Laurence 7

Hudson, W. H. 29
Hulme, T. E. 21
Jacobs, W. W. 22
James, M. R. 6
Jerome, Jerome K. 23
Johnson, Lionel 19
Kaye-Smith, Sheila 20
Kipling, Rudyard 8, 17
Lawrence, D. H. 2, 9, 16, 33
Lawrence, T. E. 18
Lee, Vernon 5
Lee-Hamilton, Eugene 22
Leverson, Ada 18
Lewis, Wyndham 2, 9
Lindsay, David 15
Lowndes, Marie Belloc 12
Lowry, Malcolm 6
Macaulay, Rose 7
MacCarthy, Desmond 36
Manning, Frederic 25
Meredith, George 17
Mew, Charlotte 8
Meynell, Alice 6
Milne, A. A. 6
Murry, John Middleton 16
Noyes, Alfred 7
Orwell, George 2, 6, 15, 31
Owen, Wilfred 5, 27
Pinero, Arthur Wing 32
Powys, T. F. 9
Richardson, Dorothy 3
Rohmer, Sax 28
Rolfe, Frederick 12
Rosenberg, Isaac 12
Ruskin, John 20
Rutherford, Mark 25
Saintsbury, George 31
Saki 3
Sayers, Dorothy L. 2, 15
Shiel, M. P. 8
Sinclair, May 3, 11
Stapledon, Olaf 22
Stephen, Leslie 23
Strachey, Lytton 12
Summers, Montague 16
Sutro, Alfred 6
Swinburne, Algernon Charles 8, 36
Symons, Arthur 11
Thomas, Edward 10
Thompson, Francis 4
Van Druten, John 2
Walpole, Hugh 5
Webb, Beatrice 22
Webb, Mary 24
Webb, Sidney 22
Welch, Denton 22
Wells, H. G. 6, 12, 19
Williams, Charles 1, 11
Woolf, Virginia 1, 5, 20
Zangwill, Israel 16

ESTONIAN
Tammsaare, A. H. 27

FINNISH
Leino, Eino 24
Södergran, Edith 31

FRENCH
Alain-Fournier 6
Apollinaire, Guillaume 3, 8
Artaud, Antonin 3, 36

Barbusse, Henri 5
Bergson, Henri 32
Bernanos, Georges 3
Bloy, Léon 22
Bourget, Paul 12
Claudel, Paul 2, 10
Colette 1, 5, 16
Coppée, François 25
Daumal, René 14
Desnos, Robert 22
Drieu La Rochelle, Pierre 21
Dujardin, Edouard 13
Eluard, Paul 7
Fargue, Léon-Paul 11
Feydeau, Georges 22
France, Anatole 9
Gide, André 5, 12, 36
Giraudoux, Jean 2, 7
Gourmont, Remy de 17
Huysmans, Joris-Karl 7
Jacob, Max 6
Jarry, Alfred 2, 14
Larbaud, Valéry 9
Leroux, Gaston 25
Loti, Pierre 11
Martin du Gard, Roger 24
Moréas, Jean 18
Péguy, Charles 10
Péret, Benjamin 20
Proust, Marcel 7, 13, 33
Radiguet, Raymond 29
Renard, Jules 17
Rolland, Romain 23
Rostand, Edmond 6, 37
Roussel, Raymond 20
Saint-Exupéry, Antoine de 2
Schwob, Marcel 20
Sully Prudhomme 31
Teilhard de Chardin, Pierre 9
Valéry, Paul 4, 15
Verne, Jules 6
Vian, Boris 9
Weil, Simone 23
Zola, Emile 1, 6, 21

GERMAN
Benn, Gottfried 3
Borchert, Wolfgang 5
Brecht, Bertolt 1, 6, 13, 35
Döblin, Alfred 13
Ewers, Hanns Heinz 12
Feuchtwanger, Lion 3
George, Stefan 2, 14
Hauptmann, Gerhart 4
Heym, Georg 9
Heyse, Paul 8
Huch, Ricarda 13
Kaiser, Georg 9
Liliencron, Detlev von 18
Mann, Heinrich 9
Mann, Thomas 2, 8, 14, 21, 35
Morgenstern, Christian 8
Nietzsche, Friedrich 10, 18
Rilke, Rainer Maria 1, 6, 19
Spengler, Oswald 25
Sternheim, Carl 8
Sudermann, Hermann 15
Toller, Ernst 10
Wassermann, Jakob 6
Wedekind, Frank 7

GHANIAN
Casely-Hayford, J. E. 24

GREEK
Cavafy, C. P. 2, 7
Kazantzakis, Nikos 2, 5, 33
Palamas, Kostes 5
Papadiamantis, Alexandros 29

HAITIAN
Roumain, Jacques 19

HUNGARIAN
Ady, Endre 11
Babits, Mihály 14
Csáth, Géza 13
Herzl, Theodor 36
Hungarian Literature of the Twentieth
  Century 26
József, Attila 22
Mikszáth, Kálmán 31
Molnár, Ferenc 20
Móricz, Zsigmond 33
Radnóti, Miklós 16

ICELANDIC
Sigurjónsson, Jóhann 27

INDIAN
Chatterji, Saratchandra 13
Iqbal, Muhammad 28
Premchand 21
Tagore, Rabindranath 3

INDONESIAN
Anwar, Chairil 22

IRANIAN
Hedayat, Sadeq 21

IRISH
A. E. 3, 10
Cary, Joyce 1, 29
Dunsany, Lord 2
Gogarty, Oliver St. John 15
Gregory, Lady 1
Harris, Frank 24
Joyce, James 3, 8, 16, 26, 35
Ledwidge, Francis 23
Moore, George 7
O'Grady, Standish 5
Shaw, Bernard 3, 9, 21
Stephens, James 4
Stoker, Bram 8
Synge, J. M. 6, 37
Tynan, Katharine 3
Wilde, Oscar 1, 8, 23
Yeats, William Butler 1, 11, 18, 31

ITALIAN
Betti, Ugo 5
Brancati, Vitaliano 12
Campana, Dino 20
Carducci, Giosuè 32
Croce, Benedetto 37
D'Annunzio, Gabriel 6
Deledda, Grazia 23
Giacosa, Giuseppe 7
Lampedusa, Giuseppe Tomasi di 13
Marinetti, F. T. 10
Papini, Giovanni 22
Pavese, Cesare 3

Pirandello, Luigi 4, 29
Saba, Umberto 33
Svevo, Italo 2, 35
Tozzi, Federigo 31
Verga, Giovanni 3

JAMAICAN
De Lisser, H. G. 12
Mais, Roger 8
Redcam, Tom 25

JAPANESE
Akutagawa Ryūnosuke 16
Dazai Osamu 11
Hayashi Fumiko 27
Ishikawa Takuboku 15
Masaoka Shiki 18
Miyamoto Yuriko 37
Mori Ōgai 14
Natsume, Sōseki 2, 10
Rohan, Kōda 22
Shimazaki, Tōson 5

LATVIAN
Rainis, Janis 29

LEBANESE
Gibran, Kahlil 1, 9

LESOTHAN
Mofolo, Thomas 22

LITHUANIAN
Krévé, Vincas 27

MEXICAN
Azuela, Mariano 3
Gamboa, Frederico 36
Nervo, Amado 11
Reyes, Alfonso 33
Romero, Jose Rubén 14

NATIVE AMERICAN
See American

NEPALI
Devkota, Laxmiprasad 23

NEW ZEALAND
Mander, Jane 31
Mansfield, Katherine 2, 8

NICARAGUAN
Darío, Rubén 4

NIGERIAN
Nigerian Literature of the Twentieth
  Century 30

NORWEGIAN
Bjørnson, Bjørnstjerne 7, 37
Grieg, Nordahl 10
Hamsun, Knut 2, 14
Ibsen, Henrik 2, 8, 16, 37
Kielland, Alexander 5
Lie, Jonas 5
Obstfelder, Sigbjørn 23
Skram, Amalie 25
Undset, Sigrid 3

PAKISTANI
Iqbal, Muhammad 28

PERUVIAN
Palma, Ricardo   29
Vallejo, César   3

POLISH
Asch, Sholem   3
Borowski, Tadeusz   9
Peretz, Isaac Leib   16
Przybyszewski, Stanisłław   36
Reymont, Włładysłław Stanisłław   5
Schulz, Bruno   5
Sienkiewitz, Henryk   3
Singer, Israel Joshua   33
Witkiewicz, Stanisłław Ignacy   8

PORTUGUESE
Pessoa, Fernando   27

PUERTO RICAN
Hostos, Eugenio María de   24

RUMANIAN
Bacovia, George   24
Rebreanu, Liviu   28

RUSSIAN
Aldanov, Mark   23
Andreyev, Leonid   3
Annensky, Innokenty   14
Artsybashev, Mikhail   31
Babel, Isaak   2, 13
Balmont, Konstantin Dmitriyevich   11
Bely, Andrey   7
Blok, Aleksandr   5
Bryusov, Valery   10
Bulgakov, Mikhail   2, 16
Bunin, Ivan   6
Chekhov, Anton   3, 10, 31
Esenin, Sergei   4
Gladkov, Fyodor   27
Gorky, Maxim   8
Hippius, Zinaida   9
Ilf, Ilya   21
Ivanov, Vyacheslav   33
Khlebnikov, Velimir   20
Khodasevich, Vladislav   15
Korolenko, Vladimir   22
Kropotkin, Peter   36
Kuprin, Aleksandr   5
Mandelstam, Osip   2, 6
Mayakovsky, Vladimir   4, 18
Merezhkovsky, Dmitri   29
Petrov, Evgeny   21
Pilnyak, Boris   23
Platonov, Andrei   14
Remizov, Alexey   27
Sologub, Fyodor   9
Tolstoy, Alexey Nikolayevich   18
Tolstoy, Leo   4, 11, 17, 28
Trotsky, Leon   22
Tsvetaeva, Marina   7, 35
Zamyatin, Yevgeny Ivanovich   8, 37
Zhdanov, Andrei   18
Zoshchenko, Mikhail   15

SCOTTISH
Barrie, J. M.   2
Bridie, James   3
Brown, George Douglas   28
Davidson, John   24
Frazer, James   32
Gibbon, Lewis Grassic   4

Graham, R. B. Cunninghame   19
Lang, Andrew   16
MacDonald, George   9
Muir, Edwin   2
Tey, Josephine   14

SOUTH AFRICAN
Campbell, Roy   5
Mqhayi, S. E. K.   25
Schreiner, Olive   9
Smith, Pauline   25
Vilakazi, Benedict Wallet   37

SPANISH
Alas, Leopoldo   29
Barea, Arturo   14
Baroja, Pío   8
Benavente, Jacinto   3
Blasco Ibáñez, Vicente   12
Echegaray, José   4
García Lorca, Federico   1, 7
Jiménez, Juan Ramón   4
Machado, Antonio   3
Martínez Sierra, Gregorio   6
Miró, Gabriel   5
Ortega y Gasset, José   9
Pereda, José María de   16
Pérez, Galdós, Benito   27
Salinas, Pedro   17
Unamuno, Miguel de   2, 9
Valera, Juan   10
Valle-Inclán, Ramón del   5

SWEDISH
Dagerman, Stig   17
Heidenstam, Verner von   5
Lagerlöf, Selma   4, 36
Strindberg, August   1, 8, 21

SWISS
Ramuz, Charles-Ferdinand   33
Spitteler, Carl   12
Walser, Robert   18

TURKISH
Sait Faik   23

UKRAINIAN
Bialik, Chaim Nachman   25
Sholom Aleichem   1, 35

URUGUAYAN
Quiroga, Horacio   20
Sánchez, Florencio   37

WELSH
Davies, W. H.   5
Lewis, Alun   3
Machen, Arthur   4
Thomas, Dylan   1, 8